Lawyers' Ethics

and

Professional Regulation

Second Edition

Alice Woolley
Richard Devlin
Brent Cotter
John M. Law

Lawyers' Ethics and Professional Regulation, Second Edition
© LexisNexis Canada Inc. 2012
August 2012

Library and Archives Canada Cataloguing in Publication

Lawyers' ethics and professional regulation, second edition / Alice Woolley ... [et al.].

Includes index.
ISBN 978-0-433-46774-8

    1. Legal ethics—Canada. I. Woolley, Alice

KE339.L39 2008   174'.30971   C2008-903831-2
KF306 L39 2008

Published by LexisNexis Canada, a member of the LexisNexis Group
LexisNexis Canada Inc.
123 Commerce Valley Dr. E., Suite 700
Markham, Ontario
L3T 7W8

Customer Service
Telephone: (905) 479-2665 • Fax: (905) 479-2826
Toll-Free Phone: 1-800-668-6481 • Toll-Free Fax: 1-800-461-3275
Email: customerservice@lexisnexis.ca
Web Site: www.lexisnexis.ca

Printed and bound in Canada.

LAWYERS' ETHICS AND PROFESSIONAL REGULATION

Editors

Alice Woolley
Faculty of Law, University of Calgary

Richard Devlin
Schulich School of Law, Dalhousie University

Brent Cotter
College of Law, University of Saskatchewan

John M. Law
Faculty of Law, University of Alberta

Authors by Chapter

Chapter 1: Introduction to Legal Ethics
Alice Woolley

Chapter 2: The Legal Profession and Lawyer Regulation in Canada
John M. Law

Chapter 3: The Lawyer-Client Relationship
Richard Devlin

Chapter 4: The Lawyer's Duty to Preserve Client Confidences
Brent Cotter

Chapter 5: The Duty of Loyalty and Conflicts of Interest
Brent Cotter

Chapter 6: Ethics in Advocacy
Trevor C.W. Farrow
Osgoode Hall Law School, York University

Chapter 7: Counselling and Negotiation
Stephen G.A. Pitel
Faculty of Law, Western University

ABOUT THE EDITORS

ALICE WOOLLEY is a Professor of Law and Director of Admissions at the Faculty of Law, University of Calgary. Professor Woolley has written academic articles and commentary on a wide variety of topics in the area of legal ethics and professional regulation. She is also the author of *Understanding Lawyers' Ethics in Canada* (LexisNexis Canada, 2011). Prior to joining the University of Calgary, Professor Woolley spent seven years working as a lawyer in Calgary, practising mainly in the areas of civil litigation and utility regulation. In 1995–1996, she was a law clerk to former Chief Justice Antonio Lamer.

RICHARD F. DEVLIN is a Professor of Law and University Research Professor at the Schulich School of Law at Dalhousie University. He has published widely in various areas, including legal theory, legal ethics, judicial education and contracts.

BRENT COTTER is a Professor and former Dean at the College of Law at the University of Saskatchewan. He was formerly a law professor at Dalhousie University and has been a visiting professor at the University of Alberta and Duke University. Prior to assuming his present position, he served for 12 years as a deputy minister with the Government of Saskatchewan in various capacities, including as Deputy Attorney General from 1992–1997. He has written in the area of ethics in public service, legal ethics and professional responsibility, including the role of professional responsibility in law school curricula and in professional legal education generally.

JOHN M. LAW is a Professor at the Faculty of Law, University of Alberta. His research interests are in the areas of administrative law, legal history, legal education and professional responsibility. Professor Law has been actively involved in the governance of the legal profession having served on numerous Law Society committees, including the committee which authored the Law Society of Alberta *Code of Professional Conduct*.

ABOUT THE CONTRIBUTORS

MICHAEL CODE received his call to the Bar of Ontario in 1981. From 1981 until 1991, he practised criminal and constitutional litigation with the Toronto firm of Ruby & Edwardh. He lectured in criminal law at Woodsworth College, University of Toronto, in evidence law at Osgoode Hall Law School and in criminal procedure at the Faculty of Law, University of Toronto during the 1980s and 1990s. He was an editor of the *Canadian Rights Reporter* from its inception in 1982 until 1996. In 1990, he went on sabbatical from his law firm and completed an LL.M. at the Faculty of Law. In 1991, he was appointed Assistant Deputy Minister, Criminal Law, Ministry of the Attorney General for Ontario. In 1996, he returned to private practice with the firm of Sack Goldblatt Mitchell. He was a visiting scholar at the Faculty of Law, University of Toronto in 2005–2006, and joined the Faculty full-time in 2006 where he taught criminal law, criminal procedure and legal ethics. He has published a number of articles and one book in these areas. In 2009, he was appointed a judge of the Ontario Superior Court of Justice.

ADAM DODEK is an Associate Professor at the University of Ottawa's Faculty of Law, Common Law Section. He teaches legal ethics, public law and a seminar on the Supreme Court of Canada. He heads the Faculty of Law's Professionalism Initiative, which includes the first Professionalism Speaker Series in Canada. His book *Solicitor-Client Privilege* will be published by LexisNexis Canada in 2013.

TREVOR C.W. FARROW is an Associate Professor at Osgoode Hall Law School in Toronto. His research and teaching focus on the administration of civil justice, including legal process, dispute resolution, professional ethics, advocacy, globalization and post-conflict development.

PAUL D. PATON is Professor of Law and Director of the Ethics Across the Professions Initiative at the McGeorge School of Law, University of the Pacific, in Sacramento, California. A Canadian lawyer with academic experience in both Canada and the United States, he formerly was a professor at Queen's University, in-house counsel to PricewaterhouseCoopers LLP, Justice and Social Policy Advisor to the Premier of Ontario and partner with a major Canadian law firm. His research interests focus on professional responsibility in corporate contexts, corporate governance and ethics in government. He was twice named a Fellow of the U.S. National Institute on Teaching Ethics and Professionalism and was a Fellow of the Keck Center on Legal Ethics and the Legal Profession at Stanford. Chair of the Canadian Bar Association's Ethics and Professional Responsibility Committee between

2008 and 2010, he was named a Reporter to the American Bar Association's Ethics 20/20 Commission in 2010. In 2012 he becomes Vice Provost of the University of the Pacific.

STEPHEN G.A. PITEL is an Associate Professor and Goodmans LLP Faculty Fellow in Legal Ethics at the Faculty of Law at Western University. His teaching and research is focused on the conflict of laws, civil procedure, torts and legal ethics. He has co-authored, edited or co-edited 11 books since 2003 including *Conflict of Laws* (2010). He was the co-developer of Canada's first mandatory first-year law school course in legal ethics and is the Director of the Lenczner Slaght Advocacy Competition in Legal Ethics. He is a member of the Chief Justice of Ontario's Advisory Committee on Professionalism and a founder of Western's Tort Law Research Group. He has received several teaching awards.

ACKNOWLEDGEMENTS

The editors and contributors thank the following people for their contribution to the preparation of this casebook: John Dickieson, Alex Hartwig, Kathryn James, David Layton, Molly Ross, Jocelyn Stacey and Linda Szeto.

A casebook on such a wide subject necessarily contains a great deal of reference to the work of others in the field, in the cases, the notes, the text and especially in the selected readings. The authors and publishers of the following articles and textbooks have been most generous in giving permission for the reproduction in this text of work already in print. References, of course, appear where necessary and possible in the text. It is convenient for us to list below, for the assistance of the reader, the publisher and authors for whose courtesy we are most grateful. The following list is organized in alphabetical order:

Georgetown University Law Center — Regan, Milton C., Jr., "Professional Responsibility and the Corporate Lawyer", Georgetown Journal of Legal Ethics, 13:2 Geo. J. Legal Ethics, 197-215, 2000. Reprinted with permission of the publisher, Georgetown Journal of Legal Ethics © 2000.

The Honourable Georgina R. Jackson, "The Mystery of Judicial Ethics: Deciphering the 'Code'" (2005) 68 Sask. L. Rev. 1 [footnotes omitted]. Reproduced with permission.

Luban, David, "The Adversary System Excuse" in *Legal Ethics and Human Dignity* (Cambridge: Cambridge University Press, 2007). Reproduced with permission.

Luban, David, "Tales of Terror: Lessons for Lawyers from the 'War on Terrorism'" in Kieran Trantler *et al.*, eds., *Reaffirming Legal Ethics: Taking Stock and New Ideas* (New York: Routledge, 2010). Reproduced with permission.

Proulx, Michel & David Layton, *Ethics and Canadian Criminal Law* (Toronto: Irwin Law, 2001). Reprinted with permission © 2001.

Wilson, Malliha, Taia Wong & Kevin Hille, "Professionalism and the Public Interest" (2011) 38 The Advocates' Quarterly 1 14-17. Reproduced with permission.

TABLE OF CONTENTS

TABLE OF CASES

[A page number in boldface type indicates that
a case has been excerpted in the text.]

CHAPTER 1

INTRODUCTION TO LEGAL ETHICS

A. INTRODUCTION

What is legal ethics? Is it a distinct set of moral obligations that arises from the lawyer's role? Is it the rules of ordinary morality applied to the practice of law? Is it the inquiry into whether the life of a lawyer can be consistent with a life well-lived? Is it the "law of lawyering" — the rules and principles that govern a lawyer's conduct of practice in the same way as the rules of court determine the process of an action? Is it market regulation — how we compensate for and regulate the imperfections associated with the market for legal services?

In this book, you will be introduced to what being an ethical lawyer requires and to how Canadian provinces (and other jurisdictions) have chosen to regulate (or not to regulate) lawyer conduct. You will be introduced to specific controversies and important questions related both to the ethical obligations of the individual lawyer and to the challenges of regulating lawyer conduct. You will be invited to consider how the life of a lawyer can be a life well-lived. Overall, we hope this book will help you to solve the ethical problems that inevitably arise in legal practice, to understand the basic structure of professional regulation and governance, to reflect on the morality of being a lawyer, and to engage critically with the most important policy questions related to the ethics of legal practice and its regulation.

This chapter provides introductory materials and discussion on lawyers' ethics and professional regulation. First, it offers a brief overview of the two main topics covered in this book: the ethical obligations of lawyers in legal practice and current approaches to regulation of lawyers' ethics. Second, it discusses the main sources of guidance and obligation for lawyers when making ethical decisions. Third, it outlines some of the ways philosophers have attempted to answer the question, "what does being ethical require?". Fourth, it examines some general and competing conceptions of the duties or qualities of the ethical lawyer: loyal advocacy; lawyers as moral agents in pursuit of justice; and integrity.

In reading these materials, you should consider the following questions and problems:

- Is legal ethics law?

- Who should decide what being an ethical lawyer means? One's self? Courts? Law societies? Other lawyers? The legislature? The general public? The reasonable person?

- What is the central quality of an ethical lawyer? What does being an ethical lawyer require as a matter of principle?

- If a lawyer's duties in an individual case conflict, how does a lawyer decide what to do?

- Is being an ethical lawyer applying the values learned in kindergarten,[1] or do different principles apply? What does a lawyer do if the values of ethical lawyering conflict with a lawyer's personal sense of what is right or wrong?

- Whose interests (clients', judges', the general public and/or lawyers') should be taken into account in deciding what is ethical?

Each of these questions can (and should) be considered through the following case.

LAW SOCIETY OF BRITISH COLUMBIA v. JABOUR

[1980] B.C.J. No. 833, 115 D.L.R. (3d) 549 (B.C.C.A.),
affd [1982] S.C.J. No. 70, [1982] 2 S.C.R. 307 (S.C.C.)
(B.C.C.A., Seaton, Lambert and Hutcheon JJ.A.)

[Donald Jabour was a senior lawyer practising in North Vancouver. He advertised the services provided by his law firm and, as a consequence, was found guilty of "conduct unbecoming" a member of the Law Society by the Law Society of British Columbia. The Law Society's ability to regulate members' advertising was challenged as contrary to federal competition legislation. That challenge was unsuccessful. In the course of its decision, the British Columbia Court of Appeal considered the powers of the Law Society of British Columbia to regulate professional misconduct.]

SEATON J.A.: —

. . . . .

Advertising by lawyers is at the root of each of the actions, but the question whether lawyers ought to be able to advertise is not before us. We are only concerned with who is to answer the question and whether it is federal or provincial legislation that is to govern the matter.

Mr. Jabour has been a member of The Law Society of British Columbia since 1959. In late January 1978 he published four advertisements in newspapers. They were in the following form:

---

1   Susan N. Turner, "Raising the Bar: Maximizing Civility in Alberta Courtrooms" (2003) 41 Alta. L. Rev. 547 at 557.

DONALD E. JABOUR Barrister & Solicitor wishes to announce the opening of a new concept of law office

LEGAL SERVICES AT PRICES MIDDLE INCOME FAMILIES can afford Buying or selling a home. Writing a will. Motor vehicle accidents or offences. Landlord/tenant problems. Family matters. Incorporations. Estates. Court appearances. These are the kinds of situations where middle income families need legal assistance. Now it is available at moderate cost, with pre-set fees for many services.

Some sample fees (excluding out-of-pocket expenses):

Simple will	$ 35
Uncontested Divorce	...from $195
Advice on Interim Agreements	$25
Purchase of home (any value)	$175
Incorporations	...from $165
Advice on Consumer Contracts	$15
Review your present will	Free

INITIAL CONSULTATION FREE

Opening February 1, 1978

The North Shore	142A W. 15th St.
NEIGHBORHOOD	North Vancouver
LEGAL CLINIC	936-4225

HOURS: 9am. to 5pm. As a convenience to clients we will also be open Wed. Eve. 7 to 9pm. Sat. from 10.30 am. to 1 pm.

Call or write for free brochure

He also mounted a large illuminated sign over his office bearing the words "The North Shore Neighbourhood Legal Clinic, Donald E. Jabour, Barrister and Solicitor".

. . . . .

... On May 12th 1978 the Committee found Mr. Jabour to be guilty of conduct unbecoming a member of the Society and on May 23rd 1978 it recommended that he be suspended from the practice of law for six months.

. . . . .

In interpreting the *Legal Professions Act* I presume, for reasons that will be given later, that freedom of speech is not lightly to be interfered with.

I set out here some of the provisions in the *Legal Professions Act* that deal with the scope of the Benchers' authority:

1. In this Act and in any rule made under this Act, unless the context otherwise requires,

...

"conduct unbecoming a member of the Society" includes any matter, conduct, or thing that is deemed in the judgment of the Benchers to be contrary to the best interest of the public or of the legal profession, or that tends to harm the standing of the legal profession;

...

(3) The Benchers or the Discipline Committee may inquire into the conduct or competence, or both, of any

(a)　member or former member...

...

48. The Benchers, or the Discipline Committee if so authorized by the Rules, may, as the result of a hearing pursuant to section 44,

(a)　dismiss the citation; or

(b)　determine whether a member or former member has been guilty of

(i)　misappropriation or wrongful conversion by him of money or other property entrusted to or received by him in his capacity as a member of the Society; or

(ii)　other professional misconduct; or

(iii)　other conduct unbecoming a member of the Society; or

(iv)　a breach of any provision of this Act or the Rules made hereunder;

...

49.(1) Where an adverse determination respecting a member is made under section 48(b), the Benchers may, by a resolution passed by the votes of at least two-thirds of the Benchers present at a duly constituted meeting of the Benchers,

(a)　fine the member an amount not exceeding one thousand dollars; or

(b)　reprimand and, in addition, fine the member an amount not exceeding one thousand dollars; or

(c)　suspend and, in addition, fine the member an amount not exceeding one thousand dollars; or

(d)　order the disbarment of the member;

and may in each case impose costs and any conditions of practice upon the member and may make such other order either on terms or otherwise as may be just.

. . . . .

The respondents say that this is an Act to provide a licensing system, to regulate competency, and to police the integrity of those entitled to practice law. I think that it is much more than that. The power given the Benchers has been held to be wide. Branca, J.A., speaking for this court in *Prescott v. Law*

Society of British Columbia, [1971] 4 W.W.R. 433 at 440, after setting out the definition of "conduct unbecoming a member of the Society", said:

> The Benchers are the guardians of the proper standards of professional and ethical conduct. The definition, in my judgment, shows that it is quite immaterial whether the conduct complained of is of a professional character, or otherwise, as long as the Benchers conclude that the conduct in question is "contrary to the best interest of the public or of the legal profession, or that tends to harm the standing of the legal profession". The Benchers are elected by their fellow professionals because of their impeccable standing in the profession and are men who enjoy the full confidence and trust of the members of the legal profession of this province. One of the most important statutory duties confided to that body is that of disciplining their fellow members who fail to observe the proper standards of conduct and/or ethics which are necessary to keep the profession on that very high plane of honesty, integrity and efficiency which is essential to warrant the continued confidence of the public in the profession.

The Benchers are not restricted to competency and integrity. Section 37(1)(a) demonstrates that. Section 48(b) (ii) and (iii), read with the definition of conduct unbecoming a member of the Society, satisfy me that it was the intention of the Legislature to vest in the Benchers very broad powers. They may prohibit any conduct that is contrary to the best interest of the public or the profession. Conduct need not be specifically prohibited before it may be the subject of disciplinary proceedings. Whether advertising as done by Mr. Jabour constitutes conduct amenable to disciplinary proceedings is a matter for the Benchers.

It must be remembered that we are not here concerned with whether the conduct warranted discipline. That matter may come before this court on appeal from the decision of the Benchers, but it is not before us at this stage.

In the judgment below and in the arguments of the respondents here, there has been frequent reference to "specific" powers. There is no specific power to prohibit advertising to be found in the Act. There are few specific powers - most are general and broad. It does not matter whether they are specific. What matters is whether they are granted. In my view the power to prohibit commercial advertising is granted as part of the broad regulatory power conferred by the Act. The Benchers are given a general power to determine what conduct is to be acceptable in the practice of law and even outside the practice for those who are members. Provided the conduct can be found to be contrary to the best interest of the public or of the legal profession, or that it tends to harm the standing of the profession, it is within the ambit of the Benchers' power.

The Benchers' powers to prohibit advertising are not wholly unlimited. I would expect, for example, that the election advertising of a solicitor running for public office would not normally come within the Benchers' scope. *Merchant v. Benchers of Law Society of Saskatchewan et al.*, [1973] 2 W.W.R. 109 [in which the Law Society sought to enjoin a lawyer from hosting a call-in radio show] offers an example of a prohibition beyond the powers of the Benchers of Saskatchewan. It would not be useful to attempt to state the outer limits of conduct that the Benchers can conclude is "contrary to the best interest of the public or of the legal profession, or that tends to harm the standing of the legal profession" (see s. 1 of the Act).

I do not intend to examine each of the rulings from The Professional Conduct Handbook. It has already been decided by this court that those rulings do not constitute regulations, breach of which is an offence. (In *Re Fan* (1977), 4 B.C.L.R. 16).

The Law Society of British Columbia and its predecessor The Incorporated Law Society of British Columbia, date back over one hundred years. Throughout that time, broad general powers of discipline have been exercised. There have been no changes in the legislation that indicate a legislative will to limit that power.

I conclude that the Benchers have the power to prohibit the type of advertising that is found here and to discipline with respect to that type of advertising. Whether they ought to exercise the power is not for us to decide in these appeals.

. . . . .

NOTES AND QUESTIONS

1. Based on the facts of this case, and thus assuming that his actions were contrary to the Law Society of British Columbia's restrictions on advertising at that time, would you describe Donald Jabour as an ethical lawyer?

2. Subsequent to this decision, and the Supreme Court's later determination that very broad advertising restrictions are contrary to the *Canadian Charter of Rights and Freedoms* (*Rocket v. Royal College of Dental Surgeons*, [1990] S.C.J. No. 65, 2 S.C.R. 232 (S.C.C.)), all Canadian law societies have loosened their restrictions on lawyer advertising. Some restrictions on lawyer advertising remain (see Chapter 3). What principle or value is protected by such restrictions?

3. The Court asserts that regulation of the legal profession includes "much more" than simply regulation of lawyer's competence and integrity, and extends to any matter that is "contrary to the best interest of the public or the profession". What interests of the public and/or the profession might be relevant to defining legal ethics? For example, is regulating to protect lawyers' economic interests a legitimate activity of a provincial law society?

Scenario One

Alex Jones and Leslie Smith are a couple living in North Vancouver in 1979 who want to buy their first home. They both work as by-law enforcement officers and have a modest family income. Neither has ever retained a lawyer previously. Would Alex and Leslie be likely to have the same assessment as the Law Society of British Columbia regarding whether Mr. Jabour's advertisement is "contrary to the best interest of the public or the profession"?

Scenario Two

In the United States, personal injury lawyers can advertise in their area with "1-800-HURT-911". The number appears on local television channels or in the yellow pages with their name, and prospective clients who call that number will reach them. Do you think it is ethical for a lawyer to participate in that type of advertising arrangement? What ethical values, if any, are implicated in a decision to advertise in this way?

B.   WHAT ARE LAWYERS' ETHICS AND PROFESSIONAL REGULATION?

The definition of "legal ethics" has engaged and troubled academic commentators for many years. For our purposes, however, it is sufficient to note some relatively uncontroversial basic features of lawyers' ethics and professional regulation. Or, to put it slightly differently, to map the landscape of what shall be covered in the rest of this casebook.

Lawyers' ethics deals with the ethical obligations of the practising lawyer, both as individuals and as members of organizations. Lawyers' ethics addresses the constraints on lawyer conduct: the rules, principles and legal obligations with which lawyers are required to comply in conducting their legal practice. It also addresses the moral or ethical aspirations of the practising lawyer — the type of decision-making processes and decisions which an ethical lawyer will employ and make. At the level of moral aspiration, of course, there is more controversy, and less agreement, as to what lawyers' ethics requires than there is at the level of legal constraint. There is, for example, far more agreement that a lawyer must not fraudulently bill a client than that a lawyer should represent only clients with a just claim. It is the task of the student and teacher of lawyers' ethics to engage, however, with both sorts of questions. This book is designed to allow you to do so. It considers specific ethical issues related to the selection and representation of clients in a variety of practice contexts, and facilitates analysis of what lawyers are required to do, and should aspire to do, in resolving those issues in those contexts. It considers these questions both as a matter of legal doctrine and as a matter of principle.

Professional regulation is also concerned with the ethics of legal practice. Its concern exists, however, at the level of regulation and governance: how do we determine and enforce ethical constraints on lawyer conduct? As presently structured, all Canadian lawyers are regulated in significant part through a form of "self-regulation" in which the rules of ethical conduct, the standards for admission to the profession, and the enforcement of those rules and standards, are set by lawyers themselves. This book also provides information about the history, current structure and future of professional regulation, and considers some of the key current issues that have arisen with respect to professional regulation.

C. SOURCES

In determining what constitutes ethical conduct, a lawyer can look to a number of sources for guidance. These include:

•   case law and legislation;

•   Rules of Professional Conduct;

•   Law Society Disciplinary Decisions; and

•   the principles or "norms" of lawyering.

1.   Case Law and Legislation

Case law and legislation (including regulations) place constraints on what lawyers can and cannot do in legal practice. The law of negligence obliges lawyers to meet certain basic standards of competence. The law of fiduciary duties obliges lawyers to act with loyalty in furthering the interests of their clients, and to put the interests of their clients before those of themselves or others. The law of contracts governs the specific obligations a lawyer has to a client under a retainer agreement (whether written or oral). In a recent case, the Supreme Court of Canada held that "the scope of the [lawyer's] retainer is governed by contract".[2] The law on taxation of legal fees, in which clients or lawyers obtain court assessment of a lawyer's bill and an order requiring the bill to be paid as assessed, provides guidance on a lawyer's ethical obligations when charging a client. Cases dealing with the law of evidence and, in particular, the doctrine of solicitor-client privilege, are essential for under-standing the lawyer's obligation of confidentiality to clients. The rules of court and the cases interpreting those rules have dealt with lawyer ethics in the conduct of an action. Finally, the inherent authority of the court to control its own processes has led to numerous cases dealing with the obligations of lawyers to avoid acting in circumstances where there is a potential conflict of interest between the lawyer and his or her client, or between the lawyers' various clients, current and former. It has also led to case law dealing with the duty of lawyers not to withdraw from a representation except with ethical justification.

Case law and legislation thus significantly guide and constrain lawyer conduct. Indeed, case law and legislation may be the most significant doctrinal source of guidance for lawyers on what is required to act ethically. Nonetheless, many issues are not addressed by case law or legislation, and direction on what lawyers may not do, or are required to do, with respect to those issues must be found elsewhere.

---

[2]   *Strother v. 3464920 Canada Inc.*, [2007] S.C.J. No. 24, [2007] 2 S.C.R. 177 at para. 34 (S.C.C.).

2. Rules of Professional Conduct

Every provincial law society has rules of professional conduct. These rules are generally enacted by the law society pursuant to its legislative authority to regulate the legal profession. The rules cover a variety of matters related to legal practice including client selection, advocacy, competence, fees, conflicts of interest, confidentiality, advising clients, interacting with judges and the business operation of a law practice. Traditionally, the provincial law societies have had distinct codes, with many (but not all) modelling their requirements on the Canadian Bar Association's *Model Code of Professional Conduct*. Now, through the Federation of Law Societies of Canada, an umbrella organization to which all the provincial law societies belong, the law societies are attempting to create a high degree of uniformity in the rules of conduct across the provinces. To that end, in 2009 the Federation published a *Model Code of Professional Conduct*. Most Canadian law societies have adopted, or are in the process of adopting, a version of the Federation's *Model Code*. This casebook references the Federation's *Model Code* when setting out what codes of conduct say about lawyers' obligations.

Despite the law societies' initiatives to create a uniform set of standards, it must be noted that in general the rules of professional conduct are not rigorously enforced by provincial law societies. In addition, the Federation's *Model Code* and its predecessors often include general and discretionary guidelines rather than specific mandatory obligations. Rules of professional conduct are therefore an important but non-exhaustive source of guidance for a lawyer in deciding what action should be taken, and what action is required to be taken, in circumstances of ethical uncertainty.

3. Law Society Disciplinary Decisions

Law society disciplinary decisions are publicly available through law society websites, Quicklaw and CanLII. Disciplinary decisions provide insight into the meaning of provisions of the Codes of Conduct. They also indicate how law societies generally define professional misconduct (misconduct by the lawyer when practising law) and conduct unbecoming (misconduct by the lawyer outside of his or her legal practice). Disciplinary decisions set out the standard of proof for establishing that a lawyer has committed professional misconduct and the sorts of sanctions that may be imposed.

Disciplinary decisions provide, however, limited guidance to lawyers because they address only a narrow range of lawyer conduct, concentrating mostly on clear legal violations such as stealing funds from clients, or on a lawyer's refusal to comply with law society regulatory requirements. Most of the vexing questions of ethics, the questions that do not lend themselves to obvious answers, are not addressed by disciplinary decisions in any meaningful way.

4.   Principles or "Norms"

Because of the wide variety of circumstances that can implicate lawyer ethics, and because of the constrained quantity and quality of the guidance provided by case law, legislation, the rules of conduct and disciplinary decisions, lawyers seeking to be ethical must look beyond those sources. A lawyer who is deciding, for example, whether to disclose information provided by a client where the rules of professional conduct say that he or she "may" do so needs to know what to consider in deciding what action to take. A lawyer who is deciding which clients to act for, when the rules of conduct and case law leave that matter almost entirely within his discretion needs to know on what basis to make that choice. A lawyer who perceives a gap between the obligations imposed by the law governing lawyers and the obligations of ordinary morality needs to know how to respond to that gap in deciding what to do, or how to reconcile her decision with a life well-lived. Where, for example, the law governing lawyers requires that information be kept confidential, but ordinary moral principles would require disclosure in order to prevent harm to third parties, a lawyer needs principles and norms to guide her response, and to allow her to determine how that response can be incorporated into a life well-lived. With respect to all these sorts of questions important sources of guidance are principles or "norms" that apply to the work that lawyers do.

Principles or norms play an additional role of importance. To act ethically, lawyers need to be sensitive to when an ethical issue has arisen; they need to have the judgment to respond to that ethical situation appropriately; and they need to have the motivation and courage to put their response into action.[3] Having these qualities requires more than that a lawyer be able to apply the law, or reason through how principles might apply to a particular situation. It requires as well that the lawyer have strong intuitions that will allow her to perceive quickly that an ethical problem has arisen, and what should be done. Developing those intuitions requires the lawyer to have a strong commitment to a principled conception of the lawyer's role, to know to the point of sensing, what being a lawyer means, and does not mean.[4]

What principles or norms best define the lawyer's role is a matter of dispute, with differing emphasis being placed on the important societal role that lawyers fulfill, on the requirements of ordinary morality, on the foundational morality of the legal system or on the possibility for incorporating a plurality of moral goods in defining what being an ethical lawyer requires in any given circumstance. In this book, we will not take a position on which principles or norms can best inform a lawyer's ethical decisions. Instead, we will present different conceptions of the lawyer's role. Students or practitioners can

---

[3]   These are the "four components" of ethical decision-making. See, in general, James Rest, *Development in Judging Moral Issues* (Minneapolis: University of Minnesota Press, 1979).

[4]   Alice Woolley, "Intuition and Theory in Legal Ethics Teaching" (2012) University of St. Thomas Law Journal [forthcoming]; David Luban, "Reason and Passion in Legal Ethics" (1999) 51 Stan. Law Rev. 873.

defensibly adopt any conception set out here, provided they do so with respect for its full complexity and the demands it actually places upon a lawyer. Moreover, students and practitioners who do this — who have a fully realized normative conception of what being a lawyer requires — will be better equipped to make morally defensible decisions in circumstances of ethical uncertainty, to reconcile their work as a lawyer with the broader goal of achieving an ethical life (a life well-lived), and to fulfill the function of the lawyer within a free and democratic society.

D. SOME WAYS OF THINKING ABOUT "NORMAL" ETHICS

The role of norms and principles means that lawyers' ethics is linked with general ways of thinking about what being ethical requires. Being an ethical lawyer is not just about applying "normal" ethics to legal practice; however, "normal" ways of thinking about ethical problems affect, and can helpfully inform, how we think about what being an ethical lawyer requires. This section provides a brief overview of the main philosophical schools of thought on ethics. In the readings listed at the end of this chapter, some of the primary sources for each of these schools of thought are also identified. In reading this overview, recall the two dimensions of ethics previously identified: ethics as a series of rules which constrain human behaviour, and ethics as a set of aspirations which, ideally, we attempt to achieve. General philosophies of ethics, like lawyers' ethics, attempt to explain and justify ethics in both senses.

1. Virtue Ethics

Aristotelian virtue ethics explains ethical action through the combination of human character, practical judgment and orientation towards human flourishing. It posits that individuals possess virtues (or vices) which orientate them towards (or away from) ethical conduct. Thus, for example, a person possessing the virtue of compassion will be disposed towards compassionate action.

The significance of virtues in virtue ethics is not that they have this effect; rather, it is that the possession and cultivation of the virtues contribute to human flourishing (*eudaimonia*). In addition, the possession of virtues is not sufficient in and of itself to ensure virtuous action. Rather, virtuous action will arise where an individual both possesses the virtues essential for such action *and* has the practical judgment (*phronesis*) essential for applying those virtues in a particular situation.

Thus, a lawyer possessed of the virtues necessary for legal practice, and faced with an ethical dilemma, will resolve that dilemma through exercising judgment about how those virtues are appropriately balanced in the circumstances. The lawyer will recognize the importance of the virtues of loyalty, honesty, care, compassion, justice and integrity to the situation, and will exercise judgment as to what those virtues require given the particular circumstances. Virtue ethics eschews the notion of specific rules as the source of ethical guidance — the Kantian position that, for example, because honesty is required by a categorical imperative, there are no circumstances in which a lie is justified — and argues instead that it is our virtues of character which, when exercised through our practical judgment, lead us to ethical action. Pursuit of the virtues is, ultimately, the precondition for human flourishing.

To understand the application of virtue ethics consider the following problem: Jack and Jane both work for a government agency responsible for combating terrorism. The agency has apprehended X, and has excellent grounds for believing that X and others have been conspiring to set off explosive devices at the Canadian National Exhibition on the following day. X's co-conspirators have not been found. If the devices are set off, many people will be injured and killed. X refuses to talk. Should Jack and Jane torture X to obtain information to prevent the execution of the conspiracy?

A virtue ethics based response to this problem would consider it through the applicable virtues which might include respect, dignity, compassion, justice and fairness. It would then assess the facts and how different responses to the facts (torture or not) would accord with the virtues. The ethical answer to the question would be that most consistent with the pursuit of the virtues as properly assessed through judgment of what the facts require.

2.   Utilitarianism (Consequentialism)

Virtue ethics clearly relies on a conception of human beings as constituted by a series of virtues and vices that motivate human action. Utilitarianism rests on starkly different premises about human nature: human beings want to maximize their self-interest and will seek to do so. Humans possess "instrumental rationality" — they can identify and will act to pursue their own interests. Utilitarianism also asserts the additional premise that a society in which overall human interests are maximized is the best society. The general aim of a society should be to achieve "the greatest good for the greatest number".

For the utilitarian, therefore, ethics is not a matter of abstract commitments to ideas of "right" or "wrong" — and certainly not to character-based assertions such as "virtue" or "vice". Rather, the most ethical action is that which is likely to do the greatest good for the greatest number or, where that is not possible, to do the least amount of harm to the fewest number of people. Utilitarianism is fundamentally and unabashedly consequentialist.

It must be noted, though, that utilitarianism does not necessarily require consequentialist analysis to occur on a case-by-case basis. "Indirect (rule) utilitarianism" posits that while it may be that the application of a particular rule does not maximize utility in a single instance, provided that the rule *in general* has that effect, then the rule is justified on utilitarian grounds. So, for example, although the requirement that lawyers keep their client's secrets in confidence may do harm in a particular case, if the overall rule maximizes social utility, the rule is justified, despite that individual case. In addition, utilitarian theory includes numerous assumptions which constrain the assessment of a particular act. For example, utilitarian theory requires "agent neutrality" — that the preferences of one person must not be privileged over the preferences of another. In addition, utilitarians such as John Stuart Mill argued that not all preferences are equal. Mill believed it reasonable to assert that some preferences were inherently more valuable than others, and thus entitled to greater weight in an assessment of an action's consequences. So, for example, Mill would suggest that a preference for providing competent legal service to a client is more valuable — worthy of greater weight in a utilitarian calculus — than a preference for sleeping in.

Further, in its most sophisticated forms, utilitarianism is not so much a means of reaching ethical decisions as it is a way of judging whether a decision is ethical. It may be that it is impossible to assess in advance the consequences of one's actions, or of a rule or policy governing human conduct. However, if after the fact it is apparent that an action has had terrible consequences, those consequences justify assessing the action as bad or unethical. For example, in the case of *R. v. Murray,*[5] excerpted later in this chapter and discussed in detail in Chapter 4, the lawyer Murray suppressed for a period of time videotapes showing his client, Paul Bernardo, and Karla Homolka committing horrific sexual violence against young women. In assessing the ethics of his act, it would be relevant in utilitarianism that one consequence of Murray's decision was that Karla Homolka escaped the criminal sanction she deserved because the Crown felt they had to offer her a favourable plea arrangement in return for her testimony against Bernardo. This consequence of Murray's choice indicates, in part, the ethical (or, more accurately, unethical) nature of that choice.

Finally, some modern consequentialists are willing to accept that consequentialism is not the only way of assessing conduct, or determining what is ethical. But they argue that any reasonable conception of what constitutes ethical action *must* take into account the consequences of that action. Even if we accept an action with horrible consequences as ultimately correct — for example, refusing to torture one person even though we know with certainty that doing so would save five others — we cannot ignore those horrible consequences in our assessment of the correctness of that action.

To understand the application of utilitarianism, consider again the Jack and Jane torture hypothetical. The utilitarian analysis of the problem would require consideration of the consequences of the torture choice. What will happen to X, to Jack and Jane, and to others if they torture X? What will happen to X, to Jack and Jane, and to others if they do not torture X? What would be the consequences of a rule permitting torture in this situation? What are the consequences of a rule prohibiting torture in this situation? The ethical response should aim to maximize the positive consequences, and minimize the negative consequences, that are possible given the facts at issue, and given the rules that could be developed to decide what to do in the face of those facts.

---

[5]   [2000] O.J. No. 2182 (Ont. S.C.J.).

3.   Kantian/Deontological Theories of Right Action

Kantian theories of right action — of deciding what is morally required — contrast starkly with both virtue ethics and utilitarianism (consequentialism). Unlike virtue ethics, Kantian theories are strongly rule-based; they assert the possibility and necessity of having universal rules that articulate what morality requires, and that can be applied to particular circumstances. Unlike consequentialism, Kantian theories reject the significance of consequences to the assessment of the morality of a course of conduct. If a rule applies to a circumstance, such as "do not torture", then that rule must be applied regardless of the consequences of doing so in a particular case.

However, like virtue ethics and consequentialism, Kantian theories rest on a particular understanding of human nature. For the Kantian, the essential relevant fact about human nature is that humans have the capacity for reasoning: freedom of choice and action. While what a particular person decides to do may be affected by personal desires or impulses, the existence of free will and the capacity to reason means that personal choice will not be *determined* by personal desires and impulses. Through the exercise of reasoning, a person can decide what to do or not do.

Any moral rule or duty must respect this fact. It must comply with what Kant calls the categorical imperative: the only principles which should guide your actions are those which could also hold as universal law, that is, those that could apply to every other free (reasoning) person. The fundamental moral requirement which follows from the application of the categorical imperative is that you must treat every person as having a free will, and you must not make any other person merely a means for the exercise of your own free will. You must treat every person as an end, and not merely as a means.

Kantian ethics also applies to Jack and Jill's ethical dilemma over whether to torture X, and unlike virtue ethics and utilitarianism, the answer it gives to the torture hypothetical would focus on articulation and application of the appropriate moral law as derived from the categorical imperative. Because the impetus for torture is entirely consequentialist, it is unlikely that a moral rule could justify it; torturing a person to achieve one's own (or society's) goal would seem a *prima facie* denial of that person's moral agency, and a treatment of him as merely a means.

4.   Postmodernism

Postmodernism is, fundamentally, a method of intellectual criticism; it does not posit a new way of ethical reasoning or a new definition of the content of ethical conduct. It simply notes the impossibility and/or implausibility of most traditional approaches to questions such as "what does it mean to be ethical?"

The central assumption of postmodernism is that the world is unknowable. It is possible to use language to describe things, but any description of the world is necessarily derived from the position of the person doing the describing (and will be understood from the position of the person hearing the description). Contrary to Kant, postmodernism asserts that a person cannot be removed from his or her desires and impulses; a person may choose not to pursue them, but their existence will necessarily shape and inform that person's analysis. Further, it is impossible to assess consequences with any degree of objectivity or certainty. Knowing what is good, even for one's self, is a situated assessment. It cannot be known in the abstract or with certainty.

Postmodernism does not reject the idea of ethics, nor does it assert that ethics is a waste of time, or that it is impossible to act ethically. What postmodernism identifies as impossible is a calculus through which moral ideas or judgments can be tested and perfected. It posits that ethical decisions must be made through individual judgment and moral intuitions, through the subjective viewpoint of the individual making them. An ethical individual will take responsibility for a decision that he or she makes, and be account-able for it, but he or she will not be aided in making that decision by abstract or objectively orientated attempts to follow a rule, or to assess the decision's consequences.

Thus, if Jack and Jill are postmodernists they must apply their individual judgment and moral intuitions to determine the ethical/rightful response to X. Further, and importantly, they must accept that they are the ones who made the decision and take responsibility for it. A postmodernist Jack and Jill must be prepared to explain why they decided to torture X (if they did so) and why they decided not to torture X (if they did not do so). No equation or analytical calculus will identify the correct solution to the problem for them — they must simply apply their intuitions and judgment, make a decision, provide justifications and take responsibility for the decision they have made.

5. Pluralism

Like postmodernism, pluralism rejects the monistic claims of consequential-ism and of Kantian deontology. It does not accept that a single premise — either as to the importance of consequences or to the importance of the human capacity to reason — can ground ethical decision-making. Rather, pluralism asserts both that there are various values, and, that there are various ways of identifying which values are important. Pluralism is *not* relativism; it does not accept that all values are equally valid or equally important. It simply asserts that the attempt to find a single unifying value or way of identifying values is misguided and impossible.

For the pluralist, the heart of ethical decision-making is not, therefore, the pursuit of a single value or source of action-guidance against which we can assess our decisions. Rather, the heart of ethical decision-making is the weighing and measuring of different — and occasionally conflicting — values in different circumstances, and the application of those values in order to decide what ethics requires given those circumstances. This may require, as did virtue ethics, the use of practical judgment. It does not necessarily do so, however. Some pluralists argue simply that in any given situation, we will scale the values and apply them: "We can work out trade-offs between different dimensions of pleasure or happiness. And when we do, we rank in a strong sense: not just choose one rather than the other, but regard it as worth more."[6]

The Jack and Jill pluralist is, like the postmodernist, also somewhat un-constrained in how to assess the torture problem. The pluralist may consider virtues, consequences and the possibility of applying a universal rule. A pluralist will not be neutral in assessing whether to torture X, but also will not be bound by one particular way of reasoning through the problem. In the end, like the postmodernist, the pluralist will be required to exercise judgment, to explain the decision and to take responsibility for what that person has done.

E.   WHAT DOES IT MEAN TO BE AN ETHICAL LAWYER?

For the remainder of this chapter, the focus is on the general question of what it means to be an ethical lawyer. In particular the following sections discuss some competing conceptions of what it means to be an ethical lawyer. In reading this section, you can consider what mode of ethical thought — virtue ethics, consequentialism, Kantianism, postmodernism or pluralism — best explains these competing conceptions, and would be most useful in attempt-ing to apply them to an actual ethical problem.

1.   Loyal Advocacy

Loyalty is the core moral requirement or value traditionally associated with legal practice. Commentators who emphasize the importance of loyalty have analogized the lawyer-client relationship to "friendship" in order to explain what loyalty requires:

> A lawyer is a friend in regard to the legal system. He is someone who enters into a personal relation with you — not an abstract relation as under the concept of justice. That means that like a friend he acts in your interests, not his own; or rather he adopts your interests as his own. I would call that the classic definition of friendship. To be sure, the lawyer's range of concern is sharply limited. But within that limited domain the intensity of the identifi-cation with the client's interests is the same.[7]

Loyalty brings two central obligations to the lawyer-client relationship. First, it requires the lawyer to place the interests of the client above those of other people. A lawyer will help the client to achieve goals despite the conse-quences for others. Second, it requires the lawyer to place the interests of the client above his or her own. As recently described by the Supreme Court: "A fundamental duty of a lawyer is to act in the best interest of his or her client to

---

[6]   J. Griffin, *Well-Being: Its Meaning, Measurement and Moral Importance* (Oxford: Clarendon Press, 1986) at 90.

[7]   C. Fried, "The Lawyer as Friend: The Moral Foundations of the Lawyer-Client Relation-ship" (1975) 85 Yale L.J. 1060 at 1071-72.

the exclusion of all other adverse interests, except those duly disclosed by the lawyer and willingly accepted by the client."[8]

Why does a lawyer have a duty of loyalty to a client? Those who place loyalty at the heart of the lawyer's ethical obligations often justify its importance for the protection of individual rights and freedoms. The thrust of this argument is that each individual in society is autonomous and, as such, is entitled to be free from unwarranted state interference. Maintaining one's autonomy from improper state interference requires every person to have the right to access the justice system. It is through lawyers that individuals access the justice system. Therefore, individuals have a right to a lawyer, and the lawyer who helps a client to access justice does an ethical act.

Further, a lawyer cannot provide meaningful help to the client without being loyal to his interests. A lawyer must do for the client what the client cannot do alone, namely, access the legal system to its full extent. Indeed, to do otherwise — to sacrifice a client to the goals of justice — is to fail to respect the autonomy of the client, and to act inconsistently with the loyalty to which the client is entitled.

More recently, the loyal advocacy position has shifted away from a focus on client autonomy. Instead, proponents of loyal advocacy emphasize the function of law as a means of achieving a civil society despite the fact that the people in any society will have deeply divergent conceptions of the right way to live. For law to function as a form of social compromise, to allow peaceful resolution of disputes and to enable, regulate or restrict individual action, it must be accessible to the citizenry. That accessibility requires lawyers, and it requires in particular lawyers who act in loyal furtherance of their client's interests.

In either case, the model of loyal advocacy does not contemplate unconstrained representation of client interests. Rather, it imposes limits on advocacy derived from the principles that justify it, namely that the purpose of advocacy is to allow clients to access the legal system. Thus, any act which does not further client access, which instead subverts or undermines the legal system, cannot be justified. Bradley Wendel, for example, argues that a lawyer's overarching ethical obligation is one of "fidelity to law". The role of the lawyer is not to substitute her moral judgment for that of a client, nor is it to simply do the client's bidding regardless of what the legal system itself requires. Instead, the lawyer's obligation is to assist her client to pursue that client's legal ends, and to do so in a manner consistent with what the legal system itself requires.

The following excerpt defends the loyal advocacy conception of the lawyer's role. Like most more recent defences of the loyal advocacy conception, it relies on the idea of law as a form of social settlement, arguing that the function of the lawyer is to help law achieve that purpose.

---

[8]   *Strother v. 3464920 Canada Inc.*, [2007] S.C.J. No. 24, [2007] 2 S.C.R. 177 at para. 1 (S.C.C.).

ALICE WOOLLEY

"In Defence of Zealous Advocacy"
Understanding Lawyers' Ethics in Canada
(Markham, ON: LexisNexis Canada, 2011) at 33-43
[footnotes omitted]

4.   THE ETHICAL JUSTIFICATION

The lawyer's role as a resolute advocate is thus both a long-standing feature of Canadian legal culture and one that flows from the norms of our legal system. Substantive legal doctrine in Canada validates the idea of the lawyer as resolute advocate but also rests on the concepts that make resolute advocacy sensible. This section considers (and rejects) the normative arguments against the lawyer as resolute advocate, and then outlines the broader normative foundations that justify resolute advocacy as a morally legitimate role for the lawyer.

A.   Arguments Against Resolute Advocacy

. . . . .

i.   *The Postmodern Objection*

[In this section Woolley critiques Trevor Farrow's "Sustainable Professionalism" article, excerpted on pages 53 to 61, arguing that it and other postmodernist articulations of the lawyer's role "try to have their ethical cake and throw it to the pigs too. They want to impose values on the lawyer, but only in a sort-of-kind-of-maybe way, one that allows the lawyer — and us — to duck the difficult questions about what we, as a society, think the right thing is for lawyers to do. Or, more individually, they duck the questions about what for the individual lawyer is the right thing to do — which choices will properly merit moral acclaim and which will properly merit moral disapprobation?"]

ii.   *The Personal Morality Objection*

Although similarly focused on the lawyer's exercise of individual judgment, the personal morality objection to zealous advocacy is not similarly reluctant to articulate what a lawyer seeking to be ethical should do. The personal morality objection starts from the premise that legality and morality are not co-terminus. There are some things that the law permits, and some that it even requires that are immoral. The law may permit a landlord to evict a tenant who has only technically violated the lease, and who has nowhere else to go. The landlord who makes that choice may nonetheless be categorized as acting immorally. And so too, the personal morality objectors argue, should the lawyer who helps the landlord to accomplish that eviction.

A lawyer is a moral agent, and does not lose his moral agency by virtue of being a lawyer. The professional obligation to be a zealous advocate within the bounds of the law may require the lawyer to assist clients pursue actions that can be judged as immoral, but to the extent that it does so the professional obligation does not give the lawyer a moral excuse; it gives the lawyer a moral problem which he has to resolve, one way or another. David Luban [excerpted on pages 36 to 50], the best of those writing from the personal morality objection, argues that while a lawyer may operate under a "presumption in favor of professional obligation" that presumption can be rebutted and, in the end, "when professional and serious moral obligation conflict, moral obligation takes precedence." Moreover, those moral obligations take precedence even where the lawyer may have to ignore legal requirements imposed on him as a lawyer: "When serious moral obligation conflicts with professional obligation, the lawyer must become a civil disobedient to professional rules." Luban acknowledges that a lawyer is unlikely to make that choice, but his point is to take apart the argument from zealous advocacy that would make that choice unnecessary.

The first difficulty with the personal morality objection is that it places an enormous trust in lawyer morality, while placing almost no trust at all in the morality of the laws and legal system within which lawyers work. Yet individual lawyer morality both reflects and influences the laws and legal system, and cannot be so neatly separated from them.

The second and related difficulty with the personal morality objection is that, in contra-distinction to the postmodernist problem, it both does not account for the possibility of deep moral disagreement amongst people, nor acknowledge the extent to which the law exists as a way of allowing people with deep moral disagreements to live in peace together. The personal morality objection does not live in a morally simplistic universe, but it does assert the possibility of universal moral claims on the basis of which lawyers can reliably make ethical decisions. Moreover, it does not give much credit to the possibility that law, as a statement of our actual compromises and joint conclusions on how we will live together, has itself a claim to respect, even where it conflicts with an individual's deeply held moral commitments. It rejects the idea that the rule of law can itself make a moral claim. It suggests, instead, that "the legal profession can properly regard itself as an oligarchy, whose duty is to nullify decisions made by the people's duly elected representatives".

The philosopher Jeremy Waldron sets out the problem with both these assertions: that which reduces the significance of our moral disagreements, and that which disregards the achievement of the law. First, while not arguing against moral agreement *per se*, Waldron questions the extent to which moral consensus exists, even within our most basic moral concepts. On matters as apparently obvious as the moral prohibition on rape, serious moral disagreement is still possible with respect to specific issues such as marital rape, consent, mistaken but honest belief in consent, the age of consent and so on. The function of law (and, Waldron argues, of political institutions which give rise to law) is to provide us with some way of resolving these difficult questions, even when we disagree, and disagree strongly about the moral perspectives that different answers reflect. Without law, we are left with nothing but our original disagreement and the need to resolve that disagreement with whatever crude and potentially violent means are at our disposal.

What follows from Waldron's analysis is the identification of law as something in and of itself worthy of our attention and respect. A lawyer's own personal disagreement with what the law permits or requires speaks to that lawyer's own personal moral values, but the whole point of law is to provide both an actual settlement to controversies over the right way to live, and to allow people the freedom, under and through the law, to live as they like. To ignore the authority of the law based on a personal assessment that a different moral answer is required, is to undermine legality altogether.

iii. The Morality-of-Law Objection

This response to the personal morality objection leads, though, to the morality of law objection to resolute advocacy. The morality-of-law objector looks to this point and says, "Yes! And the problem with resolute advocacy is that it also does not take the moral compromise of law seriously, but instead engages in legal trickery and tomfoolery, to obtain for clients results that the law does not properly permit." William Simon provides a uniquely rigorous articulation of the morality-of-law objection. Simon argues that lawyers are properly advocates for clients, but they are advocates within the context of ensuring that, in each case, the lawyer takes those "actions that, considering the relevant circumstances of the particular case, seem likely to promote justice". Simon does not view justice as a moral value existing apart from the law; he views it as part and parcel of the legal system — justice is "legal merit". Similarly, in the Canadian context, David Tanovich has argued that the obligation of the lawyer is to pursue justice:

> Justice can be defined, for the purposes of the lawyering process, *as the correct resolution of legal disputes or problems in a fair, responsible, and non-discriminatory manner.* This approach to justice has both procedural and substantive elements. The procedural component is the right to a fair and non-discriminatory process that is capable of producing the result demanded by the law. The substantive component involves assessing the merit of the legal claim as seen through the lens of the law properly interpreted. A proper interpretation is one that gives effect to the purpose behind the legal provision and which ensures that the provision is consistent with other substantive legal norms such as equality, fairness, and harm reduction. It is also one that pays special attention to our history of injustice. [emphasis in original]

On its face, this re-working of resolute advocacy has much to recommend it. It can, arguably, be interpreted as simply a direction for lawyers to do their job well, to get the law right. It takes law seriously, and also provides lawyers with a way of making decisions that they are professionally competent to make.

The problem arises, though, when we unpack a little further what is meant by "legal merit" or by the invocation of substantive norms such as "equality, fairness and harm reduction" to guide our legal interpretation. Consider this example: A lawyer is acting for a mother in a child custody and support dispute. The mother is on welfare. The father is absent much of the time, and suffers from some issues related to mental illness that compromise his fitness as a parent. In a meeting between the lawyer and his client about a week before financial disclosure is required, the client tells her lawyer that she is also working as a prostitute to better financially support herself and her son; her sister is helping with childcare so the son can be looked after while his mother is working. The client tells the lawyer that he cannot disclose her extra work to the father, welfare authorities or the court.

What does legal merit require in a case such as this? It clearly does not permit the lawyer to provide false financial disclosure to the court or to the father. It also does not permit the lawyer to disclose the client's past welfare fraud. The law with respect to false representations and maintenance of these sorts of confidences is clear. But does it permit the lawyer to avoid disclosure altogether by quickly negotiating a generous settlement with the father, one which is nonetheless less advantageous than the father would get if he had full information and went to court? The law permits this result — settlements are a legally recognized way of resolving legal disputes, and no fraud or misrepresentation is being used to achieve the settlement. But is it consistent with legal merit? Does it achieve equality, fairness and the reduction of harm? There are good arguments for and against this course of action in terms of substantial legal merit, arguments which turn on an assessment of what is in the best interests of the child (which is the applicable legal standard), what the purpose and form of the custody and support laws require, and so on.

But that means, I would suggest, that under our system of laws we have also reached the point where the decision as to what to do is properly given to the client — to the person allowed to be self-determining under and through the system of laws — not to the lawyer. If the law permits a course of action, and what constitutes legal merit is contentious, then the decision as to what should be done should be given to the person whose interests are at stake, not to the lawyer. The problem with the morality of law argument is that, in the end, it gives the lawyer the privilege of determining what can be done under and through the law, rather than leaving that privilege where it should be: with the person whose self-determination the law respects and facilitates.

B.   In Defence of the Lawyer as Resolute Advocate

By now the basis for my argument in favour of the lawyer as resolute advocate should be clear. It turns on an assertion of law as something that can make an authoritative claim against our actions, not simply by virtue of the power of the state to enforce it, but because the law, in and of itself, is worthy of our respect and attention. It is worthy of our attention because it is through the law that we achieve a civil society, one in which our disagreements are resolved through politics and adjudication, not through riots, violence and discord: "People who have grievances against one another come to lawyers as an alternative to resorting to physical violence." Whether the claim to authority that law makes is itself a moral claim, or not, is not one that I am attempting to resolve here. But I am claiming that the law is authoritative, in terms of setting out our collective decisions on what we are forbidden from doing, what we are tolerated or permitted to do, and, finally, what we are encouraged to do or facilitated in doing.

Why does this lead to resolute advocacy? Resolute advocacy has two central features. First, it places decision-making about what is to be done in a legal representation with the client. The lawyer acts to facilitate the client's accomplishment of her ends within the legal system, but it is the client who determines those ends. Second, resolute advocacy requires the lawyer to interpret and work through the law to achieve the client's goals. These features both follow from this authority claim for law. Because if law has the function of resolving disagreements between those to whom it applies, and of constraining, tolerating and encouraging conduct in those to whom it applies, then the decision about how to live within that legal framework lies with the person subject to it. If I am to decide not only how I am to live under and through the law, but also to decide how my neighbour lives under and through the law, then the law has ceased to achieve its essential function. It is not resolving disagreements between my neighbour and me; I am. And similarly for the relationship between the lawyer and the client: if the lawyer decides what the client may, must or should do, instead of simply assisting the client determine what the law permits or requires the client to do, the lawyer will have similarly usurped the law's function in resolving disagreement.

Further, to make the civil compromise of the law functional, the client must be given the means to access that civil compromise, in terms of knowing what the law means, of accessing the systems of dispute resolution that the law provides, and in terms of enforcing her legal rights and claims against others, including the state. Lawyers, in acting as resolute advocates within the bounds of the law, allow clients to achieve this access. This also means, though, that in representing a client a lawyer must engage in good faith interpretation of the law, and work within the systems of the law as they exist — if the lawyer burns documents that are properly producible in discoveries, for example, then the lawyer has not allowed the client to access the civic compromise of the law, he has helped the client to destroy it.

This leads to the other assertion that underlies the claim in favour of resolute advocacy, which is that the law is sufficiently complex that it requires the assistance of a lawyer, yet is also sufficiently capable of meaningful interpretation that the lawyer can provide assistance to the client. The first of these premises is self-evident. The second is more difficult, and requires demonstrating that the law is something which precludes certain interpretations as unreasonable, as falling outside the "range of possible, acceptable outcomes".

Providing an explanation in favour of the meaningfulness of law sufficient to convince a sceptic is not possible in this context. Suffice it to say that if meaningfully interpreting the law is impossible, then we should all — lawyers, law students and legal academics — abandon the enterprise. If meaning in law cannot be engaged with, and at minimum some interpretations of the law rejected as unsustainable and bogus — as the equivalent of asserting a belief in fairies — then there is nothing that we have to offer anyone, whether it be clients, ourselves or the public interest in general. The debates of legal ethics are meaningless, and all that is left is determining what side to take in the power struggle within which we reside. I would suggest that if that is where the argument has gone, then it has gone so far as to disprove itself.

The functioning of the legal system itself, the absence of our collapse into armed conflict to resolve our disputes, means that, one way or another, we have managed to act for a very long time as if the law does say something meaningful that we can ascertain. The law may be open to a wide range of interpretations, but the boundaries of that range are ascertainable to the ordinarily competent lawyer. The role of the lawyer is, therefore, to act within that range on behalf of her client.

What, though, of the various examples given at the beginning of this chapter, and the suggestion that at the very least a lawyer who, for example, tries to make a truthful witness look like a liar, or invites a finder of fact to draw an inference from evidence the lawyer knows is untrue, has done something that is morally doubtful? The final point to be made in favour of resolute advocacy is that the morality of an action taken within a professional role is simply not assessed at the level of the act itself. What needs to be morally justified is, instead, the professional role. What has been offered here, is that sort of moral justification. The role of the lawyer is morally justified, because of the civil compromise that is law, and because of the necessity of the lawyer to achieving that civil compromise. What this means, is that any action that is required by the lawyer's role is also morally justified.

That does not make the life of the lawyer morally uncomplicated. The tension between personally felt moral obligation and professional role is real, and cannot be reduced simply by the assertion of the moral justification for the role. To use an example given by the philosopher Timothy Chappell, suppose the officer of a wrecked ship decides, when faced with a full lifeboat, that his obligations as an officer require him to actively prevent other survivors from climbing aboard. His actions help to contribute to the death of those survivors, but protect the lives of the people on board, which would otherwise have been endangered. Let's assume, as well, that the officer is correct in his assessment of what his role requires, and that a moral justification for the role of ship's officer can be given. As Chappell notes, it would nonetheless show a comprehensive failure to understand the situation to address the officer's subsequent remorse and guilt by saying "why are you so upset? You did what your role requires." The existence of a role justification does not eliminate the moral complexity that the role brings with it. The task of the lawyer … is to learn to live with that moral complexity, as best as he or she can.

And as will be apparent throughout the remainder of this book, there are many ways in which a lawyer can manage this moral complexity, and reduce the moral tension that the role of the lawyer creates. While lawyers are constrained to act as resolute advocates for their clients, they have discretion when choosing their clients. Further, determining what a client wants — what are her ends, in fact — is in itself a complicated exercise, and a lawyer can legitimately engage in serious discussion with his client about what is an appropriate course of action within the constraints of the law. A mistake sometimes made by lawyers is to assume that they know what their client wants, and that their client wants every advantage the law permits. Finally, the lawyer does in some circumstances have the opportunity to withdraw from representation.

. . . . .

NOTES AND QUESTIONS

1.   In making this argument, Woolley on the one hand wants to deny that law can have identifiable moral values that the lawyer can protect (the Simon/Tanovich view) while on the other hand asserting that law can impose a meaningful restriction on how lawyers represent clients. Is that distinction justifiable?

2.   Assume that a lawyer is faced with a client who wants to pursue a course of conduct that the lawyer does not believe that the law, interpreted in good faith, permits. Which is more likely to influence the lawyer in that situation: the lawyer's felt loyalty to the client, or the lawyer's abstract commitment of loyalty to the law? Does this theory require that the lawyer balance personal loyalty with abstract loyalty, and is doing so realistic, or is it a model doomed to failure in practice? That is, is it likely to result in unconstrained loyal advocacy?

3.   Woolley relies on the concept of "good faith interpretation" as a core constraint on lawyers' ethics. How helpful is this tool? Are lawyers comfortable with "good faith" standards? Is "good faith" to be measured on an objective or subjective standard?

4.   Woolley seems to contemplate that lawyers simply apply or access the law. Yet it can also reasonably be argued that lawyers *make* law. If that is so, then to what should the lawyers appeal when taking steps for clients that will make law? Need the lawyers attempt to achieve justice? Or should they simply follow the client's instructions?

Compare and contrast the concept of the lawyer as loyal advocate set out by Woolley with the approach of the Supreme Court of Canada in the following case.

R. v. NEIL

[2002] S.C.J. No. 72, [2002] 3 S.C.R. 631
(S.C.C., Major, Bastarache, Binnie, Arbour and LeBel JJ.)

[The appellant brought an application for a stay of proceedings in his criminal trial on the basis that there had been an abuse of process. The abuse arose from a conflict of interest of the law firm that initially represented him and that ultimately represented a co-accused. The specific facts and legal principles arising from this case are discussed again with respect to conflicts of interest in Chapter 5.]

BINNIE J.: —

. . . . .

Appellant's counsel reminds us of the declaration of an advocate's duty of loyalty made by Henry Brougham, later Lord Chancellor, in his defence of Queen Caroline against the charge of adultery brought against her by her husband, King George IV. He thus addressed the House of Lords:

> [A]n advocate, in the discharge of his duty, knows but one person in all the world, and that person is his client. To save that client by all means and expedients, and at all hazards and costs to other persons, and, among them, to himself, is his first and only duty; and in performing this duty he must not regard the alarm, the torments, the destruction which he may bring upon others. Separating the duty of a patriot from that of an advocate, he must go on reckless of consequences, though it should be his unhappy fate to involve his country in confusion ...

These words are far removed in time and place from the legal world in which the Venkatraman law firm carried on its practice, but the defining principle — the duty of loyalty — is with us still. It endures because it is essential to the integrity of the administration of justice and it is of high public importance that public confidence in that integrity be maintained: ... Unless a litigant is assured of the undivided loyalty of the lawyer, neither the public nor the litigant will have confidence that the legal system, which may appear to them to be a hostile and hideously complicated environment, is a reliable and trustworthy means of resolving their disputes and controversies: ... As O'Connor J.A. (now A.C.J.O.) observed:

> ... the relationship of counsel and client requires clients, typically untrained in the law and lacking the skills of advocates, to entrust the management and conduct of their cases to the counsel who act on their behalf. There should be no room for doubt about counsel's loyalty and dedication to the client's case.

. . . . .

The duty of loyalty is intertwined with the fiduciary nature of the lawyer-client relationship. One of the roots of the word fiduciary is *fides*, or loyalty, and loyalty is often cited as one of the defining characteristics of a fiduciary: ... The lawyer fulfills squarely Professor Donovan Waters' definition of a fiduciary:

> In putting together words to describe a "fiduciary" there is of course no immediate obstacle. Almost everybody would say that it is a person in whom trust and confidence is placed by another on whose behalf the fiduciary is to act. The other (the beneficiary) is entitled to expect that the fiduciary will be concerned solely for the beneficiary's interests, never the fiduciary's own. The "relationship" must be the dependence or reliance of the beneficiary upon the fiduciary ... .

Fiduciary duties are often called into existence to protect relationships of importance to the public including, as here, solicitor and client. Disloyalty is destructive of that relationship.

. . . . .

The aspects of the duty of loyalty relevant to this appeal do include issues of confidentiality in the *Canada Trust* matters, but engage more particularly three other dimensions:

(i)   the duty to avoid conflicting interests ... including the lawyer's personal interest

(ii) a duty of commitment to the client's cause (sometimes referred to as "zealous representation") from the time counsel is retained, not just at trial, i.e. ensuring that a divided loyalty does not cause the lawyer to "soft peddle" his or her defence of a client out of concern for another client ... and,

(iii) a duty of candour with the client on matters relevant to the retainer ... If a conflict emerges, the client should be among the first to hear about it ...

NOTES AND QUESTIONS

1.   The context of *Neil* was a conflict of interest arising from a law firm's representation of two individuals implicated in a crime. Does the statement of the Court that a lawyer must not "soft peddle" his or her representation of a client apply more generally? Would a lawyer act ethically were he or she to refuse to cross-examine a witness having a history of psychiatric illness on that topic because the lawyer believes that the witness is speaking truthfully?

2.   The Court in *Neil* referenced the idea of "zealous representation". In Canada, however, the obligation placed on lawyers by the Federation of Law Societies is one of "resolute" advocacy. Do you think there is any meaningful distinction between being "zealous" and being "resolute"? Is there some other terminology that would be better?

In her dissenting judgment in *Strother*,[9] McLachlin C.J.C. argued that it is improper to "superimpose" a fiduciary duty of loyalty beyond that contracted for between the parties. Justice Binnie, writing for the majority, disagreed, holding that fiduciary duties "may include obligations that go beyond what the parties expressly bargained for".[10] The duty of loyalty to a client can arise under contract, but more obviously arises under the fiduciary obligation. Consider whether McLachlin C.J.C.'s or Binnie J.'s approach to a lawyer's obligations is preferable in light of the following case.

SZARFER v. CHODOS

[1986] O.J. No. 256, 54 O.R. (2d) 663
(Ont. H.C.J., Callaghan A.C.J.H.C.)

[The defendant Chodos was the plaintiff Szarfer's lawyer in a personal injury claim. In the course of his representation of the plaintiff, the defendant

9   *Strother v. 3464920 Canada Inc.*, [2007] S.C.J. No. 24, [2007] 2 S.C.R. 177 (S.C.C.).
10   *Ibid.*, at para. 34.

learned about difficulties in the plaintiff's marriage. The defendant knew the plaintiff's wife because she had worked for him occasionally as a legal secretary. In May 1981, the defendant and the plaintiff's wife had an affair, which lasted approximately six weeks. The plaintiff discovered the affair and was devastated. He had existing psychological problems of which the defendant was also aware as a result of his representation. The plaintiff and his wife ultimately reconciled.]

CALLAGHAN A.C.J.H.C.: —

Nature of claim

The plaintiff claims general, special and punitive damages from the defendant as a result of an alleged breach of fiduciary duty arising from their relationship as solicitor and client. The plaintiff claims the defendant utilized confidential information for his own advantage and placed his personal interest in conflict with his duties as a fiduciary. In addition, the plaintiff pleads that the defendant's conduct was a breach of the contract between the parties resulting in damages. In the alternative, the plaintiff claims the defendant having full knowledge of the vulnerable mental and physical condition of the plaintiff, acted in wanton disregard of such knowledge and inflicted mental suffering on the plaintiff thereby committing an intentional tort or, alternatively, the defendant acted negligently in inflicting the aforesaid injury thereby causing the damage claimed.

. . . . .

Law

The fiduciary relationship between a lawyer and his client forbids a lawyer from using any confidential information obtained by him for the benefit of himself or a third person or to the disadvantage of his client. The crucial question for decision is whether or not the defendant used confidential information for his own purposes or to the disadvantage of the plaintiff. It is conceded that the defendant was in a fiduciary relationship with the plaintiff and owed him all the duties of a fiduciary. The highest and clearest duty of a fiduciary is to act to advance the beneficiary's interest and avoid acting to his detriment. A fiduciary cannot permit his own interest to come into conflict with the interest of the beneficiary of the relationship. The equitable principle is stated in Waters, *Law of Trusts in Canada*, 2nd ed. (1984), at p. 710:

> It is a fundamental principle of every developed legal system that one who undertakes a task on behalf of another must act exclusively for the benefit of the other, putting his own interests completely aside. In the common law system this duty may be enforceable by way of an action by the principal upon the contract of agency, but the modes in which the rule can be breached are myriad, many of them in situations other than contract and therefore beyond the control of the law of contract. It was in part to meet such situations that Equity fashioned the rule that no man may allow his duty to conflict with his interest. Stated in this way, Equity has been able since the sixteenth century to provide a remedy for a whole range of cases where the person with a task to perform has used the opportunity to benefit himself.

While Equity first conceived of the rule in relation to trustees the principle applies to anyone who undertakes a task on behalf of another and is applicable to a wide and varied range of persons including lawyers ... The breadth of the application of the principle is referred to in Waters, *supra*, at p. 731:

> Private advantage gained through direct dealing with the trust property, while the most familiar abuse of the trustee's office, is not the only conduct resulting in personal benefit which Equity regards as a breach of the duty of loyalty. There are many and various ways in which trustees and other fiduciaries can derive personal benefit, as the authorities demonstrate, and they range from the acceptance of secret commissions and bribes to the use of confidential information for personal gain. In a sense these various activities cannot be distinguished. The acceptance of a bribe or a secret commission, which are examples of obvious profiteering, is a manifestation of the same wrongful act *as the exploitation of office in more sophisticated ways.*

(Emphasis added.) Once the fiduciary relationship is established, as it is in this case, the onus is on the trustee to prove that he acted reasonably and made no personal use whatsoever of the confidential information.

. . . . .

In engaging in sexual intercourse with the plaintiff's wife, the defendant was acting in his own interest and to his personal benefit. I cannot help but conclude that his actions were also to the detriment of his client's interest. Upon discovery of the affair, the client's trust in the solicitor was destroyed. Such conduct which vitiates trust, the essential element of a solicitor-client relationship, and results in physical injury to the client, is a breach of the conflict-of-interest rule referred to above. The defendant has not discharged the onus of proving that he acted reasonably in the circumstances. That in itself is sufficient to hold him liable for damages.

Furthermore, however, I am satisfied that he used confidential information for his own purposes in order to obtain the delights and benefits of the affair. The defendant had known Mrs. Szarfer since 1977 but had no sexual relationship with her until May of 1981. He did not acquire details of the Szarfers' marital and sexual problems until March or April of 1981. At that time he obtained the intimate knowledge of the emotional and mental problems of both the plaintiff and his wife. He obtained such information as part of the process of the wrongful dismissal action. The plaintiff's mental state and the plaintiff's sexual problem were issues in that action. As a solicitor he undertook to prosecute the claim for wrongful dismissal including a claim for damages for mental distress and the state of the marriage and all the information related above was an indivisible part of the task undertaken by him as a solicitor. Again, he was aware of Mrs. Szarfer's vulnerability as a result of the information he obtained about the marriage. I have not accepted the defendant's denial that he did not have any information respecting the marriage except financial nor can I overlook his denial of not knowing of the possibility of the marriage break-up even though his trial notes disclosed that he intended to examine on that very issue at trial of the wrongful dismissal action. These matters together with the time factors involved have led me to conclude that the defendant in fact did use the confidential information that he obtained from the plaintiff and his wife for his own purposes and I so find. In so doing, the defendant was in breach of his professional duty to his client, the plaintiff, and that breach was the cause of the plaintiff's post-traumatic neurosis. The breach constituted professional negligence and demonstrated an unreasonable lack of skill and fidelity in his professional and fiduciary duties as a lawyer.

. . . . .

NOTES AND QUESTIONS

1. If Chodos had no particular knowledge of the vulnerability of the Szarfers' marriage, but had simply had an affair with the wife of his client, should the result in the case have been the same? Assuming that it would not — that the breach of confidentiality was central to the finding of a breach of fiduciary duty — would Chodos' actions be considered unethical? Would the commencement of the affair in those circumstances be a violation of his duty of loyalty to his client?

2. Chodos was sued by his former client for breach of a fiduciary obligation. Should he also have been subject to discipline by the Law Society?

3. Individuals who are called to the Bar in Alberta swear the following oath:

> I will as a Barrister and Solicitor conduct all causes and matters faithfully and to the best of my ability. I will not seek to destroy anyone's property. I will not promote suits upon frivolous pretences. I will not pervert the law to favour or prejudice anyone, but in all things will conduct myself truly and with integrity. I will uphold and maintain the Sovereign's interest and that of my fellow citizens according to the law in force in Alberta.

Is this oath consistent with the identification of loyalty as a primary ethical obligation for lawyers?

Scenario Three

Alex Smith is a client of Leslie Jones. Alex retains Leslie to provide legal advice regarding Alex's plan to open a restaurant and bar and, in particular, with respect to compliance with municipal by-laws. The restaurant and bar prove to be a great success. Three years later, Leslie decides to leave legal practice and become a restaurant proprietor. Using her knowledge of municipal by-laws gained in her representation of Alex, she builds a restaurant/bar two doors down from Alex. The venture is a success and significantly undermines Alex's profitability. Are Leslie's actions ethical?

Scenario Four

Frank Johnson is a client of Hilary Smith. Frank is selling the public company in which he is a major shareholder and CEO. On Hilary's advice, he structures part of his payment from the purchaser as a "non-compete" agreement as this will result in a preferable tax treatment. The transaction is legitimate from a tax perspective; however, Frank ends up being charged with various offences under securities legislation for his failure to properly disclose the payments to shareholders. Hilary is asked to testify about the advice she gave him. During her testimony she responds honestly but makes every effort to distance herself from the transaction, and from Frank. Is Hilary's conduct ethical? See "Media execs chose to disclose payments", *Associated Press* (April 13, 2007).

2. The Lawyer as Moral Agent in Pursuit of Justice

The emphasis on loyalty as the central norm of ethical practice arguably suffers from two weaknesses. First, while there is much authority in support of the significance of loyalty to the lawyer-client relationship, there is also significant authority emphasizing the importance of other values. Notably, the word "loyalty" appears only four times in the Federation of Law Societies' *Model Code of Professional Conduct*, while the word "justice" appears 31 times. The *Model Code* imposes obligations such as: "A lawyer must encourage public respect for and try to improve the administration of justice" and "Admission to and continuance in the practice of law implies, on the part of a lawyer, a basic commitment to the concept of equal justice for all within an open, ordered and impartial system" (see Rule 4.06(1) and Commentary).

Second, the emphasis on loyal advocacy — especially its central features of advocacy for a client's interests and the absence of moral accountability for a client's aims — has been criticized for creating moral malaise and unethical conduct within the legal profession. Leading American legal ethicists, including David Luban, Robert Gordon and William Simon, have argued for a re-orientation of the model of the ethical lawyer away from loyal advocacy and towards a model under which the lawyer retains moral agency and responsibility for what she does when acting for a client. Gordon argues that lawyers must retain and use their independent judgment of whether a client's proposed course of action is just. Luban argues that an ethical lawyer cannot have an unqualified commitment either to zealous partisanship or to moral non-accountability. While the role morality of the lawyer can make a claim upon her, she can never escape the claims that ordinary moral principles make against all of us.

Simon defines the central moral principle governing lawyering as justice: "The lawyer should take those actions that, considering the relevant circumstances of the particular case, seem most likely to promote justice. This 'seek justice' maxim suggests a kind of noncategorical judgment that might be called pragmatist, ad hoc, or dialectical, but that I will call discretionary."[11] Simon defines justice as equivalent to legal merit, and argues that lawyers should only represent those clients whose cases are meritorious relative to other individuals whom the lawyer could represent. Further, a lawyer should "make her best effort to achieve the most appropriate resolution in each case".[12]

---

[11] William Simon, "Ethical Discretion in Lawyering" (1988) 101 Harv. L. Rev. 1083 at 1090.
[12] *Ibid.*

The difference between Simon and Luban is that Simon emphasizes the moral claims of the law, suggesting that the law, correctly interpreted, is co-extensive with morality. Luban, as set out in the following excerpt, sees law and morality as at points in irreducible conflict, with the result that a lawyer must choose between them. While the law has a claim that the lawyer can normally accede to, in some circumstances the lawyer can only ethically follow the dictates of morality, not of law.

The following case arguably demonstrates the strength of both Luban and Simon's point of view, insofar as it suggests that a lawyer who focuses exclusively on the interests of his client may improperly lose sight of other moral values, including the obligations imposed by the lawyer's legal duty to protect the fair administration of justice. Following the case will be an excerpt from Luban's famous critique of zealous advocacy, and his assertion of the irreducible importance of ordinary morality. When reading Luban's critique consider whether his view, or Simon's, would have better helped Murray to avoid the ethical morass in which he found himself.

R. v. MURRAY

[2000] O.J. No. 2182, 48 O.R. (3d) 544
(Ont. S.C.J., Gravely J.)

GRAVELY J.: —

The accused, Kenneth Murray, is a member of the Ontario Bar and certified as a specialist in criminal litigation by the Law Society of Upper Canada. He was retained by Paul Bernardo initially in February 1993 in regard to the "Scarborough Rapes" and on May 18, 1993, in connection with the murders of Leslie Mahaffy and Kristen French and additional related offences.

On May 6, 1993, on written instructions of Bernardo, Murray attended at the Bernardo home and removed from it videotapes which depicted gross sexual abuse of Kristen French, Leslie Mahaffy, Jane Doe and Tammy Homolka. Without disclosing their existence to the Crown, he retained the tapes for 17 months. Trial motions were to begin on September 12, 1994. On September 2, 1994, Murray, through his counsel, applied to the Law Society of Upper Canada for advice. Accepting that advice Murray appeared before the trial judge, Associate Chief Justice LeSage (now Chief Justice S.C.O.), who directed that the tapes, their integrity protected by suitable undertakings, go to John Rosen, new counsel for Bernardo, at which time Murray was given leave to withdraw as counsel. Rosen, on September 22, 1994, turned the tapes over to the police and they were used by Crown counsel at the trial. A jury found Bernardo guilty on all charges.

Murray now faces this charge of attempt to obstruct justice by concealment of the videotapes.

PART TWO - THE FACTS

. . . . .

57 BAYVIEW DRIVE

Before his arrest Bernardo lived with his wife, Karla Homolka, in a rented house at 57 Bayview Drive, St. Catharines, Ontario. Between February and April 1993 the police, for 71 days, conducted an intensive search of the premises, virtually destroying the interior of the house in the process. On April 30, 1993 the final search warrant expired and on May 4, Doyle, MacDonald and John Lefurgey (a local lawyer assisting the defence team) attended at 57 Bayview with consent of the landlords to assess the condition of the house, videotape the interior and decide what possessions of the Bernardos should be removed. The landlords agreed that the defence team could return on May 6, to remove the Bernardo belongings. They were also, at that time, to be allowed 20 minutes alone in the house in order to confer as to which of the Bernardo possessions might have some relevance to the defence and thus should be taken away.

THE REMOVAL OF THE VIDEOTAPES

On May 6, MacDonald and Doyle [who were working with Murray on the case] went to 57 Bayview at 8:30 a.m. and, with the assistance of the landlords, began to pack up the Bernardo personal effects. Murray said that on his way to 57 Bayview he got lost and, in attempting to telephone MacDonald for directions, discovered in his slipcase an unsealed envelope given to him on May 3, by MacDonald. It contained a letter from Bernardo, which was wrapped around a sealed envelope. The letter read:

> The following is to be opened only and only if you have entered 57 Bay-view. It is instructions on what is probably in the house that we need for our defence. Alone they may first appear to be irrelevant and thus overlooked but together they can be very important. Note: if we can't have access then return the letter intact.
>
> What I was worried about is I would be moved and hidden for a few days until our possession of the house was up. [underlining in original]
>
> . . . . .

Murray arrived at 57 Bayview at 11:00 a.m. and, as agreed with the landlords, the defence team was given time alone in the house. Murray then opened the sealed envelope, which contained a map and directions to assist in locating six eight-millimetre videotapes.

Referring to his note and map, Murray led the way to the bathroom and started to take apart a pot light while Doyle and MacDonald watched from the doorway. Unsuccessful in finding anything behind the light, he handed the Bernardo instructions to Doyle, who directed him to another pot light. Murray climbed onto the vanity, dismantled the light and was successful in retrieving six eight-millimetre videotapes. He then reassembled the light and placed the videotapes in his slip case. Doyle and MacDonald hugged each other and Doyle whispered to MacDonald, "what have we got?"

The defence team had lunch together on the balcony of 57 Bayview. Murray told Doyle and MacDonald that they would have to make sure that no one found out about the tapes, and the three of them would have to make a pact that they would be the only ones that ever knew what had been obtained. They shook hands, hugged, and agreed not to say anything to anyone about the tapes. Murray said in his evidence that he knew "they wouldn't tell anybody about the tapes". He felt the discovery of the tapes was a "bonanza" or "gold mine" for the defence.

Murray said MacDonald and Bernardo made up the code words on the instruction letter. "How about those Leafs?" was to be the signal that the search was unsuccessful while "How about those Jays?" meant that the tapes were found. In the afternoon of May 6, Bernardo telephoned Murray at 57 Bayview who said to him, "How about those Jays?"

With the map and directions there was a note from Bernardo that said: "... although we will have to go through them in the future. At this time I instruct you not to view them".

Murray, MacDonald and Doyle packed and removed a large number of items from the house. Murray locked the tapes in a safe or a credenza at his office.

THE HOMOLKA RESOLUTION AGREEMENT -
BERNARDO CHARGED WITH MURDERS

On May 14, 1993 Homolka's defence counsel and Crown counsel entered into a six-page written agreement. Homolka would plead guilty to two counts of manslaughter in relation to the deaths of Kristen French and Leslie Mahaffy, there would be a joint submission that she be sentenced to 12 years imprisonment and she would provide evidence to assist the Crown.

Sometime between May 14 and 17, 1993 the defence team learned about the charges against Homolka and her release on bail and made the assumption that Homolka had entered into an arrangement with the Crown.

On May 18, 1993 Bernardo was charged with two counts of first-degree murder and additional related offences. Homolka was charged with two counts of manslaughter. Murray's retainer was extended to include the additional charges against Bernardo. Bernardo signed an authorization directing Murray to review the videotapes, make copies and use the tapes as Murray deemed appropriate in Bernardo's outstanding criminal matters.

THE CRITICAL TAPES

Of the six videotapes, two ("the critical tapes") form the basis of the charge against Murray.

The critical tapes are indescribably horrible. Leslie Mahaffy was 14 years of age and Kristen French 15 when they were abducted and murdered by Bernardo, assisted by Homolka. The tapes show each of them being forced to participate with Bernardo and Homolka in the grossest sexual perversions. In the course of sexual assaults they are forced to pretend they are enjoying the experience through scripted dialogue, and, in the case of Kristen French, through being instructed to constantly smile at the camera. Obedience is obtained through physical assault and Bernardo threatens each of them with death if they do not perform as directed.

Everyone exposed to the videotapes has been deeply affected by the experience.

Doyle had to review the tapes by way of trial preparation for Rosen. In giving her evidence she broke down at the recollection and said that she saw the tapes nine times, but "a million times in my head".

Rosen, a veteran criminal defence counsel, was obliged to hesitate part way through his evidence as he recollected the images on the tapes. He described viewing the tapes on September 13, 1994 with MacDonald and Clayton Ruby. MacDonald wept beside him as the tapes were shown and Rosen said he himself was extremely upset. Murray described the tapes as "caustic", "corrosive" and "shocking". Even defence counsel, Mr. Cooper, who must in his career have been exposed to almost everything terrible the Court system has to offer, was obliged to request a brief adjournment in the course of reading in some of this evidence.

In addition to the dreadful acts perpetrated on Kristen French and Leslie Mahaffy, the critical tapes also show the drugging and sexual assaults of Jane Doe and Tammy Homolka, both 15 years of age.

The critical tapes demonstrate conclusively that Bernardo was guilty of forcible confinement, assault and sexual assault of Kristen French and Leslie Mahaffy and the sexual assault of Jane Doe and Tammy Homolka. They provide strong circumstantial evidence to prove Bernardo guilty of the murders.

. . . . .

JOHN ROSEN'S "ADVICE"

John Rosen is a senior and respected Toronto counsel. Tim Breen was the spousal companion of MacDonald and he was also a legal associate of Rosen. Breen had assisted Murray from time to time on the Bernardo case. On May 18, 1993, while visiting Bernardo and receiving his instructions to review and make copies of the tapes, Murray obtained from him some indication of their contents. That same evening he and MacDonald met with Breen to discuss tactics. The following day, May 19, Breen approached Rosen with a hypothetical question to the effect that if the defence had hard evidence that compromised Homolka's credibility, should it be revealed to the prosecution to ensure that Homolka got charged with murder, or should it be saved for trial? Rosen told Breen there was no obligation to assist in the prosecution, but that defence counsel's first duty is to the client and if the evidence would assist the defence, then it should be held in the file and used to cross-examine the witness at trial: "Hammer her with any hard evidence that compromises her plea, her deal, her credibility". Rosen warned against going to the Crown with the evidence because it would allow the Crown to prepare Homolka for cross-examination at trial.

Neither Breen nor Rosen was told anything about videotapes or the nature of the "hard evidence". Rosen assumed it was something like a diary or a letter or a card written to a friend. Both Murray and Rosen looked upon the issue as tactical rather than ethical. (At this time, Murray had not yet viewed the tapes).

THE DEFENCE PLAN

Murray testified he had to retain the critical tapes for Bernardo's defence. Bernardo admitted the crimes shown on the tapes but denied killing Leslie Mahaffy and Kristen French. The tapes, Murray said, supported this position. The Crown was going to portray Homolka as an abused, manipulated victim, while the tapes showed the reverse, that she was not afraid and was an enthusiastic participant in the sexual crimes. He was obliged to keep the existence of the tapes secret so that the Crown could not prepare Homolka for Murray's cross-examination.

It is not entirely clear how Murray planned to utilize the critical tapes. It appears there were two alternatives, to some degree conflicting:

1. Hold back the tapes, tie down Homolka's evidence at the Preliminary Inquiries and then spring the tapes on her in cross-examination at trial;

2. Tie down Homolka at the Preliminary Inquiries and then go to the Crown and attempt to negotiate a resolution of the charges against Bernardo on the basis that Murray was holding evidence that would demonstrate that Homolka was incredible. Bernardo would acknowledge guilt on most of the charges and the prosecution could extricate itself from the Homolka deal. If resolution could not be achieved, the tapes would be turned over to the prosecution. While it would be no "surprise" for Homolka at trial, at least she would have been tied down by her evidence at the Preliminary Inquiries.

Murray stated it was never his intention to "bury" the tapes and, at the very least, they would come out at the trial.

. . . . .

[Murray was ultimately acquitted of the charges on the basis that he did not have the necessary *mens rea* to be convicted of obstruction. For a discussion of the specific rules related to the disclosure of "real evidence" in criminal cases, see Chapter 8.]

DAVID LUBAN

"The Adversary System Excuse"
Legal Ethics and Human Dignity
(Cambridge: Cambridge University Press, 2007) at 32-64[*]

[Luban sets out the "standard conception of the lawyer's role", namely, that a lawyer must be a partisan advocate for his client's ends and that the lawyer has no moral accountability for those ends. Luban argues that most justifications for the standard conception arise from the adversary system or, expressed more broadly, from the role lawyers play within the justice system as a whole. In this excerpt, Luban challenges the traditional justifications given for the lawyer's role and argues that while that role may legitimately influence a lawyer's moral decisions, it cannot do so absolutely. The lawyer retains responsibility for her moral choices, whether made on behalf of a client or not.]

V.   Consequentialist Justifications of the Adversary System

A.   Truth

The question whether the adversary system is, all in all, the best way of uncovering the facts of a case at bar sounds like an empirical question. I happen to think that it is an empirical question, moreover, that has scarcely been investigated, and that is most likely impossible to answer. This last is because one does not, after a trial is over, find the parties coming forth to make a clean breast of it and enlighten the world about what *really* happened. A trial is not a quiz show with the right answer waiting in a sealed envelope. We can't learn directly whether the facts are really as the trier determined them because we don't ever find out the facts.

The kind of empirical research that can be done, then, is laboratory simulations: social psychology experiments intended to model the adversary proceeding. Obviously, there are inherent limitations on how closely such experiments can correspond to actual trials, no matter how skillfully they are done. ... Even so, the results are instructive: they show that in some situations the adversary system works better while in others the inquisitorial system does, and furthermore, that the participants cannot tell which situation they are in. This would hardly surprise us: it would be much more astounding to discover a greater difference in veracity between the Anglo-American and Continental systems, for surely such a difference would after so many centuries have become a commonplace in our folklore.

Given all this, it is unsurprising to discover that the arguments purporting to show the advantages of the adversary system as a fact-finder have mostly been nonempirical, a mix of *a priori* theories of inquiry and armchair psychology.

---

[*]   Reproduced with permission.

Here is one, based on the idea, very similar to Sir Karl Popper's theory of scientific rationality, that the way to get at the truth is a wholehearted dialectic of assertion and refutation. If each side attempts to prove its case, with the other trying as energetically as possible to assault the steps of the proof, it is more likely that all of the aspects of the situation will be presented to the fact-finder than if it attempts to investigate for itself with the help of the lawyers.

This theory is open to a number of objections. First of all, the analogy to Popperian scientific methodology is not a good one. Perhaps science proceeds by advancing conjectures and then trying to refute them, but it does not proceed by advancing conjectures that the scientist believes to be false and then using procedural rules to exclude probative evidence.

The two adversary attorneys are each under an obligation to present the facts in the manner most consistent with their client's position to prevent the introduction of unfavorable evidence, to undermine the credibility of opposing witnesses, to set unfavorable facts in a context in which their importance is minimized, to attempt to provoke inferences in their client's favor. The assumption is that two such accounts will cancel out, leaving the truth of the matter. But there is no earthly reason to think this is so; they may simply pile up the confusion.

This is particularly likely in cases turning on someone's sanity or state of mind. Out comes the parade of psychiatrists, what Hannah Arendt once called "the comedy of the soul-experts." Needless to say, they have been prepared by the lawyers, sometimes without knowing it. A clinical law teacher explained to a class that when you first contact a psychiatrist and sketch the facts of the case, you mention only the favorable ones. That way, he or she has an initial bias in your favor and tends to discount the unfavorable facts when you finally get around to mentioning them.

The other side, of course, can cross-examine such a witness to get the truth out. Irving Younger, in his time the most popular lecturer on trial tactics in the country, tells how. Among his famous "Ten Commandments of Cross-Examination" are these:

- Never ask anything but a leading question.

- Never ask a question to which you don't already know the answer.

- Never permit the witness to explain his or her answers.

- Don't bring out your conclusions in the cross-examination. Save them for closing arguments when the witness is in no position to refute them.

Of course, the opposition may be prepared for this; they may have seen Younger's three-hour, $425 videotape on how to examine expert witnesses. They may know, therefore, that the cross-examiner is saving his or her conclusions for the closing argument. Not to worry! Younger knows how to stop an attorney from distorting the truth in closing arguments. "If the opposing lawyer is holding the jury spellbound ... the spell must be broken at all cost. [Younger] suggests the attorney leap to his or her feet and make furious and spurious objections. They will be overruled, but they might at least break the opposing counsel's concentration."

My guess is that this is not quite what Sir Karl Popper had in mind when he wrote, "The Western rationalist tradition ... is the tradition of critical discussion – of examining and testing propositions or theories by attempting to refute them."

A skeptic, in fact, might try this scientific analogy: a beam of invisible electrically charged particles – charge and origin unknown – travels through a distorting magnetic field of unknown strength, then through an opposite field of unknown, but probably different, strength. The beam strikes a detector of undeterminable reliability, from which we are supposed to infer the nature and location of the beam's source. That is the adversary system at its worst.

There is, however, one legal context in which the Popperian defense of the adversary system approximates reality and in which the adversary system is indeed strongly justified. When lawyers debate purely legal questions – particularly in appellate argument, where both sides work from a fixed record and no new evidence can be introduced – we find the kind of give and take that critical rationalists favor. It makes sense to assign each advocate the task of arguing one side's interpretation of the law as forcefully as possible, and doing everything possible to undermine the adversary's arguments. With no facts to hide and everything out in the open, only the arguments and counter-arguments remain. Judges invariably attest that the better the advocates arguing before them, the better decisions they make. Adversary advocacy helps ensure that no arguments or objections get overlooked.

Now, the same thing will often be true when lawyers argue over the interpretation of evidence in a trial of facts, so it may appear that my defense of the adversary system of arguing questions of law proves too much, and provides a defense for adversary arguments about facts as well. To the extent that the lawyers are arguing the interpretation of evidence in the record, that is true. But the problems with the adversary system I have highlighted lie in the fact that trial lawyers view one of their main jobs as keeping damaging information out of the record, or – as in Younger's recommendation that lawyers disrupt their adversaries' closing arguments – clouding the decision-making process. Consider, for example, complaints by the president of a lawyers' organization about a recent American innovation in which jurors are permitted to question witnesses directly. "You work very hard to keep certain information out of the trial. Then all of your finesse and art and technique are thrown out the window when a juror comes in and asks, 'Where were you on the night in question?'" It is hard to defend adversary fact-finding on the ground that it is the best way of ensuring that judges and juries get the most information, when the lawyer's "finesse and art and technique" consists of keeping awkward facts out of court.

Even worse, adversarial tactics sometimes include efforts to ensure that cases never even make it to the stage of fact-finding. Defense counsel for corporate defendants use procedural delays to exhaust their opponents' funds. When they can, lawyers resort to intimidation tactics. A particularly egregious example occurred repeatedly during litigation over the Dalkon Shield, an intrauterine contraceptive device that pharmaceutical manufacturer A. H. Robins marketed during the 1970s to over three million women. Because of a design flaw, the Dalkon Shield caused an estimated 66,000 miscarriages and sterilized thousands of women by infecting them with pelvic inflammatory disease (PID). Faced with staggering liability exposure, Robins and its counsel decided on a scorched-earth defense. One tactic of Robins's counsel soon acquired the nickname "the dirty questions list." Defense lawyers taking depositions asked plaintiffs very specific, very graphic questions about intimate details of their personal hygiene and sexual practices – questions that one plaintiff described as "more like an obscene phone call" than a legal interrogation. Firm lawyers argued that the "dirty questions" were relevant to the law suits because they might reveal alternative sources of PID infection. The questions mainly served, however, to intimidate plaintiffs into dropping their law suits or settling them for inadequate amounts. The message was clear that they might have to answer the same questions in open court. Among other things, defense lawyers asked plaintiffs for the names of all their past and present sexual partners ("besides your husband"), with the clear implica-tion that the partners' names might be revealed and their testimony elicited for purposes of impeaching plaintiffs' answers to the "dirty questions" about what they like to do in bed. Potential plaintiffs filed affidavits indicating that they had dropped their own law suits because of the questions other plaintiffs had been asked.

A similar example is the rise of the so-called "SLAPP suit" – "Strategic Lawsuit Against Public Participation." In a typical SLAPP suit, citizens protesting corporate policies or actions are sued for defamation or tortious interference with business. Some of the alleged defamation has been based on speech as innocuous as testifying against a real estate developer at a zoning hearing, complaining to a school board about incompetent teachers, or collecting signatures on a petition. Although 80% of SLAPP suits are dismissed before trial, the aim of the suits is not legal victory but intimidation. Defendants faced with the prospect of ruinous legal bills and the risk of substantial personal liability agree to cease protest activities in return for withdrawal of the SLAPP suits.

The point of these examples is plain: you cannot defend the adversary system on the basis of its truth-finding function when it licenses (or even requires) behavior designed to ensure that the truth never comes out, because litigants are intimidated into abandoning legitimate cases.

One final difference between "pure" argument, paradigmatically appellate argument of legal issues, and the adversary system of fact-finding, appears in the ethics rules themselves. Ordinarily, lawyers are required to keep facts confidential, and in the adversary system they must never reveal damaging facts to a court unless they are compelled to do so. Matters are very different when we turn from facts to law. Here, the fundamental rule requires lawyers "to disclose to the tribunal legal authority in the controlling jurisdiction known to the lawyer to be directly adverse to the position of the client and not disclosed by opposing counsel." This rule, which law students and lawyers often find counter-intuitive ("why should I do my adversary's legal research for them?"), highlights what makes argument about legal questions different. The idea is to ensure that judges reach the best resolutions they can of questions of law. Their resolutions, after all, become precedents. Getting to the best resolutions requires total transparency, and if my adversary has overlooked a favorable case on point, the rule requires me to throw myself on the sword by telling the judge about the case, to ensure that the judge does not overlook it. By contrast, we have seen that adversarial advocacy on factual matters places lawyers at war with transparency.

[Luban then considers Lon Fuller and John Randall's justification of the adversary system in the 1958 *Joint Conference Report*. Fuller and Randall justify adversarial justice as favourable to the inquisitorial system as a basis for discovering the truth.]

. . . . .

Ultimately, the *Joint Conference Report* seems to take as a premise the idea that truth is served by self-interested rather than disinterested investigation. "The lawyer appearing as an advocate before a tribunal presents, as persuasively as he can, the facts and the law of the case *as seen from the standpoint of his client's interest*" [emphasis added]. The emphasized phrase is accurate, but it gives the game away. For there is all the difference in the world between "the facts seen from X's standpoint" and "the facts seen from the standpoint of X's interest." Of course it is important to hear the former – the more perspectives we have, the better informed our judgment. But to hear the latter is not helpful at all. It is in the murderer's *interest* not to have been at the scene of the crime; consequently, the "facts of the case as seen from the standpoint of [the] client's interest" are that the client was elsewhere that weekend. From the standpoint of my *interest*, the world is my cupcake with a cherry on top; from the standpoint of yours, its streets are paved with gold and you own the streets. Combining the two does not change folly to truth.

All this does not mean that the adversary system may not in fact get at the truth in many hard cases. I suppose that it is as good as its rivals. But, to repeat the point I began with, nobody knows how good that is.

[Luban next considers and refutes the claim that zealous advocacy is necessary to defend a client's legal rights.]

. . . . .

C.   Ethical Division of Labor

This argument is no longer that the excesses of zealous advocacy are excused by the promotion of truth or the defense of legal rights. Rather, it is that they are excused by what Thomas Nagel calls "ethical division of labor." He says, in a discussion of the peculiarly ruthless and result-oriented role morality of public officials,

> that the constraints of public morality are not imposed as a whole in the same way on all public actions or on all public offices. Because public agency is itself complex and divided, there is a corresponding ethical division of labor, or ethical specialization. Different aspects of public morality are in the hands of different officials. This can create the illusion that public morality is more consequentialist or less restrictive than it is, because the general conditions may be wrongly identified with the boundaries of a particular role. But in fact those boundaries usually presuppose a larger institutional structure without which they would be illegitimate. (The most conspicuous example is the legitimacy conferred on legislative decisions by the limitation of constitutional protections enforced by the courts.)

The idea is that behavior that looks wrong from the point of view of ordinary morality can be justified by the fact that other social roles exist whose purpose is to counteract the excesses resulting from role-behavior. Zealous adversary advocacy is justified by the fact that the other side is also furnished with a zealous advocate; the impartial arbiter provides a further check.

This is in fact one of the most commonly heard defenses for pugnacious advocacy: "he had a lawyer, too"; "I'm not supposed to do his lawyer's job for him"; or quoting Sharswood once again, "The lawyer, who refuses his professional assistance because in his judgment the case is unjust and indefensible, usurps the functions of both judge and jury."

The idea is really a checks-and-balances theory, in which social engineering or "wise legislation" is supposed to relieve some of the strain on individual conscience. A functionary in a well-designed checks-and-balances system can simply go ahead and perform his duties secure in the knowledge that injuries inflicted or wrongs committed in the course of those duties will be rectified by other parts of the system.

Will this do the trick? The answer, I am afraid, is no. Suppose that a lawyer is about to embark on a course of action that is unjustified from the point of view of ordinary morality, such as attempting to win an unfair, lopsided judgment for a client from a hapless and innocent party. Or think of our second graymailing example, in which lawyers for a corporation involved in a merger advise their client to fire employees a few at a time to blackmail federal authorities into permitting the merger to go forward. A zealous adversary advocate will do whatever she can to avoid the opposing counsel's attempt to foil her designs. For that reason, she surely cannot claim that the existence of the opposing counsel morally justifies these actions. Certainly the fact that a man has a bodyguard in no way excuses you for trying to kill him, particularly if you bend all your ingenuity to avoiding the bodyguard.

The problem is this. The checks-and-balances notion is desirable because if other parts of the system exist to rectify one's excesses, one will be able to devote undivided energy to the job at hand and do it better. It is analogous to wearing protective clothing in a sport such as fencing: knowing that your opponent is protected, you can go all out in the match. But in the adversary system the situation is different, since the attorney is actively trying to get around the checks and balances. Here the analogy is to a fencer who uses a special foil that can cut through the opponent's protective clothing. To put the point another way, the adversary advocate attempts to evade the system of checks and balances, not rely on it to save her opponents.

There is another problem with the notion of ethical division of labor. It attempts to justify a system of roles by the fact that the system is self-correcting, in other words that injuries perpetrated by one part of the system will be rectified by another. Rectification, however, carries with it high transaction costs in terms of money, time, worry, energy, and (generally) an arduous passage through the bureaucratic straits. These transaction costs create a general background "noise" in the system, a penalty imposed on one simply for becoming embroiled in it. This can be justified only if the system itself is justified, but then the checks-and-balances argument seems merely to gild the lily. Had we found a justification for the adversary system on other grounds, we would not have needed to turn to the ethical division-of-labor argument to begin with.

Division of labor arguments raise a very troubling and difficult topic. The structure of bureaucratic institutions such as the legal system lends itself to divided responsibility. Those who write the rules, those who give the orders, and those who carry them out each have some basis for claiming that they are not at fault for any wrong that results. But this is unacceptable. If moral agency divides along lines of institutional authority, it seems to me that every agent in the institution will wind up abdicating moral responsibility ... It is for this reason that division-of-labor arguments must walk a thin line between the legitimate notion that different roles have different duties and the unacceptable notion that moral responsibility is itself diminished or "divided down" by institutional structure.

· · · · ·

VI. Nonconsequentialist Justifications of the Adversary System

It may be thought, however, that assessing the adversary system in consequentialist terms of how it will get some job done misses the point. Some social institutions, such as participatory democracy, are justifiable despite the fact that – maybe even because – they are inefficient. The moral standing of such institutions has a noninstrumental basis.

I wish to consider two nonconsequentialist justifications of the adversary system. The first and perhaps boldest is an attempt to justify the adversary system in the wide sense: it is the argument that the traditional lawyer-client relation is an intrinsic moral good. The second is a cluster of related arguments: that adversary adjudication is a valued and valuable tradition, that it enjoys the consent of the governed, and that it is thus an integral part of our social fabric.

A. *Adversary Advocacy as Intrinsically Good*

When we seek out the services of a professional, it seems to me that we generally see more to the relationship than a mere quid pro quo. Perhaps this is because the quo may be of vital importance to us; perhaps it is because a lot of quid may be required to hire those services. In any event, we have the sense of entrusting a large chunk of our life to this person, and the fact that he or she takes on so intimate a burden and handles it in a trustworthy and skillful manner when the stakes are high seems commendable in itself. Nor does the fact that the professional makes a living by providing this service seem to mitigate the praiseworthiness of it. The business aspect moves along a different moral dimension: it explains how the relationship came about, not what it involves. Finally, our being able to bare our weaknesses and mistakes to the professional and receive assistance without condemnation enhances our sense that beneficence or moral graciousness is at work here. Our lawyer, *mirabile dictu*, forgives us our transgressions.

Feelings such as these are quite real; the question is whether they have merely subjective significance. If they do not, if they mean something more, that may show that Schwartz's two principles, and thus the adversary system and the behavior it countenances, are themselves positive moral goods. Such arguments are, in fact, frequently made: they are based on the idea that providing service is intrinsically good. No finer statement of this exists, in my opinion, than Mellinkoff's. He sees the paradigm client as the "man-in-trouble."

> Cruelty, oppression, deception, unhappiness, worry, strain, incomprehension, frustration, bewilderment – a sorcerer's bag of misery. These become the expected. Then the saddest of all human cries: "Who will help me?" Try God, and politics, and medicine, and a soft shoulder, sooner or later a lawyer. Too many do.
>
> The lawyer, as lawyer, is no sweet kind loving moralizer. He assumes he is needed, and that no one comes to see him to pass the time of day. He is a prober, an analyzer, a scrapper, a man with a strange devotion to his client. Beautifully strange, or so it seems to the man-in-trouble; ugly strange to the untroubled onlooker.

Charles Fried thinks of the lawyer as a "special-purpose friend" whose activity – enhancing the client's autonomy and individuality – is an intrinsic moral good. This is true even when the lawyer's "friendship" consists in assisting the profiteering slumlord to evict an indigent tenant or enabling the wealthy debtor to run the statute of limitations to avoid an honest debt to an old (and less well-off) friend.

I mention Mellinkoff's and Fried's arguments together because, it seems to me, they express similar ideas, while the unsavory consequences Fried draws from his argument exposes the limitations of Mellinkoff's. Both arguments attempt to show that a lawyer serving a client is engaged in an intrinsic moral good. Mellinkoff's, however, really shows something much weaker, that a lawyer serving a man-in-trouble is (even more cautiously: can be) engaged in an intrinsic moral good. If the client is Fried's profiteering slumlord or unscrupulous debtor, we are confronted with no man-in-trouble, and the intuitions to which Mellinkoff's argument appeals disappear. Indeed, if these were the typical clients, the real men-in-trouble – the victims of these predators – might be better off taking their chances in the war of all against all than seeking to have their "autonomy" vindicated legally. The trouble with Mellinkoff's argument is that he makes clients look more pitiable than many really are.

Fried, on the other hand, bites the bullet and argues that it is morally good to represent the man-in-no-trouble-in-particular, the man-who-troubles-others. The slumlord and the graymailing, anticompetitive multiglomerate are nobly served by a special-purpose friend who helps extract that pound of flesh. Fried constructs a "concentric-circles morality" in which, beginning with an absolute right to self-love based on our own moral standing, we work outward toward those closest to us, then to those whose connections are more remote. Fried argues that the abstract connection between a remote person (even a person-in-trouble) and the agent exercises too slight a claim on the agent to override this inclination toward concrete others. This justifies lavishing special care on our friends, even at the expense of "abstract others"; and because lavishing care is morally praiseworthy, once we grant that a lawyer is a special-purpose friend of his client, we are home free with the intrinsic moral worth of the lawyer-client relation.

Several of Fried's critics focus on the fact that the friendship analogy is question-begging: Fried builds enough lawyerly qualities into his concept of friendship that the argument becomes circular; in the words of Edward Dauer and Arthur Leff, "a lawyer is like a friend ... because, for Professor Fried, a friend is like a lawyer." It does seem to me, however, that the analogy captures some of the legitimate notion of professionals as devoted by the nature of their calling to the service of their clients. Fried's analogy contains a large grain of truth.

This does not, however, vindicate the adversary system. For the friendship analogy undercuts rather than establishes the Principle of Nonaccountability. Most of us are not willing to do grossly immoral things to help our friends, nor should we be. Lord Brougham's apology may be many things, but it is not a credo of human friendship in any of its forms. Fried realizes the danger, for he confesses that

> not only would I not lie or steal for ... my friends, I probably also would not pursue socially noxious schemes, foreclose the mortgages of widows or orphans, or assist in the avoidance of just punishment. So we must be careful lest the whole argument unravel on us at this point.

The method for saving the argument, however, proves disappointing. Fried distinguishes between *personal* wrongs committed by a lawyer, such as abusing a witness, and *institutional* wrongs occasioned by the lawyer, such as foreclosing on widows. The latter are precisely those done by the lawyer in his or her proper role of advancing the client's legal autonomy and – preestablished harmony? – they are precisely the ones that are morally acceptable. That is because the lawyer isn't really doing them, the system is.

This last distinction has not been very popular since World War II, and Fried takes pains to restrict it to "generally just and decent" systems, not Nazi Germany. With this qualification, he can more comfortably assert: "We should absolve the lawyer of personal moral responsibility for the result he accomplishes because the wrong is wholly institutional."

This last sentence, however, is nothing but the assertion that institutional excuses work for lawyers, and this should tip us off that Fried's argument will be useless for our purposes. For consider: our whole line of argument has been an attempt to justify the adversary system by showing that the traditional lawyer-client relation is an intrinsic moral good. Now it seems that this can be established by Fried's argument only if we are permitted to cancel the moral debit column by means of an institutional excuse; but that can work only if the institution is justified, and we are back where we started.

Part of the problem is that Fried considers the wrong institution: the context of the lawyer's behavior is not simply the system of laws in general, which he assumes to be just and decent, but the adversary system in particular with its peculiar requirement of one-sided zeal at the margin. It is the adversary system and not the system of laws that shapes the lawyer-client relationship.

The more fundamental problem, however, is that Fried takes the lawyer to be the mere occasion rather than the agent of morally-bad-but-legally-legitimate outcomes. The system did it; it "was just one of those things difficult to pre-visualize – like a cow, say, getting hit by lightning."

This is false in three respects: first, because it discounts the extent to which the lawyer has had a creative hand in advocating the outcome, at times even reversing the law – a skilled lawyer, after all, argues, advocates, bargains, and persuades. Second, because the system is not an abstract structure of impersonal role-descriptions but a social structure of interacting human beings, so that the actions of its agents *are* the system. Third, because the lawyer is indeed acting *in propria persona* by "pulling the levers of the legal machinery." Fried's imagery seems to trade on a Rube Goldberg insight: if the apparatus is complex enough, then the lever-puller doesn't really look like the agent. But that cannot be right. I chop the broccoli, whether I do it with a knife or merely push the button on the blender. The legal levers are pulled by the lawyer: no one else can do it.

. . . . .

VII.   The Adversary System Excuse

A.   *Pragmatic Justification*

So far the course of argument has been purely negative, a persecution and assassination of the adversary system. By this time you are entitled to ask what I propose putting in its place. The answer is: nothing, for I think the adversary system is justified.

I do not, let me quickly say, have an argumentative novelty to produce. It would be strange indeed for a social institution to be justified on the basis of virtues other than the tried and true ones, virtues that no one had noticed in it before. My justification is rather a version of the tradition argument, but purged of its ideological overtones. I shall call it the "pragmatic justification" or "pragmatic argument" to suggest its affinity with the relaxed, problem-oriented, and historicist notion of justification associated with American pragmatism. The justification is this:

First, the adversary system, despite its imperfections, irrationalities, loopholes, and perversities, seems to do as good a job as any at finding truth and protecting legal rights. None of its existing rivals is demonstrably better, and some, such as trial by ordeal, are demonstrably worse. Indeed, even if one of the other systems were slightly better, the human costs – in terms of effort, confusion, anxiety, disorientation, inadvertent miscarriages of justice due to improper understanding, retraining, resentment, loss of tradition, you name it – would outweigh reasons for replacing the existing system.

Second, *some* adjudicatory system is necessary.

Third, it's the way we have done things for at least a century.

These propositions constitute a pragmatic argument: if a social institution does a reasonable enough job of its sort that the costs of replacing it outweigh the benefits; and if we need that sort of job done, we should stick with what we have. ...

That this is a very relaxed sort of justification may be seen from the fact that it works equally well for the inquisitorial system in France and Germany. A pragmatic justification is weak as well because it crumbles in the face of a demonstration that, contrary to what we believe, the institution is awful enough to replace. The argument, in other words, does not really endorse an institution – it only endures it.

Accepting a pragmatic justification of the adversary system, it should be added, does not commit one to a blanket conservatism. One can believe that our society should be drastically changed or that our legal system is scandalously unjust and still accept that a changed society or overhauled legal system should utilize adversary adjudication. Thus, while the argument leads to a conservative conclusion, it does so in a piecemeal, nonideological way, and the conclusion extends no further than the institution for which the argument is offered.

In my opinion, many of our social institutions are like the adversary system in that they admit only of pragmatic justification. Some are not intended to serve any positive moral good; some serve it badly. That these institutions are not worth replacing may be a measure of nothing more than social lethargy and our inability to come up with a better idea; my point is that this is a real reason. A pragmatic argument is logically weak – it justifies institutions without showing that they are better than their rivals, or even that they are particularly good – but in practice it is overwhelmingly powerful. Institutions, like bodies, obey Newton's First Law.

B. *Pragmatic Justification and Institutional Excuses*

Because this is so typical of institutions it is worth asking about the effect of pragmatic argument on the moral obligations of institutional functionaries (such as lawyers). The position I want to press is roughly that a social institution that can receive only a pragmatic justification is not capable of providing institutional excuses for immoral acts. To do that, an institution must be justified in a much stronger way, by showing that it is a positive moral good. A pragmatic argument, by contrast, need show only that it is not much more mediocre than its rivals.

Let me spell this out by criticizing what I shall call the Transitivity Argument, which goes as follows:

1. The institution is justified.

2. The institution requires its functionary to do A.

3. Therefore, the functionary is justified in doing A.

This plausible-looking defense of institutional excuses can be criticized by denying the first premise; however, I am accepting the pragmatic justification of the adversary system and thus accepting the premise. Or it could be criticized by attacking the second premise: thus, William Simon and Richard Abel have argued that the role morality of lawyers is so riddled with contradictions that it is impossible to derive any coherent set of professional requirements from it. My strategy, however, is to deny that the conclusion follows from the premises. The institutional obligation is only a *prima facie* obligation, and the weaker the justification of the institution, the weaker the force of this obligation in overriding other morally relevant factors.

To get the argument underway, let us look at the way an institutional excuse might work when the institution is strongly justified, when it is a positive moral good.

Consider, as an example, a charitable organization whose sole function is to distribute food to famine-stricken people in impoverished areas of the world. We will call this the *institution*. Division of labor within it creates different jobs or *institutional tasks*, each of which has specified duties or *role-obligations*. These may be quite general: the logistics officer, for example, might have as his role-obligation procuring means of transporting food. To carry out the role-obligation, he must perform various actions, call them the *role-acts*.

Let us suppose that to get food to a remote village the logistics officer must obtain trucks from a local, very powerful gangster, P. As it happens, P is involved in a number of unsavory activities, including a plan to murder a local man, because P wants to sleep with the man's wife. Imagine further that the logistics officer overhears P dispatching a murderer to kill the man that very night, that P discovers that the logistics officer has overheard him, and that P tells the officer that if the man is warned and escapes, P will not provide the trucks.

The officer faces a terrible moral dilemma. Other things being equal, he is under a moral obligation to warn the man. Let us, at any rate, suppose that this is so. But here, if anywhere, we may wish to permit an institutional excuse. Suppose the officer complies with P's demand. Asked to justify this, he says, "My job is more important." This is an institutional excuse, the structure of which may be spelled out as follows: he points out that the role-act of complying with P is required by his role-obligation, which in turn is necessary to perform the institutional task, which (finally) is justified by the positive moral good of the institution – the saving of many innocent lives.

The general problem, which creates the dilemma, is that the propositions

> The institution is a morally good one

> and

> The institution imposes role-obligations on its officers some of which may mandate morally bad role-acts

can both be true.

In such a case, the institutional excuse, fully spelled out, will take the form I have indicated: the agent justifies the role-act by showing it is required by the role-obligation, justifies the obligation by showing it derives from the institutional task, justifies the institutional task by appealing to the structure of the institution, and justifies the institution by demonstrating its moral goodness.

. . . . .

If, on the other hand, an institution can be justified only pragmatically, the sides of the dilemma do not have equal weight and the institutional excuse collapses. For in that case it reads as follows:

It is true that I am morally wronging you. But that is required by my role-obligations, which are essential to my institutional task, which is necessary to the structure of the institution, which is justified

- because it is there.
- because it's the way we do things around here.
- because it's not worth the trouble to replace it.

This, I think, will not do. The excuse rests on an elephant that stands on a tortoise that floats in the sky. But the sky is falling.

. . . . .

The basic problem with the Transitivity Argument [from the Adversary system] is that it exempts officers of an institution from ordinary moral requirements that conflict with role-obligations, even though the institution itself is in place only because we have done it that way for a long time. The result is to place conformity to existing institutions beyond the very possibility of criticism. This, however, is no longer justified conservatism: rather, it is fetishism of tradition.

Pragmatic arguments do not really praise institutions; they merely give reason for not burying them. Since their force is more inertial than moral, they create insufficient counterweight to resolve dilemmas in favor of the role-obligation. An excuse based on institutions justified in this way is simply a "good soldier" argument with little more to be said.

VIII.   Conclusion and Peroration

It is time to summarize.

Perhaps the best way to see the import of the arguments I have been offering is not as an attack on the adversary system (for, after all, I have not suggested that it should be replaced) so much as an attack on an ideology consisting of these ideas:

1. The adversary system is the most powerful engine of justice ever devised.

2. It is a delicately poised instrument in which the generation of just outcomes depends on the regular functioning of each of its parts.

3. Hence the pursuit of justice morally obligates an attorney to assume a one-sided Broughamesque role.

4. The adversary system, in consequence, institutionally excuses lawyers from ordinary moral obligations conflicting with their professional obligations.

5. Broughamesque advocacy is, moreover, a cornerstone of our system of political liberties, for it is the last defense of the hapless criminal-accused against the awesome power of the state. To restrict the advocate is to invite totalitarianism.

I have argued against the first four of these propositions. About the fifth a more cautious conclusion is in order. The argument it offers that the criminal defense lawyer "must not regard the alarm, the torments, the destruction which he may bring upon others" (Brougham, again) is rather persuasive, but only because of two special features of the criminal context: that we have political reasons for handicapping the government in its role as enforcer, and that the criminal defendant comes closest to the paradigm of the man-in-trouble. The argument, then, countenances adversarial ruthlessness as a blanket policy only in criminal and quasi-criminal defense, and thus only in these situations is the adversary system fully available as an institutional excuse.

What does all this mean in noncriminal contexts, where this institutional excuse based on liberal fear of the state is unavailable? The answer, very simply, is this. The adversary system possesses only slight moral force, and thus appealing to it can excuse only slight moral wrongs. Anything else that is morally wrong for a nonlawyer to do on behalf of another person is morally wrong for a lawyer to do as well. The lawyer's role carries no moral privileges and immunities.

This does not mean that zealous advocacy is immoral, not even when it frustrates the search for truth or violates legal rights. Sometimes frustrating the search for truth may be a morally worthy thing to do, and sometimes moral rights are ill served by legal rights. All I am insisting on is that the standards by which such judgments are made are the same for lawyers and nonlawyers. If a lawyer is permitted to puff, bluff, or threaten on certain occasions, this is not because of the adversary system and the Principle of Nonaccountability, but because, in such circumstances, anyone would be permitted to do these things. Nothing justifies doing them on behalf of a predator.

But, it will be objected, my argument leads to a paradox, for I have claimed to offer a vindication, albeit a weak one, of the adversary system, and therefore of the duties of partisan advocacy that it entails. Am I not saying that a lawyer may be professionally obligated to do A and morally obligated not to do A?

That is indeed the conclusion, but there is no contradiction here. The adversary system and the system of professional obligation it mandates are justified only in that, lacking a clearly superior alternative, they should not be replaced. This implies, I have argued, a presumption in favor of professional obligation, but one that any serious and countervailing moral obligation rebuts. Thus, when professional and serious moral obligation conflict, moral obligation takes precedence. When they don't conflict, professional obligations rule the day. The Principle of Professionalism follows from the fact that we have an adversary system; the Principle of Nonaccountability does not. The point of elaborating the former is to tell the lawyer what, in this system, professionalism requires – to insist that it requires zeal, for example, even when cutting corners might be more profitable or pleasant. Professionalism can tell lawyers not to cut corners; my point is that it cannot mandate them to cut throats. When serious moral obligation conflicts with professional obligation, the lawyer must become a civil disobedient to professional rules.

Not that this is likely to happen. Lawyers get paid for their services, not for their consciences. But so does everyone else. As we do not expect the world to strike a truce in the war of all against all, we should not expect lawyers to. Shen Te, the Good Woman of Setzuan in Brecht's play, says:

> I'd like to be good, it's true, but there's the rent to pay. And that's not all: I sell myself for a living. Even so I can't make ends meet, there's too much competition.

That, of course, is the way the world is, and criticizing an ideology won't change the world. The point of the exercise, I suppose, is merely to get our moral ideas straight: one less ideology is, after all, one less excuse.

NOTES AND QUESTIONS

1. Had Murray had a view of the lawyer's role similar to that articulated by Luban, do you think that he might have been quicker to realize that he faced an ethical dilemma? What "ordinary" moral values are implicated by the discovery of the video tapes?

2. Is it reasonable to expect lawyers to be a "civil disobedient to professional rules"? Does this depend on whether one thinks that civil disobedience to law is generally justified? What are the conditions for the legitimate exercise of civil disobedience? Does, for example, the lawyer need to disobey publicly, accepting the consequences that the society chooses to impose? Or may the lawyer simply ignore the legal requirement, hoping that sanctions can be avoided?

3. If moral decisions are, as suggested earlier, reached normally through intuitive responses to problems, is it more likely that lawyers will have intuitions shaped by ordinary moral reasons, or by the claims of legality? In other words, is one advantage of Luban's theory that it allows lawyers to rely on the intuitions they've developed over the course of their lifetimes, rather than on ones that might have emerged only as a product of their legal training?

Scenario Five

John Smith represents a woman, M, who is claiming refugee status in Canada. Part of M's claim is that she was sexually assaulted by government soldiers in her home country. Smith has some reason to believe that M's claim is factually untrue, mostly because his assistant (who speaks the same language as M) overheard M saying that the story was "a stretch" and "more useful than true" while sitting in Smith's waiting room. He also, though, is aware that M's country of origin does not accord equal rights and freedoms to women, and that M's future there is bleak. While speaking with M, Smith learns that she has a brother who lives in Canada and is a Canadian citizen. Given what M said, the brother almost certainly would have information about whether the claim made by M is factually accurate, and is also quite likely to tell the truth (since he and M are estranged). Is it ethical for Smith not to contact the brother to find out more? In answering the question bear in mind that it is unethical to mislead a court or tribunal, or to knowingly assist your client in presenting perjured testimony to the court or tribunal. Also consider what ordinary moral values might be at play and how, if at all, those values conflict with the process or substance of the law as applied to M.

3. Integrity

As legal ethics has evolved, some scholars have come to criticize the singularity of both the zealous advocacy and moral agency conceptions of the lawyer's role. They view those conceptions as unsatisfactory because failing to capture the complex and multi-faceted emphasis on different (and sometimes competing) values by courts and professional regulators. In particular, critics note, singular normative approaches may not fully capture the moral complexity of the legal and ethical framework that governs Canadian lawyers. In a 1996 article, Alice Woolley argued that the "standard conception" of the

American lawyer differs from the standard conception of the Canadian lawyer.[13] Specifically, Canadian codes of conduct, including the new Federation of Law Societies' *Model Code*, differ from their American counterparts because they have always placed a central emphasis on lawyer "integrity". Rule 1.01 of the Federation's *Model Code* provides:

> 1.01 (1) A lawyer has a duty to carry on the practice of law and discharge all responsibilities to clients, tribunals, the public and other members of the profession honourably and with integrity.

The *Model Code* does not define integrity, but suggests in the Commentary that practising law requires being trustworthy, honourable and responsible, while always avoiding questionable conduct.

Those definitions do not, on their own, provide all that much guidance to a lawyer seeking to practise with integrity. What does maintaining integrity require? One approach, which Woolley emphasizes to some extent in her 1996 article, and again but more significantly in the excerpt above, is to see integrity as a response to the problem of conflicts between professional and personal morality. Those conflicts cannot be avoided and no fully satisfactory moral answer can be provided in circumstances where they conflict. Either professional or personal moral claims must be sacrificed. What emphasizing integrity does is assert that lawyers should, where possible, avoid circumstances where personal and professional morality are likely to conflict (by, for example, selecting clients whose moral claims the lawyer can respect). In addition, and more importantly, integrity directs the lawyer to be fully cognizant of, and responsible for, her choices in circumstances of moral conflict. Citing Gerald Postema, Woolley suggests that a lawyer must "recognize and take responsibility for the extent to which her professional life requires her to do things that conflict with what, outside of her profession, she would find morally unacceptable".[14] And, if choosing to privilege personal morality over professional obligation, she must take responsibility for that too.

An alternative approach to integrity is to suggest that it permits the incorporation of a variety of moral values within legal practice. This could look like Luban's argument, in which professional obligation is always subject to ordinary moral claims. Alternatively, it could simply incorporate a multiplicity of moral claims and values into ethical decision-making by lawyers. As set out in the following excerpt, Trevor Farrow has argued that neither traditional loyalty-based visions nor alternative justice-seeking narratives capture the current complexities of the modern practice of law, and has sought to articulate a new concept for the lawyer's role, "sustainable professionalism".

In reading Farrow's article, consider which approach to incorporating integrity into ethical decision-making — as a means of addressing the moral

---

[13]   Alice Woolley, "Integrity in Zealousness: Comparing the Standard Conceptions of the Canadian and American Lawyer" (1996) 9 Can. J.L. & Jur. 61.

[14]   *Ibid.*, at 76.

conflict created by the professional role, or as a shift in the content of the professional role — is most persuasive.

TREVOR C.W. FARROW

"Sustainable Professionalism"
(2008) 46 Osgoode Hall L.J. 51
[footnotes omitted]

The traditional narrative of the legal profession has run its course. Lawyers are looking for ethically sensitive ways to practice law that "assume greater responsibility for the welfare of parties other than clients" and that increasingly amount "to a plus for this society and for the world of our children." Lawyers are also seeking ways to practice law that allow them to get home at night and on weekends, see their families, work full or part-time, practice in diverse and "alternative" settings, and generally pursue a meaningful *career* in the law rather than necessarily a total *life* in the law. Similarly, law students are hoping not to be asked to make a "pact with the Devil" as the cost of becoming a lawyer, and are instead looking to find areas in the law that fit with their personal, political, and economic preferences. An increasing number of legal academics are teaching, researching, and writing about progressive changes to the way we view the role and purpose of lawyering. Law faculties are actively reforming their programs and creating centres and initiatives designed to make space for innovative ethics offerings and public interest programs. Law societies and other regulatory bodies are slowly chipping away at some of the time-honoured shields of ethically suspect client behaviour, while at the same time facing demands for increased accountability. The bench and the bar are taking an active interest in addressing a perceived growing lack of professionalism within the practice. The public is increasingly skeptical of the distinction that continues to be drawn between legal ethics and "ordinary standards of moral conduct." Finally, clients are not only expecting lawyers to actively canvass methods of alternative dispute resolution — the alternative to the adversarial and costly litigation process — but they are also demanding evidence of general sustainable professional practices from their legal counsel.

These current, contextual, and contested realities have become badges of modern, progressive lives in and visions of the practice of law. Taken together, they are forming a new discourse for lawyers and the profession that is seeking to become personally, politically, ethically, economically, and professionally sustainable. It is a discourse that makes meaningful space for a lawyer's own principles, interests, and life preferences by balancing them with other important interests — including, but not dominated by, those of the client — in the context of the overall calculus of what counts as the "right" course of conduct both in a given retainer as well as, more generally, in a given career. It is a discourse that seeks to make good on what has largely only amounted to aspirational promises of equality, access to justice, and the protection of the public interest. And it is a discourse that seeks both to benefit from and take seriously its obligations to address the culturally complicated makeup of the bar and our general pluralistic and globalized civil societies. This modern discourse of an ethically sustainable profession challenges the "time-honoured" centrality of client autonomy and a lawyer's unqualified loyalty to the client's interests. Specifically, it rejects stories of lawyers, collectively, as members of a relatively homogenized profession and who, individually, are single-tasked "hired guns" focused on only one interest "in all the world." According to this new model, those stories are no longer — if they ever were — sustainable.

Thinking about the profession in terms of a discourse of "professional sustainability" that takes seriously a broad range of voices and interests is surprisingly new. The label "sustainable" has not, to date, been generally applied to discussions of ethics and professionalism in the legal context. And because as a profession lawyers are still "anxiously" fearful of replacing the "spirits" of "dead generations," which continue to weigh on us "like a nightmare" (lawyers grew up and depend on stories of zeal, vigour, and role-differentiated behaviour that allow them to act for all kinds of clients, including those who they think are "reprehensible," while still being able to sleep soundly at night), a discourse of sustainable professionalism is threatening. Proponents of the dominant model borrow "names, battle slogans, and costumes": names such as "zealous advocates," "shock troops," "hired gun[s]," and "soldiers of the law"; battle slogans such as "fierce," "fearless," "resolute," and "partisan"; and costumes such as barristers' gowns, tabs, and waistcoats. They doggedly and dogmatically re-make a history under this "time-honoured disguise and this borrowed language" in a continued effort to "create a world after [their] image."

The resulting paradox created by the dominant narrative is that, although the stories that continue to be told are becoming less attractive to more people, the stories continue to be told. To my mind, given the complex realities of the current professional trajectory, lawyers need another story — a sustainable story — that captures those complex realities and provides for a meaningful prospect of broad-based buy-in. Alternative models that critique the dominant model provide another story. Those critiques, which are becoming increasingly attractive, are often framed in terms of the "moral perspective," "moral lawyering," "the moral lawyer," or "the good lawyer." These labels appear to connote some shared or required understanding of what counts as "moral" or "good," whereas the safe harbours of zealous advocacy and neutral partisanship provide sheltered role-differentiated moral refuge and continue to be preferred over alternative accounts. Further, these alternative models are typically criticized for underplaying the institutional value of the lawyer in the adversarial system, while at the same time overplaying the relevance or supremacy of the lawyer's individual moral choices or preferences that risk usurping the ethical autonomy of the lawyer's client.

In my experience, while some students and practitioners are in optimistic agreement with modern critiques, most are, at worst, put off by them and are, at best, intrigued but ultimately not persuaded by their apparent moral superiority, relativity, and sermon-like nature. ...

This article seeks to ... [provide] a new way to think about professionalism. Specifically, by tapping into and building upon the ideas and energy of many current alternative models of professionalism, I seek to assist with the project of re-conceiving our modern understanding of professionalism. It is a professionalism that, unlike traditional (dominant) accounts, makes descriptive and normative sense of the complex modern practice of law. In so doing, I do not claim to be making a radical departure from other alternative model thinkers. In fact, what this article does is simply to recalibrate many of the current (primarily alternative) models and discussions through a slightly different lens: that of sustainability.

[Farrow then reviews the competing models of zealous advocacy and moral agency for understanding the lawyer's role, and their place and justification in principle, policy and practice.]

. . . . .

III. Alternative Models of Professionalism

. . . . .

D. Competing Professionalisms

At the moment, then, students of professionalism are currently left with two broad and competing menu choices when thinking about how best to understand legal ethics, or put differently, how best to approach Atkinson's "fundamental question of professional ethics." On the one hand — speaking from principle, policy, and practice — there is clearly still robust life in the spirits of the dominant model. On the other hand, a self-conscious moral sensibility of lawyering is certainly not a stranger to the modern vision of professionalism. In fact, on each of these three indicators, there is powerful and persuasive support for those who believe that they are not guided only by law's limits in the exercise of their lawyering duties.

In my view, the principles and policies that support the alternative model fit more naturally with the modern realities of lawyering. They tend to support Tanovich's observations regarding the shift toward a "justice-seeking ethic" over the past fifteen years. Moreover, they fit more naturally with an early version of the CBA's guiding ethics principles on a lawyer's "duty": "to promote the interests of the State, serve the cause of justice, maintain the authority and dignity of the Courts, be faithful to his clients, candid and courteous in his intercourse with his fellows and *true to himself*" [emphasis added]. This vision nicely fits with the aspirations of my students when asked if they would prefer a vision of professionalism that allowed for the opportunity to maintain a meaningful sense and space for "self."

However, even if Tanovich is correct in saying that the "zealous advocacy" model is slowly being replaced by a "justice-seeking ethic," we are clearly a long way from shedding the "names, battle slogans, and costumes" of the dominant ideology. According to David Luban, one of the most vocal supporters of an alternative vision of lawyering, although those who subscribe to an alternative vision of professionalism represent "a substantial minority of the legal profession, it is a minority view nonetheless." So why do we continue to be so powerfully influenced by the dominant trend of professionalism?

. . . . .

[I think] the most persuasive reason for the continued prominence of the dominant model comes not from the strength of that model but rather from a weakness in the way that the alternative models have, to date, been presented. Specifically, the alternative models are often framed in terms of the "moral perspective," "moral lawyering," or "the good lawyer." Even though proponents of these models sometimes see things differently, these labels tend to connote some shared or required understanding of what counts as "moral" or "good." It has taken the Enlightenment three hundred years to move this understanding from the realm of the family and the personal to a collective understanding of autonomy and rights at the public level of civil society. It is an understanding that cannot, by most accounts of liberalism in a pluralistic and complex society, be defended. To avoid this apparent trap, the dominant vision of the lawyer — "aiming not to inject her own vision of the good into the representation, but simply to pursue the client's vision of the good through the maximization of the client's legal rights" (based on classic Rawlsian political liberalism that prefers the right over the good) — nicely sidesteps a search for shared values and visions of the good life through role-morality. As such, it fosters the Enlightenment project of individual freedom and autonomy.

Even if we are persuaded by, for example, Rhode's answer to the problem of shared morality, these "intolerant" labels, by their very nature, tend to characterize the "other" side as being the opposite of a "good" lawyer, a "moral" lawyer, or a "just" lawyer, which of course the "other" dominant view rejects. For example, when looking for a shared conception of the public interest, Tanovich argues that it must at least require "lawyers to act in the pursuit of justice." In turn, justice for Tanovich "can be defined, for purposes of the lawyering process, as the *correct resolution of legal disputes or problems in a fair, responsible, and non-discriminatory manner*" [emphasis in original]. This definition of justice-seeking lawyering, or any of these alternative "moral" or "good"-based labels for that matter, are not wrong. In fact, by and large they are right. The problem is that these definitions and labels could be (and are) equally and credibly claimed by both sides to describe their lawyering projects. Lawyers on both sides think of themselves as "morally reflective individuals," "better people," "better lawyers," and "correct." They just approach these labels from very different perspectives.

... What is needed is a new, persuasive lens through which to see the world not in the service of "all the dead generations," but in the service of the "living" in "this society" and in the service of "the world of our children."

What is needed is a story of professionalism that captures the energy and positive attributes of both sides of this debate. What is needed is a story of professionalism that is sustainable.

IV. Sustainable Professionalism

A key aspect of the problem is that the two stories, on their face, disagree about how to evaluate what counts as the "right" course of action in a given circumstance. Their positions on this fundamental question compete. If we continue to assert these competing positions without uncovering the interests that underlie their positions — unless we find some common ground or more specifically, a persuasive lens through which to see this potential common ground — we will maintain this gridlock. ...

. . . . .

B. *Sustainability*

My approach re-directs much of the positive energy and progressive ideas of the competing models of professionalism through a more persuasive, *sustainable* lens. This approach stems from my frustration from hearing students and lawyers say to me countless times that a new way of thinking about professionalism would be a good idea in theory, but is just not sustainable in reality. This article therefore answers those skeptics by proposing a form of professionalism that is normatively sound, is descriptively accurate, and provides the basis for broad-based buy-in from as many justice-seeking stakeholders as possible. At the moment, neither the dominant nor the alternative models satisfies all three requirements.

Interestingly, but for a handful of references to several useful but general social science initiatives looking at the role and future of professionalism, there is little meaningful discussion of "sustainability" in the academic literature on legal ethics. It is not a mantra that theories of professionalism have self-consciously embraced.

As a general matter, sustainability has come to be primarily identified with three particular approaches: "sustainability as optimal living resource exploitation"; "sustainability as respect for ecological limits"; and "sustainability as sustainable development." While all three approaches characterize the *typical* use of the concept in modern legal parlance, they do not preclude other, more general uses of the idea. ...

To my mind, the legal profession provides a new terrain for "continuing debate" about the utility of sustainability, broadly defined. ... For my purpose, a lens of sustainability provides a "powerful symbol around which diverse interests can converge," "encompasses conflicting agendas," "promises to generate continuing debate and controversy," and is open to some normative notion of "rightfulness" in the eyes of a "person or community." Also important is the consideration of both current and *future* interests.

From before, we saw that the primary conflicting agendas involved those solely of the client as compared to those of a broader range of voices. Further, the theories of professionalism disagree as to the relevance or prominence of a lawyer's individual moral opinions vis-à-vis a client's legal course of action. Therefore, a useful lens of sustainability must take into account a broad range of these competing interests, which I have grouped into four main groups: client interests, lawyer interests, ethical and professional interests (of lawyers and the profession), and the public interest. It is important to note that the following discussion purports to be neither comprehensive regarding an individual interest nor complete regarding the totality of interests. Rather, what follows is a brief treatment of a sampling of some fundamental, perhaps competing, interests.

1.   Client Interests

The dominant model of professionalism, which is described above, protects and fosters meaningful space for the interests of clients, particularly powerful and wealthy clients, typically to the exclusion of all others. As we saw, based on principle, policy, and practice-based arguments, any notion of professionalism must make robust space for the realization of a client's legal interests in a free and democratic society.

At the outset, nothing in a theory of sustainability seeks to reject the importance of a client's legal interests. In fact, as Hutchinson — a primary proponent of an alternative approach to professionalism — argues, a "directive to lawyers to take responsibility for what they do (and do not do) ought not to be viewed as an excuse to ignore the needs of clients ... ." ... Clients must play a central role in any calculus of a sustained theory of professionalism. This makes sense as a descriptive matter. It also makes sense as a freedom-seeking normative matter. Important, however, is the realization that the conversation does not end here. If we are to make sense of the further principle, policy, and practice-based arguments that so powerfully animate the alternative models of professionalism, we need to take seriously and make room for some of the other (sometimes competing) interests that are at stake in this discussion.

2.   Lawyer Interests

As a starting point, there are numerous demands of the lawyering role that engage several self-interested notions of professionalism. First, there are pecuniary interests. Lawyers want to get paid and paid fairly for the hard work that they do and for the services that they provide. Therefore, a sustainable notion of professionalism must take into account the ability of lawyers to make a fair living. As the Honourable Frank Iacobucci commented, to the "extent that lawyers ... are financially successful it is often because they effectively and efficiently serve the needs of their clients, and that is an admirable thing."

Further, non-pecuniary interests of the lawyer will also play a prominent role in a sustainable notion of professionalism. Lawyers should expect to maintain a meaningful ability to pursue activities and interests that make for a full life not only as lawyers but also as members of society. Time at work, time at home, time with friends, and time engaging in social and political affairs should all be realizable goals of a sustainable professionalism. A sustainable notion of professionalism must avoid "slavishly adhering to billable hours and client getting at the cost of overlooking the quality of the work offered by lawyers or their contributions to the profession and the community both in legal and non-legal spheres."

. . . . .

3.   Ethical and Professional Interests (of Lawyers and the Profession)

Numerous ethical and professional interests are at play when mapping out a sustainable vision of professionalism. The principles and policies that animate the alternative models provide numerous robust bases for requiring that ethical and professional considerations be a meaningful part of a sustainable vision of professionalism.

In addition to seeing the lawyer's role as one that should pursue "social justice" by avoiding "dishonourable" or "morally reprehensible conduct," several other ethical or professional interests must form part of a sustainable discourse of professionalism. As a starting point, for this discourse to include the many different faces that make up the bar today, we must first recognize and celebrate the diversity of that bar. We must reject stories of lawyers who, collectively, are members of a homogenized and unified profession. Why? First, as a descriptive matter, such stories are not reflective of reality. As numerous commentators have noticed, those who practice law make up an increasingly diverse social, political, economic, cultural, and gender-based background. Second, as an economic matter, lawyers need increasingly to make sense of diversity obligations because clients are demanding that they do so. Market-based diversity incentives, in the form of diversity checklist programs, are a further reason why diversity matters in the context of understanding modern notions of professionalism.

Third, as a normative matter, such stories act to exclude a wide range of people who are or want to be practising law in diverse and meaningful ways in society. ...

A greater understanding and openness to diversity in our notions of professionalism will provide a more welcome and meaningful home for more lawyers. It will also push the profession's understanding of and participation in a public interest that truly reflects the reality of our general pluralistic and globalized civil societies. Further, however, it will also recognize the diversity of individual lawyers, with diverse moral perspectives, which will in turn assist with the charge that by allowing lawyers to moralize about their clients' causes, we will require some sense of a shared morality. ...

Celebrating a multiplicity of voices at the bar also assists with the "last lawyer in town" objection, which is often raised by dominant model theorists as a potentially fatal concern with alternative models of professionalism. As the argument goes, if all lawyers moralize about the causes of their clients, there is a good chance that clients with unpopular causes will not be able to find lawyers to take their cases. The question then becomes even more difficult if you — as a moral lawyer — find yourself to be the last lawyer in town. Do you take the case? My first response to this question is: "show me evidence establishing this concern as a recurring problem and I will then start to worry about it." Along the lines of "hard cases make bad law," it just has not been our typical experience that unpopular causes have systematically gone unrepresented. Second, if that unlikely scenario were to materialize, a balancing of competing interests — those of the client, the lawyer, and the state to provide for an adversarial system that is open to all comers — might well lead on balance, under a sustainable theory of professionalism, to the lawyer taking the case. Third, even taking this concern at face value as a real concern (which some people do), celebrating a pluralism of voices at the bar goes a long way to mitigating this risk. With a multitude of moral backgrounds and perspectives, a diverse bar becomes more welcoming to clients with diverse legal needs.

. . . . .

4.   Public Interest

Flowing from the third group is this fourth group of interests that, taken together, focus specifically on the public interest. Again, there is a vast array of interests that could be captured as part of this discussion. A notion of sustainable professionalism must maintain meaningful room for protection of the public interest, and in particular the robust and aspirational principle and policy-based statements that animate the alternative models of professionalism in the spirit of protecting the public interest. A notion of professionalism that does not acknowledge that "[s]tandards of professional ethics form the backdrop for everything lawyers do," and further, that a "primary concern" of the profession is "the protection of the public interest," will not be sustainable on any calculus that makes good on the bargain with society to protect the public interest in return for the privilege of self-regulation.

. . . . .

... [C]ommentators also advocate a theory of professionalism that makes meaningful space for lawyers pursuing just causes with their legal skills. Duncan Kennedy, for example, makes no apologies for his view that lawyers "should avoid doing harm" with their "lawyer skills." Hutchinson, although leaving significant space for client autonomy in his alternative vision of professionalism, takes seriously the centrality of the lawyer's role by encouraging a sensibility of "critical morality" that asks: "What interests am I going to spend my life serving as a lawyer?" Each of these accounts fits with Mayer's ultimate challenge to the bar, namely, that lawyers should demand that their efforts on behalf of their clients also amount to "a plus for ... society and for the world of our children." A sustainable notion of professionalism — one that makes good on the promise of public interest protection — therefore needs to take seriously these alternative accounts. And in case this all seems far from what should reasonably be expected of the practicing bar, we should remember that calls to "maintain and advance the cause of justice and the rule of law" and to "protect the public interest" come not only from these aspirational interpretations of professional principles, but also from foundational legislative dictates that establish our very professional existence. They also, at least according to Tanovich, are already being realized.

. . . . .

C. Balance and Context

So where does this leave us? From a review of the competing principle, policy, and practice-based arguments that animate the dominant and alternative models of professionalism, and trying to make sense of these various complex, contextual, and sometimes competing interests — reminiscent of some of the interests set out at the beginning of this article — what remains is a challenge that neither the dominant nor the alternative models has fully overcome. As I argued earlier, both sides must learn to think and speak in terms that are sustainable to a wide range of voices and interests. The dominant model, through its narrow focus primarily on one interest "in all the world," misses a variety of other relevant people and interests. The alternative model, on the other hand — through its typical focus on the "good lawyer" — has been seen to be unrealistic in practice, at least in light of the continued use of "time-honoured disguise[s] and ... borrowed language."

This theory of sustainable professionalism addresses the gridlock created by these competing notions of professionalism. It purports to do so by harnessing both the energy and optimism of the alternative models as well as the tenacity of the dominant model. Even more importantly, it self-consciously identifies the myriad interests that are at stake in the context — those of the client, lawyer, profession, and public — and draws them into a theory of professionalism that is sustainable.

By moving beyond the centrality of the client's interest as championed by the dominant model, instantly we open ourselves up to competing and potentially irreconcilable interests. This theory of sustainable professionalism takes seriously the complex and pluralistic landscapes of lawyers, clients, and the public. But in order to have a chance of buy-in from those broad-based stakeholders, we need to live in the world of those complexities, not in a world of fictional simplicity. ...

. . . . .

NOTES AND QUESTIONS

1. By referencing "professionalism", Farrow's model seems to contemplate that balancing the plurality of interests inheres in the lawyer's role — that it is something that the lawyer is responsible for doing. In the context of a lawyer-client relationship, why would we have lawyers balance those interests in making decisions about representation rather than clients? What special insights might lawyers bring to the identification of, for example, the public interest? Might a client legitimately claim the ability to balance those interests herself? See Katherine R. Kruse, "Beyond Cardboard Clients in Legal Ethics" (2010) 23 Geo. J. Legal Ethics 103.

2. David Luban has argued that one way lawyers can avoid ethical errors is by
    making *ex ante* commitments — identifying ethical lines that they will never
    cross. Can Farrow's model of sustainable professionalism be reconciled with
    those sorts of commitments? What ethical lines might a lawyer following sustain-
    able professionalism want to draw?

3. Does Farrow make a convincing case for the importance of lawyer interests in
    making money and/or maintaining a reasonable work-life balance? Are there any
    lawyer interests that could not reasonably be accommodated in a model of sus-
    tainable professionalism? How does recognition of lawyer interests fit with the
    legal principle that a lawyer is a fiduciary for her client?

In reading the following judgment, consider whether following a model of
sustainable professionalism could have changed counsel for the defendant's
assessment of their obligations to the plaintiff at the point of settlement.

SPAULDING v. ZIMMERMAN

263 Minn. 346 (1962)
(Supreme Court, Thomas Gallagher, Justice.
Justice Rogosheske took no part in the
consideration or decision of this case.)

[The defendants had reached a settlement with the plaintiff for injuries he had
suffered in an automobile accident. The medical report given to the defendants indicated that the plaintiff was suffering from an aneurysm which had
not been detected by the plaintiff's own physician. The defendants did not
disclose the medical report to the plaintiff. The plaintiff later discovered the
existence of the aneurysm and sought to set aside the settlement.]

. . . . .

The principles applicable to the court's authority to vacate settlements made
on behalf of minors and approved by it appear well established. With
reference thereto, we have held that the court in its discretion may vacate such
a settlement, even though it is not induced by fraud or bad faith, where it is
shown that in the accident the minor sustained separate and distinct injuries
which were not known or considered by the court at the time settlement was
approved ... and even though the releases furnished therein purported to
cover both known and unknown injuries resulting from the accident. ... The
court may vacate such a settlement for mistake even though the mistake was
not mutual in the sense that both parties were similarly mistaken as to the
nature and extent of the minor's injuries, but where it is shown that one of the
parties had additional knowledge with respect thereto and was aware that
neither the court nor the adversary party possessed such knowledge when the
settlement was approved. ...

From the foregoing it is clear that in the instant case the court did not abuse its
discretion in setting aside the settlement which it had approved on plaintiff's
behalf while he was still a minor. It is undisputed that neither he nor his
counsel nor his medical attendants were aware that at time settlement was
made he was suffering from an aorta aneurysm which may have resulted from

the accident. The seriousness of this disability is indicated by Dr. Hannah's report indicating the imminent danger of death therefrom. This was known by counsel for both defendants but was not disclosed to the court at the time it was petitioned to approve the settlement. While no canon of ethics or legal obligation may have required them to inform plaintiff or his counsel with respect thereto, or to advise the court therein, it did become obvious to them at the time that the settlement then made did not contemplate or take into consideration the disability described. This fact opened the way for the court to later exercise its discretion in vacating the settlement and under the circumstances described we cannot say that there was any abuse of discretion on the part of the court in so doing under Rule 60.02(6) of Rules of Civil Procedure.

. . . . .

Affirmed.

NOTES AND QUESTIONS

1. Assess how each theory of legal ethics discussed here — loyal advocacy; the lawyer as moral agent in pursuit of justice; and integrity — would have affected the lawyer's decision.

2. In the judgment, the court suggests that the lawyer's ethical obligations did not require disclosure of this information. Assuming that that is correct, does it suggest a deficit in the approach to lawyer ethics, or does it suggest that the judgment here is simply limited in application to the question of when settlements should be overturned?

3. Under the applicable discovery rules, Spaulding's lawyer was entitled to request (and to receive) a copy of the independent medical examination. He did not do so. Does this affect your assessment of the ethics of the decision made by Zimmerman's counsel?

4. At the time of the accident, Zimmerman was 19 years old. Spaulding was 20 years old and riding in Zimmerman's car. The damages that Spaulding would have received would have been covered by the various insurance policies in effect given the substantive tort law then applicable. Zimmerman was not consulted about whether the disclosure should take place, and it appears that the insurance representatives were not consulted either. Does this affect your assessment of the ethics of the decision made by Zimmerman's counsel?[15]

Scenario Six

Assume that you act for a client who tested positive for HIV after negligently receiving tainted blood products from a blood services agency. You enter into settlement discussions with the agency and they provide you with a generous offer to present to your client. Prior to accepting the offer, however, your client tells you that she has just been advised that the test was in error, and

---

[15] See Roger C. Cramton & Lori P. Knowles, "Professional Secrecy and its Exceptions: *Spaulding v. Zimmerman* Revisited" (1998) 83 Minn. L. Rev. 63.

that she does not have HIV. She nonetheless instructs you to accept the settlement offer without disclosing the error. Considering only the ethical principles discussed in this chapter, what should you do?[16]

Scenario Seven

Jane Adams is a wills and estates practitioner. A couple in their sixties comes to her for legal advice. She meets with them together, and also has conversations with them on their own. During the conversation with the wife, the wife tells Jane that prior to getting married she had a child whom she gave up for adoption. She knows where the child is (the adoption was with a family member) but the child does not know she is adopted. In addition, the husband does not know about the child. The wife would like to make some provision for the child in her will, but she does not want to tell her husband. Jane believes that openness and honesty are crucial in a marriage, and that the wife's moral well-being rests on her telling the husband the truth. She also knows that under the applicable code of professional conduct she cannot continue to represent the couple unless the wife tells. Does she urge the wife to tell?

F. FURTHER READING

Arthurs, H.W., "Why Canadian Law Schools Do Not Teach Legal Ethics" in Kim Economides, ed., *Ethical Challenges to Legal Education & Conduct* (Oxford: Hart Publishing, 1999).

Bagaric, Mirko & Penny Dimopoulos, "Legal Ethics is (Just) Normal Ethics: Towards a Coherent System of Legal Ethics" (2003) 3(2) Q.U.T.L.J. 367.

Berlin, Isaiah, *The Crooked Timber of Humanity* (New York: Random House, 1991).

Blackburn, Simon, *Being Good: A Short Introduction to Ethics* (Oxford: Oxford University Press, 2002).

Dare, Tim, *The Counsel of Rogues?: A Defence of the Standard Conception of the Lawyer's Role* (Surrey, U.K.: Ashgate, 2009).

Farrow, Trevor, "Sustainable Professionalism" (2008) 46 Osgoode Hall L.J. 51.

Freedman, Monroe & Abbe Smith, *Understanding Lawyers' Ethics*, 4th ed. (New York: LexisNexis, 2010).

Fried, Charles, "The Lawyer as Friend" (1975) 85 Yale L.J. 1060.

Gordon, Robert W., "The Independence of Lawyers" (1988) 68 B.U. L. Rev. 1.

Hartwell, Steven, "Promoting Moral Development Through Experiential Teaching" (1994–1995) 1 Clinical L. Rev. 505.

---

[16] This hypothetical is adapted from Allan C. Hutchinson, *Legal Ethics and Professional Responsibility* (Toronto: Irwin Law, 1999) at 1-2.

Hursthouse, Rosalind, *On Virtue Ethics* (Oxford: Oxford University Press, 1999).

Hutchinson, Allan C., *Legal Ethics and Professional Responsibility*, 2nd ed. (Toronto: Irwin Law, 2006).

Kant, Immanuel, *The Metaphysics of Morals*, transl. Mary Gregor (Cambridge: Cambridge University Press, 1996).

Koniak, Susan P., "The Law Between the Bar and the State" (1992) 70 N.C. L. Rev. 1389.

Kronman, Anthony T., *The Lost Lawyer: Failing Ideals of the Legal Profession* (Cambridge, MA: Harvard University Press, 1993).

Luban, David, *Lawyers and Justice* (Princeton: Princeton University Press, 1988).

Luban, David, *Legal Ethics and Human Dignity* (Cambridge: Cambridge University Press, 2007).

MacIntyre, Alasdair, *After Virtue*, 2nd ed. (London: Duckworth, 1985).

Markovits, Daniel, *A Modern Legal Ethics: Adversarial Advocacy in a Democratic Age* (Princeton: Princeton University Press, 2008).

Nicolson, Donald & Julian Webb, *Professional Legal Ethics: Critical Interrogations* (Oxford: Oxford University Press, 1999).

Pepper, Stephen L., "The Lawyer's Amoral Ethics Role: A Defense, a Problem, and Some Possibilities" (1986) A.B.F. Res. J. 613.

Postema, Gerald J., "Moral Responsibility in Professional Ethics" (1980) 55 N.Y.U. L. Rev. 63.

Rhode, Deborah L., *Ethics in Practice: Lawyers' Roles, Responsibilities and Regulation* (New York: Oxford University Press, 2000).

Rhode, Deborah L., *In the Interests of Justice: Reforming the Legal Profession* (New York: Oxford University Press, 2003).

Shaffer, Thomas L. & Mary Shaffer, *American Lawyers and their Communities: Ethics in the Legal Profession* (Notre Dame: Notre Dame University Press, 1999).

Simon, William, "Ethical Discretion in Lawyering" (1988) 101 Harv. L. Rev. 1083.

Simon, William, *The Practice of Justice: A Theory of Lawyer's Ethics* (Cambridge, MA: Harvard University Press, 2000).

Stanford Encyclopedia of Philosophy, online: <http://plato.stanford.edu>.

Tanovich, David, "Law's Ambition and the Reconstruction of Role Morality in Canada" (2005) 28 Dal. L.J. 267.

Wasserstrom, Richard, "Lawyers as Professionals: Some Moral Issues" (1975) 5 Human Rights 1.

Wendel, W. Bradley, *Lawyers and Fidelity to Law* (Princeton: Princeton University Press, 2010).

Woolley, Alice, "If Philosophical Legal Ethics is the Answer, What is the Question?" (2010) 60 U.T.L.J. 983.

Woolley, Alice, *Understanding Lawyers' Ethics in Canada* (Markham, ON: LexisNexis Canada, 2011).

Woolley, Alice & W. Bradley Wendel, "Legal Ethics and Moral Character" (2010) 23 Geo. J. Legal Ethics 1065.

Williams, Bernard, *Ethics and the Limits of Philosophy* (Cambridge, MA: Harvard University Press, 1985).

CHAPTER 2

THE LEGAL PROFESSION AND LAWYER REGULATION IN CANADA

A. INTRODUCTION

The regulation of lawyers in Canada occurs in a number of ways, some more direct than others. The most direct means is self regulation, that is, the regulation of lawyers by lawyers, which is the primary subject of this chapter. That apart, regulation of lawyer conduct can occur, for example, through suits against lawyers for malpractice and breach of fiduciary duties, or criminal prosecutions for fraud. The conduct of lawyers is also regulated by the cultural practices and norms of particular firms or legal communities, and by the standards of the market for legal services.

The chief concern of this chapter is to explore lawyer self regulation in Canada through a critical consideration of: the concept, in theory and practice; its underlying purpose; the means and devices by which it is implemented; and its current scope. The chapter will also briefly address other regulatory functions of the organized profession, such as those in relation to unauthorized practice, and current forms of external regulation. Altogether, the chapter provides a critical overview of the regulatory framework for the concepts of ethics and legal ethics discussed in the preceding chapter and for the specific ethical obligations discussed in Chapters 3 to 11. In addition, it provides the necessary background information and context for the more detailed discussion of current issues in the regulation of the legal profession (Chapter 13) and access to justice (Chapter 12).

B. THE GENERAL CONCEPT OF PROFESSIONAL SELF REGULATION

The concept of self regulation is somewhat vague and imprecise. In essence, it refers to the control, direction or governance of an identifiable group by rules and regulations determined by the members of the group — in our instance, the control and direction of lawyers, an occupational group, through rules and regulations made by lawyers acting collectively, in the form of autonomous governing bodies, known as law societies in the common law provinces of Canada. Self regulation is undertaken in the public interest to ensure that legal services are provided to the public ethically and competently by only those persons qualified to do so.

Most, if not all lawyers, view self regulation uncritically, as a natural feature of law's status as a profession, an elite or privileged form of occupation which enjoys a "monopoly" or dominance over the market for legal services in Canada. Self regulation is seen as a bargain or social contract with the state, carried out by the profession in return for a state sanctioned market dominance. On this view, self regulation is deeply embedded or implicated in the concept of the practice of law as a modern profession. It is uniformly identified as one of the dominant traits or characteristics exhibited by learned professions or their members which serve to demarcate or set off professions or professionals from other less privileged occupations or workers. Among the other traits or characteristics commonly referred to in this respect are: the presence of an autonomous governing body for the purpose of regulating members' conduct; the mastery of a specialized field of knowledge acquired through an extensive period of formal education and practical training; the restriction of admission to the profession and practice to those who have demonstrated such mastery through a period of theoretical and practical training followed by successful completion of examinations and tests of competence; the presence of a first and particular responsibility to a client or patient; the provision of important services in relation to vital needs associated with the "health, freedom, spiritual state, economic well being"[1] of persons; and the use of specialized knowledge and skills in the furtherance of not only individual but the broader public interest.[2] The existence of a code of professional ethics, heightened social prestige due to the intellectual nature of the work, higher professional incomes and dominance or monopoly over the market for particular services have also been identified as traits of classic professions such as law. At the end of the day, it must be understood that these traits do not tell us why certain occupations are privileged as professions while others are not; rather, they are simply characteristics exhibited by occupations who have long claimed and been long recognized as professions.

In contrast with the dominant traits approach to defining a profession, sociologists and economists have used a number of theories to critically examine and explain the path of professions and professionalism over the course of the last century or so. Some mention of these approaches should be made to put the related concepts of "profession", "professionalism" and "self regulation" into better perspective.

One sociological approach looks at the profession from the perspective of the market.[3] On this account, professions are said to be different from other occupations in the strategies they pursue to gain advantage in a competitive marketplace with its attendant awards of social status (mobility) and heightened wealth. To begin with, the profession must construct a market, in our

---

[1]   Charles Wolfram, *Modern Legal Ethics* (St. Paul, MN: West Publishing, 1986) at 15.

[2]   *Ibid.*, at 14-16; United Kingdom, H.C. Royal Commission on Legal Services, Cmnd. 7648, Vol. 1 (1979) at 28, 30.

[3]   This view, which builds on the work of Weber, is drawn from Richard L. Abel, *American Lawyers* (New York: Oxford University Press, 1989) at 14-40.

case, the market for specialized legal services which are both valued and incapable of being produced by the consumer. Once the market is created or constructed, the profession must pursue a strategy of market closure which is designed to limit or control the number of producers (providers of legal services) in the market and to control the production by those producers within the market. Entry into the market is controlled through devices such as formal education requirements, licensing standards or qualifications and evaluations. This strategy is by nature exclusionary and, to be successful, requires in the case of the modern legal profession, co-operation between the profession, the state and the university. Control over the production by producers is designed to remedy a disorderly, chaotic, overly competitive market with its attendant threat to a professional's social status and economic benefits. The controls may be formal or informal but their purpose is clear: to protect members of the profession from competition with one another as well as from those outside of the market. A dampening of competitive activity may also allow the profession to enhance its social status by displaying an aura of disinterest and objectivity. At the end of the day, this is a fairly negative or critical account of professions, including law, which are shown to be acting out of self interest, in the pursuit of greater wealth and social status. On this view, self regulation is not undertaken in the public interest but to exclude certain persons from participation in the market for legal services, to ensure the scarcity of legal services and to dampen competition in order to keep prices for services higher than would otherwise be the case in an open, free market.

A similar view is taken by a number of economists who have criticized professions as unnecessary restraints on the operation of free markets, including that for legal services.[4] A need to ensure a certain quality of legal services is not seen as sufficient justification for the substantial restraints placed on the operations of the free market. Regulatory restraints on entry to the profession and on competition between practitioners are thought to be detrimental to consumers in the form of increased costs and unfair to competitors.

Another sociological view, labelled the "structural functional" approach,[5] takes a more positive view of professions as important contributors to order and stability in society. Professions are seen as a means whereby a society consisting of egotistical individuals can be held together. Rather than challenge society from without, individuals can compete for rewards and greater social status through structures such as those offered by professions which typically rank at the top or near the top of the hierarchy of social classes. Structural functionalists also see professions as an important source

---

[4]   For a Canadian example of a large body of work see, Phillip Slayton & Michael J. Trebilcock, eds., *The Professions and Public Policy* (Toronto: University of Toronto Press, 1978).

[5]   Richard L. Abel, *Lawyers: A Critical Reader* (New York: The New Press, 1997) at 125-28.

of community in societies marked by individualism.[6] Professional communities, such as law, are built largely around a common education, a shared sense of professional role or function and a specialized vocabulary or language. They offer a structure for self governance on the basis of a common professional culture and shared standards or norms of practice. Nevertheless, the legal profession appears to be a weak community given its significant and growing internal divisions based on clientele, type of practice and area of practice.

Under structural functional theories, professions enjoy broad autonomy which enables their members, as professionals, to use their specialized expertise and knowledge in the general welfare. Free from outside interference, from either the state or other bureaucracies, it is believed that professionals will put the interests of both their clients and the general public ahead of their own interests. While this belief has not been empirically substantiated, it would appear to underlie the claim that professions differ from other occupations in their disinterestedness and often altruistic orientation. Given the belief in autonomy, it is not surprising that structural functionalists see "self regulation" as the defining characteristic of professions. Some form of regulation is necessary to ensure both that professionals are technically qualified and that they do not abuse the power rooted in their specialized knowledge or expertise; however, professions have successfully argued that they alone must exercise regulatory control. Generally speaking, two arguments are made in this respect: first, that only the members of a profession possess the knowledge and expertise necessary to assess each others' conduct, and second, that only the profession possesses the necessary independence or autonomy from the state to regulate its members, in a disinterested fashion, in the public interest.

Historians have used the dominant traits or characteristics of legal professionalism, particularly those of qualification, admission and education, self regulation, codes of ethics and monopoly over the provision of legal services, as key reference points in their examination of the evolution of the organized legal profession in Canada. For example, Wesley Pue, a leading Canadian legal historian, has argued that lawyers in Western Canada were engaged in a culturally informed professionalism project in the first decades of the 20th century from which emerged a new and distinctive model of legal professionalism rooted in English antecedents but shaped by developments in the American legal profession.[7] This new model of legal professionalism represented significant changes to the historic structures of professionalism with a new, rigorous, university-centred model for legal education; the development of a written code of lawyers' ethics; new and expanded roles for law societies in the ethical regulation, admission, education and discipline of lawyers; and

---

[6]   Richard L. Abel, *American Lawyers* (New York: Oxford University Press, 1989) at 36-37, citing the works of Durkheim and Goode.

[7]   W. Wesley Pue, "Cultural Projects and Structural Transformation in the Canadian Legal Profession" in W. Wesley Pue & D. Sugarman, eds., *Lawyers and Vampires: Cultural Histories of Legal Professions* (Portland: Hart Publishing, 2003) at 367-91.

the assertion and attainment of a state supported monopoly over the market for legal services. Changes to the traditional structures of legal professionalism were pursued to legitimate or justify the leadership of lawyers in a new society challenged by radical impulses and social and ethnic divisions. The overall goal of this cultural project was to protect the future of lawyers and other elites and to preserve the essential "Britishness" of western Canadian society from the risk of social chaos.[8]

None of these theories or analyses completely explain the evolution of the modern profession or legal professionalism, but elements of each contribute to a better and deeper understanding of professions such as law and the power and practice of lawyer self regulation. These general views or theories about the concept of self regulation should be borne in mind when reading the following description of law as a self regulating profession.

C. THE PRACTICE OF LAWYER SELF REGULATION

In Canada, the legal profession has established a dominance or monopoly over the market for legal services; that is, only lawyers admitted to the law societies of the various provinces and territories may provide legal services to consumers or clients in these jurisdictions. This market dominance is sanctioned by the state through legislation which prohibits non-lawyers from practising law or acting as barristers or solicitors. Also, the legal profession is self regulating in regard to the admission, conduct and discipline of lawyers. This regulation is carried out through the mechanism of provincial law societies, corporations created and empowered by provincial and territorial legislation,[9] to which every practising lawyer in the various provincial and territorial jurisdictions must belong. In each jurisdiction, the management and conduct of the society's business and affairs and the exercise of its powers is vested in a largely elected body, entitled the "Benchers" of the society.

Self regulation is defended or supported by the legal profession and its members on a number of bases. First, there is an historical argument which draws on an alleged connection between the modern Canadian law society and the law guilds of medieval England, more commonly known as the Inns of Court. This appeal to history is made to legitimate, as the product of an orderly evolution, the independent and autonomous position of the contemporary Bar and its powers of self regulation. Witness the following statement taken from the submission of the Law Society of Upper Canada to the Ontario legislature's Professional Organizations Committee:

> This historical review has established that the Bar in England and Ontario grew independently of government and exercises responsibility of its own

---

[8] See also Philip Girard, *Lawyers and Legal Culture in British North America: Beamish Murdoch of Halifax* (Toronto: University of Toronto Press, Osgoode Society for Legal Publishing, 2011); Christopher Moore, *The Law Society of Upper Canada and Ontario's Lawyers, 1797–1997* (Toronto: University of Toronto Press, 1997).

[9] For example, *Legal Profession Act*, R.S.A. 2000, c. L-8, s. 2; *Legal Profession Act*, S.B.C. 1998, c. 9, s. 2; and *Law Society Act*, R.S.O. 1990, c. L.8, s. 2.

making; that it requested and obtained from government recognition and a legal framework within which it continues to discharge its functions; that this independence of the Bar is necessary to the independence of the Bench and to the freedom for the individual citizens. ... Unless there is a strong reason for change, a structure which has evolved over centuries and which is working well should not be interfered with.[10]

This argument links the independence of law as a self regulating profession with the protection of individual rights and liberties from the pervasive threat posed by the state — a key component of the Rule of Law, as a fundamental constitutional principle. Its strongest expression is to be found in the following extract from the judgment of Estey J. in *Canada (Attorney General) v. Law Society of British Columbia*:

The independence of the Bar from the state in all its pervasive manifestations is one of the hallmarks of a free society. Consequently, regulation of these members of the law profession by the state must, so far as by human ingenuity it can be so designed, be free from state interference, in the political sense, with the delivery of services to the individual citizens in the state, particularly in the fields of public and criminal law. The public interest in a free society knows no area more sensitive than the independence, impartiality and availability to the general public of the members of the Bar, and through those members, legal advice and services generally.[11]

Altogether, it is an argument which strongly resonates with lawyers who believe that law's claim to be a profession rests on its long history of self governance in the public interest. This rhetorical, somewhat politically charged argument has been challenged on the basis that it is overstated, premised on somewhat questionable history, and is not empirically true. Barton, for example, has suggested that there is "little evidence" to support this perspective and that what evidence there is suggests in fact that the bar has "regularly oppressed disfavored minority viewpoints, races and religions".[12]

A second line of argument builds on the specialized knowledge and expertise of the lawyer in relation to that of the client or consumer. Only lawyers are equipped by education and experience to understand the technical complexity involved in the regulation of lawyers or, as Arthurs puts it:

[s]econdly, there is the argument from practicality: professions must be self governing because they alone understand what their members need to know,

---

[10]   Law Society of Upper Canada, *Submission to the Professional Organizations Committee by the Law Society of Upper Canada* (Toronto: Law Society of Upper Canada, April 1979) at 7-8, cited in W. Wesley Pue, "In Pursuit of Better Myth: Lawyer's Histories and Histories of Lawyers" (1995) 33 Alta. L. Rev. 730 at 740.

[11]   [1982] S.C.J. No. 70, [1982] 2 S.C.R. 307 at 335-36 (S.C.C.).

[12]   Benjamin H. Barton, "Why Do We Regulate Lawyers?: An Economic Analysis of the Justifications for Entry and Conduct Regulation" (2001) 33 Arizona St. L.J. 429 at 484.

how they ought to behave, what constitutes deviant conduct, and which sanctions ought to be imposed when.[13]

The courts have accepted this argument as the underlying basis for self regulation. For example, in *Law Society of Manitoba v. Savino*, Monnin C.J.M. observed: "No one is better qualified to say what constitutes professional misconduct than a group of practicing barristers who are themselves subject to the rules established by their governing body."[14]

While this argument has much to recommend it, it has been challenged on several grounds: first, that the underlying information asymmetry about the appropriateness of lawyer conduct is, in fact, the product of the lawyer's monopoly over legal knowledge which can be addressed by providing more information to clients and consumers; and second, that experience shows that effective government or third party regulation, in a wide range of fields of activity, does not depend on the regulator possessing the same knowledge and expertise as the regulated — expertise can be acquired or bought, if necessary.

Self regulation is also supported, somewhat rhetorically, on the basis that it forms part of a social contract with the state; that the profession will regulate itself, in the public interest, in return for a "monopoly" or dominance over the market for legal services. This is no more than an attempt to provide an ideological basis for what exists in fact. There is no evidence that any such bargain was ever consciously entered into nor that the profession has always regulated its members in the public's interests. Indeed, it can be argued that the profession's self governance is selfishly motivated, to preclude the imposition of state or third party regulation.

Finally, it has been argued, on occasion, that self regulation by the profession is more efficient and cost effective than external regulation; as the costs of administration and enforcement are covered by the members of the regulated profession rather than by taxpayers. But, as one commentator has pointed out, total, rather than just administrative, costs must be included in any cost benefit analysis and "[a]dministrative costs ("expenses involved in operating an office, developing entry and practice standards, testing applicants, receiving and hearing complaints, conducting practice audits and holding disciplinary hearings") pale by comparison with the costs imposed on society at large from the disruption of market principles".[15] Licensing schemes limit consumer choice and access to services and make the cost of services greater.

---

13   Harry Arthurs, "The Dead Parrot: Does Professional Self Regulation Exhibit Vital Signs?" (1995) 33 Alta. L. Rev. 800 at 801.

14   [1983] M.J. No. 206, 1 D.L.R. (4th) 285 at 292-93 (Man. C.A.). See also *Pearlman v. Manitoba Law Society Judicial Committee*, [1991] S.C.J. No. 66, [1991] 2 S.C.R. 869 (S.C.C.).

15   W. Wesley Pue, "Foxes, Henhouses, Unfathomable Mysteries, and the Sufferance of the People: A Review of *Regulating Professions and Occupations*" (1996–1997) 24 Man. L.J. 283 at 287.

1.   The Structure of Self Regulation

(a)   Law Societies

Self regulation of the legal profession in Canada is carried out through the medium of provincial and territorial law societies. To practise law in a particular jurisdiction, a lawyer must be admitted to membership in the law society of that jurisdiction. Law societies are not private bodies,[16] possessed of inherent powers, rather, they are, simply the delegates of provincial and territorial legislatures, statutorily constituted and empowered for the purpose of regulating lawyers in the public interest. The powers of self regulation are, in fact, exercised by governing bodies or councils, all or the majority of whose members are elected by the profession.

As instruments of self regulation, law societies have evolved in Canada over the last 200 years starting with the Law Society of Upper Canada in 1797 which was loosely modelled after the English Inns of Court. In most instances, regulation first took the form of control over education and admission to the profession and practice, followed by further statutory delegations of power to regulate the conduct of members through rule-making and discipline. By the midpoint of the 20th century, law societies in Canada had gained extensive regulatory powers over the admission and conduct of lawyers in their respective jurisdictions, including the power to discipline. In general, these powers consisted of discretionary authority to make decisions with respect to educational qualifications, admissions applications and complaints against members for improper or unprofessional conduct. Typically, this included the power to make rules and regulations for the governance of the society and its members.

The powers of self regulation vested in the governing bodies of law societies are significant but not unlimited. The nature and scope of these powers are, of course, limited by the terms of the statutory grants of discretion. And what the legislature has given, it can amend or take away. As indicated by some of the cases excerpted elsewhere in this casebook, both the delegation of authority and its exercise may be subject to challenge on the basis of the *Canadian Charter of Rights and Freedoms*.[17] Admissions and discipline decisions which affect individual members of the profession are subject to the supervisory jurisdiction of the superior courts in each province. In some cases, the rules and regulations made by law societies in relation to matters such as discipline, accounting, education, conduct and admissions are contingent on legislative or governmental approval. Some measure of control is also provided by periodic government inquiries into the activities of occupations and professions, including that of law, which have led to some changes in powers of self regulation to provide for greater transparency and

---

[16]   *Klein v. Law Society of Upper Canada*, [1985] O.J. No. 2321, 16 D.L.R. (4th) 489 at 528 (Ont. H.C.J.).

[17]   Being Part I of the *Constitution Act, 1982*, being Schedule B of the *Canada Act 1982* (U.K.), 1982, c. 11 [hereinafter the "Charter"].

accountability in the discipline and decision-making process. For example, most provincial statutes provide for the appointment of a few non-lawyers to the governing bodies of the profession in order to provide for some sort of public oversight. The numbers of these appointments are so small that professional control of regulation is not diminished but they do ensure that "public" views are heard and that the public interest is served or, at least, is not subordinated to the interests of the profession or its members.

Even though, as a matter of constitutional law, the legal profession is regulated provincially, a type of national self regulation has emerged over the last two decades in the form of co-operative action through the Federation of Law Societies of Canada (FLSC). From an association of provincially empowered regulators, the FLSC has become the locus of a number of national initiatives designed to impart a type of "pan Canadian" regulation over Canada's lawyers in an increasingly national and international market-place. Beginning with the mobility protocol in the 1990s designed to facilitate movement between, and practice in more than one of, Canada's provincial jurisdictions, the FLSC has continued with further initiatives in legal education, legal ethics, admission and discipline to build upon and strengthen the mobility initiative through the establishment of common standards and the harmonization of provincial and territorial rules.

The impetus for the national mobility protocol was the need for a more consistent and efficient regulation of lawyer movement between the various provincial jurisdictions; mobility was not to be frustrated by differing provincial rules but to be regulated and facilitated through clear common standards and policies amongst the provincial law societies designed to ensure competent and ethical practice. Greater lawyer mobility was prompted by the growing regional, national and international focus of law practice in response to the transnational or global economic and personal activity of clients, both corporate and individual. The initiatives that followed have been undertaken to reinforce the mobility of Canadian lawyers through common or harmonized educational, admission, ethical and discipline standards and policies. For example, the Task Force on the content of Canadian common law degrees was established to set a benchmark or standard for the evaluation and accreditation of both Canadian common law and foreign law degrees. The initiative on a national or model code of legal ethics built upon the long-standing work of the Canadian Bar Association in creating and maintaining a national code or standard for lawyer practice. However, the FLSC's *Model Code of Professional Conduct* has more regulatory heft as it is the product of a national group of statutory regulators rather than the collective statement of a voluntary association of lawyers without regulatory powers. To the extent that these Federation initiatives are accepted and implemented by the various provincial law societies, a nationally constructed standard will serve as the basis for provincial regulation of lawyers.

Finally, it should be noted that self regulation has been diminished somewhat by the growing use of legislation in Canada and the United States to regulate certain aspects of law practice. To the extent that this legislation governs lawyer behaviour, the scope of self regulation, through an independent, autonomous profession is lessened. One of the areas in which this is most pronounced concerns the business activities of clients. As discussed in Chapter 9, in the United States, the *Sarbanes Oxley Act* of 2002 imposed, through Securities and Exchange Commission regulations, new obligations on lawyers "to report material violations of securities laws up the corporate ladder". Similarly, in Ontario, the Court of Appeal upheld a decision of the Divisional Court to the effect that a lawyer was not immune from proceedings under the *Securities Act* for a violation of the statute.[18]

More recently, a controversy erupted over regulations under the federal government's money laundering legislation which required lawyers to secretly report information concerning client transactions which raised suspicions. This regulation was challenged by several law societies and the FLSC on the grounds that it was an unconstitutional infringement of the independence of the Bar, and inconsistent with the lawyer's duties of loyalty and confidentiality. While lawyers were exempted from the legislation in 2003, negotiations continued over amendments to the legislation and new regulations. Subsequently, the federal government brought in changes to the legislation and regulations to address what it saw as the pressing and substantial problem of money laundering and terrorist financing. Law societies, on the basis of model rules prepared by the FLSC, adopted rules concerning cash transactions ("no cash" rule) and client identification ("client ID" rule) which in concert with law society auditing processes were designed to close any regulatory gap in dealing with the problem of money laundering. The FLSC, on behalf of Canada's law societies, then challenged the Federal legislation on the basis that it was still unconstitutional as it violated the sections 7 and 8 Charter rights of lawyers and their clients. The FLSC's position was partially sustained by the British Columbia Supreme Court in *Federation of Law Societies of Canada v. Canada (Attorney General)*,[19] where L.B. Gerow J. ruled that the legislation violated the section 7 rights of lawyers and their clients.

(b) Nature and Scope of Self Regulation

Although, in response to both internal and external pressures, the nature and scope of self regulation has expanded and become more comprehensive over the last two to three decades, entry and conduct regulation remain the core areas of concern. *Entry regulation* concerns the admission of qualified persons to the profession and practice while *conduct regulation* involves the articulation and enforcement of practice standards and norms.

Apart from these core areas, contemporary self regulation entails: the regulation of lawyers' accounts through detailed rules and enforcement practices such as audits; the operation of insurance and assurance fund schemes to compensate clients who have suffered loss as a result of lawyer

---

[18]   *Wilder v. Ontario (Securities Commission)*, [2001] O.J. No. 1017, 53 O.R. (3d) 519 (Ont. C.A.), excerpted in Chapter 9.

[19]   [2011] B.C.J. No. 1779, 2011 BCSC 1270 (B.C.S.C.).

negligence or fraud; the maintenance of quality legal services through disciplinary sanctions, continuing education programs and practice review programs; and lawyer support services, in the form of practice and ethics advice, as well as initiatives for those with personal and substance abuse problems. However, for the purposes of this chapter, the focus will be on the core areas of entry and conduct regulation.

(c) Regulation of Entry to the Profession and Practice

In order to practise law in either a provincial or territorial jurisdiction, a person must be admitted to the law society of that particular jurisdiction. Although there are some differences between the various jurisdictions in Canada, admission basically involves two matters: (1) the satisfaction of pre-admission education requirements, which include preliminary university study, the attainment of a law degree, completion of mandated period in articles (a form of apprenticeship), and completion of a bar admission course and a bar examination; and (2) the satisfaction of the "good character" requirement.[20] Each of these will now be addressed in turn.

(i) Pre-admission Education Requirements

Throughout the 19th and into the 20th century, the primary focus of law societies in Canada's provinces and territories was on the regulation of entry into the profession through means such as the establishment of educational qualifications. The avowed purpose was to restrict entry to only those persons qualified to practice competently. For most of this period the chief requirement in this respect was completion of a lengthy period of apprenticeship (three to five years) with an experienced practitioner, commonly called "articles". The education was practical in orientation and varied significantly depending on the quality and commitment of the practitioner involved. The student was to learn the law and the necessary skills from his principal in his practice. Articles also provided an excellent opportunity for the socialization and mentoring of students.[21] From time to time, law societies supplemented articles with other requirements such as entrance examinations in law or law-related subjects, keeping terms at the premises of the law society or the courts, attendance at law lectures and bar examinations. With the advent of university legal education, growing recognition was given to an academic course of study through a reduction, which varied from jurisdiction to jurisdiction, in the term of articles set for law school graduates. By the late 1950s, the three-year university degree program in law (LL.B.) had replaced

---

[20]   Some provinces, such as Nova Scotia, also require that an applicant for admission as a lawyer or an articled clerk be a "fit and proper person"; see Nova Scotia Barristers' Society, *Regulations Made Pursuant to the Legal Profession Act, S.N.S. 2004, c. 28*, rr. 3.3.2, 3.9.2. The utilization of such a standard has generated some controversy: see Jocelyn Downie, "Law Societies as Arbiters of Mental Fitness" (2001) 24 Advocates' Q. 467.

[21]   Veronica Ashenhurst, "Mentoring the Lawyer, Past and Present: Some Reflections" (2011) 42 Ottawa L. Rev. 125.

articles as the primary educational requirement for admission to practice. Over the next two decades, the educational requirements for admission to the bar became more complex and varied but typically consisted of: a period of preliminary university study of two to three years' duration; a three-year course of study at a university law school; a period in articles of least 12 months' duration; attendance at a bar admission course; and completion of a bar examination. Preparation for law practice had gained a more academic orientation although it must be admitted that, to a varying extent, the profession still exerted a measure of control or influence over the content of university legal education to ensure its practice and professional preparation orientation.

With some further variations, this basic structure of legal education remains in place to this day. The three-year LL.B. or J.D. program at a university law faculty has become the primary means of preparation for admission to the bar and law practice. In English-speaking Canada's common law programs, the first year is made up of mandatory instruction in five or six foundational subject areas such as torts, contracts, criminal law and property. Typically, some instruction is also offered in legal writing and research and legal methods or foundations. The second and third years of the program consist of an entirely, or largely, optional curriculum designed to offer students greater choice in their programs, depending on their academic or professional priorities. The optional curriculum reflects, in part, a broader view of the study of law as an intellectual enterprise beyond the traditional parameters of preparation for professional practice. In more recent years, the second and third year curriculum has also featured a more interdisciplinary approach to law study and, to a limited extent, greater attention to skills and values development.

However, despite its greater breadth and depth, the academic stage of legal education is still marked by the historic tension between preparation for professional practice and academic study. On one hand, to satisfy the views of those — chiefly practitioners — who believe that university legal education should be directed towards instruction in substantive and procedural law and skills development necessary to quality legal practice, the law school must offer instruction in core subject areas traditionally associated with law practice. On the other hand, to meet the views of others — chiefly legal academics and the wider university community — who believe that legal education should be a broader, more humanistic and inter-disciplinary study, directed to an understanding of law and its role in society, the law school must offer a wider range of courses "designed to allow students to reflect more carefully on the legal process, comparative perspectives, the role of law in international relations and law as a political, economic, philosophical and cultural phenomenon".[22]

---

[22]   John P.S. McLaren, "The History of Legal Education in Common Law Canada" in Roy Matas & Deborah McCawley, *Legal Education in Canada* (Montreal: Federation of Law Societies, 1987) 111 at 137.

Although some law societies possessed the formal power to approve or disapprove of university law programs for the purposes of admission, for nearly 50 years they did not exert any direct controls over the academic stage of legal education on the understanding that law schools would continue to allocate significant resources to instruction in the subject areas traditionally associated with law practice (the core curriculum). As a result, law school curriculum and teaching has been essentially controlled by the universities, and in particular, by the law faculties who have enjoyed a significant measure of freedom in terms of the form and content of legal education subject, of course, to the profession's concerns and sensitivities. During this period, however, despite the lack of direct controls, the profession continued to exert considerable influence over the academic stage of legal education. Members of the practising profession served both on the governing bodies of law faculties and as adjunct or sessional instructors. A professional ideology and culture that permeated the law school and the professional agenda, in terms of subject areas, course content and teaching methodology, still predominated.

In the past two years, the law societies have sought to become more actively involved in setting the content and approach to legal education in Canada, culminating in the publication in 2009 of the FLSC's *Task Force on the Canadian Common Law Degree: Final Report*.[23] Ostensibly, this Report was prompted by a growing number of persons with foreign law degrees seeking admission to practice across Canada. For the purpose of evaluating these degrees, a Canadian academic standard for admission to the bar was necessary. This standard would apply to both Canadian and foreign law degrees. The Report has been adopted by all Canadian law societies and, once fully implemented in 2015, will require law schools to certify that their graduates have successfully completed a program of study which comports with the standards set out in the Report in relation to competencies in core areas of substantive knowledge, skills, professionalism and ethics. This will not cause too much difficulty in terms of the first-year program at Canadian common law schools, a program which is very similar across the country and typically mandatory. However, some schools with optional second- and third-year programs may have to put in place mandatory courses, programs to satisfy the competency requirements set out in the report. Particularly noteworthy is the requirement that all students receive instruction in professionalism and ethics from a Canadian perspective.

At one time, greater variety in the law school curriculum was interpreted by some to mean a lack of uniformity in Canadian university law school programs and preparation for professional practice. However, in point of fact that view was mistaken as, despite optional upper-year programs, significant uniformity existed in both program form and content overall, any change was incremental, rather than radical, and often replicated in other programs. The

---

[23] See online: <http://www.flsc.ca/_documents/Common-Law-Degree-Report-C.pdf>. The joint response of the Canadian Association of Law Teachers and the Canadian Law and Society Association has been published at (2009) CLEAR 151-56.

similarity in common law university programs had long facilitated the portability of law degrees across the various Canadian provincial jurisdictions, with the possible exception of Quebec with its civil law system. This portability will be even more certain with the implementation of the FLSC's Report, which was designed in large part to replace a loose form of regulation with a national academic standard for entry into bar admissions programs and ultimately practice in Canada's common law jurisdictions. This standard will also support the interprovincial mobility of admitted lawyers under the *National Mobility Protocol*, and provide a transparent, certain standard for the evaluation and approval of new Canadian law schools and foreign law degrees.

Ironically, even though one of the primary purposes of legal education is to prepare persons for law practice, it in fact serves as a barrier to entry to that practice. For decades, the number of qualified persons seeking admission to Canadian law faculties has greatly exceeded the number of positions available. And, despite the continuing high interest in legal education, the number of available positions has not significantly expanded since 1975. As a result, a large number of interested persons have not been able to gain entry into the legal profession and practice. The profession has, for the most part, not pressed government to open new law schools or substantially enlarge existing facilities; indeed, during periodic downturns in the economy, members of the profession have campaigned to reduce the size of law school enrolments. Moreover, the cost of university legal education creates a barrier for those in lower socio-economic classes who are not able to finance the cost of their education and therefore are not able to be admitted to the bar. With significant tuition increases in Canadian legal education over the last decade, the growing cost of education continues to serve as a barrier to entry into the profession. Thus, at the end of the day, it can be argued that the high cost of legal education and the limited number of available spaces have artificially limited the number of lawyers with the result that the cost of legal services is higher than necessary and unaffordable for many.

Before admission to the profession and practice as fully fledged lawyers, law graduates must first complete a period in articles with an experienced practitioner, a truncated form of the apprenticeship used until the 20th century to prepare persons for law practice. Typically, articling is for a period of 10 to 12 months with an experienced legal practitioner in a variety of public and private practice settings.[24] During this time, the student works for and under the supervision and guidance of a seasoned lawyer, known as the principal. In theory, the purpose of the period in articles is to expose students to the practice of law and give them an opportunity to develop sound practice skills

---

[24] In the Consultation Report of the Law Society of Upper Canada Articling Task Force, dated December 9, 2011, it was reported that the bulk of articling positions (61 per cent) in Ontario are in medium to large private law firms located chiefly in the Toronto and Ottawa areas with the result that small and sole practices play an insignificant part in the articling system.

and strong professional values under the mentorship of experienced, ethical and competent practitioners.[25]

However, in many ways, it is a loose form of education that leaves much to the initiative of the individual student and the commitment of his or her principal. Overall, there is a sense that the quality of the articling experience varies significantly in terms of attaining its objectives. One commentator has described articling in the following terms:

> Articling is largely an unstructured affair in which students are supposed to learn more by osmosis than by education and to prove their mettle under the pressure of deadlines rather than acquire the professional values and skills. While there is a vast variety of experience, articling remains too much a rite of passage and not enough a period of instruction.[26]

Historically, law societies have exerted little direct control over articling beyond registering the articling contract, and ensuring that both the student and the lawyer were eligible to enter into articles. However, in recent years law societies in a number of jurisdictions have become more proactive in their superintendence of articles in response to the variable quality of the experience. They have committed themselves to greater regulation and monitoring of the articling process, through devices such as education plans and articling handbooks, and to the provision of ongoing educational support for articling students in relation to practice skills development, examination preparation, professional and personal development and instruction in the substantive and procedural aspects of core practice areas.[27] To deliver this educational support, greater resort has been made to modern electronic technology.

With a period in articles as a necessary condition to admission to the bar and full-fledged practice, the requirement has served to limit the ability of some law graduates to be admitted to practice. Even with an expansion in the number of non-traditional articling placements, the number of positions has not kept up with the demand to the extent that some graduates have had great difficulty in securing suitable articles and a growing number have not been

---

[25] In the current scheme of legal education, articling is seen as a transitional form of education designed to bridge the gap between formal university legal education and full-fledged law practice. The Law Society of Upper Canada Articling Task Force has suggested at page ii of its Consultation Report that articling is intended to address five matters:
1. Application of defined practice and problem solving skills through contextual or experiential learning.
2. Consideration of practice management issues, including the business of law.
3. Application of ethical and professionalism principles in professional practical and transactional contexts.
4. Socialization from student to practitioner.
5. Introduction to systemic mentoring

[26] Allan C. Hutchinson, *Legal Ethics and Professional Responsibility* (Toronto: Irwin Law, 1999) at 59.

[27] Bar admission programming is a continuing matter of controversy. In February 2008, the Law Society of Upper Canada Task Force on Licensing and Accreditation recommended the abolition of the four-week licensing course in light of the fact that law school curricula featured more skills training.

able to find positions at all.[28] The Law Society of Upper Canada established a Task Force in June 2011 to consider the articling shortage, the fourth review of the articling requirement in 40 years. In its consultation report, the Task Force identified the current parameters of the problem and set out for consideration a number of approaches to address it ranging from doing nothing (letting the market determine the number of positions), to subsidizing articling placements, to replacing the articling requirement for some with a third party professional legal training program or significantly enhanced clinical programs in the course of or after university legal education. Should the latter option prevail, it is likely that two categories or classes of articling students will be created, those who enter into a traditional articling arrangement with a principal in a law firm and those who complete a practice-oriented training course of up to a half-year's duration offered by a third party provider. The first class of students will be paid for their work as students at law, while the other class will pay for the course of study.

During the course of or following their articles, students must also complete the bar admission program established by the law society in their particular jurisdiction. Of varying length, structure and sophistication, these courses were created to address the uneven nature of the articling experience by providing students with a uniform measure of instruction in preparation for practice. They have not been without controversy as, for most of their history, they tended to focus on instruction in jurisdiction-specific substantive and procedural law in core practice areas which, in large respects, replicated the university legal education of many students. In response to these and other criticisms, law societies have made a variety of changes to their bar admission programs to better measure and assess the entry level competence of students seeking admission to practice in their various jurisdictions. These changes have not been uniform across the country but, in the main, they reflect a change of orientation from traditional instruction in jurisdiction specific substantive law and procedure to the development of lawyering skills and abilities associated with entry level competence. Law societies have defined this competence more broadly in recent years to include not only the possession of substantive legal knowledge but also the demonstration of practice skills, professional attitudes and judgment.

Finally, articling students are required to pass bar examinations set by provincial law societies before they are admitted to the profession and practice. Traditionally, these examinations, of varying content and structure, have not proven to be a major obstacle to admission as typically only one to two per cent of students failed the test. Aside from acting as a guarantee against sheer incompetence, the utility of these examinations has been questioned and, in recent years, as part of reforms to bar admission program-

---

[28]   In its Consultation Report, the Law Society of Upper Canada Articling Task Force reports at page iii that "[t]he unplaced rate for articling students went from 5.8% for the 2007/2008 licensing group in March 2008 to 12.1% for the 2010/2011 licensing group in March 2011. ... Moreover, the group of unplaced individuals includes those with good law school grades."

ming, law societies, in some jurisdictions, have moved to greater reliance on other assessments such as a course of practice-oriented assignments and the development of more sophisticated evaluative instruments to test not only legal knowledge but the practical and ethical application of that knowledge in a variety of practice settings.

(ii) Good Character

In addition to meeting the educational and vocational training requirements, an applicant for admission to the profession must also establish that he or she is a person of "good character" or "good character and reputation".[29] This requirement, and its related case law, is also discussed in Chapter 13, "Issues in Regulation". Its primary purpose seems obvious: to ensure that only persons worthy of trust, with moral strength or integrity are admitted to the profession and practice. Like professional discipline, the good character requirement is directed to the maintenance of a certain standard of conduct only, in the former instance, regulation takes place after admission rather than before.

> The purposes of the good character requirement are the same as the purposes of professional discipline: to protect the public, to maintain high ethical standards, to maintain public confidence in the legal profession and its ability to regulate itself, and to deal fairly with persons whose livelihood and reputation are affected.[30]

While the purposes behind the "good character" requirement are admirable, its enforcement is not. In large part, this is the product of the ambiguous nature of the term which has meant that it has often been defined in operation according to the attitudes, experiences and prejudices of the decision-maker. Its very malleability makes it "a dangerous instrument for arbitrary and discriminatory denial of the right to practise law".[31] This is borne out in a number of instances in the United States and in one reported case in Canada where its use (abuse) was motivated by racial, ethnic, gender and political biases. In *Martin v. Law Society of British Columbia*,[32] the court upheld the law society's refusal of admission of an educationally qualified applicant on the grounds that he belonged to a political party which was affiliated to communism.

---

[29]   *Legal Profession Act*, R.S.A. 2000, c. L-8, s. 40. See also Alice Woolley, "Tending the Bar: The 'Good Character' Requirement for Law Society Admission" (2007) 30 Dal. L.J. 27 for a Canadian-oriented, comprehensive discussion of the requirement.

[30]   Gavin MacKenzie, *Lawyers and Ethics: Professional Responsibility and Discipline* (Toronto: Carswell, 2000) at 23.2.

[31]   *Konigsberg v. State Bar of California*, 353 U.S. 252 at 262-63 (1957).

[32]   [1950] B.C.J. No. 94, [1950] 3 D.L.R. 173 (B.C.C.A.). In terms of the American experience, see Jerold S. Auerbach, *Unequal Justice* (Oxford: Oxford University Press, 1976) at 127-28 and Deborah Rhode, "Moral Character as Professional Credential" (1985) 44 Yale L.J. 491 at 501.

The lack of a clear statutory definition for the terms "good character" or "good character and reputation" has also led to inconsistency and unpredictability in its administration by law societies and American bar authorities. A review of "good character" decisions in Canada and the United States demonstrates that, even in the same jurisdiction, similar types of misconduct have led to different results in terms of admission decisions.[33] This makes it difficult to predict whether particular misconduct will result in a denial of admission.

The "good character" requirement is enforced in a passive manner by law societies. Applicants are required to complete questionnaires and to self report matters, such as criminal convictions, bankruptcy orders and substance abuse problems which may raise concerns about their good character or fitness to practise law. In addition, applicants are often required to file certificates of good character completed by third party referees. From a practical point of view, the value of the latter device is particularly questionable as the references are rarely if ever checked, and everyone can find someone to positively vouch for their character. The certificates appear to be nothing more than a symbolic expression of the organized profession's concern with the good character of its prospective members. Hutchinson has suggested that law societies are more concerned with the good character of their prospective members than the good character of their existing members.[34]

(d) Self Regulation of Lawyer Conduct

The second core area of self regulation concerns the control of lawyer conduct through the articulation of standards of professional practice and the enforcement of those norms by means of professional discipline. By itself, this is a very large and complex topic and given the parameters of this chapter any detailed discussion must be left to specialized works on the profession, codes of professional conduct and lawyer discipline. The focus of this section will therefore be on the development of rules of professional conduct to govern and guide lawyers' conduct in their practices and activities and on the structure and operation of the contemporary system of professional discipline.

Law societies incrementally acquired the power to discipline their members for professional misconduct at various stages across Canada during the latter part of the 19th and the early part of the 20th centuries. In most instances, the power to discipline followed the grant of authority concerning the education and admission of persons to the profession and practice, which had served as the primary responsibility of provincial law societies. Since that time, "the exercise of the discipline function has moved from the sporadic, embryonic and desultory towards the habitual and the extensive to the point

---

[33]   Gavin MacKenzie, *Lawyers and Ethics: Professional Responsibility and Discipline* (Toronto: Carswell, 2000) at 23-6 to 23-12; Alice Woolley, "Tending the Bar: The 'Good Character' Requirement for Law Society Admission" (2007) 30 Dal. L.J. 27 at 40-53.

[34]   See Allan C. Hutchinson, *Legal Ethics and Professional Responsibility* (Toronto: Irwin Law, 1999) at 61.

where ... in Canada, all but the smaller law societies have substantial organizations and resources dedicated to it".[35] Apart from formal disciplinary processes, lawyer conduct is also regulated through rules and regulations made by the law societies relating to matters such as: the keeping of accounts and records, liability insurance and the establishment of codes of ethics or conduct.

It should be noted that the discipline of lawyers for misconduct has recently taken on a national aspect. As stated, lawyer discipline is undertaken on a provincial basis by the various law societies; however, the Federation of Law Societies of Canada has embarked on a project to generate a set of national standards in relation to the handling of client complaints and the discipline of lawyers by provincial law societies. This initiative follows on others such as the *Model Code of Ethics*, the *National Mobility Protocol*, the Content of the Canadian Common Law Degree and national admissions standards all designed to put into place a form of "pan Canadian" regulation in response to the national scope and increased mobility of Canadian lawyers.

(i) Codes of Conduct

Although no law society had a written statement of standards or rules of conduct until its adoption of the Canadian Bar Association's *Canons of Ethics* promulgated in 1920,[36] codes of professional or ethical conduct are now a prominent feature of lawyer conduct regulation. Prior to the adoption of written codes, the regulation of lawyer conduct was largely a matter of compliance with standards, generally understood and accepted by the profession of the time, informed by the ethics and etiquette expected of a gentleman.

However, to many leaders of the Canadian legal profession of the time, informal regulation, based on vague community standards, was inadequate for a widely diffused profession seeking to establish its claim to privileged professional status. A written code of ethics was required. It was a means whereby the profession could solidify its national organization, assert powers of self governance, and project an image of professionalism based on notions of superior learning, ethical conduct and service in the public interest.[37]

CANADIAN BAR ASSOCIATION

Canons of Legal Ethics (1920)

Approved by the Canadian Bar Association, at the Fifth Annual Meeting, Ottawa, September 2nd, 1920, as a correct, though not exhaustive, statement

---

[35] W. William Hurlburt, *The Self Regulation of the Legal Profession in Canada and in England and Wales* (Edmonton: Law Society of Alberta and the Alberta Law Reform Institute, 2000) at 114-15.

[36] *Proceedings of the Canadian Bar Association, 1921*, 238 at 239-40.

[37] W. Wesley Pue, "Becoming Ethical: Lawyers' Professional Ethics in Early Twentieth Century Canada" (1991) 20 Man. L.J. 227.

of some of the ethical principles which should be observed by the members of the legal profession.

It is not possible to frame a set of rules which will particularize all the duties of the lawyer in all the varied relations of his professional life and no attempt has been made to do so.

The following Canons of Ethics should therefore be construed as a general guide and not as a denial of the existence of other duties equally imperative though not specifically mentioned.

The lawyer is more than a mere citizen. He is a minister of justice, an officer of the Courts, his client's advocate, and a member of an ancient, honourable and learned profession.

In these several capacities it is his duty to promote the interests of the State, serve the cause of justice, maintain the authority and dignity of the Courts, be faithful to his clients, candid and courteous in his intercourse with his fellows and true to himself.

1. *To the State*

    1. He owes a duty to the State, to maintain its integrity and its law and not to aid, counsel, or assist any man to act in any way contrary to those laws.

    2. When engaged as a public prosecutor his primary duty is not to convict but to see that justice is done; to that end he should withhold no facts tending to prove either the guilt or innocence of the accused.

    3. He should take upon himself without hesitation and if need be without fee or reward, the cause of any man assigned to him by the Court and exert his best efforts on behalf of the person for whom he has been so assigned counsel.

    4. It is a crime against the State and therefore highly nonprofessional in a lawyer, to stir up strife or litigation by seeking out defects in titles, claims for personal injury or other causes of action for the purpose of securing or endeavoring to secure a retainer to prosecute a claim therefor; or to pay or reward directly or indirectly any person, for the purpose or procuring him to be retained in his professional capacity.

2. *To the Court*

    1. His conduct should at all times be characterized by candor and fairness. He should maintain towards the Judges of the Courts a courteous and respectful attitude and insist on similar conduct on the part of his client, at the same time maintaining a self-respecting independence in the discharge of his professional duties to his client.

    2. Judges, not being free to defend themselves, are entitled to receive the support of the Bar against unjust criticism and complaint. Whenever there is proper ground for serious complaint of a judicial officer,

it is a right and duty of the lawyer to submit the grievance to the proper authorities.

3. He should not offer evidence which he knows the Court should not admit. He should not, either in argument to the Court or in address to the jury, assert his personal belief in his client's innocence, or in the justice of his cause, or as to any of the facts involved in the matter under investigation.

4. He should never seek to privately influence, directly or indirectly, the judges of the Court in his favor, or in that of his client, nor should he attempt to curry favor with juries by fawning, flattery or pretended solicitude for their personal comfort.

3.   To the Client

1. He should obtain full knowledge of his client's cause before advising thereon and give a candid opinion of the merits and probable results of pending or contemplated litigation. He should beware of bold and confident assurances to clients especially where the employment may depend on such assurances. He should bear in mind that seldom are all the law and facts on the side of his client and that *"audi alteram partem"* is a safe rule to follow.

2. He should at the time of retainer disclose to the client all the circumstances of his relations to the parties and his interest in or connection with the controversy, if any, which might influence the client in selection of counsel. He should avoid representing conflicting interests.

3. Whenever the controversy will admit of fair adjustment the client should be advised to avoid or to end the litigation.

4. He should treat adverse witnesses, litigants, and counsel with fairness, refraining from all offensive personal ties. He must avoid imparting to professional duties the client's personal feelings and prejudices. At the same time he should discharge his duty to his client with firmness and without fear of judicial disfavor or public unpopularity.

5. He should endeavor by all fair and honorable means to obtain for his client the benefit of any and every remedy and defence which is authorized by law. He must, however, steadfastly bear in mind that the great trust of the lawyer is to be performed within and not without the bounds of the law. The office of the lawyer does not permit, much less does it demand of him, for any client, violation of law or any manner of fraud or chicanery.

6. It is his right to undertake the defence of a person accused of crime, regardless of his own personal opinion as to the guilt of the accused. Having undertaken such defence, he is bound by all fair and honorable means to present every defence that the law of the land permits

to the end that no person may be deprived of life or liberty but by
due process of law.

7. He should not, except as by law expressly sanctioned, acquire by
   purchase or otherwise any interest in the subject matter of the litigation being conducted by him. He should act for his client only and
   having once acted for him he should not act against him in the same
   matter or in any other matter related thereto, and should scrupulously
   guard and not divulge his client's secrets or confidences.

8. He should report promptly to his client the receipt of any monies or
   other trust property and avoid the co-mingling with his own, or use
   of trust money or property.

9. He is entitled to reasonable compensation for his services but he
   should avoid charges which either over-estimate or under-value the
   service rendered. When possible he should adhere to established tar-
   iffs. The client's ability to pay cannot justify a charge in excess of
   the value of the service, though his poverty may require a less charge
   or even none at all.

10. He should avoid controversies with clients regarding compensation
    so far as is compatible with self-respect and with the right to receive
    reasonable recompense for services. He should always bear in mind
    that the profession is a branch of the administration of justice and not
    a mere money getting trade.

11. He should not appear as witness for his own client except as to
    merely formal matters, such as, the attestation or custody of an in-
    strument, or the like, or when it is essential to the ends of justice. If
    he is a necessary witness with respect to other matters, the conduct-
    ing of the case should be entrusted to other counsel.

4. *To His Fellow Lawyer*

1. His conduct towards his fellow lawyer should be characterized by
   courtesy and good faith. Whatever may be the ill-feeling existing between clients it should not be allowed to influence counsel in their
   conduct and demeanor towards each other or towards suitors in the
   case. All personalities between counsel should be scrupulously
   avoided as should also colloquies between counsel which cause delay and promote unseemly wrangling.

2. He should endeavor as far as possible to suit the convenience of the
   opposing counsel when the interests of his client or the cause of justice will not be injured by so doing.

3. He should give no undertaking he cannot fulfil and he should fulfil
   every undertaking he gives. He should never in any way communicate upon the subject in controversy, or attempt to negotiate or com-

promise the matter directly with any party represented by a lawyer, except through such lawyer.

4. He should avoid all sharp practice and he should take no paltry advantage when his opponent has made a slip or overlooked some technical matter. No client has a right to demand that his counsel shall be illiberal or that he shall do anything repugnant to his own sense of honor or propriety.

5. *To Himself*

1. It is his duty to maintain the honor and integrity of his profession and to expose without fear or favor before the proper tribunals unprofessional or dishonest conduct by any other member of the profession, and to accept without hesitation a retainer against any member of the profession who is alleged to have wronged his client.

2. It is the duty of every lawyer to guard the Bar against the admission to the profession of any candidate whose moral character or education unfits him for admission thereto.

3. The publication or circulation of ordinary simple business cards is not per se improper but solicitation of business by circulars or advertisements or by personal communications or interviews not warranted by personal relations, is unprofessional. It is equally unprofessional to seek retainers through agents of any kind. Indirect advertisement for business by furnishing or inspiring newspaper comment concerning causes in which the lawyer has been or is connected, or concerning the manner of their conduct, the magnitude of the interests involved, the importance of the lawyer's position, and like self-laudations defy the traditions and lower the tone of the lawyer's high calling, and should not be tolerated. The best advertisement for a lawyer is the establishment of a well-merited reputation for personal capacity and fidelity to trust.

4. No lawyer is obliged to act either as adviser or advocate for every person who may wish to become his client; he has a right to decline employment.

5. No client is entitled to receive, nor should any lawyer render, any service or advice involving disloyalty to the State, or disrespect for the judicial office, or the corruption of any persons exercising a public or private trust, or deception or betrayal of the public.

6. Every lawyer should bear in mind that the oath of office taken on his admission to the Bar is not a mere form but is a solemn undertaking and on his part should be strictly observed.

7. He should also bear in mind that he can only maintain the high traditions of his profession by being in fact as well as in name a gentleman.

Modelled on the American Bar Association's 1908 *Canons of Ethics*, the Canadian *Canons of Ethics* did not provide an exhaustive or even comprehensive statement of ethical standards or norms. Rather it was viewed as a general guide to ethical practice, "a correct ... statement of some of the ethical standards observed by members of the legal profession".[38] Short in length by today's standards, the *Canons* described the profession as an essential part of the administration of justice; identified the lawyer as a key actor with important responsibilities in the established legal order; proclaimed the superior learning, altruistic orientation and general trustworthiness of lawyers; and condemned certain practices as "unprofessional". Far from a radical document, and often short on specific ethical guidance, due to the general and hortatory nature of its language, this early code did, however, communicate a vision or ideology of professionalism to both the larger public and the profession.[39]

In 1974, the Canadian Bar Association adopted a new code, the *Code of Professional Conduct*, consisting of 17 rules or fundamental principles of conduct with written commentaries on each. While more comprehensive than its predecessor, its utility as a guide to ethical conduct in concrete situations was again limited by the aspirational tone of its language. It did not purport to offer definitive, mandatory, rules of conduct; rather, it sought to exhort lawyers to the highest standards of ethical practice. Nevertheless, it was adopted by law societies across Canada who supplemented it on occasion with their own rules.

During this time, the American Bar Association was also active in the revision of its ethics codes. Over time, its 1908 *Canons* had grown in number from 32 to 47, augmented by 1,400 interpretive opinions, which rendered it an inconsistent and unclear reference to ethical conduct.[40] To remedy this, the American Bar Association adopted the *Model Code of Professional Responsibility* in 1970 which was divided into two parts: Ethical Considerations (ECs) which were aspirational in nature, and Disciplinary Rules (DRs) which were mandatory in character. This scheme was adopted to set off ethically based questions, which were not easily codified, from minimum conduct prescriptions. Unfortunately, this *Model Code* was not successful in operation and as a result of heavy criticism the American Bar Association recommended an alternative set of standards, the *Model Rules of Professional Conduct* in 1983. The *Model Rules* represented a strong break with tradition in that the aspirational language of the past was replaced by authoritative statements of

---

[38]   W. William Hurlburt, *The Self Regulation of the Legal Profession in Canada and in England and Wales* (Edmonton: Law Society of Alberta and the Alberta Law Reform Institute, 2000) at 99.

[39]   See W. Wesley Pue & David Sugarman, eds., *Lawyers and Vampires: Cultural Histories of Legal Professions* (Portland: Hart Publishing, 2003) at 367-91; W. Wesley Pue, "Becoming Ethical: Lawyers' Professional Ethics in Early Twentieth Century Canada" (1991) 20 Man. L.J. 227.

[40]   Deborah Rhode, *Professional Responsibility: Ethics by the Pervasive Method*, 2nd ed. (New York: Aspen Publishers, 1998) at 44.

conduct and interpretative commentaries. Despite heated debates over its form and content, the *Model Rules* was ultimately adopted by a large majority of state jurisdictions.[41]

The revision of American ethics codes prompted the Canadian Bar Association to again examine its 1974 *Code*. In 1987, it adopted a substantially revised version of the 1974 *Code* made up of new material and revisions to existing chapters. That apart, the format and aspirational language of the 1974 *Code* was largely retained.

These codes served as the basis for rules of professional conduct in most Canadian provinces; some adopted the codes without amendment, while others have used the codes, with significant modifications, as the basis of their own rules of conduct. Only one province, Alberta, deviated substantially from this practice. In 1995, it adopted the most detailed code in Canada entitled the *Code of Professional Conduct*, which was divided into 15 chapters, each containing a statement of principle followed by rules and commentary. This code was unique among Canadian codes for its extensive use of mandatory language and its specific proscriptions.

Since that time, provincial law societies and the Canadian Bar Association have periodically amended their codes for purposes of clarification and to deal with new issues in largely uniform ways. However, the reliance on jurisdiction specific ethics codes by many provincial law societies suggested a "balkanization" of Canadian lawyers' ethics. This appears to have come to an end with the resurgence of national codes in the form of the 2009 Canadian Bar Association's *Code of Professional Conduct* and the 2009 Federation of Law Societies of Canada's *Model Code of Professional Conduct*. With the addition of conflicts rules by the FLSC in 2011, these codes offer comprehensive and detailed statements of lawyer ethics (165 pages in the case of the CBA *Code* and 116 pages in the case of the FLSC *Code*) remarkably similar in content and language albeit different in terms of organization. Together, these codes reflect a strong national consensus on lawyers' ethics which will be strengthened as provincial law societies adopt one or the other as the basis of their jurisdiction specific standards of lawyers' ethical conduct in the near future.

Written ethics codes are thus a prominent feature of the contemporary legal profession in Canada and the United States. Considerable time and energy has been invested by the organized profession in the periodic review and revision of these codes which are seen to serve several purposes. The first of these is essentially ideological. Written ethical codes represent and codify the collective beliefs, ideals and values of the legal community to guide the conduct of its members as legal practitioners. They also serve to make a statement to the larger public about lawyers' beliefs and values. The second function is essentially regulatory: to set out mandatory and detailed standards

---

[41] However, the work of revision continued as the *Model Rules* were amended from time to time to deal with pressing matters of contemporary concern. Continuing in this vein, in 2009 the ABA Commission on Ethics 20/20 was created to undertake a comprehensive review of the *Model Rules* and the American system of lawyer regulation.

of lawyer conduct to serve as the basis for professional discipline. The growing importance of this latter function is demonstrated in the evolution of lawyers' codes, particularly in the United States, from basic statements of aspirational ideals to detailed, specific, mandatory rules of conduct, a sort of "law for lawyers". This move towards greater reliance on detailed, specific rules in lawyer regulation has been explained a number of ways. First, it is argued that a clear statement of minimal standards provides needed clarity and certainty in a large and diverse profession which increasingly lacks the cohesion to rely on any consensus about appropriate standards. Second, it is suggested that specific, detailed rules are more useful in the resolution of some complex issues in professional responsibility, such as those relating to conflicts of interest, than general statements of principle. Third, it is asserted that lawyers are more comfortable in applying detailed rules to resolve ethical issues or concerns: "[general] ideological principles are of limited use to lawyers in answering practical questions of how they should conduct themselves in specific situations".[42] But greater reliance on detailed, specific rules comes at a price. To gain acceptance within a fragmented profession, rules often have to be formulated in highly abstract terms, such as "reasonable", which, in turn, hamper practical enforcement. Also, a concern for professional consensus may lead to the proscription of only that conduct which is generally viewed as deviant. As a result, lawyers are not encouraged to reach beyond these minimal standards in terms of their conduct. The flexibility to respond to unanticipated situations may be lost through reliance on detailed rules — "the imposition of inflexible and universal solutions is generally not the optimum approach to the resolution of complex ethical issues".[43]

Lawyers' codes of ethics have been criticized on a number of bases. A fundamental criticism relates to the concept of a written code. It has long been argued that ethics are matters for personal decision or choice and that you cannot regulate ethical behaviour through detailed, specific rules.[44] Ethics cannot be legislated; a person either acts ethically or not. Moreover, it is often argued that ethics codes actually impede moral development and deliberation; "rules" become the focus in place of rational deliberation.[45] Closely allied to this concern is the argument that lawyers' ethics codes have nothing to do with morality; that matters of morality are too indeterminate to allow professional organizations such as the CBA or the FLSC to make collective

---

[42] Gavin MacKenzie, *Lawyers and Ethics: Professional Responsibility and Discipline* (Toronto: Carswell, 2000) at 25-6 to 25-7.

[43] *Ibid.*, at 25-8. The material concerning the purposes served by ethics codes is drawn from Deborah Rhode, *Professional Responsibility: Ethics by the Pervasive Method*, 2nd ed. (New York: Aspen Publishers, 1998) at 47-48 and Gavin MacKenzie, *Lawyers and Ethics: Professional Responsibility and Discipline* (Toronto: Carswell, 2000) at 25-6 to 25-8.

[44] Margaret Ann Wilkinson, Christa Walker & Peter Mercer, "Do Ethics Codes Actually Shape Legal Practice?" (2000) 45 McGill L.J. 645.

[45] R. Elizabeth Loder, "Tighter Rules of Professional Conduct: Saltwater for Thirst" (1987–1988) Geo. J. Legal Ethics 311 at 333.

statements about the moral conduct of lawyers. Unfortunately, what remains are generalized rules that are "compromised statements of professional morality".[46] Another major criticism is that ethics codes serve the profession's interests rather than the public's interests. Codes of ethics have been seen by some as a device used by the profession to project an ethical image (that lawyers are more "ethical" because they are following a code of conduct) in support of its claim to enhanced cultural authority, or to legitimate its monopoly control over the market for legal services. Others have suggested that codes of ethics were used by legal elites to suppress those elements of the profession they did not approve of;[47] that ethics codes are an instrument of class bias.[48] Still others point to the fact that codes of ethics are promulgated by lawyers to govern lawyers without any public input. Can the profession be trusted to put the public's interests first; to rise above its own self interest on matters which affect its members' status or income? Consider the following statement:

> Lawyers are ... animated by parochial concerns. What distinguishes professionals is their relative success in packaging occupational interests as societal imperatives. In that regard, codes of ethics have proved highly useful. Seldom, of course, are such documents baldly self serving: it is not to a profession's long term advantage that it appear insensitive to the common good. But neither are any profession's own encyclicals likely to incorporate public policies that might significantly compromise member's status, monopoly, working relationships or autonomy.

> In part, the problem is one of tunnel vision. Without doubt, most lawyers ... are committed to improving the legal system in which they work. What is open to doubt is whether a body of rules drafted, approved, and administered solely by attorneys is the most effective way of realizing that commitment. No matter how well intentioned and well informed, lawyers regulating lawyers cannot escape the economic, psychological, and political constraints of their position.[49]

Still others argue that, practically speaking, written codes of conduct are ineffective instruments of regulation. Different elements of the profession, working in different contexts, sometimes view the obligations imposed on them by the rules differently. Many of the rules contained in the codes are not enforced at all. Why then are they included in the codes? For a symbolic rather than a regulatory purpose? Finally, a study of Ontario lawyers a decade ago concluded that few lawyers actually use the written code of conduct to identify or resolve issues with ethical dimensions — what then is the purpose

---

[46] Charles Wolfram, *Modern Legal Ethics* (St. Paul, MN: West Publishing, 1986) at 70.

[47] Jerold S. Auerbach, *Unequal Justice* (Oxford: Oxford University Press, 1976) at 127-28.

[48] Richard L. Abel, "Why Does the ARBA Promulgate Ethical Rules" (1981) 59 Tex. L. Rev. 639.

[49] Deborah Rhode, "Why the ABA Bothers: A Functional Perspective on Ethical Codes" (1981) 59 Texas L. Rev. 689 at 720.

of such a code, in terms of affecting lawyer behaviour, when the majority of lawyers do not even refer to it?[50]

(ii)　The Anatomy of Lawyers' Codes[51]

Having looked at lawyer's codes historically, theoretically, functionally and critically, a brief discussion of the content of these codes is now in order. This discussion will not be detailed, as an understanding of the form and content of Canadian ethics codes can best be gained through a reading of the Canadian Bar Association's *Code of Professional Conduct* (CBA Code) or the Federation of Law Societies of Canada's *Model Code of Professional Conduct* (FLSC Code). However, some sense of the general structure and content of these codes is necessary to understand the nature and scope of lawyer ethical regulation. Given the historic influence of the Canadian Bar Association's various codes on the development of provincial codes and the renewed desire for a national statement on lawyer's ethics, any difference between the various provincial law society codes, in terms of organization, degree of detail and the form of language (regulatory vs. exhortatory) utilized is likely to be minimal as either the FLSC or CBA code is adopted in the near future by provincial law societies for use in their jurisdictions.

The structure of these two codes is similar. Each purports to articulate standards for the legal profession largely in terms of a variety of obligations, duties, and responsibilities imposed on lawyers in the context of a number of general and specific relationships or practice roles and settings. For example, the FLSC Code is divided into chapters which deal with the lawyer-client relationship generally, the marketing of legal services, the lawyer's relationship as an advocate to the administration of justice, the lawyer's relationship to students, employees and others, and the lawyer's relationship to society and to other lawyers, including the profession. The CBA Code is organized somewhat differently but is built around the same kinds of relationships. Each of the codes is divided into chapters containing rules, sub-rules and principles followed by extensive commentary. The operative language varies: in the FLSC Code, the duties are set out in mandatory terms through the use of the word "must", while the CBA Code is more aspirational with the use of the word "should" in its statement of duties. For the purposes of the discussion which follows, the obligations in the codes have been loosely categorized under two headings: duties owed to clients, the courts and other lawyers; and duties owed to the profession and to the larger society.

---

[50]　Margaret Ann Wilkinson, Christa Walker & Peter Mercer, "Do Ethics Codes Actually Shape Legal Practice?" (2000) 45 McGill L.J. 645.

[51]　The title to this part is borrowed from Charles Wolfram, *Modern Legal Ethics* (St. Paul, MN: West Publishing, 1986) at 58.

A. DUTIES OWED TO CLIENTS, THE COURTS AND OTHER LAWYERS

In the representation of clients, lawyers are under a number of special obligations, some of which arise from the fiduciary nature of the lawyer-client relationship. Overall, lawyers have a duty to act honourably and with integrity in the conduct of their practices. That apart, a lawyer has a duty to be competent, and to act competently in the representation of clients whether acting as an advocate, an advisor or a negotiator. Competence is typically defined in terms of a number of fundamental characteristics: knowledge of substantive law and procedure; professional judgment and experience; legal and practice management skills and intellectual and emotional capacity. When representing clients before courts of law, statutory tribunals or other adjudicative bodies, lawyers must act resolutely and vigorously in the assertion of their clients' claims or rights or in the defence of their clients' property or interests. However, a lawyer's advocacy on behalf of a client is not unbridled; for example, a lawyer cannot abuse the process of the tribunal, deceive the tribunal through false evidence or the misstatement of either the law or the facts, or abuse witnesses. In this way, the lawyer's ethical duties to clients are bound by duties and responsibilities to the courts and society as an officer of the legal system, not to mention legal proscriptions such as those against perjury. When advising clients, lawyers are not only under a duty to act competently but they must be candid and honest in their advice. Only then can clients fully understand their legal rights and responsibilities and act accordingly. As a negotiator, a lawyer owes a client a duty to obtain the best result but again this is limited by obligations, owed to other lawyers and parties, to act in good faith, honestly and with courtesy.

Lawyers, in the representation of clients, are under a duty of confidentiality and a duty to avoid conflicts of interests. Both of these ethical duties flow from the obligations of a lawyer as a fiduciary and have been the subject of rulings by appeal and trial courts across Canada (see Chapter 4, "The Lawyer's Duty to Preserve Client Confidences" and Chapter 5, "The Duty of Loyalty and Conflicts of Interest"). For that reason, the "ethical" obligations of lawyers in these respects have been heavily influenced by the "legal" decisions of the courts with the result that the associated commentary is often the most complex and detailed of all the provisions set out in the written codes.

Specifically, lawyers must keep confidential all information concerning their clients' affairs or business acquired during the course of the professional relationship. This obligation of confidentiality is designed to facilitate free and open communication between the lawyer and his or her client, which, in turn, is thought necessary to effective representation. The duty of confidentiality is broad but it is not absolute, as in some instances, disclosure by the lawyer is not only permitted, it is mandated because of other interests at stake.[52]

---

[52]   In this respect, the CBA Code is at odds with the FLSC Code; the former requires disclosure of confidential information to prevent the death of or serious bodily harm to a

Lawyers also have a strict ethical duty to avoid conflicts of interest which may adversely affect their judgment or loyalty in the representation of a client to his or her prejudice. Conflicts can arise in a number of ways: acting for clients involved in a dispute with each other; acting for a new client against a former client; acting for more than one client in the same matter; or acting for a client in a matter where a lawyer's personal or financial interests are at stake. Conflicts can also arise as a result of the merger of law firms or lawyers transferring from one firm to another which may create the potential for misuse of confidential information. Lawyers are also under an ethical obligation to act with care and prudence when dealing with clients' property.

When representing clients, lawyers will inevitably interact with other lawyers and persons and, perhaps, even the courts. While the representation of the client is of fundamental importance, it is sometimes balanced by ethical obligations owed to other lawyers, parties and courts. Some of these have been referred to in the preceding discussion. Above all, a lawyer's dealings with other parties, lawyers and the courts must be marked by integrity, courtesy and good faith. This is essential to the effective representation of clients and the proper operation of the justice system. In particular, the lawyer must treat the court and witnesses with candour and fairness, must avoid sharp practice and must fulfill every undertaking given to another lawyer or to the court.

B. Duties Owed to the Profession and Society

Ethics codes also contain a variety of provisions concerning the lawyer's responsibilities to his or her profession and to society at large. In large part, these duties are directed towards the maintenance of public confidence in the profession as an independent, self-governing occupation. To this end, lawyers are reminded of their duty to conduct themselves in all things with integrity, "a lawyer's conduct should reflect favourably on the legal profession, inspire the confidence, respect and trust of clients and the community, and avoid even the appearance of impropriety".[53] Self governance is supported by the imposition of an obligation on lawyers, in either some or all instances, to report the misconduct and dishonesty of other lawyers to the law society. The important role played by the profession in the administration of justice is reflected in the special responsibilities imposed on lawyers in that respect. Lawyers have an obligation to act in a manner which encourages public respect for the administration of justice and, where necessary, an obligation to seek its improvement. They have a responsibility to make sure that legal services are widely available; to ensure that the legal system is accessible to as many people as possible, particularly those who are poor or disadvantaged.

---

person, whereas the latter permits but does not mandate the disclosure of confidential information by the lawyer. See Canadian Bar Association, *Code of Professional Conduct* (2009), Chapter IV, Rule 2 and Federation of Law Societies of Canada, *Model Code of Professional Conduct*, Chapter 2, Rule 2.03.

[53] Federation of Law Societies of Canada, *Model Code of Professional Conduct*, Chapter 1, Rule 1.01 Commentary.

And they have a duty to ensure that the administration of justice is conducted in an open, impartial and fair manner.

Apart from these two major categories of rules, ethics codes contain a number of provisions dealing with matters such as advertising, solicitation, fees and unauthorized practice. These latter rules are difficult to categorize, even though their stated purpose is to further the public interest in the ethical and competent provision of legal services. However, to many, these provisions are largely designed to serve the profession's interests by restricting competition in the market for legal services and by protecting the monopoly or market domination of lawyers.

Finally, the content of contemporary ethical codes reflects the profession's growing gender and racial diversity. Although the racial diversity of the profession is not well documented, some statistics are available with respect to gender balance.[54] For example, in 1995 women made up 26.2 per cent of those in private practice, while in 2000 women made up approximately 33 per cent of those in practice. By 2005, the balance had shifted again as women made up approximately 37 per cent of those in practice. The increase in the number of women practitioners parallels the steady increase in the number of women admitted to Canadian law schools over the last decade. In the 2010 admission year, 49 per cent of those admitted to Canadian law schools were male and 51 per cent of those admitted were female.

The entry of large numbers of women into the legal profession has led to serious questions about equal opportunity for women in the profession — the organization and demands of modern law practice make it difficult for women to balance their work and personal lives; the chances for promotion and advancement are often limited for female lawyers by a "glass ceiling"; and the ethics and norms of the profession are thought to represent a male ethos — a male view of law practice and professionalism. These and other issues have been studied by provincial law societies and the Canadian Bar Association with a view to addressing gender bias against women in the legal profession. One of the early initiatives was to expand the definition of professional misconduct to incorporate sexual harassment. In Ontario and Alberta, extensive ethical rules were adopted to proscribe the sexual harassment of clients, colleagues, staff and others in a professional context. This is continued in the CBA Code, which contains a lengthy description of what constitutes sexual harassment, as a form of discrimination, in its prohibition of discriminatory conduct by lawyers.[55] In contrast, the FLSC Code contains a much briefer prohibition of discrimination and harassment, as part of a lawyer's responsibility to respect and adhere to the requirements of human

---

[54] Federation of Law Societies of Canada, 1995, 2000 and 2005 Annual Statistics, online: <http://www.flsc.ca>. As the Federation changed the statistical categories during this time and as some provinces do not report in a manner consistent with the others, the comparisons are not exact and are offered only for the purposes of illustrating general trends.

[55] Canadian Bar Association, *Code of Professional Conduct* (2009), Chapter XX, Commentary 7.

rights laws in force federally and provincially.[56] The adoption of these provisions was not without debate and contest — many thought that these types of issues were not appropriate matters for ethics codes as they were already addressed under provincial human rights codes, the criminal law and perhaps even the common law. Nevertheless, sexual harassment, a form of discrimination directed towards the dignity and equality of others, is widely understood to be a serious form of professional misconduct. On a number of occasions, lawyers have been formally disciplined for such misconduct. For example, in *Re Peter Robert Ramsay*,[57] a lawyer was found guilty of professional misconduct for making inappropriate comments of a sexual nature to his client, when he suggested a reduction or cancellation of fees in return for sexual favours. Law firms, conscious of the damaging effects of this type of misconduct on the workplace, have adopted sexual harassment policies setting standards for appropriate conduct. Law societies have taken proactive steps to address the issues of discrimination and harassment through the establishment of equity ombudspersons and discipline and harassment counsel. These offices are designed to offer lawyers and the public a range of educational, counselling and mediation services. Typically, they enjoy some independence from the law society and offer their services on a confidential basis.

(iii) Discipline

Discipline is one of the primary functions of contemporary Canadian law societies. It is undertaken, as a core aspect of self regulation, not primarily for punitive purposes but to protect the public, by sanctioning the offending lawyer, and to protect the profession's reputation, by demonstrating a collective commitment to and enforcement of standards of proper conduct:

> Courts assert that the underlying purpose of disciplining lawyers is a broadly social one. The purpose is not to punish offending lawyers but to protect the public, the bar, and legal institutions against lawyers who have demonstrated an unwillingness to comply with minimal professional standards. There is reason to think, however, that a strong motivation for lawyer discipline is to reassure a doubtful public that notorious instances of lawyer depredation are being handled appropriately.[58]

Apart from protecting the public interest by dealing with the offending lawyer, professional discipline is also undertaken to deter other lawyers from breaching professional standards. To be effective in this regard, the prospect of professional discipline for misconduct must be a real possibility in the minds of lawyers — professional standards and their enforcement through

---

[56]   Federation of Law Societies of Canada, *Model Code of Professional Conduct*, Chapter 5, Rule 5.03 and Commentary.

[57]   (November 20, 1992), Law Society of Upper Canada, Order of Convocation.

[58]   Charles Wolfram, *Modern Legal Ethics* (St. Paul, MN: West Publishing, 1986) at 79. The classic statement of the purposes served by lawyer discipline is to be found in the judgment of Lord Mansfield in *Ex parte Brounsall* (1778), 2 Cow. 829, 98 Eng. Rep. 1385.

discipline must be communicated to lawyers or else the effect of discipline on lawyer behaviour and attitudes will be minimal.

A. STANDARDS OF DISCIPLINE

Canadian law societies are empowered by legislation to discipline their members for "professional misconduct", "conduct unbecoming a barrister and solicitor" or "conduct deserving of sanction". The Alberta legislation further defines "conduct deserving of sanction" as "any conduct of a member, arising from incompetence or otherwise, that (a) is incompatible with the best interests of the public or of the members of the Society, or (b) tends to harm the standing of the legal profession generally".[59] These vague and somewhat imprecise standards are employed in recognition of the discretionary nature of the decision to discipline. Whether or not alleged lawyer misconduct is sufficient to give rise to discipline is a matter for the governing bodies of each law society based on their assessment of the conduct in light of professional norms and standards, the law, and the circumstances of each case. The primacy of their role is central to self governance and has been acknowledged by the courts in several decisions:

> No one is better qualified to say what constitutes professional misconduct than a group of practicing [sic] barristers who are themselves subject to the rules established by their governing body ... .[60]

> ... a large part of effective self governance depends on the concept of peer review. If an autonomous Law Society is to enforce a code of conduct among its members, as indeed is required by the public interest, a power to discipline its members is essential. It is entirely appropriate that an individual whose conduct is to be judged should be assessed by a group of his or her peers who are themselves subject to the rules and standards that are being enforced.[61]

The use of such broad language enables governing bodies to discipline for conduct which does not constitute either a breach of law or a violation of a rule of professional conduct spelled out in codes of ethical conduct. Flexibility and creativity are necessary when dealing with misconduct which was not anticipated in the drafting of professional codes. Nevertheless, codes of conduct drawn up, published and distributed by the various law societies serve as the primary statement of professional norms and standards in their respective jurisdictions.[62] In this respect, it should be noted that some jurisdictions have defined "professional misconduct" in their codes of conduct

---

[59] *Legal Profession Act*, R.S.A. 2000, c. L-8, s. 49. See also *Law Society Act*, R.S.O. 1990, c. L.8, s. 33; *Legal Profession Act*, S.B.C. 1998, c. 9, ss. 37, 38.

[60] *Law Society of Manitoba v. Savino*, [1983] M.J. No. 206, 1 D.L.R. (4th) 285 at 292-93 (Man. C.A.).

[61] *Pearlman v. Manitoba Law Society Judicial Committee*, [1991] S.C.J. No. 66, [1991] 2 S.C.R. 869 at para. 45 (S.C.C.).

[62] In this respect, see Federation of Law Societies of Canada, *Model Code of Conduct*, Preface.

---

more specifically to better demarcate the nature and scope of proscribed misconduct. For example, Rule 1.02 of the Law Society of Upper Canada's *Rules of Professional Conduct* defines "professional misconduct" generally to include "conduct in a lawyer's professional capacity that tends to bring discredit upon the legal profession" and further specifies that such conduct includes:

(a) violating or attempting to violate one of the rules in the *Rules of Professional Conduct* or a requirement of the *Law Society Act* or its regulations or by-laws,

(b) knowingly assisting or inducing another lawyer to violate or attempt to violate the rules in the *Rules of Professional Conduct* or a requirement of the *Law Society Act* or its regulations or by-laws,

(c) knowingly assisting or inducing a non-lawyer partner or associate of a multi-discipline practice to violate or attempt to violate the rules in the *Rules of Professional Conduct* or a requirement of the *Law Society Act* or its regulations or by-laws,

(d) misappropriating or otherwise dealing dishonestly with a client's or a third party's money or property,

(e) engaging in conduct that is prejudicial to the administration of justice,

(f) stating or implying an ability to influence improperly a government agency or official, or

(g) knowingly assisting a judge or a judicial officer in conduct that is a violation of applicable rules of judicial conduct or other law.

Traditionally, "professional misconduct" has been defined in terms of "disgraceful or dishonourable conduct"; some element of moral turpitude was required but negligence, by itself, would not suffice.[63]

While in theory, the scope of professional discipline is broad, in practice it is much narrower. One leading commentator has suggested that there are basically four reasons for taking disciplinary action against lawyers:

> Essentially lawyers in Canada are subject to serious discipline for just four reasons: because they have been guilty of theft, fraud, forgery or some other criminal offence; because they have violated a fiduciary duty imposed on them by law; because they are unable to carry on their practices due to physical or mental disability or serious addiction; or because they have failed to respond to inquiries from their governing body.[64]

Studies of professional discipline in Ontario would seem to justify this assessment.[65] This means, of course, that the bulk of the provisions found in ethics codes do not serve as the basis for professional discipline. For this

---

[63] *In re Solicitor*, [1912] 1 K.B. 302; *Myers v. Elman*, [1940] A.C. 282.
[64] Harry Arthurs, "The Dead Parrot: Does Professional Self Regulation Exhibit Vital Signs?" (1995) 33 Alta. L. Rev. 800 at 802.
[65] Gavin MacKenzie, *Lawyers and Ethics: Professional Responsibility and Discipline* (Toronto: Carswell, 2000) at 26-24 to 26-25.

reason, some have suggested that regulation of lawyers through ethics codes and discipline proceedings is ineffectual; that the chief grounds of lawyer discipline can be addressed through other bodies such as courts of civil and criminal jurisdiction. Moreover, it has been argued that professional discipline has less to do with ethics or conduct codes and more to do with a lawyer's personal characteristics, the context of individual practices and the prevailing ethical concerns of the time. As a result, "[w]hile there are occasional high-profile cases involving elite lawyers and law firms, the (small) bulk of disciplinary activity occurs at the margins of the profession".[66]

Commencing in the 1970s, the scope of lawyer discipline was expanded to address incompetence in the delivery of legal services. Prior to this time, lawyer incompetence was not a matter for discipline unless the inadequate services complained of also constituted a breach of some other ethical duty or professional norm. However, with the general recognition that a lawyer owed a client an ethical duty to be competent to provide the legal services undertaken on his or her behalf, incompetence became a matter for discipline. Since that time, law societies have recognized the duty to provide competent legal services in their codes of ethics or professional conduct. For example, in Chapter 2 of the Alberta Code (modelled on the FLSC's *Model Code of Professional Conduct*), after a lengthy definition of the constitutive elements of lawyer competence, the lawyer is held to the following duty "[a] lawyer must perform all legal services undertaken on a client's behalf to the standard of a competent lawyer". Similarly, in Rule 2 of the Law Society of Upper Canada's *Rules of Professional Conduct*, a lawyer is placed under an ethical obligation to "perform any legal services undertaken on a client's behalf to the standard of a competent lawyer".

Competence is a relative concept, defined by reference to the legal knowledge, practice skills, attributes and values expected of a competent lawyer in the provision of specific services in relation to a particular matter. Lawyer incompetence is addressed through either the regular disciplinary processes or a separate track established for such matters. In addition, the normal disciplinary sanctions have been expanded to include a variety of remedial measures, such as a direction to take continuing education courses or to pass special examinations. In Ontario, the Law Society of Upper Canada has adopted practice review of junior lawyers in an attempt to be more proactive in regulating lawyer competence.

While professional misconduct is thought to refer to actions arising out of a lawyer's professional activities, the phrase "conduct unbecoming a barrister or solicitor" is generally understood to refer to the personal or private conduct of a lawyer which may give rise to professional discipline. In Ontario, "conduct unbecoming a barrister or solicitor" has been defined as the private or personal conduct of a lawyer which "tends to bring discredit upon the legal profession" and includes dishonest conduct, certain kinds of criminal conduct,

---

[66] Allan C. Hutchinson, *Legal Ethics and Professional Responsibility* (Toronto: Irwin Law, 1999) at 15.

and conduct which takes advantage of the age or the lack of sophistication of others.[67] As it involves private or personal conduct, the norms and standards set out in ethics codes will serve little or no purpose in this respect. Although it is difficult to categorize the type of private or personal misconduct which will give rise to discipline proceedings, it is suggested that the conduct must be of a type which calls into question the lawyer's integrity or ability to act competently and honestly. The commission of a crime which calls into question the lawyer's ability to practise law may well serve as the basis for discipline proceedings. However, deviant sexual behaviour, which is not criminal in nature, will not give rise to professional discipline as it does not call into question the lawyer's ability to practise and as such, proceedings would entail too great an intrusion into the private lives of others. Discipline of lawyers for "conduct unbecoming" is discussed further in Chapter 13, "Issues in Regulation".

B. DISCIPLINE PROCEEDINGS

A detailed description and discussion of the discipline processes of the various provincial and territorial law societies is beyond the scope of this chapter. Details concerning the discipline structure and processes of individual law societies are best obtained through a review of the enabling legislation, rules and regulations, and published information guidelines. Increasingly, law societies are providing this information in electronic form, online, through their websites as a greater service to the public. A review of a number of provincial jurisdictions, Alberta, British Columbia and Ontario, suggests that, despite some differences, the structure of discipline proceedings demonstrates a fair degree of uniformity. Although it needs to be acknowledged that Quebec is somewhat unique with discipline powers being exercised by discipline committees, chaired by a judge, appointed by the Lieutenant Governor in Council, with the other members appointed by the governing bodies of the profession, the general uniformity of approach facilitates the general description of discipline structures and processes in the remainder of this section.

Lawyer discipline has evolved into a fairly complex, elaborate and often formal set of proceedings with a number of distinct stages or phases. The complexity and formality of the proceedings reflects not only the seriousness of the issues but also the law society's duty to deal fairly with members whose livelihoods and reputations are at stake. It also means that law societies have to dedicate, on an ongoing basis, significant fiscal and human resources to lawyer discipline.

Discipline proceedings can be conveniently divided into three distinct stages: (1) the complaint and investigation stage; (2) the hearing stage; and (3) the penalty/sanction stage.

---

[67]   Law Society of Upper Canada, *Rules of Professional Conduct*, Rule 1.02.

Complaint/Investigation Stage

The first stage tends to be less formal than the hearing and sanction stages that follow. As lawyer discipline in Canada is largely reactive, it begins with some sort of complaint, usually from a client or former client complaining of actual or perceived lawyer misconduct. Complaints can also come from members of the judiciary, other lawyers or members of the public. Sometimes, law society investigations are prompted by random audits of members' books and accounts, media commentary, legal proceedings against lawyers or reports from law enforcement agencies. Once a complaint is received, it is reviewed and assessed by a member of the law society's administrative staff. The nature and extent of any investigation at this stage depends on the nature of the complaint and the initial assessment by law society complaints officers.

A number of criticisms have been levied at a system of discipline which depends, in large part, on complaints from either clients (or former clients) or the judiciary and other lawyers. The chief concern is the under-reporting of lawyers' ethical violations or misconduct. Few complaints are received from other lawyers, who are reluctant, despite ethical obligations to the contrary, to report the misconduct of their colleagues. Even though lawyers possess the specialized expertise to detect misconduct, most are unwilling to report it for fear of collegial hostility or retaliation, or because they do not believe they are in a good position to judge the conduct of their peers. It has been suggested that a lawyer's failure to report the misconduct of a colleague should itself lead to discipline.[68] Complaints by clients or former clients are limited by the information asymmetry which exists between lawyers and their clients. Many clients do not know what constitutes lawyer misconduct and they do not know about discipline processes. Some do not report lawyer misconduct because of the complexity of the process or because they believe that to do so would be futile.

The system is also seen to be unresponsive to a large number of client complaints about the quality of the legal services they have received. These consumer complaints are not directed at the integrity nor the competence of lawyers but rather arise out of lawyer neglect, inadequate service, or stem from unhappiness over fees or the outcome of a particular matter. A long-standing criticism of lawyer discipline is the mismatch between client needs and regulatory responses. Joan Brockman has noted the nature of complaints made about lawyers in British Columbia:

> The most common complaints to the Law Society (other than those classi-
> fied as "miscellaneous") over the twelve year period for this study (1989 -
> 2000) were dissatisfaction with legal work (14.5%), failure to communicate
> (8.5%), delay/inactivity (5.8%), conflict of interest (5.7%), unpaid creditor/
> disbursement (5.6%), fees (5%), error or negligence (4.4%) and withholding
> files or funds (3.4%). In 1999, the Law Society reported that a review of
> complaint statistics indicated that "nearly 40% of complaints are service

---

[68]   Deborah Rhode, *In the Interests of Justice: Reforming the Legal Profession* (New York: Oxford University Press, 2000) at 159 and 162-63.

related, including general dissatisfaction with legal instructions and concerns about fees, rudeness and sloppy practice.[69]

However, these types of complaints fall outside the traditional focus of discipline on lawyers' ethics and competence. As a result, law societies have typically screened out these kinds of consumer complaints on the basis that they are not appropriate for formal discipline. Or, in some cases, law societies have informally intervened with the lawyer, bringing about a partial or complete solution to the complaint. Law societies do not have the power to levy sanctions which would confer any direct benefit on clients in these kinds of situations. All the law society can do is intervene administratively to bring about a resolution of the complaint or refer the complainant to another agency which may be able to provide a remedy.

Law societies have responded to these criticisms and concerns with a greater investment of resources at the complaints stage. Complaint departments, with professional staff and trained complaints officers, have been established. Better information on the discipline process and complaints is provided through published guidelines and by means of law society websites. This information is not only designed to assist the public in making a complaint, but to get the public to screen its own complaints. For example, potential complainants are typically advised about matters which do not fall under the law society's jurisdiction or authority, such as regulating a lawyer's bills, intervening in court cases or providing compensation for losses caused by a lawyer's alleged negligence. However, increasingly, law societies are providing greater assistance in dealing with consumer complaints, such as fee mediation, realizing that a failure to do so will only heighten public skepticism about the system of self regulation, which is thought to prefer or protect lawyers. Where appropriate, administrative staff try to resolve the concern in an informal way through mediation or dispute resolution. Clients who are concerned about their lawyers' fees are referred to court taxation processes and those complaining of neglect and loss are advised to seek another lawyer's advice about a possible malpractice claim.

Complaints which are appropriate for formal discipline are reduced to writing (where necessary), reviewed by administrative staff and shared with the subject lawyer. The lawyer is required to answer any questions or provide any documents or records requested by the law society. Further investigations are then conducted if necessary. A decision is made to either dismiss the complaint or to refer the matter to either a practice standards committee (where competence is an issue) or a conduct or discipline committee (where ethics or violations of law society rules are at issue). When a decision is made at the investigative stage to dismiss the complaint, the complainant is advised in writing and is given an opportunity to appeal the dismissal to a form of appeal committee consisting of, usually, elected and lay benchers. That apart, the conduct committee (or a panel thereof) then reviews the formal complaint.

---

[69] Joan Brockman, "An Update on Self Regulation in the Legal Profession (1989–2000): Funnel In and Funnel Out" (2004) 19 C.J.L.S. 55 at 70-71.

This can include a further investigation, a referral of the matter to a conduct review committee or a bencher for a mandatory review, or a referral to a practice standards or review committee. After the review, the conduct committee must then decide whether to dismiss the complaint or to direct the preparation of a citation setting out the charges and/or alleged misconduct to be considered by a hearing committee. In Ontario, discipline proceedings are initiated only on the authorization of the Proceedings Authorization Committee, made up of five benchers (one of whom is a paralegal), appointed by convocation.

Hearing Stage

Discipline hearings are adversarial in nature, conducted before a panel of the discipline or conduct committee. The proceedings are conducted by counsel for the law society, who is either an employee of the law society or a private practitioner appointed specifically for the purpose of the particular proceedings. Law society counsel must act independently, in the public interest, even though they are paid by the law society. The burden of proof is borne by the law society, whose counsel must provide clear and convincing evidence of misconduct.

In form, discipline proceedings bear a strong resemblance to criminal proceedings although there is also some similarity to civil proceedings; indeed, it is suggested that discipline proceedings are neither criminal nor civil in nature; rather, they are *sui generis*.[70] The accused lawyer is entitled to full disclosure from counsel for the law society of all relevant documents in the law society's possession, all witness statements and expert's reports. The accused lawyer on the other hand does not have to make disclosure to a similar extent but is required to co-operate in the investigation by the law society and to produce any documents required in the investigation. Moreover, the lawyer is compellable as a witness in the proceedings.

Discipline hearings have been characterized by the courts as "judicial" or "quasi-judicial" in nature due to the potentially significant affect on the accused lawyer's reputation and livelihood.[71] Accordingly, the requirements of natural justice or fairness attach and the accused lawyer is entitled, in addition to extensive disclosure rights, to adequate notice, to be represented by counsel, and to a hearing before an impartial, unbiased adjudicator. In the latter respect, even though representatives of the law society act as "investigators, prosecutors, and judges", it is important to keep these various functions as distinct as possible. Law society counsel must represent the public, and adjudicators on hearing panels must be free from conflicts of interest and play no role in the conduct of the proceedings.

Typically, legislation or rules governing discipline hearings provide for public hearings, the taking of evidence under oath, the right of the accused

---

[70] Gavin MacKenzie, *Lawyers and Ethics: Professional Responsibility and Discipline* (Toronto: Carswell, 2000) at 26-7.

[71] *Ibid.*, at 26-34 to 26-36.1.

lawyer to make full answer and defence, and the cross-examination of witnesses. As a result, discipline proceedings are highly formal in nature, exhibiting many of the traditional elements of court processes.

As discipline proceedings are authorized by statute, they are subject to both Charter scrutiny and common law judicial review. Aspects of discipline proceedings have been challenged on the basis of both sections 7 and 11 of the Charter; section 7 would appear to apply in terms of constitutionally guaranteed procedural rights, but section 11 does not, as discipline proceedings have been held to be regulatory and not penal or criminal in nature. Given the essential nature of self regulation, which relies heavily on the expertise of lawyers in the assessment of misconduct, courts are likely to accord discipline tribunals, a fair measure of deference in any review of discipline decisions.

Discipline hearings have been characterized as "multi-stage proceedings";[72] the panel must first determine whether the facts have been established, and then it must determine whether the facts, as proven, constitute professional misconduct or conduct unbecoming a barrister and solicitor. Finally, it must decide what would be the appropriate penalty under the circumstances. The final decision of the panel must be in writing and typically, panels are under an obligation to provide reasons for their decisions, apart from those concerning the acquisition of jurisdiction.

Penalty/Sanction Stage

Having determined that the misconduct as established constitutes professional misconduct or conduct unbecoming, the hearing panel must then consider the appropriate sanction. It must be remembered that the purpose of any sanction is either the protection of the public or the profession's reputation and not the punishment of the lawyer, even though the sanction imposed has a severe effect on the lawyer's reputation and livelihood.

Hearing panels are typically empowered to impose a number of penalties and sanctions ranging in order of severity from a reprimand, which may or may not be public, a fine, suspension from practice or an area of practice, the imposition of practice conditions, to disbarment. The lawyer who has been disciplined may also be ordered to pay the costs of the investigation and the hearing. When the discipline arises from incompetence, the range of possible penalties is expanded to include remedial training and education and restrictions on practice including practice under the supervision of another lawyer.

In determining the appropriate penalty or sanction, the hearing panel will look to matters such as the nature and extent of injury to others, the blameworthiness of the offending lawyer's conduct, and penalties imposed on others for similar misconduct. The panel will also consider mitigating and aggravating factors or circumstances such as: the lawyer's general reputation or character; the lawyer's attitude towards discipline; whether or not the lawyer has made restitution; whether or not the situation was an isolated event

---

[72]   *Ibid.*, at 26-54.

or a re-occurrence; the lawyer's prior discipline record; the need for deterrence; and the lawyer's mental state.[73] The weight accorded to these factors will vary from case to case depending on the circumstances of the misconduct.

The most severe of the sanctions, disbarment or cancellation of the right to practise, is imposed the least frequently, usually in cases of deliberate, flagrant or unlawful misconduct, such as misappropriation of client funds, fraud or conviction for a serious criminal offence, and in cases of ungovernability. Suspensions are imposed for a broader range of misconduct, often of an isolated nature, such as: taking unfair advantage of clients; sexual harassment; making false submissions to courts; assisting clients in hiding assets; lying to clients; failing to account for retainers or disbursement payments; and falsifying documents. Lawyers are not allowed to practise for the term of the suspension and may have to apply for reinstatement in the case of an indefinite suspension. Depending on the length of the suspension, it can have as significant an affect on the reputation and livelihood of the lawyer as disbarment. Reinstatement is also possible in the case of disbarred lawyers but the standard for re-admission is high as the law society must be convinced that the rehabilitation of the lawyer is total and genuine. Even that may not be sufficient in some cases where the law society is of the opinion that its reputation would suffer if re-admission was allowed. For example, in a decision excerpted in Chapter 13, "Issues in Regulation", Maurice Sychuk, after serving his term of incarceration for the murder of his wife, sought reinstatement having been disbarred after his conviction. His application was denied in part due to the Law Society's concern for its reputation.[74]

Many law societies publish digests of discipline decisions online to better inform the public about their discharge of the discipline function. Publication, in electronic and written form, also serves to inform lawyers about: professional norms and standards, misconduct which is determined to breach those norms, and the consequences of such conduct. Without publication, the deterrent effect of disciplinary decisions would appear to be significantly undermined.[75]

Finally, it should be noted that, usually, a right of appeal exists from the decisions of hearing panels to either an appeal panel (or to the benchers, as a whole) or to the courts, or both. A panel's decision with respect to either professional misconduct or conduct unbecoming and with respect to the penalty imposed are subject generally to review by a court on a reasonableness standard; that is, do the reasons, taken as whole, support the decision? Is the decision intelligible, transparent and justified, and does it fall within a

---

[73] For a fuller discussion of these and other factors, see Charles Wolfram, *Modern Legal Ethics* (St. Paul, MN: West Publishing, 1986) at 119-26 and Gavin MacKenzie, *Lawyers and Ethics: Professional Responsibility and Discipline* (Toronto: Carswell, 2000) at 26-43 to 26-46.

[74] *Law Society of Alberta v. Sychuk*, [1999] L.S.D.D. No. 15.

[75] The discipline decisions of provincial law societies are published electronically by CanLII.

range of reasonable outcomes?[76] Procedural issues will be reviewed on a correctness standard.

D. OTHER REGULATORY FUNCTIONS

At this point, a brief reference will be made to some of the other regulatory functions of the modern Canadian law society. These are undertaken in the public interest and involve: (a) the protection of the profession's monopoly or dominance over the market for legal services; and (b) the operation of insurance and assurance schemes to compensate clients who have suffered loss or damage as a result of the negligent or deliberate conduct of lawyers in the representation of clients.

1. Unauthorized Practice of Law

The unauthorized practice of law simply refers to the practice of law by persons not licensed to practise or by non-lawyers. For a more detailed discussion, see Chapter 13. Practice by unauthorized persons is prohibited by provincial legislation and such activity constitutes an offence punishable by a fine and possibly even a term of imprisonment.[77] Usually, it is also an offence to misrepresent oneself as a barrister or solicitor or a person licensed to practise law. The statutory prohibition against unauthorized practice is not absolute as, typically, the legislation recognizes a number of exceptions; chiefly, the right of an individual to act on his or her own behalf, before either a court or tribunal or in the preparation of documents having legal effect,[78] but also including persons authorized by statute to appear as the agent of another in judicial or administrative proceedings, and persons enrolled as articling students, working under the supervision of licensed practitioners. Prohibitions against unauthorized practice have enabled lawyers to establish a monopoly or dominance over the market for legal services largely free from competition by others. These provisions can also be characterized as the regulation of non-lawyers, by lawyers, in the public interest.[79]

Unauthorized practice usually occurs at the margins of law practice, involving legal services of a routine nature, "areas in which the special skills and training of lawyers are least needed and thus in which it has been easiest for non-lawyers to duplicate the competence of lawyers without great expense and with high consumer acceptance".[80] Non-lawyers have acted as advocates

---

[76] *Dunsmuir v. New Brunswick*, [2008] S.C.J. No. 9, [2008] 1 S.C.R. 190 (S.C.C.).

[77] *Legal Profession Act*, R.S.A. 2000, c. L-8, s. 106; *Legal Profession Act*, S.B.C. 1998, c. 9, s. 15; and *Law Society Act*, R.S.O. 1990, c. L.8, s. 26.1.

[78] For example, *Legal Profession Act*, R.S.A. 2000, c. L-8, s. 106(2)(*h*).

[79] Interestingly, lawyers are placed under an ethical duty "to assist in preventing the unauthorized practice of law": see Federation of Law Societies of Canada, *Model Code of Professional Conduct*, Chapter 6, Rule 6.06. This is an unusual provision for a lawyers' ethics code but it does, through the Commentary, offer the organized profession an opportunity to make the "case" for the statutory prohibition of unauthorized practice.

[80] Charles Wolfram, *Modern Legal Ethics* (St. Paul, MN: West Publishing, 1986) at 828.

for persons before courts and administrative tribunals;[81] have prepared legal documents;[82] have given legal advice;[83] and have prepared and published "do-it-yourself kits" and legal forms for persons wishing to act on their own behalf.[84] Paralegal businesses have been established, offering lower cost legal services or assistance, in relation to such matters as traffic tickets, uncontested divorces, immigration, criminal pardons and civil disputes before provincial courts. Overall, non-lawyer competition has increased dramatically over the last two decades as the growing cost and complexity of lawyer services has fuelled a need for less expensive and more accessible alternatives. This increase has also been fuelled, to an uncertain extent, by modern information technology which has enabled non-lawyer businesses greater opportunities to deliver legal services directly to the public. For the most part, the profession has responded to this increase in non-lawyer activity by seeking to enforce its monopoly over the market for legal services through prosecutions for the unauthorized practise of law or applications for injunctions enjoining such activity. In the main, these legal actions are directed at those who are in the business of providing legal services. The enforcement of unauthorized practice prohibitions is usually justified on the basis that the profession is acting in the public interest by protecting clients from harmful incompetence or protecting the legal system from the deleterious consequences of incompetent or unethical non-lawyers. It is asserted that the public interest and clients are best served by lawyers whose competence and ethics are regulated by the organized profession and the courts. Also, it is pointed out that only lawyers can offer clients the benefits of confidentiality and evidentiary privilege and access to such safeguards as mandatory liability insurance and compensation funds.

The success of the profession in meeting the competitive challenge posed by non-lawyers has been mixed. Unauthorized practice by non-lawyers has not been eradicated; rather, it has increased. Enforcement efforts have been sporadic and the courts have not uniformly upheld unauthorized practice prohibitions. At times, the profession has been reluctant to pursue the zealous prosecution of unauthorized practice for fear of appearing to act solely in its members' economic interests, thereby further undermining the support of a skeptical public, many of whom value the legal services offered by non-lawyers. Moreover, the decision to seek enforcement of unauthorized practice laws in novel situations has been hampered by the uncertain and imprecise

---

[81]   *R. v. Lawrie*, [1987] O.J. No. 225, 59 O.R. (2d) 161 (Ont. C.A.); *Law Society of British Columbia v. Lawrie*, [1991] B.C.J. No. 2653, 84 D.L.R. (4th) 540 (B.C.C.A.); *Gagnon v. Pritchard*, [2002] O.J. No. 928, 58 O.R. (3d) 557 (Ont. S.C.J.); *Law Society of British Columbia v. Mangat*, [2001] S.C.J. No. 66, [2001] 3 S.C.R. 113 (S.C.C.).

[82]   *The Solicitors Act; Re Hood*, [1942] O.J. No. 468, [1942] 4 D.L.R. 505 (Ont. H.C.J.).

[83]   *Law Society of British Columbia v. Lauren*, [2012] B.C.J. No. 1004, 2012 BCSC 738 (B.C.S.C.); *Law Society of British Columbia v. Gravelle*, [1998] B.C.J. No. 2383, 166 D.L.R. (4th) 723 (B.C.S.C.).

[84]   *Law Society of British Columbia v. Burdeny*, [1996] B.C.J. No. 191, 18 B.C.L.R. (3d) 327, 6 W.W.R. 241 (B.C.S.C.); *Law Society of British Columbia v. McLaughlin*, [1992] B.C.J. No. 1300, 70 B.C.L.R. (2d) 235 (B.C.S.C.).

state of the law. Legislative proscriptions against unauthorized practice are often of little practical help given their potentially broad sweep and lack of definition. What activities constitute the "practice of law" or "practising as a barrister and solicitor"? Does the statutory definition of unauthorized practice prohibit non-lawyers from doing anything that a lawyer does? If so, the legislation would seem to proscribe wide areas of governmental and commercial activity. Conscious of the governing legislation's limitations, courts in the various provincial jurisdictions, have approached the issue of unauthorized practice on a case-by-case basis. What has emerged is a small, often inconsistent and superficial body of case law featuring conclusions, not reasoned judgments, that a particular activity does or does not amount to the practice of law by an unauthorized person: "The courts have often reached conclusions that a particular activity is unauthorized practice only after the most superficial examination of the activity, of precedent, and of the rationale for the doctrine."[85] Which, often, is of little guidance to either the profession, the courts or aspiring paralegals.

Unauthorized practice laws have been severely criticized by both legal academics and those outside of the profession. Not surprisingly, however, the large majority of the bar has historically supported vigorous enforcement of these laws. The chief focus of the critics is the largely unproven claim that unauthorized practice laws exist in the public interest to protect clients from harm caused by incompetent and unethical non-lawyers. They argue that this claim is not empirically proven and that examples of harmful non-lawyer activity can be easily matched by examples of lawyer negligence or unethical behaviour. Moreover, they point out that the public interest argument is too narrowly framed in that it fails to consider the potential benefits to consumers of paralegal services. A broader range of questions need to be asked in evaluating where the public interest lies. The issue is far more complex than protecting the public from hypothetical harms:

> In evaluating the public interest, we need to know not just whether consumer problems arise, but also how often, and compared to what? We also need to know how well the current system responds to non-lawyer abuses and at what cost. Can low income individuals realistically afford attorneys? Is lawyers' performance sufficiently superior to lay practitioners in all contexts to justify compelling the additional expense? Are unauthorized practice prohibitions well tailored to address only cases of consumer injury? Are enforcement structures adequate to deter and remedy abuse?[86]

One of the more interesting questions raised in this respect is whether many basic legal services, carried out by non-lawyers or paralegals, require the knowledge and expertise of a fully accredited lawyer. Are lawyers, in fact, overqualified to do this kind of work? Does the competent representation of a

---

[85]   Charles Wolfram, *Modern Legal Ethics* (St. Paul, MN: West Publishing, 1986) at 835 (discussing the parallel American experience).
[86]   Deborah Rhode, "Professionalism in Perspective: Alternative Approaches to Non-lawyer Practice" (1996–1997) 22 N.Y.U. Rev. of Law & Soc. Change 701 at 708.

person in traffic court or the completion of routine legal forms require the education and training of a lawyer admitted to practice? Perhaps not, as these types of matters are often delegated to paralegals in law firms working under the limited or minimal supervision of a lawyer.

Other critics decry the unnecessary limitation on competition. They point to the fact that many persons cannot afford a lawyer and that, therefore, the profession is not adequately serving the needs of the market for legal services. Independent paralegals serve this need by providing routine services at a lower cost. If lawyers are unable to provide low-cost, accessible, basic services, then why shouldn't others provide such service? Indeed, if non-lawyer assistance were more widely available, lawyers may be compelled to offer more cost-effective services in order to compete.

Finally, it is suggested that other means could be used to better achieve the goal of protecting the public from harm caused by incompetent or unethical legal services. Chief among these is imposing a regulatory frame-work on non-lawyer practitioners which better balances the public interest in consumer protection with that of consumer choice.[87] Ontario has recently moved in this direction, after a long period of debate and formal study. In 2006, acting on the recommendations of a law society committee, the Ontario legislature enacted the *Access to Justice Act, 2006*[88] which brought independ-ent paralegals under the regulatory reach of the Law Society of Upper Canada. The avowed purpose of the legislation was to protect consumers who used independent paralegals providing legal services in the following areas of practice: matters before the Small Claims Court; provincial boards and agencies; and provincial offences such as highway traffic cases. To better protect consumers, paralegals will be regulated, educated, licensed and insured. A *Paralegal Code of Conduct* has been devised by the Law Society, which will form the basis for discipline. The new scheme came into effect on May 1, 2007 and the first paralegal licences were issued in 2008.

The Ontario approach seems sensible if the real concern is the public interest in competent and ethical legal services. A regulatory scheme will provide minimum qualifications in terms of education and training and effective enforcement mechanisms. In addition, it will strengthen the profession's hand in enforcing unauthorized practice prohibitions against independent paralegals who are not licensed under the new regime. However, no other province, to date, has followed Ontario's lead. The remaining provinces and territories continue to deal with independent paralegals through unauthorized practice laws which are generally perceived by the public to serve the profession's interests and not the public's.

E. EXTERNAL REGULATION OF THE LEGAL PROFESSION

Apart from professional self regulation, lawyer conduct is regulated legally by the courts through malpractice or professional liability actions and informally

---

[87]   *Ibid.*, at 714.
[88]   S.O. 2006, c. 21.

through voluntary membership in professional organizations and groups. Judicial regulation has become particularly pronounced in relation to a lawyer's fiduciary duties of loyalty, to avoid conflicts of interest and to keep client's confidences. The decisions of the courts in these respects have significantly shaped the profession's ethical rules concerning these matters; see specifically Chapters 4 and 5.

1. Legal Liability of Lawyers

Like all providers of professional services, lawyers can be held legally liable in damages for acts or omissions which cause their clients or customers loss or injury. As the subject of malpractice or professional legal liability has been more extensively canvassed elsewhere, only a brief description of the salient features of such liability will be undertaken at this point.

Unlike self regulation, which seeks to serve the public interest and the reputation of the profession by removing the offending lawyer from practice, either temporarily or permanently, damage liability compensates the client for the loss or injury suffered. In addition, unlike the case in discipline proceedings, the client, the injured party, has control over the direction of the legal action. However, like professional discipline proceedings, damage actions serve indirectly to set conduct standards for the representation of clients. Moreover, the very possibility of such actions functions as an incentive to lawyers to act competently in the representation of clients. The duty of competence is often distinguished from professional negligence on the basis that a lawyer can be competent, in terms of possessing the requisite knowledge, skills and qualities of a competent practitioner in relation to a specific representation, and yet negligent in terms of acting carelessly or making a mistake in that particular representation. For example, Commentary to Rule 2.01(2) of the Law Society of Alberta's *Code of Professional Conduct*, modelled on the Federation of Law Societies of Canada's *Model Code of Professional Conduct*, provides:

Incompetence, Negligence and Mistakes

This rule does not require a standard of perfection. An error or omission, even though it might be actionable for damages in negligence or contract, will not necessarily constitute a failure to maintain the standard of professional competence described by the rule. However, evidence of gross neglect in a particular matter or a pattern of neglect or mistakes in different matters may be evidence of such a failure, regardless of tort liability. While damages may be awarded for negligence, incompetence can give rise to the additional sanction of disciplinary action.

Originally, lawyers' liability was based in contract; the retainer, or contract of engagement, between the lawyer and the client which authorizes and governs the representation. While the retainer can include specific terms concerning the nature and extent of the lawyer's duties, more often than not the duty of care undertaken by the lawyer is an implied, rather than an express, term of the retainer. Typically, the lawyer is under an implied duty in the representation of the client to exercise the care, skill and diligence commonly observed by other lawyers in like circumstances. Lawyers can also be concurrently liable in tort for negligence in the performance of their contractual duties; liability is simply the result of a special application of the standard negligence formula: duty, breach of duty, causation and damages. The Supreme Court of Canada, in *Central Trust Co. v. Rafuse*, decided that when a lawyer is negligent in the performance of contractual duties, he or she is open to concurrent liability in contract and tort and the client can proceed either way depending on which is most advantageous in terms of damages or limitation periods.[89] The duty is owed to the client who is in a sufficiently proximate relationship with the lawyer, although it must be appreciated that lawyers in the representation of their clients can owe duties of care to third parties whose loss or injury is foreseeable. For example, a lawyer may owe a duty of care to beneficiaries arising out of the preparation and execution of a will for his or her client, the testator. The standard of care in negligence actions is that of the "the reasonably competent solicitor, the ordinary competent solicitor, and the ordinary prudent solicitor".[90] The lawyer's conduct will be judged according to the reasonable standards of the profession. While not bound by professional codes of ethics or conduct, the courts may use them as an authoritative statement of expected norms and standards of conduct. For the most part, the standard of care does not differ between lawyers on the basis of specialized expertise or long experience as formal specialization is not generally recognized in the Canadian legal profession. What is expected is the exercise of reasonable knowledge, skill and diligence, not perfection in the representation of the client. A lawyer cannot be held liable for a result which is unfavourable to the client unless it was caused by the lawyer's negligence. Finally, the alleged negligence must be the cause of the client's loss or damage to be actionable. If the client's loss or injury would have occurred even in the absence of the lawyer's carelessness, then there will be no liability. The best example is where an action would have failed on the merits even though a limitation period was not missed.

As any work on professional negligence will reveal, liability can occur in a number of ways: through a mistake in the giving of advice; through a failure to give advice; as a result of an error in the conduct of litigation; or as a result of carelessness in non-contentious business. Where the law is clear and the matter is a common occurrence, the advice must be correct; but where the law is unclear and the issue is a matter of some complexity, the lawyer need only give advice which is reasonable and informed, where necessary, by appropriate research.[91] A lawyer is under a duty to advise a client of all material developments and all relevant information that comes to his or her attention.[92] Moreover, a lawyer is under a duty to advise a client of all potential risks

[89]   [1986] S.C.J. No. 52, [1986] 2 S.C.R. 147 (S.C.C.).
[90]   *Ibid.*, at 208.
[91]   *Ibid.*, at 208-209.
[92]   *Bailey v. Ornheim*, [1962] B.C.J. No. 159, 40 W.W.R. 129 (B.C.S.C.).

unless the client clearly knows of and understands the risks beforehand.[93] There is no immunity for lawyers in relation to negligence in the conduct of civil or criminal litigation.[94] A lawyer can be held liable for missing a limitation period,[95] or commencing an action in the wrong court or jurisdiction,[96] but, generally speaking, a lawyer will not be held liable for errors in judgment in terms of trial tactics or procedural choices so long as he or she demonstrates reasonable competence in these matters.[97] Liability for misconduct in non-contentious matters can arise where the lawyer fails to carry out the necessary searches, fails to review relevant documents[98] or fails to take the necessary steps in lending transactions to protect the client's position.[99]

In addition, it should be noted that lawyers can be held liable for misconduct which constitutes a breach of their duties as fiduciaries in the representation of clients. For example, as a fiduciary, a lawyer must keep confidential all information concerning his or her client's affairs and if this duty of confidentiality is violated for the benefit of the lawyer or others, then liability will ensue.[100]

Unlike the situation in the United States where significant numbers of practising lawyers do not carry legal malpractice insurance due to the high cost of the premiums, practising lawyers in Canada are required to participate in indemnity or insurance schemes, established and maintained by provincial law societies, to compensate clients for losses occasioned by their lawyers' negligence.[101] Commonly known as "errors or omissions" insurance, it is required as a condition of practice, although some classes of lawyers, who work as government counsel or in-house corporate counsel, are usually exempt from this requirement. By this form of regulation, law societies ensure that clients do not bear the burden of the loss caused by the negligent misconduct of their lawyers.

2.   Voluntary Professional Associations

Regulation, to an uncertain extent, occurs through voluntary membership in professional organizations, such as the Canadian Bar Association, and specialist organizations such as criminal and civil trial lawyers groups. Unlike the law societies, membership in these groups is not a prerequisite to practise.

---

[93]   *Gilkes v. Loucks*, [1989] A.J. No. 1026, 101 A.R. 25 (Alta. Q.B.), damages later varied [1991] A.J. No. 102, 79 Alta. L.R. (2d) 86 (Alta. C.A.).

[94]   *Demarco v. Ungaro*, [1979] O.J. No. 4011, 21 O.R. (2d) 673 (Ont. H.C.J.).

[95]   *Gorieu v. Simonot*, [1982] S.J. No. 691, [1982] 6 W.W.R. 221 (Sask. Q.B.).

[96]   *Re Hardy* (1871), 3 Chy. Chrs. 179.

[97]   *Heywood v. Wellers*, [1976] Q.B. 446.

[98]   *Aaroe v. Seymour*, [1956] O.J. No. 560, [1956] O.R. 736 (Ont. H.C.J.).

[99]   *Morris v. Jackson*, [1984] O.J. No. 1341, 34 R.P.R. 269 (Ont. H.C.J.); *McGrath v. Goldman*, [1975] B.C.J. No. 911, [1976] 1 W.W.R. 743 (B.C.S.C.).

[100] *Ott v. Fleishman*, [1983] B.C.J. No. 1808, [1983] 5 W.W.R. 721 (B.C.S.C.).

[101] *Legal Profession Act*, R.S.A. 2000, c. L-8, ss. 98-101; *Legal Profession Act*, S.B.C. 1998, c. 9, s. 30; and *Law Society Act*, R.S.O. 1990, c. L.8, s. 61.

However these groups do provide an opportunity for collegial activity and professional socialization.

The Canadian Bar Association (CBA) is the only national lawyer organization in Canada and has been in existence for nearly 100 years. It is organized into provincial branches whose membership varies from 100 per cent of the profession in the province to lesser amounts. The work of the CBA is carried out through national sections and provincial subsections organized around fields of law and areas of practice, such as criminal law, administrative law, labour law and taxation. The primary purpose of these section activities is the continuing education of member lawyers, but also includes law reform and lobbying on matters of professional or popular concern.

While a significant number of Canadian lawyers belong to the CBA, most do not actively participate in professional projects. Rather, "most lawyers maintain bar membership as a credential and for such fringe benefits as life and disability insurance".[102] In the main, the general membership avails itself of the educational programming and social activities organized through the sections and in conjunction with major events such as mid winter and annual meetings. The agenda for the organization is set by a small group of motivated insiders who constitute the governance committees or councils of the organization and its sections. They devise the organization's position on legal and public policy issues and they seek ratification from a rather acquiescent general membership.

The CBA has played a major role in the ongoing debate over conduct standards and their articulation in ethics codes since it adopted the first Canadian code of lawyer ethics in 1920. This code and its successors have served as the basis for many, if not most, of the provincial law societies' subsequent codes of professional conduct. Lawyers' conduct is, therefore, grounded in rules which are understood and accepted nationally. This gives these standards greater force and legitimacy in their application and helps to unite an increasingly fragmented profession. The section activities of the CBA facilitate the inculcation of practice standards and norms amongst the practitioners in a given area and provide an opportunity, when the occasion demands, for peer disapproval of questionable conduct.

In addition to the CBA, some lawyers belong to specialist groups or organizations consisting of lawyers who practise in a particular area. Across Canada, specialist organizations have been formed by criminal lawyers, Crown counsel, insolvency lawyers and civil advocates. These organizations provide an opportunity for lawyers in a particular area to network, to establish relationships and to learn from one another. Again, these groups establish, informally, community practice standards to guide lawyer conduct in particular areas which are enforced largely through peer approval or condemnation. These organizations also afford lawyers in a particular practice area a forum for the articulation of public positions on matters of professional and popular concern.

---

[102] Charles Wolfram, *Modern Legal Ethics* (St. Paul, MN: West Publishing, 1986) at 36.

F. CONCLUSION

The Canadian legal profession is a highly regulated occupation which enjoys a state-sanctioned dominance over the market for legal services. Regulation is chiefly carried out through provincial law societies which possess a large measure of independence in their regulation of lawyers in the public interest. While at one time, self regulation was directed largely towards the admission of persons to the profession and practice, this focus has shifted, as a result of the rise of university legal education, to the regulation of lawyer conduct. Apart from prescriptions and requirements found in statute, and in the by-laws and regulations of law societies, lawyer conduct is increasingly directed by detailed often mandatory codes of professional conduct governing the lawyer's conduct in a variety of roles and relationships. The legal and ethical norms of professional conduct are officially enforced through complex and formal discipline processes chiefly concerned with lawyer misconduct which poses a threat to either client interests or the reputation of the profession. Overall, with the revision and establishment of highly uniform, national codes by the Canadian Bar Association and the Federation of Law Societies of Canada, self regulation will be national or "pan Canadian" in its outlook.

The self regulation of lawyer conduct has evolved over recent decades as law societies have made significant changes to provide more accessible, accountable and transparent discipline systems. Greater organization and numbers of trained personnel have been dedicated to the task. The complaint process has been better structured. Discipline hearings are generally open to the public and greater efforts have been made to communicate more effectively with the public. Nevertheless, public dissatisfaction with the discipline process remains, grounded largely in the belief that it operates in the interests of lawyers and not those of the public. In particular, the traditional focus of discipline on professional misconduct is not seen to be responsive to the bulk of complaints about lawyers, which are consumer oriented. A system which is concerned with lawyer competence and ethics seems an ill match for complaints about delay, neglect, unreasonable fees and unfavourable outcomes. Law societies have attempted to respond to this lack of fit with better information about other means of redress and informal dispute resolution mechanisms. Only time will tell whether these efforts will satisfy public expectations. Nevertheless, the inadequacy of the discipline process in terms of addressing consumer oriented complaints will continue to present a challenge to law societies. The failure to address these types of concerns has already led to the potential diminution of self regulation and the imposition of third party oversight in other jurisdictions such as the United Kingdom and Ireland.

While self regulation, through provincial and territorial law societies, is the primary mode of controlling entry into the profession and professional conduct, it is not the only means. In addition to affording a basis of compensation, malpractice suits against lawyers for negligence in the representation of their clients give the courts an opportunity to rule on appropriate legal standards of lawyer conduct. The same can be said for legal actions concerning lawyers' failure to avoid conflicts of interest. Finally, volunteer legal organizations have made a contribution to lawyer regulation through the development of ethics codes and practice cultures with particular norms and standards of appropriate conduct.

Whatever form regulation takes, the current framework will only remain in place as long as it is seen to best secure the public interest in competent, ethical legal services. To this end, there must be greater public input into the development of lawyer codes of conduct and the operation of formal discipline processes. The obvious self-interest of the profession in setting conduct standards and in enforcing them must be better balanced through public involvement and accountability. Moreover, the regulation of non-lawyer competitors must serve the public interest in accessible, affordable legal services and not the profession's interest in excluding competition. Altogether, the regulation of the profession and its members must be directed towards, first and foremost, service in the public interest.

G. FURTHER READING

Abel, Richard L., "Why Does the ABA Promulgate Ethical Rules" (1981) 59 Tex. L. Rev. 639.

American Bar Association Commission on Professionalism, *In the Spirit of Public Service: A Blueprint for the Rekindling of Lawyer Professionalism* (Chicago: American Bar Association, 1986).

Arthurs, Harry, "The Dead Parrot: Does Professional Self Regulation Exhibit Vital Signs?" (1995) 33 Alta. L. Rev. 800.

Arthurs, Harry, Richard Weisman & Fredrick Zemans, "The Canadian Legal Profession" (1986) Am. Bar Assoc. Res. J. 447.

Auerbach, Jerold S., *Unequal Justice* (New York: Oxford University Press, 1976).

Barton, Benjamin H., "Why Do We Regulate Lawyers?: An Economic Analysis of the Justifications for Entry and Conduct Regulation" (2001) 33 Arizona St. L.J. 429.

Berry, Leanne, "Professional Negligence" in Klar, Linden, Cherniak & Kryworuk, *Remedies In Tort*, Vol. 2 (Toronto: Carswell, 2005) at 16.III-27 to 16.III-90.7.

Brockman, Joan, "Bias in the Legal Profession: A Survey of Members of the Law Society of British Columbia" (1992) 17 Queen's L.J. 91.

Brockman, Joan, *Identifying the Issues: A Survey of Active Members of the Law Society of Alberta* (Calgary: Law Society of Alberta, 1992).

Brockman, Joan, "'Resistance by the Club' to the Feminization of the Legal Profession" (1992) Can. J. Law & Soc. 47.

Canadian Bar Association, *Touchstones for Change: Equality, Diversity and Accountability* (Ottawa: Canadian Bar Association, 1993).

Cole, Curtis, *A Learned and Honorable Body: The Professionalization of the Ontario Bar, 1867-1929* (London, ON: University of Western Ontario, Faculty of Graduate Studies, 1987), Chapter 5, "To Purge the Profession of Those Who Bring Disgrace upon their Brethren: The Bar's Assumption of Autonomous Professional Self-Discipline".

Cooper, Merrill, Joan Brockman & Irene Hoffart, "Report on Equity and Diversity in Alberta's Legal Profession: Report Highlights" (January 26, 2004), online: The Law Society of Alberta <http://www.lawsocietyalberta.com/files/ equity/Equity_and_Diversity_in_Albertas_Legal_Profession_2004_Highlights.pdf>.

Fischer, James M., "External Control Over the American Bar" (2006) 19 Geo. J. of Leg. Ethics 59.

Grant, Stephen & Linda Rothstein, *Lawyers' Professional Liability* (Toronto: Butterworths, 1998).

Hagan, John & Fiona Kay, *Gender in Practice: A Study of Lawyer's Lives* (New York: Oxford University Press, 1995).

Hurlburt William, *The Self Regulation of the Legal Profession in Canada and in England and Wales* (Law Society of Alberta and the Alberta Law Reform Institute, 2000).

Iacobucci, Frank, "Striking a Balance: Trying to Find the Happy and Good Life Within and Beyond the Legal Profession" (1992) 26 L.S.U.C. Gazette 205.

Jackson, Rupert M. & John L. Powell, *Professional Negligence*, 4th ed. (London: Sweet & Maxwell, 1997).

Kay, Fiona, "Integrity in a Changing Profession: Issues of Diversity and Inclusion" (November 2005), online: The Law Society of Upper Canada, <http://www.lsuc.on ca/media/kaydiversityintegrity.pdf>.

Law, John M., "Canadian Bar Admissions" (2005) 74 The Bar Examiner 14.

Loder, R. Elizabeth, "Tighter Rules of Professional Conduct: Saltwater for Thirst" (1987–1988) Geo. J. Leg. Ethics 311.

Moore, Christopher, *The Law Society of Upper Canada and Ontario's Lawyers, 1797-1997* (Toronto: University of Toronto Press, 1997).

Orkin, Mark, *Legal Ethics* (Toronto: Cartwright & Sons, 1957).

Pue, W. Wesley, "British Masculinities, Canadian Lawyers: Canadian Legal Education, 1900-1930" in *Misplaced Traditions: The Legal Profession and the British Empire* (1999) 16(1) Law in Context 80 (symposium issue, guest edited by Robert McQueen & W. Wesley Pue).

Pue, W. Wesley, "Exorcising Professional Demons: Charles Rann Kennedy and the Transition to the Modern Bar" (1987) 5 L.H.R. 135.

Pue, W. Wesley, "In Pursuit of Better Myth: Lawyers' Histories and Histories of Lawyers" (1995) 33 Alta. L. Rev. 730.

Pue, W. Wesley, *Law School: The Story of Legal Education in British Columbia* (Vancouver: University of British Columbia, Faculty of Law, 1995).

Pue, W. Wesley, "Lawyering for a Fragmented World: Professionalism after God" (1998) 5(2-3) International Journal of the Legal Profession 125 (symposium issue on "Lawyering for a Fragmented World", edited by W. Wesley Pue).

Pue, W. Wesley, "Lawyers & Political Liberalism in 18th & 19th Century England" in Lucien Karpik & Terrence Halliday, eds., *Lawyers and the Rise of Western Political Liberalism: Legal Professions and the Constitution of Modern Politics* (Oxford: Clarendon Press; New York: Oxford University Press, 1997).

Pue, W. Wesley, "Moral Panic at the English Bar: Paternal vs. Commercial Ideologies of Legal Practice in the 1860s" (1990) 15 Law & Soc. Inquiry 49.

Pue, W. Wesley, "Rebels at the Bar: English Barristers and the County Courts in the 1850s" (1987) 16 Anglo-Am. L. Rev. 303.

Pue, W. Wesley, "Trajectories of Professionalism: Legal Professionalism after Abel" in Alvin Esau, ed., *Manitoba Law Annual, 1989-1990* (Winnipeg: Legal Research Institute, 1991).

Rhode, Deborah, "Moral Character as Professional Credential" (1985) 44 Yale L.J. 491.

Sheey, Elizabeth & Sheila McIntrye, *Calling for Change: Women, Law and the Legal Profession* (Ottawa: University of Ottawa Press, 2006).

Sibenik, Peter M., "Doorkeepers: Legal Education in the Territories and Alberta, 1885-1928" (1990) 13 Dal. L.J. 419.

Smith, Beverley G., *Professional Conduct for Lawyers and Judges*, 2nd ed. (Fredericton: Maritime Law Book, 2002).

Woolley, Alice, "Tending the Bar: The Good Character Requirement for Law Society Admission" (2007) 30 Dal. L.J. 28.

CHAPTER 3

THE LAWYER-CLIENT RELATIONSHIP

A. INTRODUCTION

In the previous chapters, we reviewed the conceptual frameworks for legal ethics and professional responsibility, and identified several governing themes and tensions. In this chapter, we translate these more abstract concerns into the day-to-day realities of legal practice by analyzing three areas of ethical concern: (a) formation of the lawyer-client relationship; (b) the obligations of competence and quality of service; and (c) terminating the lawyer-client relationship. These three broad areas generate several quite specific issues which can be best understood if we take a chronological approach to the relationship.

B. FORMATION OF THE LAWYER-CLIENT RELATIONSHIP

The core dilemma facing lawyers in the context of the formation of the lawyer-client relationship is that there can sometimes be a tension between two different visions of the lawyer. On the one hand, some commentators argue that because lawyers are the beneficiaries of a monopoly, as professionals they have an obligation to make legal services available. Other commentators, however, argue that lawyers are in essence business persons, and therefore that lawyer-client relations should be governed by the usual market norms. As we work our way through this section, consider how this tension is manifested in issues of advertising, solicitation, choice of clients and the accessibility of legal services. The starting point for the analysis is Rule 3.01(1) and (2) of the Federation of Law Societies of Canada's *Model Code of Professional Conduct*, "Making Legal Services Available":

> 3.01 (1) A lawyer must make legal services available to the public efficiently and conveniently and, subject to rule 3.01(2), may offer legal services to a prospective client by any means.
>
> 3.01 (2) In offering legal services, a lawyer must not use means that:
>
> (a)   are false or misleading;
>
> (b)   amount to coercion, duress, or harassment;
>
> (c)   take advantage of a person who is vulnerable or who has suffered a traumatic experience and has not yet recovered; or
>
> (d)   otherwise bring the profession or the administration of justice into disrepute.

How does this rule mediate the tension between the professional and business models of legal practice? Is the answer obvious from the general title of Chapter 3 of the *Model Code*, "Marketing of Legal Services"? What analytical work do the concepts of "efficiently" and "conveniently" do? How helpful are these concepts for a lawyer in the modern "legal services" marketplace?

1.   Advertising, Fee Sharing and Solicitation

Historically, there have been mixed feelings in the legal community on the question of lawyer advertising and solicitation. Some analysts (the traditionalists) were concerned that advertising and solicitation reduce the professional status of lawyers because they introduce vulgarity and commodification. Others (the modernists) claimed that advertising and solicitation are essential so as to ensure that the public has access to justice. Still others (the free marketers) argued that given the highly competitive legal market, it is important for lawyers to be able to brand and market their work (and themselves) and that, ultimately, it is an issue of consumer choice. Adherents of this third position also sometimes suggested that traditionalist arguments are often invoked by established lawyers and law firms to limit competition. As you review the following provisions, try to identify which of the foregoing approaches is embedded in the *Model Code*.

(a)   Advertising

3.02 MARKETING

Marketing of Professional Services

3.02 (1) A lawyer may market professional services, provided that the marketing is:

  (a)   demonstrably true, accurate and verifiable;

  (b)   neither misleading, confusing or deceptive, nor likely to mislead, confuse or deceive;

  (c)   in the best interests of the public and consistent with a high standard of professionalism.

Commentary

Examples of marketing that may contravene this rule include:

  (a)   stating an amount of money that the lawyer has recovered for a client or referring to the lawyer's degree of success in past cases, unless such statement is accompanied by a further statement that past results are not necessarily indicative of future results and that the amount recovered and other litigation outcomes will vary according to the facts in individual cases;

  (b)   suggesting qualitative superiority to other lawyers;

  (c)   raising expectations unjustifiably;

  (d)   suggesting or implying the lawyer is aggressive;

(e) disparaging or demeaning other persons, groups, organizations or institutions;

(f) taking advantage of a vulnerable person or group; and

(g) using testimonials or endorsements that contain emotional appeals.

Advertising of Fees

3.02 (2) A lawyer may advertise fees charged for their services provided that:

(a) the advertising is reasonably precise as to the services offered for each fee quoted;

(b) the advertising states whether other amounts, such as disbursements and taxes, will be charged in addition to the fee; and

(c) the lawyer strictly adheres to the advertised fee in every applicable case.

3.03 ADVERTISING NATURE OF PRACTICE

3.03 (1) A lawyer must not advertise that the lawyer is a specialist in a specified field unless the lawyer has been so certified by the Society.

. . . . .

NOTES AND QUESTIONS

1. From an historical perspective it seems that, increasingly, Canada has adopted the free marketer's arguments. However, is this really in the best interests of the general public or the legal profession?

2. Some argue that increased advertising increases the cost of doing business and that, inevitably, this will be passed on to clients, thereby increasing fees. Others suggest that increased advertising might reinforce the concentration of legal services in larger firms that can afford advertising to the detriment of medium and smaller sized firms. The consequence is a decrease in competition. Do you find these concerns persuasive? If so, what might be done about this?

3. Should law societies be concerned about modern forms of advertising, for example, "blawgs"? What ethical issues do you foresee in the use of such media? Is there anything law societies could, or should, do to address these concerns?

4. Apart from exceptional cases like *Jabour* (excerpted in Chapter 1), few, if any, law societies have ever disciplined a lawyer for an inappropriate advertisement. Do any of the following advertisements cross the line?

We know Everything We can do Anything We stop at Nothing	[1]

---

[1] Motto for the law firm Burchell, Smith, Jost, Willis, and Burchell, as mentioned in a book review by partner John Willis of *The Lion and the Throne* by Catherine Drinker Bowen (1958) 10 Stan. L. Rev. 782 at 784: see G. Blaine Barker, "Willis on 'Cultured' Public Authorities" (2005) U.T.L.J. 336 at 337.

Accidents happen…But don't let your choice of lawyers be one of them. |2

I may be a Son of a Bitch
But I'm your Son of a Bitch

Proven to get You Successful Results!! |3

A Chicago law firm, specializing in divorce, posted a billboard featuring the "six-pack abs of a headless male torso and tanned female cleavage heaving forth from a black lace bra". The accompanying caption announced: "Life's Short. Get a Divorce."[4] Would this run afoul of the rules in your jurisdiction? Would your opinion differ if it was an all-female or transgendered law firm?

2   Richardson's Law Office, online: <http://www.novalawyer.com>.
3   This ad was posted on the LexisNexis-powered Canadian-Lawyers.ca, online: <http://canada.lawyers.com/Ontario/Toronto/Jag-Virk-Criminal-Lawyer-42517645-f.html>.
4   The ad can be found online: <http://www.b12partners.net/mt/archives/2007/05/viagra-triangle.html> and <http://www.lifeshortgetadivorce.com>.
5   The editors thank Mr. Peter John for his permission to reproduce this advertisement.

---

6   The editors thank Mr. Peter John for his permission to reproduce this advertisement.

7   The editors thank the Honourable Michel Bastarache of Heenan Blaikie LLP for his permission to reproduce this advertisement.

(b) Fee Sharing

One important issue in the marketing of legal services is fee sharing. Consider the following Rule, and the two exceptions:

2.06 (7) A lawyer must not:

(a) directly or indirectly share, split, or divide his or her fees with any person who is not a lawyer; or

(b) give any financial or other reward for the referral of clients or client matters to any person who is not a lawyer.

Commentary

This rule prohibits lawyers from entering into arrangements to compensate or reward non-lawyers for the referral of clients. It does not prevent a lawyer from engaging in promotional activities involving reasonable expenditures on promotional items or activities that might result in the referral of clients generally by a non-lawyer. Accordingly, this rule does not prohibit a lawyer from:

(a) making an arrangement respecting the purchase and sale of a law practice when the consideration payable includes a percentage of revenues generated from the practice sold;

(b) entering into a lease under which a landlord directly or indirectly shares in the fees or revenues generated by the law practice;

(c) paying an employee for services, other than for referring clients, based on the revenue of the lawyer's firm or practice; or

(d) occasionally entertaining potential referral sources by purchasing meals, providing tickets to, or attending at, sporting or other activities or sponsoring client functions.

. . . . .

2.06 (6) If a lawyer refers a matter to another lawyer because of the expertise and ability of the other lawyer to handle the matter, and the referral was not made because of a conflict of interest, the referring lawyer may accept, and the other lawyer may pay, a referral fee, provided that:

(a) the fee is reasonable and does not increase the total amount of the fee charged to the client; and

(b) the client is informed and consents.

. . . . .

2.06 (8) Subrule (7) does not apply to;

(a) multi-discipline practices of lawyer and non-lawyer partners if the partnership agreement provides for the sharing of fees, cash flows or profits among the members of the firm; and

(b) sharing of fees, cash flows or profits by lawyers who are:

(i) members of an interprovincial law firm; or

(ii) members of a law partnership of Canadian and non-Canadian lawyers who otherwise comply with this rule.

NOTES AND QUESTIONS

1. Is there a principled justification for prohibiting fee sharing with non-lawyers, but permitting it with other lawyers?

2. Assume you are a lawyer whose main area of practice is commercial real estate transactions. Draft a letter to a client that would give effect to Rule 2.06(6). What are the challenges involved in drafting such a letter?

3. Does Commentary (d) to Rule 2.06(7) seem out of place in a *Model Code*? Is this provision in the public interest? Who ultimately pays for this type of "entertaining"?

4. Does the exception for multidisciplinary practices and inter-jurisdictional law firms create a two-tier system — one for larger firms, one for smaller firms? If so, is such a distinction justifiable? Would it be both more fair and more efficient to simply abandon the prohibition on fee sharing? Why or why not?

(c) Solicitation

Solicitation can take lawyers quite close to some ethical lines. On the one hand, there are concerns that lawyers may invade people's privacy, take advantage of vulnerable persons, engage in overreaching, succumb to opportunistic ambulance-chasing or stir up unnecessary litigation. On the other hand, it can be argued that people do not always know their rights, and do not always have a sense of the services that lawyers can provide. Solicitation, it is argued, can fill this "market gap". For example, historical research in the United States demonstrates that the NAACP in its early years "stirred up litigation" and engaged in "proselytizing" by:

- speaking before large audiences to recruit plaintiffs;

- fundraising for test cases;

- following newspaper stories about violations of rights and then writing to the victims offering to represent them; and

- staging confrontations to create facts for test cases.

All of these activities were criticized as "unethical" at that time. Consider the following Canadian example:

LAW SOCIETY OF SASKATCHEWAN v. MERCHANT

[2000] L.S.D.D. No. 24
(Law Society of Saskatchewan, Hearing Committee: B. Morgan, Chairperson, D. Plaxton and M.E. Wellsch)

[In the late 1990s, there was growing recognition that Canada's policy of residential schools for Aboriginal peoples had potentially infringed the legal rights of tens of thousands of Aboriginal people. In 1998 one law firm, the

Merchant Law Group, wrote letters to survivors of residential schools. This led to a number of consequences. The first was a discipline complaint to the Saskatchewan Law Society.]

. . . . .

On September 3, 1998, Mr. Merchant forwarded to B, of Edenwold, Saskatchewan, a letter with an attached Assignment & Retainer Agreement. ... The letter indicated that his firm acted for a number of First Nations and individual members of various Indian bands across Canada who are "suing the federal government and, in many cases, the church involved for abuse and wrongdoing at the Indian residential schools". The letter went on to state:

> "We believe the compensation that we can achieve for you will be significant and you have nothing to lose. If we do not recover anything, then you will pay nothing. If we recover, then we will receive a percentage of what we recover on your behalf".

The letter went on to explain the four areas of claim which the firm would advance, and under one of those heads, indicated that "for sexual assault, the amount of compensation could be $50,000, $75,000, or $150,000 so a lot is at stake."

The letter ended as follows:

> "If you are prepared to receive the money that we think is due to you, please write out your reflections on what happened in the school and write to me as well as sending back the authorization that is shown with your signature at the bottom. You could also contact me by telephone at 1-877-359-7777".

The letter was signed by E. F. Anthony Merchant, Q.C., under the name "Merchant Law Group".

The enclosed two page Assignment & Retainer Agreement set out the fee structure that would be claimed on a contingent fee basis, and contained the required notice under Section 64(3) of The Legal Profession Act, 1990. In addition, the Assignment & Retainer Agreement contained the following:

> "... If, after reasonable investigation of the client's claim, The Merchant Law Group determines that it is not feasible to pursue such claim, upon notification to the client of this fact, the Merchant Law Group may withdraw from its representation of the client under this Agreement. Should the client elect to change lawyers, the client will promptly pay for legal services performed up to that time at the usual hourly rates of the lawyers involved.

> If the client unilaterally decides not to pursue the claim without first getting approval from The Merchant Law Group, or if the The Merchant Law Group decides that the action ought not to be pursued, the client will be responsible for all Court costs and other out-of-pocket expenses incurred by The Merchant Law Group in the investigation and advancement of the client's claim. If the client unilaterally decides not to pursue the case without first getting approval from The Merchant Law Group, settles the case without the approval of The Merchant Law Group, or transfers the carriage of the action to another law firm, then in any of these events the client will also be responsible to The Merchant Law Group for payment forthwith of its fees at

the usual hourly rates of the lawyers who have worked on the client's file and for all legal fees for work done on the client's behalf."

On October 23, 1998, B forwarded a copy of that letter and attached Assignment & Retainer Agreement, along with her own letter ..., to Ms. Merilee Rasmussen, a lawyer with whom B was familiar, indicating that, among other things:

"I just felt offended and thought it was very bold. Even more, I've never spoke to the man and I wonder how he got my name". ...

B requested Ms. Rasmussen to "check this out."

On November 20, 1998, Mr. Merchant forwarded a letter to H ..., which was similar to the letter forwarded to B, although in this letter Mr. Merchant indicated that his firm acted "for over 1,500 different individuals with lawsuits regarding First Nation schools." Mr. Merchant's letter to H also stated: "If you know of people who ought to be suing, have them call us." The request for information contained at the end of that letter was slightly more detailed than in the letter to B, the final request being for the name and telephone number of "anyone else you think we should be contacting, which incidentally we will do on a confidential basis and they will never even know that you suggested that we call." The Assignment & Retainer Agreement contained in that letter was substantially similar to the one contained in the letter to B.

On January 6, 1999, H forwarded a formal letter of complaint to The Law Society of Saskatchewan ... Among other things, he wrote that he was "very distressed that Merchant Law Group received my name," and indicated that Mr. Merchant had no knowledge of H's personal circumstances. He also specifically objected to the suggestion that he provide Merchant Law Group "with the names of my friends who have been in these circumstances," calling that suggestion "reprehensible".

H indicated that he is a member of a First Nation and outlined his education and work experience. His evidence was that he was forty-nine years old, and had attended a residential school when he was in grade two, in approximately 1956 or 1957, had then gone to a reserve school for two years, and had returned to the residential school for grades seven and eight. He stated that he met Mr. Merchant a number of years ago in a very brief informal setting, but other than that, had had no contact with Mr. Merchant or any other members of his law firm.

He indicated that of a total membership of about 1,800 persons in his First Nation, there were probably between eight and nine hundred individuals living on the reserve. He went on to state that he was the chief executive officer for his First Nation, that unemployment was probably in the eighty to eighty-five percent range, and that his education and business experience was probably better than most other members of his First Nation.

H's evidence was that when he received the letter from Mr. Merchant, he made the assumption that Mr. Merchant had forwarded it to him based on their prior brief meeting. Although he raised some concerns about an inference in the letter that he had likely been victimized on the sole basis that he had attended a residential school, his initial plan was to throw the letter in the garbage and forget about it. However, after talking to other members of the First Nation at various functions, he understood that some other recipients of a similar letter had signed and returned the contract, at which point he decided to make a complaint.

He further specifically stated that he was not misled by anything contained in the letter, but felt others were.

In cross-examination, he acknowledged that he was unable to say whether any of the other letters he referred to had come from Mr. Merchant or from The Merchant Law Group.

The hearing committee noted that H gave his evidence in a straightforward and credible manner, and the hearing committee accepted his evidence.

The second witness called on behalf of the investigation committee was B, a forty-two year old member of a different First Nation. She indicated that in her youth she had attended a residential school, where she was the victim of sexual abuse. B had completed her grade twelve education and some university classes and was in the process of completing her University degree. She indicated that it would not be common for members of her First Nation to have a grade twelve or university education.

B testified that she was offended upon receiving the letter and stated that after receiving it, the traumatic feelings she had experienced earlier in her life came back to her. She indicated that the letter made her feel a lot of shame, and that she felt the differences between the fees referred to in the letter, and the fee structure outlined in the Assignment & Retainer Agreement, were misleading. During her cross-examination, B acknowledged that she had retained counsel to pursue her sexual abuse claim at the residential school.

She further stated during cross-examination that she was aware of at least one relative of hers who had retained Mr. Merchant for the same type of claim.

B also stated that she had become aware of other members of her First Nation who had received letters, had returned the attachments, and were expecting to get approximately $50,000 within a week or two.

. . . . .

Count 1

Count 1 of the formal complaint against the member alleges that he is guilty of conduct unbecoming a lawyer in that:

> He did correspond with B, then of Edenwold, Saskatchewan, by letter under date of September 3, 1998, which letter was likely to create in the mind of the intended recipient, an unjustified expectation about the results which the

writer may achieve, contrary to Chapter XIV of The Law Society of Saskatchewan *Code of Professional Conduct*, and did thereby breach Rule 1602(b), 1601(2)(b) and 1601(2)(c) of the Rules of The Law Society of Saskatchewan.

The essential ingredient of Count 1 that must be established in order to find that the charge is well-founded is:

1. Was the letter likely to create an unjustified expectation in the mind of the intended recipient about the results that the writer may achieve?

Mr. Merchant's letter to B of September 3, 1998 contained statements that may have been designed to create an expectation about the results which he could achieve. He spoke of claims for "cultural abuse", "a loss of a sense of family", physical abuse and sexual abuse. The paragraph concerning sexual abuse stated that "For sexual assault, the amount of compensation could be $50,000, $75,000, or $150,000 ...". No amounts were mentioned for the other types of claims.

B testified as to her personal circumstances, that is, that she was the subject of sexual abuse at a residential school. Counsel for the investigation committee did not present any evidence as to the quantum that B might have received had she pursued a claim to a successful conclusion. However, counsel for Mr. Merchant has submitted judgments, rendered subsequent to the date of the letter, awarding damages of between $80,000 and $169,500 in circumstances that may have been similar to B's.

The hearing committee has considered that, if indeed Mr. Merchant had no personal knowledge concerning B, the suggested quantum of damages contained in his letter of September 3, 1998 may have been pure speculation. However, given the subsequent judgments and the facts that are now known about B, the amounts speculated as damages are not outside the realm of possibility. In addition, B was careful to express that the letter did not create unjustified expectations, because, as she said, no amount of compensation could compensate her for "her life".

The hearing committee finds that the letter was not "likely" to create an unjustified expectation in B about the results the member may achieve, given B's circumstances.

Count 2

The amended Count 2 of the formal complaint against the member alleges he is guilty of conduct unbecoming a lawyer in that:

He did correspond with H, then of Turtleford, Saskatchewan, by letter under date of November 20, 1998, and he did correspond with B, then of Edenwold, by letter under date of September 3, 1998, which letters were reasonably capable of misleading the intended recipient, contrary to Chapter XIV of The Law Society of Saskatchewan *Code of Professional Conduct*, and did thereby breach Rule 1601(2)(c) of the Rules of The Law Society of Saskatchewan.

The rule above referred to reads:

> 1601 (1) A member may, in any medium, initiate contact with a potential client.
>
> (2) Any marketing activity undertaken or authorized by a member must not be:
>
>   (a) false,
>
>   (b) inaccurate,
>
>   (c) reasonably capable of misleading the recipient or intended recipient, or
>
>   (d) in the opinion of the discipline committee undignified, in bad taste or otherwise offensive, so as to be inimical to the best interests of the public or the members, or tending to harm the standing of the legal profession.

The committee finds that the allegation contained in Count 2 of the complaint is well founded and accordingly the member is guilty of conduct unbecoming a lawyer, in that the correspondence directed to H and the correspondence directed to B were reasonably capable of misleading the intended recipient. As stated earlier, the hearing committee has determined that the "intended recipient(s)" refer to B and H.

It is important to note the breach complained of is that the marketing activity (in this case correspondence) was reasonably capable of misleading the intended recipient. Whether or not it, in the end result, misled the recipient may be a factor in determining whether it was reasonably capable of misleading, but is not determinative of the issue, in that the prohibition is against undertaking an activity which could mislead.

We are guided in our analysis by Chapter XIV of the *Code*, entitled "Advertising, Solicitation and Making Legal Services Available," which provides:

> Lawyers should make legal services available to the public in an efficient and convenient manner that will command respect and confidence, and by means that are compatible with the integrity, independence and effectiveness of the profession.

. . . . .

We now turn our attention to the correspondence in question. In both cases, the correspondence complained of is on the letterhead of the "Merchant Law Group", which advises it is an inter-provincial law firm and lists on its letterhead in excess of 40 lawyers. The correspondence is signed "Yours truly, MERCHANT LAW GROUP Per: E.F. Anthony Merchant, Q.C."

Correspondence to B

The correspondence to B is dated September 3, 1998. The most relevant portions of same for this analysis are as follows.

At the outset, the member advises (presumably referring to the Merchant Law Group) "We act for a number of First Nations", citing that they act for over 700 individual members of various Bands from Quebec to British Columbia who are suing the federal government and, in many cases, churches for wrongdoing at Indian residential schools.

The correspondence further provides "We believe the compensation that we can achieve for you will be significant and you have nothing to lose. If we do not recover anything, then you will pay nothing." ... It then states "If we recover, then we will receive a percentage of what we recover on your behalf."

The correspondence then goes on to advise that there are four areas of claim, which the firm advances, directly quoted as follows:

1. Almost everyone was abused culturally. I call it a policy of taking the Indian out of the Indian. This cultural genocide involved stopping people from speaking their Indian language, cutting their hair, denying them an Indian culture or dance or participation.

2. Second, for almost everyone, there was a loss of a sense of family. You were not allowed to talk to or even acknowledge family members of the opposite sex. You did not see your mother and father except during the summer.

3. Almost everyone was the subject of physical abuse. This discipline gone wrong was very destructive.

4. Many were subjected to sexual abuse. If a person is sexually abused by an older student or supervisor, it is the responsibility of the government to provide a safe circumstance. They cannot force you to go into a school and take over the role of your parents without giving the kind of protection that your parents would give. For sexual assault, the amount of compensation could be $50,000, $75,000, or $150,000 so a lot is at stake.

The communication then provides "If you are prepared to receive the money that we think is due to you, please write out your reflections on what happened in the school and write to me as well as sending back the authorization that is shown with your signature at the bottom." ... The correspondence also advises that the potential client could contact the writer at a telephone number set out.

Firstly, and leaving aside questions as to the validity of claims for "cultural abuse" and "loss of sense of family", the letter is misleading in that it disregards the possibility that the recipient may not have a sustainable cause of action. Even if the recipient has a good cause of action, the letter fails to explain in even a cursory fashion the potential length and complexity of the litigation process, including preparation, possibly undergoing interviews and examinations by experts, discoveries, pre-trial procedures and the trial itself. It leaves the impression that payment will be forthcoming without any effort other than writing out "reflections" and returning the "authorization".

Further, the reader is told that he or she has "nothing to lose" and "will pay nothing" if the firm does not recover on her behalf. This representation is not only capable of misleading the reader, no matter who he or she is, but is indeed misleading when compared with the agreement attached to same. The letter itself is in larger type and for the most part employs common parlance. The agreement attached to the letter, however, is in smaller type, follows the form of a contract and employs what lay persons often refer to as "legalese". It would not be unexpected that a reader would rely on the representations made in the letter, rather than reading the agreement.

The hearing committee notes that the agreement is referred to in the letter simply as "the authorization". A recipient could legitimately conclude that this is simply a document authorizing the firm to act on their behalf. The document is in reality three documents, being a contingency fee/retainer agreement, an authorization to act on behalf of the client, and an assignment of proceeds and direction to pay proceeds of the action to the Merchant Law Group. The agreement itself is, however, more accurately entitled "Assignment & Retainer Agreement."

The hearing committee finds that referring to that document in the letter as an "authorization" is capable of misleading the intended recipient. However, the representations that the committee finds most troublesome are "you have nothing to lose" and "If we do not recover anything, then you will pay nothing."

The contingency fee agreement provides the firm will receive between 20% and 40% of amounts recovered on behalf of the client. Without reflecting upon whether these amounts are reasonable, this is consistent with the representation in the letter that the firm will receive a percentage of what is recovered.

The provisions in the agreement that are not consistent with the representations in the letter are summarized as follows:

a)   The client is responsible for all out of pocket expenses and agrees to reimburse the firm for same if billed for same. The firm may however advance some disbursements in its discretion.

b)   If the client changes lawyers, he or she is responsible to promptly pay the Merchant Law Group for all legal services performed up to that time at the hourly rates of the lawyers involved. The actual hourly rates are not disclosed.

c)   If the client decides not to pursue the claim without obtaining the Merchant Law Group's approval, or the Merchant Law Group decides the action ought not to be pursued, the client must pay for all court costs and disbursements.

d)   If the client decides not to pursue the claim without obtaining the Merchant Law Group's approval, the client is responsible forthwith for payment of fees of the lawyers at their usual hourly rates (again, the rates are not disclosed).

Although "court costs" are referred to in the agreement, nowhere in the agreement or the letter are the consequences of unsuccessful or abandoned litigation explained in terms of the nature and extent of costs that such a litigant may be liable for.

In summary, the statements referred to in the letter are misleading in that they:

- assume that the recipient likely has a valid cause of action, in the absence of any of the information as to the recipient's circumstances that would need to be known before such a representation could be made;

- fail to disclose to the recipient the rigors, potential length, and uncertainties of litigation, not to mention the personal toll it can take upon the litigant and those near him or her, especially when litigating matters as sensitive as that referred to in the letter.

- fail to disclose that the prospective client has something to lose from an economic perspective and indeed may well pay something, even if the firm recovers nothing; to the contrary, the recipient is told "you have nothing to lose." The inherent inaccuracy in that statement as compared to the terms of the attached agreement is compounded by the letter referring to the agreement simply as an authorization.

Correspondence to H

The correspondence to H is dated November 20, 1998 and has some differences when compared to the correspondence to B. This letter advises that the firm now acts for over 1,500 individuals, with suits relating to First Nations schools, with clients residing from Newfoundland to British Columbia, as well as in the Northwest Territories and the United States. It then states "If you know of people who ought to be suing, have them call us." This letter is more circumspect in its reference to potential claims, in that it relates "We also think there is some chance that you have a claim and if you want us to advance it, please call or write to me." It outlines the same four heads of possible claim as in the letter to B.

The letter refers to the document attached as an "Assignment & Retainer Agreement," which "... you should sign and send back to us as quickly as you can if you want us to act ..." The letter then states immediately after "... if you want us to act," "... you should write to me and tell me ..., and lists five requests for items in the nature of background information. The sixth item requested is "The name and telephone number of anyone else you think we should be contacting, which incidentally we will do on a confidential basis and they will never even know that you suggested that we call."

Again, as with the correspondence to B, the most bothersome representations to the recipient are "you have nothing to lose" and "If we do not recover anything, then you will pay nothing," and on that basis the hearing committee finds the correspondence to H to be reasonably capable of misleading the intended recipient.

An additional item to be addressed in the letter to H in relation to this count is the assertion that if the name and phone number of another person was supplied to the member, that person would "never even know that you suggested that we call". This is in and of itself capable of misleading, in that the source of this information may become relevant in a court or administrative proceeding. Without deciding if any privilege may apply, this evidence may be compellable and it is possible the third party would discover the identity of the person who suggested that the member call.

In argument on behalf of the member, Mr. Kuski raises the fact that evidence was not called to show that anyone was actually misled by the correspondence in question. This is correct, however this is not a defence to the allegations against the member.

The question is not whether the astute reader could or would discover any inconsistencies between the promotional letter and the retainer agreement attached, but whether the correspondence is reasonably capable of misleading the recipient. As stated above, the committee finds both letters are reasonably capable of misleading the intended recipient.

. . . . .

Count 3

Count 3 of the formal complaint against the member alleges that he is guilty of conduct unbecoming a lawyer in that:

> He did undertake a marketing activity which included correspondence with B, then of Edenwold, Saskatchewan, by letter under date of September 3, 1998, and correspondence with H, then of Turtleford, in the Province of Saskatchewan, by letter under date of November 30, [sic] 1998, which marketing activity was undignified, in bad taste or otherwise offensive, so as to be inimical to the best interests of the public or the members, or tending to harm the standing of the legal profession, contrary to Chapter XIV, of the Law Society of Saskatchewan *Code of Professional Conduct*, and did thereby breach Rule 1601(2)(d) of the Rules of the Law Society of Saskatchewan.

The rule in Chapter XIV, entitled "Advertising, Solicitation and Making Legal Services Available," is again repeated:

> Lawyers should make legal services available to the public in an efficient and convenient manner that will command respect and confidence, and by means that are compatible with the integrity, independence and effectiveness of the profession.

Commentary 2 to the Rule states in part:

> Despite the lawyer's economic interest in earning a living, advertising, direct solicitation or any other means by which the lawyer seeks to make legal services more readily available to the public must comply with any rules prescribed by the Law Society of Saskatchewan, must be consistent with the public interest and must not detract from the integrity, independence or effectiveness of the legal profession. ... They must not adversely affect the

quality of legal services, nor must they be so undignified, in bad taste or otherwise offensive as to be prejudicial to the interests of the public or the legal profession.

The Law Society's rules respecting advertisement of legal services are contained in Part 19 of the Rules, "Marketing of Legal Services."

Rule 1600, contained within Part 19, defines "marketing activity" as including:

> "any ... communication ... with any ... prospective client ... in the nature of ... an advertisement, promotional activity, or material ... or any other means by which professional legal services are promoted ..."

Rule 1601 sets out the general principles to be followed; Rule 1602 contains specific prohibitions, and Rule 1601(2)(d) specifically states that:

> (2) Any marketing activity undertaken or authorized by a member must not be:
>
> ...
>
> (d) In the opinion of the discipline committee undignified, in bad taste or otherwise offensive, so as to be inimical to the best interests of the public or the members, or tending to harm the standing of the legal profession.

The immediate questions for the hearing committee on this count are:

1) Was this a "marketing activity"?

2) If so, was it "undignified, in bad taste, or otherwise offensive" to the point of offending the rule?

3) If so, is count 3 well founded?

With respect to the first question, there can be no dispute that the letters in issue, including the attachments, Exhibits P-7 and P-9, fall within the definition of "marketing activity". There is nothing in the definition that would suggest a mass mailing is required. Indeed, one letter would constitute a "marketing activity".

With respect to the second question, the hearing committee is of the view that the letters are "undignified, in bad taste, and otherwise offensive." The letters possess these qualities to the point of offending the rule. Although each of the letters is slightly different, each has the following characteristics in common:

1. Each makes the assumption that the recipient is a member of a First Nation;

2. Each makes the assumption that the recipient attended a residential school;

3. Each makes the assumption that many or most persons meeting the criteria in (i) and (ii) above were likely to have been victims of cultural, physical and/or sexual abuse;

4.   Based on these assumptions, each letter states the belief that "the compensation that we can achieve for you will be significant".

B gave evidence, which was uncontradicted, that she had never spoken or otherwise communicated with Mr. Merchant. H gave evidence, which was uncontradicted, that he had had a brief, and chance, meeting with Mr. Merchant in an airport lounge some years earlier. The implicit assumptions in the letters:

1.   as to the likely situation of the recipient, in the absence of any knowledge as to the actual circumstances of the recipient;

2.   in disregard for the potential impact that receiving such a letter may have on a recipient;

3.   coupled as they are with a prediction of "significant compensation," in the absence of information that would be required to be known before being in a position to make that prediction;

render this marketing activity "undignified, in bad taste, or otherwise offensive".

Also meeting that criteria in the letter to H is the suggestion that, if he knows of people who ought to be suing, "have them call us".

. . . . .

[The Hearing Committee went on to find, however, that it did not have the power to subject the member to discipline for this particular breach because of a problem with the wording of the rule in question. The Committee found Merchant guilty of the second count, corresponding in a manner reasonably capable of misleading the recipient, in respect of the letters to B and H, and ordered a reprimand, a $5,000 fine, and $10,000 in costs. The judgment was affirmed by a majority of the Saskatchewan Court of Appeal in *Law Society of Saskatchewan v. Merchant*, [2002] S.J. No. 288, 2002 SKCA 60 (Sask. C.A.).]

NOTES AND QUESTIONS

1.   Do you agree with the decision of the Law Society of Saskatchewan to reprimand and fine The Merchant Law Group? If not, do you feel the fine is too harsh, or too lenient?

2.   In 1999, the Law Society of Saskatchewan adopted Rule 1602(1):

No member shall initiate contact with a prospective client who is in a weakened state for the purpose of soliciting the prospective client's legal work except by mail or advertisement. A member shall be allowed to attend any meetings arranged by a non-member or non-members to provide information to a group of prospective clients but may only attend by invitation from the prospective clients or persons arranging the meeting not connected to the member.

3.   The CBA passed two resolutions (one in 2000 and another in 2007), stating that: "lawyers should not initiate communications with individual survivors of Abo-

riginal residential schools to solicit them as clients or inquire as to whether they were sexually assaulted", and "lawyers should not accept retainers until they have met in person with the client, whenever reasonably possible". These resolutions were endorsed by the Yukon, Northwest Territories and the Law Society of Upper Canada. The other provinces and territories did not follow suit.

Do you agree with the CBA resolution? What are its strengths? What are its weaknesses? Compare it with the Saskatchewan resolution. Are both these resolutions redundant in light of the *Model Code* restrictions identified in Rule 3.01(2) and its Commentary?

Some commentators claim that some lawyers are "media hounds" who engage the media not only to promote their client's interests but also to enhance their own profile. In this regard, Rule 6.05(1) and its Commentary, "Public Appearances and Public Statements", are pertinent:

> 6.05 (1) Provided that there is no infringement of the lawyer's obligations to the client, the profession, the courts, or the administration of justice, a lawyer may communicate information to the media and may make public appearances and statements.
>
> . . . . .
>
> **Commentary**
>
> A lawyer's duty to the client demands that, before making a public statement concerning the client's affairs, the lawyer must first be satisfied that any communication is in the best interests of the client and within the scope of the retainer.
>
> Public communications about a client's affairs should not be used for the purpose of publicizing the lawyer and should be free from any suggestion that a lawyer's real purpose is self-promotion or self-aggrandizement.

Courts have also been concerned about lawyers who use the media to engage in self-promotion. Consider *Stewart v. Canadian Broadcasting Corp.*,[8] a case we will return to in Chapter 5, "The Duty of Loyalty and Conflicts of Interest".

From 1979 to 1981, Mr. Edward Greenspan served as counsel during the sentencing and appeal process for Mr. Stewart's charge and conviction of criminal negligence causing death. Ten years later Mr. Greenspan acted as a host and narrator in a televised episode of *Scales of Justice*. The episode was called "Regina v. Stewart". It revisited the crime, the trial and the public's fascination with both. Mr. Stewart was very upset that Mr. Greenspan had participated in the program, which rekindled interest in the case. He brought a claim against Mr. Greenspan for a breach of the implied terms of his contract and a breach of a fiduciary duty of loyalty. In the decision, MacDonald J. took the opportunity to comment on a lawyer's obligations to former clients when the lawyer is in the media.

---

[8] [1997] O.J. No. 2271, 150 D.L.R. (4th) 24 (Ont. Gen. Div.).

Justice MacDonald held that, in the context of public media attention directed at a former client or case, lawyers must not engage in behaviour that is motivated by self-promotion or self-aggrandizement:

> In my opinion, Mr. Greenspan's decision to involve himself in this broadcast despite Mr. Stewart's objection was motivated by self interest. I find that the substantial reason for his involvement in the broadcast was not public education about the justice system. That was assured without Mr. Greenspan's involvement. Mr. Greenspan's primary reason for involving himself in the broadcast was self-promotion, promotion on national television of his counsel practice through displaying his success on Mr. Stewart's behalf in difficult circumstances ... He re-visited and undermined the future benefits and protections which he had provided to Mr. Stewart as his counsel, for personal gain.[9]

The guiding force behind MacDonald J.'s analysis of whether or not Mr. Greenspan's actions constituted self-promotion or self-aggrandizement was Rule 6.06 of the *Code of Conduct* of the Law Society of Upper Canada, entitled "Public Appearances and Public Statements". The Commentary to this Rule reads: "Public communications about a client's affairs should not be used for the purpose of publicizing the lawyer and should be free from any suggestion that the lawyer's real purpose is self-promotion or self aggrandizement."

Justice MacDonald made further conclusions about the ways in which Mr. Greenspan promoted his personal self-interest through the program:

> There is also Mr. Greenspan's broadcast presence. To the viewer, he explained the case and its legal issues. He was thus seen by close to one million people in the role of knowledgeable professional adviser. His image and his voice were prominent throughout. His name was mentioned and displayed. In my opinion, this broadcast was not just education about the justice system. It was also education about Edward Greenspan, his role in the justice system, and his effectiveness as counsel. I find that Mr. Greenspan's primary purpose in involving himself in this production and broadcast, in which educational content was otherwise assured, was to publicize himself and his services as counsel to a national audience.[10]

Justice MacDonald ordered Mr. Greenspan to pay Mr. Stewart $2,500 for causing Mr. Stewart minor and transitory distress by participating as host and narrator in the "Regina v. Stewart" television program. Justice MacDonald also ordered Mr. Greenspan to disgorge the $3,250 profit he received for his role in the program to Mr. Stewart.

NOTES AND QUESTIONS

1. Do you agree with the decision in the case? In particular, do you agree that Mr. Greenspan breached his fiduciary obligation by discussing the former client's

---

[9]   *Ibid.*, at para. 273.

[10] *Ibid.*, at para. 234.

case for the purpose of personal self-promotion? What are the points in favour of Macdonald J.'s decision? What are the points against his decision?

2. Is the remedy imposed by Macdonald J. appropriate? What penalty would you impose?

3. Should the Law Society of Upper Canada have commenced an investigation into Mr. Greenspan's conduct? Would you encourage the Law Society to impose a penalty? If so, what penalty would you recommend?

4. What if Mr. Greenspan had published an academic article discussing the issues of legal strategy raised by Mr. Stewart's case? Should Mr. Stewart be able successfully to bring a similar claim? What reasons of law or policy would make such a claim distinguishable (or not)?

2. Choice of Client

(a) Moral Non-Accountability or "Taking it Personally"?

Having discussed the issue of marketing legal services the next question is choice of clients. Hutchinson argues that client selection

> is arguably the most important decision that any lawyer makes because, once a client is taken on, the lawyer has become committed to a whole host of ethical and moral obligations. ... Once the lawyer-client relationship is established a large part of the ethical die is cast; the lawyers' options about what they are and are not prepared to do are severely curtailed and their obligation is closely circumscribed. This is entirely reasonable because, under any realistic vision of professional responsibility, it would be unconscionable to take on clients and represent them in any incompetent or half-hearted way; that would be a travesty of any kind of ethical expectation.[11]

There is ethical consensus that a lawyer should refuse to take a client if: there is a conflict of interest; the lawyer lacks competence in the matter; there is a continuing retainer with a previous lawyer; the lawyer has the potential to be a witness in a case; or there is an illegal purpose.[12] However, beyond these scenarios there is disagreement on the ethics of accepting or refusing clients.

Broadly speaking, when it comes to the question of choice of clients the debate oscillates between two extremes of a continuum. At one end are those who advocate the principle of "moral non-accountability"; at the other end are those who advocate in favour of "taking it personally".[13] Moral non-accountability emphasizes the structural dimensions of the lawyer's role:

---

[11]   Allan C. Hutchinson, *Legal Ethics and Professional Responsibility* (Toronto: Irwin Law, 2006) at 75.

[12]   Michel Proulx & David Layton, *Ethics and Canadian Criminal Law* (Toronto: Irwin Law, 2001) at 82; Beverley Smith, *Professional Conduct for Lawyers and Judges* (Fredericton: Maritime Law Book, 1998) at 5-6.

[13]   See, *e.g.*, Stephen Pepper, "The Lawyer's Amoral Ethical Role: A Defense, A Problem, and Some Possibilities" (1986) 11 Am. B. Found. Res. J. 613; Allan C. Hutchinson, *Legal Ethics and Professional Responsibility* (Toronto: Irwin Law, 2006) at 206-18.

modern legal regimes are extremely complex and citizens need lawyers to guide them; lawyers are part of an adversary system; truth emerges through the thrust and parry of resolute advocacy; it is the task of the judge, not the lawyer, to ultimately decide the legal entitlements of parties; consequently, the lawyer is simply a neutral agent whose obligation is to represent the client's interest without regard to the morality of that client's conduct or attitude, and without necessarily having regard to that morality in deciding whether to represent the client. Moral non-accountability, in short, is a social good that promotes the fair administration of justice.

Those who espouse taking it personally acknowledge the importance of these larger systems values but, at the same time, argue that there must be limits. While structures are important, so too are human agency and human accountability. Law is an instrument of power; real people both benefit and suffer as a consequence of legal behaviour. Good and evil pervasively permeate legal practice. Consequently, lawyers must take responsibility for their choice of clients and the strategies they deploy on behalf of those clients.

The classic example of this clash of visions is the situation of the criminal defence lawyer who defends someone he or she knows to be guilty of murder, child abuse, anti-Semitism or some other morally reprehensible crime. But the dilemma can face every lawyer: tax lawyers whose task is to advise on tax avoidance; contracts lawyers who draft unconscionable contracts; environmental lawyers who seek to avoid environmental impact assessments for their client's projects; family lawyers who represent deadbeat parents.

Proulx and Layton attempt to steer a middle path between the advocates of moral accountability and taking it personally by outlining the following recommendations for the criminal defence lawyer:

- We believe that a lawyer should enjoy some discretion in deciding whether or not to take on the case of an unpopular client. The question becomes how the discretion should be exercised ...

- An overriding ethical imperative is that a lawyer must reject a retainer where personal distaste concerning the potential client or cause is so severe that the lawyer can reasonably conclude that the quality of legal representation would suffer as a result ...

- In other instances, where the client or cause is unpopular, yet the lawyer reasonably believes that the quality of representation will not suffer if the case is accepted the following guidelines are suggested:

  a. The lawyer should hold a sincere belief in the immorality of the representation.

  b. The repugnance should relate to concerns intimately connected to the representation at hand and not merely to the personality of the client.

  c. Counsel should be very slow to allow public opinion to shape his or her decision.

  d. The lawyer must take into account the importance of representation for the client.

e. A further factor is the likelihood that the prospective client can obtain competent representation from other counsel.

f. The lawyer's private opinion about the guilt of an accused person should not constitute the basis to decline employment. Once a lawyer decides to practice criminal law, choosing a client based upon the likelihood that he or she is guilty or not guilty is unacceptable.

g. A client cannot be turned away based upon an ethically prohibited ground of discrimination.

h. While uncomfortable with uncompromising refusals to represent clients who fall within a particular category of case, for instance all persons charged with a sex-related offence, we accept that a dedicated and highly competent criminal lawyer can have a profound moral objection to taking on certain types of represent-ation ...

•   Where the lawyer rejects the potential client, reasonable assistance should be provided, free of charge, in finding another competent advocate ...[14]

Hutchinson has a different suggestion:

Before taking on any clients, it seems ethically incumbent on lawyers to talk to them. This need not be a one-way lecture to the potential client about the lawyer's ethical values, but it might be a conversation in which lawyer and client outline their basic expectations of each other. Questions lawyers might ask before taking on a client include whether the objective of the case is worthy and whether the means that might be required will be allowed to be used. It is important that lawyers inform potential clients of the ethical limits they place on their provision of legal services — negotiation tactics or cross-examination style. In general, lawyers should treat their potential clients as moral persons who are capable of engaging in debate and changing.[15]

As we have seen, Rule 3.01(1) of the *Model Code* states that "[a] lawyer *must* make legal services available to the public efficiently and conven-iently ..." [emphasis added], but the Commentary adds the following:

Right to Decline Representation - A lawyer has a general right to decline a particular representation (except when assigned as counsel by a tribunal), but it is a right to be exercised prudently, particularly if the probable result would be to make it difficult for a person to obtain legal advice or representation. Generally, a lawyer should not exercise the right merely because a person seeking legal services or that person's cause is unpopular or notorious, or because powerful interests or allegations of misconduct or malfeasance are involved, or because of the lawyer's private opinion about the guilt of the accused. A lawyer declining representation should assist in

---

[14]   Michel Proulx & David Layton, *Ethics and Canadian Criminal Law* (Toronto: Irwin Law, 2001) at 110-11.
[15]   Allan C. Hutchinson, *Legal Ethics and Professional Responsibility* (Toronto: Irwin Law, 2006) at 78.

obtaining the services of another lawyer qualified in the particular field and able to act. When a lawyer offers assistance to a client or prospective client in finding another lawyer, the assistance should be given willingly and, except where a referral fee is permitted by rule 2.06, without charge.

NOTES AND QUESTIONS

1. Compare and contrast the proposals put forward by Proulx & Layton and Hutchinson, and consider whether either approach is helpful in fulfilling a lawyer's ethical obligations regarding client selection.

2. Does this Commentary on the right to decline representation lean more towards the "professional" or "business" model of lawyering?

3. What behaviour by a lawyer could lead to discipline pursuant to rules such as these?

4. When it comes to the question of choice of client, Canada does not follow the conventional English model. In theory, English barristers are governed by the "cab-rank" rule. Barristers are obliged to take the next person in line, wherever that person wants to go; barristers do not have a choice as to who their client might be, so long as the barrister is competent and available, and the client has the means to pay. (In reality, however, it is well known that English barristers have a variety of strategies by which they can filter their clients.[16]) What are the possible rationales for the English cab-rank rule? What are the possible rationales for the Canadian discretion rule? Which do you think is the better rule?

5. Not all Canadian lawyers agree with the Canadian discretion rule. In 2006, a leading Canadian advocate, Earl Cherniak, argued that lawyers have a responsibility to "take all comers" because "given the privileged position we are given in society, lawyers have a responsibility to take on those cases to which they are competent in doing".[17] Do you agree? Is the Commentary a real constraint on a lawyer's discretion? Whose interests does it really serve, clients' or lawyers'? Does it have any weight compared to the economic imperatives that tend to convert the profession of law into the business of law?

6. Is the general right to decline representation compatible with the Barrister's Oath in Ontario?

> I accept the honour and privilege, duty and responsibility of practising law as a barrister and solicitor in the Province of Ontario. I shall protect and defend the rights and interests of such persons as may employ me. I shall conduct all cases faithfully and to the best of my ability. I shall neglect no one's interest and shall faithfully serve and diligently represent the best interests of my client. I shall not refuse causes of complaint reasonably founded, nor shall I promote suits upon frivolous pretences. I shall not pervert the law to favour or prejudice any one, but in all things I shall conduct myself honestly and with integrity and civility. I shall seek to ensure access to justice and access to legal services. I shall seek to improve the administration of justice. I shall

---

[16] See, *e.g.*, H.H.A. Cooper, "Representation of the Unpopular: What Can the Profession Do about this Eternal Problem?" (1974) 22(10) Chitty's L.J. 333 at 338.
[17] Tim Wilbur, "Ethics" *The Lawyer's Weekly* (November 3, 2006) at 3.

champion the rule of law and safeguard the rights and freedoms of all persons. I shall strictly observe and uphold the ethical standards that govern my profession. All this I do swear or affirm to observe and perform to the best of my knowledge and ability.[18]

Which one of these should prevail? Should the Ontario Barrister's Oath be rewritten or abandoned?

(b) Client Selection and Discrimination

Despite the existence of a general right to decline representation, lawyers are subject to anti-discrimination norms.

5.03 (1) The principles of human rights laws and related case law apply to the interpretation of this rule.

5.03 (2) A term used in this rule that is defined in human rights legislation has the same meaning as in the legislation.

. . . . .

5.03 (5) A lawyer must not discriminate against any person.

Analyze the following scenarios based on these rules, those previously provided and the general principles related to the ethics of client selection.

Scenario One

Assume you are a member of the Board of Directors of the University Legal Aid Clinic. You have been presented with a proposal from the Executive Director, staff and students at the Clinic to adopt a policy "to represent women who are victims of violence and not to represent men charged with offences of violence against their wives or intimates".

What issues does this raise for the Board? Are there any provisions in the *Model Code* that would be of assistance? Are there other legal rules, principles or norms that would be relevant for your analysis?[19]

Scenario Two

Assume you are a patent lawyer who has been on retainer for five years with a multinational pharmaceutical corporation.

---

[18]   See Law Society of Upper Canada, *By-law 4: Licensing*, s. 21(1). Compare with the Nova Scotia Barristers' Society Oath taken at call to the Bar:

   I, [name], swear/affirm that as a lawyer, I shall, to the best of my knowledge and ability, conduct all matters and proceedings faithfully, honestly and with integrity.
   I shall support the Rule of Law and uphold and seek to improve the administration of justice. I shall abide by the ethical standards and rules governing the practice of law in Nova Scotia.

   See Nova Scotia Barristers' Society, *Regulations made pursuant to the Legal Profession Act, S.N.S 2006, c. 28*, s. 3.9.5.

[19]   See further, Mary Jane Mossman, "'Shoulder to Shoulder': Gender and Access to Justice?" (1990) X Windsor Yearbook Access to Justice 351 at 359-63.

For each of the last 10 years, between 15,000 and 20,000 people in South Africa have been dying of HIV/AIDS. Throughout that time, the government of South Africa has been negotiating with several pharmaceutical corporations, including the one you represent, to allow the manufacture of cheap generic drugs. There was no agreement.

Recently, the government of South Africa passed a law allowing for the establishment of generic drug companies in South Africa for the production of anti HIV/AIDS drugs. The stated goal of the government is to create a "high volume, no margin market".

The pharmaceutical corporation wants you to challenge the law as a breach of the World Trade Organization's Agreement on Trade Related Intellectual Property Rights (TRIPS).

What issues would you consider in deciding whether to accept this file? Having identified these issues, indicate your decision. Provide justifications for your decision.

Scenario Three

Adam Agon is a leading senior criminal defence lawyer and civil rights advocate who has been asked to represent an alleged war criminal, Ben Ban, in a hearing to decide whether Ban should be extradited to Latvia to face charges over the deaths of tens of thousands of Jews, disabled persons, gypsies, homosexuals and others during the Second World War. Adam Agon is also a prominent member of the Jewish community. His father was a Holocaust survivor who came to Canada after the Second World War. Adam is also an "out" homosexual, although he has not been active in gay politics or litigation.

Mr. Ban is 87 years old at the time of the extradition proceedings. He denies the allegation that he was an S.S. officer at a Latvian camp where 20,000 people were executed, starved or tortured. He has, however, been deported from the U.S. to Canada because of findings that he had been involved in war crimes. Ban claims that because of his blindness and prostate cancer his health is too poor for him to be extradited to Latvia. Jewish leaders claim that war criminals often claim unfitness for trial that are later proved to be unfounded. It is estimated that the extradition proceedings could last approximately 18 months if Ban could contest them. Should Adam Agon accept the retainer from Ben Ban? Provide justifications for your answer.[20]

Scenario Four

Assume you are a "marquee" criminal defence lawyer. The government has just arrested 17 alleged terrorists and charged them under the *Anti-Terrorism Act*. All the clients are relatively poor, young Muslim men who will need to rely on legal aid. You have been asked by the parents of one of the accused to

---

[20] Adapted from Christine Parker, "A Critical Morality for Lawyers: Four Approaches to Lawyers' Ethics" (2004) 30 Monash U.L. Rev. 49.

defend their son. What issues will you identify as you consider taking this case?

Scenario Five

Some firms that specialize in labour law are exclusively management firms, others are exclusively union firms. What are the ethical justifications for, and objections to, such discriminatory practices?

Scenario Six

Mary is a first-rate defence lawyer and devout Catholic. Joseph has been charged with assisting his ailing mother to commit suicide. Catholic doctrine dictates that suicide and assisting suicide are sins. Can, or should, Mary decline Joseph's request that she accept his retainer as defence lawyer?

3.   Accessibility of Legal Services

Once lawyers are given the right to choose clients based on personal judg-ments (including the client's financial circumstances) the ability of clients to access legal services becomes an issue. If lawyers do not simply represent those who come through their doors in the order in which they do so, it is clear that some clients — likely those with the fewest financial resources — will be without legal representation. This means that, necessarily, the ethical question of client selection is inextricably linked to the ethical question of access to justice.

Many students report that when they entered law school they were driven, in part, by a desire to enhance access to justice but by the time they reached third year that motivation had fallen into the background. Do you believe this is an accurate observation? If so, what are some of the causes for the abandonment of this ideal? What can be done to help students maintain their sense of self in law school? What needs to be done (both personally and institutionally) to assist those who are committed to access to justice to pursue a meaningful life in the law?

As we have seen in previous chapters, one reason proffered by the legal profession as to why it should remain a self-regulatory monopoly is because this is the best system to "protect the public interest in the practice of law".[21] This requires us to inquire what is this "public interest" that needs to be protected. This is a complex and controversial question, but most agree that, at a minimum, it requires that "legal services must be accessible". But what is meant by "accessible"?

There are many lawyers in Canada, approximately 100,000, or one law-yer for every 350 people. In spite of this, there is growing concern in the Canadian legal community that, as the 21st century unfolds, access to legal services is becoming more, rather than less, difficult. For example in 1999, Roy McMurtry, Chief Justice of Ontario, sombrely asserted:

---

[21]   *Legal Professions Act*, S.N.S. 2004, c. 28, s. 4(1).

I ... believe that the major challenge facing the justice system in the next milennium will be the absence of adequate legal advice and legal representation to our society's increasing numbers of disadvantaged.[22]

In 2007, McLachlin C.J.C. voiced similar concerns in the context of self-represented litigants:

The most advanced justice system in the world is a failure if it does not provide justice to the people it is meant to serve. Access to justice is therefore critical. Unfortunately, many Canadian men and women find themselves unable, mainly for financial reasons, to access the Canadian justice system. Some of them decide to become their own lawyers. Our courtrooms today are filled with litigants who are not represented by counsel, trying to navigate the sometimes complex demands of law and procedure.[23]

In 2011, she revisited these concerns:

We have this wonderful system of justice but the problem, we are beginning to realize, is that that is not enough. We must assure access to that system of justice. We can draft the best rules in the world. We can render the most enlightened decisions. But if people can't take advantage of that body of law, if they cannot have access to it to resolve their own legal difficulties, then it is for nought. The task of ensuring access to justice falls to this generation. They say every generation has its challenges, and our generation as lawyers, academics, judges and others interested in justice, I think, is to ensure that people can actually avail themselves of the great justice system that has been created.[24]

So the obvious ethical questions are: How has this come to pass, and what should lawyers do about it? One partial explanation is the cost of lawyers' services, fees, an issue we will return to in Chapter 12. A second explanation is the fact that the sheer complexity of law makes access to legal advice very difficult. The *Model Code* does address these questions, but only somewhat indirectly. Two prisms of analysis might be invoked: (i) a professional obligation to encourage respect for the administration of justice; and (ii) *pro bono*.

(a) The Lawyer and the Administration of Justice

The governing provisions with respect to the lawyer's obligation to the administration of justice are to be found in Rule 4.06 of the *Model Code*:

22 Roy McMurtry, C.J.O., "Report of the Court of Appeal for Ontario" (January 6, 1999), online: <http://www.ontariocourts.ca/coa/en/archives/ocs/1999.htm>.

23 Rt. Hon. Beverley McLachlin, P.C., C.J.C., "Remarks Presented at the Empire Club of Canada" (Toronto, Ontario, March 8, 2007), online: <http://www.scc-csc.gc.ca/court-cour/ju/spe-dis/bm07-03-08-eng.asp>.

24 Rt. Hon. Beverley McLachlin, P.C., C.J.C., "Access to Civil Justice Colloquium Keynote Speaker" Munk School of Global Affairs (Toronto, Ontario, February 10, 2011) at 17:16 to 18:18, online: <http://hosting.epresence.tv/MUNK/1/watch/219.aspx>.

A lawyer must encourage public respect for and try to improve the administration of justice.

. . . . .

Commentary

Admission to and continuance in the practice of law implies, on the part of a lawyer, a basic commitment to the concept of equal justice for all within an open, ordered and impartial system. However, judicial institutions will not function effectively unless they command the respect of the public, and, because of changes in human affairs and imperfections in human institutions, constant efforts must be made to improve the administration of justice and thereby, to maintain public respect for it.

Do the exhortations to "try to improve the administration of justice" and the implied "basic commitment by the lawyer to the concept of equal justice for all within an open, ordered and impartial system" impose any concrete obligations on individual lawyers? What conduct by a lawyer would constitute a violation of these rules warranting professional discipline?

(b) *Pro Bono*

The governing provision in the context of *pro bono* is the Commentary to Rule 3.01(1):

As a matter of access to justice, it is in keeping with the best traditions of the legal profession to provide services *pro bono* and to reduce or waive a fee when there is hardship or poverty or the client or prospective client would otherwise be deprived of adequate legal advice or representation. The Law Society encourages lawyers to provide public interest legal services and to support organizations that provide services to persons of limited means.

How effective is such a provision in light of the fact that, as we have seen, lawyers have "a right to decline representation", including on the basis that a client is unable to pay? What obligations do these requirements place on a lawyer, and what conduct by the lawyer would constitute a violation of these rules?

Some commentators argue that the current permissive approach to *pro bono* is ethically anemic because there is no real sense that the profession has an obligation to reduce inequality in access to justice. These arguments are explored in greater detail in Chapter 12.

4. Triggering the Lawyer-Client Relationship

The foregoing discussions presume a highly voluntaristic conception of when the lawyer-client relationship is formed — when there has been an offer and acceptance of the retainer contract. The *Model Code* defines a client as follows:

"client" is a person who

    (a) consults the lawyer and on whose behalf a lawyer renders or
        agrees to render legal services; or

(b)   having consulted the lawyer, has reasonably concluded that the
lawyer has agreed to render legal services.

Is the moment of triggering the relationship the same in situation (a) and (b)?

However, it might be possible that the lawyer-client relationship — and
the correlative ethical obligations of the lawyer — are triggered at an earlier
moment. Consider, for example, *Descôteaux v. Mierzwinski*,[25] a case we will
return to in Chapter 4. In that case, a citizen attended a legal aid office and
filled in a form titled "Application for Legal Aid". Subsequently, the police
presented themselves at the legal aid office and sought certain documents,
including the application form. The main issue in the case was whether this
form was protected by solicitor-client privilege. However, this required a
decision on a prior question — at what point is the solicitor-client relationship
formed? The Court held:

> In the case at bar the principal issue is to determine when the solicitor-client
> relationship, which confers the confidentiality protected by the substantive
> rule and the rule of evidence, arises.
>
> The Superior Court judge, as we have seen, was of the view that this
> relationship, and consequently the right to confidentiality, did not arise until
> the legal aid applicant had been accepted, that is, until the retainer was
> established.
>
> When dealing with the right to confidentiality it is necessary, in my view, to
> distinguish between the moment when the retainer is established and the
> moment when the solicitor-client relationship arises. The latter arises as soon
> as the potential client has his first dealings with the lawyer's office in order
> to obtain legal advice.
>
> The items of information that a lawyer requires from a person in order to
> decide if he will agree to advise or represent him are just as much
> communications made in order to obtain legal advice as any information
> communicated to him subsequently. It has long been recognized that even if
> the lawyer does not agree to advise the person seeking his services,
> communications made by the person to the lawyer or his staff for that
> purpose are nonetheless privileged ...
>
> Moreover, the same applies not only to information given before the retainer
> is perfected concerning the legal problem itself, but also to information
> concerning the client's ability to pay the lawyer and any other information
> which a lawyer is reasonably entitled to require before accepting the retainer.
> First, this information of an administrative nature is just as related to the
> establishment of the professional relationship as any other information; this
> is especially clear when, as in the case at bar, the legal aid applicant "*must
> set forth (his) financial means* ... and the basis of his claim." In addition,
> information of this nature that a person gives his lawyer for that purpose
> may also be highly confidential and would have been kept secret by that

---

[25]   [1982] S.C.J. No. 43, [1982] 1 S.C.R. 860 (S.C.C.).

person were it not for that person's need of the assistance of a legal adviser.[26]

NOTES AND QUESTIONS

1. Does this "first dealings" doctrine create any potential ethical problems for a lawyer?

2. Do you think that a client, having filled out an Application for Legal Aid Form, could, in the words of the *Model Code*, "reasonably conclude that the lawyer has agreed to render legal services"? Or is this precluded by "having consulted the lawyer"?

3. What if, after a 15-minute discussion at the initial interview, the potential client tells the lawyer something about another current client which constitutes a conflict of interest. What should the lawyer do?

4. Assume a 16-year-old client comes into your office wanting to hire you. She is very upset. After 10 minutes, you realize that you cannot represent her because of a potential conflict of interest. You tell her you cannot represent her but you will help her find another lawyer. At that point she pulls a bag out of her purse, and there is a bloody knife. She bursts into tears, and flees your office, leaving the knife on your desk. What do you do?

C. COMPETENCE AND QUALITY OF SERVICE

1. Introduction

Once the lawyer-client relationship is formed, its essence is that the lawyer owes the client a duty of loyalty.[27] Loyalty, however, is a somewhat abstract ideal with many dimensions. The *Model Code* attempts to substantiate this overarching principle by, for example, mandating that lawyers should be competent and render quality service to their clients. Commentators, however, often wonder how seriously these obligations are pursued and enforced by the governing bodies of the legal profession. For example, there are very few cases where lawyers have been disciplined by a law society for incompetence.[28] This is the case despite the fact, as we shall see in Chapter 13, empirical studies in other common law jurisdictions (*e.g.*, England and Australia) indicate that the major causes of client dissatisfaction with lawyers do not involve stealing from the trust funds, but rather involve the perception (or reality?) that lawyers tend to provide a poor quality service for a disproportionately high price. As we work our way through this section, one central question to consider is whether the Canadian legal profession is doing enough

---

[26] *Ibid.*, at 876-77 [emphasis added].
[27] *R. v. Neil*, [2002] S.C.J. No. 72, [2002] 3 S.C.R. 631 (S.C.C.).
[28] Harry Arthurs, "The Dead Parrot: Does Professional Self-Regulation Exhibit Vital Signs?" (1995) 33 Alta. L. Rev. 800; Gavin MacKenzie, *Lawyers and Ethics: Professional Responsibility and Discipline* (Scarborough, ON: Carswell, 1993) at 24-3, 24-8; Allan C. Hutchinson, *Legal Ethics and Professional Responsibility* (Toronto: Irwin Law, 2006) at 69.

to ensure that lawyers are competent, and that they do in fact provide quality service.

2. Competence and Quality of Service

There are two possible legal angles to address the issue of lawyers' incompetence: the law of lawyer malpractice (primarily negligence) and codes of professional conduct. The leading Canadian case on lawyers' negligence is *Central Trust Co. v. Rafuse* where the Supreme Court of Canada held that the appropriate standard of care is that "of the reasonably competent solicitor, ordinary competent solicitor and the ordinary prudent solicitor".[29]

The second, and perhaps more fruitful, angle on lawyer competence is to analyze how it is conceptualized in the *Model Code*. Traditionally, competence and quality of service were two of the least talked about issues for the legal profession, but perhaps the most significant and embarrassing. Much lip service was paid to the ideal of professionalism and inherent in that ideal was the requirement of competence, but little was done to *ensure* that lawyers were competent. The new *Model Code* has attempted to respond to this criticism by didactically specifying what it means by Competence and Quality of Service:

2.01 (1) In this rule

"Competent lawyer" means a lawyer who has and applies relevant knowledge, skills and attributes in a manner appropriate to each matter undertaken on behalf of a client and the nature and terms of the lawyer's engagement, including:

  (a) knowing general legal principles and procedures and the substantive law and procedure for the areas of law in which the lawyer practises;

  (b) investigating facts, identifying issues, ascertaining client objectives, considering possible options and developing and advising the client on appropriate courses of action;

  (c) implementing as each matter requires, the chosen course of action through the application of appropriate skills, including:

    (i)   legal research;

    (ii)   analysis;

    (iii) application of the law to the relevant facts;

    (iv)   writing and drafting;

    (v)   negotiation;

    (vi)   alternative dispute resolution;

    (vii) advocacy; and

---

[29] [1986] S.C.J. No. 52, [1986] 2 S.C.R. 147 at 208 (S.C.C.). See Chapter 2, section E.1, "Legal Liability of Lawyers".

(viii) problem solving;

(d) communicating at all relevant stages of a matter in a timely and effective manner;

(e) performing all functions conscientiously, diligently and in a timely and cost-effective manner;

(f) applying intellectual capacity, judgment and deliberation to all functions;

(g) complying in letter and spirit with all rules pertaining to the appropriate professional conduct of lawyers;

(h) recognizing limitations in one's ability to handle a matter or some aspect of it and taking steps accordingly to ensure the client is appropriately served;

(i) managing one's practice effectively;

(j) pursuing appropriate professional development to maintain and enhance legal knowledge and skills; and

(k) otherwise adapting to changing professional requirements, standards, techniques and practices.

. . . . .

Quality of Service

2.02 (1) A lawyer has a duty to provide courteous, thorough and prompt service to clients. The quality of service required of a lawyer is service that is competent, timely, conscientious, diligent, efficient and civil.

. . . . .

Commentary

A lawyer has a duty to provide a quality of service at least equal to that which lawyers generally expect of a competent lawyer in a like situation. An ordinarily or otherwise competent lawyer may still occasionally fail to provide an adequate quality of service.

. . . . .

Examples of expected practices

The quality of service to a client may be measured by the extent to which a lawyer maintains certain standards in practice. The following list, which is illustrative and not exhaustive, provides key examples of expected practices in this area:

(a) keeping a client reasonably informed;

(b) answering reasonable requests from a client for information;

(c) responding to a client's telephone calls;

(d) keeping appointments with a client, or providing a timely explanation or apology when unable to keep such an appointment;

(e) taking appropriate steps to do something promised to a client, or informing or explaining to the client when it is not possible to do so; ensuring, where appropriate, that all instructions are in writing or confirmed in writing;

(f) answering, within a reasonable time, any communication that requires a reply;

(g) ensuring that work is done in a timely manner so that its value to the client is maintained;

(h) providing quality work and giving reasonable attention to the review of documentation to avoid delay and unnecessary costs to correct errors or omissions;

(i) maintaining office staff, facilities and equipment adequate to the lawyer's practice;

(j) informing a client of a proposal of settlement, and explaining the proposal properly;

(k) providing a client with complete and accurate relevant information about a matter;

(l) making a prompt and complete report when the work is finished or, if a final report cannot be made, providing an interim report when one might reasonably be expected;

(m) avoidance of self-induced disability, for example from the use of intoxicants or drugs, that interferes with or prejudices the lawyer's services to the client;

(n) being civil.

. . . . .

NOTES AND QUESTIONS

1. Are the *Model Code* standards for competence and quality of service too low?

2. Are the standards too high? Could it be argued that the effect of these standards is to drive up the cost of legal services thereby depriving consumers of the ability to retain a lawyer? Is this an example of what economists call "the theory of negative gains"?

3. How helpful is the standard of "a competent lawyer in a like situation"? What are the strengths of such a threshold? What are the weaknesses? Does this mean that a client should have different expectations of competence and quality of service depending on whether the lawyer works in a large firm or a small firm, charges $500 per hour or $100 per hour, practices in the urban context or the rural context, is a specialist or a generalist?

4. Consider how Rule 2.01(2) of the *Model Code* conceptualizes the relationship between negligence and incompetence:

    Incompetence, Negligence and Mistakes - This rule does not require a standard of perfection. An error or omission, even though it might be actionable for damages in negligence or contract, will not necessarily constitute a failure to maintain the standard of professional competence described by the rule. However, evidence of gross neglect in a particular matter or a pattern of neglect or mistakes in different matters may be evidence of such a failure, regardless of tort liability. While damages may be awarded for negligence, incompetence can give rise to the additional sanction of disciplinary action.

In your opinion, is this the appropriate relationship? Which is the higher standard: the legal duty or the ethical duty? Which should be the higher standard?

5.   The *Model Code* says little about the relationship between competence and firm management skills merely stipulating that a lawyer should "manag[e] one's practice effectively" [Rule 2.01(1)] and "maintain office staff, facilities, and equipment adequate to the lawyer's practice" [Rule 2.02(1)(i)]. Is this sufficient? For example, the old Nova Scotia *Legal Ethics and Professional Conduct Handbook* provided:

> 2.4 The duty of competence extends to practice and firm management. Practice management comprises the knowledge, skills and attributes which a lawyer applies to the organization of his or her work, and to resources which contribute to producing the legal services required by the client. Firm management relates to the organizational structure or environment in which a lawyer works, and may include production of correct, efficient and timely legal services by the lawyer and staff members; and development of adequate organizational systems and communications. The lawyer must ensure there are in place sufficient resources and administrative support to support the practice and the work undertaken by the lawyer, and those resources must remain current with the technology required to proficiently carry out the lawyer's area(s) of practice.

Which is the more appropriate approach? Why? Does the old Nova Scotia rule go too far? What are the likely consequences of such a requirement? What impact will this have on clients? Is it another incentive to drive up legal costs?

The following two cases are illustrative of how law societies have contextualized and addressed incompetence. One is from the civil law context, the other from the criminal law context. Both were decided prior to the adoption of the *Model Code*.

NOVA SCOTIA BARRISTERS' SOCIETY v. RICHEY

[2002] L.S.D.D. No. 30
(Nova Scotia Barristers' Society, Hearing Subcommittee:
B.T. MacIntosh, Chair)

By Formal Complaint, dated October 19, 2001, the Investigative Subcommittee of the Nova Scotia Barristers' Society's Discipline Committee directed the Executive Director of the Nova Scotia Barristers' Society (hereinafter the Society) to charge Member David W. Richey (hereinafter the Member) with professional misconduct and professional incompetence ...

. . . . .

The starting point in any analysis of the application of incompetence is the legal framework. Neither the Act nor the Regulations thereunder provide any guidance on the parameters and definition of incompetence. Regulation 39(i) merely provides a circular definition of incompetence: incompetence means professional incompetence. Section 31(3)(b) of the Act specifically empowers both an Investigative Subcommittee and a Panel to investigate allegations of professional incompetence, separate and apart from the more common allegations of professional misconduct and/or conduct unbecoming. Incompetence is accordingly distinguishable in its own right. Section 31(8) of the Act specifies that the procedural, remedial, and penal provision of the Act and Regulations are applicable to professional incompetence in the same manner as professional misconduct and conduct unbecoming.

. . . . .

Incompetence in this instance is determinable by its consistent pattern. This Panel does not have to determine whether a single act of negligence, error in judgment, or professional misconduct can, by itself, constitute incompetence. The Formal Complaint as drafted, and as argued by the Society's counsel, requires evidence beyond individual acts of disciplinary default: it is in the predictability and consistency of the pattern of such acts by the member that the finding of incompetence is based.

[The Act] identifies the mandate and objects of the Society's disciplinary process: it specifically includes protection of the public by inhibiting incompetence. The public is entitled to expect that self governing legal profession will take reasonable measures to ensure that all lawyers who practise law will possess the minimum skill sets reasonably required of the circumstances. Repeated examples of the absence of specific skills - in this instance the skills of conscientious, diligent, and efficient service to client - will support a finding of incompetence.

The word "incompetence" has a distinctively negative connotation. When used to describe a lawyer, it evokes a strong negative mental image of a person who is unfit to practice law. In the opinion of this Hearing Committee, that is not the intent of the context in the Act. A finding of incompetence must inevitably bring with it professional embarrassment and a loss of confidence in the member found to be incompetent. Nevertheless, in finding that Member David W. Richey was guilty of incompetence, it is not the intention of this Panel to conclude that the Member is generally and generically incompetent. This specific finding of a disciplinary default of both incompetence and professional misconduct is fact and time specific, without any intended inference that the Member is incapable of meeting generally accepted standards of practice. To the contrary, the evidence supports the view that Mr. Richey, when he commits to doing so, can be a most competent and conscientious practitioner of law.

. . . . .

[Mr. Richey is] a senior and experienced member of the litigation bar, [whom counsel for the Society described as] "a highly intelligent, well educated and experienced lawyer who works hard in the interests of his clients and who has a significant devotion to his clients."

... Based on the evidence placed before it, this Panel concurs with that description. Nevertheless, the Member has been found guilty of professional incompetence. ... When a pattern of such poor judgment emerges, as it did in this instance, good lawyering skills on some files is no defence to incompetent lawyering on other files. When the pattern of individual acts of neglect becomes troublingly predictable, then the line is crossed from isolated acts of error in judgment to incompetence.

. . . . .

With respect to the specific allegations contained within the Formal Complaint, this Panel makes the following factual findings which contribute to the legal conclusions of professional misconduct and a pattern of conduct amounting to professional incompetence:

a. While representing AVW and DVW, David Richey failed to move the file to a settlement or trial, contrary to instructions of client;

b. While representing DVW, David Richey failed to advise his client of the reasons for not setting her case down for trial and gave frequent representations that certain commitments for moving the file forward would take place by certain dates, many of which commitments were not met;

c. While representing EP, David Richey failed to file a Pre-Trial Brief in a timely manner and failed to competently obtain and disclose all relevant medical records and information to Defence counsel as required by the Civil Procedure Rules and the directions of the Court;

d. While representing MFB, David Richey failed to commence discoveries and related applications in a timely manner and failed to be ready for trial in accordance with conventional standards of practice;

   (i)   With respect to the allegation of being late without proper excuse, this Panel finds there is not sufficient cogent evidence to support a finding of a disciplinary default. Although an error in judgment, this Panel accepts Mr. Richey's explanation that his tardiness was unintentional and an isolated oversight. This allegation is dismissed;

   (ii) This Panel finds that the filing of the Pre-Trial Brief on the installment plan was a deliberate and unacceptable breach of minimum standards of practice and constituted a deliberate breach of an undertaking to the Court, regardless of whether the specific word "undertaking" was used;

   (iii) This Panel does not have sufficient cogent evidence before it to make a finding with respect to the quality of Mr. Richey's Pre-Trial Brief to Justice Scanlan and accordingly this particular allegation is dismissed;

(iv) This Panel finds David Richey failed to disclose relevant medical information on the MFB file in a timely manner and in breach of minimally acceptable standards of practice;

(v) This Panel does not have sufficient cogent evidence before it to conclude that witness Brian Sutherland was not adequately prepared as a witness.

e. While representing other clients during the period from January 1, 1999 up to September 13, 2001, this Panel finds that David Richey failed to serve his clients in a conscientious, diligent, and efficient manner, so as to provide a quality of service at least equal to that which lawyers generally expect of a competent lawyer in like situations, and further, that he failed to advance clients' cases and expedite litigation and/or settle matters in an expeditious manner for clients. In particular:

(i) This Panel finds David Richey failed to respond to communications, requests for information, phone calls, and correspondence from clients, lawyers, and others in a timely manner;

(ii) This Panel finds that David Richey failed to maintain an adequate file management and bring forward system to ensure file matters were dealt with on a timely and efficient basis, thereby significantly impeding file progress in many instances;

(iii) This Panel finds that David Richey failed to provide full and timely disclosure of medical and other evidence by adopting an unacceptably narrow view of relevance, below the minimum generally accepted standards of practice within the profession, which failure further impeded the progress of files;

(iv) Notwithstanding the persuasive opinion evidence of the Practice Supervisor, which this Panel accepts on its face, in the absence of more specific factual evidence from clients, this Panel does not have sufficient cogent evidence before it to conclude upon the required standard of proof that Mr. Richey's clients received little or no advice regarding outcome, or that such clients had unreasonable expectations. Accordingly, this allegation is dismissed.

Based on the foregoing evidentiary findings, this Panel concludes that Member David W. Richey is guilty of both professional incompetence and professional misconduct on the grounds set forth in the Formal Complaint, excepting only those particulars aforedescribed for which there was insufficient evidence.

[The Nova Scotia Barristers' Society went on to reprimand Mr. Richey, fined him $1,000, required him to pay costs of the proceeding (almost $30,000) and required that his practice be subject to monitoring.]

NOTES AND QUESTIONS

1. Do you think that the Nova Scotia Barristers' Society has identified the proper balance between specific and generic incompetence? If not, has it set the threshold too high or too low? Does the test collapse incompetence into quality service?

2. At one point the panel notes that "Regulation 39(i) merely provides a circular definition of incompetence: incompetence means professional incompetence". Do the definitions in the *Model Code* resolve the circularity problem?

LAW SOCIETY OF ALBERTA v. SYED

[1994] L.S.D.D. No. 211
(Law Society of Alberta, Hearing Committee:
L.C. Fontaine, Q.C., Chair, V.M. May, Q.C. and F. Swanson, Q.C.)

. . . . .

The Member faced one charge as follows:

1. IT IS ALLEGED that you failed to serve your client, […] in a diligent, conscientious and efficient manner, as noted in the Report of Special Commissioner, […], and that such conduct is conduct deserving of sanction.

. . . . .

Mr. MacDonald [counsel for the Law Society], with the agreement of counsel for the Member, tendered as Exhibit 12 a document entitled Admission pursuant to Section 57 of the Legal Profession Act ("the Admission").

The Admission states as follows:

1. Mr. Syed (the "member") has been an active member of the Law Society of Alberta since 1981.

2. He is presently facing a hearing before a Conduct Committee on the following citation:

    It is alleged that you failed to serve your client […] in a diligent, conscientious and efficient manner, as noted in the Report of Special Commissioner […] and that such conduct is conduct deserving of sanction.

3. The member agrees, with respect to this matter:

    a. that he spent insufficient time interviewing the accused and did not explore with him his potential defences to the charges particularly the issue of consent;

    b. that he entered an election of provincial court judge on behalf of the client at the first court appearance without consulting the client about this election and that he had not received particulars from the Crown at this point;

    c. that he subsequently requested particulars from the Crown by letter and on August 14th he received written particulars from the

Crown by mail which are attached as Exhibit A to this Statement of Facts;

d.   that the Crown asked him on the trial date if he wanted to look at the witness statements and he did look at them but not in a detailed fashion;

e.   that he attempted to resolve this case on the date set for trial (after receiving instructions to do so from [...]) by offering to plead [...] guilty to one of the charges (Count 2) with the other charge being withdrawn. He put forward this proposal of settlement without first of all determining whether his client was guilty of the offence for which the single guilty plea was offered. He did not confirm if the complainants were under the age of 14 years. He did not attempt to interview others present that night. In other words, he did not determine from his client, before offering the guilty plea to this one charge that the client was prepared to admit to more than consensual intercourse with Ms. [...], the complainant in count two;

f.   that he left these plea negotiations until the trial date (no plea negotiations had occurred earlier) and that he was unprepared for trial if the plea negotiations did not result in a summary disposition.

4.   He agrees that his conduct in this matter is deserving of sanction.

. . . . .

Mr. Syed's Case

Counsel for the Member confirmed his agreement with the tendering of Exhibit 12 and noted that the Admission related to the conduct of the Member relating to the [...] case as conduct deserving of sanction but that it did not arise from incompetence.

. . . . .

Counsel for the Member advised that the Member takes issue with a number of statements contained in the Report of Special Commissioner [...]. In particular, counsel for the Member advised that at no time did the Member advise the accused to plead guilty to both counts as is stated in the said Report.

The Member testified on his own behalf. He reviewed his academic and professional background in Pakistan and in Alberta since his call to the Bar in 1981 and his general practice as a partner in a well-respected firm in Camrose. He advised that his criminal practice did not involve very serious cases.

The Member admitted everything contained in the Admission (Exhibit 12). He reviewed in detail the circumstances of his retainer by the Legal Aid Society of Alberta and his ultimate withdrawal as counsel for [...] when he was unable to achieve a plea bargain on the day of trial.

In Examination in Chief, the Member testified as to the following facts:

- The Member accepted a retainer from the Legal Aid Society of Alberta to represent [...] on July 3, 1991.

- The Member interviewed [...] in his office on July 15, 1991.

- The Member attended at Provincial Court with [...] on July 17, 1991 at which time he elected, without prior consultation with [...], to proceed by trial before a Provincial Court Judge. The Member explained that he did not consult with [...] because he felt that he had a successful track record before Judge [...] and considered it in the best interests of [...] to proceed with this election.

- The Member sought particulars from the Crown and received Exhibit 11.

- The Member admitted that he did not explore possible defences with [...]; in particular, he did not explore the possible defence of consent. The Member explained that he thought [...] was 21 or 22 years of age and that the two complainants whom he allegedly sexually assaulted were 14 or 15 and, as a consequence of the age difference, he did not think that consent could be a possible defence.

- The Member admitted that he always thought that he would be successful in plea bargaining with the Crown as he had been in the past. He explained that if he were not successful he could withdraw as counsel or re-elect and convert the trial to a Preliminary Inquiry. The Member stated he realized that he should have spoken to the Crown Prosecutor regarding the plea bargain prior to the date of trial.

- The Member admitted that although it was his practice to seek particulars from the Crown, he failed to review the Crown's file in any detail when same was provided to him on the day of trial. He stated that since this incident his practice has changed and he now obtains full disclosure.

Through the Member, Exhibit 13 was tendered comprising of four letters each speaking to the Member's competence and good character.

Under cross-examination, the Member testified to the following facts:

- The Member admitted that at the time in question [...] was 18 and not 21 or 22 years of age.

- The Member confirmed that although the accused has three possible elections, including to elect a trial in Queen's Bench which would give rise to the important procedural benefit to the accused of a Preliminary Inquiry, he elected to proceed by trial before a Provincial Court Judge without consulting [...]. The Member admitted that, in hindsight, [...] should have been consulted in this regard.

- The Member admitted that he was aware that consent would not be in issue if the complainants were under 14 years of age but that if the complainants were 14 years of age or over, consent could be in issue as a defence.

- The Member admitted that he received Exhibit 11 which contains particulars of the charges and indicates that the two complainants were 14 and 15 years of age thereby permitting the defence to raise the issue of consent. The Member stated that throughout, [...] had instructed him to plea bargain on the basis of a guilty plea to one of the two charges of sexual assault.

- The Member admitted that he was aware that a conviction on a major sexual assault could give rise to a sentence of three years.

- The Member stated that throughout he relied on [...]'s instructions to plea bargain and on the fact that he considered that the defence of consent was not in issue.

Under questioning by the Hearing Committee, the Member testified that on the day of the trial he learned for the first time that he may be in a position of conflict given his representation of a co-accused on unrelated charges. The Member suggested that this was a further reason for his withdrawal as counsel. The Member stated that despite the unique circumstances of the unrelated charges, he never recognized this conflict until the trial date.

Argument by Counsel for the Law Society

Mr. MacDonald submitted that the Member's conduct, which the Member admitted was deserving of sanction, arose from incompetence in his handling of the [...] matter. Mr. MacDonald submitted that Chapter 2 of the Canadian Bar Association Handbook of Professional Conduct entitled "Competency and Quality of Service" requires that a Member's conduct be sanctioned for incompetency where there is evidence of either gross neglect in a particular matter or a pattern of neglect generally. Mr. MacDonald suggested that assuming the plea bargain of guilty to one serious sexual assault had been accepted, this would have been a "travesty of justice" in the circumstances of the [...] case. Mr. MacDonald asked how this could have happened without the Member being grossly negligent in the conduct of the [...] case.

Argument by Counsel for the Member

Counsel for the Member submitted that the Hearing Committee consider that the Member is a general practitioner in a small town. He conceded that the Member did not handle the [...] matter properly.

While confirming that the Member never consulted [...] regarding the election of trial before a Provincial Court judge, counsel for the Member stressed that the Hearing Committee should keep in mind that clients rely heavily on the advice of counsel with respect to such elections. With respect to obtaining particulars of the case, Counsel for the Member submitted that prior to the *Stinchcombe* decision the Crown was reluctant to provide statements of sexual assault complainants.

Counsel for the Member did not take issue with the fact that the Member failed to realize potential defences and failed to explore these with [...].

Counsel for the Member did not take issue with the definition of incompetency proffered by Mr. MacDonald in his submission.

Counsel for the Member asked the Hearing Committee to consider the Member's conduct as coming close to, but falling just short of, incompetence and submitted that a reprimand would be an appropriate disposition of this charge.

Part III – Findings

The Hearing Committee unanimously accepted the admission as a statement of admission of guilt by the Member and, pursuant to Section 57(4) of the Legal Profession Act found that the conduct of the Member is deserving of sanction.

The Hearing Committee unanimously found that the Member's conduct arose from incompetence as it related to his handling of the […] matter. The Hearing Committee was satisfied that in his handling of the […] case the Member showed gross neglect consistent with incompetence. The Hearing Committee was struck by the Member's failure to conduct even a most cursory investigation, his failure to advise […] of his options thereby precluding the possibility of informed instructions being given, and his failure to recognize and, as a consequence, consider potential defences in a serious criminal case. The Member admitted that these should have been done by him but they were not.

Part IV - Disposition

The Hearing Committee determined that the Member should be reprimanded. The Chair administered a reprimand to the Member.

. . . . .

NOTES AND QUESTIONS

1. Does Mr. Syed's conduct fall short of any of the provisions of the *Model Code*? If so, which ones?

2. Do you think it is relevant that both Mr. Syed and Mr. Richey were relatively senior members of the profession?

3. Were the sanctions imposed upon Mr. Syed and Mr. Richey appropriate? What sanction would you impose?

4. At first blush, the conduct of both Mr. Syed and Mr. Richey seems inexplicable. If you were a member of a Hearing Panel are there any questions you would like to ask to assist you in making your decision?

5. Mr. Syed introduced four letters addressing his good character and competence. Are such letters relevant? If so, why? If not, why not?

Scenario Seven

You are a general practitioner. A potential client comes to your office asking that you draft him a will for less than $700. The client has an adult daughter who is severely disabled. You know, in general terms, that there are important issues related to leaving money to a disabled person in terms of that person's ability to continue to access government services. However, you do not know how those issues are resolved, and given your hourly rate you cannot find that out and draft a will for $700. Do you take the client? Assume that he has told you that if you cannot help him for that price he will simply use his "do your own will" kit.

Scenario Eight

Assume you are a Crown Attorney. Because of a lack of funding, your office is understaffed by 25 per cent with the consequence that a significant number of lawyers are carrying approximately 500 cases at any one time. You and your colleagues have decided that because of the excess of files you cannot properly prepare for trials, especially in the context of disclosure. Considered in light of the *Model Code*, and the *Richey* and *Syed* decisions, are you in breach of any ethical obligations? If so, what are your options?[30]

Scenario Nine

Cally is a recent law school graduate who was the top mooter in her class. Cally also has multiple sclerosis which means that she is not physically capable of working for a full eight-hour day. Cally wants to pursue a litigation practice. Is she competent to be a litigation lawyer?

Law Societies now recognize that some of the problems associated with incompetence and poor quality service are closely connected with issues of stress, depression and perhaps substance abuse. As a consequence, Law Societies often offer "Risk and Practice Management Programs" which provide "confidential support and assistance to members" as well as "Legal Assistance Programs" to help members and their families "experiencing difficulties in their personal lives". This is clearly a positive assumption of responsibility by Law Societies. But it raises an ethical question, addressed in Scenario Ten Below.

Scenario Ten

Assume that you are a member of a Legal Assistance Program and in the course of providing counselling to a lawyer with a substance abuse problem you realize that the lawyer's conduct is clearly harming his client's financial interests. Do you have a duty to report such conduct to the Law Society? Does the following provision in the Commentary to Rule 6.01(3) of the *Model Code* assist you?

> Often, instances of improper conduct arise from emotional, mental or family disturbances or substance abuse. Lawyers who suffer from such problems should be encouraged to seek assistance as early as possible. The Society supports professional support groups [such as the Lawyers' Assistance Program and the Risk and Practice Management Program] in their commitment to the provision of confidential counselling. Therefore, lawyers acting in the capacity of counsellors for professional support groups will not be called by the Society or by any investigation committee to testify at any

---

[30] "Crown Attorneys Help on its Way" *Canadian Lawyer* (May 2007) at 7.

conduct, capacity or competence hearing without the consent of the lawyer from whom the information was received. Notwithstanding the above, a lawyer counselling another lawyer has an ethical obligation to report to the Society upon learning that the lawyer being assisted is engaging in or may in the future engage in serious misconduct or in criminal activity related to the lawyer's practice. The Society cannot countenance such conduct regardless of a lawyer's attempts at rehabilitation.

Does the *Model Code* strike the appropriate balance in this Commentary?

3. Cultural Competence

In recent years, some have started to question whether we have a sufficiently inclusive conception of competence. The provisions of the *Model Code* are seen to be quite technical in nature. They do not do enough to address the deeply relational and highly contextual nature of the practice of law. Some commentators have begun to ask whether lawyers should also be required to be "culturally competent".[31] Can lawyers give competent advice if they are not in tune with the cultural context of a client? There is nothing explicit in the *Model Code* to address this question. Some argue that cultural competence is implicit in Principle 1 (Integrity) and Principle 5.03 (Harrassment and Discrimination) of the *Model Code*. Do you agree?

One commentator has argued that cultural competence has three dimensions:

KNOWLEDGE: about how "cultural" differences affect client experiences of the legal process as well as their interactions with lawyers;

SKILLS: through self-monitoring, to identify how assumptions and stereotypes influence his/her own thinking and behaviour, as well as the thinking and behaviour of others, and to work to lessen the effect of these influences;

ATTITUDE: awareness of him/herself as a cultural being and of the harmful effects of power and privilege; and the willingness and desire to practice competently in the pursuit of justice.[32]

Drawing on cultural competence initiatives in other professions such as medicine, social work and nursing, Voyvodic proposes that lawyers develop "five habits"[33] for culturally competent legal practice:

(1) take note of the differences between the lawyer and the client;

---

[31] See, *e.g.*, Rose Voyvodic, "Lawyers Meet the Social Context: Understanding Cultural Competence" (2005) 84 Can. Bar Rev. 563; Russell Pearce, "White Lawyering: Rethinking Race, Lawyer Identity and Rule of Law" (2005) 73 Fordham L. Rev. 2081.

[32] Rose Voyvodic, "Lawyers Meet the Social Context: Understanding Cultural Competence" (2004) 84 Can. Bar Rev. 563 at 582.

[33] See also Sue Bryant, "The Five Habits: Building Cross-cultural Competence in Lawyers" (2001) 8 Clinical L. Rev. 33.

(2) map out the case, taking into account the different cultural understandings of the lawyer and the client;

(3) brainstorm additional reasons for puzzling client behaviour;

(4) identify and solve pitfalls in lawyer-client communications to allow
the lawyer to see the client's story through the client's eyes; and

(5) examine previous failed interactions with the client and develop proactive ways to ensure those interactions do not take place in the future.[34]

Do you agree with this suggestion? Would you add to or subtract anything
from this list?

Should cultural competence education be mandatory? For some lawyers?
For all lawyers? Are arguments in favour of cultural competency education
reinforced by Canada's commitment in the *Charter* to embrace equality rights
and norms of multiculturalism? Read the following excerpts from a CBA
article on cultural competence and consider the questions that follow.

JATRINE BENTSI-ENCHILL

"Client Communication: Measuring Your Cross-Cultural Competence"
CBA PracticeLink In Depth, online:
<http://www.cba.org/cba/practicelink/cs/cultural.aspx>

. . . . .

Effective cross-cultural communication is the ability to communicate with
individuals from other cultures in a way that minimizes conflict, promotes
greater understanding and maximizes your ability to establish trust and
rapport. It requires lawyers to learn how to properly interpret non-verbal and
verbal cues.

. . . . .

[Ms. Bentsi-Enchill believes that the best way to determine one's cultural
competence is by way of assessment through six stages.[35]]

STAGE ONE: Denial

In this stage, lawyers are *unaware* of cultural difference.

… Lawyers in this stage of development might be so intent on the tasks at
hand that they fail to notice the cultural aspects of business relationships with
clients and colleagues. In this stage, there is a general lack of awareness about
difference.

---

[34]   Rose Voyvodic, "Lawyers Meet the Social Context: Understanding Cultural Competence"
(2005) 84 Can. Bar Rev. 563 at 586.

[35]   The stages were outlined by Dr. Milton Bennett, developer of the *Developmental Model of
Intercultural Sensitivity*.

. . . . .

STAGE TWO: Defense

Lawyers in this stage will recognize some cultural differences and view such differences negatively.

. . . . .

STAGE THREE: Minimization of Difference

It is common for lawyers in this stage to avoid stereotypes and appreciate differences in language and culture. However, many will still view their own values as universal and superior, rather than viewing them simply as part of their own ethnicity and culture.

... In dealing with clients, the lawyer is likely to misinterpret the client's behavior, opinions and reactions because the lawyer will misperceive that the client shares his or her cultural values.

. . . . .

STAGE FOUR: Acceptance of Difference

Lawyers in this stage acknowledge that identifying significant cultural differences is crucial to understanding and improving their interactions with individuals from other cultures.

. . . . .

STAGE FIVE: Adaptation to Difference

In this stage of development, lawyers are able to take the perspective of another culture and operate successfully within that culture.

... They are more likely to independently strive to understand the nuances of other cultures, which leads to openness and ability to connect with others.

STAGE SIX: Integration of Difference

In this stage, lawyers have the ability to evaluate another individual's behavior in the frame of reference of their client, opponent, colleague or staff member. They will be able to establish rapport and read the verbal and non-verbal cues of an individual from another culture.

. . . . .

[In short, cultural competence is not instantly attained and mastered, but a skill that develops over time through extensive training and exercising. Lawyers who work to attain cultural competency skills will be able to establish a greater rapport with clients from all cultural backgrounds, and thus will be better able to represent their client's interests.]

NOTES AND QUESTIONS

1.   Can you identify situations either prior to law school, or during law school, where you have experienced each of the six stages identified in the article? In retrospect, is there anything you would do differently in each of these situations?

2.   As you embark on your legal career, do you anticipate any situations where the issue of cultural competency might arise? Do you have any specific suggestions as to how you might need to prepare yourself to respond to these situations?

3.   Is the following case an example of cultural incompetence?

R. v. FRASER

[2011] N.S.J. No. 400, 2011 NSCA 70
(N.S.C.A., J.W.S. Saunders, L.L. Oland and D.R. Beveridge JJ.A.)

J.W.S. SAUNDERS J.A.:— The appellant is a former high school teacher who was accused of various sexual improprieties by a former student.

After a trial by judge and jury he was convicted of touching for a sexual purpose contrary to s. 153(a) of the *Criminal Code of Canada*, R.S.C. 1985, c. C-46 and sentenced to nine months' incarceration followed by one year probation and 50 hours of community service work and a SOIRA order.

He asks that the verdict be overturned and a new trial ordered on the grounds that he did not receive effective assistance from his trial counsel, and that the Crown breached its obligation to provide the defence with ongoing disclosure.

For the reasons that follow I would allow the appeal, set aside the conviction and order a new trial. As to the first ground of appeal, I have reached the conclusion that the legal advice and representation Mr. Fraser received was ineffective. He was denied his constitutional right to make full answer and defence and a miscarriage of justice occurred. As to the second ground of appeal, I am satisfied the Crown met its disclosure obligations.

. . . . .

On appeal, the appellant's trial counsel [Mr. Scaravelli] was granted formal intervenor status. The scope of his participation was limited to filing a factum, and an affidavit on the fresh evidence application, and to presenting oral argument restricted to the allegation concerning his competence, but not with respect to any aspect of the merits of the appeal.

. . . . .

Issues

Mr. Fraser has identified a host of specific actions, omissions or missteps which he says proves beyond any doubt that the legal representation he received from his trial counsel was ineffective and resulted in a miscarriage of justice.

The appellant's outline of complaints is detailed and comprehensive. I wish to list them verbatim before turning to a consideration of the law, the merits of such serious allegations, and their consequences:

Omissions

(i)   failing to advise the Appellant that he had the right under *R. v. Parks* to challenge prospective jurors for cause as to whether their ability to judge the evidence without bias, prejudice or partiality would be affected by the fact that the accused is a black man and the complainant is a white teenage female — especially given the concerns expressed by the Appellant to Mr. Scaravelli during their first meeting on September 23, 2008 and again both before and after jury selection on December 7, 2009 ("the Parks issue");

(ii)   failing to provide the Appellant with any information or advice regarding his statutory right to elect and re-elect his mode of trial;

(iii)   failing to conduct an effective cross-examination of the complainant at the preliminary hearing for use at trial;

(iv)   failing to adequately prepare for trial, be it as a result of his failure to: (a) conduct an effective cross-examination of the complainant at the preliminary hearing for use at trial; (b) understand the case for the defence; (c) interview potential defence witnesses; (d) know the relevant law; (e) seek disclosure of the notes of Crown Attorney Alonzo Wright relating to the complainant's "new information"; and/or (f) any combination of the foregoing such that material issues relevant to the Appellant's defence at trial were either not explored sufficiently or at all;

(v)   failing to request disclosure from the Crown of Alonzo Wright's notes from his telephone conversation with the complainant and, failing production by the Crown, to make a disclosure application;

(vi)   failing to request that the Crown obtain a formal statement from the complainant with respect to the "new information";

(vii)   failing to advise the Appellant of his right to request an adjournment of his trial as a result of the "new information" disclosed by the Crown;

(viii)   failing to understand the importance of the time line evidence and to cross examine the complainant and adduce defence evidence at trial with respect thereto;

(ix)   failing to request a copy of the statement given by Lisa Fraser to the police on Friday, December 11, 2009;

Acts

(x)   filing the Appellant's Affidavit (sworn December 4, 2009) on the s. 276 Application in circumstances where a s. 276 Application was unnecessary and where, even if it were, an Affidavit from the Appellant was not required to be filed and which, by doing so, unnecessarily exposed the Appellant to cross-examination on said Affidavit; and

(xi)   advising the trial Judge and Crown counsel on Friday, December 11, 2009, following the conclusion of the cross-examination of the Appellant and without instructions from the Appellant, that "that's the evidence for the defence".

. . . . .

Before addressing the appellant's grounds of appeal I will first consider his application to adduce fresh evidence.

Fresh Evidence

The fresh evidence before us on appeal comprises ten affidavits together with the testimony of several of those affiants during questioning under oath at the appeal hearing. I will list the affidavits filed with the Court as part of the fresh evidence application:

1.   Antoine Fraser (appellant) sworn October 18, 2010

2.   Lisa Fraser (appellant's wife) sworn October 18, 2010

3.   Erin Rose Fraser (appellant's mother) sworn October 18, 2010

4.   Reverend Wayne Desmond sworn March 22, 2011

5.   Viola Fraser (appellant's aunt) sworn October 16, 2010

6.   Rosella Fraser (appellant's aunt) sworn October 16, 2010

7.   Woo Yong Yung (appellant's son's Tae Kwon Do instructor) sworn October 15, 2020 [*sic*]

8.   Glenwood Lawrence Selig (retired police officer) sworn October 15, 2010

9.   Lawrence W. Scaravelli (intervenor) sworn November 23, 2010

10. Alonzo Wright (Senior Crown Attorney) sworn November 22, 2010.

The law governing the admission of fresh evidence on appeal is well settled and has been extensively considered by this Court in recent cases. ... In *R. v. Palmer*, [1980] 1 S.C.R. 759, at p. 775, the Supreme Court said the "interests of justice" in s. 683(1)(d) are governed by four factors:

(1)   The evidence should generally not be admitted if, by due diligence, it could have been adduced at trial provided that this general principle will not be applied as strictly in a criminal case as in civil cases. ...

(2)   The evidence must be relevant in the sense that it bears upon a decisive or potentially decisive issue in the trial.

(3)   The evidence must be credible in the sense that it is reasonably capable of belief, and,

(4)   It must be such that if believed it could reasonably, when taken with the other evidence adduced at trial, be expected to have affected the result.

I am satisfied that every factor is clearly established in this case. The second, third and fourth may be dispensed with quickly. There can be no doubt that the evidence and *viva voce* testimony is relevant. It strikes at the heart of the appellant's complaint that he suffered a miscarriage of justice at the hands of his trial counsel. The evidence relates to the acts or omissions which are said to have seriously prejudiced the appellant's ability to defend himself. The evidence is reasonably capable of belief and when considered along with the other evidence adduced at trial, it could reasonably be expected to have affected the result.

The first factor, the so-called due diligence criterion, invites a more detailed examination. After careful review, I am not prepared to say that a strict enforcement of this requirement ought to bar the admission of fresh evidence in this case. First, we know that this general principle will not be applied as strictly in a criminal case as in a civil case. Second, we know that the failure to exercise due diligence is not determinative. Third, we know that the due diligence criterion should not be applied inflexibly and will yield where its application might lead to a miscarriage of justice. ...

But even more significant is the fact that the first criterion requires any applicant seeking leave to adduce fresh evidence on appeal, to demonstrate in effect, that the exercise of reasonable diligence at trial would not have mattered. In other words, careful preparation would not have uncovered the new information. But here the principal ground of appeal is that Mr. Fraser's trial counsel was neither diligent in his preparations, nor effective in providing legal representation. Surely, in such circumstances, when an appellant bases his appeal on a claim of ineffective assistance of counsel, one will not expect that appellant to make the case for due diligence. For it is the very lack of diligence upon which he rests his complaint and pins his hope for a new trial. In such circumstances, it would hardly be in the "interests of justice" to refuse to admit evidence which forms the principal ground of appeal, simply because the applicant may have difficulty in refuting the argument that the evidence should not be admitted because it could have been adduced at trial had due diligence been exercised.

. . . . .

For all of these reasons I would exercise the wide discretion available to us under s. 683(1) and admit the new evidence on appeal in the interests of justice.

Before addressing the merits of Mr. Fraser's appeal, I wish to explain the approach I have taken when assessing credibility.

Credibility/Reliability

Nothing in these reasons should be taken to be a commentary concerning the truth of the complainant's accusations, or the appellant's guilt or innocence on the charge against him. Those questions are distinct from the issues before the Court on this appeal. They will be decided by the judge or jury trying the case whenever Mr. Fraser's prosecution on this charge is renewed.

. . . . .

In these reasons when I speak of "credibility" or "reliability" I do not mean to comment upon the "honesty" or "truthfulness" of any individual. Rather, I use those words in their broadest sense as a way to capture the overall trustworthiness of the evidence, in other words, the extent to which it can be relied upon as fact, or a basis from which reasonable inferences might be drawn.

. . . . .

After considering the intervenor's affidavit evidence and listening to his answers when questioned at the appeal hearing, it is obvious that his recollection of important matters is seriously deficient. Many of his answers were vague. Much of his evidence was internally inconsistent, and shown to be incomplete or inaccurate when contrasted with the evidence offered by the appellant and his witnesses. There was very little in the way of written records to substantiate the lawyer's testimony. I was troubled that at times his responses under questioning at the appeal appeared to reflect disdain for the process. I am not at all certain that with the benefit of hindsight the intervenor would have chosen to act any differently.

While the appellant's evidence was not without its problems, it was more detailed, and his description of his dealings with the intervenor were substantiated by the evidence of his mother, and his wife who were present at the initial meetings. Moreover, that evidence was not clearly refuted or denied by the intervenor.

I have concluded that wherever the evidence offered by the appellant and his witnesses differs in important material respects from the evidence presented by the intervenor, I prefer and accept the evidence offered by the appellant. Put simply, I find it more reliable and trustworthy.

. . . . .

Analysis

First Ground of Appeal: Ineffective Assistance of Counsel

Here again the law is well-settled. As this Court said in *West, supra*:

> [268] The principles to be applied when considering a complaint of ineffective assistance of counsel, are well known. Absent a miscarriage of justice, the question of counsel's competence is a matter of professional ethics and is not normally something to be considered by the courts. Incompetence is measured by applying a reasonableness standard. There is a strong presumption that counsel's conduct falls within a wide range of reasonable, professional assistance. There is a heavy burden upon the appellant to show that counsel's acts or omissions did not meet a standard of reasonable, professional judgment. Claims of ineffective representation are approached with caution by appellate courts. Appeals are not intended to serve as a kind of forensic autopsy of defence counsel's performance at trial. [...]
>
> [269] One takes a two-step approach when assessing trial counsel's competence: first, the appellant must demonstrate that the conduct or omissions amount to incompetence, and second, that the incompetence

resulted in a miscarriage of justice. As Major J., observed in *B.(G.D.)*, *supra*, at para. 26-29, in most cases it is best to begin with an inquiry into the prejudice component. If the appellant cannot demonstrate prejudice resulting from the alleged ineffective assistance of counsel, it will be unnecessary to address the issue of the competence.

After carefully considering the totality of circumstances in this case, I am satisfied that the appellant has demonstrated that the conduct and failures of his trial counsel amount to incompetence and that the incompetence resulted in a miscarriage of justice, necessitating a new trial.

Nothing in these reasons should be taken as suggesting that any one of counsel's failures here would, independently, establish a claim of ineffective counsel in another case. Every situation is different and requires a close examination of all of the circumstances before such a finding can be made.

Rather than analyze each and every act or omission listed by the appellant in his factum, I prefer to examine the legal representation afforded the appellant in two areas. First, I will deal with challenge for cause. Then I will undertake a broader inquiry in the area of trial preparation and performance.

Challenge for Cause

The appellant complains that despite repeated and specific inquiries, he was never advised by his trial counsel that he had a statutory right to challenge potential jurors for cause on the basis that he was black, the complainant was white, and that jurors might discriminate against him on account of those circumstances. After a thorough review of the record, I am satisfied that the appellant's complaint is justified.

No informed discussion regarding challenge for cause in a potentially race-based case can occur without considering "the *Parks* issue".

. . . . .

After a careful and detailed analysis, Doherty, J.A., on behalf of the unanimous court, wrote at para. 28:

> 28 I turn now to the principles applicable to the challenge for cause process. The accused's right to challenge for cause based on partiality is essential to both the constitutional right to a fair trial and the constitutional right, in cases where the accused is liable to five or more years' imprisonment, to trial by jury. An impartial jury is a crucial first step in the conduct of a fair trial: ... The accused's statutory right to challenge potential jurors for cause based on partiality is the only direct means an accused has to secure an impartial jury. The significance of the challenge process to both the appearance of fairness, and fairness itself, must not be underestimated.

(Underlining mine)

Justice Doherty concluded his reasons at para. 93:

> 93 I have no reason to doubt the fairness of this trial, the impartiality of this jury or the validity of their verdict. However, the appellant was denied his statutory right to challenge for cause. That right is essential to the

appearance of fairness and the integrity of the trial. The improper denial of this right necessitates the quashing of the conviction without any demonstration of actual prejudice: [...]

(Underlining mine)

Parks has since been endorsed by the Supreme Court of Canada in *R. v. Williams*, [1998] 1 S.C.R. 1128 and *R. v. Spence*, 2005 SCC 71.

Against that backdrop I will consider what transpired here. Mr. Fraser was arrested and charged on September 23, 2008. He and his family then immediately proceeded to the intervenor's office where he gave his lawyer an overview of the allegations against him as they were known to him at the time.

There was never any formal contract of legal representation. The intervenor told the appellant that his fee would be "$25,000.00 up front". It took the appellant and his relatives some time to raise the money which they turned over to the intervenor in November.

The appellant expressed his profound concerns surrounding the race issue immediately and repeatedly. As he states in his affidavit:

> I explained to Mr. Scaravelli that, being black, I was concerned and nervous about a jury. ... He also told me ... 'don't worry about it, I got lots of black guys off with all white juries before' ...

It is clear from the pre-trial conference report which the intervenor filed with the court that he did not consider the *Parks* issue to be an issue.

Following jury selection the appellant told the intervenor: "I don't like this" referring to the fact that the jury was all white. To this he swears that the intervenor told him that "there was nothing we can do about it" and repeated what he had told him during their initial meeting at his office on September 23, 2008, namely, that he had "gotten lots of black guys off before with all white juries".

The appellant's version of events is corroborated by his wife and his mother.

The appellant's affidavit goes on to say:

> 37. Mr. Scaravelli never told me that I had the right, as I have since been told by Mr. Arnold that I had, to challenge potential jurors for cause on the basis that I was black, the complainant was white and that they may discriminate against me because I was black; notwithstanding that I had raised this very point with Mr. Scaravelli when I met with him on the day I was charged.
>
> 38. Had Mr. Scaravelli told me that I had this right I would have definitely asked him to challenge each juror for cause on this basis.

(Underlining mine)

On May 31, 2010, Mr. Josh Arnold, Q.C., one of the appellant's co-appeal counsel, wrote to the intervenor and asked:

Challenge for Cause

11. What discussions did you have with Mr. Fraser regarding a challenge for cause?

On June 2, 2010, the intervenor responded:

11. Mr. Fraser and I discussed challenges for cause. He wanted to know whether he could have or expect to have jurors who were his peers i.e. Canadians from his community or elsewhere. I told him he could not insist on that. I <u>advised him that I did not find challenges for cause particularly helpful and more of a waste of time than anything else</u>. The system was set up so that people could go up to the Judge to discuss their reasons for not wanting to be at the Trial. <u>I have my own way of selecting jurors</u>. I have been very successful in the past with jury Trials. The simple system that I use seems to work. Mr. Fraser agreed that I should do whatever I thought was best.

(Underlining mine)

At the appeal hearing, the intervenor was questioned by the panel on this issue. While acknowledging that he had read the *Parks* case, he seemed confused as to whether he had read it before or after the appellant's trial, first saying that he had not read it beforehand, and then changing his evidence to say that he had read it before the appellant's trial. In any event, he admitted that he had never discussed the procedures outlined in the case with the appellant. He also said he had only ever challenged jurors for cause in one other trial.

I have no doubt that the questions raised by the appellant in his discussions with the intervenor were related to his serious concerns about being tried by a jury for a sex related offence where the complainant was a white teenage girl and he was a black school teacher. I am satisfied that the intervenor never meaningfully explained the process or objectives in challenging for cause or reviewed with the complainant his statutory right to challenge for cause based on the principles established in *Parks*.

I find that the intervenor's failure to provide advice to the appellant in response to his client's explicit and perfectly reasonable inquiries, effectively denied him his statutory right to challenge potential jurors for cause. I accept what the appellant says in his affidavit, that had he been told he had this right, he would have asked his lawyer to challenge each juror for cause on the basis that he was black and the complainant was white and that jurors might discriminate against him for those reasons.

. . . . .

While trial counsel's failing in and of itself would justify a new trial, I think it is important to undertake a somewhat broader inquiry into the area of trial preparation and performance, with specific attention paid to certain critical features.

Trial Preparation and Performance

The criticisms that follow are not intended to grade counsel's performance or serve as a primer for best practices. Such matters are generally the preserve of the Bar. I recognize that most cases dealing with ineffective assistance claims relate to trial counsel's performance during the trial itself; whereas appeals based on an alleged failure to investigate and prepare are relatively unusual. ...

I also recognize that busy trial lawyers have many other demands placed upon their professional and personal lives and do not have unlimited time and resources to expertly manage every case on their dockets. Their performance should never be gauged on a standard of perfection, nor subjected to a forensic audit whenever unfavourable results occur. The effectiveness of counsel is to be evaluated on an objective standard through the eyes of a reasonable person such that all an accused can expect of his or her defence counsel is a level of competence based on a standard of reasonableness. In other words, the lawyer is "required to bring reasonable care, skill and knowledge to the performance of the professional service which he has undertaken." (*Central Trust Co. v. Rafuse*, [1986] 2 S.C.R. 147 at para. 57.)

The appellant has met the burden of showing that the level of careful investigation and preparation one would reasonably expect of any criminal trial lawyer in such a serious matter simply did not occur in his case. Considering the variety of examples identified in these reasons, it is obvious that the legal representation afforded the appellant was largely ineffective in critical areas.

I propose to address those failings by considering several discrete examples.

First, I will review the intervenor's declared strategy. Then I will discuss his refusal to consider the importance of Antoine Fraser's wife as a material witness. Next I will comment upon his failure to effectively challenge the Crown's case on material issues, in ways that should have been obvious. Next I will describe counsel's failure to interview and call as defence witnesses persons who could be expected to seriously discredit the Crown's case. I will conclude with a discussion concerning a misguided s. 276 application, and a failure to seek an adjournment when first told the complainant had provided important last minute information to the Crown.

The intervenor described his trial strategy in his June 2, 2010, letter to Mr. Arnold as follows:

> The Trial strategy was not to question the complainant on the specific allegations of sexual assault. My strategy was to promote collateral issues, not touching her claim of specific sexual acts. In my view, you cannot win a sexual assault case that way. In addition, Antoine Fraser was denying that he had sex with the complainant so there were no new allegations to meet. ...

I will not attempt to ascribe meaning to this statement, but if the objective were to "promote collateral issues" then surely it ought to have involved carefully identifying and prioritizing what those collateral issues were; establishing the factual basis by which they could be asserted; and then finding and properly preparing defence witnesses whose evidence would then discredit (or at the very least raise a reasonable doubt about) the key issues supporting the Crown's case.

When questioned at the appeal hearing the intervenor said that his strategy "in sexual assault cases where there's a young victim" would be to "impeach the young victim's statement" but "not necessarily" to "enhance the credibility and the believability" of his own client. When asked to explain this approach, he said that all of his efforts would be to impeach the victim of the alleged sexual assault. But because this was a case that would likely turn on the issue of credibility, he would be reluctant to produce other witnesses who might support the appellant because, to his way of thinking, the jury might conclude that the appellant "was trying to damage control" such that the jury "might dwell on damage control too much".

This was the intervenor's reason for not calling the appellant's wife, Lisa Fraser, as a defence witness. During their various meetings at the intervenor's office, the appellant's wife repeatedly told the intervenor that she could disprove parts of the complainant's allegations. When asked to explain why he refused to consider her as an important material witness the intervenor replied:

> Because I was not going to call her as a witness. There was no upside to call her as a witness, only a down side. … Because I talked to her enough really to know that I would not be putting her on the stand. There was no up side to it, there was no advantage to it, only a huge disadvantage, in my opinion.

Apparently the intervenor applied the same "strategy" in either not calling other witnesses who could have supported the appellant by providing evidence which could either corroborate his version of events or seriously discredit the complainant's, or failing to seriously interview persons whose names had been provided by the appellant and his family to see if their evidence would be helpful.

I cannot conceive that a defence "theory", or its application, such as I have just described would ever pass muster on a reasonableness standard. It seems clear that trial counsel's mind was made up from the very beginning that he would never call the appellant's wife as a witness at his trial. Yet that decision was taken without ever having conducted an effective interview, from which he would have discovered the host of significant facts upon which Mrs. Fraser would have been able to give material evidence which would have both lent credence to certain aspects of her husband's testimony, and seriously discredited the complainant's evidence.

By closing his mind to the real value of Lisa Fraser's evidence, and neglecting to take steps to effectively interview her and properly prepare her as a witness, trial counsel seriously prejudiced his client's defence. His expressed concern that Mrs. Fraser would undoubtedly be questioned by Crown counsel during cross-examination as to the times her husband <u>could</u> have been alone with the complainant (for example, in driving her home after babysitting), such that she would be forced to concede that these incidents <u>could</u> have occurred without her knowledge, can hardly be a serious "down side" given the appellant's own testimony that there were occasions when he and the complainant were alone. In my opinion the real risk would be the natural tendency for the jury to wonder why Mrs. Fraser was not being called as a witness in her husband's defence.

The appellant gave a cell phone to the complainant. The circumstances surrounding it being given to J.M.; the manner and frequency of use; and the content of messages sent from one to the other all became significant during the trial. It is likely that the appellant's wife had material evidence to give relating to the phone, its use, and its origins which could reasonably be expected to have helped her husband's case.

Had trial counsel properly interviewed the appellant's wife he would have known that her evidence would contradict and could discredit the complainant's testimony in several other material respects including: that she had met the complainant a number of times, and had invited her into their home on occasions when she babysat their children; that she was present when a photograph was taken of the complainant holding the Frasers' young baby; and that it was her idea to purchase a cell phone for the complainant and that she and her husband had given that to her as a present.

At the trial, Crown counsel recognized that Mrs. Fraser was a material witness. This was the very reason the Crown attorneys instructed a police officer to take a formal statement from Mrs. Fraser. Yet the appellant's own lawyer never took the time to interview her, or prepare her as a witness for the defence, somehow caught up in the idea that her value as a witness was negligible, that she "wouldn't be believed", and that her testimony might, in fact, harm her husband's case. After observing Mrs. Fraser testify at the appeal hearing I saw nothing to indicate that she would be anything other than an impressive witness.

Just as troubling is the fact that the intervenor never asked the Crown to produce a copy of the statement Mrs. Fraser gave to the police during the course of the trial. In fact, when questioned at the appeal hearing the intervenor said that he still had not read Mrs. Fraser's statement to the police. When asked to say what affidavits forming part of the appellant's fresh evidence application he <u>had</u> read prior to testifying at the appeal, the intervenor's answers were dismissive and incomprehensible:

A.   I probably read, you know, I may have read them all. I ignored them out of hand.

Q.   I'm sorry?

A.   I ignored them out of hand because they were mostly lies, falsehoods.

If the appellant's trial counsel were intent on "producing evidence to try and impeach" the complainant, one would expect that experienced trial counsel would use the preliminary hearing as the means of laying the groundwork for later impeaching the complainant's credibility on collateral matters. Yet a review of the transcript from the preliminary inquiry reveals no such effort. The intervenor's very brief cross-examination of the complainant consists of 13 double spaced pages which really do nothing to achieve the intervenor's stated objective "I wanted to highlight any potential inconsistencies in her story." Equally, it appears that no attempt was made to pin the complainant down on material facts related to the alleged sexual incidents, or other significant collateral matters upon which the complainant's credibility might later be impugned at trial. To do that effectively, counsel would have to have already marshalled the case for the defence, by interviewing witnesses, tracking down leads, and preparing the appellant and his witnesses for direct examination and anticipated cross-examination at trial, things Mr. Fraser's trial lawyer never did.

The preliminary hearing transcript satisfies me that Mr. Fraser's trial counsel was not prepared for the preliminary hearing and, as such, conducted his cross-examination in an ineffective manner which fell well below a reasonable standard. As a result, the appellant lost the opportunity to garner critical evidence for use at trial which could then have been used for the purposes of discrediting the complainant and other Crown witnesses, and bolstering the defence case.

I need only mention one example to illustrate subject areas where effectively impeaching the complainant's credibility would seem to be elementary. The complainant never mentioned having ever attempted anal sex with the appellant during her lengthy statement to the police in June, 2008, or at the preliminary hearing on February 18, 2009. The very first time J.M. said anything about having attempted anal sex with the appellant was during the conversation she had with senior Crown attorney Alonzo Wright perhaps a day or two before the trial commenced. The complainant described the attempts she and the appellant had made to "improvise" in detail and at several points in her direct examination at trial. Yet this was an experience so painful she said that she could have screamed. And it hurt so much that she could hardly sit down for days afterwards. One would think that such a memory would be long lasting and described in some detail to the police who were interviewing her, as well as during her testimony at the preliminary hearing. I cannot comprehend why Mr. Fraser's trial counsel never even mentioned it let alone sought to attack the complainant's credibility by subjecting her to a vigorous cross-examination on the subject.

Had the appellant's trial counsel taken the trouble to interview the appellant's aunts, Ms. Viola Fraser and Ms. Rosella Fraser, he would have uncovered important evidence which could have seriously discredited the complainant. This related to evidence given by the complainant's older sister, M.M.

M.M. testified that J.M. had confided in her that she had been involved in a romantic relationship while in Grade 10. M.M. said her sister told her his name was "Ethan" "a 19-year old black guy from *". Later, when M.M. and the complainant went to their doctor's office for birth control pills she said the doctor asked her sister if she was going to go on the pill or not, and asked her if she was sexually active to which M.M. said the complainant answered in the negative. M.M. said she knew that was not the case and so she questioned her sister privately about it later. It was then that M.M. said her sister admitted that she and "Ethan" had had sex and that he had taken the complainant to a clinic in North Preston for a pap test to check for sexually transmitted diseases. The Crown's theory at trial was that "Ethan" was code for Antoine Fraser.

North Preston is a rural community on the eastern edges of the municipality with a rich and proud history as the oldest and largest black community in Canada. The area is populated mainly by African Canadians, many of whom can trace their origins to the immigration of former American slaves during the 18th and 19th centuries.

After retaining the intervenor to represent him at his trial, the appellant provided him with the names of at least 14 witnesses who could testify on his behalf. Among them were his aunts, Ms. Viola Fraser and Ms. Rosella Fraser.

Viola Fraser is 51 years of age and has been employed as a front desk administrator at the North Preston Community Centre ever since it opened in 2004. Her workstation is the focal point of the Community Centre from which she has a clear and unobstructed view of the only entrance to the Centre as well as the waiting room. Included within the facility is a walk-in medical clinic which is the only medical clinic or doctor's office in either East Preston or North Preston. To access the clinic one has to walk directly in front of Ms. Viola Fraser's workstation. Part of her duties is to keep track of the number of persons entering the Community Centre and the Wellness Centre. Her affidavit states in part:

> 8.   Included within the Wellness Centre is a walk-in medical clinic which only operates on Thursdays from 10:00 a.m. to 12:00 noon - 1:00 p.m. depending upon when Dr. Lorna J. Carter finishes her last patient.
>
>   ...
>
> 15.   I have never seen a white person (male or female) attend at the Wellness Centre to see Dr. Carter since I started working at the Community Centre when it opened in 2004.
>
> 16.   I have never seen Antoine Fraser attend at the Community Centre for the purpose of seeing Dr. Carter.
>
> 17.   I have never seen Antoine Fraser at the Community Centre with a white female for the purpose of attending at the Wellness Centre or for any other purpose.

18. I have never been told by anyone that they saw Antoine Fraser at the Community Centre with a white female for the purpose of attending at the Wellness Centre or for any other purpose.

Ms. Rosella Fraser is 48 years of age. She obtained her Bachelor of Arts degree in Sociology from St. Mary's University in 1984. She has administered all programs at the Community Centre in North Preston since it opened its doors in 2004. Her affidavit states:

7. Included in the North Preston Community Centre is the Capital Health and Wellness Clinic ("Wellness Clinic") which is located at the far end of the main hall. The actual office of the Wellness Clinic is comprised of three rooms: a waiting area which includes a reception desk, the doctor's office and an office for the registered nurse.

8. My sister, Viola Fraser, has also worked at the Community Centre since it opened. Her workstation is located immediately upon entrance to the Community Centre and from her workstation there is an unobstructed view of the only entrance door and of the main hallway of the Community Centre and the waiting room area of the Wellness Clinic.

9. The Wellness Clinic is staffed by one part-time doctor, Dr. Lorna Carter, who only works there one morning per week (Thursdays) from 10:00 a.m. until approximately 12:00 noon - 1:00 p.m.

10. I know everyone who is employed at the Community Centre and they know me.

11. The door to the Wellness Clinic is always open while the clinic is open. If the door to the Wellness Clinic is closed — the Wellness Clinic is closed.

12. I have never seen, and I have never heard, of a white person being seen by Dr. Carter at the Wellness Clinic since the Community Centre opened in 2004.

13. I have never seen, or been told, that Antoine Fraser has seen Dr. Carter at the Wellness Clinic.

14. I have never seen, or been told, that Antoine Fraser has been at the Community Centre with a white girl/woman, to see Dr. Carter or for any other reason.

Ms. Viola Fraser also testified at the appeal hearing. Her *viva voce* evidence was forceful and persuasive. For example, under cross-examination by counsel for the Crown she said:

Q. I take it then there's a possibility that you would not see a white female if she went to the Wellness Centre?

A. If a white person came through the doors of North Preston Community Centre I would have known; everyone in the facility would have known it. ...

Q. Okay. But you can't say a white girl has never gone to the Wellness Centre, can you?

A.   No, yeah, I'm saying that a white girl, a white girl and Mr. Fraser did not go to the Wellness Centre. We have white students that come in that work out at the Wellness Centre and they come in and they do greet me and I find out who they are and show them where they need to go. I haven't seen a white girl with Mr. Fraser.

Had sufficient thought and preparation been given to Mr. Fraser's defence, the significance of the evidence of Viola and Rosella Fraser would have been obvious. Their testimony could reasonably be expected to have struck a serious blow to the complainant's credibility based on the version of events she had recounted for her sister, M.M., and which M.M. described in her own testimony at trial. Yet trial counsel's failure to interview Viola and Rosella Fraser and realize how important their evidence would be to the defence, meant that a golden opportunity was lost.

Compounding the error was the fact that the intervenor did nothing to prepare his client for trial. As Mr. Fraser states in his affidavit:

57.   Prior to my taking the stand to testify in my own defence I never met with Mr. Scaravelli to discuss the specifics of my testimony nor did he discuss with me any of the areas of the evidence which I may be cross-examined on by the Crown.

...

62.   Mr. Scaravelli did not consult with me prior to making this statement in open Court nor was it my understanding that no further defence evidence would be called. To the contrary, my family and I had arranged for Reverend Desmond to be present for Mr. Scaravelli to speak to and he was, to the best of my knowledge, still in the Courthouse. I also assumed there were other defence witnesses that Mr. Scaravelli had lined up to testify from the list of witnesses I had provided to him. Moreover, I expected that Lisa would be testifying.

When questioned on his affidavit at the appeal hearing, the intervenor was asked:

Q.   You knew the Crown was going to attack him, him being Antoine Fraser, in regards to anything and everything they could ...

A.   Oh yeah, well, he — I was convinced that Antoine Fraser would hold up because he — he's an educated man, he denied having any relations with this person. He said she was lying about everything. I had no doubt that he would hold up. ...

The appellant entrusted his case to the care of the intervenor. Sadly, that trust was misplaced. Meaningful communications and updates never happened. During the 15 months that he acted for the appellant the intervenor sent his client *one* letter — it contained but one sentence which simply confirmed the date of trial.

This lack of proper preparation or effective legal representation is reinforced by another troubling example.

The intervenor filed an application pursuant to s. 276 of the *Criminal Code* asking for a determination of whether evidence of the complainant's prior sexual activity (with her father) other than the sexual activity that formed the subject-matter of the charge, would be admissible under s. 276(2). The defence alleged that the complainant had not been truthful in accusing the appellant when she gave her statement to the police in June, 2008 and that the reason she had lied to the police was that she was attempting to protect her father whom she said had molested her as a young girl. This, so the appellant argued, was relevant, and highly probative evidence which ought to be admitted to enable him to challenge the complainant's credibility both with respect to what she had told the police as well as her high school principal a few days before the police became involved.

Assuming, without deciding, that such an application was necessary in order to challenge the complainant at trial on these particular collateral issues, its handling was flawed from the beginning.

The Notice of Application filed by the intervenor on behalf of the appellant on November 20, 2009, begins:

> 1. The Applicant is charged with sexual assault contrary to s. 153(a) of the *Criminal Code* ...

This is wrong. The appellant stood charged:

> That he, between the 1st day of January 2007 and the 1st day of July 2008, at or near Eastern Passage in the County of Halifax, Province of Nova Scotia, being in a position of trust or authority towards [J.M.], a young person, did, for a sexual purpose, touch directly the body of [J.M.] with a part of his body, to wit, his penis, contrary to section 151(a) of the *Criminal Code*.

When cross-examined at the appeal hearing the intervenor admitted that he had borrowed a precedent from someone and failed to revise it to properly reflect his client's circumstances in this case. Even more startling is the fact that the intervenor had his client swear a detailed affidavit in support of the application which contained a great deal of information which could later be used (and, in fact, was used) very effectively by the Crown during its cross-examination of the appellant during the *voir dire*, and at his trial. The fact that the intervenor never prepared the appellant for trial or explained what to expect by way of cross-examination is troubling enough. Effectively forcing his client to "answer" the detailed information contained in his affidavit filed in support of the s. 276.1 application made things worse.

The intervenor did not seem to appreciate that all of this could have been avoided by simply filing a solicitor's affidavit from one of the associates in his own office. It would be a simple step to attach as exhibits suitable references from the Crown's disclosure package and provide the court with more than enough information to establish the purpose and necessity of the s. 276 application. The evidence to support the application was all easily found in the materials provided with the Crown's disclosure. Even a cursory reading of the transcript of the appellant's evidence both during the *voir dire* and at trial shows how vulnerable he appeared to be when challenged regarding the information contained in his affidavit. Such a poor showing could have been easily avoided with some careful thought and adequate preparation.

One last example will serve to illustrate the harm done by trial counsel's ineffective representation.

As noted earlier in these reasons, it was during a break in the proceedings on the first day of the appellant's trial when the intervenor told him, in the presence of his mother, father and wife, that he had just been advised by the Crown that J.M.'s story had changed. She was now making other allegations and providing further details. I am satisfied Mr. Fraser asked his lawyer whether they could get full particulars and have time to review it, but that he was told the trial had already started and there was nothing they could do about it. When pressed to explain why he had not sought an adjournment, the intervenor said his client "wanted to get this over with and behind him". I suspect that is true of anyone charged with a criminal offence who faces the prospect of a trial. But it is hardly an answer as to why an adjournment on such a serious matter was not requested, or at the very least, meaningfully discussed by the intervenor with his client.

I am also satisfied that the only details passed along by the intervenor with respect to J.M.'s new allegations were that she was now alleging attempted anal sex, and oral sex in the classroom. The appellant did not become aware of the full extent of the complainant's new allegations until he read Alonzo Wright's correspondence to his appeal counsel, the year following his conviction.

I accept the appellant's evidence that had he been informed by the intervenor of the full extent of the allegations, and had the intervenor explained to him his options including his right to request an adjournment, the appellant would have asked the intervenor to request an adjournment of his trial.

I accept Mr. and Mrs. Fraser's evidence that they became so alarmed by the poor legal representation they were getting that Mrs. Fraser was prompted to call Mr. Josh Arnold, Q.C. to seek his advice as to what options they might have. Mr. Arnold told her that if they were to dismiss the intervenor as their lawyer in mid-trial, there was a chance the trial judge might oblige Mr. Fraser to carry on alone and without counsel. They decided the risk was too great and that they had no choice but to soldier on and see things through to the end. Following his conviction, the Fraser family retained Mr. Arnold for the sentencing hearing and to launch an appeal from conviction. Messrs. Garson and Arnold soon initiated contact with the intervenor and the Crown attorney so as to establish the facts upon which their two principal grounds of appeal could be supported.

While it has not been necessary for me to comment upon each of the complaints levelled by the appellant, the few examples I have addressed clearly establish that trial counsel's actions, omissions, and choices could not have been the result of reasonable preparation or professional judgment. Their cascading effect took away the appellant's chance for a fair trial. As in *R. v. J.B.*, 2011 ONCA 404:

> [6] ... the cumulative effect of the failures of counsel undermined the reliability of the verdict and resulted in a miscarriage of justice.

. . . . .

Conclusion

There is no pleasure in writing a decision like this one. The reputations of the complainant, the appellant, and the intervenor have all been tarnished by the facts of this case. A new trial will once again subject the parties to the cold, impersonal scrutiny of our criminal justice system.

Mr. Fraser did not receive a fair trial. The legal representation he obtained fell far short of the mark reasonably expected of any defence counsel. His constitutional right to make full answer and defence was compromised. A miscarriage of justice occurred. The verdict is unsafe and must be set aside. I would allow the appeal, overturn the conviction and order a new trial.

. . . . .

NOTES AND QUESTIONS

1. Does the decision of the Nova Scotia Court of Appeal call into question Mr. Scaravelli's cultural competence in terms of knowledge, skills and attitudes?

2. In paragraph 53, Saunders J.A., quotes the *West* decision:

> There is a strong presumption that counsel's conduct falls within a wide range of reasonable, professional assistance. There is a heavy burden upon the appellant to show counsel's acts or omissions did or did not meet a standard of reasonable professional judgment. Claims of ineffective representation are approached with caution by appellate courts.

   Is such judicial defence to lawyers appropriate? If so, why? If not, why not?

3. Should the Nova Scotia Barristers' Society have investigated and laid discipline charges against Mr. Scaravelli? If so, what would be the appropriate charges and proposed penalty? If not, why not?

Scenario Eleven

You have been retained by three young black women who have been charged with possession of stolen goods. In the course of the interviews, they tell you that they were pulled over while driving a fancy car on Highway 401 just outside of Toronto. The police conducted a search of the car and found the allegedly stolen goods in the trunk. Does this situation raise any issues of cultural competence? What sorts of questions would you raise with these clients that you would not raise with other clients? Do you have concerns about being perceived to be "playing the race card"?[36]

Scenario Twelve

Assume you are a lawyer with a credit union. You are approached by an organization called the Canadian-Islamic Housing Corp. to develop a mortgage program that is compliant with sharia law. What issues does this raise for you? Identify the steps you would take to determine if you are competent to provide legal advice.[37]

Scenario Thirteen

An Aboriginal client has retained you to defend against a charge for an offence relating to hunting for food. From a technical perspective, a treaty between the client's community and the government is relevant to the case. Your client wants to use the case to draw attention to the treaty issue and to facilitate greater respect between their Aboriginal community and the government. To accomplish this your client wants you to align the legal arguments with their Aboriginal community's political stance on treaty rights.[38] Assume you are minimally aware of Aboriginal rights and culture. How would you approach the case? How would you try and connect with your client? Why is that important?

Scenario Fourteen

You are employed at a legal aid clinic. An immigrant person comes into your office seeking advice. She reveals that her spouse, another immigrant, was laid off from his work. Now the family is under considerable financial strain. The spouse has become abusive. The potential client is staunchly against filing a domestic abuse complaint or filing for divorce; they simply want the abuse to end.[39] What steps would you take? What cultural factors would be relevant, if any? Who, or which institutions, would you involve? What if the culture the immigrant comes from seems to be more tolerant of domestic abuse? What if that culture views divorce as an anathema? Does this make a difference?

---

[36] See *R. v. Belnavis*, [1997] S.C.J. No. 81, [1997] 3 S.C.R. 341 (S.C.C.); Jeffery Rosen, "The Bloods and the Crits: O.J. Simpson, Critical Race Theory, the Law and the Triumph of Color in America" *New Republic* (December 9, 1996) at 27; Frank Michaelman, "Racialism and Reason" (1997) 95 Mich. L. Rev. 723; Margaret Russell, "Representing Race: Beyond 'Sellouts' and 'Race Cards': Black Attorneys and the Straightjacket of Legal Practice" (1997) 95 Mich. L. Rev. 766.

[37] Jennifer McPhee, "Sharia mortgage comes without explicit interest" *Law Times* (June 11, 2007) at 10.

[38] Shin Imai, "A Counter-Pedagogy for Social Justice: Core Skills for Community-Based Lawyering" (2002) 9 Clinical L. Rev. 195 at 217-19.

[39] Antoinette Sedillo Lopez, "Making and Breaking Habits: Teaching (and Learning) Cultural Context, Self-Awareness, and Intercultural Communication Through Case Supervision in a Client-Service Legal Clinic" (2008) 28 Wash. U.J.L & Pol'y 37 at 58-62.

4. Continuing Legal Education

After several years of discussion, consultation and resistance, beginning in 2010 several provinces and territories have introduced compulsory continuing legal education. Most use the descriptor "Continuing Professional Development" (CPD). Several justifications have been advanced in support of such a program: it will help ensure the competence of members of the profession; it is necessary to maintain public confidence in the self-regulatory authority and capacity of the legal profession; other legal professions around the world have adopted continuing professional development; other analogous professions (doctors, dentists) have compulsory professional development; it will help keep lawyers abreast about ongoing developments and changes in Canadian society, technology pertinent to the practice of law, and the legal profession in general.

The basic model (adopted, for example, in Ontario, the Northwest Territories and British Columbia) is that lawyers are obliged to participate in 12 hours of CPD per year, two of which must focus on either practice management or professionalism and legal ethics (three in Ontario). There are variations. In New Brunswick, there are no compulsory topics or types of learning that must be studied. In Saskatchewan, the obligation is 36 hours over three years, with six "Ethics Hours". Quebec requires 30 hours of approved continuing legal education courses over two calendar years. Lawyers in Alberta do not have a minimum hourly requirement to fill. Instead, they must annually compose, record and declare a CPD plan. The plan must be kept on record for five years and must be submitted to the Law Society upon request. Similarly, Manitoba only requires yearly reports of CPD activities. There is no minimum hours requirement but 12 hours a year is recommended.

The following is a typical stipulation of the "eligible accredited activities" in which lawyers can participate. The Law Society of British Columbia approves activities for CPD credits based on the listed criteria:

(1) Significant intellectual, or practical content with the primary objective of increasing the professional competence of lawyers, paralegals, articling students and/or law students.

(2) Material dealing primarily with substantive, procedural, ethical, practice management (including client care and relations) or skills topics relating to the practice of law.

(3) Material primarily designed and focused for an audience that includes, as a principal component, lawyers, paralegals, articling students and/or law students, but not if the subject matter is targeted primarily at clients, the public, other professions, or other students.

(4) Accreditation may be obtained from subject matter relating to the law of other provinces and countries, if related to the conduct of your practice.[40]

The Law Society of Upper Canada's list of recognized accredited activities, listed below, is illustrative:

- Participation as a registrant in a college, university or other designated educational institution program, including interactive distance education

- Teaching (to a maximum of 6 hours per year). Actual teaching time will be multiplied by a factor of 3 to reflect preparation time

. . . . .

- Acting as an Articling Principal or mentoring or being mentored or supervising a paralegal field placement (to a maximum of 6 hours per year)

- Writing and editing books or articles (to a maximum of 6 hours per year)

- Participation in study groups of 2 or more colleagues

- Educational components of bar and law association meetings[41]

NOTES AND QUESTIONS

1. Do you agree with the presumption underlying these reforms that there is a causal connection between compulsory professional development and improved competence?

2. Should compulsory professional development initiatives strive to go beyond merely enhancing the competency of lawyers, to strengthening their ethical character? Is such an ambition even possible?[42]

3. Is the requirement of two hours per year on practice management, professionalism/legal ethics defensible? Desirable? Effective?

4. Is mere attendance sufficient to ensure that CPD is effective? Are there other assessment mechanisms available? For example, some Colleges of Physicians and Surgeons have a Peer Assessment Program where physicians are periodically selected to be reviewed by peers practising in the same area. Identify the arguments for and against adopting a similar system for lawyers. The LSUC has moved towards a system of peer assessment for newly admitted members to the bar. Given that almost all of the lawyers disciplined for professional misconduct are senior lawyers, not junior, is this emphasis of the Law Society warranted?

---

[40]   See, for example, Law Society of British Columbia, "Continuing Professional Development", "Approved Education Activities", online: <http://www.lawsociety.bc.ca/page.cfm?cid=261&t=Accredited-Education-Activities>.

[41]   Law Society of Upper Canada, "Continuing Professional Development", "CPD Requirement", online: <http://rc.lsuc.on.ca/jsp/cpd/index.jsp>.

[42]   See Alice Woolley, "The Character of Continuing Education in Legal Ethics" (2010) 4 Canadian Legal Education Annual Review 27.

What does it say about the law societies' views about the quality of newly admitted members?

5. How will the time and cost required by mandatory CPD affect small firms? What are some responses to these concerns? What about its effect on the trend towards specialization in law? Will CPD further isolate specialized lawyers or can it be used to develop a broader, unified legal community?

6. How will mandatory CPD affect the legal community? Is it a response to, or in furtherance of, the shift in law as a business?

D. TERMINATION OF THE LAWYER-CLIENT RELATIONSHIP

Having analyzed how the lawyer-client relationship is formed and the obligations of competence and quality of service, we are now in a position to consider how the lawyer-client relationship might be terminated. First we will consider termination in accordance with the letter of retainer, then we will assess withdrawal, both obligatory and optional.

1. The Retainer

The lawyer-client relationship, although saturated with fiduciary obligations, is primarily contractual in nature.[43] Consequently, like all contracts, the parties can anticipate the demise of the relationship. Termination may be explicit or implied. This does not normally generate any ethical concerns.

However, in recent years, as we will see in Chapter 5, Canadian courts have increasingly emphasized that lawyers have a duty of loyalty and an obligation to avoid conflicts of interest. As we shall see in *Neil* and *Strother*, the Supreme Court of Canada has made it clear that in some circumstances a business conflict can be a legal conflict, *i.e.*, that a lawyer may be retained by two clients who do not have a legal dispute with each other but may have competing business interests. Consequently one of the clients may challenge whether the lawyer is fulfilling the duty of loyalty if continuing with both representations.

The simplest way for lawyers to avoid this potential problem would be for them to send their clients an explicit termination letter once legal services have concluded. Lawyers, however, are reluctant to do this for at least two reasons: first, it is difficult to craft such letters without giving the impression that the client is being "dumped"; second, it is in a lawyer's economic interest to maintain relationships even when the particular legal service is completed because keeping a current client is easier than finding a new one. Consequently, the economic imperatives create an ethical dilemma for lawyers: in order to avoid potential conflicts when accepting new clients, lawyers should terminate their relationships with other clients once the services have been provided; at the same time, however, many clients are likely to be repeat players; therefore it is economically unwise to alienate such clients. Can you suggest a policy that would resolve this dilemma?

---

[43]   *Strother v. 3464920 Canada Inc.*, [2007] S.C.J. No. 24, [2007] 2 S.C.R. 177 (S.C.C.).

Scenario Fifteen

Draft a termination letter to a client after you have helped her to purchase a small business that she added to her three already-existing businesses.

2. Withdrawal: Obligatory and Optional

We have seen in section B.2 of this chapter that lawyers have great discretion in choosing their clients at the beginning of the relationship, and that clients (if they have the financial resources) also tend to have great choice in selecting their lawyer. This symmetry, however, does not apply when it comes to the termination of the relationship. The Commentary to Rule 2.07 of the *Model Code* explicitly states that "[a]lthough the client has the right to terminate the lawyer-client relationship at will, the lawyer does not enjoy the same freedom of action". In other words, if a lawyer accepts a client, the lawyer has a duty of fidelity and loyalty which limits the ability to end the relationship: "Having undertaken [representation] the lawyer should complete the task as ably as possible, unless there is justifiable cause for terminating the relationship. It is inappropriate for a lawyer to withdraw on capricious or arbitrary grounds." Rule 2.07 makes the same point, but negatively: "A lawyer must not withdraw from representation of a client except for good cause, and on reasonable notice to the client." The obvious questions are: What are "a justifiable cause", a "good cause" and "notice appropriate in the circumstances"?

Historically, law societies have distinguished between mandatory and permissive withdrawal, although there has not always been consensus on which circumstance falls into which category. The *Model Code* has opted for the following categorizations:

Obligatory Withdrawal

2.07 (7) A lawyer must withdraw if:

    (a)   discharged by a client;

    (b)   a client persists in instructing the lawyer to act contrary to professional ethics; or

    (c)   the lawyer is not competent to continue to handle a matter.

Furthermore, in the context of the Advocacy Rule, the *Model Code* provides:

4.01 (1) When acting as an advocate, a lawyer must represent the client resolutely and honourably within the limits of the law, while treating the tribunal with candour, fairness, courtesy, and respect.

A commentary later in the Chapter provides:

If a client desires that a course be taken that would involve a breach of this rule, the lawyer must refuse and do everything reasonably possible to prevent it. If that cannot be done, the lawyer should, subject to rule 2.07 (Withdrawal from Representation), withdraw or seek leave to do so.

. . . . .

Optional Withdrawal

2.07 (2) If there has been a serious loss of confidence between the lawyer and the client, the lawyer may withdraw.

Commentary

A lawyer may have a justifiable cause for withdrawal in circumstances indicating a loss of confidence, for example, if a lawyer is deceived by his client, the client refuses to accept and act upon the lawyer's advice on a significant point, a client is persistently unreasonable or uncooperative in a material respect, or the lawyer is facing difficulty in obtaining adequate instructions from the client. However, the lawyer should not use the threat of withdrawal as a device to force a hasty decision by the client on a difficult question.

Non-payment of Fees

2.07 (3) If, after reasonable notice, the client fails to provide a retainer or funds on account of disbursements or fees, a lawyer may withdraw unless serious prejudice to the client would result.

Commentary

When the lawyer withdraws because the client has not paid the lawyer's fee, the lawyer should ensure that there is sufficient time for the client to obtain the services of another lawyer and for that other lawyer to prepare adequately for trial.

NOTES AND QUESTIONS

1. In *Brace v. Canada (Customs and Revenue Agency)*,[44] a client swore at an employee of the law firm and accused the firm of unfitness. The lawyer sought to withdraw on the basis of a "serious loss of confidence between the lawyer and client". Chief Justice Green denied the request because of possible prejudice to the client's case. He also analogized the lawyer-client relationship to a marriage. Do you agree with Green C.J.'s decision? Is the marriage analogy helpful or confusing? Should it make a difference if the lawyer works for a large firm or is a sole practitioner?

2. In terms of non-payment of fees, is the "serious prejudice to the client" test the appropriate test? Does it give proper weight to the interests of the lawyer? Does it properly acknowledge the different economic circumstances of different lawyers and their different clienteles: corporate lawyers versus family lawyers versus criminal lawyers?

3. Rule 1.16(b)(6) of the American Bar Association's *Model Rules of Professional Conduct* permit withdrawal where continued representation "will result in an unreasonable financial burden on the lawyer". Should we adopt such a rule in Canada?

4. In 2001, Robert William Pickton was charged with murder in the case of 15 missing women in Vancouver. Pickton retained Peter Ritchie as his lawyer. While

---

[44]　[2004] N.J. No. 46, 234 Nfld. & P.E.I.R. 335 (N.L.T.D.).

Pickton and his siblings had reportedly disposed of property worth upwards of $6 million in the mid-1990s, and while his own land was worth upwards of $3 million,[45] his liquid assets left him both ineligible for legal aid and unable to afford private counsel. The police conducted the biggest investigation in the history of Canada relating to the 15 murder charges faced by Pickton, uncovering volumes of forensic evidence. Pickton's attempts to negotiate government funding for his counsel stalled immediately before the preliminary inquiry. Ritchie threatened to withdraw on the basis of Pickton's inability to pay the overwhelming costs of defending the case. Is this sufficient reason to withdraw?[46]

Scenario Sixteen

Assume you are a senior partner in a law firm. Prior to this you served as a minister in a government that was defeated a few years ago. The political party in which you were, and still are, a member retains you to defend a bill it is proposing to the House of Commons that will prohibit same-sex marriage. In particular, you are hired to defend the constitutionality of the bill.

When this retainer becomes public there is intense criticism of your firm, especially from the gay, lesbian, bisexual, transgender (GLBT) community, which attracts significant media attention. Simultaneously, potential recruits to your firm, both law students and lateral hires, decline offers because of the firm's involvement in the case. The other partners in the firm request that you terminate the retainer by the political party. What are your options?[47]

5.   The chestnut example of the ethics of withdrawal is the perjury problem. The first situation can be described as anticipated perjury, where the client indicates to the lawyer an intent to lie when put on the stand (see Scenario Seventeen below).

Scenario Seventeen

In a maintenance dispute, your client makes it clear that he is not willing to reveal the full extent of income received. Identify the various courses of action that you should consider. Do any of the above provisions on mandatory or optional withdrawal apply?

6.   The second situation is described as "surprise perjury", where the client says something on the stand which the lawyer knows to be false. The *Model Code* attempts to respond to this situation in Rule 4.01(4):

> **Disclosure of Error or Omission**
>
> 4.01 (4) A lawyer who has unknowingly done or failed to do something that, if done or omitted knowingly, would have been in breach of this

45   This land was, however, essentially valueless as the site of the ongoing forensic investigation: Jane Armstrong, "Pickton's lawyer says he'll quit over bills" *The Globe and Mail* (October 5, 2002) at A7.

46   See Robert Matas, "Lawyer quits Pickton case over legal fees" *The Globe and Mail* (October 16, 2002) at A5. Pickton (through Ritchie) eventually negotiated an agreement with the British Columbia government to cover his legal fees: Jane Armstrong, "Pickton lawyer in private talks" *The Globe and Mail* (November 7, 2002) at A13.

47   Michael D. Shear & John Schwartz, "Law firm won't defend Marriage Act" *The New York Times* (April 25, 2011), online: <http://www.nytimes.com/2011/04/26/us/politics/26marriage.html?_r=2>.

rule and who discovers it, must, subject to rule 2.03 (Confidentiality), disclose the error or omission and do all that can reasonably be done in the circumstances to rectify it.

Is this adequate guidance? What is the impact of the phrase, "subject to Rule 2.03 (Confidentiality)"? If the lawyer's knowledge of the truth is based on both what the client told her and another source, would the lawyer's duty differ?

7. Gavin MacKenzie argues that it is no part of the lawyer's duty to assist the client in misleading the court. He advances five very useful suggestions which run the gamut from a duty to remonstrate to obligatory withdrawal:

    (1) The lawyer should bear in mind the fact that clients are entitled to have issues of credibility assessed by a duty-constituted court or tribunal. Lawyers have no professional duty to refuse to call evidence except where they have actual knowledge of its falsity.

    (2) Where lawyers have actual knowledge of the falsity of evidence favourable to their client's position that their client or a witness proposes to give, lawyers should remonstrate with their client or the witness for the purpose of dissuading the client or witness from testifying falsely. The fundamental importance to our system of justice of evidence that is adduced being truthful, the possibility of criminal prosecution for perjury, the likelihood that the falsity of the evidence will be exposed on cross-examination or otherwise, possible cost consequences, and the duties of lawyers to refrain from calling false evidence and to expose perjury in many circumstances, should all form part of the remonstrance.

    (3) The effects of remonstrating for this purpose are likely to include the termination of the lawyer's retainer if the client or witness is not convinced. Withdrawal may be necessary, if permitted by the court, even though it may accomplish little except to shift the problem to another lawyer or to encourage the client or witness to be less candid with the next lawyer, and to disclose the witness's perjury to the court and other parties in many cases.

    (4) Lawyers acting as counsel in civil cases should not call witnesses who, to the lawyers' knowledge, will testify falsely. Lawyers may, however, call witnesses who will testify truthfully on some points but falsely on others if the lawyers' questions are confined to the evidence in the former category.

    (5) If false evidence is introduced unexpectedly, or if the lawyer learns of the falsity of evidence after it is introduced, the lawyer should take reasonable steps to correct it. This should be done by urging the client or witness to correct the evidence if possible, either privately or by asking questions designed to enable the truth to emerge. If the client or witness does not correct the evidence, the lawyer should do so. This may be accomplished by informing the court or tribunal in argument, without explanation, that the evidence in question cannot be relied upon. Anything short of that, including silence, is inadequate, as lawyers cannot know what

weight a court or tribunal will place on the false evidence even if lawyers make no use of it.[48]

Do you agree with these suggestions? Does (5) not convert lawyers from "trusted counsel" to snitches? Recommendation (3) counsels withdrawal for anticipated perjury, but (5) only suggests disclosure, not withdrawal, for surprise perjury. Are there any justifications for this distinction? Should MacKenzie and the *Model Code* adopt the rule in several other jurisdictions which requires withdrawal if the client refuses to correct the surprise perjury?[49]

8. Based on Gavin MacKenzie's recommendations, how would you resolve the following problem? Does this change in any way your assessment of MacKenzie?

Scenario Eighteen

What should a lawyer do if a client misrepresents to the judge that she has no prior criminal record, when the lawyer knows that such a statement is false? Would it make a difference if the lawyer's knowledge of the client's criminal record came from someone other than the client?

3.   Court Approval of Withdrawal

The ethical dilemmas generated by withdrawal are not just "private" matters between a client and a lawyer. Courts might also have to approve of a withdrawal because of their inherent jurisdiction over the orderly administration of justice. This has resulted in some checkerboard jurisprudence across Canada. In the context of withdrawal by criminal defence lawyers, for example, Proulx and Layton pointed out that in British Columbia, courts did not appear to invoke a supervisory power, but that in Alberta and Ontario they did.[50] One key question in this regard is whether, and to what extent, a lawyer must give reasons to the court to justify their withdrawal.

This question has now been addressed by the Supreme Court of Canada in the following case:

R. v. CUNNINGHAM

[2010] S.C.J. No. 10, 2010 SCC 10
(S.C.C., McLachlin C.J.C. and Binnie, LeBel
Deschamps, Fish, Abella, Charron, Rothstein, Cromwell JJ.)

[Ms. Cunningham was an employee of the Yukon Legal Services Society ("Legal Aid"). Through Legal Aid she was retained as defence counsel for an accused, Mr. Morgan, charged with three sexual offences against a young child. In order for Mr. Morgan to continue receiving Legal Aid funding, Legal

---

[48]   Gavin MacKenzie, *Lawyers and Ethics: Professional Responsibility and Discipline*, looseleaf (Scarborough, ON: Carswell, 1993) at 4, 35-36.

[49]   See Law Society of British Columbia, *Professional Conduct Handbook*, Chapter 8, Rule 8; Law Society of New Brunswick, *Code of Professional Conduct*, Part B, Rule 8; Law Society of Alberta, Chapter 10, Rule 15, Commentary 15.2.

[50]   Michel Proulx & David Layton, *Ethics and Canadian Criminal Law* (Toronto: Irwin Law, 2001) at 615-20.

Aid instructed him to update his financial information. He failed to do so. After two weeks Ms. Cunningham applied to the Territorial Court of Yukon to withdraw from the case as counsel. She provided one reason for her withdrawal: Mr. Morgan, because of the suspension from legal aid and own limited resources, was unable to pay for legal services.]

The judgment of the Court was delivered by

ROTHSTEIN J.:—

. . . . .

4. Issue

The issue in the present appeal is whether, in a criminal matter, a court has the authority to refuse to grant defence counsel's request to withdraw because the accused has not complied with the financial terms of the retainer. The reasons use the phrase "non-payment of legal fees" to refer to situations where, for example, an accused has actually defaulted on payment, where an accused has failed to provide funds on account at the agreed upon time, or where a legal aid certificate has been suspended or revoked.

5. Analysis

... The fiduciary nature of the solicitor-client relationship means that counsel is constrained in his or her ability to withdraw from a case once he or she has chosen to represent an accused. These constraints are thoroughly outlined in the rules of professional conduct issued by the provincial or territorial law societies (e.g. Law Society of Yukon, *Code of Professional Conduct*, Part One, r. 21) ... This appeal raises the issue of whether a court's jurisdiction to control its own process imposes a further constraint on counsel's ability to withdraw.

A. *Divergent Lines of Authority*

There are two lines of provincial and territorial appellate court reasoning on this issue. The British Columbia and Yukon Courts of Appeal have determined that a court has no authority to prevent criminal defence counsel from withdrawing for non-payment of legal fees. The Alberta, Saskatchewan, Manitoba, Ontario, and Quebec Courts of Appeal have taken the opposite position — a court may refuse counsel's request to withdraw. ...

. . . . .

For the following reasons, I conclude that a court does have the authority to refuse criminal defence counsel's request to withdraw for non-payment of legal fees.

B. *Jurisdiction of the Court*

[Justice Rothstein determined that superior courts have the authority, inherent and necessarily implied, to both remove counsel from cases and to refuse an application of withdrawal from a case submitted by counsel in order to protect the administration of justice.]

C. *Exercise of Jurisdiction*

[Ms. Cunningham argued that the Court should always decline to exercise jurisdiction over withdrawal applications because of solicitor-client privilege, the role of law societies, and a conflict of interest. Justice Rothstein addressed each of Ms. Cunningham's arguments. In the end he determined that none of the arguments, alone or combined, were sufficient to prevent a court from exercising its jurisdiction over applications for withdrawal based on non-fee payments.]

(1) Solicitor-Client Privilege

[Justice Rothstein noted that fee information is only *prima facie* privileged. Whether or not it is, in fact, privileged is determined by the Court. Withdrawal for non-payment of legal fees was, in this context, not privileged because it was impossible to use the fact of non-payment to speculate about the accused's activities. Even so, the Court cautioned that in other contexts, payments, or lack of, are pertinent to the case and will be protected under solicitor-client privilege. The possibility of counsel or the accused disclosing privileged information in court during an examination on the withdrawal was deemed too remote to justify imposing court deference to a counsel's unilateral decision to withdraw.]

(2) Exclusive Law Society Oversight

I am also unable to accept the argument of Ms. Cunningham and the interveners that oversight of lawyer withdrawal falls exclusively to the law societies. The law societies play an essential role in disciplining lawyers for unprofessional conduct; however, the purpose of the court overseeing withdrawal is not disciplinary. The court's authority is *preventative* – to protect the administration of justice and ensure trial fairness. The disciplinary role of the law society is *reactive*. Both roles are necessary to ensure effective regulation of the profession and protect the process of the court.

[Justice Rothstein listed a number of rules and approaches different Law Societies take to withdrawal for non-payment of fees.]

While the court is not bound to apply law society or Canadian Bar Association codes of professional conduct, these codes "should be considered an important statement of public policy" (*MacDonald Estate*, at p. 1246). These standards complement the court's discretion to refuse withdrawal where the effects on the administration of justice will be severe. For example, the Canadian Bar Association rules recognize the distinct, yet complementary, nature of the functions served by the court and law societies:

> Where withdrawal is required or permitted by this Rule the lawyer must comply with all applicable rules of court as well as local rules and practice.
> [c. XII, commentary 3]

. . . . .

Ms. Cunningham and the interveners submit that court supervision over withdrawal threatens the independence of the bar. ... I do not agree that an exceptional constraint on counsel, necessary to protect the integrity of the administration of justice, threatens counsel's independence ...

(3) Conflict of Interest

I am also unpersuaded by the Law Society of British Columbia's point that forcing unwilling counsel to continue may create a conflict between the client's and lawyer's interests. It is argued that where counsel is compelled to work for free, he or she may be tempted to give legal advice which will expedite the process in order to cut counsel's financial losses even though wrapping up a criminal matter as quickly as possible may not be in the best interests of the accused. This argument, however, is inconsistent with the Law Society's position – with which I agree – that the court should presume that lawyers act ethically. There are many situations where counsel's personal or professional interests may be in tension with an individual client's interest, for example where counsel acquires an interesting new file that requires immediate attention, or has vacation plans that conflict with the timing of court proceedings affecting the client. Counsel is obligated to be diligent, thorough and to act in the client's best interest. Similarly, if counsel agrees to be retained *pro bono*, he or she must act just as professionally as if acting for the client on a paid retainer of the same nature. Where the court requires counsel to continue to represent an accused, counsel must do so competently and diligently. Both the integrity of the profession and the administration of justice require nothing less.

. . . . .

(5) Remedy of Last Resort

Ms. Cunningham's arguments do not, therefore, support a wholesale denial of the court's jurisdiction to refuse counsel's request to withdraw.

That being said, ordering counsel to work for free is not a decision that should be made lightly. ... Refusing to allow counsel to withdraw should truly be a remedy of last resort and should only be relied upon where it is necessary to prevent serious harm to the administration of justice.

D. *Refusing Withdrawal*

The court's exercise of discretion to decide counsel's application for withdrawal should be guided by the following principles.

If counsel seeks to withdraw far enough in advance of any scheduled proceedings and an adjournment will not be necessary, then the court should allow the withdrawal. In this situation, there is no need for the court to enquire into counsel's reasons for seeking to withdraw or require counsel to continue to act.

Assuming that timing is an issue, the court is entitled to enquire further. Counsel may reveal that he or she seeks to withdraw for ethical reasons, non-payment of fees, or another specific reason (e.g. workload of counsel) if solicitor-client privilege is not engaged. Counsel seeking to withdraw for ethical reasons means that an issue has arisen in the solicitor-client relationship where it is now impossible for counsel to continue in good conscience to represent the accused. Counsel may cite "ethical reasons" as the reason for withdrawal if, for example, the accused is requesting that counsel act in violation of his or her professional obligations (see, e.g., Law Society of Upper Canada, r. 2.09(7)(b), (d) ...), or if the accused refuses to accept counsel's advice on an important trial issue (see, e.g., Law Society of Upper Canada, r. 2.09(2) ...). If the real reason for withdrawal is non-payment of legal fees, then counsel cannot represent to the court that he or she seeks to withdraw for "ethical reasons". However, in either the case of ethical reasons or non-payment of fees, the court must accept counsel's answer at face value and not enquire further so as to avoid trenching on potential issues of solicitor-client privilege.

If withdrawal is sought for an ethical reason, then the court must grant withdrawal (see *C. (D.D.)*, at p. 328, and *Deschamps*, at para. 23). Where an ethical issue has arisen in the relationship, counsel may be *required* to withdraw in order to comply with his or her professional obligations. It would be inappropriate for a court to require counsel to continue to act when to do so would put him or her in violation of professional responsibilities.

If withdrawal is sought because of non-payment of legal fees, the court may exercise its discretion to refuse counsel's request. The court's order refusing counsel's request to withdraw may be enforced by the court's contempt power (*C. (D.D.)*, at p. 327). In exercising its discretion on the withdrawal request, the court should consider the following non-exhaustive list of factors:

- whether it is feasible for the accused to represent himself or herself;

- other means of obtaining representation;

- impact on the accused from delay in proceedings, particularly if the accused is in custody;

- conduct of counsel, e.g. if counsel gave reasonable notice to the accused to allow the accused to seek other means of representation, or if counsel sought leave of the court to withdraw at the earliest possible time;

- impact on the Crown and any co-accused;

- impact on complainants, witnesses and jurors;

- fairness to defence counsel, including consideration of the expected length and complexity of the proceedings;

- the history of the proceedings, e.g. if the accused has changed lawyers repeatedly.

As these factors are all independent of the solicitor-client relationship, there is no risk of violating solicitor-client privilege when engaging in this analysis. On the basis of these factors, the court must determine whether allowing withdrawal would cause serious harm to the administration of justice. If the answer is yes, withdrawal may be refused.

Harm to the administration of justice is not simply administrative inconvenience as the interveners suggest. Harm to the administration of justice recognizes that there are other persons affected by ongoing and prolonged criminal proceedings: complainants, witnesses, jurors and society at large. Because of this, I would respectfully observe that the consideration suggested by the Alberta Court of Appeal in *C. (D.D.)* of whether allotted court time can be otherwise usefully filled is not a relevant consideration in this balancing of interests.

. . . . .

The question of whether this case meets the high threshold that must be met to refuse leave to withdraw is now moot. ... I simply emphasize that the threshold for refusing leave to withdraw is a high one and requires a proper basis in the record for its exercise.

. . . . .

6.   Conclusion

In sum, a court has the authority to control its own process and to supervise counsel who are officers of the court. The Supreme Court of the Yukon Territory correctly concluded that the Territorial Court had the jurisdiction to refuse to grant counsel's request to withdraw. This jurisdiction, however, should be exercised exceedingly sparingly. It is not appropriate for the court to refuse withdrawal where an adjournment will not be necessary, nor where counsel seeks withdrawal for ethical reasons. Where counsel seeks untimely withdrawal for non-payment of fees, the court must weigh the relevant factors and determine whether withdrawal would cause serious harm to the administration of justice.

7.   Disposition

I would allow the appeal. I would decline to grant an order as to costs.

NOTES AND QUESTIONS

1.   Do you agree with how the Supreme Court of Canada characterizes the relationship between the courts and the law societies?

2.   Has the Court been precise enough in explaining the circumstances in which lawyers can withdraw because of non-payment of legal fees?

3.   What is the point of a court asserting supervisory authority over a lawyer who seeks to withdraw if the lawyer can simply announce that there is an ethical issue, which the court must accept at "face value"?

The *Model Code* also addresses withdrawal in criminal cases:

> 2.07 (4) If a lawyer has agreed to act in a criminal case and the interval between a withdrawal and the trial of the case is sufficient to enable the client to obtain another lawyer and to allow such other lawyer adequate time

for preparation, the lawyer who has agreed to act may withdraw because the client has not paid the agreed fee or for other adequate cause provided that the lawyer:

    (a)   notifies the client, in writing, that the lawyer is withdrawing because the fees have not been paid or for other adequate cause;

    (b)   accounts to the client for any monies received on account of fees and disbursements;

    (c)   notifies Crown counsel in writing that the lawyer is no longer acting;

    (d)   in a case when the lawyer's name appears on the records of the court as acting for the accused, notifies the clerk or registrar of the appropriate court in writing that the lawyer is no longer acting; and

    (e)   complies with the applicable rules of court.

Commentary

A lawyer who has withdrawn because of conflict with the client should not indicate in the notice addressed to the court or Crown counsel the cause of the conflict or make reference to any matter that would violate the privilege that exists between lawyer and client. The notice should merely state that the lawyer is no longer acting and has withdrawn.

2.07 (5) If a lawyer has agreed to act in a criminal case and the date set for trial is not such as to enable the client to obtain another lawyer or to enable another lawyer to prepare adequately for trial and an adjournment of the trial date cannot be obtained without adversely affecting the client's interests, the lawyer who agreed to act must not withdraw because of non-payment of fees.

2.07 (6) If a lawyer is justified in withdrawing from a criminal case for reasons other than non-payment of fees and there is not a sufficient interval between a notice to the client of the lawyer's intention to withdraw and the date on which the case is to be tried to enable the client to obtain another lawyer and to enable such lawyer to prepare adequately for trial, the first lawyer, unless instructed otherwise by the client, should attempt to have the trial date adjourned and may withdraw from the case only with the permission of the court before which the case is to be tried.

Commentary

If circumstances arise that, in the opinion of the lawyer, require an application to the court for leave to withdraw, the lawyer should promptly inform Crown counsel and the court of the intention to apply for leave in order to avoid or minimize any inconvenience to the court and witnesses.

NOTES AND QUESTIONS

1.   Both the Supreme Court of Canada and the *Model Code* explicitly address court supervision of withdrawal in the criminal law context. What about the civil law context? Do different rules, principles and policies apply? Should they?

---

4. Whistleblowing, Up-the-Ladder Reporting and Noisy Withdrawal

At the end of 2001, a number of major American corporations including Enron were discovered to have engaged in massive institutionalized accounting fraud. The loss to creditors and investors in the market resulting from the Enron collapse alone was estimated to be in the range of $18.7 billion.[51] It was obvious that a significant number of lawyers were complicit in this fraud. In response in 2002, the United States revised its securities regulatory regime with the *Sarbannes-Oxley Act* to give greater powers to the Securities and Exchange Commission (SEC).[52] First, the SEC adopted a system of "up the ladder reporting". The *Model Code* also adopted this idea in Rule 2.02(8):

Dishonesty, Fraud when Client an Organization

2.02 (8) A lawyer who is employed or retained by an organization to act in a matter in which the lawyer knows that the organization has acted, is acting or intends to act dishonestly, fraudulently, criminally or illegally, must do the following, in addition to his or her obligations under subrule (7):

(a) advise the person from whom the lawyer takes instructions and the chief legal officer, or both the chief legal officer and the chief executive officer, that the proposed conduct is, was or would be dishonest, fraudulent, criminal, or illegal and should be stopped;

(b) if necessary because the person from whom the lawyer takes instructions, the chief legal officer or the chief executive officer refuses to cause the proposed conduct to be stopped, advise progressively the next highest persons or groups, including ultimately, the board of directors, the board of trustees, or the appropriate committee of the board, that the proposed conduct was, is or would be dishonest, fraudulent, criminal, or illegal and should be stopped; and

(c) if the organization, despite the lawyer's advice, continues with or intends to pursue the proposed wrongful conduct, withdraw from acting in the matter in accordance with Rule 2.07.

Commentary

A lawyer acting for an organization who learns that the organization has acted, is acting, or intends to act in a wrongful manner, may advise the chief executive officer and must advise the chief legal officer of the misconduct. If the wrongful conduct is not abandoned or stopped, the lawyer must report the matter "up the ladder" of responsibility within the organization until the matter is dealt with appropriately. If the organization, despite the lawyer's advice, continues with the wrongful conduct, the lawyer must withdraw from acting in the particular matter in accordance with Rule 2.07. In some but not all cases, withdrawal means resigning from his or her position or

---

[51] Diana B. Henriques, "Market that deals in risks faces a novel one; a jolt to the freewheeling trading of energy contracts" *The New York Times* (November 29, 2001) at C7.

[52] (2002) Pub. L. 107-204, 116 Stat. 745.

relationship with the organization and not simply withdrawing from acting in the particular matter.

Does this Rule and Commentary provide lawyers with enough guidance? Whose interests are protected by these provisions — the organization's, the lawyer's and/or the public's? Does this Rule go far enough? Does it demand too much?

The SEC also considered (but ultimately abandoned) the addition of a further step, "noisy withdrawal". This provided that if there was no response from the highest authority within the organization to the up-the-ladder reporting then not only must the lawyer withdraw, but he or she would have to do so "noisily" by: (a) informing the SEC that the withdrawal was based upon "professional considerations"; and (b) disaffirming any "tainted submissions" he or she might have made to the SEC. Identify the ethical pros and cons of this suggestion. Would noisy withdrawal be permitted, required or prohibited by the current regulatory system in Canada? Should we adopt such a rule in Canada? At the time this proposal was being considered in the United States, the President of the CBA, Simon Potter, objected, claiming that it would "turn trusted legal advisors into securities police".[53] Is this a legitimate criticism or rhetorical bluster? Whose interests would be protected by such a provision: the organization's, the lawyer's and/or the public's? Compare noisy withdrawal in this context with the rules on withdrawal in the context of client perjury.

5. Supplementary Obligations on Withdrawal

Rule 2.07(1) of the *Model Code* provides that if a lawyer withdraws he or she must give "reasonable notice". This is reinforced by:

> 2.07 (8) When a lawyer withdraws, the lawyer must try to minimize expense and avoid prejudice to the client and must do all that can reasonably be done to facilitate the orderly transfer of the matter to the successor lawyer.

Furthermore, the Commentary to Rule 2.07(1) adds:

> An essential element of reasonable notice is notification to the client, unless the client cannot be located after reasonable efforts. No hard and fast rules can be laid down as to what constitutes reasonable notice before withdrawal and how quickly a lawyer may cease acting after notification will depend on all relevant circumstances. When the matter is covered by statutory provisions or rules of court, these will govern. In other situations, the governing principle is that the lawyer should protect the client's interests to the best of the lawyer's ability and should not desert the client at a critical stage of a matter or at a time when withdrawal would put the client in a position of disadvantage or peril. As a general rule, the client should be given sufficient time to retain and instruct replacement counsel. Nor should withdrawal or an intention to withdraw be permitted to waste court time or prevent other

---

[53] Canadian Bar Association, "Client Confidentiality Needs Protection" *Bartalk* (February 2003), Vol. 15, No. 1.

counsel from reallocating time or resources scheduled for the matter in question. See subrule (8) – Manner of Withdrawal.

Every effort should be made to ensure that withdrawal occurs at an appropriate time in the proceedings in keeping with the lawyer's obligations. The court, opposing parties and others directly affected should also be notified of the withdrawal.

Does this provision provide sufficient protection for the client? Does it provide sufficient guidance for a lawyer?

There are also a series of more particular obligations which Smith characterizes as being guided by "cooperation and generosity".[54]

2.07 (9) On discharge or withdrawal, a lawyer must:

(a) notify the client in writing, stating:

  (i)   the fact that the lawyer has withdrawn;

  (ii) the reasons, if any, for the withdrawal; and

  (iii) in the case of litigation, that the client should expect that the hearing or trial will proceed on the date scheduled and that the client should retain new counsel promptly;

(b) subject to the lawyer's right to a lien, deliver to or to the order of the client all papers and property to which the client is entitled;

(c) subject to any applicable trust conditions, give the client all relevant information in connection with the case or matter;

(d) account for all funds of the client then held or previously dealt with, including the refunding of any remuneration not earned during the representation;

(e) promptly render an account for outstanding fees and disbursements;

(f) co-operate with the successor lawyer in the transfer of the file so as to minimize expense and avoid prejudice to the client; and

(g) comply with the applicable rules of court.

Are these supplementary obligations on withdrawal sufficient to protect the interests of the client?

One inherently conflictual situation arises when the client fails to pay after withdrawal by the lawyer. Can a lawyer take lien on the client's property? The Commentary to Rule 2.07(9)(a) suggests it is best not to:

If the question of a right of lien for unpaid fees and disbursements arises on the discharge or withdrawal of the lawyer, the lawyer should have due regard to the effect of its enforcement on the client's position. Generally speaking, a lawyer should not enforce a lien if to do so would prejudice materially a client's position in any uncompleted matter.

---

[54] Beverley Smith, *Professional Conduct for Lawyers and Judges*, 4th ed. (Fredericton: Maritime Law Book, 2011), ch. 7 at 51.

The obligation to deliver papers and property is subject to a lawyer's right of lien. In the event of conflicting claims to such papers or property, the lawyer should make every effort to have the claimants settle the dispute.

If it is permissible for a lawyer to breach confidentiality in order to recover his or her fees (as we shall see in Chapter 4), why are lawyers discouraged from taking a lien when they withdraw, especially if it is mandatory withdrawal caused by inappropriate client conduct?

Complications might also arise on the dissolution of a law firm. The Commentary to Rule 2.07(1) provides:

> When a law firm is dissolved or a lawyer leaves a firm to practise elsewhere, it usually results in the termination of the lawyer-client relationship as between a particular client and one or more of the lawyers involved. In such cases, most clients prefer to retain the services of the lawyer whom they regarded as being in charge of their business before the change. However, the final decision rests with the client, and the lawyers who are no longer retained by that client should act in accordance with the principles set out in this rule, and, in particular, should try to minimize expense and avoid prejudice to the client. The client's interests are paramount and, accordingly, the decision whether the lawyer will continue to represent a given client must be made by the client in the absence of undue influence or harassment by either the lawyer or the firm. That may require either or both the departing lawyer and the law firm to notify clients in writing that the lawyer is leaving and advise the client of the options available: to have the departing lawyer continue to act, have the law firm continue to act, or retain a new lawyer.

Scenario Nineteen

A client approaches you with a scheme to obtain money from lenders through fake documents in which he represents that he owns assets which he does not. You refuse and withdraw. You find out that he has gone to lawyer B. In conversations with lawyer B it becomes clear that she has not been told, and does not realize, that the documents are false and is assisting the client to obtain financing on the basis that they are accurate. What, if anything, do you tell lawyer B?

Finally, successor lawyers also have some obligations:

> 2.07 (10) Before agreeing to represent a client, a successor lawyer must be satisfied that the former lawyer has withdrawn or has been discharged by the client.

Commentary

> It is quite proper for the successor lawyer to urge the client to settle or take reasonable steps towards settling or securing any outstanding account of the former lawyer, especially if the latter withdrew for good cause or was capriciously discharged. But, if a trial or hearing is in progress or imminent, or if the client would otherwise be prejudiced, the existence of an outstanding account should not be allowed to interfere with the successor lawyer acting for the client.

6. Conclusion

Proulx and Layton provide the following synopsis of both the conceptual framework and the practical realities of withdrawal:

> First, the fiduciary nature of the client-lawyer relationship, with attendant duties of competence, loyalty, and communication, requires that counsel act in the client's best interests. As far as possible, the client should receive competent and continuing representation, without undue delay or excessive cost occasioned by termination. Second, lawyers are bound by demanding professional standards in the conduct of the client's defence. There are ethical obligations not to breach the law, mislead the court or otherwise undermine the administration of justice in representing a client. Withdrawal may be the only method by which these obligations can be met. Third, society at large and participants in the criminal justice process other than the accused and defence counsel have an interest in ensuring reasonably efficient and prompt proceedings that promote a fair and just outcome.
>
> In light of these diverse but interconnected interests, counsel is not permitted to terminate the client-lawyer relationship at will. Rather withdrawal must be for good cause, with appropriate notice to the client. In instances where withdrawal is justified, the lawyer must extricate himself or herself from the case with a minimum of prejudice to the former client.
>
> It could be argued, with convincing reference to the rules of professional conduct and case law, and despite the occasional judicial comment to the contrary, that lawyers are in fact given considerable latitude to withdraw from a case. Certainly, counsel who does not wait until the last minute to abandon a client prior to trial can choose from a panoply of grounds in engineering withdrawal, and there may be little that a client can do in response. Moreover, at the end of the day few clients will be keen to keep a lawyer who has no interest or inclination to continue with the case. These musings, though somewhat cynical, inarguably contain a kernel of validity and highlight the need for lawyers to exercise fair judgment and exhibit respect for the client and the proper administration of justice in considering the withdrawal option. Lawyers would also do well to think ahead by considering difficulties that might lead to withdrawal before accepting a case in the first place.[55]

In light of the materials reviewed in this section, do you believe that Proulx and Layton's analysis is accurate? Identify the strengths and weaknesses of the current regulatory system. Outline any revisions you would make to the system.

E. FURTHER READING

Arthurs, Harry, "The Dead Parrot: Does Professional Self-Regulation Exhibit Vital Signs?" (1995) 33 Alta. L. Rev. 800.

---

[55] Michel Proulx & David Layton, *Ethics and Canadian Criminal Law* (Toronto: Irwin Law, 2001) at 589-90.

Bryant, Sue, "The Five Habits: Building Cross-cultural Competence in Lawyers" (2001) 8 Clinical L. Rev. 33.

Cooper, H.H.A., "Representation of the Unpopular: What Can the Profession Do About this Eternal Problem?" (1974) 22(10) Chitty's L.J. 333.

Hutchinson, Allan C., *Legal Ethics and Professional Responsibility*, 2nd ed., (Toronto: Irwin Law, 2006).

MacKenzie, Gavin, *Lawyers and Ethics: Professional Responsibility and Discipline*, looseleaf (Scarborough, ON: Carswell, 1993).

Parker, Christine, "A Critical Morality for Lawyers: Four Approaches to Lawyers' Ethics?" (2004) 30 Monash U.L. Rev. 49.

Pepper, Stephen, "The Lawyer's Amoral Ethical Role: A Defence, A Problem and Some Possibilities" (1986) 11 Am. B. Found. Res. J. 613.

Proulx, Michel & David Layton, *Ethics and Canadian Criminal Law* (Toronto: Irwin Law, 2001).

Smith, B., *Professional Conduct for Lawyers and Judges*, 4th ed. (Fredericton: Maritime Law Book, 2011).

Turnball, Lorna A. (editor in chief), "Symposium on Lifelong Learning" (2010) 4 Canadian Legal Education Annual Review.

Voyvodic, Rose, "Lawyers Meet the Social Context: Understanding Cultural Competence" (2005) 84 Can. Bar Rev. 563.

CHAPTER 4

THE LAWYER'S DUTY TO PRESERVE CLIENT CONFIDENCES

A. INTRODUCTION

A lawyer's duty to preserve the confidences of his or her client is at the heart of the lawyer-client relationship. From the lawyer's point of view, comprehensive information about the client's situation is often critical to the lawyer's ability to adequately advise the client and provide appropriate representation of the client's interests. From the client's perspective, it is difficult to share information — which is often highly personal and capable of exposing a client to significant vulnerability — without great confidence that the information will be closely guarded and not disclosed without the client's permission. From the perspective of the legal profession as a whole, and the justice system itself, it is essential not only that any individual be able to trust in the confidentiality of a particular lawyer but more generally — systemically — that the general public knows that information shared with lawyers within the solicitor-client relationship will be vigorously protected.

As we shall see, the legal dimensions of lawyer-client communications — commonly referred to as solicitor-client privilege — are aggressively protected by law. As well, a central tenet of a lawyer's ethical and professional obligations, as articulated in codes of professional conduct, is the preservation of clients' confidential communications. Indeed, the ethical duty of confidentiality and the legal principle of solicitor-client privilege are among the forms of communication most highly protected in law.

From the perspective of the public, however, the lawyer's preservation of a client's confidences is often at the heart of criticisms of the profession for its disregard of a larger public interest that may suffer due to the lawyer's unwavering commitment to client interests. Attempting to identify the circumstances when a public interest value should take precedence over a foundational dimension of client representation — the preservation of client confidences — is one of the most provocative and challenging aspects of legal ethics. As we shall also see, in limited but important circumstances the protection of client confidences does yield to a greater public interest. An exploration of these exceptions to confidentiality and privilege, and the overriding public interest values imbedded in them, will show that lawyer-client confidentiality holds a very high place within the constellation of public policy values in our society. This exploration also identifies values seen to be of greater importance, as well as the evolution of confidentiality and privilege over time.

The opportunity to explore these questions has been assisted by a rapidly growing jurisprudence in Canada on the subject of lawyer-client privilege and confidentiality. In a paper on the subject of solicitor-client privilege Mahmud Jamal observed that:

> [p]rivilege has been a top priority for the Supreme Court of Canada, which largely chooses its own docket: the Court decided more cases touching on privilege in the 7 years from 1999 to 2006 than in the previous 125 years from 1875 (when the Court was created) to 1999. And, to remove any residual doubt, the Court recently declared that "the protection of solicitor-client confidences is a matter of high importance."[1]

In the course of this chapter you should give consideration to the following questions:

(a) In the jurisprudence, academic commentaries and codes of professional conduct, are the justifications for solicitor-client confidentiality and privilege sufficiently made out? Are they overstated? Understated?

(b) Is there a conceptual framework for the limited number of exceptions to confidentiality and privilege? Is this framework sound? Is it applicable to the right sort of circumstances?

(c) What are the differences between confidentiality and the various forms of privilege? What is the legal significance of these differences?

(d) To what extent ought the obligations associated with confidentiality and privilege be "discretionary" in the sense that an individual lawyer may choose to preserve confidences, or choose to disclose, according to the lawyer's judgment of the circumstances and his or her own ethical perspectives?

B.   DEFINITIONS, DISTINCTIONS AND RATIONALE

As we shall see in the cases and commentaries in this chapter, "confidentiality" and "privilege" are often used interchangeably. This produces an unfortunate conflation of two similar but legally distinct concepts, and it is important that the reader appreciate the distinctions between them. While each concept is based upon the principle that a lawyer owes a duty of loyalty to a client, including a duty to maintain a client's confidences, the source, scope and enforcement of the respective duties are distinct.

At least four features distinguish confidentiality from privilege. First, confidentiality is an *ethical* principle, whereas the duty of lawyer-client privilege is a *legal* duty. Second, the duty of confidentiality is engaged with respect to all of the client information acquired by the lawyer in the course of the

---

[1]   Mahmud Jamal, "The Supreme Court of Canada on Solicitor-Client Privilege" (Canadian Bar Association: November 2006) at para. 2.

professional relationship, whereas the lawyer-client privilege is limited to private communications that take place between lawyer and client. Third, the ethical obligation continues even if the information comes to be known by others, whereas communication of the privileged information to third parties can and often does bring to an end the lawyer's legal duties with respect to the privilege. Fourth, the privilege is a legal duty primarily associated with the law of evidence (though as we shall see in this chapter it has grown in status from an evidentiary principle to a principle of substantive law to, in appropriate circumstances, a "principle of fundamental justice"). By comparison, the ethical duty of confidentiality is a defining feature of all lawyer-client relationships.

The first two distinctions between confidentiality and privilege — confidentiality as an ethical principle and its broad scope — can best be seen in lawyers' professional codes of conduct. For example, the Federation of Law Societies of Canada's *Model Code of Professional Conduct* provides:

Confidential Information

2.03 (1) A lawyer at all times must hold in strict confidence all information concerning the business and affairs of a client acquired in the course of the professional relationship and must not divulge any such information unless:

  (a) expressly or impliedly authorized by the client;

  (b) required by law or a court to do so;

  (c) required to deliver the information to the Law Society, or

  (d) otherwise permitted by this rule.

By comparison, privilege is a concept developed by the courts, as we will see in a number of cases in this chapter.

As can be seen by the *Model Code* provision, the scope of confidentiality is clearly very broad. By comparison, Adam Dodek notes that "the privilege only applies to communications between clients and their lawyers" and that "[t]he mere fact that there is a communication to a lawyer is not enough to make the communication privileged ... [whereas] the mere fact that a communication is received from the client by the lawyer is enough to trigger the duty of confidentiality, as long as there is an existing relationship between the lawyer and client"[2].

Alice Woolley also notes that, to be privileged, a lawyer-client communication must be made for the purpose of providing legal advice, whereas any communications in the course of the professional relationship attract the lawyer's ethical duty of confidentiality.[3]

---

[2] Adam Dodek, "Solicitor-Client Privilege in Canada: Challenges for the 21st Century" (February 2011), online: Canadian Bar Association <http://www.cba.org/CBA/activities/pdf/Dodek-English.pdf>.

[3] Alice Woolley, *Understanding Lawyers' Ethics in Canada* (Markham, ON: LexisNexis Canada, 2011) at 110. She also notes (at 111) that in three different cases the Supreme Court of Canada has circumscribed lawyer-client communications that would attract privilege. For example, in *R. v. Campbell*, the Supreme Court held that advising "[w]hether or

Again, while the common law determines the circumstances when lawyer-client privilege terminates, codes of professional conduct articulate the continuing duration of the ethical duty of confidentiality. The Commentary to Rule 2.03(1) states: "The duty survives the professional relationship and continues indefinitely after the lawyer has ceased to act for the client, whether or not differences have arisen between them."

The fourth distinction, the relationship between privilege and the admissibility of lawyer-client communications as evidence, will be evident throughout this chapter, whereas confidentiality is not so limited in its application. For this reason, the Commentary to Rule 2.03(1) cautions against "indiscreet conversations and other communications, even with the lawyer's spouse or family, about the client's affairs and should shun any gossip about such things even though the client is not named or otherwise identified". The preservation of client confidences is an essential part of a lawyer's professional behaviour.

M. PROULX & D. LAYTON

Ethics and Canadian Criminal Law
(Toronto: Irwin Law, 2001)*

A. INTRODUCTION

The lawyer's duty to keep confidential all information received as a result of representing a client is a linchpin of the professional relationship. The scope of this duty is exceptionally broad, demanding that counsel take great care in handling all information pertaining to or affecting a client. At the same time, there are exceptions to the duty of confidentiality that permit, and sometimes even demand, disclosure of such information by the lawyer. Determining the instances where exceptions should apply raises some of the most controversial and daunting ethical problems facing the criminal bar today. ...

The standard justification for imposing a duty of confidentiality upon lawyers is that the client who is assured of complete secrecy is more likely to reveal to his or her counsel all information pertaining to the case. The lawyer who is in possession of all relevant information is better able to advise the client and hence provide competent service. The client's legal rights are furthered, as is the truth-finding function of the adversarial system. Additionally, the obligation to maintain confidentiality fosters the autonomy and dignity of the client by protecting his or her privacy. Finally, the duty of confidentiality is

---

not solicitor-client privilege attaches ... depends on the nature of the relationship, the subject matter of the advice and the circumstances in which it is sought and rendered": [1999] S.C.J. No. 16, [1999] 1 S.C.R. 565 at para. 56 (S.C.C.). *Campbell* involved the provision of policy advice by government lawyers. *R. v. Cunningham*, [2010] S.C.J. No. 10, 2010 SCC 10 (S.C.C.) involved lawyer-client communications related to a legal aid system's non-payment of the client's legal fees. *Foster Wheeler Power Co. v. Société intermunicipale de gestion et d'élimination des déchets (SIGED) Inc.*, [2004] 1 S.C.R. 456, [2004] S.C.J. No. 18 (S.C.C.) concerned the civil law concept of "professional secrecy" and its application to information and advice provided to municipalities by its lawyers, some parts of which met the test of "professional secrecy" and some parts of which did not.

*   Reproduced with permission.

closely connected to the overarching duty of loyalty owed by a lawyer to the client. The obligation to be loyal would be compromised if a lawyer could use information so as to cause adverse impact to the client. A complete bar on the unauthorized use of confidential information by counsel, even where no adverse impact is possible, accordingly serves a prophylactic function that helps to ensure undivided loyalty.

In promoting effective legal advice, the duty of confidentiality not only benefits the individual client but also serves a broader societal interest. As already noted, a client who is able to rely upon the assurance of confidentiality thus advances fundamental systemic goals.

C. THE PRINCIPLE AND SOME EXCEPTIONS

The scope of and justifications for confidentiality and privilege are most commonly articulated in circumstances in which someone seeks to set aside an individual's right to have confidences preserved or the privilege maintained, or where it is argued that a law requires disclosure of the information. The following cases highlight the principle and give consideration to arguments both supporting and opposing the client's confidential communications to his or her lawyer. In these cases the courts have sought to establish a framework for a consideration of confidentiality and privilege, its scope and its limitations.

1. The "Crime/Fraud" or "Criminal Communications" Exception

DESCÔTEAUX v. MIERZWINSKI

[1982] S.C.J. No. 43, [1982] 1 S.C.R. 860, 141 D.L.R. (3d) 590
(S.C.C., Martland, Ritchie, Dickson, Beetz, Estey, Chouinard and Lamer JJ.)

[In order to obtain proof that Ledoux, an applicant for legal aid, had committed an indictable offence by fraudulently reporting a lower income in order to be eligible for such services, two peace officers presented themselves at a legal aid bureau with a search warrant. This warrant related to certain documents, including an "Application for Legal Aid" form which contained, *inter alia*, information on the applicant's financial situation. The search was made in the presence of the syndic of the Bar and the police officers agreed to receive the documents in a sealed envelope without examining them. Appellants' application for *certiorari* to quash the seizure on the ground that the documents seized were protected by solicitor-client privilege was dismissed both in the Superior Court and in the Court of Appeal.

At trial and on appeal to the Quebec Court of Appeal, the documents were found not to attract the protection of lawyer-client confidentiality or privilege. The decision was appealed to the Supreme Court of Canada.

As we saw in Chapter 3, the Supreme Court of Canada found that the lawyer-client relationship commences "as soon as the potential client has his first dealings with the lawyer's office in order to obtain legal advice". The remaining part of the case, considered here, focused on whether the circumstances constituted an exception to the client's entitlement to confidentiality or privilege in relation to the documents in question.]

LAMER J.:— A citizen who lies about his financial means in order to obtain legal aid is committing a crime. This appeal concerns the right of the police to be authorized by a search warrant to search a legal aid bureau and seize the form filled out by the citizen at his interview, for purposes of proving that this crime was committed. This issue raises several others, including, in particular, the scope of and procedures for exercising the authority to search lawyers' offices, in view of the confidential nature of their clients' files. This appeal will also give everyone an opportunity to note the deficiencies in the law in this area and the limited ability of the courts to compensate for them since their role is not primarily legislative.

. . . . .

I do not intend to repeat here everything that others have said, on numerous occasions and very clearly and completely, about solicitor-client privilege, or about the issuance and execution of search warrants.

I think, however, that I should make a few remarks about the existence and effects of a person's right to have his communications with his lawyer kept confidential; I shall then deal more particularly with the search power provided for in the *Criminal Code*.

THE RIGHT TO CONFIDENTIALITY

It is not necessary to demonstrate the existence of a person's right to have communications with his lawyer kept confidential. Its existence has been affirmed numerous times and was recently reconfirmed by this court in *Solosky v. The Queen*, [1980] 1 S.C.R. 821, where Dickson J. stated (at p. 839):

> One may depart from the current concept of privilege and approach the case on the broader basis that (i) *the right to communicate in confidence with one's legal adviser is a fundamental civil and legal right, founded upon the unique relationship of solicitor and client*, and (ii) a person confined to prison retains all of his civil rights, other than those expressly or impliedly taken from him by law. (Emphasis added.)

There is no denying that a person has a right to communicate with a legal adviser in all confidence, a right that is "founded upon the unique relationship of solicitor and client" (*Solosky, supra*). It is a personal and extra-patrimonial right which follows a citizen throughout his dealings with others. Like other personal, extra-patrimonial rights, it gives rise to preventive or curative remedies provided for by law, depending on the nature of the aggression threatening it or of which it was the object. Thus a lawyer who communicates a confidential communication to others without his client's authorization could be sued by his client for damages; or a third party who had accidentally seen the contents of a lawyer's file could be prohibited by injunction from disclosing them.

. . . . .

THE SUBSTANTIVE RULE

Although the right to confidentiality first took the form of a rule of evidence, it is now recognized as having a much broader scope, as can be seen from the manner in which this court dealt with the issues raised in *Solosky*.

Solosky was an inmate at Millhaven Penitentiary. He was seeking a declaration that henceforth all properly identified items of solicitor-client correspondence would be forwarded to their respective destinations unopened.

The inmates' right to confidentiality conflicted with the *Penitentiaries Act*, ... and more particularly with s. 2.18 of the *Penitentiary Service Regulations*, allowing the director of the institution to order censorship of correspondence to the extent considered necessary or desirable for the security of the institution.

[On behalf of the Supreme Court, Dickson J. found that the solicitor-client privilege existed and that the communications between solicitor and client were to be treated as confidential subject to certain articulated exceptions or qualifications related to the safety and security of the penitentiary.]

. . . . .

It is quite apparent that the court in that case applied a standard that has nothing to do with the rule of evidence, the privilege, since there was never any question of testimony before a tribunal or court. The court in fact, in my view, applied a substantive rule, without actually formulating it, and, consequently, recognized implicitly that the right to confidentiality, which had long ago given rise to a rule of evidence, had also since given rise to a substantive rule.

It would, I think, be useful for us to formulate this substantive rule, as the judges formerly did with the rule of evidence; it could, in my view, be stated as follows:

1. The confidentiality of communications between solicitor and client may be raised in any circumstances where such communications are likely to be disclosed without the client's consent.

2. Unless the law provides otherwise, when and to the extent that the legitimate exercise of a right would interfere with another person's right to have his communications with his lawyer kept confidential, the resulting conflict should be resolved in favour of protecting the confidentiality.

3. When the law gives someone the authority to do something which, in the circumstances of the case, might interfere with that confidentiality, the decision to do so and the choice of means of exercising that authority should be determined with a view to not interfering with it except to the extent absolutely necessary in order to achieve the ends sought by the enabling legislation.

4.   Acts providing otherwise in situations under para. 2 and enabling
      legislation referred to in para. 3 must be interpreted restrictively.

. . . . .

CONFIDENTIALITY IN THE CASE AT BAR

. . . . .

The items of information that a lawyer requires from a person in order to
decide if he will agree to advise or represent him are just as much communications made in order to obtain legal advice as any information communicated
to him subsequently. It has long been recognized that even if the lawyer does
not agree to advise the person seeking his services, communications made by
the person to the lawyer or his staff for that purpose are none the less
privileged ...

Moreover, the same applies not only to information given before the retainer
is perfected concerning the legal problem itself, but also to information
concerning the client's ability to pay the lawyer and any other information
which a lawyer is reasonably entitled to require before accepting the retainer.
First, this information of an administrative nature is just as related to the
establishment of the professional relationship as any other information; this is
especially clear when, as in the case at bar, the legal aid applicant "*must set
forth (his) financial means* ... and the basis of his claim". In addition,
information of this nature that a person gives his lawyer for that purpose may
also be highly confidential and would have been kept secret by that person
were it not for that person's need of the assistance of a legal adviser.

. . . . .

I therefore do not think that a distinction should be made between information
that must be given in order to establish the probable existence of a valid claim
and that given to establish eligibility from the point of view of financial
means, since, on the one hand, information concerning the person's financial
situation may be just as highly confidential as any other information and
since, on the other hand, the fact of being unable to meet the eligibility
requirements respecting financial means is no less fatal to the ability to obtain
the services sought.

. . . . .

Confidential communications, whether they relate to financial means or to the
legal problem itself, lose that character if and to the extent that they were
made for the purpose of obtaining legal advice to facilitate the commission of
a crime.

The same is true a *fortiori* where, as in the case at bar, the communication
itself is the material element (*actus reus*) of the crime; this is all the more
evident where the victim of the crime is precisely the office of the lawyer to
whom the communication was made.

[Justice Lamer concluded that this "criminal communication" purpose
prevented the communication from attracting lawyer-client privilege.]

NOTES AND QUESTIONS

1. You will have noted that the Supreme Court of Canada in this case confirms the elevation of solicitor-client privilege to a "substantive right", and not just a rule of evidence. It will be important to observe the ways in which the Court builds upon this right in subsequent cases.

2. The Court established that this right, grounded in the solicitor-client relationship, takes effect at a very early stage. Indeed, the obligations related to client confidences are among the most significant consequences of a solicitor-client relationship commencing at such an early point. Is this appropriate? Is it manageable for lawyers who actually intend to decline to represent a person and never enter into an arrangement where they are retained by the client? What consequences for the lawyer may flow from this?

3. The Codes of Professional Conduct in a number of Canadian provinces had previously defined a client to be someone for whom a lawyer renders, or agrees to render professional services. Presumably the Codes contemplated that the lawyer-client relationship commenced at that time, with all of a lawyer's duties, including confidentiality, commencing immediately. Does this accord with *Descôteaux*? The *Model Code* now defines a client in the following way: "a 'client' means a person who: (a) consults a lawyer and on whose behalf a lawyer renders or agrees to render legal services; or (b) having consulted the lawyer, reasonably concludes that the lawyer has agreed to render legal services on his or her behalf". Is this approach closer to the Court's perspective? Would it be true to say that, by virtue of filling out the application for legal aid, Mr. Ledoux had "reasonably concluded that the lawyer has agreed to render legal services"? Can the *Model Code* definition be managed from a lawyer's perspective? Can the *Decôteaux* definition be managed?

4. *Descôteaux* is an example of the "crime/fraud" or "criminal communications" exception to lawyer-client confidentiality. Understandably, lawyers are not pleased to be used by clients to facilitate the commission of crimes, and the "crime/fraud" exception is widely accepted as a legitimate exception to confidentiality. At the same time, clients may use the instrumentality of a lawyer's services to facilitate crime without the actual communication constituting a part of the crime itself. Lying to one's lawyer in order to get the lawyer to prepare a false document would be one example. Would this be caught by Lamer J.'s articulation of the crime/fraud exception? Should it be?

5. If a client sought legal advice on whether a particular course of action was "illegal", acted on the advice and it was subsequently determined that the activity was illegal, could the information regarding the advice be required to be disclosed on the basis that it came within the "criminal communications" exception? If one part of the person's defence to the allegation of criminal misconduct was that he relied on legal advice that the actions were lawful, could the legal advice be required to be disclosed?[4]

6. As is commonly the case, the nature and importance of solicitor-client confidences is usually articulated when the right is challenged, or an exception to the right is under consideration. You will have noted that Lamer J. set out a frame-

---

[4] See *R. v. Campbell*, [1999] S.C.J. No. 16, [1999] 1 S.C.R. 565 (S.C.C.), especially paras. 55-62 and 67-71.

work for dealing with challenges and exceptions to confidentiality and privilege. Would you agree that a strong element of this framework is the expression of support for the importance of protecting client confidences and that, consequently, any interference with clients' rights in this respect should be kept to a minimum? Do you agree with this perspective? It will be important to familiarize yourself with Lamer J.'s framework, since it will make a regular appearance in subsequent cases when exceptions to confidentiality and privilege arise.

2. The "Public Safety" Exception

SMITH v. JONES

[1999] S.C.J. No. 15, [1999] 1 S.C.R. 455
(S.C.C., Lamer C.J.C. and L'Heureux-Dubé, Gonthier, Cory, McLachlin, Iacobucci, Major, Bastarache and Binnie JJ.)

CORY J. [for the majority]:— The solicitor-client privilege permits a client to talk freely to his or her lawyer secure in the knowledge that the words and documents which fall within the scope of the privilege will not be disclosed. It has long been recognized that this principle is of fundamental importance to the administration of justice and, to the extent it is feasible, it should be maintained. Yet when public safety is involved and death or serious bodily harm is imminent, the privilege should be set aside. This appeal must determine what circumstances and factors should be set aside in the interest of protecting the safety of the public.

I.   Factual Background

Solicitor-client privilege is claimed for a doctor's report. Pending the resolution of that claim the names of the parties involved have been replaced by pseudonyms. The appellant, "James Jones," was charged with aggravated sexual assault of a prostitute. His counsel referred him to a psychiatrist, the respondent, "John Smith," for a forensic psychiatric assessment. It was hoped that it would be of assistance in the preparation of the defence or with submissions on sentencing in the event of a guilty plea. His counsel advised Mr. Jones that the consultation was privileged in the same way as a consultation with him would be. Dr. Smith interviewed Mr. Jones for 90 minutes on July 30, 1997. His findings are contained in an affidavit he submitted to the judge of first instance. They set out the basis for his belief that Mr. Jones poses a continuing danger to the public.

Dr. Smith reported that Mr. Jones described in considerable detail his plan for the crime to which he subsequently pled guilty. It involved deliberately choosing as a victim a small prostitute who could be readily overwhelmed. He planned to have sex with her and then to kidnap her. He took duct tape and rope with him, as well as a small blue ball that he tried to force into the woman's mouth. Because he planned to kill her after the sexual assault he made no attempt to hide his identity.

Mr. Jones planned to strangle the victim and to dispose of her body in the bush area near Hope, British Columbia. He was going to shoot the woman in the face before burying her to impede identification. He had arranged time off from his work and had carefully prepared his basement apartment to facilitate his planned sexual assault and murder. He had told people he would be going away on vacation so that no one would visit him and he had fixed dead bolts on all the doors so that a key alone would not open them.

Mr. Jones told Dr. Smith that his first victim would be a "trial run" to see if he could "live with" what he had done. If he could, he planned to seek out similar victims. He stated that, by the time he had kidnapped his first victim, he expected that he would be "in so deep" that he would have no choice but to carry out his plans.

On July 31, Dr. Smith telephoned Mr. Jones's counsel and informed him that in his opinion Mr. Jones was a dangerous individual who would, more likely than not, commit future offences unless he received sufficient treatment.

On September 24, 1997, Mr. Jones pled guilty to aggravated assault and the matter was put over for sentencing. Sometime after November 19, Dr. Smith phoned Mr. Jones's counsel to inquire about the proceedings. On learning that the judge would not be advised of his concerns, Dr. Smith indicated that he intended to seek legal advice and shortly thereafter commenced this action.

The *in camera* hearing took place in December 1997. Dr. Smith filed an affidavit describing his interview with Mr. Jones and his opinion based upon the interview. Mr. Jones filed an affidavit in response. On December 12, 1997, Henderson J. ruled that the public safety exception to the law of solicitor-client privilege and doctor-patient confidentiality released Dr. Smith from his duties of confidentiality. He went on to rule that Dr. Smith was under a duty to disclose to the police and the Crown both the statements made by Mr. Jones and his opinion based upon them. Henderson J. ordered a stay of his order to allow for an appeal and Mr. Jones promptly appealed the decision.

The Court of Appeal allowed the appeal but only to the extent that the mandatory order was changed to one permitting Dr. Smith to disclose the information to the Crown and police ....

II.   Analysis

A.   The Nature of the Solicitor-Client Privilege

Both parties made their submissions on the basis that the psychiatrist's report was protected by solicitor-client privilege, and it should be considered on that basis. It is the highest privilege recognized by the courts. By necessary implication, if a public safety exception applies to solicitor-client privilege, it applies to all classifications of privileges and duties of confidentiality. It follows that, in these reasons, it is not necessary to consider any distinction that may exist between a solicitor-client privilege and a litigation privilege.

The solicitor-client privilege has long been regarded as fundamentally important to our judicial system. Well over a century ago in *Anderson v. Bank of British Columbia* (1876), 2 Ch. D 644 (C.A.), at p. 649, the importance of the rule was recognized:

> The object and meaning of the rule is this: that as, by reason of the complexity and difficulty of our law, litigation can only be properly conducted by professional men, it is absolutely necessary that a man, in order to prosecute his rights or to defend himself from an improper claim, should have recourse to the assistance of professional lawyers .... to use a vulgar phrase, that he should be able to make a clean breast of it to the gentleman whom he consults with a view to the prosecution of his claim, or the substantiating of his defence. ... that he should be able to place unrestricted and unbounded confidence in the professional agent, and that the communication he so makes to him should be kept secret, unless with his consent (for it is his privilege, and not the privilege of the confidential agent), that he should be enabled properly to conduct his litigation.

Clients seeking advice must be able to speak freely to their lawyers secure in the knowledge that what they say will not be divulged without their consent. It cannot be forgotten that the privilege is that of the client, not the lawyer. The privilege is essential if sound legal advice is to be given in every field. It has a deep significance in almost every situation where legal advice is sought whether it be with regard to corporate and commercial transactions, to family relationships, to civil litigation or to criminal charges. Family secrets, company secrets, personal foibles and indiscretions all must on occasion be revealed to the lawyer by the client. Without this privilege, a client could never be candid and furnish all the relevant information that must be provided to lawyers if they are to properly advise their clients. It is an element that is both integral and extremely important to the functioning of the legal system. It is because of the fundamental importance of the privilege that the onus properly rests upon those seeking to set aside the privilege to justify taking such a significant step.

· · · · ·

As the British Columbia Court of Appeal observed, solicitor-client privilege is the privilege "which the law has been most zealous to protect and most reluctant to water down by exceptions". Quite simply it is a principle of fundamental importance to the administration of justice.

B.   Limitations on Solicitor-Client Privilege

Just as no right is absolute so too the privilege, even that between solicitor and client, is subject to clearly defined exceptions. The decision to exclude evidence that would be both relevant and of substantial probative value because it is protected by the solicitor-client privilege represents a policy decision. It is based upon the importance to our legal system in general of the solicitor-client privilege. In certain circumstances, however, other societal values must prevail.

· · · · ·

(3) The Public Safety Exception

In *Solosky* ... an inmate in a federal penitentiary asked this Court to make a declaration that all properly identified correspondence between solicitors and clients would be forwarded to their destinations without being opened. The inmate's privilege was in conflict with the *Penitentiary Act* ... and with Regulation 2.18 of the Penitentiary Services Regulations, which allowed the institution's director to censor any correspondence to the extent the censor considered necessary.

In his decision, Dickson J. ruled that the inmate's privilege must yield when the safety of members of the institution is at risk. In his reasons ... he implicitly limited the solicitor-client privilege. He wrote:

> The result, as I see it, is that the Court is placed in the position of having to balance the public interest in maintaining the safety and security of a penal institution, its staff and its inmates, with the interest represented by insulating the solicitor-client relationship. Even giving full recognition to the right of an inmate to correspond freely with his legal adviser, and the need for minimum derogation therefrom, the scale must ultimately come down in favour of the public interest.

In certain circumstances, therefore, when the safety of the public is at risk the solicitor-client privilege may be set aside.

. . . . .

C. The Public Safety Exception and Solicitor-Client Privilege

The foregoing review makes it clear that even the fundamentally important right to confidentiality is not absolute in doctor-patient relationships, and it cannot be absolute in solicitor-client relationships ... When the interest in the protection of the innocent accused and the safety of members of the public is engaged, the privilege will have to be balanced against these other compelling public needs. In rare circumstances, these public interests may be so compelling that the privilege must be displaced. Yet the right to privacy in a solicitor-client relationship is so fundamentally important that only a compelling public interest may justify setting aside solicitor-client privilege.

Danger to public safety can, in appropriate circumstances, provide the requisite justification. It is significant that public safety exceptions to the solicitor-client privilege are recognized by all professional legal bodies within Canada. See, for example, Chapter 5, s. 12, of the British Columbia Professional Conduct Handbook:

> Disclosure to prevent a crime

> 12. A lawyer may disclose information received as a result of a solicitor-client relationship if the lawyer has reasonable grounds to believe that the disclosure is necessary to prevent a crime involving death or serious bodily harm to any person.

See as well the even broader Rule 4.11 of the Law Society of Upper Canada's Professional Conduct Handbook.

Quite simply, society recognizes that the safety of the public is of such importance that in appropriate circumstances, it will warrant setting aside solicitor-client privilege. What factors should be taken into consideration in determining whether that privilege should be displaced?

(1) Determining When Public Safety Outweighs Solicitor-Client Privilege

There are three factors to be considered: First, is there a clear risk to an identifiable person or group of persons? Second, is there a risk of serious bodily harm or death? Third, is the danger imminent? Clearly if the risk is imminent, the danger is serious.

These factors will often overlap and vary in their importance and significance. The weight to be attached to each will vary with the circumstances presented by each case, but they all must be considered. As well, each factor is composed of various aspects, and, like the factors themselves, these aspects may overlap and the weight to be given to them will vary depending on the circumstances of each case. Yet as a general rule, if the privilege is to be set aside the court must find that there is an imminent risk of serous bodily harm or death to an identifiable person or group.

(a) Clarity

What should be considered in determining if there is a clear risk to an identifiable group or person? It will be appropriate and relevant to consider the answers a particular case may provide to the following questions: Is there evidence of long-range planning? Has a method for effecting the specific attack been suggested? Is there a prior history of violence or threats of violence? Are the prior assaults or threats of violence similar to that which was planned? If there is a history of violence, has the violence increased in severity? Is the violence directed to an identifiable person or group of persons? This is not an all-encompassing list. It is important to note, however, that as a general rule a group or person must be ascertainable. The requisite specificity of that identification will vary depending on the other factors discussed here.

The specific questions to be considered under this heading will vary with the particular circumstances of each case. Great significance might, in some situations, be given to the particularly clear identification of a particular individual or group of intended victims. Even if the group of intended victims is large, considerable significance can be given to the threat if the identification of the group is clear and forceful. For example, a threat, put forward with chilling detail, to kill or seriously injure children five years of age and under would have to be given very careful consideration. In certain circumstances, it might be that a threat of death directed toward single women living in apartment buildings could in combination with other factors be sufficient in the particular circumstances to justify setting aside the privilege. At the same time, a general threat of death or violence directed to everyone in a city or community, or anyone with whom the person may come into contact, may be too vague to warrant setting aside the privilege. However, if the threatened harm to the members of the public was particularly compelling, extremely serious and imminent, it might well be appropriate to lift the privilege. ...

. . . . .

(b) Seriousness

The "seriousness" factor requires that the threat be such that the intended victim is in danger of being killed or of suffering serious bodily harm. Many persons involved in criminal justice proceedings will have committed prior crimes or may be planning to commit crimes in the future. The disclosure of planning future crimes without an element of violence would be an insufficient reason to set aside solicitor-client privilege because of fears for public safety. For the public safety interest to be of sufficient importance to displace solicitor-client privilege, the threat must be to occasion serious bodily harm or death.

It should be observed that serious psychological harm may constitute serious bodily harm, as this Court held in *R. v. McCraw*, [1991] 3 S.C.R. 72, at p. 81:

> So long as the psychological harm substantially interferes with the health or well-being of the complainant, it properly comes within the scope of the phrase "serious bodily harm". There can be no doubt that psychological harm may often be more pervasive and permanent in its effect than any physical harm.

(c) Imminence

The risk of serious bodily harm or death must be imminent if solicitor-client communications are to be disclosed. That is, the risk itself must be serious: a serious risk of serious bodily harm. The nature of the threat must be such that it creates a sense of urgency. This sense of urgency may be applicable to some time in the future. Depending on the seriousness and clarity of the threat, it will not always be necessary to impose a particular time limit on the risk. It is sufficient if there is a clear and imminent threat of serious bodily harm to an identifiable group, and if this threat is made in such a manner that a sense of urgency is created. A statement made in a fleeting fit of anger will usually be insufficient to disturb the solicitor-client privilege. On the other hand, imminence as a factor may be satisfied if a person makes a clear threat to kill someone that he vows to carry out three years hence when he is released from prison. If that threat is made with such chilling intensity and graphic detail that a reasonable bystander would be convinced that the killing would be carried out the threat could be considered to be imminent. Imminence, like the other two criteria, must be defined in the context of each situation.

. . . . .

(2) Extent of Disclosure

The disclosure of the privileged communication should generally be limited as much as possible. The judge setting aside the solicitor-client privilege should strive to strictly limit disclosure to those aspects of the report or document which indicate that there is an imminent risk of serious bodily harm or death to an identifiable person or group. In undertaking this task consideration should be given to those portions of the report which refer to the risk or serious harm to an identifiable group, that the risk is serious in that it involves a danger of death or serious bodily harm; and that the serious risk is imminent in the sense given to that word in para. 84 above. The requirement that the disclosure be limited must be emphasized. For example, if a report contained references to criminal behaviour that did not have an imminent risk of serious bodily harm but disclosed, for example, the commission of crimes of fraud, counterfeiting or the sale of stolen goods, those references would necessarily be deleted.

D.   Application of the Public Safety Exception to Solicitor-Client Privilege to the Case at Bar

(1)   Clarity

Would a reasonable observer, given all the facts for which solicitor-client privilege is sought, consider the potential danger posed by Mr. Jones to be clear, serious, and imminent? The answer must, I think, be in the affirmative. According to Dr. Smith's affidavit, the plan described by Mr. Jones demonstrated a number of the factors that should be considered in determining the clarity of the potential danger. They are the clear identification of the victim group, the specificity of method, the evidence of planning, and the prior attempted or actual acts that mirror the potential act of threatened future harm.

. . . . .

(2)   Seriousness

The seriousness of the potential harm, a sexually sadistic murder, is clearly sufficient. The fact that Mr. Jones has after careful and detailed planning already committed an assault upon a prostitute supports the finding that the potential harm caused would be extremely serious.

(3)   Imminence

The most difficult issue to resolve is whether the risk of serious bodily harm can be termed "imminent". ...

. . . . .

There are two important factors that indicate that the threat of serious bodily harm was indeed imminent. First, Mr. Jones admitted that he had breached his bail conditions by continuing to visit the Downtown Eastside where he knew prostitutes could be found. Second, common sense would indicate that after Mr. Jones was arrested, and while he was awaiting sentence, he would have been acutely aware of the consequences of his actions. This is of particular significance in light of his fear of being attacked while he was in jail.

Let us assume that the evidence as to imminence of the danger may not be as clear as might be desired. Nonetheless, there is some evidence of imminence. Furthermore, the other factors pertaining to clarity, the identifiable group of victims, and the chilling evidence of careful planning, when taken together, indicate that the solicitor-client privilege must be set aside for the protection of members of the public.

. . . . .

III. Disposition

The file will be unsealed and the ban on the publication of the contents of the file is removed, except for those parts of the affidavit of the doctor which do not fall within the public safety exception. Subject to this direction the order of the British Columbia Court of Appeal is affirmed and this appeal is dismissed without costs.

The reasons of Lamer C.J.C. and Major and Binnie JJ. were delivered by

MAJOR J. [dissenting in part]:—

. . . . .

The chilling effect of completely breaching the privilege would have the undesired effect of discouraging those individuals in need of treatment for serious and dangerous conditions from consulting professional help. In this case the interests of the appellant and more importantly the interests of society would be better served by his obtaining treatment. This Court has recognized that mental health, including those suffering from potentially dangerous illnesses, is an important public good: see *M. (A.) v. Ryan*, [1997] 1 S.C.R. 157 ....

Although the appellant did not go to Dr. Smith to seek treatment, it is obvious that he is more likely to get treatment when his condition is diagnosed than someone who keeps the secret of their illness to themselves. It seems apparent that society will suffer by imposing a disincentive for patients and criminally accused persons to speak frankly with counsel and medical experts retained on their behalf.

As appealing as it may be to ensure that Mr. Jones does not slip back into the community without treatment for his condition, completely lifting the privilege and allowing his confidential communications to his legal advisor to be used against him in the most detrimental ways will not promote public safety, only silence. For this doubtful gain, the Court will have imposed a veil of secrecy between criminal accused and their counsel which the solicitor-client privilege was developed to prevent. Sanctioning a breach of privilege too hastily erodes the workings of the system of law in exchange for an illusory gain in public safety.

VI. Application to the Facts

While I agree with Cory J. that the danger in this case is sufficiently clear, serious and imminent to justify some warning to the relevant authorities, I find that the balance between the public interests in safety and the proper administration of justice is best struck by a more limited disclosure than the broader abrogation of privilege he proposes. In particular, Cory J. endorses the trial judge's limitation of Dr. Smith's affidavit to those portions which indicate an imminent risk of serious harm or death. In the result, conscriptive evidence such as the accused's confession can be disclosed. In my opinion, the danger posed by the accused can be adequately addressed by the expression of that opinion by Dr. Smith without disclosing the confession.

Two principles should guide the analysis of the scope of this disclosure. First, the breach of privilege must be as narrow as possible; *Descôteaux v. Mierzwinski* ... Disclosure is justified only when it can actually accomplish something in the public interest, such as preventing injury or death. ...

. . . . .

Second, an accused's right to consult counsel without fear of having his words used against him at trial is vital to our conception of justice. ...

The public interest in cases such as this is twofold, and requires not only that the dangerous individual is prevented from harming anyone, but that they obtain treatment if needed. Appealing as it might be to force individuals in Mr. Jones's position into treatment through the criminal process, it is unlikely to happen. If there is a risk that conscriptive evidence from the mouth of the accused can be used against him, the defence bar is going to be reluctant to refer dangerous clients to the care of experts. Disclosure will be discouraged and treatment will not occur.

As the facts of this case illustrate, Mr. Jones was only diagnosed and made aware of the possibility of treatment because he felt secure in confiding to Dr. Smith. If that confidence is undermined, then these individuals will not disclose the danger they pose, they will not be identified, and public safety will suffer.

. . . . .

Accordingly, I would allow the appeal without costs, confirm the entirety of Mr. Jones's communications to Dr. Smith to be privileged, but permit Dr. Smith to give his opinion and diagnosis of the danger posed by Mr. Jones.

NOTES AND QUESTIONS

1. To what extent do the Cory J. and Major J. judgments coincide? To what extent do they diverge? To what extent do they represent fundamentally different conceptions of solicitor-client privilege and different conceptions of the lawyer's role in representing clients in criminal proceedings? Do you think that Major J. is right in his argument that greater protection accorded to solicitor-client privilege would be more likely to cause lawyers to refer their clients for professional help?

2. This case is in many ways a balancing act between (a) the public interest values inherent in the criminal justice system and the defence lawyer's role within that system in relation to his or her client; and (b) the public interest value of protecting the public from potentially dangerous people, even at the sacrifice of a privacy right. Has the Supreme Court struck the right balance?

3. This decision authorized the psychiatrist to disclose information that would otherwise have been protected by solicitor-client privilege. Does it impose an

obligation upon anyone possessed of such information (lawyer, doctor, counsellor, citizen) to make such disclosure? Should it?

4. What would have been the outcome if Mr. Jones' intentions had only been disclosed to the lawyer? The FLSC's *Model Code* provision on the future harm/public safety exception appears to reflect the outcome in the case. It provides:

> 2.03(3) A lawyer may disclose confidential information, but must not disclose more information than is required, when the lawyer believes on reasonable grounds that there is an imminent risk of death or serious bodily harm, and disclosure is necessary to prevent the death or harm.

Do you agree that this provision corresponds with the principle enunciated in *Smith v. Jones*? What criteria should guide the lawyer in determining whether to exercise his or her discretion to disclose client confidences or keep them secret? Is the deference to lawyer discretion, set out in the language of the Court that the lawyer is "authorized" to disclose or in the *Model Code* that the "lawyer *may* disclose", justified in such situations? Despite the desire for a national consensus on contentious issues such as the public safety/future crime exception, some law societies have declined to follow the *Model Code*. For example, the opening language of the comparable provision in Rule 2.03(3) of the Saskatchewan *Code of Professional Conduct* provides that "[a] lawyer *must* disclose confidential information ..." [effective July 1, 2012]. Is this provision inconsistent with *Smith v. Jones*? How does it align with your own values?

5. You will notice that the *Model Code* provision speaks of "harm" rather than "crime". Should the exception be limited to future "crimes" rather than other potentially harmful behaviour that a client may be planning, and which intention the client communicates to his or her lawyer, but which does not meet the definition of a crime? Should the primary focus be on the potential legal consequences for the client, and the protection afforded the client in those circumstances, or should we focus instead on the consequences upon others of the client's potential actions? In some cases a client may be devastated by "financial harm". If the objective is to protect the public interest from serious harm, why would "financial harm" be excluded from the exception? What does the profession's choice among these options imply with respect to the balance between a duty to clients and a duty to the wider public interest?

6. As a general rule, citizens, including those acting in a professional capacity in relation to children, are under a positive duty to report situations of child abuse or neglect pursuant to the provisions of provincial child protection legislation. Failure to report constitutes an offence under the legislation. Consider, however, the following legislative provisions as they relate to lawyers representing clients, and try to assess your obligations as a lawyer, and your own personal sentiments, in the two differing situations. In Ontario, the reporting obligations are set out in section 72 of the *Child and Family Services Act*.[5] In the more general "reporting obligation" provision a "solicitor" is included.[6] However, section 72(8) provides: "Nothing in this section abrogates any privilege that may exist between a solicitor and his or her client." By contrast, the comparable provision in the Newfoundland

---

[5] R.S.O. 1990, c. C.11.

[6] *Ibid.*, s. 72(5).

and Labrador legislation, section 11 of the *Children and Youth Care and Protection Act*,[7] imposes upon citizens, including solicitors (s. 11(5)(d)), a duty to report where a child is or may be in need of protective intervention, and provides in section 11(6) that "[t]his section applies notwithstanding that the information is confidential or privileged ..." without any specific exception being made for solicitors. What are the competing public policy motivations behind these two conflicting approaches? How would you deal with information from your client that relates to child abuse or neglect in the two different jurisdictions? How would you feel about it?

7. *Canada v. Solosky*[8] was a case in which penitentiary officials were found to be justified in opening an inmate's letters to his lawyer on the grounds of public safety, even though there appears to have been no evidence that the inmate was communicating to his lawyer about an intention to cause serious harm to anyone. Does *Smith v. Jones* suggest that the entitlement of penitentiary officials to open inmates' mail to their lawyers is circumscribed? Does the general framework for the application of legislated exceptions to confidentiality and privilege cover the situation?

8. You will have noted that the courts and the legal profession place an extremely high value on lawyer-client confidentiality, to the extent that the risk of harm to others is often a secondary concern. Now consider Rule 2.03(5) of the *Model Code*:

    > A lawyer may disclose confidential information in order to establish or collect the lawyer's fees, but must not disclose more information than is required.

    In view of the very high value of lawyer-client confidentiality, where important public interest values are often given secondary consideration, how can this exception be justified?

Scenario One

A client comes to you, ostensibly to arrange for a will to be prepared. In the course of the discussion he advises you that he is motivated to get a will because he has contracted HIV and is concerned that it could develop into AIDS. He contracted the virus through an affair and knows that if he tells his wife she will leave him and take the children. For this reason he has not told his wife of his condition and, as has been their practice, he is continuing to have unprotected sex with her. Despite your urgings, he is not immediately prepared to inform his wife of his condition or change his sexual practices. What would you do? On what basis would you justify your course of action?

Scenario Two

A client advises you, in the course of his discussions about his legal matters, that for a variety of reasons (financially and personally) his life holds no future use, and that he intends to commit suicide. In discussing the matter

---

7   S.N.L. 2010, c. C-12.2.
8   [1979] S.C.J. No. 130, [1980] 1 S.C.R. 821 (S.C.C.).

with him, you conclude that he is quite serious with respect to his intentions. What, if anything, would you do with this information?

Scenario Three

A client advises you that his elderly mother is terminally ill and is constantly in great pain. There is no hope of recovery and virtually no prospect that his mother's pain can be moderated. She wishes to end her life but is too weak to do so. She has asked her son (who is your client) for assistance and he has agreed to assist her in committing suicide. He has come to you for advice on his potential liability. You are satisfied that the son intends to assist his mother in this way and you are equally satisfied that his mother is mentally alert and clear in her own intentions. What, if anything, would you do in this situation?

3. The "Innocence at Stake" Exception

R. v. McCLURE

[2001] S.C.J. No. 13, [2001] 1 S.C.R. 445
(S.C.C., McLachlin C.J.C. and L'Heureux-Dubé, Gonthier, Iacobucci, Major, Bastarache, Binnie, Arbour and LeBel JJ.)

[McClure was charged with a number of sexual offences against former students. Another person, J.C., learned of the charges and came forward with further allegations, including that J.C. himself had been sexually assaulted. J.C. also commenced a civil action against McClure. McClure sought production of J.C.'s civil litigation file to "determine the nature of [J.C.'s] allegations first made by J.C. to his solicitor and to assess the extent of [J.C.'s] motive to fabricate or exaggerate the incidents of abuse". The trial judge allowed limited access to J.C.'s litigation file to enable McClure to make full answer and defence. The matter was ultimately appealed to the Supreme Court of Canada.]

MAJOR J.:— This appeal revisits the reach of solicitor-client privilege. This privilege comes with a long history. Its value has been tested since early in the common law. Its importance has not diminished.

Solicitor-client privilege describes the privilege that exists between a client and his or her lawyer. This privilege is fundamental to the justice system in Canada. The law is a complex web of interests, relationships and rules. The integrity of the administration of justice depends upon the unique role of the solicitor who provides legal advice to clients within this complex system. At the heart of this privilege lies the concept that people must be able to speak candidly with their lawyers and so enable their interests to be fully represented.

Interests compete within our legal system. The policy justifying the existence of solicitor-client privilege might clash with an accused's right under s. 7 of the Canadian Charter of Rights and Freedoms to make full answer and defence. This appeal raises the issue of whether the solicitor-client privilege of a third person should yield to permit an accused to make full answer and defence to a criminal charge, and, if so, when.

Solicitor-client privilege and the right to make full answer and defence are integral to our system of justice. Solicitor-client privilege is not absolute so, in rare circumstances, it will be subordinated to an individual's right to make full answer and defence. The problem is when and under what circumstances the right to full answer and defence will override the solicitor-client privilege. ...

. . . . .

III. Issues

1.   Should the solicitor-client privilege ever give way to an accused's right to full answer and defence and if so in what circumstances?

2.   If solicitor-client privilege should yield, what is the appropriate test?

3.   Should the trial judge have ordered the litigation file to be disclosed in the circumstances of this case?

IV. Analysis

A.   Evolution of Solicitor-Client Privilege

Solicitor-client privilege is part of and fundamental to the Canadian legal system. While its historical roots are a rule of evidence, it has evolved into a fundamental and substantive rule of law.

. . . . .

... The debate surrounding the origin of solicitor-client privilege while of some interest need not be resolved here. Whatever the origin of the privilege, it has clearly evolved into a substantive rule of law in Canada.

. . . . .

The existence of solicitor-client privilege as a fundamental legal right answers little. The solicitor-client privilege must be examined in the context of other types of privileges to demonstrate its unique status within the legal system.

B.   Types of Privilege

The law recognizes a number of communications as worthy of confidentiality. The protection of these communications serves a public interest and they are generally referred to as privileged.

There are currently two recognized categories of privilege: relationships that are protected by a "class privilege" and relationships that are not protected by a class privilege but may still be protected on a "case-by-case" basis. See *R. v. Gruenke*, [1991] 3 S.C.R. 263, per Lamer C.J., at p. 286, for a description of "class privilege":

The parties have tended to distinguish between two categories: a "blanket", *prima facie*, common law, or "class" privilege on the one hand, and a "case-by-case" privilege on the other. The first four terms are used to refer to a privilege which was recognized at common law and one for which there is a *prima facie* presumption of inadmissibility (once it has been established that the relationship fits within the class) unless the party urging admission can show why the communications should not be privileged (i.e., why they should be admitted into evidence as an exception to the general rule). Such communications are excluded not because the evidence is not relevant, but rather because, there are overriding policy reasons to exclude this relevant evidence. Solicitor-client communications appear to fall within this first category .... [Emphasis in original.]

For a relationship to be protected by a class privilege, thereby warranting a *prima facie* presumption of inadmissibility, the relationship must fall within a traditionally protected class. Solicitor-client privilege, because of its unique position in our legal fabric, is the most notable example of a class privilege. Other examples of class privileges are spousal privilege ... and informer privilege (which is a subset of public interest immunity).

Other confidential relationships are not protected by a class privilege, but may be protected on a case-by-case basis. Examples of such relationships include doctor-patient, psychologist-patient, journalist-informant and religious communications. ...

. . . . .

C.   Rationale of Solicitor-Client Privilege

The foregoing privileges, such as communication between a doctor and his patient, do not occupy the unique position of solicitor-client privilege or resonate with the same concerns. This privilege, by itself, commands a unique status within the legal system. The important relationship between a client and his or her lawyer stretches beyond the parties and is integral to the workings of the legal system itself. The solicitor-client relationship is a part of that system, not ancillary to it. See *Gruenke* ...:

The *prima facie* protection for solicitor-client communications is based on the fact that the relationship and the communications between solicitor and client are essential to the effective operation of the legal system. Such communications are inextricably linked with the very system which desires the disclosure of the communication [...] In my view, religious communications, notwithstanding their social importance, are not inextricably linked with the justice system in the way that solicitor-client communications surely are.

It is this distinctive status within the justice system that characterizes the solicitor-client privilege as a class privilege, and the protection is available to all who fall within the class.

. . . . .

The importance of solicitor-client privilege to both the legal system and society as a whole assists in determining whether and in what circumstances the privilege should yield to an individual's right to make full answer and defence. The law is complex. Lawyers have a unique role. Free and candid communication between the lawyer and client protects the legal rights of the citizen. It is essential for the lawyer to know all of the facts of the client's position. The existence of a fundamental right to privilege between the two encourages disclosure within the confines of the relationship. The danger in eroding solicitor-client privilege is the potential to stifle communication between the lawyer and client. The need to protect the privilege determines its immunity to attack.

D.   Scope of Solicitor-Client Privilege

Despite its importance, solicitor-client privilege is not absolute. It is subject to exceptions in certain circumstances. *Jones, supra*, examined whether the privilege should be displaced in the interest of protecting the safety of the public ...

However, solicitor-client privilege must be as close to absolute as possible to ensure public confidence and retain relevance. As such, it will only yield in certain clearly defined circumstances, and does not involve a balancing of interests on a case-by-case basis.

Not all communications between a lawyer and her client are privileged. In order for the communication to be privileged, it must arise from communication between a lawyer and the client where the latter seeks lawful legal advice. *Wigmore* ... sets out a statement of the broad rule ...:

> Where legal advice of any kind is sought from a professional legal adviser in his capacity as such, the communications relating to that purpose, made in confidence by the client, are at his instance permanently protected from disclosure by himself or by the legal adviser, except the protection be waived.

As stated, only communications made for the legitimate purpose of obtaining lawful professional advice or assistance are privileged. The privilege may only be waived by the client. See M. M. Orkin, *Legal Ethics: A Study of Professional Conduct* (1957), at p. 84:

> It is the duty of a solicitor to insist upon this privilege which extends to "all communication by a client to his solicitor or counsel for the purpose of obtaining professional advice or assistance in a pending action, or in any other proper matter for professional assistance" [...] The privilege is that of the client and can only be waived by the client.

E.   Full Answer and Defence

While solicitor-client privilege is almost absolute, the question here is whether the privilege should be set aside to permit the accused his right to full answer and defence by permitting him access to a complainant's civil litigation file. It is agreed that the file in this case qualifies for solicitor-client privilege. The solicitor-client privilege and the accused's Charter right to full answer and defence are both protected by law. Which prevails when they clash?

R. v. Seaboyer, [1991] 2 S.C.R. 577, at p. 607, opened this question:

> The right of the innocent not to be convicted is reflected in our society's fundamental commitment to a fair trial, a commitment expressly embodied in s. 11(d) of the Charter. It has long been recognized that an essential facet of a fair hearing is the "opportunity adequately to state [one's] case" ... . This applies with particular force to the accused, who may not have the resources of the state at his or her disposal. Thus ... our courts have held that even informer privilege and solicitor-client privilege may yield to the accused's right to defend himself on a criminal charge: ... . [...]

Rules and privileges will yield to the Charter guarantee of a fair trial where they stand in the way of an innocent person establishing his or her innocence ... This Court has held that informer privilege will yield in circumstances where to fail to do so will result in a wrongful conviction. Our system will not tolerate conviction of the innocent. However, an accused's right to make full answer and defence in our system, while broad, is understandably not perfect. Section 7 of the Charter entitles an accused to a fair hearing but not always to the most favourable procedures that could possibly be imagined ...

F.   Solicitor-Client Privilege vs. Full Answer and Defence

Solicitor-client privilege and the right to make full answer and defence are principles of fundamental justice. The right of an accused to full answer and defence is personal to him or her and engages the right to life, liberty, security of the person and the right of the innocent not to be convicted. Solicitor-client privilege while also personal is broader and is important to the administration of justice as a whole. It exists whether or not there is the immediacy of a trial or of a client seeking advice.

The importance of both of these rights means that neither can always prevail. In some limited circumstances, the solicitor-client privilege may yield to allow an accused to make full answer and defence. What are those circumstances?

. . . . .

H.   The Innocence at Stake Test for Solicitor-Client Privilege

... The appropriate test by which to determine whether to set aside solicitor-client privilege is the innocence at stake test, set out below. Solicitor-client privilege should be set aside only in the most unusual cases. Unless individuals can be certain that their communications with their solicitors will remain entirely confidential, their ability to speak freely will be undermined.

In recognition of the central place of solicitor-client privilege within the administration of justice, the innocence at stake test should be stringent. The privilege should be infringed only where core issues going to the guilt of the accused are involved and there is a genuine risk of a wrongful conviction.

Before the test is even considered, the accused must establish that the information he is seeking in the solicitor-client file is not available from any other source and he is otherwise unable to raise a reasonable doubt as to his guilt in any other way.

By way of illustration, if the accused could raise a reasonable doubt at his trial on the question of mens rea by access to the solicitor-client file but could also raise a reasonable doubt with the defence of alibi and/or identification, then it would be unnecessary to use the solicitor-client file. The innocence of the accused would not be at stake but instead it is his wish to mount a more complete defence that would be affected. On the surface it may appear harsh to deny access as the particular privileged evidence might raise a reasonable doubt, nonetheless, the policy reasons favouring the protection of the confidentiality of solicitor-client communications must prevail unless there is a genuine danger of wrongful conviction.

The innocence at stake test is applied in two stages in order to reflect the dual nature of the judge's inquiry. At the first stage, the accused seeking production of a solicitor-client communication must provide some evidentiary basis upon which to conclude that there exists a communication that could raise a reasonable doubt as to his guilt. At this stage, the judge has to decide whether she will review the evidence.

If the trial judge is satisfied that such an evidentiary basis exists, then she should proceed to stage two. At that stage, the trial judge must examine the solicitor-client file to determine whether, in fact, there is a communication that is likely to raise a reasonable doubt as to the guilt of the accused. It is evident that the test in the first stage (could raise a reasonable doubt) is different than that of the second stage (likely to raise a reasonable doubt). If the second stage of the test is met, then the trial judge should order the production but only of that portion of the solicitor-client file that is necessary to raise the defence claimed.

(1) Stage #1

The first stage of the innocence at stake test for invading the solicitor-client privilege requires production of the material to the trial judge for review. There has to be some evidentiary basis for the request. This is a threshold requirement designed to prevent "fishing expeditions". Without it, it would be too easy for the accused to demand examination of solicitor-client privileged communications by the trial judge. As this request constitutes a significant invasion of solicitor-client privilege, it should not be entered into lightly. On the other hand, the bar cannot be set so high that it can never be met. The trial judge must ask: "Is there some evidentiary basis for the claim that a solicitor-client communication exists that could raise a reasonable doubt about the guilt of the accused?"

. . . . .

That is then followed by a requirement that the communication sought by the accused could raise a reasonable doubt as to his guilt. This must be considered in light of what the accused knows. It is likely that the accused who, it must be remembered, has had no access to the file sought, may only provide a description of a possible communication. It would be difficult to produce and unfair to demand anything more precise. It is only at stage two that a court determines conclusively that such a communication actually exists.

. . . . .

(2) Stage #2

Once the first stage of the innocence at stake test for setting aside the solicitor-client privilege has been met, the trial judge must examine that record to determine whether, in fact, there exists a communication that is likely to raise a reasonable doubt as to the accused's guilt. The trial judge must ask herself the following question: "Is there something in the solicitor-client communication that is likely to raise a reasonable doubt about the accused's guilt?"

. . . . .

The trial judge does not have to conclude that the information definitely will raise a reasonable doubt. If this were the case, the trial would effectively be over as soon as the trial judge ordered the solicitor-client file to be produced. There would be nothing left to decide. Instead, the information must likely raise a reasonable doubt as to the accused's guilt. Also, upon reviewing the evidence, if the trial judge finds material that will likely raise a reasonable doubt, stage two of the test is satisfied and the information should be produced to the defence even if this information was not argued as a basis for production by the defence at stage one.

I.   Application to the Case at Bar

In this case, the litigation file should not have been produced to the defence.

. . . . .

The first stage of the innocence at stake test for solicitor-client privilege was not met. There was no evidence that the information sought by the respondent McClure could raise a reasonable doubt as to his guilt. Even if the chronology of events in this case — i.e. lawyer, police, therapist, civil suit — was unusual, it does not justify overriding solicitor-client privilege. ...

. . . . .

V.   Disposition

The appeal is allowed and the order for production by Hawkins J. is set aside.

NOTES AND QUESTIONS

1.   In 2002, the Supreme Court again considered the "innocence at stake" exception. In *R. v. Brown*[9] the accused sought information from a lawyer who he alleged

---

9   [2002] S.C.J. No. 35, [2002] 2 S.C.R. 185 (S.C.C.).

may have received information from the lawyer's client suggesting that the client had admitted to having committed the murder for which Brown was charged. In dismissing this application, the Court reaffirmed the *McClure* tests but added four features. First, the Court held that despite the risk that after the fact, it may be discovered that an innocent person was convicted of a crime, the most appropriate mechanism for addressing such an injustice lay with the traditional procedure of appealing to royal prerogative, as codified in section 690 of the *Criminal Code*,[10] and not by relaxing lawyer client privilege. Second, the Court was of the opinion that *McClure* applications are applicable to both oral and written communications between lawyer and client. Third, in those cases where disclosure is mandated, disclosure is to be made to the accused but not the Crown. Fourth, disclosure must be limited to the purpose of adducing information that would avoid a wrongful conviction, and cannot be used to incriminate the privilege holder, who is entitled to "immunity regarding the subsequent use of his privileged communications which would have been protected but for the operation of *McClure*".[11]

2.   As the courts note, the disclosure of client confidences will only be facilitated if the information it generates is highly relevant and likely to affect a decision with respect to charges against the "innocent party". *McClure* deals with the situation where the lawyer for an accused has some awareness of the existence of confidential client information that might assist the defence. The judgments articulate the process by which the quality of this information, and its significance to the defence, is to be determined. This is the most typical situation in which confidences are sought to be disclosed to assist a defendant in a potential "innocence at risk" situation. Does this restrictive approach to access to this information further signal the priority given by the courts and the justice system to the preservation of client confidences, except in the most compelling situations? Is this the right choice?

3.   *Brown* reinforces the limited application of this exception. Are you satisfied with Major J.'s invitation that resort be had to "wrongful conviction processes" and "moderations in the rules of evidence" as alternatives to setting aside solicitor client confidences?

4.   What about circumstances where this information is completely unknown to the accused or his or her counsel? Consider the following situation: A client discloses to you that he is the perpetrator of a serious crime. He shares with you information that confirms for you that he is telling you the truth. He does not want this information disclosed. He is not in any way a suspect. Someone else is believed to have committed this crime and the circumstantial evidence against this person is strong.

Woolley suggests that this

> demonstrates the challenges of the distinction between the lawyer's ethical duty of confidentiality and the solicitor-client privilege. Specifically, there may be circumstances where a lawyer knows that her client committed a crime of which another person has been convicted. Under the current ethical rules, a lawyer in that situation cannot disclose the existence of such information, even to trigger counsel for

---

[10]   R.S.C. 1985, c. C-46.

[11]   *R. v. Brown*, [2002] S.C.J. No. 35, [2002] 2 S.C.R. 185 at paras. 88 and 89 (S.C.C.).

the accused bringing an application under the "innocence at stake" exception. The lawyer may be compelled to produce the information if there is a successful application to involve the "innocence at stake" exception, but cannot voluntarily disclose that the information exists. As often as not this will mean that even if the "innocence at stake" exception could be invoked, the accused will not even be aware that the information exists and that he could bring a court application to obtain it.[12]

How would you deal with such information in your possession? Would it make any difference to your decision if the innocent person was on trial but not yet convicted? Convicted and now incarcerated? Convicted, served his sentence and is now released? Would it make a difference in any of these situations if your client is now deceased? Should any of these decisions be up to you? Is there any way that the issue of your obligations with respect to this information, or your discretion, could be "litigated" in some way? Is it possible to craft an ethical rule that addresses such a situation?

D. LEGISLATIVE EXCEPTIONS TO CONFIDENTIALITY AND PRIVILEGE

As we saw in *Descôteaux v. Mierzwinski*, it is not unusual for law enforcement authorities to suspect that information relevant to the commission of crimes may be in the possession of a lawyer. As we have also seen, there exists a fairly clear body of law and ethics related to the lawyer's obligation to preserve client confidentiality (including confidentiality with respect to documents). At the same time, from time to time Parliament or a provincial legislature has introduced provisions that circumscribe or set aside the client's right to confidentiality. As the following cases illustrate, such provisions are regularly the subject of scrutiny in the courts.

GOODIS v. ONTARIO (MINISTRY OF CORRECTIONAL SERVICES)

[2006] S.C.J. No. 31, 2006 SCC 31
(S.C.C., McLachlin C.J.C. and Bastarache, Binnie, LeBel, Deschamps, Fish, Abella, Charron and Rothstein JJ.)

[A journalist applied pursuant to the Ontario *Freedom of Information and Protection of Privacy Act*[13] for access to all records pertaining to allegations of sexual abuse of offenders by probation officers of the Ontario Ministry of Correctional Services in Cornwall, Ontario. The Ministry claimed solicitor-client privilege with respect to virtually all relevant documents. A Freedom of Information adjudicator ordered that 19 pages be disclosed. On appeal, Blair J. ordered that the entire private record be disclosed to the journalist's counsel to enable counsel to argue Ontario's application for judicial review, subject to

---

[12]   Alice Woolley, *Understanding Lawyers' Ethics in Canada* (Markham, ON: LexisNexis Canada, 2011) at 135.

[13]   R.S.O. 1990, c. F.31.

an undertaking that counsel not disclose the information to his journalist client. In further appeals, the matter was argued as a question of whether the court had jurisdiction to control its own process on this issue, one part of which would be the authority to order limited disclosure and thereby "ensure procedural fairness to all parties". On this basis the Ontario courts upheld the order of Blair J. On appeal to the Supreme Court of Canada, the main issue was framed differently by Rothstein J., who wrote the unanimous decision of the Court.]

ROTHSTEIN J.:—

. . . . .

There are two issues in this appeal:

(a) Can the records in issue be disclosed to counsel for the requester notwithstanding the Ministry's claim of solicitor-client privilege?

(b) Is the Divisional Court bound by the provisions of the *Access Act* such that the prohibition on the Commissioner's disclosing records applies to the court?

. . . . .

The substantive rule laid down in *Descôteaux* is that a judge must not interfere with the confidentiality of communications between solicitor and client "except to the extent absolutely necessary in order to achieve the ends sought by the enabling legislation". ...

. . . . .

(3) Meaning of Absolute Necessity

Absolute necessity is as restrictive a test as may be formulated short of an absolute prohibition in every case. The circumstances in which the test has been met exemplify its restrictive nature. In *Solosky* ... for example, it was found that subject to strict safeguards, mail received by an inmate at a penitentiary could be inspected to maintain the safety and security of the penitentiary. Similarly, in *McClure*, it was found that documents subject to privilege could be disclosed where there was a genuine danger of wrongful conviction because the information was not available from other sources and the accused could not otherwise raise a reasonable doubt as to his guilt.

While I cannot rule out the possibility, it is difficult to envisage circumstances where the absolute necessity test could be met if the sole purpose of disclosure is to facilitate argument by the requester's counsel on the question of whether privilege is properly claimed. Hearing from both sides of an issue is a principle to be departed from only in exceptional circumstances. However, privilege is a subject with which judges are acquainted. They are well equipped in the ordinary case to determine whether a record is subject to privilege. There is no evidence in this case that disclosure of records to counsel for the purpose of arguing whether or not they are privileged is absolutely necessary.

. . . . .

(5) Conclusion on Solicitor-Client Privilege

In sum, I agree with the Ministry that there is no justification for establishing a new or different test for disclosure of records subject to a claim for solicitor-client privilege in an access to information case.

I am of the respectful opinion that the Ontario courts were in error in permitting disclosure of all the documents in this case. The appropriate test for any document claimed to be subject to solicitor-client privilege is "absolute necessity". That test was not applied. Had it been, disclosure of all the records would not have been ordered.

I am mindful that openness of the court's process is a recognized principle. However, as with all general principles, there are exceptions. Records that are subject to a claim of solicitor-client privilege in an access to information case are such an exception. Absent absolute necessity in order to achieve the end sought by the enabling legislation, such records may not be disclosed. As stated, the evidence disclosed no such absolute necessity in this case.

. . . . .

LAW SOCIETY OF SASKATCHEWAN v. E.F.A. MERCHANT, Q.C.

[2008] S.J. No. 623, 2008 SKCA 128, [2009] 3 W.W.R. 279
(Sask. C.A., J. Klebuc C.J.S., R.G. Richards and Y.G.K. Wilkinson JJ.A.
Leave to appeal refused: [2008] S.C.C.A. No. 538 (S.C.C.).)

[The Law Society was investigating a complaint that Merchant, a lawyer, disobeyed a court order requiring Merchant to pay into court any funds that his client, Hunter, received from a residential school claim to secure his child support obligations. Pending Merchant's appeal from the order, the client's former wife received information that Hunter had received a settlement six months earlier. The former wife obtained court documentation to this effect. She wrote to the Law Society, indicating that Merchant had refused to discuss whether or not he had paid the funds into court as required by the order, or to her former husband, on the basis of solicitor-client privilege. She advised the Law Society that Merchant had made two payments from the settlement funds to her former husband, apparently in violation of the order. The Society began investigating the wife's complaint and requested from Merchant information about his dealings with his client. It applied for an order authorizing it to enter Merchant's offices and take possession of the records relevant to the wife's complaint. The application was refused and the Law Society appealed, arguing (i) that disclosure of privileged information to the Law Society did not constitute a breach of the privilege; and (ii) that the disclosure was "absolutely necessary" for the Law Society to fulfill its statutory responsibilities.]

R.G. RICHARDS J.A.:—

. . . . .

V. Analysis

A. Basic Principles

The essential contours of the law of solicitor-client privilege are well established and are not contested by the parties.

[The Court of Appeal rejected the Law Society's first argument to the effect that "the common law extends the envelope of solicitor-client privilege to include the Law Society".]

. . . . .

The Law Society's second submission is more conventional than its first. It contends the Chambers judge misapplied or misinterpreted the "absolutely necessary" requirement referred to in *Descôteaux v. Mierzwinski*. The Society says it has a statutory obligation to investigate Ms. Wolfe's complaint and has narrowly tailored its request for documents with the result that all the records being sought are required for its investigation. It emphasizes there is no other way of obtaining these records and, in the result, submits the absolute necessity test is satisfied.

The respondents reject this line of analysis. They say the "absolutely neces-sary" consideration cannot be satisfied on the facts at hand because the operation of the *Act* and the Rules does not fully ensure the records sought by the Law Society will be kept confidential and, in particular, do not ensure they will be kept confidential from Ms. Wolfe. This line of argument parallels the reasoning of the Chambers judge who concluded that the "absolutely necessary" standard had not been met because the *Act* and the Rules allowed "too much discretion to adequately address the protection of the solicitor-client privilege".

In my respectful view, the respondents' submissions on this aspect of the appeal are misdirected. In the present context, the "absolutely necessary" concept is concerned not with whether or how effectively the Law Society will protect the confidentiality of privileged records after they are produced. It is concerned with whether those records should be produced at all. The respondents' position, particularly in oral argument, was to the effect that solicitor-client privilege could not be overcome unless the *Act* and the Rules guaranteed the privileged information would be kept strictly confidential. However, this misconceives the "absolutely necessary" concept.

. . . . .

What then is the proper line of analysis in relation to this aspect of the appeal? It seems to me that it is ultimately quite straightforward. First, it must be determined whether the Law Society has the authority to demand the production of records subject to solicitor-client privilege. Second, if the Society has such powers, consideration must be given to whether that authority has been exercised so as not to interfere with privilege except to the extent absolutely necessary. I will examine each of these points in turn.

In assessing the nature of the Law Society's authority to demand access to privileged records, it is useful to begin with the admonishment in *Descôteaux v. Mierzwinski* that legislation which enables incursions on privilege should be interpreted restrictively. More particularly, it is important to note the Supreme Court's caution about inferring powers to abrogate privilege. Most recently, in *Privacy Commissioner of Canada v. Blood Tribe Department of Health, supra,* Binnie J. wrote as follows at para. 11:

> To give effect to this fundamental policy of the law [i.e. solicitor-client privilege], our Court has held that legislative language that may (if broadly construed) allow incursions on solicitor-client privilege must be interpreted restrictively. The privilege cannot be abrogated by inference. Open-textured language governing production of documents will be read *not* to include solicitor-client documents: *Lavallee,* at para. 18; *Pritchard,* at para. 33 ... .
> [Emphasis in original]

In the present case, the Law Society's demand for records was made pursuant to s. 63(1) of the *Act.* As noted above, it reads as follows:

> 63(1) Every member and every person who keeps any of a member's records or other property shall comply with a demand of a person designated by the benchers to produce <u>any of the member's records or other property</u> that the person designated by the benchers reasonably believes are required for the purposes of an investigation pursuant to this Act. [Emphasis added]

This provision does not authorize the Law Society, in so many words, to demand privileged documents. However, in my view, an authority to require production of "*any* of the member's records", found in the unique context of a statute dealing with the regulation of the legal profession, must be taken as referring to documents subject to solicitor-client privilege. ...

It can be readily seen that s. 63(1) stands on quite different ground than the legislation considered by the Supreme Court in the cases where it said the power to limit solicitor-client privilege should not be inferred. ...

. . . . .

... The wording of s. 63(1) of *The Legal Profession Act, 1990,* considered in its statutory context, clearly reveals a legislative intention that the Law Society be empowered to demand access to material subject to solicitor-client privilege. The phrase "... any of a member's records or other property ...", when used in reference to the professional activities of a lawyer, must necessarily include privileged material.

It is clear, therefore, that the Law Society has the authority to demand the production of privileged records. Indeed, the respondents have taken no issue with that notion. ...

As noted above, given the existence of an authority to demand privileged records, the next step in the analysis is to consider the "absolutely necessary" principle. As indicated, the question here is whether the Law Society exercised its power to request records from Mr. Merchant and his firm in a fashion which avoided interfering with privilege except, to use Lamer J.'s words, "to the extent absolutely necessary in order to achieve the end sought by the enabling legislation".

The first point to underline in this regard is that the *Act* gives the Law Society the significant responsibility of governing the legal profession in Saskatchewan and of ensuring the profession's ongoing integrity. Lebel J. explained the importance of this self-governance function in *Finney v. Barreau du Québec*, 2004 SCC 36, [2004] 2 S.C.R 17 at para. 1:

> An independent bar composed of lawyers who are free of influence by public authorities is an important component of the fundamental legal framework of Canadian society. In Canada, our tradition of allowing the legal profession to regulate itself can largely be attributed to a concern for protecting that independence and to lawyers' own staunch defence of their autonomy. In return, the delegation of powers by the State imposes obligations on the governing bodies of the profession, which are then responsible for ensuring the competence and honesty of their members in their dealings with the public.

In order to facilitate and ensure the execution of these responsibilities, the *Act*, in Part IV, lays out a comprehensive regime dealing with issues of competency and discipline. One feature of that regime places a positive obligation on the Society to investigate complaints. Section 40(1) of the *Act* states:

40(1) Where the society:

> (a) receives a complaint with respect to a member, alleging conduct unbecoming; ...

a person designated by the benchers shall review the conduct of the member.

As a result, the Society must delve into complaints in order to satisfy the objectives of the *Act*.

The scope of the demand for records made by the Law Society in this case is also significant. On this front, it is important to note that the Society has carefully framed the demand so as to limit it to matters directly related to Ms. Wolfe's complaint. It has abandoned the original, more general, request for all file material relating to Mr. Hunter's residential school claim and his matrimonial dispute with Ms. Wolfe.

In light of these circumstances, the respondents quite properly concede both that the Law Society has reasonable and probable grounds for requesting the records in question and, significantly, that those records are required for purposes of the investigation which the *Act* obliges the Law Society to conduct.

In my opinion, these concessions effectively determine the result of this appeal. The Law Society has a duty to investigate complaints and the authority to demand privileged records in the course of discharging that duty. It has framed a request which is as narrow as reasonably possible and is thus seeking only those documents necessary to investigate Ms. Wolfe's complaint. It is self-evident that there is no other way to obtain those records or to pursue the investigation. Thus, in my view, this is a clear example of what *Descôteaux v. Mierzwinski* described as "... not interfering with [privilege] except to the extent absolutely necessary in order to achieve the ends sought by the enabling legislation".

[The Appeal was allowed on this basis.]

NOTES AND QUESTIONS

1. Would clearer language in the legislation have satisfied the "absolute necessity" requirement in *Goodis*?

2. One aspect of *Goodis* included the lower court decision that confidential information be disclosed to the lawyer for the other side's counsel, subject to an undertaking that the information not be disclosed to that lawyer's client. To what extent is this justified? To what extent does it compromise the ability of the lawyer to obtain instructions from the client and for the lawyer to give frank and honest advice to the client if the lawyer cannot disclose any of the information on which that advice is based?

3. *Goodis* reminds us of the importance of the "disclosure of confidences" framework articulated by Lamer J. in *Descôteaux*. The reassertion of the principle corresponds with recent court statements of the increasing significance and legal status of confidentiality and privilege. Does this signal a restatement of more conventional lawyering values that are seen to be central to the administration of justice? In *Goodis* the "search for truth" is rendered more difficult as a result. Nevertheless, courts have historically placed some "systemic" values on a higher plane than an unrestricted search for the truth in the individual case. Does this case, as well as *McClure*, suggest that the entitlement to have one's confidences preserved is a higher value than the search for truth in the litigation process?

4. If so, what explains the willingness of the Saskatchewan Court of Appeal in *Merchant* to essentially read into the *Legal Profession Act, 1990*[14] a requirement of disclosure of client confidences, and find it to be absolutely necessary to the administration of the Act? Why would the "search for truth" in an individual lawyer discipline process be given a higher priority than the "search for truth" in *Goodis*?

5. Merchant was subsequently disciplined by the Law Society of Saskatchewan for breaching the court order and for "counselling and/or assisting his client to act in defiance of" the court order.[15]

E. LEGISLATIVE EXCEPTIONS TO CONFIDENTIALITY IN THE CONTEXT OF LAW ENFORCEMENT AND NATIONAL SECURITY

Following the terrorist attacks of September 11, 2001, Parliament sought to ensure that the safety of Canadians was not compromised by the ability of people, perceived to be threats to national security, to shelter behind the safety

---

[14] S.S. 1990-91, c. L-10.1.

[15] See online: <http://www.lawsociety.sk.ca/media/35376/merchantcasesummary.pdf>.

of the confidentiality of their lawyers. Legislation has been introduced in recent years to attempt to circumscribe the normal lawyer-client relationship and in some cases to impose upon lawyers new obligations, either of client identification or client reporting. Again, these legislative regimes have been the subject of scrutiny, including scrutiny from the courts.

Prior to the consideration of "national security" challenges to confidentiality and solicitor client privilege, it is useful to note the degree to which, even in legislation, the privilege has been respected. The issue commonly arises in the context of law office searches pursuant to the police investigation of crimes. In this context, section 488.1 of the *Criminal Code*,[16] the amendments to which were passed in 2001, sets out procedures by which a claim of solicitor-client privilege in relation to law office searches was to be assessed. A group of cases considering the constitutionality of section 488.1 reached the Supreme Court of Canada in 2002. In one of those cases, *R. v. Fink*,[17] the Supreme Court of Canada concluded that the procedures for determining claims of solicitor-client privilege regarding documents seized from lawyers' offices pursuant to search warrants were unconstitutional. The Court noted that the legislation itself acknowledged the fundamental importance of lawyer-client privilege, and that the legislative objective was not to challenge this right but to establish a process by which the evidence could be gathered and the claim of privilege tested. Writing for the majority, Arbour J. noted at paras. 24-25:

> It is critical to emphasize here that all information protected by the solicitor-client privilege is out of reach for the state. It cannot be forcibly discovered or disclosed and it is inadmissible in court. It is the privilege of the client and the lawyer acts as a gatekeeper, ethically bound to protect the privileged information that belongs to his or her client. Therefore, any privileged information acquired by the state without the consent of the privilege holder is information that the state is not entitled to as a rule of fundamental justice.
>
> It is in that context that we must ask whether Parliament has taken all required steps to ensure that there is no deliberate or accidental access to information that is, as a matter of constitutional law, out of reach in a criminal investigation.

She observed that the law sought to respect solicitor-client privilege, but the mechanisms in place for gathering the information to which the privilege might apply, as well as the procedures related to the assessment of the information more than minimally impaired solicitor-client privilege and thus amounted to an unreasonable search and seizure contrary to section 8 of the *Canadian Charter of Rights and Freedoms*[18] (at para. 38). She concluded at para. 49:

---

[16] R.S.C. 1985, c. C-46.

[17] [2002] S.C.J. No. 61, [2002] 3 S.C.R. 209 (S.C.C.).

[18] Part I of the *Constitution Act, 1982*, being Schedule B to the *Canada Act 1982* (U.K.), 1982, c. 11 [hereinafter "the Charter"].

... Solicitor-client privilege is a rule of evidence, an important civil and legal right and a principle of fundamental justice in Canadian law. While the public has an interest in effective criminal investigation, it has no less an interest in maintaining the integrity of the solicitor-client relationship. Confidential communications to a lawyer represent an important exercise of the right to privacy, and they are central to the administration of justice in an adversarial system. Unjustified, or even accidental infringements of the privilege erode the public's confidence in the fairness of the criminal justice system. This is why all efforts must be made to protect such confidences.

The minority, dissenting in part, would have upheld section 488.1 but would have found that in certain aspects of its application it violated client rights.

This provides the context for the following and much more interventionist legislative challenge to lawyer-client confidentiality and privilege.

FEDERATION OF LAW SOCIETIES OF CANADA v. CANADA (ATTORNEY GENERAL)

[2011] B.C.J. No. 1779, 2011 BCSC 1270
(B.C.S.C., L.B. Gerow J.)

[In 2001, the Government of Canada established a "Regime" intended to prevent or detect proceeds of crime that might be laundered to assist in criminal activities, in particular the financing of terrorist activities. The legislation and regulations require certain businesses and professions to collect and maintain personal and financial information in relation to their customers that can in some cases be obtained by federal authorities, often related to criminal investigations. Most aspects of the Regime are applicable to lawyers and require them to collect information from their clients and retain it so that the information can be available to law enforcement officials. The Federation of Law Societies of Canada (FLSC), the national coordinating body of the provincial and territorial governing bodies of the legal profession, obtained an injunction in 2001, preventing the legislation from being applicable to lawyers and law firms pending a trial on their petition for an order that the legislation, in its application to lawyers, contravened sections 7 (principles of fundamental justice) and 8 (unreasonable search and seizure) of the Charter and could not be rescued by section 1 (the reasonable limits provision). During the currency of the injunction, law societies in most provinces and territories implemented "client identification" and "large cash payment" or "no cash" rules intended to impede the use of lawyers' offices — either knowingly or unwittingly — for money-laundering and related illicit uses. The FLSC's position in the case was that the legislative Regime contravened section 7 by jeopardizing the liberty of lawyers and clients in a manner that failed to conform with three principles of fundamental justice, namely: (a) solicitor-client confidentiality and privilege; (b) lawyers' duty of loyalty to their clients; and (c) the independence of the bar. Section 8 arguments were not considered by the court.]

. . . . .

L.B. GEROW J.:—

Introduction

... The petitioner is challenging the anti-money laundering and terrorist financing legislation that was enacted by the federal government, insofar that it applies to lawyers, on the basis that it is unconstitutional. ...

. . . . .

The respondent takes the position that Parliament is constitutionally able to impose anti-money laundering and terrorist financing obligations on lawyers. The respondent asserts that the legislation is valid and has been adopted to address the pressing and substantial problem of money laundering and terrorist financing. Its proposed application respects both clients' and lawyers' constitutionally protected rights under the *Charter*. Therefore, the provisions impugned by the petitioner are constitutionally sound and should be permitted to operate in order to address the scourge of money laundering and terrorist financing as Parliament has intended.

The issues are: ...

   3)   Do the impugned provisions, as they apply to legal counsel and law firms, infringe ss. 7 and 8 of the *Charter*? If so, is the infringement reasonable and justified under s. 1 of the *Charter*?

   4)   If the impugned provisions infringe the *Charter*, what is the appropriate remedy?

. . . . .

Background

. . . . .

Money laundering and terrorist financing are significant public policy concerns with international dimensions. In order to address them, Parliament has enacted the *Act* which imposes anti-money laundering and terrorist financing obligations on certain businesses and professions that are vulnerable to being exploited by criminals who seek to conduct illicit transactions. These obligations include requiring financial institutions and intermediaries to conduct client identification and verification, keep records of financial transactions, establish internal anti-money laundering and terrorist financing programs and report certain transactions to the Financial Transactions Reports Analysis Centre of Canada ("FINTRAC").

As indicated by its title, the [*Proceeds of Crime (Money Laundering) and Terrorist Financing*] *Act* concerns money laundering and terrorist financing. By adopting this legislation, Canada is fulfilling its commitment to the international community to effect a coordinated response to the crimes of money laundering and terrorist financing.

The objects of the *Act* are stated in s. 3, which provides:

   The object of this Act is

(*a*) to implement specific measures to detect and deter money laundering and the financing of terrorist activities and to facilitate the investigation and prosecution of money laundering offences and terrorist activity financing offences, including

> (i) establishing record keeping and client identification requirements for financial services providers and other persons or entities that engage in businesses, professions or activities that are susceptible to being used for money laundering or the financing of terrorist activities,
>
> (ii) requiring the reporting of suspicious financial transactions and of cross-border movements of currency and monetary instruments, and
>
> (iii) establishing an agency that is responsible for dealing with reported and other information;

(*b*) to respond to the threat posed by organized crime by providing law enforcement officials with the information they need to deprive criminals of the proceeds of their criminal activities, while ensuring that appropriate safeguards are put in place to protect the privacy of persons with respect to personal information about themselves; and

(*c*) to assist in fulfilling Canada's international commitments to participate in the fight against transnational crime, particularly money laundering, and the fight against terrorist activity.

. . . . .

The petitioner asserts that the Regime violates s. 7 of the *Charter* by jeopardizing the liberty of lawyers and clients in a manner that fails to conform with the principles of fundamental justice, namely:

(a) solicitor-client confidentiality and privilege;

(b) lawyers' duty of loyalty to their clients; and

(c) the independence of the bar.

The petitioner's central complaint is that the Regime requires lawyers to collect information from their clients and retain it so that the information can be available for law enforcement officials if they wish to review it. The petitioner says this requirement turns lawyers into state agents tasked with collecting information from their own clients for potential use by the state against the clients.

. . . . .

FINTRAC is an administrative financial intelligence unit that operates independently from law enforcement agencies. It is established under the *Act* and is mandated to facilitate the detection, prevention and deterrence of money laundering and terrorist financing by collecting information, analyzing it and disclosing it to law enforcement agencies. FINTRAC is also responsible for monitoring compliance with anti-money laundering and terrorist financing obligations imposed on certain businesses and professions under the *Act*.

The petitioner agrees that requiring lawyers to take steps to deter criminals from employing them to launder money and finance terrorism is a valid societal goal. However, any system to deter money laundering and terrorist financing must respect Canada's fundamental constitutional principles. The petitioner says that the law societies have developed rules to regulate the conduct of lawyers, which ensure that the goal of deterring criminals from employing lawyers is met and which strikes the appropriate balance with Canada's constitutional structure. In this context, the impugned provisions constitute an unjustifiable infringement of ss. 7 and 8 of the *Charter*.

Lawyers were first made subject to the Regime in November 2001. As of that date, lawyers were required to report to FINTRAC "suspicious transactions"; i.e. transactions for which there were reasonable grounds to suspect they related to the commission of a money laundering offence or a terrorist financing offence.

. . . . .

Following the granting of the injunctions, the various provincial law societies have adopted rules regarding the receipt of cash, and client identification and verification [often referred to as the "No Cash" Rule and the "Client Identification" Rule].

. . . . .

The law societies have taken steps over the past few years to educate their members about the No Cash Rule and the Client ID Rule. The law societies have adopted two primary means to ensure that lawyers comply with law society rules; namely, annual reports and audits.

. . . . .

The goal of all of these activities is to ensure that the law societies discharge their primary mandate, of regulating the legal profession in the public interest.

. . . . .

Do the recording and related obligations imposed on lawyers pursuant to Part 1 of the Act infringe s. 7 of the Charter?

For the following reasons, I have concluded that the recording and related obligations imposed on lawyers pursuant to Part 1 of the *Act* infringe s. 7 of the *Charter*.

. . . . .

The analytical structure governing a s. 7 determination requires an applicant to establish that:

- the impugned legislation constitutes a deprivation of life, liberty or security of the person; and

- the deprivation does not accord with the principles of fundamental justice. ...

. . . . .

In *R. v. D.B.*, at paras. 45-46, the Supreme Court of Canada reiterated that a framework for assessing whether a principle meets the threshold required to be a principle of fundamental justice had been provided in *R. v. Malmo-Levine*, 2003 SCC 74, [2003] 3 S.C.R. 571, and *Canadian Foundation for Children, Youth and the Law v. Canada*, 2004 SCC 4, [2004] 1 S.C.R. 76. The petitioner must establish the following:

(1) there is a legal principle;

(2) there is a consensus that the rule or principle is fundamental to the way in which the legal system ought fairly to operate; and

(3) the principle is capable of being identified with sufficient precision so as to yield a manageable standard against which to measure deprivations of life, liberty or security of the person.

As stated earlier, the petitioner submits that the impugned provisions violate the principles of fundamental justice by:

- infringing on solicitor-client privilege;

- infringing the lawyer's duty of loyalty to the client; and

- compromising the independence of the bar.

The petitioner alleges that by requiring lawyers to collect information from their clients and retain it so that the information can be available for law enforcement officials if they wish to review it, the Regime turns lawyers into state agents. As a result, the Regime puts the lawyers' clients' liberty at risk.

. . . . .

The respondent states that the framers of the *Charter* did not include solicitor-client privilege as a constitutional right and therefore solicitor-client privilege is not directly protected by s. 7 of the *Charter*. The respondent asserts the statements of the Supreme Court of Canada in *R. v. National Post*, [2010] 1 S.C.R. 477 at para. 39, *R. v. McClure*, [2001] 1 S.C.R. 445 at para. 49, and *Lavallee* at paras. 49 and 51, are, at their highest point, a recognition of solicitor-client privilege as a principle of fundamental justice in the limited circumstances where the client's liberty is directly at stake. ...

. . . . .

The respondent says that therefore, absent a valid constitutional challenge to legislation either through the *Charter* or some other constitutional imperative such as the division of powers, Parliament must be seen as competent to legislate a limitation or restriction on solicitor-client privilege. The importance of the privilege, and the principles that underlie it, are protected by limiting interference with the privilege to those occasions when it is absolutely necessary, and by requiring that Parliament use clear and specific language to express its intention to abrogate the privilege.

. . . . .

... The Supreme Court of Canada has stated that the solicitor-client privilege is a "principle of fundamental justice and civil right of supreme importance in Canadian law": *Lavallee,* at para. 36. It is not an absolute right, and is subject to exceptions, but must be as close to absolute as possible to ensure public confidence and retain relevance. As such, solicitor-client privilege will only yield in clearly defined circumstances: *McLure*, at paras. 34-35.

. . . . .

It is irrelevant that the information sought to be collected is not at a level of critical secrecy. Any information that must be collected by a lawyer as a condition of providing legal advice and is solely for potential use by the state interferes to an unacceptable degree with the solicitor-client relationship.

. . . . .

The respondent's submission that the only reason lawyers are required to collect and retain information from their clients is to ensure that the lawyers are complying with their obligations under the legislation is inconsistent with its submissions that the Regime has been enacted in order to combat money laundering and terrorist financing and the need to have lawyers subject to what it describes as anti-money laundering and terrorist financing measures. In its submission at paragraphs 211 and 220, the respondent states:

> 211. The primary rationale for imposing these record keeping requirements on lawyers is to deter illicit transactions, failing which they may help establish a paper trail with respect to illicit funds that could, in appropriate circumstances and with the proper judicial authorization, be accessed by law enforcement.

> 220. FINTRAC itself cannot impose penalties. Rather, if FINTRAC becomes aware of information obtained through its compliance audits that it suspects on reasonable grounds is evidence of a contravention of the anti-money laundering requirements, it may disclose this information to the appropriate law enforcement agencies.

It is clear from the respondent's submissions that lawyers are being required to collect information from their clients to establish a paper trail for law enforcement agencies to access. In my opinion the impugned provisions infringe the solicitor-client relationship insofar as they provide that lawyers are required to obtain and retain information about their clients which can be accessed by FINTRAC and provided to law enforcement agencies.

. . . . .

[The respondent's own evidence was that] the client identification records, which are required to be kept under the Regime, "may assist law enforcement in investigating and prosecuting money launderers, and may also help detect the path that illicit funds have taken through the financial system." In other words, she deposes that the purpose of the Regime is to require lawyers to create and keep a paper trail to be used by law enforcement to incriminate the lawyers' clients.

. . . . .

To assist in meeting this purpose, the Regime provides that lawyers must:

- identify clients, and verify that identity, when the lawyer receives $3,000 or more in the course of a transaction;

- create, obtain and retain prescribed records in relation to the client and the transaction;

- produce to FINTRAC any document or information on demand, including by warrantless search, and provide FINTRAC with client names and contact information; and

- develop and maintain a regime to ensure compliance with these obligations.

Pursuant to s. 33.3 of the *Regulations*, "every legal counsel and every legal firm" is obliged to comply with the client identification and verification provisions when, on behalf of any person or entity, they receive or pay funds, or give instructions regarding the receipt or payment of funds, other than funds received or paid in respect of professional fees, disbursements, expenses or bail.

Section 33.4 of the *Regulations* provides that a "receipt of funds record" must be created when $3,000 or more funds are received in the course of a transaction. "Funds" include cash, currency or securities, or negotiable instruments or other financial instruments, in any form: s. 1(2) of the *Regulations*. The record need not be created if the funds are received from a financial entity or a public body.

. . . . .

In addition to creating a receipt of funds record, a lawyer must verify the identities of those involved. Pursuant to ss. 59.4(1) and 64-67 of the *Regulations*, a lawyer must:

- ascertain the identity of every person who conducts the transaction;

- confirm the existence of and ascertain the name and address of every corporation on whose behalf the transaction is conducted and the names of the corporation's directors; and

- confirm the existence of every entity, other than a corporation, on whose behalf the transaction is conducted.

. . . . .

In his affidavit submitted by the petitioner, Mr. Wilson deposes that some information required by the Regime goes beyond what is required under the law society rules and standard due diligence by lawyers. ...

Sections 68-70 of the *Regulations* provide that the records required by the Regime must be retained for at least five years after the completion of the transaction. The records must be kept in such a way that they can be produced to FINTRAC within 30 days after a demand.

Section 9.6 of the *Act* requires lawyers to implement a program to ensure compliance with their obligations under the Regime. A compliance program must assess the risk of a money laundering or a terrorist activity financing offence in the course of their activities. ...

While s. 10.1 of the *Act* limits the application of the reporting and disclosure requirements under ss. 7 and 9 of the *Act* where lawyers and legal firms are "providing legal services," there is no provision limiting the application of the rest of Part 1 to lawyers and legal firms that are only acting as financial intermediaries; i.e. there is no exemption under the *Act* for lawyers' recording of clients' information even if they are providing legal services.

The *Act* provides that information can be accessed by FINTRAC under ss. 62-64. The whole purpose of the Regime, as indicated by the title of the *Act*, is criminal in nature. The Regime is aimed at "combatting the laundering of proceeds of crime and combatting the financing of terrorist activities," i.e. to detect and prevent criminal activity. As a result, it is my opinion that the exemption for lawyers and legal firms contained in s. 10.1 from the reporting and disclosure requirements under ss. 7 and 9 of the *Act* does not safeguard clients' liberty interests because client information can be accessed under other provisions of the *Act* and *Regulations*.

. . . . .

As set out earlier, s. 65 provides that FINTRAC may disclose to the appropriate law enforcement agencies any information it becomes aware of under ss. 62-63.1 and that it suspects, on reasonable grounds, is evidence of a contravention of Part 1 of the *Act*.

In my view, it is clear that the clients' liberty interests are at stake. The respondent has provided extensive evidence and submissions regarding the problems and criminal activity associated with both money laundering and terrorist financing. The respondent argues that the application of the Regime to lawyers is necessary because "the use of lawyers figures prominently in criminals' efforts to launder the proceeds of their crimes."

The respondent acknowledges in its submissions that one of the purposes of the Regime is to have lawyers create a paper trail which can be used to prosecute their clients for money laundering and terrorist financing. This is consistent with Ms. Grasham's evidence that one of the policy reasons for imposing anti-money laundering measures on lawyers is that "lawyers are vulnerable to being used to effect financial transactions in aid of money laundering." It is also consistent with the object of the *Act* set out in s. 3.

It is apparent that the underlying purpose of the record keeping and record retention provisions of the Regime, as it applies to lawyers and legal firms, is to advance the criminal law interest of deterring, detecting, investigating and prosecuting crimes committed by lawyers' clients by having lawyers create a paper trail that can be used to prosecute their clients. That underlying purpose clearly puts clients' liberty interests at stake.

As noted in *Maranda*, the Supreme Court of Canada's decisions have identified that solicitor-client privilege plays a fundamental role in the criminal justice system and to the protection of the rights of accused persons. To that end, Lebel J. stated at para. 37 that: "[i]t is important that lawyers, who are bound by stringent ethical codes not have their offices turned into archives for the use of the prosecution."

In my opinion, imposing the recording and related obligations contained in Part 1 of the *Act* on legal counsel and legal firms would result in having lawyers' offices turned into archives for the use of the prosecution, and would violate the principles of fundamental justice insofar as it erodes the solicitor-client privilege. As well, as stated earlier, it is my opinion that the impugned provisions put both lawyers and clients' liberty interests in jeopardy. Accordingly, I have concluded that the record collection and related obligations pursuant to Part 1 of the *Act* as it relates to legal counsel and legal firms infringe s. 7 of the *Charter*.

[Justice Gerow found that the objectives of the legislation were valid in relation to section 1 of the Charter, but they lacked the necessary proportionality to only minimally impair the rights in question.]

As set out earlier, the law societies have adopted detailed client identification and verification requirements and restrictions on the receipt of cash, in addition to their professional conduct rules. Further, law societies undertake an extensive range of activities to promote and ensure compliance with their rules, including education, annual self-reporting, audits and investigations.

As such, to the extent that one of the purposes of the Regime is to ensure adequate client identification and record-keeping by professionals, those objectives are already being met in respect of the legal profession by virtue of the law societies' regulation of their members.

The respondent asserts that the law societies are as much a stranger to the solicitor-client relationship as the FINTRAC and that providing the law societies with access to this information is no less intrusive of the solicitor-client privilege than is the case for FINTRAC.

However, this argument does not acknowledge the role of self-regulation of the legal profession to ensure an independent bar and the protection of fundamental legal values such as the solicitor-client relationship.

For example in British Columbia the *Legal Profession Act*, S.B.C. 1998, c. 9, s. 3 states the object and duty of the law society is "to uphold and protect the public interest in the administration of justice".

The public interest has been found by the courts to be fundamentally connected to a self-regulating bar that is independent from the influence of the State. In *Canada (Attorney General) v. Law Society of British Columbia*, [1982] 2 S.C.R. 307 at 335-336, the Court stated:

... The independence of the Bar from the state in all its pervasive manifestations is one of the hallmarks of a free society. Consequently, regulation of these members of the law profession by the state must, so far as by human ingenuity it can be so designed, be free from state interference, in the political sense, with the delivery of services to the individual citizens in the state, particularly in fields of public and criminal law. The public interest in a free society knows no area more sensitive than the independence, impartiality and availability to the general public of the members of the Bar and through those members, legal advice and services generally.

It follows that, where a law society is exercising its role by regulating its members to protect the public's interests, replacement of that role with a federal statute that permits the intrusion on solicitor-client privilege is contrary to the public interest.

The protection of the solicitor-client privilege has evolved in the case law to a fundamental principle of law: *Lavallee* at para. 36. There are few reported cases in which the Courts have supported a government agency in a contest with solicitor-client privilege.

By comparison, the courts have supported law societies in their need to review otherwise privileged documents in the course of carrying out their mandate of regulating the legal profession in the public interest.

Two theories have emerged to explain why law societies are entitled to review privileged documents as part of their investigation of lawyers' conduct. On one justification, law societies may review privileged communications because the privilege extends to the law society, usually by reference to its statutory duties. Accordingly, no breach of the privilege occurs. This is sometimes referred to as the "envelope theory," i.e. that the envelope of privilege extends to the law societies. The second justification for permitting law societies to review privileged documents when investigating lawyers is that it is "absolutely necessary" for them to do so in order to meet the responsibility of self-regulation.

Solicitor-client privilege has given way to the overriding principle that members of law societies must be required to make full disclosure of their activities as professionals when under investigation for complaints by the law societies ...

In *Law Society of Saskatchewan v. Merchant*, 2008 SKCA 128 at paras. 54-58, the court found that "the *Act* gives the Law Society the significant responsibility of governing the legal profession in Saskatchewan and of ensuring the profession's ongoing integrity" including a duty to investigate complaints. As a result, Law Society review met the "absolutely necessary" test for infringing solicitor-client privilege.

. . . . .

... On a plain reading of s. 88(1) there would be no violation of solicitor-client privilege if the member were to answer the question put to him by counsel for the Law Society. He would be "deemed conclusively not to have breached any duty or obligation" to the client.

The client remains protected pursuant to ss. 88(2) and (3). The former imposes solicitor-client privilege on the recipient of the information and the latter prohibits disclosure of the information except for purposes contemplated by the Act or the Law Society Rules.

In *Stewart McKelvey Stirling Scales v. Nova Scotia Barristers Society*, 2005 NSSC 258, the right of the Nova Scotia Barristers Society to review privileged documents was confirmed even in the absence of specific legislation (although the Nova Scotia legislation did contain provisions protecting the information in the hands of the society). In reaching that conclusion, the Court relied on the unique role of law societies in regulating the legal profession.

Although the reasoning in the judgments varies, primarily on the basis of the underlying legislation in each of the provinces, the results are consistent. The decisions dealing with law societies' review of lawyers' files have consistently recognized the unique role law societies play in the regulation of the legal profession and have consistently supported the necessity of law societies' review of privileged documents as part of that role.

By contrast, there are very few instances where government agencies have been permitted to breach solicitor-client privilege, and no instances where government agencies have been permitted to impose a requirement as a condition of receiving legal advice that clients provide information to the lawyer that the government may wish to access later.

Accordingly, it is my view that the respondent has not established that the provincial and territorial law societies are as much strangers to the solicitor-client relationship as is a government agency.

I agree with the petitioner's submission that the regulation of lawyers by the law societies minimally impairs solicitor-client privilege while providing an effective and constitutional anti-money laundering and terrorist financing regime.

Having the law societies regulate lawyers and law offices in this regard, and leaving the federal government to regulate banks and other professions, is in keeping with the Constitution, which anticipates that various levels of government will cooperate to achieve common goals: Peter W. Hogg, *Constitutional Law of Canada*, loose-leaf, 5th ed., Vol. 1 (Toronto: Carswell, 2007), ch. 5 at 5-45.

Law societies are focused exclusively on regulating the legal profession in the public interest. They do so actively; for example by auditing all of their members every few years. By contrast, the evidence is that over the past five years, FINTRAC has only examined 900 of 75,000 entities subject to the Regime. FINTRAC must supervise many categories of persons and entities that are regulated under the Regime, from financial institutions to securities dealers and from casinos to money services businesses. A considerable number of these persons and entities are otherwise unsupervised, unlike lawyers.

FINTRAC concedes that if lawyers were subject to the Regime, FINTRAC would seek to enter into a Memorandum of Understanding with the law societies or the petitioner, with the aim of having law societies supervise lawyers' compliance with the Regime. In my view, this demonstrates FINTRAC's satisfaction with the law societies' abilities to ensure their members' compliance.

Law society regulation of their members imposes the least intrusion on the integrity of the solicitor-client relationship. As the authorities make clear, maintaining the integrity of the solicitor-client relationship is fundamental to the proper administration of justice in Canada. Any intrusion on that relationship must be minimized to the greatest extent possible. ...

Given the law societies' ongoing mandate and commitment to regulate their members in the public interest, including through specific measures to combat money laundering and terrorist financing, further intrusion has not been demonstrated to be necessary or appropriate.

. . . . .

To the extent that the FATF recommends that certain requirements be imposed by "law or regulation", the professional conduct rules imposed by law societies satisfy that recommendation, as the power to make the rules is conferred by legislation. For example, in British Columbia s. 11 of the *Legal Professions Act* permits the law society to "make rules for the governing of the society, lawyers, articled students and applicants, and for the carrying out of this *Act*."

In my opinion, the regulation of the profession by the law societies satisfies the FATF recommendation that proportionate and dissuasive criminal, civil or administrative sanctions be available for non-compliance with anti-money laundering requirements. The law societies' power to disbar lawyers serves as a strong incentive for lawyers to comply with law society rules, including the no cash and client identification rules. Further, a range of disciplinary options short of disbarment, including reprimands, fines and suspension, are available to the law societies. In any event, FINTRAC cannot impose criminal sanctions. Rather, FINTRAC refers such matters to the police, an option also available to law societies.

Given that the law societies have addressed the issue of client identification and verification as well as restrictions on the receipt of cash, the respondent has not established that the impugned provisions meet this part of the *Oakes* test. The respondent has not in my opinion demonstrated that there is a rational connection between the objective and infringement of the right, that the Regime interferes as little as possible with the right, or that the salutary effects of the measure outweigh its deleterious effects.

As a result, I have concluded that s. 1 does not apply to justify the infringement of the s. 7 *Charter* rights.

. . . . .

Conclusion

In summary, I have concluded that the Regime infringes s. 7 of the *Charter* insofar as it applies to lawyers and law firms because it puts both lawyers and their clients' liberty interests in jeopardy by requiring lawyers to collect and retain information about clients, and make the information available to the government to aid in combating money laundering and terrorist financing. As well, I have concluded that the infringement is not justified under s. 1 of the *Charter*.

. . . . .

NOTES AND QUESTIONS

1. Legislative attempts to circumscribe solicitor-client privilege are not limited to the field of criminal law. In *Canada (Privacy Commissioner) v. Blood Tribe Department of Health*,[19] the Privacy Commissioner for Canada sought access to documents with respect to which solicitor privilege was asserted. The Commissioner sought the right to examine the documents in order to assess the privilege assertion and complete an investigation, pursuant to her jurisdiction and responsibilities under the *Personal Information Protection and Electronic Documents Act*.[20] The initial dispute related to the dismissal of a person from employment with the Blood Tribe. In its decision, the Supreme Court of Canada noted *Pritchard v. Ontario (Human Rights Commission)*[21] and the importance of the prohibition against abrogation of solicitor-client privilege "by inference". The Court found that the Privacy Commissioner did not have status equivalent to a court with respect to access to privileged documents, and that the Privacy Commissioner's assertion that privilege be set aside must meet the same criteria established in *Descôteaux v. Mierzwinski* and *R. v. McClure*. The Court found that access to solicitor client confidences was not "absolutely necessary" to the achievement of the goals of the PIPEDA.

    Does this case represent a preservation of client rights at the expense of the legitimate ability of an officer of Parliament to carry out legislated public duties? Does it represent a choice to preserve the privilege at the expense of "the truth"?

2. When comparing the *FLSC* decision to *R. v. Murray*, excerpted on pages 260 to 268, does there appear to be a distinction drawn between "real" or "physical evidence", which must not be concealed, and "documents", to which a very strong privilege attaches? What is the justification for this distinction?

---

[19]   [2008] S.C.J. No. 45, [2008] 2 S.C.R. 574 (S.C.C.).
[20]   S.C. 2000, c. 5.
[21]   [2004] S.C.J. No. 16, [2004] 1 S.C.R. 809 (S.C.C.).

F. SPECIAL CASES

1. Lawyer-Client Confidentiality and Privilege in the Context of Withdrawal from Representation

A vexing question for lawyers is the circumstance where the lawyer wishes to withdraw from the representation of a client in a court proceeding, most commonly a criminal matter. Codes of Professional Conduct, and in some cases court-generated Rules, have sought to articulate the proper approach to this question. When withdrawing from representation, issues also arise with respect to the lawyer's duty of confidentiality to the client. An obligation of confidentiality does not cease when the representation of the client ceases. However, in some circumstances the need for the lawyer to withdraw from the representation can create challenges for the lawyer's ability to protect the client's confidentiality — the lawyer must withdraw, but must do so in a way that does not jeopardize the client's right to confidentiality. This point was addressed by the Supreme Court in the following case.

R. v. CUNNINGHAM

[2010] S.C.J. No. 10, [2010] 1 S.C.R. 331
(S.C.C., McLachlin C.J.C. and Binnie, LeBel, Deschamps, Fish,
Abella, Charron, Rothstein and Cromwell JJ.)

[As we saw in Chapter 3, "The Lawyer-Client Relationship", section D.3, "Court Approval of Withdrawal", the Supreme Court of Canada, in *R. v. Cunningham*, articulated the scope of a court's authority to refuse counsel's application for withdrawal from the representation of a client in court proceedings. Associated with this question is the degree to which the lawyer may, or must, disclose the reasons for the application to withdraw, and the degree to which such disclosure might compromise confidentiality or privilege. In *Cunningham* it will be recalled that the lawyer sought to withdraw because of non-payment of fees. The Court also offered views with respect to the lawyer's obligations of disclosure of his or her reason for withdrawal.]

ROTHSTEIN J.:—

. . . . .

Ms. Cunningham and the interveners argue that solicitor-client privilege could be violated in one of two ways: simply by disclosure of the mere fact that the accused has not paid his or her fees, or inadvertent disclosure of privileged information when engaging in a discussion with the court about the reasons for withdrawal.

Concern regarding the protection of solicitor-client privilege is warranted. It need hardly be said that solicitor-client privilege is a fundamental tenet of our legal system. The solicitor-client relationship is integral to the administration of justice; privilege encourages the free and full disclosure by the client required to ensure effective legal representation (see *Smith v. Jones*, ..., at para. 45, *per* Cory J. for the majority, and *R. v. McClure*, ..., at paras. 31 and 33, *per* Major J.).

However, revealing that an accused has not paid his or her fees does not normally touch on the *rationale* for solicitor-client privilege in the criminal context. A client must be able to rely on the confidentiality of the communications made between lawyer and client because only then can there be full and frank discussion of the facts of the case, and the giving and receiving of soundly based legal advice (see *Anderson v. Bank of British Columbia* (1876), 2 Ch. D. 644 (C.A.), at p. 649; relied on in *Smith v. Jones*, at para. 45, and *McClure*, at para. 32). There has been no explanation as to why an accused would be any more inclined to withhold information from counsel, where the court has discretion over withdrawal, than where counsel can unilaterally withdraw.

In arguing that disclosure of the mere fact that an accused has not paid or will not be paying his or her legal fees is protected by solicitor-client privilege, the Law Societies of British Columbia and Yukon rely on this Court's decisions in *Descôteaux v. Mierzwinski*, ..., and *Maranda v. Richer*, ..., where this Court held that, in the context of a law office search, an accused's financial and fee information may be privileged. In *Maranda*, the Court was concerned that fee information, specifically the amount of fees and disbursements, may appear to be "neutral" when in fact disclosure of the information could be prejudicial to the accused. In particular, LeBel J. stated that fee information

> might enable an intelligent investigator to reconstruct some of the client's comings and goings, and to assemble evidence concerning his presence at various locations based on the documentation relating to his meetings with his lawyer. [para. 24]

This information could then be used to charge and/or convict the client. Because of the potentially detrimental effect of disclosure on the client, fee information is considered *prima facie* privileged for the purposes of the search. If the Crown seeks disclosure, the ultimate decision of whether the fee information is *in fact* privileged is made by the court, not the police.

Counsel seeking to withdraw for non-payment of legal fees is a decidedly different context from a police search of counsel's accounts and records. The most significant difference is the content of the information being disclosed. The only information revealed by counsel seeking to withdraw is the sliver of information that the accused has not paid or will not be paying fees. It has not been explained how, in this case, this sliver of information could be prejudicial to the accused. Indeed, it is hard to see how this simple fact alone could be used against the accused on the merits of the criminal proceeding: it is unrelated to the information given by the client to the lawyer, and unrelated to the advice given by the lawyer to the client. It would not be possible to infer from the bare fact of non-payment of fees any particular activities of the accused that pertain to the criminal charges against him.

To be sure, this is the case where non-payment of fees is not linked to the merits of the matter and disclosure of non-payment will not cause prejudice to the accused. However, in other legal contexts, payment or non-payment of fees may be relevant to the merits of the case, for example, in a family law dispute where support payments are at issue and a client is alleging inability to pay. Or disclosure of non-payment of fees may cause prejudice to the client, for example, where the opposing party may be prompted to bring a motion for security for costs after finding out that the other party is unable to pay its legal fees. Where payment or non-payment of fees is relevant to the merits of the case, or disclosure of such information may cause prejudice to the client, solicitor-client privilege may attach.

Disclosure of non-payment of fees in cases where it is unrelated to the merits and will not cause prejudice to the accused is not an exception to privilege, such as the innocence at stake or public safety exceptions (see generally *McClure* and *Smith v. Jones*). Rather, non-payment of legal fees in this context does not attract the protection of solicitor-client privilege in the first place. However, nothing in these reasons, which address the application, or non-application, of solicitor-client privilege in disclosures to a court, should be taken as affecting counsel's ethical duty of confidentiality with respect to payment or non-payment of fees in other contexts.

In the alternative, Ms. Cunningham and the interveners argue that counsel may inadvertently disclose privileged information when explaining the reasons for withdrawing and answering questions from the judge. They argue that this risk is so unacceptable that it requires the court to decline to exercise any discretion to refuse counsel's request to withdraw. They point to *Leask* where counsel sought withdrawal due to irreconcilable differences between counsel and the accused. The provincial court judge wanted specific details to determine if the differences could be resolved (*Leask*, at pp. 318-19). The accused in *Leask* was drawn into the conversation with the judge as well. They argue that this is dangerous because the accused may unknowingly waive his or her right to privilege and disclose information that is otherwise protected.

I agree that the exchange initiated by the provincial court judge in *Leask* was inappropriate. The judge repeatedly pressed counsel for detailed reasons for withdrawal, and continued to press even when counsel attempted to rely on the professional rules of conduct. The judge bluntly asked the accused if he objected to counsel disclosing the specific reason for withdrawal. I think it is fair to say that what occurred in *Leask* was unacceptable.

… The remote possibility that a judge will inappropriately attempt to elicit privileged information in hearing the application does not justify leaving the decision to withdraw exclusively to counsel.

. . . . .

The court's exercise of discretion to decide counsel's application for with-drawal should be guided by the following principles.

If counsel seeks to withdraw far enough in advance of any scheduled proceedings and an adjournment will not be necessary, then the court should allow the withdrawal. In this situation, there is no need for the court to enquire into counsel's reasons for seeking to withdraw or require counsel to continue to act.

Assuming that timing is an issue, the court is entitled to enquire further. Counsel may reveal that he or she seeks to withdraw for ethical reasons, non-payment of fees, or another specific reason (e.g. workload of counsel) if solicitor-client privilege is not engaged. Counsel seeking to withdraw for ethical reasons means that an issue has arisen in the solicitor-client relationship where it is now impossible for counsel to continue in good conscience to represent the accused. Counsel may cite "ethical reasons" as the reason for withdrawal if, for example, the accused is requesting that counsel act in violation of his or her professional obligations (see, e.g., Law Society of Upper Canada, r. 2.09(7)(b), (d); Law Society of Alberta, c. 14, r. 2; Law Society of British Columbia, c. 10, r. 1), or if the accused refuses to accept counsel's advice on an important trial issue (see, e.g., Law Society of Upper Canada, r. 2.09(2); Law Society of Alberta, c. 14, r. 1; Law Society of British Columbia, c. 10, r. 2). If the real reason for withdrawal is non-payment of legal fees, then counsel cannot represent to the court that he or she seeks to withdraw for "ethical reasons". However, in either the case of ethical reasons or non-payment of fees, the court must accept counsel's answer at face value and not enquire further so as to avoid trenching on potential issues of solicitor-client privilege.

If withdrawal is sought for an ethical reason, then the court must grant withdrawal (see *C. (D.D.)*, at p. 328 ...). Where an ethical issue has arisen in the relationship, counsel may be required to withdraw in order to comply with his or her professional obligations. It would be inappropriate for a court to require counsel to continue to act when to do so would put him or her in violation of professional responsibilities.

. . . . .

NOTES AND QUESTIONS

1. In *Cunningham*, the Court stated that information regarding a client's non-payment of legal fees, at least in relation to a lawyer's application for withdrawal, is not privileged information. Yet the client's financial information was found to be covered by privilege in *Descôteaux*. Does this suggest that privilege is "contextual"? Or was it a matter of the Court wishing to avoid the consequences of (i) creating a new exception to privilege; or (ii) having to deal with the consequences of allowing a lawyer to "hide behind" privilege when he or she wished to get out of a case due to a dispute over fees? Is the outcome sound in light of the general language regarding the almost "absolute" sanctity of lawyer-client communications? You will recall that privilege is lost when the information comes to be known to a third party. In cases where a legal aid certificate is the basis upon which a legal aid tariff is paid (or not paid) to a lawyer, there is always "third party knowledge". Does this mean that *Cunningham* is not really about privilege but about the lawyer's overriding ethical duty of confidentiality?

2. Taking Custody and Control of Real Evidence

Defence counsel's taking custody or control of real physical evidence associated with the commission of a crime raise in a very direct way issues concerning the scope of a criminal defence lawyer's zealous advocacy on behalf of a client, along with his or her duty to the court and to the administration of justice generally. This tension is different from the nature of client communications to his or her lawyer, and therefore invites different policy and ethical considerations. Nevertheless, it is closely associated with client confidences and the lawyer's dilemmas inherent as a recipient of either confidences or "real" evidence. For this reason, the leading case in Canada, *R. v. Murray*, is considered here but receives further consideration in Chapter 8.

R. v. MURRAY

[2000] O.J. No. 2182, 144 C.C.C. (3d) 289
(Ont. S.C.J., Gravely J.)

[The relevant facts are excerpted in Chapter 1, "Introduction to Legal Ethics" at pages 31 to 35 and the case is further discussed, in the context of the limits to defence counsel's advocacy, in Chapter 8, "Ethics and Criminal Law Practice" at pages 471 to 474.]

GRAVELY J.:—

. . . . .

THE INDICTMENT

Kenneth Murray is charged:

> That from May 6th, 1993 to September 12th, 1994 inclusive in the Regional Municipality of Niagara, Central South Region, and elsewhere in the Province of Ontario, did wilfully obstruct or attempt to obstruct the course of justice by concealing certain video tapes for approximately seventeen months which are the products and/or instrumentalities of crime, those video tapes containing scenes depicting the unlawful confinement of Leslie Erin Mahaffy, unlawful confinement of Kristen Dawn French, aggravated sexual assault of Leslie Erin Mahaffy, aggravated sexual assault of Kristen Dawn French, aggravated sexual assault of Tammy Lynn Homolka, aggravated sexual assault of Jane Doe by Paul Bernardo and Karla Homolka, contrary to section 139(2) of the *Criminal Code.*

CRIME AND ETHICS

I have been supplied by counsel with voluminous material on legal ethics.

I want to make clear that my function in this case is limited to deciding if Murray has committed the crime of attempting to obstruct justice, not to judge his ethics. While ethics may integrate with the issue of *mens rea*, ethical duties do not automatically translate into legal obligations.

. . . . .

Ontario courts have uniformly applied the tendency test [as to the *actus reus* for obstruction of justice]. In *R. v. May* ..., Martin J.A. said ... that the gist of the offence:

> ... is the doing of an act which has a tendency to pervert or obstruct the course of justice and which is done for that purpose ...

. . . . .

The *actus reus* issue, therefore, is whether Murray's action in secreting the videotapes had a tendency to obstruct the course of justice.

The word "wilfully" denotes the *mens rea* of the section. This is a specific intent offence and the onus is on the Crown to prove that Murray, when he secreted the tapes, intended to obstruct the course of justice ...

. . . . .

The effect of section 139(2) is to prohibit improper interference with the functioning of any part of the justice system.

APPLICATION OF THE TENDENCY TEST

On the face of the evidence Murray's action in secreting the critical tapes had the tendency to obstruct the course of justice at several stages of the proceedings.

The tapes were put beyond the reach of the police who had unsuccessfully attempted to locate them. Secreting them had the tendency to obstruct the police in their duty to investigate the crimes of Bernardo and Homolka.

. . . . .

It would be difficult to over-estimate the evidentiary significance of these tapes. The making of them formed an integral part of the crimes. The victims were forced to participate not just in perverse sexual acts, but also actively in the videotaping of them. The resulting images amounted to the basest kind of forced child pornography. The tapes were the products and instrumentalities of crime and were far more potent "hard evidence" than the often-mentioned "smoking gun" and "bloody shirt." Once it possessed either of those items, the prosecution would still have to connect them to the accused and the accused would have room to raise issues such as self-defence. Here, jurors became eyewitnesses to Bernardo committing most of the crimes with which he was charged. Once the jury viewed the tapes, Bernardo was left with no defence to anything but the murder charges and little chance of a successful defence on those.

While Murray's conduct had a tendency to obstruct the course of justice in relation to the police and the Crown, it also influenced the way new defence counsel, Rosen, approached the conduct of Bernardo's defence. It had the further potential for a jury to be deprived of admissible evidence.

Concealment of the tapes had the potential to infect all aspects of the criminal justice system.

JUSTIFICATION

Prima facie, Murray's action in concealing the tapes is caught by the tendency test. He cannot, however, be said to attempt to obstruct justice if he had legal justification for his conduct.

There is no obligation on a citizen to help the police, but taking positive steps to conceal evidence is unlawful ...

While Mr. Cooper conceded a lay person may not conceal evidence, he argued that defence counsel's obligations to the client dictate a special status that provides reasonable justification in some cases for concealment of evidence, and while the tapes could not be permanently suppressed, these tapes had some exculpatory value and counsel was entitled to temporarily conceal them for defence purposes.

Mr. Cooper did not suggest that confidentiality of the tapes is protected under the umbrella of solicitor-client privilege and no privilege, in my opinion, attaches to this evidence. Solicitor-client privilege protects *communications* between solicitor and client ... These videotapes are not communications. They are, rather, dramatic evidence of crime and pre-existed the solicitor-client relationship. They are not similar, for example, to a sketch, which might be prepared by a client to help explain a point to his counsel, or even a videotape prepared for that purpose. Murray's discussions with his client about the tapes are covered by the privilege; the physical objects, the tapes are not. Hiding them from the police on behalf of the client cannot be said to be an aspect of solicitor-client communication.

The point is expressed well in the "bloody shirt" case. There, a lawyer was confronted with a client, wanted for murder, whose shirt was soaked in blood. Before surrendering the client to the police, the lawyer took possession of the shirt. Having some misgivings about his conduct, he retained counsel who approached the Professional Conduct Committee of the Law Society of Upper Canada for advice. He was told:

> You should not have taken the shirt. It is a piece of physical evidence. Not only that, what you saw with your eyes as opposed to what you heard with your ears, is not privileged so that you may be a witness now in this case. Our advice to you is that you must withdraw from the case and you must turn the shirt over forthwith to the Crown Attorney.

Although Murray had a duty of confidentiality to Bernardo, absent solicitor-client privilege there was no legal basis permitting concealment of the tapes. In this sense Murray had no higher right than any other citizen. Nor, in my opinion, can it be said that concealing the critical tapes was permissible because they may have had some exculpatory value. They were overwhelmingly inculpatory. Some of the United States authorities, including *The American Bar Association; Standards for Criminal Justice, Prosecution Function and Defence Function, Third Edition*, suggest counsel may retain incriminating physical evidence for a reasonable time for examination and testing. There was no testing contemplated here and, by some time in June

1993, Murray had examined the tapes and knew their contents. He chose to continue to conceal them.

In a line of United States cases ... not only is there recognition that solicitor-client privilege does not protect physical evidence, but there is a suggested obligation on counsel to turn over incriminating physical evidence to a prosecutor.

That position appears to have been supported by Canadian commentators, at least with reference to instrumentalities of crime.

I am not entirely clear why there exists this almost universal view that incriminating physical evidence must go to the prosecution. In my opinion it does not follow that because concealment of incriminating physical evidence is forbidden there is always a corresponding positive obligation to disclose. In *R. v. P. (M.B.)* (1994) ... Lamer C.J.C. said ...: "With respect to disclosure, the defence in Canada is under no legal obligation to cooperate with or assist the Crown by announcing any special defence, such as an alibi, or by producing documentary or *physical evidence*". [Emphasis of Gravely J.]

Perhaps the general view that there is a turn-over obligation to the prosecution arises from the dilemma counsel faces once improperly in possession of incriminating physical evidence. At that point, almost any step involves potential risk of criminal liability. For example, in Mr. Martin's address ... he recounts the difficulty created when the murder weapon is dropped on the lawyer's desk.

> What should the lawyer do?

> If he says, "Take the gun and come back after you have disposed of it," he has committed a criminal offence unless, of course, he can persuade a jury at his own trial that his intention was merely to instruct the client that he should leave the pistol at his residence so that it would be available to the police under a search warrant. If he takes possession of the pistol and puts it in his desk or vault a serious problem is created. Obviously, if he buried the pistol in his backyard he would be an accessory after the fact. If he puts it in his desk or vault, may it not be argued that he has just as effectively concealed it?

The American Bar Association Standards, supra, provide generally that defence counsel should return an incriminating physical item to the source after a reasonable period to allow for testing, etc.

Even if that were permissible it was not an option open to Murray. While he had no obligation to assist the police in their investigation or the Crown in its prosecution, Murray could not be a party to concealing this evidence. Having removed the tapes from their hiding place, he could not hide them again. Nor could he implement any instructions from Bernardo that would result in their continued concealment.

Once he had discovered the overwhelming significance of the critical tapes, Murray, in my opinion, was left with but three legally justifiable options:

(a) Immediately turn over the tapes to the prosecution, either directly or anonymously;

(b) Deposit them with the trial judge; or,

(c) Disclose their existence to the prosecution and prepare to do battle to retain them.

I am satisfied that Murray's concealment of the critical tapes was an act that had a tendency to pervert or obstruct the course of justice.

MENS REA

The onus is on the Crown to prove beyond a reasonable doubt that it was Murray's intention to obstruct the course of justice.

By putting the tapes beyond the reach of the police and the Crown, Murray clearly intended to impede the prosecution of the case against Bernardo. Defence strategy was based upon concealment of the tapes.

If Murray was aware concealment was unlawful, then the only reasonable inference would be, that by doing so, he intended to obstruct the course of justice.

Murray knew it was unlawful to permanently suppress the tapes. Asked by Mr. Cooper for his reaction to Bernardo's August 30, 1994 direction not to disclose the tapes, Murray said:

> It put me in a position that I was being asked to suppress evidence. I was being asked to do something that was improper, *unlawful*, unethical and something that I couldn't either under the rules of conduct or professional ethics do. [Emphasis added]

The factual questions of intent then are:

1. Did Murray intend to conceal the tapes permanently or only up to the point of resolution discussions or trial?

2. If the latter, was it his honest belief he was entitled to do so?

MURRAY'S INTENTION

Murray testified he intended to use the tapes in the defence. With the tapes he could prove Homolka to be a liar and pave the way for Bernardo to give evidence that it was Homolka who committed the murders. The tapes would be used to cross-examine her at trial or in resolution discussions with the Crown.

Mr. Scott [for the Crown] argued that Murray's evidence was a tissue of lies, that his intention was to permanently suppress the tapes and he went to Mr. Cooper for advice only when the case was so ill-prepared for trial that Rosen had to be brought in to take over and Murray was faced with giving evidence by affidavit as to his reasons for ceasing to act.

Murray was an enthusiastic witness and his answers at times on cross-examination were more combative than responsive. Perhaps that is natural for an advocate. He was casual with the truth in selling the case to Rosen. I cannot conclude from his demeanour alone that he was untruthful in his evidence. Substantial character evidence was given as to his excellent reputation for integrity and truthfulness.

I am sceptical of Murray's evidence of his intention. I am troubled by the following:

1. Murray's evidence was inconsistent as to his tactical plans to use the tapes. His primary plan seems to have been that, without disclosing them to the Crown, he would surprise Homolka with them on cross-examination at trial. Another plan was that the Crown would get the tapes as soon as serious plea negotiations occurred, or perhaps, he said, negotiations could be concluded without the Crown knowing the contents of the tapes.

2. Murray failed to disclose the existence of the tapes to Rosen.

3. Rosen testified there was nothing in the file when he took over that suggested any use of tapes in the defence.

4. In Murray's summaries of the tapes, he suggested how the non-critical tapes might be used at trial. He had no similar suggestions for the critical tapes.

5. In his resolution discussions with the Crown, Murray made no mention of the tapes.

6. The tapes were not used to tie down Homolka in cross-examination at the Kingston Prison for Women. Nor was there any mention of use of the tapes in the file prepared for that cross-examination. MacDonald conducted the cross-examination without having seen the critical tapes.

7. As of September 1, 1994, 11 days before trial motions were to begin, Doyle and MacDonald (who were said to have spent hundreds of hours preparing the case for trial) had not seen the critical tapes. The absence of consultation with co-counsel MacDonald is bizarre. In a case of this nature, one would normally expect that extensive preparation be conducted with co-counsel and very careful strategies and plans developed as to how the defence is to be approached. There was nothing of that nature apparent here in relation to the critical tapes.

   If the tapes were inevitably going to come out and probably be used at trial, MacDonald eventually had to see them. That would occur in spite of all Murray's efforts to "protect" her.

8. Murray received authorization from Legal Aid to retain not only MacDonald and Doyle, but also numbers of other individuals to as-

sist in the defence. ... There is no evidence that any of these individuals ever saw the tapes or were briefed on their contents.

Dr. Ben-Aron was expected to develop a psychiatric profile of Homolka without knowing videotapes existed that showed her apparently revelling in sexual perversions.

Professor Yarmi no doubt would have been assisted in his analysis of the psychology of the case by viewing Bernardo and Homolka engaged in these crimes.

In spite of all this preparation and all the experts and other individuals assisting in preparation for trial without knowledge of the tapes, Murray's evidence was that "the trial was the tapes" and their existence made the case a simple one.

9.   Murray on August 30, 1994 had Bernardo sign a series of directions that, if followed, would result in continued concealment of the tapes.

10. It is difficult to conceive how the critical tapes were useful to Bernardo's case. They were damning evidence against him. Murray agreed that once shown the tapes "any jury would have convicted him of sinking the Titanic". While they provided scope for the cross-examination of Homolka, as Rosen said, "the client would have been in a substantially better position if the tapes had never surfaced".

11. When asked by Mr. Cooper why he failed on September 1, 1994 to mention his ethical dilemma to LeSage A.C.J.O.C., Murray said:

> Because, as much as I was in a jackpot, the client's interests are paramount to protect. There may be an ethical issue, there may be something that I had to straighten out, but if I had gone to that meeting and said, well My Lord, the reason I want to get off is there are these video tapes that, you know, *bury his defence*, that the Crown doesn't have and he's told me to hold on to them. Well I couldn't do that ... [Emphasis added]

This hardly sounds as if Murray, at least at that point, was viewing the tapes as a defence "bonanza".

Mr. Cooper submitted that Murray's explanations should deal with my concerns. While Murray's plans to use the critical tapes at trial were unfocused, it was clear they were to be employed in some way at some stage. Much is explained, he said, by Murray's belief he had to keep the tapes strictly secret in order to retain their tactical value. Rosen could not be told because he was only conditionally on the record for Bernardo. None of the four directions was in fact followed. The tapes were not specifically used in the Homolka cross-examination because of the difficulties mentioned in the evidence and the choice was made to hold back the tapes for their surprise value in cross-examination.

Mr. Cooper argued that Murray should be believed when he says he planned to use the critical tapes for defence purposes. In a careful and detailed review of the evidence, Mr. Cooper examined the position of the defence had the tapes not existed compared to the position with the tapes available.

Without the tapes, he suggested, the evidence against Bernardo was overwhelming. In addition to other pieces of circumstantial evidence, the DNA placed Bernardo in the house and having had sexual connection with one of the victims. The defence would then be faced with Homolka, an eyewitness, who would play her role as innocent, savagely beaten wife, coerced into helping Bernardo commit his crimes. There was little potential for a successful cross-examination of her. It was a "he did it" – "she did it" case, and, with the Scarborough Rapes going in as similar fact evidence, "Bernardo the Stalker" had no chance.

The tapes, suggested Mr. Cooper, gave Bernardo a slim chance. While they show Bernardo in a terrible light, Homolka turns out to be almost as bad. The benefit to the defence was not just that Homolka could be shown as a liar, but also as a person capable of committing murder. She is shown on the tapes administering halothane to her sister and to Jane Doe, and participating in sexual assaults on both of them. The tapes also show her using items of her dead sister's clothing to sexually stimulate Bernardo. For the same purpose she employs a rose which she was then going to put on her sister's grave. Mr. Cooper conceded the tapes were "an atomic bomb" for Bernardo, but, he suggested, "it bombed both ways."

In spite of all the inferences I am tempted to draw against the credibility of Murray based on his actions as I have enumerated them, I am satisfied on the basis of Mr. Cooper's argument that a defence strategy of use of the tapes at trial was reasonably feasible. That lends support to Murray's evidence that he did not intend to permanently suppress them. In this context, I have warned myself about the dangers of hindsight.

. . . . .

Murray's evidence that he would at some time disclose the tapes is supported by the fact that MacDonald and Doyle knew they existed. Murray would know that the pact of silence, no matter how solemn, would be unlikely to survive the Bernardo trial if the tapes were ultimately suppressed.

I conclude, therefore, that Murray's explanation as to his use of the critical tapes in the defence of his client is one that might reasonably be true.

MURRAY'S BELIEF

Assuming he intended to use the tapes for defence purposes, did Murray believe he had a right to conceal them to the extent he did?

Murray testified he believed his conduct was lawful.

C.c. 139(2) casts a broad net. It does not specifically isolate as criminal the conduct Murray engaged in.

The only official guide given to lawyers in Ontario on this issue is contained in rule 10 of the Law Society of Upper Canada Professional Conduct handbook [now Rule 4.01]. It reads in part:

> 2. The lawyer must discharge this duty by fair and honourable means, without illegality and in a manner consistent with the lawyer's duty to treat the tribunal with candour, fairness, courtesy and respect.

> The lawyer must not, for example:

>> (e) knowingly attempt to deceive a tribunal or influence the course of justice by offering false evidence, misstating facts or law, presenting or relying upon a false or deceptive affidavit, *suppressing what ought to be disclosed*, or otherwise assisting in any fraud, crime or illegal conduct ..." [Emphasis of Gravely J.]

The rule provides no guidance as to the nature of evidence that "ought to be disclosed". It is of small help either to counsel or to clients who may believe that both their secrets and their evidence are safe with their lawyers.

While Murray made only a token effort to find out what his obligations were, had he done careful research he might have remained confused. The weight of legal opinion in Ontario is to the effect that lawyers may not conceal material physical evidence of crime, but how this rule applies to particular facts has been the subject of extensive discussion. ...

. . . . .

If I make the assumption Murray intended to use the tapes in the defence, I have no difficulty with the proposition that he may well have believed under the circumstances he had no legal duty to disclose the tapes until resolution discussions or trial.

PART FOUR – CONCLUSION

In summary, I find;

1. Murray's concealment of the critical tapes had the tendency to obstruct justice.

2. Murray knew it would be obstructing justice to permanently suppress the tapes.

3. He may not have intended to permanently suppress them.

4. He may have believed he had no obligation to disclose them before trial.

. . . . .

In the context of the whole of the evidence, Murray's testimony I find raises a reasonable doubt as to his intention to obstruct justice.

I find him not guilty.

NOTES AND QUESTIONS

1. Though he found that Murray's concealment of the tapes "had a tendency to pervert or obstruct the course of justice", Gravely J. also observed:

   > The weight of legal opinion in Ontario is to the effect that lawyers may not conceal material physical evidence of crime, but how this rule applies to particular facts has been the subject of extensive discussion. ...

   Is the effect of this decision that a lawyer in possession of relevant physical evidence that could implicate his or her client must make disclosure of some sort with respect to this evidence? Does this amount to a qualification, or exception, to a lawyer's obligation of confidentiality to one's client? What factors would you take into account in determining whether and how you would make disclosure in "real evidence" situations?

2. You will have noted that, following his recitation of the professional conduct rule applicable to this situation, Gravely J. stated that the rule provided "no guidance as to the nature of evidence that 'ought to be disclosed'". Following the *Murray* decision, the Law Society of Upper Canada and others struggled with the issue and attempted to formulate a workable rule with respect to relevant physical evidence that comes into the possession of a lawyer. The FLSC *Model Code* provision is set out in a Commentary to Rule 2.05(6) regarding Preservation of Clients' Property:

   > A lawyer is never required to take or keep possession of property relevant to a crime or offence. If a lawyer comes into possession of property relevant to a crime, either from a client or another person, the lawyer must act in keeping with the lawyer's duty of loyalty and confidentiality to the client and the lawyer's duty to the administration of justice, which requires, at a minimum, that the lawyer not violate the law, improperly impede a police investigation, or otherwise obstruct the course of justice. Generally, a lawyer in such circumstances should, as soon as reasonably possible:
   >
   > (a) turn over the property to the prosecution, either directly or anonymously;
   >
   > (b) deposit the property with the trial judge in the relevant proceeding;
   >
   > (c) deposit the property with the court to facilitate access by the prosecution or defence for testing or examination; or
   >
   > (d) disclose the existence of the property to the prosecution and, if necessary, prepare to argue the issue of possession of the property.
   >
   > When a lawyer discloses or delivers to the Crown or law enforcement authorities property relevant to a crime or offence, the lawyer has a duty to protect the client's confidences, including the client's identity, and to preserve solicitor and client privilege. This may be accomplished by the lawyer retaining independent counsel, who is not informed of the identity of the client and who is instructed not to disclose the identity of the instructing lawyer, to disclose or deliver the property.

If a lawyer delivers the property to the court under paragraph (c), he or she should do so in accordance with the protocol established for such purposes, which permits the lawyer to deliver the property to the court without formal application or investigation, ensures that the property is available to both the Crown and defence counsel for testing and examination upon motion to the court, and ensures that the fact that property was received from the defence counsel will not be the subject of comment or argument at trial.

Compare the Law Society of Alberta's *Code of Conduct* provision, Rule 4.01(9), Handling Evidence:

A lawyer must not counsel or participate in:

(a)   the obtaining of evidence or information by illegal means;

(b)   the falsification of evidence;

(c)   the destruction of property having potential evidentiary value or the alteration of property so as to affect its evidentiary value; or

(d)   the concealment of property having potential evidentiary value in a criminal proceeding.

Commentary

Lawyers must uphold the law and refrain from conduct that might weaken respect for the law or interfere with its fair administration. A lawyer must therefore seek to maintain the integrity of evidence and its availability through appropriate procedures to opposing parties.

The word "property" in paragraphs (c) and (d) includes electronic information.

Paragraph (a) of Rule 4.01(9) prohibits a lawyer's involvement in the obtaining of evidence or information in a civil or criminal matter by means that are contrary to law, including the Charter of Rights and Freedoms and the Criminal Code.

Paragraph (c) is not intended to interfere with the testing of evidence as contemplated by the Rules of Court.

Paragraph (d) applies to criminal matters due to the danger of obstruction of justice if evidence in a criminal matter is withheld. While a lawyer has no obligation to disclose the mere existence of such evidence, it would be unethical to accept possession of it and then conceal or destroy it. The lawyer must therefore advise someone wishing to deliver potential evidence that, if possession is accepted by the lawyer, it will be necessary to turn inculpatory evidence over to appropriate authorities (unless it consists of communications or documents that are privileged). When surrendering criminal evidence, however, a lawyer must protect confidentiality attaching to the circumstances in which the material was acquired, which may require that the lawyer act anonymously or through a third party.

There is no equivalent obligation of disclosure with respect to evidence in a civil proceeding in light of the extensive discovery process provided by the Rules of Court. However, it is improper to block disclosure of documents or other evidence duly requested pursuant to rules of production or practice.

What difference do you see between these two approaches? Is either an improvement on the Rule in *Murray*?

3. Should such a rule apply to all property having evidentiary value? For example, if your client were to bring to you the bottle of whisky from which he claims that he had only two drinks before driving his car (thus putting into dispute a breathalyzer reading, but constituting evidence that he had been drinking), what, if anything, must you do with the whisky bottle? What about hard copies of e-mails that he sent to a former lover that had potential value as evidence of harassment or stalking? Would you be required to disclose the information? Do the copies of the e-mails constitute physical evidence? If so, is there a basis for distinguishing this type of evidence from the conventional types of physical evidence? Does it make any difference that the authorities probably have access to the e-mail trail from the alleged victim's end of the e-mail chain?

4. It appears that much of what Mr. Murray claimed in his own defence constituted a disclosure of information that he had received in confidence from his client, Paul Bernardo. Assuming that Bernardo did not authorize the disclosure of this information, was its disclosure justified? See, for example, the provisions of *Model Code* Rule 2.03(4):

> If it is alleged that a lawyer or the lawyer's associates or employees:
>
> (a) have committed a criminal offence involving a client's affairs;
>
> (b) are civilly liable with respect to a matter involving a client's affairs;
>
> (c) have committed acts of professional negligence; or
>
> (d) have engaged in acts of professional misconduct or conduct unbecoming a lawyer,
>
> the lawyer may disclose confidential information in order to defend against the allegations, but must not disclose more information than is required.

5. The situation where a lawyer ends up in possession of real or physical evidence potentially related to a crime is relatively rare. But consider the following situation: A British Columbia man seized two motion-activated surveillance cameras he says the RCMP had hidden in trees near his trailer home, and they are full of images from crime scenes and investigations, as well as pictures of himself and his friends coming and going from his home. The man believed the RCMP installed the cameras in the trees because he is a graffiti artist and they wanted to track his movements.

They are now in his lawyer's possession. The lawyer said he is keeping the cameras until he gets an explanation from police. The RCMP want their cameras returned. "The fact that someone has committed a criminal act and stolen our cameras certainly is, I guess, a concern for RCMP and for our investigators", said the RCMP spokesperson.

What are the lawyer's legal and ethical duties in these circumstances?

G. FURTHER READING

Bloom, Lackland H., Jr., "The Law Office Search: An Emerging Problem and Some Suggested Solutions" (1980) 69 Geo. L.J. 1.

Davis, John E., "Law Office Searches: The Assault on Confidentiality and the Adversary System" (1996) 33 Am. Crim. L. Rev. 1251.

Dodek, Adam, "The Public Safety Exception to Solicitor-Client Privilege" (2000–2001) 34 U.B.C. L. Rev. 293.

Dodek, Adam, "Solicitor-Client Privilege in Canada: Challenges for the 21st Century" (February 2011), online: Canadian Bar Association <http://www. cba.org/CBA/activities/pdf/Dodek-English.pdf>.

Frankel, Simon, "The Attorney-Client Privilege After the Death of the Client" (1992) 6 Geo. J. Legal Ethics 45.

Freedman, Munroe, "Getting Honest About Client Perjury" (2008) 21 Geo. J. Legal Ethics 133.

Freedman, Munroe, "The Professional Responsibility of the Criminal Defense Lawyer: The Three Hardest Questions" (1966) 64 Mich. L. Rev. 1469.

Graham, Randal, *Legal Ethics: Theories, Cases, and Professional Regulation*, 2nd ed. (Toronto: Emond Montgomery, 2011), chs. 4, 5.

Ho, Hock Lai, "Legal Professional Privilege and the Integrity of Legal Representation" (2006) 9 Legal Ethics 163.

Hutchinson, Allan, *Legal Ethics and Professional Responsibility*, 2nd ed. (Toronto: Irwin Law, 2007), ch. 7.

Jamal, Mahmud, "The Supreme Court of Canada on Solicitor-Client Privilege: What Every Practitioner Needs To Know" (Canadian Bar Association: November 2006).

Layton, David, "The Public Safety Exception: Confusing Confidentiality, Privilege and Ethics" (2002) 6 Can. Crim. L. Rev. 209.

Layton, David, "*R. v. Jenkins*: Client Perjury and Disclosure by Defence Counsel" (2001) C.R. (5th) 259.

Leong, Nancy, "Attorney-Client Privilege in the Public Sector: A Survey of Government Attorneys" (2007) 20 Geo. J. Legal Ethics 163.

MacKenzie, Gavin, *Lawyers and Ethics: Professional Responsibility and Discipline* (Toronto: Thomson Carswell, 2007), Chapter 3, "Confidentiality" and Chapter 7.1, "Confidentiality and Truth".

Manes, Ronald D. & Michael P. Silver, *Solicitor-Client Privilege in Canadian Law* (Toronto: Butterworths, 1993).

Maher, Kathleen, "May vs. Must" (2005) 91 A.B.A. J. 30.

Noonan, John T., Jr., "The Purposes of Advocacy and the Limits of Confidentiality" (1966) 64 Mich. L. Rev. 1485.

Paton, Paul, "The Independence of the Bar and the Public Interest Imperative: Lawyers as Gatekeepers, Whistleblowers, or Instruments of State Enforcement?" in Lorne Sossin, ed., *The Independence of the Bar* (Toronto: Irwin Law, 2007).

Proulx, Michel & David Layton, *Ethics and Canadian Criminal Law* (Toronto: Irwin Law, 2001), chs. 4, 5.

Przypyszny, John, "Public Assault on the Attorney-Client Privilege, Ramifications of *Baltes v. Doe*" (1990) 3 Geo. J. Legal Ethics 351.

Simon, William, "The Confidentiality Fetish" *Atlantic Monthly* (November 2004) 112.

Stuart, Nancy, "Child Abuse Reporting: A Challenge to Attorney Client Confidentiality" (1987–1988) 1 Geo. J. Legal Ethics 243.

Woolley, Alice, *Understanding Lawyers' Ethics in Canada* (Markham, ON: LexisNexis Canada 2011), Chapter 5, "Lawyer-Client Trust and Confidence".

THE DUTY OF LOYALTY AND CONFLICTS OF INTEREST

A. INTRODUCTION

We saw in the previous chapter that a lawyer's duty of confidentiality is complex and sometimes morally problematic. In this chapter, we shall see that lawyers are presented with similar and equally complex obligations in relation to conflicts of interest. These obligations arise generally from the same source — the various dimensions of the duty of loyalty owed to clients. At the same time, however, a number of other public policy values are implicated in the regulation of conflicts. For example, it is reasonable to expect lawyers to try to limit the total cost of legal services to clients, to make services available as widely as possible, especially in areas where legal services are not readily attainable, and, to the greatest extent possible, to enable a client to retain the lawyer of his or her choice. In other words, these public policy values invite us to take into account other requirements of the administration of justice even when doing so creates a tension with a more pristine environment where conflicts of interest are to be avoided at all costs.

Added to this is the evolving shape of the legal profession, including the concentration of many lawyers in large law firms, the evolution of "national" and "international" law firms who serve a multitude of clients across many jurisdictions, and the development of "multi-disciplinary" firms in which lawyers and other professionals practice side by side. The lawyer's ability to provide legal representation to a client with undivided loyalty has become a much more complex enterprise in the modern-day practice of law. In her recent book, Alice Woolley suggests that "no area of the law governing lawyers consumes more lawyer time, creates more confusion and frustration, or causes lawyers more difficulty in their practices, than the rules governing conflicts of interest".[1]

Further, the lawyer personally may have interests that are not perfectly aligned with those of his or her client. These interests may be related to the issues at stake in the representation. For example, the lawyer's financial interests may be served to a greater degree by one outcome than another, outcomes over which the lawyer may have influence, but which may be at odds with the most beneficial outcome for the client. The lawyer may have an interest in entering into a potentially lucrative business relationship with a client. Or a

---

[1]   Alice Woolley, *Understanding Lawyers' Ethics in Canada* (Markham, ON: LexisNexis Canada, 2011) at 215.

lawyer may develop or have a pre-existing personal or family relationship that generates "extra-legal" loyalties in tension with accomplishment of the client's ends. Sometimes a lawyer will develop a romantic interest in a client.

While some of these circumstances lend themselves to "black and white" prescriptions, most have subtleties generated by the values embedded in the rich and complex environment in which lawyers provide legal services. Richard Devlin has described these challenges in a way that invites consideration of the issue at a more fundamental level:

> The issues generated by conflicts of interest and the duty of loyalty are multiple and complex. On one level, they raise key questions about the role of morality and ethical identity of individual lawyers, and how to manage and reconcile their own interests, those of their (various) clients and the public good. At the level of law firms, conflicts of interest and the duty of loyalty generate important issues of governance, accountability and responsibility. ... When we move to the level of regulatory authority — and legitimacy — the challenges become even more pronounced. In many jurisdictions the regulation of conflicts of interest and the duty of loyalty falls within the jurisdiction of both the courts and the law societies. If both institutions are reading from the same script and pursuing the same objectives then the challenges are likely to be minor. But if courts and legislatures are whistling different tunes, and motivated by different goals, then there are likely to be some deep structural tensions — if not contradictions. Finally, the duty of loyalty and conflicts of interests shine a spotlight on the capabilities of regulators — be they law societies or oversight bodies — to regulate in the public interest. As the business model for the practice of law gains ascendency, the temptations to maximise the economic interests of lawyers and law firms necessarily intensify. The duty of loyalty — and the correlative obligations to avoid conflicts of interest — serve as a potential bulwark against the hegemony of the business model. If that bulwark does not remain strong, the claim that regulators' primary responsibility is to serve the public interest is cast into doubt.[2]

This chapter examines the circumstances that can pull lawyers in different, and often conflicting, directions. The chapter is organized to address the two central dimensions of lawyers' conflicts of interest: those arising between or among clients ("client-client" conflicts), and those arising due to a potential conflict between the lawyer's own interests and those of the client ("lawyer-client" conflicts). However, as we shall see, these categories are not mutually exclusive; as some recent cases illustrate, client-client and lawyer-client conflicts can often converge and collide with unfortunate results for all involved.

Even a modest consideration of this topic will lead the reader to appreciate that conflicts of interest can arise in any aspect of the practice of law. Whether a person practices law in a solo practice in a small community, in a large firm with offices in multiple locations, as a lawyer in government service or as in-house counsel, it will be common for the lawyer's loyalty to be

---

[2]   Richard Devlin, "Guest Editorial: Governance, Regulation and Legitimacy: Conflicts of Interest and the Duty of Loyalty" (2011) 14 Legal Ethics at iii.

subject to competing claims. More than professional platitudes is required to deal with these issues in a professionally appropriate and principled way.

Historically, this area of lawyers' obligations was the subject of a set of ethical guidelines and little else. Codes of conduct focused on a set of general principles, perhaps honoured as much in the breach as in the observance, to guide lawyer conduct. In the last few decades, however, as has been the case with lawyer-client confidentiality and privilege, courts and disciplinary authorities have been asked to articulate standards for lawyer conduct in conflict of interest situations in more precise and meaningful ways. As a consequence, and led by the Supreme Court of Canada, there has developed a significant jurisprudence in relation to lawyers' conflicts of interest. This development has been grounded in large measure on the fundamental principles and obligations owed to clients by lawyers, and informed by the expectation that a lawyer's behaviour is (and appears to be) beyond reproach. It has given richer meaning to concepts such as loyalty. It has also generated legalistic interpretations of lawyers' obligations. In some circumstances the concept of a disqualifying conflict of interest — where a lawyer is disqualified from representing a specific client — has been turned from an honourable principle into a tool of litigation, often for less than honourable purposes. As well, these more recent developments have motivated efforts by the legal profession to articulate, or modify, the degree to which certain behaviours constitute conflicts of interest, resulting in dramatic changes to lawyers' understandings of their obligations. The materials in this chapter invite you to build an understanding of the legal and ethical dimensions of conflict of interest and to reflect on the courts' and the legal profession's efforts to breathe life into, and build precision around, such a concept. As well, you will have the opportunity to consider whether, in their efforts to balance the various competing public and professional values and interests at stake, the decision-makers have succeeded. Or have the profession's own interests been privileged in an area where lawyers themselves have a great deal at stake?

B. CLIENT-CLIENT CONFLICTS

1. Introduction

In the last generation, the Supreme Court of Canada has rendered three major judgments in the field of lawyers and conflicts of interest, referred to as its "conflicts trilogy". In these cases, in widely disparate settings, the Court has attempted to articulate a clear set of expectations of lawyer behaviour in the face of conflicting demands upon them. In each case, as we shall see, the behaviour of the lawyer in question fell short of the standard set by the Supreme Court. In one of the cases the lawyer's conduct was apparently inadvertent; in the other cases the conduct fell well short of the Court's articulated standard of ethical lawyering.

What is far more significant, however, is the work of the Court in articulating the appropriate standards, and its effort to ground these standards in fundamentally important values. Combined with the Court's decisions in other cases, a picture is emerging in relation to lawyers' duties to clients in a context where other values are both close at hand and in some circumstances influential. But this work is not uncontroversial, either within the profession or within the Supreme Court itself. Two of the cases were decided by bare majorities, and in one of these cases the minority, though concurring in the result, spoke unusually strongly about the shortcomings of the majority's decision and the degree to which the decision catered to the profession's needs at the expense of the public interest. While some of this ground has solidified despite fragile majorities in these important cases, it is likely that further refinement will occur as new and complex situations present themselves.

2.   Duties to Former Clients

The first significant case to receive comprehensive treatment in the Supreme Court of Canada in the modern era of conflicts interest is *Re Macdonald Estate*, or *MacDonald Estate v. Martin* (below). It is the quintessential "transferring lawyer" case, in which there is a conflict between the transferring lawyer's duty to his or her former client and the duties of the lawyer's new firm to its current client. In this case, Sopinka J. wrote for a bare majority of four, with Cory J. writing a concurring opinion which includes an uncompromising critique of the majority decision, perhaps the most powerful commentary he ever wrote. These diverging judgments signal the difficulty presented by these cases, and the division of opinion that exists within the Court and the legal profession itself, over the behaviour to be required of lawyers, and the principles that should govern them. As we shall see, this decision generated a great deal of work within the legal profession to establish professional standards aimed at implementing the majority's decision.

MacDONALD ESTATE v. MARTIN
[1990] S.C.J. No. 41, [1990] 3 S.C.R. 1235
(S.C.C., Dickson C.J.C., Wilson, La Forest, L'Heureux-Dubé,
Sopinka, Gonthier and Cory JJ.)

[Ms. Dangerfield, a lawyer in the Twaddle law firm in Winnipeg, was involved in the representation of Mr. Martin, the plaintiff in a lawsuit related to the MacDonald estate. She was privy to various pieces of information related to the plaintiff's case, including confidential information. Through a series of developments the Twaddle firm dissolved and Ms. Dangerfield joined another law firm which eventually merged with the Thompson Dorfman Sweatman law firm. Thompson Dorfman Sweatman represented the defendant in the lawsuit initiated by Mr. Martin. That litigation was continuing when Ms. Dangerfield joined the firm. Ms. Dangerfield was not assigned to the case and was not in any way involved in the representation of the defendant.

When the plaintiff and his counsel learned of Ms. Dangerfield's presence at Thompson Dorfman Sweatman, they made application to have the firm disqualified from continuing to represent the defendant in the litigation. Ms. Dangerfield and Thompson Dorfman Sweatman provided sworn statements that no confidential information related to the plaintiff had been shared between Ms. Dangerfield and the law firm, and gave undertakings that nothing would be shared in the future.

At the lower courts the application to remove Thompson Dorfman Sweatman was dismissed. The case was appealed to the Supreme Court.]

SOPINKA J.:— This appeal is concerned with the standard to be applied in the legal profession in determining what constitutes a disqualifying conflict of interest. The issue arose in the context of a lawsuit in which a former junior solicitor for the appellant transferred her employment to the law firm acting for the respondent.

. . . . .

The Issue

The sole issue in this appeal is the appropriate standard to be applied in determining whether Thompson, Dorfman, Sweatman are disqualified from continuing to act in this litigation by reason of a conflict of interest.

Legal Ethics — Policy Considerations

In resolving this issue, the Court is concerned with at least three competing values. There is first of all the concern to maintain the high standards of the legal profession and the integrity of our system of justice. Furthermore, there is the countervailing value that a litigant should not be deprived of his or her choice of counsel without good cause. Finally, there is the desirability of permitting reasonable mobility in the legal profession. The review of the cases which follows will show that different standards have been adopted from time to time to resolve the issue. This reflects the different emphasis placed at different times and by different judges on the basic values outlined above.

The legal profession has changed with the changes in society. One of the changes that is most evident in large urban centers is the virtual disappearance of the sole practitioner and the tendency to larger and larger firms. This is a product of a number of factors including a response to the demands of large corporate clients whose multi-faceted activities require an all-purpose firm with sufficient numbers in every area of expertise to serve their needs. With increase in size come increasing demands for management of a law firm in accordance with the corporate model. These changes in the composition and management practices of law firms are reflected in changes to ethical practices of the profession. Some of the old practices have been swept aside as anachronistic, perhaps with justification. Advertising to inform the public in a tasteful way of the services provided by a firm and of its fee schedule is but one example.

Merger, partial merger and the movement of lawyers from one firm to another are familiar features of the modern practice of law. They bring with them the thorny problem of conflicts of interest. When one of these events is planned, consideration must be given to the consequences which will flow from loss of clients through conflicts of interest. To facilitate this process some would urge a slackening of the standard with respect to what constitutes a conflict of interest. In my view, to do so at the present time would serve the interest of neither the public nor the profession. The legal profession has historically struggled to maintain the respect of the public. This has been so notwithstanding the high standards that, generally, have been maintained. When the management, size of law firms and many of the practices of the legal profession are indistinguishable from those of business, it is important that the fundamental professional standards be maintained and indeed improved. This is essential if the confidence of the public that the law is a profession is to be preserved and hopefully strengthened. Nothing is more important to the preservation of this relationship than the confidentiality of information passing between a solicitor and his or her client. The legal profession has distinguished itself from other professions by the sanctity with which these communications are treated. The law, too, perhaps unduly, has protected solicitor and client exchanges while denying the same protection to others. This tradition assumes particular importance when a client bares his or her soul in civil or criminal litigation. Clients do this in the justifiable belief that nothing they say will be used against them and to the advantage of the adversary. Loss of this confidence would deliver a serious blow to the integrity of the profession and to the public's confidence in the administration of justice.

An important statement of public policy with respect to the conduct of barrister and solicitor is contained in the professional ethics codes of the governing bodies of the profession. The legal profession is self-governing. In each province there is a governing body usually elected by the lawyers practising in the province. The governing body enacts rules of professional conduct on behalf of those it represents. These rules must be taken as expressing the collective views of the profession as to the appropriate standards to which the profession should adhere.

While there exists no national law society, the Canadian Bar Association, a national society representing lawyers across the country, adopted a Code of Professional Conduct in 1974. The Code has been adopted by the Law Society of Manitoba and by the Law Societies of other provinces. Chapter V, entitled "Impartiality and Conflict of Interest", commences with the following rule:

> The lawyer must not advise or represent both sides of a dispute and, save after adequate disclosure to and with the consent of the client or prospective client concerned, he should not act or continue to act in a matter when there is or there is likely to be a conflicting interest. A conflicting interest is one which would be likely to affect adversely the judgment of the lawyer on behalf of or his loyalty to a client or prospective client or which the lawyer might be prompted to prefer to the interests of a client or prospective client.

The rule is followed by thirteen commentaries. The most relevant of these are Commentaries 11 and 12, which state:

> 11. A lawyer who has acted for a client in a matter should not thereafter act against him (or against persons who were involved in or associated with him

in that matter) in the same or any related matter, or place himself in a position where he might be tempted or appear to be tempted to breach the Rule relating to Confidential Information. It is not, however, improper for the lawyer to act against a former client in a fresh and independent matter wholly unrelated to any work he has previously done for that person.

12. For the sake of clarity the foregoing paragraphs are expressed in terms of the individual lawyer and his client. However it will be appreciated that the term "client" includes a client of the law firm of which the lawyer is a partner or associate whether or not he handles the client's work.

A code of professional conduct is designed to serve as a guide to lawyers and typically it is enforced in disciplinary proceedings. … The courts, which have inherent jurisdiction to remove from the record solicitors who have a conflict of interest, are not bound to apply a code of ethics. Their jurisdiction stems from the fact that lawyers are officers of the court and their conduct in legal proceedings which may affect the administration of justice is subject to this supervisory jurisdiction. Nonetheless, an expression of a professional standard in a code of ethics relating to a matter before the court should be considered an important statement of public policy. The statement in Chapter V should therefore be accepted as the expression by the profession in Canada that it wishes to impose a very high standard on a lawyer who finds himself or herself in a position where confidential information may be used against a former client. The statement reflects the principle that has been accepted by the profession that even an appearance of impropriety should be avoided.

The Law

The law in Canada and in other jurisdictions has adopted one of two basic approaches in determining whether a disqualifying conflict of interest exists: (1) the probability of real mischief, or (2) the possibility of real mischief. The term "mischief" refers to the misuse of confidential information by a lawyer against a former client. The first approach requires proof that the lawyer was actually possessed of confidential information and that there is a probability of its disclosure to the detriment of the client. The second is based on the precept that justice must not only be done but must manifestly be seen to be done. If, therefore, it reasonably appears that disclosure might occur, this test for determining the presence of a disqualifying conflict of interest is satisfied.

. . . . .

In Canada, some courts have applied *Rakusen* [a prominent English Court of Appeal decision that applied a "probability of real mischief" test] but the trend is to apply a stricter test which reflects the concern for the appearance of justice. P. W. Kryworuk, op. cit., points out that Canadian courts are largely applying the stricter American test or are applying a stricter version of *Rakusen* "in light of current attitude towards 'conflict of interest, justice and the appearance of justice and even the concept of 'fairness'".

. . . . .

[I]t is evident from this review of authorities that the clear trend is in favour of a stricter test. This trend is the product of a strong policy in favour of ensuring not only that there be no actual conflict but that there be no appearance of conflict.

A number of cases have specifically addressed the question as to whether possession of confidential information on the part of one member of a firm should be imputed to the rest of the firm. The strict application of the appearance principle has led some courts to apply it so that the presumption that "the knowledge of one is the knowledge of all" is irrebuttable. ... These cases are analyzed by Graham Steele in "Imputing Knowledge From One Member of a Firm to Another: 'Lead Us Not Into Temptation'" (1990), 12 Adv. Q. 46. He concludes, at p. 58:

> Some judges (and lawyers) find the rigid application of test (2) to be too hard on lawyers and law firms, particularly in today's climate of mergers and megafirms. For the purpose of determining whether there is a conflict of interest, they would advocate what might be called a "rebuttable imputation" of a lawyer's knowledge.

The Appropriate Test

What then should be the correct approach? Is the "probability of mischief" standard sufficiently high to satisfy the public requirement that there be an appearance of justice? In my opinion, it is not. This is borne out by the judicial statements to which I have referred and to the desire of the legal profession for strict rules of professional conduct as its adoption of the Canadian Code of Professional Conduct demonstrates. The probability of mischief test is very much the same as the standard of proof in a civil case. We act on probabilities. This is the basis of *Rakusen*. I am, however, driven to the conclusion that the public, and indeed lawyers and judges, have found that standard wanting. In dealing with the question of the use of confidential information we are dealing with a matter that is usually not susceptible of proof. As pointed out by Fletcher Moulton L.J. in *Rakusen*, "that is a thing which you cannot prove" (p. 841). I would add "or disprove". If it were otherwise, then no doubt the public would be satisfied upon proof that no prejudice would be occasioned. Since, however, it is not susceptible of proof, the test must be such that the public represented by the reasonably informed person would be satisfied that no use of confidential information would occur. That, in my opinion, is the overriding policy that applies and must inform the court in answering the question: Is there a disqualifying conflict of interest? In this regard, it must be stressed that this conclusion is predicated on the fact that the client does not consent to but is objecting to the retainer which gives rise to the alleged conflict.

Typically, these cases require two questions to be answered: (1) Did the lawyer receive confidential information attributable to a solicitor and client relationship relevant to the matter at hand? (2) Is there a risk that it will be used to the prejudice of the client?

In answering the first question, the court is confronted with a dilemma. In order to explore the matter in depth may require the very confidential information for which protection is sought to be revealed. This would have the effect of defeating the whole purpose of the application. American courts have solved this dilemma by means of the "substantial relationship" test. Once a "substantial relationship" is shown, there is an irrebuttable presumption that confidential information was imparted to the lawyer. In my opinion, this test is too rigid. There may be cases in which it is established beyond any reasonable doubt that no confidential information relevant to the current matter was disclosed. One example is where the applicant client admits on cross-examination that this is the case. This would not avail in the face of an irrebuttable presumption. In my opinion, once it is shown by the client that there existed a previous relationship which is sufficiently related to the retainer from which it is sought to remove the solicitor, the court should infer that confidential information was imparted unless the solicitor satisfies the court that no information was imparted which could be relevant. This will be a difficult burden to discharge. Not only must the court's degree of satisfaction be such that it would withstand the scrutiny of the reasonably informed member of the public that no such information passed, but the burden must be discharged without revealing the specifics of the privileged communication. Nonetheless, I am of the opinion that the door should not be shut completely on a solicitor who wishes to discharge this heavy burden.

The second question is whether the confidential information will be misused. A lawyer who has relevant confidential information cannot act against his client or former client. In such a case the disqualification is automatic. No assurances or undertakings not to use the information will avail. The lawyer cannot compartmentalize his or her mind so as to screen out what has been gleaned from the client and what was acquired elsewhere. Furthermore, there would be a danger that the lawyer would avoid use of information acquired legitimately because it might be perceived to have come from the client. This would prevent the lawyer from adequately representing the new client. Moreover, the former client would feel at a disadvantage. Questions put in cross-examination about personal matters, for example, would create the uneasy feeling that they had their genesis in the previous relationship.

The answer is less clear with respect to the partners or associates in the firm. Some courts have applied the concept of imputed knowledge. This assumes that the knowledge of one member of the firm is the knowledge of all. If one lawyer cannot act, no member of the firm can act. This is a rule that has been applied by some law firms as their particular brand of ethics. While this is commendable and is to be encouraged, it is, in my opinion, an assumption which is unrealistic in the era of the mega-firm. Furthermore, if the presumption that the knowledge of one is the knowledge of all is to be applied, it must be applied with respect to both the former firm and the firm which the moving lawyer joins. Thus there is a conflict with respect to every matter handled by the old firm that has a substantial relationship with any matter handled by the new firm irrespective of whether the moving lawyer had any involvement with it. This is the "overkill" which has drawn so much criticism in the United States to which I have referred above.

Moreover, I am not convinced that a reasonable member of the public would necessarily conclude that confidences are likely to be disclosed in every case despite institutional efforts to prevent it. There is, however, a strong inference that lawyers who work together share confidences. In answering this question, the court should therefore draw the inference, unless satisfied on the basis of clear and convincing evidence, that all reasonable measures have been taken to ensure that no disclosure will occur by the "tainted" lawyer to the member or members of the firm who are engaged against the former client. Such reasonable measures would include institutional mechanisms such as Chinese Walls and cones of silence. These concepts are not familiar to Canadian courts and indeed do not seem to have been adopted by the governing bodies of the legal profession. It can be expected that the Canadian Bar Association, which took the lead in adopting a Code of Professional Conduct in 1974, will again take the lead to determine whether institutional devices are effective and develop standards for the use of institutional devices which will be uniform throughout Canada. Although I am not prepared to say that a court should never accept these devices as sufficient evidence of effective screening until the governing bodies have approved of them and adopted rules with respect to their operation, I would not foresee a court doing so except in exceptional circumstances. Thus, in the vast majority of cases, the courts are unlikely to accept the effectiveness of these devices until the profession, through its governing body, has studied the matter and determined whether there are institutional guarantees that will satisfy the need to maintain confidence in the integrity of the profession. In this regard, it must be borne in mind that the legal profession is a self-governing profession. The Legislature has entrusted to it and not to the court the responsibility of developing standards. The court's role is merely supervisory, and its jurisdiction extends to this aspect of ethics only in connection with legal proceedings. The governing bodies, however, are concerned with the application of conflict of interest standards not only in respect of litigation but in other fields which constitute the greater part of the practice of law. It would be wrong, therefore, to shut out the governing body of a self-regulating profession from the whole of the practice by the imposition of an inflexible and immutable standard in the exercise of a supervisory jurisdiction over part of it.

A fortiori undertakings and conclusory statements in affidavits without more are not acceptable. These can be expected in every case of this kind that comes before the court. It is no more than the lawyer saying "trust me". This puts the court in the invidious position of deciding which lawyers are to be trusted and which are not. Furthermore, even if the courts found this acceptable, the public is not likely to be satisfied without some additional guarantees that confidential information will under no circumstances be used. In this regard I am in agreement with the statement of Posner J. in *Analytica, supra*, to which I have referred above, that affidavits of lawyers difficult to verify objectively will fail to assure the public.

These standards will, in my opinion, strike the appropriate balance among the three interests to which I have referred. In giving precedence to the preservation of the confidentiality of information imparted to a solicitor, the confidence of the public in the integrity of the profession and in the administration of justice will be maintained and strengthened. On the other hand, reflecting the interest of a member of the public in retaining counsel of her choice and the interest of the profession in permitting lawyers to move from one firm to another, the standards are sufficiently flexible to permit a solicitor to act against a former client provided that a reasonable member of the public who is in possession of the facts would conclude that no unauthorized disclosure of confidential information had occurred or would occur.

Application to this Case

The answer to the first question in this case presents no problem. It is acknowledged that Kristin Dangerfield actively worked on the very case in respect of which her new firm is acting against her former client. She is therefore in possession of relevant confidential information.

With respect to the second question, there is nothing beyond the sworn statements of Sweatman and Dangerfield that no discussions of the case have occurred and undertaking that none will occur. In my opinion, while, as stated by the courts below, there is no reason not to accept the affidavits of apparently reputable counsel, this is not sufficient to demonstrate that all reasonable measures have been taken to rebut the strong inference of disclosure. Indeed, there is nothing in the affidavits to indicate that any independently verifiable steps were taken by the firm to implement any kind of screening. There is nothing to indicate that when Ms. Dangerfield joined the firm, instructions were issued that there were to be no communications directly or indirectly between Ms. Dangerfield and the four members of the firm working on the case. While these measures would not necessarily have been sufficient, I refer to them in order to illustrate the kinds of independently verifiable steps which, along with other measures, are indispensable if the firm intends to continue to act.

I would therefore allow the appeal ... .

. . . . .

CORY J.:— I have read with interest the reasons of my colleague, Justice Sopinka. Although I agree with his disposition of the appeal, I would impose a stricter duty upon lawyers than that which he proposes. He puts his position in this way ...:

> In my opinion, once it is shown by the client that there existed a previous relationship which is sufficiently related to the retainer from which it is sought to remove the solicitor, the court should infer that confidential information was imparted unless the solicitor satisfies the court that no information was imparted which could be relevant.

He observes that it will be difficult for a solicitor to meet that onus. He states that the position, taken by some courts, that if one lawyer in the firm cannot act, then no member of the law firm can act, is unreasonable in this era of mega-firms and mergers. Thus, he reasons that it should be open for a solicitor to show "that no information was imparted which could be relevant."

With respect, I disagree. Neither the merger of law firms nor the mobility of lawyers can be permitted to affect adversely the public's confidence in the judicial system. At this time, when the work of the courts is having a very significant impact upon the lives and affairs of all Canadians, it is fundamentally important that justice not only be done, but appear to be done in the eyes of the public.

My colleague stated that this appeal called for the balancing of three competing values, namely: the maintenance and integrity of our system of justice; the right of litigants not to be lightly deprived of their chosen counsel; and the desirability of permitting reasonable mobility in the legal profession.

Of these factors, the most important and compelling is the preservation of the integrity of our system of justice. The necessity of selecting new counsel will certainly be inconvenient, unsettling and worrisome to clients. Reasonable mobility may well be important to lawyers. However, the integrity of the judicial system is of such fundamental importance to our country and, indeed, to all free and democratic societies that it must be the predominant consideration in any balancing of these three factors.

Lawyers are an integral and vitally important part of our system of justice. It is they who prepare and put their clients' cases before courts and tribunals. In preparing for the hearing of a contentious matter, a client will often be required to reveal to the lawyer retained highly confidential information. The client's most secret devices and desires, the client's most frightening fears will often, of necessity, be revealed. The client must be secure in the knowledge that the lawyer will neither disclose nor take advantage of these revelations.

Our judicial system could not operate if this were not the case. It cannot function properly if doubt or suspicion exists in the mind of the public that the confidential information disclosed by a client to a lawyer might be revealed.

There can be no question that such a doubt would certainly be instilled if the public were to gather the perception that lawyers, by their actions, such as changing firms, create situations where the possibility of a conflict of interest exists.

Imagine a situation where a client involved in a contentious matter has divulged confidential information to a lawyer. If that lawyer practised with one partner, it would be perceived by the public as unfair and completely unacceptable if the partner were to act for the client's adversary. Similarly, if the lawyer moved to another firm which had been retained by those in opposition to the client, the most reasonable and fair-minded member of the public would find it intolerable for that firm to continue to act for those who opposed the client. In both situations the perception of unfairness would arise from the ease with which confidential information received from clients could be privately communicated between lawyers who are working together in the same firm.

Fortunately, partners rarely attempt to act for clients on both sides of a lawsuit. However, the problem more frequently arises when a lawyer, who has received confidential information, joins a firm that is acting for those opposing the interests of the former client. In such a situation there should be an irrebuttable presumption that lawyers who work together share each other's confidences with the result that a knowledge of confidential matters is imputed to other members of the firm. This presumption must apply to the members of the new firm the lawyer joins if public confidence in the administration of justice is to be maintained.

Indeed, this seems to be the purport of the Canadian Bar Association Code of Professional Conduct quoted by my colleague. The chapter entitled "Impartiality and Conflict of Interest" contains the following significant commentaries:

> 11. A lawyer who has acted for a client in a matter should not thereafter act against him (or against persons who were involved in or associated with him in that matter) in the same or any related matter, or place himself in a position where he might be tempted or appear to be tempted to breach the Rule relating to Confidential Information. It is not, however, improper for the lawyer to act against a former client in a fresh and independent matter wholly unrelated to any work he has previously done for that person.

> 12. For the sake of clarity the foregoing paragraphs are expressed in terms of the individual lawyer and his client. *However it will be appreciated that the term "client" includes a client of the law firm of which the lawyer is a partner or associate whether or not he handles the client's work.* [Emphasis added]

It is contended that it is too demanding to hold that the knowledge of one member of a law firm constitutes knowledge of all members of the firm in situations where there has been a merger of large firms or a lawyer has joined a "mega-firm". I cannot agree. It is the appearance of fairness in the eyes of the public that is fundamentally important. No matter how large the mega-firm, there will be innumerable occasions when a lawyer with a possible conflict of interest will be meeting with those lawyers in the firm who are in opposition to that lawyer's former client. Whether at partners' meetings or committee meetings, at lunches or the office golf tournament, in the boardroom or the washroom, the lawyer of the former client will be meeting with and talking to those who are on the other side of the client's case. To those who are not members of the legal profession, it must appear that the opportunities for private discussion are so numerous that the disclosure of confidential information, even if completely inadvertent, would be inevitable. Nor is it likely that disclosures of confidential information will ever be discovered. Further, if a lawyer even inadvertently discloses those weaknesses of the client that have been divulged to him or her, this may be sufficient to give the client's opponents an unfair advantage. This, I think, would be the inevitable conclusion of reasonable people.

That same conclusion would be drawn by the public no matter what form of restrictions were sought to be imposed on individual lawyers and law firms involved. No matter how carefully the Chinese Wall might be constructed, it could be breached without anyone but the lawyers involved knowing of that breach. Law has, after all, the historical precedent of Genghis Khan who, by subterfuge, breached the Great Wall of China, the greatest of Chinese walls. Nor would any system of cones of silence change the public's perception of unfairness. They do not change the reality that lawyers in the same firm meet frequently nor do they reduce the opportunities for the private exchange of confidential information. The public would, quite properly, remain skeptical of the efficacy of the most sophisticated protective scheme.

. . . . .

Let us consider again the two factors which are said to be the competing values to be weighed against the maintenance of the integrity of our system of justice. One of these was the desirability of permitting reasonable mobility in the legal profession. Yet, no matter how strong may be the current rage for mergers or how desirous the mega-firms may be to acquire additional lawyers, neither the large firms nor the lawyers who wish to join them or amalgamate with them should dictate the course of legal ethics. The latest available statistics (as of May 1990) from the Law Society of Upper Canada for the province of Ontario, where the greatest concentration of large law firms might be expected, demonstrate that lawyers in large firms do not comprise the majority of lawyers in that province. ...

[Justice Cory presents a table showing the number of lawyers practicing in Ontario in 1990, divided between those practicing law in small firms and those practicing in large law firms; the table indicates 64.3 per cent of lawyers in Ontario work in firms of 10 lawyers or less, and that outside of Toronto 82.7 per cent of lawyers work in firms of 10 lawyers or less.]

This indicates that, although the large firms may be the movers and shakers on Bay Street, they do not represent the majority of lawyers soldiering on in the cause of justice.

The judicial system and the confidence of the public in its operation are too important to be put at risk by any appearance of unfairness. Unfortunately, no matter how scrupulously ethical an individual lawyer or firm may be, the appearance of unfairness will always be present when, as in this case, one or more lawyers who had a substantial relationship with a client become members of a firm acting for an opposing party. The opportunities for disclosure, even of an inadvertent nature, are too frequent and the possibility of discovering such disclosures too minimal to permit anything less than the irrebuttable presumption that the knowledge of one member of a law firm constitutes the knowledge of all of the lawyers in that firm. Only such a test will ensure the public's confidence in the administration of justice.

This conclusion should not be taken as an impediment to the mobility of lawyers, the merger of law firms or the growth of very large firms; rather, it is a recognition of a professional responsibility owed by lawyers to the litigation process so that the process may retain the respect of the public. It is a small price to pay for mobility of lawyers, mergers of law firms and the increasing size of law firms. It is no more than the fulfilment of a duty owed by members of the legal profession to the public to preserve the integrity of, and public confidence in, the judicial system.

The other factor to be weighed against maintaining the integrity of the justice system was that litigants ought not to be lightly deprived of their chosen counsel. It seems to me that to give undue weight to this factor would unduly benefit the large corporate clients who are said by my colleague to be the raison d'être of the larger firms. It is they who would retain counsel of their choice and primarily benefit from a change in the irrebuttable presumption of shared knowledge. I can see no reason for extending any special benefit or privilege to such clients of large firms. They, like any client who must seek new counsel, will suffer from inconvenience, loss of time and the inevitable worry and concern over such a change. However, the legal profession has many able counsel. The requirement of change imposed on a client is, on balance, a small price to pay for maintaining the integrity of our system of justice.

Conclusion

Where a lawyer who has had a substantial involvement with a client in an ongoing contentious matter joins another law firm which is acting for an opposing party, there is an irrebuttable presumption that the knowledge of such lawyer, including confidential information disclosed to him or her by the former client, has become the knowledge of the new firm. Such an irrebuttable presumption is essential to preserve public confidence in the administration of justice.

. . . . .

NOTES AND QUESTIONS

1. Did the Supreme Court select the appropriate factors to be given consideration in its decision? Did it evaluate them appropriately? This will become an important question for the Supreme Court in the subsequent cases of *R. v. Neil* and *Strother v. Monarch Entertainment Ltd.*, below.

2. In many other circumstances courts accept the word of a lawyer, even when given in an unsworn statement. For example, courts will accept a lawyer's word with respect to undertakings, the reasons for delay in bringing a matter to trial and other questions related to the conduct of litigation. Here the Supreme Court of Canada takes the view that even a sworn statement setting out the lawyers' propriety is insufficient. Why? What is at stake here that seems to require a more rigorous approach? What does it say about the Court's view of the trustworthiness of lawyers when their own interests are implicated?

3. What is Sopinka J.'s justification for leaving the development of the conflict of interest regime essentially in the hands of lawyers and the legal profession? Is this an appropriate resolution of the matter?

4. Justice Cory's stinging concurrence includes what appears to be his own research on the distribution of lawyers in Ontario, a curious reference considering that the case is from Manitoba. Does this suggest that he was unusually troubled by the apparent "big law firm orientation" of the majority? Is he right to criticize the majority on the basis that the decision is unprincipled and too "lawyer-sympathetic"? Or is his judgment a desperate attempt to cling to the ideals of a bygone era, ideals now out of step with the modern day practice of law?

5. On the other hand, perhaps the majority, and Sopinka J. himself, saw that too rigorous a standard would create a powerful and dangerous litigation tool in the hands of highly zealous lawyers, who would be only too willing to threaten or proceed with disqualification motions to gain a tactical advantage in litigation. Another interpretation is that too rigorous a standard would work an unnecessary hardship on both lawyers and clients that wouldn't significantly serve the public interest.

6. The Supreme Court of Canada articulates the nature of the lawyers' obligation almost entirely in language related to "public interest" aspects of the professional role based on the public perception that a lawyer has acted with integrity. Does this ask too much of a lawyer who is, after all, attempting to act with integrity? Should he or she also have to be "appear" to act with integrity?

7. Subsequent to *MacDonald Estate v. Martin*, Canada's law societies established elaborate screening mechanisms to guide law firms so that they could: (1) minimize the risk that a client's confidential information, in the possession of his or her former lawyer, will be made known to the lawyers representing the client's adversary; and (2) at the same time enable the former lawyer to join the new oppositional law firm. The Federation of Law Societies of Canada's *Model Code of Professional Conduct* sets out these mechanisms in Rules 2.04(17)-2.04(26). Do these rules satisfactorily address and resolve the issues, and respect the values, identified by the majority in *MacDonald Estate v. Martin*?

8. Codes of Professional Conduct contemplate that a lawyer's duty to preserve client confidences continues after the representation ends. Does this case suggest that there may be other duties that continue after a lawyer-client relationship ends, including the duty not to place oneself in a position of perceived conflict of interest, or in some other situation that would be perceived to be disloyal to that former client?

9. There is no explicit reference in the judgment to Ms. Dangerfield's obligation of loyalty to her original, now former, client. Is this an oversight on the part of the Court? What are the dimensions of a lawyer's duty to a former client?

3. Duties to Current Clients

In *MacDonald Estate v. Martin*, the complaint came from Ms. Dangerfield's client, but by the time of the dispute Ms. Dangerfield was no longer representing that client. In that instance, as is clear from the judgment, the primary concern of the Court was that no confidential information with respect to the former client would pass to the current client. A different — perhaps additional — problem arises where the conflict involves two clients that a lawyer or firm is representing at essentially the same time. Even if confidential information can be protected in such a situation (for example, by protective screens placed between the two lawyers in the firm who are acting for the respective clients) it is an open question whether the law firm acting for those two clients can act in ways that still enable them to fulfill their obligations to each client, consistent with the expectations of the justice system. The following case analyzes this problem.

R. v. NEIL

[2002] S.C.J. No. 72, [2002] 3 S.C.R. 631
(S.C.C., Major, Bastarache, Binnie, Arbour and LeBel JJ.)

[Neil was accused of having committed certain criminal offences. He claimed that his lawyer had failed to adequately represent him and had essentially sold him out to the interests of another client of the firm. Neil argued that the charges against him should be stayed because of his lawyer's behaviour.

Neil operated a business as an independent paralegal in Edmonton. Lambert was his assistant. On occasion, Neil would refer clients to the Venkatraman law firm or seek the law firm's assistance. During the relevant time Lazin was a lawyer working either as an employee of the Venkatraman law firm or associated with the firm — associated in the sense that he shared office space and some facilities with the firm. Neil did some work that the Law Society of Alberta regarded as the unauthorized practice of law — essentially practising law without a licence — and a complaint led to a police investigation. Two criminal charges against Neil ultimately brought the case to the Supreme Court of Canada.

In one indictment — referred to as the "*Canada Trust*" matter — Neil and Lambert were alleged to have defrauded Canada Trust by arranging for mortgages to be signed up in Lambert's name for some of Neil's clients who did not qualify financially for a mortgage. Lazin took on the representation of Lambert in this matter at the same time that the Venkatraman firm was representing Neil. Lazin attended some consultations with Neil, essentially to obtain information that would enable him to run a "cut-throat" defence, by blaming Neil and portraying Lambert as an innocent dupe. Some time later, the Venkatraman law firm withdrew from the representation of Neil due to Lazin's representation of Lambert.

In the second indictment, the "*Doblanko*" matter, Lazin learned through the representation of one of his clients, Darren Doblanko, that Mrs. Doblanko had obtained a divorce with the assistance of Neil, allegedly on the basis of false affidavits prepared by Neil. Lazin arranged for Doblanko to report this information to the police — specifically the officer investigating Neil on the Canada Trust matter. This was said to have been done to "multiply the allegations of dishonesty" against Neil and thereby assist in Lazin's defence of Lambert. Ultimately, the charges against Lambert were dropped in exchange for her testimony against Neil.]

BINNIE J.:— What are the proper limits of a lawyer's "duty of loyalty" to a current client in a case where the lawyer did not receive any confidential information that was (or is) relevant to the matter in which he proposes to act against the current client's interest?

. . . . .

In my view, the law firm did owe a duty of loyalty to the appellant at the material time, and the law firm ought not to have taken up the cause of one of the appellant's alleged victims (Darren Doblanko) in proceedings before a civil court at the same time as it maintained a solicitor-client relationship with the appellant in respect of other matters simultaneously pending before the criminal court (the "*Canada Trust*" matters). The *Doblanko* mandate, though factually and legally unrelated to the *Canada Trust* matters, was adverse to the appellant's interest. The law firm, as fiduciary, could not serve two masters at the same time. Having said that, the appellant falls short on the issue of remedy. He may (and perhaps did) choose to take his complaint to the Law Society of Alberta, but he is not entitled to a stay of proceedings. The law firm's conduct did not affect the fairness of the *Doblanko* trial. Its involvement predated the laying of charges by the police. There was no issue of confidential information. The *Doblanko* charges were serious and would almost certainly have been laid in any event. In my view, the prosecution of the *Doblanko* charge was not an abuse of process.

. . . . .

II. Analysis

I make three preliminary observations. The first is that while misuse of confidential information is not an issue in the *Doblanko* case, in which the stay was entered, it is an issue in the *Canada Trust* matter where Lazin, acting against the appellant's interest, sat in on part of the solicitor-client interview on April 18, 1995, described above. Secondly these cases do not require the imputation of confidential knowledge from one partner of the firm to another. Here the same member of the firm (Lazin) had a finger in each of the conflict situations. Thirdly, we are not being asked to intervene based merely on an "appearance" of conflict. The conflicts were actual.

. . . . .

A. *The Lawyer's Duty of Loyalty*

Appellant's counsel reminds us of the declaration of an advocate's duty of loyalty made by Henry Brougham, later Lord Chancellor, in his defence of Queen Caroline against the charge of adultery brought against her by her husband, King George IV. He thus addressed the House of Lords:

> [A]n advocate, in the discharge of his duty, knows but one person in all the world, and that person is his client. To save that client by all means and expedients, and at all hazards and costs to other persons, and, among them, to himself, is his first and only duty; and in performing this duty he must not regard the alarm, the torments, the destruction which he may bring upon

others. Separating the duty of a patriot from that of an advocate, he must go on reckless of consequences, though it should be his unhappy fate to involve his country in confusion.

(*Trial of Queen Caroline* (1821), by J. Nightingale, vol. II, The Defence, Part 1, at p. 8)

These words are far removed in time and place from the legal world in which the Venkatraman law firm carried on its practice, but the defining principle — the duty of loyalty — is with us still. It endures because it is essential to the integrity of the administration of justice and it is of high public importance that public confidence in that integrity be maintained ... Unless a litigant is assured of the undivided loyalty of the lawyer, neither the public nor the litigant will have confidence that the legal system, which may appear to them to be a hostile and hideously complicated environment, is a reliable and trustworthy means of resolving their disputes and controversies ... As O'Connor J.A. (now A.C.J.O.) observed in *R. v. McCallen*:

> ... the relationship of counsel and client requires clients, typically untrained in the law and lacking the skills of advocates, to entrust the management and conduct of their cases to the counsel who act on their behalf. There should be no room for doubt about counsel's loyalty and dedication to the client's case.

The value of an independent bar is diminished unless the lawyer is free from conflicting interests. Loyalty, in that sense, promotes effective representation, on which the problem-solving capability of an adversarial system rests. Other objectives, I think, can be related to the first. For example, in *MacDonald Estate, supra*, Sopinka J. speaks of the "countervailing value that a litigant should not be deprived of his or her choice of counsel without good cause." Dubin J.A. remarked in *Re Regina and Speid* ...:

> We would have thought it axiomatic that no client has a right to retain counsel if that counsel, by accepting the brief, puts himself in a position of having a conflict of interest between his new client and a former one.

. . . . .

These competing interests are really aspects of protecting the integrity of the legal system. If a litigant could achieve an undeserved tactical advantage over the opposing party by bringing a disqualification motion or seeking other "ethical" relief using "the integrity of the administration of justice" merely as a flag of convenience, fairness of the process would be undermined. This, I think, is what worried the Newfoundland Court of Appeal in *R. v. Parsons* (1992), 100 Nfld. & P.E.I.R. 260, where the accused was charged with the first degree murder of his mother. The Crown sought to remove defence counsel on the basis that he had previously acted for the father of the accused in an unrelated matrimonial matter, and might in future have to cross-examine the father at the son's trial for murder. The accused and his father both obtained independent legal advice, after full disclosure of the relevant facts, and waived any conflict. The father also waived solicitor-client privilege. The court was satisfied there was no issue of confidential information. On these facts, the court concluded that "public confidence in the criminal justice system might well be undermined by interfering with the accused's selection of the counsel of his choice" ... .

. . . . .

The duty of loyalty is intertwined with the fiduciary nature of the lawyer-client relationship. One of the roots of the word fiduciary is *fides*, or loyalty, and loyalty is often cited as one of the defining characteristics of a fiduciary ... The lawyer fulfills squarely Professor Donovan Waters' definition of a fiduciary:

> In putting together words to describe a "fiduciary" there is of course no immediate obstacle. Almost everybody would say that it is a person in whom trust and confidence is placed by another on whose behalf the fiduciary is to act. The other (the beneficiary) is entitled to expect that the fiduciary will be concerned solely for the beneficiary's interests, never the fiduciary's own. The "relationship" must be the dependence or reliance of the beneficiary upon the fiduciary.

. . . . .

Fiduciary duties are often called into existence to protect relationships of importance to the public including, as here, solicitor and client. Disloyalty is destructive of that relationship.

B. *More Than Just Confidential Information*

While the Court is most often preoccupied with uses and abuses of confidential information in cases where it is sought to disqualify a lawyer from further acting in a matter, as in *MacDonald Estate, supra*, the duty of loyalty to current clients includes a much broader principle of avoidance of conflicts of interest, in which confidential information may or may not play a role ...

In *Drabinsky v. KPMG* ..., where the plaintiff sought an injunction restraining the accounting firm KPMG (of which the plaintiff was a client) from further investigating the financial records of a company of which the plaintiff was a senior officer, Ground J., grouping together lawyers and accountants, said, at p. 567:

> I am of the view that the fiduciary relationship between the client and the professional advisor, either a lawyer or an accountant, imposes duties on the fiduciary <u>beyond the duty not to disclose confidential information</u>. It includes a duty of loyalty and good faith and a duty not to act against the interests of the client. [Emphasis added.]

. . . . .

The aspects of the duty of loyalty relevant to this appeal do include issues of confidentiality in the *Canada Trust* matters, but engage more particularly three other dimensions:

(i)   *the duty to avoid conflicting interests* ...

(ii) *a duty of commitment to the client's cause* (sometimes referred to as "zealous representation") from the time counsel is retained, not just at trial, i.e. ensuring that a divided loyalty does not cause the lawyer to "soft peddle" his or her defence of a client out of concern for another client ...; and,

(iii) *a duty of candour* with the client on matters relevant to the retainer. ...

C. *The Venkatraman Law Firm's Breach of Professional Obligations*

. . . . .

(1) Did a Solicitor-Client Relationship Exist at the Relevant Time?

The Crown argues that the *Canada Trust* retainer ended before the *Doblanko* retainer began, and the relevant principles are therefore those that govern acting against a *former* client rather than the stricter and more comprehensive rules about acting against a *current* client.

The *Code of Professional Conduct* of the Law Society of Alberta defines "client" as follows, at p. viii:

> "client" generally means a person on whose behalf the lawyer renders professional services and with whom the lawyer has a current or ongoing lawyer/client relationship, but may also include a person who reasonably believes that a lawyer/client relationship exists although one or more of the customary indicia of such a relationship are absent.

[Justice Binnie rejected the argument that Doblanko was a "'former' client".]

(2) The Duty of Loyalty to an Existing Client

The Law Society of Alberta's *Code of Professional Conduct* provides that "[i]n each matter, a lawyer's judgment and fidelity to the client's interests must be free from compromising influences" (c. 6, Statement of Principle, p. 50). The facts of this case illustrate a number of important objectives served by this principle. Loyalty required the Venkatraman law firm to focus on the interest of the appellant without being distracted by other interests including personal interests. Part of the problem here seems to have been Lazin's determination to hang onto a piece of litigation. When Lazin was asked about "the ethical issue" in acting for Lambert, he said maybe "it was a question of not wanting to give up the file". Loyalty includes putting the client's business ahead of the lawyer's business. The appellant was entitled to a level of commitment from his lawyer that whatever could properly be done on his behalf would be done as surely as it would have been done if the appellant had had the skills and training to do the job personally. On learning that his own lawyer had put before the divorce court evidence of his further wrongdoing, the appellant understandably felt betrayed. Equally, the public in Edmonton, where the prosecution of the appellant had attracted considerable notoriety, required assurance that the truth had been ascertained by an adversarial system that functioned clearly and without hidden agendas.

The general duty of loyalty has frequently been stated. In *Ramrakha v. Zinner* ... Harradence J.A., concurring, observed ...:

> A solicitor is in a fiduciary relationship to his client and must avoid situations where he has, or potentially may, develop a conflict of interests ... The logic behind this is cogent in that a solicitor must be able to provide his client with complete and undivided loyalty, dedication, full disclosure, and good faith, all of which may be jeopardized if more than one interest is represented.

The duty of loyalty was similarly expressed by Wilson J.A. (as she then was) in *Davey v. Woolley, Hames, Dale & Dingwall* ...:

> The underlying premise ... is that, human nature being what it is, the solicitor cannot give his exclusive, undivided attention to the interests of his client if he is torn between his client's interests and his own or his client's interests and those of another client to whom he owes the self-same duty of loyalty, dedication and good faith.

More recently in England, in a case dealing with the duties of accountants, [*Bolkiah v. KPMG*, [1999] 2 A.C. 222 (H.L.)] the House of Lords observed that "[t]he duties of an accountant cannot be greater than those of a solicitor, and may be less" ... and went on to compare the duty owed by accountants to *former* clients (where the concern is largely with confidential information) and the duty owed to *current* clients (where the duty of loyalty prevails irrespective of whether or not there is a risk of disclosure of confidential information). Lord Millett stated ...:

> My Lords, I would affirm [possession of confidential information] as the basis of the court's jurisdiction to intervene on behalf of a *former* client. It is otherwise where the court's intervention is sought by an existing client, for a fiduciary cannot act at the same time both for and against the same client, and his firm is in no better position. A man cannot without the consent of both clients act for one client while his partner is acting for another in the opposite interest. His disqualification has nothing to do with the confidentiality of client information. It is based on the inescapable conflict of interest which is inherent in the situation. [Emphasis added.]

. . . . .

In exceptional cases, consent of the client may be inferred. For example, governments generally accept that private practitioners who do their civil or criminal work will act against them in unrelated matters, and a contrary position in a particular case may, depending on the circumstances, be seen as tactical rather than principled. Chartered banks and entities that could be described as professional litigants may have a similarly broad-minded attitude where the matters are sufficiently unrelated that there is no danger of confidential information being abused. These exceptional cases are explained by the notion of informed consent, express or implied.

The general prohibition is undoubtedly a major inconvenience to large law partnerships and especially to national firms with their proliferating offices in major centres across Canada. Conflict searches in the firm's records may belatedly turn up files in another office a lawyer may not have been aware of. Indeed, he or she may not even be acquainted with the partner on the other side of the country who is in charge of the file. Conflict search procedures are often inefficient. Nevertheless it is the firm not just the individual lawyer, that owes a fiduciary duty to its clients, and a bright line is required. The bright line is provided by the general rule that a lawyer may not represent one client whose interests are directly adverse to the immediate interests of another current client — *even if the two mandates are unrelated* — unless both clients consent after receiving full disclosure (and preferably independent legal advice), and the lawyer reasonably believes that he or she is able to represent each client without adversely affecting the other.

The Venkatraman law firm was bound by this general prohibition to avoid acting contrary to the interest of the appellant, a current client, who was a highly vulnerable litigant in need of all the help and reassurance he could legitimately get.

(3) Breaches of the Duty of Loyalty

In my view the Venkatraman law firm, and Lazin in particular, put themselves in a position where the duties they undertook to other clients conflicted with the duty of loyalty which they owed to the appellant. I adopt, in this respect, the notion of a "conflict" in s. 121 of the *Restatement Third, The Law Governing Lawyers* (2000), vol. 2, at pp. 244-45, as a "substantial risk that the lawyer's representation of the client would be materially and adversely affected by the lawyer's own interests or by the lawyer's duties to another current client, a former client, or a third person".

The initial conflict was to attempt to act simultaneously for both the appellant and his eventual co-accused in the *Canada Trust* charges, Helen Lambert. They were clearly adverse in interest. It is true that at the time Lazin and his colleague from the firm met the appellant in the Remand Centre on April 18, 1995 Lazin had not been retained by Lambert on the criminal charges. He was acting only with respect to her divorce. It is also true that in the end the appellant was eventually represented by other counsel. Nevertheless the trial judge found that on April 18, 1995, Lazin was *in fact* (if not yet officially) acting on Lambert's behalf in the criminal proceedings. Her indictment was reasonably anticipated (given her involvement in the subject matter of the *Canada Trust* charge) and, most importantly, the trial judge held that the purpose of Lazin's attendance at the Remand Centre was to get evidence to run a "cut-throat" defence against the appellant who, he found, was an ongoing client of the Venkatraman law firm. The fact that the appellant eventually looked elsewhere for a lawyer in the *Canada Trust* case, whether as a result of his choice or theirs, did not diminish their duty of loyalty. Nor does it make a difference that no professional fee was charged for that particular consultation. The Venkatraman firm (Lazin) appreciated that the appellant having been arrested, the long arm of the law would soon be laid on Helen Lambert. In fact, Helen Lambert was arrested less than two months later, on June 6, 1995.

The second conflict relates to the *Doblanko* charges. As mentioned, both Doblanko and his former wife (who had by now remarried and produced children of her second "marriage") needed their earlier divorce to be regularized. The Venkatraman firm breached their duty to the appellant in accepting a retainer that required them to put before the divorce court judge evidence of the illegal conduct of their client, the appellant, at a time when they knew he was facing other criminal charges related to his paralegal practice, in which their firm had had a long-standing involvement. It was contended that the *Doblanko* and *Canada Trust* cases were wholly unrelated in the sense that Lazin could not have obtained in the *Doblanko* mandate confidential information that would be relevant in the *Canada Trust* mandate. This, as stated, is not the test of loyalty to an *existing* client, and it is not entirely true either. While the two cases were wholly independent of each other in terms of their facts, the Lambert's cut-throat defence was helped by piling up the allegations of dishonest conduct in different matters by different complainants in a way that would make it easier for the jury to consider her a victim rather than a perpetrator. The linkage was thus strategic. The *Doblanko* application was initiated in July 1995. The Crown advised us that the *Canada Trust* criminal charges against Helen Lambert were not resolved until the spring of 1996.

In the course of the *Doblanko* application, the divorce court judge expressed the view (according to Lazin) that Lazin should report the appellant's apparent falsification of documents to the police. I think at that point that Lazin, as an officer of the court, was obliged to do so. Lazin then called the Law Society (without disclosing that the appellant was a client of his firm) who advised that Lazin *could* advise his divorce court client to report the matter to the police but he was not bound to. Lazin advised neither the trial judge nor the Law Society that the suspected forger (the appellant) was a client of his firm. Further, Lazin made a point of having the matter reported to the police officer who was responsible for investigating the appellant in connection with the *Canada Trust* and other matters.

It was the Venkatraman firm that put the cat among the pigeons by bringing the *Doblanko* application before the divorce court. Mr. Doblanko would likely have found another lawyer to make the application, and the facts might equally have eventually made their way to the police, but it was in violation of the firm's duty of loyalty to the appellant to contribute in this way to the appellant's downfall.

(4) Remedies for Breach of the Duty of Loyalty

It is one thing to demonstrate a breach of loyalty. It is quite another to arrive at an appropriate remedy.

A client whose lawyer is in breach of his or her fiduciary duty has various avenues of redress. A complaint to the relevant governing body, in this case the Law Society of Alberta, may result in disciplinary action. A conflict of interest may also be the subject matter of an action against the lawyer for compensation, as in *Szarfer v. Chodos, supra*. Breach of the ethical rules that could raise concerns at the Law Society does not necessarily give grounds in a malpractice action or justify a constitutional remedy.

. . . . .

The appellant's argument that the purity of the waters of the fountain of justice was irredeemably polluted in these cases by the action of the Venkatraman law firm (to borrow a metaphor from Lord Brougham's era) is very difficult to sustain on the facts.

[Justice Binnie ultimately declined to enter a judicial stay of proceedings, stating at paragraph 43 of the judgment that "there is nothing in the *Doblanko* verdict to contravene our fundamental notions of justice".]

NOTES AND QUESTIONS

1. To some extent the *"Canada Trust"* aspects of this case are straightforward, involving as they do a concurrent conflict (the Venkatraman law firm, including Lazin, representing both Neil and Lambert at the same time) with Lazin obtaining and making inappropriate use of confidential information from Neil in the course of his representation of Lambert. Recall the rule articulated in *MacDonald Estate v. Martin* and reinforced in *R. v. Neil* to the effect that confidential information is attributed to all members of the law firm. Assuming that there were no "screens" in place, to adequately protect this information, wouldn't the law firm normally have been disqualified anyway, whether or not Lazin had attended the interview with Neil? Does that matter in this case?

2. Conflicts of interest usually revolve around the possibility of a client's (or former client's) confidential information being shared with lawyers in opposition to that client's interests. In the *"Doblanko"* matter, however, the information was obtained in ways not associated with the client or former client, Neil. How does the Supreme Court of Canada deal with this aspect of the alleged conflict? Does this represent a significant departure from the way that conflicts of interest were viewed in *MacDonald Estate v. Martin*, not only in terms of the ultimate scope of the conflict, but, more importantly, in terms of the principles applied by the Court in reaching its conclusion? Does this explain the reconsideration by Binnie J. of the principles upon which the lawyer's responsibility to a client are based?

3. Was the part of the "bright line" rule that was highlighted by Binnie J. to the effect that it applies *"even where the matters are unrelated"* necessary to the decision? You will recall that part of Lazin's disloyalty to Neil was his use of the "Doblanko divorce" information against Neil, information that he obtained in the "unrelated" representation of Mr. Doblanko. But was it really "unrelated"? Alice Woolley argues:

    > The representation that drove the disclosure [by Lazin of the falsified documents in the Doblanko divorce] was, instead, Lazin's representation of [his client] Lambert; it was to benefit Helen Lambert that Lazin disclosed the information in the way that he did. Thus, the conduct of Lazin that was problematic was in relation to a related matter — the

> Lambert representation — and was also in relation to the very matter on which the firm was representing Neil.[3]

4. In his text *Professional Conduct for Lawyers and Judges*, written shortly before the Supreme Court of Canada's decision in *R. v. Neil*, Beverley Smith wrote:

> [T]he lawyer will be required to act in the utmost good faith toward the person for whom and on whose behalf he/she has undertaken to act. The Latin phrase *"uberrimae fidei"* aptly sums up the requirement that the lawyer act in the most trustworthy fashion. It is the existence of this duty of good faith and trustworthiness which colours all that the lawyer does during **and following** the term as the client's legal advisor and advocate.[4]

> This concept of utmost good faith seems to capture something deeper, and not limited to, a specific development in the lawyer-client relationship, such as the sharing of confidential information. Is this what the Supreme Court of Canada was trying to articulate or revive as a principle? If so, does the decision achieve this?

5. *Neil* has generated intense debate within the legal profession and significant consideration by law societies across Canada. Two aspects of conflicts of interest have been examined: conflicts related to "former clients" and conflicts concerning "current clients". The latter has dominated the debate.

4.   "Current Client" Conflicts

The *Neil* decision, and its articulation of a "bright line" rule restricting representation of current clients whose interests are directly adverse to those of other current clients, has become the most hotly debated topic in legal ethics in Canada in recent memory. We begin with some academic commentary on the matter. Shortly after the *Neil* decision, Richard F. Devlin and Victoria Rees examined the topic and came to this conclusion:

> [W]hile some commentators have dismissed the *Neil* case as an example of egregious conflict in the area of criminal law and, therefore, not of great significance, revisionists argue that this is a mistake because Binnie J. went out of his way to articulate quite carefully the Court's reflections on the duty of loyalty, echoing the biblical homily that "No man can serve two masters: either he will hate the one and love the other; or else he will hold to the one and despise the other."

> Consequently, and fifth, Binnie J. makes it clear that a business conflict can now be a legal conflict because "[l]oyalty includes putting the client's business ahead of the lawyer's business." A lawyer's desire to "hang onto a piece of litigation" is insufficient justification. As a result, retainers will have to be declined because of business conflicts. Moreover, "Chinese

---

3   Alice Woolley, *Understanding Lawyers' Ethics in Canada* (Markham, ON: LexisNexis Canada, 2011) at 267.

4   Beverley Smith, *Professional Conduct for Lawyers and Judges*, 3rd ed. (Fredericton: Maritime Law Book, 2007), ch. 2, at 3-4 [emphasis added].

walls" and "cones of silence" do not apply in the context of a breach of loyalty because their concern is confidentiality, not loyalty.[5]

This passage is significant in at least two respects. First, it highlights the point that in some respects the duty of loyalty is of greater import than the duty of confidentiality since it cannot easily be addressed through the use of prophylactic devices like "Chinese walls" and "cones of silence" or other lawyer screening mechanisms. Second, the Devlin and Rees observation about business conflicts capable of becoming legal conflicts was prescient, as we will see in *Strother*, the third case in the Supreme Court trilogy.

Of at least equal significance to those observations, however, is the degree to which *Neil* changed the standard against which "loyalty to current clients" is measured, and the degree to which previously allowed representations of clients are now off limits. This issue has largely revolved around the "bright line" prohibition against the representation of a current client whose interests are directly adverse to the interests of another client, even if the matter on which that other client is being represented is unrelated to the subject matter of the adverse representation, unless both clients consent.[6]

This has been the centrepiece of the conflicts debate.[7] Following *Neil*, the Law Societies of British Columbia and Alberta amended their Codes of Professional Conduct and adopted the "bright line" prohibition. Shortly afterward, the Federation of Law Societies of Canada undertook the development of a national *Model Code of Professional Conduct*, part of which work included a section on conflicts of interest.

Early drafts of the *Model Code* proposed the incorporation of the "bright line rule" in *Neil*. These proposals were strongly opposed by the Canadian Bar Association, which commissioned a Task Force Report on Conflicts of Interest in 2008.[8] The Task Force proposed a number of new approaches to the general subject of conflicts of interest. On the topic of "current client" conflicts, the Task Force rejected the "bright line" rule, arguing that it "was not relevant to the facts in either *Neil* or *Strother* [excerpted below] so the elaboration of the Unrelated Matter Rule was clearly obiter dicta in both

---

5   Richard F. Devlin & Victoria Rees, "Beyond Conflicts of Interest to the Duty of Loyalty" (2005) 48 Can. Bar Rev. 433 at 443-44 [footnotes omitted].

6   As Alice Woolley has noted, and as *Wallace v. Canadian National Railway*, [2011] S.J. No. 589, 2011 SKCA 108 (Sask. C.A.) demonstrates, courts have somewhat inconsistently applied the "bright line" rule. See Alice Woolley, *Understanding Lawyers' Ethics in Canada* (Markham, ON: LexisNexis Canada, 2011) at 270-72. See, also, for example, *De Beers Canada Inc. v. Shore Gold Inc.*, [2006] S.J. No. 210, 278 Sask. R. 171 (Sask. Q.B.); *Toddglen Construction Ltd. v. Concord Adex Developments Corp.*, [2004] O.J. No. 1788 (Ont. S.C.J.); and *Lotech Medical Systems Ltd. v. Kinetic Concept, Inc.*, [2008] F.C.J. No. 1595 (F.C.).

7   A comprehensive account of the debate may be found in Adam Dodek's article, "Conflicted Identities: The Battle over the Duty of Loyalty in Canada" (2011) 14 Legal Ethics 193.

8   Canadian Bar Association, Task Force on Conflicts of Interest, *Conflicts of Interest: Final Report, Recommendations and Toolkit* (August 2008) at 37, online: <http://www.cba.org/CBA/groups/pdf/conflicts_finalreport.pdf>.

cases".[9] The more than three years that followed the CBA Task Force Report were filled with conflicting legal opinions, criticisms and recriminations of *Model Code* drafts and of the CBA recommendations. Even Binnie J., the author of the unanimous judgment in *Neil* and of the majority judgment in *Strother*, entered the fray, criticizing the CBA approach.[10] The FLSC Committee tasked to develop the *Model Code* obtained a legal opinion which confirmed that its draft rule on "current client" conflicts of interest, closely tracking the "bright line" rule, was responsive to the public interest. That advice was criticized in a legal opinion, commissioned by the CBA and authored by Michel Bastarache, a retired justice of the Supreme Court of Canada who had been a member of the unanimous panel in *Neil* and a dissenting member of the panel that decided *Strother*.[11]

Ultimately, in February 2011, a majority of the Advisory Committee recommended the adoption of a "current client, unrelated matters" rule in the following terms:

> 2.04(3) A lawyer must not represent a client whose legal interests are directly adverse to the immediate legal interests of a current client – even if the matters are unrelated – unless both clients consent.[12]

In the face of strong CBA opposition, this proposed Model Rule was not adopted by the FLSC, and further work on the question was assigned to the newly created Standing Committee on the *Model Code*. The Standing Committee engaged in further consultations, obtained additional legal advice and ultimately developed a new section on conflicts of interest, introduced a new definition of a "conflict of interest", dropped the section on "current client conflicts" and proposed a new and more comprehensive rule. The principle of loyalty to clients and the "bright line rule" itself were articulated in a new Rule and associated Commentary. The Committee's recommendations were adopted by the Federation in November 2011.[13]

The relevant portions of the *Model Code* now provide:

> A "conflict of interest" means the existence of a substantial risk that a lawyer's loyalty to or representation of a client would be materially and adversely affected by the lawyer's own interest or the lawyer's duties to another client, a former client, or a third person.

---

9   *Ibid.*, at 37.

10   Ian Binnie, "*Sondage après Sondage … quelques réflexions sur les conflits d'interets*" (Speech given at Les Journees Strasbourgeoises, Strasbourg, France, July 4, 2008). See Adam Dodek, "Conflicted Identities: The Battle over the Duty of Loyalty in Canada" (2011) 14 Legal Ethics 193 at 206-208.

11   The FLSC's proposal, the Report and the conflicting legal opinions can be found in the Federation of Law Societies, Supplementary Report, Advisory Committee on Conflicts of Interest (February 14, 2011), online: <http://www.flsc.ca/_documents/Supplementary-Report-Conflicts-of-Interest-Feb-2011.pdf>.

12   *Ibid.*, at 9.

13   Federation of Law Societies of Canada, Standing Committee on the Model Code of Professional Conduct, *Report on Conflicts of Interest* (November 21, 2011), online: <http://www.flsc.ca/_documents/Conflicts-of-Interest-Report-Nov_2011.pdf>.

. . . . .

2.04 (1) A lawyer must not act or continue to act for a client where there is a conflict of interest, except as permitted under this Code.

Commentary

As defined in these rules, a conflict of interest exists when there is a substantial risk that a lawyer's loyalty to or representation of a client would be materially and adversely affected by the lawyer's own interest or the lawyer's duties to another client, a former client, or a third person. The risk must be more than a mere possibility; there must be a genuine, serious risk to the duty of loyalty or to client representation arising from the retainer. A client's interests may be seriously prejudiced unless the lawyer's judgment and freedom of action on the client's behalf are as free as possible from conflicts of interest.

. . . . .

The fiduciary relationship, the duty of loyalty and conflicting interests

The value of an independent bar is diminished unless the lawyer is free from conflicts of interest. The rule governing conflicts of interest is founded in the duty of loyalty which is grounded in the law governing fiduciaries. The lawyer-client relationship is a fiduciary relationship and as such, the lawyer has a duty of loyalty to the client. To maintain public confidence in the integrity of the legal profession and the administration of justice, in which lawyers play a key role, it is essential that lawyers respect the duty of loyalty. Arising from the duty of loyalty are other duties, such as a duty to commit to the client's cause, the duty of confidentiality, the duty of candour and the duty not to act against the interests of the client. This obligation is premised on an established or ongoing lawyer client relationship in which the client must be assured of the lawyer's undivided loyalty, free from any material impairment of the lawyer and client relationship. The rule reflects the principle articulated by the Supreme Court of Canada in the cases of *R. v. Neil* 2002 SCC 70 and *Strother v. 3464920 Canada Inc.* 2007 SCC 24, regarding conflicting interests involving current clients, that a lawyer must not represent one client whose legal interests are directly adverse to the immediate legal interests of another client without consent. This duty arises even if the matters are unrelated. The lawyer client relationship may be irreparably damaged where the lawyer's representation of one client is directly adverse to another client's immediate interests. One client may legitimately fear that the lawyer will not pursue the representation out of deference to the other client, and an existing client may legitimately feel betrayed by the lawyer's representation of a client with adverse legal interests. The prohibition on acting in such circumstances except with the consent of the clients guards against such outcomes and protects the lawyer client relationship.

Accordingly, factors for the lawyer's consideration in determining whether a conflict of interest exists include:

- the immediacy of the legal interests;
- whether the legal interests are directly adverse;

- whether the issue is substantive or procedural;

- the temporal relationship between the matters;

- the significance of the issue to the immediate and long-term interests of the clients involved; and

- the clients' reasonable expectations in retaining the lawyer for the particular matter or representation.

The Committee recommendations, also adopted, expanded upon the concept of client consent.

Adam Dodek, a proponent of the adoption of the "bright-line" rule, commented that the Report in which this new draft rule appeared

> ... essentially endorses the principles contained in previous Federation reports, although choosing to structure the rule differently. Most importantly, the Federation continues to expressly support the position of the Supreme Court of Canada and the bright-line rule of *Neil* but has also elevated the emphasis on lawyer loyalty.[14]

Whether the Model Rule is adopted by law societies in the provinces and territories remains to be seen.

Scenario One

A lawyer takes on the representation of a client, D, in a corporate takeover dispute against Company C at the same time that another lawyer in the firm is representing Company C in a wrongful death action in another country. There was no suggestion that client confidentiality was compromised. In light of *Neil*, could the law firm continue with the representation of the client in the corporate takeover dispute against C and continue the representation of C in the wrongful death case? Could the law firm drop C and continue with the representation of D in the presumably more lucrative takeover dispute? See *De Beers Canada Inc. v. Shore Gold Inc.*, [2006] S.J. No. 210, 278 Sask. R. 171 (Sask. Q.B.).

5. Former Client Conflicts

One aspect of *Neil* that has been discussed to only a limited extent is the degree to which the judgment offered insights into the standard applicable in situations of alleged conflicts of interest involving former clients. It will be recalled that *Neil* involved actions by Lazin that engaged his relationship with Neil as both a current and a former client. Is there a difference in the two situations? Should there be? Terrence O'Sullivan and Paul Michell have

---

[14] Adam Dodek, "Conflicted Identities: The Battle over the Duty of Loyalty in Canada" (2011) 14 Legal Ethics 193 at 212-13.

commented on the significance of the *Neil* decision.[15] Their assessment is that the case did not extend the duty of loyalty to former clients:

> Rather, *Neil*'s contribution has been to clarify the distinction between the duty of loyalty and the duty of confidentiality. [Earlier cases] confirm that the duty of loyalty owed to a former client is less onerous than the duty owed to a current client — a position implicitly accepted in *Neil*, and confirmed by the rules of professional conduct in several provinces. Yet one is given little help in the codes of professional conduct as to what this difference is.
>
> Generally, a lawyer should not act against a former client in the same or any related matter. Even if the duty of loyalty permits a lawyer to act against a former client, the duty of confidentiality may prevent the lawyer from doing so.[16]

In its *Model Code*, the FLSC adopted language along these lines, similar but not identical to provisions in existing provincial Codes of Professional Conduct. Rule 2.04 (10), "Acting Against Former Clients", provides:

> 2.04 (10) Unless the former client consents, a lawyer must not act against a former client in:
>
> (a)   the same matter,
>
> (b)   any related matter, or
>
> (c)   any other matter if the lawyer has relevant confidential information arising from the representation of the former client that may prejudice that client.

The Commentary to this Rule goes on to say:

> This rule prohibits a lawyer from attacking the legal work done during the retainer, or from undermining the client's position on a matter that was central to the retainer. It is not improper for a lawyer to act against a former client in a fresh and independent matter wholly unrelated to any work the lawyer has previously done for that client if previously obtained confidential information is irrelevant to that matter.

The *Model Code* extends the prophylactic use of "screens" and the application of the "interests of justice" to "former client" situations by qualifying the principle that when an individual lawyer is "conflicted" on a matter, that conflict applies to the whole firm. Rule 2.04(11) provides:

> 2.04 (11) When a lawyer has acted for a former client and obtained confidential information relevant to a new matter, another lawyer ("the other lawyer") in the lawyer's firm may act in the new matter against the former client if:

---

15   Terrence J. O'Sullivan & M. Paul Michell, "Analyzing Conflicts of Interest After *Strother*: Has Anything Changed?", Canadian Bar Association Online Continuing Legal Education Presentation (November 27, 2007) [on file with co-editors].

16   *Ibid.*, at 14-15.

(a)   the former client consents to the other lawyer acting; or

(b)   the law firm establishes that it is in the interests of justice that it act in the new matter, having regard to all relevant circumstances, including:

   (i)   the adequacy of assurances that no disclosure of the former client's confidential information to the other lawyer having carriage of the new matter has occurred;

   (ii)   the adequacy and timing of the measures taken to ensure that no disclosure of the former client's confidential information to the other lawyer having carriage of the new matter will occur;

   (iii)   the extent of prejudice to any party;

   (iv)   the good faith of the parties;

   (v)   the availability of suitable alternative counsel; and

   (vi)   issues affecting the public interest.

In considering conflicts of interest relating to "former clients", and consistent with the FLSC Rules, however, the courts appear to continue to be guided by the overriding principle of the lawyer's duty of loyalty to his or her client. One example is *Brookville Carriers Flatbed GP Inc. v. Blackjack Transport Ltd.*[17] In that case, a law firm had acted for Brookville and a number of its employees in the defence of a claim that the employees had attempted to extract bribes from one of the company's suppliers in order to get the company's business. The claim was ultimately abandoned. Shortly afterward, Brookville, represented by the same law firm, began proceedings against a number of people, including two of the employees it had represented in the previous proceeding. The allegations were that the employees had conspired against, defrauded, stolen from and breached their fiduciary duties to Brookville during a time that overlapped with the time frame of the previous proceedings. Justice Cromwell (as he then was) noted that:

> [t]he mechanisms used to accomplish these alleged depredations were not related to the specific allegations [in the earlier proceedings]. However, both actions are grounded in acts of dishonesty by the Jenkins in relation to Brookville, their employer (or former employer) during overlapping time periods.[18]

This caused the chambers judge to conclude, and the Court of Appeal to agree, that the two matters under consideration were "related matters" for the purposes of the application for disqualification. No suggestion was made that the employees' situation was compromised by the possession of confidential client information on the part of the law firm. Justice Cromwell concluded that "putting aside issues of informed consent, lawyers have a duty not to act against a former client in a related matter whether or not confidential information is at risk ...".[19] Following a comprehensive review of the authorities and,

---

[17]   [2008] N.S.J. No. 94, 2008 NSCA 22 (N.S.C.A.).

[18]   *Ibid.*, at para. 12.

[19]   *Ibid.*, at para. 17.

after repeatedly noting that this rule is grounded in the lawyer's duty of loyalty to client, he upheld the chambers judge's disqualification of the law firm from its representation of Brookville in the matter.

Scenario Two

A lawyer provided legal advice to a client on a particular issue. Then, more than 15 years later, the lawyer is approached by a different client to commence proceedings against the former client on matters related to the initial matter, though not in ways that called into question the legitimacy of the advice given to the former client at that earlier time. The commencement of the proceeding does not rely on any confidential information obtained in the course of the previous representation. Would the lawyer be disqualified from acting? See *Greater Vancouver Regional District v. Melville*, [2007] B.C.J. No. 1750, 71 B.C.L.R. (4th) 29 (B.C.C.A.), leave to appeal refused [2007] S.C.C.A. No. 561 (S.C.C.).

In 2007, the Supreme Court decided its third case in the trilogy, *Strother v. 3464920 Canada Inc.* The Court took a case in yet another area of law practice and articulated a standard of dealing with clients that promises to influence the legal profession's understanding of its ethical and legal obligations to clients. As with *MacDonald Estate v. Martin*, the issues deeply divided the Court.

STROTHER v. 3464920 CANADA INC.

[2007] S.C.J. No. 24, [2007] 2 S.C.R. 177
(S.C.C., McLachlin C.J.C., Bastarache, Binnie, LeBel, Deschamps,
Fish, Abella, Charron and Rothstein JJ.)

[Monarch Entertainment (3464920 Canada Inc.) was a film development and financing company. It was actively involved in this business through much of the 1990s, arranging the financing of Hollywood films made in Canada through the use of attractive tax advantages available to investors under Canada's income tax system. Monarch retained Davis and Company, a Vancouver law firm, to handle much of its legal business, including the film financing arrangements. Strother was a senior tax partner at Davis and Company and was responsible for much of the tax advice provided to Monarch. For the calendar years 1996 and 1997 Davis and Company entered into an arrangement whereby the firm would represent Monarch exclusively on matters related to movie financing.

During this period the government of Canada moved inexorably to eliminate the tax deduction regime that had made Monarch's work extremely lucrative. These changes in the tax laws took effect in late 1997. In 1997 Strother advised Monarch that there were no options available to it and Monarch began to wind down its business. Additional legal work was done for Monarch by Davis and Company and Strother in 1998 but no longer under the exclusive representation arrangement of the previous two years. In late 1997 or early 1998, Darc, formerly a senior employee of Monarch, approached

Strother. They discussed the development of a new submission to the tax department seeking an advance tax ruling (essentially a pre-authorization for the specific tax treatment of a proposed financing arrangement) that, if successful, would result in certain dimensions of the loophole remaining open. Strother agreed to develop the submission without a fee, but on the understanding that if the ruling was favourable he would be entitled to become a partner with Darc in the new business. Strother did not communicate any of this to Monarch. Nor did he disclose the full particulars of his arrangement to Davis and Company. Davis and Company had policies that forbade such arrangements. Late in 1998 Darc (and Strother) received a favourable advance tax ruling. Shortly afterward, Strother left Davis and Company and joined Darc and others in the venture. The venture was extremely lucrative, and the two partners earned over $60 million over the next two to three years, until the "loophole" was closed completely.

When Monarch learned of the tax ruling, and of Strother having joined Darc in their movie financing business, it commenced proceedings against Darc for violations of his obligations as a former employee, and against Strother and Davis and Company for violations of obligations allegedly owed to Monarch as their client. The proceedings against Darc were dismissed at trial and on appeal. The proceedings against Strother and Davis and Company were dismissed at trial but reversed on appeal. Strother and Davis and Company appealed to the Supreme Court of Canada.]

BINNIE J. [for the majority]:—

. . . . .

When a lawyer is retained by a client, the scope of the retainer is governed by contract. It is for the parties to determine how many, or how few, services the lawyer is to perform, and other contractual terms of the engagement. The solicitor-client relationship thus created is however overlaid with certain fiduciary responsibilities, which are imposed as a matter of law. The Davis factum puts it well:

> The source of the duty is not the retainer itself, but all the circumstances (including the retainer) creating a relationship of trust and confidence from which flow obligations of loyalty and transparency. [para. 95]

Not every breach of the contract of retainer is a breach of a fiduciary duty. On the other hand, fiduciary duties provide a framework within which the lawyer performs the work and may include obligations that go beyond what the parties expressly bargained for. The foundation of this branch of the law is the need to protect the integrity of the administration of justice: *MacDonald Estate v. Martin* ... "[I]t is of high public importance that public confidence in that integrity be maintained" ...

Fiduciary responsibilities include the duty of loyalty, of which an element is the avoidance of conflicts of interest, as set out in the jurisprudence and reflected in the *Rules of Practice of The Law Society of British Columbia*. As the late Hon. Michel Proulx and David Layton state, "[t]he leitmotif of conflict of interest is the broader duty of loyalty", *Ethics and Canadian Criminal Law* (2001) ...

In recent years as law firms have grown in size and shrunk in numbers, the courts have increasingly been required to deal with claims by clients arising out of alleged conflicts of interest on the part of their lawyers. Occasionally, a law firm is caught innocently in crossfire between two or more clients. Sometimes the claim of conflict is asserted for purely tactical reasons, an objectionable practice criticized in *Neil* at paras. 14-15, and a factor to be taken into account by a court in determining what relief if any is to be accorded ... Sometimes, however, the dilemma is of the lawyer's own making. Here the firm's position was compromised by the personal conflict of a lawyer (Strother) who, contrary to the instructions of Davis's managing partner, contracted for a personal financial interest in one client (Sentinel) whose interest he then preferred over another client (Monarch) who now sues for compensation. In that regard, Monarch relies upon the well-known proposition endorsed by Professor Waters that:

> The other (the beneficiary) is entitled to expect that the fiduciary will be concerned solely for the beneficiary's interests, never the fiduciary's own.

. . . . .

A. *The Scope of the 1998 Retainer*

A critical issue in this case is the scope of Monarch's contractual retainer with Davis in 1998. Davis acknowledges "that a solicitor's duty of single-minded loyalty to his client's interest had its roots in the fiduciary nature of the solicitor-client relationship but that duty ... 'may have to be moulded and informed by the terms of the contractual relationship'" (Davis factum, at para. 80, citing *Hilton v. Barker Booth and Eastwood*, [2005] 1 All E.R. 651 (H.L.)). At para. 30 of the *Hilton* case, Lord Walker elaborated:

> ... On this issue of liability both sides have been content for the case to be dealt with as a claim for breach of contract. However, the content of BBE's contractual duty, so far as relevant to this case, has roots in the parties' relationship of trust and confidence.

Here, too, the claim arises out of "the parties' relationship of trust and confidence" but the case is pleaded as a breach of the fiduciary duty of loyalty rather than breach of contract. ...

. . . . .

Where a retainer has not been reduced to writing (as was the case with the 1998 retainer here) and no exclusions are agreed upon, as here, the scope of the retainer may be unclear. The court should not in such a case strain to resolve the ambiguities in favour of the lawyer over the client. The subject matter of the retainer here was, as it had been for years, "tax-assisted business opportunities". It was not to sell an office building, draft an informatics contract or perform other legal services unrelated to the subject matter of the earlier advice. The trial judge exonerated Strother by placing the emphasis on

Monarch's interest in "alternative" tax opportunities, but of course Monarch only considered "alternative" tax opportunities because Strother had given categorical advice that the tax-assisted film production services business in which Strother had profitably been advising Monarch since 1993 was unequivocally dead.

I believe, as did the Court of Appeal, that the trial judge erred in drawing so narrowly the *legal* effect of his *factual* finding that the retainer dealt with tax-assisted business opportunities, alternative or otherwise. (In fact Strother's position is that what he pursued on behalf of Sentinel in 1998 *was* an alternative tax-assisted business opportunity and not the same TAPSF scheme as he had pronounced dead in 1997.) Monarch was a major Davis client of long standing. It had been Strother's biggest source of billings for years. It was in the business of marketing tax schemes whose success turned on Strother's expertise in finding a "way [to get] around the rules" ... Strother's factum emphasizes nice distinctions between tax credits, tax shelters and so on but I do not think this oral retainer can or ought to be parsed so closely.

Nor can I agree with the Chief Justice when she characterizes the legal obligation arising out of the 1998 retainer as follows:

> Only if Monarch had specifically asked Strother for advice on new film tax-shelter opportunities and Strother had agreed to give that advice, could Strother have been under any duty to provide Monarch with such advice, placing him in a conflict of interest with Sentinel Hill. ...

Monarch's tax business was in a jam. Strother was still its tax lawyer. There was a continuing "relationship of trust and confidence". Monarch was dealing with professional advisors, not used car salesmen or pawnbrokers whom the public may expect to operate on the basis of "didn't ask, didn't tell", and who collectively suffer a corresponding deficit in trust and confidence. Therein lies one of the differences between a profession and some businesses.

In my view, subject to confidentiality considerations for other clients, if Strother knew there was still a way to continue to syndicate U.S. studio film production expenses to Canadian investors on a tax-efficient basis, the 1998 retainer entitled Monarch to be told that Strother's previous negative advice was now subject to reconsideration.

It is this contractual duty that came into conflict with Strother's personal financial interest when he took a major stake in Sentinel which was, as Newbury J.A. pointed out, a competitor in a small market where experience showed that, even limited, competition could lead to a rapid erosion of market share.

B. *Breach of the 1998 Retainer*

The trial judgment, as stated, was premised on the finding that Monarch did not specifically ask about the possible revival of TAPSF-type shelters in 1998. I agree with the trial judge that *generally* a lawyer does not have a duty to alter a past opinion in light of a subsequent change of circumstances. ...

. . . . .

There are, however, exceptions to the general rule. As Deschamps J. stated in *Côté v. Rancourt* ... the "boundaries of [a lawyer's] duty to advise will depend on the circumstances" (para. 6). The issue here was not so much a duty to alter a past opinion, as it was part of Strother's duty to provide candid advice on all matters relevant to the *1998* retainer ... It appears that Lowry J. turned his mind to this exception to the general rule when he stated that a lawyer is not obligated to "alter advice given under a *concluded* retainer" (para. 121 (emphasis added)). Here Monarch's retainer of Davis was *not* a concluded retainer. The written 1997 retainer had come to an end but the solicitor-client relationship based on a continuing (if more limited) retainer carried on into 1998 and 1999. As Deschamps J. further observed in *Côté*, "the obligational content of the lawyer-client relationship is not necessarily circumscribed by the object of the mandate" ... The *Côté* approach is not consistent with the "didn't ask, didn't tell" approach taken by the trial judge. Strother was meeting with Monarch to brainstorm tax schemes and knew perfectly well Monarch would be vitally interested in Strother's re-evaluation of the tax potential of the MER. The duty to advise Monarch required Strother and Davis, as a term of the 1998 retainer, if not expressed (as claimed by Monarch) then certainly implied, to explain to Monarch that Strother's earlier advice had been overtaken by events and would have to be revisited. Indeed, Strother discussed this concern with another partner at Davis, Rowland K. McLeod who testified in cross-examination as follows:

> A. I did consider whether or not Monarch *could* be told and I guess that would include *should* be told ... And my recollection is that Mr. Strother came to me before a meeting that he was going to have with Mr. Knutson [a principal of Monarch] and we discussed and considered whether or not Monarch could be told [that the previous advice about "no fix" had been premature], and my, my recollection was that we didn't reach a consensus on what could be done and he was going to play it by ear ... He was afraid Mr. Knutson was going to ask him.
>
> Q. When was that?
>
> A. It was in, I think it was June of 1998 ... We discussed it, came to no conclusion. He went to the meeting, told me either later that day or the next day, that the issue had not arisen. [Emphasis added.]
>
> (Davis's A.R., at p. 196)

McLeod continued:

> A. The nature of the, the, the nature of the discussion was, he was going to meet with Monarch. He was concerned that Mr. Knutson would raise the question of <u>is there a way around the, whatever the change in the law was</u>. [Emphasis added.]
>
> (Davis's A.R., at p. 198)

The fact that Strother and McLeod discussed what should be said if Monarch put the right question ("is there a way around ...?") recognized that Strother appreciated that his modified view about the potential of the s. 18.1(15)(*b*) exception would likely be of continuing interest and importance to Monarch because Monarch was still looking to him for advice in rebuilding its shattered tax-related business. At that point, of course, Strother had every interest in keeping Monarch in the dark. In June of 1998, under the January 1998 agreement, he was entitled to 55 percent of the first $2 million in profits and 50 percent of Sentinel's profits on the revival of tax-assisted film production services deals, which constituted a small and select marketplace. The fewer competitors faced by Sentinel the more money Strother would make and the faster he would pocket it.

Of course, it was not open to Strother to share with Monarch any *confidential* information received from Darc. He could nevertheless have advised Monarch that his earlier view was too emphatic, that there may yet be life in a modified form of syndicating film production services expenses for tax benefits, but that because his change of view was based at least in part on information confidential to another client on a transaction unrelated to Monarch, he could not advise further except to suggest that Monarch consult another law firm. Moreover, there is no excuse at all for Strother not advising Monarch of the successful tax ruling when it was made public in October 1998. As it turned out, Monarch did not find out about it until February or March 1999. I therefore conclude that Davis (and Strother) failed to provide candid and proper legal advice in breach of the 1998 retainer.

. . . . .

1.   Davis was Free to Take on Darc and Sentinel as New Clients

Monarch claims (and the Court of Appeal agreed) that even after the expiry of the "exclusive" retainer in 1997, Davis was conflicted out of acting for Darc and Sentinel by reason of its ongoing solicitor-client relationship with Monarch. As the House of Lords recently noted in relation to conflicting *contractual* duties, "a solicitor who has conflicting duties to two clients may not prefer one to another. ... [T]he fact that he [the lawyer] has chosen to put himself in an impossible position does not exonerate him from liability" (*Hilton* ...). The same principle applies to a lawyer getting into a position of conflicting *fiduciary* duties. ... The general rule is of long standing but I do not think it applied here to prevent Davis and Strother from acting for Sentinel. As stated in *Neil* ...:

> ... An unnecessary expansion of the duty may be as inimical to the proper functioning of the legal system as would its attenuation. The issue is always to determine what rules are sensible and necessary and how best to achieve an appropriate balance among the competing interests.

This is not to say that in *Neil* the Court advocated the resolution of conflict issues on a case-by-case basis through a general balancing of interests, the outcome of which would be difficult to predict in advance. ... The "bright line" rule is the product of the balancing of interests not the gateway to further internal balancing. In *Neil*, the Court stated ...:

> The bright line is provided by the general rule that a lawyer may not represent one client whose interests are directly adverse to the immediate interests of another current client — *even if the two mandates are unrelated* — unless both clients consent after receiving full disclosure (and preferably independent legal advice), and the lawyers reasonably believes [*sic*] that he or she is able to represent each client without adversely affecting the other. [Emphasis in original.]

I agree with Strother's counsel when he writes that "[t]he retainer by Sentinel Hill was not 'directly adverse' to any 'immediate interest' of Monarch". On the contrary, as Strother argues, "Sentinel Hill created a business opportunity which Monarch could have sought to exploit" (Strother factum, at para. 66). A Sentinel ruling that revived the TAPSF business even in modified form would indirectly help any firm whose tax syndication business had been ruined by the ITA amendments, including Monarch. Representation of Sentinel was thus not "directly adverse" to representation of Monarch by Davis/ Strother even though both mandates related to tax-assisted business opportunities in the film production services field. Strother's problem arose because despite his duty to an existing client, Monarch, he acquired a major personal financial interest (unknown to Davis) in another client, Sentinel, in circumstances where his prospects of personal profit were enhanced by keeping Monarch on the sidelines. ...

(a)   *Monarch Was a Current Client*

I agree with Newbury J.A. that too much was made in argument about the shift from the 1997 written retainer to the 1998 oral retainer. The trial judge in places referred to a *concluded* retainer. However, this is not a case where *a former* client alleges breach of the duty of loyalty ... Monarch was a *current* client and was unquestionably entitled to the continuing loyalty of Strother and Davis.

(b)   *Acting for Clients with Competing Commercial Interests*

As recognized by both the trial judge and Newbury J.A., the conflict of interest principles do not generally preclude a law firm or lawyer from acting concurrently for different clients who are in the same line of business, or who compete with each other for business. There was no *legal* dispute between Monarch and Sentinel. Monarch relies on the "bright line" rule set out in *Neil* but (leaving aside, for the moment, Strother's personal financial stake) there is no convincing case for its application here.

The clients' respective "interests" that require the protection of the duty of loyalty have to do with the practice of law, not commercial prosperity. Here the alleged "adversity" between concurrent clients related to business matters. This is not to say that commercial interests can *never* be relevant. The *American Restatement* offers the example of two business competitors who seek to retain a single law firm in respect of competing applications for a single broadcast licence, i.e. a unique opportunity. The *Restatement* suggests that acting for both without disclosure and consent would be improper because the subject matter of both retainers is the same licence (*Restatement (Third) of the*

Law Governing Lawyers, vol. 2, at § 121 (2000)). The lawyer's ability to provide even-handed representation is put in issue. However, commercial conflicts between clients that do *not* impair a lawyer's ability to properly represent the legal interests of both clients will not generally present a conflict problem. Whether or not a real risk of impairment exists will be a question of fact. In my judgment, the risk did not exist here provided the necessary even-handed representation had not been skewed by Strother's personal undisclosed financial interest. Condominium lawyers act with undiminished vigour for numerous entrepreneurs competing in the same housing market; oil and gas lawyers advise without hesitation exploration firms competing in the oil patch, provided, of course, that information confidential to a particular client is kept confidential. There is no reason in general why a tax practitioner such as Strother should not take on different clients syndicating tax schemes to the same investor community, notwithstanding the restricted market for these services in a business in which Sentinel and Monarch competed. In fact, in the case of some areas of high specialization, or in small communities or other situations of scarce legal resources, clients may be taken to have consented to a degree of overlapping representation inherent in such law practices, depending on the evidence ... The more sophisticated the client, the more readily the inference of implied consent may be drawn. The thing the lawyer must *not* do is keep the client in the dark about matters he or she knows to be relevant to the retainer ...

. . . . .

(c) *The Duty of Loyalty is Concerned with Client Representation*

While the duty of loyalty is focussed on the lawyer's ability to provide proper client representation, it is not fully exhausted by the obligation to avoid conflicts of interest with other concurrent clients. A "conflict of interest" was defined in *Neil* as an interest that gives rise to a

> substantial risk that the lawyer's representation of the client would be materially and adversely affected by the lawyer's own interests or by the lawyer's duties to another current client, a former client, or a third person.

> (*Neil*, at para. 31, adopting § 121 of the *Restatement (Third) of Law Governing Lawyers*, vol. 2, at pp. 244-45).

. . . . .

Exceptional cases should not obscure the primary function of the "bright line" rule, however, which has to do with the lawyer's duty to avoid conflicts that impair the respective representation of the interest of his or her concurrent clients whether in litigation or in other matters ...

(d) *The Impact on the Representation of Monarch Was "Material and Adverse"*

The spectre is flourished of long-dormant files mouldering away in a lawyer's filing cabinet that are suddenly brought to life for purposes of enabling a strategically minded client to assert a conflict for tactical reasons. But a court is well able to withhold relief from a claim clearly brought for tactical reasons. Conflict between concurrent clients where no confidential information is at risk can be handled more flexibly than *MacDonald Estate v. Martin* situations because different options exist at the level of remedy, ranging from disqualification to lesser measures to protect the interest of the complaining client. In each case where no issue of confidential information arises, the court should evaluate whether there is a serious risk that the lawyer's ability to properly represent the complaining client may be adversely affected, and if so, what steps short of disqualification (if any) can be taken to provide an adequate remedy to avoid this result.

There is no doubt that at all material times there was a "current meaningful" solicitor-client relationship between Monarch and Davis/Strother to ground the duty of loyalty ... The availability of Strother's ongoing tax advice was important to Monarch and is the cornerstone of its claim.

Strother is dismissive of the impact his breach had on Monarch's interest (i.e. in obtaining proper legal advice). He is correct that the test requires that the impact must be "material and adverse" (as set out in the definition of conflict adopted in *Neil*, previously cited). While it is sufficient to show a possibility (rather than a probability) of adverse impact, the possibility must be more than speculation ... That test is met here, for the reasons already discussed. Once the existence of Strother's personal financial interest in Sentinel was established, it was for Strother, not Monarch, to demonstrate the absence of any material adverse effect on Monarch's interest in receiving proper and timely legal advice ...

(e)   *Sentinel's Desire to Secure the Counsel of its Choice Was Also an Important Consideration*

The evidence showed that Strother's special expertise was available from few other firms. Sentinel's Paul Darc had worked successfully with Davis and Strother for years. Our legal system, the complexity of which perhaps reaches its apex in the ITA, depends on people with legal needs obtaining access to what they think is the best legal advice they can get. Sentinel's ability to secure the advice of Davis and Strother as counsel of choice is an important consideration ... It does not trump the requirement to avoid conflicts of interest but it is nevertheless an important consideration.

2.   The Difficulty in Representing Monarch Arose from a Strother Conflict not a Davis Conflict

Davis did not appreciate what Strother was up to and had no reason to think the Sentinel retainer would interfere with the proper representation of Monarch.

. . . . .

... In general, Davis and Strother were free to take on Darc and Sentinel as new clients once the "exclusivity" arrangement with Monarch expired at the end of 1997. Issues of confidentiality are routinely dealt with successfully in law firms. Strother could have managed the relationship with the two clients as other specialist practitioners do, by being candid with their legal advice while protecting from disclosure the confidential details of the other client's business. If the two are so inextricably bound together that legal advice is impossible, then of course the duty to respect confidentiality prevails, but there is nothing here to justify Strother's artful silence. Strother accepted Sentinel as a new client and the Davis firm was given no reason to think that he and his colleagues could not provide proper legal advice to both clients.

3.   Strother was not Free to Take a Personal Financial Interest in the Darc/Sentinel Venture

The trial judge found that Strother agreed to pursue the tax ruling on behalf of Sentinel in return for an interest in the profits that would be realized by Sentinel if the ruling was granted ...

Strother had *at least* an "option" interest in Sentinel from January 30th until at least August 1998 (when he was told by Davis to give up *any* interest). This was during a critical period when Monarch was looking to Strother for advice about what tax-assisted business opportunities were open. The precise nature of Strother's continuing financial interest in Sentinel between August 1998 and March 31, 1999 (when Strother left Davis) is unclear, but whatever it was it came to highly profitable fruition in the months that followed. The difficulty is not that Sentinel and Monarch were potential competitors. The difficulty is that Strother aligned his personal financial interest with the former's success. By acquiring a substantial and direct financial interest in one client (Sentinel) seeking to enter a very restricted market related to film production services in which another client (Monarch) previously had a major presence, Strother put his personal financial interest into conflict with his duty to Monarch. The conflict compromised Strother's duty to "zealously" represent Monarch's interest ... a delinquency compounded by his lack of "candour" with Monarch "on matters relevant to the retainer" ... i.e. his own competing financial interest ...

     . . . . .

In these circumstances, taking a direct and significant interest in the potential profits of Monarch's "commercial competito[r]" ... created a substantial risk that his representation of Monarch would be materially and adversely affected by consideration of his own interests ... As Newbury J.A. stated, "Strother ... *was* 'the competition'" ... (emphasis in original). It gave Strother a reason to keep the principals of Monarch "in the dark" (*ibid.*), in breach of his duty to provide candid advice on his changing views of the potential for film production services tax shelters. I agree with Newbury J.A. that Monarch was "*entitled* to candid and complete advice from a lawyer who was not in a position of conflict" ... (emphasis in original).

Strother could not with equal loyalty serve Monarch and pursue his own financial interest which stood in obvious conflict with Monarch making a quick re-entry into the tax-assisted film financing business. As stated in *Neil*, at para. 24, "[l]oyalty includes putting the client's business ahead of the lawyer's business". It is therefore my view that Strother's failure to revisit his 1997 advice in 1998 at a time when he had a personal, undisclosed financial interest in Sentinel Hill breached his duty of loyalty to Monarch. The duty was further breached when he did not advise Monarch of the successful tax ruling when it became public on October 6, 1998. Why would a rainmaker like Strother not make rain with as many clients (or potential clients) as possible when the opportunity presented itself (whether or not existing retainers required him to do so)? The unfortunate inference is that Strother did not tell Monarch because he did not think it was in his personal financial interest to do so.

4.   Davis Did Not Participate in Strother's Disabling Conflict of Interest

[Justice Binnie found that, as Davis was unaware of Strother's financial interest in Sentinel, it was "as much an innocent victim of Strother's financial conflict as was Monarch". Davis may still be vicariously liable for Strother's "wrongful act" under s. 12 of the *Partnership Act*, as will be discussed.

Justice Binnie concluded that Strother was liable for the monies he earned from the beginning of the venture until March 31, 1999, when other business developments influenced the direction of the venture, and by which time the information on the tax ruling was fully known and Strother's links with Monarch and with Davis and Company had been severed. He found Davis and Company were innocently duped by a "rogue partner" but that Strother was nevertheless acting in the "ordinary course of the business", making Davis vicariously liable for Strother's actions pursuant to the *Partnership Act*.]

McLACHLIN C.J.C. [dissenting in part]:—

. . . . .

Insistence on actual conflicting duties or interests based on what the lawyer has contracted to do in the retainer is vital. If the duty of loyalty is described as a general, free-floating duty owed by a lawyer or law firm to every client, the potential for conflicts is vast. Indeed, it is difficult to see how a lawyer or law firm could ever act for two competitors. Consider, as in this case, a specialized tax lawyer who acts for client A and B, where A and B are competitors. Client A may ask for help in minimizing capital gains tax. Client B may seek advice on a tax shelter. The lawyer owes both A and B contractual and associated fiduciary duties. If the duty that the lawyer owes to each client is conceived in broad general terms, it may well preclude the lawyer from acting for each of them; at the very least, it will create uncertainty. If the duty is referenced to the retainer, by contrast, these difficulties do not arise. The lawyer is nonetheless free to act for both, provided the duties the lawyer owes to client A do not conflict with the duties he owes to client B.

This manner of viewing a lawyer's duties conforms to the realities of the legal profession and the needs of clients. Modern commerce, taxation and regulation flow together in complex, sometimes murky streams. To navigate these waters, clients require specialized lawyers. The more specialized the field, the more likely that the lawyer will act for clients who are in competition with each other. Complicating this reality is the fact that particular types of economic activity may be concentrated in particular regions. The obligation of the legal profession is to provide the required services. Yet in doing so, lawyers and law firms must inevitably act for competitors.

Practical considerations such as these cannot be used to dilute the rigor of the fiduciary duties that the law rightly demands of lawyers. Rather, they explain why the law has developed a precise conception of the lawyer's duty grounded in the contract of retainer. Our law rightly imposes rigorous fiduciary duties on lawyers, but it also recognizes the need to ensure that fiduciary obligations remain realistic and meaningful in the face of the realities of modern practice.

Binnie J., speaking for the Court, captured these realities when he wrote in *Neil*, at para. 29:

> ... a bright line is required. The bright line is provided by the general rule that a lawyer may not represent one client whose interests are *directly* adverse to the *immediate* interests of another current client ... [Emphasis added.]

Whether an interest is "directly" adverse to the "immediate" interests of another client is determined with reference to the duties imposed on the lawyer by the relevant contracts of retainer. This precision protects the clients, while allowing lawyers and law firms to serve a variety of clients in the same field. This is in the public interest. As Binnie J. observed in *Neil* ...:

> An unnecessary expansion of the duty may be as inimical to the proper functioning of the legal system as would its attenuation. The issue is always to determine what rules are sensible and necessary and how best to achieve an appropriate balance among the competing interests.

· · · · ·

[Chief Justice McLachlin was of the opinion that the more limited scope of Strother's obligations, defined in terms of the trial judge's interpretation of the contract of retainer, meant that Strother had not violated his duties to Monarch. On that basis she would have dismissed the claims against Strother and Davis.]

NOTES AND QUESTIONS

1. To what extent, if any, does *Strother* moderate the lawyer's obligation of loyalty to a client that is articulated in *R. v. Neil*? Had the dissenting view prevailed, would this have further moderated the lawyer's loyalty obligation to clients? Is McLachlin C.J.C. correct in her concern that the more open-ended approach of the majority will generate uncertainty for lawyers and the legal profession on the issue of conflict of interest?

2. The minority in *Strother* would have upheld the trial judge's decision that the contract of retainer delineated the core of the lawyer's responsibilities, and that Strother's conduct was not actionable. To what extent might the majority have

viewed the case as highlighting opportunistic behaviour on the lawyer's part, behaviour that might have been an embarrassment to the legal profession? As such, did the majority seek to ensure that the fiduciary net, by going beyond the mere particulars of the retainer, was cast wide enough to prevent and, in this case to some extent at least, punish such behaviour?

3.   Chief Justice McLachlin appears to assume that a law firm representing two competitors is entirely acceptable, unless there is some specific constraint imposed by the clients themselves. This argument is remarkably similar to that of Sopinka J. in *MacDonald Estate v. Martin*, advancing as it does the business reality of client and law firm needs. Yet this argument does not carry the day in *Strother*. Does this suggest that the majority decision of Binnie J. represents a noticeable shift in the Court's thinking, or a strong re-statement at least, that lawyers' obligation of loyalty to client interests is still paramount?

4.   In what ways is the situation in *Strother* different from the conflicts of interest in the earlier cases? Consider, for example, that Monarch Entertainment and Darc (and Strother in his capacity as Darc's business partner) were not in a dispute with one another, so much as they were competing for the same business? Does this make a difference to the resolution of the conflict?

5.   Note, as well, that *Strother* is different from the other cases in that the lawyer and the lawyer's personal interests are at the centre of the controversy in *Strother*. This appears to be why the British Columbia Court of Appeal referred to Strother as "the competition" for Monarch. This complicates the issue of conflict of interest, but in ways that correspond with everyday reality. In many aspects of law practice, business opportunities regularly present themselves to lawyers in ways that arise from or are associated with work on behalf of clients. Is the lawyer required to decline these opportunities? What principles should be used to distinguish the types of opportunities that could be taken up by lawyers from the ones that are off limits? These questions are addressed later in this chapter.

WALLACE v. CANADIAN NATIONAL RAILWAY

[2011] S.J. No. 589, 2011 SKCA 108
(Sask. C.A., J.G. Lane, R.K. Ottenbreit and N.W. Caldwell JJ.A.)

[In late 2008, the McKercher law firm commenced a class action on behalf of Wallace against the Canadian National Railway (CN) and others, alleging that they had systematically overcharged grain farmers in relation to grain transportation charges over the previous 25 years, and were seeking $1.75 billion in damages. McKercher had, from time to time, been one of a number of law firms used by CN in Saskatchewan. In the previous four years it had billed CN approximately $80,000 in legal fees, slightly less than one-third of the total legal fees paid by CN to Saskatchewan law firms over that time. The litigation matter in which it represented CN was one of 22 matters in which CN was a party during that period. Just prior to the commencement of the Wallace class action, McKercher was representing CN on four different matters:

•   a real estate transaction, in which McKercher, shortly after the commencement of the *Wallace* litigation, sought but was refused CN's consent to continue the representation;

- a litigation matter, from which, just prior to the commencement of the *Wallace* litigation, McKercher notified CN that it was withdrawing as counsel;

- the representation of CN in a receivership matter, from which, shortly after the commencement of the *Wallace* litigation, it withdrew (though without notification to CN); and

- the holding of powers of attorney for CN by two McKercher lawyers, which the lawyers terminated shortly after the commencement of the *Wallace* litigation.

CN did not generally give consent to law firms to act against its interests, but had not shared this policy with McKercher. None of the matters were related to the *Wallace* litigation that McKercher had commenced. McKercher had gained information about CN's "approach to litigation, its business practices and its risk perspective and tolerance" (para. 22), but was not privy to specific confidential information related to the Wallace matter.

The chamber judge disqualified McKercher on the basis that there was a substantial risk that CN's representation by McKercher had been materially and adversely affected by its decision to represent Wallace because: (a) there was a long-standing relationship between McKercher and CN; (b) CN relied primarily on McKercher as its "go-to" firm in Saskatchewan; (c) the magnitude of the Wallace claim was substantial and not minor and had the potential for significant damages; (d) the Wallace claim was a litigation matter which would necessarily be adversarial; (e) the Wallace claim was a class action, which would marshal numerous litigants against CN and the other defendants; (f) the remedy sought included aggravated and punitive damages implying reprehensible behaviour on the part of CN; (g) CN was especially sensitive to conflicts of interest among its counsel and felt betrayed by McKercher, which, in the course of acting for CN, had received information about attitudes and approaches to legal problems; and (h) because of the nature of class actions, a law firm tends to gain or lose significantly in them and have a greater interest than being purely and simply an advocate. The chamber judge also determined that there was no evidence that CN was bringing the application for tactical reasons. McKercher appealed the disqualification order.]

R.K. OTTENBREIT J.A.:—

. . . . .

B. Introduction

… [The] issues are as follows:

(1) Did McKercher possess relevant confidential information that could be used to the prejudice of CN?

(2) Is CN a professional litigant and can its consent to adverse representation be implied in the circumstances?

(3) Did McKercher breach a duty of loyalty to CN?

(4) If McKercher breached a duty of loyalty, what is the appropriate remedy?

C. The Law

[Justice Ottenbreit reviewed the *MacDonald Estate v. Martin* and *Neil* decisions on conflicts of interest, including the "bright line" rule in *Neil*, and reached the following conclusions.]

. . . . .

Neil therefore represented a conceptual shift: moving away from the negatively framed "avoidance of conflicts of interest" to the broader, more positively framed "duty of loyalty."

The three aspects of this duty of loyalty enunciated by Binnie J. at para. 19 were: (i) the duty to avoid conflicting interests, including a lawyer's personal interests; (ii) a duty of commitment to the client's cause (which includes an assurance that a lawyer's divided loyalties do not cause him or her to compromise his or her "zealous representation"); and (iii) a duty of candour with the client on matters relevant to the retainer.

. . . . .

Binnie J. adopted the following formulation of disqualifying conflict arising from a breach of the duty of loyalty at para. 31:

> In my view the Venkatraman law firm, and Lazin in particular, put themselves in a position where the duties they undertook to other clients conflicted with the duty of loyalty which they owed to the appellant. I adopt, in this respect, the notion of a "conflict" in s. 121 of the *Restatement Third, The Law Governing Lawyers* (2000), vol. 2, at pp. 244-45, as a "substantial risk that the lawyer's representation of the client would be materially and adversely affected by the lawyer's own interests or by the lawyer's duties to another current client, a former client, or a third person".

This is often referred to as the substantial risk principle.

Although *Neil* established a broad duty of loyalty, Binnie J. stated an exception to the "Bright Line" Rule at para. 28:

> In exceptional cases, consent of the client may be inferred. For example, governments generally accept that private practitioners who do their civil or criminal work will act against them in unrelated matters, and a contrary position in a particular case may, depending on the circumstances, be seen as tactical rather than principled. Chartered banks and entities that could be described as professional litigants may have a similarly broad-minded attitude where the matters are sufficiently unrelated that there is no danger of confidential information being abused. These exceptional cases are explained by the notion of informed consent, express or implied.

Binnie J. at para. 15 recognized that an application to disqualify a law firm based on a breach of loyalty involved a balancing of interests: he highlighted the link between the duty of loyalty and the policies it is intended to further, but implied that the development of the law of the duty of loyalty would be a delicate exercise:

> It is important to link the duty of loyalty to the policies it is intended to further. An unnecessary expansion of the duty may be as inimical to the proper functioning of the legal system as would its attenuation. The issue always is to determine what roles are sensible and necessary and how best to achieve an appropriate balance among the competing interests.

A legacy of *Neil* is that, in conflict analysis, primacy was given to the integrity of both the legal profession and the administration of justice over the other two competing values enunciated in *MacDonald Estate*, *i.e.* the client's choice of lawyer and lawyer mobility.

In *Strother*, the Court was divided and there was a difference in approach concerning the relationship, between a retainer agreement and fiduciary duties, in determining the origin, content and extent of obligations owed by a lawyer in a particular case. The majority superimposed fiduciary obligations on the retainer, while the minority thought the contractual terms were available to modify the existence and content of any fiduciary obligation. Binnie J. for the majority at para. 58 again explained the function of the "Bright Line" Rule:

> 58 Exceptional cases should not obscure the primary function of the "bright line" rule, however, which has to do with the lawyer's duty to avoid conflicts that impair the respective representation of the interest of his or her concurrent clients whether in litigation or in other matters ...

In addition to the case law, the analysis in this area is informed by the codes of professional conduct. While this Court is not bound by codes of professional conduct, the Supreme Court of Canada in *MacDonald Estate* recognized that "an expression of a professional standard in a code of ethics relating to a matter before the court should be considered an important statement of public policy."

The Canadian Bar Association *Code of Professional Conduct*, Chapter V, Commentary 12 and the Law Society of Saskatchewan *Code of Professional Conduct*, Chapter V, Commentary 8 allow lawyers to act against former clients in a "fresh and independent matter wholly unrelated to any work the lawyer has previously done for that person."

The substantial risk principle at para. 31 of *Neil* is consistent with the Law Society of Saskatchewan *Code of Professional Conduct*. The Law Society of Saskatchewan has never adopted the literal interpretation of the "Bright Line" Rule and does not prohibit lawyers from acting against current clients in the absence of an adverse effect upon client representation.

The CBA Task Force on Conflicts of Interest (CBA Task Force on Conflicts of Interest, *Conflicts of Interest: Final Report, Recommendations & Toolkit* (Ottawa: Canadian Bar Association, 2008)), at p. 43, pointed out the apparent conflict between the substantial risk principle (adopted in *Neil* at para. 31) and the "Bright Line"/ Unrelated Matter Rule (adopted in *Neil* at para. 29). It went on to propose a principled method for resolving the apparent conflict:

> We therefore conclude that the Unrelated Matter Rule and the Substantial Risk Principle are reconcilable. If there is a substantial risk that the lawyer's representation of the current client would be materially and adversely affected by the matter, the lawyer may not act, whether or not the matters are unrelated.
>
> ...
>
> Accordingly, we conclude that the appropriate interpretation of *Neil* and *Strother* (which also reconciles the minority reasons in *Strother*) is that, absent proper consent, a lawyer may not act directly adverse to the immediate interests of a current client unless the lawyer is able to demonstrate that there is no substantial risk that the lawyer's representation of the current client would be materially and adversely affected by the new unrelated matter.

The chamber judge adopted the CBA Task Force's report on this point at paras. 43 and 44 of his judgment. In my view, this statement of the law is an appropriate statement of the applicable approach to conflict analysis for breaches of a lawyer's duty of loyalty to clients post-*Neil* and -*Strother*.

Although a good foundation for conflict analysis has been laid, as set out earlier, the factors informing the choice of an appropriate remedy where a solicitor's duty is breached is a less developed part of the jurisprudence. The court stated in *Strother* at para. 74:

> This Court has repeatedly stated that '[e]quitable remedies are always subject to the discretion of the court.'

How that discretion should be exercised is not often clear. In *Neil*, Binnie J. said at para. 36: "It is one thing to demonstrate a breach of loyalty. It is quite another to arrive at an appropriate remedy." For example, although there had been a breach of a lawyer's duty of loyalty to the client in *Neil*, the court declined to grant the remedy requested, or indeed any remedy.

Where the adverse representation is with respect to an unrelated matter and there is no danger of misuse of confidential information, consideration can be given to an appropriate remedy, which is something other than disqualification. As the Supreme Court said in *Strother* at para. 59:

> Conflict between concurrent clients where no confidential information is at risk can be handled more flexibly than *MacDonald Estate v. Martin* situations because different options exist at the level of remedy, ranging from disqualification to lesser measures to protect the interest of the complaining client. In each case where no issue of confidential information arises, the court should evaluate whether there is a serious risk that the lawyer's ability to properly represent the complaining client may be adversely affected, <u>and if so, what steps short of disqualification (if any) can be taken to provide an adequate remedy to avoid this result.</u> [Emphasis added]

In short, in these kinds of cases, disqualification is neither automatic nor necessarily preferred.

. . . . .

The key elements informing the choice of remedy appear to be what measures are necessary to protect the interests of the complaining client and whether there is a serious risk that the lawyer's ability to properly represent the client may be adversely affected. The overarching consideration must of course be to maintain the high standard of the legal profession and the integrity of the justice system.

With this governing jurisprudence in mind, I turn now to the issues raised on this appeal.

D. Did McKercher possess relevant confidential information that could be used to the prejudice of CN?

[Following a review of the jurisprudence and the evidence, Ottenbreit J.A. concluded that CN had not met the onus of establishing "that there was an imparting of what amounts to confidential information" to McKercher, and consequently there was not a "sufficient risk of prejudice to CN in McKercher acting on the Wallace claim".]

E. Is CN a professional litigant and can its consent to adverse representation be implied in the circumstances?

. . . . .

The salient features of those exceptional cases mentioned in *Neil* when consent may be inferred or expressed to allow a law firm to act adverse in interest appear to be:

    (a) the client is a larger corporate client such as a government or bank;

    (b) the matters are sufficiently unrelated; and

    (c) there is no danger of confidential information being abused.

Binnie J.'s articulation of this exception in *Neil* implies that in those circumstances, it is reasonable to assume that the client will have a broad-minded attitude and generally accept that counsel may act adverse in interest. The corollary to this is that it is reasonable for the law firm to make such an assumption and act on it. There may be, in my view, a fourth factor bearing on when the Professional Litigant Exception will apply and that is whether, in the circumstances, its application is consistent with the high standards of the legal profession and the integrity of the justice system.

The Professional Litigant Exception is grounded in part in notions of the reasonable expectations of the lawyer and client. The reasonableness of the client's expectations must be assessed objectively, not subjectively. The client seeking to disqualify a law firm based on an allegation of breach of duty of loyalty will almost always assert a subjective expectation that the law firm would never act against them. However, the client's policy or business practice that consent is always required is not determinative. ...

. . . . .

The exception is also grounded in the notion that it may not be inimical to maintenance of the integrity of the administration of justice and the high standards of the legal profession to attenuate the rigours of the "Bright Line" where it is reasonable to do so. Certainly the context of this exception, placed as it is in *Neil* under the heading of "Duty of Loyalty to an Existing Client" and the reference to "no confidential information being abused" as a motivation for the exception, suggest such an attenuation.

Such an attenuation can be justified if one looks at the foundation of the duty of loyalty as outlined by Binnie J. in *Neil*. Two key concepts are germane. In para. 12, Binnie J. states:

> Unless a litigant is assured of the undivided loyalty of the lawyer, neither the public nor the litigant will have confidence that the legal system, which may appear to them to be a hostile and hideously complicated environment, is a reliable and trustworthy means of resolving their disputes and controversies: *R. v. McClure*, [2001] 1 S.C.R. 445, 2001 SCC 14 (S.C.C.), at para. 2; *Smith v. Jones*, [1999] 1 S.C.R. 455 (S.C.C.) [...]

. . . . .

Additionally, at para. 16 Binnie J. states:

> The duty of loyalty is intertwined with the fiduciary nature of the lawyer-client relationship. One of the roots of the word fiduciary is *fides*, or loyalty, and loyalty is often cited as one of the defining characteristics of a fiduciary [...]

In the context of these foundational ideas, the professional litigant exception can be justified on a principled basis where the client is not one "typically untrained in the law and lacking the skills of advocates", and where in fiduciary law language there is less of a relationship of "dependence or reliance of the beneficiary upon the fiduciary".

Vulnerability of the client was, for example, an important factor in *Neil*. An unsophisticated individual client who has relied exclusively or even primarily on one lawyer or law firm for his or her representation is far more vulnerable if that lawyer or law firm should choose to act against the individual than a legally sophisticated corporate client that has a large in-house legal department, employs many different outside law firms and is involved in frequent and varied litigation.

A further related rationale for the professional litigant exception is that the professional litigant often has sufficient resources and requirements for legal services that it can, by spreading its work around, materially limit without intending to do so an opposing party's choice of counsel. ...

. . . . .

It is obvious that CN is not a client which is "typically untrained in the law and lacking the skills of advocates", nor was its relationship with McKercher such that there was a substantive dependence or reliance on McKercher to do its legal work. The chamber judge therefore correctly determined that CN was a professional litigant.

However, he erred when he determined that it was not reasonable to infer consent to act pursuant to the exception. He opined that minor, non-contentious unrelated matters might lead a law firm to the conclusion that consent could be inferred. There is no indication in *Neil* that the professional litigant exception applies absolutely only to minor or non-contentious unrelated matters, nor do the principled bases for the exception imply such a limitation. Such a limitation would unduly restrict the ambit of this exception. That said, the adverse retainer and the context of the adverse representation are relevant.

. . . . .

The chamber judge suggested that CN felt a sense of betrayal because of the magnitude of the Wallace claim, the type of matter it was, the nature of the matter and the remedy sought. Although the sensitivity of CN in this case may play some part in the analysis, the real question is the vulnerability of CN given the decision of McKercher to take on the Wallace claim. Whether the acceptance of a new retainer will have an adverse effect on the client must be determined objectively on all the circumstances, not on the client's subjective reaction.

[Justice Ottenbreit rejected these conclusions as not supportable on the facts and inferences to be drawn in the case.]

Given the factual matrix in this case, it was reasonable for CN's consent to McKercher acting on even a claim as large as Wallace's to be implied. The salient features of an exceptional case are present, *i.e.*, a large corporate client, a relatively low dependency on McKercher for legal services, low vulnerability related thereto, sufficiently unrelated matters, and no danger of confidential information being abused.

The chamber judge's second reason why McKercher could not avail itself of the exception relied on several cases suggesting that consent ought not to be implied in circumstances where a party has expressly spoken out and stated that it does not consent. None of the cases dealt with lawyer disqualification.

. . . . .

An *ex post facto* objection to acting on the new retainer is not determinative. In this case, it is common ground that the express objection by CN was made after McKercher began to act for Wallace. Additionally, there was no retainer agreement between CN and McKercher which governed whether McKercher could act for another party adverse in interest to CN. There is no evidence that CN's lack of broadmindedness in allowing its counsel to act adverse in interest or that its particular sensitivity to conflicts in respect of litigation matters, was ever brought to the attention of the McKercher firm or reduced to writing in a retainer agreement at any time.

Implied consent operates in the absence of express consent, whether written or oral, where it is reasonable that it do so. Once it is concluded that implied consent is reasonable, subsequent express non-consent cannot vitiate the implied consent: otherwise the professional litigant exception would be meaningless. The situation described by the learned chamber judge at para. 57, in which a law firm could be "caught" by the retroactive express withdrawal of implied consent, would completely defeat the purpose of implied consent, for surely a client seeking to disqualify a lawyer would always play that card in circumstances where the professional litigant exception may apply. If a professional litigant takes the view that any counsel acting for it must receive <u>express</u> consent before acting adverse in interest, it should be dealt with by contract or at least made known to the lawyer.

. . . . .

Lastly, this is not a case where the public's confidence of the profession and the legal system would be diminished by the application of the professional litigant exception given the aspects of low dependency by CN on McKercher for its legal representation and the relative lack of vulnerability of CN as a client. Additionally, McKercher did very little of CN's litigation and clearly was not its primary litigation counsel. In a situation such as this, where there are relatively few CN files being handled by McKercher, it is not inimical to confidence in the profession and legal system to allow McKercher to act for other clients adverse in interest who may have specifically chosen McKercher to do so.

. . . . .

F. Did McKercher breach a duty of loyalty to CN?

Although McKercher can take advantage of the professional litigant exception respecting its continued representation of Wallace, the "Bright Line" Rule as it is conceived in *Neil* also enunciates a duty of candour and full disclosure to a client as independent and distinct aspects of the duty of loyalty described by Binnie J. in *Neil* at para. 19:

> The aspects of the duty of loyalty relevant to this appeal do include issues of confidentiality in the *Canada Trust* matters, but engage more particularly three other dimensions:
>
> . . .
>
> (ii) <u>a duty of commitment to the client's cause</u> (sometimes referred to as "zealous representation") from the time counsel is retained, not just at trial, i.e. ensuring that a divided loyalty does not cause the lawyer to "soft peddle" his or her defence of a client out of concern for another client [...] and,
>
> (iii) <u>a duty of candour</u> with the client on matters relevant to the retainer [...]
>
> If a conflict emerges, the client should be among the first to hear about it.

The client's cause in this case was the representation by McKercher on the existing files that McKercher had with CN. The chamber judge correctly pointed out at paras. 69 and 70:

> [69] Additionally, I find that "dumping" an existing client in order to clear the deck to sue that client is an ethical breach. Both the *Canadian Bar Association Code of Professional Conduct* (Ottawa: Canadian Bar Association, 2006), and the *Law Society of Saskatchewan Code of Professional Conduct* (Regina: Law Society of Saskatchewan, 1991), both contain chapters relating to the withdrawal of services:

> . . . . .

… The chamber judge was correct in characterizing the behaviour of McKercher as "dumping" CN. McKercher's peremptory termination of all of its retainers with CN but one is surely a lack of commitment to the client's cause and a breach of the duty of loyalty to CN on those matters. It was incumbent on McKercher to continue to act where it could as long as CN wanted it to do so, or at least to explore the possibility of doing so.

The failure by McKercher to advise CN in a timely manner that it intended to take the Wallace claim demonstrates a complete lack of candour by McKercher with CN. McKercher's duty of candour applied even if McKercher believed that it was justified in relying on CN's implied consent to act on the Wallace claim. It may be inferred that McKercher started acting on the Wallace claim some substantial time before it was served, but said nothing to CN. CN should have been the first to know about McKercher's intention to act on the Wallace claim and should have been kept informed of developments on this front. This would have given CN the opportunity to investigate its options for addressing the situation. These options may have included, without foreclosing other options, expressly consenting to the adverse representation (doubtful given its sensitivities) or expressly objecting to it and applying to disqualify McKercher as it has done anyway. In that case, McKercher could still have tested the applicability of the Professional Litigant Exception as it is doing in this case.

I find that McKercher breached its duty of loyalty in respect of its failure to continue to act on the CN files where it could do so and its failure to be completely candid with CN.

G. If McKercher breached a duty of loyalty, what is the appropriate remedy?

[Justice Ottenbreit concluded that the breach of loyalty did not compromise CN as far as the continued representation of Wallace by McKercher was concerned, finding that disqualification was too blunt an instrument and that it would unfairly disadvantage Wallace.]

. . . . .

CN is not without a remedy. It has the option of suing for damages for the added cost and expense of having the CN files transferred to other solicitors.

CN may also complain to the Law Society of Saskatchewan respecting McKercher's alleged ethical breaches.

As for the integrity of the system of justice, McKercher submits that the public's perception of the system of justice would be damaged more by depriving Mr. Wallace and the individual farmers he represents, litigants with far fewer resources than CN, of their counsel of choice, than it would by giving effect to CN's application to deprive Mr. Wallace of that right. This is not determinative. All of the circumstances must be considered in coming to a conclusion that the remedy other than disqualification is consistent with the high standards of the legal profession and the integrity of the system of justice.

The circumstances in their totality do not justify disqualification. In this case, the retainers are unrelated factually, legally and strategically. There is no element of confidential information which can be used to the prejudice of CN. CN is not a vulnerable client but is a professional litigant which can avail itself of its substantial legal resources in respect of the CN matters on which McKercher no longer acts and also in respect of the Wallace claim. It has not been proven that McKercher's retainer with CN will taint the fairness of the Wallace matter or prejudice CN's defence thereof. The McKercher/CN relationship is terminated. In these circumstances, the public's confidence in the legal system and the high standards of the legal profession will not be diminished by McKercher's continued representation of Wallace. The behaviour and actions of McKercher respecting the CN files and its lack of candour in respect to the Wallace claim are, in the circumstances of this case, best left to the profession's disciplinary bodies. McKercher will not be disqualified from acting on the Wallace claim.

. . . . .

NOTES AND QUESTIONS

1. *Wallace* is a decision of the highest level of court to date that has directly considered the *Neil* and *Strother* requirements in relation to "current client" conflicts, and is the first decision to apply the "professional litigant" exception. Given the competing views of the "bright line" rule, which approach does the Court appear to prefer? Was this interpretation necessary to the decision? You will recall the deference shown by the Supreme Court of Canada to the Canadian Bar Association and law societies in relation to the prospective resolution of conflicts of interest like the one that arose in *MacDonald Estate v. Martin*. Was it appropriate for the Court to be guided by the CBA's Rules and interpretation in this case? Why was there no reference to the work of the Federation of Law Societies, which is the federative body of the law societies of Canada, the entities that, unlike the CBA, are legislatively mandated to oversee and regulate the conduct of lawyers in the public interest?

2. Do you agree with the court's interpretation that McKercher, through its previous representation of CN, did not come into possession of confidential information relevant to its representation of Wallace against CN? If the court had taken a different view of the "bright line rule", might "disloyalty" alone have disqualified the McKercher firm, regardless of its possession of confidential information? Was this not what Binnie J. was trying to establish in *Neil*?

3. The court found CN to be a "professional litigant". Could there still be a "substantial risk" to the professional litigant (part of the *Neil* test) that would merit consideration, and potential disqualification, even if there was implied consent? Are professional litigants disentitled to withdraw the "implied consent" that enabled their law firms to act against them in unrelated matters where confidentiality is not compromised? If they cannot withdraw their consent, what would you advise "professional litigants" to do to prevent their law firms from being able to act against them?

4. Justice Ottenbreit concluded that the McKercher firm had engaged in unethical behaviour toward CN by failing in its duty of loyalty to CN by "dumping it" as a client on some matters and failing in its duty of candour by not informing CN of its intention to take on the Wallace representation? Is another interpretation possible? Might McKercher have been motivated to withdraw from the representation of CN on other matters because the law firm *knew* that CN was not willing to be sued by its own law firm, and the answer, from McKercher's perspective, was to try to get off these conflicting files in advance of commencing the Wallace litigation? Second, might it have been a disadvantage to Wallace for CN to be informed by McKercher of Wallace's intention to commence the class action? Might McKercher's fulfillment of its duty of candour owed to CN (according to Ottenbreit J.A.) constitute a breach of the duty of loyalty owed to Wallace? Was this the type of difficulty that Binnie J. was seeking to avoid in *Neil*?

5. The decision in *Wallace* included a finding that the McKercher firm engaged in unethical behaviour toward its client, CN. Nevertheless, since the court found that CN's interests were not directly compromised by McKercher's representation of Wallace in the litigation, but that Wallace would be disadvantaged, the court exercised its discretion not to disqualify Mckercher. Does all of this suggest the court's attempt to balance public policy factors, including the return to relevance of the "client choice" factor noted in Sopinka J.'s majority judgment in *MacDonald Estate v. Martin*?

C. LAWYER-CLIENT CONFLICTS

1. Introduction

The *Strother* case provides an excellent transition from the conflicts of interest a lawyer may encounter when the interests of present or former clients diverge, to situations where the lawyer's own interests may become entangled with those of a client. While in every lawyer-client relationship there is inherent tension between the interests of the lawyer and those of the client — for example, in the financial success of his or her law practice — the issue of "lawyer-client" conflict tend to arise in more problematic situations. These conflicts of interest have the potential to undermine the lawyer's ability to represent the client properly or, to create the perception that the client's interests have not been properly represented. The fundamental question is whether the conflict which has arisen interferes with the lawyer's duty of loyalty to the client and with his or her ability to provide uncompromised representation of the client's interests.

The most obvious example is where a lawyer takes possession of client assets. Lawyers maintain trust accounts to hold clients' money for client needs and are placed under significant fiduciary obligations to take special care of this money and to account for it appropriately. Indeed, clients' ability to place a high degree of confidence in lawyers with respect to their money facilitates transactions for clients in many aspects of their lives, from business takeovers to buying a house to settling an account. It is not surprising, therefore, that lawyers who abuse this trust by misappropriating trust moneys for their personal use are dealt with harshly by law societies and the courts. Aside from the injury to an individual client, such behaviour damages the reputation of the legal profession and has the potential to compromise the ease with which transactions are facilitated through lawyers and their management of client trust funds.

Troubling conflicts between lawyers and their clients are not, however, limited to financial matters. In some cases they arise where a lawyer is not sufficiently respectful of his or her client's circumstances and reputation when the lawyer is engaged in other activities, sometimes advancing his or her own reputation through those activities. Such cases are rarely litigated, but *Stewart v. Canadian Broadcasting Corp.*, set out below, is such a case.

Lawyer-client conflicts can also arise in the context of a personal relationship that develops between a lawyer and his or her client. We have already seen a few of these situations. Recall *Szarfer v. Chodos,*[20] a case that we considered in Chapter 1. In that case, Chodos had an affair with his client's wife and was sued by the client in negligence and for breach of fiduciary obligation for the harm he suffered. Chodos was found to be liable. This case on the surface is a case of professional negligence. But at its centre is the conflict between the lawyer's duty to his client and his own selfish interests. In rare cases the matter may come before a court. More often these cases arise in the context of law society discipline proceedings against the lawyer, where the proceedings may lead to sanctions that jeopardize the lawyer's career. A close parallel to *Szarfer v. Chodos*, and perhaps a more egregious failure by a lawyer, is *Law Society of Upper Canada v. Daboll.*[21] In *Daboll*, a lawyer while representing a client in a family law matter, became romantically and sexually involved with his client's wife.

One of those types of cases is excerpted below. When reading the decisions consider the nexus between the sexual relationship and the lawyer's ability to be loyal to his client as required by cases such as *Neil*, his obligation to act consistently with his duty of integrity and his duty to the proper administration of justice. Is loyalty the only ethical obligation undermined by this conflict, or are other ethical obligations or values also at play? In what ways?

---

[20]   [1986] O.J. No. 256, 54 O.R. (2d) 663 (Ont. H.C.J.).
[21]   [2006] L.S.D.D. No. 82, 2006 ONLSHP 79 (Ont. L.S.D.D.).

STEWART v. CANADIAN BROADCASTING CORP.

[1997] O.J. No. 2271, 150 D.L.R. (4th) 24
(Ont. Gen. Div., J. Macdonald J.)
[footnotes omitted]

J. MACDONALD J.: —

Introduction

On November 27, 1978 the plaintiff Robert Stewart ran over Judy Jordan with his automobile and dragged her to her death. He was convicted of criminal negligence causing death. Following conviction, he discharged his counsel and retained the defendant Edward L. Greenspan, Q.C. to represent him during sentencing and to appeal the conviction. The appeal was dismissed in January 1981 and Mr. Stewart began serving his sentence of three years imprisonment. He was released on parole after 11 months and began rebuilding his life.

On November 17, 1991, when Mr. Stewart believed that he had put the past behind and re-established himself, the defendant Canadian Broadcasting Corporation broadcast a one hour episode of the program known as "The Scales of Justice" on its national television network. This episode known as *Regina v. Stewart* was a re-enactment of the plaintiff's crime and trial created by the defendants Scales of Justice Enterprises Inc. and CBC. Mr. Greenspan appeared on air as the host and narrator. Mr. Greenspan had also been, with Mr. George Jonas, one of the incorporators of Scales of Justice Enterprises Inc. (hereinafter Scales) and one of the guiding minds in the development of the concept which became the television program known as "The Scales of Justice" (hereinafter the program). ...

The plaintiff instituted this action as a result of the broadcast, which was seen by close to one million viewers. I dismissed the action against CBC in oral reasons delivered earlier.

[Justice Macdonald reviewed the statements of claim and of defence in the present case (addressing claims of breach of contract founded on the retainer agreement, as well as breach of fiduciary duty), and then reviewed the facts as found at the trial of *Regina v. Stewart*. In short, after drinking some quantity of alcohol, Mr. Stewart had struck the victim, Judy Jordan, in a circular driveway in front of her building, whereupon she fell and became entangled in the undercarriage of the car. As the trial judge found, Mr. Stewart failed to stop, instead dragging her screaming for a short distance and then dragging her silent body for the remaining part of a quarter-mile.]

. . . . .

The transcript of the criminal trial shows that Mr. Stewart's first counsel took the position that Mrs. Jordan was lying in the circular driveway as a result of the actions of a third party when Mr. Stewart ran over her. He suggested in cross-examination that Mrs. Jordan had been pushed into the roadway. He questioned [the] relationship between Mr. and Mrs. Jordan, apparently attempting to implicate Mr. Jordan in her death. He also suggested that Mrs. Jordan had been killed by drug dealers with whom she was allegedly involved. An alleged friend of hers had been found murdered, supposedly as a result of involvement in drugs. These allegations were rejected out of hand by Graburn, J. in his reasons for judgment. ...

Consequently, upon conviction, Mr. Greenspan was retained. ...

. . . . .

... Mr. Greenspan knew in acting for Mr. Stewart respecting sentence that the media coverage of Mr. Stewart's crime and trial had been very negative and had gone so far as to portray him as an inhumanly cruel and wicked person, which is the relevant definition of monster from the Oxford English Dictionary. Mr. Greenspan recognized that the public abhorred Mr. Stewart because of the nature of his crime, the perception that he had attacked his victim and her family which arose from counsel's trial tactics, and the extensive and very critical media coverage. Mr. Greenspan recognized that he should address in his sentencing submissions both public abhorrence of Mr. Stewart and the public interest implicit in the objectives of sentencing. He recommended to Mr. Stewart that he authorize a public apology to the Jordan family as part of the sentencing submissions to the court, and Mr. Stewart agreed. Graburn, J. accepted the apology as genuine because he took it into account in sentencing, as described. I also accept that it was genuine. ...

. . . . .

In my opinion, the public apology made in open court and directed to members of the public taken together with Mr. Greenspan's reply to the Crown's submissions establish clearly that Mr. Greenspan went beyond submissions directed solely to sentence, and undertook the task of attempting to change through the sentencing hearing how Mr. Stewart was viewed by the public. ...

. . . . .

... I find that, in this extraordinary case, Mr. Greenspan went to extraordinary lengths as counsel to protect his client from the public. He not only addressed the public's legitimate interests and perceptions which would influence the sentence imposed by the court, he also addressed the risk that individual members of the public would sanction Mr. Stewart after his release from prison into its midst.

[Justice Macdonald reviewed and rejected the contractual claims based on express and implied terms of the retainer agreement.]

. . . . .

Mr. Greenspan's Involvement in Scales of Justice Enterprises Inc.

I find the background facts to be as follows. Mr. George Jonas is a writer, journalist, producer and director. He and Mr. Greenspan met in 1974 and they are good friends. Together they conceived of the concept which would become the program known as "The Scales of Justice" and formed the company which would produce it, the defendant described as Scales herein.

Mr. Greenspan was called to the Ontario Bar in 1970 and has been engaged since then in advocacy, primarily as criminal defence counsel. It has long been one of Mr. Greenspan's concerns that there are very few autobiographies or biographies of Canadian lawyers and Judges and as a result, Canadians get little information about Canadian law. He is committed to legal education, and spends as much time as he can teaching law students. He is also committed to legal publishing, and is the editor in chief or the associate editor of various law reports and annotated reference works. He has lectured and written frequently on subjects within his practice areas. He was co-author with Mr. Jonas of "Greenspan: Case for the Defence", a collection of his cases put together in a way which discusses social or legal issues. One of his concerns is the place of the victim in Canadian legal process.

. . . . .

... It was Mr. Greenspan choosing to involve himself, and the long standing personal and working relationships between Mr. Greenspan, Mr. Jonas and Scales, and also between Mr. Greenspan and CBC which resulted in Mr. Greenspan's involvement in the scripting, production and broadcast of *Regina v. Stewart*. The evidence establishes a long standing friendship and spirit of mutual enterprise between Messrs. Greenspan and Jonas respecting publishing or broadcasting of legal matters, and it continued despite Mr. Greenspan's resignation as a director of Scales. There was also a shorter yet substantial relationship between Mr. Greenspan and CBC based on his work in the Scales radio broadcasts. ...

. . . . .

Preparing the Regina v. Stewart Episode.

... I find that Mr. Jonas suggested the Stewart case to CBC and was instrumental in it being selected as the subject of a program. Both Mr. Jonas and George Anthony, the CBC creative head responsible for the program, thought that the Stewart case raised fascinating issues. ...

. . . . .

a) Alleged wrongful disclosure of confidential information.

. . . . .

Allegations that counsel wrongfully disclosed confidential (meaning secret) information about a client are serious allegations. It should be clearly recognized that there is no truth, not even a hint of it, in these serious allegations against Mr. Greenspan.

I accept the evidence that the script for the television broadcast was written by Mr. Tait and Mr. Jonas from publicly available materials and sources of information other than Mr. Greenspan, except as follows.

b) Mr. Greenspan's role in scripting the broadcast.

Draft scripts for the television broadcast prepared by Messrs. Tait and Jonas were forwarded to Mr. Greenspan for his review. ...

. . . . .

As a result, according to Messrs. Greenspan and Jonas, Mr. Greenspan succeeded in moderating some aspects of the portrayal of Mr. Stewart, his crime and his trial. For example Mr. Greenspan's intervention caused the deletion of a reference to the "bizarre callousness" of Mr. Stewart's crime, and the substitution of a reference to Mr. Stewart's conviction. Mr. Greenspan also intervened during filming because he found that the portrayal of Mr. Stewart on his arrival home, minutes after running over Mrs. Jordan, created a strong impression of guilt. The scene was therefore changed to give a different visual impression.

I find there is compelling evidence which proves the assertions that Mr. Greenspan had substantial control over script contents. Mr. Greenspan's impact upon the way in which Mr. Stewart's first counsel was depicted demonstrates the ability he had to determine the script contents which would be broadcast. ...

. . . . .

Mr. Greenspan testified that his reason for inserting, or seeing to the insertion of this script content was his absolute respect for the administration of justice and high regard for the lawyers who work within the process. He testified:

> And I was not prepared to do anything to cast a doubt on what was an absolutely brilliant career in [defence counsel's] case. An absolutely brilliant career. And since we were doing this case, it was very important to treat him as decently and with as much civility and with as much regard for what a great lawyer he was, and that's why those words were put in, to make sure that that was noted as fairly for him as I could. (Parentheses added).

. . . . .

How did Mr. Greenspan use his power to script the contents of the broadcast when it came to the portrayal of his former client? ...

. . . . .

[A]t no point in the broadcast was it mentioned that Mr. Stewart was not complicit in these unsavoury actions by his counsel, that he had apologized publicly for these actions or that Graburn, J. had accepted Mr. Stewart's apology as genuine, by relying on it in his reasons for sentence. In my opinion, explaining counsel's excesses and describing the benefit which Mr. Stewart could obtain from them without any reference to Mr. Stewart's lack of complicity in these unsavoury tactics and his genuine apology for them was neither sympathetic nor fair to Mr. Stewart. ...

. . . . .

In 1979, Mr. Greenspan knew that a significant part of the negative public perceptions of Mr. Stewart resulted from media reports about his first counsel's trial tactics. He knew that Mr. Stewart was seen as involved in what counsel did in his name. Mr. Greenspan therefore took steps to protect Mr. Stewart from those perceptions. Mr. Greenspan spoke to the public objectives of sentencing. He also spoke during sentencing to his objective of protecting Mr. Stewart from the effects of public revulsion in the post-sentencing period. In 1991, as part of the media, Mr. Greenspan left out of this nationally broadcast portrayal of his former client and his case the very things he had put before the public in 1979, as Mr. Stewart's counsel, to guard against public revulsion and repercussions in the years to come.

. . . . .

In addition, I find that Mr. Greenspan's narration exaggerated the distance that Mrs. Jordan was dragged screaming, and thereby exaggerated the length of time that Mr. Stewart drove on knowing that a living human being was in agony beneath his vehicle. In this fashion, Mr. Greenspan's narration portrayed his former client's conduct more negatively than the court had found it to be. ...

. . . . .

Mr. Stewart's Position Respecting the Broadcast

. . . . .

Mr. Stewart became aware of Scales' intentions when fliers explaining their filming in the area of 6010 Bathurst Street came to his attention. ...

. . . . .

I find as follows. On June 14, 1991, one week before filming or recording of Mr. Greenspan's role in the broadcast began, Mr. Stewart told Mr. Greenspan that he objected to the broadcast in issue. The precise nature of his objections is determined most reliably by the contents of his letter June 17, 1991. ... I find that Mr. Greenspan was told on June 14, 1991 that Mr. Stewart objected to any portrayal of the conduct for which he had been found guilty of criminal negligence causing death.

. . . . .

... Mr. Greenspan considered withdrawing from the production and broadcast after speaking with Mr. Stewart, to avoid a headache. However, he concluded that Mr. Stewart's lack of consent and objections posed no problem for him. He testified that he wanted to do this program because of its educational value.

. . . . .

If Mr. Greenspan Had Refrained From Any Involvement

... I find that if he had withdrawn, Mr. Jonas probably would have found another lawyer to appear on screen as host/narrator. ...

. . . . .

This leads to an important point. The Scales of Justice concept was educational. ... I find that the educational content of the *Regina v. Stewart* broadcast was fully independent of Mr. Greenspan because, if Mr. Greenspan had chosen to refrain from participation, the educational content of any broadcast of Mr. Stewart's crime and trial was nonetheless assured. ...

. . . . .

... [T]hen the small script changes for Mr. Stewart's benefit upon which Mr. Greenspan places such heavy reliance may not have been included. However, I find them to be of very little significance in terms of the overall portrayal of Mr. Stewart and his conduct which was broadcast with Mr. Greenspan's participation.

Mr. Greenspan's Loyalty to Former Counsel.

The decency and civility which are apparent in the way Mr. Greenspan portrayed former counsel are a form of loyalty to a fellow professional and to ideals based on respect for personal dignity and reputation. Mr. Greenspan chose to give that to former counsel. He could have given his former client similar benefits and protections in the broadcast, of the type I have addressed. This leads to the central questions. Did Mr. Greenspan owe a duty of loyalty to his former client in the circumstances which existed in 1991? What are the nature and extent of any such duty? Are his involvement in this broadcast and the omissions and the exaggeration in the portrayal of his former client breaches of a duty of loyalty which Mr. Greenspan owed? I will begin my analysis by considering the role of counsel.

The Role of Counsel.

. . . . .

(d) The Duties of Former Counsel.

(i) The evidence of Messrs. Greenspan and Sandler.

In considering the question of post-retainer obligations to Mr. Stewart resting on Mr. Greenspan, I return to the evidence of both Mr. Greenspan and Mr. Mark Sandler that counsel has the discretion to publicize information in the public domain respecting the case of a former client, barring contractual constraint upon such conduct.

. . . . .

I accept that there is an important benefit to society in knowing about cases before the courts, as Mr. Sandler testified. However, I reject his conclusion that counsel have the right to refer publicly to any non-confidential information respecting former clients and their cases. ...

. . . . .

I find as follows. Careful, competent and responsible criminal defence counsel should and do take into account the risk of harm to a former client in deciding whether to discuss publicly a former client or the former client's case, when all relevant information is in the public domain. That is because counsel do not wish to injure a former client by public discussion of information. If the former client may be harmed, counsel may well exercise caution and not talk about the former client or the case. Since the rules of professional conduct are not an exhaustive code of lawyer's professional obligations, and there is no rule or other standard in the profession which invariably prohibits all counsel from any mention of any information in the public domain after any retainer is over, each counsel is in the position of having to decide whether he or she will speak or write publicly about the type of information being considered. However, in my opinion, it does not follow from the need for each counsel to make decisions about his or her professional conduct in these circumstances that such decisions are never subject to legal or equitable principles and are solely personal choices.

. . . . .

Mr. Greenspan's evidence was that rule 4 of the rules of professional conduct (which I will consider shortly) bars counsel from disclosing confidential information, and that is the extent of the fiduciary responsibility respecting the affairs and business of a former client. Mr. Greenspan's position is that the rule is exhaustive respecting fiduciary responsibilities. Once the information is in the public domain, Mr. Greenspan testified that it is the lawyer's choice whether to discuss that information publicly, subject to any contractual constraint. Mr. Greenspan also testified that, respecting matters in the public domain, in a conflict between the truth and the client, "you go with the client" by perhaps not "telling it all", and that is an obligation which is broader than the rules.

. . . . .

(ii) The Rules of Professional Conduct.

There was frequent reference at trial to various rules of professional conduct and accompanying commentaries of the Law Society of Upper Canada. They play a larger part in Mr. Greenspan's defence than they do in the plaintiff's case. He pleaded that no requirement in the rules or in any other professional ethical rules made it improper for him to participate in the broadcast in issue. To the extent that the plaintiff alleged a breach of the rules, Mr. Greenspan pleaded his right to freedom of expression as guaranteed by s. 2(b) of the Charter of Rights and Freedoms, and that, if the rules infringe that right, it is not demonstrably justifiable in a free and democratic society. At trial, Mr. Greenspan's position was different. He sought shelter under the rules, arguing that they support his position that he was not bound by fiduciary duties which were breached by his actions. ...

. . . . .

In my opinion, the rules and commentaries have two limiting features which are significant here:

> 1. The Law Society Act R.S.O. 1990, c. L. 8 gives the Law Society through Convocation the power to regulate lawyers' conduct. The Act does not give Convocation the power to regulate clients or their rights. In any event, in the rules and commentaries relevant to the issues herein, Convocation has not attempted to regulate clients or their rights.

> 2. The rules and commentaries are not an all inclusive code governing lawyers' conduct in every circumstance which may arise in professional life.

They address only specific issues, and do so in a variety of ways ranging from mandatory to advisory.

[A]s of the broadcast in issue, the regulations made by Convocation did not, by their language, purport to affect the rights or protections which law and equity afford to clients. Consequently, I am of the opinion that both the Law Society Act and the regulations pursuant to it should not be interpreted so as to diminish by implication the rights and protections afforded to clients by law or equity. ... In my opinion, the intention of the Legislature manifest in the Law Society Act is to regulate the legal profession for the protection of clients. Occasionally, that enhances of [*sic*] client's rights in order to afford greater protection: see for example s. 51 respecting the compensation fund. In my opinion, the Legislature's intention was that Convocation not have the power to diminish or dissolve the legal or equitable rights or protections of clients.

[Justice Macdonald then reviewed the Law Society of Upper Canada Rules on Confidentiality of Information.]

. . . . .

Rule 21

I turn now to rule 21, paragraph 5. It is raised indirectly and partially in the pleading that one way in which Mr. Greenspan breached his fiduciary duty of loyalty to Mr. Stewart was by putting "his own self promotion or self aggrandizement before the interests of the plaintiff". This is an allegation of duty to the former client which conflicted with self interest in the form of self promotion or self aggrandizement. Rule 21, paragraph 5 contains two separate directions, not obligations. First, a public communication should not be used for the purpose of publicizing the lawyer. Second, a public communication should be free from any suggestion that the lawyers' real purpose is self promotion or self aggrandizement.

I find the facts to be as follows. Mr. Greenspan identified himself in the broadcast as Mr. Stewart's counsel during sentencing. He spoke of his work as counsel. He referred indirectly to his success on Mr. Stewart's behalf, in that he was sentenced to three years in prison when another person convicted of the same offence by the same Judge was sentenced to five years. There is also Mr. Greenspan's broadcast presence. To the viewer, he explained the case and its legal issues. He was thus seen by close to one million people in the role of knowledgeable professional adviser. His image and his voice were prominent throughout. His name was mentioned and displayed. In my opinion, this broadcast was not just education about the justice system. It was also education about Edward Greenspan, his role in the justice system, and his effectiveness as counsel. I find that Mr. Greenspan's primary purpose in involving himself in this production and broadcast, in which educational content was otherwise assured, was to publicize himself and his services as counsel to a national audience.

The second part of paragraph 5 directs that public communications "should be free from any suggestion that the lawyer's real purpose" was self promotion or self aggrandizement. The threshold is therefore not high. Was there "any suggestion" that Mr. Greenspan's "real purpose" was self promotion or self aggrandizement? The phrase "real purpose" is not synonymous with "only purpose." In my opinion, the proper interpretation is that public communications should be free from any suggestion that either self promotion or self aggrandizement was a substantial motivating factor in the lawyer engaging in that communication. In my opinion, it is only if public communication, reasonably viewed, contains either an express or implicit suggestion of either self promotion or self aggrandizement that it is capable of having the requisite degree of purpose. If the existence of "any suggestion" were left entirely in the eye of a beholder, the lawyer's "real purpose" would be made irrelevant.

The ways in which Mr. Greenspan used the broadcast to publicize himself and his professional services mean that there are both express and implicit suggestions of self promotion which fall within the second part of paragraph 5 of rule 21. The broadcast therefore was not free from "any suggestion" that Mr. Greenspan's "real purpose" was self promotion. I find that his primary purpose in involving himself in this broadcast was self promotion.

Was the broadcast free from any suggestion that Mr. Greenspan's real purpose was self aggrandizement? Self aggrandizement may mean the same as self promotion, or may mean making something appear greater than is the case, according to the Shorter Oxford English Dictionary. Since self aggrandizement is expressed to be an alternative to self promotion, I am of the opinion that Convocation intended to limit "self aggrandizement" to exaggeration of a lawyer's skills or accomplishments. In my opinion, Mr. Greenspan's description of the legal services which he provided to Mr. Stewart was somewhat restrained when compared to the superb representation which he provided to Mr. Stewart, which was in fact responsible for a moderate sentence in difficult advocacy circumstances. Leaving the apology out of the broadcast could have had the effect of making his advocacy accomplishments seem greater than they were. However the absence of this information means that it was not a "suggestion" within the meaning of the rule. Exaggeration of the distance Mr. Stewart dragged Mrs. Jordan screaming is critical to how Mr. Stewart was perceived in 1991 but that is not the issue under rule 21 paragraph 5. In my opinion, the plaintiff has failed to establish a breach of this part of rule 21 paragraph 5.

Rule 17

The rule is as follows:

> The lawyer who engages in another profession, business or occupation concurrently with the practice of law must not allow such outside interest to jeopardize the lawyer's professional integrity, independence or competence.

. . . . .

The rule is expressed in mandatory terms. A lawyer "must not allow" an outside interest to "jeopardize" the lawyer's professional integrity. ...

. . . . .

What then of counsel who broadcasts something about a former client when also engaging in the practice of law? ...

. . . . .

In my opinion, the evidence does not raise the issues in rule 17 even though it applies to a lawyer's broadcast about a former client while also engaging in the practice of law, as Mr. Greenspan was. ... This is because the plaintiff has not alleged that Mr. Greenspan breached fiduciary duties because his participation in the broadcast jeopardized his professional integrity, independence or competence. The trial did not proceed on that basis. ...

Contractual Allegations.

There are two aspects to these allegations. The first is the claim of breach of implied terms of the retainer. The second is the part which the retainer plays in the determination of fiduciary issues.

. . . . .

In my opinion, the terms of the retainer do not prevent the existence of a fiduciary duty of loyalty. The retainer term which permitted Mr. Greenspan to act as he saw it put in place certain circumstances which are fundamental to the existence of such a duty.

Fiduciary Issues.

(a) General.

Mr. Stewart's crime, trial and sentence were the subject of public controversy and widely known in 1978 and 1979. This extensive information, made known through the justice system and published by the media, was public knowledge. This information remained public knowledge in 1991 even if, with the passage of time, it had faded to the fringes of public awareness.

In 1991, Mr. Stewart did not have the legal right to preserve any decreased public awareness of this public knowledge. The law did not shield him from what he had done, or from the public's right to know how its justice system had dealt with him and his conduct, or from the media's right to remind the public about this public information. ...

Mr. Stewart's claim is narrower and more specific than an attack on media republication of public information. Mr. Stewart takes the position that, regardless of the public nature of information about his crime, trial and sentencing, and regardless of the media's right to re-broadcast it, Mr. Greenspan owed him a fiduciary duty of loyalty which arose from their concluded counsel and client relationship, which duty did not allow Mr. Greenspan to participate as he did in this broadcast.

... In my opinion, confidentiality considerations are irrelevant to the determination of fiduciary issues in this case. ...

. . . . .

In *Canadian Aero Service Ltd.* ... Laskin, J. developed the format for analysis of fiduciary claims which I will follow. He described four issues which should be determined:

  (a) The relationship between the parties.

  (b) The duty or duties owed, if any, by reason of the relationship.

  (c) Whether there was any breach of a duty owed.

  (d) The liability for any breach of duty.

Of these issues, the most significant here are whether a fiduciary duty of loyalty which arose from Mr. Greenspan's concluded counsel and client relationship with Mr. Stewart existed in 1991 and if so, whether that duty required Mr. Greenspan to refrain from his involvement in the broadcast portrayal of the subject matter of his concluded retainer. ...

[Justice Macdonald concluded that a fiduciary relationship existed between Mr. Greenspan and Mr. Stewart.]

. . . . .

(c) The duty which arises from this relationship.

It is trite but necessary, I think, to begin by noting that Mr. Greenspan was not bound to be Mr. Stewart's advocate forever. This is consistent with rule 5, commentary 13 of the rules of professional conduct which does not prohibit a lawyer from acting against a former client. It advises when a lawyer may not act, and when it is "not improper" for a lawyer to act. This standard of the profession demonstrates that a lawyer is not bound indefinitely to serve the former client's interests which were the subject of the earlier retainer. In my opinion, that obligation ends when the retainer ends. However, the end of the lawyer and client relationship as such does not end the fiduciary relationship. Duties arising from that fiduciary relationship may well restrain the lawyer from speaking about the former client's issues or business which were the subject of the concluded retainer, or from taking steps which affect them.

In my opinion, the fundamental principles which Dubin, J.A. re-stated in *R. v. Speid* (*supra*) included the nature of a lawyer's ongoing fiduciary duties to a former client. This was done through quoting part of Gale, J.'s reasons in *Tombill Gold Mines Ltd. v. Hamilton (City)* (*supra*). Gale, J. did not just speak of an existing principal and agent relationship such as an existing lawyer and client relationship, he spoke of an existing fiduciary relationship. That fiduciary relationship survives the termination of the lawyer and client relationship and the end of the duties which are solely part of it. Paraphrasing Gale, J., in a fiduciary relationship, the agent (read lawyer) is:

  -    obliged to obey instructions.

- obliged to act solely for the benefit of the principal (read client of former client) in all matters connected with the agency (read subject matter of the retainer).

- prohibited from competing with his principal (read client or former client).

- prohibited from taking unfair advantage of his position either:

    - in the use of the things acquired by him because of the agency (read retainer) or

    - in the use of the opportunities which his position affords.

- prohibited from acting disloyally in matters which are related to the agency (read subject matter of the retainer).

In my opinion, this authoritative and helpful listing of duties was not intended to be all inclusive, and the separate headings were not intended to be regarded as mutually exclusive. If regarded as all-inclusive, this list would close the categories of fiduciary obligations and stifle the ability of the fiduciary remedy to meet new fact situations. As Laskin, J. observed in [*Canadian Aero Service Ltd. v. O'Malley*] ... "new fact situations may require a reformulation of existing principle to maintain its vigour in the new setting". ... Further, Gale, J.'s prohibition against disloyalty is frequently expressed as a positive obligation of loyalty. A positive obligation of loyalty is more consistent with the positive obligation to act solely for the benefit of the principal. Consequently, in my view, these categories are best regarded as authoritative examples of underlying principle.

In determining the nature of the duty which arises from the fiduciary relationship in issue, there is an area of limited agreement in the reasons in *Hodgkinson v. Simms* (*supra*) which I believe to be relevant. In the reasons of La Forest, J. the following is quoted from the paper presented by Professor P.D. Finn, at the Professional Responsibility Seminar, University of Auckland on May 29 1987, entitled "Conflicts of Interest and Professionals" at p. 15 (see La Forest, J.'s reasons at p. 185 D.L.R.):

> In some spheres conduct regulation would appear to be becoming an end in itself and this because there can be a public interest in reassuring the community - not merely beneficiaries - that even the appearance of improper behaviour will not be tolerated. The emphasis here seems, in part at least, to be the maintenance of the public's acceptance of, and the credibility of, important institutions in society which render "fiduciary" services.

In their joint reasons Sopinka and McLachlin JJ. agreed at p. 220 with the above extract from Professor Finn's paper stating:

> We agree as well with Professor Finn at p. 15, cited by our colleague at p. 185, that imposition of fiduciary obligations in some cases may be justified on the ground of "maintenance of the public's acceptance of, and the credibility of, important institutions in society which render 'fiduciary services'".

La Forest, J.'s views are made more apparent by his statement at p. 184:

> By enforcing a duty of honesty and good faith, the courts are able to regulate an activity that is of great value to commerce and society generally.

Further, at p. 186, La Forest, J. said:

> The desire to protect and reinforce the integrity of social institutions and enterprises is prevalent throughout fiduciary law. The reason for this desire is that the law has recognized the importance of instilling in our social institutions and enterprises some recognition that not all relationships are characterized by a dynamic of mutual autonomy, and that the marketplace cannot always set the rules. By instilling this kind of flexibility into our regulation of social institutions and enterprises, the law therefore helps to strengthen them.

In my opinion, this principle is a reflection of the way in which equitable discretion traditionally has been exercised: to see done that which should be done, in the particular circumstances. Where the particular circumstances include "important institutions in society which render 'fiduciary' services", that which should be done may well include aspects of public policy because of the public importance of such institutions, the extent to which members of the public rely on them for the provision of fiduciary services, and the need for public confidence in such institutions. At the same time, the court will, in my view, be careful to take into consideration not only the many factors relevant to determining the nature of any fiduciary duty but also the nature and extent of statutory or regulatory controls upon the institution and, in the case of a self-governing profession like the Law Society, the nature and extent of the governing body's pronouncements respecting fiduciary services provided by members. The court should also take into account any other aspects of public policy which are relevant, including any which favour or support the impugned conduct.

Mr. Greenspan has raised in his defence the public benefit derived from the *Regina v. Stewart* broadcast and from his involvement. I understand the argument also to rely upon his role in developing the Scales of Justice concept and bringing it to fruition on television. A public policy purpose is said to arise from this public benefit. Mr. Jack put it this way in his written outline of argument:

> There is a very significant public policy purpose to be served by ensuring that lawyers continue to feel at liberty to take part in educational presentations which enhance the public's understanding of the legal process, and thus enhance the administration of justice in Canada.

Some evidence also addressed the advantage to the legal profession and to the public when lawyers and law students are able to learn from lawyers discussing their professional experiences.

It is also necessary to consider whether there is a public policy purpose in constraining counsel by means of a fiduciary duty for the benefit or protection of a client or former client and if so, how such policy considerations relate to the policy considerations raised on Mr. Greenspan's behalf.

I will consider first the issues raised by Mr. Greenspan. These policy issues were considered in *Edmonton Journal v. Alberta (Attorney General)* ... where the appellant, a newspaper publisher, challenged a section of the Judicature Act which prohibited publication of much information about matrimonial proceedings. In issue therefore was freedom of expression and more particularly, freedom of expression respecting matters before the court. ...

... [T]he public interest in public knowledge and understanding of the workings of courts as public institutions is well established.

. . . . .

It is clear that Mr. Greenspan played a substantial role in developing the Scales of Justice concept and the defendant Scales as a vehicle for providing both education and information to the public about the justice system. It is also clear the Scales radio and T.V. programs other than *Regina v. Stewart* impressed various members of the bench and the bar with the quality of the information they imparted about the justice system, and I accept the evidence in this regard, filed in letter form on consent, as establishing the [public] benefit of these programs. The *Regina v. Stewart* episode also provided a public benefit through education about the justice system. Nonetheless, ... Mr. Greenspan's involvement in the *Regina v. Stewart* episode was not necessary to provide the [public] benefit which is the focus of the public policy argument he raises is a significant consideration. As well, it is clear that Mr. Greenspan could have withdrawn from his involvement in the episode without any difficulty. No aspect of prior commitment or overarching duty affected his decision. He chose to carry on. In addition, Mr. Greenspan's work in preparing and presenting the *Regina v. Stewart* episode was in fact primarily self-promotion, not public education. Public education was assured without this work of Mr. Greenspan's.

What then is to be said in support of attaching a fiduciary duty to Mr. Greenspan's broadcast involvement? ... It was when he acted as Mr. Stewart's counsel that a fiduciary duty attached to Mr. Greenspan in respect of Mr. Stewart and his case. That duty was alive but inoperative through the years that Mr. Greenspan and Mr. Stewart were independent of each other. Mr. Greenspan brought himself within the sphere of that duty when, in 1991, he chose to involve himself again in the public aspects of Mr. Stewart's case. Involving himself again in the subject matter of his concluded retainer triggered the fiduciary obligation of loyalty. Mr. Greenspan's duty was to be loyal to Mr. Stewart to the extent of firstly, not taking advantage of him, and the information and issues which had been the subject of his professional services and secondly, to the extent of not undoing the benefits and protections provided by those professional services. In my opinion, the duty of loyalty itself is sufficient to ensure public confidence in the legal profession, in its relevant activities. Loyalty reciprocates the faith the client had in the lawyer respecting the information and issues which were the subject of the professional services.

In my opinion, the public policy issues raises [*sic*] by Mr. Greenspan do not materially alter these loyalty obligations and do not dissolve them, in the circumstances. ... Mr. Greenspan simply didn't understand his duty and, in the presence of self-interest, didn't ascertain it despite Mr. Stewart's objection to his intended conduct. I see no public benefit in holding that incidental public education resulting from counsel's inattention to fiduciary obligations should alter, dilute or destroy those obligations to a former client. That is particularly so when the incidental benefit to the public resulted from a substantial breach of duty to the former client.

... Since this counsel and client relationship included professional services consisting of publication of information about Mr. Stewart and public appearance on Mr. Stewart's behalf in a public forum to address public interest issues and public perceptions attended by substantial publicity, counsel's fiduciary obligation attaches to these professional services and in particular, to the information which was the subject of them. This fiduciary obligation of loyalty is not materially altered, diluted or dissolved by the public nature of Mr. Greenspan's work or by the public nature of the information with which he worked, as it might have been if the fiduciary duty depended on confidentiality. ...

. . . . .

... In a sensational case like Mr. Stewart's, particularly one involving flight to avoid prosecution, much information is public knowledge before the accused is identified and charged and often, before counsel is retained. It is noteworthy that such public information probably would not prevent the existence of a fiduciary duty based on confidentiality. Rule 4 of the rules of professional conduct indicates that a duty of confidentiality on the part of counsel may apply to information which is widely known. When the fiduciary duty is one of loyalty, unrelated to confidentiality, and in respect of the public disclosure and use of information by counsel, pre-retainer publication is of very little significance. ... The fiduciary duty in issue therefore arises in part from what Mr. Greenspan said and did in public as counsel, it applies to what he said and did in public as broadcaster and, in my opinion, it is not defeated by what others said and did publicly before that fiduciary duty of loyalty arose.

(d) Breach of Fiduciary Duty.

For the above reasons, Mr. Greenspan breached his fiduciary duty of loyalty to Mr. Stewart in the following ways:

-   He favoured his financial interests over the plaintiff's interests as alleged in sub-paragraph 25(h) of the statement of claim.

-   He put his own self promotion before the plaintiff's interests as alleged in sub-paragraph 25(i) of the statement of claim.

- By the way he publicized his former client and his former client's case in 1991, he undercut the benefits and protections he had provided as counsel, and therefore, increased the adverse public effect on the plaintiff of his crime, trial and sentencing, which falls within sub-paragraph 25(j) of the statement of claim.

It is alleged in sub-paragraph 25(f) that Mr. Greenspan breached his fiduciary duty through his speech in the production in which he identified himself as the plaintiff's solicitor. In my opinion the evidence confirming this is relevant to the above breaches, but this is not a breach in itself.

. . . . .

viii) Summary

I assess the compensation which Mr. Stewart is entitled to recover from Mr. Greenspan in the amount of $2,500.00. The amount of profit which Mr. Greenspan is obliged to disgorge to Mr. Stewart is $3,250.00.

NOTES AND QUESTIONS

1. Do you agree with the decision in the case? In particular, do you agree that Mr. Greenspan should owe a continuing fiduciary obligation to his former client, and that he breached that obligation by discussing the former client's case for the purpose of personal self-promotion? What are the points in favour of J. Macdonald J.'s decision? What are the points against his decision?

2. How significant is the fact that Mr. Greenspan misrepresented certain of the facts with respect to Mr. Stewart's case? If the broadcast had been completely accurate would/should a different result have been warranted?

3. Is the remedy imposed by J. Macdonald J. appropriate? What penalty would you impose?

4. Should the Law Society of Upper Canada have commenced an investigation into Mr. Greenspan's conduct? Would you encourage the Law Society to impose a penalty? If so, what penalty would you recommend?

5. What if Mr. Greenspan had published an academic article discussing the issues of legal strategy raised by Mr. Stewart's case? Should Mr. Stewart be able successfully to bring a similar claim? What reasons of law or policy would make such a claim distinguishable (or not)?

LAW SOCIETY OF UPPER CANADA v. HUNTER
[2007] L.S.D.D. No. 8, 2007 ONLSHP 27
(Law Society of Upper Canada, Hearing Panel: M. Sandler, Chair,
A. Alexander and S.L. Robins)
[footnotes omitted]

[A complaint of professional misconduct came before the Law Society of Upper Canada. George Hunter, a senior lawyer, a partner at a large Ottawa law firm, a prominent family lawyer, a Treasurer of the Law Society of Upper Canada and a President of the Federation of Law Societies of Canada, represented XY in acrimonious custody, access and related matters for a number of

years. In April 2003 Hunter and XY commenced a "sexual/romantic" relationship. Both Hunter and XY agreed that the relationship was consensual,
though XY claimed that Hunter made use of confidential information to take
advantage of her. Hunter denied this. Both the relationship and Hunter's representation of XY continued for approximately two and one-half more years,
when Hunter ended things. He arranged in November 2005 to meet with XY
to have her review and initial a copy of Rule 2.04 of the *Rules of Professional
Conduct* and get her to sign an Acknowledgement that he had complied with
Rule 2.04 at the commencement of their sexual/romantic relationship regarding the existence of a conflict and that she had been advised by him to obtain
independent legal advice. Hunter admitted that he had not actually done so. At
this meeting with XY, Hunter ended the relationship, also informing her that
he had been involved romantically with two other women during the period of
his relationship with XY. XY left the meeting disappointed and shocked. Subsequently Hunter e-mailed and tried to telephone XY on numerous occasions.
He attended XY's home with his lawyer, unannounced, to seek to get her to
confirm to his lawyer that the sexual/romantic relationship was as he had described, causing XY concern and emotional distress. Though other facts related to the Hunter/XY relationship were disputed, the Law Society "placed
no reliance upon any allegations made by XY that were not admitted to by the
member" (para. 15).

Hunter informed his law firm of the situation. The firm and Hunter referred the matter to the Law Society and Hunter resigned as Treasurer. Hunter
co-operated fully with the Society in its subsequent investigation, he was
charged with, and admitted to, professional misconduct in having placed himself in a "conflict of interest in relation to his client, XY, and in so doing he
failed to maintain the integrity of the profession" (para. 1). Counsel for
Hunter submitted extensive evidence of Hunter's status in the legal profession, the contributions he has made to the profession, and the devastating effect that the proceedings have had upon him, his family and his practice.
Counsel for the Law Society submitted evidence showing the effect that his
behaviour has had on the complainants.]

. . . . .

Analysis

Rule 2.04 of the *Rules of Professional Conduct* provides, in part:

2.04 AVOIDANCE OF CONFLICTS OF INTEREST

Definition

2.04 (1) In this rule,

a "*conflict of interest*" or a "*conflicting interest*" means an interest
that

(a) that would be likely to affect adversely a lawyer's judgment
on behalf of, or loyalty to, a client or prospective client ...

. . . . .

Commentary

...

Where a lawyer is acting for a friend or family member, the lawyer may have a conflict of interest because the personal relationship may interfere with the lawyer's duty to provide objective, disinterested professional advice to the client.

. . . . .

2.04 (3) A lawyer shall not act or continue to act in a matter when there is or is likely to be a conflicting interest unless, after disclosure adequate to make an informed decision, the client or prospective client consents.

Commentary

A client or the client's affairs may be seriously prejudiced unless the lawyer's judgment and freedom of action on the client's behalf are as free as possible from conflict of interest.

A lawyer should examine whether a conflict of interest exists not only from the outset but throughout the duration of a retainer because new circumstances or information may establish or reveal a conflict of interest.

...

If a lawyer has a sexual or intimate personal relationship with a client, this may conflict with the lawyer's duty to provide objective, disinterested professional advice to the client. Before accepting a retainer from or continuing a retainer with a person with whom the lawyer has such a relationship, a lawyer should consider the following factors:

a. The vulnerability of the client, both emotional and economic;

b. The fact that the lawyer and client relationship may create a power imbalance in favour of the lawyer or, in some circumstances, in favour of the client;

c. Whether the sexual or intimate personal relationship will jeopardize the client's right to have all information concerning the client's business and affairs held in strict confidence. For example, the existence of the relationship may obscure whether certain information was acquired in the course of the lawyer and client relationship;

d. Whether such a relationship may require the lawyer to act as a witness in the proceedings;

e. Whether such a relationship will interfere in any way with the lawyer's fiduciary obligations to the client, his or her ability to exercise independent professional judgment, or his or her ability to fulfill obligations owed as an officer of the court and to the administration of justice.

There is no conflict of interest if another lawyer of the firm who does not have a sexual or intimate personal relationship with the client is the lawyer handling the client's work.

While subrule 2.04(3) does not require that a lawyer advise the client to obtain independent legal advice about the conflicting interest, in some cases, especially those in which the client is not sophisticated or is vulnerable, the lawyer should recommend such advice to ensure that the client's consent is informed, genuine, and uncoerced.

. . . . .

The gravamen of the misconduct in this case is the conflict of interest arising out of the intimate relationship between the member and his client XY, the member's failure to appropriately recognize and address the issues surrounding that conflict of interest and the complainant's vulnerability, and his conduct on November 21, 2005 and thereafter to attempt to rectify the situation by pressing the complainant to confirm the member's position.

There is no doubt (and the member admitted) that the sexual/romantic relationship between the member and XY created a conflict of interest. The member had a duty to provide objective, disinterested professional advice to XY. The sexual/romantic relationship had the significant potential of jeopardizing the member's ability to provide such advice. It also had the significant potential of inhibiting the client from challenging or even questioning the advice being given by someone who was not only her lawyer, but an intimate partner. The fact that XY viewed the relationship as serious and committed reinforced this potential danger. As well, the nature of the work being performed by the member on XY's behalf — involving a dispute with XY's former husband and access issues — further underscores that danger.

The *Rules of Professional Conduct* do not create an absolute prohibition against initiating or continuing a sexual/romantic relationship with a client. This is not the case or the forum to debate whether the existing Rule is sufficiently broad or inclusive. However, it can fairly be said that any sexual/romantic relationship with a client, at the very least, raises serious questions about whether the lawyer is thereby placed in a conflict of interest or is otherwise jeopardizing the solicitor-client relationship. (In many cases, it also invites concern over whether the sexual/romantic relationship is truly consensual.)

Given the conflict of interest, the member was obligated to discuss with his client at the outset of their sexual/romantic relationship whether he should continue to act on her behalf. The member should have referred, at a minimum, to the circumstances that created the conflict of interest, and the dangers associated with that conflict of interest. The factors articulated in the Commentary to subrule 2.04(3) should have figured prominently in such a discussion.

Subrule 2.04(3) does not compel a lawyer to advise the client to obtain independent legal advice about the conflicting interest in all cases. However, where the client is unsophisticated or is vulnerable, the lawyer should recommend such advice to ensure that the client's consent is informed, genuine and uncoerced. Here, the client was emotionally vulnerable (whether as a result of the family law dispute, her new, intimate relationship with the member or both), and the member should have recommended independent legal advice. Any uncertainty on the member's part as to whether the circumstances compelled him to recommend independent legal advice should have been resolved in favour of such a recommendation.

It should be noted that, in some circumstances, the conflict of interest created by the existence of a sexual/romantic relationship will be so profound and irreconcilable with the lawyer's ability to provide objective, disinterested professional advice that the lawyer simply cannot continue to act, and must recommend that the client retain a different lawyer.

As is made clear by Rule 2.04, the member's obligation did not cease at the outset of his sexual/romantic relationship with XY. Even had an informed consent been obtained by the member at the outset of that relationship, circumstances during the relationship may have compelled the member to revisit the issue with his client.

In November 2005, the member had the client review and initial a copy of Rule 2.04 and had her sign an Acknowledgement to the effect that the member had complied with Rule 2.04. There remains some disagreement (as reflected in the agreed statement of facts) over the accuracy of some aspects of the Acknowledgement, or of the contents of the e-mails which the member subsequently sent to XY. We need not resolve that disagreement, and we draw no inference against the member in that regard. But several things are clear. First, the Acknowledgement was inaccurate in asserting that the member had complied with his obligations under Rule 2.04. As he has admitted, he did not. Second, the circumstances surrounding the initialing of a copy of Rule 2.04 and the signing of the Acknowledgement did not permit an informed decision on the part of the client. On the contrary, the circumstances advanced the interests of the member, but not those of the client. Third, the member's conduct in pressing XY to confirm the member's position to his former lawyer and law partners through e-mails and telephone calls, and through an attendance at her home without prior notification was inappropriate, contributed to the client's concern and emotional distress, and attempted to advance the member's interests, rather than those of the client.

This is a serious matter, as correctly acknowledged by some of those who acted as character references on behalf of the member. Nonetheless, the Hearing Panel recognizes the existence of a number of mitigating factors that must inform the appropriate penalty.

The member co-operated fully with the Society. He acknowledged his wrongdoing at the earliest opportunity. He self-reported to the Society. Through his counsel, an agreed statement of facts was created that spared the complainant the ordeal of testifying at these proceedings. The complainant's privacy was respected through the introduction of a summary of her psychologist's findings. A victim impact statement was filed, again on consent. The member spoke positively about the complainant's attributes. As earlier indicated, he was deeply remorseful, and did not seek to minimize, justify or excuse his misconduct.

There is no evidence before us that the member's legal work was actually affected by the conflict of interest, despite the dangers earlier articulated.

The misconduct has already taken a significant toll upon the member. We have observed his considerable fall from grace, culminating in his resignation as Treasurer of the Society. He has been unable to practise law (albeit on paid leave) since December 2005 for health and other reasons related, in large measure if not entirely, to this matter. This underscores the impact of these proceedings upon him, and is a significant factor in setting the appropriate penalty in this case.

The Society conceded that the member is in no need of specific deterrence. Its proposed disposition was based upon the need for general deterrence: in other words, to dissuade like-minded lawyers from similar misconduct.

This Hearing Panel must remain mindful of the impact of this and other decisions on the profession as a whole, and upon the confidence of the public in the profession. However, the member should not be treated more harshly as a result of his former status as Treasurer and as a bencher. Nor, of course, should he receive favoured treatment, although he is entitled to make the important point that his entire career is incompatible with this misconduct and that, therefore, this misconduct can be regarded as "out of character." We have no difficulty in so finding.

The letters filed on behalf of the member were impressive, and spoke to the member's character, integrity, and commitment to the profession. They demonstrate, in our view, that the member remains capable of serving in the future as a valuable member of his firm, and of the profession.

In *Law Society of Upper Canada v. Mark Elliott Joseph* (November 26, 1993) another panel imposed a three-month suspension for analogous conduct. We were not provided with any other decision that involves similar facts.

There were some obvious similarities and differences between the *Joseph* case and the case at bar, some favourable and some unfavourable to the member here. For example, we noted the level of vulnerability of the complainant, Ms. Doe, in that case as a result, in part, of her prior history as a victim of assault/sexual assault, and deep depression. The panel found that Mr. Joseph misused confidential information disclosed by the client in the course of seeking legal advice and representation. On the other hand, the duration of the conflict of interest in that case was far shorter than in the case at bar. Ultimately, while the principles in the *Joseph* case do inform our decision here, we make the not uncommon observation that each case spins on its own facts.

The *Joseph* decision is particularly helpful in articulating the inherent dangers when lawyers engage in sexual relationships with clients. These dangers include:

- Clients are entitled to a lawyer's independent and objective judgment, unaffected by that lawyer's conflict of interest. An ongoing sexual relationship with clients during the period of representation threatens that independence and objectivity.

- If the sexual relationship is a serious one, it is difficult for the lawyer to remain dispassionate about the client's legal issues. If the relationship is not a serious one (at least in the lawyer's mind), there is a danger that the lawyer may be exploiting the client.

- In many cases, it will also be difficult to evaluate whether a vulnerable client's purported consent to a sexual relationship is rooted, in whole or in part, in his or her dependence upon the lawyer's representation and support. Simply put, the consent may be more apparent than real.

. . . . .

[Hunter received a 60-day suspension and a fine of $2,500. The portion of the judgment dealing with the basis for this penalty is excerpted in Chapter 13.]

NOTES AND QUESTIONS

1. Are there any circumstances in which a sexual relationship between a lawyer and a client, and the lawyer's continued representation of a client, would be appropriate? What if, for example, the client was a corporation and the relationship was between the lawyer and the corporation's in-house counsel? Consider Scenario Four below.

2. Some professions have established a zero tolerance approach to professional-client (or patient) sexual relations. What should be the approach of the legal profession?

3. What do you think the appropriate penalty should be for a lawyer who takes advantage of the lawyer-client relationship and initiates sexual relations with that client? Do you think Mr. Hunter's penalty might have been different had he been a solo practitioner with no association with the Law Society? This issue is considered later in Chapter 13.

4. The judgment may imply that if Hunter had referred the file to another lawyer in the firm no Law Society discipline would have resulted. Is this result appropriate? Can you think of facts where it would not be appropriate (*e.g.*, where professional discipline would be warranted for the sexual relationship even if there was no continued representation of the client)? The *Model Code* has chosen to deal with this issue as part of the general "conflict of interest" provisions:

   > A "conflict of interest" means the existence of a substantial risk that a lawyer's loyalty to or representation of a client would be materially and adversely affected by the lawyer's own interest or the lawyer's duties to another client, a former client, or a third person.

   One Commentary to Rule 2.04(1) of the *Model Code* identifies the following example of a conflict of interest:

5. A lawyer has a sexual or close personal relationship with a client.

   Such a relationship may conflict with the lawyer's duty to provide objective, disinterested professional advice to the client. The relationship may obscure whether certain information was acquired in the course of the lawyer and client relationship and may jeopardize the client's right to have all information concerning his or her affairs held in strict confidence. The relationship may in some circumstances permit exploitation of the client by his or her lawyer. If the lawyer is a member of a firm and concludes that a conflict exists, the conflict is not imputed to the lawyer's firm, but would be cured if another lawyer in the firm who is not involved in such a relationship with the client handled the client's work.

6. What other kinds of relationships might cause serious lawyer-client conflicts? *Strother* demonstrates that conflicting financial interests between the lawyer and client might be one such conflict. Can you think of any others?

Scenario Three

Tom Thomas is the President and Chief Executive Officer of Thomas Manufacturing Ltd. His company has retained ABC Law Firm to handle its legal business. In the course of representing Thomas Manufacturing, one of the ABC lawyers, Gerry Gordon, becomes romantically involved with Thomas. Advise Gordon as to his ethical obligations in light of the relationship. Does your answer depend on how many other ABC lawyers are involved? Or whether Gordon is an associate at ABC or a partner? Or whether Gordon has disclosed his relationship to other lawyers at ABC? What if Gordon is not "out" at his law firm and does not wish to disclose the existence of the relationship to his law firm colleagues?

Scenario Four

J.J. is a lawyer in Calgary. A few years ago she persuaded a client to enter into a business transaction with her. She continued to provide legal services for the client. Ultimately the business venture collapsed, with J.J. and the client ending up in litigation for breach of contract and breach of fiduciary duty. J.J. failed to advise her client to obtain independent legal advice and should not have continued to act for him. The Law Society found, however, that the reasons for the business venture failing were largely related to the client's unreasonable behaviour. In addition, the client was sophisticated and experienced in business matters. J.J. has never been disciplined previously and has cooperated fully with the Law Society. The litigation has been settled out of court on terms that have not been disclosed. Is J.J.'s behaviour sanctionable?

Scenario Five

Janice Will is a Chinese-Canadian lawyer. She is also an active member of her local civil liberties association, and a strong believer in the importance of freedom of expression. Albert North is a white supremacist who has been convicted of hate crimes for his publication of a racist pamphlet which took particular aim at Canadians whose ethnic origins are Asian or Southeast Asian. Will has been approached by the Anti-Defamation League to act as an intervener in North's appeal and to articulate arguments in opposition to his conviction. She is uncertain whether under the *Model Code* she has a disqualifying conflict of interest, and has come to you for advice. What would you advise, and why?

D. FURTHER READING

Brenner, Susan & James Durham, "Towards Resolving Prosecutor Conflicts of Interest" (1993) 6 Geo. J. Legal Ethics 415.

Buhai, Sande, "Emotional Conflicts: Impaired Dispassionate Representation of Family Members" (2008) 21 Geo. J. Legal Ethics 1159.

Canadian Bar Association, Task Force on Conflicts of Interest *Final Report, Recommendations and Toolkit* (August 2008), online: <http://www.cba.org/CBA/groups/pdf/conflicts_finalreport.pdf>.

Devlin, Richard, "Guest Editorial: Governance, Regulation and Legitimacy: Conflicts of Interest and the Duty of Loyalty" (2011) 14 Legal Ethics at iii.

Devlin, Richard & Victoria Rees, "Beyond Conflicts of Interest to the Duty of Loyalty: From *Martin v. Gray* to *R. v. Neil*" (2005) 84 Can. Bar Rev. 433.

DiLernia, Michael, "Advance Waivers of Conflicts of Interest in Large Law Firm Practice" (2009) 22 Geo. J. Legal Ethics 97.

Dodek, Adam, "Conflicted Identities: The Battle Over the Duty of Loyalty in Canada" (2011) 14 Legal Ethics 193.

Duggan, Anthony, "Solicitors' Conflict of Interest and the Wider Fiduciary Question" (2007) 45 Can. Bus. L.J. 414.

Federation of Law Societies, Supplementary Report, Advisory Committee on Conflicts of Interest (February 14, 2011), online: <http://www.flsc.ca/_documents/Supplementary-Report-Conflicts-of-Interest-Feb-2011.pdf>.

Federation of Law Societies of Canada, Standing Committee on the Model Code of Professional Conduct, *Report on Conflicts of Interest* (November 21, 2011), online: <http://www.flsc.ca/_documents/Conflicts-of-Interest-Report-Nov_2011.pdf>.

Graham, Randal, *Legal Ethics: Theories, Cases, and Professional Regulation* (Toronto: Emond Montgomery, 2011), ch. 6, "Conflicts of Interest".

Hutchinson, Allan C., *Legal Ethics and Professional Responsibility*, 2nd ed. (Toronto: Irwin Law, 2006), Chapter 8, "Conflicts of Interest: Screens and Silences".

Loughrey, Joan, "Large Law Firms, Sophisticated Clients and the Regulation of Conflicts of Interest in England and Wales" (2011) 14 Legal Ethics 215.

MacKenzie, Gavin, *Lawyers and Ethics: Professional Responsibility and Discipline* (Toronto: Thomson Carswell, 2007), Chapter 5, "Conflicts of Interest in Litigation".

Moore, Nancy, "Regulating Law Firm Conflicts in the 21st Century: Implications of the Globalization of Legal Services and the Growth of the 'Mega Firm'" (2005) 18 Geo. J. Legal Ethics 521.

Morrison, Harvey, "Conflicts of Interest and the Concept of Loyalty" (2008) 87 Can. Bar Rev. 565.

O'Sullivan, Terrence J. & M. Paul Michell, "Analyzing Conflicts of Interest After Strother: Has Anything Changed?", Canadian Bar Association Online Continuing Legal Education Presentation (November 27, 2007).

Perell, Paul, *Conflict of Interest in the Legal Profession* (Markham, ON: Butterworths, 1995).

Proulx, Michel & David Layton, *Ethics and Canadian Criminal Law* (Toronto: Irwin Law, 2001), Chapter 6, "Conflict of Interest".

Smith, Beverley G., *Professional Conduct for Lawyers and Judges*, 3rd ed. (Fredericton: Maritime Law Book, 2007).

Stagg-Taylor, Joanne, "Lawyers' Business: Conflicts of Duties Arising from Lawyers' Business Models" (2011) 14 Legal Ethics 173.

Wolfram, Charles, *Modern Legal Ethics* (St. Paul, MN: West, 1986), ch. 7.

Woolley, Alice, *Understanding Lawyers' Ethics in Canada* (Markham, ON: LexisNexis Canada, 2011), Chapter 8, "Conflicts of Interest: Creating the Conditions for Loyalty and Confidentiality".

CHAPTER 6

ETHICS IN ADVOCACY

A. INTRODUCTION

There are many opportunities to act as an advocate in the practice of law: as a business lawyer negotiating a deal on behalf of a corporate client; as a legal aid lawyer advocating for the return to school or the safe housing of a young person in custody; as a labour lawyer negotiating the terms of a new collective bargaining agreement; as a native rights lawyer working with government representatives on a land claim settlement; as a public interest lawyer holding a press conference to raise support for a client's opposition to the creation of a local nuclear waste facility; as a collaborative lawyer seeking to work out the solution to a conflict involving the breakdown of an intimate family relationship; or as a litigator arguing on behalf of a client. All of these examples are moments of advocacy. For a code-based definition of "advocacy", see Rule 4.01(1) and Commentary of the Federation of Law Societies of Canada's *Model Code of Professional Conduct*.

What this chapter primarily deals with, specifically, is the latter example: advocacy in litigation, and in particular, in civil litigation. For related issues and discussions raised elsewhere in this book, see, for example, the professional and ethical discussions involving Confidentiality (Chapter 4), Conflicts of Interest (Chapter 5), Counselling and Negotiation (Chapter 7) and Criminal Law Advocacy (Chapter 8).

B. VISIONS OF THE ADVOCATE

The basic role of the legal advocate is to engage in advocacy on behalf of someone else, typically a client. And while the client plays a role in all visions of litigation advocacy, the centrality of his or her interests varies depending on which vision of the advocate one subscribes to. As was discussed in Chapter 1, the role of the lawyer as advocate can be defined in various ways, including by loyalty (the "loyal advocacy" model), by pursuit of the public interest (the "moral agent in pursuit of justice" model), or by seeing the lawyer as required to pursue and balance a variety of competing interests (described in Chapter 1 in the context of "integrity"). The advocacy context places particular strains on the lawyer's ability to accomplish this difficult balancing act. It is the context in which the lawyer is most strongly urged to act zealously for a client's interests, but where, as well, the lawyer can be seen as having the greatest responsibility to protect and ensure the proper functioning of the justice system.

Thus, on the one hand, modern codes of conduct, as supported by academic literature, while noting lawyers' obligations towards the administration of justice in general, continue primarily to define the litigation lawyer's role largely in terms of the zealous advocate. For example, according to Rule 4.01(1) of the *Model Code*, when "acting as an advocate", the lawyer must:

> ... represent the client resolutely and honourably within the limits of the law, while treating the tribunal with candour, fairness, courtesy, and respect ... [and]

> **Commentary**

> ... raise fearlessly every issue, advance every argument and ask every question, however distasteful, that the lawyer thinks will help the client's case and to endeavour to obtain for the client the benefit of every remedy and defence authorized by law.

This vision of the zealous advocate not only requires lawyers to emphasize their clients' views, it also requires that they de-emphasize their own views. According to the Commentary to Rule 4.01(1), when acting as an advocate, a "lawyer should refrain from expressing the lawyer's personal opinions on the merits of a client's case ...".

On the other hand, the former Chief Justice of Ontario, speaking on the topic of "advocacy in the 21st century", emphasized the various competing interests to which advocates must be faithful:

> Lawyers are not solely professional advocates or "hired guns". And while they do not surrender their free speech rights upon admission to the bar, they are also officers of the court with fundamental obligations to uphold the integrity of the judicial process, both inside and outside the courtroom. It is the duty of counsel to be faithful both to their client and to the administration of justice.[1]

Similarly, according to Lord Denning M.R., an advocate

> ... is a minister of justice equally with the judge. He has a monopoly of audience in the higher courts. No one save he can address the judge, unless it be a litigant in person. This carries with it a corresponding responsibility ... He must ... do all he honourably can on behalf of his client. I say "all he honourably can" because his duty is not only to his client. He has a duty to the court which is paramount. It is a mistake to suppose that he is the mouthpiece of his client to say what he wants: or his tool to do what he directs. He is none of these things. He owes allegiance to a higher cause. It is the cause of truth and justice. He must not consciously misstate the facts. He must not knowingly conceal the truth. He must not unjustly make a charge of fraud, that is, without evidence to support it. He must produce all the relevant authorities, even those that are against him. He must see that his client discloses, if ordered, the relevant documents, even those that are fatal to his case. He must disregard the most specific instructions of his client, if they conflict with his duty to the court. The code which requires a barrister to do all this is not a code of law. It is a code of honour. If he breaks it, he is

---

[1]   The Honourable Chief Justice R. Roy McMurtry, "Role of the Courts and Counsel in Justice", The Advocates' Society Spring Symposium 2000, Advocacy in the 21st Century (June 6, 2000).

offending against the rules of the profession and is subject to its discipline ... Such being his duty to the court, the barrister must be able to do it fearlessly. He has time and time again to choose between his duty to his client and his duty to the court. This is a conflict often difficult to resolve ...[2]

The challenges, then, when thinking about ethics in advocacy are first to iden- tify the various and often competing interests to which a litigator must be faithful; and, second, to try to sort out how to balance and resolve those com- peting interests, which is an exercise — as recognized by Lord Denning — that can be "often difficult".

For the purposes of this chapter, we will look at these competing interests and how to resolve them in several everyday contexts in which they typically arise for advocates throughout the many pre-trial and trial stages of the litiga- tion process.

C. ETHICS IN PRE-TRIAL PROCEDURES

Many, if not most, of the challenging ethical and professional issues in the context of civil litigation arise well before trial. For example, during an initial meeting with a client, considerations about conflicts of interest, confidential- ity, fees (and access to the legal system for that particular client) and other ethical issues arise.

1. Pleadings

Once a lawyer is retained and the matter is under way, many difficult advo- cacy decisions need to be made at the pleadings stage. What is my client's case? How can I best plead the case in order to "raise fearlessly every issue" and "advance every argument"? (*Model Code*, Rule 4.01(1) (Commentary)) By doing so, am I overstating the merits of the case? Is this client simply us- ing the system to extract a settlement or to "get" the other side, and if so, am I participating as an advocate in an abuse of process?[3]

Most of these considerations are the subject of pleadings rules in the various provincial rules of court. For example, if an advocate pushes zealous- ness too far by including in a client's pleading allegations that: are "unneces- sary", "scandalous", "frivolous" or "vexatious"; may "prejudice", "embar- rass" or "delay" the "fair trial or hearing of the proceeding"; or are otherwise "an abuse of the process of the court", that pleading may be struck out on

---

[2] *Rondel v. Worsley*, [1967] 1 Q.B. 443 (following note 27 and surrounding text), affd [1969] 1 A.C. 191.

[3] For a discussion of abuse of process in the context of pleadings, see, *e.g.*, *National Trust v. Furbacher*, [1994] O.J. No. 2385 (Ont. Gen. Div.), as further discussed in Trevor C.W. Farrow, "Five Pleadings Cases Everyone Should Read" (2009) 35(4) Advocates' Q. 466 at 467-73.

motion by the other party to the litigation.[4] Indeed, pursuit of an action without legal merit can place a client at risk of liability in an action for abuse of process.[5]

In addition, however, and regardless of whether or not a procedural motion is brought to strike out a pleading, all of these considerations are also at the core of professional rules governing the advocate's role. For example, according to Rule 4.01(2)(a) of the *Model Code*, when acting as an advocate, including when drafting a client's pleading, a lawyer shall not:

> abuse the process of the tribunal by instituting or prosecuting proceedings that, although legal in themselves, are clearly motivated by malice on the part of the client and are brought solely for the purpose of injuring the other party ...

These specific pleadings requirements fit within broader professional rules that prohibit the lawyer-as-advocate from pursuing unmeritorious or improper steps in the litigation process. For example, according to Rules 4.01(1) and 4.01(2)(b) of the *Model Code*, when acting as an advocate, a lawyer:

Commentary

> ... must discharge [his or her duty as an advocate in adversarial proceedings] by fair and honourable means, without illegality and in a manner that is consistent with the lawyer's duty to treat the tribunal with candour, fairness, courtesy and respect and in a way that promotes the parties' right to a fair hearing in which justice can be done. ...
>
> . . . . .
>
> ... should avoid and discourage the client from resorting to frivolous or vexatious objections, attempts to gain advantage from slips or oversights not going to the merits or tactics that will merely delay or harass the other side. ...

Rule 4.01(2)(b)

> . . . . .
>
> [must not] knowingly assist or permit a client to do anything that the lawyer considers to be dishonest or dishonourable ...
>
> . . . . .

Commentary

> ... has a duty not to mislead the tribunal about the position of the client in the adversarial process.

---

[4]   See, *e.g.*, British Columbia's Supreme Court Rules, B.C. Reg. 168/2009, Rule 9-5(1); Ontario's Rules of Civil Procedure, R.R.O. 1990, Reg. 194, Rules 21 and 25.11; Nova Scotia's Civil Procedure Rules, N.S. Reg. 420/2008, Rules 13.01(2) and 88.02(1)(e).

[5]   See, *e.g.*, *Colborne Capital Corp. v. 542775 Alberta Ltd.*, [1995] A.J. No. 538, 30 Alta. L.R. (3d) 127 at paras. 375-378 (Alta. Q.B.), affd [2000] A.J. No. 161, 250 A.R. 352 (Alta. C.A.).

Consider the ethical duties related to pleadings, and instigating a cause of action, through the following case.

D.C.B. v. ZELLERS INC.

[1996] M.J. No. 362, 138 D.L.R. (4th) 309 (Man. Q.B.),
affd [1996] M.J. No. 499, 10 W.W.R. 689 (Man. C.A.)
(Man. Q.B., Jewers J.)

JEWERS J.:— In this small claim appeal, the plaintiff sues the defendants for money she paid to them as compensation for damages the defendant Zellers (Zellers) sustained resulting from thefts committed by her young son. The issue is whether in the particular circumstances of this case having paid over the money, the plaintiff can recover it on the ground that Zellers never had a valid claim against her personally. The proceedings against the defendant Arkin have been discontinued.

A hearing officer dismissed the claim and the plaintiff appeals.

The parties filed the following agreed statement of facts. ...

[The statement of facts indicated that the plaintiff's son had been arrested for shoplifting. The goods were recovered and had a value of around $50. No damage was done to the items and they were returned for sale. After the shoplifting incident the following letter was sent to the plaintiff by Mr. Arkin, counsel for Zellers:]

"I act for Zellers to recover their damages in civil court. The civil recovery process is SEPARATE AND DISTINCT from any criminal action and the two must not be confused.

"It is alleged that on May 26, 1956 [sic] J.R.B., a young person for whose supervision my client holds you legally responsible, took unlawful possession of merchandise from Zellers, located at 969 Henderson Highway, Winnipeg, Manitoba, to the value of $59.95.

"In accordance with the Court of Queen's Bench Act of Manitoba and/or The Court of Queen's Bench Small Claims Practices Act of Manitoba, Zellers has a legal right to claim Civil Restitution from you.

"In order to eliminate additional expense to you, Zellers is willing to settle THE CIVIL CASE ONLY out of court, providing you pay the following amount by August 25, 1995:

"Restitution for cost of incident including damages and costs: $225.00

"Should you elect to ignore this demand, refuse or fail to pay the amount of the proposed out of Court settlement, Zellers will take the case before a Civil Court and claim damages, including legal costs and interest pursuant to The Court of Queen's Bench Act of Manitoba and/or The Court of Queen's Bench Small Claims Practices Act of Manitoba. Administration charges will continue to increase until the matter is concluded. Payment of the total amount demanded will be deemed full restitution and will halt the civil court action only. Any criminal court action which is, or has been undertaken, remains under the jurisdiction of the criminal prosecutor and is separate from this particular court action. Payment should be by cheque or money order made payable to CIVIL RECOVERY and sent via the enclosed postage paid envelope. Include your NAME and the CASE NUMBER, shown above.

"Any questions with regard to this matter are to be made in writing and addressed to this office. You may call (416) 234-0000 for payment enquiries only. Phone calls will be accepted between 9:00 a.m. and 4:00 p.m. Monday through Friday. (No collect calls.) NOTE; My telephone staff will not discuss the circumstances of the case.

(signed)

Harold J. Arkin 22325"

This claim is part of a loss recovery programme or policy which Zellers initiated several years ago and which commenced in their Manitoba Division in or about February 1995. Zellers wanted to recover what they called their "incremental" costs of shoplifting. These would be the costs of employing loss prevention officers and purchasing their equipment for the purpose of detecting losses (presumably mostly from theft) attributable to their customers and their employees. They concluded that the cost per incident would be approximately $310.00. They conceived the idea of claiming against the parents of children involved in thefts – obviously because it would be futile to pursue the children.

Zellers decided not to use, or hire, their own employees to process these claims but, instead, gave the job to an independent organization called Aclaim Civil Loss Recovery System. That organization reviewed the incident reports regarding the various claims and then engaged lawyers to prosecute them. If there was recovery, Aclaim would get a portion of the recovery and the balance would go to Zellers. Typically, a recovery of $325.00 would result in a fee of $125.00 to Aclaim and $200.00 to Zellers.

If necessary, the lawyers would write two demand letters and the amount claimed in the second letter would be increased somewhat over the amount claimed in the first.

In this case, because two boys were involved, the amount claimed was reduced to $225.00.

There is no general rule that parents are liable for the torts of their children by virtue of their status as parents per se. ... The parents would only be liable if they, themselves, were in some way negligent or had engaged in tortious conduct in relation to the activities of their children. There is no suggestion in this case that the plaintiff was negligent or had committed any tort in her personal capacity.

Nevertheless, counsel for Zellers submits that, whatever the validity of the underlying claim, the plaintiff voluntarily paid the compensation sought and, in effect, entered into a valid and enforceable contract with Zellers: there was consideration moving both ways; in exchange for Zellers' forbearance to bring suit against her, the plaintiff voluntarily paid to them the sum of $225.00.

Counsel for the plaintiff submits that, in the circumstances, the law will not countenance such a contract; that Zellers was never entitled to claim or get any money from the plaintiff; and that the sum in question should be returned to her on equitable principles.

It is well settled that a forbearance to sue is good consideration and that monies paid in exchange for a promise not to sue is a valid and enforceable legal contract. There are qualifications to this general rule and they are well summed up in *Chitty on Contracts*, 27th ed., vol. 1, General Principles, Articles 3-041 to 3-04-5 which are as follows:

> "3-041 *Claims known to be invalid.* A promise is not binding if the sole consideration for it is a forbearance to enforce (or a promise to forbear from enforcing) a claim which is invalid and which is either known by the party forbearing to be invalid or not believed by him to be valid.

> . . . . .

> "3-043 Two further conditions must be satisfied by a party who relies on his forbearance to enforce an invalid claim as the consideration for a promise made to him. He must not deliberately conceal from the other party (i.e. the promisor) facts which, if known to the latter, would enable him to defeat the claim. *And he must show that he seriously intended to pursue the claim.* (Emphasis mine.)

> . . . . .

In my opinion, the defendant's claim was not merely a doubtful claim – it was an invalid claim.

However, the matter is not quite so simple as that because the plaintiff has actually voluntarily paid the money over to Zellers. There was thus an executed compromise and so, ordinarily, the plaintiff would not be entitled to the return of the money. ... To establish a claim for the return of the money, the plaintiff would have to rely on other grounds.

The ground advanced by counsel for the plaintiff is under the rubric of unjust enrichment: that the money was paid over by reason of a mistake in fact or law or both.

The plaintiff testified that when she got Mr. Arkin's letter, of course she had to decide what to do about it. She thought about it and discussed the matter with her husband. It was decided that the best course would be to simply pay the claim rather than to incur the loss of time and money and the aggravation involved in defending it. Hence, the claim was paid and her son was disciplined by "grounding" him and deducting a portion of the settlement monies from his regular allowance.

The plaintiff honestly believed that the claim was a serious one and that if she did not pay it the defendant would sue her.

. . . . .

I accept this evidence. After all, the plaintiff had received a letter from a lawyer who should know something about the law and who was making an apparently serious threat of legal action if the claim was not paid. And she paid. She would not have done so if she had not believed that there was something to it.

In this belief, the plaintiff was mistaken. Whatever legal opinion or opinions Zellers might have had regarding their claims generally, I cannot believe that they seriously thought that this claim could succeed or that they seriously intended to pursue it to court if it was not paid. Mr. Arkin was not called as a witness at the trial and so we do not have the benefit of what his opinion of the claim was. But I assume that as a competent and responsible lawyer, he knew or ought to have known that the claim had no prospect whatsoever of succeeding in court and that it would be futile to pursue it.

The plaintiff subsequently took legal advice, learned of her mistake and now wants her money back.

. . . . .

The plaintiff was certainly mislead by the tone and content of the lawyer's letter. In my opinion, in the particular circumstances of this case, the plaintiff is entitled to a refund on the ground of monies paid under a mistake.

The appeal is allowed and the plaintiff's claim is allowed with interest and costs. Although the claim is a small one, and was dealt with in the small claims procedure, it appeared to have been treated as a sort of "test" case which will have a bearing on Zellers entire recovery programme. Senior counsel were engaged and I received well-researched arguments on both sides. In the circumstances, I will allow the plaintiff her costs to be assessed as if this were a Class 2 action.

NOTES AND QUESTIONS

1. Do you think the defendant's lawyer should have been disciplined by the Law Society of Manitoba? Does it matter that no pleadings were filed? Does it matter that he was (presumably) instructed to write the demand letter by his client?

2. Should the costs of this action awarded to the mother have been awarded against Zellers or against its lawyer?

3. When evaluating the conduct of the defendant's lawyer, the judge in this case mentioned the notion of a "competent and responsible lawyer". For judicial commentary on what amounts to a lawyer's "duty of competence", see, *e.g.*, *R. v. McKenzie*, [2007] O.J. No. 3222 (Ont. C.A.).

4. How weak a case should a client have before counsel are criticized or sanctioned for pursuing it? What if the case were novel — for example, the pursuit of an action in tort where, previously, liability would have only arisen in contract law

(that is, the classic case of *Donoghue v. Stevenson*, [1932] A.C. 562 (H.L.))? Traditionally, codes of conduct give some latitude to the right of lawyers to pursue novel or test cases. (See, *e.g.*, *Model Code*, Rule 2.02(7) and Commentary.) Consider the ethics of the following scenario:

Scenario One

In the residential schools litigation, damages were sought for harm done to the culture and community of former students who had been compelled to attend the schools. This was a novel cause of action. Based on principles governing pleadings set out here, how would you advise a client who approached you with this or a similarly novel claim? For similar novelty pleading issues being raised in a different legal context, see *Jane Doe v. Board of Commissioners of Police for the Municipality of Metropolitan Toronto*, [1990] O.J. No. 1584, 74 O.R. (2d) 225 (Ont. Div. Ct.). For a further discussion of *Jane Doe*, see Trevor C.W. Farrow, "Five Pleadings Cases Everyone Should Read" (2009) 35(4) Advocates' Q. 466 at 478-80.

5. Could counsel for Zellers have relied on the "novel" case argument, raised above, as a defence to the ethics of his conduct in writing the demand letter? These letters, which typically include a basic understanding of an issue or dispute and a request or demand for some kind of action or resolution essentially involve lawyers advocating on behalf of their clients. When thinking about this question, consider also the decision in *Law Society of British Columbia v. Laarakker*, [2011] L.S.D.D. No. 175, 2011 LSBC 29 (L.S.B.C.), which is included in section E, "Advocacy and Civility", near the end of this chapter. In that case, the Law Society of British Columbia was faced with a complaint about the conduct of a lawyer who acted for a client who received a demand letter very similar to the demand letter that was at issue in *D.C.B. v. Zellers Inc.*

6. In the context of drafting a pleading, at what point does an advocate's effort to "raise fearlessly every issue [and] advance every argument" (*Model Code*, Rule 4.01(1) (Commentary)) through vigorous advocacy on behalf of a client turn into an exercise of using the litigation process for purposes that are "scandalous", "frivolous" or "vexatious" (see, *e.g.*, British Columbia's Supreme Court Rules, B.C. Reg. 168/2009, Rule 9-5(1)) or that are "dishonourable" (*Model Code*, Rule 4.01(2)(b))? Consider the following scenario:

Scenario Two

You are a family law lawyer in a jurisdiction that provides for numerous causes of action in a complicated and protracted marriage breakdown involving children and a significant amount of property. You act for the husband in the relationship. You are of the view that, although technically available, only one or two of those causes of action are likely to succeed. The other causes of action are not reasonably viable under the circumstances of this case. Your client, however, says that he "hates" the other side and wants to include in his pleading "everything available under the law" to "make her life miserable". What do you do? Do the rules of professional conduct assist you with that determination? For some guidance on this issue, see, *e.g.*, *Model Code*, Rule 4.01(2)(a).

2. Discovery

Perhaps one of the thorniest areas for advocacy dilemmas, arising typically after the pleadings stage, is the discovery process. This is one of the few areas of the litigation process where parties are asked essentially to open up their offices, homes, personal files, trade secrets, *etc.*, to the scrutiny of the other side. It is a moment of apparent cooperation in an otherwise largely combative system. Clients typically do not understand the discovery process and almost invariably do not like it.

Again, as a matter of civil procedure, discovery is an area of the litigation process that is the subject of significant regulation. Provincial rules of court typically provide relatively detailed guidelines for the kinds of information that may be subject to discovery and the methods by which that information may or must be provided to the other side. Further, the same rules also typically provide litigants and the court with various remedial options for dealing with non- or improper conduct at all stages of the discovery process.[6]

However, notwithstanding these rules of civil procedure, the actual day-to-day process of discovery is largely conducted either (at the document production stage) in the privacy of the office or boardroom of a lawyer or client without the other side being present, or (when examinations for discovery are taking place) in a boardroom or court reporter's office without a judge being present. It is, therefore, largely in the hands of the parties and their lawyers, leaving significant need for rigorous ethical behaviour and significant room for unethical conduct.

The following case takes up some of these professional, procedural and ethical challenges in the context of the documentary discovery process. Although focusing primarily on the rules of court, the Court's strong language in this case applies equally to — and in fact directly engages — the professional and ethical obligations of an advocate to actively participate in the proper conduct of the discovery process (obligations that Lord Denning identified in *Rondel v. Worsley* as being part of the "difficult" balancing act of the advocacy role).[7]

GROSSMAN v. TORONTO GENERAL HOSPITAL

[1983] O.J. No. 3001, 41 O.R. (2d) 457
(Ont. H.C.J., Reid J.)

REID J.:— The action arises out of the death of Howard Grossman who is claimed to have been lost while a patient in the Toronto General Hospital ("the Hospital"). It is alleged that his body was discovered after 12 days in an air-duct shaft in the hospital.

The defence entered by the Hospital for itself and its staff amounts to a general traverse. Not even the death was directly admitted.

---

6   See, *e.g.*, Ontario's Rules of Civil Procedure, R.R.O. 1990, Reg. 194, Rules 30.08, 31.07, 34.14-15, 35.05.

7   *Rondel v. Worsley*, [1967] 1 Q.B. 443 (following note 27 and surrounding text), affd [1969] 1 A.C. 191.

That document gave a hint of what was in store for plaintiffs. The Hospital's affidavit on production (the affidavit) revealed only one thing the Hospital had no objection to producing: the deceased's hospital record. That was the only entry made in the first part of the first schedule of the form ... required by the Rules of Practice.

. . . . .

I now turn to consider the attack made on the order requiring a better affidavit on production.

Defendants' position is essentially this: plaintiffs have failed to establish that any documents exist that should be produced other than the deceased's medical record and those now described in paras. 1(a) and (b) of the master's order. When I expressed surprise that a 12-day search for a missing patient in a hospital would not have produced one scrap of paper relevant to the issues in this lawsuit Mrs. Farrer replied that any such piece of paper would be privileged, the Hospital having retained solicitors at a very early point.

That may be so. It may be a proper basis for a claim of privilege for any and all documents other than the one thing produced voluntarily and the others forced out of defendants' hands by reason of the motion before the master ... However, no one could have told from reading defendants' original affidavit whether or not that claim was justified. The answer made in the second part of the first schedule is a mere boiler-plate calculated to conceal all and any documents from inspection. The result was to deprive opposing counsel of any basis for challenging the privilege claimed. Equally, if a challenge had been made, no court could have decided it, without resorting to ordering production to the court of all the documents referred to in the second part of the first schedule. Since no one could have known from reading the schedule what documents are referred to, that would have been an order made in the dark.

The Rules of Practice are designed to facilitate production, not frustrate it.

. . . . .

Honest differences of opinion might arise over the question whether a given document should or must be produced. If that occurs, the court has power to decide the issue ... .

Notwithstanding [the rules of court] ... it becomes quickly clear to anyone setting out to practise in the courts that "production" is open to serious abuse. The integrity of the system depends upon the willingness of lawyers to require full and fair discovery of their clients. The system is, in a sense, in the hands of the lawyers. The opportunity for stonewalling and improper concealment is there. Some solicitors grasp it. They will make only such production as can be forced from them. That is bad practice. It can work real injustice. It causes delay and expense while the other side struggles to see that which they had a right to see from the first. In such a contest the advantage is to the long purse. The worst consequence is that the strategy is sometimes successful, giving its perpetrators a disreputable advantage. The practice must be condemned. If it were widespread it would undermine the trial system.

Master Sandler has written of the susceptibility of the system to abuse. ...

> I also observe that under our present system of documentary discovery, the choice as to what documents that are in a party's possession are relevant is, in the first instance, left up to the party itself, and my experience and observations have taught me that nowhere is the abuse of our rules of procedure greater than in this area of documentary production and in the failure of each party to fairly and reasonably disclose and produce to the opposite party all relevant documents, and to disclose the existence of all relevant but privileged documents. ...

The duty upon a solicitor is now, and always has been, to make full, fair and prompt discovery. Williston and Rolls, in *The Law Of Civil Procedure* (1970), vol. 2, put it this way, at pp. 892-4:

> A party giving discovery is under a duty to make a careful search for all relevant documents in his possession and to make diligent inquiries about other material documents which may be in the possession of others for him. A solicitor has a duty of careful investigation and supervision and of advising his client as to what documents should be included in the affidavit, because a client cannot be expected to know the whole scope of his obligation without legal assistance. In *Myers v. Elman* [[1940] A.C. 282] a solicitor was ordered to pay the costs of the proceedings because his managing clerk was guilty of misconduct in the preparation and filing of an incorrect and inadequate affidavit. Lord Atkin said:

> "What is the duty of the solicitor? He is at an early stage of the proceedings engaged in putting before the Court on the oath of his client information which may afford evidence at the trial. Obviously he must explain to his client what is the meaning of relevance: and equally obviously he must not necessarily be satisfied by the statement of his client that he has no documents or no more than he chooses to disclose. If he has reasonable ground for supposing that there are others he must investigate the matter; but he need not go beyond taking reasonable steps to ascertain the truth. He is not the ultimate judge, and if he reasonably decides to believe his client, criticism cannot be directed to him. But I may add that the duty is specially incumbent on the solicitor where there is a charge of fraud; for a wilful omission to perform his duty in such a case may well amount to conduct which is aiding and abetting a criminal in concealing his crime, and in preventing restitution."

Lord Wright put the matter even more bluntly:

> "The order of discovery requires the client to give information in writing and on oath of all documents which are or have been in his corporeal possession or power, whether he is bound to produce them or not. A client cannot be expected to realize the whole scope of that obligation without the aid and advice of his solicitor, who therefore has a peculiar duty in these matters as an officer of the Court carefully to investigate the position and as far as possible see that the order is complied with. A client left to himself could not know what is relevant, nor is he likely to realize that it is his obligation to

disclose every relevant document, even a document which would establish, or go far to establish, against him his opponent's case. The solicitor cannot simply allow the client to make whatever affidavit of documents he thinks fit nor can he escape the responsibility of careful investigation or supervision. If the client will not give him the information he is entitled to require or if he insists on swearing an affidavit which the solicitor knows to be imperfect or which he has every reason to think is imperfect, then the solicitor's proper course is to withdraw from the case. He does not discharge his duty in such a case by requesting the client to make a proper affidavit and then filing whatever affidavit the client thinks fit to swear to."

In the same case, there was a discussion of the duty to make further disclosure when subsequent to filing the affidavit other relevant documents were found. Viscount Maugham said:

"A solicitor who has innocently put on the file an affidavit by his client which he has subsequently discovered to be certainly false owes it to the Court to put the matter right at the earliest date if he continues to act as solicitor upon the record. The duty of the client is equally plain. I wish to say with emphasis that I reject the notion that it is justifiable in such a case to keep silence and to wait and wait till the plaintiff succeeds, if he can, in obtaining an order for a further and better affidavit. To do so is, in the language of Singleton J., to obstruct the interests of justice, to occasion unnecessary costs, and – even if disclosure is ultimately obtained – to delay the hearing of the action in a case where an early hearing may be of great importance."

Those pronouncements are clear and unequivocal. Anyone familiar with them, or with many others to the same effect, would not require a master's motion to know that the exhibits filed at the coroner's inquest would have to be produced in this case.

It has equally always been the case that sufficient information must be given of documents for which privilege is claimed to enable a party opposed in interest to be able to identify them. It is not, however, necessary to go so far as to give an indirect discovery....

. . . . .

The order made by Master Sandler is exactly in accord with the prevailing law as I understand it. I see no risk of an "indirect discovery" if defendants comply with reasonable common sense. It should be possible to describe a document sufficiently without revealing its contents.

The whole course of defendants' conduct has been to refuse to disclose anything on the ground that unless plaintiffs can prove something exists they have no right to know of its existence. The unfairness of that attitude is described by Master Sandler in *Bow Helicopters* ...:

I observe that in modern litigation, one of the most important tools in the pre-trial process is documentary discovery...and in no case is the proper use of this tool by the plaintiff more important than in a products liability case where the plaintiff must establish negligence in design or manufacture, or both, on the part of the defendant. In such a case, the defendant knows everything and usually has a large volume of documentary records, whereas the plaintiff has little or no information, except the product itself, and often, even that has been destroyed in the mishap. In this type of case, the plaintiff must try to penetrate the defendant's operation to see if it can discover records to indicate negligence in design or manufacture, and one tool to gain entry is the affidavit on production. The plaintiff's difficulty is substantially increased where the product is technologically complex, such as a helicopter.

This action is in a real sense the same as the action in *Bow Helicopters* so far as discovery is concerned, for most, if not all, of the relevant information is within the scope of defendants' knowledge, not plaintiffs'. That is what makes fair compliance with discovery obligations so acutely necessary.

Modern courts strongly favour disclosure.

. . . . .

The rule is, therefore, that a party must candidly describe in an affidavit on production not only documents for which no privilege is claimed but also those for which a privilege is claimed. It is not enough to do the one but not the other.

Litigation is, after all, a search for truth. Its processes are, we all know, imperfect. To permit advantage to be taken of its weaknesses to the point of injustice and unfairness would be wrong. Defendants' strategy in this case must not be tolerated. The appeal must be dismissed.

Plaintiffs ask for costs on a solicitor and his own client scale. That is a punitive award. Yet it was the disposition made by Master Sandler in both orders under appeal. It reveals his view of defendants' course of action.

That course of action may reflect merely excessive concern for the protection of his clients' rights or it may reveal simple stonewalling. My concern that it may be the latter is deepened by the decision of my brother Carruthers in *Fiege v. Cornwall General Hospital et al.* ... I am informed by counsel that the solicitor responsible for the defence in that case up to the point of trial is the solicitor responsible for the conduct of the defence herein. (That is not, I must add, Mrs. Farrer, whose lot it was to seek to justify someone else's conduct, and who did so with much skill and fortitude.) The failure in *Fiege* to produce an important document was strongly condemned by Carruthers J. He awarded costs on a solicitor and his own client scale against the defendant in that case because of the waste of time and money that resulted. The same may be said of this case. Time has been wasted and money thrown away. There is no merit in defendants' position.

. . . . .

Defendants' conduct in this case amounts to a deliberate refusal to comply with the notice to produce and is subject to ... sanction. But in the absence of any indication that defendants' conduct was other than as advised by their solicitor, the responsibility for it must fall on the solicitor.

The consequences for a solicitor can be severe. In *Myers v. Elman*, [1940] A.C. 282 ... (H.L.), the solicitor was ordered to pay the costs. If the course of action followed in this case were shown to be widespread an order to that effect would be appropriate as a general deterrent.

It could be argued that because this case is a repetition of conduct that has already been deplored that order should be made here. Although I have some doubt, I am satisfied to treat this case as an example of excessive zeal and to adopt Master Sandler's order. His order shall stand. The costs of the appeal shall be to plaintiffs in any event of the cause as between a solicitor and his own client. However, because this is a repetition of the same error found in *Fiege, supra*, the costs may be taxed forthwith and shall be payable forthwith thereafter.

The further affidavit, or affidavits, shall be delivered forthwith subject to any extension allowed by Master Sandler.

Appeal dismissed.

NOTES AND QUESTIONS

1. In *Grossman*, Reid J., after discussing the apparent discovery abuse that occurred on the part of the defendants (as apparently "advised by their solicitor", which was also apparently not the first time this kind of conduct involving the defendants' solicitor had occurred), was satisfied (although with "some doubt") that the discovery conduct by the defendants' counsel was "an example of excessive zeal". Justice Reid, therefore, although making a punitive solicitor-client costs award, did not order the solicitor to pay those costs personally. Do you think Reid J. was right? If subsequent proceedings before a law society discipline panel were brought against the defendants' lawyer, do you think the lawyer's conduct that was found to amount to "excessive zeal" would have offended against code of conduct provisions that regulate lawyers' actions when acting as advocates? One of the primary areas for potential difficulty in the documentary production stage is confidentiality. Consider the following scenario:

    Scenario Three

    Suppose you act for a plaintiff in a products liability case against an automobile manufacturer involving a defective seatbelt. You have been seeking information on discovery concerning unrelated litigation in which the other side is involved regarding similar problematic issues with their seatbelt manufacturing processes (that you think are relevant to the issues in your litigation). Counsel for the other side indicates that such information is irrelevant, and that in any event, if it exists, it would also be privileged. You disagree but are unable to obtain the information. Four weeks before trial, counsel for the other side's assistant sends to you — by accident — the information that you have been seeking (it was sent to you instead of their client's auditors, for whom it was intended). You still think the material is relevant. You also question the claim that it is privileged. What should you do? On what professional basis will you make your decision? In answering this question you can take into account the fact that under the *Model Code* lawyers are obliged to advise the disclosing party that they have obtained inadvertently disclosed privileged documents and, depending on the circumstances, may then need either to destroy or return them (*Model Code*, Rules 6.02(2) and (10) and Commentary). For some commentary and potential guidance on the topic, see, *e.g.*, *Firemaster Oilfield Services Ltd. v. Safety Boss (Canada) (1993) Ltd.*, [2000] A.J. No. 1466, 285 A.R. 141 at paras. 23 and 29 (Alta. Q.B.), *per* Marceau J., affd [2001] A.J. No. 1317, 293 A.R. 366 (Alta. C.A.).

3. Negotiation

Key to Reid J.'s reasoning in *Grossman* is the fact that the discovery process — because it occurs in private and out of court (and is therefore "open to serious abuse") — is "in the hands of the lawyers". Another advocacy process, again typically occurring prior to trial, which is similarly private and often in the hands of lawyers is settlement negotiation. As Armstrong J.A. has stated, "[s]ettlement discussion is something which pervades, and should pervade, almost every lawsuit".[8] And given the mounting costs and delays that are typical in the public court system, settlement negotiation is being actively encouraged not only by the courts,[9] but also by rules of civil procedure[10] and by litigants themselves.

Settlement negotiations are also increasingly being encouraged by litigation lawyers and the professional code provisions that govern them. For example, according to *Model Code*, Rule 2.02(4), in the specific context of "encouraging compromise or settlement":

> Rule 2.02(4)
>
> A lawyer must advise and encourage a client to compromise or settle a dispute whenever it is possible to do so on a reasonable basis and must discourage the client from commencing or continuing useless legal proceedings.
>
> **Commentary**
>
> A lawyer should consider the use of alternative dispute resolution (ADR) when appropriate, inform the client of ADR options and, if so instructed, take steps to pursue those options.

Most codes of professional conduct, including the *Model Code*, are still relatively silent on the professional obligations of lawyers during the conduct of a negotiation. However, the Law Society of Alberta has included some further provisions in its *Code of Conduct* that govern an advocate's conduct during the negotiation process. For example, according to Rule 6.02(2), a lawyer "must not lie to or mislead another lawyer". According to the Commentary to that Rule:

> This rule expresses an obvious aspect of integrity and a fundamental principle. In no situation, including negotiation, is a lawyer entitled to deliberately mislead a colleague. When a lawyer (in response to a question, for example) is prevented by rules of confidentiality from actively disclosing the truth, a false-

---

[8] *Ristimaki v. Cooper*, [2006] O.J. No. 1559, 79 O.R. (3d) 648 at para. 76 (Ont. C.A.).

[9] See, *e.g.*, *ibid.*

[10] See, *e.g.*, Ontario's Rules of Civil Procedure, R.R.O. 1990, Reg. 194, Rule 49.

hood is not justified. The lawyer has other alternatives, such as declining to answer. If this approach would in itself be misleading, the lawyer must seek the client's consent to such disclosure of confidential information as is necessary to prevent the other lawyer from being misled. The concept of "misleading" includes creating a misconception through oral or written statements, other communications, actions or conduct, failure to act, or silence ... .

Further, according to Rule 6.02(5) ("correcting misinformation") of Alberta's *Code of Conduct*:

If a lawyer becomes aware during the course of a representation that:

(a) the lawyer has inadvertently misled an opposing party, or

(b) the client, or someone allied with the client or the client's matter, has misled an opposing party, intentionally or otherwise, or

(c) the lawyer or the client, or someone allied with the client or the client's matter, has made a material representation to an opposing party that was accurate when made but has since become inaccurate,

then, subject to confidentiality, the lawyer must immediately correct the resulting misapprehension on the part of the opposing party.

NOTES AND QUESTIONS

1. Because settlement negotiation is discussed elsewhere in this book (see Chapter 7), it will not be significantly further developed in this section. However, because a lawyer's vigorous settlement negotiation on behalf of a client is part of an advocate's role in the adversary system, ethical considerations are as important in the settlement process as they are in any other element of the litigation system. Consider the following scenario in light of the *Model Code* and Alberta's *Code of Conduct* provisions regarding negotiation and, as well, in light of the general ethical duties of an advocate that include both zealous advocacy and fidelity to the justice system.

Scenario Four

Suppose, in the family law scenario involving the aggressive husband discussed previously, your client authorizes you to settle the matrimonial property portion of the case on the basis that he would pay the other side a lump sum of no more than $850,000. With that information in hand, are you ethically permitted to make the following statement at the settlement negotiation meeting with counsel for the other side: "Although my client would like to settle this matter, my sense is that he is not willing to pay a penny more than $600,000"?

D. ETHICS AT TRIAL

Once the pre-trial procedures are complete and the trial process has started, a new opportunity begins for ethical issues to arise (often without much time to think about or prepare for them). Again, however, most of the ethical issues that arise in the context of trials — like those that arise during the pre-trial stage of the litigation — engage the "difficult" balance that Lord Denning identified in *Rondel v. Worsley* between an advocate's "duty to his client and his duty to the court" (or more broadly to the overall administration of justice). At all times, lawyers must balance their obligations to represent their client "fearlessly" and to "advance every argument ... that ... will help the client's case" (*Model Code*, Rule 4.01(1) (Commentary)) with their similarly strong obligation not to "knowingly assist or permit a client to do anything that the lawyer considers to be dishonest or dishonourable" (*Model Code*, Rule 4.01(2)(b)). This balance is further articulated in *Model Code*, Rule 4.01(1):

> When acting as an advocate, a lawyer must represent the client resolutely and honourably within the limits of the law, while treating the tribunal with candour, fairness, courtesy, and respect.

An advocate must, therefore, establish all trial conduct on the ethical side of that difficult balance. How far from that line an advocate is personally established (*i.e.*, whether by questioning the vision of the zealous advocate the advocate is more interested in protecting the public interest than the interests of the client) is a choice that needs to be made by all lawyers (see further Chapter 1). Typically — as will be seen in the *Lyttle* case further below — the basis of these determinations is simply the conscience and good faith beliefs of the lawyer personally. But regardless of whether that line is sometimes difficult to see, it must not be crossed.

There are many aspects to the trial process that engage this balance, including representing facts and evidence to a jury in an opening statement, preparing your own witness for testimony and then taking the witness through their direct evidence, objecting to an opponent's line of questioning during the cross-examination of your client, calling reply evidence, cross-examining your opponent's witnesses, or summarizing the law in a closing argument before a judge or jury. All of these examples (several of which are discussed below) are opportunities when advocates must resist the urge to cross the line from vigorous adversarial representation to unethical conduct. They are also all addressed by various rules of professional conduct (see, *e.g.*, *Model Code*, Rules 4.01-4.04).

1. Witness Preparation

Witness preparation is a particularly important but ethically thorny aspect of the trial process. It is well accepted that, as part of trial preparation, lawyers generally are expected to prepare their witnesses. Witness preparation often starts with a blanket instruction "always to tell the truth". Lawyers will then often discuss a number of further issues, including: a review of the various parties' theories of the case; some of the basic issues and materials in the case; a review of the issues that the witness may be asked to speak about; specific areas of questioning; areas of particular interest to the other side; what the examination process will look like; what the judge might say; *etc.* Further, lawyers may also conduct some mock examinations and cross-examinations (to give the witness a feel for the process). All of that, when conducted properly and in good faith, is ethically acceptable and part of the trial preparation process.

It is also well-accepted that there is an important difference between witness preparation and witness "coaching". The distinction between the two is not always clear. However, unlike witness preparation, witness coaching (or "wood-shedding") is unethical and unprofessional. It is also illegal. Witness coaching takes preparation beyond the purpose of getting the witness comfortable with the process and with his or her own knowledge of the facts of the case, and into the terrain of evidence and witness tampering and obstruction of justice. Lawyers have a clear obligation not to assist his or her own client (or any witness) in the giving of false or misleading evidence. The rules of conduct forbid this kind of unethical behaviour. For example, according to *Model Code*, Rules 4.01(2)(b) and (k), a lawyer shall not "knowingly assist or permit a client to do anything that the lawyer considers to be dishonest or dishonourable" [or] "knowingly permit a witness or party to be presented in a false or misleading way ...". Further, according to *Model Code*, Rule 4.03, a lawyer must "take care not to subvert or suppress any evidence ...". Similar rules and principles apply for witness preparation in the context of examinations for discovery and other examinations out of court.

In *R. v. Sweezey*,[11] the Newfoundland Court of Appeal considered an appeal by a lawyer of 14 years' standing from his sentence on a conviction for attempted obstruction of justice. The lawyer had counselled a witness to be forgetful and evasive when testifying. In its majority judgment (upholding the conviction but reducing the lawyer's sentence from 18 months to 12 months), the court — in the context of protecting the integrity of the evidentiary system and the administration of justice — cited the following excerpt from the trial judgment:

> The Canadian justice system relies on the honesty and integrity of counsel who practise within it. To that end, every lawyer is made an officer of the Courts in which he will practise. Cases before such Courts are in pursuit of justice through truthful evidence. A lawyer who attempts to obstruct justice by wilfully counselling evasive evidence not only commits an offence contrary to ... the Criminal Code but also breaches his solemn duty as an officer of the Court.

This passage from *Sweezey* highlights some of the various potential avenues for sanction for misconduct on the part of an advocate, which can include: costs against a client; costs against a lawyer personally; a negative order under a given rule of civil procedure; a law society disciplinary order; and criminal sanctions. Further, and perhaps equally important, is the resulting negative reputation that will obtain in the eyes of an advocate's partners, fellow members of the bar, judges and current and future clients. Put simply, such conduct is just not worth it, for any case or any client.

Which of the following questions or statements likely amount to proper witness preparation and which amount to witness coaching? Why? Can you think of other examples?

---

[11]   [1987] N.J. No. 295, 66 Nfld. & P.E.I.R. 29 (Nfld. C.A.).

(a) "When you say you saw someone that night, wouldn't it be better to say that in fact you are pretty sure the person you saw was the defendant?"

(b) "If you are asked that question on cross-examination, I think it would be better if you were to leave out the part about having been at a bar and drinking that night. I'm worried that, by saying you were drinking, you will be less credible to the judge or jury. Instead, just say you were out with friends — it's still true isn't it?"

(c) "When you testify tomorrow, in addition to always telling the truth, make sure that you typically only answer the question you are asked."

(d) "When answering questions, don't just look at me. You should also from time to time look at the judge, and most importantly, don't forget the jury. They are the people who ultimately need to believe you."

(e) "I think you should wear a suit when you come to court — you will look more professional and maybe more credible."

(f) "I will be asking questions, the other side's lawyer will be asking questions, and from time to time the judge might ask you questions."

(g) "I think you should go down to the courthouse before your trial next week — just to get a sense of the process."

(h) "Remember that your theory of the case, as we set out in your pleading, is that the other side never agreed to the terms of the contract. So when you are asked about that on cross-examination, what are you going to say?"

(i) "Let's go through some practice questions. I have brought in one of my law partners to play the role of opposing counsel, OK?"

(j) "When the other side's lawyer asks you about the night in question, don't forget to say that it was raining."

For further discussions on the practice and ethics of witness preparation, see Bryan Finlay, Q.C. and Thomas A. Cromwell, *Witness Preparation Manual*, 2d ed. (Aurora, ON: Canada Law Book, 1999); Daniel I. Small, *Preparing Witnesses: A Practical Guide for Lawyers and Their Clients*, 3d ed. (Chicago: ABA Publishing, 2009).

2.   Cross-Examination

In the following two cases, the issue of ethics in the context of cross-examination is discussed. In the first case, *R. v. Lyttle*, the Supreme Court of Canada articulates the scope of an advocate's ethical conduct in the context of cross-examination of an opposing witness. Although the case deals with a criminal matter, the Court's statements regarding the appropriate scope of cross-examination at trial are relevant in the civil context as well. In the second case, *R. v. R. (A.J.)*, the Court of Appeal for Ontario examines the issue of Crown counsel's ethics in the context of cross-examining an accused. The comments of the court in *R. v. R. (A.J.)* on the need for counsel to be respectful of a witness during cross-examination are, again, also relevant to the civil context (see Chapter 8 for a general discussion of ethics in the criminal law context).

R. v. LYTTLE

[2004] S.C.J. No. 8, [2004] 1 S.C.R. 193
(S.C.C., McLachlin C.J.C., Major, Binnie, Arbour, LeBel,
Deschamps and Fish JJ.)

[Stephen Barnaby was beaten by five men with baseball bats, four of whom were masked. The fifth — the accused — was said to be unmasked. According to Barnaby, he was attacked over a gold chain. According to the police (in separate reports from two officers), the attack was related to a drug debt. Barnaby identified the accused in a photographic line-up. The theory of the defence's case was that Barnaby identified the accused as the man who attacked him in order to shield Barnaby's associates in a drug ring — the real assailants — from prosecution. The Crown did not plan to call the police who made the reports as witnesses. At trial, the judge ruled that counsel for the defence could only cross-examine the Crown's witnesses if she furnished "substantive evidence" of her "drug-debt" theory of the case. The defence called the officers as witnesses and, as a consequence, the accused lost his statutory right to address the jury last. No other evidence was called by the defence. The accused was convicted of robbery, assault, kidnapping and possession of a weapon. On appeal to the Ontario Court of Appeal, the Court found that the trial judge erred in allowing counsel for the accused to cross-examine only on matters for which she had a "substantive" evidentiary basis. However, the Court upheld the convictions and dismissed the appeal by resorting to the harmless error provision of s. 686(1)(b)(iii) of the *Criminal Code*. The accused appealed to the Supreme Court of Canada.]

The judgment of the Court was delivered by **MAJOR** and **FISH JJ.**:—

Cross-examination may often be futile and sometimes prove fatal, but it remains nonetheless a faithful friend in the pursuit of justice and an indispensable ally in the search for truth. At times, there will be <u>no other way</u> to expose falsehood, to rectify error, to correct distortion or to elicit vital information that would otherwise remain forever concealed.

. . . . .

In *R. v. Osolin*, [1993] 4 S.C.R. 595, Cory J. reviewed the relevant authorities and ... explained why cross-examination plays such an important role in the adversarial process, particularly, though of course not exclusively, in the context of a criminal trial:

There can be no question of the importance of cross-examination. It is of essential importance in determining whether a witness is credible. Even with the most honest witness cross-examination can provide the means to explore the frailties of the testimony. For example, it can demonstrate a witness's weakness of sight or hearing. It can establish that the existing weather conditions may have limited the ability of a witness to observe, or that medication taken by the witness would have distorted vision or hearing. Its importance cannot be denied. It is the ultimate means of demonstrating truth and of testing veracity. Cross-examination must be permitted so that an accused can make full answer and defence. The opportunity to cross-examine witnesses is fundamental to providing a fair trial to an accused. This is an old and well established principle that is closely linked to the presumption of innocence. ...

Commensurate with its importance, the right to cross-examine is now recognized as being protected by ss. 7 and 11(d) of the *Canadian Charter of Rights and Freedoms*. ...

The right of cross-examination must therefore be jealously protected and broadly construed. But it must not be abused. Counsel are bound by the rules of relevancy and barred from resorting to harassment, misrepresentation, repetitiousness or, more generally, from putting questions whose prejudicial effect outweighs their probative value. ...

Just as the right of cross-examination itself is not absolute, so too are its limitations. Trial judges enjoy, in this as in other aspects of the conduct of a trial, a broad discretion to ensure fairness and to see that justice is done – and seen to be done. In the exercise of that discretion, they may sometimes think it right to relax the rules of relevancy somewhat, or to tolerate a degree of repetition that would in other circumstances be unacceptable. ...

This appeal concerns the constraint on cross-examination arising from the ethical and legal duties of counsel when they allude in their questions to disputed and unproven facts. Is a good faith basis sufficient or is counsel bound, as the trial judge held in this case, to provide an evidentiary foundation for the assertion?

Unlike the trial judge, and with respect, we believe that a question can be put to a witness in cross-examination regarding matters that need not be proved independently, provided that counsel has a good faith basis for putting the question. It is not uncommon for counsel to believe what is in fact true, without being able to prove it <u>otherwise than by cross-examination</u>; nor is it uncommon for reticent witnesses to concede suggested facts — in the mistaken belief that they are already known to the cross-examiner and will therefore, in any event, emerge. [emphasis in original]

In this context, a "good faith basis" is a function of the information available to the cross-examiner, his or her belief in its likely accuracy, and the purpose for which it is used. Information falling short of admissible evidence may be put to the witness. In fact, the information may be incomplete or uncertain, provided the cross-examiner does not put suggestions to the witness recklessly or that he or she knows to be false. The cross-examiner may pursue any hypothesis that is honestly advanced on the strength of reasonable inference, experience or intuition. The purpose of the question must be consistent with the lawyer's role as an officer of the court: to suggest what counsel genuinely thinks possible on known facts or reasonable assumptions is in our view permissible; to assert or to imply in a manner that is calculated to mislead is in our view improper and prohibited.

. . . . .

[In] *R. v. Shearing*, [2002] 3 S.C.R. 33 ... while recognizing the need for exceptional restraint in sexual assault cases, Binnie J. reaffirmed ... the general rule that "in most instances the adversarial process allows wide latitude to cross-examiners to resort to unproven assumptions and innuendo in an effort to crack the untruthful witness." As suggested at the outset, however, wide latitude does not mean unbridled licence, and cross-examination remains subject to the requirements of good faith, professional integrity and the other limitations set out above. ...

A trial judge must balance the rights of an accused to receive a fair trial with the need to prevent unethical cross-examination. There will thus be instances where a trial judge will want to ensure that "counsel [is] not merely taking a random shot at a reputation imprudently exposed or asking a groundless question to waft an unwarranted innuendo into the jury box". See *Michelson v. United States*, 335 U.S. 469 (1948), at p. 481, *per* Jackson J.

Where a question implies the existence of a disputed factual predicate that is manifestly tenuous or suspect, a trial judge may properly take appropriate steps, by conducting a *voir dire* or otherwise, to seek and obtain counsel's assurance that a good faith basis exists for putting the question. If the judge is satisfied in this regard and the question is not otherwise prohibited, counsel should be permitted to put the question to the witness.

. . . . .

The trial judge also made reference to the case of *Browne v. Dunn* ..., as support for the proposition that an evidentiary foundation is required for questions put in cross-examination. He was mistaken. The rule in *Browne v. Dunn* requires counsel to give notice to those witnesses whom the cross-examiner intends later to impeach. The rationale for the rule was explained by Lord Herschell ... :

> Now, my Lords, I cannot help saying that it seems to me to be absolutely essential to the proper conduct of a cause, where it is intended to suggest that a witness is not speaking the truth on a particular point, to direct his attention to the fact by some questions put in cross-examination showing that that imputation is intended to be made, and not to take his evidence and pass it by as a matter altogether unchallenged, and then, when it is impossible for him to explain, as perhaps he might have been able to do if such questions had been put to him, the circumstances which it is suggested indicate that the story he tells ought not to be believed, to argue that he is a witness unworthy of credit. My Lords, I have always understood that if you intend to impeach

a witness you are bound, whilst he is in the box, to give him an opportunity of making any explanation which is open to him; and, as it seems to me, that is not only a rule of professional practice in the conduct of a case, but is essential to fair play and fair dealing with witnesses. Sometimes reflections have been made upon excessive cross-examination of witnesses, and it has been complained of as undue; but it seems to me that a cross-examination of a witness which errs in the direction of excess may be far more fair to him than to leave him without cross-examination, and afterwards to suggest that he is not a witness of truth, I mean upon a point on which it is not otherwise perfectly clear that he has had full notice beforehand that there is an intention to impeach the credibility of the story which he is telling.

The rule, although designed to provide fairness to witnesses and the parties, is not fixed. The extent of its application is within the discretion of the trial judge after taking into account all the circumstances of the case. ... In any event, the foregoing rule in *Browne v. Dunn* remains a sound principle of general application, though irrelevant to the issue before the trial judge in this case.

As long as counsel has a good faith basis for asking an otherwise permissible question in cross-examination, the question should be allowed. In our view, no distinction need be made between expert and lay witnesses within the broad scope of this general principle. Counsel, however, bear important professional duties and ethical responsibilities, not just at trial, but on appeal as well. This point was emphasized by Lord Reid in *Rondel v. Worsley* ... when he said:

> Every counsel has a duty to his client fearlessly to raise every issue, advance every argument, and ask every question, however distasteful, which he thinks will help his client's case. But, as an officer of the court concerned in the administration of justice, he has an overriding duty to the court, to the standards of his profession, and to the public, which may and often does lead to a conflict with his client's wishes or with what the client thinks are his personal interests. Counsel must not mislead the court, he must not lend himself to casting aspersions on the other party or witnesses for which there is no sufficient basis in the information in his possession, he must not withhold authorities or documents which may tell against his clients but which the law or the standards of his profession require him to produce. ... [Emphasis added.]

. . . . .

R. v. R. (A.J.)

[1994] O.J. No. 2309, 94 C.C.C. (3d) 168
(Ont. C.A., Osborne, Doherty and Laskin JJ.A.)

[The accused was charged with multiple counts of incest and sexual assault in relation to his daughter T. and his granddaughter J. The daughter T. had been given up for adoption at birth and had later sought out and found her father, the accused. When she was 20 years old, T. moved in with the accused, together with her own daughter, J. It was alleged that the sexual abuse of both

T. and J. took place over the ensuing years until T. eventually went to the police. The accused was convicted at trial and appealed.]

DOHERTY J.A.:—

. . . . .

Counsel for the appellant submits that Crown counsel's cross-examination of the appellant resulted in a miscarriage of justice. He does not base this contention on any isolated feature of the cross-examination or any specific line of questioning, but contends that the overall conduct and tenor of the cross-examination was so improper and prejudicial to the appellant, that it rendered the trial unfair and resulted in a miscarriage of justice. This argument is becoming a familiar one in this court ... [Doherty J.A. then cites four recent decisions of the Court.]

Crown counsel conducted an aggressive and exhaustive 141-page cross-examination of the appellant. She was well prepared and well armed for that cross-examination. Crown counsel is entitled, indeed, in some cases expected, to conduct a vigorous cross-examination of an accused. Effective cross-examination of an accused serves the truth-finding function as much as does effective cross-examination of a complainant.

There are, however, well-established limits on cross-examination. Some apply to all witnesses, others only to the accused. Isolated transgressions of those limits may be of little consequence on appeal. Repeated improprieties during the cross-examination of an accused are, however, a very different matter. As the improprieties mount, the cross-examination may cross over the line from the aggressive to the abusive. When that line is crossed, the danger of a miscarriage of justice is very real. If improper cross-examination of an accused prejudices that accused in his defence or is so improper as to bring the administration of justice into disrepute, an appellate court must intervene ...

After careful consideration of the entire cross-examination of the appellant in the context of the issues raised by his examination-in-chief and the conduct of the entire trial, I am satisfied that the cross-examination must be characterized as abusive and unfair.

From the outset of the cross-examination, Crown counsel adopted a sarcastic tone with the accused and repeatedly inserted editorial commentary into her questions. I count at least eight such comments in the first eight pages of the cross-examination. During that part of the cross-examination, Crown counsel referred to one answer given by the appellant as "incredible". She repeatedly asked the appellant if he "wanted the jury to believe that one too". When questioned as to how he met T., the appellant said he was told by a friend that a relative would be coming to see him, whereupon Crown counsel remarked "so I guess you were expecting some long lost cousin in the old country". After the appellant had described his reaction to being told by T. that she was his daughter, Crown counsel sarcastically said "gee, I guess everybody would react the way you did".

Crown counsel's approach from the very beginning of the cross-examination was calculated to demean and humiliate the appellant. She persisted in that approach throughout. For example, after the appellant said that he had allowed T. to move in with him shortly after they had met, Crown counsel said "you are just a really nice guy". At another point, she said "tell me sir, do fathers usually have sexual intercourse with their daughters". Still later, after the appellant had testified that his girlfriend had left him but had told him that she wished to come back, Crown counsel said "you just have all these women running after you wanting to come back".

These are but a few of a great many instances where Crown counsel used the pretence of questioning the appellant to demonstrate her contempt for him and the evidence he was giving before the jury. No counsel can abuse any witness. This self-evident interdiction applies with particular force to Crown counsel engaged in the cross-examination of an accused.

The tone adopted by Crown counsel is not the only problem with her cross-examination. Crown counsel repeatedly gave evidence and stated her opinion during cross-examination. She also engaged in extensive argument with the appellant. For example, when the appellant gave contradictory explanations in the course of cross-examination, Crown counsel announced "you were lying", and when the appellant questioned Crown counsel's description of T. as "your victim" Crown counsel replied "certainly she is". Still later, after Crown counsel had very effectively cross-examined the appellant as to when he had learned that T. was his daughter, she proclaimed "you are playing games with me, with this jury". She followed that comment with the admonition "let's try and be honest". In several instances, the cross-examination degenerated into pure argument between the appellant and Crown counsel. After one lengthy exchange, Crown counsel announced: "it is hard to keep up with you sir because you keep changing your story".

Statements of counsel's personal opinion have no place in a cross-examination. Nor is cross-examination of the appellant the time or place for argument.

. . . . .

Cases like this, where the allegations are particularly sordid, the complainants particularly sympathetic and the accused particularly disreputable, provide a severe test of our criminal justice system. It is very difficult in such cases to hold the scales of justice in balance and to provide the accused with the fair trial to which he or she is entitled. By her cross-examination, Crown counsel skewed that delicate balance. The cross-examination, considered in its totality and in the context of the entire trial, prejudiced the appellant in his defence and significantly undermined the appearance of the fairness of the trial.

. . . . .

[Appeal allowed.]

NOTES AND QUESTIONS

1. Is an advocate's assurance of his or her "good faith basis" for conducting a given line of cross-examination, as required by the Supreme Court of Canada in *Lyttle*, adequate to protect potential witnesses, as was the concern of Jackson J. in the *Michelson* case, from a "random shot at a reputation imprudently exposed or asking a groundless question to waft an unwarranted innuendo into the jury box"? Does *Lyttle* strike the right balance between the rights of the accused, the rights of a witness and the overall protection of the administration of justice? Can the decision of the court in *R. v. R. (A.J.)* be used in conjunction with *Lyttle* to make it clear what a lawyer is to do, or do the cases together simply make the lawyer's exercise of discretion more complicated?

2. As discussed above in the context of witness preparation, rules of professional conduct typically provide some guidance to advocates in the context of their participation in the evidentiary process (see, *e.g.*, *Model Code*, Rule 4.01(2)). Do these ethical requirements fit with the wide latitude given to advocates by the Supreme Court of Canada in *Lyttle* in the context of the cross-examination of an opposing witness?

3. How should lawyers balance the various obligations set out in *Lyttle* and *R. v. R. (A.J.)*? How are they similar and how are they different? Did Crown counsel in *R. v. R. (A.J.)* conduct herself in the manner explicitly permitted by *Model Code*, Rule 4.01(3), which provides that: "When acting as a prosecutor, a lawyer must act for the public and the administration of justice resolutely and honourably within the limits of the law while treating the tribunal with candour, fairness, courtesy and respect"? Does the nature of the allegations have any relevance to your thinking?

3. Representations about the Law

The *Sweezey*, *Lyttle* and *R. v. R. (A.J.)* cases are cases dealing with an advocate's ethical role in the evidentiary process. Equally important are ethical considerations regarding an advocate's obligation to inform the court about governing authorities — both positive and negative — that is an obligation to which Lord Denning M.R. referred in *Rondel v. Worsley*[12] as being part of an advocate's role as a "minister of justice".

Codes of conduct are typically sources of this obligation. See, for example, *Model Code*, Rule 4.01(2)(i), which provides that a lawyer shall not

> deliberately refrain from informing a tribunal of any binding authority that the lawyer considers to be directly on point and that has not been mentioned by another party.

The following case provides judicial treatment of this important ethical obligation of an advocate.

---

[12] [1967] 1 Q.B. 443.

GENERAL MOTORS ACCEPTANCE CORP. OF
CANADA v. ISAAC ESTATE

[1992] A.J. No. 1083, 7 Alta. L.R. (3d) 230
(Alta. Q.B., Master Funduk)

MASTER FUNDUK:— These are competing applications for summary judgment.

In June 1991 Frank and Jean Isaac, who are husband and wife, bought a car from Ken Beauchamp Chevrolet Oldsmobile Ltd. under a conditional sale contract. The dealer assigned the contract to the Plaintiff.

The evidence by a son of the Isaacs is that the father has been in an auxiliary hospital since February 1989 (so he would obviously not need a car) and the mother was diagnosed with an incurable malignant brain tumor in August, 1991, was hospitalized and later passed away.

After the mother's condition became known the family discussed what to do with the car.

[The family then decided to give up the car and indicated that they had done so by surrendering it through the dealer and the plaintiff. However, the plaintiff subsequently successfully moved to a Master for possession of the car, not by accepting the family's surrender of it or by seizure, but rather pursuant to the preservation rules of Alberta's Rules of Court. The plaintiff then sold the car.]

Counsel cited a number of cases in their written briefs and their oral submissions. Although I have read the cases I need not dwell on them. The matter can be properly disposed of based on a case not cited by either counsel in their briefs, but which was brought forward by me at the end of the application: *G.M.A.C. v. Sherwood* ... . An appeal to the Court of Appeal was dismissed from the Bench; C.A. Calgary 12743, Sept. 29, 1992.

Sherwood is also a case of a conditional sale contract assigned by the vendor to the same financier.

. . . . .

The Plaintiff in this action and the plaintiff in the *Sherwood* action are the same. In addition, counsel for the Plaintiff was also the counsel for the plaintiff in *Sherwood*.

There is a remarkable similarity between the order in *Sherwood* and the order in this action. ...

. . . . .

I am satisfied that here, as in *Sherwood*, that the Plaintiff attempts to go against the car and also to sue for the purchase price. The law is seize or sue, not seize and sue or sue and seize.

What happened here is just an attempt to get around s. 49(4) [of the Alberta *Law of Property Act*]. As in *Sherwood*, the attempt fails. In *Sherwood* the Court of Appeal uses the word "scheme" to describe what the plaintiff did. The same can be said here. This is all just a scheme by the Plaintiff to exercise its rights against the car without the limitation imposed by s. 49(4).

Decision

One

The application by the Plaintiff for summary judgment is dismissed. There will be summary judgment [for the defendant] dismissing the action.

Two

This is a case which calls for solicitor and client costs because of exceptional circumstances.

This application was heard as a special afternoon application.

Mr. Weldon, counsel for the Plaintiff, filed a written brief on October 20, 1992.

Mr. Vipond, counsel for the Defendants, filed a written brief on October 26, 1992.

Neither written brief refers to *Sherwood* although both are over a year after the chambers judge's decision and, as it turns out — over a short time after the Court of Appeal's decision.

When I read the briefs I noticed that neither referred to *Sherwood*. I was aware of the two Queen's Bench decisions in *Sherwood* but I was not aware of the Court of Appeal's decision.

I eagerly awaited to see if either counsel would bring up *Sherwood* in their oral submissions. Neither did. I assumed, wrongly as it turns out, that neither was aware of it.

At the end of the day, after I had heard the submissions of both counsel, I told them that I was reserving my decision and that I would give a written decision.

I then told counsel that there was a remarkably similar case where there was a written decision by Master Alberstat which was upheld by a written decision by a chambers judge. (I had not had the time to run down the case and I did not offhand know its name or who counsel were on it.)

My disclosure at the end of the day of my knowledge of the two Queen's Bench decisions in *Sherwood* prompted a sudden revelation by Mr. Weldon of his knowledge of the case. He quickly told me the name of the case, that he was counsel for GMAC on it and that he had been rejected by the Court of Appeal a few weeks before.

When I disclosed my knowledge of *Sherwood* it became obvious that I intended to run it down (when I got back to Edmonton) and that I would then see that Mr. Weldon was counsel for GMAC on it. The jig was up. Better a belated disclosure than not one at all.

It was Mr. Weldon's responsibility as an officer of the Court to bring *Sherwood* to my attention. Silence about a relevant decision, especially a binding one, is not acceptable.

I am satisfied that only my fortuitous knowledge of the Queen's Bench decisions in *Sherwood* and my disclosure of that knowledge were the events which triggered Mr. Weldon's disclosure of his knowledge of *Sherwood*. It is not supposed to be that way.

It would not be an answer to say that *Sherwood* is distinguishable so it need not be disclosed. That also does not work that way. The fallacy in that argument should be obvious. That would leave it to counsel to decide if a case is distinguishable. Counsel do not make that decision. The Court does.

It is proper for counsel to bring forward a relevant case and then submit that it is distinguishable for whatever reason. That is fair play. It is improper to not bring forward a relevant case on the ground that it is distinguishable. That is not fair play.

Mr. Vipond, counsel for the Defendants, did not refer to *Sherwood* in either his written brief or his oral submissions. I have no doubt he simply was not aware of *Sherwood*.

I will close my comments under this heading by a quote from *Lougheed Enterprises v. Armbruster* [[1992] B.C.J. No. 712 (C.A.)]:

> There is here an apparent conflict between two principles:
>
> 1. This is an adversarial system. That being so, every judge is generally in the hands of counsel, or where a party is not represented by counsel, in the hands of that party, on the points to be raised and decided. A judge, as has often been said, must not "descend into the arena".
>
> 2. A judge has an overriding duty, in the words of the old judicial oath, "to administer justice without fear or favour, affection or ill-will according to the laws and usages of this realm." To this extent, the judge has a duty to ensure that the law is applied, even though the litigants may not be aware of its requirements.
>
> The concept of judicial self-restraint, to which we adhere, is founded, if not wholly, at least in part, upon the assumption that counsel will do their duty, which is to do right by their clients and right by the court, and that all parties will be represented by counsel. In this context, "right" includes taking all legal points deserving of consideration and not taking points not so deserving. The reason is simple. Counsel must assist the court in doing justice according to law. When a point is deserving of consideration, the judge must have regard to all the relevant authorities.

As Lord Birkenhead, then Lord Chancellor, said in *Glebe Sugar Refining Co. v. Greenock Port & Harbours Trustees* ...:

> It was not, of course, in cases of complication possible for their Lordships to be aware of all the authorities, statutory or other, which might be relevant to the issues requiring decision in the particular case. Their Lordships were therefore very much in the hands of counsel and those who instructed counsel in these matters, and the House expected, and indeed insisted, that authorities which bore one way or the other upon the matters under debate should be brought to the attention of their Lordships by those who were aware of those authorities. That observation was irrespective of whether or not the particular authority assisted the party which was aware of it.

As Lord Chancellor's remarks arose in the following circumstance. An appeal was argued before the House of Lords in which neither party referred to a provision in an 1847 Act incorporated by reference in the 1913 statute under consideration. After argument Lord Atkinson looked at the 1847 Act and drew one of its sections, which bore on the issue, to the attention of his colleagues. A second hearing was ordered before the same panel confined to the effect of the 1847 provision. It was held to dispose of the issues before the court. In allowing the appeal ([1921] 2 A.C. 66 at 76 (H.L.)), Lord Birkenhead concluded [written judgment]:

> The appeal succeeds, not, however, upon the grounds put forward by the appellants, but upon grounds never put forward by the appellants (though they should have been); never alluded to by either of the parties in any court. It may be that this omission has brought about the entire litigation, certainly I should think it has brought about this appeal. I therefore think that both parties should bear their own costs here and below.

The term "relevant" in the context of the case before us means that counsel has a duty to be aware of all cases in point decided within the judicial hierarchy of British Columbia which consists of the Supreme Court of Canada, this Court and the Supreme Court of British Columbia, and where applicable, one of its predecessor courts, the County Court and to refer the Court to any on which the case might turn.

It is not necessary in these reasons to go into the exceptions to this duty. It is not the same as the duty to one's client to be persuasive which often requires counsel to produce authorities outside the hierarchy of British Columbia.

But these points must be made:

1. We do not expect counsel to search out unreported cases, although if counsel knows of an unreported case in point, he must bring it to the court's attention.

2. "On point" does not mean cases whose resemblance to the case at bar is in the facts. It means cases which decide a point of law.

3. Counsel cannot discharge his duty by not bothering to determine whether there is a relevant authority. In this context, ignorance is no excuse.

In the case at bar, there was a relevant authority which went to the very root of these proceedings. It said that the order sought in the petition could not be granted as a matter of law.

. . . . .

The duty to bring relevant law to the attention of the court is founded upon the proposition that counsel has an obligation to the court to assist in duly administering the law, as well as a duty to his client and that, in some circumstances, the former duty may override the latter.

In these special circumstances the Defendants will have costs of the action against the Plaintiff on a solicitor and client basis.

NOTES AND QUESTIONS

1. Notwithstanding counsel's failure to bring the *Sherwood* case to the attention of the court in *Isaac Estate*, Master Funduk ordered costs against the plaintiff, but not the lawyer, on the solicitor and client scale. Was that the correct order? If disciplinary proceedings were brought against the lawyer by the law society in your jurisdiction, what would the result be? What are the competing arguments that counsel for the law society and counsel for the lawyer would make at that disciplinary hearing? Which do you prefer? Why?

2. For a recent and particularly colourful judgment regarding a lawyer's duty to bring controlling precedents to the court's attention, see *Gonzalez-Servin v. Ford Motor Co.*, 662 F.3d 931 (7th Cir. 2011).

3. In addition to informing the court about negative legal authorities that are on point, counsel must also make sure to avoid misleading the court and the other side during the course of litigation about facts or issues relevant to the case. Further, counsel must, subject to rules of confidentiality, take steps to correct misapprehensions. For a further treatment of this issue, see *Law Society of Alberta v. Piragoff*, [2005] L.S.D.D. No. 47 (L.S.A.).

4. Consider the competing legal, personal and professional obligations in the following scenario:

Scenario Five

Assume that your practice focuses primarily on construction law, real estate and municipal regulatory matters. You are contacted by a potential client who owns a home just outside a relatively small town. She has begun renovating her home and a small cabin on her property using a local contractor. Specifically, in the cabin, which she uses as part of her bed-and-breakfast business, she is upgrading the kitchen and bathroom facilities, replacing the roof, moving some interior walls, replacing the electrical service and adding a new set of windows. The renovations to her house are smaller and simply involve painting and some plumbing repairs and upgrades to existing fixtures. At the planning stage, she asked her contractor about the need for building permits. The contractor said that, because the renovations are in the nature of "repairs" instead of "improvements", local by-laws did not require permits for the project. The contractor also indicated that the local member of town council is a friend of his with whom he regularly socializes and goes on fishing trips. With all of this, the contractor told your client "not to worry" about permits. Part way through the renovation process, your client was visited by the local building inspector (because of some complaints from the neighbours). The inspector asked to see the building permit, which of course did not exist. Shortly after the inspector's visit, your client received a "stop work" order as well as a letter indicating that if work did not stop and if a permit were not obtained, the town would consider its legal options including taking her to court. Your client is very concerned about the situation. Specifically, in order to obtain a permit, there is at least the potential concern that some of the renovation work will need to be undone and, in any event, a significant fine will likely be imposed. More importantly, however, because other work over the years has been done on the property for which permits were also not obtained, your client is concerned about the possibility of having inspectors combing the balance of the property on a re-inspection visit. Last week, the contractor was at a party with the member of council. After hearing about the situation from the contractor, the member of council indicated that your client "should just ignore the inspector. He is simply trying to flex his muscles and has no authority to be threatening law suits. The council would have to approve that kind of action, which it rarely does. And in any event, the council has no money at the moment to pursue these kinds of issues. So she has nothing to worry about". Based on your experience, you happen to know that the member of council is likely correct: although litigation is possible (particularly given the apparent multiple permit-related infractions on the property), at the moment it is unlikely that the council would pursue litigation against your client. Your client is very concerned about potential litigation. When thinking about whether to take the retainer, you look at the following *Model Code* provisions and Commentary:

Rule 4.01(1)

When acting as an advocate, a lawyer must represent the client resolutely and honourably within the limits of the law, while treating the tribunal with candour, fairness, courtesy, and respect.

Commentary

… [T]he lawyer has a duty to the client to raise fearlessly every issue, advance every argument and ask every question, however distasteful, that the lawyer thinks will help the client's case and to endeavour to obtain for the client the benefit of every remedy and defence authorized by law. …

. . . . .

The lawyer's function as advocate is openly and necessarily partisan. Accordingly, the lawyer is not obliged (except as required by law or under these rules …) to assist an adversary or advance matters harmful to the client's case …

A lawyer should refrain from expressing the lawyer's personal opinions on the merits of a client's case.

Rule 4.01(2)

When acting as an advocate, a lawyer must not: …

(b) knowingly assist or permit a client to do anything that the lawyer considers to be dishonest or dishonourable …

You are of the view that land use and municipal planning matters are important public policy initiatives. Your practice also involves a significant amount of ongoing work and contact with the local authorities. However, because you are a lawyer, you are aware that all clients deserve adequate representation. Do you take this case? On what basis? If you do, subject to rules of confidentiality and conflict of interest (discussed further in Chapters 4 and 5 of this book), which professional code of conduct provisions set out above, or others from your jurisdiction, will influence or determine the way you approach your advice or the way you will proceed to advocate on behalf of your client?

E.   ADVOCACY AND CIVILITY

"Civility" amongst lawyers has become a topic of growing discussion. It is a term that can mean many things. According to Alice Woolley (see further below), civility has two central meanings (as applied by law societies and as expressed in "civility" provisions). First, it includes a requirement that lawyers treat each other, and those participating in the justice system, with a degree of politeness. Second, it has been defined to include obligations — which are also enshrined independently in provisions of law society codes of conduct — on lawyers to act fairly, honestly and with the utmost integrity in their dealings with other lawyers and with members of the court. Civility is said to help ensure that lawyers uphold their duties as officers of the court and maintain and improve the standing of the administration of justice in the eyes of the public. Sources for this obligation are at least fourfold:

(1)   The court's inherent jurisdiction to govern proceedings in the courtroom, including lawyers' conduct within those proceedings, includes obligations for lawyer civility. This jurisdiction is exercised in the *Schreiber* case that follows.

(2)   Codes of conduct contemplate a high level of lawyer civility. In addition to Rule 4.01(5) dealing specifically with "courtesy" in the context of the lawyer's role as "advocate", *Model Code*, Rules 6.02(1) (and Commentary), 6.02(2) and 6.02(4) (dealing with "courtesy and good faith") provide that:

> Rule 6.02(1)
>
> A lawyer must be courteous and civil and act in good faith with all persons with whom the lawyer has dealings in the course of his or her practice.
>
> **Commentary**
>
> . . . . .
>
> A lawyer should agree to reasonable requests concerning trial dates, adjournments, the waiver of procedural formalities and similar matters that do not prejudice the rights of the client.
>
> Rule 6.02(2)
>
> A lawyer must avoid sharp practice and must not take advantage of or act without fair warning upon slips, irregularities or mistakes on the part of other lawyers not going to the merits or involving the sacrifice of a client's rights.

. . . . .

Rule 6.02(4)

A lawyer must not, in the course of a professional practice, send correspondence or otherwise communicate to a client, another lawyer or any other person in a manner that is abusive, offensive, or otherwise inconsistent with the proper tone of a professional communication from a lawyer.

(3) Best practice civility codes have developed that, although not formally binding, provide guidance for courts, lawyers and regulators in the area of civility. See, *e.g.*, the Advocates' Society, *Principles of Civility for Advocates*, which were referred to recently, for example, by Newbould J. in *Schreiber*, below, as well as the Canadian Bar Association, *Code of Professional Conduct*, rev. ed. (Ottawa: Canadian Bar Association, 2009) at 132-44 ("Appendix – Principles of Civility for Advocates"), both of which are referred to in the article that follows.

(4) Regardless of judicial or professional sources, lawyers' own personal ethics play an important and positive self-regulating role in the area of civility.

Although these various sources promote its importance, civility is not an un-controversial principle. Well-intentioned lawyers sometimes balk at civility, on the theory that it can at times chip away at their role as a zealous advocate. Those in favour often in turn respond that just because a lawyer decides to be civil to the other side does not mean that the lawyer is necessarily prejudicing the client's case — judges and juries can in fact derive negative impressions of bad conduct which may impair the clients' interests.[13] Clearly, there is a balance that must ultimately be struck.

The following article by Alice Woolley discusses the issue of civility. Read the article and then consider the two cases that follow, *Schreiber v. Mulroney* and *Law Society of British Columbia v. Laarakker*, both of which take up the issue of civility in different contexts.

ALICE WOOLLEY

"Does Civility Matter?"
(2008) 46 Osgoode Hall L.J. 175
[footnotes omitted]

I. INTRODUCTION

The Legal Profession cares about civility. Over the past thirty years in North America, and particularly over the past ten years in Canada, legal regulators and professional associations have undertaken initiatives to foster and encourage lawyer civility—and to discourage and even penalize lawyer incivility.

---

[13]   See, *e.g.*, Robert F. Reid & Richard E. Holland, *Advocacy: Views from the Bench* (Aurora, ON: Canada Law Book, 1984) at 28-30.

This commentary challenges the civility movement. It argues that to the extent that civility means the enforcement of good manners amongst lawyers, it is not a proper subject for professional regulation. To the extent that civility encompasses other ethical values—respect and loyalty to clients, respectfulness to the general public, and ensuring the proper functioning of the legal system—the use of "civility" as an all-encompassing ethical value obscures the real ethical principles at play. Imposing a broadly defined obligation of "civility" does not meet the goal of principles of legal ethics and professional regulation: to guide counsel as to what is required of an ethical lawyer.

This commentary develops this argument in three parts. First, it identifies how civility has been defined by the Canadian legal profession. It considers civility initiatives undertaken by organizations such as the Canadian Bar Association (CBA), as well as law society disciplinary decisions in which lawyers have been sanctioned for incivility. Second, it critiques attempts to regulate the manners of lawyers, focusing in particular on the risk that such attempts will undermine self-regulation and the pursuit of client interests. Third, it critiques the inclusion of other fundamental ethical values within the concept of "civility," arguing that rules directed at ensuring that lawyers appropriately balance and pursue honesty, loyalty, respectfulness, and justice should be identified as such. An omnibus requirement of "civility" does not give sufficient guidance to lawyers about what the duty to be ethical requires.

II. WHAT DOES CIVILITY MEAN?

As employed by the legal profession, "civility" clearly encompasses two separate areas of concern. It refers primarily to the requirement that other people, and in particular other lawyers, be treated with courtesy, manners, and politeness. Thus, the Law Society of Alberta's Office of the Practice Advisor has defined incivility as "sharp conduct or shoddy treatment of other lawyers, opposing parties and even independent witnesses." The Nova Scotia Barristers' Society 2002 Task Force on Civility defined civility as "akin to notions of courtesy, politeness, good manners and respect."

Similarly, the Canadian Bar Association and Advocates' Society *Principles of Civility for Advocates* include numerous rules directed primarily at courtesy towards others. The rules direct lawyers to "always be courteous and civil to Counsel engaged on the other side of the lawsuit," to treat witnesses with "appropriate respect," to avoid "discourteous comments," and to "avoid ill-considered or uninformed criticism of the competence, conduct, advice, appearance or charges of other Counsel."

In every provincial law society decision reported on Quicklaw in which the term "civility" is used, the allegation of incivility arose from the lawyer's use of strong, profane and/or flatly rude language towards another person. In all cases the concern about civility, and the justification for the sanction imposed on the lawyer, appears to have arisen from the lawyer's lack of courtesy or politeness. In a 2002 decision, the Law Society of Alberta discussed civility as a form of politeness, noting that "[l]aunching or exchanging insults is not professional behaviour." Similarly, the Law Society of Upper Canada has defined civility in terms of communications between counsel and others, emphasizing that while not all "strongly-worded or ill-received communications" are problematic, "[o]verwrought opinion, misplaced hyperbole, or a desire to intimidate, sully or defame have no place in communications from lawyers." Given the fine line between candour and slander, a lawyer should "err on the side of courtesy."

This first meaning of civility therefore addresses the manner in which counsels communicate with each other, specifically the politeness and courtesy, or lack thereof, in lawyer communication. The second meaning of civility is more substantial, referring generally to the conduct essential to ensure the proper functioning of the judicial process, with a specific focus on advocacy. The CBA *Principles* deal significantly with the obligation of a lawyer to ensure the expeditious and effective delivery of justice. This obligation includes duties to comply with undertakings, to ensure that draft orders "accurately and completely reflect[] the Court's ruling," to refrain from engaging in discovery merely to impose a financial burden on the other side, and to refrain from submitting perjured evidence to the court. This second class of civility obligations thus requires more than polite behaviour from a lawyer. It requires a lawyer to assist in the effective and expeditious functioning of the legal system.

The following sections assess the validity of these two categories of civility as ethical obligations.

III. IS COURTESY A MORAL GOOD?

The argument against civility as a moral good is hardly self-evident. After all, politeness, decency, and kindness to others seem like basic moral obligations with which everyone is familiar and to which everyone should adhere. One commentator has gone so far as to suggest that civility guidelines for lawyers are akin to what one might learn in kindergarten about being "nice to each other" and "kind to the teacher."

The problem, however, is that the ethical obligations of a lawyer are not the same as those of a kindergarten student. It is the unenviable job of a lawyer to argue for the guilty to be acquitted, to ask unpleasant personal questions of people who would rather not answer them, and to attempt to win even where victory imposes costs on others. Lawyers do not and should not "share and be nice" where to do so impinges either on their loyalty [to] their client or their fidelity to the legal system.

This does not mean that lawyers must be uncivil, but it does mean that disciplining lawyers for incivility—and even attempting to foster a culture of civility—may have negative ethical consequences.

Most significantly, an undue emphasis on civility has the potential to undermine the ability of law societies to fulfill their obligation to regulate lawyers' ethics. As members of a self-regulating profession, lawyers must hold each other to account. They must be actively engaged with each other's ethics and professionalism, and must be critical where necessary. Emphasizing civility has the significant potential to dampen the effect of this function, and to foster professional protectionism. If a strongly-worded criticism will subject a lawyer to discipline for incivility she will, naturally, be less likely to make that criticism even if it is well-founded. Knowing the difficulty of proving the truth of allegations of professional misconduct, she will simply refrain from making them.

In several of the disciplinary decisions lawyers were sanctioned for making allegations about the competence or ethics of other lawyers. In each case it appears that the remarks were largely unfounded, as no supporting evidence was introduced to the disciplining law society. However, assume for the moment that the allegations had a foundation in truth. Presumably information about the ethics and competence of other counsel—however rudely and impolitely expressed—is something that *should* be brought before the appropriate authorities. Had the allegations been substantiated with some evidence we could have seen examples of this in [*Law Society of British Columbia v. Goldberg*, [2007] L.S.D.D. No. 61, 2007 LSBC 40 (L.S.B.C.)] in which the lawyer being investigated for misconduct had criticized another counsel to the Court, and in [*Law Society of Upper Canada v. Carter*, [2005] L.S.D.D. No. 57, 2005 ONLSHP 24 (L.S.U.C.)] in which the lawyer had criticized another counsel to the legal aid society. Bringing forward concerns of this type is, I would argue, prima facie good and desirable. If the allegations were unfounded and untrue that is not good. But comments that are grounded in fact should be made; that they are made rudely does not warrant disciplining the lawyers who make them. Any other outcome creates the impression, as Goldberg argued in his submissions, that "the Law Society is dominated by considerations of professional courtesy and collegiality ... [that] ultimately inhibit their truth seeking function." If ensuring the appropriate airing of ethical concerns with lawyers' conduct requires occasional tolerance of incivility, rudeness, and overheated remarks, then so be it. The law of defamation still exists to give protection to lawyers who are unfairly subject to criticism by their colleagues. The addition of law society discipline fosters protectionism unnecessarily and suppresses legitimate criticism.

In addition, lawyers should not have to be civil where it undermines their ability to advocate for their client. Or, to put it differently, lawyers should not be disciplined for incivility where it occurs in the context of protecting a client's legal interests. ...

. . . . .

It may be for this reason that on two recent occasions the Ontario Court of Appeal, while deploring the lack of civility of counsel in litigation, declined to find any relationship between counsel's incivility and the fairness of the trial process. In both *R. v. Felderhof* [[2003] O.J. No. 4819, 68 O.R. (3d) 481 (Ont. C.A.)] and *Marchand v. Public General Hospital Society of Chatham* [[2000] O.J. No. 4428, 51 O.R. (3d) 97 (Ont. C.A.)], the court declined counsel's request for relief due to a trial judge's failure to control the incivility of opposing counsel.

In addition to the uncertain relationship between civility and resolute advocacy, and between civility and rigorous enforcement of lawyer ethics, civility is also problematic because it tends to lie in the eye of the beholder. One commentator has noted that in "the legal context, 'civility' does not have a precise meaning. Rather, it is a judicial construct signifying an attitude of respect." That may be an accurate statement, but it does not provide much guidance to a lawyer as to what constitutes incivility. This means that a lawyer who wishes to avoid discipline for incivility may self-censor in part because she does not know how her words will be perceived, and whether what she perceives as fair comment will be perceived by the law society as sanctionable misconduct. She may choose not to speak even though her comments would be important for calling another lawyer to account for improper behaviour, or in order to pursue the legal rights of her client.

This tendency is particularly problematic given that the historic collegiality with which civility is often associated is also connected to discrimination and intolerance for diversity. A diverse bar in which lawyers may simply have different senses of what constitutes "polite" behaviour may require greater tolerance of forms of expression than are countenanced by the civility movement. Otherwise civility would become shorthand for elitism.

This is not to say that all of the "civility" cases were wrongly decided; rather, it is to say that to the extent that those cases were correctly decided, it was because the rude behaviour of the lawyers in question implicated *other* ethical values. The lawyers behaved unethically, but not because they were rude per se. The validity of this broader definition of "civility" in the cases and civility initiatives—in which "incivility" incorporates a broad array of behaviours extending beyond simply bad manners or a lack of courtesy—is discussed in the following section.

Before turning to that discussion, however, an objection to these arguments must be addressed. The CBA *Principles* are not binding, but merely provide "an educational tool for the encouragement and maintenance of civility in our justice system." Thus, the ethical dangers identified here may be overstated and may overlook the virtue of encouraging lawyers to be polite to each other. The difficulty with this objection is that however voluntary the CBA *Principles* may be, there are numerous cases reported from law societies across the country in which lawyers have been disciplined in significant part because of the incivility of their communication. Therefore, there *is* disciplinary force to the civility movement. In addition, uncomfortable and rude speech that contributes to proper lawyer regulation, and proper client representation, is in itself a good thing, even if it occasionally results in incivility. As a consequence, to the extent that the encouragement of civility discourages that speech, it is not desirable.

IV. FUNDAMENTAL ETHICAL VALUES AND CIVILITY

A more profound objection to the preceding argument against civility arises from the incorporation of more fundamental ethical values in civility initiatives. These include the incorporation of obligations related to efficient litigation process, proper conduct in *ex parte* applications, and the general avoidance of sharp practice and improperly aggressive litigation strategies ("Rambo" litigation). The values underlying these requirements ensure that the ethics of the profession are upheld, including a lawyer's proper loyalty to his or her clients. Indeed, many if not all of the requirements of the civility initiatives are restatements or specifications of existing rules of professional conduct. They are, in other words, already an important part of lawyers' ethical obligations.

The inclusion of these fundamental ethical requirements within civility initiatives is problematic nonetheless. First, as noted, the rules of professional conduct in every province in Canada contain similar ethical obligations to those imposed by these more substantive aspects of the civility guidelines. It is not obvious that the response to the law societies' lack of rigorous enforcement of their existing rules should be the enactment of more rules, especially where the new rules specifically state that they will not be enforced.

Second, and more substantively, the emphasis on civility tends to obscure the true nature of the ethical misconduct of lawyers subject to discipline for incivility. This is most evident in the civility cases where the discipline of the lawyer was warranted not because the lawyer was rude, but rather because of the nature of his rudeness—to whom he was rude, the way in which he was rude, and the context in which the rudeness occurred. The nature of the rudeness in those cases shows how the lawyer violated both his fundamental ethical obligations of loyalty to the client and his duty to ensure the proper functioning of the legal system. Those violations arguably warranted professional discipline that the rudeness, in itself, did not. By disciplining the lawyer not for these violations, but for rudeness, the disciplining law society obscures the real ethical issues at play.

In [*Law Society of Upper Canada v. Wagman*, [2007] L.S.D.D. No. 29, 2007 ONLSHP 39 (L.S.U.C.)] for example, the lawyer was disciplined for, *inter alia*, writing a letter to a mediator with whom he was having a billing dispute in which he said "get ready because I can be ten times a bigger asshole than you. You want to fight, go ahead," and for calling a Senior Casualty Claims representative of the defendant insurer a "fucking cunt." The rudeness of these comments is indisputable. What is more significant, however, is the nature of the rudeness. In the first instance the rudeness was directed towards an individual with whom he was having a fee dispute, and could well have been viewed as a threat, or an attempt to employ non-legal, extra-judicial means to obtain a legal benefit. In the second instance the rudeness was to a participant in the litigation and, again, could have inhibited that individual's willingness to participate openly and fully in the litigation process. In other words, in both instances the rudeness was such that it arguably impacted the functioning of the justice system and had the potential to disrupt an individual's free and willing participation in that system.

In both *Law Society of Upper Canada v. Kay No. 39* [[2006] L.S.D.D. No. 39 (L.S.U.C.)] and *Law Society of Alberta v. Willis* [[1995] L.S.D.D. No. 308 (L.S.A.)], lawyers were disciplined for rudeness towards their own clients. In *Kay No. 39*, the lawyer, embroiled in a fee dispute with his client, accused her of fraud and threatened to report her to the police. He wrote her a letter in which he emphasized her recent immigration to Canada, stating, "I would like to think that any Commonwealth country, including India, takes the same dim view of your criminal activity." In *Willis* the lawyer swore at his client and ignored her instructions after he "became frustrated with what he considered to be bizarre instructions to settle a file for less than an offer the client had previously rejected." In both these cases the issue is not that the lawyers were rude and uncivil, although of course they were; it is that their incivility was contrary to the interests of their clients. Instead of facilitating their clients' autonomy in accessing the legal system, they undermined it: in *Kay No. 39* by giving the client groundless fears of criminal prosecution, and in *Willis* by interfering with her judgment as to her best course of action. That is unethical and would be unethical even had it been done politely. A polite but false indication that conduct may constitute a crime, or a polite refusal to allow a client to exercise her own judgment after receiving advice as to whether to accept a settlement, are as improper as rude and impolite versions of the same conduct.

Disciplining these lawyers for violation of their fundamental ethical obligations to clients and to the functioning of the justice system would be justifiable and is what should be at issue in the cases. To talk about the misconduct as incivility or rudeness obscures the real ethical problem with the lawyers' conduct. This is significant not just because of fairness to these lawyers, but also because it means that other lawyers reading the decisions are not properly informed as to the nature of their ethical obligations.

Being an ethical lawyer is challenging—not always, and not in every circumstance—but in general a lawyer is required to strike the difficult but proper balance between competing ethical obligations so as to make the best possible ethical decision she can. A lawyer must be loyal to her client, but she must also ensure that the justice system functions effectively. She must be honest but must also keep confidences. She must be resolute in her advocacy but also ensure that she does not interfere with the fair functioning of the justice system. She must be competent but also ensure access to justice for the disadvantaged. Deciding what to do when those obligations conflict with each other is difficult, and lawyers need all the guidance they can get: from colleagues and the courts but also from law societies and bar associations. To focus on civility, which not only fails to address these tensions but often flat out denies that they exist, provides no useful guidance for the lawyer seeking to resolve them.

The desire to improve the ethics and conduct of the legal profession is laudable. Focusing on civility does not accomplish this goal. Even defining civility as encompassing real questions of ethical importance diminishes, rather than enhances, the amount of guidance that counsel receive. Lawyers need to understand and embrace the multi-faceted roles they serve in the legal system, and learn how to resolve the difficult dilemmas those roles can present. Bar associations and law societies should focus on providing lawyers with the guidance that the civility movement cannot.

V. CONCLUSION

. . . . .

Lawyers should be free to make ... comments about each other, about the courts, and about the functioning of the justice system. Hard-hitting and unvarnished critiques are essential to working towards the justice system we should have, and to ensuring that lawyers play the role they need to play within that system. Pursuing the impossible dream of a positive public image, or seeking to soften the discomfort of hearing unpalatable and uncivil truths, is not required. What is required is strong and cogent debate about how lawyers can be ethical—how they can balance the competing values inherent in the difficult but fundamental role they play in a democratic society. The civility movement should be abandoned in favour of this more difficult but ultimately more fruitful and important task.

NOTES AND QUESTIONS

1. Do you agree with Woolley's critique of civility? Do you agree with her when she argues that "[l]awyers do not and should not 'share and be nice' where to do so impinges either on their loyalty [to] their client or their fidelity to the legal system"?

2. What view of professionalism from Chapter 1 most supports this view? Do you see any potential concerns with her approach? Is her approach consistent with the court's approach in *Schreiber* or the panel's approach in *Laarakker* (both of which are set out below)? Which do you prefer and why?

SCHREIBER v. MULRONEY

[2007] O.J. No. 3040
(Ont. S.C.J., F.J.C. Newbould J.)

F.J.C. NEWBOULD J.:— This is a motion by the defendant Brian Mulroney to set aside a default judgment obtained by Karlheinz Schreiber on July 24, 2007. Mr. Schreiber's counsel noted Mr. Mulroney in default and obtained a default judgment without any judicial intervention during litigation that was being hotly contested. For the reasons that follow, the noting of Mr. Mulroney in default and the default judgment are set aside. The actions taken to obtain the default judgment were egregious and wrong. I regret to say that counsel for Mr. Schreiber breached his obligations to the court and to counsel for Mr. Mulroney. No litigant deserves to be treated in the way that Mr. Mulroney was treated that led to the default judgment.

[Justice F.J.C. Newbould reviewed the background facts. Mr. Mulroney had been served with a statement of claim. He disputed the jurisdiction of Ontario to decide the litigation. Counsel for Mr. Schreiber agreed that while the jurisdictional issue was being resolved Mr. Mulroney would not file a statement of defence and would not be noted in default. The parties subsequently had a disagreement about whether Mr. Mulroney could be compelled to testify on an affidavit filed with respect to the jurisdictional issue. As part of that disagreement counsel for Mr. Mulroney obtained relief from Master Haberman in relation to the attempt of counsel for Mr. Schreiber to obtain a certificate of non-attendance with respect to Mr. Mulroney. Counsel for Mr. Schreiber then obtained a default judgment with respect to the original action.]

. . . . .

On July 20, 2007, Mr. Anka had a discussion with his client Mr. Schreiber. This is referred to in Mr. Sennecke's affidavit who participated in the call with Mr. Schreiber. Thus privilege was waived. Mr. Sennecke states that the options available to Mr. Schreiber at that stage were (i) they do nothing; (ii) they seek a timetable to be set for the defendant's motion or (iii) they note the defendant in default. Mr. Sennecke states that Mr. Schreiber instructed them to note Mr. Mulroney in default because Mr. Schreiber owed Mr. Mulroney no courtesy in light of the manner in which Mr. Mulroney's counsel went about obtaining the order from Master Haberman without his counsel being offered the opportunity to be present and make submissions to Master Haberman on his behalf.

This remarkable evidence is as important for what it does not say as for what it does say. There is no indication that Mr. Anka or Mr. Sennecke told Mr. Schreiber that they had an agreement in place with Mr. Prehogan [counsel for Mr. Mulroney] that Mr. Mulroney would not be noted in default. The statement that they were not offered an opportunity to be present before Master Haberman was not true. Nor was there any indication that Mr. Schreiber was told that there was a pending motion by Mr. Mulroney to extend the time to file a statement of defence.

In these circumstances it does not lie in Mr. Anka's mouth to seek to put the blame entirely upon his client for the steps that were taken. No doubt his client was more than willing to proceed with the noting of Mr. Mulroney in default and to proceed to a default judgment, but that does not excuse the matter.

On July 20, 2007, the same day that the conversation with Mr. Schreiber took place, a requisition to have the defendant noted in default was made and Mr. Mulroney was noted in default by the registrar. The memorandum of instructions given by Mr. Tingley makes clear that the court was not told of the agreement not to note Mr. Mulroney in default or of the outstanding jurisdictional motion or the motion to extend the time for filing a statement of defence.

On July 24, 2004, a requisition for default judgment was filed in which it was stated that default judgment could properly be signed because the claim was for a debt or liquidated demand in money. The default judgment was signed that day by an official in the registrar's office.

On the same day that the default judgment was signed, Mr. Anka wrote to Mr. Prehogan taking issue with the right of Master Haberman to settle the form of the order made by Master Haberman on July 5, 2007. He also took issue with what had occurred on that day in Master Haberman's office. He suggested he would be available before the registrar in the next day or two to discuss settling the order of Master Haberman. Mr. Anka did not inform Mr. Prehogan that the default judgment had been obtained that day. He said this morning that he did not know whether the default judgment had been obtained at the time he wrote the letter. He acknowledged, however, that four days earlier he had instructed people in his office to note Mr. Mulroney in default and obtain a default judgment. He ought to have given notice to Mr. Prehogan of his intention, and he ought not in his letter of July 2, 2007 have suggested that there were steps to be taken with respect to the order of Master Haberman without disclosing the true state of affairs. By that time a default judgment would render moot whatever procedural issues there were with respect to a prior interlocutory order. The letter to Mr. Prehogan was misleading in the extreme.

. . . . .

It is clear in my view that the noting of Mr. Mulroney in default and the default judgment must be set aside. I say this for a number of reasons:

(1) Throughout the litigation Mr. Mulroney indicated a clear intention to defend the action by taking the position that Ontario lacked jurisdiction over the matter. When Mr. Prehogan first learned of the default from the press on July 26, 2007, the motion to set aside the default judgment was served on the following day. There was no delay.

(2) The outstanding motion at the time of the default judgment to set aside the statement of claim on jurisdictional grounds is sufficient reason for the default proceedings to be set aside even if it could not be said that the defendant had a reasonable defensive position in the action. ...

(3) There is authority that if a plaintiff obtains default judgment to which he is not entitled, the default judgment is to be [set] aside *ex debito justitiae.* ...

. . . . .

(5) Mr. Anka breached his agreement with Mr. Prehogan when he sought default judgment. It was an egregious breach that Mr. Anka had no right to commit and Mr. Schreiber had no right to instruct his solicitor to commit.

(6) Mr. Anka did not give any advance notice to Mr. Prehogan that he was going to note the defendant in default or take default judgment proceedings. In the circumstances of this case it is quite obvious that he should have done so. It constituted sharp practice that should not be condoned. While the "Principles of Civility for Advocates" published by the Advocates' Society are not the force of law, the lack of notice to Mr. Prehogan breached those principles of civility. Incredibly, even after instructions had been given by Mr. Anka to

obtain a default judgment, he wrote on July 24, 2007 suggesting that there were still interlocutory matters to be dealt with without disclosing the default proceedings. Mr. Anka conceded that his client had not told him not to provide advance or post notice to Mr. Prehogan, so this is something that Mr. Anka took on his own behalf. This lack of frankness should not be condoned.

. . . . .

(9) Mr. Anka in his material and in argument contended that Mr. Mulroney's actions in this case have been motivated by an attempt to delay the case until Mr. Schreiber is extradited to Germany. There is nothing however in the record to substantiate this allegation. To the contrary, it is quite clear from the record that Mr. Prehogan and Mr. Holland continuously tried to move matters along in an agreeable way and that when that could not be achieved they sought unsuccessfully to have Mr. Anka agree to case management. Contrary to Mr. Anka's assertions, neither Mr. Prehogan nor Mr. Holland acted in a way other than professionally and with courtesy. The same cannot be said with respect to Mr. Anka. Mr. Prehogan was forceful in defence of his client's interests, as he was required to be, but civil. It should not be forgotten that the allegations of delay on Mr. Anka's part are on behalf of a client who waited 13 years to commence this action towards the end of his fight to avoid extradition.

Mr. Prehogan asked that if the default proceedings are set aside, there be an order restraining Mr. Schreiber or his counsel from noting Mr. Mulroney in default without express court order brought on proper notice. This request in the circumstances in this case is reasonable.

Mr. Anka on behalf of Mr. Schreiber requested that in the event that the default proceedings are set aside there be an order that Mr. Mulroney pay into court the amount of the judgment. He relies upon Rule 19.03(1) [of the Ontario Rules of Civil Procedure] that provides that the noting of default may be set aside by the court on such terms as are just. In my view it would be entirely unjust to make the order sought by Mr. Schreiber. He and his counsel are the author of the misfortune that has occurred. Mr. Anka also asked on behalf of Mr. Schreiber that he be paid the costs of the abandoned motion that was returnable on July 17, 2007. I make no such order. The motion was not abandoned nor is there any reason to be awarding Mr. Schreiber costs.

Mr. Prehogan on behalf of Mr. Mulroney has been trying for some time without success to have Mr. Anka agree to this case being case managed. It is obvious that this case cries out for case management. Mr. Anka has avoided that. However, Mr. Anka this morning agreed that the case should be case managed and he was content that there be such an order. In the circumstances I will make that order.

NOTES AND QUESTIONS

1. Is the primary issue with counsel for Mr. Schreiber one of civility, or is it a more fundamental violation of his multi-faceted ethical duties as an advocate? Do you think counsel for Mr. Schreiber should be subject to professional discipline by the

LSUC? Would the validity of his instructions from Mr. Schreiber (which the court questioned) be relevant to the determination of whether his conduct was sanctionable?

2. If dealing with counsel for Mr. Schreiber in the future, how might counsel for Mr. Mulroney conduct himself? Do you think the adage "what goes around comes around" might come into play in circumstances like this? Is the conduct of counsel for Mr. Schreiber in this matter consistent with his duties as a zealous advocate — which arise from the lawyer's obligation of loyalty and require the lawyer to act in the best interests of the client — or are they inconsistent with those duties? Do the rules of civility add anything further to those (or other) existing professional obligations?

3. Is it legitimate for the court to note that the "allegations of delay on Mr. Anka's part are on behalf of a client who waited 13 years to commence this action towards the end of his fight to avoid extradition"? What relevance, if any, would this fact have for Mr. Anka's identification of his ethical obligations to Mr. Schreiber and more generally?

LAW SOCIETY OF BRITISH COLUMBIA v. LAARAKKER

[2011] L.S.D.D. No. 175, 2011 LSBC 29
(Law Society of British Columbia, Hearing Panel: Leon Getz, Q.C., Chair,
Nancy Merrill and Alan Ross)

. . . . .

BACKGROUND

This matter arises out of allegedly discourteous and personal remarks made by the Respondent about a lawyer in Ontario (the "Ontario Lawyer").

The citation alleges:

(a) On or about November 20, 2009 the Respondent posted comments on the internet that contained discourteous and personal remarks about the Ontario Lawyer; and

(b) In the course of representing a client, the Respondent sent a fax on or about November 22, 2009 to the Ontario Lawyer which contained discourteous and personal remarks about the Ontario Lawyer.

The Respondent has admitted the evidence in the Agreed Statement of Facts. The Respondent's position is that his conduct in respect of the posting on the internet and the correspondence with the Ontario Lawyer was justified given the correspondence that the Respondent's client had received from the Ontario Lawyer.

. . . . .

FACTS

The Respondent is a sole-practitioner in Vernon, British Columbia. In or about November, 2009, a client approached the Respondent regarding a letter that she had received from the Ontario Lawyer (the "Demand Letter").

The Demand Letter sought payment of $521.97 (the "Settlement Amount") as damages from the client. The client's teenage daughter had been caught shoplifting at a retail outlet. The Demand Letter stated that the retailer took the position that it had a right to claim damages against the parent or guardian of a young person who had been caught shoplifting on the basis that the parent had failed to provide reasonable supervision.

The Demand Letter threatened that if the client did not pay the Settlement Amount, the Ontario Lawyer may receive instructions to file a civil suit against the client seeking an amount greater than the Settlement Amount.

The Respondent, for personal reasons, felt strongly about the Demand Letter.

After consulting with the client, the Respondent sent a one page fax letter to the Ontario Lawyer. The Respondent's letter read:

> I have been approached by [the client] with respect to your letter of October 30, 2009. Suffice it to say that I have instructed her not to pay a penny and to put your insulting and frankly stupid letter to the only use for which it might be suitable, however uncomfortably.
>
> It is disappointing when members of our profession lend themselves to this kind of thing. You must know that you are on the thinnest of legal grounds and would be highly unlikely to get a civil judgment against my client. That is aside from the logistics in bringing this matter to court in BC. I am also well aware that by preying on people's embarrassment and naiveté you will unfortunately be able to pry some money out of the pockets of some of the humiliated parents.
>
> I have notified the local paper of this scam. Save the postage in the future and become a real lawyer instead! You must have harboured dreams of being a good lawyer at one point. Surely bullying people into paying some small amount of money is not what you went into law for.
>
> But then again, someone has to be at the bottom of his class, practising with a restricted license as you appear to be.
>
> Good luck.

Two days before sending the letter, on November 20, 2009, the Respondent posted a comment on the "Canadian Money Advisor" internet blog. The Respondent posted the comment in response to two postings made by an individual who had received a letter similar in nature to the Demand Letter. The Respondent posted on the blog as follows:

> I am a lawyer.
>
> This guy is the kind of lawyer that gives lawyers a bad name. He is relying on intimidation and blackmail to get the lousy $500. Don't pay him. I hate these sleazy operators.
>
> Speaking as a lawyer, he would have little chance of collecting in court. He would have rto [sic] prove that a chiold [sic] was a habitual criminal. As far as an adult is concerned, he has to prove the loss.

Also remember this, he has to bring the action in a court near to where the incident took place (at least in BC) Gueuss [sic] what – that ain't going to happen.

The Respondent identified himself as a lawyer on this posting. He testified that he later received telephone calls from potential clients who read the posting.

The Ontario Lawyer made a complaint to the Law Society of British Columbia (the "Law Society") about the Respondent's remarks contained in the letter.

It is unclear when, but the Ontario Lawyer also made a complaint to the Law Society about the Respondent's blog posting.

There was a series of correspondence between the Law Society and the Respondent between February 1, 2010 and March 18, 2010. This Panel acknowledges that the Respondent was assiduous in his responses to the Law Society. When it was suggested that he should remove the blog posting, he immediately wrote to the operator of the blog and requested that the posting be removed.

In his substantive response to the Law Society's letter, the Respondent took the position that the real issue in this case was the conduct of the Ontario Lawyer. He raised several issues regarding the conduct of the Ontario Lawyer. The Respondent did concede that, if the Ontario Lawyer was found to have conducted himself professionally and ethically according to Law Society standards, then the Respondent's actions in denouncing the Ontario Lawyer were wrong and, in that case, he advised that he regretted his remarks and apologized unequivocally.

However, the entire tone of the Respondent's substantive response to the Law Society was that his letter to the Ontario Lawyer and his blog-posting were justified because the actions of the Ontario Lawyer were blameworthy.

In his oral submissions before this Panel, the Respondent indicated that he believed that he was allowed to do what he did in the face of a "rogue lawyer". He submits that none of his actions constitute professional misconduct or conduct unbecoming.

The Respondent further submitted that, if he is found to be wrong, then he would apologize.

Finally, the Respondent argued that if his conduct warranted sanction, then the Ontario Lawyer's letter constituted provocation and should be a mitigating factor.

. . . . .

The allegation of the Law Society is that the Respondent's incivility constitutes professional misconduct and/or conduct unbecoming.

TEST FOR PROFESSIONAL MISCONDUCT

"Professional misconduct" is not defined in the *Legal Profession Act*, the Law Society Rules or the *Professional Conduct Handbook*. We rely on the decisions of prior panels for the definition. In *Law Society of BC v. Martin*, 2005 LSBC 16, the panel considered the question of what constitutes professional misconduct and concluded that the test is as follows:

> Whether the facts as made out disclose a marked departure from that conduct the Law Society expects of its members; if so, it is professional misconduct. (para. [171])

The reasoning in *Martin* was revised in *Re: Lawyer 10*, 2010 LSBC 02, in which the panel decided that, in addition to the test developed in *Martin*, the conduct of the respondent must also be "culpable or blameworthy". In our opinion, the reasoning in *Re: Lawyer 10* simply provides a category of conduct that may fit within the "marked departure test", but requires a degree of personal responsibility or culpability in order to reach a finding of professional misconduct.

TEST FOR CONDUCT UNBECOMING A LAWYER

"Conduct unbecoming a lawyer" is defined in Section 1(1) of the *Legal Profession Act* LSBC 1998 c.9. That section defines "conduct unbecoming a lawyer" as conduct that is considered in the judgment of the benchers or a panel:

(a) to be contrary to the best interest of the public or of the legal profession, or

(b) to harm the standing of the legal profession.

The Benchers adopted a "useful working distinction" between professional misconduct and conduct unbecoming a lawyer (see *Law Society of BC v. Berge*, 2005 LSBC 28 (upheld on Review, 2007 LSBC 07), *Law Society of BC v. Watt*, [2001] LSBC 16). In *Watt* the Benchers stated:

> In this case the Benchers are dealing with conduct unbecoming a Member of the Law Society of British Columbia. We adopt, as a useful working distinction, that professional misconduct refers to conduct occurring in the course of a lawyer's practice while conduct unbecoming refers to conduct in the lawyer's private life.

Hence, on the facts of this case, we are of the opinion that the letter to the Ontario Lawyer cannot be considered to be conduct unbecoming a lawyer because it was undertaken within the Respondent's practice.

The blog posting, however, could be considered a mixture of conduct in the Respondent's private life and in the course of the lawyer's practice. As noted above, the blog posting was made on November 20, 2009 before the letter was sent to the Ontario Lawyer. The Respondent identified himself as a lawyer and received potential file referrals as a result of his blog posting.

Therefore, in our opinion, if it warrants sanction, the blog posting must be considered either professional misconduct or conduct unbecoming a lawyer. It was an action performed, at least in part, in the course of the lawyer's practice.

INCIVILITY

The Canons of Legal Ethics, *Professional Conduct Handbook* Chapter 1, provide the following instruction regarding a lawyer's obligations in communicating with other parties:

> A lawyer is a minister of justice, an officer of the courts, a client's advocate, and a member of an ancient, honourable and learned profession.
>
> In these several capacities it is a lawyer's duty to promote the interests of the state, serve the cause of justice, maintain the authority and dignity of the courts, be faithful to clients, be candid and courteous in relations with other lawyers and demonstrate personal integrity.
>
> ...
>
> 3. To the client
>
> (4) A lawyer should treat adverse witnesses, litigants, and counsel with fairness and courtesy, refraining from all offensive personalities. The lawyer must not allow a client's personal feelings and prejudices to detract from the lawyer's professional duties. At the same time the lawyer should represent the client's interests resolutely and without fear of judicial disfavour or public unpopularity.
>
> ...
>
> 4. To other lawyers
>
> (1) A lawyer's conduct toward other lawyers should be characterized by courtesy and good faith. Any ill feeling that may exist between clients or lawyers, particularly during litigation, should never be allowed to influence lawyers in their conduct and demeanour toward each other or the parties. Personal remarks or references between lawyers should be scrupulously avoided, as should quarrels between lawyers which cause delay and promote unseemly wrangling.

In prior decisions, the Law Society has enforced the Canons with respect to correspondence. In *Law Society of BC v. Lanning*, 2008 LSBC 31, it was held:

> A lawyer's communications must be courteous, fair, and respectful. A lawyer is to refrain from personal remarks or references, and to maintain objectivity and dignity. The purpose of a lawyer's communication is to properly advance the client's matter to a conclusion.

Further, in *Law Society of BC v. Greene* [2003] LSBC 30, the Respondent had made comments about another lawyer and members of the judiciary. The panel held (at paras. 34 and 35):

> Our occupation is one where we often deal in difficult circumstances with difficult people, and emotions often run high. It is not in the best interests of the justice system, our clients, and ourselves to express ourselves in a

fashion which promotes acrimony or intensifies the stressfulness or the difficulty of those already stressful and difficult circumstances.

Public writings or comments which promote such acrimony or denigrate others in the justice system have a negative effect upon the system as a whole. This is particularly true where it appears that the comments are made for no purposeful reason.

In both the *Lanning* and *Greene* cases, the respondent's uncivil conduct was found to be professional misconduct.

. . . . .

DISCUSSION

We set out earlier in these reasons the portions of the Canons of Legal Ethics dealing with civility. The duties described in those Canons are not restricted to situations where the lawyer agrees with the position, or the practice style, of the opposing lawyer or party. The duty of courtesy and good faith applies to all counsel, regardless of one's feelings about them. The Canons specifically note that "personal remarks or references between lawyers should be scrupulously avoided, as should quarrels between lawyers which cause delay and promote unseemly wrangling."

We accept that the Respondent may have been upset by the legal position and the allegations set out in the Ontario Lawyer's Demand Letter. However, those feelings do not justify the correspondence and blog posting drafted by the Respondent.

As noted above, the Respondent takes the position that he was allowed, perhaps even compelled, to do what he did in the face of a "rogue lawyer". Even if the Ontario Lawyer can be considered to be a "rogue", it is not the Respondent's place to pursue some form of vigilante justice against that lawyer by posting intemperate personal remarks or by writing letters that do not promote any possibility of resolution of the client's legal dispute.

Clearly, the appropriate avenue for the Respondent to take would have been to file a complaint either with the Law Society of Upper Canada or the Law Society of British Columbia. Obviously, the Respondent did not take those steps. Thus, by taking actions that he felt were protecting the integrity of the profession, he was achieving the opposite result.

The Respondent's actions were a marked departure from the conduct the Law Society expects of its members. The Respondent's belief in the correctness of his position does not relieve him of culpability.

DETERMINATION

On the basis of the reasoning set out above, we find that the Respondent's letter to the Ontario Lawyer and the blog posting constitute professional misconduct in respect of the allegations in the citation.

NOTES AND QUESTIONS

1. In its follow-up discipline hearing decision, the Law Society of British Columbia fined Mr. Laarakker $1,500 (plus costs in the amount of $3,000) for what the panel described as "professional misconduct" that was "not of the most serious nature". See *Law Society of British Columbia v. Laarakker*, [2012] L.S.D.D. No. 8, 2012 LSBC 2 at paras. 2, 10 and 15 (L.S.B.C.). Do you agree with this result?

2. Does the Law Society of British Columbia's decision in *Laarakker* fit with the court's decision in *D.C.B. v. Zellers Inc.* (set out earlier in this chapter)? Is one case saying that it is unethical for a lawyer to send a demand letter based on a dubious cause of action, and the other saying that it is unethical or uncivil for a lawyer to claim that another lawyer is doing just that? How can they be reconciled? What would Woolley say? Do you agree?

3. If law societies are not regularly going to police unprofessional demand letters (unless called upon to do so), should lawyers be allowed to play that role? If so, to what extent? Is the public's perception of civil communication the most important professional concern here? What other professional considerations are at stake?

4. For discussions of the *Laarakker* case, see Alice Woolley, "Lawyers regulating lawyers?" *ABlawg.ca* (November 3, 2011), online: University of Calgary, Faculty of Law <http://ablawg.ca/2011/11/03/lawyers-regulating-lawyers/>; Michael McKiernan, "Lawyers battle over letters to parents of shoplifters" *Law Times* (October 17, 2011), online: <http://www.lawtimesnews.com/201110178716/Headline-News/Lawyers-battle-over-letters-to-parents-of-shoplifters>.

5. In light of all of these discussions, consider what might be some costs associated with requiring lawyers to be civil in the context of the following scenarios.

Scenario Six

A Crown is prosecuting an individual for sexual assault. The alleged victim is HIV positive. On learning this fact, the judge in the case directs the Crown to have the witness testify wearing a mask, electronically from another courtroom, or from a table situated 30 feet from the judge. In submissions, the Crown loses his temper and tells the judge he has "the intelligence of a goat" and the "moral sensitivity of a member of the KKK". Do you think the Crown should be subject to professional discipline? Why or why not?[14]

Scenario Seven

Ms. Smith represents a client in a real estate purchase. Mr. Jones, the lawyer for the vendor, suggests that his client condition the sale of the property on the purchaser's ability to assume the mortgage on the property. They decline to do so. Nonetheless, on the closing of the transaction, Mr. Jones places this condition in the trust obligations. Ms. Smith objects, and ultimately Mr. Jones backs down. However, by this point the closing is delayed. Mr. Jones then seeks to require Ms. Smith's client to pay daily interest on the funds owed as a result of the delay in closing. Ms. Smith writes a letter to Mr. Jones, with whom she went to law

---

[14] The conduct of the judge in this scenario is based on "Case reveals judge's court his domain: Judge steps down amid worries over HIV-positive witness" *Law Times* (January 14, 2008).

school, stating: "I regret to say this, Jonesie, but you are clueless. I would hope that the other solicitors in your firm are not similarly clueless." Mr. Jones brings a complaint to the law society. What should the law society do?[15]

F. FURTHER READING

Atkinson, Rob, "How the Butler Was Made to Do It: The Perverted Professionalism of the Remains of the Day" (1995) 105 Yale L.J. 177.

Code, Michael, "Counsel's Duty of Civility: An Essential Component of Fair Trials and an Effective Justice System" (2007) 11 Can. Crim. L.R. 97.

Crystal, Nathan M., *Professional Responsibility: Problems of Practice and the Profession*, 3rd ed. (New York: Aspen Law & Business, 2004).

Farrow, Trevor C.W., "Five Pleadings Cases Everyone Should Read" (2009) 35 Advocates' Q. 466.

Farrow, Trevor C.W., "Sustainable Professionalism" (2008) 46 Osgoode Hall L.J. 51.

Farrow, Trevor C.W., "The Negotiator-As-Professional: Understanding the Competing Interests of a Representative Negotiator" (2007) 7 Pepp. Disp. Resol. L.J. 373.

Freedman, Monroe H., *Lawyers' Ethics in an Adversary System* (Indianapolis: Bobbs-Merrill, 1975).

Fried, Charles, "The Lawyer as Friend: The Moral Foundations of the Lawyer-Client Relation" (1976) 85 Yale L.J. 1060.

Fuller, Lon L., "The Adversary System" in Harold J. Berman, ed., *Talks on American Law* (New York: Vintage Books, 1961).

Gillers, Stephen, *Regulation of Lawyers: Problems of Law and Ethics*, 8th ed. (New York: Aspen, 2009).

Graham, Randal N.M., *Legal Ethics: Theories, Cases, and Professional Regulation*, 2d ed. (Toronto: Emond Montgomery, 2011), ch. 7.

Hanycz, Colleen M., Trevor C.W. Farrow and Frederick H. Zemans, *The Theory and Practice of Representative Negotiation* (Toronto: Emond Montgomery, 2008), chs. 2 and 5.

Hazard, Geoffrey C., Jr., *Ethics in the Practice of Law* (New Haven and London: Yale University Press, 1978).

Hazard, Geoffrey C., Jr. & Deborah L. Rhode, *The Legal Profession: Responsibility and Regulation*, 3rd ed. (Westbury, NY: Foundation Press, 1994).

---

[15] See *Law Society of Alberta v. Pozniak*, [2002] L.S.D.D. No. 55 (L.S.A.), discussed further in Alice Woolley, "Does Civility Matter?" (2008) 46 Osgoode Hall L.J. 175 at 181-82 (this portion of the article is not included in the excerpt above).

Holmes, Grace W., ed., *Excellence in Trial Advocacy* (Ann Arbor: The Institute of Continuing Legal Education, 1971).

Hutchinson, Allan C., *Legal Ethics and Professional Responsibility*, 2nd ed. (Toronto: Irwin Law, 2006).

Kaufman, Andrew L. & David B. Wilkins, eds., *Problems in Professional Responsibility for a Changing Profession*, 5th ed. (Durham: Carolina Academic Press, 2009).

Luban, David, *Lawyers and Justice: An Ethical Study* (Princeton: Princeton University Press, 1989).

Lubet, Steven, adapted for Canada by Cynthia Tape & Lisa Talbot, *Modern Trial Advocacy: Canada*, 3rd ed. (Boulder, CO: National Institute for Trial Advocacy, 2010).

McKenzie, Gavin, *Lawyers and Ethics: Professional Responsibility and Discipline* (looseleaf) (Toronto: Carswell, 1993).

Reid, Robert F. & Richard E. Holland, *Advocacy: Views from the Bench* (Aurora, ON: Canada Law Book, 1984).

Rhode, Deborah L., *Professional Responsibility: Ethics by the Pervasive Method*, 2nd ed. (New York: Aspen Law & Business, 1998).

Rhode, Deborah L., *In the Interests of Justice* (New York: Oxford University Press, 2000).

Rhode, Deborah L., ed., *Ethics in Practice: Lawyers Roles, Responsibilities, and Regulation* (Oxford: Oxford University Press, 2000).

Rhode, Deborah L. & David Luban, *Legal Ethics*, 5th ed. (New York: Foundation Press, 2009).

Simon, William H., *The Practice of Justice: A Theory of Lawyers' Ethics* (Cambridge, MA: Harvard University Press, 1998).

Smith, Beverley G., *Professional Conduct for Lawyers and Judges*, 4th ed. (Fredericton: Maritime Law Book, 2011), chs. 6-7.

White, Q.C., Robert B., *The Art of Trial* (Aurora, ON: Canada Law Book, 1993).

Woolley, Alice, *Understanding Lawyers' Ethics in Canada* (Markham, ON: LexisNexis Canada, 2011).

CHAPTER 7

COUNSELLING AND NEGOTIATION

A. INTRODUCTION

This chapter looks at the ethical rules governing two tasks frequently performed by a lawyer. The first is providing counsel by giving the client information, opinion and advice. The second is acting as a negotiator on behalf of the client. These tasks span all areas of legal practice and, in particular, are not restricted to a litigation context.

As you read this chapter, bear in mind that unlike many other tasks lawyers perform, counselling and negotiation often take place in a relatively private setting. You should consider what impact that should have on the need for ethical rules and the content of those rules. You should also consider the potential for conflict between these rules and other rules of professional conduct such as the duty of loyalty to the client.

B. COUNSELLING

It is vital that members of the public know the law, and so one of the most important services lawyers provide is telling them what the law is. The client often lacks the means of accessing the law, so the lawyer provides that access. Sometimes the law is clear and the lawyer simply communicates its content. Other times there may be doubt as to what the law is. There may be ambiguity in the wording of a statute or conflicting decisions in the reported cases. Here, the lawyer not only provides information but must also offer an opinion as to the law's true content. Further, the lawyer is frequently asked to apply the law to the client's factual situation. This too can be straightforward in some cases and more difficult in others. Finally, the client may ask the lawyer for his or her opinion on how the client should proceed.

There can be tension in the counselling process. On the one hand, lawyers should be concerned about client autonomy and respect the client's desires and decisions. On the other hand, the client is frequently looking to the lawyer for advice and guidance, which can result in lawyers expressly or implicitly making the actual decision about what is best for the client.

Counselling clients raises several important ethical issues. One is whether a lawyer can ever advise his or her client to break the law. Another is the extent to which a lawyer can provide advice that could be used by the client as a basis for a subsequent decision to break the law. These issues will be addressed in the material that follows.

In counselling clients, lawyers are not permitted to simply tell them what they want to hear. Rather, lawyers are obliged to be honest and candid. The advice must be clear and in terms that their clients can understand.

1. Counselling and Illegal Conduct

LAW SOCIETY OF UPPER CANADA v. SUSSMAN

[1995] L.S.D.D. No. 17

(Law Society of Upper Canada, Discipline Committee: D.W. Scott,
V.C. Krishna and N. Graham)

. . . . .

Background

The solicitor, Frederick Bernard Sussmann, was called to the Bar of the Province of Ontario on the 15th of June 1973. Prior to that date he was a member of the Bar of the State of New York, U.S.A., and had been since March 1944. He came to Canada to join the Faculty of Law at the University of Ottawa and upon his retirement took up practice in the City of Ottawa. The complaint in the case arises out of his representation of Jaqueline Joubarne. The solicitor is charged that:

> while acting for a wife in a matrimonial proceeding, he counselled his client to breach the terms of the Court Order respecting access.

The Facts

On November 14, 1991 the Honourable Mr. Justice McWilliam of the Ontario Court (General Division) at Ottawa issued an Order in a proceeding in which one Daniel Joubarne, the husband, was the Applicant and Jacqueline Joubarne, the wife, the Respondent. The Order was to the effect, *inter alia*, that the wife would have custody of the two children of the marriage, Jessie St. Anne Joubarne born February 29, 1980 (the child of the wife's previous marriage) and Jill Samantha Joubarne born December 28, 1983, and that the husband would have, in effect, weekend access to both children in accordance with the specific terms of the Order. ...

In accordance with the terms of the Order for access the children were with their father on Saturday and Sunday, November [30] and December 1, 1991. On Tuesday, December 3, the solicitor wrote to Richard B. Bowles, the solicitor for the husband ..., remonstrating with him with respect to his client's behaviour during access and concluded that:

> The further consequence is that, as soon as I can get the necessary affidavit from my client, I will prepare a motion for an interim restraining order barring your client's access to both children.

Some ten days later on December 13, 1991 the solicitor again wrote to Richard B. Bowles. ... His letter contained the following statement:

> The purpose of this letter is to tell you that I have instructed my client not to permit your client access to the children this coming weekend, or at any time until I can make my application for a temporary restraining order, and that you had better advise your client accordingly, since originally he was to have had access this coming weekend.

The solicitor for the husband responded ... on the same day, which was a Friday, complaining about the propriety of the position adopted by the solicitor having in mind his obligations as an officer of the Court and the terms of the existing Order. It is clear from the evidence that was tendered at the Hearing that, as a result of the position adopted by the solicitor and the advice which he gave to his client, the husband was denied access to his two children on the weekend in question, that is to say the weekend of December 14 and 15, 1991.

. . . . .

... Far from complying, or even suggesting some viable alternative, the solicitor, on August 24, 1992, wrote to Mr. Bowles ... and again made it quite clear that he was advising his client to ignore the terms of the outstanding access Order of November 14, 1991. Specifically, in this letter he notes at Point 4:

> Be advised that my client's position is that your client will be granted no further access to either child, and no further support payments for either will be accepted. This position was adopted by my client in consultation with me following consideration of your client's behaviour. ...

As a result of this communication Mr. Bowles ... reported the solicitor to the Law Society. ...

Certain matters are clear from a factual standpoint. In the first place it is conceded that the solicitor counselled his client to disobey the terms of the Order of the Honourable Mr. Justice McWilliam of November 14, 1991. Not only is this apparent from his written communications, but he admitted the same in evidence. Furthermore, it is equally clear that his client followed his advice, as she might well have done, it having been proffered by an officer of the Court. Mr. Bowles testified that access was denied during the weekend of December 14 and 15, 1991. Furthermore, Judge Desmarais concluded that access had been denied, as threatened, on [a] second occasion in August 1992.

. . . . .

... [T]he solicitor argued that he had always intended to bring a variation application and had simply never done so. This position is equally untenable. He first denied access to the children on his client's behalf on December 13, 1991. The first (and apparently only) document which he filed in support of a variation of the Order was filed some seven months later on July 17, 1992. His explanations as to why he did not make a variation application are groundless. Whether they were based on his being overburdened with work or his somewhat convoluted theory as to the onus being on the husband to apply to the Court, they provide no escape. The circumstances in which a solicitor may counsel his client to ignore the terms of a mandatory order are, not surprisingly, extremely confined. In a decision of a Discipline Committee of the Law Society in the matter of Carole Curtis (decided December 29, 1993) the Committee noted the following on the subject at page 19:

> The principle appears to be reasonably, clearly established, and we emphasize that the circumstances in which the counselling of the disobedience of a

court order can be countenanced are extremely narrow, have implicit in them the elements of reasonable and honest belief of there being imminent risk or danger to a child, and co-exist with the requirement that there be an immediate application to a court to have the issues determined forthwith. Once that application is made and the facts have been presented before a court of competent jurisdiction however briefly, if that court refuses to act to change an outstanding order, then the obligation of the client is to 'trust in the efficacy of the legal system' and adhere to the court order, and then if so advised, to seek a full hearing for a permanent change. ...

The solicitor did not suggest that there was any imminent risk or danger to the child which might have justified his behaviour. Furthermore, as pointed out by counsel for the Law Society, not only was there no immediate application to vary, there was no application by the solicitor at all. Indeed, the Committee is of the view that ... the solicitor never really intended to make an application so long as his assertions with respect to his client's decision not to follow the dictates of the Order had the intended effect upon the husband.

The complaint has accordingly been established. There will be a finding of professional misconduct against the solicitor. In particular, we find that, while acting for the wife in a matrimonial proceeding, the solicitor counselled his client to breach the terms of a Court Order respecting access.

. . . . .

... There can be no behaviour more disruptive to our system of justice and more likely to bring its administration into disrepute than a lawyer, while representing a party to a dispute, counselling his or her client to disobey the clear, unequivocal terms of a Court Order. To do so is to undermine the Court's effectiveness, contaminate the esteem with which it is held in the eyes of the citizenry and foment the law of the jungle. Behaviour of this kind is particularly troubling by reason of the highly undesirable example which it provides to ordinary citizens, lawyers and indeed law students. ...

[Mr. Sussman had an otherwise clean disciplinary record, a lengthy record of service as a lawyer, and was in ill health. He was suspended from practice for one month.]

FEDERATION OF LAW SOCIETIES OF CANADA

Model Code of Professional Conduct, Rule 2

2.02(2) When advising a client, a lawyer must be honest and candid and must inform the client of all information known to the lawyer that may affect the interests of the client in the matter.

. . . . .

2.02(7) When acting for a client, a lawyer must never knowingly assist in or encourage any dishonesty, fraud, crime or illegal conduct, or instruct the client on how to violate the law and avoid punishment.

. . . . .

2.02(8) A lawyer who is employed or retained by an organization to act in a matter in which the lawyer knows that the organization has acted, is acting or intends to act dishonestly, fraudulently, criminally or illegally must do the following, in addition to his or her obligations under subrule (7):

(a) advise the person from whom the lawyer takes instructions and the chief legal officer, or both the chief legal officer and the chief executive officer, that the proposed conduct is, was or would be dishonest, fraudulent, criminal, or illegal and should be stopped;

(b) if necessary because the person from whom the lawyer takes instructions, the chief legal officer or the chief executive officer refuses to cause the proposed conduct to be stopped, advise progressively the next highest persons or groups, including ultimately, the board of directors, the board of trustees, or the appropriate committee of the board, that the proposed conduct was, is or would be dishonest, fraudulent, criminal, or illegal and should be stopped; and

(c) if the organization, despite the lawyer's advice, continues with or intends to pursue the proposed wrongful conduct, withdraw from acting in the matter in accordance with Rule 2.07.

NOTES AND QUESTIONS

1. What rules of professional conduct did Mr. Sussman violate? How relevant is it to the analysis that his client followed his advice? For an American case with similar facts, see *In re Scionti*.[1]

2. Why might Mr. Sussman have advised his client to violate the court order concerning access to the children? In what circumstances would such advice not be unethical?

3. If a client acts illegally based on advice received from his or her lawyer, can the client rely on the advice as a defence if he or she is charged with an offence or with contempt of court?

4. In addition to prohibiting lawyers from encouraging their clients to act illegally, provincial rules of professional responsibility also prohibit lawyers from actually taking part in the illegal conduct. This is an even more serious ethical violation, and can also expose the lawyer to criminal and civil sanctions as a party to the conduct.[2]

5. Notwithstanding their duty of loyalty to the client, lawyers need to be vigilant to avoid becoming the "tool or dupe" of an unscrupulous client. The commentary to the *Model Code*'s Rule 2.02(7) tells lawyers that "if a lawyer has suspicions or doubts about whether he or she might be assisting a client in dishonesty, fraud, crime or illegal conduct, the lawyer should make reasonable inquiries to obtain information about the client and about the subject matter and objectives of the retainer". See also American Bar Association Informal Ethics Opinion 1470 (1981),

---

[1] 630 N.E.2d 1358 (Ind. 1994).
[2] See, for example, *Criminal Code*, R.S.C. 1985, c. C-46, s. 21.

which specifically addresses when a lawyer should inquire further about a client's reasons for seeking advice. Lawyers are particularly susceptible to being involved in activities like mortgage fraud and money laundering because these activities typically use commercial transactions which lawyers commonly arrange.

6.   What is the difference between a lawyer advising his or her client to dispose of a weapon used to commit a recent crime and advising the client that if the weapon was not found by the police it would be harder for the client to be convicted? For one view, see *In re Bullowa*.[3] See also Joel S. Newman, "Legal Advice Towards Illegal Ends" (1994) 28 U. Rich. L. Rev. 287 at 291.

7.   Is there a way in which Mr. Sussman could have ethically advised his client that would have led to the same actions by the client?

8.   Would it be acceptable for a lawyer to advise a client to breach a contract? Is this different from advice about breaching a court order? In *Law Society of Upper Canada v. Chojnacki* the majority stated that the Ontario equivalent of Rule 2.02(7) "on its plain reading encompasses, and was intended to encompass, both civil and criminal misconduct".[4] However, the dissent stated that "[a]ssuming ... a thorough examination of the facts and proper advice on the adverse consequences, advice that a client's best course of action is to break a contract is not, in my opinion, professional misconduct. ... To deprive the lawyer of the right to advise a client on the client's best course of action in any of these circumstances is not good public policy because it prevents the lawyer from giving any practical advice in a situation where the only advice available may be a choice between the lesser of two evils."[5]

9.   The commentary to the *Model Code*'s Rule 2.02(7) provides that "so long as no injury to a person or violence is involved, a lawyer may properly advise and represent a client who, in good faith and on reasonable grounds, desires to challenge or test a law and the test can most effectively be made by means of a technical breach giving rise to a test case". What is a "technical" breach of the law? Do you support this exception for test cases? For more on test cases see American Bar Association Formal Opinion 85-352.

10. Law societies developed rules like Rule 2.02(8) to address the role that lawyers should play in proper corporate governance. These were drafted in the wake of several high-profile corporate scandals in Canada and the United States. What do these rules require of lawyers? Do these rules strike a proper balance between the public interest in having corporations act legally and the lawyer's duty of loyalty? These rules are discussed in more detail in Chapter 9.

11. Rule 1.2(d) of the American Bar Association's *Model Rules of Professional Conduct* provides that "[a] lawyer shall not counsel a client to engage, or assist a client, in conduct that the lawyer knows is criminal or fraudulent, but a lawyer may discuss the legal consequences of any proposed course of conduct with a client". How does this rule differ from the *Model Code*'s Rule 2.02(7)? The commentary to Rule 1.2(d) provides that there is "a critical distinction between presenting an analysis of legal aspects of questionable conduct and recommending the means

---

3   229 N.Y.S. 145 (1928).
4   [2010] L.S.D.D. No. 89 at para. 82 (Law Society of Upper Canada, Discipline Committee: J. Braithwaite, B.A. Laskin and J.J. Wardlaw).
5   *Ibid.*, at paras. 144 and 154.

by which a crime or fraud might be committed with impunity". Can you explain this distinction?

12. To what extent is it acceptable for a lawyer to provide advice about a client's likelihood of being caught in any violation of the law, such as the chances of police apprehension or of a tax audit? Might not this information lead the client to choose to violate the law? See Stephen L. Pepper, "Counseling at the Limits of the Law: An Exercise in the Jurisprudence and Ethics of Lawyering" (1995) 104 Yale L.J. 1545 at 1551-52. See also American Law Institute, *Restatement of the Law Third: The Law Governing Lawyers* (St. Paul, MN: American Law Institute, 2000) at para. 94, comment c.

13. To what extent should limitations on advising clients depend on whether the client has requested particular advice from the lawyer or whether the lawyer volunteers it without a specific request? Would this give an advantage to more sophisticated or creative clients?

14. Pepper identifies several factors a lawyer should consider in determining whether to provide certain legal information to a client. They include: (i) whether the law truly prohibits the conduct or only provides consequences for it; (ii) the degree to which the law is enforced (never? rarely?); (iii) the extent to which the information is public or private; and (iv) the likelihood the client will use the information to assist in unlawful conduct. Is this sort of analysis consistent with the obligation to be honest and candid? Does it undercut the lawyer's duty of loyalty to the client?

15. Most provinces that have not adopted the *Model Code* have similar ethical rules to those set out above. See, for example, the Law Society of Upper Canada's *Rules of Professional Conduct*, Rules 2.02(1), (5), (5.1) and (5.2).

16. For further discussion of counselling and unlawful activity see Alice Woolley, *Understanding Lawyers' Ethics in Canada* (Markham, ON: LexisNexis Canada, 2011) at 61-63.

2. Other Issues in Counselling

Most provincial rules of professional conduct elaborate on the general duty of honesty and candour. The additional guidance is largely uncontroversial: the lawyer must be competent to provide the advice, must have sufficient knowledge of the relevant facts, should indicate any assumptions made and should be wary of bold or over-confident assurances.

Despite these sorts of rules, an anecdotal study of American lawyers concluded that "[l]awyers deceive their clients more than is generally acknowledged by the ethics codes or by the bar".[6] Common lies relate to the amount of work done for the client, whether certain work has been completed, the lawyer's availability to meet with the client or work on the matter, and the lawyer's degree of experience and competence. While there is a lack of empirical data, in the words of one commentator, "we all suspect strongly that many lawyers misrepresent their knowledge and experience to gain a client's

---

[6]   Lisa G. Lerman, "Lying to Clients" (1990) 138 U. Pa. L. Rev. 659 at 663.

confidence [and] exaggerate the complexity of work or the demands of skill to justify their fees".[7]

Lawyers are sometimes asked to provide business, financial or strategic advice. If they choose to do so, they should clearly differentiate between this advice and their legal advice. They should make sure the client is aware of any limitations on their ability to provide non-legal advice, such as not having financial or accounting training. If a lawyer provides non-legal advice, this opens up the possibility of the client suing him or her in negligence if the advice turns out to be incorrect. Such a claim would not likely be covered by the lawyer's professional insurance which covers claims based on providing legal services.

Some other specific ethical obligations relate to counselling clients and so should be noted. If a lawyer discovers that he or she has made an error that could damage the client's position, the lawyer should promptly notify the client and discuss how to proceed, including candidly discussing the possibility of a claim against the lawyer. The lawyer should insist that the client obtain independent legal advice (from another lawyer) before making a decision. Similarly, the lawyer should insist on independent legal advice in connection with any of the client's transactions in which the lawyer has an interest. See, for example, the *Model Code*'s Rule 2.04(29) and Rule 6.08(1).

FEDERATION OF LAW SOCIETIES OF CANADA

Model Code of Professional Conduct, Rule 2

2.02(4) A lawyer must advise and encourage a client to compromise or settle a dispute whenever it is possible to do so on a reasonable basis and must discourage the client from commencing or continuing useless legal proceedings.

Commentary

A lawyer should consider the use of alternative dispute resolution (ADR) when appropriate, inform the client of ADR options and, if so instructed, take steps to pursue those options.

DAVID LUBAN

"Tales of Terror: Lessons for Lawyers from the 'War on Terrorism'" in Kieran Tranter *et al.*, eds., *Reaffirming Legal Ethics: Taking Stock and New Ideas* (New York: Routledge, 2010) 56 at 60-61[*]
[footnotes omitted]

[Another issue that often arises for lawyers is the ethical obligation related to the advice a lawyer gives to his or her client, especially in situations where it is obvious that a client wants to be advised that a particular course of conduct is acceptable. A dramatic example arose in the context of the United States

---

[7]   Richard Uviller, "The Lawyer as Liar" (1994) 13(2) Crim. Justice Ethics 2 at 102.

[*]   Reproduced with permission.

government's dealings with detainees following the September 11, 2001 terrorist attacks. The government wanted to interrogate the detainees in as forceful and effective a way as possible without violating international law related to torture. It sought opinions from senior lawyers in the Office of Legal Counsel of the Justice Department. These opinions concluded that interrogative techniques did not amount to torture unless they posed a threat of organ failure to the detainee.

The opinions were provided to a client that presumably wanted as much leeway as possible in obtaining information from detainees in order to prevent further terrorist attacks and to capture the perpetrators of terrorist attacks. The opinions have since been discredited as having significantly overreached the legitimate interpretations of what constitutes torture and they were ultimately disavowed by the Office of Legal Counsel in 2009.

David Luban was one of the most vocal critics of these "torture memos", partly because of their content, but also because, in his view, the lawyers who provided the advice to their client failed in their ethical duties as counsellors and advisors.]

Are there lessons that lawyers can learn from this episode? The crucial question has to do with the ethical obligations of lawyers in their role as confidential counsellors, or legal advisors, to their clients. Let me set aside for the moment the most fundamental criticism of the Bybee memo, namely, that it enabled torture. The more general criticisms of the memo are two: first, it stretched and distorted the law to reach the outcome that the client wanted; and second, it nowhere indicated that its interpretations were outside the mainstream. The principles behind these criticisms apply to lawyers in private practice as well as government lawyers.

They are noteworthy criticisms, because they highlight the ethical distortion that results when lawyers bring the neutral partisan role morality of courtroom advocates into the counselling role. After all, stretching the law to reach the client's desired outcome, and disguising the fact that stretching is going on, are exactly what advocates do every day in litigation and brief-writing. The major point, then, is that the role of the counsellor and that of the advocate are fundamentally different. In the words of current US ethics rules, the counsellor is supposed to provide clients with independent and candid advice — telling the client what the law requires even if that is not what the client wants. The reason for sharply distinguishing the advocate's pro-client tilt in stating the law from the counsellor's more objective stance is straightforward. In adversary litigation, whatever exaggerations a lawyer introduces in presenting the law can be countered by the lawyer on the other side, and an impartial decision-maker will choose between the arguments. In a counselling situation, it is just the lawyers and their clients, with no adversary and no impartial adjudicator. The institutional setting that justifies an advocate's one-sided partisanship in setting forth the law is absent in the counselling role.

For that reason, the counsellor's rule of thumb should be different from the one-sided partisanship of the advocate. It is to make your description of the law more or less the same as it would be if your client wanted the opposite result from the one you know your client wants. That should be the litmus test of whether your advice is truly independent, rather than result-driven by what you know your client wants. It seems clear that the torture memos failed this test.

What should legal opinion writers do when they believe they have the law right and the mainstream has it wrong? Here, it seems to me, the rule of thumb should be this: if your view of the law is out of the mainstream, but you believe you're right, you have the responsibility to tell your client both those things: what the law, on your own best understanding, requires; *and* the fact that your own best understanding is not one that the legal interpretive community would accept.

NOTES AND QUESTIONS

1. How does *Model Code* Rule 2.02(4) restrict lawyers in the counsel they can provide to their clients? See Rules 2.02(2) and (3) in the Law Society of Upper Canada's *Rules of Professional Conduct*.

2. Why might you as a lawyer ever choose to provide non-legal advice to a client? How could you do so in a way that would best protect you from subsequent legal liability for the advice?

3. The obligation to give honest and candid advice can, in certain circumstances, include an obligation to advise a client against a legal transaction the client is otherwise committed to doing. *Neushul v. Mellish & Harkavy*[8] is routinely cited as a case in which a lawyer appears to have been held liable for failing to advise a client against a transaction on general commercial grounds. The plaintiff became romantically involved with a rogue and, when the rogue asked her for a loan, she was willing to lend him money. The plaintiff borrowed the money she needed to lend to the rogue, securing the loan with her house. For these transactions she retained a lawyer who was also the rogue's lawyer and thus knew something of his business and affairs. The rogue absconded with the money and the plaintiff sued the lawyer. The court held that a lawyer should not refrain from expressing an opinion where it is plain that the client is rushing into an unwise or disastrous transaction. The rogue's unreliability was known to the lawyer and he owed the plaintiff a duty to advise her so that she could decide what arrangements she wanted in order to protect her position.

4. Might lawyers take the duty of honesty and candour too far? In Donald C. Langevoort and Robert Rasmussen, "Skewing the Results: The Role of Lawyers in Transmitting Legal Rules" (1997) 5 S. Cal. Interdisciplinary L.J. 375, the authors argue that lawyers systematically tend to overstate legal risks. They suggest that this can be explained in economic terms, in that the overstatement can lead to lawyers being paid more for their services by their clients. They also suggest other contributing factors such as a lawyer's concern for his or her reputation in the event a transaction the lawyer opines is legal is subsequently found to be illegal.

---

[8]   (1967), 111 Sol. Jo. 399 (C.A.).

5. Do you agree with the approach to counselling outlined by Luban? Are there problems with requiring a lawyer to tell a client that he or she has views that differ from the mainstream approach? How might this affect the client's confidence in the lawyer?

Scenario One

Your client is charged with first degree murder. Your client asks you to identify countries from which extradition to Canada would be impossible or very difficult. Can you ethically comply with the client's request? How does your answer take account of the *Model Code*'s Rule 2.02(5)?

Scenario Two

Your client asks you to explain the law in Canada on assisted suicide. Would you do so? Would you insist on knowing why the client wanted this information before providing an answer? Would you confine your answer to the strict legal provisions or would you also advise as to the discretion of Crown Attorneys in laying charges and the possibility that a jury might refuse to convict? To what extent might your own moral views come into conflict with your professional obligations?

C. NEGOTIATION

One way for people to resolve disputes between them is to negotiate a solution. The process of negotiation has been extensively studied and there are many different approaches people can take to it. Books abound proposing various ways to negotiate. These books frequently discuss negotiation ethics, but very much in a non-binding sense, looking at morality and what might be perceived by others as inappropriate. See, for example, Roy Lewicki, Bruce Barry and David Saunders, *Negotiation*, 6th ed. (Toronto: McGraw-Hill, 2010) at Chapter 9; Colleen M. Hanycz, Trevor C.W. Farrow and Frederick H. Zemans, *The Theory and Practice of Representative Negotiation* (Toronto: Emond Montgomery, 2008) at Chapter 5. Subject to some relatively minimal legal restrictions imposed by the law on fiduciary duties, deceit and misrepresentation, people can act in their own best interests and are free to negotiate unethically if they so choose.

In general, negotiating parties are able to withhold material facts from each other and to make untruthful statements. This frequently happens when a party sets out his or her bottom-line position. For example, a party may state that he or she will not accept anything less than $100,000, knowing, at that time, that he or she would accept less. Under many approaches to negotiation this is not unethical, even in a moral or personal sense. Negotiation is frequently seen as a kind of "game" in which deception and bluffing are key tactics. Indeed, one commentator has claimed that "the critical difference between those who are successful negotiators and those who are not lies in [the] capacity both to mislead and not to be misled".[9] This view of negotiation has been endorsed by the courts. For example, in *Westcom TV Group Ltd. v. CanWest Global Broadcasting Inc.* the court noted that "[p]arties involved in arm's length negotiations commonly conceal their true intentions. It is part of the negotiating process that positions are advanced that do not represent what a party truly expects or is prepared to agree to in the end."[10]

Negotiating parties often employ lawyers to negotiate on their behalf. This raises two questions which will be addressed in the material that follows. The first is the extent to which the lawyer must be skilled in the process of negotiation. Lawyers are required to be competent. What does it mean to be competent to negotiate? The second question is whether the general rule about truth in negotiations, outlined above, is different when lawyers are the ones negotiating. For example, can lawyers knowingly misrepresent their clients' bottom-line position?

1. Competence to Negotiate

FEDERATION OF LAW SOCIETIES OF CANADA
Model Code of Professional Conduct, Rule 2

2.01(1)(c) ... "Competent lawyer" means a lawyer who has and applies relevant knowledge, skills and attributes in a manner appropriate to each matter undertaken on behalf of a client and the nature and terms of the lawyer's engagement, including ...

> (c) implementing as each matter requires, the chosen course of action through the application of appropriate skills, including: ...
>
> (v) negotiation; ...

NOTES AND QUESTIONS

1. Why do ethical rules make express reference to negotiation skills in defining competence?

2. Is a lawyer a competent negotiator just by virtue of being a lawyer? How many lawyers do you think would consider themselves incompetent negotiators?

3. What have you done to develop your skill at negotiation? Do you consider it sufficient?

4. Law schools offer specialized courses in negotiation, as do other educational institutions. If the people who take these courses know more about the process of negotiation than those who do not, should all lawyers be required to take such a course? Why or why not?

---

[9]   James J. White, "Machiavelli and the Bar: Ethical Limitations on Lying in Negotiation" [1980] Am. B. Found. Res. J. 926 at 927.
[10]   [1996] B.C.J. No. 1638, 26 B.C.L.R. (3d) 311 at para. 18 (B.C.S.C.).

5. Rule 2.01(1) of the Law Society of Upper Canada's *Rules of Professional Con-
    duct* is virtually identical to the above rule.

2. Regulation of Negotiations

Most provincial codes of ethics contain a requirement that lawyers must, in
their dealings with other lawyers and self-represented opposing parties, act
with integrity and in good faith. This differentiates lawyers from the negotiating parties. However, it is debatable whether these general requirements impose on lawyers an obligation not to misrepresent or conceal information in
negotiations. The orthodoxy in many provinces is that the usual degree of
deception involved in negotiations is not altered by having lawyers involved.

This may seem surprising, but there are several reasons supporting a lack
of more aggressive regulation of lawyer negotiation. One is the need to respect the lawyer's obligation to promote the interests of his or her client. The
lawyer is acting for the client, trying to achieve the most favourable result,
rather than acting with a view to the interests of both sides and the most reasonable bargain. A second reason is that if lawyers are more restricted in their
negotiation tactics, clients will be tempted to forego the use of lawyers and
either conduct the negotiations themselves or hire other professionals. Third,
concerns about misrepresentations and non-disclosure are already covered by,
and better left to, other areas of law such as the torts of deceit and misrepresentation and the doctrine of mistake in contract. Finally, even if these other
reasons could be overcome, drafting a rule about what is and is not permissible in negotiations would be a difficult exercise and it would be hard to
achieve consensus among lawyers.[11]

Proponents of greater regulation reject each of these reasons. They argue
it is too simplistic to fall back on the lawyer's fundamental duties to his or her
own client's interests. The modern regulation of lawyers involves many areas
in which those duties have to be balanced against duties to the court, the fairness of the process and the public interest. There are no compelling reasons
why a similar balancing could not happen in the context of negotiations.
There is no evidence that clients would either choose to negotiate themselves
or hire other professionals to avoid any restrictions on what lawyers could say
or do. Other areas of law at best only cover some of the conduct in negotiations which is seen as problematic, and are impractical as remedies in many
cases given the difficulties of litigating such claims through to a successful
conclusion. As to whether a workable rule about negotiation can be drafted,
the examples in the material below will allow you to judge that for yourself.

Accordingly, there is scope for a considerable debate about whether, and
to what extent, lawyers should be regulated in their conduct in negotiations.

---

[11] See Gavin MacKenzie, *Lawyers and Ethics: Professional Responsibility and Discipline*, 5th
ed. (Toronto: Carswell, 2009) at 15-1 to 15-2.

LAW SOCIETY OF NEWFOUNDLAND AND
LABRADOR v. REGULAR

[2005] N.J. No. 372, 252 Nfld. & P.E.I.R. 91
(N.L.C.A., C.K. Wells C.J.N.L., B.G. Welsh and M. Rowe JJ.A.)

[Robert Regular represented Petroleum Services Ltd. and Barrie James, who held 75 per cent of the shares of Petroleum Services Ltd. James Hughes represented Randy Spurrell, an individual who held 25 per cent of the shares of Petroleum Services Ltd. Mr. Regular and Mr. Hughes were in negotiations on behalf of their clients to ascertain the value of Mr. Spurrell's shares.]

B.G. WELSH J.A.:—

. . . . .

... Mr. Hughes wrote to Mr. Regular on December 12, 2000:

> Re: Petroleum Services Ltd.
>
> Further to the above, please be advised that we have heard that "Petroleum Services Ltd." is being sold.
>
> Rumour or not, please remind your client of Section 19 of their agreement and that Mr. Spurrell is a 25% shareholder and, even as a minority shareholder, should have input.

The letter did not request confirmation regarding the rumour. It was open to Mr. Regular simply to acknowledge receipt, and perhaps confirm that section 19 of their agreement had been drawn to his client's attention. However, Mr. Regular chose to respond on December 13, 2000, by telecopier transmittal:

> Re: Petroleum Services Ltd.
>
> Your Fax of Dec. 12/00
>
> Jim: I apologize for the delay in getting back to you. The "rumour" that Petroleum Services Ltd. is being sold is untrue. My client is committed to resolving the issues between your client and the co. (sic) As soon as I get a reply to your last correspondence I'll be back to you.

The Benchers [in the discipline proceedings below] noted that:

> [11] ... On December 14, 2000, by way of a notice of Directors dated December 12, 2000, filed by Regular as solicitor for [Petroleum Services Ltd.], Randy Spurrell was removed as a Director of [Petroleum Services Ltd.]. This was done without actual notice to Spurrell and without following the process for removal of directors set out in the Corporations Act. This was acknowledged by Regular in the hearing before the Adjudication Panel. The effective date of the removal of Spurrell as a Director pursuant to the notice of Directors was March 17, 2000. On the same date (Dec. 12/00), Regular filed a Notice with the Registry of Companies changing the registered office address of [Petroleum Services Ltd.], and Articles of Amendment changing the name of [Petroleum Services Ltd.] to Bar-Jam Holdings Limited.

This was followed, on December 19, 2000, by a sale of Petroleum Services Ltd. assets to Comstock Canada Ltd. Mr. Regular testified at the adjudication panel hearing that he was of the opinion that substantially all the assets of Petroleum Services Ltd. were not being sold. He said 50 to 60 percent of the assets were sold, while he considered 90 percent would constitute "all or substantially all the assets". However, Mr. Regular's position depended solely on a monetary calculation, without regard to the business as a going concern.

. . . . .

In a situation where less than all the assets of a company are sold, the distinction between a qualitative and a quantitative description of the sale is significant. A failure to specify which description is being relied upon is an open invitation to misunderstanding.

Accordingly, if Mr. Regular was relying on a quantitative assessment of the sale of the assets, in light of ... judicial authority which favours a qualitative analysis, it was necessary for him to identify that fact in his December 13th response to Mr. Hughes' letter. In the absence of such an explanation, it could be expected that Mr. Hughes would, in fact, be misled by Mr. Regular's blanket statement that the rumour that Petroleum Services Ltd. was being sold was untrue.

Indeed, a review of the evidence, applying a qualitative analysis to the sale of assets, leads inexorably to the conclusion that Petroleum Services Ltd. was being sold.

Commenting on this issue, the Benchers stated:

> [26] Without doubt a substantial portion of the assets of [Petroleum Services Ltd.] were disposed of, as indicated in the documentary evidence placed before the Adjudication Panel. They included contracts assigned, tools, equipment, office equipment and furniture, the company name and acronym, and the building from which [Petroleum Services Ltd.] had carried on business. While the real estate was leased rather than sold outright, we attach no particular significance to this — it was disposed of to Comstock [with an option to purchase at fair market value]. ... We agree with counsel for the Law Society that following the transaction with Comstock the company ([Petroleum Services Ltd.]) for practical purposes ceased to exist. ...

... I am satisfied that there was ample evidence to establish that substantially all the assets of Petroleum Services Ltd. were sold. Given the evidence, the members of the adjudication panel could reasonably have concluded, as two of the three members specifically did, that substantially all the assets of Petroleum Services Ltd. were sold.

. . . . .

... The question, then, is why did Mr. Regular respond with such absolute clarity that: "The 'rumour' that Petroleum Services Ltd. is being sold is untrue"? The answer to this question must be considered within the framework of all the evidence, including: the instructions from Mr. Regular's client that Mr. Hughes was not to be told about the sale of assets to Comstock in case

Mr. Hughes' client would somehow interfere with the sale; the steps taken by Mr. Regular, coincidental to the time of the sale, to retroactively, and without notice, remove Mr. Hughes' client as a director of the company; confirmation by Mr. Regular to the solicitor for Comstock, on closing the sale, that Mr. Hughes' client was not a shareholder of Petroleum Services Ltd.; the recital in the Escrow Agreement, one of the documents closing the sale, signed by Mr. Regular, stating, "AND WHEREAS the Assets and Contracts comprise all or a significant portion of the assets of [Petroleum Services Ltd.]"; and the inclusion of a "non-competition" clause as part of the sale agreement.

Considering this evidence as a whole, the inescapable inference is that Mr. Regular's response to Mr. Hughes' letter was deliberately intended to mislead Mr. Hughes. It is in this sense that the Benchers concluded that it was not critical to deciding the complaint to establish that substantially all the assets of Petroleum Services Ltd. were sold. The evidence supports the conclusion that Mr. Regular's response was calculated to deceive and to conceal the sale of the assets. On this basis it follows that Mr. Regular failed to act with integrity, failed in his responsibility to an individual lawyer, James D. Hughes, and failed to avoid questionable conduct.

· · · · ·

NOTES AND QUESTIONS

1. How would Mr. Regular's conduct be analyzed under the rules of professional conduct of your jurisdiction?

2. Does this decision undermine Mr. Regular's obligations of confidentiality and loyalty to his clients?

3. Mr. Regular and Mr. Hughes were in negotiations about the value of Mr. Hughes' client's shares in the company. Can you make an argument that Mr. Regular's December 13 statement did not relate to the value of the shares? If it did not, is this a case about ethics in negotiations? If it is not, why was Mr. Regular disciplined?

4. How strongly does this case support the argument that law societies do not need to specifically regulate lawyer negotiation, and can instead rely on more general provisions? Consider also The Advocates' Society, "Principles of Civility for Advocates" which provides that "counsel shall always be honest and truthful with opposing counsel".[12]

5. It is well accepted that settlements of disputes are to be encouraged and represent a better outcome than would be produced through litigation or arbitration. To what extent does this view depend on appropriate regulation of negotiation by lawyers?

6. Even if not considered to be unethical, deceptive or misleading conduct during a negotiation may increase the risk that a settlement will be legally invalid. See, for

---

[12]   Available online: <http://www.advocates.ca/assets/files/pdf/publications/principles-of-civility.pdf>.

example, *Spaulding v. Zimmerman*,[13] excerpted in Chapter 1. Does this change your analysis with respect to Question 2 above?

LAW SOCIETY OF ALBERTA

Code of Conduct, Chapter 6

6.02(2) A lawyer must not lie to or mislead another lawyer.

Commentary

This rule expresses an obvious aspect of integrity and a fundamental principle. In no situation, including negotiation, is a lawyer entitled to deliberately mislead a colleague. When a lawyer (in response to a question, for example) is prevented by rules of confidentiality from actively disclosing the truth, a falsehood is not justified. The lawyer has other alternatives, such as declining to answer. If this approach would in itself be misleading, the lawyer must seek the client's consent to such disclosure of confidential information as is necessary to prevent the other lawyer from being misled. The concept of "misleading" includes creating a misconception through oral or written statements, other communications, actions or conduct, failure to act, or silence (See Rule 6.02(5), Correcting Misinformation).

. . . . .

6.02(5) If a lawyer becomes aware during the course of a representation that:

(a) the lawyer has inadvertently misled an opposing party, or

(b) the client, or someone allied with the client or the client's matter, has misled an opposing party, intentionally or otherwise, or

(c) the lawyer or the client, or someone allied with the client or the client's matter, has made a material representation to an opposing party that was accurate when made but has since become inaccurate,

then, subject to confidentiality, the lawyer must immediately correct the resulting misapprehension on the part of the opposing party.

Commentary

"Subject to confidentiality" (see Rule 2.03, Confidentiality)

Briefly, if correction of the misrepresentation requires disclosure of confidential information, the lawyer must seek the client's consent to such disclosure. If the client withholds consent, the lawyer is obliged to withdraw. The terminology used in this rule is to be broadly interpreted. A lawyer may have provided technically accurate information that is rendered misleading by the withholding of other information; in such a case, there is an obligation to correct the situation. In paragraph (c), the concept of an inaccurate representation is not limited to a misrepresentation that would be actionable at law.

---

[13]   263 Minn. 346 (1962).

. . . . .

NOTES AND QUESTIONS

1. To what extent do these rules impose different obligations from the rules of your province on lawyers as negotiators? Reflecting on the debate, outlined earlier, about the appropriateness of such regulation, do you prefer the Alberta rules, the rule in your province or an alternative rule? Are you concerned that the *Model Code* does not explicitly address the obligation to be truthful in negotiations?

2. Do the Alberta rules make negotiation conducted by Alberta lawyers different from that conducted by other Canadian lawyers? What are the consequences of requiring lawyers not to lie? Are there potential problems if an Alberta lawyer enters into negotiations with a lawyer from another jurisdiction in which lawyers are not prohibited from lying in negotiations? In such a case would a client in Alberta be better off with no lawyer at all?

3. Prior to November 2011, the Alberta rules addressed negotiations even more explicitly in a chapter entitled "The Lawyer as Negotiator". The predecessor of Rule 6.02(2) stated that "[a] lawyer must not lie to or mislead an opposing party". Why has Alberta changed this provision? The commentary to the earlier rule contained some quite detailed statements about negotiating, including the following: "The process of negotiation often involves representations as to the extent of a lawyer's authority. For example, a client may authorize a lawyer to settle an action for no more than $100,000.00. The lawyer may not pretend a lack of authority to offer more than $50,000.00 or $75,000.00 or any other amount under $100,000.00. In response to a direct question about the monetary limits of the lawyer's authority, the alternatives of the lawyer are to respond truthfully or simply decline to answer. The lawyer is not entitled to offer a response intended or likely to create a misleading impression, which would be tantamount to lying." Does removing this language in any way change the lawyer's obligations?

4. Negotiation is employed to attempt to resolve a very wide range of disputes. Should the same ethical standards for negotiation apply in all contexts? As a lawyer for the government, are there important differences between negotiating with a minority rights group and negotiating with terrorists? See James J. White, "Machiavelli and the Bar: Ethical Limitations on Lying in Negotiation" [1980] Am. B. Found. Res. J. 926 at 927. Does the Alberta rule address this issue?

5. Is it unethical for a lawyer in negotiations to represent his or her client's legal position as being stronger than he or she knows it to be? Could a lawyer claim his or her client's position "has recently been confirmed by the Court of Appeal" without mentioning that the case was then reversed on appeal to the Supreme Court of Canada?

6. How context-sensitive should any obligations to be truthful be? Should they depend on the client? The client on the other side of the negotiations? The community of lawyers both negotiators are from? Whether the negotiations are proceeding on an "integrative" (cooperative) or a "distributive" (win-lose/competitive) basis? For an interesting discussion of the circumstantial reasons that might be offered for lying in negotiation, see Gerald B. Wetlaufer, "The Ethics of Lying in Negotiations" (1990) 75 Iowa L. Rev. 1219.

AMERICAN BAR ASSOCIATION

Model Rules of Professional Conduct, Rule 4.1,
"Transactions with Persons Other Than Clients"

Rule 4.1 Truthfulness In Statements To Others

In the course of representing a client a lawyer shall not knowingly:

(a) make a false statement of material fact or law to a third person; ...

[2] This Rule refers to statements of fact. Whether a particular statement should be regarded as one of fact can depend on the circumstances. Under generally accepted conventions in negotiation, certain types of statements ordinarily are not taken as statements of material fact. Estimates of price or value placed on the subject of a transaction and a party's intentions as to an acceptable settlement of a claim are ordinarily in this category, and so is the existence of an undisclosed principal except where nondisclosure of the principal would constitute fraud. Lawyers should be mindful of their obligations under applicable law to avoid criminal and tortious misrepresentation.

NOTES AND QUESTIONS

1. How high is the threshold under this rule? See American Bar Association Formal Opinion 06-439. What is the difference between a false statement of a material fact and the torts of deceit and fraudulent misrepresentation? Is this rule imposing a higher standard on lawyers than on other people? See E. Cliff Martin & T. Karena Dees, "The Truth about Truthfulness: The Proposed Commentary to Rule 4.1 of the Model Rules of Professional Conduct" (2002) 15 Geo. J. Legal Ethics 777.

2. To what extent does the commentary to this rule sanction misrepresentation in negotiations?

3. In *Virzi v. Grand Trunk Warehouse and Cold Storage Co.*,[14] the court stated, somewhat generally, that "The handling of a lawsuit and its progress is not a game. There is an absolute duty of candour and fairness on the part of counsel to both the Court and opposing counsel." Is this duty reflected in the *Model Rules*? Is it reflected in the rules in your province? Should it be? See John A. Humbach, "Shifting Paradigms of Lawyer Honesty" (2009) 76 Tenn. L. Rev. 993.

4. Is it immoral for a lawyer to make false statements during negotiations? Does it indicate a lack of respect for the person to whom the statements are made? What impact could this have on the lawyer's reputation?

5. It has been argued that requiring lawyers to be truthful in negotiations reduces the transaction costs of the negotiation process. Do you agree with this argument? See Geoffrey C. Hazard, Jr., "The Lawyer's Obligation to be Trustworthy when Dealing with Opposing Parties" (1981) 33 S.C.L. Rev. 181 at 183.

---

[14] 571 F. Supp. 507 at 512 (E.D. Mich. 1983).

6.   In *Fire Insurance Exchange v. Bell*[15] the lawyers for the defendant insurer offered
     to pay the plaintiff the full amount available under the policy, which they said
     was $100,000. This was incorrect: the policy covered losses up to $300,000. The
     plaintiff accepted the offer, even though he had suffered losses of more than
     $100,000. It was open to the plaintiff to obtain a copy of the policy and determine
     its limits for himself. Did the defendant's lawyers violate the ethical rules of: (a)
     Alberta; (b) the American Bar Association; or (c) your province? See also *In re
     McGrath.*[16]

7.   Is it ethically acceptable for a lawyer to raise a series of demands about issues
     which the client does not really care about, so that concessions can be made later
     which make the client look reasonable?

8.   There are different styles of being a negotiator. To what extent do the rules of
     professional conduct bear on negotiation style? Can a lawyer, as a tactical deci-
     sion, choose to be brusque and aggressive? See, for example, the Law Society of
     Upper Canada's Rule 6.03(1) which provides that "[a] lawyer shall be courteous,
     civil, and act in good faith with all persons with whom the lawyer has dealings in
     the course of his or her practice".

9.   Lawyers need to appreciate that they need to be concerned with more than just
     how the ethical rules impact their own conduct in negotiations. They also need to
     be concerned with the conduct of the lawyer with whom they are negotiating. A
     lawyer who chooses to always tell the truth may be less likely to violate the ethi-
     cal rules. However, depending on what the rules allow, he or she is vulnerable to
     being deceived by a less truthful lawyer, and so must be on guard to protect his or
     her client. One way to do this is by insisting that the other party confirm, in writ-
     ing, the material facts underlying the settlement and by making the settlement
     conditional on the truth of those facts.

3.   Other Issues in Negotiations

Most of a lawyer's general professional obligations apply equally in a negotiation context, such as the duties to avoid conflict of interest and to preserve
confidentiality. But there are some such obligations that specifically refer to
or concern negotiation. For example, most provincial rules of professional
conduct expressly require lawyers to work towards achieving a settlement of a
dispute. Since this will most likely be attempted through negotiation, these
rules are in a sense compelling lawyers to engage in negotiation in certain
circumstances. See, for example, the *Model Code*'s Rule 2.02(4), which states
that "a lawyer must advise and encourage a client to compromise or settle a
dispute whenever it is possible to do so on a reasonable basis". The rules may
also require that lawyers must have their client's instructions before proposing
any settlement. In their provisions on tasks which may not be delegated by
lawyers to non-lawyers or which can only be so delegated with the client's
consent, some provinces include negotiations: see, for example, the *Model
Code*'s Rule 5.01(3)(i). See also the Law Society of Upper Canada's By-Law
7.1, *Operational Obligations and Responsibilities*, sections 5(2) and 6(1)(c).

[15]   643 N.E.2d 310 (Ind. 1994).
[16]   96 A.D.2d 267 (N.Y. App. Div. 1983).

Finally, lawyers are typically restricted in the use they can make, in negotiations, of threats of starting or stopping criminal or quasi-criminal proceedings: see, for example, the *Model Code*'s Rule 2.02(5) and the Law Society of Alberta's Chapter 10, Rule 4.

Scenario Three

Lisa acts for the defendant in litigation. The defendant tells her that it wants to settle and will pay up to $250,000 to do so. The plaintiff's lawyer tells Lisa that he thinks his client would settle for $200,000 and asks Lisa whether the defendant is willing to pay that amount. This is the first time the plaintiff's lawyer has mentioned a specific settlement amount. Could Lisa ethically reply that: (a) her client would not pay that amount; (b) her client would not pay more than $150,000; or (c) she has no instructions on this issue from her client?

Scenario Four

You are defending a client charged with impaired driving. There is no evidence of your client's blood alcohol level. Since being arrested, your client has insisted, to the police and others, that he had had nothing to drink but he tells you that he had two large drinks immediately before driving. In attempting to negotiate the withdrawal of the charges, can your position with the Crown be that: (a) your client had nothing to drink; (b) he was not impaired; or (c) there is no evidence that he was impaired?

Scenario Five

You act for the plaintiff in personal injury litigation. The plaintiff's injuries are very severe. You are quite close to negotiating a substantial settlement with the defendant's lawyers, and then the plaintiff dies. The plaintiff has provided you with instructions to accept any offer of $6 million or more. Three days later the defendant's lawyer offers $6 million. Can you accept? Do you have any obligation to tell the defendant's lawyer that your client has died? Would it change your answer if instead of dying the plaintiff made a sudden and dramatic recovery?

D.   FURTHER READING

Counselling

American Law Institute, *Restatement of the Law Third: The Law Governing Lawyers* (St. Paul, MN: American Law Institute, 2000), para. 94.

Binder, David A., *et al.*, *Lawyers as Counselors: A Client-Centered Approach*, 2nd ed. (St. Paul, MN: West Publishing, 2004).

Bubany, Charles P., "Counseling Clients to Do the Right Thing in Child Custody Cases" (1996) 16 Child. Legal Rts. J. 22.

Hazard, Geoffrey C., Jr., "Lawyers and Client Fraud: They Still Don't Get It" (1993) 6 Geo. J. Legal Ethics 701.

Langevoort, Donald C. & Robert Rasmussen, "Skewing the Results: The Role of Lawyers in Transmitting Legal Rules" (1997) 5 S. Cal. Interdisciplinary L.J. 375.

Lerman, Lisa G., "Lying to Clients" (1990) 138 U. Pa. L. Rev. 659.

Luban, David, "Paternalism and the Legal Profession" [1981] Wis. L. Rev. 454.

MacKenzie, Gavin, *Lawyers and Ethics: Professional Responsibility and Discipline*, 5th ed. (Toronto: Carswell, 2009), ch. 14.

Newman, Joel S., "Legal Advice Towards Illegal Ends" (1994) 28 U. Rich. L. Rev. 287.

Pepper, Stephen L., "Counseling at the Limits of the Law: An Exercise in the Jurisprudence and Ethics of Lawyering" (1995) 104 Yale L.J. 1545.

Uviller, Richard, "The Lawyer as Liar" (1994) 13(2) Crim. Justice Ethics 2.

Woolley, Alice, *Understanding Lawyers' Ethics in Canada* (Markham, ON: LexisNexis Canada, 2011), 61-63.

Negotiation

Benson, Marjorie L., *The Skills and Ethics of Negotiation: Wisdom and Reflections of Western Canadian Civil Practitioners* (Saskatoon: College of Law, University of Saskatchewan, 2007).

Boon, Andrew & Jennifer Levin, *The Ethics and Conduct of Lawyers in England and Wales*, 2d ed. (Oxford: Hart Publishing, 2008), 376-86.

Cohen, Jonathan R., "When People are the Means: Negotiating with Respect" (2001) 14 Geo. J. Legal Ethics 739.

Craver, Charles B., "Negotiation Ethics: How to be Deceptive Without Being Dishonest/How to be Assertive Without Being Offensive" (1997) 38 S. Texas L. Rev. 713.

Hanycz, Colleen M., Trevor C.W. Farrow & Frederick H. Zemans, *The Theory and Practice of Representative Negotiation* (Toronto: Emond Montgomery, 2008), ch. 5.

Hazard, Geoffrey C., Jr., "The Lawyer's Obligation to be Trustworthy when Dealing with Opposing Parties" (1981) 33 S.C.L.R. 181.

Holmes, Eleanor Norton, "Bargaining and the Ethic of Process" (1989) 64 N.Y.U.L. Rev. 493.

Humbach, John A., "Shifting Paradigms of Lawyer Honesty" (2009) 76 Tenn. L. Rev. 993.

Jarvis, Peter R. & Bradley F. Tellam, "A Negotiation Ethics Primer for Lawyers" (1996) 31 Gonz. L. Rev. 549.

Longan, Patrick Emery, "Ethics in Settlement Negotiations: Foreword" (2001) 52 Mercer L. Rev. 807.

Lowenthal, Gary Tobias, "The Bar's Failure to Require Truthful Bargaining by Lawyers" (1988) 2 Geo. J. Legal Ethics 411.

Macfarlane, Julie, *et al.*, *Dispute Resolution: Readings and Case Studies*, 3rd ed. (Toronto: Emond Montgomery, 2011), 232-50.

MacKenzie, Gavin, *Lawyers and Ethics: Professional Responsibility and Discipline*, 5th ed. (Toronto: Carswell, 2009), ch. 15.

Martin, E. Cliff & T. Karena Dees, "The Truth about Truthfulness: The Proposed Commentary to Rule 4.1 of the Model Rules of Professional Conduct" (2002) 15 Geo. J. Legal Ethics 777.

Rubin, Alvin B., "A Causerie on Lawyers' Ethics in Negotiation" (1975) 35 La. L. Rev. 577.

Wetlaufer, Gerald B., "The Ethics of Lying in Negotiations" (1990) 75 Iowa L. Rev. 1219.

White, James J., "Machiavelli and the Bar: Ethical Limitations on Lying in Negotiation" [1980] Am. B. Found. Res. J. 926.

CHAPTER 8

ETHICS AND CRIMINAL LAW PRACTICE

A. INTRODUCTION: COUNSEL'S DUAL ROLE IN THE ADVERSARY SYSTEM

The criminal law is executed, almost exclusively, through the medium of courtroom trials. The form of trial adopted in this country is the adversary system where the case is presented to the trier by two opposing parties, each entitled to be represented by counsel.

Given this context, it is not surprising that the most important ethical duties and dilemmas in the criminal law can all be traced back to the roles that Crown counsel and defence counsel are expected to play in the adversarial system of trial. The simplistic view is that the Crown is not entitled to take a purely adversarial position, but must act as a quasi-judicial minister of justice, whereas defence counsel is entitled to take a purely adversarial approach. Thus, in the case of *R. v. Boucher*[1] Rand J. famously stated that the role of Crown counsel "excludes any notion of winning or losing", and in *R. v. Stinchcombe*[2] Sopinka J. stated that the "defence has no obligation to assist the prosecution and is entitled to assume a purely adversarial role towards the prosecution".

Although the above pronouncements are often cited as authoritative they, in fact, present only a partial picture. The modern reality of counsel's role in a criminal trial and the accompanying ethical duties is far more complex. On the Crown side, there is no longer any question that prosecuting counsel is entitled to take an adversarial position by advocating forcefully for a conviction, assuming that is a legitimate result on the evidence. As L'Heureux-Dubé J. put it in *R. v. Cook*,[3] "Nor should it be assumed that the Crown cannot act as a strong advocate within this adversarial process. In that regard, it is both permissible and desirable that it vigorously pursue a legitimate result to the best of its ability." In *R. v. Rose*,[4] Binnie J. explicitly stated that "while Crown counsel are expected to be ethical, they are also expected to be adversarial".

By the same token, it is an overstatement to say that defence counsel's role is "*purely* adversarial". In *Stinchcombe*, Sopinka J. noted "the obligation

---

[1] [1954] S.C.J. No. 54, [1955] S.C.R. 16 at 24 (S.C.C.).
[2] [1991] S.C.J. No. 83, 68 C.C.C. (3d) 1 at 7 (S.C.C.).
[3] [1997] S.C.J. No. 22, 114 C.C.C. (3d) 481 at 489 (S.C.C.).
[4] [1998] S.C.J. No. 81, 129 C.C.C. (3d) 449 at 463 (S.C.C.).

on defence counsel as officers of the court to act responsibly" and, in *Rondel v. Worsley*,[5] Lord Reid emphasized defence counsel's "overriding duty to the court, to the standards of the profession, and to the public, which may and often does lead to a conflict with his client's wishes or with what the client thinks are his personal interests".

Thus, both Crown counsel and defence counsel in fact have "dual roles" in the criminal trial. The Crown is expected to be fair, objective and dispassionate in presenting the case for the Crown but is also expected to argue forcefully for a legitimate result (which will often be a conviction). The defence is expected to vigorously represent the interests of the accused but is also expected to remain independent of the client and to be mindful of various overriding duties to the court.

In short, the proper ethical roles of Crown counsel and defence counsel in our adversarial system are complex and nuanced. Counsel on both sides must carefully hold in balance their duties to the side of the dispute that they represent as well as their competing duties to the ideals of the overall justice system.

Leading academic commentators on legal ethics have described the lawyer's purely adversarial role on behalf of the client as "neutral partisanship". The lawyer's competing role as an officer of the court or minister of justice dedicated to ideals such as truth, justice and fairness, is often referred to as "moral activism". Neither of these theoretical models for legal ethics is entirely satisfactory in the criminal law context, if they are seen as mutually exclusive. Counsel in a criminal case must be both a "neutral partisan" and a "moral activist".

In the text that follows, we will explore the most important ethical duties of Crown counsel, of "officers of the Court" (which includes both Crown and defence) and of defence counsel. As you read about each of these duties, reflect back on the "dual role" of counsel and try to situate the particular rule that emerges on the continuum between counsel's adversarial duties to the party that he or she represents and counsel's overriding duties to the court and to the ideals of the justice system. Ask yourself whether the rule favours counsel's adversarial role or whether it favours counsel's duties to the court and ask whether it strikes the right balance.

B. ETHICAL DUTIES OF CROWN COUNSEL

As noted above, Crown counsel conducts the prosecution in a criminal case and is subject to conflicting obligations that must be held in balance, namely, the duty to advocate and work hard to achieve a conviction where warranted, and the duty to be fair and objective towards the accused. In their leading text on the subject, *Ethics and Canadian Criminal Law*,[6] Proulx and Layton ex-

---

[5] [1967] 3 All E.R. 993 at 998 (H.L.).
[6] Michel Proulx & David Layton, *Ethics and Canadian Criminal Law* (Toronto: Irwin Law, 2001) at 641-44.

plain how this balancing of competing duties requires personal courage and strength of character, as well as institutional independence:

> Another aspect of the prosecutor's role as "minister of justice" that deserves special emphasis is the need for independence. Though accountable to Parliament and the courts, the attorney general and his or her agents are permitted liberal discretion in making decisions affecting the prosecution of criminal cases, and they must be secure from political or social pressures. A guarantee of independence encourages courageous decisions where needed and thus works to safeguard the public interest. Indeed, the principle of independence in the exercise of the prosecution function is an important constitutional convention that infuses the office of attorney general.

> Certainly, the prosecutor must consider public needs and community concerns in reaching a decision as to the best course of action to take in any given circumstance. But, in some matters, the prosecutor's duty clearly lies in the defiance of community pressures, though always within the confines of the law. As one commentator has noted, the only mind the prosecutor must make up is his or her own. In *R. v. Curragh Inc.*, McLachlin and Major JJ., in their dissenting opinion, remind us that since the Crown is charged with the broad duty to ensure that every accused person is treated fairly, it is "especially in high profile cases, where the justice system will be on display, that counsel must do their utmost to ensure that any resultant convictions are based on facts and not on emotions. When the Crown allows its actions to be influenced by public pressure the essential fairness and legitimacy of our system is lost."

> . . . . .

> In summary, the prosecutor's linchpin duty is to seek justice in the public interest, which encapsulates several related principles:

> 1. A prosecutor can seek a conviction but must all the while strive to ensure that the defendant has a fair trial.

> 2. The prosecutor's goal is not to obtain a conviction at any cost but to assist the court in eliciting truth without infringing upon the legitimate rights of the accused.

> 3. At each stage of the criminal justice process, the discretion vested in the prosecutor should be exercised with objectivity and impartiality, and not in a purely partisan way.

When examining the three specific prosecutorial duties discussed below, consider the extent to which their proper execution depends upon Crown counsel's personal courage, institutional independence and fidelity to the justice system.

1. Full Disclosure

Undoubtedly the most important ethical obligation that rests with Crown counsel is the duty to make full disclosure to the defence of all relevant information in the Crown's possession.

Historically, professional conduct rules qualified this duty. For example, the 1974 CBA *Code of Professional Conduct*, which was typical at the time, stated:

> ... *to the extent required by law and accepted practice*, [Crown counsel] should make timely disclosure to the accused or his counsel ... of all relevant facts and witnesses known to him, whether tending towards guilt or innocence. [emphasis added]

In light of the above formulation, the ethical duty to disclose relevant information was a malleable one that depended on the state of current case law and local practice. The case law generally was to the effect that disclosure at the pre-trial stage was entirely within the Crown's discretion and that an adjournment at trial would remedy any prejudice caused by non-disclosure.[7] At trial, the discretion passed to the judge to order disclosure upon application by the defence, but only if it was essential to the fairness of the trial.[8] In the result, there was no positive legal duty on the Crown to make pre-trial disclosure to the defence and practices varied enormously from one jurisdiction to the next and from one individual prosecutor to the next.[9]

The turning point came in 1989 when three senior judges reported, after a lengthy public inquiry, that the most significant cause of Donald Marshall, Jr.'s wrongful conviction for murder in Nova Scotia in 1971 was the failure of the Crown to make full disclosure to the defence. The Crown and the police had been in possession of significant exculpatory evidence that would likely have led to Marshall's acquittal, had defence counsel and the jury been apprised of it. The Marshall Commission recommended that Parliament enact a statutory code of procedure, requiring full disclosure at the pre-trial stage.[10] After two years of inaction by Parliament, the Supreme Court of Canada seized hold of the issue in 1991 in the seminal case of *Stinchcombe*. That case fundamentally changed the law and gave rise to the modern ethical and constitutional duty to make full disclosure.

---

[7]   *R. v. Caccamo*, [1975] S.C.J. No. 58, 21 C.C.C. (2d) 257 at 275-76 (S.C.C.); *Cunliffe v. Law Society of British Columbia*, [1984] B.C.J. No. 1514, 13 C.C.C. (3d) 560 at 571 (B.C.C.A.).

[8]   *R. v. Savion*, [1980] O.J. No. 580, 52 C.C.C. (2d) 276 (Ont. C.A.); *R. v. Bourget*, [1987] S.J. No. 14, 35 C.C.C. (3d) 371 (Sask. C.A.).

[9]   Law Reform Commission of Canada, "Disclosure by the Prosecution" (Report 22, 1984).

[10] Province of Nova Scotia, *Royal Commission on the Donald Marshall Jr. Prosecution*, Vol. 1 (1989) at 68-79 and 238-44 (the "Marshall Report").

R. v. STINCHCOMBE

[1991] S.C.J. No. 83, 68 C.C.C. (3d) 1
(S.C.C., La Forest, L'Heureux-Dubé, Sopinka, Gonthier,
Cory, McLachlin and Iacobucci JJ.)

[The accused was a Calgary lawyer charged with criminal breach of trust. It was alleged that he misappropriated trust funds deposited by one Abrams. The defence was that the accused and Abrams were partners in a business venture and, accordingly, there was no misappropriation. The Crown called the accused's former secretary, one Lineham, at the preliminary inquiry and she gave evidence favourable to the defence. The police subsequently interviewed Lineham, on two occasions, and took two statements from her. The Crown advised the defence of the fact of the two statements but refused to disclose their contents. At trial, the Crown took the position that Lineham was not credible and decided not to call her as a witness. The defence sought production of her two statements. The trial judge refused to order production and the defence decided, in the result, not to call Lineham. The accused was convicted and appealed unsuccessfully to the Alberta Court of Appeal. A further appeal was brought to the Supreme Court of Canada.

Five policy arguments were advanced by the Crown in support of the position that disclosure is not a legal right or duty but should be left to the discretion of the Crown, as follows: first, that there is value in taking an opponent's witnesses by surprise in cross-examination under our adversarial system of justice; second, the absence of reciprocal disclosure from the defence to the Crown means that "one way" disclosure unfairly skews the system; third, delays and inefficiencies will result from introducing this new procedural right at the pre-trial stage; fourth, there is a danger that defence witnesses will tailor their evidence to conform to the disclosure; and fifth, there is a danger that witnesses will be threatened or killed in certain cases if their evidence is disclosed prior to trial. The Court accepted only the last of these five arguments and held that it justified delaying disclosure, until vulnerable witnesses are safe, but did not justify completely denying disclosure. The Court then enunciated the new approach to disclosure.]

SOPINKA J.:—

. . . . .

This review of the pros and cons with respect to disclosure by the Crown shows that there is no valid practical reason to support the position of the opponents of a broad duty of disclosure. Apart from the practical advantages to which I have referred, there is the overriding concern that failure to disclose impedes the ability of the accused to make full answer and defence. This common law right has acquired new vigour by virtue of its inclusion in s. 7 of the *Canadian Charter of Rights and Freedoms* as one of the principles of fundamental justice. ... The right to make full answer and defence is one of the pillars of criminal justice on which we heavily depend to ensure that the innocent are not convicted. Recent events have demonstrated that the erosion of this right due to non-disclosure was an important factor in the conviction and incarceration of an innocent person. In the Royal Commission on the Donald Marshall, Jr., Prosecution ... the Commissioners found that prior inconsistent statements were not disclosed to the defence. This was an important contributing factor in the miscarriage of justice which occurred and led the commission to state that "anything less than complete disclosure by the Crown falls short of decency and fair play" ...

. . . . .

In my opinion, there is a wholly natural evolution of the law in favour of disclosure by the Crown of all relevant material. As long ago as 1951, Cartwright J. stated in *Lemay v. The King*, [1952] 1 S.C.R. 232, at p. 257:

> I wish to make it perfectly clear that I do not intend to say anything which might be regarded as lessening *the duty which rests upon counsel for the Crown to bring forward evidence of every material fact known to the prosecution whether favourable to the accused or otherwise* ... [emphasis of Sopinka J.]

This statement may have been in reference to the obligation resting on counsel for the Crown to call evidence rather than to disclose the material to the defence, but I see no reason why this obligation should not be discharged by disclosing the material to the defence rather than obliging the Crown to make it part of the Crown's case. Indeed, some of the information will be in a form that cannot be put in evidence by the Crown but can be used by the defence in cross-examination or otherwise. Production to the defence is then the only way in which the injunction of Cartwright J. can be obeyed.

In *R. v. C. (M.H.)* (1988), 46 C.C.C. (3d) 142 (B.C.C.A.), ... McEachern C.J.B.C. [dissenting] after a review of the authorities stated what I respectfully accept as a correct statement of the law. He said that: "there is a general duty on the part of the Crown to disclose all material it proposes to use at trial and especially all evidence which may assist the accused even if the Crown does not propose to adduce it". This passage was cited with approval by McLachlin J. in her reasons on behalf of the Court [*R. v. C. (M.H.)*, [1991] 1 S.C.R. 763]. She went on to add: "This court has previously stated that the Crown is under a duty at common law to disclose to the defence all material evidence whether favourable to the accused or not" (p. 774).

As indicated earlier, however, this obligation to disclose is not absolute. It is subject to the discretion of counsel for the Crown. This discretion extends both to the withholding of information and to the timing of disclosure. For example, counsel for the Crown has a duty to respect the rules of privilege. In the case of informers the Crown has a duty to protect their identity. In some cases serious prejudice or even harm may result to a person who has supplied evidence or information to the investigation. While it is a harsh reality of justice that ultimately any person with relevant evidence must appear to testify, the discretion extends to the timing and manner of disclosure in such circumstances. A discretion must also be exercised with respect to the relevance of information. While the Crown must err on the side of inclusion, it need not produce what is clearly irrelevant. The experience to be gained from the civil side of the practice is that counsel, as officers of the court and acting responsibly, can be relied upon not to withhold pertinent information. Transgressions with respect to this duty constitute a very serious breach of legal ethics. The initial obligation to separate "the wheat from the chaff" must, therefore, rest with Crown counsel. There may also be situations in which early disclosure may impede completion of an investigation. Delayed disclosure on this account is not to be encouraged and should be rare. Completion of the investigation before proceeding with the prosecution of a charge or charges is very much within the control of the Crown. Nevertheless, it is not always possible to predict events which may require an investigation to be re-opened and the Crown must have some discretion to delay disclosure in these circumstances.

The discretion of Crown counsel is, however, reviewable by the trial judge. Counsel for the defence can initiate a review when an issue arises with respect to the exercise of the Crown's discretion. On a review the Crown must justify its refusal to disclose. ...

[Appeal allowed.]

As Sopinka J. noted, a failure to make proper disclosure is "a very serious breach of legal ethics". The modern post-*Stinchcombe* ethical duty is, therefore, set out in the various provincial law societies' rules of professional conduct and in the Federation of Law Societies of Canada's *Model Code of Professional Conduct*. Rule 4.01(3) of the *Model Code* and the accompanying Commentary provide as follows:

> When acting as a prosecutor, a lawyer must act for the public and the administration of justice resolutely and honourably within the limits of the law ...

> **Commentary**

> When engaged as a prosecutor, the lawyer's primary duty is not to seek to convict but to see that justice is done through a fair trial on the merits. The prosecutor exercises a public function involving much discretion and power and must act fairly and dispassionately. The prosecutor should ... make timely disclosure to defence counsel or directly to an unrepresented accused of all relevant and known facts and witnesses, whether tending to show guilt or innocence.

In spite of the law societies and the Supreme Court of Canada having made it clear that the duty to disclose is an ethical obligation, most Attorneys General took the position that breaches of this duty were to be remedied through internal discipline within the prosecutor's own government department. It was argued, with some success, that the Attorney General and his or her agents (the Crown prosecutors) were immune from judicial and regulatory review when making discretionary decisions in the course of a criminal prosecution. Thus in *Hoem v. Law Society of British Columbia*,[11] the court held that decisions by the Crown to commence and continue a prosecution were immune from disciplinary review by the Law Society because of the constitutional convention concerning independence of the Attorney General. This issue of prosecutorial discretion and the independence of the Attorneys General reached the Supreme Court of Canada 10 years after *Stinchcombe* was decided.

KRIEGER v. LAW SOCIETY OF ALBERTA

[2002] S.C.J. No. 45, 168 C.C.C. (3d) 97
(S.C.C., McLachlin C.J.C., L'Heureux-Dubé, Gonthier, Iacobucci,
Major, Bastarache, Binnie, Arbour and LeBel JJ.)

[Krieger was Crown counsel in Alberta in a murder case that took place in 1994, that is, a few years after *Stinchcombe*. On May 20, approximately two weeks before the preliminary inquiry, Krieger learned that "there were preliminary results from the blood tests (from the crime scene) that implicated a different person and were accordingly favourable to the accused". Krieger did not disclose this information to defence counsel and, instead, told him in a telephone call on June 1 that "the results of DNA and biological testing conducted by the Crown of the blood found at the crime scene would not be available for the preliminary inquiry". On June 6, the preliminary inquiry commenced and defence counsel discovered the favourable preliminary results of the blood testing. Defence counsel complained to the Attorney General's office and the accused complained to the Law Society concerning Krieger's conduct. Krieger explained that he was simply delaying disclosure, presumably pursuant to the "discretion" recognized in *Stinchcombe*, while awaiting the final test results. The Attorney General's office reprimanded Krieger and removed him from the case, concluding that he had made an error in judgment. Krieger and the Attorney General then moved to stop the Law Society's processes on the basis that Krieger's exercise of prosecutorial discretion was immune from external disciplinary review. The Alberta Court at first instance upheld the jurisdiction of the Law Society but the Court of Appeal sided with Krieger and the Attorney General. The Law Society appealed to the Supreme Court of Canada.]

IACOBUCCI and MAJOR JJ.:—

. . . . .

It is a constitutional principle in this country that the Attorney General must act independently of partisan concerns when supervising prosecutorial decisions. ...

This side of the Attorney General's independence finds further form in the principle that courts will not interfere with his exercise of executive authority,

---

[11]   [1985] B.C.J. No. 2300, 20 C.C.C. (3d) 239 (B.C.C.A.).

as reflected in the prosecutorial decision-making process. In *R. v. Power* ... L'Heureux-Dubé J. said ...:

> It is manifest that, as a matter of principle and policy, courts should not interfere with prosecutorial discretion. This appears clearly to stem from the respect of separation of powers and the rule of law. Under the doctrine of separation of powers, criminal law is in the domain of the executive ...
>
> . . . . .
>
> In "Prosecutorial Discretion: A Reply to David Vanek" ... J. A. Ramsay expands on the rationale underlying judicial deference to prosecutorial discretion:
>
> . . . . .
>
>> It is fundamental to our system of justice that criminal proceedings be conducted in public before an independent and impartial tribunal. If the court is to review the prosecutor's exercise of his discretion the court becomes a supervising prosecutor. It ceases to be an independent tribunal. [emphasis of L'Heureux-Dubé J.]

The court's acknowledgement of the Attorney General's independence from judicial review in the sphere of prosecutorial discretion has its strongest source in the fundamental principle of the rule of law under our Constitution. Subject to the abuse of process doctrine, supervising one litigant's decision-making process — rather than the conduct of litigants before the court — is beyond the legitimate reach of the court. In *Re Hoem and Law Society of British Columbia* ..., Esson J.A. for the court observed ... that:

> The independence of the Attorney-General, in deciding fairly who should be prosecuted, is also a hallmark of a free society. Just as the independence of the bar within its proper sphere must be respected, so must the independence of the Attorney-General.

We agree with these comments. The quasi-judicial function of the Attorney General cannot be subjected to interference from parties who are not as competent to consider the various factors involved in making a decision to prosecute. To subject such decisions to political interference, or to judicial supervision, could erode the integrity of our system of prosecution. Clearly drawn constitutional lines are necessary in areas subject to such grave potential conflict.

. . . . .

To be a Crown prosecutor in Alberta, there are two requirements: (1) employment as such by the Attorney General's office and (2) membership in the Law Society of Alberta. To keep his or her job, a Crown prosecutor must perform to the standards of the employer, the Attorney General's office, and must remain in good standing by complying with the ethical requirements of the Law Society. All Alberta lawyers are subject to the rules of the Law Society — Crown prosecutors are no exception.

D. *Prosecutorial Discretion*

In making independent decisions on prosecutions, the Attorney General and his agents exercise what is known as prosecutorial discretion. This discretion is generally exercised directly by agents, the Crown attorneys, as it is uncommon for a single prosecution to attract the Attorney General's personal attention.

"Prosecutorial discretion" is a term of art. It does not simply refer to any discretionary decision made by a Crown prosecutor. Prosecutorial discretion refers to the use of those powers that constitute the core of the Attorney General's office and which are protected from the influence of improper political and other vitiating factors by the principle of independence.

. . . . .

As discussed above, these powers emanate from the office-holder's role as legal advisor of and officer to the Crown. In our theory of government, it is the sovereign who holds the power to prosecute his or her subjects. A decision of the Attorney General, or of his or her agents, within the authority delegated to him or her by the sovereign is not subject to interference by other arms of government. An exercise of prosecutorial discretion will, therefore, be treated with deference by the courts and by other members of the executive, as well as statutory bodies like provincial law societies.

Without being exhaustive, we believe the core elements of prosecutorial discretion encompass the following: (a) the discretion whether to bring the prosecution of a charge laid by police; (b) the discretion to enter a stay of proceedings in either a private or public prosecution, as codified in the *Criminal Code* ...; (c) the discretion to accept a guilty plea to a lesser charge; (d) the discretion to withdraw from criminal proceedings altogether ...; and (e) the discretion to take control of a private prosecution ... While there are other discretionary decisions, these are the core of the delegated sovereign authority peculiar to the office of the Attorney General.

Significantly, what is common to the various elements of prosecutorial discretion is that they involve the ultimate decisions as to *whether* a prosecution should be brought, continued or ceased, and *what* the prosecution ought to be for. Put differently, prosecutorial discretion refers to decisions regarding the nature and extent of the prosecution and the Attorney General's participation in it. Decisions that do not go to the nature and extent of the prosecution, *i.e.*, the decisions that govern a Crown prosecutor's tactics or conduct before the court, do not fall within the scope of prosecutorial discretion. Rather, such decisions are governed by the inherent jurisdiction of the court to control its own processes once the Attorney General has elected to enter into that forum.

. . . . .

Review by the Law Society for bad faith or improper purpose by a prosecutor does not constitute a review of the exercise of prosecutorial discretion *per se*, since an official action which is undertaken in bad faith or for improper motives is not within the scope of the powers of the Attorney General. As stated by McIntyre J. in his concurrence in *Nelles* ...: "public officers are entitled to no special immunities, or privileges when they act beyond the powers which are accorded to them by law in their official capacities". We agree with the observation of MacKenzie J. that "conduct amounting to bad faith or dishonesty is beyond the pale of prosecutorial discretion" ...

A finding that the Law Society does not have the jurisdiction to review or sanction conduct which arises out of the exercise of prosecutorial discretion would mean that prosecutors who act in bad faith or dishonestly could not be disciplined for such conduct. A prosecutor who laid charges as a result of bribery or racism or revenge could be discharged from his or her office but, in spite of such malfeasance, would be immune to review of that conduct by the Law Society.

. . . . .

G. *Crown Prosecutor's Failure to Disclose Relevant Exculpatory Evidence Not Within Prosecutorial Discretion*

In *Stinchcombe*, *supra*, the Court held that the Crown has an obligation to disclose all relevant information to the defence. While the Crown Attorney retains the discretion not to disclose irrelevant information, disclosure of relevant evidence is not, therefore, a matter of prosecutorial discretion but, rather, is a prosecutorial duty. Absent an explanation demonstrating that the Crown Attorney did not act dishonestly or in bad faith, it is settled law ... that "[t]ransgressions with respect to this duty constitute a very serious breach of legal ethics". This is reflected in para. (d) of the Rule which applies only to breaches of the duty to disclose which involve dishonesty or bad faith.

In this case, it would appear that the respondent Krieger failed to disclose all relevant information to the defence, but later offered an explanation. If true, the failure to disclose would constitute a violation of the duty expressed in *Stinchcombe*. The explanation would help to determine if the respondent Krieger had acted dishonestly or in bad faith. If so, this would be an ethical breach and would fall within the jurisdiction of the Law Society. The Law Society in the fulfillment of their duties will determine whether the respondent acted in conformity with the professional ethics of the Law Society of Alberta.

. . . . .

The Law Society's jurisdiction to review the respondent's failure to disclose relevant evidence to the defendant is limited to examining whether it was an ethical violation. As explained by M. Proulx and D. Layton in *Ethics and Canadian Criminal Law* ...:

> It is worth underlining that not every breach of the legal and constitutional duty to disclose constitutes a violation of an ethical duty. Non-disclosure can result, for instance, from mere inadvertence, a misunderstanding of the nature of the evidence, or even a questionable strategy adopted in good faith. These lapses may represent a denial of the accused's constitutional rights,

but an ethical violation often requires more. A finding of professional misconduct must be based on an act or omission revealing an intentional departure from the fundamental duty to act in fairness. Thus, a judicial determination that disclosure has wrongfully been withheld will not necessarily reveal a breach of ethics. Conversely, an egregious breach of ethics may in some cases have no appreciable effect on the fairness of the trial, when appropriate remedies can cure any harm suffered by the accused.

. . . . .

[Appeal allowed.]

NOTES AND QUESTIONS

1. Is the term "prosecutorial discretion" being used in two different senses in *Stinchcombe* and in *Krieger*? *Stinchcombe* expressly permits a Crown "discretion" to withhold disclosure in certain limited circumstances but makes it clear that the trial judge can review the correctness of the Crown's exercise of "discretion". *Krieger*, however, identifies certain "core elements of prosecutorial discretion" that are completely immune from judicial review, absent evidence of abuse. What distinguishes these two different kinds of Crown "discretion" in terms of the qualities of courage and independence identified by Proulx and Layton as being essential to ethical Crown conduct?

2. The Crown's modern disclosure obligation has become extremely burdensome and time-consuming, especially in large cases, because of the very broad *Stinchcombe* standard ("not ... clearly irrelevant"). Is it helpful or accurate to think of this duty to produce massive amounts of marginally relevant police investigative material as an "ethical" obligation? Or has it become more of a technical or administrative obligation, similar to the duty of a lawyer in a civil case to ensure the proper conduct of document discovery (as discussed in Chapter 6)?

3. Does the Crown fulfill its disclosure obligation by simply producing all the relevant material that is already within its possession or control? Or does the obligation include a duty to investigate the facts and discover new material which must then be disclosed? Consider the following scenario.

Scenario One

You are Crown counsel in an international drug trafficking case in which the accused raises a defence of entrapment. The key Crown witness on the entrapment hearing is a paid FBI agent, one Makdesion, who purchases cocaine from the accused and introduces him to undercover police officers. Various drug trafficking transactions are then consummated between the accused and the undercover officers. The entrapment alleged is to the effect that Makdesion demanded that the accused provide him with drugs, threatened the accused with a gun and appeared to be associated with violent organized criminals. The accused alleges that he became involved in the trafficking out of fear of Makdesion. In Makdesion's examination-in-chief you bring out his criminal record, as provided to you by the FBI and as disclosed by you to the defence, namely, one conviction for simple possession of cocaine for which he received probation. Makdesion repeatedly testifies, in-chief and in cross-examination, that this is his only criminal record. His FBI handler is in court while he gives this evidence. The trial judge rejects the accused's evidence about the threat and convicts the accused, who then appeals. While the appeal is pending, defence counsel learns from his own sources that Makdesion, in fact, has three further convictions for drug offences and for assault with a weapon, that he was sentenced to jail for two of these further convictions and that he was in the FBI's employ at the time of the further convictions. Defence counsel informs you of this more extensive and arguably more relevant criminal record and you confirm its accuracy with the police. It therefore appears to you that Makdesion committed perjury at the entrapment hearing and that the FBI may have been complicit in the perjury in that they provided you with the limited and inaccurate criminal record, which you disclosed to the defence, and that Makdesion then testified in the FBI handler's presence in accordance with the false criminal record that had been disclosed. Do you now have an obligation to commence an inquiry into the failure to make full disclosure at trial and to determine whether there was police complicity in the non-disclosure? Or are you entitled to take the position on appeal that full disclosure of the criminal record has now been made and it would not have affected the verdict at trial?[12]

Scenario Two

Like any experienced Crown counsel conducting serious criminal prosecutions, it is your practice to interview and prepare your witnesses shortly before calling them to testify at trial. You always ensure that their prior police interviews and statements have been disclosed to the defence pursuant to *Stinchcombe*. You then take the position, supported by authority, that your interview notes are privileged trial preparation, or "work product", intended only to assist you in formulating your examination-in-chief of the Crown's witnesses. If, in the course of such a Crown interview, the witness states something substantially new or different from what he or she said to the police during the earlier investigative interviews, do you now have an obligation to disclose your interview notes to the defence? If so, what form should the disclosure take and does it mean that you are now potentially a witness at trial and therefore can no longer prosecute the case?[13]

2.   The Crown's Duty to Call All Material Witnesses

It can be seen from two of the cases referred to in the previous sections of this chapter that the Crown's non-adversarial role as a "quasi-judicial minister of justice" is said to include a duty to call all credible material witnesses. In the famous passage from *Boucher*, Rand J. stated that the Crown's job was "not to

---

[12]   *R. v. Ahluwalia*, [2000] O.J. No. 4544, 149 C.C.C. (3d) 193 (Ont. C.A.).
[13]   *R. v. Harris*, [1994] O.J. No. 1875, 93 C.C.C. (3d) 478 (Ont. C.A.); *R. v. Sungalia*, [1992] O.J. No. 3718 (Ont. Gen. Div.); *R. v. Brown*, [1997] O.J. No. 6163 (Ont. Gen. Div.); *R. v. Johal*, [1995] B.C.J. No. 1271 (B.C.S.C.); *R. v. Regan*, [1997] N.S.J. No. 428 (N.S.S.C.); *R. v. O'Connor*, [1995] S.C.J. No. 98, 103 C.C.C. (3d) 1 at 45 (S.C.C.); *R. v. Elliott*, [2003] O.J. No. 4694, 181 C.C.C. (3d) 118 at 148-49 (Ont. C.A.).

obtain a conviction, [but] to lay before a jury what the Crown considers to be credible evidence".[14] In a concurring judgment in the same case, Kerwin C.J.C. said: "It is the duty of Crown counsel to bring before the Court the material witnesses."[15] Similarly, in the passage from *Lemay*, quoted with emphasis in *Stinchcombe*, Cartwright J. referred to "the duty which rests upon counsel for the Crown to bring forward evidence of every material fact known to the prosecution whether favourable to the accused or otherwise".[16] The underlying rationale for this duty to call all material witnesses was that the Crown's non-adversarial role required that he or she "bring out before the jury all the facts, those favourable as well as those unfavourable to the accused".[17]

What then is the present status of this *Lemay* and *Boucher* duty to the effect that the Crown must call all credible material witnesses? It is a duty that long preceded the modern *Stinchcombe* duty to disclose the relevant evidence. Does this historical duty to call all relevant witnesses, including those who are helpful to the defence, still exist? Or has it now been eclipsed by the Crown's duty to simply disclose their evidence, prior to trial in accordance with *Stinchcombe*, thus allowing the defence to decide whether to call the witness at trial?

The Supreme Court of Canada answered the question six years after *Stinchcombe* in the *Cook* case. If *Stinchcombe* insisted that the Crown must take a non-adversarial approach to disclosure at the pre-trial stage, consider whether *Cook* has now endorsed a more adversarial approach by the Crown at trial when calling witnesses. Has the right to full and timely pre-trial disclosure had the ironical effect of making the criminal trial more adversarial? Refer back to the short passage from *Cook* quoted earlier in this chapter in section A before reading the rest of the case.

R. v. COOK

[1997] S.C.J. No. 22, 114 C.C.C. (3d) 481
(S.C.C., Lamer C.J.C., La Forest, L'Heureux-Dubé, Sopinka, Gonthier, Cory, MacLachlin, Iacobucci and Major JJ.)

[The accused was charged with assault causing bodily harm. The alleged victim was one Dorbyson who the Crown decided not to call as a witness at trial. Instead of calling the alleged victim, the Crown relied on his former girlfriend, one R., who testified that she saw the accused assault Dorbyson with a machete which severely cut Dorbyson's arm. The Crown also called a number of pieces of circumstantial evidence which tended to support R.'s account. The New Brunswick Court of Appeal set aside the conviction, by a majority, holding that there was a duty on the Crown to call the victim of the alleged crime. The Crown appealed further to the Supreme Court of Canada.]

---

[14]   [1954] S.C.J. No. 54, [1955] S.C.R. 16 at 23 (S.C.C.).
[15]   *Ibid.*, at 19.
[16]   [1951] S.C.J. No. 42, [1952] 1 S.C.R. 232 at 257 (S.C.C.).
[17]   *R. v. Chamandy*, [1934] O.J. No. 235, 61 C.C.C. 224 at 226-27 (Ont. C.A.), *per* Riddell J.A.

L'HEUREUX-DUBÉ J.:—

. . . . .

At the outset of the analysis, I believe it is helpful to place the issue in its proper context. In essence the rule suggested by the respondent would force the Crown to call certain witnesses (assuming they were available and competent), regardless of their truthfulness, desire to testify, or of their ultimate effect on the trial. It is immediately apparent that such a duty, if it were to be established, would have a major impact upon the Crown's ability to conduct its own case. It would be a clear interference with the broad discretionary powers which are said to be within the purview of the Crown attorney, and which are at the very heart of the adversarial process. As a general principle, we have recognized that for our system of criminal justice to function well, the Crown must possess a fair deal of discretion. ...

. . . . .

[After quoting the passage from *Stinchcombe* referring to *Lemay*, already set out above, the Court continued.]

I agree with this analysis. In my view, any rationale compelling the Crown to call witnesses based on the need to bring all material facts forward was extinguished by developments in the law of disclosure. It is simply no longer correct to suggest that the defence will ever be "ambushed" by the Crown's failure to call a material witness. If, for example, the Crown becomes aware that a given witness has made a statement inconsistent with his original one, it is perfectly proper not to call the witness to testify, especially where the Crown feels that the witness is likely to mislead the court .... The defence will not be prejudiced by this decision, as the Crown will still have to turn over the statement to the defence, and the defence will have the option to call the witness.

. . . . .

The respondent also contends that if the rule is not upheld, it would force an accused to call witnesses and lose the right to cross-examine them. Ryan J.A. agreed with this proposition. In addition, he found ... that the Crown Attorney should not be making decisions about a witness' credibility and depriving the trier of fact of the evidence:

> Further, I would not be satisfied with an explanation by the prosecution that Dorbyson might be expected to testify that he fell and cut his arm on a beer bottle and therefore is an unreliable witness. Let the jury decide. It is the opportunity to cross-examine, not the fact of the cross-examination, that is crucial to the fairness of the hearing.

On this point, I must say that I much prefer the recent decision of LeBel J.A. in *V. (J.)* [(1994) (Que. C.A.)]:

> Crown counsel, of course, while bound by strict duties so as to ensure the preservation of the integrity of the criminal justice system, however must operate in the context of an adversarial procedure. Once he has satisfied the obligation to disclose the evidence, it is for him, in principle, to choose the

witnesses necessary to establish the factual basis of his case. If he does not call the necessary witnesses or evidence, he exposes the prosecution to dismissal of the charge for having failed to establish its case completely and in accordance with the reasonable doubt rule. *However, once this obligation has been met and if improper motives cannot be imputed to him, such as the desire, for example, to hide exculpatory evidence, as a general rule, he will be considered to have properly executed this part of his function in the criminal trial. The defence may, at that time, do its work and call its own witnesses, if it considers it appropriate to do so. In the tradition of the common law, on which Canadian criminal procedure is based, the case retains its adversarial nature and Crown counsel, while an officer of the court, does not act as defence counsel.* [emphasis of L'Heureux-Dubé J.]

I could not agree more. With respect, I fail to see why the defence should not have to call witnesses which are beneficial to its own case. The adversarial process functions on the premise that it is the obligation of the Crown to establish a case beyond a reasonable doubt against the accused. Once this threshold has been surpassed, however, it is up to the accused to call evidence or face conviction .... The adversarial nature of the trial process has been recognized as a principle of fundamental justice .... As such it should be construed in a way that strikes a fair balance between the interests of the accused and those of society .... In my view, placing an obligation upon the Crown to call all witnesses with information bearing on the case would disrupt the inherent balance of our adversary system. ...

. . . . .

In summary, I conclude that there is no duty upon the Crown to call witnesses nor a more specific duty to call the complainant or victim. Decisions on how to present the case against an accused must be left to the Crown's discretion absent evidence that this discretion is being abused.

. . . . .

[Appeal allowed.]

NOTES AND QUESTIONS

1. What kind of evidence would be necessary to demonstrate that the Crown's "discretion" was being abused, thereby permitting judicial review of a decision not to call a particular witness?

2. *Cook* holds that the Crown's "discretion" in this area is largely non-reviewable. What is the rationale for this deferential approach and is it similar to *Krieger* where the Court held that certain other exercises of Crown "discretion" are also generally non-reviewable? The Court in *Krieger*, however, stated that "the decisions that govern a Crown prosecutor's tactics or conduct before the court, do not fall within the scope of [non-reviewable] prosecutorial discretion". Are *Krieger* and *Cook* inconsistent on this point? In its latest pronouncement concerning this issue, *R. v. Nixon*, [2011] S.C.J. No. 34, 2011 SCC 34 (S.C.C.), the Court held that the Crown's decision to resile from a plea agreement falls within the generally non-reviewable "core" discretion.

3. Would it be appropriate for a law society to discipline a Crown for failing to call a material witness? In answering this question, consider again the Commentary to Rule 4.01(3) of the *Model Code*, which notes that "the lawyer's primary duty is not to seek to convict but to see that justice is done through a fair trial on the merits" and that the prosecutor "must act fairly and dispassionately". This kind of language, drawn from *Boucher*, is found in virtually all Canadian Codes of Professional Conduct. See, *e.g.*, Ontario's Rule 4.01(3); Alberta's Rule 4.01(4).

4. At the time of *Boucher* and *Lemay*, the Crown was in a position of great power prior to trial, as there was no disclosure obligation and only the Crown knew the real strengths and weaknesses of the case and how to fully prepare the case for trial. However, given this position of power and advantage, the courts compensated by demanding a high degree of non-adversarial behaviour from the Crown at trial, such as the duty to call all material witnesses. Now that *Stinchcombe* has created a much more level playing field, prior to trial, cases like *Cook* appear to have released the Crown from some of the old compensating constraints found in *Boucher* and *Lemay*. In the next section of this chapter, consider whether a modern trend towards excessively adversarial Crown behaviour, at trial, has emerged in the post-*Stinchcombe* and post-*Cook* era. Consider which ethical framework is more likely to further the public interest.

Scenario Three

The accused is charged with four murders, all allegedly involving the settling of accounts in the Montreal underworld. The key Crown witness is a former criminal associate of the accused, one Riendeau, who testifies that he was present when the murders were planned and when admissions were made by the accused immediately after the murders. He testifies that a second associate of theirs, one Bourgade, was also present when the accused made some of these admissions. Is it an abuse of the Crown's discretion not to call the witness Bourgade, when the Crown has twice announced to the jury that this witness will be called and has asserted, in Crown counsel's opening address to the jury, that the Crown anticipates Bourgade will corroborate Riendeau? Assuming the Crown is entitled to change his or her mind during the trial for legitimate reasons, is it legitimate not to call the previously announced witness because the Crown concluded, after Bourgade had testified at the preliminary inquiry, that he was not credible?[18]

3. Overzealous Advocacy by Crown Counsel

There is a large body of case law placing legal and ethical constraints on Crown counsel's advocacy at trial, whether in the context of jury addresses or cross-examination of defence witnesses.

The root case which explains the Crown's quasi-judicial role in a criminal trial, *R. v. Boucher*, was itself a case involving an inflammatory jury address. Chief Justice Kerwin set out two limitations on the content of Crown jury addresses:

---

[18]   *R. v. Jolivet*, [2000] S.C.J. No. 28, 144 C.C.C. (3d) 97 (S.C.C.).

In his address he is entitled to examine all the evidence and ask the jury to come to the conclusion that the accused is guilty as charged. In all this he has a duty to assist the jury, but he exceeds that duty when he expresses by inflammatory or vindictive language his own personal opinion that the accused is guilty, or when his remarks tend to leave with the jury an impression that the investigation made by the Crown is such that they should find the accused guilty. In the present case counsel's address infringed both of these rules.[19]

Justice Locke, in a concurring judgment, cited authorities that appear to place even more severe constraints on any advocacy by Crown counsel:

These are the principles which have been accepted as defining the duty of counsel for the Crown in this country.

In *Rex v. Chamandy* ... Mr. Justice Riddell, speaking for the Ontario Court of Appeal, put it this way (p. 227):

It cannot be made too clear, that in our law, a criminal prosecution is not a contest between individuals, nor is it a contest between the Crown endeavouring to convict and the accused endeavouring to be acquitted; but it is an investigation that should be conducted without feeling or animus on the part of the prosecution, with the single view of determining the truth.

In the last edition of Archbold's *Criminal Pleading, Evidence & Practice*, p. 194, the learned author says that prosecuting counsel should regard themselves rather as ministers of justice assisting in its administration than as advocates.[20]

In another concurring judgment, Taschereau J. similarly held that Crown counsel will have "fulfilled his function ... if, in a dignified fashion befitting his role, he sets aside all appeal to passion and places the evidence before the jury without going beyond what that evidence has revealed".[21] The impugned passages from Crown counsel's jury address in *Boucher*, which was a prosecution for murder, were as follows:

The doctor spoke to us about blood, — we were taken to task gentlemen because we had an analysis of the blood made. But the Crown is not here for the pleasure of having innocent people convicted.

It is the duty of the Crown, when an affair like that happens, no matter what affair, and still more in a serious affair, to make every possible investigation, and if in the course of these investigations with our experts, the conclusion is come to that the accused is not guilty or that there is a reasonable doubt, it is the duty of the Crown, gentlemen, to say so or if the conclusion is come to that he is not guilty, not to make an arrest. That is what was done here.

. . . . .

---

[19] *R. v. Boucher*, [1954] S.C.J. No. 54, [1955] S.C.R. 16 at 19 (S.C.C.).
[20] *Ibid.*, at 25-26.
[21] *Ibid.*, at 21 [translation].

Every day we see more and more crimes than ever, thefts and many another thing, at least one who commits armed robbery does not make his victim suffer as Boucher made Jabour suffer. It is a revolting crime for a man with all the strength of his age, of an athlete against an old man of 77, who is not capable of defending himself. I have a little respect for those who steal when they at least have given their victim a chance to defend himself, but I have no sympathy, none, and I tell you not to have any sympathy for these dastards who strike men, friends. Jabour was perhaps not a friend, but he was a neighbour, at least they knew each other.

In a cowardly manner, with blows of an axe. — And, if you bring in a verdict of guilty, for once it will almost be a pleasure to me to ask the death penalty for him.[22]

Justice Locke identified two principal reasons for finding the above passages from the Crown's jury address objectionable: first, it made the Crown into a witness and one who was giving inadmissible evidence; second, it employed an appeal to emotion. Justice Locke reasoned as follows:

These are statements of fact not argument and, in making them, counsel for the Crown was giving evidence. The matters stated were wholly irrelevant and, had the counsel in question elected to go into the witness box to make these statements on oath, the proposed evidence would not have been heard. In this manner, however, these facts were submitted to the jury for their consideration.

The statements were calculated to impress upon the jury the asserted fact that, before the accused had been arrested, the Crown, with its experts, had made a through investigation and was satisfied that he was guilty beyond a reasonable doubt. Introduced into the record in this manner, there could be no cross-examination to test their accuracy.

. . . . .

The Crown prosecutor, having improperly informed the jury that there had been an investigation by the Crown which satisfied the authorities that the accused was guilty, thus assured them on his own belief of his guilt and employed language calculated to inflame their feelings against him.[23]

Similar principles apply in the context of Crown counsel's cross-examination of the accused, as can be seen in the case of *R. v. R. (A.J.)*, which is found in Chapter 6, section D.2. Please re-read this case and consider the following questions and scenarios:

1. Do you think that American television programs and movies have played a role in encouraging the kind of conduct displayed by Crown counsel in the above case?

---

[22] *Ibid.*, at 30-31 [translation].

[23] *Ibid.*, at 27.

2.   Alternatively, did Crown counsel simply conduct herself in the manner explicitly permitted by modern cases like *Cook* and *Rose* namely, "as a strong advocate within this adversarial process"?

3.   The Crown's case against the accused in *R. (A.J.)* was particularly strong but the Court of Appeal, nevertheless, reversed the convictions because of Crown counsel's misconduct. In a weaker case, where the Crown's evidence is much closer to the line between conviction and acquittal, is there a risk that conduct like that exhibited by Crown counsel in *R. (A.J.)* might cause a wrongful conviction?

4.   Justice Doherty noted in *R. (A.J.)* that the problems concerning Crown misconduct in that case were already becoming "familiar" in 1994, when he wrote the judgment. The three scenarios below are drawn from cases that arose in the years immediately after *R. (A.J.)*.

Scenario Four

The accused was charged with second degree murder in the strangulation death of his wife. The accused admitted that he killed his wife; indeed, he called the police himself immediately after the homicide. The only issue in the brief trial was whether murder should be reduced to manslaughter because of provocation. The marriage had completely broken down and was characterized by constant arguments. On the day of the killing, the accused alleged that his wife had falsely accused him of incest with his daughter and had threatened to call the police. He flew into a rage and killed her. In Crown counsel's closing jury address he did the following: misstated the accused's evidence on the issue of whether he had immediately called the police; advised the jury that if the defence succeeded then "every wife ... who ... provokes their spouse, had better take cover, because it will be open season"; advised the jury that the local homicide rate "would be tripled" if provocation was allowed as a defence; compared the accused to the infamous Marc Lepine and the École Polytechnique murders in Montreal, stating that Lepine "was filled with a rage and a hatred (that Mr. Munroe felt) when he shot those 12 women to death"; and concluded by arguing that if the jury were to acquit, it would be comparable to situations where "we often read in the papers about people being assaulted, being raped, being murdered while other people stood by and allowed it to happen. And you probably thought to yourself, why didn't somebody step in and stop it or do something? Why doesn't the community do something about it? Monday morning [at the start of the trial] when you took your oath as jurors you became part of that community that can stop it." Was the Crown's jury address unethical? Why or why not?[24]

---

[24]   *R. v. Munroe*, [1995] O.J. No. 819, 96 C.C.C. (3d) 431 (Ont. C.A.), affd [1995] S.C.J. No. 91, 102 C.C.C. (3d) 383 (S.C.C.).

Scenario Five

The accused were charged with the first degree murder of one Cooper in a shooting death that occurred in the Vancouver drug underworld. The Crown's case depended primarily on the evidence of one Ivall, a cocaine and heroin trafficker with a lengthy criminal record who admitted the following: that he had procured the murder weapon, a gun, and carried it to the scene of the crime; that he had disposed of the gun after the shooting; that he was the one who had the dispute with Cooper that led to the homicide; and that he had animus against the accused S. when he went to the police and secured immunity in return for his testimony against S. and L. Defence counsel vigorously attacked Ivall's credibility and then called no defence witnesses. Crown counsel addressed the jury first and described the defence position as "driven by desperation", having "no foundation at all in the evidence", "ridiculous", "fishy", "tricky" or "laughable". Crown counsel warned the jury that the defence addresses, which they would hear next, would be "bafflegab", "smoke", "fog", "bombast" and "mudslinging". Was the Crown's jury address unethical? Why or why not?[25]

Scenario Six

The accused, a crack cocaine addict, was charged with second degree murder. He admitted killing the deceased, a drug trafficker who had attacked him and beaten him, allegedly over a small drug debt. The deceased was bigger than the accused, had forcibly entered the accused's home and had caused a number of visible injuries to the accused. The accused's account was that he fought back with a knife and hammer, killing the deceased, and then told a number of friends what had happened. He initially tried to cover up the homicide but eventually turned himself in to the police two days after the killing. The deceased's body was still in the accused's home when he went to the police. The accused testified and raised defences of provocation, self-defence and lack of intent to kill. The Crown's cross-examination of the accused included the following points: repeated questions about the accused's failure to make any statement, giving his exculpatory account, at the time of his surrender to the police; questions to the effect that the accused had obtained disclosure from the Crown and had heard the Crown's witnesses testify at the preliminary inquiry and had then tailored his story in order to make it conform to the known evidence; questions about the detailed facts underlying the accused's criminal record, especially a prior conviction for assault; and questions about alleged welfare fraud that had not resulted in any criminal conviction. Was the Crown's cross-examination unethical? Why or why not?[26]

---

[25] *R. v. Siu and Lee*, [1998] B.C.J. No. 812, 124 C.C.C. (3d) 301 (B.C.C.A.).

[26] *R. v. Schell*, [2000] O.J. No. 3633, 148 C.C.C. (3d) 219 (Ont. C.A.).

C.   THE ETHICAL DUTIES OF "OFFICERS OF THE COURT"

Both parties to a criminal proceeding, when represented by Crown counsel and defence counsel, are constrained from engaging in certain forms of highly adversarial behaviour. This is because both counsel are "officers of the court". As Mark Orkin explains in his text on *Legal Ethics*, lawyers were regarded as part of the apparatus of the courts from earliest times. Indeed, the courts and the legal profession both began to emerge in the 13th century in England, in tandem, as independent component parts of a single institution committed to the administration of justice. Orkin asserts that it is a failure to appreciate counsel's "dual role" as both "officer of the court" and "representative of the client" that has been the cause of "much misunderstanding of the lawyer's true function".[27]

The high standards of conduct imposed on both the Crown and the defence, by virtue of their status as "officers of the court", all tend to revolve around one particularly broad and poorly defined ideal to the effect that the purpose of court proceedings is to seek "justice" and "truth". As Crompton J. put it in the Irish seditious conspiracy case, *R. v. O'Connell*:

> This Court in which we sit is a temple of justice; and the Advocate at the Bar, as well as the Judge upon the Bench, are equally ministers in that temple. The object of all equally should be the attainment of justice; now justice is only to be reached through the ascertainment of the truth, and the instrument which our law presents to us for the ascertainment of the truth or falsehood of a criminous charge is the trial by Jury; the trial is the process by which we endeavour to find out the truth. ... That learned Counsel described the Advocate as the mere mouth-piece of his client; he told us that the speech of the Counsel was to be taken as that of the client; and thence seemed to conclude that the client only was answerable for its language and sentiments.
>
> Such, I do conceive, is not the office of an Advocate. His office is a higher one. To consider him in that light is to degrade him. I would say of him as I would say of a member of the House of Commons—he is a representative, but not a delegate. He gives to his client the benefit of his learning, his talents and his judgment; but all through he never forgets what he owes to himself and to others. He will not knowingly misstate the law—he will not wilfully misstate the facts, though it be to gain the cause for his client. He will ever bear in mind that if he be the Advocate of an individual, and retained and remunerated (often inadequately) for his valuable services, yet he has a prior and perpetual retainer on behalf of truth and justice; and there is no Crown or other license which in any case, or for any party or purpose, can discharge him from that primary and paramount retainer.[28]

It is perhaps not surprising, in light of pronouncements like those set out above in *O'Connell*, that counsel's duties as an "officer of the court" are

---

[27]   Mark Orkin, *Legal Ethics* (Toronto: Cartwright and Sons, 1957) at 4-13.

[28]   (1844), 7 I.L.R. 261 at 312-13 (Q.B.).

poorly understood. The duty of loyalty to the client is straightforward and easily applied but the idea that there is a competing "retainer on behalf of truth and justice" is so abstract as to offer no real guidance to counsel. Nevertheless, the case law has elucidated a number of concrete applications of the "officer of the court" ideal.

The best known modern description of the duties of an "officer of the court" is Lord Reid's famous speech in *Rondel v. Worsley*, where he stated that counsel "must not mislead the court, he must not lend himself to casting aspersions on the other party or witnesses for which there is no sufficient basis in the information in his possession, he must not withhold authorities or documents which may tell against his clients but which the law or the standards of his profession require him to produce".[29] In the same case, Lord Upjohn gave a simple illustration of how counsel's duty to the court may conflict with the client's more adversarial wishes:

> ... the client may want counsel to drag his opponent through the mire by asking a number of questions in cross-examination in the hope that the opposition may be frightened into submission. Counsel here has equally a duty to the court not to cross-examine the opposition save in accordance with the usual principles and practice of the Bar.[30]

In the leading Australian case, *Giannarelli v. Wraith*, Mason C.J. provided a further practical example of how to apply counsel's duty to the court:

> And, if he notes an irregularity in the conduct of a criminal trial, he must take the point so that it can be remedied, instead of keeping the point up his sleeve and using it as a ground for appeal.[31]

It can be seen that all of the above illustrations of counsel's broad duties as "officers of the court" tend to place a premium on counsel's honesty and integrity. The reason for this focus is that a lack of honesty and integrity, amongst lawyers who are empowered to call the case in an adversarial system of justice, will quickly undermine the search for truth and justice which is posited as the primary goal of the court system. As Lord Morris explained in his speech in *Rondel v. Worsley*:

> I think that it must be true to say, as was said in *Swinfen v. Lord Chelmsford*, that the duty undertaken by an advocate is one in which the client, the court and the public have an interest because the due and proper and orderly administration of justice is a matter of vital public concern. The advocate has a duty to assist in ensuring that the administration of justice is not distorted or thwarted by dishonest or disreputable practices. To a certain extent every advocate is an amicus curiae.[32] [emphasis added]

---

[29] [1967] 3 All E.R. 993 at 999 (H.L.).
[30] *Ibid.*, at 1035.
[31] (1988), 165 C.L.R. 543 at 556 (H.C. Aust.).
[32] [1967] 3 All E.R. 993 at 1012 (H.L.).

Two additional illustrations of the duties of "officers of the court" have been increasingly emphasized in more recent jurisprudence: the duty not to make frivolous arguments and the duty of civility. The former duty was explained in *R. v. Samra*, where Rosenberg J.A. invoked Lord Reid's speech in *Rondel v. Worsley* and stated:

> There is an erroneous premise underlying the appellant's submissions in this case — that defence counsel is but a mouthpiece for his client. His argument must be that counsel is bound to make submissions no matter how foolish or ill-advised or contrary to established legal principle and doctrine, provided that is what the client desires.[33]

Proulx and Layton, in their leading text, *Ethics and Canadian Criminal Law*, include a lengthy discussion of "the ethical rule against frivolous arguments". There are many difficulties associated with this rule, especially in the criminal context where the burden is always on the Crown to prove guilt and where creativity in mounting a defence may require novel arguments. Nevertheless, the duty has acquired renewed prominence because of the modern concern that criminal trials in the post-Charter era have been unduly lengthened by a proliferation of dubious motions and arguments.[34]

In a similar vein, a substantial body of modern case law has now emerged in both civil and criminal cases, stressing that counsel must act with "civility" due to their status as "officers of the court". The rationale for this particular duty is, once again, related to the effectiveness and fairness of adversarial trials which depends on counsel being constrained to act with honesty and integrity. The leading criminal case is *R. v. Felderhof*, where the court stated:

> Unfair and demeaning comments by counsel in the course of submissions to a court do not simply impact on the other counsel. Such conduct diminishes the public's respect for the court and for the administration of criminal justice and thereby undermines the legitimacy of the results of the adjudication.
>
> ... counsel have a responsibility to the administration of justice, and as officers of the court, they have a duty to act with integrity, a duty that requires civil conduct.
>
> ... It is a very serious matter to make allegations of improper motives or bad faith against any counsel. Such allegations must only be made where there is some foundation for them and they are not to be made simply as part of the normal discourse in submissions over the admissibility of evidence or the conduct of the trial. To persist in making these submissions does not simply

---

[33] [1998] O.J. No. 3755, 129 C.C.C. (3d) 144 at 158-59 (Ont. C.A.).

[34] See, for example: Justice M. Moldaver, "Long Criminal Trials: Masters of a System They Are Meant to Serve" (2006) 32 C.R. (6th) 316; D. Stuart, "The Charter is a Vital Living Tree Not a Weed To Be Stunted – Justice Moldaver Has Overstated" (2006) 40 C.R. (6th) 280; *R. v. Chan*, [2003] A.J. No. 1117, 15 C.R. (6th) 53 at 162-63 (Alta. Q.B.); *R. v. Elliott*, [2003] O.J. No. 4694, 181 C.C.C. (3d) 118 (Ont. C.A.); *R. v. Omar*, [2007] O.J. No. 541, 218 C.C.C. (3d) 242 at 252-53 (Ont. C.A.); *R. c. Beauchamp*, [2004] J.Q. no 3449, 24 C.R. (6th) 278 at paras. 167-183 (Que. S.C.), revd in part 36 C.R. (6th) 189 (Que. C.A.).

hurt the feelings of a thin-skinned opponent. Those types of submissions are disruptive to the orderly running of the trial. They sidetrack the prosecutor and the trial judge from the real issues at the trial.[35]

As was the case in *Felderhof,* the primary manifestation of "incivility" in criminal trials is when counsel for one side makes an unfounded or irrelevant personal attack against the honesty, integrity or motivation of counsel for the opposing party. Like the rule against frivolous arguments, the rule against "incivility" is difficult to apply because there are cases where opposing counsel's personal motivation or misconduct may be the proper subject of a motion seeking a legal remedy.[36]

Professional conduct rules generally spell out the above duties, sometimes with reasonable precision and sometimes in broad generalities. For example, Rule 4.01(5) of the *Model Code* provides that: "A lawyer must be courteous and civil and act in good faith to the tribunal and all persons with whom the lawyer has dealings."

NOTES AND QUESTIONS

1. The above discussion of the duties of "officers of the court" suggests that the adversary system sees itself as vulnerable to certain kinds of "disreputable practises" that can "distort or thwart" the search for truth and justice, as Lord Morris put it in *Rondel v. Worsley.* A lack of "honesty" and "integrity" are at the core of these "disreputable practises". The essence of the adversary system is that counsel for the two opposing parties control the calling of the case. In order to preserve the impartiality of the trier of fact and law, the judge (and any jury) remain relatively uninvolved in calling evidence, asking questions of witnesses and making argument and, instead, the trier depends upon counsel in these areas. Is it because this *laissez-faire* or somewhat unregulated characteristic of the adversary system has given counsel too much power and responsibility that the courts are now struggling to regain control over the process by emphasizing counsel's duties to the court?

2. It is obvious how a lawyer who lacks "honesty" could use the privileges given to him or her under the adversary system to subvert a true and just result in a case. "Integrity", on the other hand, is a much broader and vaguer concept than "honesty". It means, according to the *Oxford English Dictionary*, "soundness of moral principle; the character of uncorrupted virtue, especially in relation to truth and fair dealing; uprightness, honesty, sincerity". Recalling the discussion of integrity in Chapter 1, is it a manageable principle from which the courts can further develop the duties of their officers? Or is there a danger that the courts have used or will use the somewhat ill-defined concept of "integrity" in order to create a disparate set of ethical duties that undermine counsel's obligation to fearlessly defend the accused in criminal cases? This latter duty is explored in the next section.

---

[35] [2003] O.J. No. 4819, 180 C.C.C. (3d) 498 at 535-39 (Ont. C.A.).
[36] Michael Code, "Counsel's Duty of Civility: An Essential Component of Fair Trials and an Effective Justice System" (2007) 11 Can. Crim. L. Rev. 97.

Scenario Seven

Is it unethical for defence counsel in a murder case to bring 19 pre-trial motions and three mid-trial motions, alleging over 100 Charter violations, all to the general effect that numerous Crown counsel are involved in a conspiracy with the police to concoct evidence and mislead the court? Consider further that the defence counsel is young and inexperienced and that the trial judge, who has been on the bench for many years, openly encourages these defence allegations and ultimately finds that the Charter violations have been made out and then grants a stay of proceedings. Finally, consider that the numerous motions took two years to complete and that, on the subsequent Crown appeal against the stay, experienced appellate counsel for the accused conceded, and the Court of Appeal found, that the Charter motions were "baseless and frivolous".[37]

Scenario Eight

Is it unethical for defence counsel in a civil action against a senior police officer for assault and false arrest, where credibility is the key issue, to actively conceal the fact that the defendant had been demoted from the rank of chief inspector to the rank of sergeant due to a disciplinary finding of deceit in an unrelated matter? Defence counsel conceals the finding of deceit, and the penalty of demotion, by having his client appear at trial dressed in civilian clothes, by referring to him as "Mr. Fleming" rather than "Sgt. Fleming" and by omitting any questions during examination-in-chief about his client's initial promotion to chief inspector and subsequent demotion to sergeant. Plaintiff's counsel and the trial judge, however, assume throughout the trial that the defendant is a chief inspector, they refer to him as such and Fleming answers their questions falsely by stating or implying that he is still a chief inspector. Defence counsel says nothing to disabuse the court of its misconception and, in closing argument, defence counsel relies on his client's unspecified senior rank in the police force as a badge of credibility. Would your analysis be any different if Sgt. Fleming was being defended by counsel on a charge of assault, in a criminal case, rather than in a civil suit?[38]

D. THE ETHICAL DUTIES OF DEFENCE COUNSEL

1. Introduction: The Duty to the Client

The previous section of this chapter emphasizes those duties to the court, to the profession and to the administration of justice that restrain all counsel, including defence counsel, from acting in a purely partisan or adversarial

---

[37] *R. v. Elliott*, [2003] O.J. No. 4694, 181 C.C.C. (3d) 118 (Ont. C.A.). Subsequently, the Canadian Judicial Council recommended that the trial judge should be removed from office, and he resigned, while the Law Society of Upper Canada suspended defence counsel's licence to practise law for six months.

[38] *Meek v. Fleming*, [1961] 3 All E.R. 148 (C.A.).

manner. In this section, by way of contrast, the emphasis is on counsel's overtly partisan duty to the client.

In Lord Reid's famous speech in *Rondel v. Worsley*, he began by acknowledging counsel's duty to the client. Lord Reid described this function as requiring counsel "fearlessly to raise every issue, advance every argument, and ask every question, however distasteful, which he thinks will help his client's case".[39] Rule 4.01(1) of the *Model Code* requires defence counsel to "represent the client resolutely" and the Commentary to the Rule then paraphrases Lord Reid's description of the duty to the client, using the same language about fearlessly raising every issue, advancing every argument and asking every question which might help the client.

This broad partisan duty to the client is essential to the proper functioning of the adversary system. Unless the accused is resolutely defended by a skilled and loyal advocate, the innocent may be convicted. The Marshall Inquiry not only uncovered Crown misconduct, as already noted above, but also exposed serious failings by Marshall's own counsel.[40] Indeed, the gross miscarriage of justice in that case was a combined product of the Crown failing to observe its ethical duty to disclose and the defence failing to observe its ethical duty to resolutely defend the client.

One of the most important ethical rules, associated with the broad partisan duty to the client, is the duty of confidentiality. Since this duty applies in both civil and criminal matters and applies in both litigation and non-litigation contexts, it is well beyond the scope of this chapter and is dealt with separately in Chapter 4. However, the duty of confidentiality must be kept in mind when analyzing problems associated with the partisan duty to the client. Confidentiality is invariably the foundation or context in which these problems must be resolved.

In most cases, the duty to the client does not raise any great ethical difficulties. It requires loyalty, skill, industry and courage by defence counsel but, assuming counsel either has or develops these personal qualities, there should be no significant impediments to carrying out the duty to the client. However, there are a number of areas in criminal defence practice where particular problems associated with the duty to the client have arisen, and where particular ethical rules have developed. Three of these problematic areas are discussed below, all of which raise questions about the limits of counsel's partisan duty to the client.

2. Defending the Guilty Client and the Related Problem of Not Misleading the Court

Non-lawyers always ask defence counsel: "How can you defend a guilty client?" The answer to the question is that the most important ethical principle,

---

[39] [1967] 3 All E.R. 993 at 999 (H.L.).

[40] Provice of Nova Scotia, *Royal Commission on the Donald Marshall Jr. Prosecution*, Vol. 1 (1989) at 72-77.

when "defending the guilty client", is to avoid forming any opinions on the subject of guilt or innocence in the first place. In the famous case of *Boucher*, discussed above at section B.3, "Overzealous Advocacy by Crown Counsel", it is stated that Crown counsel should never express his or her personal opinion as to the accused's guilt in closing submissions at trial. By the same token, defence counsel's personal opinion as to the client's guilt or innocence is generally irrelevant and may actually cause counsel to fail in carrying out the broad partisan duty to resolutely defend the client.

In one of the most stinging criticisms found in the Marshall Inquiry Report, the three very experienced Commissioners stated that the Inquiry "heard evidence to suggest that [defence counsel] believed [their client] Marshall was guilty. Did those feelings influence the effort they put into mounting Marshall's defence?" The Commissioners did not answer this question directly but the answer is perhaps implicit in their conclusion: "Had defence counsel taken even the most rudimentary steps an accused should be entitled to expect from his or her counsel, it is difficult to believe Marshall would have been convicted."[41] The "rudimentary steps" which defence counsel never undertook on behalf of Marshall included carrying out an independent investigation of the facts, interviewing witnesses not called by the Crown, and seeking production of the Crown witnesses' prior inconsistent statements. Such steps would have revealed Marshall's innocence.

As a result of the natural human tendency to bend your efforts when you believe that your client's cause is unworthy, defence counsel must develop the discipline of not judging their clients. The adversary system assumes that the judge and jury will do the judging and that defence counsel will do the defending. As Proulx and Layton put it:

> Counsel's role in the criminal justice system is neither to judge the client nor to arrive at a personal determination as to the client's guilt. The expressions of this sentiment by distinguished lawyers and commentators are legion and frequently hackneyed. "A client is entitled to say to his counsel, I want your advocacy, not your judgment; I prefer that of the Court," stated Baron Bramwell in a much repeated quotation from *Johnson* v. *Emerson and Sparrow*. Just as famous are the comments of the defence lawyer Thomas Erskine in *R. v. Paine*:
>
>> If the advocate refuses to defend, from what he may think of the charge or the defence, he assumes the character of the judge; nay, he assumes it before the hour of judgment; and in proportion to his rank and reputation, puts the heavy influence of perhaps a mistaken opinion into the scale against the accused ...[42]

---

[41]   *Ibid.*, at 77.

[42]   Michel Proulx & David Layton, *Ethics and Canadian Criminal Law* (Toronto: Irwin Law, 2001) at 38.

One of the Commentaries to Rule 4.01(1) of the *Model Code* expressly addresses this issue of counsel's duty to defend, regardless of counsel's personal opinions about guilt or innocence:

> When defending an accused person, a lawyer's duty is to protect the client as far as possible from being convicted, except by a tribunal of competent jurisdiction and upon legal evidence sufficient to support a conviction for the offence with which the client is charged. Accordingly, and *notwithstanding the lawyer's private opinion on credibility or the merits*, a lawyer may properly rely on any evidence or defences, including so-called technicalities, not known to be false or fraudulent. [emphasis added]

Assuming counsel has properly developed the discipline of not judging the client, there nevertheless may be rare cases where counsel becomes convinced of the client's guilt. Whether it is the result of a clear and credible confession from the client, made to counsel in confidence, or whether it is due to other overwhelming evidence of guilt, the lawyer who is "convinced" of the client's guilt is subject to certain ethical constraints in the conduct of the defence. These constraints arise from the ethical duty not to mislead the court, discussed in the previous section, which always competes with the duty to the client.

The modern Canadian rule that applies in these rare cases is based on the traditional English rule. It is consistently set out, a typical example being the Commentary to Rule 4.01(1) of the *Model Code*:

> Admissions made by the accused to a lawyer may impose strict limitations on the conduct of the defence, and the accused should be made aware of this. For example, if the accused clearly admits to the lawyer the factual and mental elements necessary to constitute the offence, the lawyer, if convinced that the admissions are true and voluntary, may properly take objection to the jurisdiction of the court, the form of the indictment or the admissibility or sufficiency of the evidence, but must not suggest that some other person committed the offence or call any evidence that, by reason of the admissions, the lawyer believes to be false. Nor may the lawyer set up an affirmative case inconsistent with such admissions, for example, by calling evidence in support of an alibi intended to show that the accused could not have done or, in fact, has not done the act. Such admissions will also impose a limit on the extent to which the lawyer may attack the evidence for the prosecution. The lawyer is entitled to test the evidence given by each individual witness for the prosecution and argue that the evidence taken as a whole is insufficient to amount to proof that the accused is guilty of the offence charged, but the lawyer should go no further than that.

Two propositions emerge from the above rule, both of which have significant ethical import: first, counsel can clearly continue to defend a client, even though convinced of the client's guilt; second, counsel can only use certain means of defence in such a case, namely, those means which do not involve knowingly misleading the court.

The first proposition is illustrated by a famous Australian case where counsel appears to have believed that he could not continue to defend his client after the client had confessed to him. Worse still, counsel went on to violate the duty of confidentiality by disclosing the client's confession to the trial judge.

R. v. TUCKIAR

(1934), 52 C.L.R. 335
(H.C. Aust., Gavan Duffy C.J., Dixon,
Evatt, McTiernan and Starke JJ.)

[The accused, an aborigine, was convicted of murder and sentenced to death after a trial in the Supreme Court of the Northern Territory. He appealed successfully to the High Court. The accused was alleged to have used his spear to kill a police officer in the jungle on a remote island. When the deceased police officer's body was found, his gun had been fired three times and the spear was lying nearby. There were no eye witnesses to the murder called by the Crown. The Crown's case was based on two oral statements, allegedly made by the accused to two other aborigines, in which he admitted to killing the police officer with his spear. The two statements were different. The first statement, made to one Parriner, was more damaging. The accused was alleged to have told Parriner that the police officer, one Cst. McColl, had taken three of his wives or "lubras" into custody without apparent justification and that the accused had thrown his spear, ostensibly to free one of his wives, and that the officer had then fired his gun at the accused after being struck by the spear. The second statement, made to one Harry, was more favourable to the accused as he allegedly stated that he saw the police officer having sexual relations with his wife, that the police officer saw the accused and fired at him three times and only then did the accused throw his spear, in apparent self-defence, killing the officer.]

GAVAN DUFFY C.J., DIXON, EVATT AND MCTIERNAN JJ.:—

At the trial at Darwin, the prisoner, who understood no English, was defended by counsel instructed by the Protector of Aborigines. At the conclusion of Parriner's evidence, the Judge asked counsel for the defence whether he had put before the prisoner the story told by the witness and talked it over with him. Counsel replied that he had not done so. The Judge then asked him whether he did not think it proper to discuss the evidence with the accused and see whether it was correct. On counsel stating that he thought it desirable to take that course, the Judge arranged for him to take Paddy the interpreter and discuss the evidence with Tuckiar. The Court adjourned for half an hour to enable this to be done. On the Court resuming, Harry's evidence in chief was taken, but, before proceeding to cross-examine him, the prisoner's counsel said that he had a specially important matter which he desired to discuss with the Judge. He was in a predicament, the worst predicament that he had encountered in all his legal career. The jury retired, and the Judge, the Protector of Aborigines and counsel for the defence went into the Judge's Chambers. On their return, after some discussion of the reasons for the Crown's failure to call as witnesses other constables, trackers and the lubras, the jury were re-called and Harry's evidence was completed. Then the prosecutor obtained leave to recall a witness as to the good character of the deceased constable, McColl. This evidence was, of course, quite inadmissible, but no objection was taken to it.

. . . . .

No evidence was called for the defence. Before the Crown case was quite complete, the jury, who had heard much discussion of the Crown's failure to bring witnesses to Darwin, asked: "If we are satisfied that there is not enough evidence, what is our position?" The Judge reports that he understood them to mean, what was their position if they were satisfied that the Crown had not brought before the Court all the evidence it might have brought.

. . . . .

But it does appear that, after telling the jury that a decision on any question of fact was entirely for them and they ought not to accept any view he indicated on a question of fact unless in their own independent judgment they agreed with it, the learned Judge proceeded to condemn the story which Harry said the prisoner told him, as an improbable concoction on the part of the prisoner, and, on the other hand, said that the only conclusion from the facts which Par-riner said the prisoner narrated to him was that the homicide amounted to murder.

. . . . .

Upon the jury's finding a verdict of guilty, the Judge postponed pronouncing sentence, which, in the case of an aboriginal, is not necessarily death. The prisoner's counsel then made the following statement: — "I have a matter which I desire to mention before the Court rises. I would like to state publicly that I had an interview with the convicted prisoner Tuckiar in the presence of an interpreter. I pointed out to him that he had told these two different stories and that one could not be true. I asked him to tell the interpreter which was the true story. He told him that the first story told to Parriner was the true one. I asked him why he told the other story. He told me that he was too much wor-ried so he told a different story and that story was a lie. I think this fact clears Constable McColl. As an advocate I did not deem it advisable to put the ac-cused in the box." The learned Judge said: — "I am glad you mentioned it, not only in fairness to McColl but also because it proves that the boy Harry was telling the truth in the witness box. I had a serious doubt whether the boy Harry was telling the truth, but it now appears that he was."

When the Court resumed his Honor added: — "It did not occur to me at the time, but I think I should have stated publicly that immediately that confession had been made to you, you and Dr. Cook (the Protector of Aborigines) con-sulted me about the matter and asked my opinion as to the proper course for you, as counsel, to take, and I then told you that if your client had been a white man and had made a confession of guilt to you I thought your proper course would have been to withdraw from the case; but as your client was an aboriginal, and there might be some remnant of doubt as to whether his confession to you was any more reliable than any other confession he had made, the better course would be for you to continue to appear for him, because if you had retired from the case it would have left it open to ignorant, malicious and irresponsible persons to say that this aboriginal had been abandoned and left without any proper defence."

. . . . .

In the present case, the jury witnessed the spectacle of the prisoner's counsel, at the suggestion of the Judge, retiring to discuss with the prisoner the evidence of the principal witness against him and see whether it was correct, and of his saying after doing so, that he wished to discuss with the Judge a specially important matter, which put him in the worst predicament that he had encountered in his legal career. Afterwards, the Judge, who had to their knowledge heard counsel's communication, directed them ... which of the stories was true ... the circumstances which had occurred before them were likely to reinforce ... a well-founded surmise of what the Judge had been told by the prisoner's counsel.

. . . . .

It would be difficult for anyone in the position of the learned Judge to receive the communication made to him by counsel for the prisoner and yet retain the same view of the dangers involved in the weakness of the Crown evidence. This may, perhaps, explain his Honor's evident anxiety that the jury should not under-estimate the force of the evidence the Crown did adduce. Indeed counsel seems to have taken a course calculated to transfer to the Judge the embarrassment which he appears so much to have felt. Why he should have conceived himself to have been in so great a predicament, it is not easy for those experienced in advocacy to understand. He had a plain duty, both to his client and to the Court, to press such rational considerations as the evidence fairly gave rise to in favour of complete acquittal or conviction of manslaughter only. No doubt he was satisfied that through Paddy he obtained the uncoloured product of his client's mind, although misgiving on this point would have been pardonable; but, even if the result was that the correctness of Parriner's version was conceded, it was by no means a hopeless contention of fact that the homicide should be found to amount only to manslaughter. Whether he be in fact guilty or not, a prisoner is, in point of law, entitled to acquittal from any charge which the evidence fails to establish that he committed, and it is not incumbent on his counsel by abandoning his defence to deprive him of the benefit of such rational arguments as fairly arise on the proofs submitted. The subsequent action of the prisoner's counsel in openly disclosing the privileged communication of his client and acknowledging the correctness of the more serious testimony against him is wholly indefensible. It was his paramount duty to respect the privilege attaching to the communication made to him as counsel, a duty the obligation of which was by no means weakened by the character of his client, or the moment at which he chose to make the disclosure. No doubt he was actuated by a desire to remove any imputation on Constable McColl. But he was not entitled to divulge what he had learnt from the prisoner as his counsel. Our system of administering justice necessarily imposes upon those who practice advocacy duties which have no analogies, and the system cannot dispense with their strict observance.

In the present case, what occurred is productive of much difficulty. We have reached the conclusion, as we have already stated, that the verdict found against the prisoner must be set aside. Ordinarily the question would next arise whether a new trial should be had. But upon this question we are confronted with the following statements made by the learned trial Judge in his report — "After the verdict, counsel — for reasons that may have been good — made a public statement of this fact which has been published in the local press and otherwise broadcasted throughout the whole area from which jurymen are drawn. If a new trial were granted and another jury were asked to choose between Parriner's story, Harry's story, and some third story which might possibly be put before them it would be practically impossible for them to put out of their minds the fact of this confession by the accused to his own counsel, which would certainly be known to most, if not all, of them ... Counsel for the defence ... after verdict made, entirely of his own motion, a public statement which would make a new trial almost certainly a futility."

In face of this opinion, the correctness of which we cannot doubt, we think the prisoner cannot justly be subjected to another trial at Darwin, and no other venue is practicable.

We therefore allow the appeal and quash the conviction and judgment and direct that a verdict and judgment of acquittal be entered.

NOTES AND QUESTIONS

1. Did the trial judge's intervention and defence counsel's response, after Parriner's evidence was complete, serve to advance the search for truth and justice or did it distort the proper functioning of the adversary system? If the latter, which principles of criminal justice were undermined?

2. Once defence counsel had been reassured by the trial judge that he should continue to represent Tuckiar, it appears from the report of the case that the position he took before the jury in closing argument was that the jury should "not believe either of these stories" given by the two main Crown witnesses. Was this position ethically open to defence counsel in light of the Commentary to Rule 4.01(1), concerning the traditional constraints placed upon counsel who is "convinced" of his client's guilt? Was it misleading, in these circumstances, to challenge the truthfulness of Parriner's account?

3. Given the fact that ethical limits are placed on the conduct of the defence, once counsel becomes "convinced" of the client's guilt, some defence lawyers have adopted devices that deliberately seek to avoid this result. Some of these devices themselves raise further ethical issues, for example, advising the client not to discuss the facts of the case with counsel or advising the client of the Crown's evi-

dence and then suggesting the available defences to the client. Would it be ethical to adopt either of these approaches?

4.   Assuming that counsel has become "convinced" of the client's guilt, and that an appropriate basis exists for counsel's belief, then the Commentary to Rule 4.01(1) places reasonably clear and detailed limits on the conduct of the defence. Refer back to the Commentary and it will be seen that all of the limits revolve around counsel's ethical duty not to knowingly mislead the court. In essence, counsel has a positive duty to test and challenge the Crown's case and ensure that the Crown properly discharges its burden of proof, regardless of counsel's firm conclusion that the client is guilty. At the same time, counsel has a negative duty not to advance defences or make assertions during closing argument that are known to be false. Does this compromise approach adequately protect both the duty to the client and the duty to the court? Consider the examples below.

Scenario Nine

Your client is charged with the robbery of a jewellery store. Two store clerks identify him as one of the robbers, based on a police photo line-up. There are weaknesses in the identification evidence as neither clerk is sure of their identification of the accused and their descriptions of the robber do not match the accused in two specific ways, namely, his fluency in English and his hairstyle. Prior to trial, your client confesses to you that he is one of the robbers. At trial, assuming the accused does not testify, can you cross-examine the two chief Crown witnesses and bring out the above weaknesses in their identification of your client? Furthermore, can you call defence witnesses to testify to your client's hairstyle and fluency in English at the time of the robbery, thereby inferring that he was not one of the robbers?[43]

Scenario Ten

Your client is a federal penitentiary inmate charged with the murder of a prison guard. The main evidence against him is a series of inculpatory statements to the police, including a detailed tape-recorded confession. Your client advises you that the statements were a lie as he was trying to protect the real killer, another inmate who is a friend of your client. He refuses to name the real killer. You investigate the matter and cannot find any evidence to support your client's proposed defence and you seriously question its veracity. Your client insists on testifying, contrary to your advice. Can you continue with the defence? Can you make the following statement, prior to calling your client to testify:

> My Lord, yes, I am going to call one witness for the defence, and that will be Reginald Colpitts, the accused. And, Sir, I must — as a matter of professional ethics — do assert that this is going to happen against my better judgment and counsel. But Mr. Colpitts has decided to take the stand and I — of course — will act as examiner.

---

[43]   *R. v. Li*, [1993] B.C.J. No. 2312 (B.C.C.A.).

Is it appropriate, in defence counsel's closing jury address, to make no reference to the accused's explanation for his confession to the police?[44]

Scenario Eleven

The accused is charged with the murder of one "Boggeyman". Three eye witnesses testify at trial and describe an argument between the deceased and the accused over the sale of some car tires at a place known as "Never Dirty". The accused is then seen to draw a knife and stab the deceased in the chest. After this single stab wound the deceased is still able to walk and is taken to the hospital where he later dies. The accused reports the altercation to the police, unaware that the deceased was mortally wounded, and tells the police that "Boggeyman" threatened him and struck him. On these facts, various defences arise including provocation, self-defence and lack of intent to kill. Defence counsel conducts the defence on this basis, cross-examining the three Crown witnesses so as to suggest the various defences to them. The cross-examinations are generally unsuccessful and counsel advises the accused that he must testify. At this point, at the end of the Crown's case, the accused apparently advises defence counsel in a brief consultation in court that "Boggeyman" never threatened or struck him. Defence counsel then advises the court that he will not be calling a defence and briefly addresses the jury, simply reminding them of the burden of proof on the Crown. Has defence counsel acted ethically?[45]

3. Taking Custody and Control of Real Evidence

The second area in which defence counsel's duties to the client and to the court come into conflict is when the client asks counsel to take possession of real evidence. The classic but somewhat exaggerated example is where a murder suspect appears in counsel's office, produces a smoking gun or a bloody shirt, and asks counsel to keep these items in the defence file.

The *Model Code of Professional Conduct*, perhaps surprisingly, is largely silent or unhelpful in responding to this ethical problem. Rule 4.01(2)(e) of the *Model Code* is typical. It prohibits "knowingly" attempting to "influence the course of justice by ... suppressing what ought to be disclosed or otherwise assisting in any fraud, crime or illegal conduct".

The prohibition against "suppressing what ought to be disclosed" fails to address the problem since, in the criminal law, there is generally no reciprocal disclosure obligation placed upon the defence. In *Stinchcombe*, the Court stated that the "absence of a duty to disclose" is consistent with the "purely adversarial role" of the defence. There are three exceptions to this general rule against defence disclosure: an alibi should be disclosed in sufficient time to

---

[44] *R. v. Colpitts*, [1965] S.C.J. No. 48, 47 C.R. 175 at 188-90, 47 C.R. 146 at 176-78 (S.C.C.).

[45] *Sankar v. State of Trinidad and Tobago*, [1995] 1 All E.R. 236 (P.C.).

allow it to be properly investigated;[46] a psychiatric defence should be disclosed in time to allow a Crown psychiatrist to examine the accused;[47] and any expert opinion evidence to be relied on by the defence should be disclosed 30 days before trial.[48] The usual remedy for failing to disclose is an adverse comment on the weight of the evidence, or an adjournment of the trial to allow the Crown time to prepare, but the non-disclosed defence evidence is still admissible. In this sense there is "no legal obligation" on the defence to disclose even in these three circumstances.[49]

The main point to note, in relation to the ethical issue under discussion, is that all three of these exceptions apply narrowly to particular forms of evidence that the defence actually tenders and relies on at trial. They all share the common feature that they require time for the Crown to prepare a response, either because they are technical or are easily concocted, and so they should be disclosed in advance of their actual use at trial. These narrow and exceptional rules relating to disclosure of defence evidence have nothing to do with the ethical problem of defence counsel simply taking possession of real evidence prior to trial, in particular, real evidence that the defence may never use at any eventual trial because it is incriminating.

Not only is there no reciprocal disclosure obligation in relation to real evidence that is simply taken into defence counsel's possession but, in addition, the accused's private communications with defence counsel about the real evidence are protected by the law of privilege, assuming that the accused client is seeking legal advice about what to do with the real evidence. The limits and scope of the law of privilege and confidentiality are dealt with in Chapter 4 and will not be discussed further in relation to this particular problem.

Of course, it is precisely because the law allows the client to discuss the evidence in confidence with counsel, and because there is no general reciprocal disclosure obligation on the defence, that the client may seek out a lawyer and may ask the lawyer to deposit items like the smoking gun or the bloody shirt in the lawyer's file. From the client's perspective, the lawyer's confidential file becomes the functional equivalent of throwing the gun or the shirt into a swamp. As a matter of common sense, lawyers cannot allow their privileged status in law to be used as a vehicle for disposing of incriminating evidence. Not surprisingly, the criminal law prohibits this conduct.

As set out above, Rule 4.01(2)(e) not only deals with "what ought to be disclosed" but goes on to prohibit any attempt to "influence the course of justice by ... assisting ... illegal conduct". This broad prohibition against "illegal conduct" is a significant concern for defence counsel who take possession of real evidence because the crimes of obstruction of justice and accessory after

---

[46] *R. v. Cleghorn*, [1995] S.C.J. No. 73, 100 C.C.C. (3d) 393 (S.C.C.).
[47] *R. v. Worth*, [1995] O.J. No. 1063, 98 C.C.C. (3d) 133 (Ont. C.A.).
[48] *Criminal Code*, R.S.C. 1985, c. C-46, s. 657.3.
[49] *R. v. P. (M.B.)*, [1994] S.C.J. No. 27, 89 C.C.C. (3d) 289 at 304-305 (S.C.C.).

the fact both include the hiding of evidence and disposing of evidence within their broad *actus reus* elements. In brief, as is clear from the case that follows, the section 139 *Criminal Code* offence of attempting to "obstruct, pervert or defeat the course of justice" has been held to include hiding and disposing of real evidence within its *actus reus*. Similarly, the section 23 offence defines an "accessory after the fact" as one who "receives, comforts or assists" a person who has committed an offence and clear authority holds that hiding or disposing of real evidence also falls within this *actus reus*. The only possible defence for a lawyer who took possession of the smoking gun or bloody shirt, and then kept them in the defence file, would be a lack of *mens rea*. Section 139 requires that the accused "wilfully" intends ("attempts") to obstruct the course of justice and section 23 requires that the accused's "purpose" is to enable the escape of the principal offender. These are significant mental elements requiring close analysis of the lawyer's intentions when taking custody of real evidence.

The beginning point in this discussion, therefore, is that the lawyer who takes possession of real evidence risks criminal prosecution, depending on his or her precise state of mind or intention. This hardly seems to be a satisfactory way to resolve ethical problems, by relying on the general criminal law to enforce them, and yet it is precisely what happened in the notorious case of *R. v. Murray*, which was discussed in both Chapter 1 and Chapter 4. Re-read this case and then consider the following notes and questions.

1. From a criminal law perspective, as opposed to a legal ethics perspective, the rules that emerge from the *Murray* case can be stated fairly simply (although Gravely J. does, on occasion, appear to conflate mistake of law and mistake of fact):

   (i) defence counsel can take possession of real evidence and conceal it during the pre-trial period, if counsel honestly believes it has exculpatory uses at trial and if counsel intends to so use it at trial. In such circumstances, counsel lacks the requisite *mens rea* for the offence of obstruct justice;

   (ii) defence counsel cannot take possession of real evidence and conceal it if counsel realizes that the evidence is inculpatory. In these circumstances, possession and concealment in the defence file amounts to the offence of obstructing justice.

   The obvious shortcoming that results from this purely criminal law approach to the present problem is that it creates a large loophole because of the defence of honest mistake of fact, like the one that arose in the *Murray* case. Justice Gravely found that the true facts were that the "critical tapes" were "overwhelmingly inculpatory" and, therefore, they ought not to have been concealed by Murray. That view was shared by Rosen, Cooper and the panel of three senior lawyers convened by the Law Society to advise Mr. Cooper as all five of these experienced lawyers recommended or agreed that the tapes should be conveyed to the authorities. However, Gravely J. also found "that a defence strategy of use of the tapes at trial was reasonably feasible" and that Murray believed that he was entitled to conceal them until it came time to use them as defence evidence at trial. In other words, Murray honestly believed in a set of facts which, if true, would render his conduct lawful, which is the classic definition of a defence of mistake of fact at common law. While this defence of honest mistake, or lack of *mens rea*, may be an appropriate response to the problem in terms of criminal liability, it hardly results in a satisfactory regulatory regime for lawyers' ethics. The fact remains that defence counsel's conduct did obstruct justice and, upon an appreciation of the true facts, there was an ethical duty to hand the tapes over to the authorities.

A regulatory or legal ethics approach to the problem would insist that defence counsel who take possession of potentially inculpatory real evidence must, at a minimum, take the following steps: review the material immediately and refuse to accept instructions from the client not to review the material; advise the client that accepting such instructions and not reviewing the material is unethical; advise the client that if the material, once reviewed, turns out to be substantially or predominantly incriminatory, it is illegal and unethical for counsel to conceal it from the authorities; and finally, if the exculpatory uses of the material are not plain and obvious, or are not clearly the predominant uses of the material, counsel must consult immediately with a panel of senior lawyers convened by the relevant Law Society. In this way, the honest mistakes of individual lawyers, working in secret and in isolation, will not be allowed to obstruct the course of justice.

2.   Justice Gravely noted that the existing Law Society rules on the subject are of "small help either to counsel or clients". Many commentators responded to the *Murray* case in a similar vein by calling upon the provincial Law Societies to provide some real guidance. Proulx and Layton, in their leading text on the subject,[50] describe the existing rules as "cryptic", providing "almost nothing in the way of useful advice" and leaving lawyers "largely in the dark as to how best to respond when confronted with the incriminating physical evidence problem".

In light of this regulatory vacuum, and the strong criticism of it, some law societies responded. In Ontario, a special committee was struck by the Law Society of Upper Canada but neither the committee nor Convocation was able to reach a consensus and no new rule emerged. The Canadian Bar Association also considered the issue and they too were unable to reach any consensus on a new rule. The Crown bar and defence bar take very different views of the issue and no generally accepted regulatory compromise has emerged.[51]

3.   The one Law Society that did pass a rule expressly addressing this problem is Alberta. The Alberta rule, which largely predates the *Murray* case, is found in Rule 4.01(9) of the Alberta *Code of Professional Conduct*, and includes reasonably clear and detailed rules and commentary, as follows:

>   A lawyer must not counsel or participate in:

>   . . . . .

>   (c)   the destruction of property having potential evidentiary value or the alteration of property so as to affect its evidentiary value; or

---

50   Michel Proulx & David Layton, *Ethics and Canadian Criminal Law* (Toronto: Irwin Law, 2001) at 484-85.

51   Gavin MacKenzie, *Lawyers and Ethics: Professional Responsibility and Discipline*, 4th ed. (Toronto: Thomson Carswell, 2006) at 7-11.

(d) the concealment of property having potential evidentiary value in a criminal proceeding.

Commentary

... Paragraph (d) applies to criminal matters due to the danger of obstruction of justice if evidence in a criminal matter is withheld. While a lawyer has no obligation to disclose the mere existence of such evidence, it would be unethical to accept possession of it and then conceal or destroy it. The lawyer must therefore advise someone wishing to deliver potential evidence that, if possession is accepted by the lawyer, it will be necessary to turn inculpatory evidence over to appropriate authorities (unless it consists of communications or documents that are privileged). When surrendering criminal evidence, however, a lawyer must protect confidentiality attaching to the circumstances in which the material was acquired, which may require that the lawyer act anonymously or through a third party.

Do you think the Alberta Rule provides adequate guidance to counsel? Ask yourself whether the Rule, as drafted, is too broad? Note that the Rule itself applies to "any property having potential evidentiary value" and holds that it is unethical to "conceal" such property. Would this include exculpatory evidence? There has never been an obligation on the defence to produce exculpatory real evidence to the Crown, prior to trial, and it can quite properly be kept secret in counsel's brief. It is often in the accused's interests to disclose exculpatory evidence to the Crown prior to trial, and seek withdrawal of the charges, but there is no ethical duty to this effect.

4. The ethical problem only arises when defence counsel take possession of inculpatory real evidence, or real evidence whose effect is substantially or predominantly inculpatory. Given that most pieces of evidence can be argued to have some possible or peripheral exculpatory uses, the appropriate question to address is the predominant or substantial use of the item of real evidence that is in counsel's possession. Indeed, this is the essence of the problem in the *Murray* case as counsel focused on peripheral uses of the critical tapes while ignoring their predominant effect.

5. Does the failure of the law societies to develop a simple rule, along the lines suggested above, amount to a serious failure of leadership by the regulators of the profession? Bearing in mind the question posed at the beginning of this chapter concerning the continuum between counsel's duty to the client and counsel's duty to the court, why might provincial regulators have been reluctant to take leadership on this question? Most recently, the Federation of Law Societies of Canada tackled this problem in their October 2009 *Model Code of Professional Conduct*. The Commentary to Rule 2.05(6) provides as follows:

A lawyer is never required to take or keep possession of *property relevant to a crime* or offence. If a lawyer comes into possession of *property relevant to a crime*, either from a client or another person, the lawyer must act in keeping with the lawyer's duty of loyalty and confidentiality to the client and the lawyer's duty to the administration of justice, which requires, at a minimum, that the lawyer not violate the law, improperly impede a police investigation, or otherwise obstruct the course of justice. *Generally, a lawyer in such circumstances should,* as soon as reasonably possible:

(a) turn over the property to the prosecution, either directly or anonymously;

(b) deposit the property with the trial judge in the relevant proceeding;

(c) deposit the property with the court to facilitate access by the prosecution or defence for testing or examination; or

(d) disclose the existence of the property to the prosecution and, if necessary, prepare to argue the issue of possession of the property.

When a lawyer discloses or delivers to the Crown or law enforcement authorities property relevant to a crime or offence, the lawyer has a duty to protect the client's confidences, including the client's identity, and to preserve solicitor and client privilege. This may be accomplished by the lawyer retaining independent counsel, who is not informed of the identity of the client and who is instructed not to disclose the identity of the instructing lawyer, to disclose or deliver the property.

If a lawyer delivers the property to the court under paragraph (c), he or she should do so in accordance with the protocol established for such purposes, which permits the lawyer to deliver the property to the court without formal application or investigation, ensures that the property is available to both the Crown and defence counsel for testing and examination upon motion to the court, and ensures that the fact that property was received from the defence counsel will not be the subject of comment or argument at trial. [emphasis added]

Ask yourself whether this latest effort at regulation continues the past history of ambiguity and ambivalence, for example, by using non-prescriptive language such as: "Generally, a lawyer in such circumstances should ...". Also ask whether the *Model Code* suffers from the same overbreadth as the Alberta rule as it applies to any property of the client that is merely "relevant to a crime". This would arguably cover exculpatory materials delivered by the client to the lawyer

6.   Consider the ethical obligations of defence counsel in the following scenarios.

Scenario Twelve

In the famous "Lake Pleasant Bodies Case", the accused was charged with murder. After being promised that the information would remain confidential, he advised his lawyers, who were preparing an insanity defence, that he had killed two other persons and told his lawyers where the bodies were located. Assuming that the number and nature of homicides committed by the accused was relevant to his insanity defence, was it ethical and legal for counsel to attend at the place where the accused said he had disposed of the other bodies, discover the bodies, photograph the bodies, conceal their existence until trial and then bring out evidence of the additional homicides during the accused's evidence-in-chief? What if defence counsel was asked directly by a parent of one of the victims if he or she knew of the whereabouts of the victim's body?[52]

Scenario Thirteen

In another well-known American case, the accused was charged with murder and robbery. The accused advised his counsel that the victim's wallet was in the garbage can behind the accused's home. This location for the victim's wallet, if true, would obviously assist the prosecution in proving the identity of the accused as the perpetrator. Was it ethical for counsel to retain a private investigator to search for and retrieve the wallet? Once retrieved, was there an ethical duty to turn the wallet over to the authorities? Finally, could the prosecution call the private investigator and/or counsel at trial to testify as to the location where the wallet was found and, by inference, reveal to the jury that the wallet must have been found as a result of instructions from the accused?[53]

4. Negotiating a Guilty Plea and Sentence

The somewhat pejorative label "plea bargaining", in fact, refers to one of defence counsel's most important responsibilities; that is, the duty to appropriately negotiate a guilty plea and sentence for a client who faces inevitable conviction at trial, or for a client who simply wishes to acknowledge guilt, regardless of his or her prospects at trial.

There are many difficult ethical issues in this area, as evidenced by Proulx and Layton devoting some 60 pages to the topic in their leading text. In particular, counsel who routinely overbook their calendars and negotiate guilty pleas at the last minute, without ever properly learning the facts and law applicable to the case, are acting unethically. Similarly, counsel who pressure the client to plead guilty, for example, when counsel has to be in another court or when counsel is unprepared for trial, are acting unethically. Finally, counsel who act on a client's instructions to plead guilty for reasons of expediency, in spite of the client's confidential protestations of innocence, are arguably acting unethically.

The relevant rules of professional conduct address the issue of plea bargaining in reasonable detail. For example, Rule 4.01(7) and (8) of the *Model Code* provides as follows:

> 4.01(7) Before a charge is laid or at any time after a charge is laid, a lawyer for an accused or potential accused may discuss with the prosecutor the possible disposition of the case, unless the client instructs otherwise.
>
> 4.01(8) A lawyer for an accused or potential accused may enter into an agreement with the prosecutor about a guilty plea if, following investigation,

---

[52] *People v. Belge*, 372 N.Y.S. 2d 798 (Co. Ct. 1975), affd 376 N.Y.S. 2d 771 (App. Div. 1975), affd 359 N.E. 2d 377 (N.Y. 1976).

[53] *People v. Meredith*, 631 P. 2d 46 (Cal. 1981).

(a) the lawyer advises his or her client about the prospects for an acquittal or finding of guilt;

(b) the lawyer advises the client of the implications and possible consequences of a guilty plea and particularly of the sentencing authority and discretion of the court, including the fact that the court is not bound by any agreement about a guilty plea;

(c) the client voluntarily is prepared to admit the necessary factual and mental elements of the offence charged; and

(d) the client voluntarily instructs the lawyer to enter into an agreement as to a guilty plea.

Commentary

The public interest in the proper administration of justice should not be sacrificed in the interest of expediency.

In summary, the four main ethical rules for defence counsel, when conducting plea and sentence negotiations, are as follows:

(1) Counsel must not conclude plea and sentence discussions without first completing a thorough analysis of the facts and law applicable to the case. As Rule 4.01(8) states, such discussions can only be concluded "following investigation";

(2) Having completed the above "investigation" of the case, the client is entitled to skilled advice from counsel as to "the prospects for an acquittal or finding of guilt" if the case proceeds to trial, and as to "the implications and possible consequences of a guilty plea", again quoting from Rule 4.01(8). In other words, the client is entitled to weigh the relative merits of trial versus guilty plea on the basis of competent advice;

(3) Although the client is entitled to counsel's advice, the decision as to what plea to enter is the client's decision and it must be made freely and "voluntarily" as Rule 4.01(8) provides. There are many decisions in the course of a criminal case where counsel has considerable independence from the client and where it is counsel who makes the ultimate decision. However, even the strongest proponents of this "lawyer control" model of the solicitor and client relationship agree that it is the client who must decide what plea to enter;[54] and

(4) Although the client is entitled to make the ultimate decision to plead guilty, the plea must be based on an admission of "the necessary factual and mental elements of the offence charged", as Rule 4.01(8) provides, and the "public interest" must not be sacrificed "in the in-

---

[54] G. Arthur Martin, Q.C., "The Role and Responsibility of the Defence Advocate" (1969) 12 C.L.Q. 376 at 386-88.

terest of expediency". Section 606(1.1) of the *Criminal Code* was recently enacted and underlines this point by requiring a plea inquiry that includes "an admission of the essential elements of the offence".

The first three rules set out above are relatively straightforward. It is the fourth rule, concerning insincere guilty pleas or "pleas of convenience", that is controversial and subject to considerable disagreement, both amongst the commentators and as between the courts of Canada, the U.K. and the U.S.A. In particular, there is disagreement as to whether the accused can plead guilty, and then openly dispute the factual basis for the guilty plea in court, and, even more controversial, whether the accused can plead guilty and admit the essential facts in open court but maintain his or her innocence in confidential discussions with counsel. The predominant Canadian position, to date, is illustrated by the following case.

R. v. K. (S.)

[1995] O.J. No. 1627, 99 C.C.C. (3d) 376
(Ont. C.A., Catzman, Carthy and Osborne JJ.A.)

CARTHY J.A.:—

The appellant was originally charged with 10 counts of sexual offences against five young girls, went to trial in the youth court, and eventually pleaded guilty to four of these counts. He now seeks to set aside the plea of guilty, knowing that his sentence of 60 days' open custody and 22 months' probation has been served and that he may have to face a second trial on all 10 counts. The appellant protests his innocence and says that he has never wavered from that position. In fact, the fresh evidence tendered to this court unequivocally bears out his consistency and the question for consideration is whether this is sufficient, in the circumstances, to set aside the plea of guilty.

. . . . .

A summary of that fresh evidence can be taken from the affidavit of trial counsel which is consistent throughout with what is stated by the appellant and his father. Crown counsel had called all of his witnesses at trial and closed his case. At that point counsel for the accused discussed with the Crown the possibility of entering guilty pleas to four of the comparatively less serious assaults in return for a withdrawal of the remaining counts and, possibly, a joint submission for a non-custodial sentence. Defence counsel then spoke to the accused and his parents outlining the dangers of seeking to defend the more serious counts and the likelihood of a significant custodial sentence. He made it clear throughout that the choice was that of the accused and the trial could continue if that is what he wanted to do.

Instructions were given to proceed with the guilty pleas and in the next meeting with the Crown, agreement was reached that the appellant would plead guilty to four of the counts and that a joint submission for non-custodial disposition would be tendered. This was followed by a further discussion between counsel and the accused and his parents at which they were advised that the next step would be to have a "pre-trial" in the judge's chambers to discuss a plea resolution arrangement. That meeting followed and the trial judge indicated that he would offer no guarantees as to a non-custodial sentence if the predisposition report was not favourable.

A further meeting with the accused and his parents ensued and at this point it is worth quoting para. 13 of the affidavit of trial counsel:

> 13. During this conversation, I advised the Appellant again that the choice to enter a plea of guilty was his alone and that we would proceed with the trial, if that was his choice. As well, during this conversation, the Appellant advised me that the allegations made against him were not the truth. I advised the Appellant that criminal courts do not necessarily deal in truth, but they deal in evidence and explained to him carefully what the difference was. At the end of this conversation, the Appellant instructed me to enter pleas of guilty to the four offences we had discussed, the offences to which the Crown was prepared to accept guilty pleas.

The transcript shows that trial counsel then entered the pleas of guilty on behalf of the accused. In the cross-examination of the appellant's father it is stated that the mother questioned whether her son would have to stand up and admit guilt in front of the five girls when he was not in fact guilty and that trial counsel replied that he would do it on behalf of the accused. That seems confirmed by what did occur and is not referred to in the affidavit of trial counsel.

The judge accepted the pleas of guilty and adjourned for preparation of predisposition reports. Two such reports were prepared, one by a probation officer and the other by a psychologist, and each of them noted with concern that the accused was emphatic in declaring his innocence rendering the provision of counselling problematic.

In the transcript of the sentencing hearing itself, there is no mention of any consideration of reviewing the guilty pleas, but it is clear that both counsel were very conscious of the declaration of innocence in the predisposition reports. It is plain from the words of counsel for the accused that he recognized the threat of a custodial sentence. Crown counsel concedes the earlier submission for a non-custodial sentence but indicates that he recognizes the trial judge's difficulty in view of the content of the reports. In concluding that a custodial sentence was required, the trial judge summed up his views as follows:

> One must look at remorse and quite frankly, in this case, I see none. I saw none during the evidence that was brought forward, nor do I see any in the reports. And that is of great concern to me. Not only is there not any remorse, in both reports, not only is [*sic*] the accused, but his parents, are adamantly declaring innocence. I can only deal with the facts and the evidence as brought forward, and I do not agree with that.

The sentencing occurred on June 18th and the appellant decided to appeal on June 30, 1993, when his probation officer advised him that so long as he continued to deny the offences, he could not receive the treatment required in his probation order. That would mean he would be returned to the youth court for failing to comply with the terms of the probation order. This is confirmed in a letter from the probation officer appended to an affidavit which is part of the fresh evidence.

This is not an appeal where one need be suspicious of the motives of the appellant in seeking to set aside a plea of guilty. It was not prompted by dissatisfaction with the disposition, although I have no doubt the appellant was disappointed. It was prompted rather by the fact that the continued denial of guilt made performance of a term of probation impossible. The appellant was unaware of the contradiction between a plea of guilty and denial until he received advice from his probation officer. His state of mind was induced by his trial counsel and perpetuated by the trial judge who failed to intervene and make inquiry as to the validity of the guilty pleas when he read the pre-sentence reports. The trial judge went in the opposite direction from a review of the plea and refused to accept the joint submission for a non-custodial sentence. The system was tilted askew by the simple fact that a person protesting innocence became engaged in plea bargaining.

In the *Report of the Attorney General's Advisory Committee on Charge Screening, Disclosure, and Resolution Discussions* (1993), chaired by the Honourable G. Arthur Martin at p. 318, the committee recommends that the Attorney General seek an amendment to the *Criminal Code* ... requiring a sentencing judge to question the accused as to the validity of the guilty plea regardless of whether or not the accused is represented by counsel. It is stated at p. 320:

> As noted above, the practice in many American jurisdictions is that a plea of guilty may be accepted even though the accused maintains his or her innocence. If the plea comprehension inquiry is desirable in the American context, where ascertaining that an accused denies guilt is not fatal to the plea of guilty proceeding, it follows, in the Committee's view, that such an inquiry is even more desirable in Ontario, *where a plea of guilty cannot proceed if the accused denies guilt*. The greater scope in Ontario for the courts to decline to accept a plea of guilty heightens the importance of the courts ensuring through inquiry that a plea of guilty is sufficient in law. [Emphasis of Carthy J.A.]

No case authority is cited in the report for the emphasized clause but the conclusion seems plain from a reading of *Adgey v. R.* ...

. . . . .

> If the trial Judge chooses to hear evidence, for the purpose of satisfying himself that the charges are well founded or in order to have a factual background prior to imposing sentence, the evidence may indicate *the accused never intended to admit to a fact which is an essential ingredient of the offence* with which he is charged or he may have misapprehended the

effect of the guilty plea or never intended to plead guilty at all, in any of which events the Judge may, in his discretion, direct that a plea of not guilty be entered or permit the accused to withdraw his original plea and enter a new one. ... Statements made in the course of the inquiry following a guilty plea may, although not admitted by the Crown, justify the Court in rejecting the guilty plea and proceeding to trial. [Emphasis of Carthy J.A.]

Rule 10, Commentary 12 of the Law Society of Upper Canada's *Rules of Professional Conduct* [now Rule 4.01(9)] deals with plea bargaining and requires that the lawyer be assured, among other things, that the client is prepared to admit the necessary factual and mental elements of the guilty plea. Thus, it was proper for the trial judge to assume at the time of the plea that the appellant admitted the facts which had been put in evidence concerning the four counts but, at the second stage of the hearing when it became clear that the appellant denied the facts in evidence, the trial judge should have at least considered exercising his discretion to reject the guilty pleas and proceed with the trial.

He did not do so and this court must intervene to correct that oversight.

I have no hesitation in concluding that the guilty pleas should be set aside. This case presents a graphic example of why it is essential to the plea bargaining process that the accused person is prepared to admit to the facts that support the conviction. The court should not be in the position of convicting and sentencing individuals, who fall short of admitting the facts to support the conviction unless that guilt is proved beyond a reasonable doubt. Nor should sentencing proceed on the false assumption of contrition. That did not happen here, but worse, the sentence became impossible to perform. Plea bargaining is an accepted and integral part of our criminal justice system but must be conducted with sensitivity to its vulnerabilities. A court that is misled, or allows itself to be misled, cannot serve the interests of justice.

I would, therefore, set aside the guilty pleas, rescind the withdrawal by the Crown of the other counts, and direct a new trial on all ten counts. ...

NOTES AND QUESTIONS

1. The *K. (S.)* case is a classic example of a so-called "plea of convenience". Defence counsel and the accused, fearing the risk of convictions and a significant custodial sentence on six more serious counts, negotiated guilty pleas and the Crown's support for a non-custodial sentence on the four less serious counts. This pragmatic "plea bargain" was carried out, in spite of the accused's confidential protestations of innocence to his counsel, in order to avoid the risk of a much worse result at trial. Counsel and the accused were simply engaged in risk management and were not concerned about the more noble search for truth and justice.

    Leading American authorities support this form of plea, based on risk assessments, even where the accused openly asserts innocence in court and refuses to admit the essential facts alleged by the prosecution.[55] In the U.K., a more modi-fied "plea of convenience" is also permitted. The accused must admit the essen-tial factual ingredients of the offence, upon pleading guilty in open court, but it is ethical for counsel to proceed with the plea when the client privately insists on his or her innocence.[56]

2. Returning to the continuum of counsel's duties to the client and to the court, does the Canadian position go too far in stressing counsel's function as an "officer of the court", seeking the truth at all costs, in spite of substantial risk to the client? Or does the American or U.K. position go too far in allowing counsel to prag-matically and even cynically pursue the client's best interests without regard for the truth and while perhaps sacrificing the overriding duty not to mislead the court?

3. Does the Canadian position on this issue better protect against wrongful convic-tions or does it increase their risk? In this regard, consider the following two scenarios.

Scenario Fourteen

Your client is charged with various counts of assault and threatening against his former domestic partner, one Morales. You obtain disclosure and meet with your client who insists he is innocent. He furnishes you with various ma-terials supporting his defence, all to the general effect that Ms. Morales is of bad character, has made false allegations in the past and has now recanted the allegations against your client. You advise your client that you are only re-tained on a Legal Aid certificate, that domestic violence allegations are taken very seriously by the courts and that the defence materials, while useful, "could not secure an acquittal" because of the frequency of recantations in such cases. Your client infers from all this that he should plead guilty and you discuss this option. He agrees, a few days before the trial date, to plead guilty to one count of assault but not to the threatening charges which he continues to dispute. This proposal is not accepted by the Crown. You therefore attend at court on the trial date without clear instructions as to whether the case is proceeding to trial or whether it will be resolved in a guilty plea. You advise your client in court that you are not prepared for trial and that a guilty plea to an additional count of threatening, which the Crown is insisting on, will likely not affect the overall sentence. At this point, your client agrees to plead guilty to one count of assault and one count of threatening. He enters the two pleas personally, after being questioned by the trial judge as to the voluntariness of the pleas. The Crown withdraws the other charges and reads in the facts sup-porting the guilty pleas and your client personally admits the facts. Have you acted ethically as counsel?[57]

---

55 *North Carolina v. Alford*, 400 U.S. 25 (1970).
56 *R. v. Herbert* (1992), 94 Cr. App. R. 230 (C.A.).
57 *R. v. Ceballo*, [1997] O.J. No. 5035, 14 C.R. (5th) 15 (Ont. Prov. Div.).

Scenario Fifteen

The accused T. and D. are jointly charged with the first degree murder of a 14-year-old girl, one Gaudet, who was sexually assaulted and then strangled. The Crown's case depends on various pieces of circumstantial evidence, suggesting the accused may be the perpetrators, as well as incriminating statements to the police upon arrest in which T. admitted that he was the principal who strangled the deceased and D. admitted to being with T. and probably sexually assaulting the deceased while extremely intoxicated. The accused both call alibi defences and testify that the police had beaten and threatened them and then dictated their confessions. The jury deliberates for 14 days before convicting both accused of first degree murder. They are sentenced to life imprisonment and they appeal. The Court of Appeal dismisses T.'s appeal but allows D.'s appeal and orders a retrial on a charge of second degree murder, holding that there is no evidence D. was a party to first degree murder. On the retrial, D. pleads guilty to manslaughter and is sentenced to 12 years imprisonment. The accused D. has consistently maintained his innocence; he pleads guilty to the reduced charge of manslaughter at the re-trial only because he has "lost all hope of winning at trial". His counsel later explains: "D. decided to plead guilty for the sole reason that he no longer felt capable either of holding up through a second trial or of running the risk of a murder conviction, and not because he admitted participating in the death of Sandra Gaudet." Substantial evidence that would have been helpful to the defence, and that was never disclosed, emerges at a subsequent Commission of Inquiry into the practices of the Quebec Police Force. The two accused seek to re-open their case. Did defence counsel act ethically in pleading D. guilty to manslaughter at the re-trial and should the guilty plea be set aside?[58]

E. FURTHER READING

Boon, Andrew & Jenny Levin, *The Ethics and Conduct of Lawyers in England and Wales* (Oxford: Hart Publishing, 1999).

Burkoff, John, *Criminal Defense Ethics: Law and Liability*, rev. ed. (St. Paul, MN: West Group, 2000).

Freedman, Milton, *Lawyers' Ethics in an Adversary System* (New York: Bobbs-Merrill, 1975).

Freedman, Milton & Abbe Smith, *Understanding Lawyers' Ethics*, 3rd ed. (Lexis Nexis, 2004).

Hall, John, *Professional Responsibility of the Criminal Lawyer*, 2nd ed. (New York: Clark Boardman Callaghan, 1996).

---

[58]   *R. v. Taillefer; R. v. Duguay*, [2003] S.C.J. No. 75, 17 C.R. (6th) 57 (S.C.C.); D.M. Tanovitch, "*Taillefer*: Disclosure, Guilty Pleas and Ethics" (2003) 17 C.R. (6th) 149.

Martin, G. Arthur, "The Role and Responsibility of the Defence Advocate" (1970) 12 C.L.Q. 376.

"Panel Discussion: Problems in Advocacy and Ethics" in Law Society of Upper Canada, *Defending a Criminal Case* (Toronto: Richard DeBoo, 1969) at 279.

Proulx, Michel & David Layton, *Ethics and Canadian Criminal Law* (Toronto: Irwin Law, 2001).

Savage, C., "The Duties and Conduct of Crown and Defence Counsel in a Criminal Trial" (1958-59) 1 Crim. L.R. 164.

Schroeder, F., "Some Ethical Problems in Criminal Law" in Law Society of Upper Canada, *Representing an Arrested Client and Police Interrogation* (Toronto: Law Society of Upper Canada, 1963) at 87.

CHAPTER 9

LAWYERS IN ORGANIZATIONAL SETTINGS: CORPORATE COUNSEL

A. INTRODUCTION

While ethical issues emerge for lawyers in all practice environments, the challenges facing lawyers in organizational settings are especially complex. Lawyers working in corporate contexts build relationships with clients that may not fit neatly within the traditional paradigm of a sole practitioner or a lawyer in a law firm representing individuals. For "in-house" counsel, unique ethical challenges and often different ethical obligations can arise.

More lawyers are facing these challenges, as practice as an in-house lawyer both becomes increasingly common and increasingly attractive as a career option. Companies have found it valuable to have dedicated legal expertise resident within their walls, with professionals who know both the law and the organization intimately. Hiring corporate counsel can also be far more cost-efficient than paying outside law firms on a case-by-case basis. For many lawyers, in-house practice can offer the combined attractions of interesting work, a lifestyle often perceived as more accommodating than that offered by private practice, greater job security, and significant financial reward through both substantial salaries and the chance to participate in the success of the company through compensation plans that include stock options or other incentives tied to company success.

Despite this shift towards greater numbers of corporate counsel and the transformation of their practice environment, increased public and scholarly attention to the ethical challenges facing corporate counsel is a relatively recent phenomenon. The spectacular financial scandals of the late 1990s and early 2000s, and the collapse in 2001 of what was then the world's largest publicly traded corporation, Enron, in particular, led to both the most radical transformation of business law in the United States since the 1930s in the *Sarbanes-Oxley Act of 2002*[1] and to changes in rules of professional conduct for American lawyers to respond specifically to what was seen as lawyer responsibility for failing to prevent the scandals from occurring. Canada has not been immune from corporate scandal, with home-grown examples of corporate fraud involving companies traded on stock exchanges in Canada in the late 1990s such as Bre-X Minerals, Livent and YBM Magnex. The implosion in 2001–2002 of Nortel Networks (which at the time had the largest market

---

[1] Pub. L. 107-204.

capitalization of any publicly traded Canadian company), and of Sino-Forest (at the time Canada's largest publicly traded forestry company) in 2011 both served as reminders that corporate scandal was not just an American phenomenon. Rules of professional conduct for lawyers in organizational settings were changed in Canada in the wake of the Enron scandal but, as will be detailed below, in significantly different ways than those changes made to rules in the United States.

One question that emerged on both sides of the border in the wake of these scandals was whether lawyers should be seen as "gatekeepers", responsible for protecting the public against malfeasance by their corporate or organizational clients. This conception challenged the traditional understanding of lawyers as "zealous advocates" responsible for loyalty only to their clients. A number of issues specific to corporate environments flow from this clash of ideas. Should lawyers ever be responsible for reporting on their clients to a government agency or regulator? Should a lawyer ever be permitted to do so to prevent financial harm to investors or others? These questions are important for lawyers in all settings, but the consequences of decisions about them are especially acute for a lawyer who is "in-house", working for a single corporate client or organization as its employee.

In addition, lawyers in corporate settings also face the challenges of maintaining independence and integrity as professionals while simultaneously functioning as employees of the organization they are advising. Lawyers working in-house are valued for their in-depth knowledge of the organization's activities and culture, and aspire to become a "trusted advisor". But to whom do they owe their loyalty? Who is the client? The senior executive to whom the lawyer might report will of course have responsibility for providing instructions, directions and often evaluations of the lawyer-employee's performance (and related decisions about compensation), but in a corporate setting the "client" is the organization itself rather than the individual.

Lawyers working in corporate environments need to be especially careful when their advice and counsel is sought for business matters as well as legal ones. Do the usual rules of privilege and confidentiality apply? For in-house counsel in Europe, a 2010 decision of the European Court of Justice, discussed later in this chapter, reconfirmed the European perspective that in-house lawyers there lacked independence because of their employment relationships and therefore did not have privilege. Can an in-house lawyer give business advice? Should he or she? How is legal advice delineated from business advice, if at all? And what impact might that have on privilege?

Further complicating matters, many lawyers in corporate settings also function as "corporate secretaries" or "compliance officers", sometimes while also serving as general counsel or lawyers for the organization, but often just as a member of the management team and not in a legal capacity. The wearing of multiple hats, and the transformation of the role of corporate secretary over the last decade, raise additional ethical concerns.

Finally, in-house lawyers have to be especially aware of the challenges to their independence, and the phenomenon described as "cognitive dissonance". As many legal ethics experts have noted, in cases of client misconduct, lawyers' professional norms of client loyalty often conflict with personal norms of honesty and integrity. To reduce the "cognitive dissonance", lawyers will often unconsciously dismiss or discount evidence of misconduct and its impact on third parties. This becomes even more of a problem when lawyers bond socially and professionally with other employees, including senior management. The more a lawyer blends into insider culture, the greater the pressures to conform to the organization's cultural norms. That can in turn lead lawyers to underestimate risk and to suppress compromising information in order to preserve internal solidarity. In the long run, this dynamic can create problems for everyone: clients lose access to disinterested advice; lawyers lose capacity for independent judgment and moral autonomy; and the public loses protection from organizational misconduct. While this is a problem for all lawyers, the challenge is especially strong for corporate counsel. Although the financial and other consequences of terminating a relationship with a major client can be significant for lawyers in law firms, they pale in comparison to the consequences faced by an in-house counsel who is in essence walking away from his or her job and the attendant financial security. The pressures — personal and professional — are enormous.

This chapter provides an introduction to the important roles lawyers play in corporate organizations, together with an overview of the many ethical challenges they encounter. It then sets out the background to the Enron scandal and introduces the actions of lawyers in that debacle that led directly to moves by the United States Congress not only to directly legislate new rules for lawyers in organizational settings, but to give responsibility for policing that conduct to a government agency, the Securities and Exchange Commission. It considers the debate over whether lawyers should simply have to report malfeasance "up the ladder" within an organization, or engage in "noisy withdrawal" and report to authorities. The extent to which those changes have or have not been adopted in the Canadian context is also assessed. Finally, the problems of privilege, issues for lawyers functioning in multiple roles within an organization, and the European approach to privilege and independence for company lawyers are also introduced.

B. ETHICAL OBLIGATIONS OF CORPORATE COUNSEL

1. Introduction

Who are corporate counsel? What is their role? As you consider these two readings, reflect on whether the ethics issues you have studied so far apply generally to lawyers in all contexts, or whether special attention and special rules are required to address the particular corporate environments in which these lawyers are working.

MILTON C. REGAN, JR.

"Professional Responsibility and the Corporate Lawyer"
(2000) 13 Geo. J. Legal Ethics 197[*]
[footnotes omitted]

... [C]orporate law practice continues to raise important and complex questions of professional responsibility that have implications for all lawyers. In the most immediate and concrete terms, changes in corporate use of legal services in the past twenty-five years or so have dramatically altered relationships between law firms and clients, partners and associates, partners and partners, and among law firms. Increased reliance on in-house legal departments has brought inside the corporation much work that previously served as the foundation of long-term relationships between firms and clients. Corporations now tend to seek specialized expertise rather than general services from outside counsel. They also exert more vigorous controls over how those services are provided and how they are priced.

. . . . .

Aside from the importance of corporate practice for the ways in which modern legal services are provided, certain features of that practice are notable for the important ethical issues that they raise. First are the complexities of representing an organization rather than an individual. That undertaking can be especially challenging because ethical provisions for the most part implicitly are premised on a relationship between an attorney and an individual client. The lawyer who represents a corporation represents an abstraction: her client is the corporate entity rather than any of the individuals who act on its behalf. Such lawyers deal daily with managers and officials who are authorized to speak for the corporation, yet they must not mistake those individuals for the entity itself. Even in the normal course of events, actors in a large organization may not be in full agreement on various matters. Lines of authority are not always clear; the organization chart may obscure as much as reveal who wields power and influence. The lawyer thus often must become familiar with the dynamics of the bureaucratic milieu in order to discern just which actors speak for the corporation on what issues.

The difficulty is compounded when there is reason to question whether an official is acting in the best interests of the corporation. Ethical provisions, along with the business judgment rule, suggest that the lawyer should defer to the manager in most instances, even when she might have charted a different course under the circumstances. That presumption of deference evaporates, however, when the lawyer knows that a corporate official is violating a duty to the entity or is acting illegally so as to threaten the corporation with serious harm. The problem is that this transformative moment can be quite difficult to recognize. One reason is that knowledge often is fragmented in large modern organizations. Information sufficient to ensure that a lawyer "knows" of mis-

---

[*]   Reproduced with permission.

conduct may be scattered among several offices and people, no one of whom has the complete picture. It is tempting in such situations to conclude that one lacks the certitude necessary to challenge the corporate decisionmaker, even when such ignorance is the product of diligent avoidance of unpleasant facts.

. . . . .

In sum, it is increasingly the case that lawyers in many kinds of modern practice represent organizations rather than individuals. Such a phenomenon calls for a more sophisticated understanding of the organizational milieu and the distinctive ethical issues that it generates. Corporate lawyers have significant experience with such representation, and often are acutely aware of how little guidance ethical rules can provide in this setting. A focus on corporate practice thus can generate insights that are becoming important for an ever larger proportion of lawyers.

A second disjunction between corporate practice and ethical rules is the fact that the latter traditionally have been formulated primarily with the litigator in mind. Yet transactional work, a staple of corporate practice, raises questions that do not always fit easily within this paradigm. Should a party with whom the lawyer is negotiating a joint venture, for instance, be regarded more as an adversary or as a cooperative partner? The answer may be important in determining the attorney's duty of confidentiality, as well as in identifying conflicts of interest that could arise from simultaneous or successive representation of other clients.

Similarly, should the fact that business negotiations typically take place outside the supervision of a court place a greater or lesser responsibility on lawyer and client to disclose information that other parties might regard as relevant to the negotiations? Litigation is marked by both judicial oversight and relatively stringent disclosure duties because of concern about the integrity of legal proceedings. By contrast, disclosure obligations are relatively relaxed in transactional settings, despite the absence of any constraining judicial involvement. They are based primarily on common law fraud standards, which in turn look to conventional expectations of typical parties engaged in negotiation. Yet reliance solely on such expectations as the touchstone of legality has the potential to create a downward spiral, as aggressive practices provoke even more aggressive responses. The cumulative effect may be to lower expectations of fair dealing, increase bargaining costs, and secure judicial validation of provisions formerly regarded as unenforceable. Corporate lawyers historically have had to navigate the transactional terrain with minimal guidance from ethical rules. This does not mean, however, that the ethical issues that arise in this form of practice are of negligible importance. Rather, it highlights the fact that law practice requires a cultivated sense of judgment that goes beyond mere rule compliance.

A third notable dimension of corporate practice is the fact that many corporate lawyers not only represent organizations, but are employed by them. The widely-noted rise in the visibility and prestige of inside counsel in the last two decades or so has fueled the continuing debate over the meaning of lawyers' professional independence. Here again, corporate lawyers have firsthand experience with a growing phenomenon: the increasing number of lawyers who are employees in various types of organizations. To what extent is it possible to preserve a sense of identification with a distinct professional legal culture while being immersed in an organizational culture as well? Is it easier to invoke ethical constraints on company conduct if the lawyer is familiar with corporate operations and is regarded as a member of the "team?" Or does her dependence on a single client who is her employer tend to make her excessively deferential toward company officials?

Many lawyers and commentators suggest that in-house counsel are in a position to provide a unique combination of business and legal advice that helps the organization plan for, rather than simply react to, a tumultuous global economy. Rather than merely passing judgment on the legality of measures that management proposes, counsel help frame strategy with an eye toward anticipating and preventing legal issues from arising in the first place. This "proactive" approach to practice expands the boundaries of legal practice to include functions not traditionally characterized as strictly legal in nature. It also calls into question the traditional assumption that the client determines the ends of representation and the lawyer selects the means to achieve those ends. This dichotomy generally is an important premise of ethical rules, which conceptualize the lawyer as distant from the substantive objectives of the client. If in-house counsel do indeed become integrally involved in formulating company goals and structuring company operations, it may be unrealistic to insist they nonetheless remain legal technicians morally unaccountable for the consequences of those activities.

. . . . .

Another development in which corporate lawyers are the advance troops is the increasingly global nature of law practice. National boundaries pose no obstacle to modern corporate activity. A parent firm may be in one country, its subsidiaries in several others, and its joint venture partners or licensees in still others. Furthermore, its products and services may well be available in most countries around the world. Corporate counsel may have her office in New York, consult long-distance about Italian law with a subsidiary in Italy that is entering into a licensing agreement with a South African company, or travel to Japan to negotiate with a Japanese bank about financing for a project that will engage in manufacturing in several Asian countries and sell its products mainly in North America and Western Europe.

Aside from the need to master the interplay among the substantive legal provisions of the different jurisdictions that may assert an interest in such corporate activities, counsel also must navigate through a thicket of differing and sometimes conflicting rules that purport to govern the conduct of lawyers. There is no common set of ethical provisions that apply to lawyers engaged in cross-border practice. Indeed, there is no uniform definition of what constitutes the practice of law in various countries, or of what is permissible activity for foreign lawyers who are authorized to practice in a jurisdiction. Once these threshold issues are resolved, the lawyer must determine which country's ethical standards — and standards of malpractice liability — are applicable. An example of the striking differences that can exist between legal regimes is the Court of Justice of the European Communities' decision that in proceedings brought by the European Commission the attorney-client privilege may not be invoked with respect to communications between a client and its in-house counsel. The difficulty of reconciling ethical obligations under different state regimes in the United States already creates unpredictability for the large number of lawyers engaged in multistate practice. That complexity is magnified exponentially in the arena of transnational practice, and corporate lawyers are the ones who increasingly must respond to it.

. . . . .

... The fact that corporate lawyers are strategically placed in positions of influence with respect to regulated activities has led some to maintain that they have an obligation to serve as "gatekeepers" who restrain misconduct or even "whistleblowers" who report it. Such roles are in tension with the notion that the attorney's sole obligation is to the client, and the claim that self-regulation by the legal profession offers the best assurance of ethical legal practice.

This leads to a final feature of corporate law practice that has particular significance for ethical purposes. This is the fact that corporations are not simply private actors pursuing their own goals along with other interest groups in society. Rather, as Charles Lindblom has noted, a market-based economy delegates to corporations substantial authority over matters of wide-ranging social importance, such as employment, the availability of consumer goods, and investment decisions that determine how and when resources will be used. This arguably places the business firm at the intersection of private and public domains. In light of this, it is not surprising that the nature and purposes of the corporation have been fiercely contested questions since at least the latter part of the nineteenth century. The debate has taken on even greater urgency as sprawling global operations and the rapid emergence and obsolescence of new technology have intensified the dynamism of corporate enterprise at the dawn of the twenty-first century.

This generates special challenges for corporate lawyers because it requires that they play two roles that to some degree are in tension. The rapid pace of change in the corporate world demands that lawyers create new legal forms and arrangements to address unprecedented circumstances. Such creativity has always been necessary for those who represent corporations, from the lawyers who devised trusts and holding companies in the late nineteenth century to those who fashioned various "poison pills" to deter takeover activity a century later. As Michael Powell has observed, business lawyers create law "from the ground up" by developing novel legal structures and casting them in a vocabulary that confers on them the status of legitimate extensions of traditional legal categories. As activities outrun the legal paradigms meant to contain them, the alert lawyer exploits "loopholes" and pushes against the limits of the law in an effort to secure advantage for her client.

Yet the corporate lawyer must also be mindful that the integrity of the legal system is a form of social capital in a market society. A competitive economy requires cooperation and trust in order to flourish … . Law cannot be seen merely in instrumental terms, as an obstacle to be overcome with the help of professionals who are trained to capitalize on its ambiguity. In such a world, "abiding by the 'rule of law' is only for wimps: the smart, powerful people opt out of law by means of lawyers, and thereby provoke others to do likewise." It is difficult for legal and social norms in such a world to persist beyond the next shift in the balance of power. The effectiveness of law in a democratic polity depends heavily on voluntary compliance, and such compliance in turn requires the perception that law has at least some intrinsic normative force.

How corporate lawyers present legal provisions to their clients, and how far they are willing to push the letter of the law regardless of its spirit, cumulatively has the potential to have a profound effect on attitudes toward the legal system. Performance of this quasi-public role means that lawyers at times may have to prevail upon their clients to forbear from exploiting every possible legal advantage, for the sake of both the client's long-term interest and that of society as a whole. The distinctive function and influence of business corporations in a market democracy thus means that the corporate lawyer's work unavoidably has both private and public dimensions whose tensions are not always easily mediated.

PAUL D. PATON

"Corporate Counsel as Corporate Conscience: Ethics and
Integrity in the Post-Enron Era"
(2005) 84 Can. Bar Rev. 533
[footnotes omitted]

The transformation of corporate, or in-house, counsel practice in recent years has rightly garnered considerable attention. Once considered by some to be the refuge of those unable to sustain the intense pressure of a private major firm practice, an in-house lawyer now occupies a privileged position in the "corridors of power." The misperception of corporate counsel as lawyers lacking the "stern stuff required to fill the vast quotas of billable hours and sustain the great partnerships," and occupying "the lesser part of our profession" is mercifully in decline. Moves of senior practitioners in Canada from private law firms to prominent general counsel positions at major Canadian corporations, as well as similar transitions at more junior levels, have signaled that corporate counsel positions are increasingly attractive as a career option for ambitious lawyers, and that in-house posts are providing both compensation and levels of sophistication sufficient to challenge the cream of the profession. Several American studies have tracked the transformation of the in-house stereotype over the last forty years: from a lawyer who, having been passed over for partner, left private practice to do "routine, repetitive corporate work, while everything interesting was farmed out to private firms" to a near-total reversal, with corporate counsel managing major transactions, complex litigation, and hiring outside lawyers only on an as-needed basis. A seminal 1985 U.S. study asserted that a "new breed of general counsel has left this stereotype behind. Not only have the offices grown in size, but in importance as well. The General Counsel sits close to the top of the corporate hierarchy as a member of senior management."

. . . . .

In a post-Enron era the tensions and demands on in-house lawyers to ensure compliance with new corporate governance rules and shifting internal and external requirements and expectations of regulators, directors, officers, shareholders, employees, pensioners, and creditors have made the role of in-house counsel an even more important and ethically complex one. This has prompted some caution amongst those considering a move in-house. Beyond simply managing litigation, the emphasis in ethics and compliance positions in-house has been described as "more strategic than tactical." In-house counsel now have a role that extends beyond providing technical legal services and litigation management into matters at the heart of proper governance of organizations. Building on whatever experience they have ordinarily gained in a variety of private practice settings, in-house lawyers layer focused legal knowledge with the broader insight into a client or corporate environment that a perch inside an organization affords. That poses unique ethical challenges for lawyers seeking to maintain professional integrity within the confines and constraints of their corporate client, particularly as they typically occupy multiple roles within the organization.

The professional and ethical failings of those in-house counsel involved in the Enron scandal have been the subject of particular attention, but lawyers were involved in most of the major corporate scandals now synonymous with corporate governance reform in the United States — Tyco, Worldcom, Adelphia, Global Crossing, Qwest, Dynegy, Vivendi, Sprint and HealthSouth. These scandals are significant not only for the fact of internal and external lawyer involvement, but as the impetus behind major U.S. reforms, including a direction from the U.S. Congress in the *Sarbanes-Oxley Act* of 2002 to the Securities and Exchange Commission (SEC) to develop standards of professional conduct for attorneys ... . The development of these standards has already had, and will continue to have, a significant impact on both U.S. and Canadian in-house lawyers.

Focusing on work in legal ethics that takes "account of the particular contexts in which lawyers practice" is both necessary and important. As one British study has noted, while "core values" "may survive at a symbolic level, their role as a starting point for the formulation of detailed rules of professional conduct may become more difficult to sustain as the discreet arenas which help shape ethical norms and form the context of regulation become increasingly diverse."

. . . . .

Practicing with integrity in an in-house position, whether in the private or public sector, has always required special skill; but along with the advantages of the insider's perspective come particular challenges. The fact of having one client — the corporation or the government — means that an in-house lawyer is particularly vulnerable when there is challenge from within the organization. Telling senior officers "no" to their proposed plans and schemes may be the right legal and ethical answer, but it can bring a particularly high price, especially if the lawyer finds that he or she has to exercise the ultimate professional recourse and withdraw from representation. Losing a major client in a law firm can have significant consequences, to be sure, but withdrawing from your one client as an in-house lawyer equates to a loss of status, income and employment, raising the ethical stakes for in-house practitioners that much further. Remaining ethical, independent, and professional in an in-house practice requires a level of personal sacrifice and dissociation from the company or the team not demanded of almost any other corporate player.

Yet the response of Canadian regulators to the challenges faced by in-house counsel has been inadequate, and merits review. In addition to providing the assistance of an imperative — a rule of professional conduct — to which in-house counsel might point when faced with client misconduct, the lesson of the United States experience has been that legislators and regulators are no longer content simply to permit the self-regulating legal profession autonomy when it comes to rectifying an obvious failing.

In introducing the amendment to *Sarbanes-Oxley* that directed the SEC to draw up "Rules of Professional Responsibility for Attorneys," Senator John Edwards said that for "the sake of investors and regular employees, ordinary shareholders, we have to make sure that not only the executives and the accountants do what they are responsible for doing, but also that the lawyers do what they are responsible for doing as members of the bar and as citizens of the country." Senator Mike Enzi said "[l]awyers have just as much responsibility as accountants and corporate executives to protect the best interest of the shareholder. It is not unreasonable to expect attorneys to play it straight with their clients, especially when we are talking about restoring corporate integrity." While the perspectives of Senators Edwards and Enzi might be controversial (and, indeed, they are ones with which Canadian law firms and lawyers have vehemently disagreed), their comments signal that public representatives are no longer willing to let the profession determine for itself the boundaries of appropriate lawyer conduct where a greater public interest is identified. That has ramifications for the future of self-regulation of the legal profession as a whole.

NOTES AND QUESTIONS

1.   Which features of the corporate environment are particularly important for lawyers working with and for corporate organizations? What impact does globalization have on the practice environment in which corporate counsel operate?

2.   What strategies might an in-house counsel employ to reduce the pressure for compliance?

3.   Is there a difference between the challenges faced by "in-house" lawyers and those faced by lawyers in law firms representing corporations? Should there be different ethics rules for lawyers in the separate environments, or one code for all?

Scenario One

You work as in-house counsel for an international oil and gas company. You discover that the corporate CEO has made "financing arrangements" with a foreign government that, if scrutinized, are essentially bribes to allow the company to obtain development rights. You suspect that the General Counsel (your direct boss) knows about the "financing arrangements" but that the Board of the company, and in particular the Board's external directors, do not. You know that the bribes violate the United States' *Foreign Corrupt Practices Act*, 15 U.S.C. §§78 dd-1 and that that legislation applies to foreign issuers of U.S. securities, like your employer. They may also violate Canadian law. What do you do?

2.   The Legacy of Enron for In-House Counsel

As noted earlier, the focus upon and transformation of the rules for lawyers in corporate settings flows directly from the spectacular financial scandals of the late 1990s and early 2000s. The collapse of Enron was a seminal event for corporations around the world, and many of the key changes to both corporate and securities laws generally and to the laws concerning lawyer conduct in particular can be traced to the chronology of events for that one company. The next excerpt provides an introduction to the corporate story of Enron, and to the conduct of the lawyers inside and outside the company prompting changes in the rules. As you consider this story, reflect on what you might have done had you been in the position of the junior lawyer within the company. How would you have acted if you had been faced with the same circumstances?

DEBORAH L. RHODE & PAUL D. PATON

"Lawyers, Ethics and Enron"
(2002) 8 Stan. J.L. Bus. & Fin. 1
[footnotes omitted]

Despite the risks of oversimplifying an extraordinarily complex saga, a brief summary of key facts is necessary to understand the role of lawyers involved with Enron. The company was formed in 1985 from a merger of Houston Natural Gas and Internorth. This merger created America's first nationwide natural gas pipeline network. Over time, the firm's business focus shifted from regulated transportation of natural gas to energy trading in an increasingly deregulated environment. During this evolution, top management ventured away from traditional approaches to the core business in order to generate higher financial returns. ...

. . . . .

A Special Investigation Committee of Enron's Board of Directors (the "Powers Committee") was established in late October 2001 as the scandal was nearing the height of public exposure. Chaired by University of Texas School of Law Dean William Powers, Jr., the Committee concluded in its February 2002 report (the "Powers Report") that as financial problems arose in operations outside its core energy business, Enron had used Special Purpose Entities ("SPEs") or Special Purpose Vehicles ("SPVs") and off-balance-sheet partnerships to enter into transactions generally considered too risky or controversial for ordinary commercial entities. These SPEs and partnerships were not consolidated with Enron's other activities on Enron's financial statements; as a result, Enron's significant losses and debts could be concealed from public disclosure.

In hindsight, the rules governing accounting treatment of SPEs have become a key issue, underscoring the need for unbiased professional judgment by lawyers as well as by accountants. ...

... Whether Enron's SPEs should have been consolidated, and whether they ought to have been disclosed, were not only accounting issues but also key legal questions. For answers, Enron relied on assistance not only from accountants and auditors at [accounting firm Arthur] Andersen, but also from its in-house lawyers and outside counsel at Vinson & Elkins. These attorneys all played an important role in the process of drafting and certifying disclosure statements, and in advising whether the legal and accounting requirements governing SPEs and SPVs had been met.

The Powers Report noted that in some cases, transactions were designed specifically for the results they would produce on financial statements, not for legitimate economic objectives. Nor were the transactions adequately disclosed. Further, even though Enron's public filings revealed the existence of Enron's transactions with the partnerships, "the disclosures were obtuse, did not communicate the essence of the transactions completely or clearly, and failed to convey the substance of what was going on between Enron and the partnerships." ... The SPEs were terminated in September 2001, resulting in a surprise announcement that was the first public disclosure even hinting at the severity of the problems.

This announcement came on October 16, 2001, and marked the beginning of formal confirmations that matters had gone awry. Enron confirmed that it was taking a $544 million after-tax charge against earnings related to transactions with an investment partnership created and managed by Andrew Fastow, Enron's former Executive Vice President and Chief Financial Officer, and by other Enron employees who worked with Fastow. About a month later, on November 8, 2001, Enron announced in an SEC filing that it was restating its financial statements for the years 1997 through 2001 because of "accounting errors relating to transactions with a different Fastow partnership ... and an additional related-party entity." The restatements reduced Enron's reported net income by a total of $1.5 billion, reduced reported shareholder equity by over $2 billion, and shattered the confidence of the market and investors in the company. In November, Enron also revealed for the first time that it had learned that Fastow had received more than $30 million from two of the partnerships; other Enron employees involved in the partnerships had been enriched at Enron's expense "in the aggregate, by tens of millions of dollars they should not have received." On November 28, 2001, major bond rating agencies downgraded Enron's debt to junk bond status. The company filed for Chapter 11 bankruptcy on December 2, 2001.

. . . . .

The Role of the Lawyers

On the basis of the facts now publicly available, lawyers' activities in three contexts merit particular attention. The actions of Enron's in-house counsel, Enron's primary outside counsel Vinson & Elkins, and Andersen's in-house counsel all raise important concerns.

A. Enron's In-House Counsel

The role of Enron's in-house counsel in structuring critical transactions and advising the firm on disclosure requirements reflects longstanding issues about conflicts of interest and professional independence. The Powers Report's detailed references to these lawyers make clear their integral contribution to the creation and operation of the various partnerships and SPEs; to the negotiations between Enron and the partnership entities; and to the preparation of related-party proxy disclosure statements. In assessing that conduct, the Report criticized "an absence of forceful and effective oversight by Senior Enron Management and in-house counsel" in the failure to disclose meaningful information about the SPEs and the essential nature of the transactions in issue.

Of still greater concern was the Powers Report's finding that one of the company's in-house lawyers, Kristina Mordaunt, not only gave advice on the SPE transactions, but also invested her own money in one of the entities. She did so without obtaining the consent of Enron's Chairman and CEO, in violation of Enron's Code of Conduct. Mordaunt reportedly received $1 million in return for a $5,800 investment. That investment may also have violated bar disciplinary rules concerning conflicts of interest. The Powers Report itself notes, though, that Mordaunt later admitted that her participation in the SPE was an error in judgment and that "she did not consider the issue carefully enough at the time."

By contrast, at least two Enron attorneys had serious concerns about the company's financial conduct, but were stymied by other Enron lawyers or managers in efforts to respond. A case in point involves a September 2000 memo by an Enron North America attorney expressing concern about the possibility that "the financial books at Enron are being 'cooked' in order to eliminate a drag on earnings that would otherwise occur under fair value accounting." More senior attorneys who received the memo did not believe the factual assertions on which the memo's conclusions were based, but conducted no investigation to verify their belief and took no further action. A second example involves an Enron attorney who reportedly asked the law firm of Fried Frank Harris Shriver & Jacobsen to review the legality of the partnerships and SPEs. After Fried Frank recommended that Enron halt the practice of using such structures, the Enron attorney sent written internal memoranda to company executives to the same effect. The failure by more senior counsel and by Enron executives to follow such advice, or to investigate its factual basis, suggests greater problems with the corporate culture — one that prized aggressive behavior, put a premium on risk and "valued appealing lies over inconvenient truths."

B. Enron's Outside Counsel: Vinson & Elkins

Of equal concern is the role of Vinson & Elkins lawyers, Enron's primary outside legal counsel, in structuring transactions and providing legal advice on public disclosure documents. ... Indeed, the Powers Report concludes that Vinson & Elkins

> provided advice and prepared documentation in connection with many of the [problematic] transactions. ... It also assisted Enron with the preparation of its disclosures of related-party transactions in the proxy statements and the footnotes to the financial statements in Enron's periodic SEC filings. Management and the Board relied heavily on the perceived approval by Vinson & Elkins of the structure and disclosure of the transactions. Enron's Audit and Compliance Committee, as well as in-house counsel, looked to it for assurance that Enron's public disclosures were legally sufficient. It would be inappropriate to fault Vinson & Elkins for accounting matters, which are not within its expertise. However, Vinson & Elkins should have brought a stronger, more objective and more critical voice to the disclosure process.

Vinson & Elkins's leaders have denied that the firm acted improperly. In their view, outside lawyers may assist in a transaction that is not illegal and that has been approved by company management. In so doing, "the lawyers are not approving the business decisions made by the clients." Yet not only is that an unduly circumscribed understanding of the lawyer's ethical responsibilities, it also begs the question of who is the "client." [T]he firm's response also raises a question that has become central to debates over regulatory reform: when do lawyers have an obligation to bring dubious conduct to the attention of more senior management or the board of directors?

A related issue involves the responsibility of Vinson & Elkins when it was asked to investigate initially anonymous allegations by Sherron Watkins. In August 2001, Watkins, Enron's vice president of corporate development, wrote an anonymous six-page memo to Kenneth Lay, Enron's Chairman and CEO, detailing her concerns about the propriety of Enron's disclosure statements and accounting treatment of the SPE and partnership transactions. Watkins recommended that Enron's Chief General Counsel hire an independent law firm to investigate the transactions, and specifically advised against using Vinson & Elkins. As she noted, "(Can't use V&E due to conflict —

they provided some true sale opinions on some of the deals)." In agreeing to take on this investigation, Vinson & Elkins placed itself in the position of evaluating its own work. The firm also agreed to highly restrictive limitations on the scope of its review, which further circumscribed the value of its advice. At a minimum, as most legal ethics experts have suggested, Vinson & Elkins's lawyers should have discussed the possible conflict with Enron executives and directors and secured a written conflicts waiver. It is, however, by no means clear that a waiver would have solved the problem. Prevailing bar ethical rules prohibit lawyers from representation that would be "materially and adversely affected" by the lawyers' own interests, unless the client gives informed consent and the lawyer reasonably believes the representation will not be adversely affected. ...

As it was, the nine-page report that the firm provided to Enron's General Counsel on October 15, 2001 left much to be desired. Although Vinson & Elkins characterized its investigation as "preliminary," the report recommended no additional scrutiny. After a notably inadequate review of the facts, the law firm's report concluded that they did not "warrant a further widespread investigation by independent counsel and auditors." Without meaningful discussion of the substance of the transactions at issue, the report primarily focused on their "bad cosmetics," namely "a serious risk of adverse publicity and litigation." To that end, Vinson & Elkins recommended "some response should be provided to Ms. Watkins to assure her that her concerns were thoroughly reviewed, analysed, and although not found to raise new or undisclosed information, were given serious consideration."

Despite that recommendation, the Powers Committee was established just two weeks later to undertake precisely the sort of detailed investigation that Vinson & Elkins had found unnecessary. The Powers Committee retained a different law firm for assistance, and in February 2002 released a report of some 200 pages. That report criticizes Vinson & Elkins's actions with respect to many aspects of the investigation. Because Enron's General Counsel had instructed Vinson & Elkins that a detailed examination of the relevant transactions and discussions with accounting advisors need not be part of the law firm's review, the "result of the V&E review was largely predetermined by the scope and nature of the investigation and the process employed." By contrast, the Powers Report notes that its own investigation was able to identify the most serious problems at Enron only after making the detailed inquiries that Vinson & Elkins had agreed were unnecessary. In reaching that conclusion, Vinson & Elkins's lawyers had interviewed only "very senior people" at Enron and Andersen, who "with few exceptions, had substantial professional and personal stakes in the matters under review." So did Vinson & Elkins, given its advice on the events under scrutiny and its ties to the key players. ...

C. Andersen's In-House Counsel

Nancy Temple, in-house counsel at Andersen, emerged as a key figure in Andersen's demise, and her actions have been a controversial centerpiece in discussions of lawyers' social responsibilities. As noted earlier, Andersen played a crucial role in creating and auditing questionable investment vehicles, and in certifying Enron's financial statements and public disclosures. Accordingly, Andersen's documents regarding those matters could be critical to government investigators and civil litigants. The firm's detailed document retention policies called for the destruction of all nonessential draft documents or conflicting documentation relating to an audit, including the e-mails, voicemail messages, and desk files of Andersen personnel working on the audit. The policy itself was not unusual; what created problems was the timing and manner of Temple's calls for compliance with the policy.

Temple's actions became the subject of a highly unflattering Congressional hearing in January 2002. Committee members were left incredulous by her characterization of actions concerning Andersen's document retention and destruction as customary housekeeping duties. She admitted awareness, prior to October 8, of allegations by an Enron employee of inappropriate accounting procedures, as well as an investigation by Vinson & Elkins. She also admitted that between September 28 and October 12, she provided legal advice about specific documentation and retention issues. The SEC placed Enron under investigation in early October, and it confirmed that fact publicly in an October 22 press release. Temple's notes from a conference call on October 8 anticipated that outcome: "Highly probable some SEC investigation."

Despite her knowledge, Temple sent an email on October 12 to Andersen's Houston practice director making reference to the firm's document retention and destruction policy: "It might be useful to consider reminding the engagement team of our documentation and retention policy. It will be helpful to make sure that we have complied with that policy." On October 23, David Duncan, Andersen's lead engagement partner on the Enron audit, ordered his team to comply with Andersen's policy and gathered all of the documents relating to Enron. Andersen officials later admitted that significant numbers of documents were shredded between this time and November 10. Media reports chronicled the accumulation of more than eighteen trunks and thirty boxes of documentary debris on only one of the days at one of the offices. Not until November 10, after the SEC had subpoenaed documents from Andersen concerning its Enron investigation and after Andersen had received a second subpoena in a related lawsuit, did Temple instruct the Enron engagement team "to preserve documents, computer files and other information relating to Enron."

Andersen officers were clearly alert to problems with Enron in September 2001. By October 9, the accounting firm had retained lawyers at Davis, Polk & Wardwell ("Davis, Polk") to "help with the complex issues that were going on in the third quarter." Temple admitted that she had discussed documentation and retention issues with Davis, Polk as early as October 16. In testimony during a Congressional subcommittee hearing, Andersen's Senior Executive, C.E. Andrews, initially disclaimed any expectation of litigation on October 9. However, a few minutes later, in response to a different question, Temple acknowledged that as soon as she was aware that Enron would be restating its prior financials, she concluded that Andersen "would likely be sued." Almost immediately thereafter, Andrews conceded that Davis, Polk had been hired "for purposes to help [Andersen] with the financial reporting and possible litigation." Accordingly, a "reminder" about the audit firm's document shredding policies in early October 2001 could plausibly be interpreted as encouraging destruction of background papers that might be relevant to its liability or to the regulatory investigation of its client.

In a televised interview on *Meet the Press*, Andersen's CEO Joseph Berardino attempted to discount this possibility: "Nancy just told people to use their judgment. She did not instruct them to do anything, to my knowledge." Yet despite the insistence that Temple had made no error, legally or ethically, Andersen fired David Duncan, its Enron team leader, for similar conduct. According to Andersen's CEO, in the same interview, Duncan "displayed extremely poor judgment in the destruction of documents' issue" after he learned of the SEC investigation. The attempt to scapegoat Duncan while exonerating Temple did not sit well with Congressional investigation. As the Subcommittee Chairman noted, "common sense gets a little lost here."

. . . . .

In a *New York Times* article [after the conviction of Andersen for obstruction of justice], Stephen Gillers, a prominent legal ethics expert, defended Temple's actions as "the kind of advice that lawyers routinely give." Other ethics experts take a different view. Under the statutes and ethics rules of most jurisdictions, it is unethical to destroy documents if they are subject to discovery or relevant to a "clearly foreseeable" legal action. The facts currently available permit the inference that Temple knew or should have known that a proceeding was clearly foreseeable at the time that she reminded Andersen partners and employees about document retention policy. Her failure to clarify the need to preserve critical Enron-related materials was highly problematic. Her instructions on revising a characterization of financial disclosure was problematic as well, particularly if part of the motivation was her own self-interest in avoiding involvement in the government's investigation. In any event, whether or not Temple violated bar ethical rules, it is troubling that so many lawyers, including ethics experts like Gillers, assumed that such actions are "routine." If current norms and standards of conduct permit complicity in frustrating federal investigation, then reform initiatives are clearly appropriate.

. . . . .

NOTES AND QUESTIONS

1.   Part of the Enron tale is the story of Enron attorneys who attempted to prevent the wrongdoing from occurring and/or continuing. Does the failure of those lawyers' efforts suggest that it may be impossible for a lawyer to prevent an organization set on illegal/unethical behaviour? What strategies would be most likely to encourage reporting by subordinate lawyers? What obligations do senior lawyers have to respond to such reports or situations, if any?

2.   In the article, Rhode and Paton note Stephen Gillers' defence of Nancy Temple in the *New York Times*. Do you agree or disagree with Gillers' assessment of her conduct?

3.   Note that Temple was counsel to Arthur Andersen, an accounting firm. Do you think any relevant differences exist for a lawyer providing in-house legal advice to a partnership of other professionals, where there are no external shareholders and no corporate board? Is this lawyer's circumstance ethically distinct from that of a lawyer working in a more traditional corporate context? Could Temple or someone working in a similar position legitimately rely on the professional ethics of the accountants for whom she worked to inform or modify her own ethical obligations?

4.   Should Vinson & Elkins have accepted the retainer to investigate the allegations Sherron Watkins raised? Was Enron's waiver of any conflict of interest enough? How does the alleged conflict here relate to that discussed in the *Strother* case in Chapter 5?

3.   The American Response to Enron

The collapse of Enron spawned exploration of all levels and layers of activity inside and outside of the organization, as legislators and regulators attempted to find out what had gone wrong and how future catastrophes might be prevented. The United States Congress and the Securities and Exchange Commission made various and numerous legislative and regulatory changes to improve corporate governance.

While the accountability of auditors was especially important, lawyers working with corporations were not immune from scrutiny. Significant legal and regulatory changes to the ethical and other obligations of corporate counsel in the United States were introduced in 2002 and 2003. Specifically, the United States Congress passed the *Sarbanes-Oxley Act*. Described by Senator John Corzine as incorporating the "most far-reaching reforms of American business practices since the time of Franklin Delano Roosevelt", *Sarbanes-Oxley* was the culmination of a series of earlier and separate efforts in both the House of Representatives and in the Senate to respond to the Enron crisis and to restore investor confidence. In a remarkable show of unity, the Act cleared the House by a vote of 423-3 and, a few hours later, cleared the Senate by a vote of 99-0. It included a provision that obligated lawyers to report corporate fraud and rules that required the U.S. Securities and Exchange Commission to establish "minimum standards of professional conduct" for lawyers who practice before the Commission. These features had aroused little public debate or controversy when they first appeared (and passed unanimously) in an earlier iteration of what became *Sarbanes-Oxley*, despite vehement opposition from the American Bar Association.

Sarbanes-Oxley also obligated lawyers to report "evidence of a material violation of securities law or breach of fiduciary duty", first to a company's general counsel, then to its CEO and ultimately to its board of directors. The statute also directed the SEC to adopt rules to interpret and implement this legislation.

Legislative attention in the aftermath of Enron had focused first on independent auditors, then on employees, directors, investment dealers and consultants, together with boards of directors and audit committees. *Sarbanes-Oxley* contained sweeping reforms to corporate governance rules for all of these groups. Gradually the roles and responsibilities of lawyers engaged in corporate misconduct moved toward centre stage as well. An October 2002 U.S. Senate Committee Report on Financial Oversight of Enron highlighted the important role lawyers play as "gatekeepers", particularly in public securities markets, and suggested that the "role of lawyers and law firms as gatekeepers should not be overlooked".

The next section sets out the language of *Sarbanes-Oxley* relating to lawyer conduct. This is followed by the story of both the implementation of new rules by the SEC and the subsequent response by the American Bar Association with changes to its *Model Rules of Professional Conduct*. As you consider this material, reflect on whether lawyers should be seen as "gatekeepers": are lawyers responsible for their clients' conduct? Should they be?

SARBANES-OXLEY ACT OF 2002

Pub. L. 107-204

Sec. 307. Rules Of Professional Responsibility For Attorneys

Not later than 180 days after the date of enactment of this Act, the Commission shall issue rules, in the public interest and for the protection of investors, setting forth minimum standards of professional conduct for attorneys appearing and practicing before the Commission in any way in the representation of issuers, including a rule —

(1) requiring an attorney to report evidence of a material violation of securities law or breach of fiduciary duty or similar violation by the company or any agent thereof, to the chief legal counsel or the chief executive officer of the company (or the equivalent thereof); and

(2) if the counsel or officer does not appropriately respond to the evidence (adopting, as necessary, appropriate remedial measures or sanctions with respect to the violation), requiring the attorney to report the evidence to the audit committee of the board of directors of the issuer or to another committee of the board of directors comprised solely of directors not employed directly or indirectly by the issuer, or to the board of directors.

PAUL D. PATON

"Corporate Counsel as Corporate Conscience: Ethics and
Integrity in the Post-Enron Era"
(2005) 84 Can. Bar Rev. 533
[footnotes omitted]

Debates over where the balance between candor and confidentiality ought to lie are important for all professionals in corporate practice. The particular challenge for regulators and for the profession after Enron lies in resolving the choice between disclosure to public officials of corporate misconduct and the traditional requirement of loyalty to the organizational client. In the United States, there was a firestorm over Section 307 of the *Sarbanes Oxley Act* of 2002 and the [Securities and Exchange Commission, or "SEC"] rule proposals implementing that legislation, and also in response to proposals and eventual changes to the [American Bar Association, or "ABA"] ABA Model Rules of Professional Conduct pertaining to the Organization as Client (MR 1.13) and Confidentiality (MR 1.6). In stark contrast, an amendment to the Rules of Professional Conduct in Ontario in March 2004 took place with virtually no public input or debate, with [the Law Society of Upper Canada] proceeding after having been prompted by a query from the [Ontario Securities Commission] about the need for the same type of rules on lawyer conduct as had been mandated for the SEC under *Sarbanes-Oxley*.

In contrast to the uncertainty created by other sections of the *Sarbanes-Oxley Act* of 2002, which introduced the most substantial reform of corporate governance in the United States in decades, Section 307 of the legislation has from the start been seen as clear, if extremely controversial. It has two dimensions. First, Section 307 of the Act instructs the SEC to adopt a rule of practice establishing "minimum standards of professional conduct" for lawyers "appearing or practicing before the Commission." Second, the Section specifically directs the SEC to include a rule requiring all such lawyers to report evidence of fraud and other corporate misconduct in the companies they represent "up the ladder" to the company's senior management, and if necessary, to the board of directors. The SEC published a proposed rule (Part 205) on November 21, 2002 and closed its comment period on December 18, 2002. The Act required the final rule on this section to be issued on or before January 26, 2003. On January 23, 2003, the SEC passed rules implementing Section 307 of *Sarbanes-Oxley* and published the rule text the following week.

Regardless of the contours of the final rule, the fact the SEC would begin regulating attorney conduct represented a significant shift away from deference to the self-regulatory tradition of the bar. It was also a signal that lawyers were attracting critical attention in the aftermath of Enron, and that legislators view the public interest to be best served by having lawyers more responsible to the public for their clients' conduct. As Senator Michael Enzi, an accountant and a co-sponsor of the amendment to *Sarbanes-Oxley* that became Section 307 noted:

As we beat up on accountants a little bit, one of the thoughts that occurred to me was that probably in almost every transaction there was a lawyer who drew up the documents involved in that procedure. It seemed only right there ought to be some kind of an ethical standard put in place for the attorneys as well.

... The Rule casts a very wide net, defining "appearing and practising before the Commission" to include those "preparing, or participating in the process of preparing" essentially anything filed with or incorporated into any communication with the SEC. The definition also includes advising a party that something should *not* be filed with the Commission. The ABA criticized the definition as "inappropriately encompass[ing] non-securities specialists who do no more than prepare or review limited portions of a filing, lawyers who respond to auditors letters or prepare work product in the ordinary course unrelated to securities matters that may be used for that purpose, and lawyers preparing documents that eventually may be filed as exhibits." Others criticized the Rule as not going far enough, by not including law firms as well as individual lawyers in the Commission's disciplinary sights. They encouraged the SEC to broaden the scope to impute knowledge within law firms and hold the law firm responsible for the acts of its lawyers as agents of the law firm entity.

The fact that the definition also applies to foreign lawyers on an equal basis prompted additional cause for concern. In particular, the reporting requirements raised the spectre that foreign lawyers would be required to violate their domestic bar rules concerning privilege and confidentiality of client communications or risk breaching the SEC rules and possibly invite U.S. criminal sanction. The International Bar Association issued a strong call to the SEC to exempt non-U.S. lawyers from the proposed Rule. The ABA argued that "especially in the case of foreign attorneys, the extraordinary breadth of the term "appearing and practising" is likely to lead to confusion as to who is subject to the obligations of the rules, and to its sanctions in the event of non-compliance." This concern was partly self-motivated, as the ABA worried "that subjecting foreign attorneys to regulation by the SEC could result in foreign agencies seeking to regulate the conduct of U.S. attorneys representing U.S. companies abroad or foreign companies."

Others were uncompromising in supporting the proposal's extra-territorial reach. The submission to the SEC by three leading law school professors, endorsed by at least 53 others, unapologetically applauded the rule, reflecting a "U.S.-first" mood not limited to Section 307 alone: *"No foreign country, lawyer or corporation has a "right" to participate in our securities markets on their own terms. They have a choice: to play by our rules or not"* [emphasis added]. The professors argued that exempting foreign lawyers would simply open a loophole for many large corporations to skirt the SEC's rules, resulting in "violence to the legislative scheme, harm to investors, and harm to the domestic securities bar who would be placed at a competitive disadvantage vis-à-vis their foreign counterparts." They concluded:

The arguments made by foreign bars are virtually indistinguishable from those made by the ABA to ward off SEC regulation of domestic lawyers. What we know of foreign enforcement efforts against securities lawyers suggests that their arguments are as illusory as those advanced by domestic lawyers in the effort to ward off effective federal regulation. The Commission should maintain its principled, wise and legislatively justified stance to regulate foreign and domestic lawyers equally.

The particularly vexing part of the proposed rule (and the legislation) for both domestic and foreign lawyers was a proposal that would have required "noisy withdrawal." In addition to requiring a lawyer to report potential violations "up the ladder" within a company to its chief legal officer or CEO and then to the audit committee, an independent committee, or the board of directors, the original proposal for Part 205 mandated that a lawyer take further steps if the company failed to act to rectify the situation. Where a lawyer believed the company had not adequately responded to reported "evidence of a material violation" of the securities laws, "a material breach of fiduciary duty, or a similar material violation," the lawyer would then be required to 1) withdraw from representation; 2) notify the SEC of the withdrawal, indicating that it was based on professional considerations, and 3) disaffirm any filing with the SEC that the attorney has prepared or assisted in preparing that the attorney believes is or may be materially false or misleading. Noted as going "to the heart of the attorney-client relationship," this part was criticized as "almost deputiz[ing] attorneys to become quasi-governmental inspectors," and for turning all "lawyers into junior regulators, surveillance operatives, whistle-blowers." The ABA said the rule contradicted legislative intent, relying on comments by Senator John Edwards (one of the principal architects of Section 307) that in *Sarbanes-Oxley* there "is no obligation to report anything outside the client — the corporation." The President of the American Corporate Counsel Association noted, "There's a very real fear that the rules will change the relationship [with the client]."

These comments overlooked the fact that even in the absence of the "noisy withdrawal" requirement, lawyers in forty-one states were, at the time, permitted (but not obliged) to report evidence of a continuing crime or fraud by a client. The ABA had, prior to this point, twice rejected proposals by its own Ethics 2000 Commission to tighten this requirement. The SEC proposal stepped into that breach and would have made this conduct mandatory; a more rigorous SEC standard would in effect pre-empt state rules.

Other provisions in the Rule further exacerbated these concerns about the attorney-client relationship. Section 205.3(e)(2) allows an attorney to disclose confidential information to the Commission without the issuer's consent:

i)   to prevent the issuer from committing an illegal act that the attorney reasonably believes is likely to result in substantial injury to the financial interest or property of the issuer or investors;

ii) to prevent the issuer from committing an illegal act that the attorney reasonably believes is likely to perpetrate a fraud upon the Commission; or

iii) to rectify the consequences of the issuer's illegal act in the furtherance of which the attorney's services had been used.

Section 205.3(e)(1) allows an attorney to use any report under this section in self-defence. Section 205.3(e)(3) provides that sharing of information with the Commission by an issuer through its attorney does not constitute a waiver of any privilege or protection as to other persons. Nonetheless, the ramifications of this part in respect of the lawyer-client relationship, as well as the relationship of lawyers to the SEC, are significant and fundamental: the traditional conception of loyalty and fealty to the client or organization may be infringed upon for the greater public good.

The final Rules implementing Section 307 provisions of *Sarbanes-Oxley* on attorney conduct took a considerably different turn from the original proposals and constituted a major retreat by the SEC. The Final Rule maintained the "up the ladder" reporting requirement for evidence of material violations of securities laws, but changed the test for "evidence of a material violation" from a relatively straightforward determination to a standard which is considerably more difficult to enforce because the definition of what constitutes "evidence of a material violation" is now far more complex than in the proposed rule. Further, even if a lawyer finds such evidence under the new standard, he or she can back down from pressing the company to change the behavior if another lawyer opines that there is a "colorable defence" for the company's actions.

The Commissioners also backed down on the "noisy withdrawal" requirement so strongly advocated by the group of law professors and strongly resisted by the practicing bar. The SEC extended the comment period on this issue for a further 60 days, and suggested a possible alternative rule requiring a lawyer to withdraw from representation but requiring the client, rather than the lawyer, to publicly disclose the withdrawal or written notice that the lawyer did not receive an appropriate response to a report of a material violation. While formally never concluded, for the time being it appears this fight is over. The CBA called the changes a positive step, but insisted that they did not go far enough to preserve lawyer-client relationships. More importantly, the CBA press release signalled again a more fundamental debate: "The CBA continues to stress that it is unacceptable for any government agency to dictate ethical standards for Canadian lawyers."

NOTES AND QUESTIONS

1. In the SEC Regulations implementing *Sarbanes-Oxley*, a lawyer is required to report evidence of a "material violation of an applicable United States federal or state securities law, a material breach of fiduciary duty arising under United States federal or state law, or a similar material violation of any United States federal or state law" subject to certain exceptions and qualifications. What should

a lawyer's obligation be when he or she has reservations about the morality or legality of a company's conduct, even though that conduct might not constitute "material violations" of securities laws? Does your answer change if the lawyer is acting as in-house counsel rather than as an attorney from an outside law firm?

2.   Is "noisy withdrawal" by lawyers ever appropriate or necessary? If auditor resignations serve to protect the public by signalling to the market that corporate conduct is awry, why should lawyers be exempted from similar requirements?

3.   Are the American Bar Association's objections to SEC regulation of lawyer conduct warranted? Who should regulate lawyers? Who should be able to decide? Is the Canadian Bar Association right when it says that it is "unacceptable for any government agency to dictate ethical standards for Canadian lawyers", or just that it is inappropriate for American authorities to do so? Consider these questions in light of the arguments for and against self-regulation discussed in Chapters 2 and 13.

In the eyes of many key U.S. lawmakers, the American Bar Association and all bar regulators had failed to take appropriate steps to ensure that lawyers representing corporate clients were upholding the highest standards of conduct. The introduction of section 307 and the granting of authority to the SEC for the regulation of lawyer conduct reflected this concern. The American Bar Association eventually responded with changes to the *Model Rules of Professional Conduct* to address concerns about lawyers in organizational settings, prompted in particular by the March 2003 report of the ABA Task Force on Corporate Responsibility on the role of lawyers for public corporations. As you review these Rules, consider whether they are sufficient to ensure that lawyers representing corporate clients will uphold the standard of ethical conduct. The Canadian approach, considered further below, leaves out key components of these Rules, notably the "crime-fraud exception" to confidentiality in Rule 1.6. Consider why the Canadian regulators might have done so, and which approach has greater merit.

AMERICAN BAR ASSOCIATION

Model Rules of Professional Conduct

Rule 1.13 Organization as Client

(a) A lawyer employed or retained by an organization represents the organization acting through its duly authorized constituents.

(b) If a lawyer for an organization knows that an officer, employee or other person associated with the organization is engaged in action, intends to act or refuses to act in a matter related to the representation that is a violation of a legal obligation to the organization, or a violation of law that reasonably might be imputed to the organization, and that is likely to result in substantial injury to the organization, then the lawyer shall proceed as is reasonably necessary in the best interest of the organization. Unless the lawyer reasonably believes that it is not necessary in the best interest of the organization to do so, the lawyer shall refer the matter to higher authority in the organization, including, if warranted by the circumstances, to the highest authority that can act on behalf of the organization as determined by applicable law.

(c) Except as provided in paragraph (d), if

(1) despite the lawyer's efforts in accordance with paragraph (b) the highest authority that can act on behalf of the organization insists upon or fails to address in a timely and appropriate manner an action, or a refusal to act, that is clearly a violation of law, and

(2) the lawyer reasonably believes that the violation is reasonably certain to result in substantial injury to the organization,

then the lawyer may reveal information relating to the representation whether or not Rule 1.6 [Confidentiality of Information] permits such disclosure, but only if and to the extent the lawyer reasonably believes necessary to prevent substantial injury to the organization.

(d) Paragraph (c) shall not apply with respect to information relating to a lawyer's representation of an organization to investigate an alleged violation of law, or to defend the organization or an officer, employee or other constituent associated with the organization against a claim arising out of an alleged violation of law.

(e) A lawyer who reasonably believes that he or she has been discharged because of the lawyer's actions taken pursuant to paragraphs (b) or (c), or who withdraws under circumstances that require or permit the lawyer to take action under either of those paragraphs, shall proceed as the lawyer reasonably believes necessary to assure that the organization's highest authority is informed of the lawyer's discharge or withdrawal.

(f) In dealing with an organization's directors, officers, employees, members, shareholders or other constituents, a lawyer shall explain the identity of the client when the lawyer knows or reasonably should know that the organization's interests are adverse to those of the constituents with whom the lawyer is dealing.

(g) A lawyer representing an organization may also represent any of its directors, officers, employees, members, shareholders or other constituents, subject to the provisions of Rule 1.7 [Conflicts of Interest]. If the organization's consent to the dual representation is required by Rule 1.7, the consent shall be given by an appropriate official of the organization other than the individual who is to be represented, or by the shareholders.

Rule 1.6 Confidentiality of Information

(a) A lawyer shall not reveal information relating to the representation of a client unless the client gives informed consent, the disclosure is impliedly authorized in order to carry out the representation or the disclosure is permitted by paragraph (b).

(b) A lawyer may reveal information relating to the representation of a client to the extent the lawyer reasonably believes necessary:

(1) to prevent reasonably certain death or substantial bodily harm;

(2) to prevent the client from committing a crime or fraud that is reasonably certain to result in substantial injury to the financial interests or property of another and in furtherance of which the client has used or is using the lawyer's services;

(3) to prevent, mitigate or rectify substantial injury to the financial interests or property of another that is reasonably certain to result or has resulted from the client's commission of a crime or fraud in furtherance of which the client has used the lawyer's services;

(4) to secure legal advice about the lawyer's compliance with these Rules;

(5) to establish a claim or defense on behalf of the lawyer in a controversy between the lawyer and the client, to establish a defense to a criminal charge or civil claim against the lawyer based upon conduct in which the client was involved, or to respond to allegations in any proceeding concerning the lawyer's representation of the client; or

(6) to comply with other law or a court order.

---

4. The Canadian Response

Though the focus on changes to the rules and regulation of lawyer conduct has been developed most publicly in the United States, the same issues and concerns about the ethics of lawyers advising corporations has been important in Canada. The Law Society of Upper Canada, the self-regulatory body responsible in Ontario for lawyer discipline and conduct, introduced amendments to the *Rules of Professional Conduct* in 2004 without public deliberation or debate. The Federation of Law Societies of Canada's *Model Code of Professional Conduct*, new in 2010–2011, adopted the same language first introduced in Ontario, omitting an ABA-style "crime-fraud" exception to the professional conduct rules on confidentiality. As you review these changes, consider why Canadian legal regulators might have taken a different approach.

As in the United States, there has been some debate in Canada about what role, if any, securities regulators should be playing in the regulation of lawyer conduct. Does such regulation contradict or complement the acts of the law societies? Under provincial Securities Acts, provincial securities regulators (rather than a national regulator like the SEC) exercise responsibilities comparable to those of the SEC for oversight of participants in the Canadian capital markets. Section 1 of the Ontario *Securities Act*,[2] for example, provides that the purposes of the Act are "to provide protection to investors from unfair, improper or fraudulent practices" and "to foster fair and efficient capital markets and confidence in capital markets". The Ontario Securities Com-

---

[2]   R.S.O. 1990, c. S.5.

mission (OSC) is given the mandate and responsibility for administering the Act and for enforcement of its provisions. While the OSC exercises jurisdiction over the practices of lawyers in relation to the Commission's statute and regulations accordingly — and did so prior to the Enron scandal — the extent of its commitment to this oversight, and the merits of having the OSC responsible for disciplining lawyers at all has been questioned. As you read *Wilder v. Ontario (Securities Commission)*[3] excerpted in this chapter, consider whether the approach the court adopts will be sufficient to ensure ethical practice by those lawyers appearing before the OSC. Are Law Society concerns about regulatory encroachment by securities regulators warranted?

(a) Law Society Rules

FEDERATION OF LAW SOCIETIES OF CANADA

Model Code of Professional Conduct

When the Client is an Organization

2.02 (3) Although a lawyer may receive instructions from an officer, employee, agent or representative, when a lawyer is employed or retained by an organization, including a corporation, the lawyer must act for the organization in exercising his or her duties and in providing professional services.

. . . . .

Dishonesty, Fraud, when Client an Organization

2.02 (8) A lawyer who is employed or retained by an organization to act in a matter in which the lawyer knows that the organization has acted, is acting, or intends to act dishonestly, fraudulently, criminally, or illegally, must do the following, in addition to his or her obligations under subrule (7):

(a) advise the person from whom the lawyer takes instructions and the chief legal officer, or both the chief legal officer and the chief executive officer, that the proposed conduct is, was or would be dishonest, fraudulent, criminal, or illegal and should be stopped;

(b) if necessary because the person from whom the lawyer takes instructions, the chief legal officer or the chief executive officer refuses to cause the proposed conduct to be stopped, advise progressively the next highest persons or groups, including ultimately, the board of directors, the board of trustees, or the appropriate committee of the board, that the proposed conduct was, is or would be dishonest, fraudulent, criminal or illegal and should be stopped; and

(c) if the organization, despite the lawyer's advice, continues with or intends to pursue the proposed wrongful conduct, withdraw from acting in the matter in accordance with Rule 2.07.

---

[3] [2001] O.J. No. 1017, 53 O.R. (3d) 159 (Ont. C.A.).

Commentary

The past, present, or proposed misconduct of an organization may have harmful and serious consequences, not only for the organization and its constituency, but also for the public who rely on organizations to provide a variety of goods and services. In particular, the misconduct of publicly traded commercial and financial corporations may have serious consequences to the public at large. This rule addresses some of the professional responsibilities of a lawyer acting for an organization, including a corporation, when he or she learns that the organization has acted, is acting, or proposes to act in a way that is dishonest, fraudulent, criminal or illegal. In addition to these rules, the lawyer may need to consider, for example, the rules and commentary about confidentiality (Rule 2.03).

This subrule speaks of conduct that is dishonest, fraudulent, criminal or illegal. Such conduct includes acts of omission. Indeed, often it is the omissions of an organization, such as failing to make required disclosure or to correct inaccurate disclosures that constitute the wrongful conduct to which these rules relate. Conduct likely to result in substantial harm to the organization, as opposed to genuinely trivial misconduct by an organization, invokes these rules.

In considering his or her responsibilities under this section, a lawyer should consider whether it is feasible and appropriate to give any advice in writing.

A lawyer acting for an organization who learns that the organization has acted, is acting, or intends to act in a wrongful manner, may advise the chief executive officer and must advise the chief legal officer of the misconduct. If the wrongful conduct is not abandoned or stopped, then the lawyer must report the matter "up the ladder" of responsibility within the organization until the matter is dealt with appropriately. If the organization, despite the lawyer's advice, continues with the wrongful conduct, then the lawyer must withdraw from acting in the particular matter in accordance with Rule 2.07. In some but not all cases, withdrawal means resigning from his or her position or relationship with the organization and not simply withdrawing from acting in the particular matter.

This rule recognizes that lawyers as the legal advisers to organizations are in a central position to encourage organizations to comply with the law and to advise that it is in the organization's and the public's interest that organizations do not violate the law. Lawyers acting for organizations are often in a position to advise the executive officers of the organization, not only about the technicalities of the law, but about the public relations and public policy concerns that motivated the government or regulator to enact the law. Moreover, lawyers for organizations, particularly in-house counsel, may guide organizations to act in ways that are legal, ethical, reputable, and consistent with the organization's responsibilities to its constituents and to the public.

Recall the discussion of the lawyer's duty of confidentiality in Chapter 4, and the future harm/public safety exception to confidentiality. The Federation of Law Societies of Canada's *Model Code* provision on this exception provides:

Future Harm/Public Safety Exception

2.03 (3) A lawyer may disclose confidential information, but must not disclose more information than is required, when the lawyer believes on reasonable grounds that there is an imminent risk of death or serious bodily harm, and disclosure is necessary to prevent the death or harm.

NOTES AND QUESTIONS

1. What would it mean for a lawyer to "withdraw from acting" as required by Rule 2.02(8)(c) if the lawyer is employed by the corporation? Rule 2.07 which governs withdrawal provides no guidance in this respect, concentrating exclusively on directing lawyers in private practice as to when and in what manner they should withdraw. Is it reasonable to require a lawyer to quit his or her employment as an ethical duty? Should a lawyer who followed the chain of upward reporting but did not withdraw be subject to professional discipline?

2. Compare ABA Model Rule 1.6(b)(1)-(4) and the FLSC *Model Code* Rule 2.03(3). The U.S. approach contains provisions that permit (but do not require) disclosure in the event of fraud as well as for incidents involving imminent death or serious bodily harm. Does it matter that the U.S. approach is permissive, not mandatory? Given the impact of corporate fraud on the investing public, should the provision be added to the Canadian rules?

3. The rules refer to the organization acting "dishonestly, fraudulently, criminally, or illegally". How does a lawyer know an organization's conduct is illegal? Is illegality simply a matter of the lawyer's own judgment, such that if the lawyer suspects that the conduct might be found to be illegal that triggers the obligation, or does the lawyer need some tangible basis — arising from legislation or judicial decision — to justify the assertion of illegality? Consider the following scenario.

Scenario Two

Jack works as in-house counsel for an automotive manufacturer. The manufacturer has discovered that its construction of a recent vehicle has a design flaw which in a certain number of cases will cause the vehicle to explode in even minor rear-end collisions. The manufacturer does an actuarial calculation which shows that the cost of civil tort claims arising from such explosions will be lower than the cost of a vehicle recall to repair the design flaw. Jack is asked to provide a legal opinion about the likelihood of a plaintiff obtaining a judgment against the manufacturer in tort and as to the likely quantum of damages that would result. Based on the actuarial calculation, and on Jack's opinion, the manufacturer decides not to recall the vehicles. Does Jack have any obligations under the FLSC *Model Code* as a result of his knowledge of the manufacturer's decision?[4]

---

[4]   This example is adapted from David Luban's discussion of the infamous *Pinto* case in *Lawyers and Justice* (Princeton: Princeton University Press, 1988) at 206-10.

(b) The Role of the Securities Regulators

The question of whether securities regulators in Canada should have authority or responsibility for regulating lawyer conduct was addressed in a case that pre-dated the Enron scandal. The Law Society of Upper Canada vehemently objected to an effort by the Ontario Securities Commission to reprimand a law firm lawyer representing a corporate client for his alleged misconduct in filing misleading materials with the Commission.

WILDER v. ONTARIO (SECURITIES COMMISSION)

[2001] O.J. No. 1017, 53 O.R. (3d) 519
(Ont. C.A., Abella, Goudge and Sharpe JJ.A.)

SHARPE J.A.:— This appeal calls into question the authority of the Ontario Securities Commission (the "OSC") to reprimand the appellant, Lawrence D. Wilder ("Wilder"), a solicitor, for alleged misconduct in connection with his representation of a client before the OSC. The appellants, Wilder and Cassels Brock and Blackwell ("Cassels"), supported by the intervenor, The Law Society of Upper Canada ("The Law Society"), submit that the OSC lacks a statutory mandate to reprimand Wilder for his conduct. They argue that the allegations against Wilder must be dealt with either by way of quasi-criminal proceedings before the Ontario Court of Justice or by The Law Society. They appeal, with leave of this Court, the order of the Divisional Court dismissing their application for judicial review, asking for an order that the OSC be prohibited from continuing proceedings against the appellants and quashing a Notice of Hearing.

FACTS

Wilder is a solicitor and a partner in the Cassels firm. At all relevant times, YBM Magnex International Inc. ("YBM") was a client of Cassels and Wilder in connection with the filing of a preliminary prospectus with the OSC. Wilder is not and never has been an officer, director, shareholder or promoter of YBM. In all of his dealings with the OSC on behalf of YBM, Wilder acted exclusively as YBM counsel.

The proceedings at issue before the OSC were commenced by a Notice of Hearing, dated November 1, 1999, naming Wilder, YBM, the directors of YBM, its CEO and CFO, and the co-lead underwriters for a YBM financing. The Notice advises the named parties of a hearing to determine whether various orders should be made against them pursuant to ss. 127 and 128 of the *Securities Act*, R.S.O. 1990, c. S.5. With respect to Wilder, the Notice of Hearing states that at the hearing the OSC will consider:

1. whether in its opinion it is in the public interest to make an order pursuant to s. 127(1), para. 6 of the Act to reprimand Wilder; and

2. whether, if the OSC determines that Wilder has not complied with Ontario securities law, application should be made to the Superior Court of Justice for a declaration that Wilder has not complied with

Ontario securities law, pursuant to s. 128(1) of the Act, and/or a remedial order against Wilder, pursuant to s. 128(3) of the Act.

The Statement of Allegations of the Staff of the OSC, served in support of the Notice of Hearing, provides details of the specific allegations. The Staff alleges that a letter to the OSC written by Wilder on behalf of YBM contained misleading or untrue statements of fact:

> Wilder made statements in a letter dated July 4, 1997 to Staff of the Commission that in a material respect, and at the time and in the light of the circumstances under which the statements were made, were misleading or untrue or did not state a fact that was required to be stated or that was necessary to make the statements not misleading; specifically, statements concerning the result of due diligence conducted in respect of YBM. In doing so, Wilder acted in a manner contrary to the public interest.

The allegations against the other named parties relate to alleged non-disclosure by YBM in prospectuses filed with the OSC and to YBM's alleged failure to comply with its continuous disclosure obligations. The allegations against these parties concern contraventions of duties and obligations imposed by Ontario securities law.

LEGISLATION

The *Securities Act*, Part XXII provides for three methods of enforcement that are available to the OSC in carrying out its mandate to regulate the securities industry. ...

[The court reviewed the availability of: i) quasi-criminal proceedings in provincial court leading to conviction and fines or imprisonment for false or misleading statements made in materials filed with the OSC; ii) the power of the OSC to apply for a declaration from superior court that a person or company is not complying with securities laws; and iii) the power of the OSC to hold its own administrative proceedings and make an "order in the public interest". This "public interest" power, in s. 127(1) of the Act, provides for a broad range of possible sanctions, including restrictions from participating in the market for securities.]

JUDGMENT OF THE DIVISIONAL COURT ...

Before the Divisional Court, the focus of the appellants' attack on the OSC proceedings was the submission that s. 127(1) should be interpreted so as not to apply to lawyers acting in their professional capacity. It was further submitted that if the provision does apply to lawyers acting in their professional capacity, it is to that extent unconstitutional and should be read down.

Swinton J., writing for the Court, rejected the appellants' submission. She observed that there was nothing in the language of s. 127(1) nor in its legislative history to suggest that it should not apply to lawyers. Indeed, she noted ... adoption of the provision indicated a legislative intention "to broaden the powers of the [OSC] to make orders in the public interest" and that the legislature "chose words which do not preclude their application to lawyers." The

Divisional Court rejected the contentions that The Law Society has exclusive jurisdiction to regulate the professional conduct of lawyers, and that to allow the OSC to involve itself in the professional conduct of lawyers would have a chilling effect upon the ability of members of the public to obtain independent legal representation.

The Divisional Court found that the OSC's proposed exercise of jurisdiction over Wilder was not inconsistent with the important role of The Law Society in regulating the legal profession. Both The Law Society and the OSC exercise public interest functions, but ... "the public interests which they seek to protect are not the same." The Law Society's role ... is "to govern the legal profession in the public interest, and to ensure that members of the profession do not engage in professional misconduct or conduct unbecoming a barrister and solicitor." The role of the OSC, on the other hand, was described ... as "that of protecting investors and the proper functioning of Ontario's capital markets. Ensuring proper disclosure and maintaining the integrity of its processes are an important part of this role." The Divisional Court concluded ... that there was no basis for holding lawyers immune from the regulatory powers of the OSC:

> In proceedings such as these, the [OSC] is not usurping the role of the Law Society, as its objective is not to discipline the lawyer for professional misconduct; rather its concern is to remedy a breach of its own Act which violates the public interest in fair and efficient capital markets, and to control its own processes.

Finally, the Divisional Court rejected the contention that by exercising jurisdiction over Wilder, the OSC would infringe the rule of law by interfering with the independence of the bar. The Divisional Court observed ... that all the OSC was seeking to do was "to ensure that lawyers, among others, do not mislead" it and that the exercise of that jurisdiction "will not interfere with the ability of lawyers who practice securities law to continue to provide excellent and vigorous representation to their clients."

. . . . .

ISSUES

1. Does the OSC have jurisdiction, as a matter of statutory interpretation, to reprimand Wilder for the alleged misconduct?

2. Does the OSC have jurisdiction to reprimand lawyers for their conduct as solicitors before the OSC?

ANALYSIS

Issue 1: Does the OSC have jurisdiction, as a matter of statutory interpretation, to reprimand Wilder for the alleged misconduct?

[The court held that the OSC has the requisite jurisdiction as a matter of statutory construction and interpretation, noting that the arguments raised on this issue had "nothing to do with Wilder's status as a solicitor or member of The Law Society. They are based entirely upon the wording of the relevant provisions of the Act and would apply to any person or corporation alleged to have provided misleading or untrue information to the OSC".]

Issue 2: Does the OSC have jurisdiction to reprimand lawyers for their conduct as solicitors before the OSC?

The appellants submit that s. 127(1) should be interpreted so as not to apply to lawyers acting in their professional capacity and that the attempt by the OSC to assert of [*sic*] jurisdiction with respect to Wilder's conduct collides with the authority of The Law Society to discipline lawyers. The appellants further submit that the assertion of jurisdiction by the OSC infringes the constitutional principle of the rule of law.

In my view, these arguments were fully and correctly dealt with in the reasons for judgment of Swinton J., writing for the Divisional Court. I cannot improve upon her analysis of these issues and for the reasons she gave, I would dismiss this aspect of the appeal.

I would, however, add this caveat with respect to the importance of ensuring that solicitor-client privilege is maintained and protected.

Solicitor-client privilege was described by Dickson J. in *Canada v. Solosky* ... as a "fundamental civil and legal right and more recently by Major J. in *R. v. McClure* ... as "fundamental to the justice system in Canada." It is an important substantive right, long recognized as essential to ensuring that citizens have access to full and candid advice about their legal rights. The rationale for the privilege was explained in *Anderson v. Bank of British Columbia* ... in terms that have been quoted by the Supreme Court of Canada ...

> The object and meaning of the rule is this: that is, by reason of the complexity and difficulty of our law, litigation can only be properly conducted by professional men, it is absolutely necessary that a man, in order to prosecute his rights or to defend himself from an improper claim, should have recourse to the assistance of professional lawyers, and it being so absolutely necessary, it is equally necessary, to use a vulgar phrase, that he should be able to make a clean breast of it to the gentleman whom he consults with a view to the prosecution of his claim, or substantiating his defence against the claim of others; that he should be able to place unrestricted and unbounded confidence in the professional agent, and that the communications he so makes to him should be kept secret, unless with his consent (for it is his privilege, and not the privilege of the confidential agent), that he should be enabled properly to conduct his litigation. That is the meaning of the rule.

Members of the public engaged in activities in the capital markets and subject to the authority of the OSC need to be able "to place unrestricted and unbounded confidence" in their legal advisors.

However, I do not accept the contention of the appellants and The Law Society that the need to respect solicitor-client privilege requires a blanket preclusion, preventing the OSC from reprimanding lawyers in all cases, provided the OSC pays adequate heed to the importance of solicitor-client privilege.

Where a lawyer is threatened with a reprimand by the OSC, there are two important interests at stake. On the one hand, the lawyer is entitled to be dealt with fairly and to be permitted to answer the allegations that have been made. On the other hand, where the lawyer's answer involves revealing the confidence of the client, the client's interest in confidentiality is invoked. In this regard, the lawyer's promise of confidentiality is not absolute. It is recognized by The Law Society's *Rules of Professional Conduct*, Rule 2.03(4), there are situations in which a lawyer may be entitled to reveal the confidence of a client to defend against allegations of criminal misconduct, claims of civil liability or allegations that the lawyer is "guilty of malpractice or misconduct". It seems to me that a lawyer facing a reprimand for making an untrue or misleading statement is facing an allegation of "misconduct". The Law Society's Rules of Professional Conduct define the terms upon which a lawyer's promise of confidentiality is made. They contain a general provision allowing for disclosure of confidential information where necessary to defend the lawyer's legal interests, and there is no reason that provision should not apply to an allegation of misconduct by the OSC.

However, this exemption for the lawyer does not, in my view, allow the OSC to ignore the importance of solicitor-client privilege in the exercise of its enforcement powers. The OSC, like any other public body exercising statutory authority, must ensure on a case-by-case basis that the substantive legal right to solicitor-client privilege is respected. In my view, the OSC must exercise particular caution where it decides to proceed against both the lawyer and the lawyer's client. Such a situation creates an inherent danger that the lawyer will have to reveal the client's confidence in order to mount a full defence. The OSC should avoid creating a dynamic where the lawyer is placed in the dilemma of either forgoing the right to defend his or her own interests or harming the interests of the client by disclosing privileged information. In such a case, it may well be that the OSC will have to decide to forgo proceeding against the lawyer or, at a minimum, ensure that adequate steps are taken to ensure that the proceedings are conducted in a fashion that fully respects the procedural rights of the lawyer and the substantive legal rights of the client. Failure to do so could well result in a situation where it would not be in the public interest to continue the proceedings against both the lawyer and the client.

I hasten to add that as the application for judicial review amounted to a preemptive strike against the OSC's intended hearing, there is nothing in the record as it now stands to indicate either that Wilder will argue the need to reveal privileged information in his own defence or, if that be the case, how the OSC will protect the client's interest.

CONCLUSION

For these reasons, I would dismiss the appeal with costs.

NOTES AND QUESTIONS

1. Should Canadian lawyers be concerned with regulation by both Canadian and U.S. authorities? For which lawyers is this most likely to be a concern?

2. In *Wilder*, the Divisional Court notes that both the Law Society and the OSC exercise public interest functions, but that "the public interests which they seek to protect are not the same". Do you agree? Should Wilder be subject to discipline by both the OSC and the Law Society for the same act(s)?

3. What are the goals of lawyer regulation in the corporate context? What remedies or sanctions will be effective in achieving them? Who should impose discipline where more than one regulator might govern? Consider the OSC investigation and proceedings against Sally Daub, Vice President and General Counsel for ATI Technologies Inc., a publicly traded Canadian technology company. During the OSC investigation of a company press release about lower than expected financial performance, Daub provided a letter to the OSC setting out a chronology of material events. In preparing the letter she relied upon information from members of senior management and a member of the company's board. Daub did not take sufficient steps to confirm that information for herself, and the letter to the OSC was misleading. The Settlement Agreement noted that Daub "did not intend to mislead" OSC staff in the letter, cooperated with the investigation, and "no longer works at ATI". Daub was reprimanded under s. 127(1) of the *Securities Act* and ordered to pay $5,000 in respect of the cost of the investigation and hearing. Should the case have been prosecuted? Should the Law Society have taken action as well?

(c) Privilege for Corporate Counsel and the European Approach

Because in-house counsel are not just lawyers — they are also employees and sometimes hold non-legal management or officer positions or have non-legal duties in addition to their legal ones — one of the challenges for in-house lawyers working for organizations is to carefully manage divergent roles and responsibilities both as legal advisors and as members of the management team. Often these lawyers are relied upon and expected to provide both business and legal advice; lawyers working for law firms may be asked to do the same by their corporate clients, but the intertwining of the advice is especially pronounced when a lawyer is working in an in-house capacity. While all lawyers need to be careful to ensure that privilege and confidentiality are protected, this is especially important for corporate counsel.

In *Pritchard v. Ontario (Human Rights Commission)*, the Supreme Court of Canada wrote:

> Owing to the nature of the work of in-house counsel, often having both legal and non-legal responsibilities, each situation must be assessed on a case-by-case basis to determine if the circumstances were such that privilege arose. Whether or not the privilege will attach depends on the nature of the relationship, the subject matter of the advice, and the circumstances in which it is sought and rendered.[5]

---

[5]   [2004] S.C.J. No. 16, [2004] 1 S.C.R. 809 at para. 20 (S.C.C.).

The Saskatchewan Court of Queen's Bench had considered this issue in *Potash Corp. of Saskatchewan v. Barton* and held that:

> ... when corporate counsel works in some other capacity, such as an executive or board secretary, information is not acquired in the course of the solicitor/client relationship and no privilege attaches.[6]

So, where in-house counsel is playing an executive role that is not necessarily a legal role, the safest course is to assume that privilege will not apply. But subject to the kinds of cautions noted in these two cases, Canadian jurisprudence still affords privilege for the legal advice and communications between corporate counsel and their organizational clients. This is not the case in Europe, where at least in the context of regulatory investigations conducted by the European Commission, communications between European in-house lawyers and their corporate clients are not considered privileged as those lawyers have been held to lack the requisite independence that the European Court of Justice found to be necessary as a prerequisite for recognizing privilege between lawyer and client.

PAUL D. PATON

"The Future of Privilege"
The Lawyers Weekly In-House Counsel (2011) at 8

Should in-house counsel be treated the same as their law firm counterparts, especially when it comes to solicitor-client privilege? A recent European case and Canadian Bar Association (CBA) report have reignited the debate.

The European Court of Justice decision [in September 2010] in *Akzo Nobel Chemicals, Ltd. and Akcros Chemicals Ltd. v. Commission* offered a rare opportunity for the European Court of Justice (ECJ) to revisit two previous landmark decisions from 1982 and 1984 that privilege was not available to prevent disclosure of communications involving in-house lawyers in competition law investigations. In addition to reaffirming that principle, *Akzo* set back perceptions of the role of in-house lawyers in Europe by 30 years or more, and put into question the protections available for any communications between North American in-house counsel and their European counterparts or company executives.

In *AM&S*, a 1982 decision, the European Commission (EC) seized documents emanating from in-house counsel during surprise raids on the company and used them as evidence of infringement of European Union (EU) competition law even though the documents contained only legal advice to company management. The ECJ established that a "legal professional privilege" exists in the EU where i) the communication was made for the purpose of and in the interest of a client's defense, and, ii) where the communication involves an

---

[6]   [2002] S.J. No. 484, 219 D.L.R. (4th) 513 at para. 26 (Sask. Q.B.).

"independent lawyer, that is to say one who is not bound to his client by a relationship of employment."

In *John Deere*, a 1984 case, the document seized during a similar raid was a memorandum from Deere and Co.'s American general counsel to company managers in Europe in which he expressed the view that company policies may have been violating EU law. The EC rejected the company's privilege claim and used the memo as evidence that the company was engaging in competition law violations willingly *and* knowingly.

Akzo Nobel was the latest round in this battle. The case arose out of raids by the EC in 2003 on the premises of Akzo and its subsidiary Akcros during an investigation of suspicions that the companies were participating in a cartel. The documents seized included two emails between a company executive and Akzo's in-house counsel for competition law, who was admitted to the Netherlands Bar. The in-house lawyer had signed an agreement with Akcros specifically acknowledging his independence, which would have permitted the company to assert privilege under Dutch law.

In its September 14, 2010 decision, the ECJ reconfirmed *AM&S* and held that legal professional privilege did not apply to communications with in-house lawyers in competition law investigations conducted by the EC under EU law, despite the independence agreement the Dutch lawyer had signed with the company. The language the ECJ adopted in coming to this conclusion had both practical and symbolic implications. In particular, the court focused on the in-house lawyer's "economic dependence" and "close ties" with his employer to find that he "does not enjoy a level of professional independence comparable to that of an external lawyer." Despite the fact that an in-house lawyer is enrolled with a Bar or law society and has professional ethical obligations which flow as a result, he "occupies the position of an employee which, by its very nature, does not allow him to ignore the commercial strategies pursued by his employer, and thereby affects his ability to exercise professional independence."

While the [U.S.] Association of Corporate Counsel (ACC) attempted to diminish the impact of the decision in a September 2010 member briefing by noting that in "concrete terms ... the overwhelming majority of potential legal privilege cases or incidents will not be affected by the *Akzo* ruling at all," and that the decision "has limited legal effect outside EU competition law investigations conducted by the EC," an ACC press release suggested much more grave consequences.

The ACC quoted J. Daniel Fitz, former ACC board chair in London, as saying that the ruling "has serious ramifications as it denies in-house attorneys and multinational businesses in Europe and elsewhere the critical legal counsel on competition law matters that companies working in today's global legal marketplace require. The Court has locked into place the notion that in-house lawyers are not capable of independent judgment under EU professional standards." The ACC's General Counsel was even stronger in her condemnation.

Susan Hackett said the court ignored "the realities of modern in-house practice. In-house counsel are top legal practitioners who are just as capable as their outside counsel counterparts; the idea that professional independence stems from the type of office a lawyer works in, rather than from their moral and professional compass, evidences a deep misunderstanding of legal professionalism and lawyers."

And while *Akzo Nobel* started as a competition investigation, language in the judgment signals that the same result may be applied beyond the narrow confines of competition law and perhaps to other European Union (EU) regulations and institutions. The decision creates a direct conflict with privilege that might otherwise be accorded at a national level to in-house counsel (in England, for example). Further, the European Advocate General's opinion in the case, though not binding, took the position that privilege does not extend to external counsel who are not admitted to the Bar of an EU member state.

For practical purposes, then, all communications between North American corporate counsel and the offices and subsidiaries in Europe are potentially at risk. The decision could drive company management to ensure that any communications with in-house lawyers about EU competition law are oral, not written; North American corporate counsel will need to remember that their conversations with European counterparts may not be privileged for certain purposes in Europe; and the possibility exists that challenges might arise in Canadian and U.S. courts to privilege claims over inter-company communications: can a communication with in-house lawyers arise with a "reasonable expectation of confidentiality" when such communications are subject to seizure by the European Commission?

A February 2011 discussion paper prepared for the Canadian Bar Association entitled "Solicitor-Client Privilege: Challenges for the 21st Century" raises curious questions about privilege in corporate contexts within its broad sweep. The paper's author, ... Professor Adam Dodek, notes that Canadian law has "only begun to address the multiplicity of issues that can arise in the corporate context" and that the Supreme Court of Canada "has only determined the most fundamental question," that privilege applies to advice given in the corporate context. Yet in a previous 2010 article upon which much of the CBA paper is based, Dodek concluded that "[w]hen the client is an organization, the privilege should not apply" and argued for reduced protection for privilege in organizational contexts. Such a radical recommendation both misunderstands the importance of privilege within corporations and — like *Akzo* — could consequently cast corporate counsel into a lesser status within the profession. In contrast, a 2010 CBA report [the CBA's Ethics Committee's November 2010 "FAQs on Solicitor-Client Privilege and Confidentiality"] offers both practical tools for corporate counsel and reaffirms the importance of privilege to the lawyer-client relationship in all practice environments.

Akzo Nobel shows there is a need for a better understanding of the rationale for privilege and of the professional ethics and role of in-house counsel. Becoming more aware of both the domestic and international challenges, substantive and symbolic, is only the first step.

NOTES AND QUESTIONS

1. What practical steps might in-house counsel in Canada take to ensure that privilege is protected?

2. The European Court of Justice found that because an in-house lawyer has "economic dependence" upon and "close ties" with his employer, he "does not enjoy a level of professional independence comparable to that of an external lawyer". Do you agree? How does the role of the corporate counsel differ from that of the external lawyer? How might an in-house counsel ensure that his or her independence is protected and maintained?

C. CONCLUSION

In providing an introduction to the important roles lawyers play in organizations, together with the ethical challenges they encounter, this chapter has sought both to raise questions about how lawyers practise law in such settings and about the rules that guide them in doing so. The Enron scandal and responses to it by legislators and regulators in the United States set the stage for fundamental changes not only to those rules, but also to the assignment of responsibility for creating and enforcing them. The broader debate over whether lawyers are "gatekeepers" continues, and is especially important for lawyers in corporate or organizational settings. Differences in Canadian and U.S. approaches to regulating lawyer conduct in this area remain, for the time being, though for Canadian lawyers working in organizational settings the influence of globalization and cross-border practice means that knowing about U.S. rules and approaches is especially important. And as *Wilder* and *Daub* indicate, Canadian lawyers are not immune from scrutiny and discipline by regulators other than their own law societies.

Knowing the general rules concerning client relationships, privilege and confidentiality, and the distinction between legal and business advice are also of particular importance for lawyers in organizational settings, even though the general guidance provided in Rules of Professional Conduct may not specifically address in-house settings. Who is the client? When does privilege apply? Where is the line drawn between legal and business advice? How might the answers change because of the corporate context?

With these challenges come opportunities. Lawyers in organizational settings can serve as the "corporate conscience", aiding their organizational clients to situate and assess the daily business challenges and economic imperatives with broader and longer-term concerns, and to establish an organizational culture of compliance and integrity. In order to do so, however, these lawyers need to be aware of the pressures to compromise their own independence and integrity. Understanding and appreciating the underlying personal and professional pressures is the necessary prerequisite to informing thoughtful rule development.

Rules alone are not enough, however. Recognizing the unique ethical challenges corporate counsel in Canada face, acknowledging the increasing importance of corporate counsel in Canada, and taking constructive steps to support them as they face their personal and organizational tests, are all part of the solution. In the end, lawyers, corporations and the public will all be better served by corporate counsel who have the broader bar's understanding of — and empathy for — the social and professional reality they occupy within the complex set of fiduciary and professional responsibilities to their clients and to the public in the post-Enron era.

D. FURTHER READING

Anisman, Philip, "Regulation of Lawyers by Securities Commissions: Sarbanes-Oxley in Canada" (Toronto: Capital Markets Institute, March 2003).

American Bar Association, Task Force on Corporate Responsibility, *Final Report* (March 31, 2003), online: <http://www.abanet.org/buslaw/corporate responsibility>.

Daly, Mary C., "The Cultural, Ethical and Legal Challenges in Lawyering for a Global Organization: The Role of the General Counsel" (1997) 46 Emory L.J. 1057.

DeMott, Deborah A., "The Discrete Roles of General Counsel" (2005) 74 Fordham L. Rev. 955.

Hazard, Geoffrey C., Jr., "Ethical Dilemmas of Corporate Counsel" (1997) 46 Emory L.J. 1011.

Kraakman, Reiner, "Gatekeepers: Anatomy of a Third-Party Enforcement Strategy" (1985) J.L. Econ. & Org. 53.

Langevoort, Donald, "Where Were the Lawyers? A Behavioral Inquiry into Lawyers' Responsibility for Clients' Fraud" (1993) 46 Vand. L. Rev. 75.

Le Mire, Suzanne, "Testing Times: In-House Counsel and Independence" (2011) 14(1) Legal Ethics 21.

Le Mire, Suzanne & Christine Parker, "Keeping it In-House: Ethics in the Relationship between Large Law Firm Lawyers and their Corporate Clients through the Eyes of In-House Counsel" (2008) 11(2) Legal Ethics 201.

Painter, Richard W. & Jennifer E. Duggan, "Lawyer Disclosure of Corporate Fraud: Establishing a Firm Foundation" (1996) 50 SMU L. Rev. 225.

Paton, Paul D., "Corporate Counsel as Corporate Conscience: Ethics and Integrity in the Post-Enron Era" (2005) 84(3) Can. Bar Rev. 531.

Paton, Paul, "Navigating the Investigation Minefield" *The Lawyers Weekly In-House Counsel* (2011) 8.

Paton, Paul, "Who's Your Client?" *The Lawyers Weekly In-House Counsel* (2011) 8.

Paton, Paul, "In-House Counsel Under Fire" *The Lawyers Weekly In-House Counsel* (2009) 8.

Paton, Paul, "The Company Moral Compass" *The Lawyers Weekly In-House Counsel* (2008) 8.

Rosen, Robert Eli, "The Inside Counsel Movement, Professional Judgment and Organizational Representation" (1989) 64(3) Ind. L.J. 479.

Simon, William H., "Whom (or What) Does the Organization's Lawyer Represent? An Anatomy of Intra-client Conflict" (2003) 91 Cal. L. Rev. 57.

CHAPTER 10

GOVERNMENT LAWYERS

A. INTRODUCTION

The dominant model of the Canadian lawyer is the lawyer in private practice, specifically the advocate, representing his or her client's rights against the state or another adversary. We have raised generations of lawyers on the inspirational words of Lord Brougham: an advocate "knows but one person in all the world, and that person is his client" and "[t]o save that client by all means and expedients, and at all hazards and costs to other persons, and, among them, to himself, is his first and only duty; and in performing this duty he must not regard the alarm, the torments, the destruction which he may bring upon others".[1]

This model is problematic in various ways. As set out in Chapter 1, many critics, such as David Luban and Trevor Farrow, criticize the ethical foundations of this approach. Further, on a descriptive level, it does not accurately reflect what most Canadian lawyers actually do. The model of the lawyer as a strongly zealous advocate tends to be invoked most frequently in relation to the criminal defence lawyer, yet only a small percentage of Canadian lawyers can be described as engaging in criminal defence work. In particular, the dominant model does not fit very well when applied to public sector lawyers.

Public sector lawyers include lawyers who work for one of the three levels of government or for one of the many public entities that have been created with the rise of the administrative state in Canada since the 1960s. These include lawyers for hospitals, schools boards, public utilities, securities commissions, Crown corporations, human rights commissions, legal aid clinics and like bodies. In 1961, 6.7 per cent of all Canadian lawyers worked in the public sector. By 1986, that figure had increased to 10.8 per cent[2] and by 2008–2009, an estimated 15-25 per cent of Canadian lawyers worked in the public sector, depending on the jurisdiction.[3] Think about that for a moment: if you are an aspiring lawyer in Nova Scotia, one in four of you will likely work in the public sector.[4] In British Columbia or Ontario, that figure is

---

[1] J. Nightingale, ed., *Trial of Queen Caroline*, vol. 2 (London: J. Robins & Co., 1821) at 8.

[2] David A.A. Stager with Harry W. Arthurs, *Lawyers in Canada* (Toronto: University of Toronto Press, 1990) at 158 (Table 6.12).

[3] There are no available comprehensive figures but the range of 15-25 per cent is taken from statistics from the individual Law Societies.

[4] See Nova Scotia Barristers' Society, "Statistical Snapshot – September 2011", online: <http://nsbs.org/sites/default/files/cms/menu-pdf/snapshot2011.pdf> (25.3 per cent of lawyers in Government/Public Sector).

about one in six. Yet, references to public sector lawyers are almost entirely absent from most codes of conduct and discussions of legal ethics in Canada. For these reasons, Allan Hutchinson rightly called government lawyers "the orphans of legal ethics" because so "little energy has been directed towards defining and defending the role and duties of government lawyers".[5]

In this chapter, we are concerned with a subset of public sector lawyers: the government lawyer. The government lawyer works for one of the three levels of government: federal, provincial or municipal. In fact, we might consider the federal Department of Justice to be Canada's largest law firm, although they do not describe themselves as such. The "DOJ" or "Justice" employs over 5,200 persons, more than half of whom are lawyers. With over 2,700 lawyers, it is more than twice the size of the largest Canadian law firm.[6] It has offices in 17 cities across Canada and has 42 practice groups specializing in tax, Aboriginal law, transportation, immigration, civil litigation, terrorism, international law and many other areas. It is the most frequent litigator in the Supreme Court of Canada and it advises cabinet ministers and government agencies.[7]

In this chapter, we explore some of the unique ethical issues relating to and experienced by government lawyers. In the first part, we examine the issue of whether government lawyers owe "special obligations" that would lead to those lawyers being held to higher ethical duties. In the second part, we examine what the nature of such special obligations would be. Then in the third part we examine some of the organizational pressures faced by government lawyers.

B.   SPECIAL OBLIGATIONS?

Canadian lawyers who work for the government do so in a wide variety of contexts, just a few of which include: advising government on the legality of public policy; bringing or defending civil actions to which the government is a party; prosecuting criminal or regulatory offences; working for regulatory agencies or tribunals; negotiating government contracts; advising government on foreign affairs and international law; and designing and drafting legislation.

---

5   Allan C. Hutchinson, "'In the Public Interest': The Responsibilities and Rights of Government Lawyers" (2008) 46 Osgoode Hall L.J. 105 at 106. For notable exceptions, see the references at the end of this chapter. The paucity of attention to government lawyers in Canada compares poorly with the attention given to the subject in the United States.

6   These figures are current as of March 31, 2010. See Canada, Department of Justice, *Workforce Representation and Availability as of March 31, 2010* (Ottawa: Department of Justice, 2010) (on file with author).

7   See Canada, Department of Justice, *Canada's Department of Justice*, online: <http://canada.justice.gc.ca/eng/dept-min/pub/about-aprop>. The DOJ has a budget of $900 million. It has 17 regional offices and sub-offices and 42 Departmental Legal Services Units (DLSUs) co-located with client department and agencies. See Canada, Department of Justice, *Report on Plans and Priorities 2009-10*, online: <http://www.tbs-sct.gc.ca/rpp/2009-2010/inst/jus/jus00-eng.asp>.

The question considered here is this: to what extent does the fact that a lawyer's client is "the Crown" affect the nature of his or her ethical obligations? Is the lawyer required to be more critical of what he or she is being asked to do? Does he or she have broader and deeper ethical obligations to the administration of justice and/or the protection of the public interest? Some of these questions were touched upon in Chapter 8 with respect to Crown counsel prosecuting criminal trials, but they arise more generally for all lawyers working for federal or provincial governments. In Canada, there has been very little discussion of whether government lawyers owe a "higher" ethical duty than other lawyers. The *Everingham* case below provides one of the few judicial considerations of this issue. Consider the contrasting perspectives of Borins J. and the Divisional Court.

EVERINGHAM v. ONTARIO

[1991] O.J. No. 3578, 84 D.L.R. (4th) 354, 3 C.P.C. (3d) 87
(Ont. Gen. Div., Borins J.)

[Denis LePage was a patient in the Social Behaviour Program at the Oak Ridge division of the Mental Health Centre in Penetanguishene, Ontario. He and other patients had brought an application alleging that they had been subject to Charter rights violations and were entitled to relief pursuant to section 24(2) of the Charter. Mr. LePage was due to be cross-examined by attorneys for the Crown. The day before his cross-examination he had a conversation with Thomas Haldane Wickett, the lawyer for the Crown who was to cross-examine Mr. LePage the following day. Mr. LePage's own counsel was not present when the conversation took place. The content of that conversation was disputed. However, it was found by Borins J. that Mr. Wickett did tell Mr. LePage that he was the lawyer who was going to cross-examine him the next day, that Mr. LePage stated that he understood that his lawyer was going to be present during the cross-examination, that Mr. Wickett "did not obtain any information from Mr. LePage which he could use in questioning him the next day" but that "Mr. LePage was sufficiently concerned and upset ... that he reported the incident to his lawyer, Mr. Taman". Mr. LePage and the other applicants brought a motion seeking to have the Attorney General for Ontario removed as solicitor of record.]

BORINS J. (orally):—

. . . . .

The starting point is Rule 10, Commentary 14, of the Rules of Professional Conduct of The Law Society of Upper Canada. Rule 10 states:

> When acting as an advocate the lawyer, while treating the tribunal with courtesy and respect, must represent the client resolutely and honourably within the limits of the law.

The relevant portion of Commentary 14 reads:

> An opposite party who is professionally represented should not be approached or dealt with save through or with the consent of that party's lawyer.

I have no doubt that what occurred in this case represented a breach of the rule and the commentary by Mr. Wickett. The consequences which should flow from this breach represent a more difficult question. In this regard, the obvious alternatives which I have are to dismiss or allow the motion. A further alternative would be to disqualify Mr. Wickett from any further involvement in the case as solicitor for the respondents. This alternative arises from the inherent jurisdiction which this court has to control and supervise barristers and solicitors who are, of course, officers of the court in respect of their conduct in legal proceedings. Should it be necessary to cite authority for this proposition, I would rely upon the decision of the Supreme Court of Canada in *MacDonald Estate v. Martin*, [1990] 3 S.C.R. 1235.

Notwithstanding the comprehensive submissions of Mr. Taman, I am of the view that it would not be appropriate in the circumstances of his case to remove the Attorney General for Ontario as solicitor of record for the respondents. I base this conclusion on a number of grounds. First, this is not a case in which a lawyer deliberately sought out and spoke to a party behind the back of the party's lawyer. The meeting of Mr. LePage by Mr. Wickett was purely coincidental. Second, in speaking to Mr. LePage, Mr. Wickett had no oblique motive. He simply wanted to alleviate Mr. LePage's concern with respect to his identity and why he was there and what was to occur in respect to his cross-examination the next day. Third, nothing concerning the application was discussed and Mr. Wickett obtained no information confidential, or otherwise, from Mr. LePage. Fourth, this is not a case - being a *Charter* application - in which there are conflicting interests in the usual sense of that term as encountered in private litigation. Fifth, the meeting was brief and innocent in its nature. Sixth, other than the loss of confidence which Mr. LePage may now have if Mr. Wickett is to be permitted to continue as counsel for the respondents, and I do not minimize this, no prejudice was caused to Mr. LePage by the interview.

It remains to be decided, however, whether in the circumstances Mr. Wickett should be permitted to continue as counsel for the respondents. In my view, he should not. Although the spirit of Rule 10, Commentary 14, was not breached because Mr. Wickett did not obtain any advantage in the conduct of the litigation by talking to Mr. LePage, nevertheless what he did constituted a serious indiscretion on his part. He should have been more sensitive to the circumstances and the situation in which he found himself. In this regard, I trust it goes without saying that Ms. Regenstreif committed no indiscretion. Being aware of the litigation and the pending cross-examination of Mr. LePage and the other applicants, Mr. Wickett should not have toured the hospital. However, he did. When he came into contact with Mr. LePage he should not have talked to him. If it was necessary for Mr. Wickett to explain his presence in the ward to Mr. LePage, he should have asked Dr. Jones or somebody else to do so. However well motivated he was, it is now obvious that what he did seriously affected Mr. LePage and has so undermined his confidence in the system that I feel that I must, to restore that confidence, disqualify Mr. Wickett from any further participation in this litigation.

Although the Rules of Professional Conduct of The Law Society of Upper Canada must necessarily apply to all lawyers, it is my view that one who is a lawyer employed by the government must be particularly sensitive to the rules which govern his or her professional conduct. Such a lawyer may be said to have a higher obligation than lawyers generally. The government lawyer, to use the expression employed by counsel, is usually one who is a principal legal officer of a department, ministry, agency or other legal entity of the government, or a member of the legal staff of the department, ministry, agency or entity. This lawyer assumes a public trust because the government in all of its parts, is responsible to the people in our democracy with its representative form of government. Each part of the government has the obligation of carrying out, in the public interest, its assigned responsibility in a manner consistent with the applicable laws and regulations and the Charter of Rights. While the private lawyer represents the client's personal or private interest, the government lawyer represents the public interest. Although it may not be accurate to suggest the public is the client of the government lawyer as the client concept is generally understood, the government lawyer is required to observe in the performance of his or her professional responsibility the public interest sought to be served by the government department, ministry or agency of which he or she is a part. That is why I believe there is a special responsibility on the part of government lawyers to be particularly sensitive to the Rules of Professional Conduct, a responsibility which, regrettably, Mr. Wickett overlooked in this case.

Therefore, there will be an order disqualifying Mr. Wickett from any further involvement directly, or indirectly, in the conduct of this litigation on behalf of the respondents.

EVERINGHAM v. ONTARIO

[1992] O.J. No. 304, 88 D.L.R. (4th) 755
(Ont. Gen. Div., Callaghan C.J.O.C., Hartt and Campbell JJ.)

THE COURT:—

The application

The Attorney General for Ontario appeals, with leave, against an order disqualifying a Crown solicitor from any further involvement in a lawsuit brought against the Ontario government by a number of patients at the Oak Ridge Mental Health Centre.

The issue

Should a solicitor acting against a patient confined in a mental hospital be disqualified from continuing because he met privately with the patient in the institution without the presence or knowledge of the patient's counsel?

The facts

[The court reiterated the facts and findings of the motions court judge, and quoted Rule 10, Commentary 14 of the *Rules of Professional Conduct* of the Law Society of Upper Canada.]

The legal findings

Because the solicitor did not intend or obtain any advantage in the conduct of the litigation by talking to the patient, the learned judge found that the solicitor had not breached "the spirit" of Rule 10, Commentary 14 of the Law Society of Upper Canada.

The judge, however, concluded that the solicitor had breached Rule 10, Commentary 14, that lawyers employed by the government have a higher professional obligation to observe the Rules of Professional Conduct than other lawyers and that the solicitor's conduct in breaching the rule had so seriously undermined the patient's confidence in the system that it was necessary to disqualify the solicitor from further participation in the litigation.

Was the rule breached?

The judge erred in law in concluding that the solicitor had breached Rule 10, Commentary 14. Having found the meeting coincidental, innocent, unprejudicial, motivated solely out of concern to alleviate the patient's concern, having additionally found that the solicitor did not discuss the lawsuit or obtain any information, confidential or otherwise, and having further found that the spirit of the rule was not breached, there was no basis for the motions court judge to conclude that the rule was breached.

A purposive interpretation of the rule requires consideration of the purpose, intent, content and setting of the contact between the solicitor and the opposite party. No lawyer can completely avoid all contact, casual or otherwise, with every party against whom he or she acts. The words "approached or dealt with" must mean approached or dealt with in relation to the subject-matter or process of the litigation itself.

Having regard to the findings above and the fact that the solicitor did not approach or deal with the client in relation to the subject-matter or process of the litigation, there is no basis for a finding that the rule was breached and it cannot fairly be said that the solicitor breached the rule in this case.

The professional standard of Crown solicitors

Central to the conclusion of the learned judge was his view that lawyers employed by the government have a higher professional obligation than other lawyers to observe the Rules of Professional Conduct. There is no basis for this conclusion in the laws or traditions that govern the bar of this province.

All lawyers in Ontario are subject to the same single high standard of professional conduct. It is not flattering to the lawyers of Ontario to say that most of them are held to a lower standard of professional conduct than government lawyers.

The Ministry of the Attorney General Act, R.S.O. 1990, c. M.17, and the *Law Society Act*, R.S.O. 1990, c. L.8, codify some of the special public obligations of the Attorney General in relation to the public interest in the legal profession and the conduct of government business according to law. The unique obligations of Crown counsel in the conduct of public prosecutions are well known. Because of these public obligations and the traditions associated with the Crown office in this province, the courts have come to expect a particular level of conduct and expertise from Crown counsel in various types of judicial business.

It is one thing to say that a particular branch of the Crown law office or a particular law firm or lawyer has earned a reputation for a high standard of professional conduct. It is quite different to say that any lawyer or group of lawyers is subject to a higher standard of liability than that required of every lawyer under the Rules of Professional Conduct.

In respect of their liability under the Rules of Professional Conduct, as opposed to the public interest duties associated with their office, Crown counsel stand on exactly the same footing as every member of the bar.

It is therefore an error of law to exact from government lawyers a higher standard under the Rules of Professional Conduct than that required of lawyers in private practice.

Subjective or objective standard

The standard for the removal of counsel is objective. The standard is that of a reasonably informed member of the public: *MacDonald Estate v. Martin*, [1990] 3 S.C.R. 1235, ... at pp. 1259-60 S.C.R. ... The personal feelings of the litigant are only one element in the application of an objective standard.

The motions court judge applied a subjective standard by requiring the solicitor's removal on the grounds that his conduct "seriously affected the patient and undermined his confidence in the process". By applying a subjective rather than an objective standard, the motions court judge erred in law.

Should the removal order stand?

Notwithstanding the error in finding a breach of the rule, the error in requiring a higher standard of professional conduct from government lawyers and the error in applying a subjective standard, should the removal be upheld?

In our view, it should.

It is within the inherent jurisdiction of a superior court to deny the right of audience to counsel when the interests of justice so require by reason of conflict or otherwise. This power does not depend on the rules of professional conduct made by the legal profession and is not limited to cases where the rules are breached.

The issue here is not whether or not the rule was breached or whether the solicitor worked for the government. Nor is it solely whether the patient lost confidence in the process.

The issue is whether a fair-minded reasonably informed member of the public would conclude that the proper administration of justice required the removal of the solicitor.

It is simply a matter of common sense that mental patients confined in institutions are in a vulnerable position. The administration of justice requires not only that confined mental patients be treated fairly in the legal process, but that they also be seen to be treated fairly in the legal process.

There is an obvious appearance of unfairness when a lawyer acting against a confined mental patient conducts a private meeting with the patient in an interview room in the institution without the presence or even the knowledge of the patient's counsel. This is particularly so when the meeting takes place at the arrangement and authority of the very custodians whose authority is challenged by the patient in the legal proceeding.

There is an obvious appearance of compulsion and an obvious apprehension of oppression in the very fact of such a meeting. The patient, with no notice to his counsel or access to legal or other advice or assistance, was under a custodial compulsion to meet privately with his legal opponent in an inter-view room in a closed institution hidden away from any public or judicial scrutiny, with no record kept of what was said. There is an obvious appear-ance that the patient's right to counsel is being undermined.

It is irrelevant that the solicitor's innocent version of the meeting is eventually found by a court to be preferable to the patient's version of the meeting. Apart from the obvious appearance of compulsion, oppression and deprivation of counsel, it is inevitable that such a meeting will produce different versions of the conversation. That is the mischief to be avoided, yet that is the very mischief that occurred here in the patient's version of what happened and the impression left with him that the meeting was pre-arranged with a view to gaining an advantage over him.

The public interest in the administration of justice requires an unqualified perception of its fairness in the eyes of the general public. This is particularly so when the rights are at stake of powerless and vulnerable litigants like detained mental patients. The appearance of unfairness, oppression and deprivation of counsel is not, as noted above, cured by an eventual finding that a court prefers the evidence of the solicitor to the evidence of the detained mental patient. The goal is not just to protect the interests of the individual litigant but even more importantly to protect public confidence in the administration of justice: *Goldberg v. Goldberg* (1982), 141 D.L.R. (3d) 133 ... (Ont. Div. Ct.), per Callaghan J., at pp. 135-36 D.L.R. ... The sine qua non of the justice system is that there be an unqualified perception of its fairness in the eyes of the public: *MacDonald Estate, supra*, at p. 1256 S.C.R., ... quoting *O'Dea v. O'Dea* (1987), 68 Nfld. & P.E.I.R. 67, ... (Nfld. U.F.C.), aff'd Nfld. C.A., June 6, 1988.

No reasonably informed member of the public would think it fair for any lawyer, about to cross-examine a detained mental patient, to take the patient into a closed institutional interview room under the authority of the very custodians whose legal authority over the patient is challenged, and conduct a private unrecorded conversation without any notice to the patient's counsel either before or after the interview.

The objective appearance of unfairness, oppression and deprivation of counsel is too blatant to be tolerated.

Notwithstanding the errors of law in the judgment appealed from, the order removing the lawyer must be upheld for the reasons stated above. The appeal is dismissed.

NOTES AND QUESTIONS

1. What did the lawyer for the Government do wrong according to Borins J.? Are there any circumstances in which it would be acceptable for a lawyer to speak with the opposing client without their counsel present? What features would such circumstances have in common?

2. How would you describe the key differences in the approaches of Borins J. and the Divisional Court to the question of whether government lawyers have special ethical duties? Which approach is preferable? Why?

3. If the Divisional Court found there was no conflict, why did it confirm the order of Borins J. to remove the lawyer? In answering this question consider in particular the court's statement that "no reasonably informed member of the public would think it fair" to act as the Crown did when examining Mr. LePage. If no reasonably informed member of the public would think it fair, does it make sense to describe the Crown's conduct as nonetheless ethically satisfactory?

4. In Chapter 5, dealing with conflicts of interest, you read in *MacDonald Estate v. Martin* that where one lawyer is found to be in a conflict of interest, that lawyer's firm is also disqualified. Does this apply when a Government lawyer is found to be in a conflict of interest? Can it? Should it? What rule should apply when an individual government lawyer is found to be in a conflict of interest?

5. The heart of the debate in *Everingham* is whether government lawyers owe "a higher duty". The readings that follow take different approaches to this issue. In reading each excerpt recall the facts and judgments in the two *Everingham* cases. Which approach would best resolve the problem that case presented?

ADAM DODEK

"Lawyering at the Intersection of Public Law and Legal Ethics:
Government Lawyers as Custodians of the Rule of Law"
(2010) 33 Dal. L.J. 1 at 18-28
[footnotes omitted]

. . . . .

As a matter of public law, government lawyers should owe higher ethical duties than private lawyers because they exercise public power ...

. . . . .

[Exercising public power] is what it means to be lawyers for the Crown because the Crown is the concept that personifies the exercise of state power. As discussed below, government lawyers are not just passive vessels implementing the instructions of their political masters. Government lawyers interpret, advise and advocate on the powers and duties of the Crown. In so doing, government lawyers exercise public power. This exercise of public power is therefore the key distinction between government lawyers and all other lawyers. This is why it is an oversimplification, an understatement and is misleading to characterize government lawyers as lawyers for an organization. The source of this heightened ethical duty is therefore to be found in public law, specifically in the constitutional responsibilities of the Attorneys General.

All government Lawyers are agents of the Attorney General and under the *Carltona* doctrine, it is recognized that the Attorney General can only fulfill the duties of the office through delegation to his or her agents. Government lawyers' higher duty therefore derives from the duties and responsibilities of the Attorney General. That office has a unique constitutional status in Canada. It has been described as "the guardian of the public interest" or "the defender of the Rule of Law." ... [In *Secession Reference*, [1998] 2 S.C.R. 217 at para. 70, the Supreme Court of Canada held that] "At [its] most basic level, the rule of law vouchsafes to the citizens and residents of the country a stable, predictable and ordered society in which to conduct their affairs. It provides a shield for individuals from arbitrary state action."

With this understanding of the rule of law, the case for the Attorney General as its defender becomes more straightforward. The Attorney General has a statutory duty to "see that the administration of public affairs is in accordance with the law." As former Ontario Attorney General Ian Scott explained,

> the Attorney General has a positive duty to ensure that the administration of public affairs complies with the law. Any discussion of the Attorney General's responsibilities must keep this fundamental obligation in mind.

In the landmark 1968 McRuer Report into Civil Liberties in Ontario, Commissioner McRuer explained that

> [t]he duty of the Attorney General to supervise legislation imposes on him a responsibility to the public that transcends his responsibility to his

colleagues in the Cabinet. It requires him to exercise constant vigilance to sustain and defend the Rule of Law against departmental attempts to grasp unhampered arbitrary powers, which may be done in many ways.

Government lawyers operate within a matrix of a rule of law triangle. Their higher duties are a result of operating at the intersection of three axes: as delegates of the Attorney General, as public servants and as members of the legal profession.

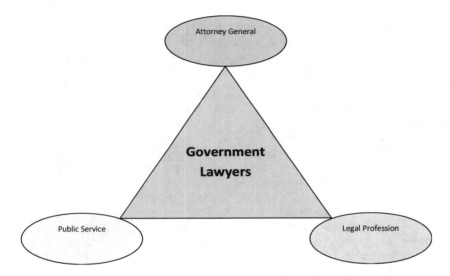

The Attorney General has a clear duty to uphold the rule of law. At its most basic level, this requires the Attorney General to ensure that all government action complies with the law. The Attorney General can only fulfill this duty through his or her agents, government lawyers. Government lawyers therefore have a delegated responsibility for fulfilling this public law duty. This is a critical point which distinguishes government lawyers from other lawyers who do not have such an express duty to ensure that their client complies with the law. While ethical codes prohibit lawyers from actively assisting or facilitating their client's commission of illegal conduct, they do not generally require lawyers to prevent their client from committing illegal acts. As delegates of the Attorney General, government lawyers have an affirmative duty that extends far beyond this minimal general duty of all lawyers. Government lawyers must ensure that all actions of government comply with all laws: civil, criminal and administrative. The ramifications of this duty are discussed below.

As public servants, government lawyers also have a duty to uphold the rule of law. As Chair of the Task Force on Public Service Values and Ethics, former Deputy Minister of Justice John Tait, Q.C. explained:

> One of the defining features of public service organizations, especially in
> Canada, is that they are established under law and have as one of their chief
> roles the administration and upholding of the laws of Canada. In order to do
> this well, the public service and individual public servants should be
> animated by an unshakable conviction about the importance and primacy of
> law, and about the need to uphold it with integrity, impartiality and
> judgement.

Elsewhere Tait asserted that public servants must remember some of the basic
purposes of government "such as democratic accountability, the rule of law,
and fairness and equity." In short, all public servants have a duty to uphold
the rule of law and government lawyers *qua* public servants share in this duty.

As lawyers, government lawyers are part of a profession devoted to the Rule
of Law, but the perspectives of the profession and of Government are
different. As the Law Society of Upper Canada's Task Force on the Rule of
Law and the Independence of the Bar asserted, "[a]n independent Bar works
in tandem with an independent judiciary in the implementation of the Rule of
Law." The conceptual problem for government lawyers is that at first glance
their position as lawyers for the government is inimical to most conceptions
of an independent bar. These include the notion that lawyers are able to put
their clients' interest first without fear of constraint *especially by the state*. It
also includes the asserted "right of the public who need legal assistance to
obtain it from someone who is independent of the state and can thereby
provide independent representation." The other element of independence of
the bar that is problematic for government lawyers is the idea of independence
from client control: lawyers "should have autonomy to decide which clients
and causes to represent and how to conduct that representation." As members
of the legal profession, government lawyers are part of a profession dedicated
to preserving the rule of law; however in the work that they do as government
lawyers, the bar's conception of independence does not accurately describe
their work.

When the three elements of government lawyers' identity — public servants,
lawyers and delegates of the Attorney General — are combined, the unique
relationship between government lawyers and the rule of law begins to
appear. The core meanings of independence for the bar involve independence
from the state, either in terms of interference with the lawyer-client relationship by the state or in terms of regulation by the state. For government
lawyers, their client is the state. And as lawyers for the state, government
lawyers are not only tasked with ensuring that the state and its officials
comply with the law, but they are also involved in creating law in a way that
private sector lawyers are not. Government lawyers are involved in protecting
the rule of law from the inside. Moreover, what fundamentally distinguishes
government lawyers from their non-government counterparts is that they
exercise state power.

Government lawyers exercise state power in everything they do. There are
some who will challenge this assertion and claim that government lawyers do
not exercise state power but rather they represent the interests of those who

do. This assertion fails to adequately capture the nature of government lawyers' work. We no longer live in a legal culture dominated by formalism where we believe that legal reasoning is the process of finding one true "correct" answer. Rather, we have come to acknowledge the indeterminacy of law and to acknowledge that there are subjective influences on legal interpretation. Government lawyers who are advising their clients on the law exercise power given to them under law. In many cases, they exercise significant discretion in providing legal advice. The act of giving legal advice, of interpreting the law, is itself an exercise of power. It can have a broad impact on people's lives – sometimes equal to or exceeding that of a Crown counsel in a criminal prosecution. Nowhere is this more the case nor more important than in the area of human rights and constitutional law.

The American example of the torture memos is the best example of the powerful impact that legal advice can have on people's lives. The act of legal interpretation can be used to constrain or to authorize power. In this instance, government lawyers used the law not as a constraint on power, but as "the handmaiden of unconscionable abuse." In the words of legal ethicist David Luban, the government lawyers spun their legal advice because they knew that "spun advice" is what their clients wanted. Lawyers in the Office of Legal Counsel in the Department of Justice interpreted law to authorize a host of heightened interrogation methods which most people would identify as torture. Moreover, lawyers in the Office of Legal Counsel used legal interpretation to create an entire category of persons who would not be protected by the rule of law (enemy combatants) and their advice supported the attempt to create a rule of law-free zone (Guantánamo). While this American example may be extreme, an important Canadian example demonstrates how the act of legal interpretation is itself an exercise of state power.

Under the *Canadian Bill of Rights*, the Minister of Justice is required to examine every draft regulation and every government bill introduced in the House of Commons "in order to ascertain whether any of the provisions thereof are inconsistent with the purposes and provisions" of the *Bill of Rights* and the Minister "shall report any such inconsistency to the House of Commons at the first convenient opportunity." An analogous provision of the *Department of Justice Act* requires the Minister to examine every draft regulation and every Government Bill introduced in the House of Commons

> in order to ascertain whether any of the provisions thereof are inconsistent with the purposes and provisions of the *Canadian Charter of Rights and Freedoms* and the Minister shall report any such inconsistency to the House of Commons at the first convenient opportunity.

Since 1960 when the *Canadian Bill of Rights* was enacted and since 1982 when the *Charter* was enacted, there has never been a single report made to the House of Commons by any Minister of Justice. Some think this is negative while other are less concerned about it. Here my point is that every time a decision is made not to make a report to the House of Commons, there has obviously been an act of interpretation. Indeed, this was made clear when a Department of Justice lawyer disclosed at a house committee that the standard used to trigger the reporting requirement was "manifestly unconstitutional." This phrase is itself an act of legal interpretation and a highly discretionary one at that. If lawyers in the Department had chosen a standard of "arguably unconstitutional," it is likely that many more bills would have been reported as under these provisions. This could have had a very different effect on legislation and the relationship between the courts, the legislature and the executive, to say the least of the potential impact of such legislation on affected groups.

These arguments for the higher duty of government lawyers as custodians of the rule of law are supported by existing duties of the Crown in other areas, government statements and some judicial pronouncements. In fact, if we examine the conduct expected of government lawyers, we find that they are already subject to a higher duty than private lawyers. The standards of conduct expected of government lawyers in areas outside of criminal law demonstrate that there are a whole host of areas where a higher duty is expected of government lawyers. Outside of criminal law, there are other areas where the Attorney General is expected to act independently, that is without political considerations or involvement. These include public interest injunctions and interventions. Other areas where the Attorney General represents the public interest include *parens patriae* jurisdiction, child protection, expropriation and charities. In Aboriginal Law, the honour of the Crown doctrine requires the Crown to consider Aboriginal interests in dealings with Aboriginal peoples.

When government lawyers are dealing with vulnerable parties who are represented by counsel, a higher standard of conduct may be expected of them than if the case simply involved two private parties. Thus, in the public inquiry into wrongful conviction of Donald Marshall, the Commission was critical of how the government handled the negotiations with Mr. Marshall's counsel over compensation. Counsel for Nova Scotia negotiated what would objectively be considered a good deal for the government to settle Mr. Marshall's claims for the sum of $270,000. However, the public inquiry did not view it in this manner. The Commissioners did not analyze government counsel's actions through the traditional paradigm of the adversarial model of litigation. Instead, the Commission stated that the Deputy Attorney General "should have realized that the Donald Marshall, Jr. compensation question was not merely a routine piece of civil litigation and the question of fairness needed to be considered. It was not." No further explanation was given as to why this was not an ordinary piece of civil litigation. If it was because of Crown wrongdoing, then the Commission did not make clear why counsel for the Crown owed a higher duty than in other cases of Crown wrongdoing.

In essence, when we put aside the situations where it is recognized that government lawyers do owe higher duties, we are left with two types of government lawyering activities: civil litigation against a non-vulnerable party and advisory functions, including legislative drafting and policy development. In ordinary civil litigation, government lawyers often do not behave like their private counterparts. For example, in the area of costs, the Crown routinely foregoes its right to seek costs against the losing party in litigation or seeks significantly less in indemnification than what a private party would.

A more recent decision addressing the conduct of government lawyers against a non-vulnerable party is perhaps more illuminating than the Hickman Inquiry's statements regarding government counsel's conduct *vis à vis* Donald Marshall. In a decision unsealed in 2010 involving the disclosure of a privileged report, Justice Michael Code of the Ontario Superior Court of Justice made the express connection between counsel's conduct and the government's duty under the rule of law. According to Justice Code, it is not enough for a public sector lawyer to take an adversarial stance in litigation because opposing counsel's argument is not well-framed. The government lawyer has a duty to ensure that the government complies with the law: "the importance of the rule of law as constitutional precept in Canada does not permit this approach to public administration at any level of government." Justice Code's statements involved the conduct of a lawyer for the City of Toronto. They have stronger force in the case of lawyers for the provincial or federal government because of the constitutional responsibilities of the federal and provincial Attorneys General.

If the statements of Justice Code are representative of a wider judicial attitude towards government lawyers, it is likely that many judges expect more from government counsel — even in ordinary civil litigation cases where the adversary is a well-resourced private lawyer. I would suspect that many government lawyers similarly hold themselves to a higher standard and take very seriously the moniker that they are lawyers for the Crown. In fact, the mandate, mission and values of the Department of Justice provide that its lawyers should "provide high-quality legal services" while "upholding the highest standards of integrity and fairness." Thus, the official policy of the Department of Justice would seem to support the idea of a higher duty. In policy and in practice, government lawyers are committed to a higher duty and not simply to the minimal standards of ethical conduct prescribed in law society rules.

MALLIHA WILSON, TAIA WONG & KEVIN HILLE

"Professionalism and the Public Interest"
(2011) 38 Advocates' Q. 1 at 14-17[*]
[footnotes omitted]

Dodek argues that government lawyers are subject to a higher ethical duty because they operate at the intersection of three axes …

[*] Reproduced with permission.

But the fact of operating within that matrix does not necessarily or easily translate into higher ethical standards for government lawyers. In litigation against major corporate or institutional litigants, for example, wouldn't the public interest be best served by government lawyers who avail themselves of whatever arguments they can within the bounds of the law in order to achieve the government's goals? The matrix within which government lawyers operate may indeed be unique, but it is not monolithic. Instead, government lawyers advise on and litigate a wide range of matters involving a broad spectrum of litigants. Imposing higher ethical duties on government lawyers without regard to the diversity of their practice and the needs and obligations of the ministries and agencies they serve would impede the delivery of legal services in government.

Moreover, Dodek's suggestion that government lawyers owe a higher ethical duty as a result of their exercise of public power is difficult to reconcile with government decision-making processes involving significant matters, in which only certain public officials have the legal authority to decide matters on behalf of the Crown. These public officials wield and exercise public power, not the government lawyers who advise them. The government lawyer provides legal advice on proposed courses of action that government officials may wish to take, but he or she does not have decision making authority either directly or indirectly, as legal considerations are only one factor, along with policy and political considerations, that influence official decision-making.

While it may be true that, as Dodek suggests, government lawyers exercise discretion in providing legal advice and that the act of giving legal advice, of interpreting the law, is itself an exercise of power, that discretion and power is circumscribed by the institutional and constitutional confines within which the government lawyer works. The role of the government lawyer is to state what the law is, thereby enabling the Attorney General to discharge his or her obligations to defend the rule of law and safeguard the public interest. In a democratic, post-Charter society, government lawyers cannot decide what constitutes the public interest and enforce the rule of law themselves by pre-emptively acting inconsistently with the legitimate goals of a democratically-elected government, particularly when their advice is cloaked in secrecy and protected by solicitor-client privilege. Rather, government lawyers are responsible for empowering the Attorney General to discharge his or her responsibilities of upholding the rule of law and protecting the public interest by providing advice that is thorough, balanced and independent of partisan political consideration. The suggestion that government lawyers owe higher ethical duties because they exercise public power therefore collapses the roles of the government lawyer and the Attorney General, when in fact constitutional norms, the institutional hierarchy of government and democratic ideals require their separation. The government lawyer's job is fundamentally to give the best legal advice about what is required by the rule of law. There is no need for a higher ethical obligation for that to occur.

Some legal theorists have taken the fact that regulatory codes are silent on the difference between government lawyers and private counsel as an indication that the expectations of the former are not substantially different than those of the latter. Other theorists have suggested, however, that even where a higher standard of conduct is not contained in extrinsic codes of conduct, it is nevertheless derived intrinsically from the position of a government lawyer as a public official. They argue that the oath of loyalty taken by government lawyers, to the Crown and to the public interest, along with the public interest obligations inherent in their office, is enough to elevate the standards of ethical and professional conduct by which government lawyers must govern themselves.

These theorists reason, as did the motions judge in *Everingham*, that there is a positive obligation on government lawyers to advance the public interest in litigation and to seek a fair result beyond the interests of their government client. As representatives of a sovereign whose interest is to seek justice, these theorists reason that government lawyers must also seek justice. This mandate could require a government lawyer to not bring forth unmeritorious or undeserving cases, exploit legal or factual errors made by the court or the opposing party, call attention to mistakes or take advantage of procedural lapses without regard to the actual merits of a party's position. For such theorists, seeking justice could also mean disclosing confidential information if it were in the democratic interests of preserving open and transparent government.

According to these commentators, the key difference between the government lawyer and the private lawyer is that the government lawyer serves the public interest exclusively, if indirectly and derivatively, over and above any private interests. The public interest, however, is a concept that is itself amorphous, representing a plurality of interests and conflicting values. It is therefore difficult to translate the service of such dynamic interests into clear ethical obligations. Moreover, some commentators suggest that the way in which government lawyers ultimately interpret their role with respect to these obligations to the public will no doubt influence the types of arguments that they make and the litigation strategies that they employ, such as asserting technical defences to defeat meritorious claims, accepting erroneous court decisions and pursuing costly litigation of questionable merit for political purposes. For instance, Catherine Lanctot has argued that the public interest is sufficiently served by government lawyers advocating the interests of their agency clients with the same zeal as private counsel:

> If the bar truly believes its own rhetoric that zealous advocacy on behalf of a client serves the highest purposes of the American justice system, and if the bar expects government lawyers to "seek justice," then logically the bar should demand of government lawyers that they be at least as zealous as their private counterparts, if not more so.

Accordingly, there is no need for additional, elevated standards of ethical conduct in order for the public interest to be served. Government lawyers serve the public interest by representing "their clients to the best of their ability, asserting whatever arguments they can in order to achieve their clients' goals."

NOTES AND QUESTIONS

1. What do you think of Dodek's argument that government lawyers exercise public power? If you agree, do you think this necessarily imposes a higher obligation on government lawyers?

2. How do Wilson, Wong & Hille respond to Dodek? Which account of the work of government lawyers do you prefer and why? Which account would best explain the reasonable person's reaction that the Crown's conduct in *Everingham* was not "fair"? Does the answer to that question affect your assessment of which account is preferable?

3. What is at stake in the debate over whether government lawyers owe a higher duty? Two government lawyers have asserted that the debate is "academic" because in practice government lawyers are held to a higher standard than other lawyers, by themselves and by courts. See Michael Morris & Sandra Nishikawa, "The Orphans of Legal Ethics: Why Government Lawyers are Different – And How We Protect and Promote that Difference in Service of the Rule of Law and the Public Interest" (Paper presented at the Osgoode Professional Development Administrative Law Conference, October 17, 2011).

C. NATURE OF THE GOVERNMENT LAWYER'S DUTY

As noted by Dodek, developments in the United States in the first decade of the 21st century brought the issue of the ethical obligations of government lawyers to the fore. Specifically, the question of whether government lawyers have particular ethical obligations, and as to the nature of those obligations, became the subject of considerable discussion in response to the participation of lawyers in designing and authorizing the Bush administration's use of torture in its pursuit of the "War on Terror". The Bush administration used a variety of methods of torture to obtain information from detainees and terrorism suspects, including waterboarding, which has been described as "slow motion suffocation with enough time to contemplate the inevitability of black out and expiration — usually the person goes into hysterics on the board".[8]

As discussed in detail by David Luban, amongst others, the lawyers advising the Bush administration and the Central Intelligence Agency (CIA) were willing to go to extraordinary lengths to justify torture of this type. Not only were numerous legal opinions provided by government lawyers in support of the use of torture, the opinions provided were notable for their willingness to stretch legal doctrine and analysis in order to endorse the government's goals. Luban, in analyzing the various opinions, goes so far as to describe one memo's conclusions as ranging "from the doubtful to the

---

[8]   W. Bradley Wendel, "Executive Branch Lawyers in a Time of Terror" (2008) 31 Dal. L.J. 247, citing an article by Malcolm Nance from *Small Wars Journal*.

loony".[9] This was the "Bybee" memo, in which Jay Bybee and John Yoo, lawyers at the Office of Legal Counsel, advised the CIA on how far it could go in abusing detainees. In the memo, Bybee and Yoo concluded that "inflicting physical pain does not count as torture until the pain reaches the level associated with organ failure or death" and that "utilizing techniques known to be painful is not torture unless the interrogator specifically intends the pain to be equivalent to the pain accompanying organ failure or death".[10] As described by Luban, Bybee and Yoo relied in defending this conclusion on a domestic Medicare statute:

> The statute defines an emergency medical condition as one in which someone experiences symptoms that "a prudent lay person ... could reasonably expect" might indicate "serious impairment to bodily functions, or serious dysfunction of any bodily organ or part." The statute specifies that severe pain is one such symptom. In an exquisite exercise of legal formalism run amok, the Memo infers that pain is severe only if it is at the level indicating an emergency medical condition. The authors solemnly cite a Supreme Court decision to show that Congress's use of a phrase in one statute should be used to interpret its meaning in another.[11]

Luban goes on to argue that this and other memos written in justification of torture violated the ethical standards that should apply to lawyers providing advice to government or, indeed, to anyone. The lawyers were not candid or independent, they simply acted to provide "cover" to the agencies receiving the advice, and their conduct in writing the memos did not represent an act of good faith legal interpretation.

In this analysis Luban focuses primarily on the way in which the torture lawyers violated basic and common norms of legal ethics; in the main he argues that the torture lawyers were unethical because they were bad lawyers as measured against the normal standard which applies to lawyers, not because they were government lawyers pursuing a wicked end. Luban does go on, however, to argue that the fact that the violation of the lawyer's ethical obligations was in pursuit of state-sanctioned torture is itself significant:

> I have focused on ... the procedural side of the subject: the requirements of honesty, objectivity, and non-frivolous argument regardless of the subject-matter on which lawyers tender their advice. But that does not mean the subject-matter is irrelevant. It is one thing for boy-wonder lawyers to loophole tax laws and write opinions legitimizing financial shenanigans. It is another thing entirely to loophole laws against torture and cruelty. Lawyers should approach laws defending basic human dignity with fear and trembling.[12]

---

9   David Luban, *Legal Ethics and Human Dignity* (New York: Cambridge University Press, 2007) at 175.
10   *Ibid.*
11   *Ibid.*, at 178-79.
12   *Ibid.*, at 205.

Luban does not generalize from this argument to conclude that government lawyers have a heightened or different ethical obligation. As discussed in the previous section, however, it is certainly arguable that government lawyers do have such an ethical obligation. As Luban notes, there is a difference between the sorts of legal matters addressed by government lawyers and those addressed by lawyers in private practice. Government lawyers have the power — inescapably — to facilitate and endorse the exercise of state power against individuals. A government lawyer may be asked to provide an opinion on the ethics of, for example, using surveillance against participants in a regulatory proceeding; this is simply not an ethical issue likely to be faced by a lawyer in private practice. It is also, of course, not an ethical issue that raises the same moral and legal stakes as advising on the legality of torture. Nonetheless, like opining on the legality of torture, it places the government lawyer at the intersection between the rights of the citizenry and the power of the state, and raises moral, political and ethical dimensions to the lawyer's conduct that are not obviously present for the lawyer in private practice. It is for this reason that, as Dodek suggests, government lawyers can reasonably be understood to be ethically distinct from the profession in general.

Assuming that that is correct, of what would government's special ethical obligation consist? What, ethically speaking, would be the difference between being a government lawyer and not? In the following excerpt Brent Cotter argues that government lawyers have a special "duty of fair dealing" which should inform their conduct.

In reading this excerpt, consider how a duty of fair dealing would apply to a lawyer such as Jay Bybee. Consider as well how the existence of such a duty might have changed the conduct of the government lawyer in *Everingham*, or changed the Court's response to that conduct.

BRENT COTTER

"Lawyers Representing Public Government and a Duty of 'Fair Dealing'"
Canadian Bar Association, Alberta Law Conference (March 2008)

Introduction

The aim of this short paper is to give broad brush consideration to the ethical framework of lawyers in government service, and those retained to represent governments, and to suggest that this framework differs in one significant respect from that of lawyers in private practice. This difference is based on the nature of the client — public government — and on certain unique responsibilities of that client. I argue that these unique responsibilities inform the ethical obligations of lawyers in their representation of government interests and impose upon those lawyers "public interest" responsibilities in ways that are noticeably different from those of lawyers with private sector clients.

Some commentators have claimed that lawyers retained to represent government are required to serve the "public interest"; or that their client is "the public". I argue that while there is a set of public interest obligations imposed upon these lawyers, the idea that one "serves the public interest" is a vacuous concept, and a potentially dangerous one if "public interest" obligations are not given a clear framework. Equally, the idea that the government lawyer's client is "the public" amounts to an operational impossibility in any conventional understanding of a lawyer's role and responsibilities. As a lawyer, try to imagine taking instructions from "the public", or honouring one's obligations of confidentiality to "the public". Just stating the circumstance exposes the absurdity of the concept.

Rather, I argue that such a lawyer does have a client in the conventional way, but in the representing public government, the lawyer owes obligations to the community of interest in opposition to the government — obligations that are not owed by lawyers for private clients. These greater obligations derive their shape from the duties owed by the government itself to the public interest. They can be articulated in general ways, though I readily concede that it may not always be easy to fulfill them perfectly. I shall call this set of responsibilities the "duty of fair dealing", and try to give it some preliminary shape.

The Conventional Paradigm

The standard conception of a lawyer's representation of a client is that this representation is significantly "client-centred". This orientation, and the lawyer's concomitant duty of loyalty, is certainly the governing paradigm in the representation of private clients. This orientation reinforces the entitlement of the client to pursue actions favourable to himself or herself, with the aid of a lawyer, despite the consequences for others. Indeed, the only limitations suggested to qualify this pursuit of self-interest are that the objective and the means used to pursue it not be unlawful or require the lawyer to engage in unethical conduct. Indeed, from a lawyer's perspective, the adversary system — a civilized conflict between adversaries in the pursuit of interests at odds with one another — relies on this contest of self-interest to justify conventional lawyering roles in many of our legal and judicial processes. In large measure this approach is based on the sense that the individual entity owes a duty only to himself or herself or itself. The lawful pursuit of enlightened self-interest is a central tenet of our society and of the consequent design of our legal system.

The Nature of "Representational Entities"

Is this orientation appropriate for "representational entities"? By representational entities, I mean those organizations with a different purpose than the pursuit of self-interest. Organizations that seek to "represent" the interests of a larger community with one or many objectives related to the community of interest it seeks to represent.

There are many types of "representational" entities. In certain respects corporations are representational. Many organizations designed to advance the interests of their members have a "representational" dimension. And it is surely the case that public government has a representational dimension.

Indeed, one might argue that its "representational" role — the representation of the interests of its citizens — is the raison d'être for public government to exist. To get at the question of the role and responsibilities for a government lawyer, it is necessary to consider the question of who exactly does the 'representational' entity, government, represent.

This appears to be a straightforward question. The conventional understanding is that public government represents all of its citizens. As a consequence the conventional understanding of the ambit of legal and ethical duties naturally extends to "all citizens" — the public, from which it is argued that lawyers representing public government therefore represent "the public" or "the public interest". This concept presents two significant problems. One is practical. It is pretty much impossible to consult or take instructions from "the public" or "the public interest", except through some legally authorized representative of "the public". It also goes without saying that some of the standard understandings of a lawyer's duties would be rendered meaningless if one is required to consider "the public" to be the client. It also renders meaningless the significance of "representative government", as the entity which actuates the public's wishes. To assume that the lawyer owes client-like duties to "the public" or "the public interest" makes a mockery of representative government and invites the lawyer to determine what the public interest is. Surely no one contemplates this outcome.

A second difficulty is the one related to the complicated nature of government itself. One of the critical responsibilities of governments is to make choices among scarce public resources in pursuit of public policy objectives. By definition, this involves a choice between or among competing interests, as a consequence of which not all of the citizens will be satisfied all of the time. Similarly, governments have a duty to protect taxpayers' resources, in the form of government revenues and government assets, from claims upon them, even from their own citizens. This may require a choice on the part of government to protect the collective interests of citizens against the claims of one individual citizen. These situations will often lead to conflict between the government and its representatives, on the one hand, and one or more of the citizens it exists to represent. These conflicts may arise in a variety of forms and forums. Legislators may be required to choose among conflicting legislative approaches. Decisions will be made to use the financial resources of the government in ways that embrace some policy choices and that reject other choices. The government will choose to acknowledge some citizens' claims and resist the claims of others. The representatives of public government will be called upon to make these choices and to direct their agents, including lawyers, to pursue the choices, resist the claims, as the representatives deem appropriate.

From this set of examples it is clear that the government in its representative capacities will of necessity place itself in conflict with individual citizens or groups of citizens. This happens to individuals and private actors all the time. When it does occur, within the limits of law and the moral choices of the

private actor, self-interest is entitled to prevail without any special consideration of the interests of the "other". Is this the case with public government in
terms of duties owed to the "other" — citizens with whom it is in conflict? Is
there a particular set of obligations owed to those who are part of the collective, representational interest of government but who are also its adversaries
in one or other context?

I argue that governments do owe duties to that "other". To take a different
view would require us to accept the proposition that a citizen in conflict with
his or her government is somehow diminished in his citizenship by virtue of
the conflict. This does not mean that government is somehow required to
accede to the claims of citizens in conflict with government. Rather, the real
question is the nature of the duties owed by the government, as a "representational" entity, to the members of its "representational" community with whom
it might be in disagreement or conflict. It is here that I believe the roles and
responsibilities of a lawyer representing public government diverge from
those of a lawyer representing a private interest.

The Dimensions of this "Representational" Duty

I propose to examine the nature of this duty from the perspective of a citizen
in a legal conflict with his or her government. It is often the case that citizens
make claims upon governments that are not well founded in law, or that are in
direct conflict with the policy direction that the government wishes to pursue.
In these situations governments are surely entitled, on behalf of the collective
interest of their citizens, to resist these claims, to stay the course. Sometimes,
however, citizens make claims that are entirely or at least partly well founded.
Is government entitled, in advancing the collective interest of their citizens, to
resist the legitimate claims of its citizens? The answer in my view is "no". I
make this assertion from two perspectives; first, from analogies drawn from
the criminal law and the responsibilities owed by public prosecutors to
defendants in criminal proceedings; second, from the perspective of a set of
duties owed by representative governments to it citizens.

(a) The Public Prosecutions Analogy

Prosecutors represent the state in criminal proceedings. They are legally
styled as "agents of the Crown". Their role is to review and prosecute
allegations of criminal conduct. They are required to do so in the pursuit of
fair and just outcomes. This requires an assessment of whether there is
sufficient evidence in a case to justify laying charges or proceeding with
them, and an assessment of whether the public interest is served in pursuing
the charges. As a matter of policy, and perhaps law, prosecutors are not
entitled to proceed with charges that do not meet this standard. As well, as a
matter of good policy and law [*R. v. Stinchcombe*] prosecutors are required to
disclose to the defence all relevant information in relation to the criminal
proceedings, whether it helps or hurts the prosecution's case. This is intended
to ensure that a person who is the subject of a prosecution gets a fair trial. It is
part of the obligation placed upon the Crown of 'fair dealing' with its citizens

in criminal proceedings. This has the consequence of ensuring full disclosure of everything relevant to a prosecution, and of ensuring that, as far as a system can do so, the Crown acknowledges and concedes everything in an accused person's favour that should legitimately be acknowledged or conceded in a proceeding, to ensure that justice is done.

Criminal cases have potentially serious implications for those who are accused of crimes, and in that sense may require certain values — including constitutional values — to be given priority; values that are not directly implicated in other proceedings between the Crown and its citizens. However, the consequences for citizens of a wide variety of non-criminal dealings with government are likely as profound as many criminal matters. Is a citizen any less entitled to this standard of fair dealing because the matter does not involve criminal proceedings against him or her? Or because the conflict between a citizen and the government does not involve a court proceeding?

(b) A Duty of "Fair Dealing"

The government serves in a "representational" capacity with respect to all of its citizens. Indeed, we often refer to our form of government as "representative government". This "representativeness" includes those who support its policies and those who oppose them. It includes those who may benefit from the political choices politicians and governments make, and those who are adversely affected. And it includes those who may be in legal conflicts with the government. A "representational" entity, and particularly government, understandably owes a duty to the collective interest of all of its citizens. With respect to government, this may require the government to do its best to ensure that chosen public policies are not derailed, or that illegitimate claims upon the public purse are resisted, or that other actions or claims seen to be contrary to the public interest are opposed. These are all perfectly legitimate, even required, roles for a government to undertake. And as a general rule they benefit the public interest as defined at the time.

But what duty is owed to the claimant in opposition to the government. In this respect the government, as a "representational entity", is in a different position from others. One aspect of that "representativeness" includes a duty to the very citizen who brings the challenge, or makes the claim, against his or her own government. What is the nature of that duty?

I argue that at the very least it requires a standard of "fair dealing" with its citizens in these positions, a standard that exceeds the requirements of private persons. This governmental standard of fair dealing should, for example, exceed the minimum requirements one finds in legal proceedings. Aside from making the disclosures required by law to claimants, it should include admitting what should reasonably be admitted, conceding what should reasonably be conceded, accommodating what should reasonably be accommodated. In its "representational" duties to one of its citizens with whom it is in conflict, a duty of fair dealing requires nothing less. This requires the accommodation of the legitimate interests of citizens whenever those interests are reasonably known to be legitimate.

This does not mean that governments must accede to any allegation made by a claimant, or acquiesce in the face of every challenge to its policies. To do so would subjugate, illegitimately, the representative responsibilities of government to its larger public interest. I concede that in some cases the role of a government's legal representative will be difficult in trying to ensure a fair outcome without giving away too much, and being constrained in the use of certain legal tools available to the private litigant. It does require however, that in the interests of legitimate claimants the larger public interest defers to and accommodates these legitimate claims. Not grudgingly, but in a fair and timely way. In this way, "fair dealing" with its citizens does not detract from the representative nature of public government. Rather, it advances and enriches it for all.

Conclusion

There is a fundamental "public" value at stake here that does not have the same resonance when conflict arises between private claimants. Simply put, largely un-moderated self-interest — justified within our systems of dispute resolution for private disputants — has no place in where a government finds itself in conflict with its citizens. Governments owe "just" outcomes to all of their citizens, including the ones with whom they are in conflict. This can only be achieved through a moderation of zealous advocacy, in much the same way that this moderation is required in criminal prosecutions in order to achieve just outcomes. Governments, and their lawyers, owe to their citizens a duty of fair dealing.

NOTES AND QUESTIONS

1. Do you find Cotter's argument that a general duty to the public interest is not an appropriate obligation to place on a government lawyer, but that a duty of fair dealing is, compelling?

2. How significant a constraint on government conduct is a duty of "fair dealing"?

3. Dodek is sympathetic to Cotter's argument but ultimately finds it difficult to translate on a practical level as to what lawyers should do. Instead, Dodek falls back on the explanation offered by former Deputy Minister of Justice of Canada, John Tait, who asserted that government lawyers owed a number of unique duties including being "guardians of the rule of law as it applies within government in a parliamentary democracy".[13] Tait asserted that government lawyers have a higher duty to the law and to the Constitution.[14] In practical terms, this means that government lawyers must provide objective and independent advice. Tait explained:

---

[13] John C. Tait, "The Public Service Lawyer, Service to the Client and the Rule of Law" (1997) 23 Commonwealth L. Bull. 542 at 543.

[14] *Ibid.*, at 548.

The duty to promote and uphold the rule of law means that there is a quality of objectivity in the interpretation of the law that is important to the public service lawyer. There must be a fair inquiry into what the law actually is. The rule of law is not protected by unduly stretching the interpretation to fit the client's wishes. And it is not protected by giving one interpretation to one client and another to another department.[15]

Dodek asserts that in advising the Crown, government lawyers must provide a fair interpretation of the law: "Moreover, as custodians of the Rule of Law, they cannot use the law as a sword to batter their opponents, for the Rule of Law is intended as a shield against arbitrary government action not as a weapon in the Government's arsenal. Thus, unlike private sector lawyers, government lawyers should not exploit loopholes in the law in sanctioning government action or rely on technicalities in litigation." Dodek also argues that being custodians of the Rule of Law imposes a special obligation on government lawyers to support other institutions crucial to the maintenance of the Rule of Law like the independence of the judiciary and the independence of the bar.

Do you find conceptual or practical differences between Cotter's and Dodek's approaches? Which do you find more helpful?

4.   What would the effect of an obligation of fair dealing be on lawyers asked to provide an opinion on the legality of waterboarding? Or, to put it slightly differently, would Cotter provide a different explanation for the ethical failure of the torture lawyers than that provided by Luban?

5.   Who should fall within the category of government lawyers? Would the lawyers who acted for the Toronto General Hospital in *Grossman v. Toronto General Hospital*, [1983] O.J. No. 3001 (Ont. H.C.J.), excerpted in Chapter 6, count? If so, would you describe their conduct as consistent with the obligation of fair dealing? What would fair dealing have looked like in a case like that one?

Scenario One

You act for the government in litigation brought by an Aboriginal band alleging that the government violated its fiduciary obligations in relation to natural resources on reserve lands. The band alleges that the government failed to maximize the value of the resources, and profited at the band's expense. In substance your assessment of the claim is that the band is likely correct — the conduct of the government did breach its fiduciary obligations. However, a significant portion of the band's claim likely falls outside the applicable limitation periods and is, as a consequence, statute barred. Is it ethical for you to apply for the claim to be struck on that basis? Is doing so consistent with your obligation of fair dealing or your duty as a custodian of the Rule of Law? See: *Canada (Attorney General) v. Lameman*, [2008] S.C.J. No. 14, 2008 SCC 14 (S.C.C.); *Wewaykum Indian Band v. Canada*, [2002] S.C.J. No. 79, [2002] 4 S.C.R. 245 (S.C.C.).

---

[15]   *Ibid.*, at 543-44.

D. ORGANIZATIONAL PRESSURES

Another significant ethical issue for government lawyers arises from the fact that they, like corporate counsel, are employees in organizations. As discussed at the beginning of Chapter 9, working within an organization can heighten the risk that lawyers engage in cognitive dissonance, and as a consequence cease to be independent and candid in the advice they provide. They can also become socially and culturally embedded in the norms of their organization, regardless of whether those norms are consistent with their broader ethical obligations as lawyers. In addition, and again like corporate counsel, because "withdrawal" for a government lawyer means quitting her job, it can seem costly and perhaps impossible for a lawyer to dissent from the positions being taken by her organization more generally.

One particular manifestation of these organizational pressures can be excessive commitment to the client's goals. This arguably was one factor at work for the "torture lawyers" — that those lawyers simply became psychologically committed to the policy goals of the government entities with which they were organizationally associated. Consider whether organizational pressures — such as, for example, ensuring that goals of taxation authorities are realized — provide a possible explanation for the ethical violations of the Crown lawyer in his conduct of the tax case excerpted below.

In addition, in reading the case consider whether the Crown lawyer acted consistently with a duty of "fair dealing" outlined previously by Cotter or a duty as "custodian of the Rule of Law" outlined by Dodek and whether his conduct would be considered unethical regardless of whether he is a Crown, and, alternatively, whether the fact that he is renders the conduct more offensive.

GENERAL MOTORS OF CANADA LTD. v. CANADA

[2008] T.C.J. No. 80, 2008 TCC 117 (T.C.C.),
affd [2009] F.C.J. No. 447 (F.C.A.)
(Tax Court of Canada, Campbell T.C.J.)

[General Motors (GM) appealed a Goods and Services Tax assessment made pursuant to the *Excise Tax Act*, R.S.C. 1985, c. E-15. One issue in the case was whether the respondent Crown had acted improperly in pleading that, in making its assessment of GM, it had assumed a particular fact. In tax litigation cases if the Minister of National Revenue, at the time of making an assessment, relies on an assumption of fact then the onus is on the taxpayer to demonstrate that the fact is not true. Conversely, if the Minister of National Revenue does *not* make an assumption of fact then the Crown bears the onus of proving that the fact is true. In this case the respondent Crown stated in its pleadings that the Minister of National Revenue had assumed a particular fact: that the "investment management services", which were part of the matters in dispute, were not a "service" as defined by the legislation. The Appellant GM argued that the Minister of National Revenue (the Respondent) had never made any such assumption. It argued that the Crown had wrongfully and inaccurately pled the assumption which it had not made in order to obtain a tactical advantage about the burden of proof.]

CAMPBELL T.C.J.:—

. . . . .

Preliminary Matter #2 — Improper Pleading of Assumption 5(f) ...

Paragraph 5(f) of the Reply states:

> 5. In assessing the Appellant ... the Minister of National Revenue (the "Minister") relied on, *inter alia*, the following assumptions or findings of fact ...
>
> (f) the investment management services were not a service listed in paragraphs (a) to (m) of the definition of a financial service under the *Act*; ...

This is not the first time I have considered this assumption of fact. In a pre-hearing Motion, the Appellant [GM] requested the Court to either instruct the auditor, Aaron Wong, to answer questions posed to him during the examination for discovery concerning paragraph 5(f) or to strike paragraph 5(f). Although I concluded that it would be premature to strike the paragraph, I ruled that those questions posed to Mr. Wong by Appellant counsel had been properly put to him and that the examination for discovery should be continued to give Mr. Wong an opportunity to respond. I also concluded that Respondent counsel's objections were inappropriate and amounted to interference by counselling and cuing the witness to give essentially the same response of "the services are taxable" to all of those questions.

It was the Appellant that called Mr. Wong as a witness. It is clear from his evidence that the voluntary disclosure provided by [GM] to CRA was the sole basis of the initial assessment. However, this disclosure made no reference to whether the supply of Investment Management Services was a financial service as referenced in paragraph 5(f) of the Reply. Instead it dealt only with the subsection 169(1) issue. In response to questioning by both Appellant and Respondent counsel, it is evident that Mr. Wong never considered or addressed in any manner whether these services were exempt financial services under the *Act*. His repeated parroting of the response that "the services were taxable" was entirely non-responsive. It comes nowhere close to a consideration of whether those Investment Management Services fell within each of the paragraphs (a) through (m) of subsection 123(1) of the *Act*. It was apparent that Appellant counsel was frustrated with this response, and with good reason, particularly given my directions subsequent to the hearing of the Motion. What is conspicuously offensive here is the approach which Respondent counsel took with this issue. After hearing the Motion, I concluded that counsel's actions were tantamount to cuing and coaching Mr. Wong to state that "the services were taxable". Mr. Wong was true to this response and kept to his script during the hearing of the appeal.

Respondent counsel argued that the Appellant's position [that the Respondent filed improper pleadings] is both "irrelevant and wrong" ... I am quite frankly shocked by the Respondent's position. Essentially the position of the Respondent was that since sufficient evidence was adduced during the hearing, issues of assumptions and burden of proof became merely academic. While this, on its face, is true, it cannot transform the Crown's actions, which I consider to be intrinsically appalling, into something that is right and therefore acceptable.

Respondent counsel argued that the cross-examination of Mr. Phillips elicited sufficient facts pertaining to the specifics of the Investment Management Services to enable the Court to determine whether those services are a financial service as contemplated by subsection 123(1). While this may be true, it does not assist the Respondent in defending its position that in fact this assumption was made.

In reviewing the transcripts, I believe I have sufficient testimony together with documentary evidence to make a determination on whether the supply was a financial service. However, this line of reasoning does not negate the fact that the Crown was wrong in pleading assumption 5(f) in the first place which became more blatantly evident after the Motion and the continuation of the examination for discovery.

. . . . .

[Tax Court Justice Campbell then addressed the Respondent Crown's argument that the assumption was pled legitimately because the assumption was implicit in the tax assessment. Justice Campbell held that the evidence given by Mr. Wong in discovery demonstrated that this argument was not supportable.]

. . . . .

Paragraph 5(f) of the Reply explicitly refers to the various sub-provisions of the definition of financial services. This undoubtedly gives the impression that the Minister had put his mind to the various components of the definition, going through each and every subparagraph, before finally concluding that the service in question did not fall under each individual subcomponent of that definition. Although Mr. Wong's testimony for the most part was simply of no assistance, he did admit that he did not review each of the paragraphs (a) through (m) of subsection 123(1) and therefore did not consider whether the Investment Management Services fit under any of them. At page 113 of the Transcript, the following exchange occurred between Appellant counsel and Mr. Wong:

> Q: ... I am putting to you [you] did not ask yourself that question. I want you to answer the precise question I am asking. Not that you thought it was taxable. I know you thought it was taxable. That is not what the assumption says. The assumption doesn't say it is taxable. The assumption speaks specifically as to whether it is a financial service under (a) to (m). You did not ask yourself that question, did you, sir?
>
> A: No.
>
> Q: Your answer was no, I think?

A: No.

Q: In fact, sir, you did not open the sections, the definition in 123, and say to yourself, what is the investment management service and then ask yourself does it fit in (a)? What is the investment management service, does it fit into (b)? You didn't do that because your audit was only about the input tax credit. Would you agree with me, sir?

A: Yes.

I believe that my directions were very clear in the Order issued in the pre-hearing Motion and as a result the Respondent should have been on notice of the impugned assumption.

At the subsequent examination of Mr. Wong, it should also have been abundantly clear to Respondent counsel, if it was not previously, that Mr. Wong never considered in any manner the financial service issue. The proper next step was to amend the Reply to delete this assumption of fact. This step was not taken and I consider this to be a very serious matter.

The Respondent cannot be permitted to trivialize the inclusion of assumption 5(f) in its pleadings and I am not persuaded by any of its arguments. There were ample warning signs along the way. They were all ignored. The fact that there is sufficient evidence before me to make a factual determination of the issue does not negate the Respondent's duty to honestly plead assumptions at the outset or to amend the pleadings once it becomes abundantly clear that an assumption had not been made. Assumptions relied upon in pleadings must be stated fairly, honestly and accurately. That was not done here.

So what is the appropriate remedy where the Minister improperly pleads an assumption of fact, but where there is sufficient evidence before the Court to make a determination of the issue? ...

. . . . .

Although this may be a case akin to what Justice Bowman in *Holm* described as "flagrant and reprehensible behavior," I believe that I can and should address this issue pleaded in the alternative, based on the evidence adduced through Mr. Phillips, and that I can best deal with the seriousness of the Respondent's actions and the attempt to trivialize this issue through an award of elevated costs. ...

NOTES AND QUESTIONS

1. Tax Court Justice Campbell thus found that the Crown in this case had improperly pled an assumption of fact where the assumption was not made; improperly coached his witness on discovery in order to avoid the Respondent finding out unfavourable information; and maintained the pleading even once it was clear that it was false. Would this conduct be ethical in any advocate, whether Crown counsel or otherwise? Is it more egregious because the counsel in question was a Crown?

2.   What would a duty of fair dealing have required of the Crown here? At what point would such a duty have required the Crown to amend the pleading, or otherwise admit that no such assumption had been made? What would Dodek's theory of government lawyers as "custodians of the Rule of Law" have required here?

3.   Is an order of costs against the Crown a sufficient sanction? Why or why not?

4.   Would you advise the Law Society of Upper Canada to bring disciplinary proceedings against this Crown? On what basis? Note in analyzing this question, Campbell T.C.J.'s statements that the Crown's conduct was akin to "flagrant and reprehensible", was "intrinsically appalling" and that the Crown was "counselling and cuing" his witness during discoveries.

Scenario Two

You are a lawyer at a provincial regulatory agency. The agency is conducting a hearing into the proposed construction of a 500 kV electricity transmission line. The provincial government has publicly stated its commitment to developing the transmission grid in the province, and congestion on the transmission grid has been a significant problem since at least 1999. Landowners who may be affected by the line are, however, strongly opposed to its construction, and the hearing into the construction of the facility can fairly be said to have gone badly. In a report filed with the provincial Privacy Commission about what happened at the hearing the following information was provided:

> In the first incident ... an individual approached one ... [agency] employee and swung twice at the employee's head with a closed fist. The ... employee was able to duck and none of the punches landed ... [A] news video ... showed a second incident involving an individual raising his hand close to another ... [agency] employee's neck and then grabbing the employee's arm and pushing the employee aside. The ... third incident occurred later that same day when a group of landowners attempted to prevent a lawyer from approaching the podium to give evidence by physically standing between the lawyer and the podium.[16]

The agency has adjourned the hearing while it considers how to respond. After some discussion it is suggested that it would be appropriate to segregate the landowners and other interveners in a separate facility where they can watch the proceedings through closed circuit televisions. It is also suggested that private investigators be retained to observe the interveners and report back on any suspicious activities.

You are asked to advise as to the legality of these suggestions. It is clear to you that the agency wants you to affirm this proposal. And it is also clear to you that by relying on a very doctrinal analysis of the law on procedural fairness you can probably do so. In reading the law, however, you are also of the view that the proposed steps are in substance unfair, and may well later be found by a court to have been problematic at best. How do you advise the

---

16   Alberta Information and Privacy Commissioner, Investigation Report F2007-IR-005 at 3.

agency? If you advise the agency not to take these steps, and they do so anyway, what are your ethical obligations, if any? (See Alice Woolley, "Enemies of the State? — The Alberta Energy and Utilities Board, Landowners, Spies, a 500 kV Transmission Line and Why Procedure Matters" (2008) Journal of Energy and Natural Resources Law 234.)

Scenario Three

As lawyers, government lawyers have an ethical duty to keep confidential "all information concerning the business and affairs of a client acquired in the course of the professional relationship" (*Model Code*, Rule 2.03(1)). Each Law Society has a limited public safety exception which permits or requires lawyers to disclose confidential information in certain circumstances. For example, the Federation of Law Societies of Canada's *Model Code of Professional Conduct* provides:

Future Harm / Public Safety Exception

2.03(3) A lawyer may disclose confidential information, but must not disclose more information than is required, when the lawyer believes on reasonable grounds that there is an imminent risk of death or serious bodily harm, and disclosure is necessary to prevent the death or harm.

This does not necessarily accord with federal public servants' whistleblowing provisions. Under the *Public Servants Disclosure Protection Act*, a public servant may make a public disclosure if there is not sufficient time to make a report to the relevant official and:

> ... the public servant believes on reasonable grounds that the subject-matter of the disclosure is an act or omission that
>
> (a) constitutes a serious offence under an Act of Parliament or of the legislature of a province; or
>
> (b) constitutes an imminent risk of a substantial and specific danger to the life, health and safety of persons, or to the environment ...[17]

Imagine that you are a lawyer working for the federal government and you discover that a public official has been defrauding the government of millions of dollars. If you exercise your whistleblowing rights as a public servant, would you be violating your ethical duties under Law Society Codes of Conduct? Could a federal justice lawyer be disciplined by a Law Society for breaching his or her duty of confidentiality in such circumstances? Conversely, if a lawyer complied with the ethical duty of disclosure under Law Society rules, would he or she be violating her oath of confidentiality as a public servant and be subject to discipline by his or her Government employers?

Consider the same scenario if the government lawyer discovered that a government agency or official was ignoring the dumping of hazardous waste

---

[17]   R.S.C. 2005, c. 46, s. 16(1).

into a river which was likely to cause serious damage to the surrounding ecosystem.

E. FURTHER READING

Badgerow, Nick J., "Walking The Line: Government Lawyer Ethics" (2003) 12(3) Kan. J.L. & Pub. Pol'y 437.

Bell, Griffin B., "Office of Attorney General's Client Relationship" (1981) 36 Bus. Law. 791.

Berenson, Steven K., "Hard Bargaining on Behalf of the Government Tortfeasor: A Study in Governmental Lawyer Ethics" (2005) 56(2) Case W. Res. L. Rev. 345.

Edwards, John L.I.L., *The Attorney General, Politics and the Public Interest* (London: Sweet & Maxwell, 1984).

Hammond, Kristina, "Plugging the Leaks: Applying the Model Rules to Leaks Made by Government Lawyers" (2005) 18(3) Geo. J. Legal Ethics 783.

Hemingway, Anna P., "Conflicting Obligations" (2000) 9(2) Widener J. Pub. L. 227.

Hutchinson, Allan C., "'In the Public Interest': The Responsibilities and Rights of Government Lawyers" (2008) 46 Osgoode Hall L.J. 105.

Keyes, John Mark, "The Professional Responsibilities of Legislative Counsel" (2009) 3 JPPL 453.

Lederman, Marty, "Principles to Guide the Office of Legal Counsel" (December 18, 2004) (with other posts on the torture lawyers at "balkinization"), online: <http://balkin.blogspot.com/2005/09/anti-torture-memos-balkinization-posts.html>.

LeDonne, Gregory B., "Revisiting the McDade Amendment: Finding the Appropriate Solution for the Federal Government Lawyer" (2007) 44(1) Harv. J. on Legis. 231.

Lefcourt, Gerald B., "Fighting Fire With Fire: Private Attorneys Using the Same Investigative Techniques as Government Attorneys: The Ethical and Legal Considerations for Attorneys Conducting Investigations" (2007) 36(2) Hofstra L. Rev. 397.

Leong, Nancy, "Attorney-client Privilege in the Public Sector: A Survey of Government Attorneys" (2007) 20(1) Geo. J. Legal Ethics 163.

Levinson, Sanford, "Identifying the Compelling State Interest: On 'Due Process of Lawmaking' and the Professional Responsibility of the Public Lawyer" (1994) 64 Hastings L.J. 1035.

Luban, David, *Legal Ethics and Human Dignity* (New York: Cambridge University Press, 2007).

MacNair, Deborah, "The Role of the Federal Public Sector Lawyer: From Polyester to Silk" (2001) 50 U.N.B.L.J. 125.

MacNair, Deborah, "In the Service of the Crown: Are Ethical Obligations Different for Government Counsel?" (2005) 84 Can. Bar Rev. 501.

Paulson, M.S., "Hell, Handbaskets and Government Lawyers: the Duty of Loyalty and its Limits" (1998) 61 Law & Contemp. Probs. 83.

Sanders, Maureen A., "Government Attorneys and the Ethical Rules: Good Souls in Limbo" (1993) 7 B.Y.U.J. Pub. L. 39.

Scott, Ian, "Law, Policy and the Role of the Attorney General: Constancy and Change in the 1980s" (1989) 39 U.T.L.J. 109.

Shpall, Jessica, "A Shakeup for the Duty of Confidentiality: The Competing Priorities of a Government Attorney in California" (2008) 41(2) Loy. L.A. L. Rev. 701.

Symposium, "Legal Ethics for Government Lawyers: Straight Talk for Tough Times" (2000) 9 Widener J. Pub. L. 199.

Tait, John C., "The Public Service Lawyer, Service to the Client and the Rule of Law" (1997) 23 Commonwealth L. Bull. 542.

Webb, Duncan, "Keeping the Crown's Conscience: A Theory of Lawyering for Public Sector Counsel" (2007) 5(2) N. Z. J. Pub. & I. L. 243.

Wendel, W. Bradley, "Executive Branch Lawyers in a Time of Terror" (2008) 31 Dal. L.J. 247.

Wendel, W. Bradley, "Government Lawyers, Democracy, and the Rule of Law" (2009) 77(4) Fordham L. Rev. 1333.

Wilner, Joshua, "Service to the Nation: A Living Legal Value for Justice Lawyers in Canada" (2009) 32 Dal. L.J. 177.

Woolley, Alice, "Enemies of the State? The Alberta Energy and Utilities Board, Landowners, Spies, a 500 kV Transmission Line and Why Procedure Matters" (2008) 26(2) Journal of Energy & Natural Resources Law 234.

Note, "Government Counsel and their obligations" (2008) 121(5) Harv. L. Rev. 1409.

Note, "Rethinking the Professional Responsibilities of Federal Agency Lawyers" (2002) 115(4) Harv. L. Rev. 1170.

CHAPTER 11

JUDGES' ETHICS, LAWYERS' DILEMMAS

A. INTRODUCTION

Judges are lawyers, but they are not members of law societies. Furthermore, the roles and responsibilities of judges are distinct from those of lawyers. Consequently judges inhabit a discrete and distinctive ethical domain from that of lawyers. In Chapter 1, it was suggested that three core principles structure the lawyer's world: loyal advocacy, lawyers as moral agents in the pursuit of justice and integrity. For judges there are five core principles: impartiality, independence, integrity, diligence and equality.

The range of potential issues to be discussed under the rubric of judicial ethics is quite large, ranging from pre-appointment behaviour, through conduct while serving as a judge (including matters arising in both one's public and private life), to post-retirement activities. It is not possible to cover all such issues in one chapter; therefore, this chapter will focus on a number of key issues that address the relationship between judges and lawyers and how the conduct of the former can create challenges, even dilemmas, for the latter.

The dilemmas can arise on two levels. First, at the level of principle, lawyers are "officers of the court" and therefore they owe judges a measure of courtesy and respect. However, lawyers also have duty of loyalty to their clients and a duty to promote the administration of justice. Sometimes these duties might conflict. Second, at the level of practical reality, many legal communities are small, the lawyers and judges are well known to each other and the norms of collegiality are strong. However, the relationship between judges and lawyers is often hierarchical. This may create a disincentive for lawyers to challenge a judge whose conduct appears to be potentially unethical.

B. THE GOVERNING REGIME

Judicial ethics are governed by three key mechanisms: constitutional norms, case law and ethical guidelines. First, key ethical ideas such as judicial independence and impartiality are said to be part of the constitutional order, both written and unwritten. Second, the courts have sought (with some difficulty) to develop legal rules to govern judicial behaviour, most significantly in the realm of bias and recusal. Third, the Canadian judiciary itself has articulated a series of principles to guide the ethical conduct of judges. While all three dimensions are important, for the purposes of this chapter we will focus on the third.

Canadian judges fall into one of two categories: those who are appointed by provincial or territorial governments, and those who are appointed by the federal government.[1] Most judges in the first category are not bound by a code of conduct. In fact only two provinces have a code of conduct for judges: Quebec and British Columbia. Is this surprising to you? Is it justifiable? Consider the *Judicial Code of Ethics* for Quebec judges:

1. The judge should render justice within the framework of the law.

2. The judge should perform the duties of his office with integrity, dignity and honour.

3. The judge has a duty to foster his professional competence.

4. The judge should avoid any conflict of interest and refrain from placing himself in a position where he cannot faithfully carry out his functions.

5. The judge should be, and be seen to be, impartial and objective.

6. The judge should perform the duties of his office diligently and devote himself entirely to the exercise of his judicial functions.

7. The judge should refrain from any activity which is not compatible with his judicial office.

8. In public, the judge should act in a reserved, serene and courteous manner.

9. The judge should submit to the administrative directives of his chief judge, within the performance of his duties.

10. The judge should uphold the integrity and defend the independence of the judiciary, in the best interest of justice and society.[2]

How helpful is such a code of conduct? Is it better than no code at all, or is it so general that it provides little assistance to those in need?

Federally appointed judges are in a different situation. In 1998, the Canadian Judicial Council created a 52-page handbook called *Ethical Principles for Judges.*[3] Compare this document with the Quebec Code of Conduct. Which is the better document? Why? The second paragraph of the *Ethical Principles* is especially important. It states:

> The Statements, Principles and Commentaries are advisory in nature. Their goals are to assist judges with the difficult ethical and professional issues which confront them and to assist members of the public to better understand the judicial role. They are not and shall not be used as a code or a

---

[1] Provincial judges are appointed under the authority of s. 92(14) and federal judges are appointed under the authority of s. 96 of the *Constitution Act, 1867* (U.K.), 30 & 31 Vict., c. 3, reprinted in R.S.C. 1985, App. II, No. 5.

[2] R.S.Q., c. T-16, r. 4.1, ss. 1-10.

[3] Available online: <http://www.cjc-ccm.gc.ca/cmslib/general/news_pub_judicialconduct_Principles_1998_en.pdf>.

list of prohibited behaviours. They do not set out standards defining judicial conduct.

The following extract, by a judge of the Saskatchewan Court of Appeal, provides four justifications in support of this position.

THE HONOURABLE GEORGINA R. JACKSON

"The Mystery of Judicial Ethics: Deciphering the 'Code'"
(2005) 68 Sask. L. Rev. 1*
[footnotes omitted]

There are four policy reasons that support this interpretation [in the *Ethical Principles*]. First and foremost, it is not necessary to interpret the *Ethical Principles* as creating standards of conduct. The *Ethical Principles* booklet is written for an independent judiciary. Canadian judges have earned their status first through rigorous training, and then by the respect and approval of their peers prior to appointment, A disciplinary code may be more important in a judicial system where judges are elected or enjoy less status than Canadian judges, but it is not needed for a judiciary that is free from political and financial pressures.

Second, it is commonly believed that the test for sanctionable conduct is now established at a level that maximizes the exercise of impartial judicial thought. If the *Ethical Principles* are interpreted as creating a standard of conduct for disciplinary purposes, the ambit of what is considered sanctionable conduct may be broadened. This may result in an increase in complaints. As Professor Morissette indicates, "a series of complaints is likely to affect the judge where he or she is most vulnerable, namely in the ability to make impartial decisions with the appropriate degree of detachment on questions of general interest that are both very difficult and very controversial."

Third, one can, in my opinion, accomplish more with ethical principles than with a code of prohibited behaviours. Ethical principles are, by their nature, more stringent than any standard of conduct can ever be. They represent the ceiling to which judges strive. Justice Thomas states:

> Some standards can be prescribed by law, but the spirit of, and quality of the service rendered by, a profession depends far more on its observance of ethical standards. These are far more rigorous than legal standards ... They are learnt not by precept but by the example and influence of respected peers. Judicial standards are acquired, so to speak, by professional osmosis. They are enforced immediately by conscience.

In *Ruffo v. Conseil de la magistrature*, Gonthier J., speaking for the majority in the Supreme Court of Canada, makes the same point:

> Ethical rules are meant to aim for perfection. They call for better conduct not through the imposition of various sanctions, but through compliance with the

---

*   Reproduced with permission.

personally imposed constraints. A definition, on the other hand, sets out
fixed rules and thus tends to become an upper limit, an implicit authorization
to do whatever is not prohibited. There is no doubt that these two concepts
are difficult to reconcile, and this explains the general nature of the duty to
act in a reserved manner: as an ethical standard, it is more concerned with
providing general guidance about conduct than with illustrating specifics and
the types of conduct allowed.

Ethical principles leave more to the individual good conscience of the judge
than a code that can lead simply to a legalist ritual.

Fourth, any attempt to use the *Ethical Principles* as a standard of behaviour
for discipline overlooks the fact that the booklet omits matters that we take for
granted as sanctionable conduct and addresses matters which could be
considered innocuous. For example, there is no mention of gifts, but there is
extensive treatment of the circumstances in which a judge can give a letter of
reference.

NOTES AND QUESTIONS

1. Do you find these arguments persuasive? Could the same justifications be applied
    to the Federation of Law Societies of Canada's *Model Code of Professional Con-
    duct*? What are some of the challenges faced by lawyers in dealing with judges
    governed by non-binding statements of principle as opposed to a binding code of
    conduct?

2. Does this mean that Canadian judges have even greater self-regulatory authority
    than Canadian lawyers? Why might this be the case? Is it appropriate?

3. Do the *Ethical Principles* achieve the right balance between judicial indepen-
    dence and judicial accountability? What changes would you make to them?

In the remainder of this chapter, we will use the five core principles from the
Ethical Principles for Judges — impartiality, independence, integrity,
diligence and equality — to structure our analysis.[4]

C. IMPARTIALITY

Impartiality is the most significant of the *Ethical Principles for Judges*. The
Statement is very straightforward:

> Judges must be and should appear to be impartial with respect to their
> decisions and decision-making.

However, the principles and commentaries elaborating upon this statement
continue for another 25 pages and are subdivided into five categories:
General; Judicial Demeanour; Civic and Charitable Activities; Political
Activity; and Conflicts of Interest. The following decision of the Canadian
Judicial Council illustrates both how this self-regulatory body interprets the

---

[4] The *Ethical Principles for Judges* puts the chapter on Impartiality last. For the purposes of
our analysis in this book, we have put it first because we understand impartiality to be the
capstone of judicial ethics.

impartiality principle and the operation of the complaints process against judges.

CANADIAN JUDICIAL COUNCIL

Report of the Canadian Judicial Council to the Minister of Justice in the Matter Concerning Justice Cosgrove (March 30, 2009), online: <http://www.cjc-ccm.gc.ca/cmslib/general/ Report_to_Minister_Justice_Cosgrove.pdf>

INTRODUCTION

... After inquiring into the conduct of the Honourable Paul Cosgrove, we find that he has failed in the due execution of his office to such an extent that public confidence in his ability to properly discharge his judicial duties in the future cannot be restored. In the result, we conclude that a recommendation be made to the Minister of Justice that Justice Cosgrove be removed from office.

BACKGROUND

. . . . .

From 1997 to 1999, Justice Cosgrove presided over the murder trial of Julia Elliott. A stay of proceedings was granted on 7 September 1999 after Justice Cosgrove concluded that there had been over 150 violations of Ms Elliott's rights under the *Canadian Charter of Rights and Freedoms*. On appeal, the stay of proceedings was set aside, and a new trial was ordered. The Court of Appeal remarked ...:

> ... The trial judge made numerous legal errors as to the application of the Charter. He made findings of misconduct against Crown counsel and police officers that were unwarranted and unsubstantiated. He misused his powers of contempt and allowed investigations into areas that were extraneous to the real issues in the case.

. . . . .

In its review of the judge's conduct, the Inquiry Committee adopted the reasoning of the Supreme Court of Canada in *Moreau-Bérubé v. New Brunswick* ...:

> In some cases, however, the actions and expressions of an individual judge trigger concerns about the integrity of the judicial function itself. When a disciplinary process is launched to look at the conduct of an individual judge, it is alleged that an abuse of judicial independence by a judge has threatened the integrity of the judiciary as a whole. The harm alleged is not curable by the appeal process.

The Inquiry Committee found that the judge's conduct included: an inappropriate aligning of the judge with defence counsel giving rise to an apprehension of bias; an abuse of judicial powers by a deliberate, repeated and unwarranted interference in the presentation of the Crown's case; the abuse of judicial powers by inappropriate interference with RCMP activities; the misuse of judicial powers by repeated inappropriate threats of citations for contempt or arrest without foundation; the use of rude, abusive or intemperate language; and the arbitrary quashing of a federal immigration warrant.

The members of the Inquiry Committee then agreed unanimously as follows ...:

> In our opinion, the evidence we have characterized as lack of restraint, abuse of judicial independence, or abuse of judicial powers fully warrants a recommendation for removal from office, subject to whatever effect may be given to the judge's statement [of apology] of 10 September 2008.

After considering the judge's statement and the submissions, four out of the five members of the Inquiry Committee concluded as follows ...:

> ... [Justice Cosgrove's words and conduct] give rise to a reasonable and irremediable apprehension of bias. ...

. . . . .

In his statement to Council, Justice Cosgrove confirmed that his personal statement of 10 September 2008 to the Inquiry Committee was intended to be an unqualified recognition of his judicial misconduct and an unqualified apology. He repeated these sentiments in his statement before us. ...

. . . . .

ISSUES

. . . . .

... There can be no doubt that Justice Cosgrove engaged in serious judicial misconduct, within the meaning of the *Judges Act*.

Accordingly, it remains for Council to proceed to the second stage and determine if public confidence in the judge's ability to discharge the duties of his office has been undermined to such an extent that a recommendation for removal is warranted. In this regard, we adopt the standard identified by Council in the Marshall matter and widely applied in other cases since then:

> Is the conduct alleged so manifestly and profoundly destructive of the concept of the impartiality, integrity, and independence of the judicial role, that public confidence would be sufficiently undermined to render the judge incapable of executing the judicial office?

. . . . .

The Apologies

. . . . .

As found by the Inquiry Committee, the judge's conduct included: giving rise to an apprehension of bias; repeated and unwarranted interference in the presentation of the Crown's case; inappropriate interference with RCMP activities; inappropriate threats of citations for contempt or arrest without foundation; the use of rude, abusive or intemperate language; and the arbitrary quashing of a federal immigration warrant. These are not mere judicial errors.

. . . . .

... [W]e must consider an additional – more important – aspect in deciding whether a recommendation for removal is warranted: the effect upon public confidence of the actions of the judge in light of the nature and seriousness of the misconduct.

For Council, therefore, the key question is whether the apology is sufficient to restore public confidence. ...:

> ... In discharging its function, the Council must be acutely sensitive to the requirements of judicial independence, and it must ensure never to kill the expression of unpopular, honestly held views in the context of court proceedings. It must also be equally sensitive to the reasonable expectations of an informed dispassionate public that holders of judicial office will remain at all times worthy of trust, confidence and respect.

. . . . .

In this case, it is our conclusion that the misconduct by Justice Cosgrove was so serious and so destructive of public confidence that no apology, no matter its sincerity, can restore public confidence in the judge's future ability to impartially carry out his judicial duties in accordance with the high standards expected of all judges. This was not a single instance of misconduct but, rather, misconduct that was pervasive in both scope and duration.

. . . . .

While it is not strictly necessary to address this issue, given the decision just made, we make the following points. It was open to Justice Cosgrove to offer, at any time, an apology about his conduct but he did not. It appears that the judge did not, for years after the fact, appreciate that he had engaged in serious misconduct.

. . . . .

The tardiness of the judge's apology reveals both his lack of insight and his lack of appreciation of the impact of his egregious misconduct on public confidence in the judiciary.

. . . . .

DECISION

We agree with the conclusions reached by the majority of the members of the Inquiry Committee, as outlined in paragraph 189 of their report, which we now repeat:

> For the reasons given above, the words used and the conduct engaged in by Justice Cosgrove, over a prolonged period of time, constitute a failure in the due exercise of his office by abusing his powers as a judge. They give rise to a reasonable and irremediable apprehension of bias. Regrettably, his statement is insufficient to offset the serious harm done to public confidence in the concept of the judicial role, as described in the Marshall test. He has rendered himself incapable of executing the judicial office.

We find that Justice Cosgrove has failed in the execution of the duties of his judicial office and that public confidence in his ability to discharge those duties in future has been irrevocably lost. We find that there is no alternative measure to removal that would be sufficient to restore public confidence in the judge in this case. Therefore, we hereby recommend to the Minister of Justice, in accordance with section 65 of the *Judges Act*, that Justice Cosgrove be removed from office.

NOTES AND QUESTIONS

1. Justice Cosgrove resigned from the bench before the Minister of Justice exercised his authority to commence removal proceedings.

2. What options are open to a lawyer if you believe that a judge is:

    (a) inappropriately aligning herself with counsel for the other side;

    (b) deliberately, repeatedly and unwarrantedly interfering in your presentation of the evidence;

    (c) inappropriately threatening you with citations for contempt or arrest without foundation; or

    (d) using rude, abusive or intemperate language?

If a lawyer has concerns about the impartiality of a judge, the lawyer can ask the judge to recuse herself from the case. It is up to the individual judge to decide whether to accede to this request. Identify the challenges that this might create for a lawyer. Should Canadian judges adopt a rule which requires that recusal requests be heard by another judge?

If self-recusal is the most appropriate process when a judge sits alone, is it also the most appropriate process in a multi-person court, for example, a court of appeal or the Supreme Court of Canada? Consider the following two decisions from the Supreme Court of Canada.

ARSENAULT-CAMERON v. PRINCE EDWARD ISLAND

[1999] S.C.J. No. 75, [1999] 3 S.C.R. 851
(S.C.C., Bastarache J.)

[Parents in a Prince Edward Island town demanded the French Language Board provide a facility that offered French-language instruction at the primary level in the community. The Government of P.E.I. refused and offered transport services to a nearby community that had the desired facility. The case reached the Supreme Court of Canada. Sitting on the case was Bastarache J. Justice Bastarache was a long-time supporter of French-language rights.

The respondent filed a motion directed at Bastarache J. The motion claimed that, because of Bastarache J.'s history of promoting French-language rights, his presence on the bench gave rise to a reasonable apprehension of bias. Justice Bastarache heard the motion and, alone, decided whether or not he should recuse himself.]

BASTARACHE J.:— I have considered the notice of motion of the applicant as if it was addressed to me in the form of an application for recusal on the basis of apprehension of bias. I deny the motion.

The test for apprehension of bias takes into account the presumption of impartiality. A real likelihood or probability of bias must be demonstrated ... I find nothing in the material submitted by the applicant that would cause a reasonable person who understands the complex and contextual issues to believe that I would not entertain the various points of view with an open mind.

Given the nature of the aforesaid material, it is fitting to quote Cory J. in *S. (R.D.)* ..., on the relevance of past experience to the question of apprehension of bias:

> ... There is no human being who is not the product of every social experience, every process of education, and every human contact with those with whom we share the planet. Indeed, even if it were possible, a judge free of this heritage of past experience would probably lack the very qualities of humanity required of a judge. Rather, the wisdom required of a judge is to recognize, consciously allow for, and perhaps to question, all the baggage of past attitudes and sympathies that fellow citizens are free to carry, untested, to the grave.

> True impartiality does not require that the judge have no sympathies or opinions; it requires that the judge nevertheless be free to entertain and act upon different points of view with an open mind.

> (Canadian Judicial Council, *Commentaries on Judicial Conduct* ...).

. . . . .

The writings referred to by the applicant do not reveal any prejudgment of the issues in this case. As formulated by Le Dain J. in *Valente v. The Queen*, ... partiality is "a state of mind or attitude ... in relation to the issues and the parties in a particular case", a real predisposition to a particular result. The applicant would have to show wrongful or inappropriate declarations showing a state of mind that sways judgment in order to succeed.

In conclusion, I find that no evidence was adduced demonstrating that my beliefs or opinions expressed as counsel, law professor or otherwise would prevent me from coming to a decision on the basis of the evidence.

For these reasons, I would deny the motion.

WEWAYKUM INDIAN BAND v. CANADA

[2003] S.C.J. No. 50, 2003 SCC 45
(S.C.C., McLachlin C.J.C. and Gonthier, Iacobucci, Major,
Bastarache, Arbour, LeBel and Deschamps JJ.)

[Two Indian bands filed a motion to have a decision of the Supreme Court of Canada set aside. The judgment was written by Binnie J. and received unanimous approval from the other eight justices. The motion was filed after the decision. It was only then that one of the bands learned Binnie J. was previously involved with the same case, as an Associate Deputy Minister in the Department of Justice, during its early stages in the 1980s. The bands claimed his prior involvement produced a reasonable apprehension of bias that warranted disqualifying the Court's decision.

Once the motion was received, Binnie J. recused himself from further proceedings. The remaining eight justices examined whether or not a reasonable apprehension of bias was raised and, if it was, what impact it could have on the decision of the Court.]

The following is the judgment delivered by **McLACHLIN C.J.C.** and **GONTHIER, IACOBUCCI, MAJOR, BASTARACHE, ARBOUR, LeBEL** and **DESCHAMPS JJ.:—**

. . . . .

II. Factual Background

. . . . .

C. *Results of the Access to Information Request*

... On May 23, 2003, the Assistant Deputy Attorney General, James D. Bissell, Q.C., wrote the Registrar of the Supreme Court of Canada to inform her that as a result of the preparation of the Department's response to the access to information request, it appeared "that Mr. W.I.C. Binnie in 1985 and early 1986, in the course of his duties as Associate Deputy Minister of Justice, participated in discussions with Department of Justice counsel in the *Wewaykum* [Campbell River] *Indian Band* case".

. . . . .

D. *The Motion for Directions*

. . . . .

Produced with the motion for directions were the documents referring to Mr. Binnie while in the employ of the Department of Justice and Campbell River's claim in relation to Reserves Nos. 11 and 12. Upon receipt of the motion by the Court, Binnie J. recused himself from any further proceedings on this matter and, on May 27, 2003, filed the following statement with the Registrar of the Supreme Court:

. . . . .

> It is a matter of public record that between September 1982 and July 1986 I was Associate Deputy Minister of Justice responsible for all litigation for and against the federal Crown except tax matters and cases in Quebec. This included Indian claims. At any given time, the responsibility covered several thousand cases.
>
> When this appeal was pending before the Court in 2002, I had no recollection of personal involvement 17 years earlier at the commencement

of this particular file, which was handled by departmental counsel in the Vancouver Regional Office.

I do not recall anything about any involvement in this case to add to what is set out in the departmental file.

I recuse myself from consideration of the pending motion.

. . . . .

IV. Analysis

A. *The Importance of the Principle of Impartiality*

The motions brought by the parties require that we examine the circumstances of this case in light of the well-settled, foundational principle of impartiality of courts of justice. There is no need to reaffirm here the importance of this principle, which has been a matter of renewed attention across the common law world over the past decade. Simply put, public confidence in our legal system is rooted in the fundamental belief that those who adjudicate in law must always do so without bias or prejudice and must be perceived to do so.

The essence of impartiality lies in the requirement of the judge to approach the case to be adjudicated with an open mind. Conversely, bias or prejudice has been defined as

> a leaning, inclination, bent or predisposition towards one side or another or a particular result. In its application to legal proceedings, it represents a predisposition to decide an issue or cause in a certain way which does not leave the judicial mind perfectly open to conviction. Bias is a condition or state of mind which sways judgment and renders a judicial officer unable to exercise his or her functions impartially in a particular case. [*R. v. Bertram*, quoted by Cory J. in *R. v. S. R.D.*]

Viewed in this light, "[i]mpartiality is the fundamental qualification of a judge and the core attribute of the judiciary" [*Ethical Principles for Judges*]. It is the key to our judicial process, and must be presumed. As was noted by L'Heureux-Dubé J. and McLachlin J. (as she then was) in *S. (R.D.)*, *supra*, at para. 32, the presumption of impartiality carries considerable weight, and the law should not carelessly evoke the possibility of bias in a judge, whose authority depends upon that presumption. Thus, while the requirement of judicial impartiality is a stringent one, the burden is on the party arguing for disqualification to establish that the circumstances justify a finding that the judge must be disqualified.

In Canadian law, one standard has now emerged as the criterion for disqualification. The criterion, as expressed by de Grandpré J. in *Committee for Justice and Liberty v. National Energy Board* [at 394] is the reasonable apprehension of bias:

> ... In the words of the Court of Appeal, that test is "what would an informed person, viewing the matter realistically and practically — and having thought the matter through — conclude. Would he think that it is more likely

than not that [the decision-maker], whether consciously or unconsciously, would not decide fairly."

. . . . .

B. *Reasonable Apprehension of Bias and Actual Bias*

... Here, as in many cases, it is conceded by the parties that there was no actual bias on Binnie J.'s part, and his statement that he had no recollection of involvement is similarly accepted by all concerned ... Nevertheless, it is said, the circumstances of the present case are such as to create a reasonable apprehension of bias on his part. Since the two propositions go hand in hand, to understand what is meant by reasonable apprehension of bias, it is helpful to consider what it means to say that disqualification is not argued on the basis of actual bias.

Saying that there was "no actual bias" can mean one of three things: that actual bias need not be established because reasonable apprehension of bias can be viewed as a surrogate for it; that unconscious bias can exist, even where the judge is in good faith; or that the presence or absence of actual bias is not the relevant inquiry. We take each in turn.

. . . . .

... [I]n the present instance, no one suggests that Binnie J. was consciously allowing extraneous influences to affect his mind. Consequently, it would appear that reasonable apprehension of bias is not invoked here as a surrogate for actual bias.

. . . . .

As framed, some of the arguments presented by the parties suggest that they are preoccupied that Binnie J. may have been unconsciously biased despite his good faith.

... [W]hen parties concede that there was no actual bias, they may be suggesting that looking for real bias is simply not the relevant inquiry. In the present case, as is most common, parties have relied on Lord Hewart C.J.'s aphorism that "it is not merely of some importance but is of fundamental importance that justice should not only be done, but should manifestly and undoubtedly be seen to be done" [*The King v. Sussex Justices, Ex parte McCarthy*] ...

Of the three justifications for the objective standard of reasonable apprehension of bias, the last is the most demanding for the judicial system, because it countenances the possibility that justice might not be seen to be done, even where it is undoubtedly done – that is, it envisions the possibility that a decision-maker may be totally impartial in circumstances which nevertheless create a reasonable apprehension of bias, requiring his or her disqualification. ... The reasonable person is asked to imagine the decision-maker's state of mind, under the circumstances. ...

. . . . .

D. *Reasonable Apprehension of Bias and Its Application in This Case*

The question, once more, is as follows: What would an informed person, viewing the matter realistically and practically – and having thought the matter through – conclude? Would this person think that it is more likely than not that Binnie J., whether consciously or unconsciously, did not decide fairly?

. . . . .

As the parties acknowledged, Binnie J.'s past status as Associate Deputy Minister is by itself insufficient to justify his disqualification. The same can be said of his long-standing interest in matters involving First Nations. The source of concern, for the bands in these motions to vacate the judgment, is Binnie J.'s involvement in this case, as opposed to his general duties as head of litigation for the Department of Justice in the mid-1980s.

. . . . .

… [W]hat is germane is the nature and extent of Binnie J.'s role. The details of Binnie J.'s involvement in this case, as outlined in the earlier part of these reasons and which should be viewed in the context of his broad duties in the Department of Justice, would convince a reasonable person that his role was of a limited supervisory and administrative nature.

Admittedly, Binnie J.'s link to this litigation exceeded *pro forma* management of the files. On the other hand, it should be noted that he was never counsel of record, and played no active role in the dispute after the claim was filed. …

. . . . .

To us, one significant factor stands out, and must inform the perspective of the reasonable person assessing the impact of this involvement on Binnie J.'s impartiality in the appeals. That factor is the passage of time. Most arguments for disqualification rest on circumstances that are either contemporaneous to the decision-making, or that occurred within a short time prior to the decision-making.

. . . . .

In the present instance, Binnie J.'s limited supervisory role in relation to this case dates back over 15 years. This lengthy period is obviously significant in relation to Binnie J.'s statement that when the appeals were heard and decided, he had no recollection of his involvement in this file from the 1980s. …

. . . . .

… The question is whether the reasonable person's assessment is affected by his statement, in light of the context – that is, in light of the amount of time that has passed, coupled with the limited administrative and supervisory role Binnie played in this file. In our view, it is a factor that the reasonable person would properly consider, and it makes bias or its apprehension improbable in the circumstances.

574 Lawyers' Ethics and Professional Regulation

Binnie J.'s lack of recollection is thus relevant. Yet it is not decisive of the issue. This is not a case in which the judge never knew about the relevant conflict of interest, which would be much easier, but a case in which the judge no longer recalls it. Without questioning his recollection, the argument can be made that his earlier involvement in the file affected his perspective unconsciously. Nevertheless, we are convinced that the reasonable person, viewing the matter realistically, would not come to the conclusion that the limited administrative and supervisory role played by Binnie J. in this file, over 15 years ago, affected his ability, even unconsciously, to remain impartial in these appeals. ...

We thus conclude that no reasonable apprehension of bias is established and that Binnie J. was not disqualified in these appeals. The judgment of the Court and the reasons delivered by Binnie J. on December 6, 2002, must stand. It is unnecessary to examine the question whether, in the event that the Court had found that Binnie J. was disqualified, the judgment of the Court in these appeals would have been undermined. Nevertheless, because of the importance of the issue, we offer a few comments in this respect.

The decision-making process within the Supreme Court of Canada, while not widely known, is a matter of public record. ... Each member of the Supreme Court prepares independently for the hearing of appeals. All judges are fully prepared, and no member of the Court is assigned the task to go through the case so as to "brief" the rest of the panel before the hearing. After the case is heard, each judge on the panel expresses his or her opinion independently. Discussions take place on who will prepare draft reasons, and whether for the majority or the minority. Draft reasons are then prepared and circulated by one or more judges. These reasons are the fruit of a truly collegial process of revision of successive drafts. In that sense, it can be said that reasons express the individual views of each and every judge who signs them, and the collective effort and opinion of them all.

Here, the nine judges who sat on these appeals shared the same view as to the disposition of the appeals and the reasons for judgment. Cases where the tainted judge casts the deciding vote in a split decision are inapposite in this respect. In the circumstances of the present case, even if it were found that the involvement of a single judge gave rise to a reasonable apprehension of bias, no reasonable person informed of the decision-making process of the Court, and viewing it realistically, could conclude that it was likely that the eight other judges were biased, or somehow tainted, by the apprehended bias affecting the ninth judge.

V. Conclusion

We conclude that no reasonable apprehension of bias is established. Binnie J. was not disqualified to hear these appeals and to participate in the judgment. As a result, the motions to vacate the judgment rendered by this Court on December 6, 2002, are dismissed. The Crown's motion for directions is also dismissed. ...

NOTES AND QUESTIONS

1. Which process is more legitimate: for the allegedly tainted judge to make the decision whether to recuse herself, or for her colleagues to do so? Which system would be preferred by lawyers?

2. Would it be better for another independent Panel composed of judges from the same court to make the recusal decision?[5]

3. If such a Panel could not be constituted would it be wise to create an ad hoc panel of other judges? How does one balance the demands of judicial impartiality with norms of efficiency and accountability? Do you think that the "fully informed reasonable person" test is analytically strong?

4. A judge may decide to recuse himself or herself based completely on the judge's own decision. There are no standards apart from those general standards that exist under the Ethical Principles and under case law. A survey of provincially appointed judges across Canada showed wide variation in both how judges approached issues of recusal and the actual decisions that they made on whether or not to recuse themselves. See P. Bryden & J. Hughes, "The Tip of the Iceberg: A Survey of the Philosophy and Practice of Canadian Provincial and Territorial Judges Concerning Judicial Disqualification" (2011) 48 Alta. L. Rev. 569. What dilemmas does this pose for counsel when they might not even know if or how a judge recused themselves?

5. How would you as a lawyer decide whether to bring a motion to recuse a judge? What would you do if you discover that the judge had some involvement with one of the parties prior to being appointed to the bench but you do not think it rises to the level of being "a reasonable apprehension of bias"? What would you do?

6. After *Wewaykum*, the Supreme Court enacted Rule 25(1)(d) which states that "if a judge's previous involvement or connection with the case may result in it being inappropriate for that judge to take part in the adjudication on the proceedings in the Court"[6] counsel must file a certificate in Form 25C setting out the issues. Does this Rule go far enough?

Scenario One

You represent a group of 16 Hispanic employees of We-Rent-A-Car who are alleging racial discrimination against We-Rent-A-Car. You are co-counsel with the Hispanic Canadian Civil Liberties Association. On the first day of trial, your case is assigned to Judge Reyes. You know that Judge Reyes used to be involved with the Hispanic Canadian Civil Liberties Association but ceased her involvement once she was appointed to the bench. Judge Reyes' spouse, however, is on the board of the Hispanic Canadian Civil Liberties Association Trust, which is a charitable organization that raises money for the Association. Judge Reyes has a reputation as a judge who is skeptical of discrimination lawsuits. You are uncertain whether in law her associations raise an apprehension of bias but you think it would be advantageous to your

5   *In re Pinochet*, [1999] UKHL 1, [2000] 1 A.C. 119 (H.L.).
6   Rules of the Supreme Court of Canada, SOR/2002-156.

client to have another judge preside at the trial of their claims. What do you do?

Scenario Two

Assume you are the lawyer for an intervenor group, Family Values for All, who are objecting to an action to legalize same-sex marriage. The trial judge found for the plaintiffs, legalized same-sex marriage and rejected your client's arguments. Two months later you discover that the trial judge is gay. What do you do? Would your answer be different if the judge was not only gay, but himself entered into a same-sex marriage within two months of making the decision to legalize gay marriage?[7]

Scenario Three

Assume you are the lawyer for an intervenor group, Mums Against Guns, who are objecting to an action to eliminate the "Long-Gun Registry". The trial judge found for the plaintiffs, struck down the Long-Gun Registry as unconstitutional and rejected your client's arguments. Two months later you discover that for the last 10 years the trial judge has been a member of the Canuck Hunters' Association, which also objects to the long-gun registry, but was not part of the litigation. What do you do? Would your answer be different if the judge was not just a member of the Association, but was himself an avid collector of long-guns?[8]

Practising law, either as a lawyer or as a judge, can lead to moments of stress, frustration, exasperation and even anger. Occasionally, judges and lawyers cross swords and the consequences can be disturbing. The Impartiality Principle attempts to address this as follows:

1. Judges should strive to ensure that their conduct, both in and out of court, maintains and enhances confidence in their impartiality and that of the judiciary.

. . . . .

Judicial Demeanour

1. While acting decisively, maintaining firm control and ensuring expedition, judges should treat everyone before the court with appropriate courtesy.

The following case illustrates the failure of a judge to fulfill these obligations, the riposte of the lawyer, the admonition of the Canadian Judicial Council to the judge and the Barreau du Québec's disciplining of the lawyer.

[7]   Linda Greenhouse, "Recuse Me" *New York Times: Opinionator* (May 4, 2011), online: <http://opinionator.blogs.nytimes.com/2011/05/04/recuse-me/>.

[8]   See also Beverley Smith, *Professional Conduct for Lawyers and Judges*, 4th ed. (Fredericton: Maritime Law Book, 2011), at ch. 14, para. 52.

DORÉ v. BARREAU DU QUÉBEC

[2012] S.C.J. No. 12, 2012 SCC 12
(S.C.C., McLachlin C.J.C. and Binnie, LeBel, Fish, Abella,
Rothstein and Cromwell JJ.)

ABELLA J.:— The focus of this appeal is on the decision of a disciplinary body to reprimand a lawyer for the content of a letter he wrote to a judge after a court proceeding.

. . . . .

Background

Gilles Doré was counsel for Daniel Lanthier in criminal proceedings. On June 18 and 19, 2001, Mr. Doré appeared before Boilard J. in the Superior Court of Quebec seeking a stay of proceedings or, in the alternative, the release of his client on bail. In the course of Mr. Doré's argument, Justice Boilard said about him that [TRANSLATION] "an insolent lawyer is rarely of use to his client". In his written reasons rejecting Mr. Doré's application on June 21, Boilard J. levied further criticism (*R. v. Lanthier*, 2001 CanLII 9351). He accused Mr. Doré of [TRANSLATION] "bombastic rhetoric and hyperbole" and said that the court must "put aside" Mr. Doré's "impudence". Justice Boilard characterized Mr. Doré's request for a stay as "totally ridiculous" and one of his arguments as "idle quibbling". Finally, he said that "fixated on or obsessed with his narrow vision of reality, which is not consistent with the facts, Mr. Doré has done nothing to help his client discharge his burden".

On June 21, Mr. Doré wrote a private letter to Justice Boilard, stating:

[TRANSLATION]

WITHOUT PREJUDICE OR ADMISSION

Sir,

I have just left the Court. Just a few minutes ago, as you hid behind your status like a coward, you made comments about me that were both unjust and unjustified, scattering them here and there in a decision the good faith of which will most likely be argued before our Court of Appeal.

Because you ducked out quickly and refused to hear me, I have chosen to write a letter as an entirely personal response to the equally personal remarks you permitted yourself to make about me. This letter, therefore, is from man to man and is outside the ambit of my profession and your functions.

If no one has ever told you the following, then it is high time someone did. Your chronic inability to master any social skills (to use an expression in English, that language you love so much), which has caused you to become pedantic, aggressive and petty in your daily life, makes no difference to me; after all, it seems to suit you well.

Your deliberate expression of these character traits while exercising your judicial functions, however, and your having made them your trademark concern me a great deal, and I feel that it is appropriate to tell you.

Your legal knowledge, which appears to have earned the approval of a certain number of your colleagues, is far from sufficient to make you the person you could or should be professionally. Your determination to obliterate any humanity from your judicial position, your essentially non-existent listening skills, and your propensity to use your court - where you lack the courage to hear opinions contrary to your own - to launch ugly, vulgar, and mean personal attacks not only confirms that you are as loathsome as suspected, but also casts shame on you as a judge, that most extraordinarily important function that was entrusted to you.

I would have very much liked to say this to your face, but I highly doubt that, given your arrogance, you are able to face your detractors without hiding behind your judicial position.

Worst of all, you possess the most appalling of all defects for a man in your position: You are fundamentally unjust. I doubt that that will ever change.

Sincerely,
Gilles Doré

P.S. As this letter is purely personal, I see no need to distribute it.

. . . . .

The next day, June 22, 2001, Mr. Doré wrote to Chief Justice Lyse Lemieux, with a copy to Justice Boilard. He made it clear that he was not filing a complaint with her against Justice Boilard. Instead, Mr. Doré respectfully requested that he not be required to appear before Justice Boilard in the future since he was concerned that he could not properly represent his clients before him.

On July 10, 2001, Mr. Doré complained to the Canadian Judicial Council about Justice Boilard's conduct. On July 13, Chief Justice Lemieux sent a copy of the letter Mr. Doré had sent to Justice Boilard to the Syndic du Barreau, the body that disciplines lawyers in Quebec.

In March 2002, the Assistant Syndic filed a complaint against Mr. Doré based on his letter to Justice Boilard. The complaint alleged that Mr. Doré had violated both art. 2.03 of the *Code of ethics of advocates*, R.R.Q. 1981, c. B-1, r.1, and Mr. Doré's oath of office. Art. 2.03 stated: "[T]he conduct of an advocate must bear the stamp of objectivity, moderation and dignity."

In the interval between the filing of the Assistant Syndic's complaint against Mr. Doré and the actual proceedings against him, a committee of judges appointed by the Judicial Council to look into Mr. Doré's complaint communicated its conclusions to Mr. Doré and Justice Boilard in letters sent on July 15, 2002. The committee found that Justice Boilard had made [TRANSLATION] "unjustified derogatory remarks to Mr. Doré" stating, in part:

[TRANSLATION]

... to use the words "bombastic rhetoric and hyperbole" and "impudence" in referring to counsel arguing a case before you, quite clearly in good faith, is unnecessarily insulting. To reply to counsel who submits that you have not allowed him to argue his case "that an insolent lawyer is rarely of use to his client" not only is unjustified in the circumstances, but could tarnish counsel's professional reputation in the eyes of his client, his peers and the public. To say to counsel arguing a case before you that "I have the impression this is going to be tiresome" is to gratuitously degrade him. To describe a procedure before the court as "totally ridiculous" is unnecessarily humiliating. It is the panel's opinion that such comments would seem to show contempt for counsel not only as an individual but also as a professional.

The evidence reveals a flagrant lack of respect for an officer of the court, namely Mr. Doré, who was nevertheless at all times respectful to the court. The evidence also shows signs of impatience on your part that are surprising in light of every judge's duty to listen calmly to the parties and to counsel. It is the panel's opinion that in so abusing your power as a judge, you not only tarnished your image as a dispenser of justice, but also undermined the judiciary, the image of which has unfortunately been diminished. The panel reminds you that your independence and your authority as a judge do not exempt you from respecting the dignity of every individual who argues a case before you. Dispensing justice while gratuitously insulting counsel is befitting neither for the judge nor for the judiciary.

Having also read the judgments of the Quebec Court of Appeal in *R. v. Proulx*, *R. v. Bisson* and *R. v. Callochia*, the panel observed that you tend to use your platform to unjustly denigrate counsel appearing before you. The transcript of the hearing of April 9, 2002 in *Sa Majesté la Reine v. Sébastien Beauchamp*, which contains evidence of personal attacks on another lawyer, also confirmed that the case raised in Mr. Doré's complaint is neither unique nor isolated, but shows that extreme conduct and comments seem to form part of a more generalized attitude. In the panel's view, the fact that such an attitude could persist despite warnings from the Court of Appeal is troubling.

The panel finds that the impatience you showed and the immoderate comments you made to an officer of the court, Mr. Doré, are unacceptable and merit an expression of the panel's disapproval under subsection 55(2) of the Canadian Judicial Council By-Laws.

The panel notes that you have deferred to its decision and assumes that the fact that Mr. Doré has made a complaint will lead you to reflect on this and will remind you of your duty as a judge to show respect and courtesy to all counsel who appear before you.

On July 22, 2002, after receiving this reprimand, Justice Boilard recused himself from a complex criminal trial involving the Hell's Angels, a trial related to the trial of Daniel Lanthier in which Mr. Doré had acted. As a result of this recusal, the Attorney General of Quebec requested the Canadian Judicial Council to conduct an inquiry. The Judicial Council concluded that Justice Boilard's recusal had not constituted misconduct.

As for Mr. Doré, the proceedings before the Disciplinary Council of the Barreau du Québec took place between April 2003 and January 2006. In its January 18, 2006 decision, the Disciplinary Council found that Mr. Doré's letter was [TRANSLATION] "likely to offend and is rude and insulting"

(2006 CanLII 53416, at para. 58). It concluded that his statements had little expressive value, as they were "merely opinions, perceptions and insults" (para. 62). The Disciplinary Council rejected Mr. Doré's submission that his letter was private, since it was written by him as a lawyer. It also concluded that Justice Boilard's conduct could not be relied on as justification for the letter.

. . . . .

Analysis

Mr. Doré's argument rests on his assertion that the finding of a breach of the *Code of ethics* violates the expressive rights protected by s. 2(*b*) of the *Charter*. Because the 21-day suspension had already been served when he was before the Court of Appeal, he did not appeal the penalty. The reasonableness of its length, therefore, is not before us.

[The Court then engaged in a lengthy discussion of the relationship between the *Charter* and administrative bodies such as the Barreau du Quebéc and concluded the following.]

If, in exercising its statutory discretion, the decision-maker has properly balanced the relevant *Charter* value with the statutory objectives, the decision will be found to be reasonable.

Application

The *Charter* value at issue in this appeal is expression, and, specifically, how it should be applied in the context of a lawyer's professional duties.

At the relevant time, art. 2.03 of the *Code of ethics* ... stated that "[t]he conduct of an advocate must bear the stamp of objectivity, moderation and dignity". This provision, whose constitutionality is not impugned before us, sets out a series of broad standards that are open to a wide range of interpretations. The determination of whether the actions of a lawyer violate art. 2.03 in a given case is left entirely to the Disciplinary Council's discretion.

No party in this dispute challenges the importance of professional discipline to prevent incivility in the legal profession, namely "potent displays of disrespect for the participants in the justice system, beyond mere rudeness or discourtesy" ... The duty to encourage civility, "both inside and outside the courtroom", rests with the courts and with lawyers (*R. v. Felderhof* (2003), 68 O.R. (3d) 481 (C.A.), at para. 83).

As a result, rules similar to art. 2.03 are found in codes of ethics that govern the legal profession throughout Canada. ...

But in dealing with the appropriate boundaries of civility, the severity of the conduct must be interpreted in light of the expressive rights guaranteed by the *Charter*, and, in particular, the public benefit in ensuring the right of lawyers to express themselves about the justice system in general and judges in particular ...

In *Histed v. Law Society of Manitoba*, 2007 MBCA 150, 225 Man. R. (2d) 74, where Steel J.A. upheld a disciplinary decision resulting from a lawyer's criticism of a judge, the critical role played by lawyers in assuring the accountability of the judiciary was acknowledged:

> Not only should the judiciary be accountable and open to criticism, but lawyers play a very unique role in ensuring that accountability. As professionals with special expertise and officers of the court, lawyers are under a special responsibility to exercise fearlessness in front of the courts. They must advance their cases courageously, and this may result in criticism of proceedings before or decisions by the judiciary. The lawyer, as an intimate part of the legal system, plays a pivotal role in ensuring the accountability and transparency of the judiciary. To play that role effectively, he/she must feel free to act and speak without inhibition and with courage when the circumstances demand it. [Emphasis added; para. 71.]

Proper respect for these expressive rights may involve disciplinary bodies tolerating a degree of discordant criticism. As the Ontario Court of Appeal observed in a different context in *R. v. Kopyto*, the fact that a lawyer is criticizing a judge, a tenured and independent participant in the justice system, may raise, not lower, the threshold for limiting a lawyer's expressive rights under the *Charter*. This does not by any means argue for an unlimited right on the part of lawyers to breach the legitimate public expectation that they will behave with civility.

We are, in other words, balancing the fundamental importance of open, and even forceful, criticism of our public institutions with the need to ensure civility in the profession. Disciplinary bodies must therefore demonstrate that they have given due regard to the importance of the expressive rights at issue, both in light of an individual lawyer's right to expression and the public's interest in open discussion. As with all disciplinary decisions, this balancing is a fact-dependent and discretionary exercise.

In this case, the 21-day suspension imposed on Mr. Doré is not before this Court, since Mr. Doré did not appeal it either to the Court of Appeal or to this Court. All we have been asked to determine is whether the Disciplinary Council's conclusion that a reprimand was warranted under art. 2.03 of the *Code of ethics* was a reasonable one. To make that assessment, we must consider whether this result reflects a proportionate application of the statutory mandate with Mr. Doré's expressive rights.

Lawyers potentially face criticisms and pressures on a daily basis. They are expected by the public, on whose behalf they serve, to endure them with civility and dignity. This is not always easy where the lawyer feels he or she has been unfairly provoked, as in this case. But it is precisely when a lawyer's equilibrium is unduly tested that he or she is particularly called upon to behave with transcendent civility. On the other hand, lawyers should not be expected to behave like verbal eunuchs. They not only have a right to speak their minds freely, they arguably have a duty to do so. But they are constrained by their profession to do so with dignified restraint.

A reprimand for a lawyer does not automatically flow from criticizing a judge or the judicial system. As discussed, such criticism, even when it is expressed robustly, can be constructive. However in the context of disciplinary hearings, such criticism will be measured against the public's reasonable expectations of a lawyer's professionalism. As the Disciplinary Council found, Mr. Doré's letter was outside those expectations. His displeasure with Justice Boilard was justifiable, but the extent of the response was not.

The Disciplinary Council recognized that a lawyer must have [TRANSLATION] "total liberty and independence in the defence of a client's rights", and "has the right to respond to criticism or remarks addressed to him by a judge", a right which the Council recognized "can suffer no restrictions when it is a question of defending clients' rights before the courts" (paras. 68-70). It was also "conscious" of the fact that art. 2.03 may constitute a restriction on a lawyer's expressive rights (para. 79). But where, as here, the judge was called [TRANSLATION] "loathsome", arrogant and "fundamentally unjust" and was accused by Mr. Doré of "hid[ing] behind [his] status like a coward"; having a "chronic inability to master any social skills"; being "pedantic, aggressive and petty in [his] daily life"; having "obliterate[d] any humanity from [his] judicial position"; having "non-existent listening skills"; having a "propensity to use [his] court — where [he] lack[s] the courage to hear opinions contrary to [his] own — to launch ugly, vulgar, and mean personal attacks", which "not only confirms that [he is] as loathsome as suspected, but also casts shame on [him] as a judge"; and being "[un]able to face [his] detractors without hiding behind [his] judicial position", the Council concluded that the "generally accepted norms of moderation and dignity" were "overstepped" (para. 86).

In the circumstances, the Disciplinary Council found that Mr. Doré's letter warranted a reprimand. In light of the excessive degree of vituperation in the letter's context and tone, this conclusion cannot be said to represent an unreasonable balance of Mr. Doré's expressive rights with the statutory objectives.

I would dismiss the appeal with costs.

NOTES AND QUESTIONS

1. Do you agree that the letter was not a private letter?

2. To what extent does this decision encourage or discourage lawyers from criticizing judges? Are you relieved to discover that you do not have to behave like a "verbal eunuch"? Do you think lawyers typically act with "dignified restraint"?

3. Rule 4.01(5) of the *Model Code* provides that a "lawyer must be courteous and civil and act in good faith to the tribunal and all persons with whom the lawyer has dealings". The Commentary adds: "Legal contempt of court and the professional obligation here are not identical, and a consistent pattern of rude, provocative or disruptive conduct by a lawyer, even though unpunished as contempt, may constitute professional misconduct."

Does Mr. Doré's letter meet the thresholds identified in this Rule and Commentary? Rather than treating this as a disciplinary matter, would it have been better for Boilard J. to cite Mr. Doré for contempt of court?

4.   In what way was the decision of the Barreau to discipline Mr. Doré in the public interest?

5.   Do you agree with the sanction imposed by the Barreau?

Scenario Four

In *R. v. Ewanchuk*,[9] the Supreme Court of Canada decided that there was no defence of implied consent to the charge of sexual assault. Justice L'Heureux-Dubé wrote a very strongly worded concurrence. The Alberta Court of Appeal judge who wrote the decision at issue, McClung J.A., took offence and took the unusual step of writing a letter to the editor in a national newspaper defending himself and attacking L'Heureux-Dubé J. He was sanctioned by the Canadian Judicial Council for his actions. Numerous lawyers came to his defence and criticized L'Heureux-Dubé J. Consider the excerpt from the following op-ed penned by a leading Canadian barrister. In light of *Doré*, do you think that the lawyer criticized the judiciary "with dignified restraint"? If you were a member of a law society discipline panel, how would you have measured the lawyer's criticism "against the public's reasonable expectations of a lawyer's professionalism"?

EDWARD L. GREENSPAN

"Judges Have No Right to Be Bullies"[*]
(*National Post*, March 2, 1999)

. . . . .

When the Supreme Court judges swore their oath, they were not given the right to be bullies. They were not given the right to pull a lower court judge's pants down in public and paddle him. The job description does not permit them to say mean, gratuitous, and terrible things about lower court judges that will be recorded forever in Canadian legal history.

By labelling Judge McClung, in effect, the male chauvinist pig of the century, the chief yahoo from Alberta, the stupid, ignorant, ultimate sexist male jerk, Judge L'Heureux-Dubé did an unnecessary and mean-spirited thing. It was undignified and very wrong. I am not surprised that Judge McClung reacted angrily by writing a letter and giving an interview to the *National Post*.

... But make no mistake about this, Judge L'Heureux-Dubé drew first blood and whatever he said will not be recorded in Canadian judicial history like her vicious comments about him will. She tagged him with a label that she has no

---

9   [1999] S.C.J. No. 10, [1999] 1 S.C.R. 330 (S.C.C.).

*   We have produced an edited version of the article. If interested, the full article can be found online: <http://www.fact.on.ca/newpaper/np990301.htm>.

right to tag him with. She was intemperate, showed a lack of balance, and a terrible lack of judgment.

· · · · ·

Judge L'Heureux-Dubé was hell-bent on re-educating Judge McClung, bullying and coercing him into looking at everything from her point of view. ... But don't talk of removing him from office. Don't talk of censure. Likewise, don't censure her and don't remove her. Let the record show that she is not a very nice person and let the public debate ask the only question that matters: Does the Supreme Court of Canada care so little about its own reputation that it could not persuade Judge L'Heureux-Dubé to rewrite her judgment before she issued it, so as not to disgrace the court?

NOTES AND QUESTIONS

1. What do you think *Doré* says about lawyers criticizing each other? Rule 6.02(4) of the *Model Code* provides:

    A lawyer must not, in the course of a professional practice, send correspondence or otherwise communicate to a client, another lawyer or any other person in a manner that is abusive, offensive, or otherwise inconsistent with the proper tone of a professional communication from a lawyer.

2. Recall the *Laarakker* case in Chapter 6 where a British Columbia lawyer was disciplined for sending a strongly worded letter to an Ontario lawyer and posting a negative comment on a blog. In light of *Doré*, do you think Laarakker should have been sanctioned for his comments?

Scenario Five

Two lawyers are members of the listserv of the Law Union, a progressive lawyers group. There is a heated discussion of the Israel-Palestine conflict and one lawyer writes to the listserv accusing the other of being "an idiot know-nothing who spews vile anti-Semitic hatred under the guise of reasoned analysis". Does *Doré* permit or prohibit such remarks? What is the role of the law society in regulating political discussions of this sort between lawyers in a public forum?

D. INDEPENDENCE

Independence is a foundational principle for judges:

Statement:

An independent judiciary is indispensable to impartial justice under law. Judges should, therefore, uphold and exemplify judicial independence in both its individual and institutional aspects.

Principles:

1. Judges must exercise their judicial functions independently and free of extraneous influence.

2. Judges must firmly reject any attempt to influence their decisions in any matter before the Court outside the proper process of the Court.

3. Judges should encourage and uphold arrangements and safeguards to maintain and enhance the institutional and operational independence of the judiciary.

4. Judges should exhibit and promote high standards of judicial conduct so as to reinforce public confidence which is the cornerstone of judicial independence.

An important question for lawyers is whether some judges might take advantage of judicial independence to advance their own view of the world. Consider how the following case discusses the balance between judicial independence and judicial accountability.

RE RUFFO

[2005] Q.J. No. 17953, 2005 QCCA 1197
(Que. C.A., Paul-Arthur Gendreau J.C.A., Thérèse Rousseau-Houle J.C.A.,
Jacques Chamberland J.C.A., France Thibault J.C.A. and
Pierrette Rayle J.C.A.)
[footnotes omitted]

[Andrée Ruffo was a Court of Quebec judge for 15 years. During that time, she breached Quebec's *Judicial Code of Ethics* on several occasions. In doing so she received a number of reprimands from the Quebec Judicial Council. The Court of Appeal considered these incidents and Ms. Ruffo's reactions to them when determining an appropriate sanction in this case.

The particular complaint that gave rise to these proceedings was over Ms. Ruffo's relationship with an expert witness. The complainant alleged, and the court affirmed, that Ms. Ruffo was friends with an expert witness, a psychologist named Claire Jodoin, whom she knew was going to testify at a trial Ms. Ruffo was hearing. Even so, Ms. Ruffo did not inform the parties of her friendship with the expert witness.]

. . . . .

REPORT OF THE COURT OF APPEAL

On December 3, 2004, the Minister of Justice asked this Court to hold an inquiry and to submit a report on the conduct of the Honourable Andrée Ruffo, judge of the Court of Quebec. This request was filed pursuant to section 95 of the *Courts of Justice Act* (C.J.A.):

The Government may remove a judge only upon a report of the Court of Appeal made after inquiry at the request of the Minister of Justice.

The request by the Minister of Justice followed upon the recommendation of the Conseil de la magistrature du Québec (the Conseil), whose Committee of Inquiry found that Judge Ruffo is no longer able faithfully to carry out her functions as a judge of the Court of Quebec because her conduct is [TRANSLATION] "manifestly and totally contrary to the impartiality, integrity and independence of the judiciary, and undermines the confidence of individuals appearing before her or of the public in its justice system".

Since her appointment to the bench in 1986, Judge Ruffo has demonstrated an interest in children's rights.

The complaints against her are unrelated to such matters. Rather, they relate to judicial ethics. Did she breach her obligations as set out in the *Judicial code of ethics* (*Code of ethics*)? If so, do these breaches justify recommending her removal?

This report is essentially an assessment of Judge Ruffo's conduct in light of the *Code of Ethics* with a view to determining the most adequate recommendation in the circumstances. ...

[The Court then reiterated the provisions of Quebec's *Judicial Code of Ethics*.]

. . . . .

B.   RECOMMENDATION OF THE CONSEIL DE LA MAGISTRATURE

. . . . .

The Committee of Inquiry concluded its report by stating that the breaches of the *Code of Ethics* it found in its study of Ms. Sonia Gilbert's complaint are significant, that the allegations against her are serious, and that past appeals to Judge Ruffo to change her behaviour had been urgent. In its opinion, Judge Ruffo's prior record in ethical matters, her behaviour in the present case, and her public comments on March 29, 2004 all demonstrate that she does not wish to change or that she is incapable of doing so and that a reprimand is clearly no longer an appropriate, credible or effective measure.

. . . . .

At its meeting on November 17, 2004, the Conseil acknowledged the Committee of Inquiry's report and, on November 18, 2004, recommended that the Minister of Justice present a request to the Court of Appeal pursuant to section 95 of the C.J.A.

C.   LEGAL FRAMEWORK OF THE MANDATE OF THE COURT OF APPEAL

. . . . .

The public's confidence in its justice system, which every judge must strive to preserve, is at the very heart of the present inquiry and must dictate the Court's final conclusion. Therefore, to borrow the terms used by Justice Gonthier in *Therrien*, it is necessary to determine whether the conduct at the origin of the complaints against Judge Ruffo "is so manifestly and totally contrary to the impartiality, integrity and independence of the judiciary that the confidence of individuals appearing before the judge, or of the public in its justice system, would be undermined, rendering the judge incapable of performing the duties of [her] office". If this is the case, the only possible recommendation to the Minister of Justice is removal. Indeed, the C.J.A. sets out only two options, a reprimand or a recommendation of removal. ...

. . . . .

E. CONSTITUTIONAL ARGUMENTS

. . . . .

The ethical procedure governing judges of the Court of Quebec has on a number of occasions been carefully analyzed by the Supreme Court and the Quebec courts in light of the principles of judicial independence and the security of tenure of judges. For example, in *Ruffo v. Conseil de la magistrature*, the Supreme Court, affirming the decisions of the Court of Appeal and the Superior Court, held that the structure of the C.J.A., pursuant to which the Conseil receives and deals with complaints against judges, does not undermine judicial independence and that there is no reason to believe that the legislative framework is in itself inherently or inevitably biased.

. . . . .

The procedure contemplated in the C.J.A. strikes a balance between judicial independence and judicial ethics, as it permits the removal of a judge only where the results of a complete inquiry on the facts so justify.

. . . . .

F. ETHICAL DUTIES OF JUDGES

. . . . .

In *Le Regime juridique du pouvoir judiciaire*, Luc Huppe identifies the fundamental elements of the ethical framework outlined by Justice Gonthier in *Therrien*. These are: 1) the judge's commitment to the law; 2) his or her adherence to typically judicial modes of operation and thought; 3) the preservation of his or her impartiality; and 4) the prohibition against using the prestige associated with the judicial function for purposes other than what it is meant to serve.

These fundamental rules, which are the tools used in a disciplinary inquiry to gauge the conduct of a judge who is reproached for acts or speech that threaten the integrity of the judiciary, are the very ones that form the foundation of the *Code of ethics*. This code can accurately be described as a code of values. Such codes do not prescribe precise behaviours to embody the founding values of the practice or the professional relationship, which is why it is difficult to determine, in particular situations where values may clash, what behaviour is unacceptable according to judicial ethics.

The document entitled *Ethical Principles for Judges*, published in 1998 by the Canadian Judicial Council, may be useful when examining the contours of the behavioural standards applicable to judges. It makes recommendations to help judges find answers to thorny ethical questions they may come up against, while also fostering a better understanding of the role of judges in society.

This document sets out five fundamental values associated with the judicial function, which are the very same values articulated in the form of mandatory rules in the *Code of ethics*. The document prepared by the CJC, however, has the advantage of setting out concrete principles of application for each of the values. These are worth reviewing here. The principles linked to *judicial independence* urge judges to follow high standards of conduct and to shelter the performance of their duties from any outside influence. Judicial independence does not constitute a free pass or the immunity to say anything without discernment or moderation. The concept of judicial independence is the foundation of judicial impartiality and is a constitutional right to the benefit of every citizen. It is therefore not a right that belongs personally to the judge. It is only by following these very elevated standards of conduct that judges may preserve their own independence and warrant the confidence of the public upon which respect for their decisions rests. As for *integrity*, judges are urged to behave in a manner that is above reproach in the view of a reasonable, fair-minded and informed person. The obligation of *diligence* implies that judges should take measures to perform their duties with reasonable promptness and that they should maintain and enhance the knowledge, skills and personal qualities necessary for the judicial office. Regarding *equality*, the document recommends that judges strive to be aware of differences arising from gender, race, religious conviction, ethnic background, sexual orientation or physical or intellectual disability. Finally, principles relating to *impartiality* address primarily the way in which judges should conduct their personal affairs and participate in public activities so as to minimize the possibility of conflict of interest and, therefore, of recusation.

.....

The reconciliation both inside and outside the courtroom of the principle of impartiality and the respect for the values of judicial independence and integrity raises the important question of the scope of the duty of judges to act in a reserved manner and the limits they must accept on their freedom of expression.

.....

For judges, then, the implementation of the right to freedom of expression, which is recognized for all citizens, requires it to be reconciled with and, as needed, prioritized in relation to the constitutional right to judicial independence and the institutional protection of the judiciary as a whole. This arises from the fact that the integrity of the judiciary includes both values, which may sometimes be in conflict.

The freedom of expression of judges in the performance of their duties is an essential attribute of judicial independence. The judges must be free to render judgment without any manner of external pressure or influence whatsoever, and they must be perceived to be so.

Protecting the integrity of the judiciary may, however, justify certain restrictions on the right of judges to express themselves freely in the performance of their duties. Inevitably, there are cases where their acts and words are called into question because they sow doubt regarding the integrity of the judicial function. Through the disciplinary process, which permits inquiries concerning judges, judges may be reprimanded or their removal recommended if their conduct is likely to threaten the integrity of the judiciary as a whole.

Judges who express themselves outside of the courtroom must also be aware of the risks arising from the problem of identifying potentially conflicting values and the interrelationship between them. The institutional protection of the judiciary and compliance with a guarantee of genuine judicial independence ... requires that the comments of judges not undermine public confidence in their impartiality by creating a reasonable apprehension that they do not feel "free to entertain and act upon different points of view with an open mind".

Drawing particular inspiration from the *Ethical Principles for Judges*, it is appropriate to set out certain concrete propositions that, in the view of the Court, permit a harmonious reconciliation of judicial integrity and the freedom of expression of judges outside the courtroom. In principle, then, and insofar as the active role of judges does not undermine the appearance of impartiality or give rise to an excessive number of recusations, the following activities are permitted:

- taking part in continuing professional development programs for legal professionals and judges and in activities aimed at improving the public understanding of the law and legal proceedings;

- defending judicial independence;

- making observations, in an appropriate forum, on certain ill-defined points of law or insufficiencies of the law, while refraining from giving an opinion on the legality or constitutional validity of a bill or an act and from giving the impression of participating in the activities of lobby groups;

- denouncing, in an appropriate forum, gaps in the administration of justice when they are directly related to the proper functioning of the court and to the execution of its orders;

- participating in civic, charitable or religious activities, provided that their goal is not the economic or political profit of their members and that they do not risk impeding the performance or dignity of the judicial function.

By contrast, the following instances of public speech and behaviour seem to be irreconcilable with the institutional protection to be afforded the judiciary as a whole:

- a judge commenting on his or her own decisions, except when the judge attempts to share opinions with the public regarding his or her role, without discussing the merits of the decision;

- refusing to accept an ethical sanction, except to exercise the right to legally contest it;

- being a member of associations whose activities risk hindering the performance or dignity of judicial functions;

- engaging in public fund-raising;

- being a member of a political organization;

- participating in a public debate on controversial subjects, except those that directly concern the functioning of the courts, judicial independence or fundamental elements of the administration of justice;

- signing petitions that aim to influence a political decision;

- making vexatious remarks regarding the behaviour of persons appearing before the court.

Generally speaking, any public statement made outside the context of a hearing must be examined in light of certain factors, including the manner in which the statement was made, the fervency of the judge's intervention, its appropriateness at the time, the forum selected, and the degree of visibility. In matters of freedom of expression, it is all a question of degree, and a judge must exercise great restraint in all circumstances.

· · · · ·

[The court recommended to the government that Ruffo J. be removed from office. In making this decision, the court echoed the conclusion of the Committee of Inquiry and Conseil in the Quebec Judicial Council, which found that Ruffo J.'s behaviour was manifestly and totally contrary to the impartiality, integrity and independence of the judiciary and undermined the confidence of the public in its justice system. As a result, her ability to perform judicial functions as a judge of the Court of Quebec ceased.

Of importance in the conclusion is that the court lauded Ruffo J.'s concern with and efforts at defending children and their rights. Still, the court was emphatic in stating that no cause can override or justify a breach of judicial obligations and professional conduct. Tied to this, the court asserted that a judge's conduct must project, above all else, an image of impartiality. In practice this means avoiding controversy and conduct that may vitiate that image.]

PART THREE: CONCLUSION

The Conseil found that Judge Ruffo should be removed because, according to the conclusions of the Committee of Inquiry, she could no longer usefully perform her functions as a judge of the Court of Quebec, as her behaviour was manifestly and totally contrary to the impartiality, integrity and independence of the judiciary and undermined the confidence of the public in its justice system.

After carrying out its inquiry, the Court finds itself obliged to reach the same conclusion and recommend to the Government that Judge Ruffo be removed.

. . . . .

Care must be taken not to confuse the cause that Judge Ruffo has been defending on all platforms for nearly 20 years now and her record in matters of professional conduct as a judge of the Court of Quebec. The first, however laudable and popular it may be, cannot overshadow or still less justify or excuse the second.

. . . . .

Respect for and confidence in the judicial task and the correlative duty to act in a reserved manner demand that judges remain apart from any turmoil or controversy that is likely to taint the image of impartiality that their conduct must project.

In short, Judge Ruffo could have supported the cause of children while conscientiously carrying out her functions as a judge. The two are not mutually incompatible goals; indeed, far from it. Doing so, however, would have required her to carry out her judicial tasks with discrimination and skill.

Since her appointment to the bench, Judge Ruffo has broken a number of rules set out in the *Code of Ethics*, sometimes repeatedly ...

. . . . .

Each of these ethical breaches constitutes a breach of one of the four fundamental elements of the ethical framework described above.

Taken in isolation, these ethical breaches are serious and justify the reprimands that the Conseil de la magistrature has imposed on Judge Ruffo over the years. Taken together, they constitute an aggravating factor that must be taken into consideration.

. . . . .

Judge Ruffo's attitude toward the disciplinary process cannot be ignored.

. . . . .

Judge Ruffo seems unable to accept the rules of the disciplinary process. Reprimands have had no effect on her behaviour. Apart from one occasion when she was obliged to recuse herself following her comments on a case that was before her, Judge Ruffo has never expressed any regret for her actions that have earned her reprimand after reprimand from the Conseil. On the contrary.

A few weeks after being reprimanded by the Conseil for having made orders that deliberately breached her duty to "render justice within the framework of the law", Judge Ruffo once again affirmed her intention to continue to render only the decisions she deemed acceptable, regardless of their legality.

Nearly fifteen years later, Judge Ruffo still has not mended her ways. In the television interviews she gave in March 2004 during the Conseil's inquiry into the Gilbert complaint, she mocked the complaint against her even though the allegations were serious, as we have seen. She also ridiculed the reprimand she received following the television advertisement for a railroad company in which she had allowed her name and title to be used. ...

Like the Conseil de la magistrature, therefore, the Court finds that the conduct for which Judge Ruffo has been reproached for nearly 20 years now is "so manifestly and so totally violates the impartiality, integrity and independence of the judiciary, that it undermines the confidence of individuals appearing before [her], or of the public in its justice system, and renders [her] incapable of performing the duties of [her] office".

THEREFORE, THE COURT:

Recommends to the government that the Honourable Judge Ruffo be removed from her functions as Judge of the Court of Quebec.

NOTES AND QUESTIONS

1. Is the "public perception/public confidence" test the same as the "fully informed reasonable person" test? If it is not, which is the better test? Why?

2. When you read this case, is your sense that this case is primarily about Ruffo J.'s relationship with the psychologist, or is it motivated by a broader concern about how she is fulfilling her judicial responsibilities?

3. If you were a lawyer who represented a father accused of sexually assaulting his daughter, would you have asked Ruffo J. to recuse herself from the case?

4. Sometimes judges make decisions that receive very strong, sometimes mistaken, responses from the general public and the media. Because a judge is functus after she issues her reasons for her decision, the judge cannot respond to such criticisms. Is there any obligation on a lawyer, and in particular the lawyers in the case, to address these criticisms? See Commentary to Rule 4.06(1) of the FLSC's *Model Code*.

Scenario Six

Assume you are a lawyer taking a case to the Court of Appeal in your province. The firm representing the other side has recently hired a former Court of Appeal judge who, three years ago, sat on a Panel which issued the leading precedent on the matter in dispute. Does this raise any concerns for you? Would it make a difference if the prior decision had been unanimous? Was it a majority decision, with the retired judge writing for the majority? Was the judge who wrote the dissenting decision? Would it make a difference if that retired judge argues the case before her former colleagues?

E. INTEGRITY

The third principle of judicial ethics is Integrity.

Statement:

Judges should strive to conduct themselves with integrity so as to sustain and enhance public confidence in the judiciary.

Principles:

1. Judges should make every effort to ensure that their conduct is above reproach in the view of reasonable, fair minded and informed persons.

2. Judges, in addition to observing this high standard personally, should encourage and support its observance by their judicial colleagues.

NOTES AND QUESTIONS

1. In Chapter 1 of this book we discussed the importance of a lawyer's obligation to act with integrity. This is reinforced by Rule 1 of the *Model Code*, which also imposes an obligation to act with integrity. Are there any similarities or differences in the meaning and purposes of integrity as used in these governing documents?

2. Re-read *Ruffo*. Do you think that Ruffo J. was acting with integrity? How helpful is the "reasonable, fair-minded and informed person" standard as a test to determine if someone lacks integrity?

3. Media reports from the period indicate that Ruffo J. was very popular with the general public because of her outspoken ways and defence of vulnerable children. Should this be relevant for the Court of Appeal in deciding whether to recommend her removal from the bench?

Scenario Seven

When a lawyer is appointed to the bench, her membership with the law society is held in abeyance while she is a judge. If she wants to return to practice after ceasing to be a judge, she must apply to the law society to have her membership and her licence to practise law restored.

Justice Jones was appointed to the Provincial Court of British Columbia in 1999. Between 2006 and 2008, the Judicial Council launched complaints about Mr. Jones' behaviour on the bench. The complaints centred on improper sexual touching and inappropriate remarks made by Mr. Jones. In 2008, Mr. Jones was also charged with sexual assault. He was later acquitted. The same year, the Judicial Council issued its decision. It concluded that Mr. Jones engaged in misconduct. Before the Judicial Council was able to issue a penalty, Mr. Jones resigned from the bench.[10]

Less than two months later, Mr. Jones applied to the Law Society to have his membership as a lawyer in the law society restored. A restoration hearing has

---

[10]   See *Law Society of Upper Canada v. Evans*, [2007] L.S.D.D. No. 27 (L.S.U.C.).

been set up and proceedings commenced. Should the law society restore Mr. Jones' licence to practise law? The factors for consideration of restoration of one's licence are similar to the "good character" requirements discussed in Chapter 13.

Scenario Eight

You are Crown counsel in a highly publicized murder trial. The trial is by jury and has been going on for a number of months at considerable financial and emotional cost to taxpayers and the parties involved. Suddenly, the trial judge recuses herself from the case. In explaining her decision, the trial judge simply states that she considered the matter with care and was fully aware of the consequences of her decisions. She also indicates that she will retire. With that, she directs the case to be adjourned in order for an alternative judge to preside over the case.

What will you do? Were the judge's actions acceptable? Should she have done more? If so, what? Do you anticipate any disciplinary action against the trial judge? If so, of what nature? What do you think should happen to the trial judge and why? Does it matter that this was a trial by jury? What if it were only a trial by judge?

An alternative judge takes over and quickly decides not to resume the trial. A month later, you appear in court in an unrelated case. Arriving at court, you notice the trial judge is the same one who recused herself from the murder trial. Contrary to her earlier suggestion, the trial judge has resumed her judicial duties. What will you do?[11]

Scenario Nine

You are acting as the Crown in a spousal murder case. The details of the case are grave. The trial was emotionally exhausting for the victim's family. The trial ends in a first-degree murder conviction of the husband. When the judge releases his decision, you read the following:

> A scream from the victim: an emission of agony. A knife with blood and prints: an admission of guilt. September 24, 2010. At dusk, with the light dimming in the sky and on her life, Mrs. Smith came home from work. A 12-hour shift. Exhausted. As she entered the kitchen what she didn't expect was exactly what Mr. Smith had planned. A hand brandishing a blade. An arm set on auto-stab. A heart pierced. Fatally. The end of a marriage. The end of a life.

---

[11]   Canadian Judicial Council, Past News Releases, *Report of the Canadian Judicial Council to the Minister of Justice of Canada Under ss. 65(1) of the Judges Act concerning Mr. Justice Jean-Guy Boilard of the Superior Court of Quebec* (2003), online: <http://www.cjc-ccm.gc.ca/cmslib/general/conduct_inq_boilard_ReportIC_200312_en.pdf>.

What are your thoughts on how this decision was written? As a representative of the victim's family, how would you react? To whom or to what institutions would you file a complaint, if you had one?[12]

Scenario Ten

You are a practising lawyer. Twenty years ago, when you first entered law school you became best friends with Pat. Throughout law school you both worked hard and played hard, including smoking marijuana on a relatively frequent basis. Your friendship has continued over the years and once a month you and Pat continue to meet socially, usually at each other's houses or cottages. More often than not you both have a joint or two at these get-togethers. Six months ago, Pat was appointed to the Federal Court. Pat continues to smoke marijuana when you get together. Does this raise any ethical issues? What options, or responsibilities, do you have? Would your analysis be different if Pat was using cocaine?

Scenario Eleven

Justice Al has been a member of the Ben Beag golf club for 25 years. This club excludes from its membership GLBT persons. Despite pressure from his peers, Justice Al refuses to resign from the club, arguing that for the last 10 years he has pleaded with the Board to change its policy and he has sponsored a leading gay activist for membership. He admits that both these efforts have failed, but he claims he will continue to "fight from within". Furthermore, Justice Al has supported the work of EGALE for the last 10 years by speaking at conferences and fundraisers. You are counsel for EGALE in a case that has been assigned to Justice Al. EGALE Board policy is to oppose discriminatory clubs and to seek recusal of all judges who belong to such clubs. What do you do?

Scenario Twelve

Judge Bob loves the street he lives on. The municipal transit authority has recently decided to build a station at the end of this street. All the residents are opposed to the project, including Judge Bob. At a community meeting, Judge Bob agrees to take a leadership role in protesting the development project. Judge Bob writes letters to the municipal council, the Attorney General, the local newspaper and makes several media appearances.

You are a lawyer representing the transit authority in litigation involving a different development project. When you arrive in court, you discover that

Judge Bob is the assigned judge. Identify the challenges that this creates for you. What do you do?[13]

F. DILIGENCE

Diligence is the fourth of the ethical principles for judges:

Statement:

Judges should be diligent in the performance of their judicial duties.

Principles:

1. Judges should devote their professional activity to judicial duties broadly defined, which include not only presiding in court and making decisions, but other judicial tasks essential to the court's operation.

2. Judges should take reasonable steps to maintain and enhance the knowledge, skills and personal qualities necessary for judicial office.

3. Judges should endeavour to perform all judicial duties, including the delivery of reserved judgments, with reasonable promptness.

4. Judges should not engage in conduct incompatible with the diligent discharge of judicial duties or condone such conduct in colleagues.

Judging can be a burdensome, even tiresome, job. Occasionally, a judge might fall asleep during the course of a trial. What do you do if you are one of the lawyers appearing in front of a judge who falls asleep? Given your duty of loyalty to your client, would it make a difference if the judge is sleeping during the arguments of opposing counsel, but not your arguments? Consider the following case.

LEADER MEDIA PRODUCTIONS LTD. v. SENTINEL HILL ALLIANCE ATLANTIS EQUICAP LIMITED PARTNERSHIP

[2008] O.J. No. 2284, 90 O.R. (3d) 561 (Ont. C.A.),
leave to appeal refused [2008] S.C.C.A. No. 394 (S.C.C.)
(Ont. C.A., M. Rosenberg, J.L. MacFarland and D. Watt JJ.A.)

[The trial concerned a contractual dispute between two businesses. There was an appeal. The appellant claimed there was new evidence to suggest the trial judge did not follow substantial portions of the trial. Specifically, the appellant claimed the trial judge fell asleep throughout the course of the trial. The court went on to discuss how the allegations impacted and were relevant to a trial.]

J.L. MacFARLAND J.A.:—

. . . . .

---

[13] Canadian Judicial Council, Inquiry Committee Decision, *Proceedings and reports regarding Mr. Justice Theodore Matlow of the Ontario Superior Court of Justice* (December 2008), online: <http://www.cjc-ccm.gc.ca/cmslib/general/CJC_20080528.pdf>.

3.   Trial Judge's Inability to Follow the Evidence (Fresh Evidence Application)

The appellants have moved in this court to admit fresh affidavit evidence showing that the trial judge was unable to follow the evidence because he fell asleep repeatedly during the trial. The fresh evidence consists of five affidavits authored by appellants' trial counsel and others. These affidavits suggest the trial judge fell asleep frequently, but for only very brief periods of time.

. . . . .

Despite the respondent's argument, I would admit the fresh evidence because it relates to the validity of the trial process. ...

. . . . .

However, even where the fresh evidence is admissible, on the particular facts of this case, in my view, it does not assist the appellants.

At trial, the appellants deliberately did not raise with the trial judge their concern that he might have been sleeping. Instead they made a deliberate tactical decision to in effect – as respondent's counsel put it – "hedge their bets". Instead of confronting the trial judge, after discussions among appellants' counsel (including a senior litigator at the firm who remained at the office and was not directly involved in the trial *per se*), they made a deliberate decision not to raise the issue. As Mr. Bradley Sherman put it in his affidavit, they decided to "wait and see how things played out". Presumably, if the trial result was in their favour they would do nothing; if not, they would have this additional evidence to use as a basis for appeal arguing that they were denied the right to a fair trial.

Even after the reasons for judgment were released, the appellants did not base their motion for a mistrial on the drowsiness of the trial judge nor did they even raise the issue. The mistrial motion was based solely on the fact that the appellants had been denied the opportunity to make oral argument in addition to written argument. Only in this court, for the first time, is the issue raised that the trial judge was inattentive to the evidence.

There appears to be little case law on point. In fact, the parties have only drawn the court's attention to two similar cases. The first is a case decided by the Australian Queensland Court of Appeal. The second is a recent decision from the Alberta Court of Appeal which was only released several weeks after this appeal was argued.

In the Queensland Court of Appeal case, *Stathooles v. Mount Mines Limited*, ... the allegations were that the trial judge had dozed off or slept during part of the evidence. In making its decision, the court stressed the fact that the alleged drowsiness was not raised with the trial judge at any time during the trial, and dismissed the appeal. Macrossan C.J. noted ...:

> A broad discretion does exist for an appellate court to order a new trial in civil cases where a first trial has been unfair ... In civil, as in criminal cases, the discretion can be exercised when the first trial has resulted in a miscarriage of justice.

...

The exercise of the discretion to order a new trial on the basis that a miscarriage of justice has occurred may require a wide view to be taken of the circumstances but it is necessary to remember that our adversarial system requires parties to proceedings to accept responsibility for their own actions deliberately and consciously taken. Decisions taken by parties with a full awareness of relevant matters can strongly influence the way in which the discretion in cases of an alleged miscarriage of justice will be exercised.

Macrossan C.J. then went on to quote from a joint judgment of the High Court of Australia in the case of *Vakauta v. Kelly* ...:

[A] party who has legal representation is not entitled to stand by until the contents of the final judgment are known and then, if those contents prove unpalatable, attack the judgment on the ground that, by reason of those earlier comments, there has been a failure to observe the requirement of the appearance of impartial judgment. By standing by, such a party has waived the right subsequently to object. The reason why that is so is obvious. In such a case, if clear objection had been taken to the comments at the time when they were made or the judge had then been asked to refrain from further hearing the matter, the judge may have been able to correct the wrong impression of bias which had been given or alternatively may have refrained from further hearing. It would be unfair and wrong if failure to object until the contents of the final judgment were known were to give the party in default the advantage of an effective choice between acceptance and rejection of the judgment and to subject the other party to a situation in which it was likely that the judgment would be allowed to stand only if it proved to be unfavourable to him or her.

The appellant's argument in *Stathooles* was that the determination of the case turned on the credibility of witnesses and that the judge had been especially inattentive during the cross-examination of Stathooles, yet made a finding adverse to him. It was argued that the conclusion may have been different had there been no failure on the part of the trial judge to observe and listen to that witness throughout his testimony, in reaching a conclusion, Macrossan C.J. noted:

The lack of reaction here by counsel fully aware of the situation is of importance from a different point of view. It cannot be accepted that there is an entitlement to do nothing at the time, hold the point in reserve until the decision is given and then, since it has proved to be adverse to the appellants, seek to set it aside.

...

In the present case, if what is alleged to have occurred is sufficient to constitute a significant defect in the proceedings, it should have been drawn to the attention of the trial judge at the time it occurred. To experienced counsel there should have been no difficulty other than perhaps some slight embarrassment in being required to draw the judge's attention to the concern that was felt that he may be missing an important feature of the evidence. Experienced professional advocates may be called on to display conduct which will need to be more robust than that in their day to day practice in the courts. There should have been no fear that what needed to be done could not have been handled with the customary courtesy that should, and usually does, prevail between judge and counsel in the hearing of cases.

The second case, *R. v. Chan*, ... was only released by the Alberta Court of Appeal after this appeal was heard. In this case, during the sentencing hearing, court staff noticed that the trial judge appeared to be sleeping during the appellant's testimony. The judge was awakened and adjourned the proceedings. The appellant then applied for a mistrial.

During argument on the mistrial, the trial judge advised that he had fallen asleep because of a medical condition. The appellant then filed an affidavit alleging that the trial judge's posture while sleeping was the same as it had been during critical points of the trial. The trial judge refused to grant a mistrial, stating that lawyers are obligated to raise inattentiveness in a judge when they notice it. He directed another judge to deal with sentencing. The appellant appealed.

Although the Court of Appeal ultimately allowed the appeal on other grounds, it rejected the appellant's inattentiveness argument for the same reasons discussed above. Speaking for the court, Ritter J.A. stated:

> [19] We conclude that Nicholas has failed to demonstrate that he suffered prejudice at the trial stage of these proceedings. The trial judge fell asleep during the testimony at the sentencing stage of the trial, several months after all evidence relating to Nicholas' guilt had been adduced. An accused person must, at a minimum, show a real danger of prejudice before judicial inattentiveness, that is sleeping, will call for the results of his trial to be set aside. In this case, Nicholas' affidavit accomplishes, at most, speculation that the trial judge's similar posture during the trial must mean he was asleep.

> [20] Nicholas' affidavit does not identify exactly when he noticed this posture, so it is impossible to determine whether any crucial issues were being dealt with at the time. Moreover, it is incumbent upon counsel to immediately draw a trial judge's inattentiveness to his attention, so as to permit replacement testimony or other corrective procedures during the course of the trial. It is not enough, nor is it appropriate, to note the inattentive episode and then hold it on reserve in the event the result at trial was less than what is hoped for. We do not suggest that is what occurred here, but the effect is the same, whether the withholding of the concern was advertent or inadvertent.

In my view, the same reasoning must apply here. While appellants' trial counsel was not experienced (this was her first trial), the record discloses that she did consult with senior litigation counsel in her firm about the judge's inattention. Together they made the decision to do nothing about it at the time but to, as respondent's counsel put it, "roll the dice".

Counsel was obliged to bring the trial judge's inattention home to him at the time. Not having done so, and having decided to wait and see what happened, they cannot now raise that inattention for the first time as a ground of appeal on either a substantive or contextual basis. I would dismiss this ground of appeal.

In the result, I would dismiss the appeal.

. . . . .

NOTES AND QUESTIONS

1.   In light of the fact that a lawyer has a responsibility to "bring the judge's inattention home to him" at the moment it is happening, describe exactly how you would go about fulfilling this responsibility? What sort of responses might your approach elicit from the inattentive judge? Does your answer change if you are a second-year associate or a senior partner? Does your answer depend upon whether the judge appeared distracted or sleepy or whether the judge was clearly asleep (*e.g.*, snoring)?

Scenario Thirteen

Assume you are a lawyer representing a client and the other party is self-represented. When the judge issues her written decision, your client wins and the judge substantially reproduces 80 per cent of your written arguments as part of her reasons for decision. Do you have any ethical obligations?[14]

Scenario Fourteen

In the course of your work as a law clerk, you interact with Justice Jones on a regular basis. Recently, you have noticed that he has become forgetful and confused. He frequently forgets your name and sometimes calls you by the wrong name. He never used to do this before. At times when you are discussing cases or issues with him, he seems to get lost and refer to wrong information. You are supporting Justice Jones in work on a bench-bar committee and attend the meeting of the committee. At one point, Justice Jones appears to be distracted and says something that is completely irrelevant. You notice that some of the lawyers on the committee appear quite concerned. Several days later, you receive a phone call from your friend Lois who is a reporter with the *Thunder Bay Telegram*. Lois tells you that a colleague of hers is writing a story about recent actions of Justice Jones in court that may indicate that he has some condition that might impact his ability to do his job. Lois tells you that that she is not asking you to provide any information. All she is asking you is to tell her if her colleague is way off base to spare the paper, and the judge, potential embarrassment. Lois assures you that she won't tell anyone about your conversation. You completely trust Lois as you grew up together in Smallville. What do you tell Lois? What are your responsibilities? What should you do about Justice Jones?

---

14   See also *Cojocaru (Guardian ad litem) v. British Columbia Women's Hospital and Health Center*, [2011] B.C.J. No. 680, 2011 BCCA 192 (B.C.C.A.), leave to appeal granted [2011] S.C.C.A. No. 253 (S.C.C.).

G. EQUALITY

Equality is the fifth of the ethical principles for judges.

Statement:

Judges should conduct themselves and proceedings before them so as to assure equality according to law.

Principles:

1. Judges should carry out their duties with appropriate consideration for all persons (for example, parties, witnesses, court personnel and judicial colleagues) without discrimination.

2. Judges should strive to be aware of and understand differences arising from, for example, gender, race, religious conviction, culture, ethnic background, sexual orientation or disability.

3. Judges should avoid membership in any organization that they know currently practices any form of discrimination that contravenes law.

4. Judges, in the course of proceedings before them, should disassociate themselves from and disapprove of clearly irrelevant comments or conduct by court staff, counsel or any other person subject to the judge's discretion which are sexist, racist or otherwise demonstrate discrimination on grounds prohibited by law.

Do you believe that the Quebec Court of Appeal gave sufficient weight to the equality of rights of children in the *Ruffo* case?

Equality according to law is, undoubtedly, a social good. But what is the relationship between equality and impartiality? Sometimes equality and impartiality are seen to be mutually supporting, at other times they are seen to be in tension. The Supreme Court of Canada has addressed this issue in the following case.

R. v. R.D.S.

[1997] S.C.J. No. 84, [1997] 3 S.C.R. 484
(S.C.C., Lamer C.J.C. and La Forest, L'Heureux-Dubé, Sopinka, Gonthier, Cory, McLachlin, Iacobucci and Major JJ.)

[Justice Sparks heard the case at trial. There were two witnesses: the accused, R.D.S., and the arresting constable. Justice Sparks found R.D.S.'s testimony to be more honest and accurate than the constable's. This finding raised a reasonable doubt about what happened and led to R.D.S. being acquitted. When Sparks J. provided her oral reasons, she noted:

The Crown says, well, why would the officer say that events occurred the way in which he has relayed them to the Court this morning. I am not saying that the Constable has misled the court, although police officers have been known to do that in the past. I am not saying that the officer overreacted, but certainly police officers do overreact, particularly when they are dealing with non-white groups. That to me indicates a state of mind right there that is questionable. I believe that probably the situation in this particular case is the case of a young police officer who overreacted. I do accept the evidence of [R.D.S.] that he was told to shut up or he would be under arrest. It seems to be in keeping with the prevalent attitude of the day.

These comments formed the basis of subsequent appeals, which focused on whether or not Sparks J.'s remarks raised a reasonable apprehension of bias.

At the Nova Scotia Supreme Court (Trial Division) (see [1995] N.S.J. No. 184), Glube C.J.S.C. held the comments were made without evidence. This led her to determine that, based on what a reasonable, right-minded person with knowledge of the facts would conclude, Sparks J.'s remarks gave rise to a reasonable apprehension of bias. In a 2-1 decision the majority at the Nova Scotia Court of Appeal agreed with both the test Glube C.J.S.C. applied and her conclusions. They dismissed the appeal. The dissent did not find a reasonable apprehension of bias and would have allowed the appeal.

At the Supreme Court of Canada, six of the nine judges found in favour of the appellant. There was, however, a plurality of reasons. Chief Justice Lamer, Sopinka and Major JJ. dissented although relying on the same approach as Cory and Iacobucci JJ., who would have allowed the appeal. Justices L'Heureux-Dubé and McLachlin, with concurrence from Gonthier and La Forest JJ., applied a different approach although also allowing the appeal.]

The reasons of Lamer C.J.C. and Sopinka and Major JJ. were delivered by

MAJOR J. (dissenting):— I have read the reasons of Justices L'Heureux-Dubé and McLachlin and those of Justice Cory and respectfully disagree with the conclusion they reach.

. . . . .

… In spite of the submissions of the appellant and interveners on his behalf, the case is primarily about the conduct of the trial. A fair trial is one that is based on the law, the outcome of which is determined by the evidence, free of bias, real or apprehended. Did the trial judge here reach her decision on the evidence presented at the trial or did she rely on something else?

. . . . .

In view of the manner in which this appeal was argued, it is necessary to consider two points. First, we should consider whether the trial judge in her reasons, properly instructed herself on the evidence or was an error of law committed by her. The second, and somewhat intertwined question, is whether her comments above could cause a reasonable observer to apprehend bias. The offending comments in the statement are:

(i)   "police officers have been known to [mislead the court] in the past";

(ii)   "police officers do overreact, particularly when they are dealing with non-white groups";

(iii) "[t]hat to me indicates a state of mind right there that is question-able";

(iv)   "[i]t seems to be in keeping with the prevalent attitude of the day"; and,

(v)   "based upon my comments and based upon all the evidence before the court I have no other choice but to acquit."

. . . . .

In addition to not being based on the evidence, the trial judge's comments have been challenged as giving rise to a reasonable apprehension of bias. ...

. . . . .

The life experience of this trial judge, as with all trial judges, is an important ingredient in the ability to understand human behaviour, to weigh the evidence, and to determine credibility. ... It is of no value, however, in reaching conclusions for which there is no evidence. ... There was no evidence before the trial judge to support the conclusions she reached.

The trial judge could not decide this case based on what some police officers did in the past without deciding that all police officers are the same. As stated, the appellant was entitled to call evidence of the police officer's conduct to show that there was in fact evidence to support either his bias or racism. No such evidence was called. The trial judge presumably called upon her life experience to decide the issue. This she was not entitled to do.

. . . . .

In my opinion the comments of the trial judge fall into stereotyping the police officer. She said, among other things, that police officers have been known to mislead the courts, and that police officers overreact when dealing with non-white groups. She then held, in her evaluation of this particular police officer's evidence, that these factors led her to "a state of mind right there that is questionable". The trial judge erred in law by failing to base her conclusions on evidence.

. . . . .

The following are the reasons delivered by

L'HEUREUX-DUBÉ and McLACHLIN JJ.:—

I.   Introduction

. . . . .

We endorse Cory J.'s comments on judging in a multicultural society, the importance of perspective and social context in judicial decision-making, and the presumption of judicial integrity. However, we approach the test for reasonable apprehension of bias and its application to the case at bar somewhat differently from our colleague.

In our view, the test for reasonable apprehension of bias established in the jurisprudence is reflective of the reality that while judges can never be neutral, in the sense of purely objective, they can and must strive for impartiality. It therefore recognizes as inevitable and appropriate that the differing experiences of judges assist them in their decision-making process and will be reflected in their judgments, so long as those experiences are relevant to the cases, are not based on inappropriate stereotypes, and do not prevent a fair and just determination of the cases based on the facts in evidence.

We find that on the basis of these principles, there is no reasonable apprehension of bias in the case at bar. ... [W]e disagree with Cory J.'s position that the comments of Judge Sparks were unfortunate, unnecessary, or close to the line. Rather, we find them to reflect an entirely appropriate recognition of the facts in evidence in this case and of the context within which this case arose – a context known to Judge Sparks and to any well-informed member of the community.

II.   The Test for Reasonable Apprehension of Bias

The test for reasonable apprehension of bias is that set out by de Grandpré J. in *Committee for Justice and Liberty v. National Energy Board* ... Though he wrote dissenting reasons, de Grandpré J.'s articulation of the test for bias was adopted by the majority of the Court, and has been consistently endorsed by this Court in the intervening two decades ... De Grandpré J. stated ...:

> ... the apprehension of bias must be a reasonable one, held by reasonable and right-minded persons, applying themselves to the question and obtaining thereon the required information ... [T]hat test is "what would an informed person, viewing the matter realistically and practically – and having thought the matter through – conclude. Would he think that it is more likely than not that [the decision-maker], whether consciously or unconsciously, would not decide fairly."
>
> The grounds for this apprehension must, however, be substantial and I ... refus[e] to accept the suggestion that the test be related to the "very sensitive or scrupulous conscience".

... The presumption of impartiality carries considerable weight, for as Blackstone opined at p. 361 in Commentaries on the Laws of England, Book III ..., "the law will not suppose a possibility of bias or favour in a judge, who is already sworn to administer impartial justice, and whose authority greatly depends upon that presumption and idea". Thus, reviewing courts have been hesitant to make a finding of bias or to perceive a reasonable apprehension of bias on the part of a judge, in the absence of convincing evidence to that effect ...

Notwithstanding the strong presumption of impartiality that applies to judges, they will nevertheless be held to certain stringent standards regarding bias – "a reasonable apprehension that the judge might not act in an entirely impartial manner is ground for disqualification" ...

In order to apply this test, it is necessary to distinguish between the impartiality which is required of all judges, and the concept of judicial neutrality. ...

. . . . .

... As the Canadian Judicial Council noted in *Commentaries on Judicial Conduct* ... "[t]here is no human being who is not the product of every social experience, every process of education, and every human contact". What is possible and desirable, they note, is impartiality:

. . . . .

> True impartiality does not require that the judge have no sympathies or opinions; it requires that the judge nevertheless be free to entertain and act upon different points of view with an open mind.

III. The Reasonable Person

The presence or absence of an apprehension of bias is evaluated through the eyes of the reasonable, informed, practical and realistic person who considers the matter in some detail. The person postulated is not a "very sensitive or scrupulous" person, but rather a right-minded person familiar with the circumstances of the case.

It follows that one must consider the reasonable person's knowledge and understanding of the judicial process and the nature of judging as well as of the community in which the alleged crime occurred.

A.   The Nature of Judging

As discussed above, judges in a bilingual, multiracial and multicultural society will undoubtedly approach the task of judging from their varied perspectives. ... The reasonable person does not expect that judges will function as neutral ciphers; however, the reasonable person does demand that judges achieve impartiality in their judging.

. . . . .

At the same time, where the matter is one of identifying and applying the law to the findings of fact, it must be the law that governs and not a judge's individual beliefs that may conflict with the law. Further, notwithstanding that their own insights into human nature will properly play a role in making findings of credibility or factual determinations, judges must make those determinations only after being equally open to, and considering the views of, all parties before them. ...

... There is more to a case than who did what to whom, and the questions of fact and law to be determined in any given case do not arise in a vacuum. Rather, they are the consequence of numerous factors, influenced by the innumerable forces which impact on them in a particular context. Judges, acting as finders of fact, must inquire into those forces. In short, they must be aware of the context in which the alleged crime occurred.

Judicial inquiry into the factual, social and psychological context within which litigation arises is not unusual. Rather, a conscious, contextual inquiry has become an accepted step towards judicial impartiality. In that regard, Professor Jennifer Nedelsky's "Embodied Diversity and the Challenges to Law" ... offers the following comment:

What makes it possible for us to genuinely judge, to move beyond our private idiosyncracies and preferences, is our capacity to achieve an "enlargement of mind". We do this by taking different perspectives into account. This is the path out of the blindness of our subjective private conditions. The more views we are able to take into account, the less likely we are to be locked into one perspective ... It is the capacity for "enlargement of mind" that makes autonomous, impartial judgment possible.

Judicial inquiry into context provides the requisite background for the interpretation and the application of the law. ... [Such an] inquiry provide[s] the Court with a larger picture, which [is] in turn conducive to a more just determination of the case.

An understanding of the context or background essential to judging may be gained from testimony from expert witnesses in order to put the case in context: *R. v. Lavallee* ... from academic studies properly placed before the Court; and from the judge's personal understanding and experience of the society in which the judge lives and works. This process of enlargement is not only consistent with impartiality; it may also be seen as its essential precondition.

A reasonable person far from being troubled by this process would see it as an important aid to judicial impartiality.

B.   The Nature of the Community

The reasonable person ... is an informed and right-minded member of the community, a community which, in Canada, supports the fundamental principles entrenched in the Constitution by the Canadian Charter of Rights and Freedoms. ... The reasonable person must be taken to be aware of the history of discrimination faced by disadvantaged groups in Canadian society protected by the Charter's equality provisions. These are matters of which judicial notice may be taken. ...

The reasonable person is not only a member of the Canadian community, but also, more specifically, is a member of the local communities in which the case at issue arose (in this case, the Nova Scotian and Halifax communities). Such a person must be taken to possess knowledge of the local population and its racial dynamics, including the existence in the community of a history of widespread and systemic discrimination against black and aboriginal people, and high profile clashes between the police and the visible minority population over policing issues ... The reasonable person must thus be deemed to be cognizant of the existence of racism in Halifax, Nova Scotia. It follows that judges may take notice of actual racism known to exist in a particular society. Judges have done so with respect to racism in Nova Scotia. ...

. . . . .

We conclude that the reasonable person contemplated by de Grandpré J., and endorsed by Canadian courts is a person who approaches the question of whether there exists a reasonable apprehension of bias with a complex and contextualized understanding of the issues in the case. The reasonable person understands the impossibility of judicial neutrality, but demands judicial impartiality. The reasonable person is cognizant of the racial dynamics in the local community, and, as a member of the Canadian community, is supportive of the principles of equality.

Before concluding that there exists a reasonable apprehension of bias in the conduct of a judge, the reasonable person would require some clear evidence that the judge in question had improperly used his or her perspective in the decision-making process; this flows from the presumption of impartiality of the judiciary. ... Awareness of the context within which a case occurred would not constitute such evidence; on the contrary, such awareness is consistent with the highest tradition of judicial impartiality.

IV. Application of the Test to the Facts

. . . . .

Judge Sparks was faced with contradictory testimony from the only two witnesses, the appellant R.D.S., and Constable Stienburg. Both testified as to the events that occurred and were subjected to cross-examination. As trier of fact, Judge Sparks was required to assess their testimony, and to determine whether or not, on the evidence before her, she had a reasonable doubt as to the guilt of the appellant R.D.S. It is evident in the transcript that Judge Sparks proceeded to do just that.

. . . . .

While it seems clear that Judge Sparks did not in fact relate the officer's probable overreaction to the race of the appellant R.D.S., it should be noted that if Judge Sparks had chosen to attribute the behaviour of Constable Stienburg to the racial dynamics of the situation, she would not necessarily have erred. As a member of the community, it was open to her to take into account the well-known presence of racism in that community and to evaluate the evidence as to what occurred against that background.

That Judge Sparks recognized that police officers sometimes overreact when dealing with non-white groups simply demonstrates that in making her determination in this case, she was alive to the well-known racial dynamics that may exist in interactions between police officers and visible minorities. ...

Given these facts, the question is whether a reasonable and right-minded person, informed of the circumstances of this case, and knowledgeable about the local community and about Canadian Charter values, would perceive that the reasons of Judge Sparks would give rise to a reasonable apprehension of bias. In our view, they would not. The clear evidence of prejudgment required to sustain a reasonable apprehension of bias is nowhere to be found.

Judge Sparks' oral reasons show that she approached the case with an open mind, used her experience and knowledge of the community to achieve an understanding of the reality of the case, and applied the fundamental principle of proof beyond a reasonable doubt. Her comments were based entirely on the case before her, were made after a consideration of the conflicting testimony of the two witnesses and in response to the Crown's submissions, and were entirely supported by the evidence. In alerting herself to the racial dynamic in the case, she was simply engaging in the process of contextualized judging which, in our view, was entirely proper and conducive to a fair and just resolution of the case before her.

V.   Conclusion

In the result, we agree with Cory J. as to the disposition of this case. We would allow the appeal, overturn the findings of the Nova Scotia Supreme Court (Trial Division) and the majority of the Nova Scotia Court of Appeal, and restore the acquittal of the appellant R.D.S.

The judgment of Cory and Iacobucci JJ. was delivered by

CORY J.:—

. . . . .

III.   Issues

Only one issue arises on this appeal:

>   Did the comments made by Judge Sparks in her reasons give rise to a reasonable apprehension of bias?

IV.   Analysis

. . . . .

B.   Ascertaining the Existence of a Reasonable Apprehension of Bias

(i)   Fair Trial and The Right to an Unbiased Adjudicator

. . . . .

… Fairness and impartiality must be both subjectively present and objectively demonstrated to the informed and reasonable observer. If the words or actions of the presiding judge give rise to a reasonable apprehension of bias to the informed and reasonable observer, this will render the trial unfair.

. . . . .

The question which must be answered in this appeal is whether the comments made by Judge Sparks in her reasons give rise to a reasonable apprehension that she was not impartial as between the Crown and the accused. …

. . . . .

(iii) What is Bias?

It may be helpful to begin by articulating what is meant by impartiality. In deciding whether bias arises in a particular case, it is relatively rare for courts to explore the definition of bias. In this appeal, however, this task is essential, if the Crown's allegation against Judge Sparks is to be properly understood and addressed. …

... In a more positive sense, impartiality can be described — perhaps somewhat inexactly — as a state of mind in which the adjudicator is disinterested in the outcome, and is open to persuasion by the evidence and submissions.

In contrast, bias denotes a state of mind that is in some way predisposed to a particular result, or that is closed with regard to particular issues. ...

. . . . .

(v) Judicial Integrity and the Importance of Judicial Impartiality

Often the most significant occasion in the career of a judge is the swearing of the oath of office. ... The oath requires a judge to render justice impartially. ...

Courts have rightly recognized that there is a presumption that judges will carry out their oath of office. ... This is one of the reasons why the threshold for a successful allegation of perceived judicial bias is high. However, despite this high threshold, the presumption can be displaced with "cogent evidence" that demonstrates that something the judge has done gives rise to a reasonable apprehension of bias. ... The presumption of judicial integrity can never relieve a judge from the sworn duty to be impartial.

. . . . .

... It is obvious that good judges will have a wealth of personal and professional experience, that they will apply with sensitivity and compassion to the cases that they must hear. The sound belief behind the encouragement of greater diversity in judicial appointments was that women and visible minorities would bring an important perspective to the difficult task of judging. ...

Regardless of their background, gender, ethnic origin or race, all judges owe a fundamental duty to the community to render impartial decisions and to appear impartial. It follows that judges must strive to ensure that no word or action during the course of the trial or in delivering judgment might leave the reasonable, informed person with the impression that an issue was predetermined or that a question was decided on the basis of stereotypical assumptions or generalizations.

(vi) Should Judges Refer to Aspects of Social Context in Making Decisions?

... Whether or not the use of references to social context is appropriate in the circumstances and whether a reasonable apprehension of bias arises from particular statements will depend on the facts of the case.

. . . . .

Certainly judges may, on the basis of expert evidence adduced, refer to relevant social conditions in reasons for judgment. In some circumstances, those references are necessary, so that the law may evolve in a manner which reflects social reality. ...

. . . . .

Similarly, judges have recently made use of expert evidence of social conditions in order to develop the appropriate legal framework to be utilized for ensuring juror impartiality. ...

Other cases have applied and extended these principles on the basis of expert knowledge of the social context existing in the particular community, or in the particular relationships between parties to the case. ...

In *Parks* and *Lavallee*, for instance, the expert evidence of social context was used to develop principles of general application in certain kinds of cases. These principles are legal in nature, and are structured to ensure that the role of the trier of fact in a particular case is not abrogated or usurped. It is clear therefore that references to social context based upon expert evidence are sometimes permissible and helpful, and that they do not automatically give rise to suspicions of judicial bias. However, there is a very significant difference between cases such as *Lavallee* and *Parks* in which social context is used to ensure that the law evolves in keeping with changes in social reality and cases, such as this one, where social context is apparently being used to assist in determining an issue of credibility.

(vii) Use of Social Context in Assessing Credibility

... It is the highly individualistic nature of a determination of credibility, and its dependence on intangibles such as demeanour and the manner of testifying, that leads to the well-established principle that appellate courts will generally defer to the trial judge's factual findings, particularly those pertaining to credibility. ...

. . . . .

When making findings of credibility it is obviously preferable for a judge to avoid making any comment that might suggest that the determination of credibility is based on generalizations rather than on the specific demonstrations of truthfulness or untrustworthiness that have come from the particular witness during the trial. ... Neither the parties nor the informed and reasonable observer should be led to believe by the comments of the judge that decisions are indeed being made based on generalizations.

. . . . .

In some circumstances it may be acceptable for a judge to acknowledge that racism in society might be, for example, the motive for the overreaction of a police officer. This may be necessary in order to refute a submission that invites the judge as trier of fact to presume truthfulness or untruthfulness of a category of witnesses, or to adopt some other form of stereotypical thinking. Yet it would not be acceptable for a judge to go further and suggest that all police officers should therefore not be believed or should be viewed with suspicion where they are dealing with accused persons who are members of a different race. Similarly, it is dangerous for a judge to suggest that a particular person overreacted because of racism unless there is evidence adduced to sustain this finding. ...

If there is no evidence linking the generalization to the particular witness, these situations might leave the judge open to allegations of bias on the basis that the credibility of the individual witness was prejudged according to stereotypical generalizations. ... The difficulty is that reasonable and informed people may perceive that the judge has used this information as a basis for assessing credibility instead of making a genuine evaluation of the evidence of the particular witness' credibility. ...

To state the general proposition that judges should avoid making comments based on generalizations when assessing the credibility of individual witnesses does not lead automatically to a conclusion that when a judge does so, a reasonable apprehension of bias arises. In some limited circumstances, the comments may be appropriate. Furthermore, no matter how unfortunate individual comments appear in isolation, the comments must be examined in context, through the eyes of the reasonable and informed person who is taken to know all the relevant circumstances of the case, including the presumption of judicial integrity, and the underlying social context.

. . . . .

C.   Application of These Principles to the Facts

Did Judge Sparks' comments give rise to a reasonable apprehension of bias? In order to answer that question, the nature of the Crown's allegation against Judge Sparks must be clearly understood. At the outset, it must be emphasized that it is obviously not appropriate to allege bias against Judge Sparks simply because she is black and raised the prospect of racial discrimination. ...

Similarly, her finding that she could not accept the evidence of Constable Stienburg cannot raise a reasonable apprehension of bias. ... An unfavourable finding relating to the credibility of Constable Stienburg could only give rise to an apprehension of bias if it could reasonably be perceived to have been made on the basis of stereotypical generalizations, or as Scalia J. put it in *Liteky, supra*, on the basis of "wrongful or inappropriate" opinions not justified in the evidence.

. . . . .

Before finding that a reasonable apprehension of bias did arise Glube C.J.S.C. found that Judge Sparks conducted an acceptable review of all the evidence before making the comments that are the subject of the controversy. She concluded that if the decision had ended after the general review of the evidence and the resulting assessments of credibility, there would be no basis on which to impugn Judge Sparks' decision. I agree completely with this assessment. It is with the finding of a reasonable apprehension of bias that I must, with respect, differ.

A reading of Judge Sparks' reasons indicates that before she made the challenged comments, she had a reasonable doubt as to the veracity of the officer's testimony and had found R.D.S. to be a credible witness. She gave convincing reasons for these findings. ... None of the bases for reaching these initial conclusions on credibility was based on generalizations or stereo-types. ...

... The statement that police officers have been known to mislead the court, or to overreact is not in itself offensive. Police officers are subject to the same human frailties that affect and shape the actions of everyone. The remarks become more troubling, however, when it is stated that police officers do overreact in dealing with non-white groups.

The history of anti-black racism in Nova Scotia was documented recently by the Royal Commission on the Donald Marshall Jr. Prosecution (1989). It suggests that there is a realistic possibility that the actions taken by the police in their relations with visible minorities demonstrate both prejudice and discrimination. ...

However, there was no evidence before Judge Sparks that would suggest that anti-black bias influenced this particular police officer's reactions. Thus, although it may be incontrovertible that there is a history of racial tension between police officers and visible minorities, there was no evidence to link that generalization to the actions of Constable Stienburg. The reference to the fact that police officers may overreact in dealing with non-white groups may therefore be perfectly supportable, but it is nonetheless unfortunate in the circumstances of this case because of its potential to associate Judge Sparks' findings with the generalization, rather than the specific evidence. ...

There is a further troubling comment. After accepting R.D.S.'s evidence that he was told to shut up, Judge Sparks added that "[i]t seems to be in keeping with the prevalent attitude of the day". Again, this comment may create a perception that the findings of credibility have been made on the basis of generalizations, rather than the conduct of the particular police officer. Indeed these comments standing alone come very close to indicating that Judge Sparks predetermined the issue of credibility of Constable Stienburg on the basis of her general perception of racist police attitudes, rather than on the basis of his demeanour and the substance of his testimony.

... It is necessary to read all of the comments in the context of the whole proceeding, with an awareness of all the circumstances that a reasonable observer would be deemed to know.

The reasonable and informed observer at the trial would be aware that the Crown had made the submission to Judge Sparks that "there's absolutely no reason to attack the credibility of the officer". She had already made a finding that she preferred the evidence of R.D.S. to that of Constable Stienburg. She gave reasons for these findings that could appropriately be made based on the evidence adduced. A reasonable and informed person hearing her subsequent remarks would conclude that she was exploring the possible reasons why Constable Stienburg had a different perception of events than R.D.S. Specifi-cally, she was rebutting the unfounded suggestion of the Crown that a police officer by virtue of his occupation should be more readily believed than the accused. Although her remarks were inappropriate they did not give rise to a reasonable apprehension of bias.

. . . . .

... The reasonable and informed observer would know that the Crown at all times bore the onus of proving the offence beyond a reasonable doubt. It was obvious that Judge Sparks had a reasonable doubt on the evidence. As long as she had a reasonable doubt regarding the veracity of the officer's testimony, R.D.S. was entitled to an acquittal. Judge Sparks' remarks could reasonably be taken as demonstrating her recognition that the Crown was required to prove its case, and that it was not entitled to use presumptions of credibility to satisfy its obligation.

. . . . .

Finally, she concluded that "[a]t any rate", on the basis of her comments and all the evidence in the case, she was obliged to acquit. A reasonable, informed person reading the concluding statement would perceive that she has reached her determination that R.D.S. should be acquitted on the basis of all the evidence presented. The perception that her impugned remarks were made in response to the Crown's suggestion that she should automatically believe the police officer is reinforced by her use of the words "[a]t any rate".

A high standard must be met before a finding of reasonable apprehension of bias can be made. ... Although her comments, viewed in isolation, were unfortunate and unnecessary, a reasonable, informed person, aware of all the circumstances, would not conclude that they gave rise to a reasonable apprehension of bias. Her remarks, viewed in their context, do not give rise to a perception that she prejudged the issue of credibility on the basis of generalizations, and they do not taint her earlier findings of credibility.

. . . . .

V. Conclusion

In the result the judgments of the Court of Appeal and of Glube C.J.S.C. are set aside and the decision of Judge Sparks dismissing the charges against R.D.S. is restored. I must add that since writing these reasons I have had the opportunity of reading those of Major J. It is readily apparent that we are in agreement as to the nature of bias and the test to be applied in order to determine whether the words or actions of a trial judge raise a reasonable apprehension of bias. The differences in our reasons lies in the application of the principles and test we both rely upon to the words of the trial judge in this case. The principles and the test we have both put forward and relied upon are different from and incompatible with those set out by Justices L'Heureux-Dubé and McLachlin.

NOTES AND QUESTIONS

1. All the judges agree in *R.D.S.* that the appropriate test is the "reasonable person" test, but when they apply it to the facts they reach three very different conclusions. In light of this, how helpful is the reasonable person test for lawyers?

2. If you had been the Crown prosecutor in *R.D.S.* would your decision as to whether or not to appeal the acquittal be affected by the fact that Sparks J. was the only African-Nova Scotian female judge in the province? See also Rule 4.01(3) of the *Model Code*.

3. In light of the competing views of the judges in *R.D.S.*, do you think the judges crossed the line when they made the following comments? More particularly, if you were the lawyer representing the parties who are the subjects of each of these following quotes, what would you do (a) immediately in the courtroom; (b) at the next recess; (c) when the case is finished?

   A. Justice Moreau-Bérubé made the comments below after hearing a breaking and entering and theft case that featured two repeat offenders and allegations of drug use. Within days of making the comments Moreau-Bérubé J. informed the Judicial Council about her remarks and issued an apology at a hearing. Her apology was in reference to the following comment:

   > These are people who live on welfare and we're the ones who support them; they are on drugs and they are drunk day in and day out. They steal from us left, right and centre and any which way, they find others as crooked as they are to buy the stolen property. It's a pitiful sight. If a survey were taken in the Acadian Peninsula, of the honest people as against the dishonest people, I have the impression that the dishonest people would win. We have now got to the point where we can no longer trust our neighbour next door or across the street. In the area where I live, I wonder whether I'm not myself surrounded by crooks. And, that is how people live in the Peninsula, but we point the finger at outsiders. Ah, we don't like to be singled out in the Peninsula. And it makes me sad to say this because I live in the Peninsula now. It's my home. But look at the honest people in the Peninsula, they are very few and far between, and they are becoming fewer and fewer. And do you think these people care that it cost hundreds and thousands of dollars to repair that? They don't give a damn. Are they going to pay for it? No, not a dime. All the money is spent on coke. These people, they don't give a damn. It doesn't bother them one bit, they just – do you think you are going to arouse their sorrow and sympathy by saying that it costs hundreds and thousands of dollars. We, it bothers us because we are the ones who pay, because we have to wake up every morning and go to work. When we receive our paycheck, three quarters are taken away to support these people. They, don't care. They have nothing to do. They party all day and party all night and that's all they do. They don't care, not one bit. We on the other hand, we have to care because it is our property. These people, if they don't have enough they go to welfare and they get even more and that is how it works. So, I do not want to interrupt you, but I understand what you mean when you say that it cost thousands of dollars and counsel here understand, but the type of people we are dealing with here today in this courtroom, they couldn't care less. Whether it cost one thousand dollars to repair it or whether it cost only two cents, whether it requires six police officers to investigate, they find it

funny. Their mentality is that "The pigs will not be at Tim's while they are chasing after us."[15]

B.   The following comments were made by a judge to an accused convicted of murder during the sentencing proceedings:

> It has always been said, and correctly so, that when women – whom I have always considered the noblest beings in creation and the noblest of the two sexes of the human race – it is said that when women ascend the scale of virtues, they reach higher than men, and I have always believed this. And it is also said, and this too I believe, that when they decided to degrade themselves, they sink to depths to which even the vilest of man could not sink.

> Alas, you are indeed the image of these women so famous in history: the Delilahs, the Salomes, Charlotte Corday, Mata Hari and how many others who have been a sad part of our history and have debased the profile of women. You are one of them, and you are the clearest living example of them that I have seen.

> At the Auschwitz-Birkenau concentration camp in Poland, which I once visited horror-stricken, even the Nazis did not eliminate millions of Jews in a painful or bloody manner. They died in the gas chambers, without suffering.[16]

C.   Writing for a majority that dismissed the Crown's appeal in a sexual assault case, McClung J.A. of the Alberta Court of Appeal made the following remarks:

> (i)   [I]t must be pointed out that the complainant did not present herself to Ewanchuck or enter his trailer in a bonnet and crinolines.

> (ii)   [S]he was the mother of a six-month-old baby and that, along with her boyfriend, she shared an apartment with another couple.

> (iii) There is no room to suggest that Ewanchuk knew, yet disregarded, her underlying state of mind as he furthered his romantic intentions. He was not aware of her true state of mind. Indeed, his ignorance about that was what she wanted. The facts, set forth by the trial judge, provide support for the overriding trial finding, couched in terms of consent by implication, that the accused had no proven preparedness to assault the complainant to get what he wanted.

---

15   *Moreau-Bérubé v. New Brunswick*, [2000] N.B.J. No. 368, 2000 NBCA 12 at para. 5 (N.B.C.A.).

16   Canadian Judicial Council, Inquiry Committee Decision, *Inquiry Committees' Report to the Minister of Justice Regarding Mr. Justice Bienvenue of the Superior Court of Quebec* (June 1996) at 25-26, online: <http://www.cjc-ccm.gc.ca/cmslib/general/conduct_inq_bienvenue_ReportIC_199606_en.pdf>.

(iv) [Describing the sexual assault]: [Ewanchuk's actions were] clumsy passes ... [actions that] would hardly raise Ewanchuk's stature in the pantheon of chivalric behaviour.

(v) [E]very advance he made to her stopped when she spoke against it. ... there was no evidence of an assault or even its threat. ... [T]he sum of the evidence indicates that Ewanchuk's advances to the complainant were far less criminal than hormonal.

(vi) In a less litigious age going too far in the boyfriend's car was better dealt with on site — a well-chosen expletive, a slap in the face or, if necessary, a well-directed knee.[17]

D. An accused was convicted of sexual assault, including forced intercourse. The Crown requested a sentence of three years in jail. The judge issued a conditional sentence. In justifying the lesser sentence the judge indicated that the accused is not as culpable as other rapists because "he was a clumsy Don Juan", "sex was in the air [that night]", and that the "victim was wearing a tube top without a bra, high heels and plenty of make-up".[18]

E. On May 10, 1983, the Court of Appeal rendered its judgment in an appeal investigating the wrongful conviction of Donald Marshall, Jr. for murder. The court quashed Marshall's conviction and directed an acquittal. At the end of its judgment, the court makes the following comments:

Donald Marshall, Jr. was convicted of murder and served a lengthy period of incarceration. That conviction is now to be set aside. Any miscarriage of justice is, however, more apparent than real.

In attempting to defend himself against the charge of murder Mr. Marshall admittedly committed perjury for which he still could be charged.

By lying he helped secure his own conviction. He misled his lawyers and presented to the jury a version of the facts he now says is false, a version that was so far-fetched as to be incapable of belief.

By planning a robbery with the aid of Mr. Seale he triggered a series of events which unfortunately ended in the death of Mr. Seale.

By hiding the facts from his lawyers and the police Mr. Marshall effectively prevented development of the only defence available to him, namely, that during a robbery Seale was stabbed by one of the intended victims.

He now says that he knew approximately where the man lived who stabbed Seale and had a pretty good description of him. With this

17 *R. v. Ewanchuk*, [1998] A.J. No. 150, 1998 ABCA 52 at paras. 4, 5, 8, 11, 15 and 21 (Alta. C.A.).
18 Mia Rabson, "Board raps judge for comments – Council lets Dewar stay on bench" *Winnipeg Free Press* (November 10, 2011).

information the truth of the matter might well have been uncovered by the police.

Even at the time of taking the fresh evidence, although he had little more to lose and much to gain if he could obtain his acquittal, Mr. Marshall was far from being straightforward on the stand. He continued to be evasive about the robbery and assault and even refused to answer questions until the court ordered him to do so.

There can be no doubt but that Donald Marshall's untruthfullness through this whole affair contributed in large measure to his conviction.[19]

F. The following comment was said by a judge to a Crown Attorney while walking to the judge's chambers:

> A couple of Greek restaurant owners are claiming very large damages for alleged faulty construction. [I] have not been able to believe any Greeks on matters such as this to date – perhaps this time will be the exception to the rule.

The judge defended the comment by stating it was made in frustration, "without malice" and occurred "in the sanctuary of [his] Chambers".[20]

4. The foregoing comments indicate that sometimes judges engage in stereotyping. What do you do if, for example, you are representing a client and you know that if you can stereotype the opposing client that will play to a judge's (or a jury's) prejudices?[21] See also Rules 4.01 and 5.03 of the *Model Code*.

Scenario Fifteen

Assume you are a criminal defence lawyer. Your client has been charged with assault. Your client is an indigent street person, a veteran of the Afghanistan war, and exhibits signs of post-traumatic stress disorder and depression. Your client is being held in remand. You are informed that the trial will be heard by Judge Fortuna. In the local community, Judge Fortuna has a reputation for being pro-prosecution and decidedly unsympathetic to persons with mental disabilities who appear as accuseds. Moreover, in the last few years, Judge Fortuna has been overruled on appeal on at least five occasions. Each time, the appellate court was very critical of the quality of Judge Fortuna's reasons for deciding to convict. You believe that your client has a good argument against a conviction but you are worried about Judge Fortuna's pattern of decision-making. Should you advise your client to plea bargain with the prosecutor? Consider Rule 4.01(8) of the *Model Code*.[22]

---

19 *Mackeigan v. Hickman*, [1989] S.C.J. No. 99, [1989] 2 S.C.R. 796 at para. 35 (S.C.C.).
20 *Jordash Co. v. Arvanitis*, [1992] O.J. No. 2257 (Ont. Gen. Div.).
21 See *e.g.*, Abbe Smith, "Nice work if you can get it: 'Ethical' Jury Selection in Criminal Defence" (1998) 67 Fordham L. Rev. 523.
22 Kirk Makin, "Ontario Court judge upbraided again: Judge John Ritchie taken to task again, this time for convicting a mentally ill man after Crown backed off case" *The Globe and Mail* (February 23, 2012) at A9.

H. FURTHER READING

American Bar Association, *Model Code of Judicial Conduct*.

Alfini, James, *et al.*, *Judicial Conduct and Ethics*, 4th ed. (Newark: Matthew Bender & Co., 2007).

Devlin, Richard, Adèle Kent & Susan Lightstone, "The Past, Present and Future of Judicial Ethics in Canada" (2013) 14 Legal Ethics [forthcoming].

Dodek, Adam & Lorne Sossin, *Judicial Independence in Context* (Toronto: Irwin Law, 2010).

Friedland, Martin, *A Place Apart: Judicial Independence and Accountability in Canada* (Ottawa: Canadian Judicial Council, 1995).

Mahoney, Kathleen & Sheilah Martin, *Equality and Judicial Neutrality* (Toronto: Carswell, 1987).

Marshall, The Honourable Mr. Justice T. David, *Judicial Conduct and Accountability* (Scarborough, ON: Carswell, 1995).

Shetreet, Simon, *Judicial Independence: The Contemporary Debate* (Dordrecht: Nijhoff, 1985).

Smith, Beverley, *Professional Conduct for Lawyers and Judges*, 4th ed. (Fredericton: Maritime Law Book, 2011).

Thomas, The Honourable Mr. Justice, *Judicial Ethics in Australia* (Agincourt: Carswell, 1988).

CHAPTER 12

ACCESS TO JUSTICE

A. INTRODUCTION

In an earlier chapter of this book, Chapter 3, we discussed the obligation of the individual lawyer to foster access to justice. In this chapter, we revisit the question of access to justice but do so at the general level of professional obligation. That is, rather than looking at what individual lawyers should do to foster access to justice, we look at what the profession as a whole should do, and at what it does do, to foster access to justice.

We start out by briefly considering the nature of the "access to justice" problem in Canada and the general societal obligation to address that problem. We then consider the arguments in favour of lawyers having a special obligation to foster access to justice, and the difficulties with those arguments. Finally, we look at the efforts lawyers have made to foster access to justice.

In reviewing these materials, you should consider the following questions:

1. Do Canadians have sufficient access to justice?

2. What is the most effective way to address the access to justice problem; *i.e.*, to ensure individuals can access the justice system?

3. Is access to justice better fostered by reducing the need for lawyer services or by making lawyer services available at low or no cost?

4. How convincing are the arguments in favour of lawyers having a special obligation to foster access to justice?

5. If lawyers have a special obligation to foster access to justice, is that obligation best satisfied by lawyers providing free services to low-income individuals or by lawyers paying a fee or tax to an organization like legal aid?

6. Who should decide what the obligations of lawyers are with respect to access to justice?

B. CONSTITUTIONAL RIGHT OF ACCESS TO JUSTICE?

The following case considers whether there is a constitutional obligation to foster access to justice.

BRITISH COLUMBIA (ATTORNEY GENERAL) v. CHRISTIE

[2007] S.C.J. No. 21, 2007 SCC 21
(S.C.C., McLachlin C.J.C., Bastarache, Binnie, LeBel, Deschamps,
Fish, Abella, Charron and Rothstein JJ.)

[Dugald Christie was a lawyer in British Columbia who provided legal services at low or no cost to individuals in downtown Vancouver. In the years 1991–1999, his income never exceeded $30,000. Mr. Christie's practice ran into financial difficulties after the imposition of a seven per cent tax on legal services by the British Columbia government. Because his clients did not pay him, Mr. Christie was unable to meet his tax payments as they became due, and the government seized funds from his bank account. Mr. Christie also had difficulties affording the cost of setting up an appropriate accounting system to manage the tax. Mr. Christie brought a constitutional challenge to the tax. He was successful at trial and partially successful at the Court of Appeal. The British Columbia government appealed to the Supreme Court of Canada and Mr. Christie cross-appealed.]

The following is the judgment delivered

BY THE COURT:—

. . . . .

II. Analysis

The respondent's claim is for effective access to the courts which, he states, necessitates legal services. This is asserted not on a case-by-case basis, but as a general right. What is sought is the constitutionalization of *a particular type of* access to justice — access aided by a lawyer where rights and obligations are at stake before a court or tribunal ... In order to succeed, the respondent must show that the Canadian constitution mandates this particular form or quality of access. The question is whether he has done so. In our view, he has not.

We take as our starting point the definition of the alleged constitutional principle offered by the majority of the Court of Appeal ... the right to be represented by a lawyer in court or tribunal proceedings where a person's legal rights and obligations are at stake, in order to have effective access to the courts or tribunal proceedings.

We will first discuss what the proposed right entails. We will then ask whether the right, thus described, is prescribed by the constitution.

This general right to be represented by a lawyer in a court or tribunal proceedings where legal rights or obligations are at stake is a broad right. It would cover almost all — if not all — cases that come before courts or tribunals where individuals are involved. Arguably, corporate rights and obligations would be included since corporations function as vehicles for individual interests. Moreover, it would cover not only actual court proceedings, but also related legal advice, services and disbursements. Although the respondent attempted to argue otherwise, the logical result would be a constitutionally mandated legal aid scheme for virtually all legal proceedings, except where the state could show this is not necessary for effective access to justice.

This Court is not in a position to assess the cost to the public that the right would entail. No evidence was led as to how many people might require state-funded legal services, or what the cost of those services would be. However, we do know that many people presently represent themselves in court proceedings. We also may assume that guaranteed legal services would lead people to bring claims before courts and tribunals who would not otherwise do so. Many would applaud these results. However, the fiscal implications of the right sought cannot be denied. What is being sought is not a small, incremental change in the delivery of legal services. It is a huge change that would alter the legal landscape and impose a not inconsiderable burden on taxpayers.

The next question is whether the constitution supports the right contended for. In support of this contention, two arguments are made.

First, it is argued that access to justice is a fundamental constitutional right that embraces the right to have a lawyer in relation to court and tribunal proceedings. This argument is based on *B.C.G.E.U. v. British Columbia (Attorney General)*, [1988] 2 S.C.R. 214, where this Court affirmed a constitutional right to access the courts, which was breached by pickets impeding access. It is argued that a tax on legal services, like pickets, prevents people from accessing the courts. It follows, the argument concludes, that a tax on legal services also violates the right to access the courts and justice.

The right affirmed in *B.C.G.E.U.* is not absolute. The legislature has the power to pass laws in relation to the administration of justice in the province under s. 92(14) of the *Constitution Act, 1867*. This implies the power of the province to impose at least some conditions on how and when people have a right to access the courts. Therefore *B.C.G.E.U.* cannot stand for the proposition that every limit on access to the courts is automatically unconstitutional.

A second argument is that the right to have a lawyer in cases before courts and tribunals dealing with rights and obligations is constitutionally protected, either as an aspect of the rule of law, or a precondition to it.

. . . . .

The rule of law embraces at least three principles. The first principle is that the "law is supreme over officials of the government as well as private individuals, and thereby preclusive of the influence of arbitrary power" ... The second principle "requires the creation and maintenance of an actual order of positive laws which preserves and embodies the more general principle of normative order" ... The third principle requires that "the relationship between the state and the individual ... be regulated by law" ...

It is clear from a review of these principles that general access to legal services is not a currently recognized aspect of the rule of law. However, in *Imperial Tobacco*, this Court left open the possibility that the rule of law may include additional principles. It is therefore necessary to determine whether general access to legal services in relation to court and tribunal proceedings dealing with rights and obligations is a fundamental aspect of the rule of law.

Before examining this question, it is important to note that this Court has repeatedly emphasized the important role that lawyers play in ensuring access to justice and upholding the rule of law ... This is only fitting. Lawyers are a vital conduit through which citizens access the courts, and the law. They help maintain the rule of law by working to ensure that unlawful private and unlawful state action in particular do not go unaddressed. The role that lawyers play in this regard is so important that the right to counsel in some situations has been given constitutional status.

The issue, however, is whether *general* access to legal services in relation to court and tribunal proceedings dealing with rights and obligations is a fundamental aspect of the rule of law. In our view, it is not. Access to legal services is fundamentally important in any free and democratic society. In some cases, it has been found essential to due process and a fair trial. But a review of the constitutional text, the jurisprudence and the history of the concept does not support the respondent's contention that there is a broad general right to legal counsel as an aspect of, or precondition to, the rule of law.

The text of the *Charter* negates the postulate of the general constitutional right to legal assistance contended for here. It provides for a right to legal services in one specific situation. Section 10(*b*) of the *Charter* provides that everyone has the right to retain and instruct counsel, and to be informed of that right "on arrest or detention." If the reference to the rule of law implied the right to counsel in relation to all proceedings where rights and obligations are at stake, s. 10(*b*) would be redundant.

Section 10(*b*) does not exclude a finding of a constitutional right to legal assistance in other situations. Section 7 of the *Charter*, for example, has been held to imply a right to counsel as an aspect of procedural fairness where life, liberty and security of the person are affected ... But this does not support a general right to legal assistance whenever a matter of rights and obligations is before a court or tribunal. Thus in *New Brunswick*, the Court was at pains to state that the right to counsel outside of the s. 10(*b*) context is a case-specific multi-factored enquiry. ...

Nor has the rule of law historically been understood to encompass a general right to have a lawyer in court or tribunal proceedings affecting rights and obligations. The right to counsel was historically understood to be a limited right that extended only, if at all, to representation in the criminal context ...

We conclude that the text of the constitution, the jurisprudence and the historical understanding of the rule of law do not foreclose the possibility that a right to counsel may be recognized in specific and varied situations. But at the same time, they do not support the conclusion that there is a general constitutional right to counsel in proceedings before courts and tribunals dealing with rights and obligations.

. . . . .

[Appeal allowed and cross-appeal dismissed.]

NOTES AND QUESTIONS

1. What if the government imposed a $20,000 fee on anyone who sought the services of a lawyer in any matter not related to criminal, family or immigration law? Could such a fee be constitutionally justified in light of the *Christie* decision?

2. The social services tax at issue in the *Christie* case applied only to legal services and not to other professional fees. The government claimed that the tax would be used to increase funding for legal aid, although revenues from the tax were put in the government's general revenues account and were not specifically earmarked for legal aid funding. Accepting the Court's conclusion that the British Columbia government was constitutionally permitted to put such a tax in place, do you think it was good public policy for it to have done so? Is the tax likely to foster or impede access to justice?

3. Does the Court's emphasis on the cost of the right claimed suggest a position on the importance of the right claimed; that is, if the Court was more impressed by the significance of the need to access justice would it have been less concerned about the cost of an obligation on the government to ensure that access occurs?

4. The Canadian Bar Association (B.C. branch) was very active in resisting the Social Services tax.[1] Do you think that this campaign was an appropriate one for the CBA to undertake (bearing in mind that the CBA is distinct from the Law Society of British Columbia but at the time membership in the CBA was compulsory for all British Columbia lawyers)?

5. How could the government of British Columbia have structured this tax so as to generate revenues for legal aid but to avoid the negative effect on lawyers like Mr. Christie and their clients?

C. WHAT IS THE "ACCESS TO JUSTICE" PROBLEM?

When we state that there is an issue or "problem" with respect to access to justice we make a number of important assumptions. First, we assume that accessing the justice system is important — that individuals need to be able to appear before courts and/or administrative tribunals to ensure their rights are protected and respected by other individuals and by the state. Second, we assume that to access the justice system effectively individuals need, or at minimum will benefit from, the assistance of legal counsel. Finally, we assume that lawyers are not accessible to everyone — that hiring a lawyer costs more than at least some people can afford. From these assumptions we can identify the problem: there are individuals in society who need a lawyer to exercise and/or protect their legal rights but who cannot afford one.

While at the fringes these assumptions can be debated and qualified, their basic truth is difficult to dispute. While a person who is fortunate will never

---

[1] See *Canadian Bar Association v. British Columbia (Attorney General)*, [1993] B.C.J. No. 407, 101 D.L.R. (4th) 410 (B.C.S.C.) and *Canadian Bar Association v. British Columbia (Attorney General)*, [1994] B.C.J. No. 981, 91 B.C.L.R. (2d) 207 (B.C.S.C.).

need to go to court to protect their legal rights, many are not so lucky. The tenant whose landlord unjustly refuses to return her damage deposit, the husband and wife who get divorced, the landed immigrant who has difficulties obtaining citizenship and the mother of a disabled child who is wrongfully denied benefits which legislation makes available for that child, all have legal rights that have been infringed or denied. To protect or establish those rights they at least need to be able to access the justice system to ensure that those rights are protected (that is, the wrongdoer needs to at least see a reasonable possibility that the individual being wronged will access the justice system to prevent the wrongdoing).

Further, while every Canadian jurisdiction has attempted to make the justice system accessible, legal counsel is very helpful, and may be crucial, in ensuring effective protection of one's legal rights. The Supreme Court of Canada recognized as much in its 1999 decision in *New Brunswick (Minister of Health and Community Services) v. G. (J.)*,[2] in which it held that a mother against whom a child custody order was being sought could not effectively protect her security of the person without the assistance of counsel. The *Christie* case affirmed this point when it noted (at para. 22) that "lawyers are a vital conduit through which citizens access the courts, and the law".

The final assumption — that not everyone can afford a lawyer — is also difficult to refute. In Canada in 2007, 75 per cent of the population had income under $50,000.[3] Median family income in 2007 was $66,550.[4] Canadians are, by world standards, wealthy. However, it is still the case that for most Canadians, paying for a lawyer requires sacrificing something else of importance, or going into debt. According to the 2010 Canadian Lawyer survey, lawyers called to the bar in 2009 (*i.e.*, with only one year of experience) had an average hourly rate of $185/hour, while lawyers called to the bar in 2000 had an average hourly rate of $317/hour. Although this data is obviously very limited from a statistical point of view, it does indicate a significant gap between the amount of money earned by the average Canadian family — at its median in 2007 $1,279/week — and the amount of money charged by an average Canadian lawyer. The access to justice problem arises in this gap.

D. SOLVING THE ACCESS TO JUSTICE PROBLEM

1. Introduction

How do we ensure that people have access to justice? How do we ameliorate the difference between the cost of legal services and the need for such services? In the following article, Brent Cotter analyzes the assumptions that underlie the access to justice problem, and identifies things that could or

---

2   [1999] S.C.J. No. 47, [1999] 3 S.C.R. 46 (S.C.C.).
3   Statistics Canada Table, "Individuals by total income level, by province and territory (Canada)", online: <http://www40.statcan.gc.ca/l01/cst01/famil105a-eng.htm>.
4   Statistics Canada Table, "Median total income, by family type, by province and territory", online: <http://www40.statcan.gc.ca/l01/cst01/famil08a-eng.htm>.

should be done by different actors in the legal system — legal educators, the judiciary, the legal profession, government — to improve access to justice.

BRENT COTTER

"Thoughts on a Coordinated and Comprehensive Approach to
Access to Justice in Canada"
(2012) U.N.B.L.J. [forthcoming]

INTRODUCTION

I propose ... to address the question of Access to Justice in a broad, holistic way. I will begin by defining the topic broadly ... [and] will then set out five assumptions about ... Access to Justice that seem to me to be essential foundational dimensions of the subject and our ability and willingness to tackle it. ... I will offer a brief examination/critique of the four critical 'actors' in relation to the challenge of Access to Justice and in so doing, offer some relatively controversial approaches that I believe are required by all of us in the various sectors of the legal system — in partnership — to improve access to justice for Canadians in a meaningful and sustainable way ...

A DEFINITION

... [W]e do not have hope for success if we are not able to identify the issue we are addressing, or if we are unable to determine the nature of the problem. [Justice Cromwell] described 'access to justice' in terms of a state of affairs where "in general terms, members of our society would have appropriate access to civil and family justice if they had the knowledge, resources and services to deal effectively with civil and family legal matters". Justice Cromwell's focus, and the subject matter of his talk was "Access to Civil and Family Justice" and his definition was accordingly focussed on access to justice in that context. In my opinion, the definition he offers, with one slight modification, is applicable to the whole range of issues within the broad scope of access to justice.

When we talk about the legal needs of our citizenry in any area, whether it be advice about the drafting of a will, dealing with one's immigration or refugee status, sorting out a landlord-tenant dispute, making a claim for employment insurance or dealing with a criminal charge, or a host of other matters, the 'knowledge, resources, services' conception is equally applicable. I would only add this. The range of needs of our citizens in relation to access to justice in any of these or other areas varies. Some people need meaningful, perhaps comprehensive legal service so that they can be represented in court or before an administrative agency in order to obtain justice. Others may need less: perhaps access to a mediator or to other resources that can facilitate a resolution of a legal problem on their own. Still others may only need more information, thereby enabling them to make decisions or plan their lives and careers in ways that suit them best. For this reason, and in its broad application to the spectrum of circumstances in which people need assistance, I am inclined to the view that Access to Justice means access to '*knowledge, resources or ser-*

vices', as needed, to address the individual's particular circumstances. Sometimes 'access to justice' will mean full scale legal representation; in some cases it will mean no more than providing a person with the information he or she needs to sort things out without resort to additional resources or services.

FIVE ASSUMPTIONS OR PRESUMPTIONS

. . . . .

There is little doubt that access to justice is a serious problem across a wide spectrum of our society. On the basis of this uncontrovertible premise I turn to five 'assumptions' about the fundamental nature of the 'problem' and about the orientation we need to bring – collectively – to the challenge in order to make a meaningful impact. The five 'assumptions' are:

1   Not only 'justice' but 'access to justice' is itself fundamental to how citizens live their lives in a respectful society governed by the rule of law.

2   Lack of access to justice undermines our society and our confidence in its essential fairness and justness, undermining our confidence in the rule of law itself.

3   Ensuring access to justice gets harder every day.

4   No one person alone can solve the problem of access to justice, but every single one of us has a responsibility to contribute to the solutions, even when those solutions are and must be 'uncomfortable' for us.

5   Each of us associated with law has been given an opportunity, and a 'trust' in relation to the justice system, and we have an obligation to preserve and strengthen access to justice as part of that 'trust'.

THE ROLES AND RESPONSIBILITIES OF THE 'LEGAL ACTORS' IN RELATION TO ACCESS TO JUSTICE

1   LEGAL EDUCATION

I start with … legal education. My sense of legal education a generation ago, when I was a student and a junior professor, is that there was in those years a greater commitment to 'public service' in our law schools. We learned then, and should be learning still, that service in the law is an important calling, a calling to 'public service' in whatever way that we make use of our law degree. To some extent we have lost that orientation to public service and we must get it back again.

How might we do this? First, we must teach our students about the importance of 'access to justice' and the role of the law and lawyers in facilitating rather than impeding this goal. This means the incorporation of 'access to justice' themes in our law school courses, from the start. For example, in most of our courses we study significant cases and legal decision-making processes without acknowledging or appreciating the implicit assumption that legal representation was in place for the participants. The significance of the role of the lawyers in these processes, or the consequences that may have befallen a person who couldn't draw upon his or her lawyer's skills, are taken for granted. They are almost never acknowledged in law school classes. We need meaningful educational strategies at our law schools to incorporate these understandings – and their significance to the administration of justice in our society – into our law school curricula. To date this is a 'hit or miss' proposition, and it is simply too important a matter for it to be allowed to 'miss'. This is a role for law schools and they should show leadership, appropriate to their important place in the firmament of society-building institutions.

Second, we must be more pro-active in our expectations that law students learn about 'public service' through experience, ideally through facilitating access to justice experiences writ large. In my opinion this can only be achieved by law schools mandating that, as a prerequisite to obtaining their law degrees, students must participate in at least a limited amount of pre-scribed, structured public service during their time at law school. This calls for change. It imposes, and makes demands of law schools and law students. But it can be done – look at the public interest requirement at Osgoode Hall Law School. And if Chief Justice McLachlin is correct about the challenge our society faces, it must be done if law schools are going to do their part in preparing strongly oriented, self-aware students and graduates to do their part.

Third, we must begin to rethink our law school curriculum with greater emphasis on service. I am still in favour of our students learning a little law. But we have to teach it less for its own sake and more as a set of tools designed to enable those who study it to make use of that learning to solve people's problems. Legal understanding must be seen as part of the toolkit for access to justice. This calls for more contextual learning, more experiential learning and more clinical education. Here, students can learn the law and contribute to access to justice at the same time. Once again this calls for change. It makes demands on law schools and on students, but it can be done. It must be done.

Fourth, we need to think of the ways in which laws can be changed to facilitate access to justice and at the same time ensure that legal education is responsive to those changes. A small example of this occurred in Saskatchewan in the 1990s. When the Government of Saskatchewan introduced a 'mandatory, front end exploratory mediation' requirement for nearly all civil litigation undertaken in the province, it also funded a position at the College of Law to enable the development of an educational program aimed at teaching law students about dispute resolution approaches other than litigation to solve their clients' problems. These measures have been successful both in terms of the 'mediation' project itself and in terms of a rich academic undertaking to strengthen the legal problem-solving skills of students and graduates.

Fifth, we need to attract candidates for law school – most of whom will become lawyers – at least in part on the basis of their genuine inclination toward service and in their belief in and desire to foster access to justice. Canada's law schools have a remarkable pool of talent of applicants from which to draw. We should include in our criteria for selection, from this talented pool, an expectation that they be committed to service and to the betterment of our legal system. After all, these will be the lawyers of Canada's future.

2   LAWYERS AND THE LEGAL PROFESSION

. . . . .

Despite obvious challenges to access to justice, we have not, as lawyers, used all the tools at our disposal to address these issues ... I note the work of the legal profession in relation to 'unbundling of legal services', where a lawyer may be retained to provide a portion of the legal services in relation to a matter, either because this is all that the client requires or it is all that the client can afford. Courts are becoming more accepting of this arrangement and law societies, at least in British Columbia and Ontario, have modified their Rules of Professional Conduct to accommodate the efforts of lawyers to assist clients in this limited way, particularly in pro bono representations, without them or their law firms encountering intractable conflict of interest problems as a result of a limited representation of a client in need.

This is a positive development, but I think we need to be bolder. In remarks at the University of Manitoba shortly after his retirement, Chief Justice Brian Dickson said:

> [T]he external aspect – the other side of the coin – is our special obligation to ensure that the less fortunate have access to the legal system and justice – the cost of legal advice should not put it beyond the reach of have-nots and have-little who claim the protection of the law.

In my view, we in the legal profession, as people who make our livings – generally decent livings and in some cases very good livings – within and through the justice system, and to whom a certain authority and public trust is granted in relation to the justice system – owe it to that system, when it is struggling, to help make it better. This is captured in our Codes of Professional Conduct. For example, the Federation of Law Societies Model Code of Professional Conduct provides, under the heading "Encouraging Respect for the Administration of Justice", the following Rule:

> 4.06 (1) A lawyer must encourage public respect for and try to improve the administration of justice ...

The following two suggestions would take this hortatory and aspirational message and make it a reality. Neither suggestion is novel, but both of them, a challenge to our profession, would make a lasting difference in terms of access to justice and would immensely improve the public's regard for the legal profession. I put these suggestions in the context of the role and responsibilities of our self-governing law societies, but in each case their goal is to improve access to justice for those in need.

First, each of us as lawyers should be required to provide a modest portion of our time, or money's worth of our time, to support a pro bono program. Such a program could be established and overseen by our respective law societies and should be applicable to all of the members of the profession including articling students, those in government service and those working as in-house counsel. I acknowledge that this requires a 'bureaucracy' and that it asks lawyers to contribute to the solution of a problem that they have not themselves directly created. But when we face a problem of the present magnitude, so important to our society and so close to home, so to speak, we all have to contribute to the solution, even if we are not paid to do so. The exact amount of time [or money's worth] required of each of us each year is something to be determined by those who best appreciate the challenge that a mandatory pro bono program would present – and who best know the 'access to justice' needs in our society. But to stand idly by and declare that 'it is not my problem' would signal that we are only interested in the justice system for what we can gain from it rather than what we owe to it.

Second, we must begin to contemplate a fundamental redesign of the ways in which we deliver legal services. We need to engage in this in ways that are not 'lawyer-centric'. This requires that we be less focussed on what is referred to in other professions as 'scope of practice', in other words, the scope of the monopoly in the delivery of legal services. We need to imagine ways in which suitably qualified people – *who are non-lawyers* – can deliver certain legal services competently and at lesser cost. Law remains one of the few professions in our society that has not undertaken a meaningful consideration of how it might be possible to redesign delivery systems for legal services that best serve the public interest by better aligning client needs with the skill sets of service providers.

It is possible for us to do this if the leaders of the legal profession's governing bodies take a broad, societal view of their mandate to govern in the public interest. Specifically, they must embrace as their mandate not just the governance of lawyers but the governance of the provision of legal services.

In Justice Cromwell's Viscount Bennett Lecture he ended with this question:

> [W]hat will be said about the contributions to improved access to justice by the legal profession – judges, practitioners, academics – of the early twenty-second century?

While we may not regard access to justice as 'our problem', I greatly fear that if we do not, as a profession, begin to offer meaningful solutions to what seem today to be society's intractable problems of access to justice, the 22nd Century answer will be a negative and uncharitable one. Simply put, we lawyers have a monopoly on the delivery of legal services for a reason. And that reason is not about us. If we don't begin to imagine and implement ways by which affordable access to one of the great social goods of our society can be achieved, others will do it for us. And I can guarantee that we will not like it.

3   THE JUDICIARY

Despite the improvements that these changes would generate in addressing the challenge of access to justice, many are pessimistic about the prospects for fundamental change. In 2005 Rollie Thompson wrote:

More lawyers for civil cases in our superior courts will not be forthcoming. There is no chance that our market system for allocating lawyers, based upon the wealth of parties, will be changed. Legal aid gives a low priority to civil matters outside family law. Even if there were more money for legal aid lawyers in civil matters, the real priority should be poverty law – like income assistance, residential tenancies, public housing, mental health, etc. – which takes place outside the superior courts. Given these legal aid priorities, duty counsel will likely never be allocated to civil matters in superior courts.

While recognizing these constraints does not mean that it is not possible for the judiciary to look for and implement ways by which access to justice can be enhanced for litigants. I make four suggestions, the last of which is drawn from Thompson's observations. First, court processes, and our explanations of these processes, can be simplified. We have rightly valued fairness and due process in court proceedings. However, our commitment to these values can sometimes cause us to lose sight of other values of equal or greater importance to the parties – the people, after all, for whom the process exists. Often litigants want timely, inexpensive and accessible processes to resolve their problems and procedural perfection is itself a less important value to them. For many, rough but affordable justice is better than no justice at all. We need to be mindful of the need for litigants' interests to be given priority in the design and operation of our dispute resolutions systems.

Second, we need to be open to dispute resolution processes that are less focussed on the legal framework of the dispute and more focussed on addressing the interests of the parties. This may mean that we use judges less and other dispute resolution professionals more in the resolution of certain kinds of conflict.

Third, judges need to be mindful in the exercise of their authority to order that certain parties receive government-funded representation in individual cases that it is highly likely that these directives – often in significant cases but at disproportionately high levels of legal cost – will be funded out of government resources that would otherwise be dedicated to other forms of subsidized legal services for citizens. In terms of cost-benefit analysis, it is likely that many deserving clients will go wanting in terms of access to legal advice and representation as a result of every single court-ordered, government-funded litigant.

Fourth, in some cases we need to reconsider the role of the judge in certain proceedings involving unrepresented litigants. To the credit of the Canadian Judicial Council, it has begun to examine the role of the judge in cases where one or both parties are unrepresented. Thompson called for a fundamental reconsideration of the role of the judge in addressing the needs of unrepresented parties in court proceedings. This approach has merit. It admittedly challenges one of the fundamental principles of our adversary system of dispute resolution that the parties are responsible for the advancement of their case, with the associated values of judicial independence and judicial neutrality. Nevertheless, it is possible to envisage that, in certain cases where the parties know and agree to a different approach, the judge might be expected to take on a significantly different role in court proceedings. In such cases where justice requires it, the judge would be much more engaged in the process. For example, Thompson argues that where both parties are unrepresented:

> [T]here should be different rules for the conduct of the trial or hearing. We should recognize the need to shift to a more inquisitorial procedure in such cases, with the judge examining witnesses, proving documents, retaining experts, suggesting possible arguments to the parties, etc.

This is a very different role for the judge, and the design of such a judicial role is both challenging to our conventional thinking and potentially complicated in its implementation. Whether he is right in the details is less important than whether he is right in principle. That is, in order to provide better justice to unrepresented litigants should we not begin to consider less conventional judicial approaches and roles that can achieve this objective of meaningful access to justice for the unrepresented?

4 GOVERNMENTS

I begin by repeating the foundational point that access to justice is a critical feature of the rule of law and a cornerstone of people's confidence in a fair and just society. Governments have a great interest in the preservation of the rule of law and people's confidence in our society's fairness and justness. It is therefore critical that governments not only respect these principles but advance them in their actions, investments and policies.

Obviously greater financial support is both justified and needed to facilitate access to justice for citizens. With respect to Legal Aid, that case has been powerfully made by Len Doust in Foundation for Change. As he noted, in Recommendation 6 of his Report:

> The provincial and federal governments must increase funding for legal aid and provide this funding through a stable, multi-year granting process. The provision of essential public legal services is a governmental responsibility and the delivery of core services should not depend upon charitable contributions from the Law Foundation, the Notary Foundation, community groups, and pro bono efforts of the legal profession, paralegals and others.

Similarly, legal information services often perform a significant access to justice role at modest cost and deserve the government's support and investment. Similarly, court-based services that can assist unrepresented litigants in basic ways and in the explanation of court processes have the ability to serve litigants, courts and the process of justice at modest cost.

Beyond funding, governments can make a contribution in other important ways. First, they can make a real commitment to the crafting of laws and procedures in clear, simple, understandable ways. This means that not only precision but simplicity and clarity should be articulated objectives of government drafting. Second, governments should develop 'policy screens' as a means of assessing whether any particular policy, law or administrative practice facilitates or impedes access to justice for citizens. The mandate would be to review critically, and with a view to modification, any that impede access. Such screens would operate in ways that are similar to the assessment of laws and government policies used to determine whether they contravene the Charter of Rights. Laws that impede access to justice would require special justification, or the compensating financial or policy support to ameliorate the impediment created.

CONCLUSION

I have suggested that access to justice is a critical dimension of our society in the sense that it is fundamental to citizens' confidence in the rule of law and on our confidence that we live in a fair and just society. Absent access to justice, law appears to be available for only the powerful or the wealthy. We live in a country where the rule of law is fundamental to our belief in a civilized society. Where citizens have little or no access to law to enable them to understand and, if necessary, advance our rights, their confidence in a just society based on law will be eroded. This is not just a question of who 'has' and who 'has not' in our society. It is a recipe for the diminishment of our society as a whole.

The challenge to providing access to justice for citizens is so broad and so diverse that its solutions can only be achieved through the concerted efforts of many sectors of our society. While the 'law' sector is not the only dimension of our society that should be called upon, we have a special place in the 'system' and bear a 'trust' with respect to that system. As Justice Cromwell noted in his Viscount Bennett Lecture:

> We in the profession are trustees of our legal system; we not only function within it and know how it works, we are also primarily responsible for its preservation.

If we do not care enough to invest our time, energy, ideas, expertise and sometimes our resources to address this problem, why should we expect that others will?

NOTES AND QUESTIONS

1. In his article, Cotter sets out a broad variety of mechanisms for improving access to justice. Which do you think are most likely to occur? Which are most likely to be effective?

2. In his article, Cotter advocates for a requirement that law students be required to engage in "at least a limited amount of prescribed, structured public service during their time at law school". Does your law school have such a requirement? Should it?

3. In its *Access to Justice Act*,[5] the Government of Ontario adopted a system of formal regulation of paralegals, and gave the task of regulating paralegals to the Law Society of Upper Canada. Do you think that formalizing the role played by legal

---

[5]   S.O. 2006, c. 21.

professionals other than lawyers will improve access to justice? What costs and benefits might be associated with doing so? Should those other legal professionals be regulated by the Law Society of Upper Canada?

The following sections consider in more detail solutions to the access to justice problem, looking first at what governments could do differently and then at whether lawyers should have an obligation to perform a certain amount of *pro bono* service.

2. Government

The Supreme Court's decision in *Christie* indicates that apart from fundamental legal rights, there is no constitutional obligation on the state to ensure access to justice. As a matter of public policy, however, every Canadian jurisdiction has attempted to close the gap between the cost of legal services and the inability of many individuals to pay for them. Thus, while political theorists may still argue about whether there is a general social obligation to foster access to justice, it is clear that Canadian society has accepted the existence of that obligation. The only remaining issue is whether governments have gone far enough in filling that gap. The following extract questions the sufficiency of legal aid in British Columbia.

PUBLIC COMMISSION ON LEGAL AID IN BRITISH COLUMBIA

*Foundation for Change: Report of the Public Commission on
Legal Aid in British Columbia* (March 8, 2011) at 5-11

Executive Summary

The Public Commission on Legal Aid (the "Public Commission") was launched in June of 2010 for the purpose of engaging British Columbians regarding their views on the future of legal aid in the Province of British Columbia.

In the course of the Public Commission process, submissions were made by both individuals and organizations, detailing their stories and experiences and sharing constructive proposals for the improvement of the legal aid system in the future. The overwhelming majority of submissions spoke to the general failure of our legal aid system, the negative repercussions for needy individuals and families, and the consequent adverse impact on our communities and justice system. There were also many representations made by organizations and groups involved in the process of the delivery of legal aid services — those who were extremely knowledgeable and were able to point clearly to the deficiencies, and the consequences of the deficiencies, and to assist me in terms of making recommendations for reform. The range of individuals and organizations included legal aid clients, legal services providers, and those representing the broader public interest.

The representations constituted a cross-section of views on a province-wide basis. The response was outstanding and the Public Commission was called upon to sit for extended hours on a number of occasions. There can be no doubt that the public was indeed engaged; many of the submissions were made passionately and out of a clear sense of the need for reform.

. . . . .

Legal Aid in British Columbia

Until the 1960s, legal aid in British Columbia was provided through the pro bono efforts and volunteer services rendered by the legal profession to those who could not afford, but required, legal services. In the early 1970s the federal and provincial governments began to contribute to funding for legal aid. In 1979 the Legal Services Society ("LSS") was established by provincial statute.

Since then, the present legal aid system in British Columbia has experienced many highs and lows and has been the subject of numerous government reports. The demand for legal aid services has grown steadily while government contributions have been inconsistent. In the mid-1990s British Columbia had one of the most comprehensive programs in Canada, but the continued increasing demand consistently outpaced budget allocations, giving rise to shortfalls in service.

Reductions in government commitment to legal aid became evident through the 1980s and 1990s when the federal government capped transfer payments and reconfigured its cost-sharing for civil legal aid and moved to a general transfer of funds to the provincial government rather than a transfer specifically designated for legal aid. The commitment of the provincial government has also gradually eroded and in 2002, the budget of LSS was reduced by close to 40 percent over a three year period. Budget reductions have necessitated changes in service delivery by LSS including the closure of approximately 45 branch offices, which were replaced by seven regional centres, and services from local agents. In 2010 the number of regional centres was further reduced to two. Most notably, poverty law services and many family law services were eliminated.

. . . . .

While LSS has prioritized the protection of its core services in an environment of insufficient and uncertain funding, it is clear to me that the legal aid system is failing to meet even the most basic needs of British Columbians. Additional reductions in service occurred in 2009 — on top of what was then an unsustainable and highly volatile legal aid system.

Based on the evidence presented to me, I cannot come to any conclusion other than the services provided in British Columbia today are too little, their longevity or consistency too uncertain. This result is the consequence of the cutbacks and lack of sufficient and consistent financing, even though LSS has done its very best, and in my view has done everything possible, to accommodate the needs within their limited budgetary restrictions.

Other groups have attempted to fill the gaps within the system, but have largely fallen short in their efforts. The lawyers through Access Pro Bono as well as the Law Foundation of British Columbia have made considerable efforts, but at the end of the day, I am satisfied that we have fallen from being a leader in legal aid provision to seriously lagging behind other jurisdictions. We can no longer avoid the fact that we are failing the most disadvantaged members of our community, those for whom legal aid exists within our province.

What the Commission Heard

The submissions received by the Public Commission clearly evidenced the gaps — the inability of the present system to respond to what can only be characterized as the obvious and dire needs of many of the disadvantaged, their inability to obtain even the basic benefits to which they are legally entitled because of the lack of assistance.

The submissions also outline the downstream consequences—the economic and social costs of this failure. The submissions and representations made it abundantly clear that the system is failing. They provided constructive and thoughtful ideas with respect to reform and assisted me significantly in coming to my conclusions and recommendations in this report. On the basis of the evidence presented before me, I have made seven overarching findings:

- The legal aid system is failing needy individuals and families, the justice system, and our communities.

- Legal information is not an adequate substitute for legal assistance and representation.

- Timing of accessing legal aid is key.

- There is a broad consensus concerning the need for innovative, client-focused legal aid services.

- Steps must be taken to meet legal aid needs in rural communities.

- More people should be eligible for legal aid.

- Legal aid should be fully funded as an essential public service.

Specific Areas of Concern

I have no hesitation in concluding that legal aid is an essential public service in our society. For the reasons contained in this report it is my view that in a just society, it is a public service that is as essential as education, healthcare, and social assistance. There must be a broad consensus on this point. Indeed, the significance of the legal aid system is that it picks up where our other social systems fail and timely legal aid can often significantly reduce the strain on healthcare and social assistance.

Legal aid is essential in criminal matters where persons are accused of serious crimes and they cannot otherwise afford to pay for a lawyer. Their liberty is at stake. Timely and appropriate criminal legal aid actually results in significant cost savings to the system. Over 80 percent of all criminal trials in the province are resolved before trial. However, when a litigant in a criminal trial is unrepresented it is extremely difficult, if not impossible, to either resolve the matter without a trial or to even expedite the trial process.

Legal aid is necessary in many other situations where, once again, the provision of timely and adequate legal advice and representation results in justice and satisfaction of the basic necessities of life; it also provides downstream economic and social benefits to society. Timely legal aid may prevent additional healthcare costs, the commission of criminal offences as a response to the failure to properly access legal benefits, and further burden on the social welfare system.

In the child protection context, parents face the threat of losing custody and care of their children to state authorities. The implications of this are obvious not only to the parents but to the well-being of the children.

Individuals who are involuntarily committed to a provincial health facility have the right to have their detention reviewed at specific intervals—this is an important safeguard given they are being deprived of their liberty. These individuals face insurmountable barriers in representing themselves but all too frequently the process grinds to a halt without the assistance of legal aid or legal representation.

Similarly, refugees seeking asylum in British Columbia are faced with adversarial state representation and must deal with a complex process. The fairness of this process depends absolutely upon adequate representation and the stakes for the individual are high, including risk of life, family separation, and possible return to a country to which a refugee may have no connection whatsoever or may face serious wrongful political persecution.

Legal aid is absolutely essential in family law and poverty law matters. The family law regime provides important legal rights and protections to address the consequences of the breakdown of a marriage or long term relationship, including those pertaining to child custody, access and child support, division of property and spousal support. These issues relate to the most fundamental aspects of their lives, their relationship with their children, and their ability to provide their families with adequate housing and other necessities of life.

The need for legal aid for poverty law matters is perhaps the least well understood but is clearly a pressing area of concern. Poverty law problems include issues such as debt, access to social assistance and housing, worker's compensation claims, access to pension benefits, and many other social welfare benefits to which individuals are legally entitled.

Those on the margins of our society are unable to deal with ruthless and unscrupulous landlords with respect to their housing needs. Debt left unattended can lead to loss of housing and/or the ability to meet basic needs; such losses may contribute to the breakdown of relationships, giving rise to a whole new range of legal aid and social assistance requirements.

The list of poverty law requirements is set out more fully in this report.

Summary of Recommendations

I have made nine recommendations in this report based on my analysis of the evidence, information and material provided to the Public Commission, and my best effort to address the deficiencies of our legal aid system.

Without adequate legal aid, we all fail in our social obligation to ensure that every citizen of our province has available at least the basic necessities of their lives so they can adequately sustain themselves and their families. My recommendations are designed to overcome what I perceive to be the deficiencies that exist, addressed in the representations made to me in the course of the hearings and a complete review of the written submissions provided. ...

Recommendation 1: Recognize legal aid as an essential public service

The *Legal Services Society Act* should be amended to include a statement clearly recognizing legal aid as an essential public service and the entitlement to legal aid where an individual has a legal problem that puts into jeopardy their or their family's security — be it their liberty, health, employment, housing, or ability to meet the basic necessities of life — and he or she has no meaningful ability to pay for legal services.

Recommendation 2: Develop a new approach to define core services and priorities

A new approach to defining core public legal aid services and priorities should be developed which merges the traditional legal categories approach (e.g., criminal law, family law, and poverty law) with an approach based on the fundamental interests of the most disadvantaged clients, where the need is most pressing and the benefit is likely to be the greatest. At a minimum this will require reinstating coverage for many family law and poverty law matters.

Recommendation 3: Modernize and expand financial eligibility

(a) Financial eligibility criteria should be modified so that more needy individuals qualify for legal aid and the criteria should be linked to a generally accepted measure of poverty such as Statistics Canada's Low-Income Cut-Off or Market Basket Measure.

(b) Legal aid should be made available to the "working poor", defined as those earning up to 200 percent of the poverty rate through a sliding scale contribution system.

(c) Basic legal aid services such as legal information and limited legal advice should be available to all residents of British Columbia, but only to the extent that the entitlements under (a) and (b) to comprehensive legal aid is fully met.

Recommendation 4: Establish regional legal aid centres and modernize service delivery.

Legal aid service delivery should be modeled on evidence-based best practices, which take into account the needs of economically disadvantaged clients for lasting outcomes and the geographic and cultural barriers they face in accessing public services. This model should include the following nine features:

1. Establishment of Regional Legal Aid Centres across the province to serve as the point of entry hub of legal aid service delivery for all core services to facilitate early intervention in resolving legal problems;

2. Mobile outreach services to individuals who cannot access the Centres due to geographic, cultural and/or other barriers;

3. Enhanced team approach to the delivery of legal aid services with greater emphasis on the role of community advocates and legal advocates acting with adequate support, training and supervision by lawyers;

4. Gradual expansion of the role of duty counsel and staff lawyers where monitoring and evaluation demonstrate the effectiveness of these modes of service delivery in meeting client needs;

5. Greater integration of legal aid services with other support services to meet client needs in a more holistic manner;

6. Enhanced case management of large criminal cases and in other situations, where warranted;

7. Targeted strategies to meet the needs of under-served communities including Aboriginal communities, women leaving abusive relationships, individuals with mental or cognitive disabilities, migrant workers and the elderly;

8. Re-establishment and expansion of LawLINE; and

9. Cautious expansion of information technology in delivering legal aid services bearing in mind the proven barriers to accessing and using legal information, particularly by the most disadvantaged.

Recommendation 5: Expand public engagement and political dialogue

Justice system stakeholders, including those that established this Commission and members of the Coalition for Public Legal Services, should continue to take steps to expand public engagement and political dialogue on the urgent need to renew the legal aid system in British Columbia.

Recommendation 6: Increase long-term, stable funding

The provincial and federal governments must increase funding for legal aid and provide this funding through a stable, multi-year granting process. The provision of essential public legal services is a governmental responsibility and the delivery of core services should not depend upon charitable contributions from the Law Foundation, the Notary Foundation, community groups, and pro bono efforts of the legal profession, paralegals and others.

Recommendation 7: The legal aid system must be proactive, dynamic, and strategic

The legal aid system should be more proactive, dynamic and strategic in its approach, which requires enhanced research, policy development, monitoring, and evaluation capacities.

Recommendation 8: There must be greater collaboration between public and private legal aid service providers

Mechanisms to facilitate collaboration between public legal aid providers and private service providers, such as an "Access to Justice Committee", should be established on both a province-wide and regional basis. These committees could also play an important function in providing input to broader court reform and access to justice initiatives.

Recommendation 9: Provide more support to legal aid providers

Steps should be taken to develop, support, and recognize community advocates, legal advocates, paralegals, and lawyers who provide both public and private legal aid services in order to ensure the quality of these services. These steps should include: increased training and professional development opportunities, increased informational resources and other forms of support, quality assurance mechanisms, and ensuring that remuneration is sufficient to make it economically feasible for lawyers and others to perform these essential services.

NOTES AND QUESTIONS

1. In its full report, the Public Commission compares legal aid to publicly funded health care and states (at 13): "Thus, there is a critical distinction between health care and legal aid. It is not a distinction in terms of need, but rather only in terms of the public's awareness and understanding of the necessity of providing legal aid." Do you agree with this characterization? If the equivalency is not fair, what does that mean for the conclusions and recommendations of the Commission?

2. What metric should be used to assess the sufficiency of legal aid? One metric might be whether the outcomes in legal cases are affected by the absence of legal counsel for all parties. What are the strengths and weaknesses of that metric? What other metrics might be used?

3. Does the Commission tend to conflate access to justice and access to lawyers? Is this necessarily the most effective and efficient solution to the problems of access to justice?

4. Would the existence of legal aid be a means for a government to resist a constitutional challenge such as that brought by Dugald Christie?

5. In the United States, there is a federal legal aid program. However, that program was gradually subjected to significant funding cuts commencing with the Reagan presidency. Some Canadian lawyers have used the existence of Canada's much more generous legal aid program to reject the application of American arguments in favour of mandatory *pro bono* work in Canada.[6] Given the findings of the Commission, does that argument make sense?

6. When you read the analysis of *pro bono* later in this chapter, consider whether lawyers doing work for legal aid should be considered to be doing *pro bono* work or not. To provide some context for your analysis, consider that in Manitoba legal aid lawyers may charge fees, depending on the nature of the offence of $310–$890 for entering a guilty plea before a hearing, $825–$1,610 for a half-day trial, with rates of $175–$375 for each additional half-day, and $480–$890 for a preliminary hearing. In civil cases, fees are set at $57/hour with maximum amounts for each matter dealt with (*e.g.*, a maximum of $1000 for a trial).[7]

7. Who provides legal aid funding in your province?

3.   Lawyers and the Legal Profession

Legal aid goes some distance to reduce the access to justice problem. But as the Public Commission documents, there are some obvious gaps even after the operation of the program. Legal aid does not cover every type of legal claim. It operates only for individuals with very limited financial resources, leaving many individuals who cannot afford a lawyer without financial assistance. It pays lawyers much less than the market rate for legal fees in most jurisdictions, and normally does not pay for all of the work necessary to ensure effective resolution of legal disputes. This means that lawyers are either reluctant to do legal aid work or, if they do, must choose whether to do a less than complete job or provide some necessary services at their own time and expense.

Given these gaps, it is important to address the role of lawyers in fostering access to justice. The following excerpts offer different arguments in favour of the existence of such an obligation. In reading the excerpts, consider whether you think the arguments offered are plausible and, if so, which arguments are the most convincing. Also, review Cotter's article again. Do you think that mandatory *pro bono* is the most effective change the legal profession could make to improve access to justice?

---

[6] See Law Society of Alberta, Stakeholder Consultation on the Proposed Alberta *Pro bono* Network Final Report (June 1, 2006) at 11, online: <http://www.lawsociety.ab.ca/files/pbla/Stakeholder_Consultation_on_the_Proposed_PBAN_2006.pdf>.

[7] See Legal Aid Regulation, Man. Reg. 225/91 (under the *Legal Aid Manitoba Act*, C.C.S.M. c. L105).

RICHARD DEVLIN

"Breach of Contract?: The New Economy, Access to Justice and the Ethical
Responsibilities of the Legal Profession"
(2002) 25 Dal. L.J. 335
[footnotes omitted]

[After assessing the empirical data indicating an unmet need for access to
justice, the author considers the arguments in favour of a special obligation on
lawyers to meet that need. The focus of the argument is on whether lawyers
should be required to perform *pro bono* work.]

3. *Arguments for mandatory pro bono*

Several different types of argument can be mobilized in favour of mandatory
pro bono. As Deborah Rhode points out, both rights-based and utilitarian arguments can be developed in support of mandatory *pro bono*. The primary
rights-based argument suggests that there is an unmet right to legal assistance
and that, contractually, the legal profession is obliged to respond to that need
because of its privileged monopoly situation. Utilitarian arguments depend
more on the distributive benefits and instrumental consequences of mandatory
pro bono. I will address each of these in turn.

a. *The Rights Based Argument: Monopoly and the Juridical Contract*

Building on Locke's social contract theory, advocates of mandatory *pro bono*
suggest that we need to be aware of three potential contracts. First, there is the
contract whereby the citizenry agree among themselves to leave the state of
nature in the pursuit of mutual self interest. Second, there is the contract between the citizens and the sovereign whereby the latter agrees to protect the
rights of the citizens and to enforce the rule of law. In contrast to conventional
Lockean theory, which had a relatively narrow and negative conception of
rights and the rule of law, modern Canadian society has a broader conception
of what these concepts mean. In several recent cases the Supreme Court of
Canada has attempted to delineate what is encompassed by the rule of law.
Crucial to this exercise is the idea of equality before the law, that "[t]here is,
in short, one law for all." In Canada, we have adopted an expansive definition
of what equality means. Section 15(1) of the Charter provides:

> Every individual is equal before and under the law and has the right to the
> equal protection and equal benefit of the law without discrimination and, in
> particular, without discrimination based on race, national or ethnic origin,
> colour, religion, sex, age or mental or physical disability.

This approach to equality rights is much more encompassing than the American ideal of "equal justice under the law." For good or ill, lawyers are the
gatekeepers to providing equal access to the law. The state has given the legal
profession a nationalized monopoly in this regard: lawyers regulate admission
to the profession, engage in legal practice to the exclusion of all others and
self-regulate for misconduct. Thus we come to the third contract—the juridical contract—that in exchange for their monopoly, autonomy and indepen-

dence there is a corresponding obligation on the legal profession to ensure that there is equal access to law for all members of the community. Indeed, lawyers swear to honour this obligation when they take their oath. As David Luban has argued:

> The lawyer's lucrative monopoly would not exist without the community and its state; the monopoly and indeed the product it monopolizes is an artifact of the community. The community has shaped the lawyer's retail product with her in mind; it has made the law to make the lawyer indispensable. The community, as a consequence, has the right to condition its handiwork on the recipients of the monopoly fulfilling the monopoly's legitimate purpose.

The idea of special status engendering special responsibilities is given even more concrete, quasi-economic form in Lubet and Stewart's "public assets theory." They argue that lawyers are essentially concessionaires, in that the state grants to them exclusive access to certain publically created commodities — including rights of confidentiality, loyalty, lawyer-client privilege, and conflict of interest rules — which they then sell for profit to clients. In other words, a significant portion of the legal profession's income is based upon these specially designated lawyer commodities, which should be compensated by way of a user fee or commission in the form of a contribution to the public good. This monopoly has directly translated into the fact that lawyers, as a group, tend to be extremely well paid relative to other members of the public. Moreover, as I have indicated, a significant portion of many lawyers' salaries comes from the public purse, either as a consequence of contracting out or as recipients of legal aid disbursements.

Furthermore, the education of most Canadian lawyers has been subsidized by the state. Until recently, law school fees have been quite low, accounting for a fraction of the cost of the education provided. While it is true that there has been a significant increase in fees over the last few years, the vast majority of lawyers have been able to maximize their private wealth on the basis of a public investment in their professional training.

In short, the practice of law in Canada is not, and never has been, a private practice freely playing in the competitive marketplace; on the contrary, it is a state created and facilitated privilege and advantage. As Katzman summarizes the argument:

> The state grants ... autonomy, an effective monopoly, in exchange for lawyers, as officers of the court, discharging their duty to further equality before the law ... A lawyer's duty to serve those unable to pay is thus not an act of charity or benevolence, but rather one of professional responsibility, reinforced by the terms under which the state may grant to the profession effective control of the legal system.

A similar point has been made by Dickson J. [as he then was] when he argued: "[i]mplicit in the legislative grants of self government and monopoly is concern for the protection of the public interest. Monopoly is only a means to an end, and that end is service to the public."

Despite this monopoly situation, there are no distinct rules of professional conduct which require lawyers to provide legal services to those of lesser means. Rather there are just aspirational propositions. As MacKenzie notes:

> Canadian rules of professional conduct recognize that lawyers have a general duty to break down barriers to equal access to legal services, but fall short of prescribing such specific duties as acting for reduced or no fees to accomplish that objective. Thus, while lawyers are enjoined to 'encourage respect for and try to improve the administration of justice' (CBA Code, chapter XIII, rule; Ontario rule 11), to have 'a basic commitment to the concept of equal justice for all' (CBA Code, chapter XIII, commentary 1; Ontario rule 11, commentary 2), and to 'make legal services available to the public in an efficient and convenient manner' (CBA Code, chapter XIV, rule; Ontario rule 12(1)), the rules make it clear that lawyers have a general right to decline a particular employment' (CBA Code, chapter XIV, commentary 6; Ontario rule 12, commentary 5), and that whether they wish to participate in legal aid plans and other programmes designed to provide legal representation or public education or advice, is entirely up to them (CBA Code, chapter XIV, commentary 5; Ontario rule 12, commentary 3).

Moreover, lawyers have not been passive recipients of such a monopoly but have proactively encouraged it. Lawyers have resented and resisted paralegals and other non-lawyer agents and this is reflected in legislation in many provinces. It might be possible to deregulate a significant number of legal services (wills, probate, real estate closing, uncontested divorces, title searches) so that they could be performed either by other professionals or even laypersons at significantly reduced costs, thereby increasing access to justice for at least some matters. As one American commentator has suggested, lawyers cannot have it both ways:

> they may accept their roles as public servants and shoulder the burden of bridging the gap between needs and services; or they may characterize themselves as business people and yield their monopoly of the legal services market, thus opening up to competition from non-lawyers and fostering a more available, more affordable market.

b. *Utilitarian Arguments: Distributive and Instrumental Benefit*

Deborah Rhode has succinctly summarized the possible distributive benefits of mandatory *pro bono* as follows:

> promoting more just outcomes in legal disputes; enabling more individuals to enforce their entitlements to crucial benefits; enhancing the legitimacy of the legal system; increasing public regard for lawyers; and expanding attorneys' awareness of how the law functions, or fails to function, for subordinate groups.

From a different perspective, several commentators have argued that there are a number of instrumental values for individuals and institutions to be gained from *pro bono* work. For example, the Brookings Institution in the United States has argued that *pro bono* can be in the self-interest of both lawyers and law firms. For individual lawyers, the quality of their lives can be improved, their morale can be boosted, legal skills can be developed and enhanced, networks can be created, and social capital can be increased. Moreover, it can be argued that *pro bono* is also beneficial for law firms because it enables them to recruit talented junior lawyers who aspire to something more than the treadmill of maximizing billable hours; intensify the productivity of a more experienced, mature, imaginative, responsible and talented staff; enhance employee satisfaction with, and loyalty to, the firm; and project a positive public image that can be a marketing asset in a competitive environment. One English commentator has characterized such arguments as motivated by "enlightened self-interest."

However, as I will discuss in the next section, not everyone is persuaded by such arguments.

4. *Arguments Against Mandatory Pro bono*

Opponents of mandatory *pro bono* have identified at least eight possible objections. While several raise legitimate concerns, others are premised upon mistaken assumptions. None, however, are fatal to the idea of mandatory *pro bono*, properly understood and flexibly institutionalized.

a. *Autonomy*

This rights-based argument is often advanced in response to the monopoly argument outlined previously. Lawyers have rights too; they should neither be conscripted to provide services without remuneration nor compelled to work for someone who is not of their choosing, for this infringes their right of self determination. It is inappropriate to put the burden of access to justice on lawyers alone: "[i]f society wishes to expand legal access, society as a whole should pay the cost."

This is an important argument that requires careful consideration. Usually it is bolstered by analogies to doctors or cab drivers who are also said to be beneficiaries of state-created monopolies, but do not face any *pro bono* requirements. However, several counterarguments might be made. First, arguing that lawyers should not have to perform *pro bono* because doctors or cab drivers do not simply avoids the issue. Second, neither doctors nor cab drivers have the same "public assets" of confidentiality and privacy as lawyers. Third, and closely related, the legal profession's power of self-regulation is distinct from other professions in that it is explicitly justified on the basis of the public interest. Fourth, the analogy to doctors might backfire. Recently, in response to a shortage of doctors in emergency wards, Quebec introduced Bill 114 which empowers the government to force doctors to provide services in emergency rooms on the basis of social necessity. Fifth, the argument relies on an impoverished conception of autonomy. Several relational theorists have rejected "the autonomy as freedom from" metaphor to demonstrate that autonomy is always relational and contextual and therefore embedded in obligations of interdependence and reciprocity. Lawyers are never truly autonomous as they are only free to practice law in the context of the society in which they operate, a society which makes legal relations and lawyers' services not just possible but unavoidable.

Other opponents of mandatory *pro bono* have questioned the assumption of whether lawyers truly exercise a monopoly. To bolster this argument, they argue that litigants can be self-represented, that the large number of lawyers in the marketplace makes for strong competition, that there has been an easing of the restraints on internal competition, and that some other market players do provide legal services. Such arguments are unpersuasive: the vast majority of self-represented litigants are clearly at a disadvantage, and while it may be true that there is some competition within the legal profession, this has not kept the cost of legal services down. Furthermore, these arguments ignore the reality that only lawyers can provide legal advice on the vast majority of legal issues. Indeed as one African-American lawyer has recently noted, "few, if any, attorneys will compete to represent indigent clients ... [and] no amount of competition will provide assistance to the truly indigent."

b. *Necessity*

It is often suggested that the economics of law practice make demands for *pro bono* unrealistic. Such an argument is usually made by way of assertion rather than through empirical proof. However, one cautious (and admittedly limited) study of large firms in the United States found that *pro bono* is "not incompatible with the flourishing of the large law firm." Another commentator has argued that the real costs are greatly exaggerated and do not factor in the intangible benefits. Smaller firms are said to face particularly high costs because of tighter profit margins, higher administrative costs and minimal flexibility. However, as I shall argue later, there may be ways of designing *pro bono* programmes that do not unduly burden small firm lawyers and may redistribute the cost of providing legal services for the disadvantaged to some of the deeper pockets within the legal profession. Indeed, my approach explicitly recognizes and values the contributions — both in kind and financial — of lawyers who work at the lower end of the stratified legal profession and, as such, will not add to their burdens.

c. *Unfairness*

There are two aspects to this argument. The first is connected to the necessity argument just analyzed. It is sometimes suggested that given the fragmentation and inequalities within the legal profession it is unfair to impose mandatory *pro bono* on all lawyers. It has been argued that it is easier for larger firms and wealthier lawyers to absorb the cost of *pro bono* than for smaller firms and less affluent lawyers. Moreover, there is already a significant cadre of lawyers, particularly in the criminal, family and immigration fields, who are already helping the disadvantaged. There is merit in this concern. However, it seems to me that if, as I suggest later, we can devise a flexible system of mandatory *pro bono* — for example, by pro rating to salary/seniority, allowing for buy outs or *pro bono* credits — then this is not an absolute bar. Indeed, mandatory *pro bono* can be viewed as a way of redistributing the burden within the profession, from the lower echelons to the higher echelons, thereby marginally decreasing the inequalities. Coombs characterizes this as a form of "professional cross-subsidization".

The second unfairness argument is that the costs of *pro bono* will not really be borne by lawyers but will be redistributed to paying clients. This consequence would be unfair not only because it would be an arbitrary and unprincipled imposition of a tax upon those who pay, but also because this additional cost would make access to legal services unattainable for even more people. This "robbing Peter to pay Paul" argument is a real danger, but on a redistributive justice basis it can be argued that this disadvantage will be offset by the benefits reaped from a mandatory *pro bono* scheme that also helps to redistribute some of the wealth generated by the new economy from the top of the social hierarchy to those further down.

d. *Competence*

Codes of ethics impose a responsibility on lawyers to engage only in practice where they are suitably competent. As a result of specialization, it may be that some lawyers have little they can offer to the disempowered. Consequently, it is argued that it is inappropriate to foist low quality service on the disadvantaged. It is probably true that a tax lawyer who specializes in international transactions can be of little assistance to a disabled person with an accessibility issue, and they are likely to be inefficient. But there are three responses to the competency objection. First, competency is a comparative concept — would not limited competency be preferable to no legal representation at all? Despite specialization, many lawyers do have the general skills required by many of the disadvantaged. Second, many of the legal problems of the disadvantaged can be addressed if the lawyer is at all competent and is willing to invest some time in developing new skills and knowledge. Such skills can probably be utilized with other similarly disadvantaged persons. Third, as I will suggest later, *pro bono* need not be the actual provision of in-kind legal services, but could be based upon a tax on lawyers or buy out options.

e. *Inefficiency/Impractical*

Deborah Rhode nicely summarizes this objection as follows:

> *Pro bono* obligations are not an efficient way of realizing the benefits of broadened access. Lawyers who lack expertise and motivation to serve under-represented groups will not provide cost-effective representation. Requiring lawyers to provide a minimal level of services of largely unverifiable quality cannot begin to meet [the] nation's massive problem of unmet legal need. Worse still, such token responses to distributional inequalities may deflect attention from the fundamental problems that remain and from more productive ways of addressing them. Preferable strategies might include simplification of legal procedures, expanded subsidies for poverty law programs, and elimination of the professional monopoly over routine legal services.

Moreover, it is suggested that it would be administratively impractical to co-ordinate the provision of *pro bono* services, monitor the quality of the service provided by a lawyer or to ensure there is compliance with any minimal requirements. Unlike most of the previous arguments, these objections come from the left, from those who are skeptical of over-emphasizing the role of lawyers at the expense of a more profound re-organization of legal services. Again, these are legitimate concerns, but it seems to me that realistically large scale reorganization is highly unlikely in the current politico-economic environment. More specifically, some of the criticisms only apply if *pro bono* is assumed to be in kind. However, as I will argue in Part IV, *pro bono* can be more flexible than this. Moreover, the coordination problem may be resolvable by building upon the *Pro bono* Net initiatives already underway in British Columbia and Ontario.

f. *Inherently Contradictory*

Opponents of mandatory *pro bono* often suggest that the term is an oxymoron, as the essence of *pro bono* is its voluntary quality. The coercive and conscriptive dimensions of a mandatory system undercut the moral ideals of personal growth and fulfillment. Two counterpoints can be made. First, *pro bono* has no necessary essence; it need not be conceived of as being about the interests of lawyers, but rather about the impact on recipients. Second, the evidence from the United States indicates that voluntary initiatives systematically fail. In several American jurisdictions mandatory *pro bono* has been resisted and legal organizations have argued that voluntary initiatives can fill the gap. However, the pattern appears to be that while there is a spike in voluntary *pro bono* when mandatory *pro bono* is proposed, within a few years volunteer rates drop significantly. As the Marrero Report in New York commented:

> … the 'voluntarism' so eloquently extolled and advocated by the organized Bar may well amount to little more than a rallying cry for the status quo. When all is said and done, only the same disappointingly small proportion of practicing attorneys who can contribute *pro bono* efforts to the poor would be counted upon to continue bearing the full load for the rest of the legal profession.

g. *Scope*

It may be argued that there are a significant number of lawyers who do not fit nicely with either the monopoly analysis or public assets theory. These might include in-house corporate counsel, government lawyers and law professors. Because they are not providing direct legal advice or selling privacy, they are outside the equation. In response, it can be suggested that these lawyers are still direct beneficiaries of the legal regime. In-house counsel and government lawyers still provide some legal advice or have skills that are directly related to their legal training; and law professors, to be blunt, are parasites whose professional existence is dependent upon the continued market demand for legal services. As beneficiaries, they too must accept their burden.

h. *The Soup Kitchen Argument: Why Legal Services?*

The final argument against mandatory *pro bono* legal services is not an argument in principle against mandatory *pro bono*, but asks whether a lawyer's *pro bono* contributions should necessarily be funnelled into legal services.

Why cannot other socially positive contributions — for example, helping in a soup kitchen — be adequate?

Again, several counterarguments might be suggested. First, there is nothing about mandatory *pro bono* legal services which precludes lawyers from engaging in other additional *pro bono* contributions. Second, because legal *pro bono* need not be in kind, lawyers can have sufficient opportunities to engage in other services, if they choose to do so. Third, lawyers have unique — indeed exclusive — skills and rights as officers of the court that other members of the public do not possess and which the disempowered need. Fourth, and finally, the assumption underlying this view is that *pro bono* legal services are a charitable donation, and therefore *morally* fungible with other charitable contributions. However, in this paper I have assiduously avoided characterizing *pro bono* legal services as charitable in nature; rather, they are a duty that emerges from the special privileges that are given to lawyers ...

ALICE WOOLLEY

"Imperfect Duty: Lawyers' Obligation to Foster Access to Justice"
(2008) 45 Alta. L. Rev. 107
[footnotes omitted]

[In her article, Woolley rejects many of the arguments offered by Devlin on the basis that they do not give a sufficiently accurate portrait of the lawyers' role in the legal system. She argues, however, that there is nonetheless conceptual justification for the imposition of a special obligation on lawyers to foster access to justice based on the imperfections in the market for legal services.]

. . . . .

3. Imperfections in the Market for Legal Services

A. What are the imperfections?

In order to be perfectly competitive, an economic market must have five central attributes: 1) numerous buyers and sellers, so that no part of the market can exercise market power; 2) product homogeneity so that producers are meaningfully competitive with each other; 3) complete information held by all economic actors in the market so that, for example, demand cannot be manipulated by producers; 4) free entry and exit, so that there is supply and demand responsiveness; and 5) an absence of externalities, so that producers bear the costs of production and consumers bear the costs of consumption. With the exception of the first criterion — as already noted there are numerous sellers and buyers of legal services — the market for legal services satisfies none of these criteria.

1) Product homogeneity

First, legal services are inherently non-homogeneous. The services offered by the most intelligent, practical, diligent and experienced counsel in closing a corporate transaction are not the same as those offered by her less qualified counterpart. The differences relate to the time which is put into a matter; the quality of the legal reasoning brought to bear upon a problem; the prior experience of the lawyer in resolving similar difficulties in the past, perhaps to the point of specialization in the area; the inter-personal skills of the lawyer in dealing with other individuals involved in the issue; and a myriad of other relevant skills and qualities. An hour of one lawyer's time may have radically different value than an hour of another lawyer's time.

Further, even were one lawyer much like another, the demands placed on lawyers by their clients are not. The needs of a client litigating a contractual dispute are entirely different from the needs of a client doing an initial public offering for a company. And even the needs of a client litigating a contractual dispute may not be the same of those of another client who is also litigating a contractual dispute. While not all demands are highly variable – one residential house closing is generally much like another – more often than not what one client needs from her lawyer is quite different from what is needed by another client.

The absence of homogeneity in legal goods is exacerbated by the "winner-takes-all" or "tournament" quality of much legal work. In many legal contexts, including most obviously litigation but also to some extent transactional work, the essence of the lawyer's work is not only to obtain good outcomes, but is also to obtain *better* outcomes than those obtained by the lawyer on the other side. In litigation a lawyer needs to win; in a contract negotiation they need to get the best of the deal; in a purchase they need to ensure that their clients' rights and interests are protected relative to the other side. The client thus has a significantly greater stake in the nature of the legal services purchased than does the purchaser of, for example, dental services. As long as a dentist acts within the bounds of professional competence that will usually be sufficient; she does not need to be better than the dentist down the street. By contrast, I need my lawyer not only to be good and competent; I need him to be better and more competent than the lawyer on the other side. Markets with tournament features tend to be associated with price escalation.

Thus, the "product" of legal work is significantly non-homogeneous. What one lawyer is capable of providing is inherently dissimilar to that which another lawyer can provide and what one client needs is inherently dissimilar to what another client needs. Moreover, non-homogeneity is material: the nature of the legal service provided has a significant impact on the client's ability to achieve her goals.

2) Information Insufficiency and Asymmetry

Second, and certainly most importantly, the market for legal services is notable for the total absence — and actual impossibility — of informational sufficiency and symmetry with and between participants in the market. This arises most obviously from the fact that any person who needs a lawyer — who does not have himself the relevant qualifications and abilities — self-evidently lacks knowledge about what needs to be done to solve his problem. He must rely on the lawyer not only to do the work, but also to tell him what it is that needs to be done and how best to do it. A client often does not know, for example, whether writing a will should take one hour or five; he depends on the lawyer to provide an honest answer as to which it is, and to do no more work than is necessary to get the job done.

This informational asymmetry in the market for legal services leads to "agency costs" (the costs arising from the client's need to rely on his lawyer as his agent) and to the characterization of legal services as a "credence good" (in which clients depend on lawyers to tell them how much of the good they need). The point in any event is simply that in general, clients are both relatively and deeply uninformed relative to the lawyer they are retaining: clients know less than their lawyers and what they do not know is significant, going to the essence of the commodity which they are purchasing.

Further, the client's lack of sufficient information is not only relative, it is also absolute. Because legal outcomes are significantly determined by factors outside the control of either the lawyer *or* the client, it may be impossible to determine how much work will be required to resolve a particular problem, or whether even with a great deal of work the problem will be capable of successful resolution. In addition, even after the fact it may be difficult to determine whether an unsuccessful outcome arose from a lack of effort of counsel or from bad luck with respect to the judge, other relevant third parties (a regulator or financial institution), the conduct of other counsel, or a myriad of other factors. As one commentator asked rhetorically, "If the intrinsic quality of the service does remain unobservable, as there are factors outside the lawyers' control which contribute to the outcome, how does the consumer react? In other words is a good reputation consistent with a long run of bad luck?" Or, conversely, should a long run of good luck warrant a good reputation?

The information problems are, obviously enough, an issue more for some types of legal work than for others, and more for some types of clients than for others. The greater the homogeneity and simplicity of the work product in question — closing of a real estate transaction or drafting a will — in general the greater the client's ability to obtain information about what is needed to perform the task. And even for less homogeneous and more complex legal work, a corporate client, who may have in-house experts, and who is far more likely to be a repeat player in the legal services market, is better able to obtain good information about the quality of the legal services which it is purchasing. Corporate clients are less likely to be influenced by "spurious" signals of a lawyer's quality such as fancy offices in a prestigious location than are less sophisticated non-repeat players in the legal services market. They are more likely to have accurate information against which to assess the likelihood that they will be provided with competent and sufficient (but not excessive) service.

Even sophisticated corporate clients are, however, unable to eradicate entirely the information problem when purchasing legal services. As noted, the absence of information is to some extent absolute — *ex ante* predictions about whether a lawyer will be able to achieve the desired legal result are necessarily uncertain and even *ex post* it may not be clear that a good result flowed from a lawyer's high quality efforts. Further, given the "unobservable" quality of legal services even sophisticated clients have to rely on "signals", and particularly status, in deciding whether a lawyer is likely to provide them with high quality service in solving their legal problem. While far from spurious, signals related to status are also not entirely reliable in indicating the quality of the legal services being purchased. The relationship between status and quality is stochastic: "Not every shift in quality at a given level will be detected, not every detected shift will be communicated to the same number of potential future users, and not every communication between users will occur at the same rate".

In addition, a lawyer may have attained high status because of performance in the past, but may not provide quality service consistent with that status because she is now subject to too many demands on her time from a broad client base, or may no longer be capable of the same level of performance as she once was. For example, in a well documented case, Robert Stewart was represented in his initial trial for manslaughter by a lawyer "who had been a formidable leader of the criminal defence bar for many years". At the time of Mr. Stewart's trial, however, this lawyer was almost certainly suffering "from a degenerative brain disorder" and, it appears as a consequence, provided highly doubtful legal services for his client. He arguably made his client's already difficult legal situation considerably worse. Simply put, shifts in quality may not always be reflected in status.

Further, status may be achieved through relationships rather than through actual ability. Association with a particular firm might lead even sophisticated clients to conclude that the lawyer has "quality" which he does not have. A relationship between a corporate client's employee and an individual lawyer may convince that employee of the lawyer's ability, in addition to or in substitution for actual demonstration of it.

Thus, the legal services market is characterized by relative and absolute informational insufficiency. The client knows less than the lawyer, and what he does not know is significant. Further, because quality can only be judged indirectly and imperfectly, obtaining the information relevant for making a rational consumption choice may be impossible.

[Woolley then discusses the imperfections related to market entry/exit and externalities. She suggests that these exacerbate the product non-homogeneity and informational asymmetry/insufficiency problems but are not, in and of themselves, as important.]

. . . . .

B. The consequences of market imperfections — conceptual

Analysts of the market for legal services, or other markets with similar imperfections, generally see two economic consequences as likely to arise. The first is that the imperfections will result in a diminution in the quality of legal services: "consumers may follow price rather than quality, in an unregulated 'race to the bottom';" the "professional service could be 'diluted' to meet a lower price or effectively bilk the client." Under this model, consumers do not know that quality is important, believe that quality is guaranteed by the lawyer's professional qualification or view price as more significant than quality, perhaps because they "assume the worst" with respect to the quality they are going to receive. As a consequence, they purchase the cheapest legal services available. They then, though, are vulnerable to those services being low quality and insufficient to meet their legal needs. Further, and over the profession as a whole, lawyers will be highly competitive with respect to the price they charge and not especially competitive with respect to the quality. They will attempt to lower their prices regardless of the impact on quality which results.

The second identified possible economic consequence of the imperfections in the market for legal services is that they will lead to price escalation and the extraction of economic rents by the profession. A consumer who recognizes that quality is important — and especially if he recognizes that it is disproportionately important because of the winner-takes-all quality of legal services — will prioritize quality over price in making consumption choices. He will be willing to "pay a lot for a little" and will choose the "best" lawyer whose fees are within his budget (rather than the cheapest lawyer he can find). Further, the consumer will assess quality based on signals indicative of quality, particularly status, but also other signals which can, ironically, include price: a higher priced lawyer is likely to be viewed as higher quality than one who is less expensive.

The second economic consequence can occur even where market participants are sophisticated and knowledgeable. In the market for legal services, corporate consumers may be sensitive to costs, and may have better information against which to judge quality, but even they will tend to view outcomes and quality as more important than cost, particularly where the work is "deemed important to the company's business strategy". They will be willing to accept price escalation in a quest for quality. Assume that a corporation is involved in $2 million litigation. Assume that the corporation is skeptical and well-informed, and determines that the top end partner at a local law firm, who bills at $800/hour, will only provide a 10% quality advantage over a junior partner, who bills at $400/hour. Until the lawyer has spent 500 hours on the file, it is more cost effective to retain the top lawyer, even though the difference in quality between the two is much smaller than the difference in price. And where the amount of money at issue is more significant — in a major corporate acquisition, for example — almost any conceivable difference in fees will be rationally incurred to obtain even a minor improvement in quality.

Lawyers' ability to extract economic rents might also arise from the tendency of agent controlled markets to lend themselves to differentiation and specialization. Lawyers who can plausibly assert that the services they provide are unique, or highly specialized, can potentially create sub-markets in which competitive forces relative to price are even less pronounced, and economic rent seeking is heightened.

. . . . .

At least conceptually, then, the imperfections in the market for legal services provide the opportunity for lawyers to obtain economic windfalls — they have the ability to obtain overcompensation relative to the quality of service they provide, whether that quality is high or low. This could, in turn, impede access to justice ....

The question is, though, has this occurred? While lawyers may theoretically be able to extract economic rents, is there any reason to believe that they have actually done so?

[Woolley concludes that the empirical evidence indicating that lawyers are extracting economic rents is weak. There is no evidence to support the race to the bottom scenario (and, in fact, evidence to suggest it is incorrect). There is some evidence to support the price escalation scenario but it is weak and problematic. Thus, Woolley argues that while a public policy response giving effect to lawyers' special obligation to foster access to justice is warranted, that response should be modest in scope.]

NOTES AND QUESTIONS

1. Which author provides a more persuasive argument in favour of lawyers having a special obligation to foster access to justice, whether in the form of a mandatory *pro bono* obligation or otherwise?

2. Do you think analysis of the imperfections in the market for legal services could be meaningfully applied to other ethical questions raised in this book? For example, do market imperfections explain or justify the lawyer's obligation to keep her client's secrets?

3. In her article, Woolley criticizes the monopoly/social contract argument advanced by Devlin on the basis that lawyers are no different from any other licensed service provider who simultaneously meets an important human need (whether dentistry or dispute resolution) and who does so under an exclusive licence from the state (whether as a dentist or as a lawyer). Is this criticism convincing? Or does it simply indicate that the obligations identified for lawyers should be extended more generally?

4. In her article, Woolley also questions voluntary *pro bono* initiatives, such as that described in the following section, suggesting that a rational actor will recognize that (a) those initiatives do not do much to solve the access to justice problem; and (b) the awareness that others may be free riding on efforts means that an individual lawyer will not rationally choose to participate in *pro bono* activities. Do such arguments affect your own assessment of whether *pro bono* activities are worthwhile? Why or why not?

E. INITIATIVES TO FOSTER ACCESS TO JUSTICE

Whatever the arguments for or against such an obligation, Canadian law societies have traditionally accepted that lawyers have a special obligation to foster access to justice. For example, the Commentary to Chapter 1 of the *Professional Code of Conduct* that was formerly used in Alberta (and which has now been superseded by the Federation of Law Societies of Canada's *Model Code of Professional Conduct*) adopted the "monopoly" argument in favour of such obligations:

> ... The *Legal Profession Act* provides that no person other than a lawyer is authorized to practise law.
>
> As a consequence of this position of privilege, lawyers have certain enhanced responsibilities to society. The first is to ensure that competent and high-quality legal services are readily available at a reasonable cost to those who require them. Lawyers also have an obligation to ensure that legal services are generally available to those who require them, and have an obligation to support legal aid plans and referral services, and to act on a *pro bono* basis in appropriate cases.

While not referencing lawyers' monopoly on the provision of legal services, the Commentary to Rule 3.01 of the Federation's *Model Code* similarly provides:

> As a matter of access to justice, it is in keeping with the best traditions of the legal profession to provide services *pro bono* and to reduce or waive a fee when there is hardship or poverty or the client or prospective client would otherwise be deprived of adequate legal advice or representation. The Law Society encourages lawyers to provide public interest legal services and to support organizations that provide services to persons of limited means.

No Canadian law society has taken the position that such activities should be mandatory (*i.e.*, that lawyers who do not do these things should be subject to law society discipline). However, the law societies and Canadian lawyers do participate in a variety of activities to foster access to justice. All interest earned on lawyers' trust accounts is paid into provincial "law foundations" that undertake various justice-related activities, such as financial support for legal aid. Some law societies sponsor lawyer referral services. In Alberta, for example, through the lawyer referral service, the law society refers individuals to three lawyers with some knowledge in the area of concern. The lawyer contacted then provides half an hour of free advice to the individual. The law societies of British Columbia and Ontario also participate in "dial-a-law", "lawline" or other like initiatives in which individuals can obtain some basic legal advice over the phone at no cost. A similar service is available in other jurisdictions but is not provided by the law societies. Finally, a number of law societies have undertaken *pro bono* initiatives to foster lawyers' provision of free legal services to the public. The following excerpt from the *Pro Bono* Committee of Law Society of Alberta indicates how law societies have approached the issue of *pro bono*.

"PRO BONO PUBLICO — FOR THE PUBLIC GOOD"

Report of the *Pro Bono* Committee of the Law Society of Alberta
(April 2003), online: <http://www.lawsociety.ab.ca/files/pbla/
Pro_Bono_Publico_For_the_Public_Good_2003.pdf>
[footnotes omitted]

INTRODUCTION

At the April 2002 Convocation, Alan Hunter Q.C. implored the Benchers to address the professional obligation of lawyers to provide *pro bono* legal services particularly to those who have an inability to pay for those services. The Benchers directed the *Pro Bono* Committee to consider the issues and report to the Benchers with its "thoughts and recommendations".

. . . . .

REASONS FOR DOING *PRO BONO* WORK

First, the Committee considered the reasons to promote the provision of *pro bono* services.

Discussion: It was agreed that there are many compelling reasons for doing *pro bono* legal work. Primarily, it is important to ensure access to legal representation for those who require it, regardless of ability to pay. There are many collateral benefits as well. *Pro bono* service achieves the moral satisfaction derived from helping others, and thus improves the quality of professional life that a firm can offer to lawyers and students alike. Further, it offers a method of training articling students and junior associates by giving them the opportunity to work on files of interest, including, potentially, large and complex matters. It improves the reputation of the legal profession and the individuals and firms who participate in it.

Decision: *Pro bono* services should be encouraged among legal practitioners.

THE ROLE OF THE LAW SOCIETY AND THE *PRO BONO* COMMITTEE

The Committee then turned to the proper role of the Law Society in the promotion of *pro bono* services.

1. *What is the proper role of the Law Society, with respect to the provision of pro bono legal services, in light of its mission statement?*

Discussion: The Committee viewed the promotion of *pro bono* services as in accordance with the mission of the Law Society of Alberta, which is to serve the public interest by promoting a high standard of legal services and professional conduct through the governance and regulation of an independent legal profession.

By promoting access to legal services, the public interest in obtaining high quality professionally delivered services is advanced. By promoting access through the vehicle of a self-governing profession, the public interest in the maintenance of a self-governing profession is demonstrated, and potential challenges to the independence of the profession are convincingly met. For both of these reasons, the Committee agrees with the view recently expressed by the Access to Justice Committee of the Law Society of Upper Canada that access to justice, including through the provision of *pro bono* legal services, "is an integral part of the values of the Law Society as the governing body of an independent, self-governing profession, acting in the public interest."

The Code of Professional Conduct provides in Chapter 1, Rule 4 that: " A lawyer should support and contribute to the profession's efforts to make legal services available to all who require them, regardless of ability to pay." The Statement of Principle in Chapter 5 states: "The profession has a duty to ensure that the public has information regarding the nature and availability of legal services and access to the legal system." The Commentary elaborates on this general principle as follows:

> The *Legal Profession Act* provides that no person other than a lawyer is authorized to practise law. As a result, the profession must ensure that legal services are readily available to those who require them. Lawyers therefore have an obligation to support legal aid plans and referral services and **to act on a *pro bono* basis in appropriate cases.** (emphasis added)

At the same time, the Committee also agreed with the following statement made by the Treasurer of the Law Society of Upper Canada:

> Not all solutions are in the power of the Law Society as a regulatory body. What we can do is provide a structure, offer leadership and encouragement to promote a culture of *pro bono* legal services in Canada.

This qualification does not affect the mandate of the Law Society regarding *pro bono* services, but may affect the methods by which the Society promotes their provision.

Decision: The Law Society of Alberta should take a leadership role in the promotion of *pro bono* legal services among members of the legal profession of Alberta. ...

. . . . .

PRO BONO SERVICE AND LEGAL AID FUNDING

4. *Will an increase in pro bono schemes result in the decline of government funded Legal Aid programs?*

Discussion: While this is a debatable issue, it is not the intention of the Committee that *pro bono* services would in any way replace an adequate Legal Aid system. Rather, it is meant to address areas where the legal aid system does not apply; it is meant to merely complement legal aid programs. It was agreed that an express statement to this effect should be made.

Decision: The Law Society of Alberta should make a statement that *pro bono* programs are not meant to replace Legal Aid programs. Instead *pro bono* programs are meant to complement properly funded Legal Aid programs.

DEFINITION OF *PRO BONO* LEGAL SERVICES

The Committee turned to the definition of *pro bono* services.

. . . . .

B. The Beneficiaries of Pro bono Services

7. *Should the definition of pro bono service restrict the possible recipients of services?*

Discussion: The Committee discussed whether the definition should be limited to the provision of services to persons of limited means. Ultimately, the Committee agreed that, for the reasons set out above, the definition should be broad and inclusive in terms of recipients of services, as well as in other respects. This would not prevent the Committee or the Law Society from developing programs focused on specific projects or needy groups.

Decision: The definition of *pro bono* should not limit the recipients of such services. However, the Law Society in encouraging the development of *pro bono* programs may wish to focus its efforts on *pro bono* legal services for the most needy members of society.

C. Are Pro bono Services Free Services?

8. *Does pro bono service include legal services provided at a substantially reduced fee?*

9. *In order to constitute pro bono service; must there be a lack of expectation of payment on the part of the legal practitioner? If legal services are rendered, and then the client is unable to pay, has the lawyer provided a pro bono service?*

Discussion: It was decided that if the legal service is provided and then the client is unable to pay, this does not constitute providing *pro bono* legal services. The Committee determined that *pro bono* services must be provided in a spirit of charity. It would not be appropriate to include the provision of services at reduced rates within the definition as this practice is common and not exclusively or even predominantly associated with charitable purposes. However, the Committee recognized that there are circumstances where *pro bono* services are rendered and a fee is paid by a client as a mere token of payment. Under such circumstances, the services would be considered to be *pro bono* service.

Decision: There must be a lack of expectation of payment on the part of the legal practitioner. Working for reduced fees is not providing a *pro bono* service, unless the fee is a mere token of payment and the services has been provided in a spirit of charity.

10. *Is working on a Legal Aid file providing a pro bono service in light of the relatively low fees paid?*

Discussion: Again, Legal Aid work is not exclusively or predominantly provided in the spirit of charity.

Decision: Working on a Legal Aid file is not providing a *pro bono* service.

11. Is working on a contingency basis providing a pro bono service?

Discussion: Working on a contingency basis is not exclusively or predominantly provided in the spirit of charity.

Decision: Working on a contingency basis is not providing a *pro bono* service.

D. Are Pro bono Services Legal Services Only?

12. Is community volunteer work considered pro bono work?

Is sitting on the board of directors of a non-profit society *pro bono* work?

Is assisting/consulting with law students at legal clinics a *pro bono* service?

Is instructing bar admission or continuing education courses providing a *pro bono* service?

Discussion: The Committee decided that all community volunteer work involving a degree of legal content should be included in the definition of *pro bono* legal services. Community service without any legal content (e.g., coaching a sports team, canvassing for a charity) would not be included, but work that involves legal issues as well as other issues would be included. Thus service on a board might be *pro bono* service, if it is at least partly legal in nature. With regard to the teaching of bar admission or continuing education courses, as this is legal in nature, and provided it is performed without a fee or expectation of a fee, it should be considered as *pro bono* service. This is consistent with the approach that there should be no restriction regarding the recipients of *pro bono* service. The Committee is of the opinion that the definition of *pro bono* should not include non-legal community service work. This approach is consistent with the LSBC *Pro Bono* Report and other *pro bono* programs in Ontario and throughout Canada.

Decision: Community volunteer work that is legal in nature is providing a *pro bono* service.

E. Voluntary vs. Mandatory Issue

13. Should the definition include a mandatory number of pro bono hours to be completed annually?

Discussion: The Committee decided unanimously that the Law Society should encourage, but not mandate *pro bono* services. If the Law Society chooses to encourage *pro bono* work, and does so effectively, then *pro bono* service should not have to be mandated.

Decision: Pro bono service should not be mandatory.

14. Should the definition refer to a target or desired number of hours?

Discussion: Committee members expressed differing opinions on this issue. Some Committee members felt that it would be useful to include a target number of hours that practitioners or firms could aspire to. If, in the future, the Law Society of Alberta and the *Pro Bono* Committee choose to recruit the assistance of law firms in promoting *pro bono*, then a target number of hours may provide a helpful guide. However, other Committee members felt that inserting a target number into the definition of *pro bono* services would be a step down the path towards mandatory *pro bono* work.

The Committee concluded that a target number may not have to appear in the definition, but could be incorporated into a specific program; this system would allow target numbers to be developed in consultation with firms or practitioners to meet the objectives of the specific program.

Decision: The definition of *pro bono* should not include a target or desired number of *pro bono* service hours to be achieved. In relation to particular programs that may be developed in consultation with firms and practitioners, target numbers could be developed to meet the objectives of the specific program.

15. Are monetary donations providing a pro bono service?

Discussion: The Committee felt that monetary donations should not replace the professional responsibility to provide *pro bono* legal services. In formulating a definition of *pro bono*, the Committee recognized that no person, other than a lawyer is authorized to practise law. Therefore, it is the provision of a lawyer's knowledge and skills that is the essence of the *pro bono* service not a monetary donation. The Committee also recognizes the importance of monetary donations to charitable purposes which may include donations to organizations that provide *pro bono* legal services.

Decision: Monetary donations do not constitute *pro bono* services. ...

G. *Reporting of Pro bono Services*

19. Should the reporting of pro bono services rendered be voluntary or mandatory?

Discussion: The Committee noted that it would be valuable for the Law Society to have statistical information regarding the number of hours that lawyers spend doing *pro bono* work; this would be proof that the legal profession is shouldering its responsibility to those less fortunate in society. Ultimately, however, it was concluded that reporting does not have to be mandated in the definition of *pro bono*. Instead this could be encouraged through the various programs the Committee decides to support or spearhead.

Decision: The Committee is opposed to mandatory reporting of *pro bono* services rendered. ...

NOTES AND QUESTIONS

1. The recommendations of the *Pro Bono* Committee were accepted by the Benchers. Further, as part of its 2007 centenary celebrations, the Law Society has launched "Pro Bono Law Alberta" which is described on its website <http://pbla.ca> as follows:

    Pro Bono Law Alberta's Mission:

    To improve access to justice by increasing the scope and availability of pro bono legal services for Albertans of limited means. Pro bono legal services are intended to complement, not replace, a properly funded legal aid system.

    . . . . .

    ... It undertakes activities relating to these specific goals:

    1. Create opportunities for Alberta lawyers to discharge their professional responsibilities to provide pro bono legal services.

    2. Improve the overall delivery of pro bono legal services by facilitating the integration and co-ordination of services provided by pro bono organizations throughout the province of Alberta.

    3. Ensure province-wide access to high-quality pro bono legal services to persons of limited means by: (i) supporting and improving the quality of existing pro bono programs; (ii) working with existing pro bono legal clinics to assist them in providing pro bono services; and (iii) fostering the development of new pro bono programs where needed.

    4. Enhance the growth of a pro bono culture within the Alberta bar.

    5. Raise general public awareness of pro bono legal services to community organizations and persons of limited means who require legal services.

    6. Raise the awareness of Alberta lawyers of the need for pro bono services and of the resources available to lawyers who are prepared to provide pro bono services.

    What difference will this program likely make to the access to justice problem for Albertans, and in particular for Albertans earning the median income for Canadian families? What would Devlin's analysis say about these Alberta initiatives? Why? What would Woolley's analysis say? Why? What is your own analysis? Provide reasons.

2. In its report, the Committee suggests that if the Law Society "effectively" encourages *pro bono* work then a mandatory program should not be "necessary". Is this a sufficient reason to have a voluntary program only?

3. The Committee also rejects the idea of a reporting requirement. Do you think the Committee gives enough justification for that refusal? Would a reporting requirement affect participation in *pro bono* initiatives? What about the costs associated with a reporting requirement both for lawyers and for the Law Society?

4. In its report, the Committee suggests that *pro bono* work "improves the reputation of the legal profession and the individuals and firms who participate in it". Is this a legitimate reason for the Law Society to emphasize *pro bono*?

5. As previously mentioned, interest on lawyers' trust accounts is used to fund a variety of justice/law-related activities. Does this constitute an effort by lawyers to foster access to justice or by their clients?

6. Who ultimately pays for a lawyer's *pro bono* work, the lawyer or the lawyer's other (paying) clients?

7. Do you think law students should have a *pro bono* obligation? Osgoode Hall Law School requires students to complete 40 hours of public service as a requirement for graduation.[8] In some American jurisdictions, while state bar associations have rejected the imposition of such an obligation on lawyers they have endorsed it for law students.[9] David Luban has also argued that law professors should be subject to a mandatory *pro bono* obligation.[10] Do you agree? Which of the arguments of Devlin or Woolley best supports (or opposes) the imposition of such an obligation on law students?

Scenario One

John Jones operates a private legal clinic just outside of downtown Calgary. He provides services to people of very limited means. He bills his clients but only receives full payment about 30 per cent of the time, and about 20 per cent of his bills are not paid at all. Anne Franklin is also a lawyer in Calgary, working as a partner at a large downtown firm. In her spare time, Anne sits on the Board of her daughter's exclusive private school and provides the Board with legal advice on various governance matters. Which of Anne and John is properly described as doing *pro bono* work? When answering this question, consider the definition of *pro bono* given by the Alberta Committee.

Scenario Two

You have just been named Executive Director of your province's law society. Assume that your province has a legal aid program but as yet has undertaken no other formal program for fostering access to justice. The Benchers have asked that, as your first task in your new position, you advise them as to what initiatives the law society should undertake to foster access to justice. How would you advise them? Use the following chart to guide you in your answer. You may check "yes" to as many features as you like.

---

8   See online: <http://www.osgoode.yorku.ca/programs/jd-program/upper-year-program/opir>.

9   See, in general, Deborah L. Rhode, "Cultures of Commitment: *Pro bono* for Lawyers and Law Students" (1999) 67 Fordham L. Rev. 2415.

10 David Luban, "Faculty *Pro bono* and the Question of Identity" (1999) 49 J. Leg. Educ. 58.

PLAN FOR FOSTERING ACCESS TO JUSTICE[11]

FEATURE	YES	NO
Voluntary *pro bono*		
Mandatory *pro bono*		
Expand Legal Aid offices (*e.g.*, hire more government-employed lawyers)		
Legal fee stamps (like food stamps)		
Public interest law firms		
Reducing the need for lawyers to access the law		
Change the focus of legal education		
Non-profit groups		
Other ideas?		

F.　FURTHER READING

Cramton, Roger, "Mandatory *Pro Bono*" (1991) 19 Hofstra L. Rev. 1113.

Hadfield, Gillian, "The Price of Law: How the Market for Lawyers Distorts the Justice System" (2000) 98 Mich. L. Rev. 953.

Luban, David, *Lawyers and Justice: An Ethical Study* (Princeton: Princeton University Press, 1988).

Lubet, Steven & Cathryn Stewart, "A 'Public Assets' Theory of Lawyers' *Pro bono* Obligations" (1997) 145 U. Pa. L. Rev. 1245.

Millemann, Michael, "Mandatory *Pro Bono* in Civil Cases: A Partial Answer to the Right Question" (1990) 49 Md. L. Rev. 18.

"*Pro Bono Publico* — Lawyers Serving the Public Good in British Columbia", Report of the *Pro Bono* Initiative Committee, a joint Committee of the Law Society of British Columbia and the Canadian Bar Association (B.C. Branch) (June 2002), online: <http://www.lawsociety.bc.ca/docs/publications/reports/ProBono_02-06.pdf>.

Silverman, Ronald H., "Conceiving a Lawyer's Legal Duty to the Poor" (1991) 19 Hofstra L. Rev. 885.

Woolley, Alice, *Understanding Lawyers' Ethics in Canada* (Markham, ON: LexisNexis Canada, 2011), ch. 10.

---

[11]　Adapted from a matrix developed by Innis Christie.

CHAPTER 13

ISSUES IN REGULATION

A. INTRODUCTION

Chapters 1 and 2 provided an introduction to, and overview of, the key questions of legal ethics and the core elements of the Canadian regulatory regime. This final chapter brings us full circle. In light of the analysis and discussions generated by the previous 12 chapters, this final chapter asks whether the right balance has been struck for the regulation of Canadian lawyers. In the opinion of some analysts there is excessive regulation of the ethical conduct of Canadian lawyers; others, however, assert that there is far too little regulation. To focus this debate, this chapter identifies five key issues that can help us reflect upon our own opinions on these matters: the good character requirement; the regulation of extra professional misconduct; sanctioning lawyers for misconduct; the policing of the unauthorized practice of law; and possible alternatives to self-regulation.

As you approach each of these issues, assume that you are a member of the governing body of your law society and this topic has been brought to it for an open discussion of both the issues and potential solutions. Be prepared to: (a) identify the competing values at stake; (b) weigh the pros and cons of the potential arguments available; (c) take a position on the issues; and (d) provide rational and defensible justification(s) for your ultimate decisions.

B. THE "GOOD CHARACTER" REQUIREMENT

A traditional emphasis in regulating the legal profession has been on "inputs" — on determining whether applicants for law society admission are suitably qualified for the practice of law. The main input requirements imposed by provincial law societies relate to questions of competence: whether the applicant has achieved the prescribed educational and licensing requirements — normally that he or she has graduated from an approved Canadian law school, has passed his or her bar examinations and completed a period of articles. In addition, however, all Canadian law societies (along with other jurisdictions) require that applicants for bar admission be of "good character". Or, more accurately, the law societies require applicants to demonstrate an absence of conduct indicating bad character such as prior criminal convictions, academic dishonesty or attempting to deceive the law society. Also, if such behaviour has occurred, the law societies are concerned to ensure applicants are repentant and rehabilitated; applicants must have recovered from the conduct which gives rise to a negative inference about their character.

The purposes of the good character requirement are to protect the public, maintain high ethical standards and maintain public confidence in the legal profession.[1] Its ability to accomplish these purposes rests, however, on the truth of a specific underlying assumption: that character determines conduct, and that an applicant of bad character who becomes a lawyer is more likely to act unethically and more likely to pose a risk to an unsuspecting public.

In reading the next two cases consider the following questions:

(1) How plausible is the assertion that character determines conduct?

(2) Assuming character does determine conduct, how likely is it that a panel of the law society will be able to gauge accurately an applicant's character?

(3) Does the conduct which led to the character inquiry in each of these cases suggest that the law society is appropriately concerned with the applicant's character?

(4) Does it matter that good character is determined through an absence of bad character, as opposed to a positive determination that the applicant's character is good?

PREYRA v. LAW SOCIETY OF UPPER CANADA

[2000] L.S.D.D. No. 60
(Law Society of Upper Canada, Hearing Panel: C. Curtis, Chair,
B. Wright and A. Coffey)
[footnotes omitted]

Introduction

The purpose of this hearing is to determine whether the applicant is of good character (under section 27(2) of the Law Society Act, R.S.O. 1990, c. L.8, as amended), and should now be admitted to the Bar. The applicant is Alan Preyra, a 33-year-old student-at-law who has completed the Bar Admission Course and his articles.

The applicant completed law school at Queen's University in 1994 and completed Phase One of the Bar Admission Course in June 1994. He was unable to find an articling job and in August 1994, in his attempt to find an articling job, the applicant intentionally falsified his law school marks and other academic credentials and pursuits to prospective employers, as follows:

-   He altered 11 grades on the transcript.

-   He sent the altered transcript to at least five law firms.

-   His resume falsely indicated he was a candidate for the Rhodes scholarship.

---

[1] *Re Rajnauth and Law Society of Upper Canada*, [1993] O.J. No. 999, 13 O.R. (3d) 381 (Ont. Div. Ct.).

- The cover letter falsely indicated he intended to pursue a Master of Laws degree at Harvard but could not do so because of financial reasons.

- He misrepresented that he had submitted two lengthy research papers in various different areas to several law journals for publication (including papers on international taxation and intellectual property, competition law and intellectual property, competition law and liability in tort, mergers and monopolies and law and economics).

- He falsely stated that he had been offered five or six articling interviews during articling week.

- He falsely told one law firm that another law firm had told him they would rank him if he ranked their firm.

These misrepresentations were uncovered in August 1994. ... Even after his misrepresentations were exposed, the applicant continued to misrepresent what had happened in significant ways.

- He told the Dean of his law school that he sent false transcripts to only one or two firms.

- He did not disclose the full extent of the misrepresentations to the mentor assigned him by the Law Society (Chuck Magerman), and told the mentor that he had reported it to the Law Society himself.

- In a document prepared by him to be given to prospective employers in January 1998, he did not disclose the full extent of the misrepresentations, but continued to claim that he self-reported, not that he had been caught.

- He continued to misrepresent the extent of his behaviour, even to his own lawyer (Derek Freeman), and his articling employer (David Diamond) until November 1998, when he was finally honest with them about the details of his misrepresentations.

The Test for Admission

The applicant's counsel acknowledged that all of the applicant's behaviour ... dealt directly with honesty and integrity.

These misrepresentations go to the very heart of who lawyers are and what lawyers do. Integrity is fundamental to the competence of a lawyer; competence necessarily includes integrity. The applicant was not of good character from at least 1994 through to at least late 1998. The question for the admissions panel is whether the applicant has changed since November 1998 and is now of good character.

The purpose of the good character requirement is to ensure that the Law Society can protect the public and maintain high ethical standards in the lawyers the Law Society admits to practice. Any decision about this Application must serve to protect the public and maintain high public confidence in the Law Society's self-governance.

The definition of good character is set out in previous decisions of Law Society admissions panels, and is an evolving definition. The definition is not exhaustive, and refers to a bundle of attributes which, when taken together, amount to good character:

> Character is that combination of qualities or features distinguishing one person from another. Good character connotes moral or ethical strength, distinguishable as an amalgam of virtuous attributes or traits which would include, among others, integrity, candour, empathy and honesty.

The onus is on the applicant to prove that he is of good character at the time of the hearing of the application. The standard of proof is the balance of probabilities. The relevant test is not whether there is too great a risk of future abuse by the applicant of the public trust, but whether the applicant has established his good character at the time of the hearing on a balance of probabilities. The test does not require perfection of certainty. The applicant need not provide a warranty or assurance that he will never again breach the public trust. The issue is his character today, not the risk of his re-offending.

It is important not to confuse the good character requirement for admission with notions about forgiveness or about giving an applicant a second chance. The admissions panel is not in the forgiveness business, the test to be applied is clear, and the admissions panel is to determine if the applicant is of good character today. The Law Society Act does not permit an admissions panel to apply any test other than that relating to the applicant's good character at the time of the hearing.

The Evidence

The Applicant's Evidence

The applicant comes from a success-oriented family of ten children, all of whom have achieved significant academic and vocational success. He explained his behaviour in altering his transcript as motivated by his belief that "some of my grades weren't competitive, I wasn't competitive". He described himself as without a safety net in 1994, and having no one he could turn to and rely on when he felt out of control (although his brother was at law school with him in the same class at law school).

The applicant described a healing process for himself that began in September 1994 with a breakthrough at the end of 1998, when he says he fully accepted the extent of his wrongdoing. The applicant says that until the end of 1998 he was still running away from the other details of his wrongdoing. The applicant says that he became an honest person with the Law Society in late 1998, and that he became an honest person before that in other aspects of his life.

The applicant entered therapy from December 1998 to March 1999 with a psychologist, Dr. Leon Steiner. Dr. Steiner treated the applicant with a technique known as brief dynamic psychotherapy during six sessions over a three-month period. There is no therapy, although there is ongoing therapeutic contact (telephone calls). It is the position of the applicant and Dr. Steiner that the applicant's behavioural patterns of misrepresentation and deception, which lasted for at least four years, have now been treated in the six sessions.

The applicant has had some very good things happen to him in the last few years. He married in May 1999, and had two very positive work relationships with the lawyers who acted as his articling principals (Winfield Corcoran and David Diamond). In two major areas of his life (home and work), the applicant has some very good supportive relations.

The Articling Principals' Evidence

Both Winfield Corcoran and David Diamond gave evidence on the applicant's behalf. They were each his articling principals (one after the other) and are now his friends. They were straightforward and supportive. They testified that he had demonstrated honesty and integrity in their offices and in the handling of his files, and that he was a very competent articling student. The applicant was still working for David Diamond at the time of the hearing.

Competence, however, does not prove good character. As well, even his articling principals didn't learn all the details of the applicant's misbehaviour and misrepresentations when they hired him. The applicant was not entirely honest with either of them about what he had done. Both articling principals admitted that they learned of some of the details of the applicant's behaviour for the first time at the hearing.

The Medical Evidence

The medical evidence was detailed, complicated, extremely technical, often contradictory, and in some respects inconclusive. There were five medical reports prepared by three different doctors: Two psychologists (Dr. Leon Steiner and Dr. Percy Wright) and a psychiatrist (Dr. Philip Klassen). All three doctors were present when the applicant gave his evidence, and all three doctors gave evidence.

. . . . .

Evidence of Dr. Klassen

Dr. Klassen is a forensic psychiatrist, who works with issues dealing with the legal process, and conducts assessments and prepares reports for the Law Society and other professional disciplinary bodies. Both his report and his oral testimony were extremely detailed. He found no mental illness in the applicant, but described him as experiencing, in 1994, grandiosity, a sense of being special or unique, with a need for admiration and, perhaps most significantly, a sense of entitlement. The medical evidence established that the applicant had been very angry throughout law school and in the period immediately after law school.

The fact that the applicant came from a high-achieving, and success-oriented family, coupled with the fact that he struggled at law school, resulted in anger, a sense of injustice, and a sense of entitlement in the applicant. He felt that others had an easier time, and that he was being treated unfairly. The sense of failure was a blow to his self-esteem, which resulted in a counterattack. Dr. Klassen described the applicant in 1994 as an angry man who was going to take control of the profession that had treated him badly.

Dr. Klassen's analysis was that the applicant had been involved with serious transgressions in 1994 and had continued behaving in duplicitous and fraudulent ways for a number of years after that.

Only in late 1998 or early 1999 did the applicant decide to discontinue his struggle with the Law Society. Dr. Klassen expressed doubt that this was the result of his therapy. He noted that the therapeutic contacts had been brief. He noted that of the six sessions with Dr. Steiner, it was not clear how many sessions were assessment sessions. He described the result of the sessions as more confession than treatment. Dr. Klassen's skepticism about Dr. Steiner's therapy was related to the applicant's history of duplicity over a long period of time, which appeared to be caused by a personality of character deviation which, in turn, was a foundation of lying.

Dr. Klassen described the relationship between character and behaviour, stating that behaviour flows from character. In 1994, the applicant displayed bad behaviour from which an inference could be drawn about bad character. In 1999, the applicant displayed good behaviour. The question for Dr. Klassen was whether this was the result of a conscious decision on the part of the applicant to change his behaviour without an underlying change in character (in which case, his earlier behaviour was related to transient factors), or whether that good behaviour flowed from the applicant's bad character as yet unchanged.

. . . . .

Decision

Being a lawyer is a great privilege; it is a gift, not a right. It is not automatic, and does not necessarily follow from passing law school and the Bar Admission Course. More than simply meeting the academic standards, the statutory scheme is clear that an applicant must also be of good character.

The applicant engaged in duplicitous behaviour over a long period. He failed to be entirely honest about it for four years. This was not a single lapse of judgment resulting from a stressful situation. Even after being caught, the applicant had several opportunities to admit his misrepresentations to all that he should have. He did not do so. As recently as one year before the hearing, the applicant was still misrepresenting the truth to people close to him, and was still failing to be honest with his articling principal, and even with his own lawyer.

The transition from being a person not of good character to one of good character is a process, not an event. It may or may not happen to someone who was not of good character. It may or may not happen to this applicant. The applicant asserts that he has been in the process of change since 1994. Central to the task of the admissions panel is to determine whether that process is concluded. ...

The applicant has not satisfied the onus of proof, on the balance of probabilities, that he is now of good character.

LAW SOCIETY OF UPPER CANADA v. BURGESS

[2006] L.S.D.D. No. 81
(Law Society of Upper Canada, Hearing Panel: P. Copeland, Chair,
A.F. Coffey and J.M. Potter)

... The purpose of this hearing was to determine whether the applicant is of good character and should now be admitted to the bar. The applicant is Aidan Christine Burgess, a 27-year-old law student who has completed the Bar Admission Course and her articles.

· · · · ·

As revealed in the Agreed Statement of Facts, Ms. Burgess was found to have committed plagiarism in regard to an essay she handed in during her fourth year at the University of Toronto. That event, which occurred in the spring of 2001, standing alone, would not have precluded us from making a finding five years later that Ms. Burgess was of good character.

What is of much more serious weight are the ongoing and persistent lies told by Ms. Burgess to the Law Society of Upper Canada and to various persons who provided her with character references.

As revealed in the [University] Discipline Case Report ... received by the Law Society, Ms. Burgess was caught having submitted an essay for credit that was substantially based on material taken verbatim from an internet source without appropriate sourcing.

In her letter to the Law Society, dated November 11, 2003, Ms. Burgess gave a false account of the U of T incident:

> While attending the University of Toronto, there was a claim made against me for academic misconduct in PHL382 "Death and Dying," for handing in a paper that was deemed to be too similar to a paper that I had handed in for another course. Although the claim was the result of a misunderstanding, I did not proceed with a hearing because I was graduating. I failed the course and was cautioned for academic misconduct.

· · · · ·

By letter dated January 4, 2005 Ms. Burgess provided a 2 1/2 page letter to the Law Society. In that letter, in great detail, Ms. Burgess in effect repeated her original lie to the Law Society, the same lie that she had given to her two personal character references and to her two professional references. In that letter (a portion is reproduced below) Ms. Burgess explained why she had not obtained the requested letter from her Articling Principal.

Reproduced below is a significant portion of the letter (with footnotes omitted.) The letter was addressed to Kim Bailey, an investigator at the Law Society.

> This is in response to your letter dated November 29, 2004 in which you requested that I provide a written explanation of the circumstances surrounding my academic record at the University of Toronto and at Queen's University.
>
> 1.   University of Toronto
>
> At the University of Toronto I was cautioned for academic misconduct under the University's Code of Behaviour on Academic Matters. This Code states in section B.I.1 that it "shall be an offence for a student knowingly: e) to submit, without the knowledge and approval of the instructor to whom it is submitted, any academic work for which credit has previously been obtained or is being sought in another course or program of study in the University or elsewhere." I was enrolled in both PHL 382 – Death and Dying, and PHL 407 – Seminar in Ethics. I wrote a paper for both courses.
>
> For the Ethics course, I wrote a paper regarding the use of "slippery slope" arguments within ethical debates. I maintained that such arguments are not valid and should not be used to substantiate ethical norms. I received an A- in this course, and there was no issue with respect to the authorship or proper referencing of any materials. In the course on Death and Dying, I wrote a paper on the euthanasia debate which incorporated the illegitimate use of slippery slope arguments when arguing against euthanasia. This paper was focused on arguments for and against euthanasia, and only used slippery slope arguments as one example. I did, however, use portions of my paper from the Ethics course. I did not think this would be a problem since I was only using a portion of the paper and they were significantly different papers with different substantive arguments using different philosophers. Because I did not think it would be a problem to use sections of a paper that I had written when writing another paper, I did not ask for permission from my instructor to use my previous paper.
>
> The instructor in my Death and Dying course believed that I had committed an academic offence by submitting similar academic work for two courses, and reported the matter to the department chair and the Dean. The Dean called me in for a meeting where we discussed the situation and the various options available to me. The Dean advised me that if I did not admit the alleged offence, my case would proceed to a tribunal for decision. He stated that the University tried to avoid such costly and lengthy proceedings, and indicated that if I were to be found guilty at such a proceeding, the penalty could range from suspension to expulsion from the University. The Dean said that if I were to admit to the offence, I would fail the course with 40% and would have a notation on my transcript for 6 months. This notation would say that I had been cautioned for academic misconduct. After the 6 months, the notation would be removed.
>
> I decided to admit to the offence even though I did not think I had violated the University's policy. Despite my certainty that the papers were substantially and significantly different and did not constitute the same academic work, I was not sure how a tribunal would respond, especially if it

included members who were not familiar with philosophical papers and arguments. I was about to graduate and did not want to risk facing suspension or expulsion from the University. At the time, I thought that since I had already been accepted into law school, having one failed course on my transcript was better than risking my entire degree. After coming to this conclusion, I admitted to the offence, failed the course and was cautioned for academic misconduct with a six month notation on my transcript.

[The portion of the letter addressing her alleged plagiarism at Queen's University is redacted.]

3.   My Thoughts on Plagiarism and My Actions

I recognize that plagiarism is a very serious academic offence and appreciate that the functioning of the academic system relies on students properly referencing materials. I think that it is dishonest to attempt intentionally to pass off someone else's work as your own, and that stealing ideas is just as wrong as stealing anything else. Although there is a lot of pressure on students to get good marks, I think that grades must be earned and be an accurate reflection of a student's ability. Students should not receive grades for work that they did not do.

I would definitely handle my situation at the University of Toronto differently today.

. . . . .

On April 21, 2005 the Law Society Investigator, Yvonne Skilton telephoned Ms. Burgess to enquire about the apparent discrepancy between the explanation contained in Ms. Burgess' letter dated November 11, 2003 and the Discipline Case Report that had been received from the University of Toronto. That Discipline Case Report had been received by the Law Society on September 30, 2004.

In oral evidence, Ms. Burgess said that at the time of the incident she had been given a handbook and Rules regarding the situation at the University of Toronto. From reading the handbook and Rules she knew that handing in a paper that was too similar to another paper that had been handed in was treated as plagiarism. She testified that as a result of gathering that knowledge she created her original (false) story. She was aware that she had to give some explanation to the Law Society about the nature of the plagiarism.

It was only when confronted with the discrepancy that Ms. Burgess acknowledged to the Law Society the correct facts concerning the plagiarism incident at the University of Toronto.

. . . . .

On April 25, 2005 Ms. Burgess had spoken with Lorne Abugov and Patricia Brady [her professional references] and explained what actually happened in the plagiarism incident at the University of Toronto.

By letter dated May 4, 2005 Mr. Abugov and Ms. Brady advised the Law Society that notwithstanding the lie told to them by Ms. Burgess about the U of T plagiarism incident, they continue to stand by her in support of her as a person of good character.

By letter dated August 9, 2005, Ms. Burgess advised Professors Pardy and Baines [her academic references] of the U of T incident.

By e-mail dated August 12, 2005 Professor Baines acknowledged receipt of the letter from Ms. Burgess and indicated "I have no intention of amending the character reference that I provided".

By letter dated September 30, 2005, Professor Pardy stated, in part, to Ms. Skilton as follows:

> At the time I wrote my January 2005 letter, I was not aware of this incident of plagiarism. The fact that Ms. Burgess was found guilty of plagiarism at the University of Toronto does not change the observations that I made in my letter. However, I am surprised and disappointed that Ms. Burgess did not communicate this fact to me earlier. I would have expected, in a request for a reference letter, complete disclosure of circumstances surrounding the investigation.

Ms. Burgess' August 9, 2005 letter to Professors Pardy and Baines acknowledged a plagiarism incident at the U of T but did not, in any way, reveal to those Professors that Ms. Burgess had lied to the Law Society about the nature of that plagiarism incident.

The oral evidence of good character given by Blair Williams and by Lorne Abugov was very thoughtful and impressive. Lorne Abugov, in particular, had taken very seriously his responsibilities in regard to providing a letter of character reference for Ms. Burgess.

He testified that Ms. Burgess had made disclosure (albeit a false disclosure) of the U of T plagiarism incident to Mr. Abugov on April 1st. Mr. Abugov indicated that his initial view of Ms. Burgess had been that she was one of the best articling students he had seen.

Mr. Abugov testified that he had come to the Law Society and talked to them about his responsibilities and to help him figure out his responsibilities to all of the various stakeholders. Mr. Abugov testified that it took him 18 days to write the first character letter for Ms. Burgess. He said he was stunned and shocked by the first disclosure.

Even after the second disclosure, Mr. Abugov continued to support Ms. Burgess and to regard her as a person of good character. Both Mr. Abugov and Ms. Burgess testified that Ms. Burgess withdrew her name from consideration for hire-back by Osler, Hoskin and Harcourt.

Ms. Burgess testified as to the six counselling sessions that she had taken through the Osler, Hoskin & Harcourt Employee Assistance Program which paid for counselling services at Warren Shepell Consultants Corp. Mr. Abugov testified that he was aware Ms. Burgess had attended those counselling sessions.

The Panel was provided with the counselling note from those six sessions. They were quite minimal and of little to no assistance to the Panel.

Ms. Burgess testified that both for economic reasons and because in the counselling session she had dealt with the issue of putting forward the false account of plagiarism, that she felt the six counselling sessions were sufficient.

There was evidence presented to us of many varied positive things that Ms. Burgess had done in the community, including volunteer work for Amnesty International, extensive coaching of soccer, and assistance to other students.

It is also of significance to the Panel that Melanie Polowin, the counsel for Ms. Burgess was from the Ottawa branch of Osler, Haskin & Harcourt. We regard that as another indication of the support that firm is giving to Ms. Burgess.

The issue for the Panel is whether or not, on a balance of probabilities, Ms. Burgess has established that she is of good character today.

It is very clear that she was not of good character up until August 25, 2005. Ms. Burgess lied to the Law Society over an extended period of time and lied to her references. The sophistication of the lie, describing a very different type of activity that still fit within the definition of plagiarism at the University of Toronto, is of great significance to this Panel.

We note that there was no psychiatric or psychological evidence called at this hearing. Such evidence was called in the second *Preyra* case and was called in the *Miller* character hearing. ...

. . . . .

In Ms. Burgess' case we do not think that there has been sufficient passage of time for us to be able to conclude that Ms. Burgess has established that she is a person of good character and suitable for admission as a member of the Law Society.

Given the serious nature of the deception engaged in by Ms. Burgess, the Panel would have found it helpful if we had had some psychiatric and/or psychological evidence presented to us concerning Ms. Burgess and concerning the behaviour that she engaged in, up until as recently as 17 months ago.

The Panel references the comments from paragraph 42 of the first *Preyra* decision.

> The transition from being a person not of good character to one of good character is a process, not an event. It may or may not happen to someone who was not of good character. It may or may not happen to this applicant. The applicant asserts that he has been in the process of change since 1994. Central to the task of the admissions panel is to determine whether that process is concluded.

It is urged before us that the applicant's serious deception resulted from her embarrassment and shame over the plagiarism incident at the University of Toronto.

As noted above, the deceptions to the Law Society and Ms. Burgess' references continued until April 25, 2005.

Central to the task of this Panel it is to determine whether the process of change since April 2005 has concluded. We do not believe that there has been sufficient passage of time for us to find that the bad character exhibited by Ms. Burgess up until April 2005 has changed.

In our view the applicant has not satisfied the onus of proof on the balance of probabilities that she is now of good character.

It gives us no pleasure to make this decision. From the references it appears that Ms. Burgess is a very intelligent and competent individual. Perhaps in future she will be able to establish to the satisfaction of a Panel that she is of good character and a suitable person to be admitted to the Law Society.

NOTES AND QUESTIONS

1. Preyra was ultimately admitted to the Law Society of Upper Canada: *Law Society of Upper Canada v. Preyra*, [2003] L.S.D.D. No. 25 (L.S.U.C.). In the subsequent decision, the panel noted the improved evidence of rehabilitation. It also noted the evidence of Preyra's law firm employers under whose supervision he worked in an essentially legal capacity (these lawyers also gave evidence in the first hearing).

2. In *Preyra* and *Burgess*, the bad conduct of the applicants concerned misrepresentations to the Law Society and to prospective employers as well as, in Burgess' case, academic misconduct. How significant should the nature of the applicant's misconduct be in determining whether or not the applicant is of good character? In answering the question, consider the following three cases from 2011. In *Law Society of Upper Canada v. Manilla*, [2011] L.S.D.D. No. 39, 2011 ONLSAP 10 (L.S.U.C.), the Law Society rejected Manilla's application for admission on the basis that he was not of good character. Manilla had engaged in a protracted dispute with his condo board and had shouted, made ethnic slurs, written and posted defamatory letters about board members purportedly written by someone else, and engaged in other offensive conduct. He was charged criminally but the charges were withdrawn after he agreed to sell his condominium unit, refrain from any further statements about the board and made a charitable contribution in the names of the complainants. In *Law Society of Upper Canada v. Smithen*, [2011] L.S.D.D. No. 60, 2011 ONLSHP 44 (L.S.U.C.), the Law Society accepted Smithen's application for admission on the basis that she was of good character. Smithen had, *inter alia*, 38 convictions for fraud-related offences between 1979 and 1993; made misrepresentations to immigration authorities and the Canada Revenue Agency in 2000; had worked in the sex-trade industry as an escort from 1992–1999 and from 2002–2004; and had made misrepresentations in a family law proceeding in 2005. In *Law Society of Upper Canada v. Bornmann*, [2011] L.S.D.D. No. 141, 2011 ONLSHP 130 (L.S.U.C.), the Law Society accepted Bornmann's application for admission on the basis that he was of good character. In 2004 Bornmann had admitted to paying bribes to government officials in British Columbia and had agreed to provide evidence against the government officials in a criminal investigation in exchange for immunity from prosecution. When applying for articles Bornmann only told the law firm that he was going to

be a witness in a criminal trial; when the firm found out about his admission of bribery they requested that Bornmann resign.

3. In *Preyra* the applicant argued that he should be admitted subject to conditions. The Law Society held that it had no power to impose conditions on an applicant for admission. Should such a power be granted to the Law Society? What kind of conditions should be imposed?

4. In an early case on the good character requirement, the Law Society of Upper Canada rejected the relevance of evidence of future good conduct to the decision. The panel said that the applicant in that case "did not need to demonstrate good character beyond a reasonable doubt, nor was he obligated to provide a warranty or assurance that in the future he would not breach the public trust".[2] This position was also noted in *Preyra*. Is this limitation on the consideration of character consistent with the accomplishment of the requirement's stated purpose of protecting the public and ensuring the maintenance of ethical standards?

5. In applying the good character requirement, law societies do not independently investigate applicants. They rely on self-reporting and on being contacted by third parties about applicants' issues of character. Is this sufficient? Does it potentially result in some applicants being unfairly singled out for scrutiny? See *Law Society of Upper Canada v. Shore*, [2006] L.S.D.D. No. 63 (L.S.U.C.). Or does it simply convert the law societies' monitoring of good character into a "fig leaf"?

6. How appropriate is the weight given by the panel to the psychological evidence filed in the *Preyra* case and to the absence of such evidence in the *Burgess* case?

7. In every reported case on good character, positive character evidence is filed. Indeed, in the first published case of a person denied admission to the Law Society of Upper Canada — whose character was at issue because of his conviction for crimes related to his sexual assault of two children — one witness testified that it would be "a tragedy for him and the legal profession if such a talented person were to be shut out".[3] What weight should the Law Society give such evidence?

C. EXTRA-PROFESSIONAL MISCONDUCT

In addition to regulating the character of applicants for admission to the bar, law societies also assert jurisdiction over misconduct by lawyers outside of their legal practice. At its narrowest this jurisdiction allows a law society to regulate ethical misconduct which is substantially, but not technically, related to the lawyer's conduct within legal practice. Thus, for example, in *Adams v. Law Society of Alberta*,[4] excerpted below, the Law Society of Alberta disbarred Adams for soliciting sex with his young (16-year-old) prostitute client. The victim was also the girlfriend of another of Adams' clients. Adams' misconduct was squarely within the conduct of his legal practice (as the court noted, soliciting sex from her was a considerable abuse of his client's trust).

---

[2] *In the Matter of an Application for Admission to the Law Society of Upper Canada by Joseph Rizzotto*, Reasons of Convocation (September 14, 1992) at para. 32.

[3] *Re P. (D.M.)*, [1989] O.J. No. 1574 (L.S.U.C.).

[4] [2000] A.J. No. 1031 (Alta. C.A.).

However, had the girl not been his client — but simply the vulnerable young girlfriend of his client — Adams' abuse would still have been related to his conduct of his legal practice. It would have been technically, but not substantially, outside of his legal practice. The power of the law societies to discipline for extra-professional misconduct ensures that a technical argument that the misconduct occurred outside of the lawyer's legal practice is unavailable to lawyers who have behaved unethically in this way.

At its broadest, however, the power of the law societies to regulate for extra-professional misconduct extends much further. It allows the law societies to discipline a lawyer for any behaviour which the law society believes constitutes "conduct unbecoming" a member of the law society. Canadian lawyers have been disciplined (albeit in some cases mildly) for "conduct unbecoming" as varied as public nudity, failing to care for animals at the lawyer's farm and writing a bad cheque to a landlord.

The lawyers in the following two excerpts were disciplined by the law societies for far more serious incidents of extra-professional misconduct: murder and sexual exploitation of minors. In reading the excerpts consider the following questions:

(1) Is it legitimate to take away someone's ability to practice his or her profession because failing to do so would "compromise the public's respect for the law and the legal profession"?

(2) Where there is no evidence to indicate that the lawyer has acted unethically within the confines of his or her legal practice, is it nonetheless reasonable to conclude that lawyer's unethical behaviour outside of his or her practice casts doubt on that lawyer's future ability to practice law ethically?

(3) What types of extra-professional misconduct should concern law societies? What types of extra-professional misconduct should not?

LAW SOCIETY OF UPPER CANADA v. BUDD

[2009] L.S.D.D. No. 141, 2009 ONLSHP 111
(Law Society of Upper Canada, Hearing Panel: Thomas G. Heintzman, Q.C. (Chair), Patrick G. Furlong, Q.C., Catherine Strosberg)

. . . . .

The Notice of Application seeks a determination, pursuant to s. 34(1) of the *Law Society Act*, that Peter Brian Budd (the "Lawyer") has contravened s. 33 of the *Law Society Act* by engaging in conduct unbecoming a licensee.

. . . . .

III. EVIDENCE

(i) Admission and Finding of Conduct Unbecoming

[The parties signed an Agreed Statement of Facts that indicated that the lawyer has been convicted of criminal conduct in relation to his sexual exploitation of two girls, sisters with whom the accused had sexual relationships when they were in their teens (ages 14 and 16 when they first had sexual intercourse with the lawyer). The girls and their mother were friends with the lawyer prior to the sexual relationships beginning.]

In his Reasons for Sentence the trial judge stated as follows:

> This case is unique. Convictions were registered against Peter Budd on two charges of sexual exploitation relation to two D. sisters ...

> In 1985, s. 153 of the Criminal Code was introduced by the then Minister of Justice, the Honourable Ray Hnatyshyn. He is quoted by Mr. Justice Cosgrove in *R. v. Palmer* [1990] O.J. No. 51, as follows:

>> "We have a responsibility to protect children from sexual abuse and exploitation and to deter those who seek to victimize them."

> While both girls had sex with Peter Budd when they were in the formative and still-maturing youth, it is difficult in this case to find "true victims" in the ordinary sense of the word.

> The Victim Impact Statements of both sisters seem to indicate that they relate their victimization to either, as in A's case, not being able to see Peter Budd any longer, or in K's case, losing him as a friend. Letters of reference in this case are numerous and glowing. Peter Budd has no criminal record and until this matter was exposed, was a major, positive contributor to society and apparently still may be.

> He is relied upon by his sons for moral and financial support and by his former wife for financial support to some degree. His friends and acquaintances to [*sic*] continued to rely upon him for assistance and advice.

> But, he is guilty of a breach of trust.

> . . . . .

> Little remorse has been shown as indicated by the letters of reference, and the actions of Peter Budd throughout.

> I do believe that serious consideration must be given to the fact that society places a premium on the predictability of our relationships with each other, and it must be shown that a breach of trust is not to be treated lightly. Deterrence of others must be given some prominence. On the other hand, the acts were consensual and the girls were over 14.

> In my view, but for the breach of trust, all other sentencing factors to be considered are mitigating.

> . . . . .

We were advised by counsel for the Law Society and counsel for the Lawyer that the transcript at the criminal trial indicates that an oral apology was offered by the Lawyer when the family was informed about the events.

(iv) The Evidence Tendered by the Lawyer

The Lawyer led considerable evidence to address the appropriate conduct order and mitigating circumstances. The evidence fell into three categories:

medical evidence; evidence of his professional career and competence; and evidence from friends and from neighbours in the community where his farm and the farm of the D. family were located.

Dr. John Bradford is the Associate Chief of the Healthcare Group, Forensic Section of a major civic hospital. Dr. Bradford examined the Lawyer and subjected him to a number of tests for the purpose of determining whether the Lawyer had a likelihood of reoffending. He concluded that the Lawyer did not have any deviant sexual preference. He agreed with the trial judge's statement the likelihood of the Lawyer re-offending was very remote.

Dr. Bradford said the Lawyer took responsibility for the fact that he should have morally behaved in a better way. He was of the view that the Lawyer would be at the low end of risk for future sexual problems of any difficulty.

Under cross-examination Dr. Bradford agreed that, in order for a person to be remorseful, the person had to have insight into what he had done wrong, and the more selective one is about the facts that one is willing to accept the less insight one generally has about one's behaviour, and the less insightful one is the less remorse one can have. He agreed that when the Lawyer was speaking with him there was some minimization of these facts. Dr. Bradford agreed that the Lawyer told him the evidence that occurred in court was not what actually happened, and that the Lawyer was minimizing the relationship and the exploitation concerning A.D.

Dr. Bradford acknowledged that the crimes the Lawyer committed were not as a result of any disorder or mental illness and that the Lawyer was a normal, heterosexual man who happened to have access to teenage girls and was found guilty of abusing their trust and that of their parents.

Dr. Bradford agreed that, if he had administered his tests to the Lawyer 10 years ago, he would have received the same results. Indeed, Dr. Bradford said that, had he conducted his test 10 years ago, he would have found the Lawyer was a low risk for offending.

In re-examination, Dr. Bradford said that there was nothing to indicate that the Lawyer could not learn from his mistakes and that taking responsibility morally was a step forward. He said that the "other side of it" is the consequences of the actions have been severe to the Lawyer and he is very sensitive to that. Dr. Bradford also stated that he had been given by the Lawyer examples of testimony at the criminal trial which the Lawyer felt were unfair.

[The decision then summarizes extensive evidence from Budd's colleagues and family testifying to his legal abilities and his character. The witnesses generally viewed Budd's sexual relationships with K.D. and A.D. as an error of judgment that was aberrational relative to the conduct of the rest of his professional and personal life.]

. . . . .

The Lawyer filed as Exhibit 5 a booklet containing: letters from the Lawyer's brother, his sons and former wife; letters from friends and from persons living near the Lawyer's farm; letters from persons who know the Lawyer from business or professional circumstances; and articles about the Lawyer and his legal specialty in the energy field.

The letters from the Lawyer's brother, two sons and former wife describe a person who is generous and has a passion for helping others both professionally and personally and one who has a loving relationship with his sons. The letters from his friends and acquaintances again describe a person who is generous and loving and a leader in his community. The letters from business acquaintances attribute the same qualities to the Lawyer. Included within those letters is one from Dr. Nathan Pollock indicating that counselling was provided to the Lawyer as a result of the emotional impact of his criminal conviction and incarceration and the implications for his career and personal relationships, with the counselling focused primarily on helping the Lawyer adjust emotionally to the destruction in his life.

(v) Impact on the D. Family

The impact on the D. Family of the Lawyer's sexual relations with the three D. girls, and the criminal proceeding is described in the Impact Statements tendered at the criminal trial and the Impact Statements filed in this proceeding.

In her Victim Impact Statement tendered to the criminal trial K.D. indicated that after returning to high school in 2004 she felt "as though everyone was watching and judging me feeling that they all knew what I had done and been through. It was a stressful and constant worrying time that drove me to exhaustion." K.D. said that in April 2004 she was admitted to the psychiatric ward of the Victoria Hospital in London, Ontario for having suicidal thoughts and attempts. She was in the hospital for five days. After returning home she was unable to return to school. Her statement indicates that she has been on an emotional rollercoaster for two and a half years having feelings of doubt and worry or being completely and totally embarrassed and ashamed of what she had caused her family and herself. As the trial judge noted, K.D. expressed a feeling of loss of the Lawyer to herself and her family. Her statement demonstrates an ambiguous feeling of loss of friendship.

In her current Victim Impact Statement in this proceeding, K.D. expresses the guilt she had in May 2006, and still has, saying that "There is no easy way of reminding myself that it was not my fault and that he was the grown adult, and he knew what he was doing." Her statement reveals the anxiety, relief, confusion and disappointment surrounding the double life she had lived with the Lawyer and its revelation.

A.D.'s Victim Impact Statement at the criminal trial demonstrated her opposition to the charge laid against the Lawyer and her continued attachment to the Lawyer. In her statements in this proceeding, A.D. strongly expresses her opposition to the charges laid against the Lawyer, her continued affection for the Lawyer and her opposition to the Lawyer losing his right to practise law as a result of the events in which she was involved.

. . . . .

IV. LEGAL ISSUES, ANALYSIS AND REASONS

Rule 1.02 of the *Rules of Professional Conduct* defines "conduct unbecoming a barrister or solicitor" to mean as follows:

> [C]onduct, including conduct in a lawyer's personal or private capacity, that tends to bring discredit upon the legal profession including, for example, (a) committing a criminal act that reflects adversely on the lawyer's honesty, trustworthiness, or fitness as a lawyer, (b) taking improper advantage of the youth, inexperience, lack of education, unsophistication, ill health, or unbusinesslike habits of another, or (c) engaging in conduct involving dishonesty or conduct which undermines the administration of justice.

The commentary to this definition of "conduct unbecoming a barrister or solicitor" states in part as follows:

> Dishonorable or questionable conduct on the part of a lawyer in either private life or professional practice will reflect adversely upon the integrity of the profession and the administration of justice. If the conduct, whether within or outside the professional sphere, is such that knowledge of it would be likely to impair the client's trust in the lawyer, the Society may be justified in taking disciplinary action.

The well-established criteria determining the appropriate conduct order are: the protection of the public, the preservation of the public's confidence in the legal profession, and the maintenance of high professional standards. In determining the just and appropriate conduct order to serve those disciplinary objectives we are required to consider the gravity of the misconduct and the need for both specific and general deterrence and the particular circumstances of the offending lawyer and the context of the misconduct.

In determining the appropriate conduct order, an essential exercise is to ensure that the conduct order imposed upon the Lawyer is comparable to the conduct order imposed in other similar cases. As Justice Cory said in *Re Stevens v. Law Society of Upper Canada*:

> Any sentencing involves an onerous exercise of will that involves a conscious act of balancing and comparison. How bad is the wrongdoer presently before the tribunal compared first, to the non-wrongdoer and, secondly, to other wrongdoers. Sentencing requires a consideration of the accused and the facts of the case presently before the Court. A conscious comparison should be made between the case under consideration and similar cases wherein sentences were imposed. If the comparison with other cases is not undertaken, there may well be such a wide variation in the result as to constitute not simply unfairness but injustice. Considerations of such a nature should have as great a significance for professional discipline bodies with the power to impose onerous penalties as they do for courts of appeal and of first instance dealing with sentences upon conviction of criminal offences.

A determination of similar cases can start with a broader or narrower range of conduct considered to be comparable. A narrow range of comparisons in this case could involve sexual relations between a lawyer and persons under 18 years of age and involving a breach of trust. Comparisons on a wider basis could include sexual relations between a lawyer and any persons, including adults, and involving circumstances of a solicitor-client relationship and/or mental incapacity or depression. We will first examine discipline cases which bear the most immediate comparison to the present one. We will then examine cases which fall within a broader range of comparability.

[The panel reviewed the case of *Law Society of Upper Canada v. Johnston*, in which a member was disbarred for having sex with underage prostitutes he met during the course of his employment as a Crown Attorney.]

. . . . .

In the *Johnston* case, the lawyer was disbarred. Certain features of that case are more serious than the present one, but other features of the present case are more serious. The fact that the lawyer in the *Johnston* case was a crown attorney was found by the Hearing Panel to be an aggravating factor since the lawyer had access to a captive "client" pool of prostitutes over whom he could exercise his power. The lawyer called no evidence on his behalf and relied on only written materials. No character evidence was called nor any character letters filed on his behalf. No evidence concerning the lawyer seeking or receiving psychiatric help, alcohol counselling and drug counselling was tendered and there was no evidence that the lawyer wanted rehabilitation or was capable of rehabilitation. Those factors are very different from the present circumstances where there was no power relationship arising from a court setting and abundant evidence has been led on behalf of the Lawyer in this case with respect to his character and the unlikelihood of repeat conduct.

Certain features of the present case are, however, more serious than those in the *Johnston* case. In the present case, the Lawyer has been convicted of offences in relation to K.D. and A.D. over a prolonged period of time. The Reasons of the trial judge indicate that the relationship between the Lawyer and A.D. commenced at an even younger age, but the Agreed Statement of Facts before us establishes that the Lawyer and A.D. began their sexual relationship in the summer of 2000 when she was 16 years of age and he was 39 years old. It continued up to the summer of 2002 when A.D. was 18 years old and she moved in to live with the Lawyer and the relationship continued. The relationship between K.D. and the Lawyer commenced in the fall of 2002 when she was 16 and continued until November 2003. On one occasion K.D. had sexual relations with the Lawyer when A.D. and D.D. were in the Lawyer's home. K.D. and the Lawyer had sexual relations on several more occasions over the following year. So these sexual relations between the Lawyer and these two young persons were not single occurrences but conduct which continued repeatedly, over at least three years.

The second distinguishing feature in the present case is the relationship of trust and confidence, which the Lawyer breached, both with respect to the mother, D.D. and the young persons themselves. In paragraphs 1 to 7 of his judgment dated May 16, 2006, the trial judge described how the Lawyer worked his way into the D. family life, became a confidante and friend and abused the trust which had been placed upon him, particularly by the mother, D.D. As the trial judge said: "D.D., K.D. and the accused all knew that this encounter only took place because of the privileged position in which the accused found himself and the reliance of the mother on his integrity ... The accused permitted sex to take place knowing that he had been entrusted with K.D.'s safety and well-being. K.D. knew it as well."

The third aspect of the present case which distinguishes it from *Johnston* is the way in which the Lawyer employed A.D. in order to create a relationship of dependency, reliance and trust. As the trial judge noted:

> A.D. worked for the accused at his home, cottage and as a receptionist in his law office. She lived at his home as a tenant, sometimes free of rent ... He looked after her in the big city. He got permission from her parents to take her to England in November 2001. He employed and housed her. And he had sex with her. There is no doubt that the accused deceptively camouflaged the sexual nature of his relationship with A.D., at least at the beginning, and capitalized upon the trust position in which he found himself with A.D. just as he had with K.D ... [H]e was entrusted with their safety and protection and he violated it.

A fourth element of the present case is the purposeful, secretive and deceptive nature of the Lawyer's conduct. As the trial judge noted in his judgment of May 16, 2006, "the accused deceptively camouflaged the sexual nature of this relationship with A.D.". In his Reasons for Sentence the trial judge stated that: "This abuse lasted over a period of time. It was premeditated. Mr. Budd continually deceived Mrs. D at least, and perhaps Mr. D., in order to facilitate the sexual acts ... [the sexual exploitation was] carried on over a prolonged period and was accompanied by repeated acts of deceit permitting it to continue ... the incidents were premeditated and for [the lawyer's] personal gratification." In her Victim Impact Statement to the criminal trial K.D. describes breaking "our promise and told the secret that he and I shared."

The breach of trust inherent in the Lawyer's conduct and his criminal conviction strikes at one of the most important characteristics of the stature of lawyers and the confidence in which they are held by the public. Such a prolonged breach of trust in relation to young people made vulnerable by their age and the imbalance in the nature of the relationship between them and the Lawyer renders this case equally serious, and in our view more serious, than that in *Johnston*.

[The decision considered other sexual exploitation cases.]

. . . . .

With respect to the issues of specific and general deterrence, counsel for the Lawyer and for the Society both submitted that specific deterrence was not an issue in this case. Counsel for the Lawyer referred to the fact that the trial judge found the likelihood of the Lawyer re-offending was very remote. Dr. B came to the same conclusion. There is nothing on the record before us that would support the conclusion that the Lawyer will in the future commit sexual misconduct. Having said that, the fact that the Lawyer acted in such disregard for the well-being of young persons, and by way of breach of trust and deceptively, does leave us with some lingering concerns about his care towards other people notwithstanding his otherwise exemplary conduct. Notwithstanding those concerns, we do not conclude that specific deterrence is a material element in the determination of the appropriate conduct order in this case.

So far as general deterrence is concerned we consider that factor to be one of importance in this case. Lawyers must know that to act in the fashion in which the Lawyer acted in this case amounts to unacceptable conduct that deserves and will receive a severe response from the Law Society. In our view the protection of the public interest merits no less a response.

The issue of general deterrence is an important factor by itself, but it also has a connection to the maintenance of the standing and integrity of lawyers before the public. We return to that issue later in these Reasons. In our view, general deterrence of lawyers from engaging in exploitative sexual behaviour, and maintaining the public's confidence in the status of lawyers and their entitlement to practise as a self-regulating profession, are two sides of the same coin.

. . . . .

Placing the present facts in that context, here we have convictions for sexual misconduct involving a breach of trust with young persons over a lengthy period of time. That conduct - a criminal act, a breach of a lawyer's trustworthiness, and the taking advantage of youth - are all elements specifically referred to in the definition of "conduct unbecoming" in Rule 1 of the *Rules of Professional Conduct*. The penalty for professional misconduct of this kind has invariably been disbarment (or now, revocation) or permission to resign. In this context a consideration of the historical conduct and the issue of mitigation will now be addressed.

[The Panel then considered mitigating factors.]

. . . . .

As counsel for the Law Society has pointed out, no evidence of remorse was given by the Lawyer during these proceedings. While the Lawyer's counsel sought to have him make a statement not under oath, this Panel held that any such statement should be made under oath, and no such evidence was given.

... The difficulty in the present circumstances is that the acknowledgement by the Lawyer has been accompanied by a reluctance to accept that the evidence was properly presented to the criminal trial. Moreover, there is force to the submission of counsel for the Law Society that, to a considerable extent, the Lawyer's acknowledgement of his "mistake", and the witnesses' evidence about that acknowledgment, has been about the consequences to the Lawyer himself, rather than to the D. family.

. . . . .

In the present case, as already noted, there is no evidence that the conduct of the Lawyer can be explained by a medical or psychiatric disorder or substance abuse from which he had been successfully rehabilitated. To the contrary, the Lawyer was apparently an outstanding citizen before and after the events in question. If Mrs. D had been asked for her opinion about the character, reputation and standing of the Lawyer before the instances in question, she would have spoken as eloquently as have the witnesses who have testified before us and written letters on the Lawyer's behalf. As counsel for the Law Society submitted, it may be that the Lawyer's conduct is only explainable as greedy and lustful conduct, or as the trial judge said "personal gratification". In the absence of medical, scientific or other appropriate evidence, it is not appropriate for the Panel to give weight to an explanation as a mitigating factor.

Moreover, the character evidence given on behalf of the Lawyer was given by persons who knew the Lawyer during the very years that he was engaging in the sexual conduct with the D. girls. They were totally unaware of it. They were as misled as Mrs. D. If an explanation is sought by way of mitigation, none arises from the character evidence. While it may relate to the unlikelihood of the repetition of the conduct, that conclusion cannot be wholly justified if it does not explain the original conduct.

In our view, the absence of any meaningful expression of remorse removes that factor and the related factor of acknowledgement of misconduct as mitigating factors in relation to the proper conduct order to be imposed upon the Lawyer.

. . . . .

We are unable to find any condition from which the lawyer suffered at the time and for which he has been rehabilitated, and true remorse. We are left with a lawyer who has had an outstanding career, but who has committed a crime, and serious misconduct for a member of a profession that is based upon principles of trust and the protection of the weak and vulnerable.

We return to the criteria for determining the appropriate conduct order: the protection of the public, the preservation of the public's confidence in the legal profession, and the maintenance of high professional standards; and in that context and to serve those objectives, the gravity of the misconduct, the need for both specific and general deterrence and the particular circumstances of the offending lawyer and the context of the misconduct. It is in that context that the evidence of mitigation and the character evidence must be considered.

We consider the gravity of the misconduct to be of a high order. In our view, while specific deterrence is not necessary in this case, general deterrence of this sort of conduct is of great importance both for the legal profession and the public. There are no circumstances of the offending solicitor which explain or can give a mitigating context to the misconduct. In these circumstances, it is our view that the conduct order of revocation is an appropriate one. In other comparable cases of similar misconduct that has been the conduct order which has been imposed.

In considering the appropriate conduct order we have given consideration to two other potentially mitigating factors: the consent of the D. daughters to the sexual exploitation which occurred; and the criminal proceedings and conviction and the suffering that the Lawyer has endured by reason of those proceedings. Neither factor is, in our view, a mitigating factor.

. . . . .

... We recognize and have considered the outstanding career which the Lawyer has had, the contribution which he has made to society and the other factors in his favour referred to in paragraphs 91 and 92 of these Reasons. However, those factors do not sufficiently address and mitigate the distrustful, deceptive and prolonged nature of the sexual exploitation of the two young persons in this case. ... [T]hey do not adequately address, nor do they displace, the need in the present case to address the maintenance of the collective reputation of the legal profession and the public's confidence in the membership and regulation of that profession.

Accordingly, we conclude that revocation is the appropriate conduct order in this case. It has been the order in similar cases and is the appropriate order having regard to the gravity of the Lawyer's misconduct. No sufficient reason or mitigating factors have been shown to us to depart from that conclusion.

In the result, an order for the revocation of the Lawyer's licence is made.

. . . . .

[In its decision upholding this decision, an appeal panel of the Law Society of Upper Canada concluded: "The Appellant brought opprobrium upon the profession. Revocation of licence is deserved as a matter of general deterrence and of maintaining public confidence in the legal profession" (*Law Society of Upper Canada v. Budd*, [2011] L.S.D.D. No. 6, 2011 ONLSAP 2 at para. 89 (L.S.U.C.)). This case was affirmed: [2012] O.J. No. 577 (Ont. Div. Ct.).]

LAW SOCIETY OF ALBERTA v. SYCHUK

[1999] L.S.D.D. No. 15
(Law Society of Alberta, Hearing Committee: A.D. Macleod,
F. Swanson and W. Willier)

This is an application for reinstatement pursuant to the above sections of the Legal Profession Act and the Law Society Rules. The Applicant was disbarred on October 18, 1990 following his conviction of Second Degree Murder for which he was sentenced to life imprisonment without eligibility for parole for ten years.

. . . . .

On October 13th, 1998, the Applicant applied for reinstatement as a member of the Law Society of Alberta. Under the Legal Profession Act, a person who has been disbarred shall not be reinstated as a member except by an Order of the Benchers.

. . . . .

Events Leading up to Disbarment

One only has to read Mr. Sychuk's curriculum vitae as of October, 1986 and which is attached to his affidavit (Exhibit C) to appreciate how tragic and dramatic was his fall from grace. He was a very well known professor of law at the University of Alberta. He was frequently consulted by other lawyers, companies and individuals because of his reputation as an expert in oil and gas law and land titles matters. He was a Bencher of the Law Society of Alberta.

However, while the Applicant was a very high achiever, signs of a troubled person emerged. He was a heavy drinker. On November 10th, 1985, the Applicant became inebriated and quarrelled with his wife. When he went down to the basement, she locked the basement door and he subsequently blew the lock off the door with a shotgun. He entered a plea of guilty to a charge of using a firearm without lawful excuse and without reasonable precautions for the safety of other persons and received a conditional discharge. One of the conditions was to continue therapy for alcohol abuse.

On December 31st, 1987, Mr. Sychuk and his wife, Claudia, went out with friends to a New Years Eve Party. They quarrelled. The Applicant was intoxicated and when they returned home, the quarrel continued. The following is a quote taken from the Reasons for Judgment of the Honourable Mr. Justice MacKenzie delivered on January 27th, 1989 in the case of Her Majesty the Queen vs. Maurice Sychuk:

> "On the early morning of January 1st, 1988, a total of twenty-two stabs wounds were inflicted upon the wife of the accused. In addition, her left arm had been broken by a twisting motion requiring considerable force coupled with blunt trauma. Her hands had cuts indicating efforts to defend herself from a knife attack. She was also struck with considerable force on the mouth and on the left eye. Of the twenty-two stab wounds, nine of them were life-threatening and, indeed, the wounds caused her death. There is no question but that the accused inflicted the injuries and caused her death."

On behalf of the Applicant, it was argued that because of his intoxication, a conviction of manslaughter was appropriate, but the Applicant was convicted of second degree murder and this conviction was upheld by the Alberta Court of Appeal on January 9th, 1990. Leave to appeal to the Supreme Court of Canada was refused on June 14th, 1990. Although he sought to resign, the Applicant was disbarred on October 18th, 1990.

Applicant's Testimony at the Hearing

Most of the evidence was admitted by agreement in written form. The only witness was the Applicant and we had the benefit of his lengthy testimony in addition to his affidavit in support of his application, statutory declaration and other materials authored by him.

As one might expect, the events of January 1st, 1988 were devastating to the entire Sychuk family. The Applicant attempted suicide following the murder and deep feelings of agony, guilt, remorse, self-loathing, and depression plagued him for years. Of the three children, the two older ones do not have a relationship with the Applicant. Fortunately, the Applicant and his youngest son Bruce have developed a close relationship and early on, he promised Bruce that he would not take his own life. Since then he has embarked upon a long and difficult journey of rehabilitation. His progress has been remarkable and admirable. He has received a lot of psychiatric and psychological treatment and counselling. He is a recovering alcoholic and has not had a drink since that fateful evening. He states that he has gotten in touch with his feelings and has developed coping mechanisms and methods of monitoring which are designed to enable him to manage his anger and remain sober. Whereas before the tragedy, he was unable to get in touch with his feelings including his deep-seated hatred of his father, he is now sensitive to his feelings and is able to deal with them without drinking or venting his feelings in the form of anger.

While in prison, he participated in a number of programs and indeed, he has designed and led programs dealing with rehabilitation from addictions.

The Applicant acknowledges the enormity of the crime he has committed and states that over the last eleven years he has grown as a person and believes that he has a great deal to contribute as a member of the Law Society of Alberta. He says that the prime motivation for his wanting to be reinstated is not to practice his specialty which is oil and gas law, but to help others who have problems with respect to addictions and related problems. His evidence on this point is significant. When asked why he applied in October of 1998 for reinstatement, he responded in part:

"I have made that application because of all of the difficulties that I had been having in my efforts to share my knowledge with members of the public.

Unfortunately there is still a tremendous degree of hypocrisy, and while people purport to worship at the shrine of rehabilitation, when push comes to shove, that is not the manner in which they act.

...

It is my firm belief that the process that I am going through and that the attendant vetting of my rehabilitation by the Law Society of Alberta will give me both an accessibility and an acceptability to participate in the kinds of programming that I want to do that is otherwise very difficult for me to do."

While the practice of law is part of it, he made it very clear that it was not his prime motivation.

The Applicant has developed a new relationship with a lady friend and is presently living in Calgary with her. She was one of the witnesses interviewed by Mr. Busch and her interview is contained in Exhibit D. She is, of course, supportive and it appears that their relationship is excellent.

. . . . .

Responses to the Law Society's Notice

This application is controversial. Letters were received from over ninety people, most of them members, and they were still coming in during the course of the hearing. All but a handful expressed opposition to the Applicant's reinstatement. The opposition had a common theme, which was unrelated to the issue of rehabilitation. It had to do with the public's perception of the Law Society and public respect for the law and the rule of law. Typical of the responses is the following:

> "I read with concern the Notice in this matter dated June 2nd, 1999. Although I do not have any evidence relating to Mr. Sychuk's application for reinstatement, I do know of a reason why he should not be reinstated, and that is simply this: As lawyers, we are sworn to uphold the law. The rule of law is so vital to a civil society, yet so fragile, and under so much attack in today's world. Violent responses to emotionally charged situations are becoming more commonplace. Many people (especially our young people) are being bombarded with influences against the law and the rule of law in society. Assuming for the moment that Mr. Sychuk has completely reformed himself and has overcome his psychological problems, it would still be problematic to allow reinstatement of his membership in the Law Society because of the mixed message we would be sending to the general public. By allowing Mr. Sychuk, a convicted killer, to again practise law, the importance of the rule of law to lawyers and the importance of keeping oaths is minimized, and this will erode the confidence of the public in our profession. As a former high profile member of the legal community, Mr. Sychuk and his criminal conduct have already reflected badly on lawyers in this province: let us not make the mistake of throwing aside justice, integrity, and morality, and allow him to once again be reinstated as a certified member of our profession."

A response was received from eleven members of the Faculty of Law of the University of Alberta. The letter said in part:

> Thirdly, an exercise of self-governance cannot be proper if it brings the entire practice and philosophy of self-governance into disrepute. In our view, a decision to readmit Mr. Sychuk would work just such a result. The public whom we serve and on whose trust we finally depend would loudly and widely condemn the decision and the independence which made it possible, and this response would be entirely justified. Quite simply, there exists no defensible theory of self-governance or of legal ethics which would ground a decision to re-admit a person under a life sentence or a person who has been proven, in a court of law, guilty of committing an act in violation of the most basic human right, morally and at law, namely, the right to life.

Applicant's Position

In addition to the voluminous evidence, we were also grateful to receive a large volume of authorities filed on behalf of the Applicant and the Law Society. The argument on behalf of the Applicant was structured around three issues:

1. Whether a conviction for a serious offence was an absolute bar and on that issue, the Applicant, through Mr. Craig, submitted authority to the effect that it was not.

2. Whether an individual can be a member, even though he is on parole, and it was submitted that the rules contemplated this possibility and that unless the Applicant reoffends, the restrictions of parole do not interfere with the functions of a barrister and solicitor.

3. If the answer to the first two issues was in the Applicant's favour, then the only remaining question is whether there is clear and convincing evidence of rehabilitation.

We have chosen not to deal with those three issues separately. First of all, the answer to any or all of those questions is not necessarily determinative of the issue before us which is whether this Applicant ought to be reinstated. Second, the issues ought not to be considered separately and in isolation. The Applicant's overall position is summarized in the following three paragraphs.

A number of authorities support the proposition that there is no per se bar to readmission because of the seriousness of the crime. Moreover, there is no per se bar to readmission on the basis that the Applicant is on parole. The controlling factor to an application for readmission at law is rehabilitation. While the seriousness of the crime is a legitimate consideration, it speaks to the amount of proof the benchers should require of complete rehabilitation. In other words, the more serious the crime, the more clearly it has to be demonstrated that rehabilitation has been complete. Rehabilitation is a core precept in our society and it is a principle that should be honoured and respected by the Law Society. Disbarment is not a life sentence. The Law Society should not be less forgiving than society at large if the evidence of rehabilitation is clear and compelling, and there is no danger that the Applicant will reoffend. The Applicant, through dint of hard work and the endurance of a lot of pain and agony, has made tremendous progress on his road to redemption and right thinking people with knowledge of the facts and the applicable principles of rehabilitation would reinstate Mr. Sychuk. Indeed, it would be wrong to deprive society from the benefits of the Applicant's considerable talent and the benefit of his difficult experience.

The letters received in response to the Law Society notice ought to be in large measure discounted because all of the responses opposing his reinstatement are authored by people who have had no contact with the Applicant since his disbarment.

While the Law Society acted entirely appropriately in disbarring Mr. Sychuk in 1990, the Applicant had met the criteria at law for reinstatement because the evidence of rehabilitation was overwhelming and uncontradicted.

. . . . .

Discussion

The textbook, *Lawyers and Ethics*, by Gavin MacKenzie of the Ontario Bar was cited to us. At page 23-2, it states:

> "The purposes of the good character requirement are the same as the purposes of professional discipline: to protect the public, to maintain high ethical standards, to maintain public confidence in the legal profession and its ability to regulate itself, and to deal fairly with persons whose livelihood and reputations are affected."

At page 26-61, the author states under the heading Readmission:

> A former lawyer who has been disbarred or given permission to resign may apply to be readmitted. As the Alberta Court of Appeal pointed out in a 1988 case, '[t]he removal of a lawyer from the rolls of the Society is not "a life sentence".' Applications for readmission in Ontario are heard by a panel of three benchers sitting as a quorum of the admission committee, which makes a recommendation to Convocation.
>
> In Ontario, the standard that an applicant for readmission must meet has been articulated as follows:
>
> 1. As a general rule, an order of disbarment for serious professional misconduct is intended to be permanent. Readmission should be the exception rather than the rule.
>
> 2. Applicants must show by a long course of conduct that they are persons to be trusted, who are in every way fit to be lawyers.
>
> 3. Applicants must show that their conduct is unimpeached and unimpeachable, and this can only be established by evidence of trustworthy persons, especially members of the profession and persons with whom applicants have been associated since disbarment.
>
> 4. A sufficient period of time must have elapsed before an application for readmission will be granted.
>
> 5. Applicants must show by substantial and satisfactory evidence that it is extremely unlikely that they will misconduct themselves in future if permitted to resume practice.
>
> 6. Applicants must show that they have entirely purged their guilt.
>
> 7. Applicants must show that they have remained current in the law through participating in continuing legal education since the termination of their membership in the Law Society, or at least that they have a plan acceptable to the Law Society that will enable them prior to readmission to become sufficiently current in the law to fulfil their responsibilities as lawyers."

. . . . .

Understandably, counsel for the Applicant stressed three cases in which individuals convicted of homicide were admitted to the bar.

. . . . .

It must be noted that in none of these cases was the crime committed while the Applicant was a member of the bar. Indeed, in *Manville*, the Court made it clear that had the crime been committed while the Applicant was a member, the disbarment would be permanent. Moreover, in at least two of the cases, the crimes were committed by the Applicants when they were young. While the age of Mr. Brousseau is not revealed in the decision, it seems likely that he too was young. In only one of the cases (the English case) was the Applicant on parole. With respect to the Brousseau case, it would appear that there may be mitigating factors of which we are not aware because the sentence of fifty-eight months was a light one, given the nature of the crime, and the Applicant only served one year of that sentence.

We agree with counsel for the Applicant that as a Committee of Inquiry, we must carry out our mandate and make our recommendation in accordance with the law. In our view, however, the lists of criteria contained in the textbooks and cases cited on behalf of the Applicant are not very helpful in this particular case. In a case such as this, certain principles come to the forefront making other considerations pale in significance. We agree with counsel for the Law Society that rehabilitation cannot be the paramount factor at the expense of the standing of the legal profession.

As a starting point, Section 47 of the *Legal Profession Act* defines "conduct deserving of sanction" as:

> "any conduct of a member, arising from incompetence or otherwise, that:
>
> (a) is incompatible with the best interests of the public or of the members of the Society, or
>
> (b) tends to harm the standing of the legal professional generally."

Clearly, then, the statute under which the Applicant applies for reinstatement recognizes the importance of the standing of the legal profession. Moreover, under Section 39, people are not admitted as students at law unless they are "of good character and reputation". Good character without a good reputation is insufficient.

An independent legal profession is an important part of a democratic society. Along with an independent judiciary, it serves the Rule of Law. More than that, each of our members takes an oath which includes the following:

> I will not pervert the law to favour or prejudice anyone, but in all things will conduct myself truly and with integrity. I will uphold and maintain the Sovereign's interest and that of my fellow citizens according to the law in force in Alberta.

While he was not there dealing with reinstatement, it is useful to read the words of Stevenson, J.A. [in] *Achtem v. Law Society of Alberta* ...

> "Indeed, it may be thought to be unseemly to permit someone to practise law who has been found guilty of a serious violation of the law which he is bound to uphold. The legislature may have recognized the undesirability of

permitting a serving prisoner the privilege of membership in the Law Society."

Then, later on at the same page:

"The status of convict is *prima facie* inconsistent with the privileged office a lawyer occupies."

Fundamental to the role of lawyers in society and the administration of justice is the need to uphold the law. In our view, this principle becomes even more critical when the legal profession is self-governing and independent from the state. In Alberta, unlike some other jurisdictions throughout the world, the legal profession is not supervised directly by the courts or by the state. As a self-governing profession, we are all too aware that the public sometimes sees us as self-serving rather than fulfilling our mandate which is to govern in the public interest and to protect the public interest.

Moreover, many of the authorities cited to us by the Applicant support the view that respect for the legal profession and the law is a paramount consideration. For example, in the *Hiss* case, supra, the court noted at pp. 441 and 442 that:

"Indeed, the counsel of the Boston Bar Association, the organization which filed the information leading to disbarment, voted to communicate the opinion to the Board that Hiss' resumption of practice would not adversely affect the standing and integrity of the bar or the public interest."

. . . . .

In our view, an application for reinstatement is much different from an application for admission to the Bar. The Applicant in this case, in addition to committing the most serious of crimes, has broken faith with his oath, his role as an officer of the court, and as a member of our Law Society. As Deborah Rhode wrote in her article "Moral Character as a Professional Credential" ...

"Clearly the rationale for monitoring practitioners' personal behavior is somewhat stronger than the justification for screening candidates' conduct. Attorney actions, unlike much applicant misconduct, cannot be discounted as remote in time or the product of youthful indiscretion. Moreover, violations of the law assume a different symbolic dimension when committed by those sworn to uphold it."

Ultimately, the Benchers must assess the effect of the admission to the bar of this Applicant on public respect for the legal profession and the law in Alberta.

. . . . .

Mr. Sychuk was convicted of a brutal crime, one of the most serious crimes one can commit. It was not a product of youthful indiscretion. Two years prior to killing his wife, he discharged a shotgun in his own home in the presence of his wife and children while drunk. This case has achieved widespread notoriety. For the crime of murder, he was sentenced to life imprisonment. We have received a great deal of evidence as to Mr. Sychuk's difficult journey to rehabilitation. However, rehabilitation is not the only principle at play here. In

Regina v. C.A.M. ... the Court discussed principles of sentencing and said at
p. 369:

> "[81] Retribution, as well, should be conceptually distinguished from its
> legitimate sibling, denunciation. Retribution requires that a judicial sentence
> properly reflect the moral blameworthiness of that particular offender. The
> objective of denunciation mandates that a sentence should also communicate
> society's condemnation of that particular offender's conduct. In short, a
> sentence with a denunciatory element represents a symbolic, collective
> statement that the offender's conduct should be punished for encroaching on
> our society's basic code of values as enshrined within our substantive
> criminal law. As Lord Justice Lawton stated in *R. v. Sargeant* ... 'society,
> through the courts, must show its abhorrence of particular types of crime,
> and the only way in which the courts can show this is by the sentences they
> pass.' The relevance of both retribution and denunciation as goals of
> sentencing underscores that our criminal justice system is not simply a vast
> system of negative penalties designed to prevent objectively harmful
> conduct by increasing the cost the offender must bear in committing an
> enumerated offence. Our criminal law is also a system of values. A sentence
> which expresses denunciation is simply the means by which these values are
> communicated. In short, in addition to attaching negative consequences to
> undesirable behaviour, judicial sentences should also be imposed in a
> manner which positively instills the basic set of communal values shared by
> all Canadians as expressed by the Criminal Code."

Largely because of his exemplary conduct as a prisoner and his success at
rehabilitation, the Applicant was granted day parole effective March 4th, 1996
and full parole effective January 1st, 1998. However, while he is on parole, he
is at law still serving his sentence for life. ...

. . . . .

The life sentence imposed upon the Applicant reflected society's denunciation
of the crime he committed. Moreover, at the time, he was an officer of the
court sworn to uphold the law and this exacerbating factor calls for increased
denunciation by the Law Society which governs the legal profession in the
public interest. In our opinion, this denunciation by the public and the Law
Society would be compromised or undermined if the Law Society were to
reinstate him. One of the main reasons he seeks reinstatement is to improve
his acceptability; in other words, his respectability in the community. Implicit
in that is that membership in the Law Society and the Bar of Alberta carries
with it a badge of respect, but that brings us full circle. In our view, the Applicant's admission to the Bar of Alberta would tarnish that badge, not because he is a bad person, but because of the enormity of the crime he committed while a member of the bar. In reaching this view, we are not rejecting the
principle of rehabilitation or the qualities of forgiveness and mercy. Indeed,
we recognize them as valid considerations. In the circumstances of this case,
however, it is our view that these considerations cannot prevail where reinstatement may compromise the public's respect for the law and the legal profession.

Even if we are wrong, however, and rehabilitation is the controlling factor, we would not have recommended that the Applicant be admitted to the bar. We concede that the evidence of rehabilitation is substantial, and we concede that the Applicant has developed new ways to deal with his anger and his addiction. Nevertheless, he has only been out on full parole since January 1, 1998, and in our view, insufficient time has passed to provide us with sufficient comfort of complete rehabilitation.

Conclusion:

We are all of the opinion that the application for reinstatement should not be granted.

. . . . .

... While our recommendation is against his reinstatement, we wish to assure Mr. Sychuk that we very much admire the inner strength he has demonstrated on his continuing journey to personal redemption and rehabilitation. We wish him well.

. . . . .

NOTES AND QUESTIONS

1. The 2007 Calendar of Seminars for the Canadian Association of Petroleum Landmen contains the following entry for one of its instructors:

    Maurice J. Sychuk, B.A.; LL.B.; M.C.L.; Q.C.

    Mr. Sychuk taught Oil and Gas Law for 22 years at the Universities of Alberta and Saskatchewan. He also taught Land Titles, Company Law, Real Property Law and Contracts.

    Mr. Sychuk practiced law for 24 years and was a member of the Law Societies of Alberta, Saskatchewan and the Northwest Territories. His principal area of expertise was the negotiation, drafting, interpretation and litigation of contracts used in the oil and gas industry, but he acted as Counsel, Advisor, Consultant, Expert Witness and Arbitrator on a myriad of oil and gas law issues. His expertise in oil and gas law has been recognized internationally. ...

    Mr. Sychuk is now semi-retired and has been working part-time as a Consulting Landman where his work has involved him in all aspects of the oil and gas business. He teaches in the Canadian Association of Petroleum Production Accounting Program at Mount Royal College and teaches the CAPL seminars on The Law of Pooling: Voluntary and Compulsory and The Alberta Limitations Act.

    Is it acceptable for Mr. Sychuk to be permitted to teach and to work as a Consulting Landman? If not, then what prospect is there for someone convicted of a serious offence to re-establish a life after imprisonment? If so, then what is the distinction which warrants excluding him from the practice of law but which permits him to work as a Landman?

2. Is it a legitimate regulatory function of a law society to "denounce" the immoral conduct of a lawyer where that immorality occurs outside of the context of the law-

yer's legal practice? Does this denunciation potentially duplicate the denunciatory effect of the legal sanctions imposed on Sychuk elsewhere in the legal system? Do you think that the decision in *Budd* was similarly motivated by a desire to denounce his conduct?

3. In *Budd* the panel placed considerable reliance on the importance of maintaining the reputation of the legal profession. Is that a legitimate basis for revoking a lawyer's licence?

4. What empirical connection, if any, might exist between the type of misconduct engaged in by Budd or Sychuk and the lawyer's ability to fulfill the legal and ethical obligations he owes to the client and the legal system? Is a lawyer who has done the sort of things done by Budd or Sychuk less likely to fulfill his professional obligations? Why?

5. Would requiring a lawyer who had been convicted of an offence to list that conviction on her website, or in her advertising materials, be a reasonable regulatory approach to this problem?

6. Both Budd and Sychuk were convicted of crimes involving serious moral turpitude. What is more relevant in determining whether they should be allowed to continue to practise law: the immorality of their actions or the closeness of their misconduct to the practice of law? What if, for example, a lawyer through negligence — as a result of being overcommitted — fails to keep proper accounts for the high-level amateur sports team she coaches and operates? As a result, there are funds unaccounted for and the team has financial difficulties, which result in it being placed on probation by its league. The lawyer is not charged criminally but she is fired. Is this a matter which should concern the law society?

Scenario One

John Jones, a lawyer, is a white supremacist. He has published materials casting aspersions on racialized minorities. Specifically, he has published pamphlets which identify certain activist groups and accused them of conspiratorial activities to "infiltrate" the "corridors of power" in government and business. Jones has not been charged with any crime. However, his local law society has asked you for guidance as to whether they should nonetheless prosecute him for conduct unbecoming. What would you advise?

D.   SANCTIONING LAWYERS FOR MISCONDUCT

One of the difficult challenges faced by law societies is the question of the appropriate sanction to impose on lawyers. As noted earlier, sanctions imposed can range from a reprimand through to fines, suspension and outright disbarment. In both *Sychuk* and *Budd* the lawyers were disbarred. In other cases excerpted in this case book lawyers have been fined (*Merchant*[5]) and suspended (*Richey*[6]). In the following two cases lawyers are disciplined for having sexual relations with their clients. Compare the facts of the cases, the

---

[5]   *Law Society of Saskatchewan v. Merchant*, [2000] L.S.D.D. No. 24 (L.S.S.), affd [2002] S.J. No. 288 (Sask. C.A.).

[6]   *Nova Scotia Barristers' Society v. Richey*, [2002] L.S.D.D. No. 30 (N.S.B.S.).

nature of the ethical violation committed by the lawyers, and the sanction imposed by the Law Society of Alberta and the Law Society of Upper Canada respectively. Consider whether, in light of each other, the sanctions are justifiable. If not, in each case what sanction would be appropriate, and why? How can law societies determine what sanctions are appropriate? What factors were used by the two Law Societies in deciding the sanction? What factors should be relevant for determining an appropriate sanction? Should law societies have "penalty guidelines" similar to the sentencing guidelines occasionally imposed on criminal courts?

ADAMS v. LAW SOCIETY OF ALBERTA

[2000] A.J. No. 1031, 2000 ABCA 240
(Alta. C.A., Fraser C.J.A., Bracco and McFadyen JJ.A.)

THE COURT:— This is an appeal by Adams from the Decision of the Benchers of the Law Society of Alberta dismissing his appeal from the Decision of the Hearing Committee that he be disbarred from the practice of law. There were dissenting opinions at both the Committee and Bencher levels regarding the disbarment order.

The matter arose regarding four complaints. The first two counts concerned Adams' conviction for sexual exploitation of his 16-year-old client.

. . . . .

With respect to the first two counts relating to the 16-year-old client, Adams admitted the facts that had been filed in criminal court. When facing the criminal charges, Adams pled guilty to the indictable offence of s. 153(1)(b), namely sexual exploitation, and received a 15-month conditional sentence. He likewise admitted to the Hearing Committee that he breached his fiduciary duty to his client, and that his conduct with respect to both counts brought the profession into disrepute and was deserving of sanction. However, he contended before the Benchers and before us that disbarment was manifestly unreasonable.

The grounds of appeal are that the Benchers failed to conclude that the Hearing Committee had committed errors in principle and failed to conclude that the penalty of disbarment is demonstrably unfit. In particular, Adams argued that the Hearing Committee overemphasized the harm to the reputation of the legal profession; failed to accord sufficient weight to good character evidence; erred in rejecting expert evidence as to the risk of Adams' re-offending; erred in relying on aggravating factors that were not proven; and finally, imposed a penalty that is a marked departure from penalties imposed on similar offenders for similar offences, and is manifestly unreasonable.

. . . . .

Before addressing the specific grounds of appeal, it may be helpful to consider the context of a professional disciplinary hearing. Professional bodies are those to whom the government has seen fit to grant monopoly status. With this monopolistic right comes certain responsibilities and obligations. Chief amongst them is self-regulation. Self-regulation is based on the legitimate expectation of both the government and public that those members of a profession who are found guilty of conduct deserving of sanction will be regulated - and disciplined - on an administrative law basis by the profession's statutorily prescribed regulatory bodies. Thus, a professional disciplinary hearing is not a criminal hearing; it is an administrative hearing. Admission or proof of the alleged professional misconduct (or incompetence) is not the same as a plea or finding of guilt in a criminal matter. Rather, it is a finding of conduct deserving of sanction or incompetent practice based on administrative principles, including applicable evidentiary rules. A professional misconduct hearing involves not only the individual and all the factors that relate to that individual, both favourably and unfavourably, but also the effect of the individual's misconduct on both the individual client and generally on the profession in question. This public dimension is of critical significance to the mandate of professional disciplinary bodies.

In the context of the legal profession, a lawyer is required to complete stringent academic and professional studies as well as successful articles before being admitted to the Bar. The character and integrity of the applicants are relevant factors for admission to the profession. A member of the legal profession having successfully met all of the prerequisites of the profession is accepted into the profession on the basis that he or she has full knowledge and understanding of the responsibilities, duties and obligations of that office.

. . . . .

Historians may question the origin and the history of the oft-repeated statements about the honour and integrity of the legal profession, but it cannot be denied that the relationship of solicitor and client is founded on trust. That fundamental trust is precisely why persons can and do confidently bring their most intimate problems and all manner of matters great or small to their lawyers. That is an overarching trust that the profession and each member of the profession accepts. Indeed, it is the very foundation of the profession and governs the relationships and services that are rendered. While it may be difficult to measure with precision the harm that a lawyer's misconduct may have on the reputation of the profession, there can be little doubt that public confidence in the administration of justice and trust in the legal profession will be eroded by disreputable conduct of an individual lawyer.

It is therefore erroneous to suggest that in professional disciplinary matters, the range of sanctions may be compared to penal sentences and to suggest that only the most serious misconduct by the most serious offenders warrants disbarment. Indeed, that proposition has been rejected in criminal cases for the same reasons it should be rejected here. It will always be possible to find someone whose circumstances and conduct are more egregious than the case under consideration. Disbarment is but one disciplinary option available from a range of sanctions and as such, it is not reserved for only the very worst conduct engaged in by the very worst lawyers.

. . . . .

Adams' first ground of appeal is that the Hearing Committee overemphasized the harm to the reputation of the legal profession. The question of what effect a lawyer's misconduct will have on the reputation of the legal profession generally is at the very heart of a disciplinary hearing and is clearly best considered by elected members of that profession and the lay benchers appointed to assist in that task and others. It is one of the prime reasons why professional discipline hearings are entrusted to the profession itself.

In this case Adams, twice the age of his young client, and fully aware of her strong desire to have her boyfriend released from jail, persuaded her to have sex with him. At the Committee Hearing, he admitted that his arranging to have sex with his client was "inappropriate". He also admitted that he knew that he was in a trust position with her. He expressed remorse for his conduct and acknowledged to the Hearing Committee that he had dishonoured his profession as a result of his misconduct.

Adams was correct in his assessment that this conduct brought dishonour on the legal profession, as this type of behaviour can lead the public to believe that lawyers are prone to abusing their position of trust. Members of the legal profession must earn the trust of their clients and the public generally, and conduct such as Adams' completely undermines that trust. As such, on reviewing the record, the report of the Hearing Committee and the decision of the Benchers, we are not persuaded that there was an overemphasis of the harm to the reputation of the legal profession.

Adams submits that the Committee failed to give sufficient weight to the good-character evidence. The record shows that the Committee did hear and consider all of the character evidence and referred to those "glowing character references" but decided that those references did not displace or support the facts as found and admitted by Adams as to what had occurred. This ground fails.

In the next ground of appeal, Adams submits that the Committee erred in rejecting expert evidence as to the risk of his re-offending. Dr. Pugh, the psychologist who assessed Adams, stated that there was little likelihood that Adams would re-offend, but he suggested that Adams needed to review articles regarding ethical conduct and dual relationships and also meet, more than once, with a respected criminal lawyer to discuss the underlying problem with such relationships. It was also apparent that Adams was not fully candid with Dr. Pugh in his recounting of what happened. As they were entitled to do, the majority of the Committee stated that they found nothing in Dr. Pugh's report and testimony that gave assurance that there would be no recurrence. In the dissenting Reasons, there was no discussion of Dr. Pugh's evidence nor any issue taken with the majority's assessment of it. We find no error regarding this ground of appeal.

Adams further contends that the Committee erred in relying upon aggravating factors that were not proven; specifically, it is alleged that the Committee:

(a) speculated as to the complainant's motives and vulnerability;

(b) misapprehended the evidence as to whether Adams offered consideration for sexual favours; and

(c) exaggerated the prevalence of the risk of the sexual misconduct similar to that of Adams.

Adams adopted the dissenting view that the vulnerability of the 16-year-old complainant referred to in the majority Decision was not proved. She did not testify. However, there is no dispute as to her age and the disparity between the ages of Adams and the complainant. Nor is there any dispute as to her anxious desire to have her boyfriend released from jail. While the majority focussed on the impropriety of a lawyer pursuing a dual relationship, one personal or sexual and one professional, with a client, they also considered the likely effect on the client's perception or expectation regarding the legal services she would receive. This would be a valid consideration regarding any client's finding herself in that situation and perhaps more so if the client is young. Dr. Pugh characterized the solicitor-client relationship as very special ...:

> ... lawyers are perceived by clients to be very special people with very special powers, and this means that the client then is in a very vulnerable position ... in his or her relationship with the lawyer, and it's incumbent upon the lawyer to recognize that nature of this very special trust relationship.

> Mr. Adams set that aside, the almost sanctity of this relationship, and minimized it and discounted it and took advantage of this young woman ... .

The understanding that Dr. Pugh had of the importance of the solicitor-client relationship would certainly be within the knowledge of the majority of the Committee. It was in the context of their understanding of that relationship that they spoke of the vulnerability of the young client. We find no error in their discussion of the solicitor-client relationship and the vulnerability of a young client in these circumstances.

Both Adams and the dissenting member of the Committee miss the mark when they focus on the complainant's motive and vulnerability. She did not initiate the proposition of a sexual encounter. It was Adams' desire, despite his acknowledgment that what he proposed was inappropriate, and despite the complainant's reminding question about his having sex with clients.

It does not appear that the Committee misapprehended the evidence as to whether Adams offered consideration for sexual favours. The majority Report correctly stated: "[w]hether there was to be payment or not is unclear on the evidence." Regarding Adams' suggestion that the majority of the Committee wrongly believed that Adams was also guilty of an offence under s. 212(4) of the Criminal Code, communication for the purpose of obtaining sexual services, the Benchers, in the majority Decision rejected that suggestion. They stated at A.B. 204:

> When put in context, it appears to us that the Majority referred to s. 212(4) in order to point out the seriousness of the offence under s. 153(1)(b) in that both could be proceeded with by way of indictment.

We agree.

We also agree with the majority of the Benchers' view that the Committee's majority Report was an expression of opinion that there was no evidence that sexual misconduct by lawyers was a serious problem. The discussion was focussed less on prevalence than on the comparative seriousness of Adams' misconduct in proposing a sexual relationship with his client as opposed to misappropriating trust funds. The majority contended that perhaps the breach of trust involved in a proposed sexual relationship was even more serious than converting trust funds, for money can be restored but honour cannot. The minority expressly contended that Adams' misconduct was less serious than a case of misappropriation of trust funds, which "in virtually every case ... calls for disbarment." This suggestion is troubling, as it implies that the integrity of the person is somehow less important than the integrity of the dollar. We do not diminish the seriousness of the offence of absconding with a client's trust funds. However, we have surely come to a point in our understanding of individual respect where the violation of a person's dignity is at least as important as the value of a bank account. As Wilson J. said in *Frame v. Smith ...*

> [t]o deny relief because of the nature of the interest involved, to afford protection to material interests but not to human and personal interests would, it seems to me, be arbitrary in the extreme.

Finally, Adams argued that the penalty of disbarment is much more severe than penalties that have been imposed in other similar cases, and that disbarment in this case is manifestly unreasonable. We acknowledge that considering the dispositions in disciplinary matters in other cases and in other jurisdictions can be helpful. But this assessment must be undertaken with due respect to contemporary values in Canadian society. In this regard, we observe that in the past, there has sometimes been a tendency to minimize and excuse misconduct of a sexual nature between the members of some professions and their clients. Further, and in any event, because the relevant facts vary greatly from case to case, care must be taken to consider each complaint in the context of its particular circumstances. As stated earlier, we do not accept the proposition still often invoked in criminal cases, that the most serious disciplinary sanction, disbarment, should be reserved for the most serious misconduct by the most serious offender. In this case, the majority of the Hearing Committee correctly addressed the relevant factors and held that disbarment was the appropriate disposition. Likewise the majority of the Benchers reviewed that disposition and agreed that disbarment was the appropriate order. We do not find that disposition to be manifestly unreasonable. Pursuant to s. 79(1)(c) of the Legal Profession Act, the order of the Benchers disbarring Adams is confirmed.

LAW SOCIETY OF UPPER CANADA v. HUNTER

[2007] L.S.D.D. No. 8, 2007 ONLSHP 27
(Law Society of Upper Canada, Hearing Panel: M. Sandler, Chair,
A. Alexander and S.L. Robins)
[footnotes omitted]

[George Hunter was disciplined by the Law Society for his sexual relationship with a client and the resulting conflict of interest. The part of the decision related to conflicts of interest is excerpted in Chapter 5. This excerpt deals only with the issue of penalty.]

. . . . .

ADDITIONAL EVIDENCE TENDERED ON BEHALF OF THE MEMBER

On the issue of penalty, additional documentary evidence was filed, on consent of both parties.

On behalf of the member, a brief containing 27 character letters was introduced. The letters came from fellow lawyers, and from others who know the member in a variety of ways. Each was made aware of the misconduct that brings the member before the Society.

The authors describe the member as "highly professional", "ethical, "well liked", "honourable" and as a person of the "highest integrity". He was known within his firm as its "conscience" in his principled approach to professional obligations and clients' interests. A number of authors indicate that this misconduct can only be regarded as "out of character" and as representing "human fallibility in an intrinsically good lawyer and person, rational judgment clouded by emotion." One author states that "[t]he allegations against him, which he admits, are serious and represent dishonourable, unprofessional conduct showing flawed judgment — they are also utterly inconsistent with the kind, principled, honourable man and lawyer he has been throughout his legal career."

It should be noted that several of the authors expressed opinions concerning the appropriate disposition in this case. No objection was taken to these letters being received by the Hearing Panel, despite the inclusion of these opinions. Each letter did also contain properly admissible character evidence in support of the member. We respectfully place no reliance on any such opinions. The determination of penalty is exclusively our function.

Several of the letters came from current benchers. No doubt, this was a reflection of the fact that the member's professional life was deeply connected with his role as a bencher and, later, as Treasurer. There is no legal impediment that prevents benchers from providing such letters. However, there may be a concern that such letters can contribute to a perception that the member is differently situated than others, and unfairly so. Ultimately, it is unnecessary for us to comment on the role that bencher letters should play in these kind of cases. The Society conceded that the member was of prior good character and acknowledged his contributions to the profession. This concession conformed to the wealth of unchallenged evidence on this point, most of which came from non-benchers.

Dr. John Bradford, Professor and Head of the Division of Forensic Psychiatry at the University of Ottawa provided an assessment of the member. He concluded:

CONCLUSIONS AND RECOMMENDATIONS:

Mr. George Hunter has had an exemplary professional career reaching the post of Treasurer of the Law Society of Upper Canada. For approximately 12 to 24 months prior to December 2005, he suffered varying degrees of depression that gradually worsened with time. In addition, probably as a complication of the depressive disorder, he neglected his insulin-dependent diabetes mellitus with significant risk to his physical health.

Although very successful in his professional career, his marriage had been in difficulty for more than 10 years. Personal attempts and marital counseling failed to resolve the situation. While Mr. Hunter was very unhappy in his private life, he was reluctant to terminate the marriage because of his deep concern about the potential ill effects on his children. The emptiness of his marriage led to him to seek out other intimate relationships to escape feelings of depression and loneliness. Although, Mr. Hunter was confused as to why he became involved in three relationships, in the fall of 2005, he felt he could no longer live in the way he had been living and therefore disclosed his relationships to his wife; his long-term relationship partner; and the other two women. By doing so, he brought about a series of events that have had a profound effect on his life. It led to the dissolution of his marriage; it led to employment difficulties at his law firm; and also led to his resignation as Treasurer of the Law Society of Upper Canada and discipline proceedings against him.

There are various potential psychological explanations for his behavior, one of which can be that his behaviour became increasingly self-destructive, most likely arising from the underlying depressive disorder, Mr. Hunter also had extreme difficulty accepting the failure of his marriage; his professional and other successes exacerbated this difficulty of failing to accept and manage the deep failings in his personal life.

By December 2006, Mr. Hunter had successfully worked through many of these issues and is trying to move on with his personal life, deal with his mental health and physical health issues, continue and strengthen his relationship with his children; return to his professional work and hopes to have a long-standing relationship in the future.

In my opinion, Mr. Hunter has experienced deep personal embarrassment as a result of these events and it is extremely unlikely that Mr. Hunter will breach the rules of professional behaviour ever again.

The Hearing Panel was also provided with a list of Committees sat on or chaired by the member while he was a bencher. Suffice it to say, the member was a very active, highly engaged bencher who served in a wide range of capacities before he became Treasurer.

Finally, the member made a statement to the Hearing Panel. He articulated deep remorse for his misconduct, and recognition of the impact of this misconduct on those around him, and upon the profession as a whole. He also acknowledged the complainant's hurt and pain, and her positive attributes. The member did not attempt to minimize, justify, or excuse his misconduct.

ADDITIONAL EVIDENCE TENDERED ON BEHALF OF THE SOCIETY

As a result of the member's conduct, the complainant XY was referred for individual psychotherapy to a qualified psychologist. She was examined on November 20, 2006. A summary of the psychologist's report was admitted, again on consent. No issue was taken with its accuracy. It reflects that, at the time XY was examined, she was experiencing a considerable level of distress, was diagnosed with Anxiety Disorder, NOS (Subsyndromal Post-Traumatic Stress Disorder) and was expected to require prolonged psychotherapy.

A victim impact statement on behalf of XY was also filed on consent. The complainant indicates that after November 21, 2005, she developed rapid weight loss, sleep deprivation, fatigue, chills, shivering, increased heart rate and elevated blood pressure. The member's revelations on November 21, 2005 caused her to seek counselling from a physician and later from a psychologist as earlier noted. She is now fearful, irritable, depressed and stressed. She is given to frequent bouts of tearfulness and anxiety. This has affected her work performance. She worries that she has been less attentive and responsive to her daughter because of the symptoms arising from the events involving the member. It should be noted here that the member, in his statement to the Hearing Panel, extolled the complainant's virtues and abilities as a mother.

In fairness, XY's ongoing distress is explained not only by that part of the member's actions that constituted professional misconduct, but also by his revelations to XY on November 21, 2005 that effectively spelled the end of a relationship that XY regarded as serious and committed. This does not mean that XY's distress should be discounted as a relevant consideration on the issue of penalty. Distress was a foreseeable byproduct of the nature of the misconduct involved here.

SUBMISSIONS

Counsel for the Society, Mr. Hunt, submitted that the appropriate disposition was a suspension for four months, together with costs in the range of $1,500 to $2,500. Counsel for the member, Mr. Paliare, submitted that the appropriate disposition was a reprimand or, in the alternative, a very short suspension. He did not disagree with the imposition of costs.

. . . . .

The gravamen of the misconduct in this case is the conflict of interest arising out of the intimate relationship between the member and his client XY, the member's failure to appropriately recognize and address the issues surrounding that conflict of interest and the complainant's vulnerability, and his conduct on November 21, 2005 and thereafter to attempt to rectify the situation by pressing the complainant to confirm the member's position.

. . . . .

[The panel found that there had been an improper conflict of interest.]

This is a serious matter, as correctly acknowledged by some of those who acted as character references on behalf of the member. Nonetheless, the Hearing Panel recognizes the existence of a number of mitigating factors that must inform the appropriate penalty.

The member co-operated fully with the Society. He acknowledged his wrongdoing at the earliest opportunity. He self-reported to the Society. Through his counsel, an agreed statement of facts was created that spared the complainant the ordeal of testifying at these proceedings. The complainant's privacy was respected through the introduction of a summary of her psychologist's findings. A victim impact statement was filed, again on consent. The member spoke positively about the complainant's attributes. As earlier indicated, he was deeply remorseful, and did not seek to minimize, justify or excuse his misconduct.

There is no evidence before us that the member's legal work was actually affected by the conflict of interest, despite the dangers earlier articulated.

The misconduct has already taken a significant toll upon the member. We have observed his considerable fall from grace, culminating in his resignation as Treasurer of the Society. He has been unable to practise law (albeit on paid leave) since December 2005 for health and other reasons related, in large measure if not entirely, to this matter. This underscores the impact of these proceedings upon him, and is a significant factor in setting the appropriate penalty in this case.

The Society conceded that the member is in no need of specific deterrence. Its proposed disposition was based upon the need for general deterrence: in other words, to dissuade like-minded lawyers from similar misconduct.

This Hearing Panel must remain mindful of the impact of this and other decisions on the profession as a whole, and upon the confidence of the public in the profession. However, the member should not be treated more harshly as a result of his former status as Treasurer and as a bencher. Nor, of course, should he receive favoured treatment, although he is entitled to make the important point that his entire career is incompatible with this misconduct and that, therefore, this misconduct can be regarded as "out of character." We have no difficulty in so finding.

The letters filed on behalf of the member were impressive, and spoke to the member's character, integrity, and commitment to the profession. They demonstrate, in our view, that the member remains capable of serving in the future as a valuable member of his firm, and of the profession.

In *Law Society of Upper Canada v. Mark Elliott Joseph* (November 26, 1993) another panel imposed a three-month suspension for analogous conduct. We were not provided with any other decision that involves similar facts.

There were some obvious similarities and differences between the *Joseph* case and the case at bar, some favourable and some unfavourable to the member here. For example, we noted the level of vulnerability of the complainant, Ms. Doe, in that case as a result, in part, of her prior history as a victim of assault/sexual assault, and deep depression. The panel found that Mr. Joseph misused confidential information disclosed by the client in the course of seeking legal advice and representation. On the other hand, the duration of the conflict of interest in that case was far shorter than in the case at bar. Ultimately, while the principles in the *Joseph* case do inform our decision here, we make the not uncommon observation that each case spins on its own facts.

. . . . .

DISPOSITION ON PENALTY

Having regard to all of the circumstances, we cannot agree that a reprimand is in the public interest. Such a disposition would fail to reflect the seriousness of the misconduct here. That being said, we also do not accept the necessity for a suspension of a length recommended by the Society. Such a suspension fails to adequately take into consideration the accumulation of mitigating factors that we find to be present in this case.

The Hearing Panel orders as follows:

1. The member is suspended for 60 days to commence on February 5, 2007 or such other date as may be agreed upon by the Society and the member.

2. The member shall pay costs to the Society in the amount of $2,500.00, payable upon completion of the period of suspension.

We wish to commend all counsel for their assistance in this difficult matter. They advanced the interests of the public, and of the member with great skill, while demonstrating a high level of co-operation. It was much appreciated.

NOTES AND QUESTIONS

1. Subsequent to this decision XY commenced a lawsuit against Hunter, his law firm and the Law Society of Upper Canada for the harm she suffered as a result of his actions.

2. Should consistency in result be a factor in the decisions of discipline panels dealing with similar offences? In considering the widely divergent penalties in *Adams* and *Hunter*, how significant is the fact that the client in *Adams* was a minor and that Adams was convicted criminally for soliciting her? Recall as well that Budd was disbarred in part because his victims were minors.

3. Adams was a sole practitioner. Hunter was a practitioner at a national law firm. Many commentators have noted that most individuals subject to law society dis-

cipline are sole practitioners or from small law firms. Do you think that the differing practice circumstances of Adams and Hunter had anything to do with the variation in the sentences? Should they have?

4.   Leaving aside the comparative difference between the treatment of Adams and Hunter, what do you think the appropriate penalty should be for a lawyer who takes advantage of the lawyer-client relationship to initiate sexual relations with the client? Should the law society intervene when a relationship was consensual between adults?

5.   Note that in *Hunter* the issue was a conflict of interest; presumably, if Hunter had referred the file to another lawyer in the firm no law society discipline would have resulted. Is this result appropriate? Can you think of facts where it would not be appropriate?

E.   REGULATING THE UNAUTHORIZED PRACTICE OF LAW

As we have seen in Chapter 2, legislation in every Canadian province confers a monopoly on lawyers to practise law. In addition, provincial law societies are granted the responsibility to police the unauthorized practice of law. The following case illustrates this issue and provides an example of the sort of penalty that might be imposed by a law society, and ultimately by a court, in such a case. When reading the case consider whether this regulation protects the public interest. In particular, consider its effect in light of the discussion of issues related to access to justice and competence in previous chapters.

LAW SOCIETY OF UPPER CANADA v. BOLDT

[2006] O.J. No. 1142
(Ont. S.C.J., P.C. Hennessy J.)

P.C. HENNESSY J.:— The Law Society of Upper Canada (LSUC) brings a motion for contempt against Maureen Boldt for breaching the injunction Order of Bolan J. dated September 1, 2000.

History

Ms. Boldt is not and has never been a member of the LSUC or licensed to practice law in Ontario. At the time these proceedings were initiated, she carried on business as a paralegal and mediator.

The LSUC prosecuted Ms. Boldt in 1995 and 1998 for the unauthorized practice of law contrary to s. 50 of the *Law Society Act*. The 1995 proceedings ended following a successful motion for non-suit. That decision was appealed and a new trial was ordered. Just prior to trial, which was scheduled for April 1998, the parties entered into an agreement. As a result of the pre-trial agreement, Maureen Boldt pleaded guilty to one count of unlawfully acting or practicing as a barrister and solicitor. The agreement included the following additional terms:

1.   An admission that Maureen Boldt had unlawfully offered legal services in the areas of wills, divorces and incorporations.

2. An admission that Maureen Boldt had represented clients in Ontario Court (General Division) including the preparation of court documents and pleadings.

3. An admission that Maureen Boldt had provided legal advice when preparing wills and separation agreements.

4. An acknowledgement by Maureen Boldt that her actions constituted a breach of s. 50 of the *Law Society Act*.

5. A fine of $100.00.

6. An undertaking by Maureen Boldt not to engage in the offering or delivering of legal services of any kind except those specifically authorized by statute and not to commit further breaches of s. 50 of the *Law Society Act*.

7. An agreement by the LSUC to drop the balance of the charges.

In 1999, the LSUC made an application for an injunction against Maureen Boldt to prohibit her from practicing law. After a five-day hearing, Bolan J. issued a permanent injunction.

In October 2003, the Labbe incident, which is central to this case, came to the attention of the LSUC. In September 2004, the LSUC initiated these contempt proceedings. They were adjourned once before this hearing.

The Issue

The LSUC argues that Ms. Boldt has violated the injunction and has carried on the unauthorized practice of law. In particular, the LSUC claims that Ms. Boldt has prepared separation agreements, provided legal advice for the separation agreement and offered to institute and complete divorce proceedings.

Ms. Boldt's response to the motion was that she engaged in the mediation of memoranda of understanding between parties in domestic relationships. She submits that neither mediators nor mediation are regulated by the LSUC and that therefore she has not violated the terms of the injunction or her undertaking to the court.

The first issue in this case is whether Ms. Boldt's conduct constitutes the unauthorized practice of law as prohibited by the injunction. If this question is answered in the affirmative, the next question is: "What is the remedy"?

The Injunction and Reasons of Bolan J.

The Order of Bolan J. included the following terms:

1. A finding that Maureen Boldt had been acting as a barrister and solicitor in contravention of s. 50 of the *Law Society Act* in contravention of the 1998 Agreement.

2. A permanent injunction restraining Maureen Boldt from acting or practicing as a barrister or solicitor.

3. A permanent injunction restraining Maureen Boldt from performing the following:

    (a) preparing and drafting separation Agreements and Petitions for divorce in uncontested matters and contested matters;

    (b) offering and providing services in the preparation and drafting of Wills and Incorporations.

In reasons accompanying the permanent injunction, Bolan J. set out the facts on which he based his decision. Maureen Boldt had advertised that she offered various paralegal services, including the preparation of legal documents which intended to have a legal operation and services related to uncontested divorces, which is the service at issue in these proceedings.

Bolan J. reviewed a number of agreements prepared by Maureen Boldt setting out terms of separation. He received evidence from the couples who had gone to Maureen Boldt for the purpose of obtaining a binding agreement. In each case, Ms. Boldt charged the couple $1,000 for the separation agreement. The final documents prepared for them by Maureen Boldt were entitled "Agreements." A number of exhibits from the proceeding before Bolan J. were made exhibits in this proceeding, including these Agreements and witness statements.

The clients, referred to above, believed they had signed final and binding separation agreements. In at least one of the cases before Bolan J., Maureen Boldt had described her role as mediator.

Bolan J. found that Maureen Boldt did, in fact, act and practice as a solicitor by, among other things, preparing legal documents, including the above noted separation agreements, which were intended to have a legal operation.

The Labbe-Lowney Agreement

Ms. Labbe wished to obtain a legally enforceable agreement with her husband.

Ms. Labbe gave evidence about her professional relationship with Ms. Boldt and the professional services she obtained from Ms. Boldt.

She first went to see Maureen Boldt in September 2002. She had known Maureen Boldt as a childhood friend and was aware of her position as a city councillor.

Ms. Labbe had seen Maureen Boldt's advertisements and believed that Maureen Boldt could "fashion" written documents in matrimonial matters that would have a legally binding effect. It was Ms. Labbe's evidence that she communicated to Maureen Boldt that she wanted a legal separation and that she needed an agreement that would bind her husband to the terms of his departure from the matrimonial home by a specific date. Ms. Labbe described the household situation as very messy, and she told Ms. Boldt that she had received threats of violence from her husband. She also told Ms. Boldt that she wanted Mr. Lowney [her husband] to leave the house by a fixed and certain date. Ms. Labbe hoped that if she and Mr. Lowney could come to an agreement on the property issues, Mr. Lowney would leave the house without violence.

Ms. Labbe was asked on cross-examination if she wanted mediation. Ms. Labbe was clear and unequivocal. She did not want mediation; she wanted and needed a separation agreement.

Maureen Boldt advised that she could perform these services and quoted her a fee of $1,000 for the work. At this first meeting, Ms. Boldt provided a booklet, which Ms. Labbe took home and used to make a first draft of an agreement.

Ms. Labbe met with Ms. Boldt two or three times over the next couple of months to provide financial and personal information. On the basis of the information provided, Maureen Boldt advised Ms. Labbe that the legal separation date was in or about September 2002 and that Ms. Labbe would have no obligation to pay legal support. Ms. Boldt provided Ms. Labbe with a draft document setting out the respective obligations of the parties on property, support, debt responsibility, Canada Pension and financial releases. After each visit, Ms. Labbe would return home and discuss certain terms with her husband and obtain his agreement.

Ms. Labbe testified that she never showed these draft agreements (entitled Memorandum of Understanding) to her husband. At no time did Mr. Labbe attend at Maureen Boldt's office with Mr. Lowney. Ms. Labbe recalled that Maureen Boldt made a telephone call to Mr. Lowney one time during a visit. The purpose of that telephone call was to set up a meeting with Mr. Lowney to attend at the office to sign the agreement.

Ms. Labbe drove Mr. Lowney to Maureen Boldt's office on November 14, 2002 so he could sign the Memorandum of Understanding. Ms. Labbe waited in the car while he did this. Beside his signature is a signature of Maureen Boldt, also dated November 14, 2002. Ms. Labbe did not go into Maureen Boldt's office that day. Because Ms. Labbe had been told that Maureen Boldt would not give her the signed agreement until the full $1,000 fee was paid, Ms. Labbe waited until November 19, 2002 to attend for signature. It was on that day that she signed and dated the document and paid the final installment on the fee.

Ms. Labbe testified that she did not sign an Agreement to Mediate, even though such a document with an illegible signature was shown to her on cross-examination. The Agreement to Mediate document was signed by Mr. Lowney on November 14, 2002 and by Ms. Boldt.

Ms. Labbe took the signed Memorandum of Understanding, believing that she had a legally enforceable separation covering the following matters:

1. That Mr. Lowney would receive the proceeds of the sale of a property owned by Ms. Labbe as full and final settlement of all financial claims.

2. That Ms. Labbe would retain title and equity in the matrimonial home and assume all debt and liability associated with it. Mr. Lowney released all claim to the home and its equity.

3. Division of house contents.

4. That Mr. Lowney did not require spousal support.

5. Mr. Lowney provided a release with respect to two vehicles.

6. Ms. Labbe agreed to assume all specified debt.

7. Ms. Labbe was to have exclusive possession of the matrimonial home.

8. Full and final releases.

Ms. Labbe gave evidence about the document entitled, "Memorandum of Understanding." She stated that the document was created by Maureen Boldt on the basis of information provided to her by Ms. Labbe. The document includes a statement that the separation date was September 1, 2001. That date was suggested by Maureen Boldt after a discussion with Ms. Labbe about the facts relevant to her relationship with Mr. Lowney, even while the couple continued to reside in the same house.

Ms. Labbe also testified that Maureen Boldt did not, at any time, recommend that she or Mr. Lowney obtain independent legal advice. Ms. Labbe was in touch with another solicitor during this time. He was doing her real estate work. Ms. Labbe denied that she ever sought advice or received any advice from this solicitor regarding her separation.

During the meetings between Maureen Boldt and Ms. Labbe, certain terms were discussed. For example, Ms. Labbe had originally proposed to include a term requiring her to pay to Mr. Lowney spousal support in the amount of $250. On Maureen Boldt's recommendation, Ms. Labbe decided not to include a provision for spousal support.

Similarly, Maureen Boldt advised Ms. Labbe regarding Mr. Lowney's pension and the distribution of proceeds from the sale of property. Ms. Labbe followed this advice. Ms. Labbe testified that the wording of the financial release clause came from Maureen Boldt.

Ms. Labbe testified that Maureen Boldt explained that the document was a final agreement and that both Ms. Labbe and Mr. Lowney were under the impression that it was a binding agreement. There was no suggestion that anything further had to be done to make the agreement binding. Ms. Labbe understood that she had a final agreement that would ensure Mr. Lowney's departure from the home on December 31, 2002 and that was what did happen.

On Ms. Labbe's last attendance at the office, after she had signed the document, Ms. Boldt told her that if she brought in her marriage certificate and paid an additional $1,200, Maureen Boldt would complete the matter by obtaining a divorce. There was no mention of a lawyer's involvement in this procedure.

Mediation in the Context of Family Law in Ontario

The LSUC called Susan Healey as a witness. She was qualified to give opinion evidence.

Susan Healey is a member of the LSUC and the president of the Ontario Association of Family Mediators. At the time of the Labbe-Lowney incident, she was practicing full time in the area of family law. From 2000 to 2004, Ms. Healey was practicing as a mediator in Family law matters and practicing law. She is an accredited mediator with OAFM and has completed the Advanced Family Law Mediation Course at Harvard, among other courses.

OAFM is a voluntary association of family mediators and those otherwise involved in the family law community. To some extent, the Association tries to regulate the conduct of its members in the practice of mediation through its *Code of Conduct and Practice*. Individuals who wish to become accredited members of OAFM must demonstrate that they have followed 100 hours of approved mediation training and must apply to the Board.

At the time of the Labbe-Lowney incident, Maureen Boldt was an associate member of OAFM. There are only two conditions of this class of membership in the Association. One must pay annual fees and one must agree in writing to be bound by the *Code of Ethics*. At no time has Maureen Boldt applied for accredited member status with OAFM. As a member of OAFM, Ms. Boldt was automatically a member of a national organization, Family Mediation Canada.

Ms. Healey was approached by Ms. Boldt, after the LSUC instituted these proceedings. Ms. Boldt called her and told her that the LSUC was trying to regulate mediation, was using Ms. Boldt as an example and suggested perhaps that the OAFM might contribute to her defence costs. Ms. Healey agreed to review the motion materials that were provided to her by counsel for Ms. Boldt and bring the matter to the attention of the OAFM Board.

Ms. Healey reviewed the materials and, as a result of her summary and recommendation, the Board permanently revoked Ms. Boldt's membership from the Association. Ms. Healey then contacted the LSUC and filed an affidavit in these proceedings.

Ms. Healey was qualified as an expert in family law for the purposes of giving opinion evidence on certain questions including: the purpose of mediation, and how mediation is generally carried out by members of her association in the province of Ontario.

Ms. Healey was asked to describe the purpose of mediation in the context of negotiating a separation agreement. She explained that the mediation practice approved by OAFM results in an agreement to agree. The mediator meets with parties, who are advised to obtain independent legal advice and who agree to participate in the mediation subject to certain conditions. One of those conditions is that the parties agree to make full financial disclosure. The terms of the mediator's retainer is usually set out in a signed document entitled, Agreement to Mediate.

At the end of mediation, the mediator signs a document which sets out the items on which the parties have agreed. The document is ordinarily entitled a Mediator's Report or a Memorandum of Understanding. Members of OAFM are strongly cautioned to avoid doing anything throughout the process that would mislead the participants into believing that the end product of mediation is a legally binding agreement. The purpose of the Mediator's Report or Memorandum of Understanding is to record the agreement of the parties for the purpose of instructing counsel.

In Ms. Healey's experience, she or the client delivers the document to the parties' solicitors who then draft a separation agreement. Section 55(1) of the *Family Law Act* requires that, in order for a separation agreement to be enforceable, it must be in writing, signed by the parties and witnessed.

When a mediator is a lawyer, the final product of the mediation may also be a separation agreement. Lawyers who conduct mediations, however, are prohibited by the LSUC *Code of Conduct* from giving legal advice and must ensure that the parties have independent legal advice.

Mr. David Jarvis has been practicing law in Toronto for over 25 years. He has also been appointed as a Dispute Resolution Officer with the Ontario Superior Court of Justice for ten years and has been involved in teaching, examining and mentoring in family law. He was qualified as an expert in family law to give expert opinion evidence on certain questions, including the difference between a separation agreement and the outcome of mediation.

Mr. Jarvis often receives Mediation Reports or Memorandum of Understanding from mediators directly or via his clients, who then seek his advice and assistance to negotiate and/or draft a final separation agreement. In his experience, mediation reports are not signed by the clients. Where clients execute a Separation Agreement, their signatures attest to the fact that the parties agree to be bound by the terms contained in it. A Mediation Report, in his view, is not designed to be binding, is not signed by the parties and does not contain the usual hallmarks of a final agreement between parties. For instance, Mr. Jarvis testified that he has never seen a Memorandum of Understanding from a mediator that contained releases. The end product of mediation is a document drafted by the mediator that simply records the agreements reached by the parties through that process. These agreements are not binding on the parties. Hence, the parties do not sign the document. It is expected that the parties, through counsel, will take the agreements reached through a mediation process and finalize a separation agreement, which will create binding legal rights and obligations and may also include waivers of legal rights and obligations.

Mr. Jarvis has also been qualified as an expert in the injunction proceeding. For that application, he had reviewed and was familiar with the three files referenced above. Mr. Jarvis was of the view that these three agreements all shared the same characteristics with the Labbe-Lowney document: a place for the parties' signatures, provisions dealing with custody and access rights, child and spousal support obligations, ownership and division of property, and possession of the matrimonial home. The documents all contain final releases.

None of the agreements indicate that the parties have obtained independent legal advice.

. . . . .

The Law

Section 50(1) of the *Law Society Act* provides as follows:

> Except where as otherwise provided by law,
>
> (a) no person, other than a member whose rights and privileges are not suspended, shall act as a barrister or solicitor or hold themself out as or represent themself to be a barrister or solicitor or practices as a barrister or solicitor.

There is no statutory exception allowing non-lawyers to draft separation agreements, provide legal advice with respect to separation agreements, or prepare court documents for an uncontested divorce.

In the injunction proceedings against Maureen Boldt, Bolan J. relied on the definition of "acting as a solicitor" drawn from the reasons in *R. v. Campbell and Upper-Canada Business Administrators Ltd.* ...

> A person who "acts as a solicitor" is one who conducts an action or other legal proceeding on behalf of another, or advises that other persons on legal matters, or frames documents intended to have a legal operation, or generally assists that other person in matters affecting his legal position.

I agree that this statement represents the current state of the law. Counsel for Maureen Boldt did not raise any challenge to this definition.

The law on contempt was stated in *British Columbia Government Employees' Union v. British Columbia Attorney General* ...:

> Contempt ... embraces "where a person, whether a party to a proceeding or not, does any act which may tend to hinder the course of justice or show disrespect to the court's authority," "interfering with the business of the court on the part of a person who has no right to do so" ...

The overriding concept of contempt is that of public respect for the orders of our courts.

The LSUC is not obliged to show that Maureen Boldt intended to put herself in contempt; it need only demonstrate that she knowingly, or willfully or deliberately did some act which was calculated to result in a disturbance or an interference with the judicial process: *British Columbia Government Employees Union, supra* at 234.

It must be shown that the alleged contemner had knowledge of the court order and had the opportunity to comply with it. A person charged with contempt has the right to call witnesses and the right to be presumed innocent.

Analysis

The practice of law in Ontario is regulated by the governing body of the LSUC, the *Law Society Act* and regulations as administered. When a government provides a profession with exclusive use of a particular title, for example, barrister and solicitor, and provides that profession with the exclusive right to perform specific professional services for members of the public, the return obligation of those professionals is to govern themselves in the public interest.

Among other things, the LSUC requires its members to carry professional liability insurance and it administers an indemnity fund for victims of a lawyer's dishonest conduct. In addition, in order to deal with public complaints, the LSUC operates a rigorous complaints and discipline process in which members of the public participate. These processes are designed to ensure that lawyers who have the exclusive right to practice law also have the heavy and costly burden of doing so in a manner that is in the public's interest.

On the other hand, if an individual who is not a member of the LSUC and is not entitled to practice law in Ontario provides legal advice to members of the public and prepares documents that purport to define legal entitlements and obligations, the members of the public are not protected in any way from service which is below standard.

Maureen Boldt has operated a paralegal business for eight years. On discovery in these proceedings, Maureen Boldt acknowledged that, since the injunction, she has handled approximately two-dozen "mediations" per year at the usual fee of $1,000. By rough estimate, therefore, she has earned approximately $130,000 in revenue from this service between September 2000 and March 2006.

Counsel for Maureen Boldt, who did not give evidence, argued that the Labbe-Lowney Memorandum of Understanding [and others] are the results of mediations and that they are not separation agreements. This argument is based largely on the title of the document. Counsel for Ms. Boldt argued that the title "Memorandum of Understanding" demonstrates that the document was the product of mediation and was not intended to be binding. However, it is the substance of the document that must be considered in determining the central issue in this case.

I find that these documents, notwithstanding their title, were prepared with the intention of affecting the legal rights and obligations of the parties who signed them. The evidence of Ms. Labbe is uncontradicted. She sought and believed she obtained an agreement which would finally resolve the issues of exclusive possession, division of property and spousal support.

I am of the view that, in substance, the documents in the Labbe-Lowney case [and other] case are separation agreements. In these documents, the parties agree to grant one another certain rights to property, support, exclusive possession and parenting. Equally, they waive rights to these things. They also make these agreements acknowledging the intended legal effect by incorporating releases into the appropriate clauses, putting a final catch-all release paragraph at the end of the agreement, and signing their names.

In the Labbe-Lowney Memorandum of Understanding, the separation date is defined as September 14, 2001. This date becomes the valuation date for the fixing of asset and debt values and the start date for the determination of grounds for a divorce. To advise someone in Ms. Labbe's position of the separation date is to give legal advice. This legal advice is dependent upon an application of the existing case law to the relevant facts. Similarly, Maureen Boldt's recommendation that there be no provision for spousal support constitutes the provision of legal advice.

The Labbe-Lowney Memorandum of Understanding constitutes a separation agreement in both form and substance. In form, the technical requirements of a separation agreement have been met. It is in writing, signed by the parties and witnessed. It addresses those matters that must be resolved at the end of a marriage. The parties acknowledge that they agree to certain rights and obligations arising at the end of a marriage and confirm that they are releasing the other party from any further obligation.

In [all cases] these members of the public paid for a service that was not protected by statute. There is no recourse by either of these couples to an indemnity fund or an insurance plan if it is determined that their rights have not been protected.

. . . . .

The practice of mediation, as defined by OAFM and other voluntary associations, is a valuable service to the public. Mediation in the family law context is a non-adversarial approach to the resolution of matters arising out of the break up of a marital or domestic relationship. It is a process that suits the circumstances and conditions of many couples that are separating. However, its form cannot and will not be used as a shield to protect those who are carrying on the unauthorized practice of law. Family law mediators, if successful, may assist a couple in coming to an agreement on all matters arising from the breakdown of the marriage and separation. They can do this based on their sound knowledge of the necessary law, a commitment from the parties to make full disclosure throughout the process and with the assurance that the parties are receiving independent legal advice.

Ms. Healey was candid in her view of the risk to Ms. Labbe in this case. Ms. Labbe is a person of modest income, who needed a binding separation agreement in order to ensure that her husband would leave the home and allow her to deal with her property. Ms. Labbe was asked if she would have been prepared to pay $1,000 for anything other than a final separation agreement. She answered clearly in the negative. She could not afford anything other than an agreement.

In Ms. Healey's view, Ms. Labbe's funds would have been better spent, from the onset, by having a lawyer negotiate and prepare a separation agreement. Ms. Healey suggested that a mediator who was properly serving her client would have so advised. However, it appears that Ms. Labbe thought that Maureen Boldt provided a legitimate alternative to a lawyer for the purpose of obtaining a separation agreement. This was a false hope.

The problems with access to justice are the subject of current comment within the profession and the community generally. It is a well-known fact that low and middle income persons often find the cost of legal services beyond their means. There are alternatives to the legal process for the resolution of disputes. Mediation is one of these alternatives. However, mediators should not be seen as a low-priced alternative to lawyers. The mediation process cannot be a shield for those who are illegally providing legal advice and leading clients to believe that their legal rights and entitlements are fixed. Where individuals seek advice about creating documents that are legally binding and enforceable and will have an impact on their rights and entitlements, they are entitled to that advice only from lawyers who are regulated in the public interest.

Ms. Boldt did not call any evidence in her defence. The evidence of the LSUC is uncontradicted. Drafting separation agreements was a lucrative enterprise for Ms. Boldt, who carried on her practice as if there had been no injunction at all. In substance, her practice did not change from 1993-2003, notwithstanding the significant injunction proceedings where she was wholly unsuccessful in advancing her positions.

Maureen Boldt was fully aware of the terms of the injunction Order made by Bolan J. She had every opportunity to observe the restrictions. Although there was some suggestion that there is a blurring of the line between mediating and giving legal advice or drawing up separation agreements, there was no evidence to support it. This position does not have the air of reality. In any event, it is a moot point, because Maureen Boldt did not engage in mediation as it is commonly understood. Her practice was not consistent with the *Code of Ethics* of the OAFM, of which she was a member.

I find that Maureen Boldt breached the terms of the injunction dated September 1, 2000 by engaging in the unauthorized practice of law contrary to s. 50 of the *Law Society Act* and more particularly, that she dispensed legal advice, prepared separation agreements and offered to undertake divorce proceedings. I, therefore, find that Maureen Boldt carried on the unauthorized practice of law in direct contradiction to the clear and plain terms of the injunction. It is obvious from the transcript of the discovery, read in for these proceedings, that she fully understood the terms of the injunction. It is regrettable that she thought she could ignore the injunction simply by changing the title on her document. This is a flagrant breach of the Order of Bolan J.

I find Maureen Boldt to be in contempt of court. The trial coordinator, in consultation with the parties, will set a date for further submissions on penalty and costs.

NOTES AND QUESTIONS

1. In a separate proceeding, Boldt was sentenced to four months of house arrest, was prohibited from working as a paralegal and was ordered to pay costs of $35,000. The court noted past issues with Boldt and the fact that "Ms. Boldt showed deliberate and wilful contempt of the court's Order. She profited from her continued violations of the court Order. Her unauthorized practice of law has had serious and prejudicial consequences for some of her clients."[7] Given the sanctions imposed on Adams and Hunter, does the sanction for Boldt seem appropriate? To what extent is the sanction justified by the fact that she was in contempt of court? To what extent is it justified by the fact that she was engaged in unauthorized practice of law?

2. In 2011 Boldt applied for reinstatement as a paralegal but was refused. See "Boldt Denied Paralegal Reinstatement Bid", online: <http://www.moosefm.com/cfxn/news/7256-boldt-denied-paralegal-reinstatement-bid>.

The regulation of unauthorized practice raises significant issues of public policy. Specifically, how should we appropriately balance the need to protect people from the harm that may be done by a person providing legal services who is unqualified to do so, while at the same time ensuring access to justice. In the decision, P.C. Hennessy J. notes (at para. 70) that "[i]t is a well-known fact that low and middle income persons often find the cost of legal services beyond their means" but emphasizes the need for protection of the public and the statutory monopoly that lawyers enjoy. Is this the right balance? Consider that question in light of the following case. In particular, note the role played by lawyers in controlling unauthorized practice. Do you think that non-lawyers would approach the issue in the same way?

LAMEMAN v. ALBERTA

[2011] A.J. No. 966, 2011 ABQB 396
(Alta. Q.B., K.D. Yamauchi J.)

K.D. YAMAUCHI J.:—

I. Introduction

The Plaintiffs apply on behalf of certain lawyers from Tooks Chambers, UK (the "Tooks barristers") for a right of audience to assist the Plaintiffs in their case against Defendants. The Plaintiffs claim to be impecunious and unable to

---

[7]   *Law Society of Upper Canada v. Boldt*, [2007] O.J. No. 3757 at para. 5 (Ont. S.C.J.).

prosecute the case without substantial *pro bono* assistance. The Tooks barristers have agreed to provide this assistance.

The Defendants brought applications ("Applications to Strike") pursuant to rule 129 of the *Alberta Rules of Court*, Alta. Reg. 390/68 (*"Old Rules"*). The Plaintiffs sought an adjournment of the Applications to Strike, based on their impecuniosity. This Court heard the adjournment application in the fall of 2010 and granted the Plaintiffs their adjournment. ...

The Plaintiffs first broached with this Court the prospect of retaining the Tooks barristers during their adjournment application. During that application, the Plaintiffs advised this Court that their request was restricted to obtaining the Tooks barristers' assistance in the preparation of their briefs, which they would file to challenge the Applications to Strike. Since then, the Plaintiffs have expanded their request to include Tooks barristers' assistance in other capacities, including a request for the right of audience, and questioning of witnesses in the absence of Canadian counsel of record.

No one takes exception to Tooks barristers participating "behind the scenes," such that they would assist the Plaintiffs' counsel of record in the conduct of research and preparation of briefs, provided any documents that the Plaintiffs place before the court are under the signature of the Plaintiffs' counsel of record. However, the Law Society of Alberta ("Law Society") and the Defendants argue that questioning witnesses and otherwise having a right of audience constitute "practising law." For the Tooks barristers to undertake the practise of law in this case, they must comply with s. 106 of the *Legal Profession Act*, R.S.A. 2000, c. L-8 (the *"LPA"*).

. . . . .

III. Background

The Plaintiffs claim that the federal and provincial Crowns have infringed their treaty rights by taking up so much of their traditional territory that no meaningful right to hunt, trap or fish remains.

Garry Benson, instructing counsel for the Plaintiffs, in his affidavit that he affirmed on November 3, 2010, deposes that the Beaver Lake Cree Nation does not have sufficient funds to cover the cost of completing this litigation. Gerald Whitford, administrator for the Beaver Lake Cree Nation, in the affidavit he affirmed on October 5, 2010, deposes that Beaver Lake Cree Nation:

(a) has very little discretionary funding;

(b) the costs for appropriately and adequately presenting an argument in response to the Applications to Strike would amount to around $100,000; and

(c) this cost would put considerable strain on Beaver Lake Cree Nation's community education, health, social and cultural programs.

Tooks barristers have offered to provide services on a purely voluntary and completely *pro bono* basis, as indicated in an exhibit attached to Garry Benson's affidavit. All of the lawyers in question are trained as barristers in England, have been called to the bar of England and Wales, and are experienced. None is a member of the Law Society.

IV. Legislation and Rules

LPA ss. 102(2) and 106 provide:

> 102(2) Active members are officers of the Court of Queen's Bench and all other courts of record in Alberta and have a right of audience in those courts.
>
> 106(1) No person shall, unless the person is an active member of the Society,
>
> > (a) practise as a barrister or as a solicitor,
> >
> > (b) act as a barrister or as a solicitor in any Court of civil or criminal jurisdiction,
> >
> > (c) commence, carry on or defend any action or proceeding before a Court or judge on behalf of any other person, or
> >
> > (d) settle or negotiate in any way for the settlement of any claim for loss or damage founded in tort.

New [Alberta Rules of Court] rr. 1.2(1)(b) and 2.23 provide:

Purpose and intention of these rules

> 1.2(1) The purpose of these rules is to provide a means by which claims can be fairly and justly resolved in or by a court process in a timely and cost-effective way.
>
> (2) In particular, these rules are intended to be used
>
> …
>
> > (b) to facilitate the quickest means of resolving a claim at the least expense
>
> …

Assistance before the Court

> 2.23(1) The Court may permit a person to assist a party before the Court in any manner and on any terms and conditions the Court considers appropriate.
>
> (2) Without limiting subrule (1), assistance may take the form of
>
> > (a) quiet suggestions,
> >
> > (b) note-taking,
> >
> > (c) support, or
> >
> > (d) addressing the particular needs of a party.
>
> (3) Despite subrule (1), no assistance may be permitted
>
> > (a) that would contravene section 106(1) of the *Legal Profession Act*,

(b) if the assistance would or might be disruptive, or

(c) if the assistance would not meet the purpose and intention of these rules.

The Information Note for *New Rules* r. 2.23 states:

> Under section 106(1) of the *Legal Profession Act* assistance permitted by this rule must fall short of "acting as a barrister or solicitor" or "commencing, carrying on or defending an action or proceeding before a Court or judge on behalf of another person".

Old Rules r. 5.4 provided:

> 5.4 With the permission of the Court, a person may be represented before the Court by an agent other than a solicitor.

V. Plaintiffs' Position

The Plaintiffs concede that Tooks barristers are not permitted to practise law in Alberta within the meaning of *LPA* s. 106. However, they submit that they do not seek the permission of the Court for Tooks barristers to practise law in Alberta. The Plaintiffs' written brief that they filed on May 13, 2011, in support of this application gives a clearer sense of what they are seeking. The written brief says:

> 30 The Plaintiffs respectfully request that this Court grant the Agents a right of audience to permit the Agents to address the Court as representatives, agents and advocates on behalf of the Plaintiffs ...

> 31 More specifically, the Plaintiffs submit that the Agents be granted a right of audience subject to such conditions or arrangements as deemed appropriate by this Court. The order will allow them to appear as advocates on behalf of the Plaintiffs, to examine witnesses, and to make submissions on the law and facts, under the direction and approval of Alberta Lawyers who are lawfully instructed by the Plaintiffs. The Agents will also be able to assist the Alberta Lawyers with legal research and the drafting of legal submissions when necessary.

"Agents" are Tooks barristers.

The Plaintiffs argue that this proposed arrangement does not contravene *LSA* s. 106(1) because:

(a) the Plaintiffs will instruct, at all times, Alberta lawyers until the conclusion of the case, and the Alberta lawyers will direct, control and supervise Tooks barristers' work;

(b) Tooks barristers will only be assisting the Plaintiffs, so they will not be practising law in Alberta; they will not execute pleadings, swear affidavits, make admissions or give undertakings, and they are not expecting a fee; and

(c) by having Alberta lawyers overseeing Tooks barristers at all times, public policy concerns are addressed since the Alberta lawyers are accountable to the Plaintiffs, the court and the Law Society.

The Plaintiffs argue that despite the wording of *LSA* s. 106, this Court has inherent jurisdiction to allow Tooks barristers such a right of audience before this Court ...

. . . . .

Finally, the Plaintiffs argue that if this Court were to allow their application, it would promote a timely and cost-effective resolution of the claim, as encouraged by *New Rules* r. 1.2. This Court could address any lingering concerns through conditions or arrangements, as it deems appropriate.

VI. Law Society's Position

The Law Society argues that *LPA* s. 102 does not grant a right of audience to Tooks barristers who are not members of the Law Society. As well, *New Rules* r. 2.23 does not extend to represented litigants. Further, if this Court has a residual jurisdiction in relation to represented litigants, then this is not an appropriate case for it to exercise its inherent jurisdiction to grant Tooks barristers a right of audience. The Plaintiffs are represented and have counsel of record, and if this Court were to grant the Plaintiffs' application, this would require the Court to usurp the regulatory role of the Law Society and would allow Tooks barristers to do indirectly what they are prohibited by *LPA* s. 106 from doing directly.

. . . . .

The *LPA* and this Court's inherent jurisdiction govern and define the right of audience before the court. The *New Rules* govern and define a non-member's ability to assist a litigant before the court. The Law Society argues that *New Rules* r. 2.23 applies only where the party before the court is unrepresented. Therefore, the sole basis on which the Plaintiffs may ask this Court's permission for an audience for Tooks barristers is this Court's inherent jurisdiction to grant a right of audience beyond that contemplated by the *LPA*.

. . . . .

The Woodco lawyers, as active members of the Law Society of British Columbia who have not been admitted in Alberta, are "visiting lawyers" as defined by the *Rules of the Law Society of Alberta* (the "*Rules*"). The *Rules* rr. 71 - 73 describe the conditions precedent to any visiting lawyer providing legal services in Alberta, as well as the visiting lawyer's obligations. By complying with these inter-jurisdictional practice rules, Woodco's lawyers, who are not members of the Law Society, are entitled to practice law in Alberta, including a right of audience before the court. However, the Tooks barristers are not visiting lawyers within *Rules* r. 71(1)(k) nor are they members of the Law Society. Therefore, they do not qualify for the right of audience extended to Alberta lawyers and visiting lawyers by *LPA* s. 102(1) and are prohibited from carrying out those actions detailed in *LPA* s. 106.

The Law Society explains that *New Rules* r. 2.23(1) codifies the decision of the English Court of Appeal in *McKenzie v. McKenzie*, [1970] 3 All E.R. 1034 (C.A.) ...

The assistance referred to in *New Rules* r. 2.23 mirrors that suggested in *McKenzie*: a person may attend as a friend of either party, take notes, quietly make suggestions, and give advice. *New Rules* r. 2.23(3)(a) expressly states that the assistance cannot contravene *LPA* s. 106, i.e. it cannot be in the nature of acting as a barrister or solicitor. The rationale for allowing a McKenzie friend is fairness to self-represented litigants ...

The Plaintiffs argue that *New Rules* r. 2.23(1) is drafted more widely than its predecessor *Old Rules* r. 5.4. The Law Society argues that the contrary is true. *Old Rules* r. 5.4 dealt with a right of audience, conferring greater rights on a non-lawyer than the more limited right of assistance permitted by *New Rules* r. 2.23(1). ... *New Rules* r. 2.23(3) specifically refers to *LPA* s. 106(1), which prohibits persons who are non-members from acting as barristers and solicitors in any court of civil jurisdiction.

The Law Society argues that this is not an appropriate case in which this Court should invoke its inherent jurisdiction to grant audience to Tooks barristers. ... Where a party has counsel, there is generally no need to ask the court to grant a right of audience to someone other than the litigant's counsel. There may be unusual and emergent circumstances in which this could be necessary, such as where the litigant's counsel is unavailable for an emergency application, bail hearing, or similar interlocutory application. In those circumstances, a represented litigant may seek assistance to fill the gap caused by its counsel's unavailability. This is not the case here. ...

. . . . .

VIII. Analysis

The Alberta Court of Appeal in *Pacer Enterprises*, held that whether a non-lawyer is practising law is a question of degree. As mentioned earlier, no one takes issue with Tooks barristers providing support to Woodco through research and drafting, provided Woodco, as counsel of record, assumes ultimate responsibility for the work product.

Beyond this area of consensus, there was little agreement. Significant time was spent in oral argument on what constitutes the "practice of law." It is not the task of this Court to delineate the limits of the practice of law; nor would it be desirable so to do. The law, as a profession, evolves along with societal needs and desires.

However, we are dealing here with represented Plaintiffs proposing to engage trained foreign lawyers who are non-members. This Court finds that the proposed involvement of Tooks barristers, including questioning of witnesses, preparation of argument, and advocacy before the Court, clearly encompasses matters in respect of which law students receive training and which the public understands to form part of a litigator's stock and trade. It involves acts which in the usual course, if performed improperly, might appropriately draw comment or sanction from the Law Society. If these tasks do not form part of the practice of law, what does?

The Alberta Legislature has chosen to grant the privilege of self-regulation to the legal profession in Alberta. The Alberta Legislature enacted *LPA* s. 106(1) for the purpose of ensuring, among other things, that lawyers practising in Alberta be competent and proficient, adequately insured by the Alberta Lawyers' Insurance Association, and bound by the *CPC*. While Tooks barristers may well be competent and proficient, there was no evidence before this Court that they are insured, nor did the Plaintiffs present evidence to establish that Tooks barristers would be bound by the *CPC*.

The Plaintiffs rely heavily on *Professional Signcrafters*. That decision addressed *Old Rules* r. 5.4. It is noteworthy that the issue before O'Leary J., as he then was, was whether the director of the plaintiff corporation had contravened the *LPA* by commencing an action on behalf of the plaintiff corporation. The director had already lost on an appeal of a Master's decision denying him standing to make representations on behalf of the plaintiffs at the hearing of the motion to strike out the plaintiffs' pleadings. Although O'Leary J. in *obiter dictum* distinguished between the right of audience in *Old Rules* r. 5.4, and the right to practice law under the equivalent of *LPA* s. 106(1), there is no suggestion that he intended his comments to extend so as to allow trained lawyers to circumvent the regime of self-regulation established by the Alberta Legislature, particularly where the party seeking this relief is already represented by counsel of record.

Further, *New Rules* r. 2.23 speaks not of "represent" and "representation," but of "assist" and "assistance." While the list of forms of assistance set forth in *New Rules* r. 2.23(2) is not exhaustive, *New Rules* r. 2.23(3) is absolutely clear that, despite the apparent broadness of *New Rules* r. 2.23(1), a court has no discretion to permit assistance where the court's ruling would contravene *LPA* s. 106(1). This Court has no inherent jurisdiction to make an order negating the unambiguous expression of the will of the Alberta Legislature: *Baxter Student Housing Ltd. v. College Housing Co-Operative Ltd.*, [1976] 2 S.C.R. 475 at 480. If this language left any room for doubt, the Information Note that one finds in the *New Rules* emphasizes that the "assistance" must fall short of "acting as a barrister or solicitor." This Court need not determine the broadness (or narrowness) of *New Rules* r. 2.23. In particular, it need not determine whether *New Rules* r. 2.23 is or is not limited to self-represented litigants by virtue of the fact that *New Rules* r. 2.22 is headed "Self-represented litigants," *New Rules* r. 2.23 is headed "Assistance before the Court," and there is no mention of self-represented litigants in the title of the division of the *New Rules* in which *New Rules* r. 2.23 appears.

This Court also notes that *LPA* s. 106(2)(m) creates a very limited exception to *LPA* s. 106(1). That paragraph allows a person holding professional legal qualifications obtained in a country outside Canada in respect of services permitted to be provided by that person in accordance with the rules in giving legal advice respecting the laws of that country. That exception does not apply here. *Rules* r. 74(e) says "practise as a foreign legal consultant" means to carry on a practice as a legal advisor with respect to the laws of a foreign country or of a political subdivision of a foreign country, and "the practice of a foreign legal consultant" has a corresponding meaning. *Rules* rr. 74 to 80 require foreign legal consultants to apply to the Law Society for licences, pay annual licensing fees and provide services, only in accordance with the conditions imposed by the licences. In this case, Tooks barristers is not intending to practice as a foreign legal consultant, as it is not advising on the laws of the foreign country. It intends to advise on and apply Canadian law.

This Court finds that the *LPA* and *New Rules* r. 2.23 prohibit Tooks barristers' proposed expanded participation in these proceedings and, in particular, in the Applications to Strike. The *LPA* and *New Rules* r. 2.23 do not provide an alternative basis for this participation.

The Plaintiffs assert that Woodco's active representation will come at a price which is beyond the Plaintiffs' means. The Defendants took issue with the affidavit evidence regarding the Plaintiffs' alleged impecuniosity. Although that issue is not squarely before this Court, it is acutely aware of the resources likely spent to date on court appearances since the first adjournment application in the fall of 2010. Nothing can be inferred solely from that fact. It may reflect the Plaintiffs' available resources. At the same time, it might support the argument that the Plaintiff cannot continue to fund the litigation at the current rate.

Having considered all of the arguments presented, this Court can come to no other conclusion but that under the current circumstances the proposed participation of Tooks barristers, beyond the supporting role conceded by the Law Society and the Defendants, are prohibited by *LPA* ss. 102 and 106. Further, this Court declines to exercise its inherent jurisdiction to grant an order for expanded participation beyond that to which the parties have agreed.

. . . . .

NOTES AND QUESTIONS

1. The judgment was upheld on appeal: See *Lameman v. Alberta*, [2012] A.J. No. 180, 2012 ABCA 59 (Alta. C.A.).

2. In "Unauthorized Practice and Access to Justice", *ABlawg.ca* (August 3, 2011), online: University of Calgary, Faculty of Law <http://ablawg.ca/wp-content/uploads/2011/08/blog_aw_tooks_aug2011.pdf>, Alice Woolley said the following:

   Justice Yamauchi's reasons seem compelling given the clear terms of the *LPA*, and the constrained language of the Rules of Court. The case does raise, though, the question of whether lawyers in Alberta should be given a monopoly over the provision of legal services as extensive as the one they enjoy.

   It is true that the lawyers from Took Chambers may not carry Canadian insurance, and may not be technically bound by the Code of Professional Conduct. It is also true that they have not been trained – at law school, through articles or otherwise – in the substantive content of Canadian law. However, these barriers do not seem especially substantial, or to undermine the point that the firm's services would provide real and tangible benefits to the Nation in the prosecution of their action at little cost. The terms of English codes of conduct are in substance similar to those that apply in Canada. In the event that their services prove to be negligent or in breach of contract, it seems likely that the firm has resources to cover claims made against them by their clients. Further, those clients are not unsophisticated, and could make the decision themselves as to whether to be represented by an uninsured firm. After all, most American lawyers are not legally required to carry insurance, and yet the US legal services market seems to carry on regardless. Lawyers are rarely sued successfully for their conduct of litigation.

Further, what information I could obtain on them from the web suggests that lawyers from Took Chambers are likely to provide outstanding service to their clients, whether in Canada or elsewhere. They have a practice that they describe as "unashamedly political" and have been involved in a wide variety of domestic and international matters raising questions of access to justice and civil rights. In one article that mentioned them they were described as "Left-wing legal Chambers presided over by the wildly grand Michael Mansfield QC" (Mail Online, Quentin Letters, "Vera the Amazon is back as Bar maid", January 23, 2011). Mansfield represented those wrongfully convicted in the IRA's Guildford and Birmingham pub bombings, amongst other high profile cases.

On the specific facts of this case it seems likely that the benefits of the Took Chambers representing the National significantly outweigh the costs and risks with their doing so.

The arguments against the representation are likely to operate at the level of generality and policy – that even if it might be a good thing for the Took Chambers to act for the Nation, it is nonetheless a bad thing to allow people who are not members of the Law Society of Alberta (or, given our new mobility rules, another Canadian law society) to practice law here. Non-members may not be competent, and their practice cannot be regulated by the law society; they may inflict costs on their clients and the functioning of the administration of justice while not meaningfully improving access to justice.

These general arguments undoubtedly have considerable weight. One of the reasons why we license certain activities and restrict who may participate in them is to protect the public against incompetent or unscrupulous persons to whom they might otherwise be vulnerable. But their weakness in the particular case of Took Chambers does suggest that we should be careful in simply assuming that those arguments are sufficient to justify the blanket prohibitions contained in the *LPA*. Can there not be a more nuanced or careful approach to the provision of legal services, in which consumer and public interests are protected, but the availability of competent and helpful legal advice is not irrationally restricted? I have to think that there could be; the facts of this case invite us to try.

Do you agree with this analysis? What, in your view, would a more careful and nuanced approach to these issues look like?

F.   ALTERNATIVES TO SELF REGULATION

In the previous sections, and in previous chapters of this book, we have looked at the regulation of lawyers by lawyers in the areas of advertising, solicitation, exercise of prosecutorial discretion and otherwise. We have also seen, arguably, regulation of lawyers by the courts with respect to confidentiality, conflicts of interest and advocacy. An underlying theme which arises from this case law and discussion is as to whether the regulation of lawyers by lawyers is an appropriate regulatory mechanism, or whether some other approach would be better. The following excerpt provides consideration of the question of the present and future of lawyer self-regulation.

R. DEVLIN & P. HEFFERNAN

"The End(s) of Self Regulation(?)"
(2008) 45 Alta. L. Rev. 169
[modified, footnotes omitted]

Introduction

All around the world jurisdictions are reconsidering and ultimately abandoning self regulation as a model for the governance of the legal profession. Whether it be Australia, New Zealand, Scotland, England and Wales, South Africa or Ireland a wide range of advanced liberal democratic societies have assessed self regulation and found it wanting as a defensible regime. By contrast, in Canada self regulation by the legal profession appears to be a sacred cow. Governments, the general public, the judiciary and the profession itself all appear to believe that self regulation is *de facto* and *de jure* the only game in town and that substantive consideration of alternatives would be unnecessary, fruitless and pointless.

It is time to consider whether such complacency is warranted in Canada. Have there been any failures by the regulatory bodies in Canada? Have law societies in Canada established all the appropriate standards, adequately monitored lawyers' conduct and enforced suitable penalties? Do we have all the ethical rules and principles that we need in Canada? Are there any rules and principles that are missing? Are there any rules and principles that are superfluous?

Comparative Developments

A look at the regulation of the legal profession throughout common law countries confirms that pure self-regulation has increasingly become an endangered species. It appears, in fact, that Canada may soon be the only country in the Commonwealth where the profession remains self-governing. The type of regulatory intervention and the degree of authority lost by the professional bodies varies among jurisdictions. Some common threads are apparent, however. In most cases an independent regulatory agency has been created, one which is appointed not by the law society (or its equivalent) but by the government. Frequently the state reclaims responsibility for complaints handling and discipline and assigns it to this body, but leaves the law society to establish codes of conduct and standards of practice, and even to govern admissions and qualification. Finally, the new mechanisms that are introduced often provide for significant lay participation in the disciplinary process.

Australia and the United Kingdom are leading the charge against self-regulation, with other jurisdictions following close on their heels. In Australia, reforms to the regulation of the profession have been unfolding for more than a decade. Because the legal profession is regulated at the state, rather than the federal level, the regulatory structures are not traditionally uniform. Part of the reforms involves an effort to unify the regulatory systems across the country, and to improve the mobility of lawyers. The reforms are otherwise broadly similar: in most states the reforms provide for an independent, government-appointed body to handle the complaints and discipline process, usually with some supervised involvement by the Law Society. The Law Society does retain the authority to establish rules and standards for practice, but it is subject to supervision in this regard. Provision is also usually made for significant lay involvement in the regulatory process.

England and Wales

In United Kingdom, reforms to the governance of solicitors in England and Wales have provided an example which the governments of other jurisdictions have watched with interest. Over the last decade, the Law Society of England and Wales has repeatedly restructured its complaints handling process in response to pressure from government and consumer groups, each time seeking and claiming increased independence for the complaints division from the rest of the Law Society. The most recent round of reforms, which at the time of writing remain before the British Parliament, would establish a Legal Services Board to oversee the regulation of legal practitioners throughout England and Wales, and would separate the complaints handling process completely from the jurisdiction of the Law Society. In addition, the reforms would provide for the provision of legal service under alternative business structures, including both multi-disciplinary practices and larger commercial practices, meaning, for example, that "retailers could offer legal services" (i.e. "Tesco law firms").

Scotland

Scotland has also passed similar reforms, providing for an independent regulatory agency with substantial lay representation which would take over some authority from the Law Society and Faculty of Advocates. The new structure involves a split between professional service complaints and low-level negligence complaints on the one hand, and professional misconduct and discipline complaints on the other. The new Scottish Legal Complaints Commission will handle the former independently of the profession, while the Law Society and Faculty of Advocates will continue to handle the latter. The new body provides for substantial lay participation in the process: it will be chaired by a non-lawyer, with four lawyer and four non-lawyer members. Details of the structure of the new Commission will be released as its launch target of mid-2008 draws closer.

Other Jurisdictions

Reforms are underway in other countries as well: in Ireland, recent reforms have provided for more lay involvement in the professional regulatory bodies, without actually removing regulation from the hands of the profession. Legislation is presently under consideration which would create the office of the Legal Ombudsman to review the claims of those dissatisfied with the professional bodies' own complaints handling processes. In New Zealand, reforms have been introduced requiring the Law Society to split its representative and regulatory functions. These will supplement previous reforms which established the office of the Lay Observer, who has the responsibility for reviewing the handling of complaints by the Law Society. Finally, in South Africa the local professional bodies retain powers of self-regulation, but debate continues over reforms to establish a more independent national regulatory body.

Taken together, these international developments portray Canada as increasingly unique in its continued reliance on almost completely unhindered self-regulation for the legal profession. Independent of the specific reasons for concern raised in the last section, it seems either naïve or obtuse to imagine that there is no need even for debate about the issue in Canada. Virtually every other similarly situated jurisdiction in the world is at least exploring other options, if not already reworking their regulatory regime. In the absence of clear and unequivocal evidence, it is difficult to believe that the Canadian profession is not affected by the same factors motivating reforms in other jurisdictions. On what basis could one sustain the claim that Canadian lawyers are better at regulating themselves than their Australian, British, Scottish or New Zealand counterparts? The next section will identify and consider some of the traditionally proferred justifications.

The Well-Tilled Field: Arguments Pro and Con Self Regulation

The arguments pro and con self regulation have been developed over many decades, by many authors, in many different fora. It is therefore unnecessary to rehearse them in detail. However, a brief overview is helpful in order to set the context for the remainder of this section and to highlight the complexity of the problem of designing a suitable regulatory regime. Regulation is not just about techniques and institutions, it is also about the underlying values of the society in which it operates: democracy, accountability, equality, transparency, effectiveness and efficiency. Consequently it is incumbent on analysts to both question their taken-for-granted assumptions and avoid overly hasty conclusions.

The essence of the argument in favour of self regulation can be captured in a formula, A+E=I: autonomy plus expertise = independence from state regulation and market forces. The essence of the critique is the old latin maxim: *quis custodiet*, or more polemically: should we allow the fox to guard the chickens … or is it wise to put Dracula in charge of the bloodbank?

These larger propositions can be broken down into a more specific series of claims.

Arguments in Favour

Independence of the Bar

It is often argued that the independence of the bar is an unqualified social good and that, of necessity, such independence requires self governance. For example, in *Jabour*, excerpted in Chapter 1, Justice Estey argued:

> The independence of the Bar from the state in all its pervasive manifestations is one of the hallmarks of a free society. Consequently, regulation of these members of the law profession by the state must, so far as by human ingenuity it can be so designed, be free from state interference, in the political sense, with the delivery of services to the individual citizens in the state, particularly in fields of public and criminal law. The public interest in a free society knows no area more sensitive than the independence, impartiality and availability to the general public of the members of the Bar and through those members, legal advice and services generally. The uniqueness of the position of the barrister and solicitor in the community may well have led the province to select self-administration as the mode for administrative control over the supply of legal services throughout the community.

In *Pearlman* Justice Iacobucci quoted with approval the following extract from a report commissioned by the Attorney General of Ontario:

> The regulation of professional practice through the creation and the operation of a licensing system, then, is a matter of public policy; it emanates from the legislature; it involves the creation of valuable rights; and it is directed towards the protection of vulnerable interests.
>
> On the other hand, where the legislature sees fit to delegate some of its authority in these matters of public policy to professional bodies themselves, it must respect the self-governing status of these bodies. Government ought not to prescribe in detail the structures, processes, and policies of professional bodies. The initiative in such matters must rest with the professions themselves, recognizing their particular expertise and sensitivity to the conditions of practice. In brief, professional self-governing bodies must be ultimately accountable to the legislature; but they must have the authority to make, in the first place, the decisions for which they are to be accountable.
>
> Stress was rightly laid on the high value that free societies have placed historically on an independent judiciary, free of political interference and influence on its decisions, and an independent bar, free to represent citizens without fear or favour in the protection of individual rights and civil liberties against incursion from any source, including the state.

Justice Iacobucci concluded after this quote that:

> "On this view, the self-governing status of the professions, and of the legal profession in particular, was created in the public interest."

These claims are often backed up with reference to international norms, such as the United Nations *Basic Principles on the Independence of the Judiciary* (1985) or the United Nations *Basic Principles on the Role of Lawyers* (1990).

Independence of the Judiciary

This argument is a follow on from the previous claim. The bar is the nursery for the judiciary and an independent legal profession helps to foster the independence and impartiality so essential to the judicial role.

Democracy, Freedom and the Rule of Law

Because a free and democratic society requires an independent judiciary to maintain the rule of law, that free and democratic society of necessity also needs an independent legal profession as a linchpin to secure the public good. Pue, for example, has recently argued that there can be an organic relationship between the independence of the legal profession and the emergence of a "liberal constitution." The nexus is that an independent legal profession can only exist if it is self-regulating.

Public Confidence in the Legal Profession

Proponents of self-regulation argue that if the general public had the perception that lawyers were subject to the control of the state then that public would not have the confidence that lawyers will resolutely pursue the interests of their client against the state. The independence of the legal profession should not only be done, but manifestly and undoubtedly be seen to be done.

Tradition

Self-regulation by the legal profession can be traced all the way back to at least the fifteenth century, if not further. For some this means that self-regulation is a fundamental aspect of our legal heritage and perhaps even an aspect of our unwritten constitution. If self government were lost the legal profession would be "a mere trade or business," rather than a pillar of our liberal social order.

Expertise

This claim proposes that only lawyers have the relevant expertise and knowledge to formulate appropriately nuanced rules and assess other lawyers' compliance with, or deviation from, such rules. For example in *Jabour* Estey opined that "The nature of the services [lawyers bring to the public] makes the valuation of those services by the unskilled very difficult."... and that "the general public is not in a position to appraise unassisted the need for [or effectiveness of] legal services." Similarly in *Pearlman* the Supreme Court of Canada indicated that only lawyers have the "particular expertise and sensitivity to the conditions of practice" to assess other lawyers. A more poignant version is Justice Finlayson's proposition that "No one knows better than a fellow lawyer whether or not a brother lawyer has become a transgressor."

Efficiency

This argument is closely connected to the previous argument. The advocates of self regulation argue that the costs of regulation are internalized to the profession because they are borne by membership through the payment of fees. Consequently there is no additional bureaucracy that needs to be bankrolled out of the taxes paid by the general public. Moreover, the cheapest and most efficient way to protect a victimized member of the public is to internalize the cost to the profession via mandatory insurance and reimbursement from liability funds.

Higher Standards

This argument advances the claim that the profession can more finely calibrate the responsibilities of lawyers, and tailor penalties more appropriately than government regulation, or blunt instruments such as criminal prosecution or civil suits. Moreover, the law societies are able to develop complaints resolution procedures that deal with the real and specific concerns of clients without invoking draconian disciplinary processes and deploy other regulatory devices that fulfill the public interest. In other words, the profession in order to both protect the public and promote its reputation "funnels in" conduct that would otherwise go unchecked.

Commitment to the Public Good

This is essentially a psychological argument — because lawyers recognize that they have been entrusted with a sacred privilege they tend, both as individuals and a group, to contribute to the public good by, for example, seeking to maintain high standards of "professional purity" and moral reasoning among themselves. Others also suggest that self regulation encourages lawyers to enhance access to justice through reduced fees for those who are in need, or even participation in *pro bono* activities. To remove self regulation would be to undercut this psychological motivation to promote the public good, and alienate the profession from its traditional commitments.

Arguments Against

There are, however, a significant number of arguments that cast doubt on the foregoing claims. The essence of the critique is that self regulation is a privilege (not a right) that was granted to the legal profession as part of a "regulative bargain" and in return the profession would promote and protect the public interest. The legal profession, the critics claim, has failed to live up to the regulative bargain on a number of levels.

Conflict of Interest

The key concern of the conflict of interest claim is that it is not possible for a single organization to fulfill both a representative function and a regulatory function. According to the critics it is just too convenient that the public interest in accessing legal services should be presumed to dovetail with the professional interest in providing such services. The legal profession prohibits individual lawyers from benefitting from conflicts of interest, but is oblivious to its own constitutive conflict of interest. For example, if one analyses the sorts of pitches that are made by candidates seeking election to bar council they overwhelmingly reflect the interests and concerns of lawyers, not the public.

Critics of self-regulation, just like the defenders, also play the public perception card: even if there is no actual conflict of interest and the profession does successfully put the public interest ahead of its own, the public is not likely to see it that way and that perception is just as important as reality. If confidence in the rule of law really is at stake, then it should be beyond doubt that the guardian of the rule of law, the legal profession, must itself be free of the taint of impartiality.

Seneviratne points out that in the English context there were some lawyers who agreed that regulation and representation should be separated for several reasons: first, law societies could then focus on their representative role; second, lawyers would not be burdened with the increasing bureaucratic costs of regulation; third, it would potentially enhance the legitimacy of the profession in the eyes of the public; and fourth, it might lead to more efficient complaints systems in which both lawyers and the public would benefit.

To buttress this criticism, reference is often made to other professions, for example doctors, who have two very distinct organizations, the Canadian Medical Association (representative), the College of Physicians and Surgeons (regulatory).

Monopoly/Market Control

Although this argument is informed by the economic analysis of law, it is worth noting that it is embraced by critics on both the left and right of the political spectrum. On this view the legal profession is a "conspiratorial cartel" and self regulation is anti-competitive because it limits the supply of legal services thereby artificially inflating prices. Many legal services could be supplied by others, for example paralegals, and there is no empirical evidence to suggest that the removal of self regulation would either diminish the quality or availability of legal services. More specifically, comparative empirical research confirms that in many jurisdictions there is a fundamental "lack of a consumer orientation" on the part of the legal profession and, more importantly, that law societies have done little to try to improve this. Thus it is argued that competition might well increase both the possibility of lower prices and improve the quality of services. In short, it engenders competitiveness in quality control. In the long run this should enhance the level of consumer satisfaction. Other analysts go further and suggest that we are witnessing the phenomenon of "regulation-for-competition" whereby regulatory innovation is seen to be a competitive asset in an increasingly globalized world.

Independence: Really ... and From Whom?

Critics of self-regulation tend to make three broad claims in response to the independence argument: the first calls for analytical clarity; the second suggests a reality check; and the third pleads for historical accuracy.

First, a number of recent studies of the independence of the bar have been very careful to make a distinction between "the independence of the bar" and "self-governance." While most suggest that there may be a relationship between the two, they are all very explicit that "independence" does not necessarily entail "self-governance." Indeed, a Task Force of the Law Society of Upper Canada suggests that the "independence of the bar" is best "understood as a right enjoyed by the public and as a mechanism for maintaining and defending the rule of law ..." Monahan, for example, argues that the independence at stake is independence from the executive branch of government and that this can be achieved by means other than self-regulation. He claims that self-regulation is simply a policy choice in pursuit of the public interest and that other regulatory instruments in pursuit of that interest might be constitutionally legitimate. To butress this claim Monahan also invokes *Jabour* to highlight various dicta of Justice Estey that are not usually mentioned by the defenders of self-regulation:

> The general public is not in a position to appraise unassisted the need for legal services or the effectiveness of the services provided in the client's cause by the practitioner, and therefore stands in need of protection. It is the establishment of this protection that is the primary purpose of the Legal Profession Act. *Different views may be held as to the effectiveness of the mode selected by the Legislature, but none of the parties here challenged the right of the province to enact the legislation. It is up to the Legislature to determine the administrative technique to be employed in the execution of the policy of its statutes.* I see nothing in law pathological about the selection by the provincial Legislature here of an administrative agency drawn from the sector of the community to be regulated. Such a system offers some immediate advantages such as familiarity of the regulator with the field, expertise in the subject of the services in question, low cost to the taxpayer as the administrative agency must, by the statute, recover its own expenses without access to the tax revenues of the Province. One the other hand, to set out something of the other side of the coin, there is the problem of conflict of interest, an orientation favourable to the regulated, and the closed shop atmosphere. In some provinces some lay Benchers are appointed by the provincial governments; in other provinces the Attorney General is seized with the duty as an ex officio Bencher of safeguarding the public interest; a right of appeal from decision affecting members is given to the Court; and the confirmation by the Provincial Executive, the Lieutenant Governor in Council, of all regulations adopted by the Society as a prerequisite to their validity. *It is for the Legislature to weigh and determine all these matters and I see no constitutional consequences necessarily flowing from the regulatory mode adopted by the province in Legislation validly enacted within its sovereign sphere as is the case here* ... (emphasis added).

The uniqueness of position of the barrister and solicitor in the community may well have led the province to select self-administration as the mode of administrative control over the supply of legal services throughout the community. *Having said all that, it must be remembered that the assignment of administrative control to the field of self-administration by the profession is subject to such important protective restraints as the taxation officer, the appeal to the courts from action by the Benchers, the presence of the Attorney General as an ex officio member of the Benchers and the legislative need of some or all of the authority granted to the Law Society. In any case this decision is for the province to make.* (emphasis added).

In short, to confuse independence of the legal profession with self-regulation is a subtle, but indefensible legerdemain.

Second, critics call for a reality check. Traditional arguments for independence focus on the threat of the state, but in the modern world the state is not the only, or even major, centre of power and control in society. Corporations also wield great influence. Not only are in-house counsel especially vulnerable to their economic masters, so too are law firms that service corporations, especially corporations who are repeat clients ... he who pays the piper ... as the aphorism goes. The independence of the legal profession, in other words, is more apparent than real.

Third, from a historical perspective, critics point out that the legal profession has been somewhat less than enthusiastic in its pursuit of independence than it is often asserted. Many of the elements of self-regulation cannot be traced back to the mystical origins of the common law but are relatively recent, i.e. twentieth century, developments. Furthermore, at times the profession has been aligned with repressive forces as much as with democracy and the rule of law. During the Winnipeg General Strike some members of the legal profession engaged in outrageous behaviour. In Quebec during the Duplessis regime many lawyers refused to provide legal services to Mr. Roncarelli, a Jehovah's Witness, to fight the padlock laws. Many lawyers did little to protest the invocation of the War Measures Act and, currently, there are allegations that a significant number of marquee criminal defence lawyers made themselves scarce when the Toronto 17 were arrested. And then again there is Ms Finney who only got *pro bono* assistance when the case went to the Supreme Court of Canada. As to the argument that there is threat to the independence of the judiciary it has been noted that a significant number of judges come from government or universities, yet there is nothing to indicate that they are less independent or impartial.

Undemocratic

In response to the claim that self regulation is essential for democracy, critics point out that the causal connection is missing: there are many liberal democratic societies where there is no self government by the legal profession, yet they seem to be flourishing as well as Canada. Conversely, there are jurisdictions that have a self-regulating legal profession but are deeply authoritarian, for example, Singapore. Moreover, critics insist that the demand for self regulation comes from the profession itself, not the general public and as such is, in fact, an exercise in "regulatory imperialism." The concern that the public will lose confidence in the legal profession if self regulation is abolished is conjecture, devoid of any empirical support. To the contrary, at least one commentator suggests that self-regulation may be only a contingent and transitional moment in the development of a profession as it seeks to establish its legitimacy, but once that legitimacy has been consolidated, self-regulation can be relinquished as the profession becomes more mature. Moreover, it is argued that the governors within the legal profession are rarely representative of a cross section of an increasingly diversified and fragmented profession, let alone society. Given this, it is difficult to imagine how their conception of the public interest could authentically and democratically capture the (increasingly complex) reality of the public interest.

Protection Racket

There are a couple of dimensions to this concern. The first is that despite the fact that Codes of Conduct both allow and demand whistle blowing on fellow lawyers, it is very rare for lawyers to report the misconduct of other lawyers. So, while it is true that lawyers may have the expertise to distinguish between proper and improper conduct, that does nothing to ensure that they will in fact exercise that expertise in the public interest. It is not just high profile cases such as the *Pilzmaker* case where there is a failure to report. Just speak to members of the profession after a successful discipline prosecution and many will tell you "sure, everybody knew he was a bad apple but …"

Moreover, critics also argue that when discipline proceedings are instituted the penalties are too lenient because lawyers are too sensitive to their colleague's situation … "there but for the grace of god go I…." The previous discussion of Mr. Hunter is but one example of this. Another concern is that few lawyers are ever disciplined for excessive billing, a common practice that is the most significant complaint from clients.

Still others argue that the complaints processes run by law societies are not especially consumer friendly. Furthermore, even if people do pursue their concerns, the disciplinary system occupies the field, crowding out other remedial avenues (civil or criminal). The consequence is that discipline is a sop, it funnels complaints away and often, miscreant lawyers get off the hook, or receive only minimal discipline.

Reactive and Inefficient Institutional Culture

Because the self-regulatory process is beholden to the lawyers themselves in the form of fees, law societies are significantly underfunded and understaffed. Consequently they operate reactively, primarily on the basis of complaints, rather than actively seeking out problematic behaviour, before it is too late. While law societies are empowered to conduct spot audits and can commence an investigation without a complaint, these actions are the exception rather than the rule.

From a slightly different perspective it might also be suggested that law societies' regulatory structures are inefficient/sub-optimal. While it is true that the costs are internalized to the profession, some [commentators] indicate that the bureaucracies created by law societies may not be particularly efficient. The argument is that they are run by lawyers, not professional regulators, and consequently they do not get the best bang for the regulatory buck. An independent regulatory body can provide greater professionalism, rationality, accessibility and efficiency.

Psychological Critique

Some critics also claim that self-governance is not just about enhancing the economic monopoly of lawyers, but also to "bid up the value of their intellectual cultural capital." The goal is to enhance the psychic esteem of the legal profession.

Public Relations Exercise

Finally, critics also argue that self governance is essentially a public relations exercise, it is symbolic and ideological and it creates the appearance of responsibility and accountability but not the reality. Harry Arthurs takes this claim one step further by claiming that "regulation is not a major determinant of professional culture .... Professional conduct is ... shaped by three important factors, the personal characteristics of the lawyer, the professional circumstances of his or her practice, and the ethical economy of the profession."

Enlarging the Regulatory Imagination: Calibrated Regulation and Its Options

Analysts frequently note that regulation of the professions is a complex and multifaceted process, covering at least three distinct aspects: admission to the profession, the establishment of ethical and quality standards, and discipline for breach of such standards. The contemporary theory and practice of regulation in many professions in many jurisdictions now recognize that effective regulation must be able to identify and respond to such complexities. Within the literature this is variously described as "the new regulatory state," "smart regulation," "decentred regulation," "dynamic regulation," "responsive regulation," "reflexive regulation," "nimble regulation," "meta-regulation," "regulatory pluralism," or "the regulatory web."

While there are many significant differences between these various conceptions of regulation they all agree on three key points: pure self-regulation is both normatively indefensible in a liberal democratic society and strategically ineffective in achieving its goals; the traditional alternative, i.e. the conventional state-centred command and control model of regulation, is much too blunt an instrument to effectively and efficiently get results; the only viable strategy is to develop a hybrid and nuanced constellation of civil society/market/state based regulatory instruments that can be synergistically deployed (in an increasingly intensified way from co-operation to coercion) in a contextually sensitive manner. For the purposes of this chapter, we will call this "calibrated regulation." One common metaphor is that there should be a "pyramid of regulatory controls." Another is that the state should "steer" rather than "row."

If one stands back and looks at the various regulatory functions relevant to the legal profession it becomes apparant that "calibrated regulation" is indeed an apt characterization of the beast. William Hurlburt, for example, has provided a very helpful cartography of seventeen various and complex regulatory devices that might be used by the legal profession:

> The devices employed by the law societies to promote the competence and ethical motivation of lawyers (the uplift side) are as follows:
>
> 1. Influence on or control of the pre-legal and legal education of incoming lawyers.
> 2. Apprenticeship or supervision (articling, pupilage, and training contracts).
> 3. Vocational training (vocational courses, bar admission courses, and bar admission examinations).
> 4. Requirements of good character.
> 5. Promulgation and promotion of ethical standards (general).
> 6. Promulgation and promotion of ethical standards (duty of competence).
> 7. Practice advisory services.
> 8. Certification of specialists.
> 9. Encouragement of continuing legal education or the establishment of mandatory continuing legal education.
>
> The devices on the policing and punishment side are as follows:
>
> 1. Discipline and sanctions (general).
> 2. Discipline and sanctions (competence).
>
> Devices which have both uplift and policing aspects and which therefore occupy a middle ground between the promotion of standards, on the one hand, and discipline and sanctions, on the other, are as follows:
>
> 1. Practice review.
> 2. Remedial continuing legal education.
> 3. Supervision.
> 4. Restrictions on practice.
>
> A fourth element, devices which do not directly affect professional standards but which are part of a system for the protection of the public, are as follows:
>
> 1. Schemes for the compensation of clients for dishonesty and misappropriation of funds.
> 2. Schemes for the compensation of clients for negligent or incompetent service.

Hurlburt argued in 2000 that all of these functions can be fulfilled by self-regulation. However, in light of the arguments offered by the critics, such optimism may no longer be valid in Canada because there have been significant (perhaps even systemic) failures in establishing standards, monitoring behaviour, and enforcement. In the remainder of this chapter we will attempt to expand the Canadian regulatory imagination by offering four regulatory models each of which attempts to respond to the reality of "calibrated regulation." In each case, a simplified chart is included as an illustration of the structure described.

If the traditional model of self-regulation places full regulatory authority over all of Hurlburt's factors in the hands of the law societies [as represented in Figure 1], then the models of calibrated regulation described here all involve the splitting of such authority along one or more lines. Where self-regulation grants the Law Society unfettered and unsupervised regulatory authority, these models involve other agents in the process, narrow the Law Society's authority, and strip it of responsibility over some functions. None of these models envision the total removal of the Law Society from the process. Each recognizes that the expertise and experience of the profession in regulating itself is not to be disposed of lightly, and seeks a workable and effective compromise in the division of authority. It is worth noting also that these models represent points on a continuum and not watertight compartments. They are not presented as mutually exclusive, but rather as broadly overlapping illustrations of a few recurring categories of regulatory reform.

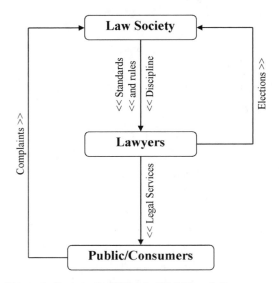

Figure 1: Prototypical Model of Self Regulation

The first, and perhaps most straightforward of these reforms splits the regulation of the profession along the rule creation/rule enforcement line [See Figure 2]. Under this model, the responsibility for rule-creation, or the first nine 'uplift' factors of Hurlburt's list, remains in the hands of the Law Society. The Society sets standards of ethical behaviour and competence, it governs the rules for admission and stipulates the pre-admission educational requirements, and it sets the program of articling or apprenticeship and any professional training, including bar courses and exams. The rule enforcement side of regulation, or Hurlburt's policing and punishment, is removed from the hands of the Law Society. An independent body is created with the responsibility for hearing and determining complaints against practicing lawyers, and for administering discipline.

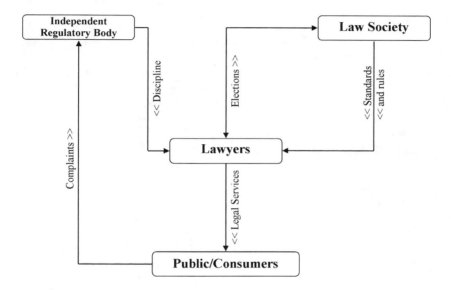

Figure 2: Coregulatory Option 1: Authority split between rule-making and rule-enforcement

Looking to reforms in other parts of the world … this fairly basic change to the structure of professional regulation is common. In England and Wales, pending reforms will take responsibility for complaints and discipline away from the Law Society, while also introducing more comprehensive oversight and more effective lay participation into the system, two changes which we will consider shortly. The reforms recently completed or underway in most Australian states are similar. The states of New South Wales, Queensland, and Victoria all provide for an independent body to administer complaints against lawyers, while the Law Society retains varying degrees of authority to set the standards of practice and ethical rules against which those lawyers will be judged.

The problem of a conflict of interest — real or perceived — is at the heart of this reform, and in a large measure is why it is so common. Whether accurate or not, there is an appearance of a conflict of interest in lawyers judging their own for compliance with ethical and competency standards they have set. Transferring the judging function to another body eliminates this conflict. This particular division has the additional advantage of allowing the Law Societies to continue to set rules and standards of practice, a task which arguably requires a great deal of experience with the practice of law and its ethical pot-holes and deadfalls. Some argue that allowing the profession to retain this function is not enough, however. They claim that this same experience is a necessary prerequisite to determining whether lawyers have complied with the ethical standards, or demonstrated an appropriate level of competence. The following co-regulatory compromise in some measure addresses this claim.

A second common type of co-regulatory reform is to split the disciplinary process itself [See Figure 3]. Leaving Hurlburt's 'uplift' factors aside for the moment, reforms of this sort divide the disciplinary and complaints process in some way, for example between a) conduct complaints alleging breaches of ethical standards, and b) competence complaints alleging poor quality of service [as in Figure 3]. An independent body such as that described above takes over responsibility for one genre of complaints, while the law society retains jurisdiction to deal with the other.

This structure should be familiar to Canadian practitioners. All Canadian jurisdictions already provide for some division in complaints, even while remaining wholly self-governing. We are referring, of course to the jurisdiction of the courts over civil complaints, including both fee disputes and professional negligence claims.

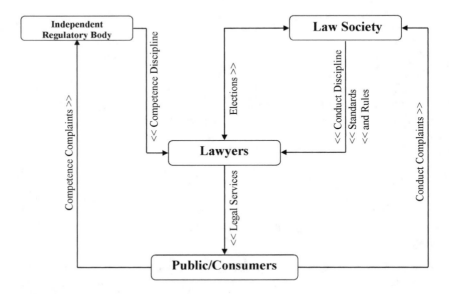

Figure 3: Coregulatory Option 2: Authority split by category or discipline

Internationally, several jurisdictions distinguish between competence and conduct complaints in their reformed discipline process. In Scotland, the forthcoming reforms distinguish between the two, leaving conduct issues to the law society to deal with, while the Scottish Legal Complaints Commission will hear claims of incompetence and poor service. In New South Wales, a distinction is drawn between three types of complaints: consumer disputes, unsatisfactory professional conduct complaints, and misconduct complaints. In all cases, as discussed above, complaints are brought initially to the Office of the Legal Services Commissioner, who has the authority to remit the complaint back to the Law Society for resolution. The category of complaint determines the scope of the Law Society's authority.

The next two regulatory options are essentially two ends of the same spectrum. The first model can be described as oversight regulation. It is common to many of the reforms underway internationally and, in fact, it frequently predates the most recent round of reforms. It seems to be a common first step in reforming professional regulation. Rather than withdrawing authority from the Law Society, this model places a check on that authority through the creation of an independent body to oversee the operation of some or all of the Society's regulatory functions [See Figure 4]. While the body is frequently at

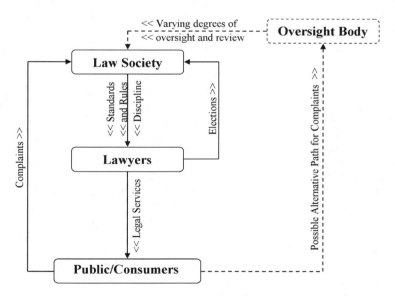

Figure 4: Coregulatory Option 3: Oversight Regulation

least partly made up of lay persons, its precise composition and extent of its powers of review over the actions of the Society varies by jurisdiction. Most commonly, the body provides some protection for complainants dissatisfied with the operation of the Law Society's complaints handling process. This may be through a formal review and reconsideration of individual decisions, or through general monitoring and operational review. The body may be empowered to overturn decisions of the Society, or only to request that the Society review and reconsider a particular matter. Furthermore, the oversight body may hear complaints directly from consumers in certain circumstances, for example where the complaint is with regards to the Law Society's discipline processes, or where it implicates the Law Society itself.

This model has been introduced in one form or another in virtually all of the jurisdictions reviewed in Section II, above. The long process of reform in England and Wales has involved several forms of oversight culminating in the forthcoming Legal Services Board, which shades from oversight into full independent regulation, a topic which will be addressed shortly. In all of the Australian states which have instituted some reforms to the governance of the profession, some form of strong oversight has been created, including notably New South Wales. Even in New Zealand, where reforms to professional regulation have been relatively restrained, the Complaints Review Office has been created, with the jurisdiction to hear complainants dissatisfied with the Law Society's handling of their case, and to bring disciplinary prosecutions itself where it sees fit.

There are no guarantees that oversight bodies will work perfectly. For example, Quebec is alone in Canada in having an Office of the Professions which has both regulatory and research capacity over the professions, including law, and yet this failed to prevent the *Finney* case. Similarly, in England and Wales a series of different oversight bodies have failed to satisfy both consumers and regulators. None of the regulatory options presented here are in fact offered as a definitive answer to the criticisms of the present system. Each branch of reform has its own particular strengths and weaknesses, which together warrant a full and frank discussion of the available options.

Where oversight shades into the withdrawal of actual power or ultimate decision-making authority from the Law Society, the structure may more appropriately be called one of full independent regulation. The move to fuller models of independent regulation seems to have arisen in some jurisdictions out of dissatisfaction with the effectiveness of oversight regulation. Under a model of independent regulation, all regulatory authority is withdrawn from the Law Society and assigned to an independent appointed regulatory agency [See Figure 5]. In many cases the Law Society will not be cut completely out of the regulatory process: the independent regulator may delegate some authority back to the Society to act as a front line regulator, for instance receiving complaints at first instance, or drafting codes of ethics and standards of practice. This is a very limited form of co-regulation. The regulatory body retains the power to withdraw what authority it delegates should it see fit. This may be by requiring the Society to hand over investigation or prosecution of a complaint, or by amending the rules of practice on its own motion, for example.

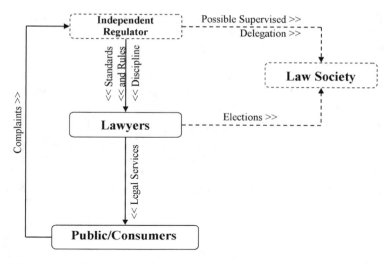

Figure 5: Prototypical Independent Regulation

A number of countries have introduced reforms which will take their regulatory regimes closer to an independent model. The closest regulatory system presently operating, however, is that in the Australian state of Victoria. As mentioned above, many Australian states incorporate elements of oversight into their regulatory structures. In Victoria, the government has taken oversight one step further. Ultimate authority for all aspects of the regulation of the profession rests with the Legal Services Board. While the Law Institute may still set standards and rules of practice, they are subject to the approval of the Board. The chair of the Board, who sits as the Legal Services Commissioner, has authority over the complaints and discipline process. This involves receiving complaints at first instance and making the decision in each case. While the Commissioner can delegate some responsibility back to the Law Institute, this is only with respect to the investigation of complaints. The Commissioner retains the responsibility to decide each case. In summary, in Victoria what few regulatory powers the Law Institute retains are subject to close supervision, and ultimately exercised at the pleasure of the independent regulator.

The final category of reforms which bears mentioning is the inclusion of a greater role for lay participants in the regulatory process. While most Canadian law societies provide for some lay participation in the discipline process, a common feature of regulatory reforms in other jurisdictions has been to enhance the number or role of lay participants. Although this is not *per se* a regulatory regime, it is an important element of reforms, one which has been adopted even in jurisdictions which have so far been reluctant to introduce the other models of coregulation discussed above. Lay participation takes different forms, forms which are varied enough that there is little point illustrating an example. In some systems, the situation is the same as that in Canada: limited representation of lay persons on discipline and hearing committees. In other jurisdictions, however, provision is made for lay representatives to form a majority on either body. Lay participation is also a common feature of over-sight regulation mechanisms, for example in the form of a Legal Ombudsman, or Lay Observer. Whatever the role of the lay participants, there is clearly an international trend toward enhancing their number and effectiveness in the regulation of the profession.

There are of course serious questions to be considered about lay representa-tives: a) the necessary qualifications for appointment; b) who has authority to appoint them; and c) their relative numbers so that they offer an effective and critical mass. Similar debates have already taken place in the context of Judi-cial Appointments Committees and, for a time at least in some jurisdictions, it seemed like progress was being made.

The foregoing is, obviously, an abstract schematic of various regulatory re-gimes envisioned by calibrated regulation. There are potential weakness in every regime — complexity, inefficiency, inaccessibility, alienation, confu-sion, ignorance, expense, inconsistency — and there is always the possibility of what the economists call negative gains. The point we do want to empha-size, however, is that all of these systems recognize that there are a number of competing public goods at stake.

Traces of Calibrated Regulation

Advocates of self-regulation portray calibrated regulation as fundamentally incompatible with the norms and traditions of the Canadian legal system. If we stand back from the details, however, there is a sense that quietly, almost unnoticeably, Canada has already taken a few steps away from self regulation towards calibrated regulation. First, it is important to note that Canada does not have a system of pure self-regulation, rather we have delegated self-regulation. Pure self-regulation would characterize private, contractually based organizations, for example, the Portuguese Water Dogs Association. In Canada, the legal profession has been statutorily authorized to regulate itself. Indeed in some jurisdictions as a matter of law, the Executive does have some authority to regulate the profession. For example, s. 13 of the Ontario *Law Society Act* identifies the Attorney General as "the guardian of the public in-terest in all matters within the scope of the Act, or having to do with the pro-fession in any way." In Nova Scotia, s. 7 of the *Legal Profession Act* provides that the Attorney Generals of Canada and Nova Scotia or their representatives must sit on Bar Council.

Second, courts do fulfill an important regulatory role, for example, when they impose criminal liability on lawyers for theft or fraud. More importantly they can also impose civil liability for contractual, tortious or fiduciary breaches. One need only consider cases such as *Martin v. Gray (MacDonald Estates)*, *Neil* and *Strother* to witness how the Supreme Court of Canada's decisions had an impact on forcing the profession to develop its standards, particularly in the realm of conflicts of interest. ... In some jurisdictions, courts police the withdrawal of lawyers. Occasionally, but rarely, courts impose costs on lawyers if they have engaged in egregious behaviour. Finally, as we noted earlier, assessment officers who adjudicate fee disputes between lawyers and clients are judicial officers under the control of the judiciary, not the law societies.

Moreover, other bodies have also assumed modest regulatory authority over lawyers. In *Wilder* the Ontario Court of Appeal held that the Securities Commission can reprimand a lawyer under the authority of s. 127(1) of the *Securities Act*, and that this did not threaten the independence of the bar because the goal was to protect the public interest in fair and efficient capital markets. In *Kreiger* the Supreme Court of Canada held that "the Attorney General's office has the ability to discipline a prosecutor for failing to meet the standards set by that office, but that is a different function from the ability to discipline the same prosecutor in his or her capacity as a member of the Law Society." The court also pointed out that the remedies available to each were quite different … for example, the Attorney General could not disbar a member.

Finally, and perhaps most interestingly, from a calibrated regulation perspective, there is the situation in British Columbia. British Columbia established an Ombudsman in 1977 to hear consumer complaints about the actions of public bodies. From the outset, the Ombudsman has had jurisdiction to hear complaints about the conduct of professional associations in British Columbia, including the Law Society. The Ombudsman has in fact received between 30 and 60 complaints per year about the Law Society for the last ten years. Most of these have been declined or determined to be unsubstantiated, but a number have been settled as a result of consultation between the Ombudsman, the complainant and the Law Society. It seems that the Ombudsman has not only practical authority to review the actions of the Law Society, but a willingness to exercise it as well.

This has important implications for the self-regulation debate. Despite passionate objections to the very idea of calibrated regulation, British Columbia has been quietly, and apparently effectively, operating a functional system of oversight regulation for over thirty years. This has resulted neither in the collapse of democracy in the province, nor even in government influence over the actions of individual lawyers or the Law Society. The Ombudsman is independent of the government, and in fact must be so in order to be effective, as she also has review powers over government bodies. As such, it is difficult to make out the argument that her powers of review represent a government incursion on the independence of the legal profession.

The British Columbia Ombudsman model certainly bears further study. Its long history of apparently peaceful coexistence with the Law Society should be reviewed in combination with a critical assessment of its effectiveness as a means of addressing consumer dissatisfaction, a project which is beyond the scope of this paper. Whatever the long-term value of the British Columbia model, however, it provides immediate illustration of the point that the Canadian legal profession may not be as purely self-regulating as is often claimed.

These four examples are, of course, relatively modest incursions on self-regulation but they are important in that they acknowledge that pure self regulation is a chimera, and that practically Canada has already embarked upon the project of calibrated regulation. The real questions are whether we should go any further, and if so, in which direction(s)?

A Modest Proposal

The authors argue that the way forward is to create a National Task Force, The Sponsors' Table on the Regulation of the Legal Profession to consider the present state and future possibilities for the recalibrated regulation of the legal profession in Canada. In the following extract they describe how they came to this proposal and delineate some key characteristics of the Sponsors' Table.

The key question is, of course, where would one find an institutional home for a "structure-revising-structure" of this nature. There are several possibilities. Option One might be the Federation of Law Societies because it is an obvious unifying institution for the legal profession. The problems, however, are a) historically it has seen its role as more of a "structure-preserving-structure" (witness its role in *Finney*); and b) it is likely to be too closely aligned with the interests of the profession to be sufficiently impartial. Option Two might be a governmental review along the lines of Clementi. Such a suggestion is not unprecedented. In Ontario in 1977, the Professional Organizations Committee of the Ministry of the Attorney General issued a Report entitled *Regulation of the Practice of Law in Ontario*. The problems with this option are threefold: a) because this is provincially based it would not encompass a national vision; b) governments might have their own agendas that would threaten the impartiality of the Task Force; and c) the necessary resources are likely to be beyond the resources of all but a few jurisdictions. Option Three might locate the Task Force within a Law Reform Commission initiative. For example, in 1994 the Manitoba Law Reform Commission issued a report on *Regulating Professions and Occupations*. However again there are the problems with a) scope, and b) resources. Option Four, our preferred option, requires us to think outside the box and create a new type of institution, The Sponsors' Table. The idea for this comes from the recently created Sponsors' Table for Human Research Participant Protection in Canada. The goal of a Sponsors' Table is twofold: a) to bring together all the key players who share a common interest in a particular area of social policy that raises questions of governance, transparency and public accountability; and b) to support and encourage a thoughtful consideration of the issues in question.

Mapping this onto the issue of the regulation of the Legal Profession we would propose the following template:

GOAL

- To bring together all the key players who have a common interest in ensuring that the regulation of the legal profession complies with the principles of good governance, transparency and accountability.

REPRESENTATION

- Federation of Law Societies Representatives.
- Government Representatives.
- Consumer Representatives.
- Judicial Representatives.
- Canadian Council of Law Deans Representatives.
- Regulatory Specialists.

TERMS

- All members will facilitate the work of an Experts Committee to ensure that it completes its work with integrity and efficiency.
- The Table will be chaired by an "eminent person".
- The Table will meet at the request of the Chair.
- The tenure of the Table will be three years.

TASKS

- Establish an Experts Committee to conduct original empirical, historical, comparative and conceptual research into the regulation of the legal profession.
- Reach out to other organizations that might have an interest in the regulation of the legal profession.
- Provide Terms of Reference to the Experts Committee.
- Facilitate the work of the Experts Committee through funding and in-kind support as appropriate and within the financial capacity of each member.
- At its request, provide advice and support to the Experts Committee. The Experts Committee has full authority with regard to the substantive elements of its work.
- Monitor the progress of the Experts Committee and require that it meets its timelines as set within its workplan.
- Establish a Virtual Secretariat.
- Develop a communications strategy for the Sponsors' Table and the Experts Committee.
- Make recommendations for the future regulation of the legal professions in Canada.

NOTES AND QUESTIONS

1. This excerpt sets out numerous arguments for and against self-regulation. Which set of arguments do you consider to be the most persuasive? Give reasons. How many of the arguments of the defenders of self-regulation and their critics are based upon empirical claims? How many are conceptual claims? How many are ideological claims? How do you plan to resolve each of these different types of disputes? What sorts of skills are required to engage in analysis of this nature? Has your legal education provided these skills?

2. The authors set out four alternative regulatory models. Are there any models of regulation that the authors have not identified? If so, briefly describe them and develop your own charts. Which model do you prefer? Provide reasons. What additional information would you need to determine which model would be appropriate in Canada? Should every jurisdiction in Canada have the same model or might there be reasons why some jurisdictions would be suited to one model, while others would be better served by a different model?

3. Which regulatory model do you think is optimal given the various arguments for and against self-regulation provided earlier in the excerpt? That is, which of the models best preserves the advantages of self-regulation while removing some of the notable disadvantages?

4. Does the discussion of traces of calibrated regulation in Canada change your opinion: (a) on whether the defenders or critics of self-regulation are right; or (b) on which model of regulation you would prefer? Can you think of any other examples which indicate that we have already abandoned self-regulation in Canada? Would it be a good idea to expand the regulatory authority of the judiciary, as most American jurisdictions have done? Do you think the Canadian judiciary would be in favour of adopting such a role? What objections might they advance? What weight would you give to such objections?

5. Identify the strengths and weaknesses of the proposal for a Sponsors' Table. Is it the proper way to proceed or is it a recipe for a feckless bureaucracy? What would be a better alternative? Justify your proposal.

G. FURTHER READING

American Bar Association Commission on Professionalism, *In the Spirit of Public Service: A Blueprint for the Rekindling of Lawyer Professionalism* (Chicago: American Bar Association, 1986).

Arthurs, Harry, "The Dead Parrot: Does Professional Self Regulation Exhibit Vital Signs?" (1995) 33 Alta. L. Rev. 800.

Arthurs, Harry, Richard Weisman & Fredrick Zemans, "The Canadian Legal Profession" (1986) Am. Bar Assoc. Res. J. 447.

Barton, Benjamin H., "Why Do We Regulate Lawyers?: An Economic Analysis of the Justifications for Entry and Conduct Regulation" (2001) 33 Arizona St. L.J. 429.

Devlin, Richard & Albert Cheng, "Re-Calibrating, Re-Visioning and Re-Thinking Self-Regulation" (2011) 17(3) International Journal of the Legal Profession 233.

Hurlburt, William, *The Self Regulation of the Legal Profession in Canada and in England and Wales* (Law Society of Alberta and the Alberta Law Reform Institute, 2000).

Fischer, James M., "External Control Over the American Bar" (2006) 19 Geo. J. Legal Ethics 59.

Orkin, Mark, *Legal Ethics* (Toronto: Cartwright & Sons, 1957).

Rhode, Deborah, "Moral Character as Professional Credential" (1985) 44 Yale L.J. 491.

Sheey, Elizabeth & Sheila McIntrye, *Calling for Change: Women, Law and the Legal Profession* (Ottawa: University of Ottawa Press, 2006).

Smith, Beverley G., *Professional Conduct for Lawyers and Judges*, 2nd ed. (Fredericton: Maritime Law Book, 2002).

Turriff, Gordon, "Self-Governance as a Necessary Condition of Constitutionally Mandated Lawyer Independence in British Columbia" (September 17, 2009), online: <http://www.lawsociety.bc.ca/docs/publications/reports/turriff-speech.pdf>.

Webb, Duncan, "Are Lawyers Regulatable?" (2008) 45 Alta. L. Rev. 233.

Woolley, Alice, "Tending the Bar: The Good Character Requirement for Law Society Admission" (2007) 30 Dal. L.J. 28.

Woolley, Alice, "Rhetoric and Realities: What Independence of the Bar Requires of Lawyer Regulation" (2011) 45 U.B.C. L. Rev. 145.

INDEX

COUNSELLING
alternative dispute resolution, 418
business vs. legal advice, 418
contractual breach, 416
desired outcomes, advice re, 418-420
duty of loyalty, 415, 417
generally, 411
honesty and candour, duty of, 417, 420
illegal conduct and, 412-417
• disobebience of court order, 414
• duty of loyalty and, 415, 417
• *Law Society of Upper Canada v. Sussman*, 412-414
• *Model Code* rules re, 414-416
independent and candid advice, 419
issues raised, 411
Model Code rules, 414-416, 418
scope/limits of, 417

CRIMINAL LAW PRACTICE
adversary system, dual role in, 435-436
Crown counsel. *See* **CROWN COUNSEL**
defence counsel. *See* **DEFENCE COUNSEL**
generally, 435-436
"neutral partisanship" role, 436
officers of the court. *See* **OFFICERS OF THE COURT**

CROSS-EXAMINATION. *See* **ADVOCACY**

CROWN COUNSEL
advocacy and objectivity, dual roles of, 436-437
full disclosure duty, 437-447
• Charter right to make full answer and defence, 439
• historical approach to, 438
• independence of Attorney General, 442-446
• *Krieger v. Law Society of Alberta*, 442-446
• *Model Code* rule, 441
• modern constitutional duty, 438
• prosecutorial discretion re, exercise of, 440-441, 442-446
• *R. v. Stinchcombe*, 439-441
generally, 436-437

justice in the public interest, duty to seek, 437
material witnesses, duty to call all, 447-451
• discretion re, reviewability, 450-451
• full disclosure vs., 448
• *R. v. Cook*, 448-450
• rationale for, 448
overzealous advocacy, 451-455

CULTURAL COMPETENCE. *See* **COMPETENCE**

DEFENCE COUNSEL
client, duty to, 460-461
confidentiality, duty of, 461
custody and control of real evidence, 469-475
• Alberta Code rule re, 472-473
• assistance of illegal conduct, 470
• disclosure duty, 469-470
• mistake of fact defence, 471-472
• *Model Code*, absence of rule, 469, 470, 473-474
• obstruction of justice, CC provision re, 471
• *R. v. Murray*, 471
• scenarios, 474-475
guilty client, defence of, 461-469
• confessions of guilt, disclosure of, 464-467
• non-judgmental approach, 462
• opinion re guilty, avoidance of, 462
• *R. v. Tuckiar*, 464-467
• when convinced of guilt, 463
misleading court, avoidance of, 463
partisan duty of, 461
plea/sentence bargaining, 475-482
• generally, 475
• main ethical rules re, 476
• *Model Code* rule, 475-476
• pleas of convenience, 477-481
• *R. v. K. (S.)*, 477-480
• scenarios, 481-482

DILIGENCE. *See* **JUDGES' ETHICS**

DISCIPLINE
codes of conduct and, 100, 101
"conduct unbecoming", meaning of, 2-6, 101-102

JUDGES' ETHICS — *cont'd*
- apprehension of bias, test re, 569, 571-574
- *Arsenault-Cameron v. Prince Edward Island*, 568-569
- civility, principle of, 580
- Cosgrove case, 565-568
- *Doré v. Barreau du Québec*, 577-583
- importance of principle, 571
- judicial demeanour/courtesy, 567-583
- judicial misconduct, example, 565-568
- principle stated, 564
- *Wewaykum Indian Band v. Canada*, 569-575
independence, 584-592
- freedom of expression, 588
- principle stated, 585-592
- public confidence in judicial system, 586, 592
- public speech and behaviour, limitations on, 589-590
- *Re Ruffo*, 585-592
integrity, 593-596
- *Model Code* provision, 593
- principle stated, 593
- scenarios, 593-596
Quebec *Judicial Code of Ethics*, 562
removal of judge, justification, 585-592
statement of, 587

LAW SOCIETIES
access to justice initiatives, 654, 655-656
Charter issues and, 75, 76
conduct. *See* **CONDUCT REGULATION**
discipline. *See* **DISCIPLINE**
entry to profession, regulation of. *See* **ENTRY TO PROFESSION**
extra-professional misconduct. *See* **EXTRA-PROFESSIONAL MISCONDUCT**
Federation of Law Societies of Canada, 75
generally, 74-76
historical context, 74
ineffeciency of, 735
judicial review of, 74

money laundering legislation, reaction to, 76
national mobility protocol, 75
powers of, scope, 74, 99, 101
public oversight, 75
regulatory devices available to, 737
statutes re, disclosure provisions, 237-241
statutory regulation and, 75-76
unauthorized practice of law. *See* **UNAUTHORIZED PRACTICE OF LAW**

LAWYER LIABILITY
competence, duty of, 112
contractual basis of, 112
duties to client, 112-113
errors and omissions insurance, 114
fiduciary breaches, 114
malpractice, 112
negligent conduct, 114
reasonable standards of care, 113
sources of liability, 113
tort basis for, 113-114

LAWYER REGULATION. *See* **LAW SOCIETIES; SELF REGULATION**

LAWYER-CLIENT RELATIONSHIP
accessability of legal service, 147-149
administration of justice, duties re, 148
advertising, 122-125
- examples, 124-125
- FLSC *Model Code* rule, 122
- issues re, 123
availability of legal services, tension re, 121
choice of client, 141-147
- criminal lawyers, ethical issues of, 142-143
- discrimination and, 145-147
- English "cab-rank" rule, 144
- generally, 141
- "moral non-accountability", 141-142
- refusing client, grounds for, 141-145
- "taking it personally", 141-142

SELF REGULATION — *cont'd*
Rule of Law justification for, 72
Scotland, in, 727
South Africa, in, 728
specialized knowledge and expertise
  justification, 72-73
traditional model of, 738

SETTLEMENT. *See*
  NEGOTIATION

SEX
conflicts of interest, 331, 347-353
misconduct sanctions, 701-705
sexual exploitation, 676-685, 696-700
sexual harassment rules, 97-98

SOLICITATION. *See* **LAWYER-
CLIENT RELATIONSHIP**

**SOLICITOR-CLIENT
PRIVILEGE**. *See*
CONFIDENTIALITY DUTY

**TERMINATION OF LAWYER-
CLIENT RELATIONSHIP**. *See*
**LAWYER-CLIENT
RELATIONSHIP**

TRIALS. *See* **ADVOCACY**

**UNAUTHORIZED PRACTICE OF
LAW**
access to justice vs. statutory
  monopoly, 717
"assistance" vs. "practice", 717-725
competition issue, 111
enforcement of laws re, 109-110
forms of, 108-109
generally, 108
increase in, 109
Lameman v. Alberta, 717
*Law Society of Upper Canada v.
  Boldt*, 706-717
mediation, practice of, 711-713
paralegals, increase in, 111
public interest issue, 110
statutory provisions re, 713, 718-724

VOLUNTEER
community work, 658
professional associations, 114-115

ZEALOUS ADVOCACY. *See*
**ADVOCACY; CROWN
COUNSEL; LEGAL ETHICS**